S
MAN

CONCEPTS AND
EXPERIENCES

Vanessa Vaughan
60, Mooiland Road
Bargoed
Mid Glam
CF8 8UJ

McGraw-Hill Series in Management

FRED LUTHANS AND KEITH DAVIS, CONSULTING EDITORS

Allen: The Management Profession
Arnold and Feldman: Organizational Behavior
Benton: Supervision and Management
Buchele: The Management of Business and Public Organizations
Cascio: Managing Human Resources: Productivity, Quality of Work Life, Profits
Cleland and King: Management: A Systems Approach
Cleland and King: Systems Analysis and Project Management
Dale: Management: Theory and Practice
Davis and Newstrom: Human Behavior at Work: Organizational Behavior
Del Mar: Operations and Industrial Management: Designing and Managing for
   Productivity
Dobler, Lee, and Burt: Purchasing and Materials Management: Text and Cases
Dunn and Rachel: Wage and Salary Administration: Total compensation Systems
Feldman and Arnold: Managing Individual and Group Behavior in Organizations
Finch, Jones, and Litterer: Managing for Organizational Effectiveness: An Experiential
   Approach
Flippo: Personnel Management
Frederick, Davis, Post: Business and Society: Management, Public Policy, Ethics
Gerloff: Organizational Theory and Design: A Strategic Approach for Management
Hampton: Management
Hampton: Inside Management: Readings from *Business Week*
Hicks and Gullett: Management
Hichs and Gullett: Organizations: Theory and Behavior
Hodgetts: Effective Supervision: A Practical Approach
Jauch and Glueck: Business Policy and Strategic Management
Jauch and Glueck: Strategic Management and Business Policy
Jauch and Townsend: Cases in Strategic Management and Business Policy
Johnson, Kast, and Rosenzweig: The Theory and Management of Systems
Karlins: The Human Use of Human Resources
Kast and Rosenzweig: Experiential Exercises and Cases in Management
Knudson, Woodworth, and Bell: Management: An Experiential Approach
Koontz, O'Donnell, and Weihrich: Essentials of Management
Koontz and Weihrich: Management
Kopelman: Managing Productivity in Organizations: a Practical, People-Oriented
   Perspective
Levin, McLaughlin, Lamone, and Kottas: Production/Operations Management:
   contemporary Policy for Managing Operating Systems
Luthans: Organizational Behavior

STRATEGIC MANAGEMENT

CONCEPTS AND EXPERIENCES

SECOND EDITION

Leslie W. Rue

Professor of Management
College of Business Administration
Georgia State University

Phyllis G. Holland

Associate Professor of Management
School of Business Administration
Valdosta State College

McGRAW-HILL BOOK COMPANY

New York   St. Louis   San Francisco   Auckland   Bogotá   Caracas   Colorado Springs
Hamburg   Lisbon   London   Madrid   Mexico   Milan   Montreal   New Delhi   Oklahoma City
Panama   Paris   San Juan   São Paulo   Singapore   Sydney   Tokyo   Toronto

STRATEGIC MANAGEMENT:
Concepts and Experiences
INTERNATIONAL EDITION

Copyright © 1989
Exclusive rights by McGraw-Hill Book Co. - Singapore
for manufacture and export. This book cannot be re-exported
from the country to which it is consigned by McGraw-Hill.

3 4 5 6 7 8 9 0 CMO PMP ' 9 4 3 2 1 0

This book was set in Times Roman by the College Composition Unit in
cooperation with Better Graphics Inc.
The editors were Kathleen L. Loy, Cynthia L. Phelps, and Larry Goldberg;
the production supervisor was Louise Karam.
The drawings were done by Accurate Art, Inc.

Library of Congress Cataloging-in-Publication Data

Rue, Leslie W.
    Strategic management: concepts and experiences/Leslie W. Rue,
    Phyllis G. Holland. - 2d ed.
    p. cm. - (McGraw-Hill series in management)
    Includes bibliographies and index.
    ISBN 0-07-054308-9
    1. Strategic planning. I. Holland, Phyllis G. II. Title.
III. Series.
HD30.28.R84 1989
658.4'012-dc19   88-27386

When ordering this title use ISBN 0-07-100290-1

Printed in Singapore.

ABOUT THE AUTHORS

LESLIE W. RUE (Georgia State University) is a professor of management at Georgia State University. Dr. Rue was formerly on the faculty of the School of Business, Indiana University at Bloomington, Indiana. He has worked as a data processing project officer for the U.S. Army Management Systems Support Agency, in the Pentagon, and as an industrial engineer for Delta Airlines. In addition, Dr. Rue has worked as a consultant and trainer for numerous private and public organizations in the areas of planning, organizing, and strategy.

Dr. Rue is the author of over 40 articles, cases, and papers that have appeared in numerous academic and practitioner journals. In addition to this book, he has coauthored seven other textbooks in the field of management. Several of these books have gone into multiple editions.

Dr. Rue has just celebrated his twentieth wedding anniversary and has three teenage children. His hobbies include the restoration of antique furniture and antique wooden speedboats.

PHYLLIS G. HOLLAND (University of Georgia) is an associate professor of management at Valdosta State College. She previously taught at Georgia State University. She is the author of a number of cases which appear in strategic management texts, and her articles on family business have appeared in *Business Horizons* and *The Director*. She serves as a consultant on strategic planning for not-for-profit organizations.

To Penny and Mike

CONTENTS

PREFACE

As is the case with most authors, we have made some significant changes in the second edition of this book. The field of strategic management has continued to evolve, and we have learned some lessons from the first edition.

As in the first edition, this text is organized around what we think is a simple, yet logical model of the strategic management process. We believe that use of this model makes the concepts easy to comprehend for the reader and easier to teach for the instructor. Building on the positive feedback from the first edition, we have used even more real-life examples and illustrations in this edition. It is our hope that these examples and illustrations will add a dimension of realism not usually found in college textbooks. Other significant changes in this edition include a new chapter on international and global strategies. Also, the first edition chapter covering financial analysis has been placed in an appendix following Chapter 12.

In the first edition, we placed two cases at the end of each chapter. The idea was to provide cases that could be used to directly reinforce the major ideas in the respective chapters. While we think this approach was successful, many users found it to be overly restrictive. Therefore, in this edition, all the cases are numbered sequentially and placed in alphabetical order at the back of the book. In the instructor's manual we have provided a matrix which clearly indicates which cases we think can best be used with each chapter. We feel that this approach will give instructors much more latitude without compromising our major intent.

We believe that our instructor's manual is one of the best available. It contains suggested course syllabi, summaries, and detailed outlines of each chapter, suggested answers to the chapter review and discussion questions, transparency masters, exam questions, and detailed analyses of each case. It should also be pointed out that each case is analyzed using a similar format. For those users who have access to a personal computer, the supplemental McGraw-Hill manual, *Strategic Case Analysis Using the Personal Computer,* by Benjamin

Harrison has been completely revised. This manual and software were written for analyzing the cases in this book.

We realize that our goals for this book are high. We have sincerely tried to meet these goals, and we hope you will agree that we have been at least partially successful.

Like most authors, we are indebted to numerous friends, family, students, and colleagues. First and foremost, we would like to acknowledge the support of our spouses to whom we have dedicated this book. Additionally, we would like to thank the following people for their very frank and helpful reviews: William D. Fitzpatrick, Villanova University; William B. Gartner, Georgetown University; George J. Gore, University of Cincinnati; Joseph G. P. Paoullo, University of Mississippi; Michael T. Quinn, California State University; Peter Ring, University of Minnesota; Sidney R. Siegel, Drexel University; Scott Traxler, Averett College; and Frank C. Wright, California State University.

We would also like to thank each person who contributed one or more cases to the book. These individuals are acknowledged at the beginning of their respective cases. Thanks are extended to Thomas B. Clark, Chairman, Department of Management at Georgia State University and John Oliver of Valdosta State College for providing environments which actively supported this project. Special thanks go to Caron St. John of Clemson University who wrote most of Chapter 12 and to Vidyarana Gargeya and Howard Hopewood who provided assistance in many phases of this project. Last, but not least, our sincere thanks go to Loyce McCarter for her typing and editing assistance. Loyce is simply the best with whom we have ever worked.

Leslie W. Rue
Phyllis G. Holland

CASE METHODS

A GUIDE FOR STUDENTS PREPARING CASE ASSIGNMENTS

The problems of strategic management are often unstructured. It is clear that *something* is wrong in the organization, but defining the problem is as much of a challenge as is finding a solution. In an actual business or agency, strategists are constantly receiving information, trying to discern patterns in the information, and taking action based on their perceptions of these patterns. A case provides the student with a similar situation. There is a mass of information which must be digested and sorted into problems to be solved. The student, like the manager, will find that while irrelevant information is included in the case, some key facts are not available and the time and/or cost involved in obtaining those facts is prohibitive.

The purpose of this case methods guide is to provide some guidance for those unfamiliar with the analysis of cases. Subsequent sections will discuss reading a case, analyzing the materials presented, and presenting the results of the analysis in written and oral form.

HOW TO READ A CASE

It may seem obvious that one reads a case by starting at the beginning and reading each sentence in turn until the end. The physical process of reading the case is, of course, the same as that for any other written material, but some alterations in this process can make the next step, analysis, go more smoothly.

For all readings (yes, plan several), have a pad and pen handy for note taking. Highlighting doesn't work well for cases unless you use several colors, because you need to categorize information. A pad with several columns marked off will be much more helpful. To begin with, read the case for the two C's: chronology and characters. List major events with their dates in a column, and make notes about the people in the case: personal characteristics, background, position and experience, relationships, and perceptions of the situation. This first reading should give you a feeling for the setting, major events, and people that make up the context of the case. You *should not* draw any conclusions without further analysis, no matter how obvious the problems and solutions may first appear.

ANALYSIS OF CASE MATERIAL

Analysis of a compound in chemistry means breaking the compound down so that the elements that make it up can be identified. Analysis of a case means "taking the case apart" to identify cause-and-effect relationships and make feasible recommendations. A case is like a complex puzzle, and analysis corresponds to finding the clues and fitting them together so that the puzzle can be solved. You must read a case to analyze it, but reading is only the first step.

Quantitative Analysis

Many of the "clues" in most cases are given in the balance sheet and income statements, and ratios must often be calculated to reveal these clues. This information can also be used to calculate break-even points, contribution ratios, and rates of growth which can be funded internally.

Other quantitative data (unit sales, industry advertising expenses, consumption patters, etc.) are likely to appear also. Always convert such information into percentages if possible. Percentage figures are more informative than absolute numbers because they do not allow problems to hide behind growth. In the following simple example, Brand B has shown increased sales for the 3 years shown and has been the sales leader each year. However, because of the rate of market growth, it is actually losing ground. This can be shown by calculating the market share for each brand each year or by calculating the growth rate for each brand and for the market as a whole.

SALES ($1000s) Example:

	1986	1987	1988
Brand A	25	35	40
Brand B	50	55	60
Brand C	25	30	40
Total	100	120	140

	Market share				% Change from previous year		
	1986	1987	1988		1986	1987	1988
Brand A	25%	29%	28.5%	Brand A	—	+ 40%	+ 14%
Brand B	50	46	43	Brand B	—	+ 9	+ 9
Brand C	25	25	28.5	Brand C	—	+ 20	+ 33
	100%	100%	100 %	Total	—	+ 20%	+ 17%
				Average	—	+ 23	+ 19

As you study a case, take time to manipulate the quantitative data in any way that seems appropriate and informative. This will help you spot trends and focus on strengths and weaknesses.

Beyond Quantitative Analysis

Other analytical methods used will vary with the case. The text provides descriptions of many tools, including industry analysis, portfolio analysis, determination of competitive advantage, etc., as well as checklists of questions to evaluate the functional areas. Always be alert for ways to apply concepts that you have discussed in class or read about in the text.

A columnar list is a simple but useful tool for organizing your analysis. The format below is one possibility:

Facts and Opinions	Problems	Alternatives
—	—	—
—	—	—
—	—	—

The facts and opinions are supplied from your reading and analysis. Note in this column anything that appears unusual (positive or negative). If the entry is not objectively verifiable, note the person on whose opinion the entry is based. An example of a fact would be, "Sales growth below market growth for previous 2 years." An opinion would be, "Sales manager says sales force not pushing product B." In a creative but careful fashion, you must group facts and opinions into underlying problems. Several alternatives should be considered for each problem.

A strengths, weaknesses, opportunities, and threats (SWOT) analysis is an aid for both generating and evaluating alternatives. Again, the format is simple. Using a matrix, list the internal strengths and weaknesses of the organization in the upper-left and -right quadrants and list the external environmental

Strengths: *Weaknesses:*

Opportunities: *Threats:*

opportunities and threats in the lower-left and -right quadrants. Alternatives which capitalize on strengths to take advantage of opportunities are generally the most attractive. An alternative whose success depends on an identified weakness is suspect.

Keep in mind that all cases are not problem-oriented. You need to be able to recognize a company that is successful and to identify through analysis the causes of its success as well as any potential threats. When the Facts and Opinions column is mostly positive, a better heading for the Problems column might be "Threats to Continued Success."

Pros and Cons

In evaluating alternatives (always think of more than one), think through the implementation of each alternative by listing pros and cons. No solution is perfect, and consideration of positive and negative aspects will give you a feel for the trade-offs among alternatives. Being able to demonstrate that you are aware of these trade-offs indicates that you have done a thorough analysis.

PRESENTING THE RESULTS OF ANALYSIS

Reading and analyzing the case provides the raw material from which you will present your case evaluation. In typical courses in strategic management, presentations may be oral or written and may be made by individuals or groups. Written and group oral presentations tend to be more structured than open class discussion, in which students may interject their comments into an on-going discussion. All these situations reflect important ways of surfacing ideas and studying problems in organizations, and they present opportunities for you to develop useful skills.

Class Discussion

The oral discussion of a case—with individual students contributing insights to issues as they arise and challenging the remarks of others—can be intimidating as well as stimulating. The following hints are intended to help reduce the intimidation surrounding this approach:

1 Be prepared with the facts of the case and be as specific as possible in your comments.

Typical: The company has grown steadily in the last few years.

Better: The 10 percent annual growth experienced in 1985 and 1986 increased slightly in 1987 and 1988 to 11 percent.

2 Provide comparative data to add dimension to your comments.

Example: The slight increase in growth rate (from 10 percent annually in 1985 and 1986 to 11 percent in 1987 and 1988) has been achieved during a general recession and in an industry growing at about 8 percent annually.

3 Enter the discussion early. Taking a position and defending it adds to interest, catches the attention of the other students, and will result in a better evaluation for you.

4 Know when to drop an issue or retreat from a position. You will not always be right and will make a better showing by gracefully conceding a point than by defending it to death.

5 Don't hesitate to challenge an error, a misinterpretation of fact, or an opinion with which you disagree, but do it with tact. Never interrupt or belittle another student. Listen to the discussion. Some students get so involved in thinking about what they are going to say next that they repeat material previously discussed because they didn't hear the point being made earlier.

6 Build on other students' comments. Don't abruptly shift the discussion unless asked to do so. Try to relate your comments to those that immediately preceded them.

7 Don't worry about saying you don't know some detail or hadn't thought of something when asked a direct question that you can't answer. Do offer some opinion or information that you think is relevant, even if it is not the exact information sought.

Written Case Reports

In addition to oral discussion, you will probably be responsible for written analysis and recommendations for some cases. Your task is to present your reader with the results of your thinking in a form which is easy to follow and reflects the quality of your effort. The following suggestions should help you produce a report that achieves these aims:

1 Be very clear about the assignment and its constraints and strictly adhere to length, format, and content instructions. If at all possible, type reports and be very particular about spelling and grammar. A paper with a sloppy or carelessly written appearance is a liability to its contents. Allow enough time to produce a paper with a finished appearance.

2 Be direct about your conclusions and recommendations. Tell the reader early in the paper where you are going and how the material you are presenting in the report supports your conclusions. The element of surprise is vital to a whodunit, but no manager wants to have to read through several pages of material just to find out the major points of the report. Often, the manager doesn't really want to read it at all, and if you can save him or her valuable time by the way you structure reports, you will be performing a real service.

3 Use subheadings to organize your paper. This will help the reader follow your thoughts, save space by making lengthy transitions unnecessary, and help you to see whether you have covered all the points you intended to cover in a logical sequence.

4 Use lists, charts, tables, flowcharts, and diagrams where appropriate. Financial analysis lends itself to tabular presentation. Simply refer the reader to a table of ratios which you attach to the report, rather than taking up space with a tedious recital of financial results. Similarly, a diagram of a distribution system, a listing of alternatives with pros and cons, a time line, or an organizational chart conveys much information in a limited space. These graphic representations are also easily transformed into transparencies when more formal presentations are required.

5 Beware of summarizing the case. You can safely assume (unless instructed otherwise) that your instructor is familiar with the facts of the case and does not want to read an extensive summary of the case. If you find that your report repeats case material without manipulating it or presenting new insights, you are probably summarizing. This frequently results from moving directly from case reading to case writing without performing adequate analysis. Remember, you must take the case apart and put it back together again so that problems are defined and solutions presented.

6 Recommendations should be specific actions addressed to individuals who have the authority and responsibility to carry them out.

Typical: This company needs to get a better idea of its market.

Better: Mr. Pickett, vice president of marketing, should conduct studies of specific consumer groups to determine how the product is being used.

Best: Ms. Johnson, sales manager, and Mr. Weiss, marketing research manager, should meet with the sales force each quarter to discuss (1) specific complaints, (2) adaptations of the product to new uses by customers, and (3) orders lost to competitors. The results of this meeting should be summarized by Mr. Weiss and reported to Mr. Pickett.

Oral Reports

You may be asked to present a case analysis to your classmates. This gives you an opportunity to practice making formal presentations, a skill you will frequently use in most organizations. Assuming you have done a thorough job of case analysis and made feasible and creative recommendations, the critical aspects of an oral presentation are catching and holding the interest of your audience so that your listeners are receptive to the information you wish to convey. Very seldom is the case itself or your analysis so intrinsically fascinating that they carry themselves. Some suggestions are presented below for gaining and holding attention.

1 Time your presentation, and make cuts so that you fall within the allotted time. If you are not accustomed to making presentations, you will be amazed at how time flies when you are talking about something to which you have devoted a lot of effort.

2 If you are talking more than 5 minutes, you will need to jog your listeners periodically. This can be done by soliciting their active involvement (have them write something down or ask a direct question) or by doing something different yourself (move across the floor, change your voice, introduce props or aids).

3 Don't read. Maintain eye contact with the audience at all times. Put in the time it takes to become familiar enough with your material to be able to look mostly at your audience. Speak clearly, audibly, and distinctly.

4 Use props, audiovisual aids, and handouts. Be sure the aids you choose are appropriate; are easily seen from the back of the room (transparencies typed in standard-sized typeface don't usually meet this criterion); and en-hance, rather than distract from, your presentation. Practice will prevent fum-bling with unfamiliar objects.

5 Appearance counts. You probably don't have to go all out in your job interview finery, but you should be neatly dressed and well groomed. Avoid items of dress that would distract the audience from what you are saying.

6 If your group is large, consider having one or two of the best speakers make the presentation (with your instructor's permission). Switching speakers can be awkward and distracting.

CONCLUSION

Case preparation and presentation is one of the most challenging and reward-ing aspects of the course. As you develop and refine your skills, you will find that they apply to numerous situations in your professional and personal life. Remember that each case requires significant amounts of time. If you do not allocate your time wisely, you may find that you are expending considerable energy without receiving commensurate rewards.

STRATEGIC MANAGEMENT

CONCEPTS AND EXPERIENCES

THE ROLE OF STRATEGIC MANAGEMENT

LEARNING OBJECTIVES

After studying this chapter, the reader should be able to:

1 Introduce and define the concept of strategy and the process of strategic management
2 Clarify terminology related to strategic management
3 Define the different levels and types of strategy
4 Relate strategic management to business policy and long-range planning
5 Discuss the benefits of strategic management

CHAPTER OUTLINE

DEALING WITH CHANGE: STRATEGY AND STRATEGIC MANAGEMENT

BENEFITS OF STRATEGIC MANAGEMENT

PLAN OF THE BOOK

VOCABULARY OF STRATEGIC MANAGEMENT
  Objective
  Goal
  Mission
  Strategy
    • Levels and Types of Strategies
  Policy
    • Procedures and Rules

AN EXAMPLE

STRATEGIC MANAGEMENT AND PLANNING
  Long-Range Planning vs. Short-Range Planning
  Formal Planning vs. Informal Planning
  Strategic Planning vs. Tactical Planning

STRATEGIC MANAGEMENT AND THE INTERNATIONAL
SETTING
STRATEGIC MANAGEMENT AND YOU
SUMMARY
REVIEW QUESTIONS
DISCUSSION QUESTIONS
REFERENCES
APPENDIX: SUMMARY OF STUDIES INVESTIGATING THE
RELATIONSHIP OF STRATEGIC MANAGEMENT AND
ORGANIZATIONAL PERFORMANCE

The greatest challenge for a successful organization is change. Many good
ideas about which products and services should be offered, how they should
be produced and delivered, and which customers would find them most useful
have suddenly become obsolete in the face of change. For example, consider
the impact that the hand-held electronic calculator had on the demand for slide
rules. Change also challenges managers. Many find themselves unable to cope
with an environment or an organization which has become substantially different from the one in which they received their training and gained their early
experience. Other managers find that they are unable to transfer their skills to
a new assignment in a different industry. A growing company, a new assignment, and changing customer needs or technology are frequently encountered
in a manager's career.

Organizations are beset by change, and the casualties are well documented:

• International competition has decimated certain sectors of the American
electronics industry and the American watch industry, and it has severely
weakened the steel industry. The number and type of competitors have
changed.

• Changing age distribution in the population has sent soft drink, beer, and
baby products companies scrambling to diversify, often with costly mistakes.
The preferences of major customer segments are changing.

• The U.S. automotive industry was hard hit in the mid- and late 1970s because it was not geared to the production of fuel-efficient cars.

• Deregulation in the airline, trucking, and banking industries has caused
major shake-ups and realignments in each of these industries.

All threatening changes are not external. The loss of key people, for example,
introduces a number of internal problems for an organization.

It is not surprising that the concept of "strategy," which provides a way to
deal with change, was developed in military settings. Rapid change and its accompanying uncertainty and complexity are probably at their maximum in
times of war. A strategy gives direction to diverse activities, even though the
conditions under which those activities are carried out are rapidly changing.
As the conditions under which businesses and not-for-profit organizations operate become more "warlike" (with increasing competition), as the range of
responses becomes more constrained (by government intervention), and as the

survival stakes become higher (with slowing economic growth), strategy is relevant to sound management.

DEALING WITH CHANGE: STRATEGY AND STRATEGIC MANAGEMENT

As organizations of all sizes adopt the strategic management process, it is important for all managers to understand both the concept and the process. When used in the context of the organization as a whole, *strategy* describes the way that the organization will pursue its goals, given the threats and opportunities in the environment and the resources and capabilities of the organization. As suggested by this definition, three factors that have a significant influence on strategy are the external environment, the internal resources, and the goals that are being pursued. In essence, an organization's strategy provides a basic understanding of how the organization will compete. *Strategic management* is the process by which top management determines the long-run direction and performance of the organization by ensuring that careful formulation, proper implementation, and continuous evaluation of the strategy takes place.

When starting a new business the determination of strategy is obviously critical. Decisions must be made concerning what products and/or services to offer, what markets to pursue, and how the products and/or services will compete. Keeping the strategy current is no less critical for an ongoing organization. When these fundamental changes in the environment, the internal situation, or the goals of the organization occur, it may be necessary to change the strategy itself. The strategic management process must be in place to ensure continuous reevaluation of these key elements to determine whether changes are needed.

Napoleon Bonaparte developed a successful strategy for conquering Europe. He used his large but mostly unprofessional army to overwhelm better-trained but less committed foes. He used artillery skillfully, joined battles so that the terrain would aid his cause, and attempted to outnumber the enemy forces 2 to 1. The approach worked well in the European environment, but Russia and Spain were very different settings. In both disastrous campaigns, Napoleon was unable to get the quick, decisive battles his strategy depended on, and the protracted campaigns led to his ultimate defeat.

Napoleon was a great strategist but did not practice strategic management. He failed to evaluate the appropriateness of his strategy when the environmental determinant changed. The difference between having a strategy and practicing strategic management can be the difference between success and failure. Many organizations are successful with their original concept of how they will deliver a product or service to their chosen market. However, when changes occur that make the original concept outmoded, they fail to adjust their concept of competition to the new situation.

Strategic management does not ensure that the best match will be made or that ideas will be executed properly. We believe, with the support of considerable research, that an orderly approach to change improves the odds for good performance in both large and small organizations. The practice of strategic management ensures a continuous assessment of internal and external changes and an adjustment of competitive approach on the basis of that assessment.

BENEFITS OF STRATEGIC MANAGEMENT

Many empirical studies have been conducted to measure the relationship of strategic management (or some closely related variable such as long-range or strategic planning) and the performance of organizations. The appendix at the end of this chapter presents a summary of several of these studies. The following paragraphs describe some of the most significant of these. Several of these studies do support a positive relationship between strategic management and good performance.

One of the pioneering research efforts was reported in 1970 by Ansoff, Avener, Brandenburg, Portner, and Radosevich.[1] In comparing formal planners who took a strategic management approach with nonplanners in 93 U.S. manufacturing firms, they found that the planners were more accurate in predicting the outcome of major strategic actions and outperformed nonplanners in terms of several financial criteria. Similar results were reported by Thune and House in the petroleum, food, drug, steel, chemical, and machinery industries, and by Herold in the drug and chemical industries.[2]

More recently, Robinson found that strategic planning had favorable impact on the performance of 101 small businesses.[3] Similar results were obtained by Sapp and Seiler in their study of 302 U.S. commercial banks, by Welch (1984) in his study of 49 varied firms, and by Bracker and Pearson in their study of 188 small firms in the dry cleaning business.[4]

A recent study by Rhyme of 210 Fortune 500 firms investigated whether firms conforming to strategic management theory outperformed firms which did not.[5] Rhyme found that firms with planning systems more closely resembling strategic management theory exhibited superior long-term financial performance both relative to their respective industry and in absolute terms.

Based on the evidence, organizations that successfully implant a strategic management approach can reasonably expect improved financial performance. While many of the studies reported in the appendix to this chapter found a positive relationship between planning and financial performance, those reporting mixed results should not be particularly surprising or discouraging in view of the fact that so many other variables can have a significant impact on an organization's financial success. In fact, a recent review of 18 empirical studies relating to the relationship between formal strategic planning and financial performance concluded that the inconsistent findings were due to shortcomings in the methodologies employed.[6] Others have suggested that the mixed results are because most studies have focused on the differences in performance between planners and nonplanners and not on the degree to which companies conform to strategic management theory.[7] An additional point that should be made is that the success of strategic planning and strategic management should be measured by factors other than just financial measures.[8]

A primary benefit of strategic management is that it provides an organization with consistency of action. A sound strategic management process helps ensure that all organizational parts are working toward the same objectives and purposes. Without the guidance provided by strategic management, individual organizational units often have a tendency to go off in different directions.

We believe that one of the major benefits of strategic management is the *result* of the process itself as opposed to the outputs produced by the process. In other words, the mental revelations that take place as a result of engaging in strategic management are as valuable as the actual plans that might be produced by the process. The strategic management process forces managers to be more proactive and conscious of their environments. It gets managers into the habit of thinking in terms of the future.

Another real benefit of strategic management is the opportunity to involve different levels of management in the process. Not only does this encourage commitment on the part of participating managers, but it also reduces resistance to proposed change. People tend to resist anything they don't understand. On the other hand, most people accept decisions when they understand the limiting factors and possible alternatives and when they participate in the process of making decisions.

While strategic management tends to be more formalized in large organizations, it can be just as necessary and valuable in small organizations. Statistics show that of the approximately 600,000 new businesses started in the United States each year, approximately 40 percent fail within the first year, 60 percent fail by the end of the second year, and a staggering 90 percent fail within 10 years.[9] Philip Thurston, a small business expert at the Harvard Business School, has observed:

> The smaller companies weathering the current difficult economic times seem to be those following an ideal—call it a no-frills, down-to-earth but clear plan—of how to take advantage of the environment and how to allocate resources. And in either the lean or prosperous years ahead, I think the planner will increasingly have the edge.[10]

While strategic management will never be a cure-all, especially for incompetent management, it can go a long way toward improving an organization's long-term performance. As the old adage says, "If you don't know where you're going, any road will get you there." A sound strategic management program can help provide the necessary direction.

PLAN OF THE BOOK

In our view the strategic management approach to the problem of change requires:

1 Understanding the concepts and processes which have been developed and adopted by practitioners of strategic management

2 Appraising the current situation of the organization and of the prospects for its future

3 Making a careful determination of the future course of action for the organization

4 Translating the desired future direction into specific actions and communicating these desired actions throughout the organization

Chapters 1 through 3 of this text deal with the basic concepts of strategy and the strategic management process. These chapters introduce the vocabulary of strategic management and discuss administrative aspects of the process.

Chapters 4 through 7 provide tools for appraising the current situation as well as for evaluating the critical environmental and internal determinants of strategy. It is necessary to understand where the organization is and how it achieved that position in order to make a reasonable assessment of how environmental changes will affect it. It is also necessary to understand the capabilities for response which the organization has developed, as well as any weaknesses that may be present.

Chapter 8 presents tools and concepts to assist in determining which response to change, from the variety of responses available, is the most appropriate. Chapters 9 through 11 address the difficult and complex issues of implementing strategic changes in an organization. Chapter 12 emphasizes the importance of international and global environments in today's world. An appendix which discusses financial analysis follows Chapter 12.

VOCABULARY OF STRATEGIC MANAGEMENT

The first prerequisite for learning about a subject is learning to "speak the language." Strategic management, like any subject area, has terminology which identifies important aspects of the process. Unlike other subject areas, however, strategic management has no universally accepted definitions for many key terms. For example, you might read two textbooks, an article in a practitioner's journal, and an article in *Business Week,* and find that each author gives a slightly different meaning to the term "corporate strategy." We will define our terms precisely and use them consistently. If you become familiar with these meanings and interrelationships, you should not be confused. Each of the following definitions is amplified and supplemented with additional examples in subsequent chapters.

Objective

An *objective* is a statement of what is to be achieved. Objectives are normally stated in terms of a desired level of attainment within a specific time frame. For example, one objective might be "to increase sales revenues to $8 million by the end of the current fiscal year."

Ideally, objectives are quantifiable, simply stated, and measurable. Exhibit 1.1 presents several examples of poorly stated objectives and shows how these same examples might be better stated.

Objectives can be classified as either short-range or long-range. Normally, objectives which have a time span of 1 year or less are classified as short-range; objectives spanning more than 1 year are classified as long-range. While many managers use only short-range and long-range objectives, some also utilize intermediate-range objectives. In this context, intermediate-range usually means 1 to 3 years, and long-range means anything over 3 years.

Objectives can also be classified according to their breadth of influence in

EXHIBIT 1.1   POOR AND BETTER STATEMENTS OF OBJECTIVES

Poor:	To minimize our costs
Better:	To reduce our departmental costs by 10 percent within the next 6 months
Poor:	To increase the quality of our work
Better:	To reduce the number of rejects to an average of 5 per month by the end of the current fiscal year
Poor:	To follow up more quickly on all sales inquiries
Better:	To follow up on all sales inquiries within 48 hours after the initial contact
Poor:	To become a socially responsible company
Better:	To hire at least 4 minority employees within the next year and to donate $1000 to the United Way campaign
Poor:	To increase sales
Better:	To increase sales by 20 percent by the end of September of this year
Poor:	To upgrade employee morale
Better:	To decrease employee absenteeism to an average of 2 days per year per employee and to reduce tardiness to an average of 2 days per year per employee by the end of the current fiscal year

the organization. For example, objectives that apply to the entire organization are called *corporate,* or *organizational, objectives.* Objectives that apply only to a certain division within an organization are referred to as *divisional objectives;* those that apply to a certain department within an organization are referred to as *departmental objectives.*

Goal

Many authors and managers use the term "goal" interchangeably with "objective." Others envision goals as being somewhat broader and having longer range than objectives. Still others refer narrowly to specific targets as goals. The problem with differentiating between goals and objectives is deciding just what the difference is. In other words, when does an objective become a goal, and vice versa? The terms "objective" and "goal" are used interchangeably in this text.

Mission

An organization's mission is actually the broadest and highest level of its objectives. *Mission* defines the basic purpose or purposes of the organization (for this reason, the terms "mission" and "purpose" are often used interchangeably). Basically, an organization's mission outlines why the organization exists. A mission statement usually includes a description of the organization's basic products and/or services and a definition of its markets and/or sources of revenue. Example 1.1 presents the mission statement of ADP, Inc.

Strategy

The word "strategy" is derived from the ancient Greek word "strategia," which connoted the art and science of directing military forces.[11] A more recent definition is provided by a 1974 survey which asked corporate planners what the word "strategy" meant to them. The conclusion of the respondents was, "It includes the determination and evaluation of alternative paths to an already established mission or objective and eventually, choice of the alternative to be adopted."[12] In other words, *strategy* outlines how management plans to achieve its objectives.

In almost all situations there are many ways in which an objective or a set of objectives can be pursued. A strategy outlines the fundamental steps—the pathway—that management plans to follow in order to reach an objective or set of objectives. Strategy is the product of the strategic management process. Throughout this book, we typically refer to the organization's top-level or *corporate strategy*. However, in reality, strategies also exist for individual units or individual members of an organization. A first-line supervisor, for example, may very well formulate strategy for meeting the weekly production quota.

Levels and Types of Strategies   Strategies may be classified according to their focus. Corporate strategies are established at the highest levels in the organization and address what businesses an organization will be in and how resources will be allocated among those businesses. Corporate strategies generally involve a long-range time horizon, relate to the entire organization, and direct financial investment.

EXAMPLE 1.1

The Mission Statement of Automated Data Processing (ADP)

ADP's mission is to help an ever-increasing number of businesses improve their performance by regularly using ADP's computing services to meet their ongoing needs for computing-based solutions. ADP computing includes recordkeeping, data communications, and information services, with single-source ongoing support for all of the client's needs that relate to these areas. ADP offers high quality computing services that can be efficiently and profitably mass marketed and mass produced at low cost with recurring revenues.

Source: ADP, Incorporated.

Business strategies focus on how to compete within a given business. They determine the competitive approach for companies which have a single product or are units of a multiproduct organization. Business strategies are established for each *strategic business unit* (SBU). An SBU is a distinct business, having its own set of competitors, which can be managed in a manner reasonably independent of other businesses within an organization.[13] For example, Borg-Warner is engaged in five separate major businesses, each of which makes up an SBU. From a financial standpoint, an SBU is almost always treated as a separate profit center. Business strategies are usually formulated by business-level managers via negotiation with corporate managers. Obviously, business strategies must be derived from and supportive of corporate strategies.

Functional strategies are narrower in scope than business strategies. As the name suggests, functional strategies primarily are concerned with the activities of the functional areas of a business (such as operations, finance, marketing, and personnel). Functional strategies may also be established by product line, by geographic area, or by type of customer. Normally, functional strategies span a relatively short period of time—usually 1 year or less. While functional strategies must directly support business strategies, they are primarily concerned with "how to" issues.

Business-level managers typically delegate the development of functional strategies to functional area managers. Functional managers must work closely with their business-level managers when developing strategy to ensure that the different functional strategies mesh and mutually support their respective business strategies. Exhibit 1.2 summarizes some of the important characteristics of corporate, business, and functional strategies.

EXHIBIT 1.2 CHARACTERISTICS OF CORPORATE-, BUSINESS-, AND FUNCTIONAL-LEVEL STRATEGIES

	Corporate	Business	Functional
Level of management responsibility	Top: corporate-level managers	Upper middle: business- or division-level managers; or top in a single-business or single-product company	Operating: functional-level managers
Scope	Entire organization	SBU or single-business or single-product company	Functional area, geographic area, product area, customer area
Time span	Long-range (3–5 years)	Intermediate-range (1–3 years)	Short-range (0–1 year)
Specificity	General statements of direction and intent	Concrete and operationally oriented	Action and implementation oriented

Example 1.2 presents some example strategies for Blue Bell, the maker of Wrangler Jeans, Maverick Active Wear, Jantzen Sportswear, and Red Kap Occupational Apparel.

Policy

A *policy* is a broad, general guide to action which constrains or directs goal attainment. Policies do not normally dictate what action should be taken, but they do provide the boundaries within which the objectives must be pursued. Thus policies serve to channel and guide the implementation of strategies. Exhibit 1.3 presents several examples of possible organizational policies.

Policies exist at all levels of an organization. A typical organization has some policies that relate to everybody in the organization and some policies that relate only to certain parts of the organization. A policy such as "This company will always try to fill vacancies at all levels by promoting present employees" would relate to everyone in the organization. On the other hand, a policy which states "Salespeople may negotiate up to a 5 percent discount off the suggested manufacturer's price" relates only to salespeople.

Procedures and Rules Procedures and rules differ from policies in degree of specificity. Policies, procedures, and rules all seek to limit opportunities for individuals to make bad decisions or take undesired action. A *procedure* is a series of related steps or tasks expressed in chronological order to achieve a specific purpose. Procedures specify in step-by-step fashion the manner in which a recurring activity must be accomplished. Procedures generally do not

---

EXAMPLE 1.2

Example of Strategy Statements

Corporate Strategy

Blue Bell will concentrate on strengthening its position in its current core businesses. These core businesses consist of jeans, sports and other casual wear in the U.S. and Europe, and occupational apparel in the U.S.

Business Strategy

Although long regarded as having among the lowest manufacturing costs in the industry, Blue Bell must strive for a superior quality product with a low *total* cost. In addition to reducing manufacturing costs, striving for a low total cost includes reducing working capital needs, overhead costs, and distribution costs.

Functional Strategy

Implement a compensation system whereby management compensation is closely linked to profit center and individual performance.

Source: 1983 Annual Report of Blue Bell.

EXHIBIT 1.3   EXAMPLES OF ORGANIZATIONAL POLICIES

1. *Policy.* To distribute at least 50 percent of net earnings to stockholders (e.g., *policy of any organization*)
2. *Policy.* To accept all returns that are accompanied by a sales slip (e.g., *policy of retail store*)
3. *Policy.* To require a minimum down payment of 10 percent of the purchase price (e.g., *policy of a mortgage company*)
4. *Policy.* To pay the shipping costs of all goods bought from the company (e.g., *policy of a mail-order company*)
5. *Policy.* To answer all written customer complaints in writing (e.g., *policy of a firm's public relations department*)

allow much flexibility and deviation. A company's policy may be to accept all customer returns submitted within 1 month of purchase; company procedures would outline exactly how a return should be processed by the salespeople.

Well-established and formalized procedures are often known as *standard operating procedures,* or SOPs. For example, SOPs may be established for handling customer complaints.

Rules require that specific and definite actions be taken or not taken with respect to a given situation. Rules leave little doubt about what to do. They permit no flexibility and no deviation. Unlike procedures, rules do not necessarily specify sequence. For example, "No smoking in the conference room" is a rule.

Procedures and rules are subsets of policies. All provide guidance in certain situations. The differences lie in the range of applicability and the degree of flexibility. A no-smoking rule is much less flexible than a procedure for handling customer complaints, which is likewise less flexible than a hiring policy.

Exhibit 1.4 summarizes the key definitions discussed in this section.

AN EXAMPLE

The following hypothetical example illustrates, in a realistic setting, how objectives, strategies, and policies relate to each other. In addition, it demon-

EXHIBIT 1.4   VOCABULARY OF STRATEGIC MANAGEMENT

Objective. A statement of what is to be achieved

Goal. Synonymous with objective; a statement of what is to be achieved

Mission. Defines the basic purpose or purposes of the organization; usually includes a description of the organization's basic products and/or services and a definition of its markets and/or sources of revenue

Strategy. Outlines the fundamental steps that management plans to undertake in order to reach an objective or set of objectives

Corporate strategies. Address what businesses an organization will be in and how resources will be allocated among those businesses

Business strategies. Focus on how to compete in a given business

Functional strategies. Focus on the short run, "how-to" issues of implementing strategies

Policies. Board, general guides to action which contain or direct goal attainment

strates different levels of objectives and strategies. The example relates to Borg-Warner, which successfully altered its business mix to emphasize higher-profit SBUs.[14]

Mission:	Borg-Warner will concentrate on delivering high-quality products and service in four major manufacturing areas: transportation equipment, air conditioning, energy and industrial equipment, and chemicals.
Long-range objective:	Borg-Warner will reduce its dependency on the auto industry as reflected in percent of corporate profit from 67% to 20% during the next 15 years.
Short-range objectives:	1. Reduce auto contribution to profit from 67% to 57% of total in the next 12 months. 2. Increase profit margin from 5% to 7% in the next 12 months.
Corporate strategy:	Diversify by acquisition of non-auto-related firm(s).
Policies:	Acquisition candidate must have expected annual profit of at least 10% of sales (allows flexibility as to industry, maximum size, etc.). Change from centralized control of marketing expense and purchase agreements to decentralized at business level. (Business can maintain present policy or change.)
Business-level objective—auto:	Increase profit margin 2% this year.
Business strategy—auto:	Decrease cost by purchasing from local suppliers to take advantage of local competition.
Functional strategy—manufacturing:	Negotiate new purchase agreements.
Functional strategy—marketing:	Revise commission schedule.
Business-level objective—Unit B:	Increase profit 67% this year.
Business strategy—Unit B:	Increase sales 67%. Policy change to allow overnight trips for salespeople. (Respond to market opportunity.)
Functional strategy—marketing:	Raise price. Enlarge territory.
Functional strategy—manufacturing:	Rev up output.

STRATEGIC MANAGEMENT AND PLANNING

Strategic management as we know it today has evolved from, and is still very closely related to, the planning function of management. *Planning* is the process of deciding which objectives to pursue within a specific future time period and how to achieve those objectives. Planning, at any level in an organization, is primarily concerned with the future implications of current decisions rather than with decisions to be made in the future. Planning is such a fundamental activity in human enterprise that many terms exist to describe various kinds of planning.

Long-Range Planning vs. Short-Range Planning

Planning can be either long-range or short-range. *Long-range planning* typically pertains to a period which starts at the end of the current fiscal year and extends 3 to 7 or more years into the future. Circumstances vary from organization to organization and from industry to industry and so the appropriate time frame for a long-range plan changes with the nature of the specific environment and activity. For example, "long-range" for lumber companies may be the decades needed to grow trees, while "short-range" may cover the several years necessary to clear a major section of land. In contrast, "long-range" in certain parts of the electronics industry might mean anything over 6 months. As is the case of objectives, some people utilize the term "intermediate-range planning." When used, *intermediate-range planning* normally covers a span of 1 to 3 years.

Formal Planning vs. Informal Planning

Almost all managers plan. The difference lies in the methods they employ and the structure they impose on their planning activities. *Informal planning* is planning that is carried out on a casual basis. Informal planning occurs when managers do not engage in an identifiable process and do not record their thoughts but rather carry them around in their heads. *Formal planning* refers to "a planning system that operates on the basis of some systematic and/or orderly set of procedures."[15] Formal planning almost always results in some type of written plan. However, the plan does not necessarily have to be comprehensive and long; a formal plan can vary from a one-page document to a massive planning manual.

There are many reasons why formal planning is preferable to informal planning. Probably the most important reason is that unless a formal system has been established, daily problems almost always take precedence over planning. The result is that little, if any, planning is done. Another reason is that formal planning forces collaboration among different managerial levels and different organizational units. A significant amount of informal planning will occur even when a formal system is in place. The point is not to attempt to eliminate informal planning but rather to ensure that some formal planning exists.

Strategic Planning vs. Tactical Planning

Strategic planning is an orderly process by which top management determines organizational objectives, strategies needed to reach these objectives, and short-range, top-level actions necessary to implement the strategy properly.[16]

Strategic planning is, in actuality, top-level long-range planning. Strategic planning is also sometimes called *corporate planning*.

Tactical planning refers to short-range planning that is oriented toward operations and is concerned with specific and short-range details. Planning is employed in the strategic management process to consider the future implications of current decisions. It is used to determine objectives as well as courses of action. Strategic management requires planning at all management levels and uses plans as a means of coordination and communication. A number of key terms related to planning are summarized in Exhibit 1.5.

STRATEGIC MANAGEMENT AND THE INTERNATIONAL SETTING

The manager who believes the only difference between the company's domestic operations and those of its Brazilian subsidiary is that the latter's sales force speaks Portuguese is surely the relic of a more isolated era in business. Managers are becoming less insular, ethnocentric, and prone to cultural shock whenever national boundaries are crossed. Operating internationally requires more than sensitivity to obvious locational differences such as climate, food, and language. Managing in an international setting means cultivating an awareness of:

• Views about the proper role of business and its conduct in a society which may vary significantly from the culture of the manager's origin
• Different views of what constitutes an acceptable rate of change
• The presence in a single country of different views about the rights and responsibilities of business

EXHIBIT 1.5　DEFINITIONS OF MAJOR TERMS RELATED TO PLANNING

Planning. Function of management which involves deciding which objectives to pursue within a specific future time period and how to achieve those objectives

Long-range planning. Planning which can vary in its time frame according to the situation; typically pertains to a period which starts at the end of the current fiscal year and extends 3 or more years into the future

Intermediate-range planning. Planning which typically covers a span of 1 to 3 years

Short-range planning. Planning which typically covers a period of up to 1 year

Formal planning. Planning system that operates on the basis of some systematic and/or orderly set of procedures; almost always results in some type of written documentation

Strategic planning. Process which sets forth organizational objectives to be achieved, strategies and policies needed to reach the objectives, and short-range plans to make sure that the strategies are properly implemented; for all practical purposes, analogous to top-level long-range planning

Tactical planning. Short-range planning that is oriented toward day-to-day business operations

- Cultural biases rooted in the historical development of the country
- Labor pools which have developed with unique skills and deficiencies[17]

There is growing evidence that strategic planning is an important element for helping companies break into new international markets.[18] In view of the complexity of international operations, the orderly approach to preparing for the future provided by strategic management requires more discipline to enforce but is also more useful. Strategic management should provide the organization with:

- A tool for coordinating and integrating operations which are geographically distant and operationally diverse
- A means of anticipating and preparing for change
- A way to ensure more meaningful involvement of nondomestic affiliates in global concerns
- The critical link between formulation and implementation of strategy[19]

All firms with international operations do not organize to pursue international business the same way. Several terms are employed to make major distinctions among these firms.[20] A *multinational corporation* (MNC) is one which has significant markets and assets outside its home country. An MNC has operations which function simultaneously in several different countries. Assets are likely to be completely or partially owned by the MNC. An MNC may be classified as either a multidomestic or a global company. A *multidomestic company* is comprised of relatively autonomous units which typically operate as independent profit centers. Decision making is likely to be decentralized. In contrast, a global company competes against other global companies on a worldwide basis. Its national subsidiaries are interdependent and require a unified strategy. A company which has all its assets based in one country but sells to others is called an *international export company*. A *domestic company* locates all operations and markets in a single country.

While the concept of strategy and the practice of strategic management apply to all organizations regardless of geographic location, we will occasionally point out some of the special problems and challenges of the MNCs. The last chapter of this book addresses some of the special challenges presented by international and global environments.

STRATEGIC MANAGEMENT AND YOU

We feel that an understanding of strategic management and the concept of strategy can be as important to a manager embarking on his or her career as it is to the upper-level executive who guides the organization. Understanding an organization's strategy should be part of the process of evaluating any job offer that an organization may make to you. The offer is only as good as the organization's prospects for the future. Also, the understanding of the strategic management process is an aid in understanding the relationship of an individual to the whole organization. Knowledge of strategy can help you see ways to advance your career by making important contributions to the organization. Finally, because formulating strategy applies to how an individual, as well as an organization, deals with change, the strategic management approach is useful for career planning and many other areas of life.

SUMMARY

Both organizations and managers are subject to changes which render once-effective approaches to competition ineffective. The concept of strategy and the process of strategic management provide a way to deal with change. A strategy gives steady direction to diverse activities even though the conditions under which those activities are carried out are rapidly changing. A strategy describes the way the organization will pursue its goals, given the threats and opportunities in the environment and the resources and capabilities of the organization. This strategy provides a basic understanding of how the organization will compete. Three determinants of strategy are the external environment, the internal situation, and the goals that are being pursued. Strategic management is the process by which top management determines long-run direction and performance of the organization by ensuring that careful formulation, proper implementation, and continuous evaluation of strategy takes place. Several studies have shown that the practice of strategic management improves the odds for good performance.

The benefits of practicing strategic management include:

1 *Consistency of action.* Ensures that all organizational parts are working toward the same objectives and purposes

2 *Raised managerial consciousness.* Requires environmental awareness and proactive approach

3 *Multilevel involvement.* Encourages better commitment and reduces resistance to decisions

In this book the concepts and terminology of strategic management are introduced in the first three chapters as a background for the in-depth exploration of the tools and techniques of strategic management which are presented in the remaining chapters.

Strategic management, like many other subjects, has developed terminology to identify important concepts. We do not claim that our definitions are universally accepted, but we believe that learning them and using them consistently will enable you to talk intelligently about strategic management with most practitioners.

Strategic management, as we know it today, evolved from and is still very closely related to the planning function. Planning is a function of management, and top management is very much involved in several kinds of planning. The strategic management process uses the function of planning in determining objectives and in choosing and describing specific actions to achieve those objectives. The process also requires planning by individuals at all levels and uses the plans as a means of communication and coordination.

Because formulating strategy applies to how an individual, as well as an organization, deals with change, the strategic management approach is useful in many aspects of life.

CHAPTER 1 REVIEW QUESTIONS

1 What is strategic management?
2 Explain the time frame used to differentiate short-range, intermediate-range, and long-range objectives.
3 Is an organization's mission the same as its objectives?
4 Where did the term "strategy" originate? Explain how strategy relates to objectives and mission.
5 Distinguish between corporate, business, and functional strategies.
6 Define "procedure" and "rule" in relation to policy. How does policy relate to business policy?
7 Distinguish between strategic planning and tactical planning.
8 What is a multinational corporation?

CHAPTER 1 DISCUSSION QUESTIONS

1 Go to the library and research and compare Delta Airlines' and Eastern Airlines' responses to deregulation in terms of the strategic management process. How do you think their effectiveness in coping with deregulation is related to strategic management?
2 Would the use of standardized terminology improve the implementation of strategic management by business? Explain why or why not.
3 Get one or two recent issues of a major business journal like *Business Week* or *Forbes*. Read the featured article, and try to pick out evidence of strategic management. Use specific terms with your examples.

CHAPTER 1 REFERENCES

1 H. I. Ansoff, J. Avener, R. G. Brandenberg, F. E. Portner, and R. Radosevich, "Does Planning Pay? The Effect of Planning on Success of Acquisition in American Firms," *Long Range Planning,* December 1970, p. 207.
2 Stanley S. Thune and Robert J. House, "Where Long-Range Planning Pays Off," *Business Horizons,* August 1970, pp. 81–87; and D. M. Herold, "Long-Range Planning and Organizational Performance," *Academy of Management Journal,* March 1973, pp. 91–102.
3 Richard B. Robinson, Jr., "The Importance of 'Outsiders' in Small Firm Strategic Planning," *Academy of Management Journal,* March 1982, pp. 80–93.
4 Richard W. Sapp and Robert E. Seiler, "The Relationship between Long-Range Planning and Financial Performance of U.S. Commercial Banks," *Managerial Planning,* September–October 1981; Jonathan B. Welch, "Strategic Planning Could Improve Your Share Price," *Long Range Planning,* April 1984, pp. 144–147; and J. S. Bracker and J. N. Pearson, "Planning and Financial Performance of Small, Mature Firms," *Strategic Management Journal,* November –December 1986, pp. 503–522.
5 John A. Pearce II, Elizabeth B. Freeman, Richard B. Robinson, Jr., "The Tenuous Link between Formal Strategic Planning and Financial Performance," *Academy of Management Review,* October 1987, pp. 658–673.
6 Lawrence C. Rhyme, "The Relationship of Strategic Planning to Financial Performance," *Strategic Management Journal,* September–October 1986, pp. 423–436.
7 Lawrence C. Rhyme, "The Relationship of Strategic Planning to Financial Performance," *Strategic Management Journal,* September–October 1986, pp. 423–436.

8 Pearce, Freeman, and Robinson, op. cit.

9 Jeffrey A. Timmons, Leonard Smollen, and Alexander Dingee, *New Venture Creation,* 2d ed., Richard D. Irwin, Inc., Homewood, Ill., pp. 3–4.

10 Philip H. Thurston, "Should Smaller Companies Make Formal Plans?" *Harvard Business Review,* September–October 1983, p. 184.

11 George A. Steiner, *Top Management Planning,* Macmillan, New York, 1969, p. 237.

12 James K. Brown and Rochelle O'Connor, *Planning and the Corporate Planning Director,* National Industrial Conference Board, New York, 1974.

13 George A. Steiner, John B. Miner, and Edmond R. Gray, *Management Policy and Strategy,* 2d ed., Macmillan, New York, 1982, p. 189.

14 This example was provided by a reviewer.

15 George A. Steiner, "Formal Strategic Planning in the United States Today," *Long Range Planning,* March 1983, p. 12.

16 Ibid.

17 N. K. Sethi, "Strategic Planning System for Multinational Companies," *Long Range Planning,* June 1982, p. 81.

18 Scott L. Weeden, "Strategic Planning: Experts Agree It's Still the Most Important Element in Breaking into International Markets," *Oil Daily,* April 6, 1987, p. 9.

19 Sethi, op. cit., p. 82.

20 Definitions are based on J. Daniels, E. Ogram, and L. Radebaugh, *International Business: Environment and Operations,* Addison-Wesley, Reading, Mass., 1976; and T. Hout, M. E. Porter, and E. Rudden, "How Global Companies Win Out," *Harvard Business Review,* September–October 1982, p. 103.

Chapter 1   Appendix

SUMMARY OF STUDIES INVESTIGATING THE RELATIONSHIP OF STRATEGIC MANAGEMENT AND ORGANIZATIONAL PERFORMANCE

			Criteria used			
			Qualitative		Quantitative	
Studies	Types of firms studied	No. of firms studied	Evidence to support a positive relationship	Little evidence to support a positive relationship	Evidence to support a positive relationship	Little evidence to support a positive relationship
Najjar (1966)[a]	Small mfg. companies	94	—	X	—	—
Thune & House (1967)[b]	Varied small mfg. firms	36	—	—	X	—
Henry (1966)[c]	Unspecified mfg. firms	45	X	—	—	—
Guynes (1969)[d]	Small mfg. firms	160	X	—	—	—
Ansoff et al. (1970)[e]	Mfg. firms	93	—	—	X	—
Herold (1972)[f]	Small mfg. firms	10	—	—	X	—
Rue (1973)[g]	Mfg. & service firms	386	—	—	—	X
Karger & Malik (1975)[h]	Mfg. firms	90	—	—	X	—

			Criteria used			
			Qualitative		Quantitative	
Studies	Types of firms studied	No. of firms studied	Evidence to support a positive relationship	Little evidence to support a positive relationship	Evidence to support a positive relationship	Little evidence to support a positive relationship
Malik & Karger (1975)[i]	Mfg. firms	38	—	—	X	—
Grinyer & Norburn (1975)[j]	Mfg. firms in U.K.	21	—	X	—	—
Ang & Chua (1979)[k]	Large mfg. firms	113	—	—	X	—
Wood & LaForse (1979)[l]	Banks	61	—	—	X	—
Kudla (1980)[m]	Fortune 500 firms	328	—	—	—	X
Sapp & Seiler (1981)[n]	Commercial banks	302	—	—	X	—
Robinson (1982)[o]	Varied small firms	101	—	—	X	—
Welch (1984)[p]	Varied firms	49	—	—	X	—
Bracker & Pearson (1986)[q]	Small dry cleaning firms	188	—	—	X	—
Rhyme[r]	Fortune 500					

[a]Mohamed A. Najjar, "Planning in Small Manufacturing Companies: An Empirical Study," unpublished doctoral dissertation, Ohio State University, 1966.

[b]Stanley S. Thune and Robert J. House, "Where Long-Range Planning Pays Off," *Business Horizons,* August 1970, pp. 81–87.

[c]Harold W. Henry, *Long Range Planning in 45 Industrial Companies,* Prentice-Hall, Englewood Cliffs, N.J., 1967.

[d]Carl S. Guynes, "An Analysis of Planning in Large Firms," unpublished doctoral dissertation, Texas Tech University, 1969.

[e]H. I. Ansoff, J. Avener, R. G. Brandenberg, F. E. Portner, and R. Radosevich, "Does Planning Pay? The Effect of Planning on Success of Acquisition in American Firms," *Long Range Planning,* December 1970, p. 207.

[f]D. M. Herold, "Long-Range Planning and Organizational Performance," *Academy of Management Journal,* March 1972, pp. 91–102.

[g]Leslie W. Rue, "Theoretical and Operational Implications of Long-Range Planning on Selected Measures of Financial Performance in U.S. Industry," unpublished doctoral dissertation, Georgia State University, 1973.

[h]Delman Karger and Zafar Malik, "Long Range Planning and Organizational Performance," *Long Range Planning,* December 1975, pp. 60–64.

[i]Zafar Malik and Delman Karger, "Does Long-Range Planning Improve Company Performance?" *Management Review,* September 1975, pp. 27–31.

[j]P. H. Grinyer and D. Norburn, "Planning for Existing Markets: Perceptions of Chief Executives and Financial Performance," *The Journal of the Royal Statistical Society,* 1975, 138, Series A, pp. 70–97.

[k]J. S. Ang and J. H. Chua, "Long Range Planning in Large U.S. Corporations," *Long Range Planning,* April 1979, pp. 99–102.

[l]D. Robley Wood, Jr., and R. Lawrence Laforse, "The Impact of Comprehensive Planning on Financial Performance," *Academy of Management Journal,* September 1979, pp. 516–526.

[m]Ronald J. Kudla, "The Effects of Strategic Planning on Common Stock Returns," *Academy of Management Journal,* March 1980, pp. 5–20.

[n]Richard W. Sapp and Robert E. Seiler, "The Relationship between Long-Range Planning and Financial Performance of U.S. Commercial Banks," *Managerial Planning,* September–October 1981, pp. 32–36.

[o]Richard B. Robinson, Jr., "The Importance of 'Outsiders' in Small Firm Strategic Planning," *Academy of Management Journal,* March 1982, pp. 80–93.

[p]Jonathan B. Welch, "Strategic Planning Could Improve Your Share Price," *Long Range Planning,* April 1984, pp. 144–147.

[q]J. S. Bracker and J. N. Pearson, "Planning & Financial Performance of Small, Mature Firms," *Strategic Management Journal,* November–December 1986, pp. 503–522.

[r]Lawrence C. Rhyme, "The Relationship of Strategic Planning to Financial Performance," *Strategic Management Journal,* September–October 1986, pp. 423–436.

THE STRATEGIC MANAGEMENT PROCESS

LEARNING OBJECTIVES

After studying this chapter, the reader should be able to:

1 Demonstrate that all organizations engage in the strategic management process either implicitly or explicitly and that the degree of
formality of the process can vary considerably
2 Emphasize that several different levels of management have
responsibilities relating to the strategic management process
3 Discuss the different stages involved in the evolution of a mature
strategic management process
4 Present a model of the strategic management process

CHAPTER OUTLINE

FORMALITY OF THE PROCESS
RESPONSIBILITY FOR STRATEGIC MANAGEMENT
    The Role of the Chief Executive Officer (CEO)
    The Role of the Corporate Planner
    The Role of Line Managers
    The Role of the Board of Directors
EVOLUTION OF STRATEGIC MANAGEMENT
    Phase 1: Financial-Based Planning
    Phase 2: Forecast-Based Planning
    Phase 3: Externally Oriented Planning
    Phase 4: Strategic Management
A STRATEGIC MANAGEMENT MODEL
    Analyzing the Current Status
      • Identifying Mission • Identifying Past and Present Strategies
      • Diagnosing Past and Present Performance

In Chapter 1, the strategic management process was described as the process by which top management determines the long-run direction and performance of the organization by ensuring that careful formulation, proper implementation, and continuous evaluation of the strategy takes place. Setting the organization's mission; defining what business or businesses the organization will be in; setting objectives; developing, implementing, and evaluating strategies; and adjusting these components as necessary are all involved in this process.

While the basic process is similar in most organizations, differences exist in the formality of the process, levels of managerial involvement, and degree of institutionalization of the process. This chapter explores the dimensions of the strategic management process. This chapter explores the dimensions of the strategic management process which give it variety and also introduces a model which provides a basic description of the common components and sequence of the process.

All organizations engage in the strategic management process either formally or informally. Organizations that consciously engage in strategic management generally follow some type of formalized process for making decisions and taking actions that affect their future direction. In the absence of a formal process, strategic decisions are made in a piecemeal fashion. An informal approach to strategy, however, does not necessarily mean that the organization doesn't know what it is doing. It simply means the organization does not engage in any type of formalized process for initiating and managing strategy. Although it is unlikely that an organization will continue to grow successfully and to branch out into new ventures without a real understanding of the pattern of decisions which produced success, many firms are unaware of the strategy that underlies their initial success. This is why many established companies fail miserably when they attempt a program of corporate acquisition, product diversification, or market expansion. The formality of the process is understandably quite important.

FORMALITY OF THE PROCESS

For those organizations that do consciously engage in strategic management, the degree of formality can vary considerably. The more explicit the procedure to be followed, the more formal the process is.

Henry Mintzberg has described three distinct approaches, or modes, for making strategy: (1) the entrepreneurial mode, (2) the adaptive mode, and (3) the planning mode.[1] Of these three modes, the entrepreneurial mode is least formal and the planning mode is most formal. The mode most likely to be used by an organization is largely a function of its size and maturity. Larger and more mature organizations are more likely to use the planning mode, while smaller and younger firms are likely to use the entrepreneurial mode.

Exhibit 2.1 outlines the major characteristics of each of Mintzberg's three modes.

RESPONSIBILITY FOR STRATEGIC MANAGEMENT

Successful strategic management involves the cooperation of several levels in the organization. Our definition of strategic management emphasizes the cen-

 EXHIBIT 2.1   THREE MODES OF STRATEGY MAKING

Entrepreneurial mode

1. Strategy-making is dominated by active search for new opportunities.
2. Power is centralized in the hands of the chief executive.
3. Strategy making is characterized by dramatic leaps forward in the face of uncertainty.
4. Growth is the dominant goal.
5. Lends itself to organizations that are small and/or young.

Adaptive mode

1. Clear goals do not exist; strategy-making reflects a division of power among members of a complex coalition.
2. The strategy-making process is characterized by the "reactive" solution to existing problems rather than the "proactive" search for new opportunities.
3. Makes its decisions in incremental, serial steps.
4. Decisions are disjointed.
5. Lends itself to large established organizations with great sunk costs and many controlling groups holding each other in check.

Planning mode

1. Analyst or planner plays a major role in strategy-making.
2. Focuses on systematic analysis, particularly in the assessment of the costs and benefits of competing proposals.
3. Characterized above all by the integration of decisions and strategies.
4. Lends itself to organizations of reasonable size that do not face severe and unpredictable competition.

Source: Henry Mintzberg, "Strategy-Making in Three Modes," *California Management Review,* Winter 1973, pp. 44–53. © 1973 by the Regents of the University of California. Reprinted/condensed from the *California Management Review,* vol. 16, no. 2, by permission of the Regents.

tral role that top management plays in the process. What top management's role should be, and how it relates to the corporate planning staff (where one exists) and to line managers, is discussed in the following sections. The role of the board of directors in the strategic management process is also explored.

The Role of the Chief Executive Officer (CEO)

George Steiner, a nationally recognized expert on strategic management, has stated, "there can and will be no effective formal strategic planning in an organization in which the chief executive does not give it firm support and make sure that others in the organization understand his depth of commitment."[2] This statement leaves little room for doubt concerning the importance of the CEO's involvement. In addition to being personally committed to the process, the CEO must make sure that others in the organization are aware of his or her commitment. This emphasizes the fact that a CEO's commitment must include hands-on involvement. A good example is J. C. Penney, Inc., which is known for the excellence of its planning process. Donald V. Siebert, Penney's former chair and CEO, described the system and his commitment to it in these words: "We did our first formal five-year planning around 1963, and since then, our projections have been updated annually.... Our goal is to set guidelines for delegated decision-making to give our operating managers an idea of what (top) management expects."[3]

Exhibit 2.2 summarized the role of the CEO in strategic management. As can be gleaned from Exhibit 2.2, the CEO is the one person most responsible for strategic management. Many attempts at strategic management have failed because a CEO professed commitment but never became personally involved. Other members of the organization take their cues from the CEO. If he or she demonstrates involvement, others are likely to follow. Unfortunately, the re-

EXHIBIT 2.2 ROLE OF THE CEO IN STRATEGIC MANAGEMENT

1. The CEO must understand that strategic management is his or her responsibility. Parts of this task, but certainly not all of it, can be delegated.
2. The CEO is responsible for establishing a climate in the organization that is congenial to strategic management.
3. The CEO is responsible for ensuring that the design of the process is appropriate to the unique characteristics of the company.
4. The CEO is responsible for determining whether there should be a corporate planner. If so, the CEO generally should appoint the planner (or planners) and see that the office is located as close to that of the CEO as practical.
5. The CEO must get involved in doing the planning.
6. The CEO should have face-to-face meetings with executives for making plans and should ensure that there is a proper evaluation of the plans and feedback to those making them.
7. The CEO is responsible for reporting the results of the strategic management process to the board of directors.

Source: Adapted from George A. Steiner, *Strategic Planning: What Every Manager Must Know*, Free Press, New York, 1979, pp. 93–94.

verse is also true: if the CEO exhibits a lack of involvement, others will interpret this as a sign of disinterest. The importance of the CEO's active involvement cannot be overstated.

The Role of the Corporate Planner

As organizations become larger and more complex, staff personnel are often added to assist in the strategic management/planning process. Usually these staff personnel are known as *corporate planners.*

When a corporate planning staff exists, what are its duties? Naturally, the specific duties of any corporate planning staff are going to vary from organization to organization. In general, however, these responsibilities can be grouped into five major areas:[4]

1 Helping the CEO discharge the strategic management responsibilities of that office
2 Coordinating divisional plans
3 Helping top management devise the planning system
4 Preparing environmental analyses for divisions and giving them overall guidance
5 Developing overall corporate plans for top management for such matters as acquisitions and divestitures

Note that in none of the above items is the planning staff responsible for the total development of plans at any level. Rather, the planning staff primarily serves as a coordinator, adviser, and evaluator.[5]

The presence and influence of corporate planners grew steadily from the 1960s through the early 1980s (see Exhibit 2.3).

EXHIBIT 2.3* THE USE OF CORPORATE PLANNERS AND PLANNING GROUPS

Study	No. of firms in study	Used planning staff or individual planner	
		No.	Percent
Newell (1962)	118	Many	3
Litschert (1967)	40	5	13
Business Mgt. (1967)	101	11	11
Holmberg (1967)	111	20	18
Rue (1973)	398	164	41
Boulton et al. (1982)	142	75	53
Diffenbach (1983)	90	66	73

*Due to the manner in which the question was posed, it was determined that at least the number indicated used some type of corporate planner or planning group; the actual number could have been higher.
Source: Leslie W. Rue, "Theoretical and Operational Implications of Long Range Planning on Selected Measures of Financial Performance in U.S. Industries," unpublished dissertation, Georgia State University, 1973, Atlanta, Ga.

However, beginning in the early to mid-1980s, many CEOs became disenchanted with the role that many of their corporate planners were fulfilling.[6] In these companies the size of the corporate planning staffs and their demands on operating managers had grown out of control. This often resulted in hostility between the corporate planners and the operating managers. In some companies, operating managers were made to feel like second-class citizens when compared to the corporate planners. As the chasm between corporate planners and operating managers widened, strategic planning often grew further and further away from the real world of customers and competitors. As a result of these and similar problems, many companies have reduced the size and influence of their corporate planning staffs. Example 2.1 discusses some of the actions taken by General Electric.

There is nothing inherently wrong with having a corporate planning staff. It is often very desirable, provided it operates as it is intended. Corporate planners should function as coordinators, catalysts, and advisers for top and line managers. They should not do the planning *for* any level of management.

The Role of Line Managers

In many cases line managers do not have to be concerned about how to design and manage the planning system, as this is done at the corporate level.[7] However, in many companies that have cut back on the number and influence of corporate planners, line managers are being asked to assume a more active role in the strategic management process. Daniel Gray, a strategic consultant, recently made the following statement: "It is now widely accepted that strategic planning is a line management function in which staff specialists play a supporting role."[8] Michael E. Naylor, General Motors' general director of corporate strategic planning, reinforces this point: "Planning is the responsi-

---

EXAMPLE 2.1

Reducing the Planning Staff at GE

After taking over at General Electric, Chairman John F. Welch, Jr. cut the corporate planning group from 58 to 33. Scores of other planners were also purged in operating sectors, groups, and divisions. For example, Roger W. Schipke, head of GE's Major Appliance Business Group, reduced his planning staff from 25 to 0. Schipke now takes his "visions" for the group to his top operating managers who "hash out a consensus" and oversee its implementation. Schipke strongly believes that for any strategy to succeed, operating people need to "understand it, embrace it, and make it happen."

Source: "The New Breed of Strategic Planner," *Business Week,* September 17, 1984, pp. 62–68.

bility of every line manager. The role of the planner is to be a catalyst for change—not to do the planning for each business unit."[9]

At the very least, line managers must understand the strategic management process and system well enough to be able to provide the inputs required of them. These inputs naturally vary from situation to situation, but they often relate to operating capabilities. For example, are there enough machines to supply the demand for the product? Line managers typically provide information to corporate planners (or the CEO) relating to the internal and external analyses and to the selection of long- and intermediate-range objectives. The most visible involvement of line managers is in implementing the chosen corporate and business strategies by formulating the necessary functional strategies.

Line managers should know what role they are expected to play in the strategic management process. They should also be aware of corporate-level plans so that their operating plans can be properly formulated. Involving line managers in the strategic management process not only provides needed information but also greatly reduces resistance to any changes resulting from the process.

The Role of the Board of Directors

A board of directors can be characterized as either an inside or an outside board. On an inside board a majority of the members hold management positions in the organization; on an outside board a majority of the members do not hold or have not held a position with the organization. While insiders who are members of a board will ordinarily have other duties related to the strategic management process by virtue of their corporate position, the role played by the board as an entity should be basically the same for both types. A 1983 survey of 119 large companies found that 100, or 84 percent, of their boards had a majority of outside directors.[10] However, there are signs that this is changing. For the first time since the mid-1960s, the makeup of boards is shifting toward inside boards.[11] The reason for this is increased concern for legal liabilities and the time required to serve on a board. It has been estimated that today directors have a 1-in-5 chance of being party to a shareholder suit.[12] Reflecting this trend, the cost of liability insurance for directors jumped tenfold in the period from 1984 to 1986. Most directors will not serve unless some form of liability insurance is provided by the company.

To quote Harvard Professor Kenneth Andrews, "The strengthening of the corporate board of directors has not yet produced a clear or widely accepted conclusion about the board's role in formulating, ratifying, changing, or evaluating corporate strategy."[13] Traditionally, boards of directors have been rather passive groups that rubber-stamped the proposals of the CEO. However, recent lawsuits against boards of directors, concerning their liabilities to their respective organizations, have caused board members to become somewhat more active than in the past and to be more concerned about the activities of their companies. In spite of this trend, little evidence exists to indicate that directors have become appreciably more involved in the strategy process.[14] There are many possible reasons for this:[15] many CEOs do not engage in comprehensive strategic management and therefore have no process in which to involve board members (in these instances, the CEO manages on a short-term basis and uses an intuitive approach to planning and decision making); other CEOs do not believe their outside directors know enough or have enough time to be effectively involved in the strategy process; still other CEOs deliberately do not involve their boards for fear of losing power.

Just what role should a board play in the strategic management process? Professor Andrews has provided the following answer: "A responsible and effective board should require of its management a unique and durable corporate strategy, review it periodically for its validity, use it as the reference point for all other board decisions, and share with management the risks associated with its adoption."[16] An important implication of this statement is that the board does *not* formulate strategy but reviews it and monitors the process that produces the strategy. Of course, inside members of the board may, through their corporate positions, be involved in the formulation of corporate strategy. However, the board as an entity does not normally formulate strategy. By serving in a review capacity, the board is in a position to ask questions and require justification for the proposed strategies. One significant advantage of this system, especially with an outside board, is that the board is able to provide a different and objective evaluation of management's proposals. In this same light, one author has stated, "the major role of the Board as it relates to strategy is to replace the CEO if results over a reasonable period of time do not confirm the existence of a successful strategy."[17] Thus, while the board does not formulate strategy, it can and should play an important role in the strategic management process.

There are several additional reasons why a board should concern itself with the specific content of the corporate strategy:

1 The board needs evidence that its management has a process for developing, evaluating, and choosing among strategic alternatives.

2 Independent directors need to understand the nature of the company's industry and business.

3 Being familiar with the company's strategy can give the board a reference point for other decisions that it may face.

4 Understanding the content of corporate strategy enables the board to evaluate the performance of the management team.[18]

The argument is often made that strategy is, by nature, less explicit in smaller organizations and, therefore, that board members of smaller organizations should not expect precise definitions of objectives and plans.[19] Similarly, the same argument holds that board members of small organizations should not expect the CEO (who is often the owner) to share his or her thinking with them. While there is no doubt that this argument is fostered in some organizations, there is no justification for its acceptance. Board members should have many of the same responsibilities and duties in a small organization that they have in a large organization. They certainly are subject to the same legal liabilities. Example 2.2 describes one unusual manner in which PepsiCo has used its board.

EVOLUTION OF STRATEGIC MANAGEMENT

Three members of McKinsey & Company systematically studied the evolution of strategic management in 120 companies.[20] They concluded that although

---

EXAMPLE 2.2

Board Members as Traveling Salesmen

In January of 1986, PepsiCo Chairman Donald Kendall turned his board of directors into a band of high-class traveling salesmen. Kendall took three inside directors and seven of ten outside directors on an eight-day, four-city tour of China with the express purpose of using the directors to help sell PepsiCo's products to the Chinese leaders. Because the Chinese are impressed with successful people, Kendall felt that board members could accelerate Pepsi's acceptance by the Chinese leaders. The hope was to cut through months or even years of bureaucratic tape by building personal relationships with the Chinese leaders. The tour mostly consisted of working lunches and dinners and back-to-back meetings with different Chinese leaders.

Source: Louis Kraar, "Pepsi's Pitch to Quench Chinese Thirsts," *Fortune,* March 17, 1986, pp. 58–61.

---

strategic management may evolve at varying rates, it does indeed evolve along similar lines in different organizations. As shown in Exhibit 2.4, the researchers segmented the evolutionary process into four sequential phases. Each phase is marked by clear advances over the previous one in terms of explicit formulation of issues, quality of preparatory staff work, readiness of top management to participate in and guide the strategic decisions process, and effectiveness of implementation.[21]

Phase 1   Financial-Based Planning

It is rare today to find a manager in any type of organization, at any level, who is not involved in some phase of the budgeting process. Organizations in phase 1 emphasize preparing and meeting annual budgets. Financial targets are established and revenues and costs are carefully monitored. Generally speaking, most organizations in this phase exhibit few other characteristics relating to the future. The emphasis is short-term, and the primary focus is on the functional aspects of the organization. It should be pointed out that organizations in phase 1 may very well have developed more sophisticated strategies which have not been formalized. Usually, such strategies have been formulated by the CEO and remain in his or her mind. This is especially true in organizations that are young and relatively small. Organizations that wish to remain relatively small often never progress beyond phase 1. However, organizations that desire a longer-range view of things advance to phase 2.

Phase 2   Forecast-Based Planning

The first evidence of phase 2 is usually an extension of the time frames covered by the budgeting process. Capital expenditure planning often initiates this

EXHIBIT 2.4 FOUR PHASES IN THE EVOLUTION OF STRATEGIC MANAGEMENT

	Phase I Basic financial planning	Phase II Forecast-based planning	Phase III Externally oriented planning	Phase IV Strategic management
Effectiveness of formal business planning				Orchestration of all resources to create competitive advantage
		More effective planning for growth	Increasing response to markets and competition	Strategically chosen planning framework
		Environmental analysis	Thorough situation analysis and competitive assessment	Creative, flexible planning processes
	Operational Control	Multi-year forecasts	Evaluation of strategic alternatives	Supportive value system and climate
	Annual budget	Static allocation resources	Dynamic allocation of resources	
	Functional focus			
Value system	**Meet budget**	**Predict the future**	**Think strategically**	**Create the future**

Source: Frederick W. Gluck, Stephan P. Kaufman, and A. Steven Walleck, "Strategic Management for Competitive Advantage," *Harvard Business Review,* July–August 1980, p. 157. ©1980 by the President and Fellows of Harvard College; all rights reserved. Reprinted by permission of *Harvard Business Review.*

decision. As the time frame is extended, managers tend to seek more sophisticated forecasts and to become aware of their external environment and its effect on their organizations. The resulting multiyear view of the future often improves the effectiveness of the planning process. Two useful results are more effective resource allocation and more timely decisions relating to the organization's long-range competitive position.

As might be suspected, certain problems are associated with phase 2. The new interest in long-term events may conflict with the organizational reward systems, which often focus on short- or intermediate-term performance. Also, the desire for sophisticated forecasts can cause major issues to be buried under masses of data. A very real danger of phase 2 is that the planning process can become merely a slightly altered repeat of the previous year's plan.

Phase 3 Externally Oriented Planning

Organizations progress to phase 3 after they have become frustrated with the forecasting approach emphasized by phase 2. Phase 3 is characterized by the attempt to understand basic marketplace phenomena. The emphasis shifts from perfecting forecasting techniques to being responsive to customers and market shifts. Planners in phase 3 begin to search for new ways to define and satisfy customer needs. At the same time, managers consider altering their current products and services to meet customer needs better. This causes management to take a much more dynamic view of the resource allocation process.

Phase 3 differs from the earlier phases in that businesses usually are formally grouped into strategic business units (SBUs). The SBU managers are asked to engage in strategic planning, which requires that they answer strategic questions about the external environment. The most significant difference of phase 3 is that the corporate planners are expected to generate a number of alternative courses of action for top management. This process signals the beginnings of true "strategic" thinking. It is in phase 3 that top management first begins to evaluate strategic alternatives in a formalized manner. Until this time, such evaluations, if considered at all, were undertaken informally by one or more members of top management. The major weakness of phase 3 is that the planning efforts of the different organizational units are often splintered and not thoroughly integrated.

Phase 4   Strategic Management

Phase 4 is characterized by the merging of strategic planning and management into a single process. The strategic planning process is directly linked to operational decisions. This integrated approach to planning and actions is accomplished through the presence of three elements:

1 *Pervasive strategic thinking.* Managers at all levels have learned to think strategically; all managerial levels, including the supervisory level, are involved in strategic management in some way.

2 *Comprehensive planning process.* The planning process is comprehensive, yet flexible and creative. Special care is taken to ensure that strategic planning does not degenerate into a meaningless bureaucratic, number-crunching exercise.

3 *Supportive value system.* The value system held by top management must establish a supportive climate. It is this value system that reflects the attitude of top management toward such critical issues as teamwork, entrepreneurial spirit, open communication, and the destiny of the organization.

While larger organizations tend to have more sophisticated planning systems, there is certainly nothing to prevent smaller companies from reaching phase 4. Looking at the evolution of strategic management from an historical perspective, phase 1 approximated the state of the art in the 1950s, phase 2 in the 1960s, phase 3 in the 1970s, and phase 4 in the 1980s.

A STRATEGIC MANAGEMENT MODEL

Different organizations may use somewhat different approaches to the strategic management process; fortunately, however, most successful approaches share several common components and a common sequence. Furthermore, the components and sequence can be represented in model form, as shown in Exhibit 2.5. This model is applicable to both single-business and multibusiness firms. As indicated by the categories listed in the center of Exhibit 2.5, the strategic management process has been divided into five major segments:

EXHIBIT 2.5   THE STRATEGIC MANAGEMENT PROCESS

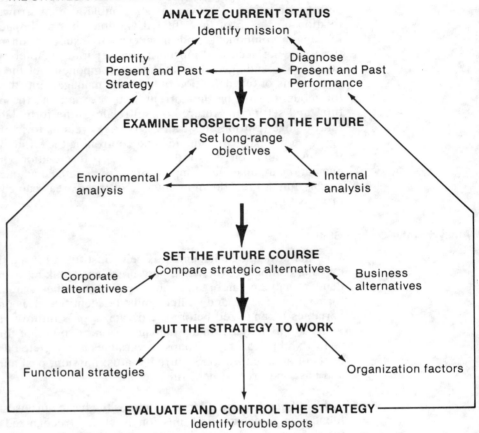

1. Analyzing the current status
2. Examining the prospects for the future
3. Setting the future course
4. Putting the strategy to work
5. Evaluating and controlling the strategy

The logic behind this breakdown is as follows. Any organization must first analyze and clearly understand its current status. Once an organization has a firm grip on its present status, it is in a position to examine its prospects for the future. After its prospects have been identified, the organization must set its future course through careful evaluation and choice of alternatives. In the next stage, the organization implements the chosen strategy. In the final stage, the organization evaluates and controls the selected strategy. It should be noted that the strategic management process is presented as an iterative process, as indicated by the arrows leading from the bottom of the model back to the top.

The implication is that the process is never-ending and requires constant evaluations, updating, and revising. The double-headed arrows indicate a two-way relationship: each of the affected variables has an impact on the other. The four major components and their respective subcomponents are introduced in the following sections. Furthermore, separate chapters in the book are devoted to expanding each of the major components of the model.

In terms of our definition of strategic management, the first three stages of the model (analyzing the current status, examining the prospects for the future, and setting the future course) relate to the formulation of strategy. The fourth stage (putting the strategy to work) relates to implementation of strategy. The fifth stage (evaluating and controlling the strategy) relates to the continuous evaluation of strategy. Strategy formulation, implementation, and evaluation are all equally important for the strategic management process to be successful. A breakdown in any one of these areas can easily cause the entire process to fail.

Analyzing the Current Status

Whether strategic management is being instituted for the first time in a new or existing company, whether a new president is taking over, or whether a student is analyzing an organization from a case, the organization's current performance, mission, and strategy must be identified. It is only logical that these variables be analyzed before the organization's future is mapped out. As obvious as this may be, many managers appear to ignore this step.

In Exhibit 2.5, three groups of variables are depicted as the major determinants of an organization's current status: mission, past and present strategies, and past and present performance.

Identifying Mission   *Mission* defines the basic purposes of the organization. Ideally, an organization's mission is clearly recognized and widely known throughout the organization. Even when this is the case, however, an organization may wish to alter or redefine its mission. Thus an organization should periodically evaluate its mission to ensure that the mission is current. In situations where the mission has not been clearly defined, it is absolutely necessary to do so. In small organizations this normally requires that the owner or owners define exactly what the organization is trying to produce and/or sell and what market or markets it is trying to serve. In large organizations these same issues must be agreed upon by top management and the board of directors.

Identifying Past and Present Strategies   It is a well-known fact that Sears, Roebuck and Company embarked on a conscious strategy to upgrade its quality image in the 1960s. Prior to implementing this new strategy, Sears first had to identify clearly what its strategy had been in the past. In other words, before a strategic change can be developed and implemented, the past and present strategies must be clarified.

General questions to be addressed include the following: Has past strategy been consciously developed? If not, can past history be analyzed to identify what implicit strategy has evolved? If so, has the strategy been recorded in written form? In either case, a strategy or series of strategies, as reflected by the organization's past actions and intentions, should be identified.

Diagnosing Past and Present Performance In order to evaluate how past strategies have worked and to determine whether strategic changes are needed, the organization's performance record must be examined. How is the organization currently performing? How has the organization performed over the last several years? Is the performance trend moving up or down? These are all questions that the strategist must address before attempting to formulate any type of future strategy. Evaluating an organization's performance usually involves some type of in-depth financial analysis and diagnosis. In Exhibit 2.5 an arrow has been drawn from the bottom of the model to present and past performance. This indicates that the present and future performance of an organization is affected by its present and past strategies and that the strategic management process is a never-ending process.

Examining the Prospects for the Future

The first step in looking toward the future is to decide what the long- and intermediate-range objectives should be in light of the current mission. However, these objectives cannot be accurately established without examining the internal and external environments. Thus establishing the long- and intermediate-range objectives and analyzing the internal and external environments are concurrent processes which influence one another. These circular relationships are shown by the two-way arrows in Exhibit 2.5.

Setting Long-Range Objectives Given the mission, what does the organization hope to achieve and accomplish over the long range? In establishing long-range objectives, the emphasis is on corporate- and divisional-level objectives, as opposed to departmental objectives.

The first step is to decide which areas of the organization's business should be covered by objectives. Common choices include sales, market share, costs, product introductions, return on investment, and societal goals. Once the areas for objectives have been decided upon, the next step is to determine the desired magnitudes and associated time frames for accomplishment.

Conducting an Internal Analysis The basic idea in conducting an internal analysis is to perform an objective assessment of the organization's current status. What things does the organization do well? What things does the organization do poorly? From a resource perspective, what are the organization's strengths and weaknesses? Additional areas that should be investigated include the organization's structure and its culture. It is usually desirable to analyze structure in terms of the lines of authority, communication patterns, and work flow. With regard to culture, the first step is usually to identify corporate norms and mores.

As emphasized earlier, the process of setting long-range objectives is influenced by the results of the internal analysis. Similarly, the internal analysis should focus on factors affected by the long-range objectives. Thus there is a circular relationship between these variables.

Assessing the External Environment   An organization's external environment consists of everything outside the organization, but the focus of the assessment is on the external factors that have an impact on the organization's business. Such factors are classified by their proximity to the organization: they are either in its *broad environment* or in its *competitive environment*. Broad environmental factors are somewhat removed from the organization but can still influence it. General economic conditions and social, political, and technological trends represent common factors in the broad environment. Factors in the competitive environment, which is also referred to as the task environment, are close to and come in regular contact with the organization. Stockholders, suppliers, competitors, labor unions, and customers represent members of the competitive environment. The external analysis, like the internal analysis, has a circular relationship with the long-range objectives. This portion of the model concludes the reflective part of the strategic management process. Having analyzed its current status and examined its prospects for the future, the organization is then in a position to consider its future course.

Setting the Future Course

Setting the future course involves generating possible strategic alternatives, based on the mission and long-range objectives, and then selecting the best alternative.

Comparing Strategic Alternatives   The goal in this phase of the process is to identify the feasible strategic alternatives, in light of everything that has been done up to this point, and then to select the best alternative. Given the mission and long-range objectives, what are the different feasible strategic alternatives? The internal and external environmental analyses also place specific limitations on the feasible strategic alternatives. For example, the results of an internal financial analysis could severely limit an organization's options for expansion. Similarly, the results of an external analysis of population trends might also limit an organization's expansion plans. Once a set of feasible alternatives has been defined, the final strategic choice must be made.

The evaluation and final choice of an appropriate strategic alternative involves the integration of the mission, objectives, internal analysis, and external analysis. In this phase an attempt is made to select the overall, or grand, strategy that offers the organization its best chance to achieve its mission and objectives through actions that are compatible with its capacity for risk and its value structure. Once the grand strategy has been identified, additional substrategies must then be selected to support it.

In the case of diversified, multi-industry organizations, comparing strategic alternatives involves assessing the attractiveness of each of the different businesses as well as the overall business mix. The next step is to evaluate specific alternative strategies for each business unit. Thus the emphasis in this phase of the model is on the need for generating strategic alternatives at both the corporate level and the business level.

Putting the Strategy to Work

The fourth section of the model emphasizes the importance of translating planned strategy into organizational actions. Given that the grand strategy and supporting substrategies have been clearly identified, what actions must be taken to implement these strategies? Strategy implementation involves everything that must be done to put the strategy in motion successfully. Necessary actions include determining and implementing the most appropriate organizational structure, developing short-range objectives, and establishing functional strategies.

Implementing Strategy: Organizational Factors   Not only does an organization have a strategic history, but it also has existing structures, policies, and systems. Although each of these factors can change as a result of a new strategy, each must be assessed and dealt with as part of the implementation process.

Although an organization's structure can always be altered, the associated costs may be very high. For example, a reorganization might result in substantial hiring and training costs for newly structured jobs. Thus, from a very practical standpoint, an organization's current structure places certain restrictions on how a strategy should be implemented.

The strategy must fit with current organizational policies, or the conflicting policies must be modified. Often, past policies heavily influence the extent to which future policies can be altered. For example, it has been the policy of the A. T. Cross Company (manufacturers of the world-renowned writing instruments) to unconditionally guarantee its products for life. This policy is well-known and has come to be expected by many of the company's customers. Because of these expectations, it would now be very difficult for Cross to discontinue its guarantee policy.

Similarly, organizational systems that are currently in place can affect how the strategy might best be implemented. These systems can be either formal or informal. Examples include information systems, compensation systems, communication systems, control systems, and planning systems.

Implementing Strategy: Functional Strategies   Functional strategies are the means by which the business strategy is operationalized. Functional strategies outline the specific short-range actions to be taken by the different functional units of the organization (production, marketing, finance, personnel, etc.) in order to implement the business strategy. The purpose of functional strategies is to make the corporate- and business-level strategies a reality.

The formulation of functional strategies plays a major role in determining the feasibility of the corporate- and business-level strategies. If sound functional strategies cannot be formulated and implemented, it may be that the corporate- and/or business-level strategies need to be reworked. As the old saying goes, the functional strategies are the point where "the rubber meets the road."

Evaluating and Controlling the Strategy

After things have been put into motion, the next challenge is to monitor continuously the organization's progress toward its long-range objectives and mission. What types of managerial controls are needed to ensure that acceptable progress is being made? Is the grand strategy working, or should revisions be made? Where are problems likely to occur? The emphasis here is on making the organization's strategists aware of the problems that are likely to occur and of the actions that should be taken if these problems do occur. As mentioned earlier, the arrows looping back up from this last component of the model indicate that the strategic management process is continuous and never-ending.

SUMMARY

All organizations engage in the strategic management process, although not always by design. Organizations that consciously engage in strategic management generally follow some type of formalized process for making decisions and taking actions that affect the direction of the organization. For such organizations, the degree of formality can vary considerably. In general, the more detailed the procedures to be followed, the more formal the process is. Mintzberg's three modes or degrees of formality for making strategy are the entrepreneurial, the adaptive, and the planning modes.

The CEO is the person who has ultimate responsibility for strategic management. The CEO must be personally involved in the strategic management process and he or she must clearly communicate this involvement to other in the organization. The planning staff should primarily serve as coordinators, catalysts, and advisors in the strategic management process. Line managers should be actively involved in the strategic management process by providing inputs to top management and implementing the chosen strategy. The primary responsibilities of the board of directors in the strategic management process are to review the strategy and monitor the process that produces the strategy.

Although strategic management may evolve at varying rates, it almost always evolves through a series of four separate phases: (1) financial-based planning, (2) forecast-based planning, (3) externally oriented planning, and (4) strategic management. Each phase is marked by clear advances over the previous phase in terms of explicit formulation of issues, quality of preparatory staff work, readiness of top management to participate in and guide the process, and effectiveness of implementation.

While different organizations may take somewhat different approaches to the strategic management process, most successful approaches share several common components and a common sequence which can be represented in model form. The model presented in this book divides the strategic management process into five major segments: (1) analyzing the current status of the organization, (2) examining the prospects for the future, (3) setting the future course, (4) putting the strategy to work, and (5) evaluating and controlling the strategy. The logic behind this breakdown is as follows: any organization must first analyze and clearly understand its current status. Once an organization has a firm grip on its present status, it is in a position to examine its future prospects. After its prospects have been identified, the organization must set its future course through careful evaluation and choice of the alternatives. The organization then implements the selected strategy. In the final stage, the organization evaluates and controls the strategy after it has been implemented. Each of these major segments of the strategic management model was introduced and briefly discussed.

CHAPTER 2 REVIEW QUESTIONS

1 What are Mintzberg's three modes for making strategy? Identify, by size, the types of organizations that are most likely to use each mode.
2 What role does the CEO play in the strategic management process?
3 What role does the corporate planner play in strategic management? What role does the line manager play?
4 Describe the role that the board of directors should normally fill in the strategic management process.
5 Name and briefly describe each of the four phases in the evolution of strategic management.
6 What are the variables that are the major determinants of an organization's current status?
7 According to the strategic management model, what are the major factors that must be evaluated in examining the prospects for the future? In what order should these factors be evaluated?

CHAPTER 2 DISCUSSION QUESTIONS

1 Use McKinsey & Company's research on the phases of the evolutionary process to illustrate how the strategic management process develops according to the model presented in Exhibit 2.2.
2 Relate Henry Mintzberg's three modes for making strategy to the formality of the strategic management process.
3 Use your knowledge of a major firm and its CEO (use library sources) to defend or refute the following statement: "The primary responsibility for strategic management lies with top management, specifically the CEO."

CHAPTER 2 REFERENCES

1 Henry Mintzberg, "Strategy-Making in Three Modes," *California Management Review*, Winter 1973, pp. 44–53.
2 George B. Steiner, *Strategic Planning: What Every Manager Must Know*, Free Press, New York, 1979, p. 80.

3 Chester Burger, *The Chief Executive: Realities of Corporate Leadership,* CBI, Boston, 1978, p. 110.

4 Steiner, op. cit., p. 72.

5 Ibid.

6 "The New Breed of Strategic Planner," *Business Week,* September 17, 1984, pp. 62–68.

7 Peter Lorange, *Corporate Planning: An Executive Viewpoint,* Prentice-Hall, Englewood Cliffs, N.J.: 1980, p. 264.

8 Daniel H. Gray, "Uses and Misuses of Strategic Planning," *Harvard Business Review,* January–February 1986, p. 91.

9 "The New Breed of Strategic Planner," op. cit., p. 62.

10 Ahmad Tashakori and William Boulton, "A Look at the Board's Role in Planning," *Journal of Business Strategy,* Winter 1983, p. 66.

11 "The Job Nobody Wants," *Business Week,* September 8, 1986, p. 56.

12 Ibid.

13 Kenneth R. Andrews, "Director's Responsibility for Corporate Strategy," *Harvard Business Review,* November–December 1980, p. 30.

Journal of Business Strategy, Fall 1986, pp. 87–95.

15 Andrews, op. cit.

16 Ibid, p. 30.

17 Joseph Rosenstein, "Why Don't U.S. Boards Get More Involved in Strategy?" *Long Range Planning,* June 1987, p. 33.

18 Andrews, op. cit., p. 31.

19 Kenneth R. Andrews, "Corporate Strategy as a Vital Function of the Board," *Harvard Business Review,* November–December 1981, p. 182.

20 Frederick W. Gluck, Stephen P. Kaufman, and A. Steven Walleck, "Strategic Management for Competitive Advantage," *Harvard Business Review,* July–August 1980, pp. 154–161. Much of this section is drawn from this work and from the Blass synopsis of this work, Walter P. Blass, "Optimizing the Corporate Planning Function," in Kenneth J. Albert (ed.), *The Strategic Management Handbook,* McGraw-Hill, New York, 1983, pp. 6-4–6-8.

21 Ibid., p. 155.

GENERIC STRATEGY ALTERNATIVES

LEARNING OBJECTIVES

After studying this chapter, the reader should be able to:

1 Introduce and define the different possible strategy alternatives at both the corporate level and the business level
2 Discuss the pros and cons of the different strategy alternatives
3 Present numerous examples of the way in which different strategy alternatives are used by actual companies

CHAPTER OUTLINE

GENERIC CORPORATE STRATEGY ALTERNATIVES
Growth Strategies
  • Concentration • Vertical Integration • Diversification • Vehicles for Realizing Growth
Stability Strategies
  • Harvesting
Defensive Strategies
  • Turnaround • Divestiture • Liquidation • Filing for Bankruptcy
  • Becoming a Captive
Combination Strategies
GENERIC BUSINESS-LEVEL STRATEGIES
Overall Cost Leadership
Differentiation of the Product or Service
Focus of the Product or Service

SUMMARY
REVIEW QUESTIONS
DISCUSSION QUESTIONS
REFERENCES

There are numerous distinctly identifiable basic strategies that an organization may choose to follow. Which of these is most appropriate naturally depends upon several factors, such as the mission and long-range objectives, the growth rates of the related markets, and the competitive position of the company. The most appropriate strategy may, and often does, change from time to time. The purpose of this chapter is to introduce and define the different possible strategy alternatives at both the corporate level and the business level. The selection of the most appropriate strategy for a given set of situations cannot be made until the specifics of the situation, as outlined in the strategic management model, have been determined and evaluated. This is done in subsequent chapters of this book.

GENERIC CORPORATE STRATEGY ALTERNATIVES

Keep in mind that corporate strategy is concerned with which businesses an organization will be in and how its resources will be distributed among those businesses. Numerous corporate strategy alternatives exist, which can all be placed into one of four basic categories: (1) growth, (2) stability, (3) defensive, or (4) a combination of the previous three. Exhibit 3.1 presents a brief comparison of the different categories.

EXHIBIT 3.1   FOUR BASIC CATEGORIES OF STRATEGIC ALTERNATIVES

Strategy	Frequency of use, %*	Goals	Uses
Growth Concentration Vertical integration Diversification	54.2	To increase sales and earnings	High market growth, economic prosperity
Stability	9.2	To increase profitability	In mature industry, stable environment
Defensive Turnaround Divestment Liquidation	7.5	Survival, to cut costs and eliminate losses	In crisis, severe losses, etc.
Combination	28.7	To increase earnings and cut costs	In economic transition, multidivision companies

*From a study of 358 Fortune companies over 45 years, as reported in William F. Glueck, *Business Policy and Strategic Management*, 3d ed. McGraw-Hill, New York, 1980, p. 290.
Source: Adapted from Donald F. Harvey, *Business Policy and Strategic Management*, Merrill, Columbus, Ohio, p. 131.

Growth Strategies

As shown in Exhibit 3.1, growth-oriented strategies are used by U.S. businesses more often than all the other strategies put together. The growth rates experienced by some companies are phenomenal. For example, the hundred fastest-growing smaller (sales or revenues were less than $25 million in 1976) publicly held companies in the United States in 1987, as ranked by *Inc.* magazine, all experienced an average growth in sales of more than 1200 percent over the previous 5 years.[1] Why is it that so many companies follow a growth strategy? While there is no single reason, several different possibilities exist:

(1) Growth has been ingrained in Americans as "the path of success." Since childhood, many Americans have held the dream of starting and expanding their own businesses. This has always been, and still is, viewed as the quickest way to get rich.

(2) Managers are often given bonuses, salary increases, and continued employment for achieving growth in sales and profits. For example, it is not unusual for a bonus based on growth in profits to be written into a top-level manager's employment contract (see Example 3.1).

(3) Managers who did not start, and may not even own, a significant interest in the company want to be remembered as having made significant contributions to the company. More often than not, making "significant contributions" is interpreted as having expanded the company.

(4) Pressures from investors and others with a financial interest in the company stress high growth. Stockholders, security analysts, and bankers like to invest in and support growth-oriented companies.

(5) A belief exists that the company must grow if it is to survive. In certain volatile industries, an organization does not have the option of remaining stable if it is to survive.

EXAMPLE 3.1

Relating Executive Pay to Earnings

Increasingly boards of directors are tying executive incentive pay and bonuses directly to a company's earnings. For example, Reebok International's chairman, Paul Fireman, gets 5% of any pretax corporate profits exceeding $20 million. In 1986 that amounted to a $12.7 million bonus on top of his $363,931 base pay. Similarly, Disney's Chief Executive, Michael D. Eisner, receives an annual bonus of 2% of the company net income exceeding a 9% return on equity. In 1986 that amounted to a $2.6 million bonus on top of his $750,000 salary.

Source: "Executive Pay: Who Got What in '86," *Business Week*, May 4, 1987, pp. 50–58.

Several different generic strategies fall into the growth category. The most frequently encountered and clearly identifiable of the growth strategies are discussed in the following sections.

Concentration A *concentration strategy* is one that focuses on a single product or service or on a small number of closely related products or services. This is the strategy followed when an organization concentrates on extending the sales of its current business. The list of companies that initially became successful by following a concentration strategy includes Coca-Cola, Coors, Kellogg, and McDonald's.

Following a concentration strategy does not necessarily mean that an organization must continue to do the same things in exactly the same ways. It does, however, mean that whatever is done will be related directly to the current product(s) or service(s). As evidenced by the previously cited examples, a concentration strategy does not keep a company from growing. However, it does limit the types of growth opportunities that can be pursued. This usually results in a slower but more controlled and stable growth. There are basically three approaches to pursuing a concentration strategy—market development, product development, and horizontal integration.

• *Market development*. The thrust under a market development approach is to expand the markets of the current business. This can be done by gaining a larger share of the current market, expanding into new geographic areas, or attracting new market segments. Coca-Cola has continued to follow a market development strategy since its inception. It amassed its impressive market share through large-scale advertising programs, and it has continued to expand into new geographic areas (most recently, international markets such as China). Similarly, Dr. Pepper sought a new market segment by promoting the idea of heating its product and drinking it "hot."

• *Product development*. The thrust under a product development approach is to alter the basic product or service or to add a closely related product or service that can be sold through the current marketing channels. Successful product development strategies often capitalize on the favorable reputation of the company or related products. The telephone companies' introduction of numerous styles of phones and additional services, such as call forwarding and call holding, is an example of a product development strategy. Yet another example would be Levi-Strauss's decision to make and sell designer clothes.[2]

• *Horizontal integration*. Horizontal integration occurs when an organization adds one or more businesses that produce similar products or services and that are operating at the same stage in the product-marketing chain. Almost all horizontal integration is accomplished by buying another organization in the same business. Unilever's acquisition of Chesebrough-Pond's and International Paper's acquisition of Hammermill Paper in 1986 are both examples of horizontal integration. The major advantage of horizontal integration is that it provides immediate access to new markets and, many times, eliminates a competitor.

A concentration strategy usually has the advantage of low initial risk because the organization already has much of the knowledge and many of the resources necessary to compete in the marketplace. A second advantage is that a concentration strategy allows the organization to focus its attention on doing a small number of things extremely well. One does not have to look very far to find examples of companies that have failed because they spread their talents and resources in too many different directions. The major drawback to a concentration strategy is that it places all or most of the organization's resources in the same basket. If sudden changes occur in the industry, the organization can suffer significantly. One of the most obvious examples in this area is the U.S. railroad industry. Because the railroads had always followed a concentration strategy, they were severely hurt by the introduction of the automobile and airplane.

Vertical Integration *Vertical integration* occurs when a business moves into areas that serve either as suppliers to or as customers for its current products or services. If a business integrates by moving into an area that serves as a supplier, the process is referred to as *backward integration*. A decision by Coca-Cola to enter into the manufacture of glass bottles would be an example of backward integration. Example 3.2 describes backward vertical integration at Anheuser-Busch. If a business integrates by moving into an area that serves as a customer or user of its products or services, the process is referred to as *forward integration*. The decision of the Florsheim Shoe Company to establish retail stores in many of the nation's malls is an example of forward integration.

There are many reasons why a business might want to follow a vertical integration strategy. The primary reason for utilizing backward integration is to

---

EXAMPLE 3.2

Backward Vertical Integration at Anheuser-Busch

Anheuser-Busch is a company committed to growth. To ensure that growth is maintained along with a competitive edge, Busch uses a backward vertical integration strategy. The company acquired container manufacturing facilities about 1966, brewing ingredients production capability in 1974, a container recovery corporation in 1978, and a metal labeling factory in 1979. Busch produces about 40% of its own cans as well as a significant portion of its malt and labeling. The result is greater control over costs and an increased knowledge of the economics of the brewing business. As a result, industry analysts rate Anheuser-Busch as having the highest per-barrel profit in the industry. This strategy has helped Anheuser-Busch strengthen its leadership position in the beer industry. For example, Anheuser-Busch experienced a 5.8% sales increase in 1984 while industry sales fell .8%.

Source: Annual report, Anheuser-Busch Company, Inc., 1966, 1974, 1975, 1978, 1979, 1981, 1984, and "The Five Best Managed Companies," *Dun's Business Month,* December 1982, p. 48.

ensure the availability and quality of supplies. For example, if Coca-Cola were to produce its own bottles, it would have much more control over availability and quality. A second frequently encountered reason for engaging in backward integration is to control costs and improve overall profits.

Similarly, a primary reason for following forward integration is to realize additional profit potential. For example, A. G. Bass, the manufacturer of the famous Bass Weejuns and other sport shoes, has recently opened retail stores. Another reason for engaging in forward integration is to ensure quality of the final product. Truett Cathy, the founder of the fast-food chicken chain, Chic-fil-A, Inc., initially sold his chicken through other restaurants. The basic agreement was that Chic-fil-A, Inc., would provide the chicken, a special batter, and the cooking method. Much to Mr. Cathy's disappointment, many of the restaurants took shortcuts and did not carefully follow the prescribed cooking method. The result was that the quality of the chicken suffered. Subsequently, Mr. Cathy withdrew from this approach and began opening his own retail outlets. Tandy Corporation achieved increased profits and product quality at Radio Shack through forward vertical integration, as described in Example 3.3

The primary reason why vertical integration is not pursued by a great many firms is that it usually requires a significant financial commitment and managerial talents that organizations may not possess. For example, not many firms have the financial means that were required for the vertical integration by Anheuser-Busch, described in Example 3.2.

EXAMPLE 3.3

Forward Vertical Integration at Radio Shack

Charles D. Tandy, founder of the Tandy Corporation, and master marketer, began to implement a forward vertical integration strategy soon after acquiring the Radio Shack chain in the mid-1950s. Because he was interested in long-term growth and the bottom line, Mr. Tandy set out to make Radio Shack stores a more reliable and profitable retail outlet of the Tandy line of electronic products than its competition (small independent retailers). As of 1985, Tandy had 6069 company-owned stores and 3048 dealer/franchise locations in 83 countries. Radio Shack outlets carry a broad range of products from stereos to microcomputers, walkie-talkies, spare parts, and tools for hobbyists. The company also owns 226 technical repair centers nationwide. This forward vertical integration strategy has paid off in that Radio Shack is renowned as one of the (if not the) best in the consumer electronics industry.

Source: "Five Best-Managed Companies," *Dun's Business Month,* December 1981, p. 76; and Annual Report, Tandy Corporation, 1985.

Diversification *Diversification* occurs when an organization moves into areas that are clearly differentiated from its current businesses. The reasons for embarking on a diversification strategy can be many and varied, but one of the most frequently encountered is to spread the risk so that the organization is not totally subject to the whims of any one given product or industry. For example, as shown in Exhibit 3.2, both Philip Morris and R. J. Reynolds have diversified significantly since the time that cigarettes were first linked to cancer. A second reason to diversify is that management may believe the move represents an unusually attractive opportunity, especially when compared with other possible growth strategies. Possible reasons for this attractiveness could be that the markets for current products and services are saturated or, if current markets are not saturated, that the profit potential of diversification looks greater than that of expanding the current business. A third reason to diversify is that the new area may be especially intriguing or challenging to management. A fourth reason why diversification can be attractive is to balance out seasonal and cyclical fluctuations in product demand.

Most diversification strategies can be classified as either concentric diversification or conglomerate diversification. *Concentric diversification* occurs when the diversification is in some way related to, but clearly differentiated from, the organization's current business. *Conglomerate diversification* occurs when the firm diversifies into an area(s) totally unrelated to the organization's current business.

Concentric Diversification The basic difference between a concentric diversification strategy and a concentration strategy is that a concentric diversification strategy involves expansion into a related, but distinct, area whereas concentration involves expansion of the current business. A concentric diversification can be related through products, markets, or technology. Coca-Cola's entry into the orange juice business through its purchase of Minute

EXHIBIT 3.2   DIVERSIFICATION BY MAJOR TOBACCO COMPANIES

	Percentage of operating revenues	
	1972	1986
Philip Morris		
Tobacco related	84	50
Food products	0	38
Beer	10	12
Other	6	0
R. J. Reynolds*		
Tobacco	83	37
Foods and beverages	0	63
Other	17	0

*Changed name to RJR Nabisco, Inc., in 1985 following the acquisition of Nabisco Brands, Inc.
Source: Annual Report, Philip Morris, 1972, 1986; and Annual Report, R. J. Reynolds, 1972, 1986.

Maid is an example of a product-related diversification. Although orange juice is clearly different from carbonated soft drinks, they are both consumer beverages. Anheuser-Busch's introduction of Eagle Brand snack foods is an example of a diversification based on related markets. Beer and snack foods have no relationship as far as product characteristics, but they are both consumed by many of the same customers. The decision of 3M to enter the sandpaper business was based on the company's knowledge of coating and bonding technology. Holiday Inns, Inc., combined gaming with its hotel business, as described in Example 3.4

A concentric diversification strategy can have several advantages. The most obvious is that it allows the organization to build on its expertise in a related area. It also can have the advantage of spreading the organization's risks. In their study to identify common characteristics of successful U.S. companies, Thomas Peters and Robert Waterman, Jr., concluded, "Organizations that do branch out but stick very close to their knitting outperform the others."[3]

Conglomerate Diversification   Most conglomerate diversifications are based on the rationale that expansion into the area under consideration has a very attractive profit potential. Many large companies, such as ITT, Gulf & Western, Litton Industries, and Textron, were built during the 1950s and 1960s by following a conglomerate diversification strategy. More recently, however, conglomerate diversification strategies have received considerable criticism and have fallen into general disfavor.

EXAMPLE 3.4

Concentric Diversification at Holiday Inn

Holiday Inns, Inc., is the world's largest innkeeper with the best occupancy rate in the industry in their 300,000 + rooms throughout the world. Green is the color that is associated with their signs and other logos and green is also the color of the gaming tables and money in their casinos. Michael Rose, Chairman of the Board and CEO, reported in 1981: "We got into gaming mainly to diversify from hotels but we wanted to get into something where our technical expertise was relevant....That's synergy, taking two elements that are somewhat similar and combining them to make something greater than the sum of the parts." Holiday Inns, Inc., is in all the major gaming markets: Reno, Lake Tahoe, Las Vegas, and Atlantic City. Since first getting into the gaming business in 1978, Holiday Inns reports contributions to earnings as follows: 1979—7%, 1980—14%, 1981—21%, 1982—28%, 1983—40%,1984—37%, 1985—30%. Rose says: "Again it was synergy; it was something we could understand fairly rapidly."

Source: Steven S. Anreder, "Color Me Green," *Barron's*, Dec. 21, 1981, pp. 29–30; and Annual Reports, Holiday Inns, Inc., 1982, 1985, and 1986.

Not only have some well-known conglomerates (such as LTV and Bangor Punta) experienced difficulties but research studies have concluded that conglomerate diversification is not generally as profitable as other forms of growth.[4] This is not surprising, as conglomerate diversification might involve getting into not only an unrelated business but also one which the organization knows very little about. A recent study of 33 large, prestigious U.S. companies over the 1950–1986 period found that these companies ended up divesting a startling 74 percent of all unrelated acquisitions.[5]

Evidence shows that conglomerate firms which limit their diversification to three or four major business categories are generally more successful than those that don't.[6]

There is little doubt that the right diversification strategy, whether concentric or conglomerate, can produce profitable results. However, experience, supported by research, tends to favor concentric diversification over conglomerate diversification especially when the diversification controls the sharing of activities (such as distribution channels) and the transferring of skills among the old and new businesses.[7]

Vehicles for Realizing Growth   All the previously discussed growth strategies can be implemented either through internal growth or through acquisition, merger, or joint venture.

Internal Growth vs. Acquisition or Merger   When a company expands its current market share, its markets, or its products through the use of internal resources, *internal growth* takes place. An *acquisition* occurs when one company purchases the assets of another and absorbs them into its own operations. A *merger* occurs when two or more companies combine into one company. In an acquisition one company clearly acquires another; in a merger neither participant acquires the other, but rather both companies merge together, combining operations.

Whether it is wiser to grow through internal development of new activities or through acquisition or merger depends on many factors. Internal growth is generally slower and less traumatic for the organization. It usually takes place over an extended period of time, allowing time to adjust to the change. Of course, if an organization is in a particular hurry to enter an area, the shorter time required by an acquisition or a merger might be considered an advantage. Growth through acquisition or merger can also help avoid or eliminate many barriers to entry, such as patents, costly promotions, and broad recognition. Although exceptions do exist, internal growth is generally less risky than an acquisition or a merger. This is because growth, through internal means, is incremental and can be terminated at almost any time. Thus, if an organization determines that an expansion is not working out, the project can be dropped. On the other hand, growth through acquisition or merger is not incremental, and it requires a total financial commitment from the start.

Generally speaking, internal growth strategies work well for companies whose products or services are in the early or middle stages of the product-service life cycle.[8] Most firms following a concentration strategy via product or market development would fall into the latter stages of the life cycle. As mentioned earlier, almost all horizontal integration is through acquisition or merger. Growth through vertical integration can be obtained by internal means or by acquisition or merger. The best method is entirely dependent on the situation. Growth through concentric diversification is similar to growth through vertical integration because it can be successfully realized either by internal means or by acquisition or merger. Entry into new, unrelated businesses (conglomerate diversification) is usually more successful through acquisition than through internal growth.[9] The main problem with trying to develop new businesses through internal means is that the organization usually does not possess the core skills required. Because of this, it is usually better to enter an unrelated business through an acquisition or a merger. Exhibit 3.3 summarizes the appropriateness of growth through internal versus external (acquisition or merger) means. Acquisitions and mergers are discussed further in Chapter 9.

Joint Venture   A *joint venture* occurs when two or more organizations pool their resources for a given project or a business product. There are a number of reasons why a joint venture may be attractive to the respective participants:

1 By pooling their resources, the organizations may be capable of doing things that they could not do separately.

2 By joining with another firm or firms, the companies share the risks of the venture.

3 Certain government-sponsored projects have aggressively encouraged joint ventures for the purpose of involving minority businesses.

4 International companies are often encouraged by host countries to enter into joint ventures with local companies.

A joint venture can be on either a temporary or a permanent basis. For example, a construction company might enter into a temporary joint venture with another construction company for purposes of erecting a specific building. On the other hand, two or more companies might enter into a permanent arrangement such as jointly owning a business. Example 3.5 describes a joint venture between General Motors and Toyota.

As indicated by item 4, joint ventures are especially popular between firms in different countries. What makes joint ventures so attractive in the international setting is that both the host firm and the entering firm benefit. Under a joint venture, the host firm does not have to fear that foreigners are taking

EXHIBIT 3.3   DESIRABILITY OF INTERNAL GROWTH VS. GROWTH THROUGH ACQUISITION OR MERGER

Generic growth strategy	Generally preferred method of growth
Concentration	Internal
Vertical integration	Internal, or acquisition or merger
Concentric diversification	Internal, or acquisition or merger
Conglomerate diversification	Acquisition or merger

EXAMPLE 3.5

General Motors/Toyota Joint Venture

In February 1983, General Motors and Toyota Motor Company inked an agreement to jointly produce 200,000 subcompact cars per year for Chevrolet at GM's then idle Fremont, California assembly plant. In GM's initial announcement Chairman Roger Smith said the new car "...is not a copy of any car being offered in this country. It will be a specific design for Chevrolet." Smith also predicted that the joint venture would provide as many as 12,000 U.S. jobs, about 3,000 at the Fremont plant with the rest at support facilities. The initial agreement was for a period of 12 years and was to begin in late 1984. The car was planned for 50 per cent local content and 50 per cent foreign content.

Source: Automotive News, February 21, 1983, p. 1.

---

over, and the entering firm is afforded much more confidence that its products and services will be accepted. An additional benefit for both parties is that less individual investment is required. It is not surprising that joint ventures in the international setting work best when the cultures and economic conditions of the different partners are similar.[10]

Stability Strategies

In certain situations an organization may desire to pursue a *stability,* or *neutral, strategy*. This occurs most often when an organization is satisfied with its current situation and wants to maintain the status quo. A stability strategy is not a "do-nothing" approach; rather, it is a "do-the-same-thing" approach. Under a stability strategy, a company makes few changes in its products, markets, and production methods. Growth is possible under a stability strategy; however, when growth exists, it will be slow, methodical, and nonaggressive. Although stability strategies do not usually produce glamorous or news-making results, many companies use a stability strategy at some point in their corporate life cycle. Probably more organizations elect a stability strategy by default than by any conscious decision process. Specific reasons for using a stability strategy are outlined below:

1 The company is doing well and subscribes to the theory: "If it works, don't fix it."

2 The company is performing at an acceptable level or better and management does not want to be bothered by the additional hassles often associated with growth. This attitude is found especially in small, privately owned organizations.

3 "Staying the course" often minimizes the risk taken by the company.

Change inherently is accompanied by a certain degree of risk, and this can be minimized by not changing.

4 Managers become so caught up in their routines and in the way they have always done things that they never even consider doing things differently.

5 Management believes that the prospects for growth are low but that the company can maintain its present position.

6 The company has exhausted its financial or managerial resources through rapid growth and must "regroup" before a new round of growth can begin.

Small, privately owned companies make up the largest group of firms likely to adopt a stability strategy. These companies are not subject to pressures for growth from outside stockholders. Another potential group consists of large, dominant companies in mature industries. The goal of these companies is usually to maintain their current position. A third category includes regulated industries such as alcoholic beverages, pharmaceuticals, tobacco products, nuclear energy, and public utilities. Typically, companies in highly regulated industries are limited to a stability strategy by law. It should be pointed out that a stability strategy is often employed only for a relatively short period of time. For example, a company may temporarily opt for a stability strategy to "catch its breath" following a period of rapid growth. Example 3.6 describes a company that has followed a stability strategy for years.

Harvesting   Most products and services eventually reach a point where future growth appears doubtful or not cost-effective. This may be because of

---

EXAMPLE 3.6

Stability Strategy at E. L. McIlheney—The Maker of Tobasco Sauce

Tobasco Sauce, first produced commercially in 1868 by E. L. McIlheney & Company, has been manufactured and marketed in much the same way since the company's first factory opened in 1905. The overall strategy taken by the family firm has been one of stability. In fact, a new factory was not added until 1980. Between 1918 and 1928 McIlheney consolidated its position through various legal actions fighting use of the name, Tobasco, and label by rivals. By 1931, the name and label were patented and remain uniquely their own. The sauce's ingredients, recipe, and the way the sauce is manufactured (bottling, labeling, packaging, and materials handling) and distributed have remained stable. The company controls production of the basic ingredients and the formula so quality control is no problem. McIlheney has operated in international markets since the beginning. As a result of this stability strategy, Tobasco Sauce has a 95% share of the market. Only one price increase was made between 1928 and 1980!

Source: Phil Patton, "Tobasco Sauce: Hot Peppers and History in Every Bottle," *Companion*, July 1977, pp. 8–11.

new competition, changes in consumer preferences, or some other similar factor. When this occurs, organizations often attempt to "harvest" as much as they can from the product or service. The usual approach is to limit additional investment and expenses and to maximize short-term profit and cash flow. Ideally, organizations using a harvesting strategy will maintain market share at least over the short run. A harvesting strategy should be considered under the following conditions:[11]

1 The business is in a saturated or declining market.
2 The business's current market share is small, and it is not cost-effective to try to increase it.
3 The profit prospects are not especially attractive.
4 The organization has more attractive uses for any freed-up resources.
5 A decrease in expenses and investment will not cause a sharp decline in sales.
6 The business is not a major contributor of sales, stability, or prestige to the organization.

Naturally, the more of the above characteristics that are present, the more likely that the business is a candidate for harvesting.

Defensive Strategies

Defensive strategies, sometimes referred to as *retrenchment strategies*, are used when a company wants or needs to reduce its operations. Most often, defensive strategies are used to reverse a negative trend or to overcome a crisis or problem situation. Consequently, defensive strategies usually are chosen as a short-term solution or because no better alternative exists. Specific reasons for using defensive strategies include:

1 The company is having financial problems. These problems can stem from the fact that all or only certain parts of the organization are doing poorly.
2 The company forecasts hard times ahead. This can be caused by such factors as new competitors entering the market, new products, or changes in government regulations.
3 Owners either get tired of the business or have an opportunity to profit substantially by selling.

Defensive strategies include turnaround, divestiture, liquidation, filing for bankruptcy, and becoming a captive.

Turnaround A *turnaround strategy* is designed to reverse a negative trend and to get the organization back on the track to profitability. Turnaround strategies usually try to reduce operating costs, either by cutting "excess fat" and operating more efficiently or by reducing the size of operations. Specific actions that can be taken to operate more efficiently include eliminating or cutting back employee compensation and/or benefits, replacing higher-paid employees with lower-paid employees, leasing rather than buying equipment, reducing expense accounts, and even cutting back marketing efforts. Examples of ways to reduce the size of operations include eliminating low-margin or unprofitable products, selling buildings or equipment, laying off employees, and dropping low-margin customers. Companies that employ a turnaround strategy are usually forced into it and do so with the hope that it will be only a temporary measure until things improve. Example 3.7 describes how Polaroid has employed a turnaround strategy.

Divestiture A *divestiture* occurs when an organization sells or divests itself of a business or part of a business. There are many reasons why an organization may adopt a divestiture strategy, but probably the most frequently encountered one is that a previous diversification did not work out. For example, Singer Company, the maker of sewing machines, went on a diversification binge in the 1960s and early 1970s. Heavily laden with debt and a number of poorly fitting acquisitions, Singer subsequently divested itself of a dozen different businesses between 1975 and 1979.[12]

Certain businesses may have an indefensible market position, poor profitability, or anemic growth prospects.[13] In such cases, divestiture may be nec-

---

EXAMPLE 3.7

Turnaround Strategy at Polaroid

What can a company do to rebound from midlife crisis? Polaroid, the picture-in-a-minute pioneer, has revived with a hot product and a new emphasis on marketing. Now it is betting on floppy disks and electronic cameras.

Not long ago, consumers had grown disenchanted with instant photography, and Polaroid sales suffered from a bad case of miniaturization. Now the company suddenly is up and moving again. Revenues for the first nine months of 1986 rose 29% to $1.1 billion, and profits more than quintupled to $64 million. The turnaround strategy has the following elements:

1 Reduce the workforce from 20,000 to 13,000.
2 Reorganize the company into three profit centers (consumers, industrial, and magnetics).
3 Create an entrepreneurial atmosphere by paying profit-based bonuses to the rank and file employees.
4 Rebuild morale—the CEO emphasizes his willingness to listen to new ideas.
5 Insist on a more sophisticated approach to marketing.
6 Introduce new products such as the Spectra camera, floppy disks for personal computers that will hold much more information than hard disks, an electronic still camera, and the Freeze Frame which can make an instant photographic print from any scene on a videotape.

Wall Street must have had these events in focus when Polaroid stock jumped 55% over a 12-month period.

Source: "How Polaroid Flashed Back," *Fortune*, February 16, 1987, pp. 72–74.

essary for survival. Sometimes a company's situation has deteriorated to the point that the only chance for survival is to sell major components and thereby raise sufficient capital to put the remaining parts on firm footing. Baldwin-United was forced to sell major parts of the company, including the original piano division, in 1983 in hopes of raising enough capital to shore up the remaining business.[14]

Sometimes companies successfully fend off an unfriendly takeover attempt by buying up large blocks of stock. Often this leaves the company with unacceptably high levels of debt. The solution is then to sell some of the company's assets. Example 3.8 discusses why Goodyear Tire and Rubber Company has had to sell certain assets.

A final reason for engaging in divestiture is government antitrust action—or fear of such action. American Telephone & Telegraph (AT&T) was forced by the courts to break up into eight separate companies as of January 1, 1984. This was the country's largest divestiture ever and one which AT&T calculates cost it $1.23 billion.[15]

Often, the decision to divest a business is very difficult for management to make. Divestiture is frequently interpreted as a sign of failure or even mismanagement. This is especially true when a divestiture decision is faced by the same management team that either started up or acquired the business in question. For this reason, many divestment strategies are immediately preceded or instigated by changes in top management. For example, the divestitures at Singer Company were instigated shortly after Joseph B. Flavin took over as chair and chief executive officer in 1975.[16] Similarly, when Martin S. Davis took over Gulf & Western Industries in 1982, he immediately dumped twenty-five businesses.[17] Immediately after taking over as chief executive of RJR Nabisco, Inc., in January 1987, Ross Johnson sold off the company's

EXAMPLE 3.8

The Costs of Fending Off a Takeover Attempt

In November 1986 Goodyear Tire and Rubber Company fought off a takeover raid by Sir James Goldsmith, the Anglo-French financier. Goodyear was able to fend off Goldsmith by buying out his stake and 41 percent of its other shareholders at a cost of nearly $2.7 billion. In order to finance this enormous debt, Robert E. Mercer, Goodyear's chairman, is selling off most of the company's nontire operations. Sell off candidates include Celeron Corporation, its blimp-making aerospace subsidiary, a wheelmaker, an Arizona resort hotel, and a recently completed $1 billion pipeline that stretches from California to West Texas.

Source: James B. Stewart and Philip Rerzin, "Sir James Goldsmith, as Enigmatic as Ever, Bails Out of Goodyear," *The Wall Street Journal,* November 21, 1986, pp. 1, 19; and Subrata N. Chakravarty, "Merci, Jimmy," *Forbes,* June 15, 1987, pp. 114–116.

Heublein, Inc. wine and spirits business. Johnson has hinted that other divestitures may be coming.[18]

Liquidation *Liquidation* occurs when an entire company is either sold or dissolved. The decision to sell or dissolve may come by choice or force. When liquidation comes by choice, it can be because the owners are tired of the business or are near retirement. Similarly, the chance to "get rich quick" has lured many owners of small, privately held organizations into selling. In other situations, management may have a negative view of the organization's future potential and, therefore, desire to sell while the business can still fetch a good price.

When an organization is forced to sell out, or to liquidate its assets, the decision often occurs because of a deteriorated financial condition. Obviously, such circumstances leave the seller in a weak bargaining position. Liquidation of assets is usually a last-resort measure and generally is forced by an organization's financial backers. Example 3.9 describes the situation surrounding the liquidation of the DeLorean Motor Company.

Filing for Bankruptcy *Filing for bankruptcy* under Chapter 11 of the Federal Bankruptcy Act has recently emerged as a type of defensive strategy. The Bankruptcy Reform Act, which took effect on October 1, 1979, was the first major alteration of the bankruptcy law in 40 years. Chapter 11 of the act allows a company to protect itself from creditors and from enforcement of executory contracts, which legally are those not yet completed, including labor contracts. The reasoning behind Chapter 11 is that a company should have an opportunity to rehabilitate itself and avoid insolvency. The degree of financial soundness which may prevent a company from filing bankruptcy under Chapter 11 is established by the bankruptcy court on an individual case-by-case basis. A prime factor used by several companies in the decision to file for bankruptcy under Chapter 11 is the desire to void current labor contracts which management feels are "onerous and burdensome" to the point of threatening the solvency of the company. Many people believe that this was the principal reason Continental Airlines filed for bankruptcy under Chapter 11 in September 1983. Another reason for filing for bankruptcy under Chapter 11, demonstrated by the Manville Corporation in 1982, is to protect the company from lawsuits. Example 3.10 describes the situation leading to Manville's decision.

Most companies that file for bankruptcy under Chapter 11 eventually return to operation.[19] Some return in a different form, while others return in the same business but under a new name.

Becoming a Captive Becoming a captive of another organization occurs when an independently owned organization allows another organization's management to make certain decisions for it in return for a guarantee that the managing organization will buy a certain amount of the captive's product or service. More often than not, such arrangements are made between a small to medium-sized manufacturer or supplier and a larger retailer. A captive organization may give up decisions in the areas of sales, marketing, product design, and even personnel. A company can make a conscious decision to do

---

EXAMPLE 3.9

Liquidation of the DeLorean Motor Company

John Z. DeLorean, former "golden boy" at General Motors, seemed to have everything he had always wanted. He owned 82% of the DeLorean Motor Company and was selling his $22,000 stainless steel, gull-winged sports car for $26,000. By March 1982, everything was a disaster and he was lucky to sell the few cars he could get his hands on to a liquidator for $8,000 to $13,500 apiece.

Great Britain provided $115 million in grants, loans, and equity plus unlimited access to other funds when an agreement was reached to produce the cars in Belfast. Bank of America provided financing to ship the cars to waiting dealers. Show business figures like Johnny Carson and Sammy Davis, Jr., invested in the American dream. But by February 1982, the plant was in receivership and the survival of the company hinged on whether or not DeLorean would manage a public stock offering. A whole series of disasters led up to the final scenario—bad weather, recession, but most of all mismanagement on the part of the president, chairman, major stockholder, and founder, DeLorean. In order to break even, forecasts projected sales of 10,000 with a 12,000 per year maximum market forecast. DeLorean pushed production up to 80 cars per day or 20,000 per year with untrained workers and not enough new orders. The result was insolvency and cars which spent more time at the repair shop than in the new owner's garage.

Ignoring all constraints, John DeLorean spent most of his time on private projects and schemes. Defaulting on his Bank of America funding for car delivery and refusing to reimburse the dealers for mounting repair bills was the last straw. Arrogance, bad management, and alleged criminal activity took the company out of John DeLorean's hands. The result was liquidation of what had been considered a dream-come-true enterprise.

Source: Ann Morrison, "How DeLorean Dashed His Dream," *Fortune*, May 3, 1982, pp. 140–142, 144ff.

---

business as a captive, or it can become a captive over a period of time (the company does more and more business with one other company until it no longer has a choice about becoming a captive). Although becoming a captive can work out well for both parties, it usually occurs either by default or because of a long and gradual increase in the dependence of one company on another. Once a company has become a captive, it is very difficult to break away from the controlling company.

Combination Strategies

A *combination strategy* is used when an organization simultaneously employs different strategies for different organizational units. As was shown in Exhibit

---

EXAMPLE 3.10

Why the Manville Corporation Filed for Bankruptcy under Chapter 11

Manville Corporation and 19 of its subsidiaries filed separate petitions for bankruptcy (Chapter 11) on August 26, 1982. Although by 1981 asbestos accounted for just 6½ percent of total revenue, Manville had been the world's largest producer for 50 years. At the time of the petition, the corporation faced 16,500 asbestos lawsuits, with about 500 new ones filed per month. The downturn in construction, net losses in the first 2 quarters of 1982, and the lawsuits combined to make bankruptcy and reorganization a strategic alternative. A drastic cost-cutting program had been in effect since 1981 which included hiring freezes, layoffs, reduction in administration expenses (in 9 countries), cutting capital expenditures, leasing the headquarter's jet, and using the executive dining room to store the ever-mounting legal paperwork. At the time Manville was the largest firm ever to file for bankruptcy under Chapter 11.

Source: "Stockholders Meeting Briefs: Manville Corp.," *The Wall Street Journal*, May 10, 1982, p. 36, and "Manville's Reorganization Plan Resolves Nothing," *Business Week*, Dec. 5, 1983, pp. 72–73.

3.1, a combination of strategies is used more often than any single generic strategy with the exception of growth strategies. In fact, most multi-business organizations use some type of combination strategy, especially when they are serving several different markets. Certain generic strategies lend themselves to being used in combination with other strategies. For example, harvesting, divesting, and liquidating strategies are usually used in combination with one or more strategies for other parts of the organization. Coca-Cola was pursuing a combination strategy in 1983 when it divested its Wine Spectrum at the same time that it was expanding Columbia Pictures and its soft drink business.

GENERIC BUSINESS-LEVEL STRATEGIES

As previously noted, corporate-level strategies identify which businesses the organization intends to be in and how the resources will be allocated among those businesses. Business-level strategies outline how each business will compete within its respective industry.[20] For purposes of this discussion, an *industry* is defined as "the group of firms producing products [or services] that are close substitutes for each other."[21]

By nature, business-level strategies tend to be much less generic than corporate-level strategies. This is because most business-level strategies must be fitted to a unique business situation in terms of the organization's position in the industry and the competition. Although all business-level strategies are tailored in some degree to a specific situation, it is nevertheless possible to categorize most business-level strategies according to three major types: (1) overall cost leadership, (2) differentiation of the product or service, and (3) focus of the company.[22]

Overall Cost Leadership

The idea behind an *overall cost leadership strategy* is to be able to produce and deliver the product or service at a lower cost than the competition. Cost leadership is usually attained through a combination of experience and efficiency. More specifically, cost leadership requires close attention to production methods, overhead, marginal customers, and overall cost minimization in areas such as sales and research and development (R&D). There are a number of reasons why a cost leadership strategy can be attractive.[23]

1 It can give the firm above-average returns even in the face of strong competitive forces.

2 It can defend the firm against rivalry from competitors because it is difficult for competitors to force the firm out on the basis of price.

3 It can defend the firm against powerful buyers because buyers can exert pressure only to drive prices down to the level of the next most efficient competitor.

4 It can defend the firm against powerful suppliers by providing flexibility to deal with input cost increases.

5 The factors contributing to a low-cost position can provide substantial barriers to entry (such as expensive production equipment).

6 It can put the firm in a favorable position to fend against substitutes from the firm's competitors.

Achieving an overall low-cost position usually requires that the company develop some unique advantage or advantages over its competitors. Examples include a high market share, favorable access to raw materials, use of state-of-the-art equipment, or special design features which make the product easy to manufacture. Example 3.11 summarizes how Timex became successful in the watch industry by using an overall cost leadership strategy.

Differentiation of the Product or Service

A *differentiation strategy* involves doing something so that the product or service is perceived as unique in the industry. There are many general approaches for accomplishing differentiation: brand image (Izod or Polo in sportswear), design image (Lalique in glassware), technology (Hewlett-Packard in small computers), quality image (Mercedes or Rolls Royce in cars, Kitchen Aid in appliances), features (the Jenn-Air cook top), customer service (IBM in office equipment and computers, Sears Roebuck in home appliances), dealer network (Caterpillar and John Deere), or any combination of these. Product differentiation in the fashion industry is described in Example 3.12.

EXAMPLE 3.11

How Timex Has Used an Overall Cost Leadership Strategy in the Watch Industry

Timex, long the leader in the watch market through the use of a low-price strategy, owed its advantage to Joakim Lehmkuhl, a Norwegian engineer. His idea for low-cost timekeeping was a completely mass-produced watch. Integral to the low-price strategy were hard alloy bearings, far less costly and more rugged than the jeweled bearings previously used. Lehmkuhl's manufacturing mechanization and engineering system made him the Henry Ford of the watch industry and the Timex watch the Model A. When fine jewelry stores refused to carry Timex watches, Timex sought outlets in drugstores, hardware stores, and even cigar stands. Today Timex has 100,000 outlets, down from a high of 250,000. By limiting production to 85% of demand, Timex kept dealers and prices firmly in line. In the 1960s, every second watch sold was a Timex!

Source: Myron Magnet, "Timex Takes the Torture Test," *Fortune,* June 27, 1983, pp. 112–115, 118ff.

EXAMPLE 3.12

Product Differentiation in the Fashion Industry

The "lifestyle image" is the brand differentiation strategy used in the mass-market designer clothing industry by such names as Ralph Lauren, Calvin Klein, Bill Blass, Pierre Cardin, and Christian Dior. These designers build an image consistent with quality that caters to a special audience. Designers like Lauren design only the *right clothes for the right people*. Their fashions speak for them in advertising campaigns which often use a single model or type. The clothes are seen as the enactment of a lifestyle to be emulated—a continuation of the ad into real life. The name and logo may be all that is needed to portray the message of the special brand strategy. The result for Ralph Lauren's "Polo Club" is to convey understated elegance, quality, status, and exclusivity. Not only are these brand names highly recognizable as a special "lifestyle" label, but also they mean healthy, growing profits.

Source: Anna Sobezynski, "Evoking the Image of a Stylish Life," *Advertising Age,* Sept. 6, 1982, pp. M20–M21; and "Those Who are *Haute* in the World of Fashion," *Advertising Age,* Sept. 6, 1982, pp. M20–M21.

Following a differentiation strategy does not imply that the business should have little concern for costs but, rather, that the major competitive advantage sought is through differentiation. Differentiation has several potential advantages:[24]

1 It can provide protection against competition because of brand loyalty by customers and their resulting willingness to support higher prices for brand items.

2 It can increase margins because of the ability to charge a higher price.

3 Through higher margins, it can provide flexibility for dealing with supplier power (such as raising the cost of raw materials).

4 It can mitigate buyer power because there are no comparable alternatives.

5 It can provide entry barriers for competitors as a result of customer loyalty and the need for a competitor to overcome the product or service uniqueness.

6 Because of customer loyalty, it can put the company in a favorable position to fend against substitutes from competitors.

Depending on what is required to achieve differentiation, a company may or may not find it necessary to incur relatively high costs. For example, if high-quality materials or extensive research is necessary, the resulting product or service may be priced relatively high. When this is the case, the idea is that the uniqueness of the product or service will create a willingness on the part of the customers to pay the premium price. While such a strategy can be very profitable, it may or may not preclude gaining a high share of the market. For example, Rolex demands a very high price for its watches and makes a profit, but it has a very small market share. On the other hand, IBM generally demands a higher price than its competitors and still maintains a large market share.

Focus of the Product or Service

A third generic competitive strategy is to focus on a particular market segment. The segment sought may be defined by a particular buyer group, a geo-

EXHIBIT 3.4   COMPARING THE THREE GENERIC COMPETITIVE STRATEGIES

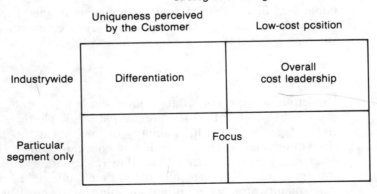

Source: Michael Porter, *Competitive Strategy: Techniques for Analyzing Industries and Competitors,* Free Press, New York, 1980, p. 39. Reprinted/adapted with permission of The Free Press, a Division of McMillan, Inc., from *Competitive Strategy* by Michael E. Porter. ©1980 by The Free Press.

EXAMPLE 3.13

How Frederick's of Hollywood Uses a Focus Strategy

Frederick's of Hollywood, established in 1946, is an innovative firm, founded by Frederick Mellinger, designer and retailer of provocative fashions. Mellinger has always followed a focus strategy which identifies the firm's market niche, targeting Frederick's of Hollywood fashions toward women (and men) concerned with a "total look." Quoting Mellinger: "You see, fashion changes. But sex is always in style. I don't carry anything—no matter how fashionable—that doesn't make women (and men) look sexy. I sell a look!"

Source: "Making Mountains out of Molehills," *Forbes,* Mar. 15, 1974, p. 36.

---

graphic market segment, or a certain part of the product line. As opposed to low-cost and differentiation strategies, which have industrywide appeal, a *focus strategy* is based on the premise that the firm is able to serve a well-defined but narrow market better than competitors who serve a broader market. The basic idea of a focus strategy is to achieve a least-cost position or differentiation, or both, within a narrow market. Exhibit 3.4 illustrates how a focus strategy relates to overall low-cost and differentiation strategies. Frederick's of Hollywood (see Example 3.13) has followed a focus strategy by targeting that segment of the lingerie industry which is attracted by a sex-appeal approach. In the small-tool industry, Black and Decker has focused on the home market.

The key to employing a successful business-level (competitive) strategy is knowing which strategies work under which conditions. Each of the three generic competitive strategies has certain associated risks. Each requires different skills and resources and different organizational settings to be successfully implemented. Exhibit 3.5 summarizes some of the specific requirements for each strategy. How to select and implement a competitive strategy for a given situation is covered in Chapters 8, 9, and 10.

SUMMARY

Numerous generic corporate- and business-level strategic alternatives exist and can be identified. Corporate-level strategic alternatives fall into four general categories: growth, stability, defensive, and combination strategies. Growth-oriented strategies, including concentration, vertical integration, and diversification, were defined and illustrated with specific examples. Growth strategies are the strategic alternatives most often used by U.S. businesses.

A stability strategy is not a do-nothing approach. It is a do-the-same-thing approach and is adopted by organizations that want to maintain the status quo.

In the case of defensive strategic alternatives, the choice of strategy may or

EXHIBIT 3.5   SKILLS, RESOURCES, AND ORGANIZATIONAL REQUIREMENTS OF GENERIC
COMPETITIVE STRATEGIES

Generic strategy	Commonly required skills and resources	Common organizational requirements
Overall cost leadership	Sustained capital investment and access to capital Process engineering skills Intense supervision of labor Products designed for ease in manufacture Low-cost distribution system	Tight cost control Frequent, detailed control reports Structured organization and responsibilities Incentives based on meeting strict quantitative targets
Differentiation	Strong marketing abilities Product engineering Creative flair Strong capability in basic research Corporate reputation for quality of technological leadership Long tradition in the industry or unique combination of skills drawn from other businesses Strong cooperation from channels	Strong coordination among functions in R&D, product development, and marketing Subjective measurement and incentives instead of quantitative measures Amenities to attract highly skilled labor, scientists, or creative people
Focus	Combination of the above policies directed at the particular strategic target	Combination of the above policies directed at the particular strategic target

Source: Michael Porter, *Competitive Strategy: Techniques for Analyzing Industries and Competitors,* Free Press, New York, 1980, pp. 40–41. Reprinted/adapted with permission of The Free Press, a Division of Macmillan, Inc., from *Competitive Strategy* by Michael E. Porter. Copyright © 1980 by The Free Press.

may not be up to the organization. If things are not going well, one alternative is to implement a turnaround strategy by reducing operating costs. The organization might choose to divest itself of business units that are unprofitable or just don't fit. Sometimes the only alternative is to liquidate (sell or dissolve) the organization. This is one strategic alternative which can be forced on an unprofitable organization by its stockholders or outside creditors. Following a bankruptcy strategy can be a means of defending against threats like burdensome labor contracts or lawsuits. It gives the organization protection and relief, with provision for reorganization if approved by the courts. Becoming a captive is not always a conscious strategic choice. If a firm has only one customer, becoming a captive can evolve slowly over time. Although the choice may not be conscious, once the captive relationship is developed, it is very difficult to dissolve.

A combination strategy is used when an organization simultaneously employs different strategies for different organizational units.

Strategic alternatives are also available at the business level. These alternatives outline how each business will compete within its respective industry. Business-level strategies are categorized into three major types: overall cost leadership, differentiation of product or service, and focus of the product or service.

CHAPTER 3   REVIEW QUESTIONS

1 Why are growth strategies such popular strategic choices? Name and define the different types of growth strategies.

2 Differentiate between the market development concentration strategy and the product development concentration strategy. When would each most likely be used?

3 Give the conditions under which a firm might adopt a vertical integration strategy. What determines whether vertical integration is backward or forward?

4 How does concentric diversification differ from concentration? What advantage does the concentric diversification alternative offer?

5 Under what circumstances will an organization use an internal growth strategy? Why might an external growth strategy be used?

6 Would it be correct to say that a stability strategy is a do-nothing strategy? Why or why not?

7 Define the various defensive strategies, including circumstances under which each is likely to occur.

8 Define and distinguish between the three basic types of business-level strategies.

CHAPTER 3   DISCUSSION QUESTIONS

1 In addition to the examples given in the text, identify at least one other company using each of the generic corporate strategies discussed in this chapter.

2 Identify at least one company using each of the generic business-level strategies discussed in this chapter. (Do not use the examples given in the text.)

3 Identify two major companies that were at some point forced to implement a turnaround strategy and that subsequently went on to bigger and better things. What type of corporate strategy were they following prior to implementing the turnaround strategy?

4 Would you classify Dr. Pepper's acquisition of Canada Dry in 1982 as part of a concentration strategy or part of a concentric diversification strategy? Justify your answer.

CHAPTER 3   REFERENCES

1 "The Inc. 100," *Inc.*, May 1987, pp. 46–54.

2 "Levi Forms Unit to Make and Sell Designer Clothes," *The Wall Street Journal*, Jan. 18, 1984.

3 Thomas J. Peters and Robert H. Waterman, Jr., *In Search of Excellence*, Harper & Row, New York, 1982, p. 293.

4 For example, see Richard Rumelt, *Strategy, Structure, and Economic Performance*, Harvard University Press, Cambridge, Mass., 1974.

5 Michael E. Porter, "From Competitive Advantages to Corporate Strategy," *Harvard Business Review*, May–June 1987, pp. 43–59.

6 Kenneth N. M. Dundas and Peter R. Richardson, "Implementing the Unrelated Product Strategy," *Strategic Management Journal*, October–December 1982, pp. 287–301.

7 Porter, op. cit.

8 William F. Glueck and Lawrence R. Jauch, *Business Policy and Strategic Management*, 4th ed., McGraw-Hill, New York, 1984, p. 217.

9 Dundas and Richardson, op. cit., p. 293.

10 R. Wright and C. Russel, "Joint Ventures in Developing Countries: Realities and Responses," *Columbia Journal of World Business,* Summer 1975, pp. 74–80; and R. Peterson and J. Shimada, "Sources of Management Problems in Japanese-American Joint Ventures," *Academy of Management Review,* October 1978, pp. 796–804.

11 Philip Kotler, "Harvesting Strategies for Weak Products," *Business Horizons,* August 1978, pp. 17–18.

12 "Singer Sewing Machines Finally Take a Backseat as It Expands into Aerospace," *Business Week,* January 13, 1983, p. 66.

13 "Conglomerate Managers Fall into Step, Too," *Business Week,* February 6, 1984, pp. 50–51.

14 "Why Baldwin Will Have to Sell MGIC," *Business Week,* October 3, 1983, p. 51.

15 "Expensive Divorce," *Time,* February 6, 1984, p. 51.

16 "Singer Sewing Machines Finally Take a Backseat," op. cit.

17 "Conglomerate Managers Fall into Step, Too," op. cit., p. 50.

18 Bill Saporito, "Handy Guy with a Razor," *Fortune,* Aug. 3, 1987, p. 53.

19 "Where Are They Now?" *Financial World,* November 15, 1987.

20 Much of this entire section is drawn from Michael Porter, *Competitive Strategy: Techniques for Analyzing Industries and Competitors,* Free Press, New York, 1980.

21 Ibid., p. 5.

22 Ibid., p. 35.

23 Ibid., pp. 35–36.

24 Ibid., pp. 37–38.

IDENTIFYING MISSION AND STRATEGY

LEARNING OBJECTIVES

After studying this chapter, the reader should be able to:

1 Define organizational mission and explain the role of mission in strategic management
2 Write a mission statement
3 Explain why it is necessary to identify strategy
4 Distinguish among the three levels of strategy
5 Write business- and corporate-level strategy statements

CHAPTER OUTLINE

MISSION
  Mission and Stakeholders
    • Name • Public Statements • Slogans
  Mission and Management
  Changing the Mission
IDENTIFYING OBJECTIVES
STRATEGY
IDENTIFYING A STRATEGY
ANALYZING A STRATEGY
  A Note on Usage
  Determining the Level of Strategy
  Identifying the Components of Strategy
    • Corporate Strategy Patterns • Business Strategy Patterns

The strategic management process should begin with an analysis of the current situation of the organization. Only by a careful review of the current performance of the organization and the decisions which resulted in that performance can the strategist make reasonable choices about the future.

Three fundamental aspects of this analysis are discovering why the organization exists, what the organization is trying to achieve, and how it intends to achieve its desired ends. The *mission* of the organization tells why it exists; the *objectives* relate what the organization is trying to achieve; and *strategy* identifies the means that the organization will use to achieve its objectives. This chapter explains the role of mission and strategy in the strategic management process and provides guidelines for identifying current mission, objectives, and strategy(ies). The appendix reviews tools for analyzing financial performance, which is an important indicator of how effective strategies have been in achieving objectives.

If analysis of the current situation reveals that the organization is operating without mission, objectives, and/or strategy, these omissions are a priority for action. Often the absence of a strategic direction accounts for poor performance.

MISSION

Whether it is called the mission, the business definition, or the purpose, all organizations have a fundamental reason for existence. This mission "sets a business apart from other firms of its type and identifies the scope of its operations in product and market terms."[1] While many organizations explicitly record their mission statements, mission may also be implicit. The term "mission" is used to refer to an explicit statement or implicit understanding of why the organization exists. When this understanding is shared and agreed upon by top management, it provides a common framework for decision-making which provides direction for the organization. A written mission statement should identify the product, market, and technological scope of the organization and any pervasive aims, designs, or thrusts which indicate the fundamental character and role of the organization. Example 4.1 gives examples of mission statements for a single-product-line firm (ADP, Inc.) and a more general statement of purpose and beliefs for IBM Corporation.

An explicit mission guides a variety of decisions which insiders, as well as outsiders, make regarding their association with, support of, and actions for

---

EXAMPLE 4.1

Mission Statements for ADP, Inc., and IBM Corporation

Automatic Data Processing, Inc. (ADP)

ADP's mission is to help an ever-increasing number of businesses improve their performance by regularly using ADP's computing services for record keeping and management information services. We will offer computing services that can be efficiently and profitably mass marketed and mass produced with recurring revenues.

Source: "Corporate Philosophy," ADP brochure.

IBM Corporation

IBM's statement of purpose is found in its basic beliefs:

- Respect for the individual. Respect for the dignity and the rights of each person in the organization.
- Customer service. To give the best customer service of any company in the world.
- Excellence. The conviction that an organization should pursue all tasks with the objective of accomplishing them in a superior way.

In addition to these basic beliefs, there is a set of fundamental principles which guide IBM management in the conduct of the business. They are:

- To give intelligent, responsible, and capable direction to the business.
- To deal fairly and impartially with suppliers of goods and services.
- To advance our technology, improve our products, and develop new ones.
- To enlarge the capabilities of our people through job development and give them the opportunity to find satisfaction in their tasks.
- To provide equal opportunity to all our people.
- To recognize our obligation to stockholders by providing adequate return on their investment.
- To do our part in furthering the well-being of those communities in which our facilities are located.
- To accept our responsibilities as a corporate citizen of the United States and in all the countries in which we operate throughout the world.

Source: Corporate documents.

---

the organization. While a formal mission state is typically simple and straightforward, mission is an important and multifaceted concept. Exhibit 4.1 shows the mission as an important determinant of direction and commitment. Mission is communicated to outsiders through public statements, corporate mottoes or slogans, and the name and image of the organization. These outsiders become *stakeholders* in the organization if the purpose of the organization attracts them as customers, investors, or employees. Mission is communicated to in-

EXHIBIT 4.1 USES OF MISSION FOR INSIDERS AND OUTSIDERS

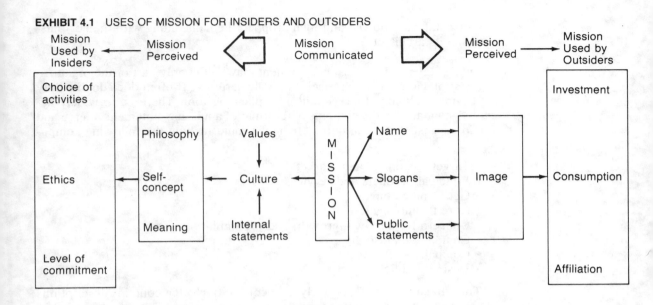

siders through the written and oral statements of management as well as through the value and culture systems of the organization. Mission sets the limits within which the organization will operate, and it influences ethical, personal, and strategic decisions made by managers and employees.

Mission and Stakeholders

Many individuals and groups outside the organization make decisions which are crucial to organizational success. The investment community makes judgments concerning the level of financial support it will provide; customers judge whether to support the organization by purchasing goods and services; and potential employees determine whether or not their individual goals will be furthered by joining the organization. The image, or identity, of the organization can affect these decisions. There is little doubt that potentially valuable supporters can be lost if they do not approve the organization mission.[2] It is important, therefore, that the mission be explicitly communicated to avoid misunderstanding of the fundamental purpose of the organization.

Name Often, an organization's name gives some information about its mission. Names like Toys 'R' Us and the Salvation Army are not only colorful and memorable, they are also informative. As mission changes with the addition of new products/services, markets, or technologies, names may also be changed. Cox Broadcasting Corporation became Cox Communications to reflect a wider product and service range.[3] United Airlines became Allegis to shed a restrictive identity as they moved into a broad spectrum of travel services (rental cars, hotels) and then dropped the name along with the new mission and its architect.[4]

Public Statements   Mission statement may be the only part of the organization's strategic plan which receives public scrutiny. It often does double duty as a public relations tool as well as a planning tool. There is no widely accepted standard for the contents and format of a mission statement. Pierce and David suggest that a mission statement should include the following components:

- Target customers and markets
- Principal products and services
- Geographic domain
- Core technologies
- Concern for survival, growth, and profitability
- Company philosophy
- Company self-concept
- Desired public image[5]

The annual report of a publicly held corporation often contains descriptions of the company's products, markets, and technologies. This statement is frequently labeled a *business definition*. Together with statements the organization may provide about its philosophy and direction, these business definitions provide considerable insight about the organization's mission. Example 4.2 provides examples of some business definitions.

Slogans   Organizational slogans or mottoes can be memorable indicators of mission. Du Pont used the phrase "Better things for better living through chemistry"; for many years General Electric's motto was "Progress is our most important product." Both mottoes associated the organizations with advancement through technology without being specific enough to be restrictive. Many slogans are temporary advertising phrases, but these phrases may contain clues as to the fundamental purpose of the organization.

Mission and Management

Mission must be communicated to and internalized by managers and employees. This is accomplished through the explicit statements of top management as well as through the value and culture system of the organization.

Mission provides criteria for strategy selection by executives. Many potential acquisitions or diversification moves have been ruled out because the new business was not within the framework established by the mission. Mission defines the boundaries or domain within which the organization will operate. These boundaries may be defined as industries or types of activities.

When a mission is recognized and accepted by managers and employees, it becomes a common framework for making decisions and setting priorities. It is something that everyone in the organization is aware of, and employees can relate their activities to other activities through the mission. The IBM beliefs

EXAMPLE 4.2

Public Statements

PepsiCo, Inc.

PepsiCo, Inc., is a worldwide consumer products and service company. Through its divisions and subsidiaries, both domestic and international, PepsiCo operates in three major business segments: beverages, food products, and food service. It is also actively involved in sporting goods. PepsiCo has achieved a leadership position in each of these lines of business.

Source: From *Annual Report,* 1985.

Flowers Industries, Inc.

We call ourselves the Flowers family because we are committed to one another and to our company.

We believe in the family spirit, a concept founded on the realization that we must support each other as we strive to achieve our individual ideals, goals, objectives, and dreams. Working together with cooperative enthusiasm, feeling, a sense of pride in what we do and fostering a genuine concern for our fellow employees are essential elements of the family spirit. Each day we want to further establish in our Flowers family that sense of caring, sharing, and giving which is such an important ingredient in our personal families.

We value the integrity, ability, opinion, and contributions of each of our family members to the success of our company. Cultivating and developing our individual skills, experiences, knowledge, leadership, and creativity strengthens each of us as individuals as well as our entire corporate family. We share the responsibility for our company's success, recognizing the value of sharing information, accountability, and opportunity.

We are committed to a perpetual quest for excellence in every aspect of our personal and business lives. We must always be mindful of this dedication to excellence and of our primary reason for being in business—to provide long-term economic opportunity for our family members and a meaningful return for our shareholders. To do this, we must

- meet the needs of our customers and consumers,
- maintain the highest quality and value in our products,
- produce our products at the lowest possible cost,
- increase the profitability of our company on a consistent and predictable basis through internal and external expansion, and
- develop an atmosphere in which each of us lives daily the tenets of the "Flowers Family Philosophy."

Source: Annual Report, Flowers Industries, Inc., 1987.

(see Example 4.1) are an example of a mission effectively in place. Their belief in service conveys priorities and attitudes toward customers that apply to the newest technician as well as the most experienced vice president.

Mission does not prevent change, it simply provides direction for seeking new opportunities. Many years ago, IBM enlarged its scope from producing business machines to serving information processing needs. This opened a wide range of options, but is still restrictive enough to keep IBM in fields in which it has developed or could readily develop expertise. A good mission statement is broad enough to allow exploration of new opportunities but specific enough to prevent the organization from going too far afield.

Finally, mission conveys to employees the philosophy of the company and gives their jobs meaning beyond the immediate physical or mental activity in which they are engaged. The perceived meaningfulness of the job can in turn affect the level of employee commitment to the organization.

Changing the Mission

Mission is so fundamental to most organizations that it is viewed as fixed and is seldom reconsidered in any systematic fashion. Mission is most likely to be a given in the strategy formulation process, but it should not be viewed as unchangeable. In certain circumstances the mission itself must be reevaluated if the organization is to survive.

An organization which has fulfilled its mission must reevaluate its reason for existence. Another reason for changing the mission of an organization occurs when the long-term prospects for an organization's core business are not good and the organization decides to redirect its activities. In the packaging industry, several companies have undergone such a redirection. Continental Can became the Continental Group with the addition of insurance, natural gas, forest products, and other businesses to its packaging business. American Can undertook a change of mission which took it out of the packaging business entirely. Example 4-3 reproduces an advertisement widely run by the company to explain its change in mission and introduce its new name. The ad was accompanied by a picture of John Wayne, who had also once changed his name (from Marion Morrison).

IDENTIFYING OBJECTIVES

The mission provides a framework for organization activities and decisions by answering the question of why the organization exists. Other important questions must be answered as we try to analyze the current status of an organization. The first of these is that of what the organization is trying to do. To answer this question, we must identify the organization's objectives and compare these with actual performance. (See the appendix which follows Chapter 12 to review some tools of financial analysis for assessing performance trends.) Objectives are frequently discussed in annual reports and other public documents after they have been achieved. However, it is less common to find ex-

EXAMPLE 4.3

American Can Changes Its Mission and Its Name

John Wayne was born Marion Morrison. When he broke into movies, he changed his name—"Marion" just didn't seem to fit him anymore.

Sometimes the name you grow up with doesn't fit you anymore.

That's why American Can has changed its name to Primerica.

When we redirected American Can Company out of manufacturing and into financial services and specialty retailing, our name just didn't fit us any longer. Which is why we sold it along with our packaging business last year.

After all, it doesn't make much sense to go on calling yourself American Can when you no longer make cans.

Primerica (pronounced pry-MER-i-ca) is our new name. It provides a link to our proud heritage, yet gives us flexibility to enter new businesses in the future. It also better suits what we have become.

We are the country's number one underwriter of individual life insurance. One of the largest originators of home mortgages. And one of the nation's top managers of mutual funds and pension assets.

We're also the largest retailer of recorded music and audio/video products in the U.S. And one of the country's largest direct-mail marketers.

Over the past six years, as we redirected the company, our shareholders have been rewarded with substantial increases in the value of their stock. From a low of 25¾ in 1982, our common stock price hit an all-time high of 107 in early 1987, prior to a two-for-one stock split.

We're Primerica. A company with prime growth prospects and the resources to fund that growth. A name to be reckoned with.

NYSE symbol: PA.

PRIMERICA

Primerica Corporation. Greenwich, Connecticut 06830

Financial Services: American Capital Management & Research, Inc.; Berg Enterprises, Inc.; Insurance Marketing Corp. of America (a co-venture); Mass. Indemnity and Life Ins. Co.; Margaretten & Co., Inc.; National Benefit Life Ins. Co.; PennCorp Financial, Inc.; Penn. Life Ins. Co.; RCM Capital Management (a partnership); Satellite Conference Network, Inc.; Transport Life Ins. Co.; Triad Life Ins. Corp.; Voyager Group, Inc. **Specialty Retailing:** Current, Inc.; Dunham's Athleisure Corp.; Figi's, Inc.; Fingerhut Companies, Inc.; Michigan Bulb Co.; The Musicland Group, Inc.

Primerica is a service mark and a trademark of Primerica Corporation

Photo © 1978 David Sutton

71

plicit targets with time frames which show what is being attempted for the future. For purposes of analysis, it is reasonable to assume that management wants to perform at least as well in the future as it has in the past in key results areas like growth and profitability. When no specific objectives can be determined, an analysis of growth and profitability trends for the immediate past can serve as a proxy for objectives. These can be adjusted based on other information about desired performance which may be available. The next chapter is devoted to the process of establishing objectives.

STRATEGY

By identifying the strategy of an organization, we can answer the last question about the current status of the organization: How is the organization trying to achieve its objectives and carry out its mission? The need to identify strategy and to state it explicitly exists in a number of situations. An organization using the informal strategy-making mode may have no strategy documented at all, but even key managers have an awareness of strategy without any written statement. Identification of the strategy would be most important for newcomers who need to understand where the organization is headed and how their own responsibilities relate to the chosen method of competition. If the organization has operated in an adaptive strategy-making mode, a survey of successful decisions over time may reveal a pattern of which executives are only intuitively aware but which constitutes a strategy. Any new chief executive needs to discover this pattern of decisions as part of his or her orientation. When an organization experiences a decline in performance which is not well understood, articulation of strategy is a first step in problem solving. An individual considering a job with a particular organization might better evaluate his or her prospects by analyzing the organization's past and current strategies to see whether they afford opportunities for growth and advancement. For example, the experience and opportunities in an organization engaged in a turnaround will be very different from those in an organization which is following a concentration strategy.

Outsiders can also benefit from such an exercise. Consultants, members of the financial community, and students analyzing cases all improve their ability to make recommendations by starting with an understanding of the past and current strategies of the organization.

IDENTIFYING A STRATEGY

One approach to identifying the presence of a strategy is summarized in the flowchart in Exhibit 4.2.[6] The numbers beginning the following paragraphs refer to branches in the flowchart.

1 An organization which has no explicit strategy is relatively easy to identify. Its activities usually don't have a common thread, and executives leap at every opportunity as equally attractive or turn down all new ideas as equally risky. Lack of strategy does not always show up on the bottom line, especially

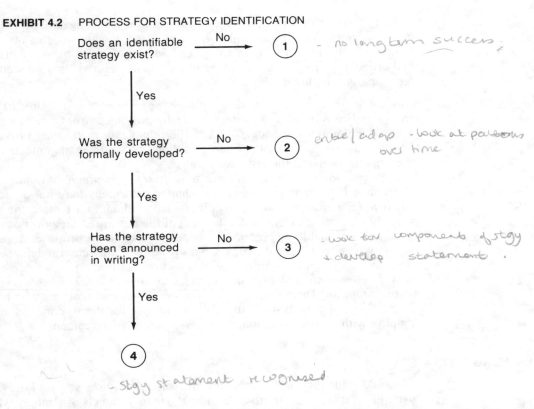

EXHIBIT 4.2   PROCESS FOR STRATEGY IDENTIFICATION

Does an identifiable strategy exist? → No → (1) — no long term success.

↓ Yes

Was the strategy formally developed? → No → (2) entre/adap - look at patterns over time

↓ Yes

Has the strategy been announced in writing? → No → (3) - look for components of stgy + develop statement.

↓ Yes

(4)

— stgy statement recognised

in the short run. However, the probabilities of long-term success are greatly reduced without a consciously developed strategy.

(2) Strategy may exist even when it is not formally developed and explicitly communicated. Entrepreneurs, for example, may have an intuitive understanding, which they have never really recorded or even verbalized, of how their company can successfully compete. Similarly, larger organizations may develop a strategy through a trial-and-error process without really articulating why they are able to exploit certain products and markets and are not able to be successful with others. The process of identifying strategy in the entrepreneurial or adaptive mode is similar to a detective process. The clues are provided by key decisions made over time. Similarities in these decisions allow the analyst to find patterns. These patterns constitute strategy.

(3) If the strategy has been developed but not written, it becomes necessary to look for evidence (or components) of strategy rather than for a statement of the strategy itself. The evidence is then used to construct a strategy statement. This may occur when an organization is in the early phases of the planning mode.

(4) In this situation, a formally developed, written strategy makes identification simply a process of locating the statement of strategy or an individual who can divulge it. The situation usually occurs when an organization is in the later phases of planning.

Identification of strategy involves elements of investigative work, clinical analysis, and scholarly reasoning. In view of the demands of this task, the rationale for the undertaking is worth considering. The purpose of identifying and articulating the current strategy of an organization as the first step in strategic analysis is threefold:

1 *To provide an understanding of how the organization reached its present status and current level of performance.* Identifying current strategy also tells a great deal about the background of the organization and may provoke preliminary questions about the appropriateness of strategic alignments between the organization and the environment.

2 *To provide the first alternative for any set of strategic alternatives.* That alternative is to "continue as is." A change in strategy may not be desirable. Even when a change is necessary, incremental changes are often the most favorably received. A clear understanding of the current strategy is necessary to generate reasonable incremental changes as well as to propose more drastic shifts. When necessary, drastic changes usually require careful defense and robust support based on knowledge of the current situation.

3 *To communicate with other analysts to come to a common understanding of the situation.* Discussion of a strategy statement with others who have performed a similar analysis is an excellent vehicle for discovering disparities of opinion without dwelling unnecessarily on areas of agreement.

ANALYZING A STRATEGY

The task of identifying a firm's current strategy requires several kinds of analysis. First, it is necessary to determine the level or levels of strategy which are found in the organization. Next, the components of strategy(ies) for each level must be identified and patterns must be found in those components. Finally, a statement (or statements) of strategy should be written.

A Note on Usage

It is important to recognize that the terms "corporate" and "business" have been given special definitions to serve as terms to distinguish levels of specificity and differences in focus among two types of organizational strategies. The special use of these terms may be confusing, since both words also have common meanings which are more frequently encountered. In common usage *corporate* refers to a legal form of organization (common stock corporation vs. single proprietorship or partnership). *Business* is used to designate any profit-seeking enterprise. When these terms are used by strategists, however, they have different meanings. *Corporate strategy* defines what businesses an organization will be in and how its resources will be allocated among those businesses. In this context, even a single-business company must decide to remain a single business. It must then decide how to compete in the chosen business. *Business strategy* indicates how the company or unit has chosen to compete in its specific industry and how resources will be allocated on the functional level to achieve competitive advantage. A multiproduct company will have only one corporate strategy but will have as many business strategies as it has different industries in which it competes.

Determining the Level of Strategy

Strategic decisions on the corporate level are different in several ways from strategic decisions on the business level. A corporate strategy involves a choice of competitive arenas (usually called businesses or industries) for an organization which wishes to be active in more than one competitive arena to spread risk or grow more rapidly. Strategic decisions on the corporate level also require choices about how corporate resources will be allocated among these competitive arenas. This level of strategy indicates *where* the organization will compete. It identifies corporate investment opportunities and is often called portfolio strategy. Only organizations which compete in more than one industry need to be concerned about how they will distribute scarce corporate resources among their individual businesses and whether there are attractive businesses they should enter.

BCI Holdings, Inc. (formerly Beatrice Foods) has a number of unrelated product lines. On the level of corporate strategy, the major concern is determining how corporate resources can be allocated to achieve corporate goals of growth and profitability. This requires determining what types of opportunities each business presents and what the relationship among these businesses should be. It also requires establishing and implementing criteria for acquiring new lines and for divesting those which do not contribute to goal achievement. A business strategy focuses on how to compete in a particular product line. BCI would have one corporate strategy to define the businesses the company would be in and how resources would be allocated among those businesses, but each business would require a separate strategy to guide it. Business strategy deals with competition and must be tailored for the competitive situation of each industry. Stieff Lamps is one BCI unit. It competes and distributes its products differently than Samsonite Luggage, another unit. A strategy that would be general enough to cover the competitive activities of both would not be specific enough to guide operations.

Preparation of a corporate strategy statement is necessary when the organization being analyzed competes in more than one industry. If there is more than one product-market-process configuration, a corporate strategy statement is necessary to indicate how businesses are chosen and which businesses are given investment support. If the unit for analysis is a subunit of a corporation (a strategic business unit, or SBU) or if it is an independent business having a single product or product line, a business strategy statement must be prepared. In all organizations a third level of strategy which is even more specific is present. This is called *functional strategy* and indicates how particular units or departments (such as marketing or operations) will allocate resources to achieve the objectives of that unit.

Strategy is hierarchical. This means that the levels of strategy have a relationship to each other. Corporate strategy is the broadest statement of how objectives will be achieved and it sets constraints for business strategies. Business strategies in turn set constraints for functional strategies. For example, many cigarette manufacturers have made the corporate strategic decision to diversify away from their tobacco businesses because of the long-term outlook for tobacco consumption. This corporate decision constrains the efforts of executives of the tobacco units to compete in their industry. They know that the corporate strategy will probably not support projects which require large investments or have long payback periods. Other units in these companies also know that the corporate strategy calls for them to position their units for long-term growth and to plan their business strategies accordingly.

Identifying the Components of Strategy

— Value chain link

Simply stated, identifying strategy requires examining strategic decisions to identify patterns. These patterns may be described using the generic strategies described in Chapter 3. For example, if we learn that Fuqua Industries has established a pattern of acquiring companies that are well run, maintaining current management, and holding the company only as long as performance standards are met, we could conclude that Fuqua is pursuing a corporate strategy of conglomerate diversification. The reliance on maintaining current management is a strong clue, as is the notable absence of any criteria that relate new businesses to current business activities (operational fit). However, this identification of the generic strategy of conglomerate diversification does not give us the complete picture, and an analyst should seek more specific information about what types of companies are acquired, how corporate resources are allocated, and which companies are divested. This information would bring us closer to being able to write a corporate strategy statement which defines the unique approach of this organization.

If we were analyzing the Snapper unit (manufacturer and distributor of lawn care equipment) of Fuqua Industries, we would be interested in the corporate strategy because it defines the limits within which the unit must operate, but we would also want to identify the specific business strategy of Snapper in the manufacture and distribution of lawn mowers and other related equipment. This would require an examination of strategic decisions on the business level to discover a pattern which would define Snapper's approach to competition. An understanding of generic business strategies helps here. We would probably conclude that Snapper is using a product differentiation strategy. We would then have to delve more into the specifics of competition to write a strategy statement which would accurately portray Snapper's competitive strategy.

Corporate Strategy Patterns   A collection of businesses requires a concept of strategy different from that of a single business. Strategy provides guidance for resource allocations among businesses for a multiproduct firm and also indicates standards for adding new businesses or deleting existing ones. Identifying past or current strategy at the corporate level requires tracking resource allocations and acquisitions and/or divestiture decisions. Clues to corporate strategy are found in similarities among existing businesses, criteria for acquisitions, and characteristics of units which are divested.

[handwritten margin notes: Comp Bus Fun; Porter Value chain; growth into similar business]

Organizations pursuing concentric diversification usually have a common feature among their businesses which, when identified, becomes an important component of the corporate strategy statement. The Coca-Cola Company maintains that it is in businesses which market packaged consumer products. Avon at one time was involved in a number of businesses which sold directly to the consumer. The cosmetic and jewelry lines were distributed by the Avon Lady, plastic party ware was sold in home parties, and clothing was marketed by mail-order catalogs. All these businesses were united by the common feature or corporate theme of direct sales. Blue Bell's Apparel manufactures only clothing that is nonseasonal such as blue jeans and work clothes.

Acquisition criteria are also useful in formulating a corporate strategy statement. ConAgra and Penn Central both seek to grow by acquisition. ConAgra's corporate strategy is to acquire food companies at bargain prices and turn them around. Penn Central is targeting a number of industries where growth and return prospects are good. Both companies are growing by acquisition, but the types of acquisition they seek show real differences in their corporate strategies. (See Example 4.4.)

Divestitures also show patterns which can be useful in determining corporate strategy. Characteristics of units which have been divested may indicate what types of activities did not constitute a strategic fit or meet performance objectives.

Business Strategy Patterns Business strategy answers the question: How do we compete in the _____ business? Clues are found in the patterns of resource allocations to the functional areas to create and maintain competitive advantage. These key decisions might include:

Product or service offered
Market or markets served
Process or service delivery technology utilized
Distribution channels
Promotion emphasis
Financing practices and preferences
Organizational climate and leadership style
Research stance

Identification of each of these key decisions yields a list of decisions or facts about the organization. It is also useful to look at how resources are allocated across the functional areas. Which department has the largest budget? How is it used? Where are the most capable people located in the organization? Where will the next chief executive come from? What does top management spend most of its time doing? It is a creative process to take this information and shape it into a strategy statement by discovering and articulating decision patterns. Example 4.5 illustrates this process with the long-distance telephone company MCI Inc.

Writing a Strategy Statement

When the process of gathering information about the components of corporate and/or business strategy has been completed, a statement of strategy should be formulated. This final step is necessary for three reasons:

EXAMPLE 4.4

Acquisition Criteria at ConAgra and Penn Central

ConAgra Inc.

Since 1982, ConAgra, a diversified food company, has made almost 50 acquisitions under the leadership of CEO Charles M. Harper. These acquisitions have diversified the product line and made ConAgra the second largest producer of chicken and the third largest beef producer. Sales for fiscal 1987 were expected to be $7 billion. Average return of equity for the years 1980 to 1987 was 23 percent. Harper has targeted for acquisition companies that are in trouble either because of sluggish growth in their industry or because of the need for internal adjustments to changing markets. These companies are bought at the lowest possible price, and Harper's management team makes the necessary adjustments to restore or improve profitability. Acquisitions must return 20 percent on equity.

Penn Central

Having shed its railroad business in 1976 and its Pennsylvania location in 1978, Penn Central went on to diversify into a number of unrelated businesses. It emerged from Chapter 11 bankruptcy in the late 1970s to begin an acquisition spree. Subsequently many of these businesses were divested and by 1987, Penn Central had unused cash of $1.1 billion and a new CEO—financier and investor Carl Lindner. In addition to the cash, Penn Central had $1.4 billion in unused tax credits and a debt-to-capital ratio of 5 percent. The company is targeting companies in telecommunications, food service, media, and financial services as investment and growth vehicles. Management skills in investment and control are in place.

Source: Based on information in "How ConAgra Grew Big and Now, Beefy," *Business Week,* May 18, 1987, p. 87; and "With Lindner in Charge, Penn Central Is on the Prowl," *Business Week,* April 20, 1987, p. 80.

---

1. To compare conclusions about company strategy with direct statements in company documents or pronouncements by executives
2. To compare your conclusions about the strategy with that of other observers
3. To summarize your understanding of the current situation

Corporate Strategy A corporate strategy statement will be more general and probably shorter than a business strategy statement. Example 4.6 provides an example of a corporate strategy statement for Penn Central and ConAgra.

Business Strategy A good business strategy statement should:[7]

1. Be stated in active and precise terms
2. Explicitly relate to the organization's goals

EXAMPLE 4.5

Components of MCI, Inc.'s Strategy

MCI Communications Corporation broke into the AT&T monopoly of long-distance telephone service with lower rates. The effects of deregulation have been lower rates across the board, and MCI no longer has an edge in price of service. In 1986, the company recorded its first deficit in 10 years, a loss of $448 million. MCI is taking the actions listed below to recover:

Since January, 1986, the work force has been reduced by 16 percent.

Its capital budget has been cut by 12 percent.

Through loan refinancing, interest payments were cut by $15 million in 1987.

A joint marketing venture with IBM is under way which will package long-distance services with computers for big business customers.

Advertising is being revised to target corporate customers.

Its TV ad budget has been cut 50 percent, while its print ad budget has increased by 30 percent.

Computerized network phone services have been introduced to attract business customers.

Digital transmission lines, which work well for computer communications, are being added.

A successful bid was made for the first competitively bid federal contract for 800 service for a government agency.

Phone service is being provided for Western Europe and Japan.

Obviously a turnaround strategy is in place at MCI, with efforts directed at both cost cutting and increasing revenue. More specifically, MCI is refocusing its efforts to win business customers and to penetrate new markets. Advertising shifts to print media will reach the business market more effectively than television. Changes which are pending in the software used in switching 800 calls will open that market to MCI. These moves are made to restore profitability and ensure that MCI will maintain its number 2 position in the industry. In the meantime, there is speculation about a possible merger between MCI and the number 3 Sprint.

Source: Adapted from information in "The Long-Distance Wars Get Hotter," *Business Week,* March 23, 1987, pp. 150–154.

3) Indicate how the business is competing with regard to products or services, markets, and processes

4) Include any unique functional area, corporate climate, or leadership approaches which characterize the organization and provide it with advantages

A strategy statement for an independent single-product-line firm in the cosmetics industry (Estée Lauder) and for an SBU competing in the same industry (Avon Beauty Products) is given in Example 4.7.

Sample Corporate Strategy Statements

The corporate emphasis of *ConAgra Inc.* is the food industry. ConAgra seeks acquisitions in slow-growth segments of the industry which carry attractive price tags and require the services of our management team, which is skilled in cost cutting and product repositioning. Resources are directed to building the managerial skills needed for these activities. Businesses must achieve a 20 percent return on equity.

The corporate emphasis of *Penn Central* is investment. Acquisitions which can produce attractive returns and growth are sought in industries such as telecommunications, food service, media, and financial services. Resources are directed toward analysis and control to achieve corporate goals of stock appreciation and return on investment.

Strategy statements derived from information in Example 4.5.

Sample Business Strategy Statements

Estée Lauder, Inc., provides high-quality, science-based products for affluent men and women. Distribution is exclusively through better department stores. Product development focuses on anticipating trends with formulations which will produce long-term sales potential.

To ensure desired growth and leadership status in the industry, the company will continue to allocate resources to R&D in excess of industry averages and to cultivate relationships with independent research laboratories. Senior management will continue the personal involvement in operations, which allows quick decision making in response to market feedback. The company will remain privately held and family-managed.

The Beauty Products Division of Avon, Inc., manufactures and distributes cosmetics, fragrances, and fashion jewelry through a network of independent sales representatives to women in 32 countries. A cost-efficient manufacturing process and person-to-person distribution process provide unique service, quality, and cost benefits to customers. In order to improve short-term performance, the division will emphasize its image with more advertising and less discounting. It will also focus on improvement in representative productivity. In order to improve profitability, a brand management approach will be adopted. In addition, new channels of distribution which do not directly compete with independent representatives will be explored. To achieve a consumer focus in operations, a decentralized structure will be adopted which will make the division more responsive to the consumer.

SUMMARY

To understand the current situation which an organization faces, it is useful to begin by identifying mission, objectives, and strategy. These three concepts tell why the organization exists, what the organization is trying to do, and how it is going about it. The final element of analysis of the current situation is a diagnosis of current performance. (See appendix for review of the highlights of financial analysis.)

Mission, also called purpose or business definition, is the fundamental concept which defines the organization's reason for existence. Mission may be either implicit or explicit; an explicit mission is useful to people both inside and outside the organization. Mission is conveyed to outsiders through name, public statements, and slogans. Insiders have internal statements, values, and culture as sources of information about mission. Although mission is so fundamental that it is rarely changed, it should not be viewed as totally inflexible. Systematic reconsideration of mission is part of the strategic management process.

Objectives may not be explicitly stated. If not, it is usually safe to assume that the organization is seeking to maintain or improve its historical rates of growth and profitability.

In an organizational setting, identification of strategy may be difficult, especially when the strategy is not written down, or formally developed. It is important to attempt to identify the current strategy of an organization to learn about the organization as a whole, to recommend possible changes, and to communicate effectively with other organizational observers.

The task of identifying organizational strategy and writing a strategy statement begins with the determination of the level or levels of strategy which the organization has. A corporate strategy indicates which businesses a multi-product or multiproduct-line organization will be in and how resources will be allocated among those businesses. A business strategy focuses on how to compete in a single product or product line. A functional area strategy applies to one part or function of the organization, such as marketing or personnel.

If there is more than one product-market-process configuration, a corporate strategy statement is necessary to indicate how businesses are chosen and which businesses are emphasized. If the unit for analysis is a subunit of a corporation (an SBU) or if it is an independent business having a single product or product line, a business strategy statement must be prepared. Functional strategies are found in all organizations. Corporate strategy is different in focus and content from business strategy.

Components of business strategy include product or service offered, market or market segments served, process or service technology utilized, distribution channels, promotion emphasis, financing practices and preferences, organizational climate and leadership style, and research stance. Areas of expenditure also provide clues to the strategy.

A good business strategy statement should be (1) stated in active and precise terms, (2) relate explicitly to goals, (3) indicate how goals will be reached, and (4) include unique features of the business.

Because the vocabulary of strategic management is specialized, it is important to understand the concepts underlying terms such as "corporate strategy" and "business strategy."

CHAPTER 4 REVIEW QUESTIONS

1 Define "organizational mission." In what ways can stakeholders in the organization use the mission?
2 What circumstances would require an organization to change its mission?
3 Under what circumstances might a strategy exist but not be written down?
4 What is the purpose of writing a strategy statement?
5 What are the differences between corporate and business strategies?
6 What are the relationships among corporate, business, and functional strategies in a multiproduct organization?
7 What is an SBU?
8 How would you determine how many levels of strategy are present in an organization?
9 What information would you seek to discover what an organization's business strategy is? What would you need to know to determine corporate strategy?
10 What are the characteristics of a good business strategy statement?

CHAPTER 4 DISCUSSION QUESTIONS

1 Both mission and strategy statements begin with products, markets, and processes or technology. Why? What is the difference between these two statements?
2 Think of an organization with which you would like to be affiliated. What is the mission of that organization? Does its mission have anything to do with your attraction to it?
3 Defend or refute: Mission is just a PR tool; it has no real significance for organizational operations.
4 Defend or refute: Failure to have a written strategy statement is a sign of bad management in an organization.
5 Choose an organization with which your classmates are likely to be familiar. Be prepared to identify the levels of strategy in that organization in class discussion.
6 How could the concepts of business, corporate, and functional strategy be applied to an organization like the Boy or Girl Scouts? To a local hospital? To the United Way?

CHAPTER 4 REFERENCES

1 John A. Pearce II, "The Company Mission as a Strategic Tool," *Sloan Management Review*, Spring 1982, pp. 14–24.
2 W. Marguilies, "Make the Most of Your Corporate Identity," *Harvard Business Review*, July–August 1977, pp. 66–74.
3 "Why Companies Keep Changing Their Names," *U.S. News & World Report*, July 12, 1982, p. 73.
4 "Allegis: The Unraveling of an Idea," *Business Week*, June 22, 1987, p. 42.
5 J. A. Pearce and F. David, "Corporate Mission Statements: The Bottom Line," *Academy of Management Executive*, vol. 1, no. 2, 1987, p. 109.
6 Henry Mintzberg, "Strategy-Making in Three Modes," *California Management Review*, Winter 1973, pp. 44–53.
7 In *Strategy Formulation: Analytical Concepts*, West, St. Paul, Minn., 1978, Charles W. Hofer and Dan Schendel provide an extensive discussion of the evaluation of strategy statements.

THE DECISION ENVIRONMENT AND THE ESTABLISHMENT OF OBJECTIVES

LEARNING OBJECTIVES

After studying this chapter, the reader should be able to:

1 Gain an appreciation and an understanding for many of the factors that can have an impact on the decision environment of the strategic manager
2 Introduce the hierarchies of objectives that exist within the strategic management process
3 Illustrate how long-range objectives are established or formulated by designating key result areas, determining the time frame and magnitude, and putting these into written form
4 Discuss the role that social responsibility plays in today's organizations

CHAPTER OUTLINE

THE DECISION-MAKING ENVIRONMENT
    The Role of Managerial Values
    The Role of Ethics
      • Current Trends
    Lower-Level Participation
    The Role of Politics and Power Relationships
      • Power-Base Determinants • Implementing Power
THE ESTABLISHMENT OF OBJECTIVES
    Hierarchies of Objectives

Previous chapters covered have dealt, almost exclusively, with decisions and actions taken in the past. The thrust has been to identify and analyze the current status of the organization as shaped by earlier decisions. Now that we have a picture of the organization's current status, it is time to shift to a future orientation. Long-range objectives must be set, strategies must be chosen, and these strategies must then be implemented. The first part of this chapter is designed to examine those factors in the strategic manager's environment that can influence the decision process. The second part of the chapter deals with one of the first areas in which the strategic manager must make decisions—the establishment of long-range objectives.

THE DECISION-MAKING ENVIRONMENT

There are a multitude of internal and external environmental factors that can have an impact on decisions made by strategic managers. This chapter will introduce several of the most significant of these.

The Role of Managerial Values

Few people would be surprised if, for a given set of resources, a group of clergy members defined objectives different from those of a group of military commanders; in fact, most people would expect different objectives. A large part of the expected differences would be attributable to differences in values. A *value* is a conception, explicit or implicit, defining what an individual or group regards as desirable.[1] People are not born with values but rather acquire and develop them early in life. Parents, teachers, other persons, and personal experiences influence an individual's values. Because of this, every manager brings a certain set of values to the workplace.

Undoubtedly, an infinite number of different value sets exist. However, the majority of value sets fall into certain basic categories. Exhibit 5.1 presents a value classification scheme developed by William Guth and Renato Taguiri. Exhibit 5.2 presents a somewhat different classification scheme developed by George England.

EXHIBIT 5.1   GUTH AND TAGUIRI'S VALUES CATEGORIES

Theoretical. Primarily interested in the discovery of truth and knowledge

Economic. Primarily interested in what is useful and economically practical

Aesthetic. Primarily interested in the artistic aspects of life

Social. Primarily interested in the love of other people

Political. Primarily interested in acquiring power

Religious. Primarily interested in relating to the universe

Source: Reprinted by permission of the *Harvard Business Review*. Excerpt from William D. Guth and Renato Taguiri, "Personal Values and Corporate Strategy," *Harvard Business Review,* September–October 1965, pp. 124–125. Copyright © 1965 by the President and Fellows of Harvard College; all rights reserved.

Research has shown that the value set of top management does have a significant influence over the direction of an organization. For example, Guth and Taguiri reported, "It is quite clear, on the basis of both observations and systematic studies of top management in business organizations, that personal values are an important determinant of the choice of corporate strategy."[2] Further, in assessing the values of over 4000 managers and administrators, George England reported the following findings:[3]

1 There are large individual differences in personal values within every group studied.

2 Personal values of managers are relatively stable and do not change rapidly.

3 Personal value systems of managers are related to and/or influence the way managers behave on the job.

4 Personal value systems of managers are related to their career success as managers.

5 There are differences and similarities in the value systems of managers within the different countries studied.

6 There are both differences and similarities in the value systems of managers in different countries.

Bamberger has recently supported the findings of England and hypothesized that strategic behavior can also determine values.[4] Bamberger's reasoning is that a certain type of strategy and associated environment may require or mold a certain value profile of managers. Ideally, the value sets of the different

EXHIBIT 5.2   ENGLAND'S MAJOR CATEGORIES OF VALUES

Pragmatic. View ideas and concepts in terms of whether or not they work or are successful

Ethical-moral. View ideas in terms of being right or wrong

Feeling. View ideas in terms of whether or not they are pleasant

Source: George England, "Personal Value Systems of Managers and Administrators," *Academy of Management Proceedings,* August 1973, pp. 81–94.

people who may influence the strategic management process are consistent. However, when the value sets of the different influences are not consistent and/or when other differences exist, conflicts often arise.

The Role of Ethics[5]

The question of what is ethical behavior has existed since people began to work together in primitive societies. In those societies, what was right and what was wrong became an integral part of tribal customs, practices, and mores. Life was simpler and, consequently, ethical decisions were simpler. As societies became complex, ethical issues became more complex. Today with rapidly changing technology, increased worldwide communication, and a community that encompasses the entire globe, we can no longer have customs, practices, and mores that provide the "correct" answer to every ethical issue. As managers and employees, we must try to develop within us an ethical discipline that helps guide us and the companies for whom we work to the most ethically "correct" answer possible.

Exhibit 5.3 presents a matrix which illustrates many potential decisions that may be affected by the ethical standards of the strategic manager.

Current Trends During the 1960s and 1970s the American public became increasingly concerned with ethical issues. Some of the most significant events during this time which heightened the general concern for corporate and government abuse were:

- The electrical price conspiracy cases and television quiz scandals (1960–1961)
- The mounting concern for equal employment opportunities (mid-1960s)
- The Watergate era (early 1970s)
- Iran-Contra Hearings (mid-1980s)

This concern was not just an erroneous perception of the public because of increased media attention; it was real. "During the 1970s, 11 percent of the largest U.S. firms were convicted of bribery, criminal fraud, illegal campaign contributions, tax evasions, or some sort of price-fixing."[6] Several of these firms had two or more convictions, with Braniff International, Gulf Oil, and Ashland Oil having at least four convictions.

By the end of the 1970s, a study of managers at several firms showed that 59 to 70 percent of the managers felt "pressured to compromise personal ethics to achieve corporate goals."[7] However, corporations were beginning to respond to the pressures of the public and their own values, and by the end of that decade, almost three-fourths of all U.S. firms had a code of ethics, and more than 100 boards of directors of large firms had established a committee concerned with ethics, social responsibility, and/or public policy.[8] This same trend was confirmed by a 1984 survey which found that 80 percent of the respondents were taking steps to incorporate ethical values and concerns into their daily operations.[9]

Even though there has been increased emphasis on good ethical behavior,

EXHIBIT 5.3   ETHICS MATRIX

	Internal		External	
	I. Employers and employees	**II. Management and stockholders**	**III. Corporations and consumers**	**IV. Corporations and community**
A. Personnel	1. Discrimination 2. Sexual harassment 3. Financial protection of executives 4. Reverse discrimination 5. Quality of work life 6. Equal opportunity 7. Unions, testing, and job security 8. Executive compensation 9. Privacy	1. Electing board members 2. Equal opportunity proxy		1. Social organization dictating personnel policies 2. Insider trading 3. Public service 4. Integration
B. Operations	1. Job redesign 2. Quality of work life 3. Plant closing 4. Plant layoffs 5. Overtime allocation 6. Worker safety 7. Job assignment/ promotions 8. Theft 9. Performance evaluation	1. Plant closing/ modernization 2. Asset mismanagement 3. Pollution 4. Products liability 5. Products safety		1. US govt. vs. foreign govts re: production of goods 2. Bribery in site selection 3. Plant closing/ modernization 4. Bribery in contracts 5. Govt. assistance in site selection 6. Pollution 7. Supplier relations 8. EPA and site selection
C. Engineering	1. Theft of company secrets	1. Products liability 2. Products safety	1. Products reliability 2. Products liability 3. Products safety 4. Consumers dictating product design 5. Consumer monitoring	1. Govt. restriction on product design 2. Product safety 3. Free design service/ bribery
D. Finance/ accounting	1. Unethical accounting/financial practices 2. Expense accounting 3. Theft	1. Campaign contributions		1. US govt. bailout 2. Social organization dictating how/where to spend
E. Marketing	1. Product choice	1. Product choice	1. Service, quality, and safety	1. Price fixing 2. Distributor relationships 3. Product distribution 4. Product choice 5. Bribery 6. Advertising

Source: Richard W. Deane and Valerie Mock, unpublished paper, Georgia State University, 1987.

ethical misconduct has not been eliminated. Routine overcharges in defense and government contracts and incidents like the Ivan Boesky insider stock trading scandal remind us that there are still many areas in which we can improve our ethical decision making. Two ways to help improve this activity are: (1) understanding those areas where an ethical issue may be involved and (2) making ethical considerations an integral part of decision making.

Lower-Level Participation

Ultimately all decisions made by strategic managers must be interpreted and implemented through many individuals throughout the organization. If this process is to be successful, the different individuals must not only understand the decisions but also accept them.

A good way to get individuals to understand and accept decisions is to involve them in the strategic management process. As discussed in Chapter 2, the primary responsibility for determining corporate strategy usually rests with some combination of top management, the board of directors, and corporate-level planners. However, this does not mean that other levels in the organization cannot and should not participate in this process. On the contrary, it is good management practice to involve directly affected lower-level managers. From a practical standpoint, it usually works well to involve the next lower level of management. For example, when setting the corporate-level objectives, top management should normally involve the affected divisional managers in the process. Likewise, when setting divisional objectives, a division manager should involve the affected department managers. Actively involving the next lower level of management does not alter who is ultimately responsible, but it does generate additional inputs, ensure consistency, and foster commitment.

The Role of Politics and Power Relationships

One of Webster's definitions of politics is "of measures, plans, etc., shrewdly contrived, especially with regard to self-interest." Webster defines power as "ability to act; capacity for action of being acted upon; capability of producing or undergoing an effect." There is no doubt that organizational politics and power can, and often do, play a significant role in influencing decisions. The old saying "It's not what you know but who you know" reflects the general belief in the importance of politics. In a study of twenty-five strategic decision situations, Henry Mintzberg and his colleagues found that power and politics played a significant role in eight of the cases and were influencing factors in all the situations.[10] For purposes of this discussion, the external political environment is composed of those forces in the external environment which may influence decision processes. Obvious members of this group include lenders, stockholders, labor unions, pressure groups (such as consumer advocates, environmental advocates, civil rights groups, etc.), political parties, and government officials. The internal political environment is composed of those internal forces which may influence the strategic choice process. Members of this environment include employee groups and individuals in power positions. All forms of internal conflict and power struggles are manifestations of the internal political environment. Example 5.1 summarizes how some of these forces affected the Caterpillar Tractor Company in 1983. The end result of changes in the political environment is that management must find ways of involving and influencing the decision processes of other interests that have the power to prevent its strategies from being successfully implemented.

Power-Base Determinants The extent to which strategic decisions are influenced by politics depends on the power bases of those making the strategic choice. In this context, a *power base* consists of the resources available to a manager that give him or her the ability to convince others to go along with his or her ideas.[11] The resources contributing to a strategic manager's power base include such factors as the manager's professional reputation, his or her relationships with other managers (both superiors and subordinates), the manager's ownership position, and the manager's ability to recognize and use the available resources.

A manager's professional reputation is very much influenced by his or her past performance record. For example, a chief executive officer (CEO) who has a well-documented and successful track record is going to be in a much better position to exert influence than a newly appointed CEO. A manager's relationships with other managers can have a tremendous impact on the manager's power base. Relationships with the chairperson and the board of direc-

---

EXAMPLE 5.1

How Certain Forces in the Political Environment Affected Caterpillar Tractor Co.

In the face of tough competition from Japan's Komatsu Ltd., Caterpillar Tractor Company has been having a rough time. A major reason for this is that Komatsu's labor costs are about one-half of CAT's. After a bitter and financially damaging 7-month strike, CAT relented in its battle to keep labor costs from rising further. Faced with first fiscal quarter losses of $172 million and mounting inventory shortages, CAT dropped many of its demands for concessions and offered its 20,400 hourly workers a substantial raise. Despite the union's apparent victory, the settlement could have a long-term negative effect on both sides. Many believe that the settlement will make it even more difficult for CAT to compete against lower-cost producers. Ironically, the union leadership was not satisfied with the agreement and the company-union relationship has only become more hostile.

Source: Adapted from "A Strike-Weary Caterpillar Knuckles Under," *Business Week*, May 2, 1983, pp. 30–31.

tors are two of the most crucial factors in determining the manager's power base. A CEO who is at odds with the chairperson and/or the board is generally not in a position to exercise much influence.

A manager who owns a significant portion of an organization is naturally in a much more powerful position than one who doesn't, but what constitutes a "significant portion" depends on the size of the organization. In large organizations, owning a small percentage may be significant. For example, Alfred Sloan, who once controlled General Motors, owned only 1 percent of its stock.[12] In small organizations, however, a 51 percent interest is generally required for control. Finally, it is possible for a manager to have many of the above-described power bases and yet not know how to use them effectively. Effective use of power requires certain strategic maneuvers which some managers seem to grasp more readily than others. The following section describes some of the maneuvers a manager can undertake to successfully use his or her power.

Implementing Power   Recognizing that every situation is unique, a manager can do many things to better his or her chances for influencing others.[13]

- *Present a nonthreatening image.* Most people do not respond to threats, and even when they do, the threats create a negative environment.
- *Ask for input from others.* Everyone likes to be asked his or her opinion. Doing so increases the likelihood of employee support.
- *Diffuse opposition by bringing it out into the open.* It is usually better to bring the opposition out into the open and to confront it than to try to stifle it.
- *Align with others in power.* As the old saying goes, "Don't argue with the man whose name is on the building!"

There is little doubt that both values and power relationships have a significant impact on the formulation of organizational objectives. These relationships are often evidenced through top-level turnover and power struggles that are made public. One highly publicized case involved the Bendix Corporation in 1982. William Agee, who was chairman of Bendix, attempted a hostile takeover of the Martin Marietta Corporation. The end result, after much maneuvering by several parties, was that Bendix was itself acquired by Allied Corporation. After a few short months as the number 2 man at Allied, Agee resigned.

THE ESTABLISHMENT OF OBJECTIVES

As defined in Chapter 1, an objective is a statement of what is to be achieved. Once the mission has been established, objectives specify the results that are expected in the pursuit of the mission. In essence, objectives provide a means of transforming a broad mission or purpose into specific actions. Clearly stated objectives also provide a basis for monitoring progress toward the mission. Without clear objectives it is difficult for an organization to know what it should be doing to achieve its mission. Similarly, without measurable objectives it is difficult for an organization to realize just how it is progressing toward its mission. Objectives fit into the strategic management process in the following hierarchical manner.

Hierarchies of Objectives

Hierarchies of objectives exist in almost all organizations. One hierarchy is based upon the *breadth of influence* of the objectives. An organization's mission is in one sense the broadest and highest-level objective. The next level is composed of objectives that affect the entire organization; these are called *corporate,* or *organizational, objectives. Divisional objectives* are those derived from the corporate objectives, *departmental objectives* are derived from the divisional objectives, and so forth, right down to the individual level. Exhibit 5.4 illustrates this hierarchy of objectives.

In addition to the hierarchy based on breadth of influence, organizations also have a hierarchy based on *time span* of the objectives. What is long-range and short-range is not absolute but rather depends on the industry and its environment. For example, long-range in the electronics industry might be 2 years, whereas long-range in the brick-manufacturing industry might be 8 years. However, most companies consider long-range to be anything over 3

EXHIBIT 5.4 HIERARCHY OF OBJECTIVES BASED ON BREADTH OF INFLUENCE

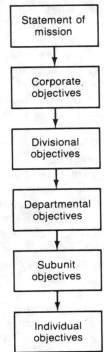

years, intermediate-range to be 1 to 3 years, and short-range to be 1 year or less.

These two hierarchies of objectives are not mutually exclusive of each other. In general, the wider the breadth of influence, the longer-range the objectives tend to be. For example, most corporate objectives are long-range. However, it is possible to have a mix of time span objectives for a given level of the organization. For instance, a department may have some long-range and some short-range objectives.

Formulating Objectives

Formulating meaningful objectives at any level in the organization involves at least four stages:

1. Identifying the different key result areas to be covered by objectives
2. Determining the time frame covered by the objectives
3. Determining the magnitudes of the objectives ← size
4. Putting the objectives in written form

Key Result Areas The most difficult and critical stage of the objective formulation process is identifying the areas that are vital to the success of the organization. These areas are referred to as *key result areas*. In general, each key result area should be covered by an objective. Key result areas exist for the organization as a whole and for the different subunits of the organization. For example, corporate growth objectives would represent a key result area for the organization as a whole. On the other hand, output per machine objectives would represent a key result area for a manufacturing department. Key result areas answer the question: What areas should be monitored to determine whether the organization (or the organizational unit) is doing a good, average, or poor job? In other words, key result areas should reflect the performance of the organization or the organizational unit in question.

Corporate Key Result Areas Exhibit 5.5 presents a list of some of the most commonly used corporate key result areas. It should be noted that the list in Exhibit 5.5 is not exhaustive but rather is intended to illustrate potential corporate key result areas. Naturally, the key result areas appropriate for a given organization are dependent on the specific business and industry. Research has shown that profitability and market-related objectives tend to be the most frequently used.[14] When selecting corporate-level long-range objectives, the strategist should attempt to answer the question, "What factors should be measured to know how the organization is performing?" Objectives should usually be set to reflect each of these factors.

Multiple Objectives Research studies accentuate the fact that most firms today are emphasizing performance in multiple key result areas as opposed to a single area. For example, Shetty reported that most of the companies in his study of eighty-two companies had five or six objectives.[15] Bhatty reported

EXHIBIT 5.5   POTENTIAL CORPORATE KEY RESULT AREAS

1. *Profitability.* Measures the degree to which the firm is attaining an acceptable level of profits; expressed in terms of profits before or after taxes, return on investment, earnings per share, or profit-to-sales ratios, among others.
2. *Markets.* Reflects the firm's position in its marketplace; expressed in terms of share of the market, dollar or unit volume in sales, or niche in the industry.
3. *Productivity.* Measures the efficiency of internal operations; expressed as a ratio of inputs to outputs such as number of items or services produced per unit of time.
4. *Product.* Describes the introduction or elimination of products or services; expressed in terms of when a product or service will be introduced or dropped.
5. *Financial resources.* Reflects goals relating to the funding needs of the firm; expressed in terms of capital structure, new issues of common stock, cash flow, working capital, dividend payment, and collection periods.
6. *Physical facilities.* Concerned with the physical facility needs of the firm; expressed in terms of square feet of office or plant space, fixed costs, units of production, or other similar measurements.
7. *Research and innovation.* Reflects the research, development, and/or innovation aspirations of the firm; usually expressed in terms of dollars to be expended.
8. *Organization objectives.* Describes objectives relating to changes in the organizational structure and related activities; expressed in terms of a desired future structure or network of relationships.
9. *Human resources.* Concerned with the human assets of the organization; expressed in terms of absenteeism, tardiness, number of grievances, and training.
10. *Social responsibility.* Refers to the commitments of the firm regarding society and its environment; expressed in terms of types of activities, number of days of service, or financial contributions.

that 80 percent of the companies in his study of medium-sized companies in the United Kingdom developed a set of multiple objectives.[16] When multiple objectives are being pursued, it is not unusual for some of the objectives to be in conflict with another, for example, production objectives and output objectives versus quality objectives. A good approach is first to rank and then to balance the different key result areas. Thus it is usually unwise to emphasize production output totally, with little regard for quality. On the other hand, overemphasizing quality can result in unacceptably low levels of production output. The need to strike a balance between production output and quality is obvious but in practice difficult. Example 5.2 lists the primary objectives of Automatic Data Processing, Inc., as spelled out in a company publication.

Determining the Time Frame Covered by Objectives

The time frame covered by an objective of increasing sales by 10 percent within the next 3 months is very different from one of increasing sales by 10 percent within the next 3 years. As discussed earlier, objectives are often categorized as short-range or long-range depending on the time horizon covered. Generally, short-range objectives are not established until the overall strategy has been formulated and is ready to be implemented. As a result, short-range objectives are usually established during the strategy implementation phase of

---

EXAMPLE 5.2

Objectives for ADP, Inc.

For our clients: to earn their continuing loyalty and respect. Client service is #1 at ADP. Our growth objectives leave little room for losing clients. Each of our clients is precious. They need us only if we provide them with accurate, efficient and responsible service. The client is pre-eminent and should be treated accordingly.

For our stockholders: to increase the value of their investment by continuing our historical growth of at least 15% per year, every year, in revenues and earnings. Our Return on Investment (ROI) should exceed external investment alternatives to ensure that our stockholders get a satisfactory return on ADP's retained earnings which are not paid out as dividends.

For our employees: to offer participation in ADP's success in which they play an important role...by offering challenges, opportunities for creativity, rewards, security, personal skills development and performance feedback. Our rewards should include competitive wages, above average opportunities for promotions, supplemental gain from ADP's stock participation plans and psychic income from accomplishment in an informal, apolitical, fast-paced environment.

Source: ADP Corporate Philosophy, rev. ed., Automatic Data Processing, Inc., Roseland, N.J., 1986, pp. 2–3. Used by permission.

---

the strategic management process. Therefore, this chapter is primarily concerned with the establishment of long-range objectives. When asked in 1978 what time horizon was covered by his company's planning, Samuel B. Casey, Jr., chairman of Pullman, Inc., answered:

> It depends on the individual business area. Some of the technological horizons in our divisions are out 12 or 15 years. Some of the product development systems are out seven years. Some of the other systems are out three or four years. For convenience of pulling it together and making it make sense, our strategic plan right now runs out seven years. There's nothing magical about the number of years; all we wanted to do was run the horizon out far enough so that an intelligent guy could not say to us without thinking, "It's going to look in 1985 just the way it does now." We simply set the horizon far enough so that if indeed change is likely, he's going to think about it and he's going to talk about it and we can interact on how we are going to respond to the change.[17]

Unfortunately, there are no firm rules which dictate the most appropriate time horizon for the different levels of objectives. As mentioned earlier in this chapter, the wider the breadth of influence, the longer-range the objectives generally tend to be. The important point is to recognize that every objective, with only a few possible exceptions, should be assigned a time horizon for accomplishment. Determining the magnitude of a given objective must be done in conjunction with establishing its time frame.

3. Determining the Magnitude of Objectives

The key point in setting the magnitude of an objective is to make it challenging but realistic. Determining the magnitude involves assigning specific values for objectives; for example, "In the next 6 months, the firm will hire ten new salespeople." Some people believe that the best approach to setting an objective is to set it just slightly higher than can be achieved. The theory behind this approach is that it keeps everybody stretching and avoids a letdown should an objective be attained.

The problem with this approach is that people almost always realize that the objective is unattainable, and therefore they say, "Why try? I know the objective is impossible to reach." Additionally, this approach ignores the fact that most people become more motivated when objectives are attained. The magnitude and accompanying time horizon of corporate objectives should be set so that the organization as a whole is challenged.

However, making the objectives realistic is just as important as making them challenging. Once the corporate-level objectives have been established as challenging and realistic, these same characteristics should cascade down through the different levels of objectives in the organization.

This leads to the next logical question: How does one know what is challenging yet realistic? Several factors can be analyzed to help determine the answer. The first thing to do is to look at historical results. For example, if a selected key result area is sales growth, at what rates have the company's sales grown over the previous several years? Another helpful approach is to analyze, wherever possible, how competitors have fared in the key result area. Industry and trade publications will often provide information relating to market share and sales volume. A source that is always available is the advice of others. Talk to key managers in the organization and solicit their ideas. Once each of the above sources—and any others that might be readily available—has been researched, challenging and yet realistic objectives can be developed for practically every situation.

4. Putting Objectives into Writing

If an adequate amount of thought has gone into selecting the key result areas, determining the time frame covered, and establishing the desired magnitude, committing the information to written form is a fairly easy task. Chapter 1 presented a few brief examples of both well-written and poorly written objectives. Exhibit 5.6 lists several guidelines that should be followed when objectives are being put into written form.

A good question to ask after an objective has been written is, "When the stated time period has passed, will there be any doubt or room for argument

EXHIBIT 5.6 GUIDELINES FOR PUTTING OBJECTIVES INTO WRITTEN FORM

A written statement of objectives should be:
1. Clear, concise, and unambiguous
2. Stated in a form that facilitates their use in measuring results at a future time
3. Accurate in terms of the true end-state sought
4. Consistent with the policies of the organization
5. Actionable and able to motivate
6. Conform to the ethical and social codes of society

concerning whether or not this objective has been reached?'' If the answer is yes, then the objective should be rewritten. For example, suppose a decided-upon objective is "to minimize the marketing costs over the next 6 months." At the end of the 6 months, there will probably be considerable room for debate concerning whether or not costs were truly "minimized." In the strictest sense of interpretation, the only real way to minimize costs is to spend zero dollars. On the other hand, if the objective has been "to reduce marketing costs by $150,000 over the next 6 months," there would be little room for doubt as to whether the objective has been achieved. Although there might be considerable debate as to why the objective *had* or *had not* been achieved, there should be no debate as to *whether* it had been achieved.

Unfortunately, not all objectives lend themselves to quantification. In such cases a *subjective* is used. A subjective is expressed in terms of a number of specific and verifiable activities which, when accomplished, lead to the desired future state or condition.[18] Exhibit 5.7 presents examples of subjectives. Thus, even when subjectives are properly used as goals, it should not be difficult to determine whether or not the stated activities have been accomplished.

The Role of Social Responsibility

Most firms are much more conscious of the societal impact of what they do than they were 20 years ago. Although no universally accepted definition of

EXHIBIT 5.7 EXAMPLES OF SUBJECTIVES

To improve public relations with the community:
a. Publish and distribute a districtwide newsletter to all parent, teacher, and student groups each month.
b. Conduct "open house" at least once a year at each school in the district.
c. Conduct weekly "rap" sessions for student representatives in each intermediate and high school.

To improve communications in the plant:
a. Conduct weekly staff meetings with all department heads.
b. Publish a monthly employee newsletter beginning in March of this year.
c. Have lunch at least once a month with two or three randomly selected foremen.

Source: Anthony P. Raia, *Managing by Objectives,* Scott, Foresman, Glenview, Ill., 1974, p. 25. Used by permission.

social responsibility currently exists, it has been defined as "the moral and ethical content of managerial and corporate decisions over and above the programmatic requirements imposed by legal principle and the market economy."[19] In other words, social responsibility refers to actions taken above and beyond those required by law and/or those that are directly financially beneficial. Some actions that might be classified as socially responsible are listed in Exhibit 5.8.

Many authors have argued that organizations must learn to achieve a certain level of corporate social responsibility if the present society and economy are to survive and flourish.[20] The basic tenet of this argument is that the *long-run* social usefulness of a business organization is a necessary condition for its continued existence.

People who argue against the active role of business in social responsibility are usually not opposed to the idea of social responsibility per se but rather question the appropriateness of business involvement. Subscribers to this viewpoint argue that the primary purpose of business is to maximize profit for shareholders and that anything which potentially detracts from profits should be shunned.

The biggest single obstacle to organizations assuming more social responsibility is pressure by financial analysts and stockholders. These groups push for steady increases in earnings per share on a quarterly basis. These pressures make it difficult to invest in areas that cannot be accurately measured and which may not produce immediate returns. Furthermore, most companies' performance appraisal systems are geared to short-term profit goals. Budgets and objectives are often based on short-run considerations. Management may state a willingness to forego some short-term profit in order to achieve certain social objectives. However, managers who sacrifice profit in their own departments and seek to justify it on the basis of corporate social goals often find superiors unsympathetic. The long-term orientation of a formal strategic management process can certainly help overcome these problems.

Regardless of how one feels, there is little doubt that social responsibility is considered a key result area by an increasing number of organizations. Example 5.3 outlines an innovative socially responsible program undertaken by Levi Strauss and Company. Example 5.4 describes a program ini-

EXHIBIT 5.8   SAMPLE SOCIALLY RESPONSIBLE ACTIONS

- Hiring the hard-core unemployed
- Hiring minorities
- Contributing human resources and/or money to charitable organizations
- Contributing money to educational institutions
- Supporting community projects such as renovating urban areas
- Maintaining a stable work force
- Supporting the efforts of minority groups in the community
- Ensuring the quality of products and services produced
- Installing modern pollution abatement equipment

EXAMPLE 5.3

Social Responsibility and Levi Strauss

Levi Strauss & Company, the maker of Levi jeans, is the largest garment maker in the world, with 44,000 employees in 140 plants worldwide, and is also widely recognized for its philanthropic activities. In recent years, Levi has donated approximately 2.4% of its pretax earnings to various worthwhile causes and has an innovative program to involve its employees in its philanthropic activities. About 10,000 Levi's employees belong to as many as 90 Community Involvement Teams throughout the world. Through these teams, the company has provided people and money to help correct a variety of problems in over 100 communities. Some of the community projects worked on include building an orphanage in Argentina and installing wells in the Philippines. Closer to home, the Community Involvement Teams have helped to create public health clinics and volunteer rescue squads.

Source: Adapted from ''Levi's Chief Urges Corporate Responsibility,'' *Management Review,* May 1, 1986, p. 8.

[handwritten margin note: love of mankind]

tiated in 1978 by Norton Simon, Inc., to relate bonuses directly to social responsibility.

SUMMARY

There are a multitude of internal and external environmental factors that can have an impact on decisions made by strategic managers. Some of the most significant of these factors include the values held by the managerial team, the ethical codes followed by the managerial team, the degree of lower-level participation in decisions, and the politics and power relationships present. A value is a conception, explicit or implicit, defining what an individual or group regards as desirable. People are not born with values but rather acquire and develop them early in life. Managers must try to develop an ethical discipline that helps guide them and their organizations toward the most ethical decisions. Several types of decisions influenced by the ethical standards of the strategist were presented. A good way to get individuals to understand and accept decisions is to involve them in the strategic management process. There is no doubt that organizational politics and power can, and often do, play a significant role in influencing decisions.

Objectives, which provide a means of transforming a broad mission or purpose into specific actions, exist within the framework of the strategic management process in hierarchical form. The hierarchies are organized in terms of both breadth of influence and time span. These two hierarchies are not mutually exclusive but are interactive. Generally, the wider the breadth of influence, the longer-range the objectives.

EXAMPLE 5.4

An Example of a Socially Responsible Firm

Social Responsibility at Norton Simon, Inc.—Norton Simon, Inc.,* whose subsidiaries include Avis, Inc., and Max Factor and Co., has even gone so far as to tie the annual bonuses of its managers to their performance in the area of social responsibility. Good performance on objectives relating to social responsibility can boost a manager's annual bonus as much as 20 percent; poor performance can reduce it by a similar amount. Considering the fact that annual bonuses often run as high as 50 percent of basic salary, the incentive has clearly been established. To use the words of David Mohoney, Norton Simon's Chairman and President, "Moral pressure is not enough to make managers behave in a socially responsible way."

Norton Simon concentrates its social responsibility efforts in four major areas: (1) equal employment opportunity; (2) the encouragement of minority businesses; (3) charitable contributions; and (4) the involvement of managers in community organizations. When calculating bonuses, Norton Simon takes into account performance in all of the above areas. Philip Davis, a Corporate Vice-President in charge of social responsibility, has said, "We try not to weigh particular areas of social responsibility. You have to be a full corporate citizen. We work on a spread of activities." Because of the difficulty of measuring socially responsible activities in some areas, bonuses are based roughly half on meeting numerical objectives and half on other factors.

As an example of how the program has worked out at Norton Simon, as of 1978, ethnic minorities made up 30 percent of the work force. This was about double the national average. Ethnic minorities also comprised about 11 percent of the managers compared with a national average of only 6 percent. About 22 percent of managers and professional employees are women. This was up from only 18 percent in just over a year since the bonus scheme was initiated.

*Norton Simon, Inc., was acquired by Esmark Apparel, Inc., in 1983 and Esmark was subsequently acquired by Beatrice Companies, Inc., in 1984.

Source: "Bonuses Pay-Outs Linked to Social Responsibility," *International Management,* August 1978, pp. 49–52. Reprinted with special permission from *International Management.* Copyright © 1978 McGraw-Hill Publications Company. All rights reserved.

Four stages are involved in formulating long-range objectives:

1 Identifying the different key result areas to be covered by objectives
2 Determining the time frame covered by the objectives
3 Determining the magnitudes of the objectives
4 Putting the objectives in written form

Once the corporate long-range objectives have been established, specific objectives are derived for different subunits of the organization. Primary responsibility for determining objectives rests with a combination of top management, the board of directors, and corporate-level planners, but directly affected managers in the next lower level should participate in the process. For example, when corporate-level objectives are being set, it is good management practice to involve the affected divisional managers, and so on down the line.

The establishment of objectives is clearly an interactive process which is influenced by many factors outlined in this chapter. An increasingly important key result area, social responsibility, was explored. This particular key result area remains quite controversial, however.

CHAPTER 5   REVIEW QUESTIONS

1 How can managerial values influence the decision-making process? Name the six categories of values established by Guth and Taguiri.
2 Describe at least three significant events that occurred during the 1960s and 1970s that contributed to the public's concern with corporate and government abuse of ethics.
3 Explain why it is good management practice to involve lower-level managers in the objective formulation process.
4 List and briefly discuss four possible actions a manager can take to implement power effectively.
5 What two hierarchies of objectives exist within the strategic management process? Are they mutually exclusive? Why or why not?
6 What steps are involved in the formulation of long-range objectives? Briefly outline each step.
7 Differentiate an objective from a subjective. When are subjectives used?
8 Define "social responsibility" and summarize the major arguments for and against it.

CHAPTER 5   DISCUSSION QUESTIONS

1 How would managerial values influence whether or not a company sees social responsibility as a key result area? Be specific in documenting which values would most likely result in a very socially responsible organization and which would lead to a more traditional bottom-line orientation.
2 How does the organization's mission influence the selection of key result areas?
3 Go to the library and look for illustrations of key result areas that are currently most important to some of our most successful corporations. Give specific examples, and make comparisons between companies. (Possible sources include annual reports and periodicals such as *The Wall Street Journal, Fortune,* and *Business Week.*)

CHAPTER 5   REFERENCES

1 William D. Guth and Renato Taguiri, "Personal Values and Corporate Strategy," *Harvard Business Review,* September–October 1965, pp. 124–125.
2 Ibid., p. 123.
3 George W. England, *The Manager and His Values: An International Perspective*

from the United States, Japan, Korea, India, and Australia, Ballinger, Cambridge, Mass., 1975.

4 I. Bamberger, "Values and Strategic Behaviour," *Management International Review,* vol. 26, no. 4, 1986, pp. 57–67.

5 The authors are indebted to Valerie Mock for much of the material in this section.

6 Gerald F. Cavanaugh, *American Business Values,* Prentice-Hall, Englewood Cliffs, N.J., 1984, p. 127.

7 Archie Carroll, "Managerial Ethics: A Post-Watergate View," *Business Horizons,* April 1975, pp. 75–80.

8 *Chronicle of Higher Education,* August 6, 1979, p. 2; and "Business Strategies for the 1980's," *Business and Society: Strategies for the 1980's,* U.S. Department of Commerce, Washington, D.C., 1980, pp. 33–34.

9 The Center for Business Ethics, "Are Corporations Institutionalizing Ethics?" *Journal of Business Ethics,* April 1986, pp. 85–91.

10 Henry Mintzberg et al., "The Structure of Unstructured Decision Processes," *Administrative Science Quarterly,* June 1976, p. 262.

11 Adapted from Virginia E. Schein, "Strategic Management and the Politics of Power," *Personnel Administrator,* October 1983, p. 56.

12 Alfred Sloan, Jr., in John McDonald and Catherine Stevens (eds.), *My Years with General Motors,* MacFadden-Bartell, New York, 1965.

13 Part of this list is adapted from Schein, loc. cit.

14 William R. Bolton, Stephen G. Franklin, William M. Lindsay, and Leslie W. Rue, "How Are Companies Planning Now?—A Survey," *Long Range Planning,* February 1982, p. 83; Y. K. Shetty, "New Look at Corporate Goals," *California Management Review,* vol. 16, no. 2, p. 73; and Egbert F. Bhatty, "Corporate Planning in Medium-Sized Companies in the U.K.," *Long Range Planning,* 1981, p. 65.

15 Shetty, loc. cit.

16 Bhatty, loc.cit.

17 Reprinted, by permission of the publisher, from Darryl J. Ellis and Peter P. Pekar, Jr., *Planning for Nonplanners,* AMACOM, New York, 1980, p. 95. Copyright ©1980 AMACOM, a division of American Management Associations, New York. All rights reserved.

18 Anthony P. Raia, *Managing by Objectives,* Scott, Foresman, Glenview, Ill., 1974, p. 25.

19 Robert H. Bork, "Modern Values and Social Responsibility," *MSU Business Topics,* Spring 1980, p. 7.

20 For example, see Henry Mintzberg, "The Case for Social Responsibility," *The Journal of Business Strategy,* Fall 1983, pp. 3–15; and Jacob Naor, "Planning and Social Responsibility," *Journal of Business Ethics,* vol. 1., 1982, pp. 313–319.

6

ASSESSING THE ENVIRONMENT

LEARNING OBJECTIVES

After studying this chapter, the reader should be able to:

1 Define the sectors of an organization's environment and to identify key issues in each sector
2 Explain the role of environmental analysis in the strategic management process
3 Locate appropriate sources of environmental information
4 Select and use appropriate tools for environmental analysis
5 Produce assumptions from environmental analysis and explain the importance of assumptions as an output of the analysis process

CHAPTER OUTLINE

CHARACTERISTICS OF THE ENVIRONMENT
  Uniqueness
  Dynamic Nature
  Variability of Control
REQUIREMENTS OF ENVIRONMENTAL ANALYSIS
  Defining the Broad Environment
    • The Economic Sector   • The Technological Sector   • The Social Sector
    • The Political Sector
  Defining the Competitive Environment
    • Analyzing Industry Structure   • A Closer Look at Competitors

The most promising path for an organization to follow in pursuit of its objectives depends on its internal capabilities (Chapter 7) and on a complex series of interactions and relationships with forces external to the organization. These external forces, conditions, situations, events, and relationships over which the organization has little control are referred to collectively as the organization's *environment*. The increasing influence of the environment on contemporary organizations has been widely discussed and documented.[1]

Environmental analysis is a critical component of strategic management because it produces much of the information which is required to assess the outlook for the future. The environment is a significant source of change. Some organizations become victims of change, while others use change to their advantage. Organizations are more likely to be able to turn change to their advantage if they are forewarned. This is a major purpose of the environmental analysis process. Example 6.1 shows how Alcoa Aluminum is responding to perceived change in consumption patterns for basic materials to position itself for long-term growth and profitability.

CHARACTERISTICS OF THE ENVIRONMENT

Before beginning environmental analysis, the strategist should understand some characteristics of the environment. Organizational environments are unique and dynamic and can be influenced in some cases.

Uniqueness

No two organizations face exactly the same external environment. Even competitors like Gerber and Heinz, who provide baby food to similar customers, do not face the same external conditions. Exhibit 6.1 compares the environment faced by Gerber with that faced by Heinz. Both companies are

---

EXAMPLE 6.1

Alcoa Responds to a Changing Environment

In 1987, the Aluminum Company of America (Alcoa) received 85 percent of its revenues from aluminum, but a program is underway to decrease that percentage to 50 by 1995 and to shift the product offerings in the aluminum line to more profitable lines. Alcoa hopes to "transform itself from a 100-year-old metals company into the leading Space Age materials producer of the 21st century." The company employs over 1000 researchers and is prepared to spend billions to achieve this transformation.

The company is responding to trends in materials usage which threaten its basic business. Materials use in general is declining as engineers and designers search for ways to use less steel, concrete, and aluminum in products and structures. In most cases both cost and weight are factors in the changes in materials. There is also a shift to alloys, composites, and new forms of plastics and ceramics. In addition, materials manufacturers are working more closely with customers to design materials that will meet specific needs to capture markets and higher profits. If materials have life cycles, it appears that steel has followed its predecessor iron into decline and that aluminum and cement may not be far behind. Alcoa is moving to build new businesses before it is too late.

Source: Adapted from information in "Alcoa: Recycling Itself to Become a Pioneer in New Materials," *Business Week,* February 9, 1987, pp. 56–58; "The Future Belongs to the Light Stuff," *Business Week,* February 9, 1987, p. 57.

---

leading producers of baby foods. Competitors in the same industry face unique environments, and analysis must be tailored specifically for the organization for which strategy is formulated.

Dynamic Nature

The relationships, events, and conditions which make up the unique environment of any organization are not static. Very few organizations face the same set of factors at the same magnitudes of importance for many years. Customer needs and tastes change; legal obligations and restraints change; or the organization simply grows and establishes a different position relative to competitors. The financial services industry and the firms which comprise it have been faced with a succession of environmental changes. Some of these environmental changes are so fundamental that they may affect the long-term survival of organizations, while others are only temporary and may be ignored. The dynamic nature of the environment means that environmental assessment must be continuous.

EXHIBIT 6.1   THE UNIQUE ENVIRONMENTS OF GERBER AND HEINZ

Gerber Products Co. and H. J. Heinz are the leading producers of baby foods in the United States. Both use similar processes to produce high-quality products for safe consumption by babies. Both are affected by changes in birthrate trends, which each watches very closely. These and other similarities do not provide these competitors with identical environments. Each company must identify the most relevant aspects of the environment for its own unique situation.

	Gerber	Heinz
Supply sector	Purchases food for processing	Some backward integration into vegetable growing.
Buyer sector	Retail shelf space is tight; premium price has quality image with mothers (buyers are not the consumers).	Underprices Gerber slightly; image lower accordingly.
Substitutes	Both companies vulnerable to increase in nursing mothers and to use of home processed baby food.	
Competitors	Holds dominant position; 71% share seen as difficult to increase.	A distant second to Gerber.
Geographic scope	International forays less successful; e.g., left Venezuela because of price controls.	Leading international baby food manufacturer; product line wider internationally than in U.S.
Political sector	Subject to regulations concerning content, sanitary processing, and advertising domestically.	Exposure to different political systems and regulations worldwide.
Social/economic sector	U.S. birthrate to rise 1% annually till 1990; U.S. per capita use of baby foods rising; 42% of U.S. babies first born.	Birthrate dropping in EEC; less worldwide acceptance of prepared foods.

Conclusions: The international scope of Heinz' baby food business presents a different set of threats and opportunities from that of Gerber, which is primarily a domestic company and is also diversified into other baby products.

Source: Adapted from "Gerber Concentrating on Babies Again for Slow, Steady Growth," *Business Week,* August 22, 1983, p. 80.

Variability of Control

Organizations are not helpless in the face of environmental factors, but certainly some aspects of environmental change are more amenable than others to control or influence. The political sector on all levels is notoriously open to influence by interest groups. In contrast, the weather must be taken as it comes and is not even predictable for more than the very short term. This variability in control means that an organization may work to shape parts of its environment but that it may also have to alter strategy or even objectives when faced with insurmountable environmental obstacles. When cable television and VCRs threatened the box office revenues of the American film industry in the 1980s, the industry simultaneously sought to adapt to and shape the new environment:

1 *The competitive environment.* Several studios have entered into joint ventures for film production with services which compete with the leading cable company, Home Box Office. These joint ventures helped finance and spread the risk of filmmaking as well as ensured pay television distribution outlets. Disney created its own cable outlet, the Disney Channel.

2 *Legal action.* MCA, Inc., sued Sony in what became known as the "Betamax Case." The Supreme Court declared that home taping of television material, including movies, is legal. The film industry then began to seek a surcharge on the machines and blank tapes in compensation for what the industry claimed was copyright infringement. This effort has not been successful.

3 *Lobbying.* The Motion Picture Association of America lobbied to stiffen copyright infringement penalties in the United States from a misdemeanor to a felony, carrying a maximum penalty of 5 years in jail and a $25,000 fine.[2]

The influence of an industry or of a specific organization over its environment varies. Although some events must be accepted as givens, there is often room for response which can mitigate their effects.

REQUIREMENTS OF ENVIRONMENTAL ANALYSIS

The environmental analysis phase of the strategic management process seeks to uncover *relevant* information rather than *extensive* information; it rewards the pursuit of quality rather than quantity. Furthermore, the process must be future-oriented to provide for adequate response time, whether the desired response is to capitalize on a trend or to influence its direction. Finally, the information must be translated into a form that facilitates its use in strategic planning. From these requirements, environmental analysis can be divided into three major steps:

1 *Defining.* Determining the bounds and relevant sectors of the environment.

2 *Scanning and forecasting.* Ensuring that information is available concerning the defined environment.

3 *Interpreting.* Packaging information into forms that are useful for planning.

The next sections of the chapter deal with each step in detail.

Defining the Broad Environment

Every organization is subject to general trends which are felt in many industries and which are not usually amenable to influence by a single organization. These trends can be classified as technological, economic, social, and political, according to the sector of the environment from which they come. The force of trends varies with the geographical scope of competition, so it is helpful to identify the scope of the sector which requires scanning. For example, a local restaurant is much more influenced by local and to a lesser extent regional trends than a national chain of fast-food restaurants would be. A fast-food company such as McDonald's, which is international in scope of operations, has a still wider range of environmental influences to which it must respond.

The Economic Sector The fluctuations of local, national, and world economies are related in many ways, but it is still important to make separate assessments based on organizational scope. Local conditions can moderate or deepen the effects of national economic trends. The decline in oil prices in the mid-1980s was beneficial for many areas, but Texas and Louisiana suffered a recession in the midst of national economic prosperity because their economies were dependent upon oil. To assess the local situation, an organization might seek information concerning the economic base and future of the region and the effects of this outlook on wage rates, disposable income, unemployment, and the transportation and commercial base.[3] On the national level, trends in growth, income levels, inflation, balance of payments, and taxation are only a few of the indicators of the ability of the economy to produce and consume goods and services.

The international economy can be divided into four economic categories: (1) the western democracies (including Japan), (2) the eastern bloc, (3) the underdeveloped nations, and (4) the developing nations. In the western democracies, growth is concentrated in the service, high-technology, and leisure industries. Population growth is slow, causing more and more businesses to rely on segmentation of markets. The political situation is usually stable. The eastern bloc is following the path of the western democracies, but has not made as complete a shift to service. The underdeveloped nations are characterized by rising populations, low standards of education, and lack of a transportation and commercial base. The standard of living in these countries has changed only marginally throughout their history. In the developing nations, gross national product (GNP) is rapidly increasing, but wages are low and consumer goods scarce. Most critical is the unevenness of income and wealth, the rapidity of change, and the political instability which can threaten organizations operating in such areas. Thus it is possible for an international organization to be operating in or dealing with as many as four different economic environments.

The Technological Sector *Technology* refers to the means chosen to do useful work. "Technological trends include not only the glamorous invention that revolutionizes our lives, but also the gradual painstaking improvements in methods, in materials, in design, in application, in diffusion into new industries and in efficiency."[4] It includes hardware, software, and "liveware." For centuries, the simple process of handling business correspondence has involved dictation, transcription, and final review and signature. Technological improvements which made the process more efficient include the creation of a standardized shorthand writing system, the invention of the typewriter, the use of voice recording machines for dictation, and the use of the microcomputer for transcription and editing. All four represent technological change even though only the typing, recording, and word processing activities involve machines.

The effects of technological changes are felt in all the following ways:

- *New products or services.* The development of the internal combustion engine produced new products, from automobiles to lawn mowers to motorcycles, as innovators began to visualize better work methods and leisure applications for the engine.
- *Alternate processing methods, raw materials, and service delivery.* The introduction of robotics to assembly line work has altered mass production technology in some sectors of the automobile industry, while the development of alloys and plastics has made cars lighter and more fuel-efficient.
- *Changes in complementary products or services.* Blacksmiths have all but disappeared, but van customization has become a significant business in some areas of the country. Both related to the development and applications of the internal combustion engine.

All companies feel the effects of "progress," but the dramatic shifts in technology which render whole sectors of the economy almost obsolete are rare. Foreseeing technological change is probably not as critical a skill for the strategist as choosing the proper time frame for reacting to and determining the implications of changes. It is less important to track every possible change which may affect the organization than to consider only several of the most important changes.

The Social Sector   The behavior patterns of individuals and groups reflect their attitudes, beliefs, and values. The social environment includes the attitudes and values of society as well as the behavior which is motivated by those values. A community's attitude toward legalized gambling, the composition of families and households, and the preference for fast food over home cooking are all manifestations of the social environment. The impact of the social sector is felt in changing needs, tastes, and preferences of consumers, in relations with employees, and in the expectations of society about how the organization should fulfill its citizenship role. Expectations concerning responsible use of the physical environment have greatly increased in business organizations since the 1960s. The attitudes of employees and, consequently, the relationship of employees to the firm are also changing. The willingness to put forth an all-out effort to earn more money is less evident than it was in the past, as employees opt for more leisure and depend less on work to meet their needs for esteem and fulfillment.[5]

Societal attitudes that are strongly held are often expressed as laws. For example, the value placed on human life is expressed in legislation dealing with homicide. A wave of antialcohol feeling in the early years of the twentieth century led to the national institution of Prohibition and is still expressed in "dry" counties and municipalities. Recently, many states have passed harsher laws dealing with the problem of driving under the influence of alcohol. The increasing concern over the physical environment in the 1960s and 1970s led to a multitude of pollution laws and regulations and a cleaner environment in the 1980s.

The Political Sector   The political sector of the environment presents actual and potential restrictions on the way an organization operates. These restrictions can take the form of (1) laws which require or prohibit certain actions, (2) regulations which interpret and detail laws, or (3) avenues for reporting relationships and oversight functions. The differences among local, national, and international subsectors of the political environment are often quite dramatic. Political instability in some countries makes the very form of government subject to revolutionary change. For example, the overthrow of Ferdinand Marcos in the Philippines and the return of Hong Kong to the Peoples' Republic of China raise serious questions about the rules for doing business in those areas.

In addition to the basic system of government and the laws the system promulgates, the political environment might include such issues as monitoring government policy toward income tax, relative influence of unions, and policies concerning utilization of natural resources.[6]

The political environment is probably most subject to influence exerted by organizations or groups of organizations with common goals. Political action committees are one method used for political influence by a single organization, while industry lobbying groups represent combinations of interested parties. Public opinion may be used to influence the political environment as well.

Defining the Competitive Environment

Exhibit 6.2 shows the organization's interaction with the broad environment and the competitive environment. While the organization is affected by trends in the broad environment, these trends are often felt by the organization's competitors also. In the political environment, for example, laws generally regulate whole industries rather than singling out individual companies for regulation unless the industry is a regulated monopoly. In the competitive environment, however, events often have unequal impact. Because of this unequal impact, it is the competitive environment in which strategy can be most useful. For example, in the American wine industry, all competitors are subject to changing consumption trends which originate in the social environment. As the population ages and has a higher average level of education, it turns away from "hard" liquor, wine becomes more popular. The wine cooler, a mixture of wine and fruit juice, with high consumer appeal and high margins, was introduced in the mid-1980s and soon became the fastest growing product in the industry. Gallo wine, the dominant competitor in the industry, was in the best position to capitalize on this opportunity. Gallo's introduction and promotion of their Bartles' and James' wine cooler had a significant impact on their competitors. In less than a year, B&J had reached number 1 status in the industry while the other brands, including the original wine cooler, California Coolers, lost share. The effect of the broad environmental trend on wine producers was shaped by Gallo's response to that trend.

The competitive environment is the arena in which goals and objectives are actually pursued. Constraints on strategic choices come from the structure of the industry, the competitors' strategies, and the market.

Analyzing Industry Structure Michael Porter has popularized the technique of industry analysis in a number of articles and two books.[7] Porter ar-

EXHIBIT 6.2   AN ENVIRONMENTAL SCHEMATIC

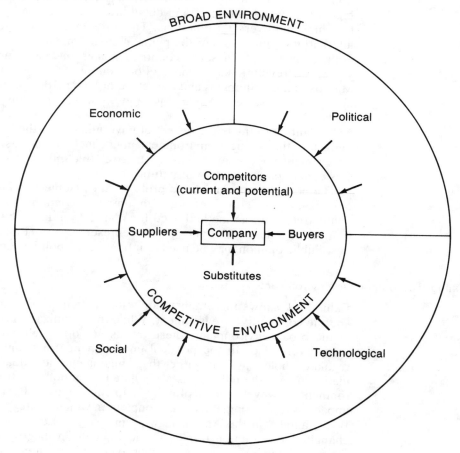

gues that there are five forces which work together to determine the type and direction of pressures on profitability that will be found in a given industry. When these forces of competition are favorable, there will be less downward pressure on profitability, and the industry should have a higher average level of profitability (measured by return on investment). When the structural factors are unfavorable, there will be more downward pressure on profitability and a correspondingly lower average level of profitability. A company which is competing in an industry with an unfavorable structure must find a way to gain an advantage over its competitors which will allow it to earn above-average levels of profitability. If no competitive advantage can be developed, it may be possible to change the structure of the industry. If changing the structure is not a viable alternative, the company should consider exiting the industry. A company which is operating in an industry with a favorable structure should work to maintain the structure.

Exhibit 6.3 lists the five forces of competition and shows how each affects profitability, all other things being equal. It is important to remember, however, that all other things are seldom equal. That is, each of these forces operates simultaneously with the others so that the stronger forces will predominate. For example, if the force of rivalry is very strong, average profitability may be low even if all the other forces are mildly favorable.

Rivalry   The force of rivalry reflects the interactions among competitors who produce products or services that are close substitutes for each other. These competitors are collectively known as an industry. An industry which is characterized by firms trying to edge out each other for market share is said to be experiencing rivalry. Rivalry is more intense than ordinary competition. Firms take actions which may damage their own profitability in the short run with the idea that it will hurt competitors more, and in the long run, the initiating firm will gain some advantage over the others. Rivalry is usually exhibited in price wars (a series of retaliatory price cuts), advertising barrages (characterized either by the disparaging tone of the advertisement itself or by a significant increase in the amount of advertising), and product proliferation (each competitor matches the other with new product introductions). Rivalry is damaging to industry profitability because it is costly. Businesses generally try to minimize rivalry within the bounds of law; however, many factors can create or escalate rivalry in an industry and they should be carefully monitored as part of the environmental analysis process.

As rivalry increases, average profitability is pushed down, all other things being equal. Rivalry is greater when:

- There are many small firms in an industry or when there is no clearly dominant firm to set and enforce standards for competition.

EXHIBIT 6.3   FIVE FORCES OF COMPETITION AND THEIR EFFECTS ON AVERAGE INDUSTRY PROFITABILITY
(All other things being equal)

Forces	Effect on
Rivalry ↑	Average profitability ↓
Power of suppliers ↑	Average profitability ↓
Power of buyers ↑	Average profitability ↓
Threat of new entrants ↑	Average profitability ↓
Threat of substitutes ↑	Average profitability ↓

(b) • Market growth rate slows because each firm must begin to take sales from competitors if it wishes to maintain historic growth rates.

(c) • It is difficult to leave the industry. This occurs when there is no market for assets of the industry or when government regulation prohibits exit.

(d) • There is chronic overcapacity, high fixed costs, and/or perishable products. In each of these situations, there is great incentive to cut prices to move products and provide some contribution toward fixed costs. Industrywide, this practice can lead to price wars.

(e) • Industry products/services are undifferentiated. When price is the only distinguishing factor for the buyer, there is great incentive to gain share by lowering price, a practice which can also result in price wars.

(f) • Competitors are diverse. A new company, acquisitions, or changes in management can introduce new values, ideas about competition, and practices to an industry. As current competitors respond to new strategies, rivalry may escalate.

2 _Power of Suppliers_ Suppliers provide the inputs necessary for the production of the product or delivery of the service by the industry. Organizations within an industry compete with each other as well as with organizations outside the industry for labor, raw materials, and capital. When suppliers are able to dictate the terms on which supplies will be obtained, and the industry is not able to pass the cost of these terms along to the customer, there is downward pressure on industry profitability. If suppliers are in a position to dictate such terms, they are said to be powerful.

Powerful suppliers can reduce industry profitability by influencing cost, quality, and/or availability of inputs. Suppliers are powerful if

1 • There are no substitutes for the input they provide
2 • The industry does not generate significant volume for the suppliers
3 • The supplier industry is concentrated
4 • The supplied input makes a significant contribution to the final appearance or function of the industry product
5 • The suppliers provide a credible threat of forward integration
6 • The industry would incur switching costs if they change supply sources
7 supplier doesn't contend with other products.

3 *Power of Buyers* The term ''buyers'' refers both to the immediate customer for the product (such as the soft drink bottler who buys soft drink concentrate from the major soft drink concentrate manufacturers like Coca-Cola and Pepsi) as well as the final consumer (the individual who orders a Coke at a restaurant or purchases a Pepsi from a vending machine). In some industries there may be several intermediate customers between the industry and the final consumer; in others the industry sells directly to the consumer of the product. The more buyers are able to dictate the terms under which they will make their purchases, the more powerful they are.

Powerful buyers can exert bargaining leverage in their dealings with the industry or because of price sensitivity they may curtail purchases. Buyers are powerful when

1 • They are concentrated

8 - low profits ∴ low purchasing costs
9 - buyer not concerned about quality
10 - buyer - product doesn't save money

2 • They generate significant volume for the industry
3 • They are informed about the product or service
4 • They provide a threat of backward integration
5 • Substitute products exist
6 • Purchases from industry constitute a large percentage of total purchases
7 • Product/service is undifferentiated — plenty of substitutes.

4¾ ***Entry Barriers*** An analysis of the prospects for the beer industry in 1970 would have presented a comfortable picture for companies producing brands like Schlitz, Falstaff, and Carling—if the forces of rivalry, buyers, and suppliers had been considered. Each of the companies had a respectable share of a growing national market. Anheuser-Busch held the leading position, but there seemed to be opportunities for all. The acquisition of Miller (then makers of a premium beer called Highlife) by the international conglomerate Philip Morris was the key change that caused disaster, or near disaster, for several national brands. Miller, backed by the resources of Philip Morris, began an aggressive fight for position in the industry, and Anheuser-Busch responded with equal vigor. Many lesser competitors were lost as the giants battled for market share. As the previous example illustrates, the competitive environment can be dramatically altered by the acquisition of one of the competitors or by the development of competitive capabilities by an organization not previously competing in the industry. Such situations make it necessary to consider entry barriers. *Entry barriers* are the factors which put new entrants at a cost disadvantage relative to competitors already established. When new entrants are subject to higher operating costs than established competitors, they may find other more attractive opportunities. Even if they persist with their plans for entry, current competitors can defend their positions from a position of strength (lower costs).

Entry barriers are higher when

1 • Economies of scale exist for current competitors in the industry. New entrants must incur the capital costs of large production facilities to keep their unit costs down and maintain competitive prices, or they may forego the large capital investment but have higher unit costs and higher prices. Higher prices, in turn, make it difficult to gain share from established competitors who enjoy a more favorable cost position.

2 • Absolute cost advantages exist for current competitors in the industry. Absolute cost advantages exist when current competitors (regardless of the size of their operations) have lower costs. This may be due to patents, favorable long-term supply contracts, or experience in operations.

3 • Brand loyalty and product differentiation are present in the industry. Users view the product/service as unique and are less price sensitive. This makes it difficult for new competitors to establish a market position.

Airline industry deregulated → caused more competition

4 • Government regulations limit new competitors.

5 • Start-up costs (including both fixed and working capital) are high.

6 • Current competitors move to make it difficult for new entrants to establish themselves. This may be done by cutting prices in markets where new products are being tested as long as such pricing is not predatory.

plus 7. access to dist. channels

It should be noted that entry barriers are most effective against start-ups. The only entry barrier which seems to be consistently effective against entry by acquisition is the reaction of existing competitors.[8]

Substitute Products   Industry sales and profitability are limited by what the customer will pay for a given level of quality or service when alternatives are available. Commercial baking companies often switch from high-fructose corn sweeteners to sugar when the price of sugar decreases and switch back when the price of sugar increases. As a result profits in the high-fructose corn syrup industry are limited by the price of sugar. When there is a strong threat of substitution, average profitability can suffer.

The threat of substitution holds down industry profits by allowing buyers options. The threat of substitution is greater when

- Switching costs are not significant
- Substitutes provide about the same value for cost
- Buyers are in the habit of substituting

A Closer Look at Competitors   Exhibit 6.4 summarizes in graphic form the key elements of industry analysis. This approach provides an understanding of the broad competitive forces which influence average industry profitability. The strategist must also take a closer look at competitors. The first step in this process is to identify them. This requires defining the industry in functional terms (what the product or service does) rather than physical terms (what the product or service is). This allows the strategist to work with a list of competitors which is broad enough to include the key competitors but not so broad that valuable resources are wasted in analysis of noncritical competitors. Using a functional rather than a physical definition of the industry will yield a broad industry definition. Taking care to formulate a precise definition will provide the needed focus. Exhibit 6.5 provides examples of functional and precise industry definitions.

EXHIBIT 6.4   PORTER'S MODEL OF INDUSTRY ANALYSIS

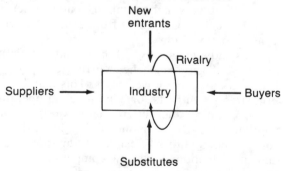

Source: Michael Porter, *Competitive Strategy: Techniques for Analyzing Industries and Competitors,* Free Press, New York, 1980. Reprinted with permission of The Free Press, a Division of Macmillan, Inc. © 1980 by The Free Press.

EXHIBIT 6.5   EXAMPLES OF INDUSTRY DEFINITIONS

	Product	Function
General	Telephone service	Information transmission
Precise	Long-distance telephone service	Immediate long-distance information transmission

(a)

	Product	Function
General	Railroad	Transportation
Precise	Long-haul, coal-carrying railroad	Long-distance transportation of high-density, low-value products

(b)

The definition in Exhibit 6.5a would include close substitutes to long-distance telephone service such as facsimile transmission and would be more useful for strategy analysis.

There may be hundreds of companies that make products that are close substitutes and thus should be considered competitors. All are not equally important to the environmental analysis of a particular organization. Key competitors may fall in several categories. The dominant company in an industry should receive careful scrutiny. A company may be dominant by virtue of its cost position, its research and development skills, its marketing clout, its customer service, or any of a number of ways that competitive advantage can be achieved. Anheuser-Busch, Coca-Cola, and IBM have all played this role in their industries. Another category of key competitors is those who are pursuing strategies similar to the company of interest. Companies which pursue the same strategy in an industry are known as a *strategic group*. They have answered the question of how to compete in the same way and should be carefully monitored. Finally, companies in the industry may change from one strategic group to another and firms should watch for trends which indicate changing strategies by competitors. Exhibit 6.6 provides a format for identifying and assessing key competitors. Exhibit 6.7 provides a format for analysis of key competitors.

EXHIBIT 6.6   FORMAT FOR IDENTIFYING KEY COMPETITORS

List competitors with product line(s) most similar to that (those) of your company:

1. _____

2. _____

3. _____

List competitors who serve customer needs most similar to yours:

1. _____

2. _____

3. _____

List competitors with geographic scope similar to yours:

1. _____

2. _____

3. _____

List competitors who provide a price/performance value similar to yours:

1. _____

2. _____

3. _____

List competitors in order by market share until your market share is reached:

1. _____

2. _____

3. _____

List as many competitors as are necessary to complete the category. Key competitors will be those that appear in the top three of any one list and those that reappear on more than one list.

EXHIBIT 6.7 FORMAT FOR ANALYSIS OF KEY COMPETITORS
(Rate each key competitor on the categories below.)

Category	Competitor names				
	A	B	C	D	E
Growth capacity					
Cost position					
Customer franchise					
Management style					
Scope of operations					
Product performance					
Market responsiveness					
R&D capabilities					
Image of quality					
Market share					
Financial strength					

Note: Summary ratings such as strong, weak, and not applicable may be used, but there should be documentation for these summaries.

Identifying Markets and Market Segments A final but critical element of the competitive environment is the market or market segments served by the company. Many have suggested that it is almost impossible to know too much about or be too close to one's customers. An organization should know what needs are being met by their product and should attempt to define what the value of their product or service is to their customer. This information is the basis for generating strategic alternatives for both product development and market development. Exhibit 6.8 provides a format for market identification and assessment.

Scanning and Forecasting

In order to obtain accurate information concerning current events and reasonable assessments of future trends, an intelligence function must be in place. It may be informal and impressionistic or part of a sophisticated information system. The intelligence function must be designed and judged on the basis of the benefit to the organization rather than the size, sophistication, or cost of the effort. In the face of information overload, many argue that it is more important to pick up a few key trends and incorporate them into strategy formulation

EXHIBIT 6.8   CUSTOMER PROFILE

Consumer markets	Commercial markets
Age	Industry
Income levels	Purchasing procedures
Education	Product specifications
Buying preferences	Price sensitivity
Family type/household arrangements	Cost structure
Sex	Performance standards
Purchase rationale	

Prepare a customer profile for each market segment served.

than to amass a vast collection of detailed information which no one knows how to use.[9]

Research indicates that organizations often overlook important sources of information if they fail to maintain contacts with customers, suppliers, and competitors. However, maintaining these contacts is not enough; the information gleaned must reach the place in the organization where its significance can be evaluated.

How Much Is Enough?   One method of organizing the environmental scanning function is to adopt either the "inside-out" or the "outside-in" approach.[10] With the inside-out approach, an organization selects areas for intelligence gathering that are based on those areas of the organization's activities which are most sensitive to environmental change. A personal computer software producer, for example, might concentrate most of its environmental intelligence effort on the changes in microprocessor technology and on the activities of key competitors. This approach has the advantage of focusing the effort and expending resources on proven areas of critical influence. With the outside-in approach, an organization would take a broad-based look at many environmental areas, without initial reference to the organization's particular areas of vulnerability. The advantage of this approach is that threats frequently come from new sectors which have not necessarily been important in the past. The disadvantage is that much information of marginal usefulness may also be acquired. Which approach to follow should be a conscious decision by top management and should periodically be reevaluated.

Who Will Do It?   Gathering information about the environment may be done by top managers, corporate staff, line middle managers, or consultants. While staff and consultants have the advantage of specialization and concentration in intelligence gathering, top management and line participation is necessary to ensure that the information is incorporated into strategic planning in a meaningful way. Employees on all levels can be particularly valuable sources of information when they have their direct contact with distributors, end users, raw-materials suppliers, substitute-product manufacturers, machinery suppliers, advertising agencies, investment bankers, and analysts.[11] Top management can encourage the upward flow of information by using the information rather than ignoring it, preventing negative consequences for passing along information, and providing suitable rewards for useful information.[12] Other managers can enhance their ability to contribute by:

- Maintaining an awareness of the strategy of the organization
- Cultivating contacts who have needed information
- Keeping current in their own functional areas
- Passing on information in a form that is likely to be accepted (brief and through proper channels)

What Are the Available Sources of Information? Published data are plentiful and can provide insights into environmental events and trends. The appendix to this chapter lists some of these sources. Forecasts are also available for selected sectors of the environment. Forecasters have been most active in projecting events in the economic sector and the social sector through demographic projections. Economic forecasts are in plentiful supply from many university business scholars, the federal government, and various private agencies. Demographic forecasts may be prepared by consultants for special purposes or may be available from a variety of public and private sources concerning general trends such as age distribution of the population.

The use of forecasts requires special caution. Quantitative forecasts are not predictions, they are projections. The difference is critical. Historical trends are projected into the future. If the future is discontinuous with the past, projections will not provide accurate pictures of the future. For example, in the 1940s demographers did not spot the coming postwar baby boom because it reversed a trend toward a declining birth rate. Also they did not spot the end of the baby boom in the late 1950s because it reversed the newly established trend of rising birth rates. Qualitative or judgmental forecasts can be useful because they augment projection with individual or group judgment. Exhibit 6.9 summarizes and evaluates several different forecasting techniques.

Even when a forecast is available in which confidence can be placed, caution should be taken. This is because different trends may interact to affect the behavior of interest and because there may be trends hidden in trends. For example, the average size of the American home has been decreasing for a number of years. Over the same time period, the percentage of working women has steadily increased. These two trends impact each other to affect the appliance needs of the family. While the average house size decreased, the size of the kitchen and the bath have increased in average size. All these trends together explain the popularity of large refrigerators. People have less time to shop and want to make fewer trips to the grocery store and have large kitchens in which to place large refrigerators to store their purchases.[13]

EXHIBIT 6.9 SUMMARY AND EVALUATION OF FORECASTING TECHNIQUES

Technique	Short description	Cost	Popularity	Complexity	Association with life-cycle stage
Quantitative:					
Econometric models	Simultaneous systems of multiple regression equations.	High	High	High	Steady state
Single and multiple regressions	Variations in dependent variables are explained by variations in the independent one(s).	High or medium	High	Medium	Steady state
Time series:					
Trend extrapolation	Linear, exponential, S curve, or other types of projections.	Medium	High	Medium	Steady state
	Forecasts are obtained by smoothing (averaging) past actual values in a linear or exponential manner.	Medium	High	Medium	Steady state
Qualitative (judgmental):					
Sales force estimate	A bottom-up approach aggregating salespersons' forecasts.	Low	High	Low	All stages
Juries of executive opinion	Marketing, production, and finance executives jointly prepare forecasts.	Low	High	Low	Product development
Anticipatory surveys; market research	Learning about intentions of potential customers or plans of businesses.	Medium	Medium	Medium	Market testing and early introduction
Scenario	Forecasters imagine the impacts of anticipated conditions.	Low	Medium	Low	All stages
Delphi	Experts are guided toward a consensus.	Low	Medium	Medium	Product development
Brainstorming	Idea generation in a noncritical group situation	Low	Medium	Medium	Product development

Source: Adapted from J. A. Pearce, II, and R. B. Robinson, Jr., "Environmental Forecasting; Key to Strategic Management," *Business,* July–September 1983, p. 6. Used by permission.

Interpreting Environmental Information

The forecasts and predictions which result from environmental scanning provide the raw material from which assumptions about the future are developed. The importance of making these assumptions explicit is described in the following statement:

No one can be sure of the future, but it is possible to construct a logical plan based on assumptions about the future. This, of course, is done all the time by all managers, but the assumptions are seldom explicitly defined or their implications fully understood. Not only are explicit assumptions defined after proper study more likely to be correct, but the fact that they are explicit means that they can be monitored and significant deviations advised promptly so that any necessary changes can be made to the plan.[14]

 Assumptions should provide a consistent planning base throughout the organization. This is particularly important for a multiproduct firm because, without guidance, different divisions may make plans on the basis of different assumptions. Such a situation makes it difficult to compare plans across divisions for resource allocation decisions. Examples of assumptions for the various environmental sectors are shown in Exhibit 6.10

Even the most carefully focused environmental analysis is likely to result in a multitude of assumptions which are of varying degrees of importance. The last step in translating environmental information into useful strategy inputs is the ranking of assumptions.[15] Two systems are described here. The first is a single ranking system which separates assumptions into threats and opportunities and ranks by some estimate of magnitude. The second is a dual ranking method which considers both impact and probability of occurrence.

Threats and Opportunities   This ranking rests on the premise that assumptions have either negative or positive consequences for the organization. As-

EXHIBIT 6.10   EXAMPLES OF ENVIRONMENTAL ASSUMPTIONS FOR SECTORS OF THE BROAD ENVIRONMENT

Economic sector

- Interest rates will remain in the 9 to 11 percent range until the next presidential election
- GNP growth will average 2.5 percent annually for the next 5 years.
- New housing starts in our standard metropolitan statistical area will fall for the next year until the current housing stock is depleted.

Political sector

- Political instability in Korea will continue or worsen.
- Tax laws will be revised by Congress to allow deductibility of IRAs.
- Activities of the lobby against drunk driving will result in a local ordinance which will close at midnight all establishments which sell alcohol.

Social sector

- Work will play an increasingly peripheral role in the lives of hourly workers in our company.
- Fertility levels will continue to decrease, producing a long-term labor shortage.
- Families with one child will predominate by the year 1995. Family spending per child will increase in areas such as education and apparel.

Technological sector

- Superconductor technology will be available for consumer uses by 1995.
- Plastic will be available at the necessary strength and flexibility to replace the metal in our product in the next 5 years.

EXHIBIT 6.11 EXAMPLES OF THREATS AND OPPORTUNITIES

Threats
• Annual growth in laundry detergent of only 2 percent
• Consumer paper goods market maturing
• Coca-Cola and Pepsi-Cola entering juice and food markets aggressively
• Consumers increasingly responsive to price
• Supermarket industry increasingly concentrated

Opportunities
• Electronic price scanning systems provide data to speed up test marketing
• Consumers accepting product alterations well
• Convenience food sectors growing more rapidly than industry as a whole

Source: Adapted from "Why Procter and Gamble Is Playing It Even Tougher," *Business Week,* July 18, 1983, pp. 176–186.

sumptions which carry potentially positive consequences are called opportunities; those carrying potentially negative consequences are called threats. Once the assumptions are sorted as to consequences, they can then be ranked for significance. Exhibit 6.11 presents such a ranking for Procter and Gamble.

Dual Ranking This system requires consideration of each assumption along two dimensions: the potential impact on the organization and the likelihood of actual occurrence. Exhibit 6.12 illustrates this ranking system.

While each of these assumption-ranking procedures could be completed with knowledge of the environment alone, it is necessary to incorporate information concerning the internal resources. Threats and opportunities are relative to the resources that are available to deal with them. In this regard, one company's threat is often another company's opportunity. The next chapter addresses the critical issue of internal analysis.

EXHIBIT 6.12 A SIMPLIFIED EXAMPLE OF RANKING THREATS AND OPPORTUNITIES BY IMPACT AND PROBABILITY OF OCCURRENCE

Event	Impact on company	Probability of occurrence
Major technological breakthrough that renders our product obsolete within 10 years.	High	Low
Economic growth continues at 5% annually.	Medium	High
Economic growth falters and stops within 5 years.	Medium	Medium
Legislation to free our product from credit restrictions.	Low	Low

Source: J. Argenti, *Practical Corporate Planning,* Allen & Unwin, London, 1980. Used by permission.

SUMMARY

The most promising path for an organization to follow in pursuit of its objectives depends, in part, on external forces, conditions, events, and relationships. These complex factors over which the organization has little control are called environmental factors and seem to be increasing in influence.

Analysis of the environment should be directed by an awareness of the uniqueness, dynamism, and interaction which characterize organizational-environmental relationships. The most relevant parts of the environment differ from industry to industry and among competitors in the same industry. Therefore, each organization's environment is unique. The environment is constantly changing for a given organization, and this dynamic nature means that assessment must be continuous, or, at least, periodic. Finally, organizations interact with their environments and are often able to influence the external situation favorably.

Environmental analysis requires information that is relevant, future-oriented, and usable. Three steps in producing such information are:

1 Defining the environment by determining its boundaries and relevant sectors
2 Collecting information and forecasting the changes in the environment
3 Interpreting the information for the organization's use

The broad environment influences many organizations in similar ways. Sectors of this environment are technological, economic, social, political, and ecological. Trends also vary by geographic region in the broad environment. The competitive sector of the environment includes organizations and forces which interact with the organization and its industry directly. The competitive environment includes the industry, suppliers, buyers, potential entrants, producers of substitutes, and current competitors.

Environmental scanning and forecasting systems must be based on the benefit the organization will derive from the activities. Inside-out scanning focuses on areas of proven vulnerability; outside-in scanning takes a much broader look at the environment. Regardless of who gathers intelligence, top management and line participation is necessary to ensure meaningful use of the information.

Forecasts and predictions provide the raw material from which assumptions are developed. Assumptions are statements about the environment which give the organization a consistent planning base. Assumptions must be ranked so that the key threats and opportunities can be identified.

CHAPTER 6 REVIEW QUESTIONS

1 Describe the environmental characteristics which influence the environmental analysis process.
2 What distinctions can be made between the broad environment and the competitive environment?
3 How does location and scope of a business's activities affect its definition of the economic sector of the environment?
4 Which areas of the technological sector require the most careful management attention?
5 How do the social and political sectors of the environment interact?

6 Why must potential entrants to an industry be considered in the analysis of the competitive environment?

7 What are the major components of the competitive environment and how does each affect the average level of profitability in the industry, all other things being equal?

8 Contrast the inside-out approach with the outside-in approach to environmental scanning. When would you recommend that each be used?

9 What internal sources of environmental information are available?

10 What are environmental assumptions? Why are explicit assumptions necessary?

CHAPTER 6 DISCUSSION QUESTIONS

1 Consider two small businesses. Business A is a car wash, and business B is a small bar. Both are located in a college town. Which sectors of the environment would be most relevant? How could these sectors be influenced by each of the businesses? How much organizational effort should be devoted to environmental scanning and forecasting by each business?

2 The graying of America is a fact, but determining its implications for a given organization is more complicated. Translate the demographic data below into a set of assumptions for (a) a small community hospital, (b) an urban school system, and (c) General Motors.

PERCENTAGE INCREASE IN POPULATION BY AGE GROUPS, 1980–1990

Ages	1980–1985	1985–1990	1980–1990
Under 15	3.4	70	10.6
15–17	− 11.6	− 10.3	− 20.1
18–24	− 5.4	− 9.7	− 14.6
25–34	10.2	3.0	13.5
35–44	22.2	16.6	42.4
45–54	− 0.9	12.4	11.5
55–65	2.4	− 4.1	− 1.9
Over 65	9.6	9.1	19.6

How does this demographic data rank in importance with other environmental trends which might affect each of these organizations?

CHAPTER 6 REFERENCES

1 R. E. Emery and E. L. Trist, "The Causal Texture of Organizational Environments," *Human Relations,* vol. 18, 1965, pp. 21–32; P. R. Lawrence and J. W. Lorsch, "Differentiation and Integration in Complex Organizations," *Administrative Science Quarterly,* vol. 12, 1967, pp. 1–47; J. D. Thompson, *Organizations in Action,* McGraw-Hill, New York, 1967; and J. Pfeffer and G. Salancik, *The External Control of Organizations,* Harper & Row, New York, 1978.

2 "How TV is Revolutionizing Hollywood," *Business Week,* February 21, 1983, pp. 78–89.

3 John Argenti, *Practical Corporate Planning,* Allen & Unwin, London, 1980, pp.133–134.

4 Ibid., p.139.

5 J. B. Whitaker, *Strategic Planning in a Rapidly Changing Environment*, Lexington Books, Lexington, Mass., 1978, p. 22.

6 Ibid., pp. 23–24.

7 Michael Porter, *Competitive Strategies*, Free Press, New York, 1980; Michael Porter, "How Competitive Forces Shape Strategy," *Harvard Business Review*, March–April 1979, pp. 84–88. The discussion of the competitive environment is based on Porter's work.

8 George S. Yip, *Barriers to Entry*, Lexington Books, Lexington, Mass., 1982, p. 130.

9 Robert E. McAvoy, "Corporate Strategy and the Power of Competitive Analysis," *Management Review*, July 1983, p. 11.

10 C. W. Hofer and Dan Schendel, *Strategy Formulation: Analytical Concepts*, West, St. Paul, Minn., 1978, p. 91.

11 McAvoy, op. cit., p. 19.

12 L. W. Rue and L. L. Byars, *Management: Theory and Application*, Irwin, Homewood, Ill., 1980, p. 281.

13 "The New Breed of Strategic Planner," *Business Week*, September 17, 1984, pp. 62–68.

14 D. E. Hussey and M. J. Langham, *Corporate Planning: The Human Factor*, Pergamon, New York, 1979, p. 167.

15 Whitaker, op. cit., p. 27.

Chapter 6   Appendix

PUBLISHED SOURCES FOR ENVIRONMENTAL INFORMATION

*General
Environment*   Technological Sector

- *Technology Assessment*—focuses on the business relevance of changing technology.
- *Contracts Monthly.*
- *The Research and Development Directory*—indicates what competitors are doing and what research the government is supporting, as well as provides new technology updates.

Economic Sector

- *Monthly Economic Indicators* and *Annual Reports*—economic statistics from the Council of Economic Advisors.
- *Statistical Abstract of the U.S.**—population, housing income, price, etc., information from the Department of Commerce, Bureau of the Census. Other reports from the Department of Commerce which contain some general economic data include *Business Conditions Digest, U.S. Industrial Outlook,* and *Survey of Manufacturers.*
- Economic newsletters of national and regional banks—one which is recommended is that of Morgan Guaranty Trust in New York.

Social Sector

- *Social Indicators.*
- *Social Reporting.*

- Polls—such as the University of Michigan Survey, Yankelovitch Monitor, Gallup Poll, and Harris Poll.
- *American Demographics*—applies census and demographic data to business purposes.

Political Sector

- *Public Affairs Information Services Bulletin.*
- *Congressional Information Index.*
- *Federal Register**—for pending regulations.

Competitive Environment

National

- *Guide to Consumer Markets.*
- *Current Sources of Marketing Information: A Bibliography of Primary Market-Data*—by Gunther and Goldstein.
- Robert Morris annual statement studies.
- *Almanac of Business and Industrial Financial Ratios*—by Troy.
- *Enterprise Statistics.**

  Statistical Abstract of the U.S.*
  U.S. Census of Manufacturers.*
  Survey of Current Business.
  Predicasts.

Specific Industries

- Industry surveys.
- Trade magazines.
- Industry association publications.
- *Barron's*—occasional in-depth look at an industry.
- *Wall Street Transcript*—analysts discuss specific industries.
- *Forbes.*
- *Fortune.*
- Investment services directories—such as *Moody's, Standard & Poor's,* and *Dun and Bradstreet.*

Specific Companies

- Business press—*Fortune, Business Week, Wall Street Journal,* and *Advertising Age.*
- Annual reports and 10-K reports—available from individual companies and on microfiche through Disclosure, Inc.
- The business and trade press can be accessed by several indexes. The most widely available are the *Business Periodicals Index,* which lists articles by subject and title, and the *Funk and Scott Index,* which lists articles by companies and industry and which provides a one-line synopsis of the contents of each article referenced. *The Wall Street Journal Index* carries only articles in that publication by company name, title, and subject.

By Geographical Area

* Local
    State industry surveys.
    County Business Patterns.
    County and City Data Book.
    Market Guide—1500 U.S. and Canadian cities.
    Census data—also broken down by locale.

* International
    *Statistical Yearbook.***
    *Yearbook of International Trade Statistics.***
    World Development Report.
    World Bank Atlas.
    The U.S. Department of Commerce—publications dealing with many aspects of international trade: *Guide to Foreign Trade Statistics,* Overseas Business Reports,* Foreign Economic Trends,* Business America,* Foreign Traders Index.**

*Government publications, available from Superintendent of Documents, Government Printing Office, Washington, D.C. 20401, or from libraries which serve as repositories for government documents.
**U.N. Publishing Service, One Dag Hammarskjold Plaza, New York, NY 10017.
Source: Adapted from J. A. Pearce and R. B. Robinson, Jr., "Environmental Forcasting: Key to Strategic Management," *Business,* July–September 1983, pp. 8–9; and D. J. Ellis and P. P. Pekar, Jr., *Planning for Nonplanners,* AMACOM, New York, 1980, pp. 84–90.

INTERNAL ANALYSIS: ACTION CAPABILITIES AND CORPORATE CULTURE

LEARNING OBJECTIVES

After studying this chapter, the reader should be able to:

1 Explain the role of internal analysis in the strategic management process
2 Classify and evaluate organizational capabilities and vulnerabilities in organizations of interest
3 Distinguish between business- and corporate-level capabilities
4 Define and assess corporate culture as an organizational asset
5 Recommend whether strategy or culture should be adjusted

CHAPTER OUTLINE

ORGANIZATIONAL STRENGTHS AND RESOURCE ALLOCATIONS
CLASSIFYING ACTION CAPABILITIES ON THE BUSINESS LEVEL
    Competitive Advantages
    Business Requirements
    Key Vulnerabilities
CORPORATE RESOURCES AND ACTION CAPABILITIES
    New Business Capability
    Economies among Existing Businesses

128

An organization's ability to achieve its desired levels of performance can be enhanced or diminished by its environment. However, an organization is not helpless in the face of environmental threats nor is it guaranteed success by the presence of opportunities. The ability to parry threats and capitalize upon opportunities depends upon the actions that the organization can take in the face of environmental trends. These action capabilities may be thought of as strengths with strategic significance. It is impossible to consider an organization's fitness for the future without enumerating the organization's strengths and evaluating the significance of those strengths. It is also necessary to determine areas of vulnerability.

Internal analysis begins with identification of the organization's resource allocations. This analysis should produce an enumeration of organizational strengths—what the organization does well. Strengths must then be analyzed for their strategic significance. It is also necessary to identify areas of weakness and to determine whether these weaknesses have strategic significance—that is, whether they make the organization vulnerable. All these assessments are relative; they must incorporate environmental information.

ORGANIZATIONAL STRENGTHS AND RESOURCE ALLOCATIONS

Organizational strengths are produced by conscious managerial decisions which are called resource allocations. *Resource allocations* convert financial resources into organizational, human, and physical resources and ultimately into the ability to interact with the market. Successful market interaction generates more financial resources, which can be used to generate still more financial resources and begin the cycle again. Obviously resource allocation which produces ability to successfully interact with the market is most desirable in that it gives the organization the ability to meet its objectives. Exhibit 7.1 depicts the resource conversion process. Example 7.1 uses Federal Express as an example of how the process works. Resource allocations that do not result in successful market interactions must be carefully examined to be sure that resources are not being wasted.

EXHIBIT 7.1   THE RESOURCE CONVERSION PROCESS

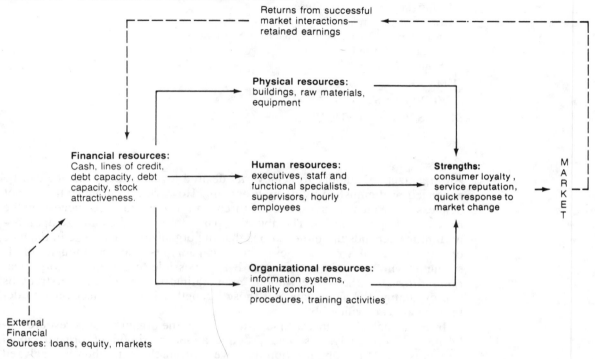

Source: Adapted from C. Hofer and D. Schendel, *Strategy Formulation: Analytical Concepts,* West, St. Paul, Minn., 1978, p. 146.

CLASSIFYING ACTION CAPABILITIES ON THE BUSINESS LEVEL

Organizations which survive and prosper over the long term are those which distinguish themselves in a way that continually generates resources which can be used to improve the current strategic capabilities or to create new ones. It is not enough that an organization does things well; an organization must do those things well that count in the marketplace. The things that an organization does well may be identified by a functional audit. A *functional audit* is an exhaustive appraisal of the organization by functional areas. Exhibit 7.2 lists some standards which can be used as part of a functional audit to identify an organization's strengths and weaknesses. Environmental information must be coupled with information gained from the functional audit to determine which strengths have strategic significance and where the organization is vulnerable to attack.

Strengths have strategic significance when (see Exhibit 7.3):

1. They provide a competitive edge. This is called a *competitive advantage* and occurs when an organization is able to do something which competitors

---

EXAMPLE 7.1

Resource Conversion Process at Federal Express

Frederick Smith, the founder of Federal Express, started the company with $3.5 million he had inherited. With this as "seed" money, he was able to raise another $79 million. Financial resources were quickly converted into physical facilities (planes, hangar space, and package-sorting equipment); human resources (primarily students at Memphis State University who wanted part-time night work, managers, and pilots); and organizational resources (scheduling and sorting systems and a system to track the location of all packages). These resources, in concert, provide the company with the ability to guarantee overnight delivery of a package anywhere in the United States and to report the location of any package in the pipeline within half an hour of the initial inquiry. These capabilities have generated a tremendous volume of business, which ensures that more financial resources are available for conversion into capabilities which the market requires.

---

cannot do or cannot do nearly as well. A competitive advantage is analogous to having a head start in a foot race.

(2) They allow the organization to maintain its position by performing the activity in question at the same level as other organizations in the industry. This is called a *business requirement* and is a function of the type and level of competition in the industry. It is analogous to starting a foot race at the starting line.

Weaknesses may also have strategic significance. All organizations must concentrate their efforts because they do not have unlimited resources and as a result will not be able to maintain a position of strength in all facets of operations. When an organization has a weakness in an area of operation that is a business requirement, or where another organization in the industry has a competitive advantage, a *key vulnerability* exists. Resources should be reallocated as part of the strategic management process to remove key vulnerabilities. A key vulnerability is analogous to starting a foot race five steps behind the starting line.

Competitive Advantages

In the production of jug wine for the mass market, national advertising has become a necessity, but quality control and consistency are also important. The top five wineries have developed strengths in all these areas. What has kept Gallo on top of the industry, however, is its tight control of its distributors and its cost control through vertical integration.[1] These are Gallo's competitive advantages; existence of strengths in these areas gives Gallo an edge over the competition.

While strengths and weaknesses are usually expressed in terms of specific

EXHIBIT 7.2   STANDARDS FOR FUNCTIONAL AUDIT

Marketing

1. Application of the marketing concept to produce a sense of mission and integrated effort.
2. Appropriate means of identifying customer needs and meeting them with new or improved products.
3. Appropriate segmentation and targeting of markets.
4. Ability to select and manage distribution channels.
5. Appropriate selection and mix of promotion techniques for cost-effectiveness in target market or markets.
6. Pricing flexibility used as competitive weapon.
7. Ability to describe customer behavior in relation to new product introductions.
8. Ability to predict shifts in customer needs and to formulate new segments.
9. Productive, motivated sales force.
10. Effective advertising promotion.
11. Good product planning based on product life cycles, style, and fashion cycles.

Operations

1. Facilities are located close to raw materials, transportation hubs, and/or customers.
2. Facilities have up-to-date equipment and are well maintained.
3. Process is designed for efficiency and workers.
4. Product is consistently at the chosen level of quality.
5. Routing, scheduling, inventory, and purchasing techniques minimize production delays.
6. Maintenance is performed with a minimum of downtime.
7. Production costs are consistently close to or below budget.
8. Deadlines are consistently met; orders are filled on time with few returns.

Finance

1. Cost of capital is at or below industry average.
2. Working capital is readily available to finance growth.
3. Stockholder relations are good.
4. Relations with funding institutions are good.
5. The capital structure provides leverage, security, and flexibility.
6. Short-term creditor relations are good, and short-term credit is readily available from suppliers.
7. Financial control, budgeting, and allocation techniques are used appropriately.
8. Sources and uses of funds are appropriately matched.

Personnel

1. Job descriptions exist for all jobs and are up to date.
2. Recruitment and selection methods are appropriate and yield qualified employees.
3. Desirable employees are not lost to competitors with better salary and/or benefits.
4. New employees receive appropriate orientation and training.
5. Turnover and absenteeism are at or below industry levels.
6. Layoffs are rare because of planning and cross-training.
7. The organization is a good source for middle- and upper-level managers because of employee development programs.
8. Labor relations are rarely disruptive.
9. The organization is in compliance with relevant legislation.

R&D, engineering, and technical

1. The technical focus is appropriate.
2. The technical focus produces results in new and improved products and/or new and improved processes.
3. The technical focus yields advances ahead of or close after competitors.
4. Technical efforts are cost-effective, and all cost-effective sources of technical improvements are utilized.
5. Technical efforts are strategically sound.
6. Technological changes are forecasted.
7. A critical technical mass exists and is respected by peers.

132

EXHIBIT 7.3   FLOWCHART FOR DETERMINING STRATEGIC SIGNIFICANCE OF STRENGTHS AND WEAKNESSES

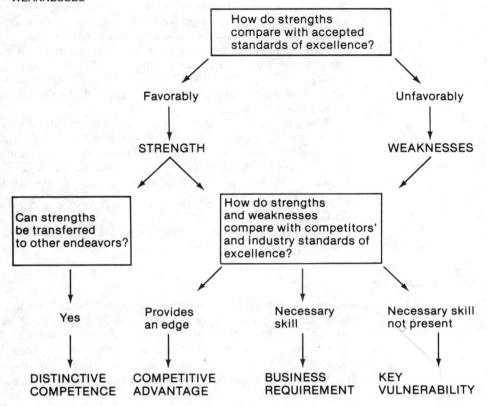

Strengths: what the organization does well
Competitive advantage: what the organization does better than competitors
Business requirements: what all competitors must do to succeed
Key vulnerability: what is subject to competitor attack
Distinctive competence: transferable skill

functional areas, competitive advantages frequently result from the integration of several functional areas. Therefore, competitive advantages are best expressed as the ability to do something which competitors cannot do or at least cannot do nearly as well. Examples of such statements are:

• We are the lowest-cost producer in the industry and can resist any attempt to win share by cutting our price.
• We are able to respond to market changes with product modifications more quickly than our competitors 8 times out of 10.

Business Requirements

In most consumer-oriented businesses, marketing skills are requirements for survival. In the mass market for wine, soft drinks, and fast foods, the ability to design and execute marketing and promotional campaigns must be present for companies to maintain their positions. Occasionally, a particularly effective campaign will provide a short-term boost such as Wendy's scored with its legendary "Where's the Beef?" spots or Coca-Cola achieved with Max Headroom. In general, promotional skills simply keep the organizations even; they do not provide an edge.

Business requirements are determined by the dynamics of the competitive environment. They are the factors which are critical to success in the industry and which competitors cannot afford to ignore for very long. They can be identified by asking the question, "What skills must competitors possess in order to survive in this business?" Some examples of answers are:

- We must maintain consistency of service from location to location (lodging, fast foods).
- We must maintain efficient operations for low operating costs (airlines, meat packing).

Key Vulnerabilities

While an organization tries to do as many things well as possible, it is inevitable that an organization will not have strengths in all areas. When a given weakness is being evaluated, the key question to ask is, "How does this area of weakness compare with the competition?" A weakness becomes a key vulnerability when it is a capability which is held by most competitors and is necessary for success in that competitive environment. For example, lack of cost-efficient facilities is a key vulnerability for many American steel manufacturers because of international competition. A weakness can become a key vulnerability when environmental changes redefine the business requirements in the industry. Domestic airlines once depended on their ability to obtain favorable route and rate structures from the Civil Aeronautics Board; they were less concerned about cost control. With the deregulation of the airlines industry, the "old" airlines found that unionized work forces and high fixed costs made them vulnerable to competition from "new" airlines with streamlined operations and lower labor costs.

CORPORATE RESOURCES AND ACTION CAPABILITIES

The strengths or action capabilities of particular interest on the corporate level are:

- The capability of entering and succeeding in new businesses
- The achievement of synergy among existing businesses

New Business Capability

New business capability is developed in a number of ways. One way is the use of *distinctive competences* in existing businesses to provide springboards for the acquisition or development of new businesses. A distinctive competence exists when a strength can be used advantageously in areas beyond the current business. Example 7.2 describes how Sears has transferred a strength to other areas. A second approach is to use available *financial resources*. These financial resources may be produced by the generation of excess cash from existing businesses, from a financial situation that makes the stock of the company attractive, or from the existence of additional debt capacity. For example, the cash generated by its lodging business provided Holiday Inns with the financial resources necessary to enter the gaming and casino business. Finally, *managerial skills* may provide new business capability. Some of these skills are the ability to evaluate acquisition opportunities, the ability to promote entrepreneurship internally, and the ability to integrate the operations of new businesses (whether acquired or developed internally) into the existing operations of the organization. Probably the best indication of these capabilities is the track record of the organization with its new business activities. A company which is just beginning a diversification program will not have such a track record, and for this reason, its initial efforts are critical in establishing its future.

Economies among Existing Businesses

Joint effects which increase the output of combined activities over the output of individual activities are called *synergistic effects*. Synergy occurs when the whole offers benefits greater than the sum of the individual parts. Synergy can occur among corporate units when several units can use the same facilities, staff, or systems. Hewlett-Packard, for example, maintains a corporate research and development (R&D) unit. Synergy is present if this unit provides more new products and processes as a result of combining all R&D efforts

---

EXAMPLE 7.2

Distinctive Competence at Sears

Sears Roebuck and Company has recognized and applied a distinctive competence in information systems. Sears has an information system which supplies data on its 40 million retail customers and enables the company to target groups such as appliance buyers, gardening enthusiasts, and mothers-to-be. This targeting ability provides Sears with a competitive advantage as a retailer and with a distinctive competence because the same system can be used to generate sales leads for Sears' subsidiaries in the insurance, real estate, and stock brokerage areas. Sears' strength in information process gives it both an edge against retail competitors and a capability that is transferable to other competitive realms.

Source: Adapted from "Business Is Turning Data into a Potent Strategic Weapon," *Business Week*, August 22, 1983, p. 93.

than would be provided if each SBU maintained its own R&D effort. It is difficult to evaluate the synergistic effects of a given situation without making other confounding changes in the organization. Because of this difficulty, there is little hard evidence of synergy.[2]

An objective assessment of strengths and weaknesses to identify competitive advantages, distinctive competences, and key vulnerabilities provides the strategist with an understanding of the organization's capabilities for dealing with the threats and opportunities in the environment. There is another, more fundamental aspect of the organization's ability to deal with the uncertainties of the environment which must also be examined. That aspect is known as corporate culture.

Established culture constrains the organization's ability to respond to the demands of the environment. Culture is often cited as both a strength and a source of problems. The remainder of the chapter will examine this phenomenon and suggest a method for assessing corporate culture for purposes of strategic management.

CORPORATE CULTURE: THE INTANGIBLE ASSET

Corporate culture is a pervasive influence in organizations. Schein lists the following meanings of culture obtained from organizational research:

1. Observed behavioral regularities when people interact, such as the language used and the rituals around deference and demeanor.
2. The norms that evolve in working groups, such as the particular norm of "a fair day's work for a fair day's pay" that evolved in the Bank Wiring Room in the Hawthorne studies.
3. The dominant values espoused by an organization, such as "product quality" or "price leadership."
4. The philosophy that guides an organization's policy toward employees and/or customers.
5. The rules of the game for getting along in the organization; "the ropes" that a newcomer must learn in order to become an accepted member.
6. The feeling or climate that is conveyed in an organization by the physical layout and the way in which members of the organization interact with customers or other outsiders.[3]

All these are actually manifestations of culture. *Culture* can be defined as the beliefs which pervade the organization about how business should be conducted and how employees should behave and should be treated.[4] These beliefs are made manifest in a number of ways. Example 7.3 illustrates some of these.

Culture is important to strategic management because it is a stabilizing influence on organizational activities. A strong culture makes activities predictable. Management knows how employees will react in certain situations and vice versa. Strategic change which requires activities different from those suggested by the culture may be doomed before it is begun unless explicit attention is given to matching strategy and culture. While this is to a certain extent an implementation issue, the wise strategist is aware of the culture and this awareness shapes

---

EXAMPLE 7.3

Manifestations of Corporate Culture

Anheuser-Busch

Aggressive marketing built Anheuser-Busch's domestic beer market share to 38% by 1987. Company insiders say the pressure in the marketing department in the 1980s was extreme in the pursuit of increased share. Performance standards were exceptionally tough although the rewards were lavish including perks like first class airline tickets and hotel suites. A former regional sales manager called the situation "a golden nose ring." A sports marketing specialist said, "You lived on the edge. If you screwed up, you got shot."

Source: "Anheuser-Busch: The Scandal May Be Small Beer After All," *Business Week,* May 11, 1987, pp. 72–73.

Banco Brasiliero do Descontos S.A.

Teamwork is the philosophy of the Banco Brasiliero do Descontos S.A. founder, Amador Aguiar. This philosophy is made visible in the physical arrangement of the bank. There are no offices. Executives work around large tables in rooms from 7 AM to 7 PM. The long hours allow small farmers who are the target market to conduct business before or after their labor in the fields. Open desks at the front of each branch make management more approachable to prospective clients. There is little or no privacy as telephones, meals, and business affairs are shared among executives. The teamwork concept has a physical manifestation in this organization.

Source: Lynda Schuster, "At a Bank in Brazil, Stress on Teamwork Pays Big Dividends," *The Wall Street Journal,* August 22, 1985, p. 1.

---

his or her strategic alternatives and choices. When a shift in strategy requires a shift in culture, it should be explicitly planned (see Example 7.4).

Identifying Corporate Culture

Culture in an organization is analogous to personality in an individual and is transmitted in many ways:

> Long-standing, and often unwritten rules and regulations; a special language that facilitates communication among members; shared standards of relevance as to the critical aspects of the work that is to be done; matter-of-fact prejudices; standards for social etiquette and demeanor; established customs for how members should relate to peers, subordinates, superiors and outsiders, and other traditions that clarify to members what is appropriate and "smart" behavior within the organization and what is not.[5]

In short, culture determines "how we do things around here." Example 7.5 describes contrasting cultures at two large corporations.

EXAMPLE 7.4

Changing Culture at AT&T

AT&T faced a shift in environment that required a shift in culture when the Justice Department's antitrust suit was settled in 1982 with a divestiture agreement. The logistics of the split were staggering; one employee compared the process of divesting without interrupting phone service to disassembling a 747 and reassembling it into two 707s—in flight. While redeploying personnel, restructuring management systems, and redistributing decision-making roles, AT&T also had to deal with an increasingly competitive and constantly changing environment. A former marketing executive assessed the situation as follows.

> Their relative success in making that transition from a monopoly to a competitive enterprise, from a telephone company to an information systems supplier will be determined by their ability to shift the culture.

The culture that predominated at AT&T before the divestiture was well suited to the regulated, monopolistic environment in which the company operated for over a century. The mission of providing high-quality, low-cost, universal telephone service was simple; it attracted committed managers who appreciated the structured organization that promoted this mission.

But the security of the structured environment disappeared. The organization has shifted its structure to push more responsibilities to middle management and is struggling to give those managers new values. The new emphasis is on teamwork, flexibility to compete, risk taking, increased responsibility, faster action, and appropriate rewards for those who adapt and succeed in the new environment. The transition has not been an easy one, as one consultant acknowledged: "If you move too slowly, the current culture moves around anything new and engulfs it. If you do it too quickly, you can get a reject."

By 1988, AT&T had made a painful transition. It had experienced problems in its new computer and overseas telephone businesses, it had dealt with issues of turf protection and empire building, it had jeopardized union relations but had emerged from these traumas with a team spirit and an understanding of the cooperation needed by all units. James E. Olson, the chairman of the board, described the situation under the new culture: "Now, we're paying much more attention to outside forces, we're totally market driven, we know what the customer wants, what he's willing to pay, and what our competitors are offering."

Source: Adapted from "Culture Shock Is Shaking the Bell System," *Business Week,* September 23, 1983, p. 113; and "AT&T: The Making of a Comeback," *Business Week,* January 18, 1988.

EXAMPLE 7.5

Contrasting Cultures at PepsiCo and J. C. Penney

Since 1960, PepsiCo has systematically changed its culture from passive to aggressive. Competition, both inside and outside the company, has become the accepted behavior, and winning has become the path to success. Not only has Pepsi challenged Coca-Cola's number one position in soft drinks with aggressive advertising, but Pepsi has also encouraged managers to vie with each other for increases in market share, profits, and product volume. Former Pepsi President John Scully described the pressure put on managers: "Careers ride on tenths of a market share point." A former manager reemphasized this point: "Everyone knows that if the results aren't there, you had better have your resume up to date."

The competitive corporate culture at Pepsi is the result of many factors:

- Managers are moved to new jobs often, and management staff is minimized.
- The chair of the board provides an example of the behavior he expects by actions such as coming to work by snowmobile in a blizzard.
- The company employs four physical fitness experts and encourages individual as well as interdepartmental competition in a variety of sports.
- Less competitive managers are weeded out, while those who remain are reported to thrive on the atmosphere.

The aggressiveness of Pepsi's culture is reflected in inroads into Coca-Cola's market share, but it may have negative consequences as well. There is little company loyalty built into the competitive culture, and managers are easily lured away, sometimes by competitors.

One company that would not be attractive to the Pepsi "tigers" is J. C. Penney. Long-term loyalty on the part of customers and employees is the cornerstone of Penney's culture. The average executive tenure is 33 years, while the average tenure at Pepsi is 10 years. A number of factors are cited as contributing to this atmosphere:

- Adhering to the seven guiding principles established by founder James Cash Penney
- Avoiding taking unfair advantage of anyone
- Providing participation in decision making
- Avoiding layoffs and providing less demanding jobs for employees who have problems handling duties

While Penney's has been cited by two national magazines as one of the ten best places to work, its culture has also made it slower to change.

Source: Adapted from "Corporate Culture: The Hard to Change Values That Spell Success or Failure," *Business Week,* October 27, 1980, pp. 148–160.

Origins of Culture

Many organizations trace their beliefs to an individual who envisioned and provided a living example of how the business should be run and how people should be treated. Robert Wood Johnson of Johnson & Johnson, Harley Procter of Procter & Gamble, Walt Disney of Walt Disney Productions, and Thomas J. Watson, Sr., of IBM Corporation were all founders or top managers who left their imprint on the organization they founded or headed. Research on values in new companies indicates, however, that fewer than half of a new company's values reflect the values of the founder or chief executive.[6] The rest appear to develop in response to the specific environment in which the business operates and to the needs of the employees. In general, four origins of organizational culture can be identified: (1) history, (2) environment, (3) staffing, and (4) socialization.[7]

History   Employees are aware of the organization's past, and this awareness reinforces culture. Much of the "way things are done" is a continuation of the way things have always been done. The existing values which may have been established originally by a strong leader are continuously and subtly reinforced by experiences. The status quo is also protected by the human tendency to embrace beliefs and values fervently and to resist changes. Executives for Walt Disney Productions reportedly pick up litter on the grounds unconsciously because Disney's vision of an immaculate Disneyland became so habitual. Similarly, Thomas Watson's views on employee dress and compensation are still very much in evidence at IBM Corporation—more than 30 years after his death. As a final example, many attribute the formality at the University of Virginia to the influence of the founder, Thomas Jefferson, two centuries ago.

Environment   Because all organizations must interact with their environments, the environment has a role in shaping culture. In the case of AT&T (see Example 7-5), the highly formalized and risk-averse culture was in large part a product of the regulatory environment in which the company operated for so many years. Today, the company is no longer sheltered by its monopoly power, and the culture is no longer appropriate. The shift from a culture of consistent service at any cost to a culture which promotes market responsiveness and internal cost cutting is still in progress.[8]

Staffing   Organizations tend to hire and retain individuals who are similar to current employees in important ways. A person's ability to "fit in" can be an important criterion in the selection process. This "fit" criterion ensures that current values are accepted and that potential challengers of "how we do things" are screened out. For example, a study by the U.S. Federal Trade Commission indicated that in hiring decisions for attorneys, more importance was placed on regional background, prep school and college associations, and political connections than on grades or quality of law school attended. In many organizations, hiring and promotion decisions relate more to how people fit organizational norms than to more objective measures.

Socialization Companies with strong cultures attach great importance to the process of introducing and indoctrinating new employees. While values, norms, and beliefs may be widely and uniformly held, they are seldom written down. The new employee is least familiar with the culture and therefore is most likely to challenge it. It is important to help the newcomer to adapt to, as well as to adopt, the organization's culture. This is the socialization process. Not only does socialization reduce threats to the organization from newcomers, but it also indicates to newly hired employees what is expected of them. Socialization may be handled in a variety of ways, ranging from the informal, individual, sink-or-swim approach to the lengthy, structured approach characterized by programs for groups of employees in large companies. The more formal and structured the approach, the more likely it is that the desired learning will occur. An IBM training program is described in Example 7.6. Less formal approaches will leave more room for individual creativity and for influence by informal work groups.

The Cultural Audit

In order to assess the cultural constraints on strategy formulation, it is necessary to make the beliefs which are the basis of culture explicit and visible. Managers should be aware of beliefs prior to dealing with environmental

[handwritten margin note: —not implying stating in exact terms.]

EXAMPLE 7.6

In Training at IBM Corporation

IBM is one of the most frequently cited examples of a company with a strong culture. Achievement, loyalty, and discipline are virtues which training instills in new employees, company structure and rules (written and unwritten) reinforce, and subsequent training renews. The pattern is simple: goals are set high for new trainees, they are supervised closely, evaluated frequently, and rewarded for their achievements. Then new, higher goals are set and the cycle continues. Sales training schools immerse trainees in work and pressure to perform. Rooms must be left spotlessly clean. A trainee who fails inspection may be called back to finish the job or the trainee's manager may be charged for cleaning. Instructors observe who is studying late at night and which students finish their work in time to help struggling classmates. Class officers are elected (the high achievers have the best shot at such offices) and officers often get the best sales territories when they return to the field. Instructors are responsible for evaluating trainees on both content of learning and attitudes displayed. High marks go to those who display product knowledge, enthusiasm, confidence, sincerity, cooperation, working with others, and desire to learn.

Source: Adapted from Susan Chance, "The Corporate Culture at IBM: How It Reinforces Strategy," *The Wall Street Journal,* April 18, 1982.

changes which may challenge these beliefs. A cultural audit is an exercise by which top management develops a consensus about their shared beliefs. The process is a simple one but not always easy, since the beliefs may be so internalized they are not easily recognized.[9] First, top management develops individual answers to the questions, shown in Exhibit 7.4. Next these individual answers are compared and discussed with the objective of reaching a consensus. There are several cautions which should be observed in this process:

1. Belief statements should be based on actual practices of the organization, not some idealized version which sounds good but doesn't reflect reality.

2. Top management commitment is required. Both the individual response process and the reaching of consensus are likely to be time-consuming.[10]

3. A facilitator may be necessary. Insiders may take the beliefs for granted to such an extent that those beliefs are invisible to them. An outsider is needed to probe for explanations and interpretations of organizational events.[11]

Changing Culture

Because organizational culture is difficult to change, it is important to consider events in the environment in relation to the organizational culture to determine what responses may be feasible for a particular organization. The Management Analysis Center (MAC), a consulting group which specializes in corporate culture, has developed a matrix for evaluating the risk associated with attempting to implement a new strategy within the existing culture (see Exhibit 7.5).[12] A planned change resulting from a proposed new strategy is positioned on the matrix with regard to its compatibility with the existing culture and its importance to the strategy. According to MAC, any proposed change that shows up on the matrix as being higher in strategic importance than cultural compatibility is seen as involving an unacceptable level of risk. In these cases, MAC advises that less dangerous (less risky) tactics be used, that the proposed strategy be reevaluated, or, as a last resort, that the culture be changed.

Executives who have successfully reoriented organizational cultures suggest allotting up to 15 years for the process.[13] Such an undertaking requires careful justification. Allan Kennedy, co-author of the best-selling *Corporate Cultures,* lists five reasons that can justify large-scale cultural change:

1 Company has strong values that don't fit a changing environment.
2 Industry is very competitive and moves with lightning speed.
3 Company is mediocre or worse.   *neither good nor bad*
4 Company is about to join the ranks of the very largest companies.
5 Company is small but growing rapidly.[14]

While massive cultural reorientation may be unreasonable in most situations, it is possible to strengthen, or fine-tune, the culture. A statement of corporate mission which is consistently reinforced by systems, structures, and policies is a useful tool for strengthening the culture. Special attention to people who exhibit key values also spreads the message effectively.

EXHIBIT 7.4   CULTURAL AUDIT

	Questions	Examples
Beliefs about goals	About what financial objectives do we have strong beliefs based on traditions and history?	Return on assets Rate of growth Debt/equity ratio Bond rating Dividend policies
	How, if at all, are those beliefs about financial goals related to each other?	Growth should be financed internally, which means no long-term debt and limited dividends.
	What other goals do we believe to be important?	To be in the top quartile of Fortune 500 companies.
		To be the best in our country.
		To be a responsible corporate citizen.
		To be an "all-weather" company.
Beliefs about distinctive competences	What do we believe to be the appropriate scope of our competitive activity?	We can manage any business.
		We can succeed in domestic consumer products.
		We can succeed with products based upon our technological expertise.
		We can only succeed in the paper industry.
		We can manage our business worldwide.
	To what earlier experience can we trace these beliefs?	
	Do they reflect a realistic assessment of the competence of management and the company?	
Beliefs about product market guidelines	What broad guidelines do we believe should guide our managers in competing in product markets?	Have one or two share in each market.
		Provide the best quality product.
		Compete on service, not on price.
	Can these principles be traced to earlier historical events?	
	Are these guidelines valid today in our various businesses?	
Key beliefs about management employees*	What do we believe employees want and/or deserve in exchange for their effort?	Safe working conditions
		Stable employment
		High wages
		Share of profits
		Equity ownership
	What beliefs do we hold about the importance of employees to company success?	Our scientists are key to innovation.
		We want managers and employees to work as one big team.
		Committed employees lead to satisfied customers.

*While these are not strategic beliefs, strictly speaking, they are important to understand because they are so closely related to strategic premises.

Source: Jay Lorsch, "Managing Culture: The Invisible Barrier to Strategic Change," California Management Review, Winter 1986, pp. 95–109. Originally published in Gaining Control of the Corporate Culture, ed. Ralph H. Kilmann, Mary J. Saxton, and Roy Serpa, Jossey-Bass, San Francisco, 1985. Used by permission.

EXHIBIT 7.5 CULTURAL RISK MATRIX

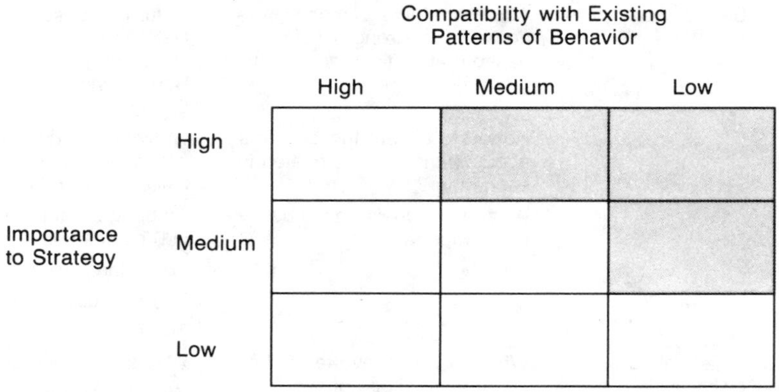

Compatibility with Existing
Patterns of Behavior

		High	Medium	Low
Importance to Strategy	High			
	Medium			
	Low			

Tactics are placed in the matrix and those that are higher in strategic importance than in cultural compatibility are considered unacceptable risks. These are shown as shaded areas. The attempt to instill risk-taking propensities at AT&T might fall into a shaded area because it has high importance but low capability.

MAC has developed and successfully used the following six-step process for changing culture:

1 Start by having senior managers reexamine the company's history, culture, and skills, as well as the traits of the business they are in.

2 Have the CEO announce a vision of the new strategy and the shared values to make it work. The CEO should then spread the gospel through speeches, memos, and informal contracts.

3 Confront mismatches between present behavior patterns and those required by the future strategy. This may entail designing new organizational incentives and controls to encourage different behavior.

4 Have executives promulgate and reinforce the new values in everything they do.

5 Reshuffle power to elevate people who implement the new ways, including outsiders hired mainly for their values.

6 Use levers of change such as the budgeting process and internal public relations to keep people moving toward the desired behaviors.[15]

Because of the cost, time, and difficulty involved in changing people by changing culture, some argue that it is easier to change the people directly. That is, replace employees steeped in the old beliefs with new employees who already display the appropriate beliefs. While changes in key leadership positions can be very influential, wholesale changes in the composition of the management are usually not feasible.

SUMMARY

The difference between an environmental threat and an opportunity often lies in the resources that an organization can muster to deal with trends in the environment. Internal analysis enumerates an organization's strengths and weaknesses; it also determines whether it possesses competitive advantages and distinctive competences, and whether it is hampered by key vulnerabilities. Internal analysis also requires making visible the organizational belief system known as culture.

Organizational strengths are produced by the conversion of financial resources to organizational, human, and physical resources, which together produce the ability to interact with the market. To survive and prosper over the long term, organizations must allocate resources to produce strengths which will in turn generate more resources. The effectiveness of the resource allocation process can be determined by an internal audit.

Strengths have strategic significance on the business level when they provide a competitive edge, allow the organization to maintain a competitive position, or put the organization at a disadvantage relative to competitors.

On the corporate level, the activities of business units rather than functional areas must be managed in a way that provides advantages to the combined corporate entity. Corporate advantages may derive from the ability to enter new businesses or to produce synergy among existing units.

Corporate culture is an important factor in the organization's ability to act. It is the underlying beliefs that determine how business is done and how employees are treated and are supposed to act. Culture originates in history and the environment; it is reinforced by staffing decisions and the socialization process.

A cultural audit is a tool that can be used to make beliefs visible in an organization. This is important for strategic management because the culture of the organization is an important influence on how the organization can respond to changes in the environment. Changing culture is costly, time-consuming, and difficult. However, culture can be strengthened by leadership and consistency.

↑ viability

CHAPTER 7 REVIEW QUESTIONS

1 What is the relationship of internal analysis to environmental analysis? To the strategic management process?
2 How is an internal audit conducted? What is the purpose of such an audit?
3 How does a competitive advantage differ from a business requirement?
4 What makes a weakness a key vulnerability?
5 What capabilities have strategic significance on the corporate strategy level?
6 How can the existence of synergy be determined?
7 How is corporate culture developed and maintained?
8 What is a cultural audit? What cautions should be employed when conducting a cultural audit?
9 Under what circumstances would you advise a change in corporate culture?
10 What types of actions can change culture?

CHAPTER 7 DISCUSSION QUESTIONS

1 Choose a not-for-profit organization of which you are a member (church, sorority, campus club, or professional group) and analyze its culture. How is your behavior as a member shaped by the organization's culture? How are expectations transmitted to new members?

2 How does internal analysis for a single-product organization differ in focus and scope from internal analysis for a multiproduct organization?

3 Research studies have shown that internal analysis is more often neglected in the strategic management process than is environmental analysis. Why might this be the case? What procedures could you recommend to the president of a medium-sized business to ensure adequate internal analysis?

CHAPTER 7 REFERENCES

1 "The Wine Wars Get Hotter," *Business Week,* April 11, 1983, pp. 61, 65, and "How Gallo Crushes the Competition," *Fortune,* September 1, 1986, pp. 24–31.

2 W. F. Glueck and L. R. Jauch, *Strategic Management and Business Policy,* 4th ed., McGraw-Hill, New York, 1984, p. 227.

3 E. H. Schein, *Organizational Culture and Leadership,* Jossey-Bass, San Francisco, 1985, p. 6.

4 J. W. Lorsch, "Managing Culture: The Invisible Barrier to Strategic Change." *California Management Review,* Winter 1986, p. 95; and J. B. Barney, "Organizational Culture: Can It Be a Source of Sustained Competitive Advantage?" *Academy of Management Review,* July 1986, p. 656.

5 S. P. Robbins, *Essentials of Organizational Behavior,* Prentice-Hall, Englewood Cliffs, N.J., 1984, p. 173.

6 "The Corporate Culture Vultures," *Fortune,* October 17, 1983, p. 72.

7 The discussion of origins of culture closely follows Robbins, op. cit., pp. 174–176.

8 M. Lefkoe, "Why So Many Mergers Fail," *Fortune,* July 20, 1987, p. 113.

9 Barney, op. cit., p. 661.

10 Lorsch, op. cit.

11 Schein, op. cit., p. 113.

12 "Corporate Culture Vultures," op. cit., p. 70.

13 Ibid.

14 T. Deal and A. E. Kennedy, *Corporate Cultures,* Reading, Mass., Addison-Wesley, 1982.

15 Ibid.

GENERATING, EVALUATING, AND CHOOSING STRATEGIC ALTERNATIVES

LEARNING OBJECTIVES

After studying this chapter, the reader should be able to:

1 Explain the concept of the performance gap and determine whether one is present in an organization
2 Apply tools for generating and evaluating strategic alternatives at both the corporate and business levels of strategy
3 Discuss the pros and cons of popular approaches for comparing strategy alternatives
4 Explain the steps in preparing contingency strategies

CHAPTER OUTLINE

Industry Evolution
- Emerging Industry • Maturing Industry • Declining Industry
- Fragmented Industry

STRATEGIC CHOICE

CONTINGENCY STRATEGIES

Identifying Key Variables

Establishing Trigger Points

Planning Appropriate Action

SUMMARY

REVIEW QUESTIONS

DISCUSSION QUESTIONS

REFERENCES

Having gained an understanding of the current situation of the organization and having made an assessment of the organization's prospects for the future, the strategist must now consider strategic alternatives. One of two directions may be taken by the strategist. One direction involves only incremental adjustment or fine-tuning of the current strategy. The other direction represents a shift from one generic strategy to another or the addition of new generic strategies. If change rather than adjustment is needed, further analysis will utilize a variety of tools which have been developed for the purpose of generating and evaluating generic alternatives. If only adjustment is needed, further analysis will focus on functional strategies and on the implementation phase. These relationships are diagramed in Exhibit 8.1. This chapter will introduce the tools for generating and evaluating strategic alternatives, while Chapters 9 and 10 will discuss strategy implementation.

THE PERFORMANCE GAP

To determine which direction to take in considering strategic alternatives, it is necessary to project the results that will be achieved if no changes are made in the current strategy. The projection of future performance under the current strategy takes into account environmental trends and internal resources. When projected performance under the current strategy will not achieve objectives set for the planning period, a *performance gap* exists. Exhibit 8.2 diagrams a performance gap, and Example 8.1 provides examples of gaps faced by several companies. The reason (or reasons) for the gap are: the current strategy is not appropriate for changing environments; the current strategy is not appropriate because of changing internal configurations of resources; and/or the current strategy is not being implemented properly.

Gap analysis may be performed at the corporate level or business level. For each objective of importance (at least growth and profitability objectives should be analyzed), the projected performance is subtracted from desired performance for each year of the planning period. In Exhibit 8.3, which is a simplified example of a gap matrix, the analysis indicates that in year 1, the company will exceed total sales goals by $2.5 million but will fail to meet sales

EXHIBIT 8.1   DIRECTIONS TO TAKE IN GENERATING STRATEGIC ALTERNATIVES

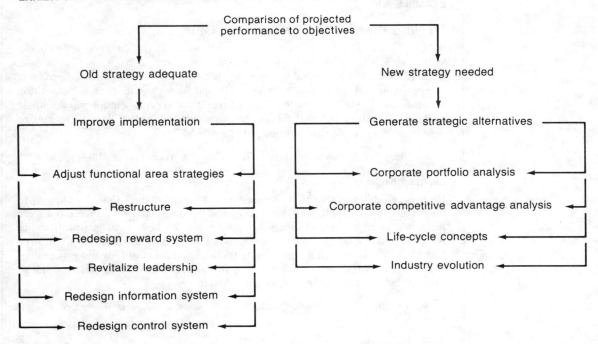

EXHIBIT 8.2   THE PERFORMANCE GAP

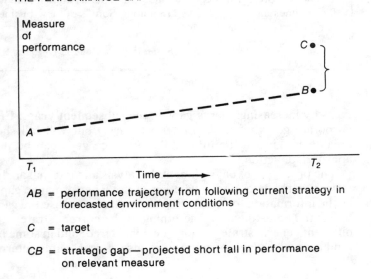

AB = performance trajectory from following current strategy in forecasted environment conditions

C = target

CB = strategic gap—projected short fall in performance on relevant measure

---

EXAMPLE 8.1

Organizations with Performance Gaps

General Electric

GE CEO John F. (Jack) Welch observed that many of GE's diversified products competed in mature industries where demand was stagnating and competition was increasing. He believes that high tech and the service sectors will dominate in the next century and that GE needed to adjust its product lines to be able to maintain the type of growth it desired.

Source: "Can Jack Welch Reinvent GE?" *Business Week,* June 30, 1986, pp. 62–67.

Eastman Kodak

Eastman Kodak was essentially a one-product company until 1984. By clinging to their highly profitable film business, they had become a household word but were facing a mature market with high cost operations. Without a change, profitability would continue a downward pattern. Kodak began internal cost cutting, acquired Fox Photo to strengthen its hold on its traditional market of film and processing, and began to introduce a number of new products such as the "point and shoot" camera and a digitized medical imaging device.

Source: "Kicking the Single-Product Habit at Kodak," *Business Week,* December 1, 1986, pp. 36–37.

Sony Corporation

The decision was made at Sony to reduce dependence on the consumer electronics division because of threatening trends in that business. Competitors in consumer electronics were cutting the time it took to produce look-alike products, had lower costs, and were able to match quality. Continuance of these trends threatened Sony's strategic advantage and ability to maintain its targeted profits. Telephones and floppy disks are among Sony's 20 new businesses that account for 25 percent of sales.

Source: "Sony's Challenge," *Business Week,* June 1, 1987.

---

goals by increasingly large gaps in the subsequent years. EPS will also exceed corporate goals in the short term (year 1) but will fall short by greater and greater margins in the future. Performance gaps can be prevented by taking appropriate action.

The processes of environmental analysis and internal analysis provide the information for determining whether or not a performance gap may occur as well as the information for generating alternatives to close the gap. The first alternative is the adjustment or fine-tuning of the current strategy; next, one or more different generic strategies may be considered; and in some instances, the more fundamental change of mission is also a reasonable alternative to consider.

EXHIBIT 8.3   EXAMPLE OF A GAP MATRIX

Time periods in
planning horizon

	Year 1	Year 2	Year 3	Year 4	Year 5
Total sales revenue ($ millions)	+ 2.5	− 7.3	− 10.9	− 18.7	− 28.3
EPS ($ per share)	+ 0.05	− 0.11	− 0.31	− 0.80	− 1.35

Corporate goals

Source: K. J. Cohen and R. M. Cyert, "Strategy Formulation, Implementation, and Monitoring," *Journal of Business,* vol. 46, no. 3, 1973. Used by permission.

Adjusting Current Strategy

Often a performance gap may be closed by more careful implementation of the current strategy. The internal analysis process and the identification of the current situation should provide insight into whether fine-tuning or more dramatic change is necessary. Changing strategy is generally more difficult than tightening operations, and the strategist should be relatively certain that operating changes are not sufficient to close the performance gap before embarking on a change of strategy.

A performance gap may be closed by improving the internal alignment of resources for increased efficiency (improving margins) or by improving competitive position for increased effectiveness (improving market share). Generally, it is possible to improve margins without provoking a response from competitors. Efforts to win market share, however, are more likely to provoke a reaction from others. Feasibility of these alternatives also depends on how far from the break-even point the organization is operating. Improving margins through cost cutting (retrenchment) will usually yield the greatest benefits to a business whose sales are just below or just above the break-even point. More drastic measures, such as asset reduction, may be necessary if the firm is well below the break-even point. Exhibit 8.4 depicts these situations.

Strategic Alternatives

Generic strategic alternatives (see Chapter 3) provide an aid to strategists by reducing to a relatively few categories of strategies the multitude of options which are available. The analytical tools which produce general strategy recommendations typically use one or two dimensions to summarize both the in-

EXHIBIT 8.4   STRATEGIC ALTERNATIVES FOR CLOSING PERFORMANCE GAPS

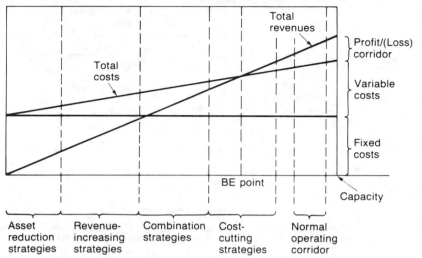

ternal and external situations. The techniques then suggest that certain generic strategies are appropriate alternatives for certain types of external environments and internal situations. For example, when an organization faces an environment in which demand for its primary product is falling, the environment might be labeled as low in growth or unattractive. If the organization is the leading company in that industry and has significant resources, it might be typed as a dominant company. Strategy alternatives for a dominant company in a low-growth environment might include growth or stability strategies. For a weak company in the same industry, only defensive strategies should be considered according to most generic strategy systems.

Aids to generating strategic alternatives on both the corporate level and the business level are presented in this chapter. These aids are analytical in nature. They are based on economic analysis and assume a competitive strategy is desirable. Strategists may also turn to political and cooperative solutions for performance gaps.

CORPORATE STRATEGY ANALYSIS

Corporate Portfolio Analysis

Corporate strategies are usually a combination of generic strategies guided by the desire to diversify operations. Diversification provides growth opportunities when the original market has matured and reduces other risks associated with a single product or service. The benefits of diversification are accompanied by administrative difficulties, as corporate executives must make corporate resource allocations among businesses which are difficult to compare using traditional capital budgeting techniques. Several techniques have been developed to facilitate the comparison of different businesses. These portfolio analysis techniques summarize important strategy influences (usually the environment and the internal solution in two dimensions of a matrix). Strategic business units (SBUs) are then compared on these dimensions and strategy prescriptions can be made.

General Electric Planning Grid   General Electric (GE) was a pioneer among diversified companies in the development of a portfolio approach to strategic planning. The approach was inspired by the need to perfect a way of evaluating the plans of approximately forty businesses in order to fund the plans with the greatest potential for success. Net present value analysis was not sufficient because of the necessity to assume that all projects to be compared had equivalent levels of risk. The two dimensions chosen to evaluate the business units were business strengths and industry attractiveness. In order to arrive at a rating of low, medium, or high for business strengths, a number of factors are considered. These factors may include size of unit, growth rate of unit, market share held, profitability, competitive position, image, and people. Industry attractiveness is also judged on a number of factors—size of market, market growth rate, industry profitability, competitive structure, pricing practices, etc.—and is also rated low, medium, or high. The choice of factors and the weight assessed factors may vary from business unit to business unit. For example, in some industries technology is a key to success; in others, image is critical. Considerable expertise and research goes into the rating process, and this process is valuable because it requires management to examine the critical success factors in their own industry and judge where their operations stand in relationship to these factors.[1] (Example 8.2 shows this process for a hypothetical business unit.)

All units can be placed on the same portfolio planning grid and their relationship to each other graphically represented. (See Exhibit 8.5.) By placing all units on the same grid, the organization has achieved the difficult task of comparing projects with varying degrees of risk on the same dimensions. The best alternatives for each unit are narrowed down and the organizational resource allocation process is simplified. The best opportunities for corporate investment are likely to be in those units which hold strong positions in attractive industries. On the other extreme, investing in units with weak positions in industries of low attractiveness would be squandering resources which could be better used elsewhere. For a unit of only medium attractiveness and strengths or in which a high on one dimension is balanced by a low on the other, the selected investment of resources to increase strengths or a stability strategy to take advantage of a strong position should be considered. If an organization finds a high proportion of its units in the lower right-hand portion of the grid, the model suggests there is a need for acquisitions or development of new businesses in order to bring the portfolio into better balance.

EXAMPLE 8.2

Rating of a Business Unit for Placement on GE Business Screen SBU A

Managers of a manufacturer of consumer goods with a strong market position in a declining market might choose the criteria for industry attractiveness and competitive position to be:.

Industry Attractiveness	Competitive Position
Growth rate	Cost control capability
Average return of equity	Brand recognition
Intensity of competition	Process improvement ability
Capacity utilization	Promotional capability

The criteria would be weighted according to the perceptions of the managers about their importance for that industry and rated according to the situation of the SBU. That process might produce the following scores:

Factor	Weight	×	Rating (1–10) =	Score
Industry attractiveness				
Growth rate	3		5	15
Average return/equity	4		3	12
Intensity of competition	2		4	8
Capacity utilization	1		1	1
Total	10			36
Competitive position				
Cost control capability	3		10	30
Brand recognition	3		9	27
Process improvement ability	2		8	16
Promotional capability	2		9	18
Total	10			91

The total score would be used to determine whether the SBU was high, medium, or low on each dimension and the SBU's position on the Business Screen is determined by plotting the summary assessment of each dimension. The score of 36 out of 100 would be in the low to medium range, while the score of 91 is in the high range. This unit would rate low on industry attractiveness but high on competitive position, which would put it in the Stability/Growth sector of the matrix.

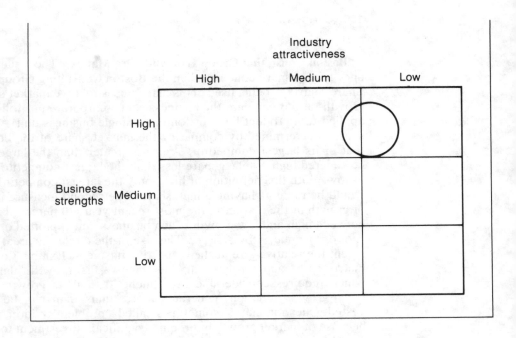

EXHIBIT 8.5   GE PLANNING GRID

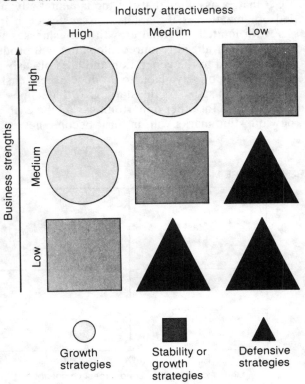

Boston Consulting Group Growth-Share Matrix The issue of portfolio balance is of primary concern when the Boston Consulting Group (BCG) Growth-Share Matrix is being used. This matrix uses relative market share and market growth rate to compare the businesses in a corporate portfolio (it may also be applied to a product line portfolio in a single business unit).[2] Relative market share is determined by comparing the market share of the business unit with that of its largest competitor. A share greater than the largest competitor is considered high, while a share less than the largest competitor would be rated as low. With this definition of high, only the largest competitor in the industry would be rated as having a high share. The second measure is the percentage of growth of the market in the most recent year; 10 percent is the cutoff point between high and low growth. Each business unit is plotted on the appropriate spot on the matrix by a circle. The size of the circle (its area) is drawn to represent the relative size of the respective business. Exhibit 8.6 shows the BCG matrix with each cell labeled. The star is a fast-growth, high-share business which requires considerable investment to fund its growth. The cow, in a lower-growth situation, generates more funds than can be profitably reinvested. Question marks (sometimes called "problem children") have potential because of market growth but require significant investment to gain star status. The dogs are viewed as having no future. They are in a poor position in a stagnant market; divestiture is usually the recommended alternatives.

The BCG matrix assumes that the fundamental advantage to be found in a diversified organization is the ability to transfer cash from highly profitable businesses with limited potential growth to businesses which have better future potential.[3] Centralized resource allocation will produce a portfolio which is balanced in regard to the generation and uses of cash. In a balanced portfolio, there should be cows available to produce excess cash to invest in question marks to make them stars. As the stars' growth declines, they become cows—new sources of cash for other opportunities. As the cash generation cycle continues, new question marks will, in turn, become new stars. A balanced port-

EXHIBIT 8.6 BCG GROWTH-SHARE MATRIX

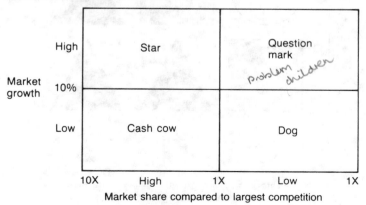

Market share compared to largest competition

folio may emphasize growth with a preponderance of stars or margins with a preponderance of cows. There is little room in a balanced portfolio for dogs, which use cash with no potential for improved cash flow.

Assumptions and Precautions   Both the GE Planning Grid and the BCG Growth-Share Matrix assume that business units are independent. General Electric used the term "strategic business unit" to apply to groupings of products or services with interdependent prices, similar competitors, similar customer groups, and the potential for sharing research and development, manufacturing, or marketing experience.[4] When these interdependencies cross business units (i.e., a dog and a cow share production or distribution facilities), neither matrix is appropriate.

Because of the perceived importance of the ability to transfer cash at the corporate level, the dimensions used to position businesses on the Growth-Share Matrix are assumed to be related to the ability of a business to generate cash as well as the cash-use requirements of the business. The association of market share with the ability to generate cash is based on the experience curve concept. The experience curve suggests that costs can be reduced and margins improved (generating cash) by cumulative experience in manufacturing, distribution, procurement, etc. Cumulative experience is gained through increased market share, thus greater market share should provide greater cash flow. Market growth is related to the use of cash because a growing market requires significant investments to establish primary demand as well as to create a customer franchise. A third assumption is that all funds for financing unit operations are generated internally.

Corporate portfolio approaches such as the BCG Growth-Share Matrix, the General Electric Planning Grid, or the Royal Dutch Shell Directional Policy Matrix (similar to the GE Grid), have advantages which relate in large part to the process of using the matrices. These advantages are listed in Exhibit 8.7. However, there are also some problems with the specific matrices as well as with the general approach. The existence of these problems requires that they be used very carefully, with full understanding of the underlying assumptions. If products are differentiated, if SBUs share costs, or if product lines cannot be divided into a reasonable number of SBUs, the matrices may not produce

---

EXHIBIT 8.7   ADVANTAGES OF PORTFOLIO PLANNING

- Provides an easily graspable, informative framework
- Results in differential treatment of businesses (resource allocation, management evaluation and compensation, risk assessment)
- Gives a CEO support to divest a cash-draining business
- Enhances the quality of plans
- Promotes long-run thinking
- Aids in monitoring competitors
- Nurtures the entrepreneurial spirit

Source: K. Giddens-Emig, "Portfolio Planning: A Concept in Controversy," *Managerial Planning,* November–December 1983. Used by permission.

good alternatives.[5] Portfolio models should be viewed as one tool for generating strategic alternatives, but choice should be tempered by managerial judgment, not by mechanical application of planning matrices.

Competitive Advantage and Corporate Strategy

One critic of portfolio approaches to corporate strategy analysis is Michael Porter of Harvard University. He characterizes portfolio strategy as follows:

> The corporation acquires sound, attractive companies with competent managers who agree to stay on.... The acquired units are autonomous and the teams that run them are compensated according to unit results. The corporation supplies capital and works with each to infuse it with professional management techniques. At the same time, top management provides objective and dispassionate review of business unit results. Portfolio managers categorize units by potential and regularly transfer resources from units that generate cash to those with high potential and cash needs.[6]

He argues that portfolio management does little to create or increase shareholder value because portfolios are not unique sources of advantages. Capital markets are so well developed and sound strategies so easily funded that the cash transfers which are the hallmark of portfolio management are easily arranged outside the corporation. Also the autonomy given business units and the separation of their operations from each other may actually erode performance.

Porter proposes three other approaches as a basis for generating corporate-level strategy alternatives. These approaches are restructuring, transferring skills, and sharing activities.[7] Restructuring adds value by actually changing the business and possibly the industry by shifting strategy, replacement management, or redeploying assets. Organizations using the restructuring approach will seek out companies which are underdeveloped or industries on the brink of change. The transferring-skills approach is viable when businesses can share expertise that will yield competitive advantages for each of the businesses. The sharing-activities approach seeks to exploit relationships among business units that lower costs or increase differentiation for the units. Example 8.3 illustrates each.

These three approaches present a contrast to portfolio analysis in several ways:

1 They emphasize and capitalize on relationships among business units and between the corporate and business levels, while portfolio analysis emphasizes and requires independence of strategic business units and objective analysis of corporate-level managers.

2 These relationships are difficult to measure, while portfolio analysis relies on more objective criteria for assessing business units.

3 These approaches do not lend themselves to graphic presentation.

Porter suggests a seven-step approach to generating strategic alternatives:

1 Identifying interrelationships among already existing business units

EXAMPLE 8.3

Restructuring, Transferring Skills, Sharing Activities as Basis for Corporate Competitive Advantages

Restructuring (Del Monte)

RJR purchased Del Monte, a producer of canned fruits and vegetables, in 1979 for $618 million. During the next 4 years, 12 businesses were divested, 38 plants were closed, and $55 million written off. Under the new ownership, product lines were pared, production efficiency increased, and market responsiveness emphasized. The company has shifted its product line into low-sugar and low-salt items and has made significant contributions to RJR profits.

Source: "The Consumer Drives RJR Again," *Business Week*, June 4, 1984, pp. 92–93.

Transferring Skills (Weight Watchers)

Heinz's acquisition of Weight Watchers gave Heinz an entrée into the low-calorie food market with a well-known name. Weight Watchers was able to use Heinz's product development skills and supermarket distribution clout to introduce a line of frozen low-calorie entrées and desserts.

Sharing Activities (Nabisco and Standard Brands)

Nabisco and Standard Brands merged in 1981 to form Nabisco Brands. The intent was to exploit each company's resources to enhance the food industry clout of the combination. The results become evident when the Great Cookie War was begun in 1983 by food giants, Procter & Gamble and Frito-Lay. Both introduced soft, "home-style" cookies in take-home packages at the grocery. The expertise of Standard Brands was tapped by Nabisco for new product development. Market share in all areas is growing.

Source: "Do Mergers Really Work?" *Business Week*, June 3, 1985, p. 91.

2 Selecting the core businesses that will be the foundations of the corporate strategy

3 Creating horizontal organizational mechanisms to facilitate interrelationships among core businesses and lay the groundwork for future related diversification

4 Pursuing diversification opportunities that allow shared activities

5 Pursuing diversification through transfer of skills if opportunities for sharing activities are limited or exhausted

6 Pursuing a strategy of restructuring if this fits the skills of management or no good opportunities exist for forging corporate interrelationships

7 Paying dividends so that the shareholders can be the portfolio managers[8]

The ability to identify competitive advantages and distinctive competences on the business level is a skill critical to these corporate strategy alternatives.

LIFE CYCLE CONCEPTS FOR BUSINESS STRATEGY

A basic limitation to the ability of the organization to shift strategy results from the nature of the demand for its product or service. Changing demand patterns often require new strategic alternatives. The vacuum tube, the integrated circuit, and the silicon chip are three generations of products with similar applications in electronics. The vacuum tube and the integrated circuit no longer compete for consumer electronics applications, but they still have specialized uses. Early tube manufacturers, like Raytheon, were forced to rethink strategic alternatives because of the dynamics of product demand. In order to meet growth objectives, Raytheon was forced to turn to other products. Strategic alternatives became severely limited in tube manufacturing because of the decline in demand. Similarly, the competitive requirements of an industry evolve over the life of the product and with the strategic moves made by competitors in the industry. The product life cycle, experience, learning, and technology curves, and the industry evolution concept all provide analytical tools for formulating business-level strategies.

The Product Life Cycle

The product life cycle describes the hypothetical passage of a product or service through a series of stages, beginning with introduction and culminating in saturation. The introduction stage is characterized by slow growth while primary demand for the product is established and buyer resistance is overcome. When this has been achieved, demand accelerates rapidly. As primary demand is satisfied, the curve flattens to approximately the growth rate of the buyer group. The market may remain saturated and sustain the level of demand, or new products may appear and cause demand to decline sharply. Technological innovation may put the product in another period of rapid growth.

The product life cycle captures the dynamics of product and market evolution and can be used for generating strategic alternatives. Specifically, the product life cycle has the following analytical uses:

1 To suggest appropriate functional area emphasis by stages of the life cycle (see Exhibit 8.8). In the early development stage, R&D requires significant attention and resources and is the most likely source of competitive advantage. In the shakeout stage, resource allocations to improve efficiency of operations usually yield the greatest competitive benefits.

2 To suggest appropriate generic strategy alternatives. Growth strategies are usually pursued early in the cycle, while retrenchment is more appropriate as the product reaches maturity. When the product life cycle is coupled with an assessment of competitive position (see Exhibit 8.9), more specific strategic alternatives emerge.

3 To time strategy changes. Hofer and Schendel suggest that the points of inflection on the curve provide the best opportunities to attack industry leaders.[9]

4 To assess the balance of a corporate portfolio of business units to ensure that developing products are introduced as others pass through growth to maturity.

EXHIBIT 8.8 PRODUCT LIFE CYCLE

Stage	Development	Growth	Shakeout	Maturity	Saturation		
					Saturation	Decline	Petrification
Market growth rate	Slight	Very large	Large	GNP growth	Population growth	Negative	Slight to none
Change in growth rate	Little	Increases rapidly	Decreases rapidly	Decreases slowly	Little	Decreases rapidly, then slow. May increase, then slow.*	Little
Number of segments	Very few	Some	Some	Some to many		Few	Few
Technological change in product design	Very great	Great	Moderate	Slight	Slight †	Slight	Slight
Technological change in process design	Slight	Slight/ moderate	Very great	Great/ moderate	Slight	Slight	Slight
Major functional concern	Research and development	Engineering	Production	Marketing, distribution, finance		Finance	Marketing and finance

*The rate of change of the market growth rate usually only increases during the decline stage for those products that do not die, i.e., that enter the petrification stage of evolution.

†Although the rate of technological change in the basic design of the product is usually low during this stage of market evolution, the probability of a major breakthrough to a different kind of product that performs the same function increases substantially during this period.

Source: C. W. Hofer, "Conceptual Constructs for Formulating Corporate and Business Strategy," Boston: Intercollegiate Case Clearing House, 9-378-754, Boston, 1977, p. 7.

161

EXHIBIT 8.9 STRATEGIC GUIDELINES BASED ON PRODUCT MATURITY AND COMPETITIVE POSITION

Competitive position	Stage of product life cycle			
	Embryonic	Growing	Mature	Aging
Dominant	All-out push for share Hold position	Hold position Hold share	Hold position Grow with industry	Hold position
Strong	Attempt to improve position All-out push for share	Attempt to improve position Push for share	Hold position Grow with industry	Hold position or harvest
Favorable	Selective or all-out push for share Selective attempt to improve position	Attempt to improve position Selective push for share	Custodial or maintenance Find niche and attempt to protect	Harvest or phased withdrawal
Tenable	Selective push for position	Find niche and protect it	Find niche and hang on or phased withdrawal	Phased withdrawal or abandon
Weak	Up or out	Turnaround or abandon	Turnaround or phased withdrawal	Abandon

Source: Based on P. Patel and M. Younger, "A Frame of Reference for Strategy Development," *Long Range Planning,* April 1978, p. 10.

Learning/Experience/Technology Curves

The learning curve is a representation of the relationship between the hours of labor required to produce a product and the number of units produced. The hours of labor required to produce a product or service usually declines as a function of the units produced. It is theoretically possible to predict how long it will take to make the one-hundredth product if the time for making the first and the tenth is known. The application of the learning curve concept to all costs was the work of the Boston Consulting Group (BCG). The BCG consultants found that in some of their clients, every time production doubled, unit costs fell between 25 percent and 30 percent. They maintained that this had implications for generating strategic alternatives. If cost per unit decreases with the number of units produced, the company that has the lowest marginal cost for a particular product is the one that has made the most of that product over the time the product has been in production. Producing the most means selling the most and, thus, market share became the strategic focus of experience curve advocates. The company with the largest market share is in the best position to continue to increase share because it has the lowest marginal costs and is in a better position to cut price to gain share longer than its competitors can. A company that foregoes margin to gain share will be able to establish a position that no other competitor will challenge because of the impossibility of matching cumulative experience.

Difficulties with applying this concept to strategy formulation should be noted:

- Costs do not *automatically* decline with experience.
- Competitors also cut prices, and cutthroat price wars may result and hurt all competitors.
- Anticipated margins may not appear if customers choose substitutes when prices are raised.[10]

While the concept of the experience curve may be a useful tool in considering strategic alternatives, it probably should not be used as the only analytical tool. Exhibit 8.10 shows an experience curve for random access memory (RAM) chips.

A third concept related to and an extension of the previous curves is the technological S curve, which plots the life cycle of a technology. The technological S curve is based on the idea that each technology has a limit (or point of diminishing returns) and that there are common danger signals of when the limit is being approached. Technologies follow a curve which reflects the relationship between worker-hours invested and product performance. Early in the cycle, considerable R&D effort is required to achieve small gains in performance. Eventually, effort begins to pay off and large gains are achieved with small incremental effort. At some point, the returns begin to diminish and

EXHIBIT 8.10   EXPERIENCE CURVE FOR DYNAMIC RAMs

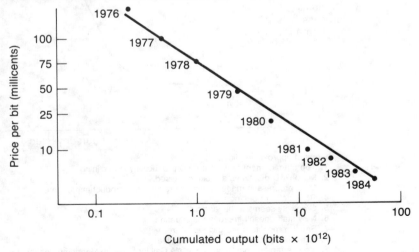

Source: P. Ghemawat, "Building Strategy on the Experience Curve," *Harvard Business Review,* March–April 1985. From Integrated Circuit Engineering Corporation. Used by permission.

as in the beginning, considerable effort is required for small gains in performance. At this point the product is vulnerable to substitution by another product technology which is at an earlier stage in its life cycle but which starts the cycle at a higher performance level. As shown in Exhibit 8.11, the curves tend to overlap and the implications for strategy derive from this overlap. Dependence on a single technology places an organization in a dangerous situation. It is necessary to be alert to the danger signals which indicate the approach to the limits of the current technology. When this occurs, the strategist should prepare to deal with potential substitutes or be a part of the development of these substitutes. Product development and diversification strategies are generic strategies which reduce dependence on particular products.

Industry Evolution

Strategic alternatives for an SBU or a single-product or service organization must be generated within the constraints of the industry in which the SBU or company competes. The constraints vary over time with changes in the nature of the industry and the relationship of the organization to dominant competitors.[11] Competitive interaction, determined by the forces described in Chapter 6, may be classified into five types of industries: emerging, maturing, declining, fragmented, and global. An *emerging* industry is a new formation of

EXHIBIT 8.11   TECHNOLOGICAL S CURVES

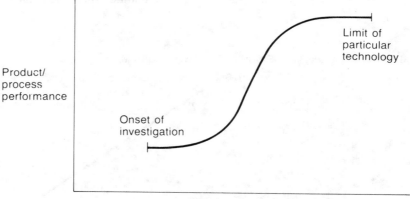

Signs of approaching limits:
1. Top management feels that R&D productivity is declining.
2. More R&D deadlines are being missed.
3. Most progress is made in process rather than product improvements.
4. R&D staff not getting along well.
5. Creativity seems to be lagging.
6. New staff doesn't improve the situation.
7. Small competitors are gaining share.
8. Small competitors are more innovative.
Source: Adapted from R. N. Foster, "A Call for Vision in Managing Technology," *Business Week,* May 24, 1982, p. 26.

a group of competitors around a technological innovation, cost shift, or other environmental change that creates a new product or service. In this situation, the key result areas and business requirements will be established as firms achieve success and establish defensible positions. The biotechnology industry, in which gene splicing is applied to health and agricultural problems, was such an industry in the mid-1980s. A *maturing* industry is one whose period of rapid growth has passed. Slower growth is reflected in greater competition for market share, a growing number of experienced buyers who are brand-oriented, a greater emphasis on cost and service, overexpansion of capacity, and increasing international competition. Fast foods, soft drinks, home appliances, and hand-held calculators are produced by industries exhibiting characteristics of maturity. An industry is said to be *declining* when it has suffered an absolute decline in sales over a long period of time. Some causes of decline include technological substitution, demographic shifts, or shifts in buyers' needs or preferences. The brown liquor and cigarette industries are declining. A *fragmented* industry is one in which no dominant competitor exists. No one firm has a dominant market share. Instead of a recognized leader with a number of followers, there are numerous small and medium-sized companies. Examples include the service, retailing, distribution, wood and metal fabrication, and agricultural products industries. A *global* industry is one in which competition in a given geographic area is influenced by the worldwide position of the competitors. In a global industry, it is necessary to look at international relationships even when only a national market is of concern. Global industries are discussed in more detail in Chapter 12. Exhibit 8.12 summarizes the characteristics of the generic industry types and gives examples of each.

Emerging Industry   The absence of established bases of competition distinguished emerging industries and results in considerable uncertainty for both

EXHIBIT 8.12   GENERIC INDUSTRY TYPES

	Characteristics	Examples
Fragmented industries	No dominant competitor Numerous small and medium-sized companies	Health spas Restaurants Retailers Travel agencies
Maturing industries	End period of rapid growth	Fast foods Meat packing Soft drinks
Declining industries	Absolute decline in sales over long period	Dry cleaning
Emerging industries	New products or services Key success factors not established No dominant competition	Biotechnology
Global industries	Competition in given geographic area is worldwide	Automobiles Steel

customers and competitors. Product standards for the industry have not been set. Prices are likely to fall, since great cost reductions are possible. Buyers are usually not very knowledgeable, competitor information is scarce, and there are many new and spin-off companies. Some competitors may be subsidized. The only certainty is that the current situation will change and the greatest rewards will be reaped by those who shape the change. The personal computer field exhibited emerging industry traits until IBM's entry into the market with the PC established product standards.

A central concern in emerging industries is the timing of market acceptance. A market which develops early shows rapid customer acceptance. Such acceptance is likely when the product or service provides a clear performance or cost advantage or has reached the state of the art required to achieve significant benefits. Markets which develop slowly prolong uncertainty.

Because of the uncertainty and the lack of defined competitive rules which characterize emerging industries, good strategic choices made early can provide great benefits. In an emerging industry, it is important to create demand for and confidence in the product or service itself rather than for the product or service of one competitor. This can be achieved through product standardization and industry cooperation to create and enforce quality standards. It is important to remember that it is the ultimate structure of the industry, not its initial growth rate, that determines attractiveness. Many companies entered the market for home video games in the early 1980s as growth rates soared only to find by 1984 that growth could not be sustained.

Maturing Industry Growth can mask strategic errors, but as growth slows, the failure to position the organization properly has more severe consequences. Issues of concern when the growth rate declines include:

- Costing appropriately to prune unprofitable products
- Pricing appropriately to assess contribution of individual products
- Assessing the role of process innovation
- Increasing product or service offerings to existing customers
- Assessing opportunities to buy cheap assets of failed or marginal firms
- Expanding internationally

An organization should consider divestment as an option at the onset of maturity. An organization which has limited resources for transition to slower growth, one which faces determined competitors with greater resources, or one which faces a situation of extended-transition turmoil and only modest prospects for profits should plan a phase-out.

Declining Industry Strategic alternatives in declining industries depend on calculations of how rapidly the current competitors will leave the industry and how vigorously those remaining will defend their positions. In addition, the perceived certainty and speed of the decline, as well as the structural characteristics of the remaining segments, will affect competitive decisions. The exit option may not be very attractive because the assets have a greatly diminished liquidation value. This can occur because of the special nature or location of the assets, because fixed costs such as labor settlements are high, because cancellation penalties for long-term contracts exist, because of synergy among other businesses, or because of a reduction in the financial credibility of the firm. Government regulations and perceptions of social responsibilities can also make it difficult to exit a declining industry.

When capacity is not retired but is merely shifted (employee buy-outs, for example) or when weak but financially well-backed competitors try to improve position as demand declines, a price war is likely to result. This threatens the entire industry.

Kathryn Harrigan has provided a series of analytical questions to ask to generate feasible strategic alternatives in a declining industry.[12]

1 How desirable is it to remain in the industry? What is the certainty and speed of the decline? What is the projected profitability of the remaining sectors?

2 What will competitors do? Are there significant exit barriers? What strengths exist in the remaining sectors?

3 What is the position of the firm? Are there significant exit barriers? What strengths does the firm have in sectors where demand remains?

Fragmented Industry In a fragmented industry, where no dominant competitor exists, the establishment of dominance will yield great returns. The competitor that achieves economies of scale in manufacturing, distribution, or service; standardizes the product or components of the product; or combines functions where economies exist is establishing a defensible position in the industry. If fragmentation cannot be overcome, specific approaches to the cost leadership, differentiation, and focus strategies should be considered. Some alternatives and examples from the grocery industry are listed in Example 8.4.

EXAMPLE 8.4

Strategies in a Fragmented Industry

1 Southland Corporation, which owns 7-Eleven convenience stores, maintains tight controls over a decentralized operation.
2 National grocery chains such as Safeway or Kroger use "formula" facilities in multiple locations and take advantages of economies of scale in buying and distribution.
3 Luxury groceries (Bruno's in Atlanta, Bocage in Baton Rouge) provide increased value added through more service and specialized services.
4 Specialty shops such as butcher shops or seafood stores provide specialized products or serve particular market segments.
5 Wholesalers who serve only commercial customers specialize by customer segment.
6 Regional chains segment the market by geographical area.
7 Warehouse groceries provide no frills (bags, separate pricing, carry-out, etc.) and maintain lower prices.

Fragmented industries are often characterized by small competitors whose motivation and aspirations are highly individualistic. The ownership and operation of a small business may be a reward in itself for these individuals. The level of returns for the industry as a whole may be lower because competitors continue in business even when economic analysis suggests that they exit. Battles for market share can be disastrous in this setting.

STRATEGIC CHOICE

The analytical tools and conceptual models presented in this chapter represent only a few of the approaches which are available to the strategist. Consultants are active in creating these approaches, practicing managers develop tools, and academicians also churn out models and matrices. Some general guidelines for evaluation and choosing analytical tools are listed below:[13]

• Be sure to identify and understand all assumptions upon which the analytical model is based.

• Be sure that the characteristics of your organization and industry meet those assumptions.

• Don't forget to ask questions about implementation in your own competitive setting.

• Consider carefully the accuracy of the information upon which analysis is based and the dynamics of your situation to determine the useful life of that information.

• Use several tools rather than one.

• Don't advertise your approach; it makes it easier for competitors to figure out your next move.

Exhibit 8.13 provides some guidance for choosing the appropriate analytical tool(s).

EXHIBIT 8.13   GUIDELINES FOR APPLICATION OF STRATEGY ANALYSIS TOOLS

Level of strategy	Tool	Precautions
Business	Product life cycle	May be difficult to assess position
	Experience curve	Can lead to price wars; costs do not automatically decrease with increased share
	Technological S curves	Probably restricted in usefulness to industries with significant R&D
	Industry evolution	May be obvious to competitors
Corporate	GE Planning Grid	May be manipulated; assumptions must be met
	BCG Growth Share	Measures too limited; assumptions restrictive
	Competitive advantage analysis	Exact analysis difficult

Techniques for generating strategic alternatives, if used properly, provide only a starting point for the choice process. In the final analysis, the right strategy is one that works. To work, a strategy must have the support of top management (reflect managerial preferences and values), fit the resources of the organization and the realities of its environment, and be "doable." Fashioning a strategy that has these characteristics is the point at which strategic management moves from the realm of science to the realm of art.[14]

CONTINGENCY STRATEGIES

The comparison of strategic alternatives and the final choice are based on the strategist's best forecast of the internal and external environments. However, the possibility always exists that this forecast or some other key assumption will not be accurate. Naturally, the risk associated with specific forecasts and assumptions varies with the situation. Because the possibility of error does exist, it is wise to develop alternative strategies to be followed in the event that certain key assumptions and forecasts do not hold.

Implementing a contingency process includes three steps:

1. Identifying the key variables
2. Establishing the trigger points that will determine when something needs to be done
3. Planning the appropriate actions[15]

Identifying Key Variables

There are many forecasts and assumptions that can cause a strategy to become inappropriate. Some of the most common include deviations from expected sales or costs, interruptions in supplies and raw materials, changes in laws and regulations, and unanticipated competing products. The most critical step in developing a contingency strategy is to identify the key variables. Key variables are, naturally, the variables that are most important to the success of the strategy. Key variables reflect the critical assumptions about the environment and the internal situation upon which the strategy is based.

Establishing Trigger Points

Once the key variables have been identified, the next step is to establish how much deviation should be allowed a given key variable before a contingency strategy is activated. For example, how far behind the forecast for demand does total industry sales have to fall before a contingency strategy (such as upgrading advertising efforts) is implemented? Naturally, the answer to this question depends on the situation. However, it is important that *specific* trigger points be established, for example, "If the prime interest rate reaches 11 percent..." rather than "We'll watch the prime rate." A major consideration when a trigger point is being established is to provide sufficient time for the contingent actions to be perfected and implemented.

Planning Appropriate Action

The reason for the deviation in the key variable or variables will influence what the appropriate response should be. However, this does not preclude planning what the response will be if certain potential scenarios develop. One company's approach to developing a set of strategies for use if the primary strategy proved unsuccessful is given in Example 8.5.

The level of detail of contingency actions can vary from "We need to take another look" to very detailed and specific actions extending all the way down to the bottom levels of the organization. However, because the original strategic choice is based on the strategist's best forecasts, contingent actions are usually not drawn up in extreme detail until the trigger point has been reached. Ideally, the trigger point allows sufficient time for response to the changed conditions.

The major advantages of developing contingency strategies are to make the strategist more cognizant of when changes might be required and to shorten the resulting reaction time. In all too many instances, top management insists on implementing a previously chosen strategy in spite of significant environmental changes. Detroit's refusal to shift to smaller, more fuel-efficient cars in the early 1970s is a good example of this behavior.

In most instances, it is much more important to identify clearly the key variables and assumptions and to establish specific trigger points than to develop extremely detailed actions. If the first two steps are properly done, then sufficient lead time should be provided to perfect the contingency actions.

EXAMPLE 8.5

Contingency Strategies

If current divestiture strategy is not successful in achieving complete divestiture, implement alternative strategies for complete withdrawal from this business through the following strategies:

1 Sell segments of the business; or
2 Gradually phase out segments that cannot be sold; or
3 Close down segments that cannot be sold or phased out; or
4 If none of the above are achievable at an acceptable cost in the near future, make whatever management changes and investments are required to achieve improved performance until economic and political circumstances change so that we can withdraw at an acceptable cost.

Source: William R. King and David Clelland, *Strategic Planning and Policy,* Van Nostrand, New York, 1978, pp. 55–56.

SUMMARY

When projected future results of following the current strategy fall short of desired results, a performance gap exists. A performance gap is identified through environmental and internal analyses and may require a change in current strategy. The alternatives for this change can be generated in a systematic fashion using various models and concepts. The performance gap may require only fine-tuning of the current strategy, which is done by examining functional area strategies and implementation efforts.

The difficulty of making resource allocations among dissimilar businesses in a corporate setting provided the impetus for the development of portfolio planning techniques. The General Electric Planning Grid compares business units on dimensions of industry attractiveness and competitive position. The Boston Consulting Group Growth-Share Matrix compares units on market growth rate and market share in relation to the largest competitor. Investment recommendations are based on the placement of individual units on the grids created by these two dimensions. These techniques should be used only when assumptions underlying the techniques are met.

Another way to consider corporate strategy is to analyze the ability of the corporation to build competitive advantage. This may be done through restructuring, transferring skills, and/or sharing activities. The life cycle concepts suggest shifts in strategic emphasis which are based on cycles of development. The product life cycle describes the hypothetical passage of a product or service through a series of stages characterized by different demand growth rates. This concept suggests appropriate areas of functional emphasis, generic strategy alternatives, timing for strategy shifts, and ways to balance a corporate portfolio.

Experience curves, which are based on learning-curve concepts, describe decreases in unit costs which accompany the accumulation of experience. They suggest pricing strategies to gain market share and ultimate market dominance. Technology curves provide a tool for analyzing R&D performance and suggest a shift to new technology as the old technology reaches the limits of its performance.

When a performance gap is projected for a strategic business unit or a single-product organization, it may be possible to close the gap by improving profit margins or improving market share. Break-even analysis is an aid in judging the feasibility of these alternatives. Alternatives for changing strategy must be generated within competitive constraints. The industry evolution concept provides a means to do this.

In applying tools and techniques for generating strategic alternatives, it is crucial to see that assumptions hold, that information is accurate, that implementation is considered, and that mechanical application of models is avoided.

Because the possibility always exists that key forecasts or assumptions will not be accurate, it is wise to develop contingency strategies. Implementing a contingency process involves three steps: (1) identifying the key variables, (2) establishing the trigger points that will determine when something needs to be done, and (3) planning the appropriate response.

CHAPTER 8 REVIEW QUESTIONS

1 Under what circumstances might a company currently enjoying satisfactory performance project a performance gap?

2 How does a performance gap differ from current poor performance?

3 What are the alternative approaches for dealing with a performance gap?

4 What assumptions must be met in order to properly use the GE Planning Grid? The BCG Growth-Share Matrix?

5 What are the ways that competitive advantage can be gained at the corporate level?

6 How does the product life cycle help generate strategic alternatives for an organization?

7 Compare and contrast technology curves and the product life cycle.

8 How does the idea of industry evolution differ from the product life cycle curve?

9 List the generic industry types and the characteristics of each which are most relevant for generating strategic alternatives.

10 What is a contingency strategy? How would you implement one effectively?

CHAPTER 8 DISCUSSION QUESTIONS

1 Given the following information about higher education, determine the generic industry type which applies, and generate strategic alternatives for the institution you are attending.
* Total number of 18-year-olds: 4.2 million in 1975, 3.6 million in 1985, and 3.2 million (projected) in 1992.
* The percentage of high school graduates going to college is increasing.
* Undergraduate student characteristics:

	1960 (%)	2000 (projected %)
Women	37	52
Minorities	4	25
Part time	30	45
Two-year	26	41
Commuters	60	85
Over 22	30	50

* Expected changes in enrollment by region: −10 percent, East; −10 percent, Midwest; +5 percent, South; and +10 percent or more, Southwest or West.
* Role of private postsecondary institutions in 1982: 22 percent of 12 million students were enrolled in private institutions and 54 percent of 3270 were private.
* Colleges and universities employ 2 million people, including one-fourth of the nation's scientists and engineers.

2 Using a copy of your college or university's catalogue, decide whether portfolio concepts might apply. Be sure to review the assumptions that must be met. Are there the equivalent of SBUs?

CHAPTER 8 REFERENCES

1 J. K. Ryans and W. L. Shanklin, *Strategic Planning,* Random House, New York, 1985, p. 202.

2 See G. S. Day, "Diagnosing the Product Portfolio," *Journal of Marketing,* April 1977, pp. 29–38.

3 A. C. Max and M. S. Majiluf, "The Use of the Growth-Share Matrix in Strategic Planning," *Interfaces,* February 1, 1983, p. 50.

4 P. Patel and M. Younger, "A Frame of Reference for Strategy Development," *Long Range Planning,* vol. 11, no. 4, 1978, pp. 6–12.

5 K. Giddens-Emig, "Portfolio Planning: A Concept in Controversy," *Managerial Planning,* November–December 1983, p. 11; M. B. Choate, "Pitfalls in Portfolio Planning," *Long Range Planning,* vol. 16, no. 3, 1983, p. 51; and R. A. Bettis and W. K. Hall, "The Business Portfolio Approach—Where It Falls Down in Practice," *Long Range Planning,* April 1983, pp. 95–104.

6 M. Porter, "From Competitive Advantage to Corporate Strategy," *Harvard Business Review,* May–June 1987, p. 51.

7 Ibid., pp. 52–59.

8 Ibid., pp. 58–59.

9 C. Hofer and D. Schendel, *Strategy Formulation: Analytical Concepts,* West Publishing, St. Paul, Minn., 1978, p. 107.

10 W. Kiechel III, "The Decline of the Experience Curve," *Fortune,* October 5, 1981, pp. 139ff.

11 This section summarizes chapters 9 through 13 in M. Porter, *Competitive Strategies,* Free Press, New York, 1980.

12 Ibid., pp. 254–274.

13 List drawn from Choate, op. cit., pp. 47–56; Giddens-Emig, op. cit., pp. 4–14; and G. S. Omura and M. B. Cooper, "Three Strategic Planning Techniques for Retailers," *Business,* January–March 1983, pp. 2–8.

14 See W. Kiechel III, "Three (or Four, or More) Ways to Win," *Fortune,* October 19, 1981, pp. 181–188, for a discussion of some of these.

15 J. L. Cooley, Jr., *Corporate and Divisional Planning,* Reston Publishing, Reston, Va., 1984, p. 436.

IMPLEMENTING STRATEGY: COMMUNICATION AND TACTICAL ISSUES

LEARNING OBJECTIVES

After studying this chapter, the reader should be able to:

1 Discuss the differences between the implementation and formulation phases of the strategic management process
2 Discuss the pros and cons of using direct communication of strategy as a tool of implementation
3 Assess the implications of changing business level strategy for the functional areas
4 Evaluate merger and acquisition tactics

CHAPTER OUTLINE

LINKING ACTIONS TO IDEAS
COMMUNICATING STRATEGY
  Issues in Strategy Communication
    • Proprietary Nature of Strategy • Political Impact of Strategy
    • Expectations Aroused by Strategy • Motivational Impact of Strategy
    • Decisional Impact of Strategy
FUNCTIONAL AREA STRATEGIES
  Marketing Issues
  Operations Issues
  Financial Issues

174

In this chapter and the next, we consider some important aspects of strategy implementation. On the business level, these include specifying the requirements of the business strategy for each of the functional areas and resolving any functional area conflicts in the interest of the organization as a whole. On the corporate level, a number of issues arise around the merger tactic to implement growth and/or diversification strategies. Corporate strategy implementation also requires proper alignment of the organization's structuring mechanisms, its control systems, its reward systems, and management's approach to leadership. Exhibit 9.1 shows factors which affect strategy implementation.

EXHIBIT 9.1   COMPONENTS OF STRATEGY IMPLEMENTATION

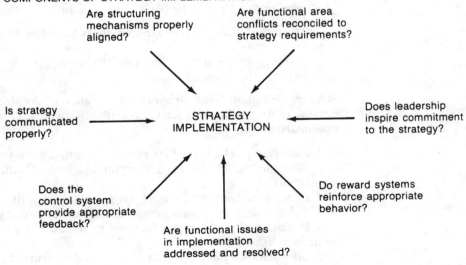

Are structuring mechanisms properly aligned?

Are functional area conflicts reconciled to strategy requirements?

Is strategy communicated properly?

STRATEGY IMPLEMENTATION

Does leadership inspire commitment to the strategy?

Does the control system provide appropriate feedback?

Are functional issues in implementation addressed and resolved?

Do reward systems reinforce appropriate behavior?

LINKING ACTIONS TO IDEAS

The strategist has a number of tools which can be used to put strategy into action. These tools should be utilized in a manner that is both comprehensive and consistent. *Comprehensive* implementation refers to the range of techniques employed. An organization which seeks an increased reliance on new products and customers to broaden its revenue base has a wide selection of techniques available to make the shift. A typical approach might include increased resource allocations to both research and development (R&D) and marketing, a shift in the reward system to encourage the extra attention needed by new activities, and a change in the way activities are grouped as well as in reporting relationships. Furthermore, it is necessary to track the progress of new endeavors, compare progress with original plan, and provide the resulting information to those parts of the organization which can take appropriate action. The use of functional area strategies, the organization structure, the reward systems, the control systems, and the information systems to implement changes in strategy constitutes a more comprehensive approach than, say, the shift in functional area strategy alone. *Consistent* implementation minimizes conflicting signals when several techniques are being used. A conflict could occur, for example, when a shift in structure to allow for managerial attention to new products is implemented under a reward system which focuses sales force attention on repeat sales to current customers.

Lack of comprehensiveness and consistency are manifest in different ways. Failure to implement comprehensively is wasteful because all techniques are not used. The danger of contradictory signals is that individuals are left to resolve contradictions on their own and the unifying power of a common direction for effort is dissipated in numerous uncoordinated decisions.

Whether an organization seeks improved implementation of its current strategy or must adjust current implementation techniques to the requirements of a new strategy, the same basic concerns must be addressed:

1 The requirements of the strategy must be defined for groups and individuals.

2 These groups and individuals must receive organizational support necessary to fulfill the requirements.

Strategy definition results from communication of the strategy and explicit discussion of its implications for various units. This is accomplished through several instruments:

1 Leadership which clarifies strategy through word and example

2 Structure which divides and groups tasks and defines authority and responsibilities

3 Control systems which track progress and identify problems

4 Reward systems which motivate individuals to carry out strategy

5 Policies and procedures which define the limits within which results must be accomplished

6 Information systems which provide the information needed for decision making

Implementing strategy is the work of the entire organization. Top managers must work through others rather than taking actions directly. This requires skills in administration, an understanding of what motivates human behavior, and a grasp of how the parts of the organization interact. These skills are not so much learned as developed.

COMMUNICATING STRATEGY

Before a strategy can be implemented it must be clearly understood. A clear understanding of strategy gives purpose to the activities of each organization member. It allows the individual to link whatever task is at hand to the overall organizational direction. This is mutually enhancing and gives meaning to the task. It also provides the individual with general guidance for making decisions and enables him or her to direct efforts toward activities that count. For example, the manager of a strategic business unit (SBU) slated for divestment would not waste effort preparing a proposal to fund additional capacity. On the other hand, knowledge of the pending divestment might be so demoralizing that the organization would lose the manager's best efforts while the manager seeks employment elsewhere. Thus, there may be disadvantages as well as advantages to communicating strategy. Several issues which should be considered in deciding how or whether to announce strategic decisions are discussed in the following paragraphs.

Issues in Strategy Communication

The desirability of the direct announcement of a strategy depends on several factors:[1]

- Proprietary nature of the strategy
- Political impact of the strategy
- Expectations aroused by the strategy
- Motivational impact of the strategy
- Decisional impact of the strategy

Proprietary Nature of Strategy   The wider the dissemination of information concerning strategic decisions, competitive moves, or shifting emphasis, the greater the likelihood that it will reach a competitor who could subvert the move, decision, or shift. A strategy which will provide or exploit an unpublicized advantage may be best kept undisclosed. The advantages of organizational commitment would be offset by the loss of surprise. If the strategy will divulge proprietary information, it should be shared only on a need-to-know basis.

Political Impact of Strategy   It is not always possible to achieve consensus concerning the appropriate strategic directions for an organization. If a number of top managers participate in the formulation process, it is not unlikely that there will be differences of opinion about the final choice. The differences of opinion may have been settled in a way that created animosity in the "losers." In an organization where relationships are strained, factions may form around strong individuals, and the strategy may be judged and supported according to who is backing it rather than upon its own merits. In such a situation it may be more efficient to communicate the strategy piecemeal rather than as a whole. Strategy communication that sparks infighting will hinder implementation more than it will help.

Expectations Aroused by Strategy   The announcement of a strategy gives all organizational stakeholders a means of evaluating operations and performance. It also raises and defines expectations about the future of the organization which may prove embarrassing to management if unforeseen circumstances arise and diminish performance. For this reason, many public announcements of strategy are retrospective, indicating what has been attempted and how well the objectives have been met.

An organization which announces strategy is subject to criticism from security analysts, to fluctuations in stock prices, to government scrutiny, and to buyer and supplier moves, as well as to union responses. Communication of strategy should be preceded by consideration of the expectations and resulting responses by stakeholders that may be generated.

Motivational Impact of Strategy   A clear statement of strategy may either inspire or demoralize. The effect of a given communication must be considered in light of the personal implications for the individuals required to implement it. Growth strategies have enjoyed popularity because, among other things, the rewards—both financial and career—are perceived as greater for all concerned. Retrenchment strategies are full of financial and personal unpleasantness even though they may be necessary to maintain long-term viability.

At the corporate level, considerable differences may exist among the strategies of various business units. These differences may make some units much more attractive than others. The use of the term "dog" with the attendant divestiture strategy is likely to have negative effects on SBU morale.

If communicating strategy is more likely to reduce morale or drive away good managers than to inspire action, a comprehensive strategy announcement is usually undesirable.

Decisional Impact of Strategy   Strategy is often an evolving understanding of where the organization is going and how it plans to get there. An announced strategy brings closure to the formulation question and focuses on implementation. This closure is not always desirable, because lower levels of management can make significant contributions to the strategy as they work through the implementation process. Therefore, before top management announces a strategy, they should be certain that closure of the formulation phase is desired.

Whether or not organizationwide communication is chosen as the first step in implementation, it is necessary to relate each level of strategy to the level below it. Corporate strategies are implemented through business strategies, and business strategies are implemented through functional-level strategies and tactics. Strategies on all levels are constrained by organizational policies and resource allocations, and they are supported by leadership, structure, and organizational systems.

FUNCTIONAL AREA STRATEGIES

A myriad of details about how the organization will act to implement its overall strategy must be resolved on the functional level. Resolving these details also clarifies and defines the strategy for most parts of the organization. Functional area strategy implementation communicates strategy, but only that part which is relevant to the specific functional areas. A number of strategic and tactical issues are likely to arise in the functional areas during this process. Some of the most common are discussed below.

Marketing Issues

The familiar "four P's" of marketing (product, price, place, and promotion) provide a good starting point for consideration of the requirements of strategy implementation in the marketing function. In general, the mix of these marketing elements should be appropriate, and the plans for each of the elements must also be appropriate.

The marketing function is consumer-oriented. Marketing decisions are based on the careful identification of consumer needs and on the design of marketing strategies to meet those needs. Some observers have suggested that a shift is occurring in the underlying nature of markets so that a "mass market" no longer exists.[2] This theory holds that markets have been fragmented into a number of segments and that ability to target products and services has become critical to the success of all organizations.

Products or services are characterized by number, diversity, and rate of change. A limited product line with few new products being introduced is not likely to implement a growth strategy, unless the product is in the early stages of the product life cycle. A wide line is often pruned in a retrenchment strategy so that only the most profitable items remain, even though market share may be lost. In a product development strategy, the rate of new product development may be the single most important strategic issue.

A number of *pricing* options are available. A lower price will be desirable to increase volume. However, in the early stages of the product life cycle, a "skim the cream" approach may be justified to establish image. Pricing is a complex issue because it is related to cost-volume-profit trade-offs and because it is frequently used as a competitive weapon. Pricing policy changes are likely to provoke competitor response. Using price to jockey for position can lead to price wars, which usually hurt all participants.

The benefits of well-conceived pricing include increasing sales to current customers, attracting new customers, maximizing short-run cash flow, and maintaining an established position. The particular benefit or benefits sought should be defined by the business strategy, and the various pricing options should be considered so that the most appropriate approach is selected. Pricing must be considered in relation to costs, to consistency, and to potential inflation.

The *distribution* system brings the product or service to the place where it can best fill customers' needs. Access to distribution can mean all the difference between success and failure for a new product. Because many products require support from distribution channels in the form of prompt service, rapid order processing, or parts inventory, the choice of distributors, wholesalers, and jobbers is extremely important. The increasing costs of transportation as a percentage of total costs must also be factored into the choices made concerning distribution.

The choice of markets, market segmentation, and targeting decisions are closely related to distribution. A focus or differentiation strategy requires careful segmentation and targeting with matching distribution. A cost leadership strategy requires weighing benefits and costs of wide versus intensive distribution approaches.

Promotion is more than advertising. *Promotion* refers to the methods which are used to put products and services in the public eye. Products and services may be promoted through personal selling, print and electronic media, displays, use of logos on related or unrelated products, and sponsorships. The location, size, and nature of markets which the business strategy defines will guide promotion-mix decisions and should indicate the content of promotional material as well.

A new strategy should raise a number of questions for managers of the marketing function. The following list is suggestive rather than exhaustive:

• What changes in product or service offerings are required by the new strategy?
• Is the pace and success rate of new product development adequate for the strategy?
• Are distribution arrangements in place and efficient? Are new channels needed?
• Is the sales force ready to implement the strategy? Is adequate support available?
• Are advertising and other promotional methods in line with the new strategy?
• Are product adaptations required for international markets?

Operations Issues

The operations (or production) function has responsibility for the procurement and transformation of raw materials into products or services. This involves securing raw materials, making decisions to make or buy parts and components, maintaining adequate inventory, designing and scheduling production, ensuring quality control, and making capacity adjustments. Decisions in the operations area determine a large proportion of the organization's costs and are reflected in measures of efficiency and productivity. Decisions in this area also affect the performance and reliability of the product. Operations issues related to a changing strategy include the following questions:

• Is capacity adequate for projected sales under the new strategy? What is the most timely and cost-effective method for matching capacity with demand? How does the strategy affect current methods of matching seasons and cyclical shifts in demand with operations flexibility?

• What degree of vertical integration makes sense under the new strategy?

• Are production methods and processes adequate to meet the cost and quality requirements of the strategy?

• Are inventory levels adequate? Is inventory control properly maintained?

• Are sources of raw materials and employees adequate for the change? Will new training be needed?

The operations function often receives the brunt of international competition. Nondomestic producers have cost advantages because of lower wage rates. Many large and small companies are turning to outsourcing, off-shore manufacturing, and importing. *Outsourcing* shifts component manufacturing to overseas suppliers while maintaining domestic assembly. *Off-shore manufacturing* shifts the entire production function overseas. *Importing* is the purchase and subsequent resale of products produced by foreign companies.

Financial Issues

The finance function provides the financial resources necessary to implement strategy. Changes in strategy often involve adjustments to financial policies. Product and market development strategies, for example, may require an increase in working capital as well as in fixed capital. A change in strategy will raise the following financial questions:

• Are sources of long-term and short-term financing available to support the new strategy?

• How will the change in strategy affect the company's standing with suppliers of capital?

• How will the change in strategy affect the cost of capital?

• Does the new strategy change uses of funds in such a way that new sources of capital are needed?

• Is dividend policy appropriate for the new strategy?

Additional questions for organizations with international operations include:

• Are sources of local funding available and properly developed for nondomestic operations?

• How will the strategy be affected by currency depreciation and/or inflation?

• How can overall tax be minimized?

• How should the transfer of profits from foreign subsidiaries to headquarters be handled for optimum capital structure?

The timing and amount of cash inflows and outflows are shown by a projection called a cash budget. Cash budgeting assists in strategy implementation by showing what cash needs are involved in implementing a new or adjusted strategy. Cash budgets are done on a monthly or even weekly basis if flows are volatile or seasonal. Cash budgets for more stable situations may cover longer time periods.

The steps in cash budgeting are as follow:

1 Prepare or obtain the sales forecast for the period of the budget.

2 Determine the cash receipts from these sales and when they will be received.

3 Determine whether any asset sales are planned for the period and include cash to be realized.

4 Determine disbursements based on production plans, capital expenditures, dividend payments, federal income taxes, etc.

5 Compare receipts with disbursements for each period to determine whether there will be a surplus or a deficit.

6 If there will be a deficit, make arrangements to finance it or adjust tactics in operations and/or marketing.

Pro forma statements forecast assets and liabilities as well as income statement items for a selected future date. The pro forma balance sheet can be prepared in several ways. One method is to use a cash budget for the period covered. The cash budget provides figures or allows extrapolation of the balance sheet accounts. In another approach, historical ratios of assets and liabilities to sales and production are projected into the future. The pro forma income statement begins with a sales forecast and projects revenues and expenses on the basis of plans and historical relationships.

Pro forma statements, if properly prepared, allow analysis of the changes in financial condition and performance for the period covered. Access to personal computers and spreadsheet programs greatly simplifies the calculations required but does not relieve the analyst from the responsibility of understanding the financial relationships which underlie the figures. Pro forma statements are not substitutes for cash budgeting, because it is entirely possible for a company to show a healthy profit on its income statement and still experience cash-flow problems. This can happen when cash inflow is delayed because of collection problems or when the organization has large, upfront expenses such as those associated with rapid expansion.

Because the availability of financial resources is one of the key constraints which limits strategic choice, proper implementation of all strategies requires consideration of financial issues. In certain strategies, considerable functional expertise in finance is necessary. For example, retrenchment requires careful long- and short-term asset management. Diversification through acquisition requires the ability to evaluate another company using, for the most part, publicly available financial data. In organizations that compete globally, international funds management is a key factor in maintaining profits against currency shifts.[3]

Research and Development Issues

The need to develop or improve products and production processes is met by the research and development (R&D) function. The more important innovation is to the strategy of the organization, the more implementation will require consideration of strategic issues in R&D.

The focus of R&D may be basic research which advances knowledge with no particular commercial application in mind, or it may be applied research which seeks marketable products from basic knowledge. Only organizations with considerable financial resources undertake basic research to implement strategy. Not only is the payback period considerably longer, but the success rate is very low and considerable investment is usually required to capitalize on the output of the research.[4]

The division of R&D effort between product and process research is relevant to strategy. Growth strategies, such as product development, clearly require R&D emphasis on providing new products. With a cost leadership strategy, the production processes should be under constant scrutiny by R&D to make efficiency improvements.

The desired status in relation to competitors is another component of R&D. Some organizations maintain an offensive R&D stance so that leadership in new product introductions or process improvements is maintained. Others choose to let industry leaders bear the cost and risks of R&D leadership.

R&D also involves a "make or buy" decision. While internal R&D can yield tremendous returns, the costs and risks can strain the resources of many organizations. In these cases companies often turn to licensing, contract research, or joint ventures. The strategic questions related to R&D include:

• Does the strategy require a change in the focus of R&D, the division of R&D effort, or the desired status in relation to competitors?

• Can the strategy succeed with the current method of doing research (internally or externally)?

• Can the strategy succeed with the current level of R&D funding? Does internal allocation of funds need to be adjusted?

Personnel Issues

An important issue which involves all the functional areas is the availability of human resources to implement the strategy. Personnel questions include:

• Does the strategy require significant new skills? If so, how can they be obtained in a timely and cost-effective manner?

• Are salary and benefits administered in a way that will promote implementation of the strategy?

In many organizations, a separate but related function is that of industrial relations. Few strategies can successfully be implemented in the face of union opposition. Retrenchment, for instance, requires a high degree of union management cooperation. Strategic questions relating to labor relations include:

• Is the new strategy likely to provoke union resistance? Will the resistance extend to strikes, slowdowns, or other work disruptions?

• Can the changing strategy be presented in a way that will enhance cooperation?

Cross-Functional Implications of Strategy Implementation

The following story emphasizes the importance of integrating the different functional strategies. The owner and manager of a small business decided to diversify his business by distributing a new product line. The payment schedule for the product was such that the burden of financing accounts receivable would be high during the first 6 months of sales. The owner was so enthused about the product and so caught up in making preparations to market it that the finance problem did not emerge until customers took delivery of the products. The customers did not have to pay the business, but the owner had to pay his suppliers immediately. The business did survive the short-term financial crisis, but the owner was horrified at what a close call it had been. The owner of this business performed both the finance and marketing functions and yet failed to consider the effects of the strategic decision on both functions. It is easy to imagine the problem of functional integration in organizations which are large and complex.

Failure to integrate functional area strategies is failure to consider the cross-functional implications of strategy when the critical issues of strategy are appraised. Functional area specialists have goals and objectives which, if carried to maximization, are likely to conflict. Exhibit 9.2 illustrates some areas of potential conflict. A classic example is the desire of operations to maintain efficiency by having as few different production runs as possible. Marketing, on the other hand, wants to provide the customer with as many options as possible. Operations personnel fight for narrow product lines with few variations, while marketing personnel are likely to argue for wider product lines with numerous options for color, accessories, and so on. In each case the functional specialist may be doing his or her best for the organizations in relation to the function he or she represents. However, this can lead to unnecessary conflict and poor strategy implementation unless it is explicitly managed.

Cross-functional implications of strategy can be identified by considering the following:

• *Formulation.* Careful consideration of the strengths and weaknesses of the organization includes a review of the functional areas which should alert managers to potential conflicts.

• *Trade-offs.* A strategy which is comprehensive should spell out certain major trade-offs.

• *Communication.* Communication of the strategy is a way of giving functional areas the same information.

• *Participation.* Functional managers who have some part in the process of formulating and implementing strategy are in a better position to understand what is required of them.

EXHIBIT 9.2 SOURCES OF FUNCTIONAL AREA CONFLICT IN A MANUFACTURING FIRM

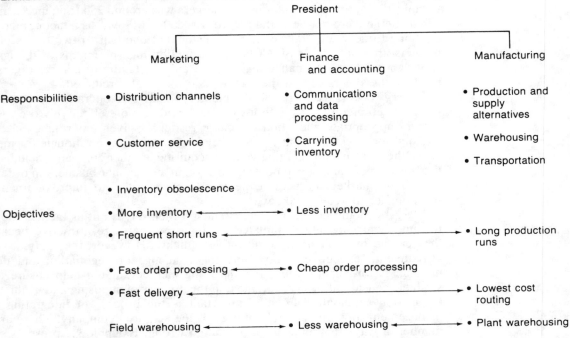

Source: John F. Stolle, "How to Manage Physical Distribution, *Harvard Business Review*, July/August 1967, p. 95. Used by permission.

- *Close lateral relations.* As functional specialists have closer contact with each other, trade-offs can be better assessed.
- *Multifunctional experience.* Many organizations require that managers spend part of their tenure in functions other than their own specialty. "Walking in the other's shoes" gives tremendous insight into the practices and problems of others.
- *Coordination.* As part of the implementation process of identifying strategic issues for each of the functional areas, the cross-functional implications of a change in strategy should be addressed.

IMPLEMENTING CORPORATE STRATEGIES: MERGERS AND ACQUISITIONS

Although the conflicting priorities of functional areas are not trivial, they seem almost dwarfed by the problems of meshing the operations of entire organizations. Corporations seeking to implement growth strategies have a number of tactical options from which to choose. Mergers or acquisitions, joint ventures, and internal product or business development are ways of implementing growth strategies. Mergers and acquisitions are frequently chosen. Through the mid-1980s, the annual number of mergers was around 2500 and increasing.[5] While mergers are not new (the record was 6000 in 1969),[6] as a tactic, mergers continue to generate controversy. An estimated one-half to two-thirds of all mergers are not successful. Critics also mention high premiums paid, significant debt incurred to finance high prices, and the failure of many mergers to produce the synergies that the architects of the deals predicted.

Synergy occurs as the result of a merger, when "two operating units can be run more efficiently (i.e., with lower costs) and/or more effectively (i.e., with a more appropriate allocation of scarce resources given environmental constraints) together than apart."[7] Synergy is often cited as a rationale for mergers. Other reasons for merging with or acquiring another company include improving or maintaining competitive position in a particular business in order to enter new markets or acquire new products rapidly, to improve financial position,[8] or to avoid a takeover.

Mergers should not be viewed as ends in themselves but as tactical moves to implement carefully formulated strategy. Mergers are attractive because they can accomplish strategic objectives quickly. However, they may also be attractive to executives who enjoy the challenge of negotiation and deal-making. A formal procedure for analyzing mergers should help ensure that strategic considerations are foremost in the process of choosing and evaluating acquisition candidates. Equally important is the process of integrating the management, operations, and cultures of the acquired company. There are a number of ways that an acquisition can go wrong. Example 9.1 presents several situations when acquisitions have not worked out. When acquisition is chosen as a tactic to implement a growth strategy, the chances of failure can be minimized by giving attention to the major phases of the acquisition process: identification and evaluation of prospective acquisitions, negotiation of the acquisition, and integration of the acquisition into operations.

Identifying and Evaluating Prospective Acquisitions

Acquisition can be a good way of entering new markets or new businesses or of improving competitive positions in existing businesses. Performance gaps in both growth and earnings can be closed by acquisitions. On the other hand, profitability gaps can be reduced by divesting less profitable enterprises. Acquisition alternatives may be identified through a research approach, an opportunistic approach, or a combination of the two.[9]

Research Approach This approach involves the analysis of broad sectors of the economy, with a successive narrowing of industries and of choices within industries.[10] The first cut should eliminate industries which fail to meet upward limits on sales. For example, if $100 million in sales is the upper limit for consideration, mainframe computing or basic mining should not be considered, because they would exceed these limits. Managerial preferences should be reviewed at this point in the process also. When a broad group of acceptable sectors has been identified, each should be reviewed for the strength and

---

EXAMPLE 9.1

Ways an Acquisition Can Fail

Coca-Cola built the Wine Spectrum through a series of acquisitions including Taylor Wine, Sterling Vineyards, and Monterrey Vineyards. The intention was to transfer soft drink marketing skills to wine, but Coke misread the competition and failed to understand the cyclicality of the business. The Wine Spectrum was sold in 1983 to Seagram's, who sold it again in 1987.

Fluor served as a white knight for St. Joe Minerals. Almost immediately, the market for minerals softened. Fluor paid a high premium for a company with incompatible culture.

Mobil acquired unfamiliar businesses (retailing and containers) with Marcor. They also acquired problems that were not apparent in the preacquisition analysis.

Schlumberger paid a premium for Fairchild Camera and Equipment. The two cultures did not mesh and many of Fairchild's key personnel left. Product development was set behind and performance plummeted.

The proposed acquisition of Schlitz by Heilman Brewing was stopped by regulatory requirements.

Shareholders failed to approve the acquisition of Colt Industries by Penn Central.

Source: Compiled from D. R. Willensky, "Making It Happen: How to Execute an Acquisition," *Business Horizons,* March–April 1985, pp. 38–45; and "Do Mergers Really Work?" *Business Week,* June 3, 1985, pp. 88–100.

---

position of existing competition. Industries in which the leading firms are strong and aggressive or in which the leading competitor has taken and can defend a strong position are not attractive—except in the unlikely event that these major competitors can be acquired. More attractive is a situation in which the leader is losing its market share to an upcoming competitor and that competitor is available for acquisition. A second consideration is favorable trends in the industry's market. While mature industries may contain reasonable candidates, the better opportunities are more likely to be in industries in earlier life cycle stages.

With a few sectors chosen, the next step is to identify promising candidates. The industry position of candidates must be evaluated to determine whether strong competitive positions can be established. This analysis requires some understanding of the key success factors of the industry and of the way the candidate competes. However, it is the combined ability of the acquirer and the candidate that must be considered.

The final consideration is future financial performance. The levels of performance, as well as their predicted variability, are important. If the industry analysis has been carefully done, there should be a good appreciation of the events that can produce variability in performance.

This approach is not likely to produce conglomerate mergers or acquisitions. The emphasis on competitive dynamics and position of the combined entity rather than on current financial performance is most appropriate for implementing concentric diversification or horizontal or vertical integration. Example 9.2 outlines two diversification thrusts at Procter & Gamble which were accomplished by acquisitions.

Opportunistic Approach Prescriptive approaches to mergers emphasize the acquisition decision as a result of the strategic management process and propose a rigorous analysis process in which candidates are chosen from a broad pool of industries and organizations. This does not mean that candidates which appear from other sources should not be considered. Merger and acquisition opportunities arise from a variety of personal contacts as well as from the financial entrepreneurs who serve as brokers, bringing together potential

---

EXAMPLE 9.2

Concentric Diversification at Procter & Gamble

Both Charmin Paper Mills and Eaton-Norwich pharmaceutical division of Morton Norwich illustrate the way P&G uses acquisitions to extend strategic thrusts and thereby create value. P&G's largest distribution outlet, the supermarket, provides considerable shelf space for tissue products. P&G had some knowledge of tissue technology through its Buckeye Cellulose Laboratory. What it needed was manufacturing capability and a product line to match its product technology and distribution clout. The acquisition of Charmin Paper Mills filled these requirements nicely. The tissue products proved profitable and even with maturity and price pressure continue to generate cash. In addition, the base and manufacturing technologies led to the Pampers line of disposable diapers, which may be the most successful consumer disposable ever introduced.

The Eaton-Norwich acquisition seems to fill a missing distribution channel. Because of its work with soaps and detergents, P&G has considerable expertise in the behavior of calcium in water. This is called surfactant technology and has led to the introduction of bone disease drugs. P&G's supermarket clout was no help with the pharmaceutical market, however. With Eaton-Norwich, the company acquired a field sales force and the broader distribution it required as well as a successful firm with established products.

Source: Adapted from H. W. Ebeling, Jr., and T. L. Doorley III, "A Strategic Approach to Acquisitions," *Journal of Business Strategy,* Winter 1983, p. 54.

partners. Rather than having several candidates to compare against each other on predetermined criteria, an organization is likely to be faced with a succession of candidates requiring individual evaluation without comparison against other candidates. Some basic questions may be used to screen such opportunities:[11]

1 How would the acquired company be run? The acquiring organization must be prepared to provide managerial time and talent to a merger or an acquisition that is not performing well or where current management is likely to leave as a result of the purchase. If the managerial expertise is not available in-house or cannot be easily gained, an important aspect of the merger negotiations must be the future of the acquisition's key managers. Steps must be taken to ensure that these managers remain with the organization.

2 What synergies exist between the firm and the acquisition candidate? Economies which are expected to result from the merger should be precisely identified and the probability of achieving them carefully estimated. The possibility of negative synergies should also be raised. Will the difficulties of combining the operations of two separate organizations outweigh the benefits?

3 What types of weaknesses can be tolerated in the acquired companies? An acquiring organization with well-developed marketing skills may be able to tolerate poor marketing planning in an acquisition because the skills to remedy it are readily available. Poor labor relations, on the other hand, might be so difficult for the acquiring company to deal with that the combination should not occur.

4 Is timing crucial to the success of the merger? A prospective turnaround must be acquired before it is too late to save the company. A growth company should be acquired before the price becomes too high but after it is clear that the company will survive. Other prospective buyers for an acquisition may also create time pressures.

Negotiating the Acquisition

When an acquisition candidate is chosen, the delicate process of making the initial contact, negotiating, and reaching a final agreement must be planned. While the acquiring company may have reached the conclusion that the merger is an appropriate move for them, it will still be necessary to convince the candidate. The acquirer should be prepared with a rationale for the merger which shows how the combination will benefit both parties. The way in which initial contact with the target company is made can be very important. It is important to reach the real decision makers in the target organization and to reach them in a way that does not offend. Example 9.3 demonstrates some poor ways to make initial contact.

The negotiation phase should first seek broad agreement between the parties about how the two companies will mesh and how the transaction will be handled. Later stages of negotiation should focus on working out the details of price and transition. Putting agreements in writing is beneficial to ensure identification and discussion of major issues.[12]

EXAMPLE 9.3

Results of Poor Initial Contacts for Merger Negotiations

Seagram Company was interested in St. Joe Minerals and proceeded to file the required documents with government agencies. This filing was the way that St. Joe found out that a bid was being made for the company. The St. Joe Chairman, Jack Duncan, was quoted as saying "If Seagram had talked to us first, we might have reached agreement." Instead, another company was successful in acquiring St. Joe.

A large consumer-oriented company was interested in a large soft drink bottler. The chairman of the consumer company called his counterpart at the bottling company and began to explain the takeover plan over the phone. The bottling company executive was angry at the bluntness of the approach and began to take steps to find a white knight. The consumer company lost the battle which ensued for the bottler.

Source: D. R. Willensky, "Making It Happen: How to Execute an Acquisition," *Business Horizons,* March–April 1985, pp. 38–45.

A key decision is the price of the acquisition. Price is a function of what the buyer feels the combined operations will be worth, and the supply and demand for this type of company in the merger market. Usually some type of discounted cash flow analysis is used to determine valuation of the merger candidate. This type of analysis requires a number of assumptions and is very sensitive to the assumptions. Assumptions about time period, cash flow, residual value, and discount rate should be very carefully reached. Overly optimistic estimates of cash flow, for example, can radically change the valuation.[13]

Management of the acquisition target does not always support the acquisition. Reasons to fight acquisition range from managers' fear of losing their jobs to disagreement with the plans of the acquiring company. An industry has arisen around the drive to acquire and the need to defend against acquisition. More than $1 billion of merger-related fees were paid to investment bankers and law firms in 1984. By 1987, the securities industries derived 30 to 35 percent of its profits from mergers and acquisitions. One attorney who specializes in takeover advice is retained by 200 corporations to ensure that he will not work against them. The value of these retainers is estimated at $10 million annually. Exhibit 9.3 lists some typical defenses against unfriendly takeovers.

Integration of the Acquisition

A transition plan should be part of the negotiation process, especially if the acquiring company wishes to retain top management of the acquired company. The transition plan should address the following issues:[14]

EXHIBIT 9.3   DEFENSES AGAINST UNFRIENDLY TAKEOVERS

1. *Self-protection*. Maintain a relationship with legal and/or financial advisers who have special knowledge of mergers.
2. *Pac-Man*. Buy your attacker's stock. The most famous Pac-Man maneuver is the response of Martin-Marietta to Bendix's takeover bid.
3. *Self-tender*. Offer to buy your own stock.
4. *Dilution*. Dilute the voting power of current stock by issuing more stock to shareholders of record.
5. *Shark repellents**
   - Revise the corporate bylaws to stagger the terms of directors so that it takes several years to get a majority of board members.
   - Adopt a bylaw requiring a supermajority to approve a tender offer.
   - Reincorporate in a state which has rules that favor existing management.
6. *White knight*. Find a more compatible buyer that will make a better offer.
7. *Poison pill*. Take on large amounts of debt.
8. *Greenmail*. Buy stock from raiders at a premium over market.

*These are of questionable legality.

1 How will systems (accounting, personnel, budgeting, planning, etc.) be merged?

2 What degree of autonomy will the acquired unit have?

3 What reporting relationships and requirements will be created by the merger? How will previously independent executives relate to their new superiors?

4 How will compensation, benefits, and company perks be handled?

A successful merger is the exception rather than the rule. Exhibit 9.4 lists some pitfalls to avoid in evaluating, negotiating, and integrating an acquisition into an existing operation.

To successfully implement a merger, it is important to consider the expectations and the preferences of the acquired firm concerning how the merger is to be implemented as well as the objectives of the acquiring organization. Factors which should be considered are the degree to which members of the acquired firm wish to preserve their own organizational culture and the perceived attractiveness of the acquiring firm to the acquired firm. An acquired

EXHIBIT 9.4   SEVEN DEADLY SINS IN MERGERS AND ACQUISITIONS

1. Paying too much.
2. Assuming a boom market won't crash.
3. Leaping before looking.
4. Straying too far afield.
5. Swallowing something too big.
6. Marrying disparate corporate cultures.
7. Counting on key managers staying.

Source: "Do Mergers Really Work?" *Business Week*, June 3, 1985, p. 90.

company with a strong preference for their own culture and a strong dislike for the culture of the acquiring firm may create severe problems in implementation.[15]

SUMMARY

The goal of strategy implementation is to take plans for how the organization should compete and to turn these plans into actions that produce results. Strategy implementation is action-oriented, requires the efforts of all organization members, and is based on behavioral precepts. Implementation should be comprehensive, using all feasible techniques, and consistent, using techniques that are mutually supportive. Implementation involves defining the responsibilities of the strategy for groups and individuals and providing the support necessary for meeting these responsibilities.

The strategy may be defined explicitly or in parts for various groups. Explicitly defining strategy provides motivation and meaning for employees, but the benefits should be weighed against possible disadvantages. Strategy may be appropriately communicated in parts when the complete strategy might provide proprietary information to competitors, when it might precipitate political conflict, when it might be demoralizing to some groups, when undesirable expectations might be aroused, or when the announcement might bring premature closure to the formulation process.

Strategy is further defined by determining how it will work or is working in the functional areas. Changes in strategy may require marketing adjustment in products or services offered, pricing practices, mix of promotional methods, and arrangement for distribution. Operational issues include raw-material and component acquisition, process and product design, production scheduling, quality maintenance, inventory maintenance, and capacity utilization. The finance function must provide resources for strategy implementation as well as analysis of financial information for control and appropriate resource allocation techniques. A new strategy may require a shift in R&D focus. Availability of human resources for strategy implementation is the responsibility of the personnel function. The presence or potential presence of an organized union can also affect the ways that strategy changes can be made.

The interests of the functional areas do not automatically coincide. As each function pursues efficiency and effectiveness in its particular sector, cross-functional conflicts may arise. These conflicts can be minimized by careful formulation of strategy, use of a comprehensive strategy, functional participation in strategy formulation, and use of a system that provides managers with experience in more than one function.

Mergers are means to an end rather than an end in themselves. A successful merger requires a strategic rationale, careful evaluation and analysis of potential candidates, negotiation of price and other transaction details, and a transition plan. A majority of mergers fail but that hasn't dampened the enthusiasm of managers for merger as a tactic.

CHAPTER 9   REVIEW QUESTIONS

1 How does the process of strategy formulation differ from that of strategy implementation?
2 Distinguish between comprehensive strategy implementation and consistent strategy implementation. Why is each important?
3 List the pros and cons of announcing a new comprehensive strategy to the entire organization.
4 What roles do the functional areas play in strategy definition?
5 What issues in marketing, operations, finance, and personnel would be raised by the choice of a strategic alternative that is significantly different from the current strategy?
6 How can cross-functional conflicts be identified and resolved?
7 Compare and contrast the research and opportunistic approaches to evaluation of merger candidates.
8 What are the major elements of a transition plan for a merger?

CHAPTER 9   DISCUSSION QUESTIONS

1 The newly hired marketing specialist at a company that operates retail specialty shops supplying camping and outdoor equipment has an idea for a promotional campaign which will increase sales by 50 percent in the normally slow season between January and March. What would the implications of such an increase be for store managers? How should top management judge such an idea?
2 Do library research on a corporate divestiture (GE–Utah International and Avon Products–Tiffany's are two possibilities). Was the acquired company a good choice originally? Why did the divestiture occur? What conclusions can you draw from your analysis about mergers?

CHAPTER 9   REFERENCES

1 Based on discussions in J. B. Quinn, *Strategies for Change*, Irwin, Homewood, Ill., 1980; and B. B. Tregoe and J. W. Zimmerman, *Top Management Strategy*, Simon & Schuster, New York, 1980.
2 Marketing shift is described in "Marketing: The New Priority," *Business Week*, November 21, 1983, pp. 86–106.
3 F. R. Johnson, "Specialist vs. Generalist: Who Runs the Company?" *Management Review*, January 1980, pp. 43–45.
4 B. Schorr, "Many New Products Fizzle, Despite Careful Planning, Publicity," *The Wall Street Journal*, April 5, 1981.
5 "Do Mergers Really Work?" *Business Week*, June 3, 1985, p. 88; and "A New Strain of Merger Mania," *Business Week*, March 21, 1988, pp. 122–126.
6 L. L. Fray, D. H. Gaylin, and J. E. Down, "Successful Acquisition Planning," *Journal of Business Strategy*, vol. 5, no. 1, Summer 1984, p. 47.
7 M. Lubatkin, "Mergers and the Performance of the Acquiring Firm," *Academy of Management Review*, November 2, 1983, p. 218.
8 M. Lubatkin, "Merger Strategies and Stockholder Value," *Strategic Management Journal*, vol. 8, 1987, pp. 39–53.

 9 J. L. Frier, "Acquisition Search Program," *Mergers and Acquisitions,* Summer 1981, pp. 35–39.
10 H. W. Ebeling, Jr., and T. L. Doorley III, "A Strategic Approach to Acquisitions," *Journal of Business Strategy,* Winter 1983, pp. 44–54.
11 C. Hofer and D. Schendel, *Strategy Formulation: Analytical Concepts,* West, St. Paul, Minn., 1978, pp. 95–98.
12 D. R. Willensky, "Making It Happen: How to Execute an Acquisition," *Business Horizons,* March–April 1985, pp. 38–45.
13 Fray, Gaylin, and Down, op. cit.
14 Ibid.
15 A. Nahavandi and A. R. Malekzadeh, "Acculturation in Mergers and Acquisitions," *Academy of Management Review,* January 1988, pp. 79–90.

IMPLEMENTING STRATEGY: LEADERSHIP, SYSTEMS, AND STRUCTURE

LEARNING OBJECTIVES

After studying this chapter, the reader should be able to:

1 Explain the relationship between organizational leadership and strategy implementation
2 Show how management control systems are related to the implementation of strategy
3 Explain the strategic aspects of reward systems design
4 Determine whether an organization's structural arrangements are appropriate for its strategy

CHAPTER OUTLINE

Structural Options
- Job Specifications • Grouping • Linking Organizational Units
- Decision Making

IMPLEMENTATION: THE CHALLENGE

SUMMARY

REVIEW QUESTIONS

DISCUSSION QUESTIONS

REFERENCES

The tools of strategy implementation are not limited to directives from the top of the organization and functional area strategies. Other implementation tools include (1) leadership (both symbolic and substantial), (2) control systems, (3) information systems, (4) reward systems, and (5) organization structure.[1] *Leadership* refers both to symbolic and decisional roles of top management. *Control systems* direct the activities of the organization. *Information systems* collect data and integrate information to support management decision making. *Reward systems* establish provisions for compensation and benefits as well as policies for conveying recognition, status, and perquisites. *Organization structure* reflects decisions made about the grouping of key tasks and the definition of lines of authority and responsibility.

Each of these tools is a means of influencing members of the organization to follow the course determined by strategic choice. Two things should be noted about the relationship of these tools to effective strategy implementation. First, the direction of influence may be two-way. That is, the choice of strategy may be influenced by the type of information provided to the decision maker, by the rewards associated with various types of strategies, or by the grouping of organizational activities. Second, there are a number of influences on human behavior other than the tools mentioned here. We have oversimplified the relationships in order to discuss them more easily. Exhibit 10.1 shows a few of the past experiences, present influences, and future desired states that can affect the behavior of people in organizations. It is the sheer complexity of these relationships that makes strategy implementation so important and so difficult.

LEADERSHIP

The behavior and activities of top management, especially the CEO (chief executive officer) contribute to strategy implementation in at least two ways. Top management supports the strategy and builds the culture of the organization by example. Top management also makes decisions based on skill, personality, and experience, which determine the approach that implementation will take.

Symbolic Leadership

The values demonstrated by the organization's most visible executives provide a point of reference for other organization members as they carry out their du-

EXHIBIT 10.1   SOME INFLUENCES ON HUMAN BEHAVIOR IN IMPLEMENTING STRATEGY

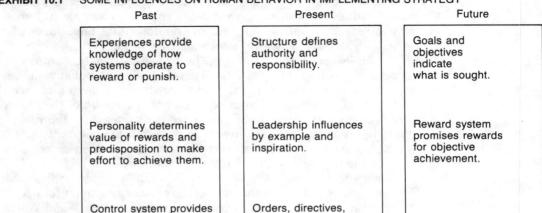

ties. In small organizations, frequent personal contact with top managers is likely. However, because of sheer size and physical separation in medium and large organizations, the process of instilling values is often dependent on public acts rather than direct contact. One accepted method of appraising leadership is to determine how well the public and quasi-public acts of recognized organization executives mesh with the strategic thrust of the firm.

Lee Iacocca, the architect of the Chrysler turnaround, received $1 in salary for his first year's employment at Chrysler. Even though his signing bonus was $400,000, much of his financial compensation was tied to Chrysler's performance. Iacocca began the turnaround by asking all levels of Chrysler employees to make financial sacrifices—and set an example himself. In 1986, as a result of Chrysler's performance, Iacocca was the highest-paid executive in the United States when salary and bonuses were combined. By 1987, Chrysler though profitable was losing market share and earnings, and layoffs were announced. Iacocca continued to appear as one of the top ten in executive compensation surveys. It is much easier to promote austerity in the ranks of the organization if there is austerity at the top.

The actions of executives are transmitted to distant employees by the media, by word of mouth individually, and by the grapevine. Executives seem to get employees' attention either by dramatic gestures or by repeated emphasis on one or two themes. A CEO at Dana Corporation emphasized his intention to streamline operations by tearing up the organization's rather thick policy manual at one of the first meetings of his management team. This rather dramatic gesture was worth many words. In contrast, Example 10.1 shows how a retailing executive quietly but regularly reinforced the importance of customer service—a key component of the company's strategy.

Not all leaders have the personality to make dramatic gestures like a Lee Iacocca or a René Macpherson (at Dana Corporation), but anyone can provide the type of quiet, consistent attention to detail of a Richard Rich (see Example 10.1). All CEOs should be aware of the symbolic nature of their behavior and avoid actions that appear to be counter to the strategy and the values they are trying to promote. One executive who was preaching austerity and cost control to his managers was discovered in a check of expense accounts to have charged the company with a $1000 dinner for two.

Leadership provides values for the organization. Values indicate what is important and, as values are shared, energize the organization for accomplishing its purpose. In their study of excellent companies, Peters and Waterman observed:

> We are struck by the explicit attention (excellent companies) paid to values, and by the way in which their leaders have created exciting environments through personal attention, persistence, and direct intervention—far down the line.[2]

Matching Leader Skills and Strategy

The CEO and top management team are more than symbols of strategy. They also contribute knowledge and skills to the implementation of strategy. While it has been argued that general managers should be able to lead different types of organizations, there are some strong arguments for ''specialization'' of general managers. The basic argument is that different strategies require different knowledge and skills to properly implement. Individuals are limited in their ability to implement strategy because of this requirement. If all managers are not equally able to implement strategy, it makes sense to match strategy with the individual who is best suited for the task.[3] The ability of executives to meet

---

EXAMPLE 10.1

Leadership as Symbolic Behavior

The largest department store in Atlanta, Georgia, is Rich's. For many years, the president was Richard Rich, and the theme that he embraced was customer service. He visited the sales floor and talked to customers frequently. During busy seasons, he could be found carrying parcels to cars for shoppers. Rich's presence on the sales floor and his performance of customer service activities gave his employees a clear example of what was important. Seeing Mr. Rich spend an extra minute to be sure a customer had found what he was looking for made an impression which carried over into employees' daily activities.

the leadership requirements of a particular strategy depends on their training, experience, and personality. Because these characteristics are not easily changed, a change in strategy is often accompanied by a change in leadership.

A. K. Gupta contends that the requirements of the strategy depend on the level of implementation, the objective desired, and the competitive approach. On the corporate level of strategy implementation, knowledge about financial management and the ability to exert impersonal financial control over a number of businesses are necessary to the CEO. By contrast, implementing strategy on the business level requires familiarity with the firm and the industry, expertise in at least one functional level [research and development (R&D), manufacturing, or marketing], and interpersonal skills. On the corporate level, leadership and strategy implementation is much less a "hands-on" process than on the business level.

The skills and knowledge needed to successfully implement the strategies that result in growth are different from those needed for strategies which maintain stability. Entrepreneurial behavior and a risk-taking attitude are necessary attributes of a growth-oriented leader. Growth strategies require a long-term view and the ability to make the investments that will pay off in the long run. Product and market innovation must be encouraged, and development of people in the organization is a priority. Stability-oriented strategies require a short-term view because the immediate cash generation is the purpose of the strategy. Skills in production and accounting or finance are at a premium in such a strategy. Executives should be able to resist risk and innovation. Defensive strategies have an even more short-term orientation. Immediate cash is necessary to the short-term survival of the business, yet generating that cash usually involves decisions with painful human consequences (layoffs, plant closings, divestitures). Example 10.2 recounts the experiences of some executives who have specialized in turnarounds.

Choice of competitive focus also affects leadership requirements. Differentiation and cost leadership strategies direct organization efforts in very different paths. Differentiation requires industry knowledge, marketing and R&D skills, and the ability to encourage and promote creativity among subordinates. To capitalize on the customer's ability to see differences in the product is not usually compatible with a tight cost control. On the other hand, cost leadership requires both tight operating controls and tight financial controls. The ability to design and use these controls is critical to successful implementation.

Closely matching executives with the strategy they are to implement may not be appropriate in all situations. Gupta lists four situations in which matching may *not* be the best approach:

1. Matching may interfere with the need for strategic flexibility. In some instances adherence to the strategy of choice is undesirable. When the organization is subject to unpredictability of some environmental factor or when the strategy may need significant adjustment, a CEO who is best suited for one strategy may be a hindrance to the adjustment process rather than a help.

2. Matching can interfere with management development. Particularly on the strategic business unit level, the transfer of executives from unit to unit is

---

EXAMPLE 10.2

Turnaround Artists

There is a growing group of executives in the United States who specialize in turning around corporations in trouble. They are likely to be called in when creditors become alarmed about a company's deteriorating financial position. As a condition of employment they are likely to demand complete authority to take the actions needed. Often they specialize in specific industries. Turnarounds often require painful cost-cutting measures, and an outsider is viewed as being better able to be objective about what is right and what is wrong with a company's operations. The salaries and bonuses commanded by these specialists are not the only tangible rewards of success. Often, turnaround artists invest their own money and reap substantial returns on their investments.

Q. T. Wiles specializes in high-tech turnarounds. He rescued 12 corporations in 15 years. He believes in discipline and weekly reports on market and profits, and he is willing to embarrass those who don't deliver. One of his efforts, a disk-drive maker called Miniscribe Corporation, increased sales 70 percent under his direction and increased equity 10 times. At 67, Wiles had no plans for retirement.

Jerry Goldress specializes in a different way. He provides short-term stabilization and usually stays in a job less than a year before making way for a new CEO to implement the recovery plan he has devised. He believes he has a 90 percent success rate in cutting costs quickly. His compensation averages $1.4 million annually. He logs considerable air time because he often works on more than one turnaround at once.

Source: "The Green Berets of Corporate Management," *Business Week,* September 21, 1987, pp. 110–114.

---

part of the management development process. This provides experience for executives which helps them to appreciate the interrelationships among units in the organization and also provides experience for those on the way up. Matching would limit the ability to rotate assignments in this way.

(3) Matching can create motivation problems for executives in some strategies. Studies have shown that executives who are rated as good performers in harvest strategies do not feel as satisfied with their efforts or feel that they are rewarded to the extent that other strategists are.

(4) Matching cannot overcome the influence of other factors on successful implementation. There are many factors which determine how effectively a chosen strategy will be implemented. Managers are only one of these factors, and in some instances a minor one.

This discussion is summarized in a series of guidelines given in Exhibit 10.2. This flowchart first addresses the issue of whether the executive has much in-

EXHIBIT 10.2 GUIDELINES FOR ANALYZING NEED TO MATCH EXECUTIVES TO STRATEGY

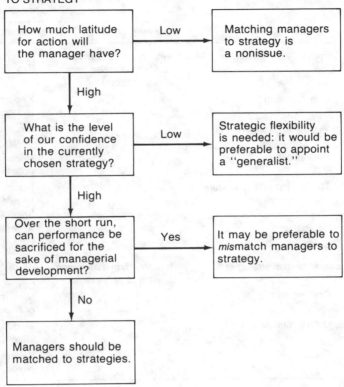

Source: A. K. Gupta, "Matching Managers to Strategies: Point and Counterpoint," *Human Resource Management*, Summer 1986, vol. 25, no. 2, pp. 215–234. Used by permission.

fluence on the outcome. If not, the more critical factors should be addressed and matching won't make any difference. Next, the question of whether the current strategy may need to be changed arises. If there is uncertainty about how permanent the current strategy is, matching is not the best way. Next, we consider whether we can afford to risk performance for the sake of management development. If so, deliberate mismatching will have educational value for the executive and long-term payoffs for the organization. Only when the executive can have a significant impact on performance, when the chosen strategy will be maintained, and when short-term performance is critical should managers be matched to strategy.

If matching is appropriate for the situation, the level of strategy, the goals of the organization, and the competitive focus of the strategy are important variables in making the right match. Some specific skills and attributes required by generic strategies are listed in Exhibit 10.3. This exhibit is intended to serve as

EXHIBIT 10.3   SKILL/KNOWLEDGE REQUIREMENTS FOR EXECUTIVES

	Skills/knowledge	
	For level	**For strategy**
Corporate-level strategies	Financial management; ability to exercise impersonal control	
Concentration		Knowledge of market and technical aspects of business
Vertical integration		Learn new business; financial analysis
Diversification		Measurement and control; portfolio approach
Turnaround and divestiture		Financial control; technical knowledge; ability to make tough decisions
Liquidation		Asset valuation and disposal
Bankruptcy		Legal knowledge
Business-level strategies	Industry, firm experience; interpersonal skills	
Cost leadership		Measurement and control of costs
Differentiation		Market knowledge; ability to foster creativity
Focus		Knowledge of market niche needs

a basis for thinking about the appropriate match between leadership and strategy and for diagnosing mismatches, *not* as a statement of absolute requirements. Executives do not change radically; however, they can adapt and learn. Example 10.3 relates how Victor Posner, a well-known corporate raider, made some adjustments in his approach.

CONTROL SYSTEMS

Control is necessary for goal achievement. Progress toward desired ends must be periodically monitored and evaluated in order to take corrective action in a timely fashion. The control process has three steps: (1) setting standards for performance, (2) measuring actual performance, and (3) taking corrective action when performance does not fall within an acceptable range. Control is one of the functions of management and is needed on all levels and in all activities of an organization. Components of management control systems include budgets, statistical reports, policies/procedures, and performance appraisal.[4] While we often speak of *the* organizational control system, most organizations

EXAMPLE 10.3

Victor Posner Adjusts His Leadership Style

Corporate raider Victor Posner has been known for his "slash and burn" approach to his acquisitions. He has used cash from acquisitions to finance other acquisitions rather than to reinvest. His relationships with managers of acquisitions have been stormy. Tight financial controls created problems with suppliers because of slow payment of accounts. He has drawn large salaries and acquired equally large amounts of debt in the companies he controls. His empire fell on hard times in 1985, with two bankruptcies, a staggering amount of debt, and a trial for income tax evasion.

Observers report that he has backed off of his hard-driving style; this change is attributed to various causes, including the influence of friend and fellow financier Carl Lindner. He has provided cash for businesses rather than draining off cash, left management to manage in the businesses they know well, loosened financial controls, and accepted a ceiling on his salary. His new approach has resulted in three turnarounds: RC (a soft drink company), Arby's (a fast food chain), and Graniteville (a textile manufacturer). These turnarounds may be divested to put the financial status of Posner's holding company in better shape.

Source: "Three Sparkling Turnarounds: Can This Really Be Victor Posner?" *Business Week,* July 27, 1987, pp. 56–57.

have *many* control systems which may or may not be coordinated with each other. In addition to the formal control systems most often associated with operations and accounting, many informal controls may also be in place. These departmental and individual efforts at control can help or hinder the strategy implementation process.

Control-oriented behavior is a term which describes behavior that is of importance for strategy implementation. This phenomenon occurs when employees prioritize their activities to protect themselves from unpleasant feedback. When employees are measured on activities, they ascribe importance to these activities and may seek to maximize performance while neglecting other activities where shortfalls in performance are less likely to be noticed or traced to the individual. If control systems are biased toward certain activities, employees interpret these activities as being the most important. Salespersons measured on the number of new accounts opened each quarter may neglect proper servicing of existing accounts. Machine operators measured solely on the rate of output per day are not likely to be quality-conscious. Managers who are measured on short-term profits may neglect investments for long-term growth. Organizations which emphasize quantitative measures of performance may find their employees engaging in unethical practices in order to meet objectives.

Control-oriented behavior creates the need to match the design of the control systems of the organization with the requirements of strategy. These systems are powerful implementation tools. Many times employees pay more attention to control systems than to formal communication. It is imperative that key control systems in the organization be consistent with the requirements of the strategy even through the systems are designed for functional area management. Among the design factors to be considered are:

1 *Loose vs. tight controls*. Tight controls ensure standard responses but leave little room for creative responses. Loose controls may postpone recognition of a problem, but they can also result in greater flexibility.

2 *Time emphasis*. Frequency of measurement affects employee time horizons.

3 *Quantitative vs. qualitative measures*. The balance between quantitative and qualitative measures can affect the employee's orientation toward the organization. The more quantitative the measures, the more the employee is likely to focus on the task at hand. The introduction of qualitative measures forces consideration of how the task at hand interfaces with other organizational considerations (such as ethics).

Exhibit 10.4 presents business-level strategies and shows how the organizational control systems associated with each might differ.

One difficulty in determining the design of control systems is that different individuals react differently to similar controls. Problems related to control systems can result from both overcompliance and outright resistance.[5] People may adhere to the behavior prescribed by control systems even when such behavior is inappropriate. A salesperson who will not vary from prescribed procedures to satisfy a customer complaint may be acting correctly according to the system but may not be implementing the strategy. Problems stemming from resistance to controls arise when people attempt to preempt, circumvent, or sabotage control systems. Distorting a report or padding the budget is a form of control resistance.

Departmental and individual control systems are important aspects of strategy implementation. Another aspect of control is the evaluation and control of the strategy itself, which is part of the strategic management process and may be thought of as control of the performance of the organization as a whole. Control as a phase of strategic management is discussed in Chapter 11.

EXHIBIT 10.4 CONTRASTS IN ORGANIZATIONAL CONTROL EMPHASIS BY BUSINESS STRATEGIES

Strategy	Control approach
Cost leadership	Tight cost control Frequent, detailed reports Output-oriented
Differentiation	Control of input by selection of creative people or skilled labor Subjective evaluation Input- and output-oriented
Focus	Market-related combination of the above

INFORMATION SYSTEMS

The information system of an organization provides support for internal decision making and for monitoring the progress of strategy implementation. It is important that the information system provides information that is timely, relevant, and complete and that the system itself is accessible to the user.[6]

Two variables in the design of an information system which should fit strategy are the focus of the system (cost and/or profit) and the relationship of organizational units (shared resources vs. independent units). When firms follow a concentration, and to a certain extent market or product development strategy, organizational units are defined as cost centers and profit is measured at the corporate level. When diversification or horizontal or vertical integration occurs, profit responsibility is usually given to individual units and the information system must be adjusted to provide this information. In a turnaround situation, it may be necessary to develop an information system which can assess profitability of products or customer groups.

Complicating the design process in a multibusiness organization is the existence of shared resources. When this happens, the information system must correctly allocate costs across division. Often, transfer pricing is the mechanism for this cost allocation and if not done carefully, it becomes a bone of contention among managers.

Information systems may also serve to build and/or protect a competitive advantage. Electronic information process technology has been used by a number of retailers to create cost advantages. Example 10.4 describes such a system at Wal-Mart.

EXAMPLE 10.4

Electronic Data Interchange at Wal-Mart

Mr. Sam Walton may drive a beat-up truck and espouse old-fashioned values, but his Wal-Mart discount chain is frequently in the vanguard of using information systems for competitive advantage. As a result of electronic data interchange (EDI) arrangements with suppliers, Wal-Mart can improve its selection on seasonal products, increasing sales, and cutting inventory costs. For example, Wal-Mart has an EDI with Seminole Manufacturing Co., which produces men's slacks. This means that the Wal-Mart inventory control system can send purchase orders direct to the Seminole computer. This eliminates human error in data entry, decreases delivery time for orders, frees salespeople from routine paperwork, and lowers inventory levels. As a result of its arrangement with Seminole, Wal-Mart was able to offer 64 size and color combinations of pants and to have them available when customer demand was greatest. This produced a 31 percent increase in pants sales in 9 months.

Source: "An Electronic Pipeline That's Changing the Way America Does Business," *Business Week*, August 3, 1987, p. 80.

Information systems must also provide information about external trends in markets, political, economic, and technological environments. Often this information will be qualitative rather than quantitative. As important as computerized information handling can be, there is no substitute for the more traditional sources of information such as customers, suppliers, consultants, and personal observation. In fact, computerized information systems can free managerial time for obtaining the type of information that only people can perceive, interpret, and apply.

REWARD SYSTEMS

The way that management recognizes outstanding performance—or fails to recognize it—sends signals throughout the organization about what is desired and what it is worth to try to achieve it. These signals should support the overall strategic direction of the firm. An organization which bases its increases in compensation on overall performance of the company and distributes raises equitably across ranks when the company is doing well is signaling that cooperation and loyalty are important. The company which provides high rewards for top performance and nothing for "second place" is sending a very different set of signals. The correctness of the signals can be determined only in relation to the requirements of the strategy.

There has been considerable research concerning how to design and administer reward systems. Many organizations find it useful to employ consultants for this complex task. An executive reward system is described in Example 10.5. This example explains how bonuses are awarded at Flowers Industries, a

---

EXAMPLE 10.5

Executive Bonus System at Flowers Industries

The performance share plan is available just to our top management...the plant presidents and the top people at Corporate. A grant of performance shares is made by the Compensation Committee of the Board at the beginning of an award period, which covers four years. Payment is made at the end of the award period, and the value of the performance shares is based on the value of the Company's stock at the time of payment. The total amount of the grant is paid if we have a compounded increase in earnings per share of at least 15 percent over the four-year period. (That's a difficult goal, but it's been achieved.) A percentage of the grant is payable on a sliding scale if the increase in EPS is less than 15 percent but at least 8 percent; if the increase is less than 8 percent the payment is zero. Payment for performance shares has been made one-half in cash and one-half in stock; this is so recipients can have the cash to pay the taxes on the award.

Source: Presentation at Georgia State University.

company which has experienced rapid growth in sales and profitability since 1968.

The control system is often viewed as distributing sanctions, and the reward system provides positive feedback. In theory, the two should be coordinated so that rewards are derived from superior performance on control measures. Information systems should be designed to support both. In practice, the reward system can be effected by nonstrategic factors such as the market wage rate of specialists or government regulations. Nonmonetary rewards are especially useful because they can be tied directly to strategy.

Long-Term vs. Short-Term

The timing and criteria used to determine wage increments and bonuses can focus attention on immediate improvement or on building for future performance. While most strategies require a balance between the two, there are situations in which one or the other is desired. A harvest strategy, for example, requires that rewards should be immediate and based on short-term performance. The harvest strategy is designed to generate as much cash from the business as possible without making any long-term financial commitments to the business. Implementing growth strategies, on the other hand, may require sacrifice of immediate returns in order to establish position and competences for the future.

Corporate Considerations

In a corporate strategy there will likely be a combination of strategies. The use of SBUs or profit centers for measurement and control allows different evaluation measures for individual units and requires reward systems appropriate for the unit's strategy. Example 10.6 illustrates the weighted strategic factors approach to the design of a reward system for a diversified organization.

At the same time, the reward system should send the appropriate signals concerning the desired amount of cooperation among the separate units. Conglomerate diversification yields a collection of businesses which ask or require little cooperation other than sharing corporate staff and benefit plans. Concentric diversification, in contrast, may include substantial sharing of facilities, the marketing force, and information systems. The reward systems should discourage power struggles among units. This can be accomplished by basing at least a portion of executives' bonuses or incentives on performance of the organization as a whole.

Nonmonetary Rewards

Status, recognition, and attention are highly prized by most individuals. They can be conveyed in support of a strategy throughout the organization. Management is limited only by its own creativity in devising these types of rewards. While formal rewards are often distributed on a schedule that corre-

---

EXAMPLE 10.6

Weighted Strategic Factors Approach to Compensation

An organization with several business units is likely to be pursuing more than one strategy. Some units might be pursuing growth strategies, some stability strategies, and others defensive strategies. The weighted strategic factors approach is an attempt to recognize the differences in performance that such strategies will produce to design a reward system that is both equitable and consistent with strategic requirements. The organization would choose several factors which would be applied across all units. Examples of such factors include return on equity, cash flow, market share, and progress on strategic projects. The weights accorded each factor would differ with the strategy of the unit. A manager of a business unit pursuing a growth strategy might have the following weights:

Return on equity	10%
Cash flow	00%
Market share	45%
Progress	45%

A manager of a stability strategy business might have very different weights:

Return on equity	50%
Cash flow	50%
Market share	00%
Progress	00%

Source: Adapted from P. J. Stonich, "Using Rewards in Implementing Strategy," *Strategic Management Journal,* vol. 2, 1981, pp. 345–352.

---

sponds with accounting cycles, nonmonetary rewards can be given immediately to reinforce desired behavior.

STRATEGY AND STRUCTURE

The importance of a fit between strategy and structure has been verified in a number of research studies.[7] Achieving this fit is a complex process involving decisions about how activities will be grouped and how groups will be coordinated. This section addresses issues in the strategy-structure relationship.

Complex Interactions

Structure is defined by Henry Mintzberg as "the sum total of the ways in which (the organization) divides its labor into distinct tasks and then achieves coordination between them."[8] Clearly, strategy implementation requires division of tasks so that strategic functions are given high visibility and close attention. It also requires coordination of all an organization's efforts, including the most mundane. All strategic functions are important, but many nonstrategic, routine functions are also important.

The division of labor and regrouping of tasks often begins with a one-dimensional diagram of boxes and lines representing a particular structural type. Structural types and sample diagrams are presented in Exhibit 10.5. The grouping process depicted in such diagrams provides terminology to identify structural types but is only one aspect of the structural problem of the strategist. It represents the flow of formal authority in the organization but does not adequately show other flows which are important to successful strategy implementation. Materials in the work process, control information, and decisions often follow paths different from those represented by the formal lines of authority. In addition, a network of informal communication exists which channels important information. Exhibit 10.6 shows how these flows can differ in relation to the flow of formal authority.

Because the structuring of an organization involves more than redrawing the organization chart, the formal division and regrouping of authority should always be carefully monitored for implementation problems. The strategist should be aware of the full range of options for achieving the necessary fit between strategy and structure.

Structural Options

Job Specifications   In order to implement strategy, it is necessary to identify the strategic tasks that must be performed as well as the more routine tasks which support and facilitate the organization's operations. Individual behavior is shaped by specialization of tasks, by job descriptions, by rules, and by training. In small to medium-sized businesses, the task of job specification may, on occasion, be completed "from scratch." On the other hand, most job specification is done incrementally. As the burden of work increases, a position is split and two new jobs are created, or an individual expands his or her job by seeking new tasks. In large organizations the specification of individual jobs based on new strategy would be formidable and likely to impede implementation rather than enhance it. Strategic implementation issues within large organizations are more likely, of necessity, to be concerned with groups of jobs.

Grouping   Job specification results in thousands of individual positions whose activities must be coordinated. One way to achieve this coordination is to group activities into primary work units and then to group these units into more comprehensive units, until the hierarchical ordering of the organization is complete. Since "organizational design is much less common than organization redesign," the implementation of strategy usually involves the shifting of groups rather than of individual positions.[9] The fundamental choice to be made is whether to group by the characteristics of the markets served (clients),

EXHIBIT 10.5   STRUCTURAL TYPES

Primitive, or Entrepreneurial, Type

All employees report to the President.
Duties may vary with daily requirements
of business.

Organization is dependent on the skills
of the top manager but is quite flexible.

Divisional Type

This type is usually found in organizations facing
diversity in markets, products, and/or technologies.
At least two levels of general management
make it possible for top management to
delegate some responsibility for profits.

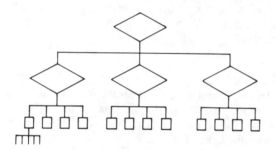

An SBU is a group of several divisions
with common strategies.

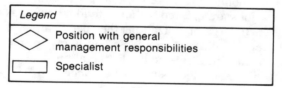

Legend	
⬦	Position with general management responsibilities
▭	Specialist

Functional Type

Employees are grouped by
function and report to superiors
in the same area of functional
expertise, who report to the President.

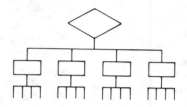

Specialization provides efficiency
but may decrease response time
as the organization grows.

Matrix Type

Employees in this type are
responsible both to functional
executives and to product
or market executives. The
dual responsibility ensures
both specialization and quick
market response.

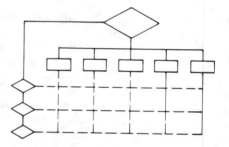

This type is frequently
criticized for its ambiguity.

may not be significant

by the means used to serve markets (activities), or by the end product or service (output).[10] Market grouping provides an environmental orientation for the organization and may be based on products, customers, or geographic location. These groupings promote responsiveness to environmental change in that they facilitate both the recognition of key shifts and the ability to adjust to them. Grouping by means of service (activities) creates an internal orientation and is based on work processes, skills, and the knowledge used to produce products or services. Grouping by end product or service facilities product

EXHIBIT 10.6   STRUCTURE AND FUNCTION IN A SMALL MEAT PROCESSOR

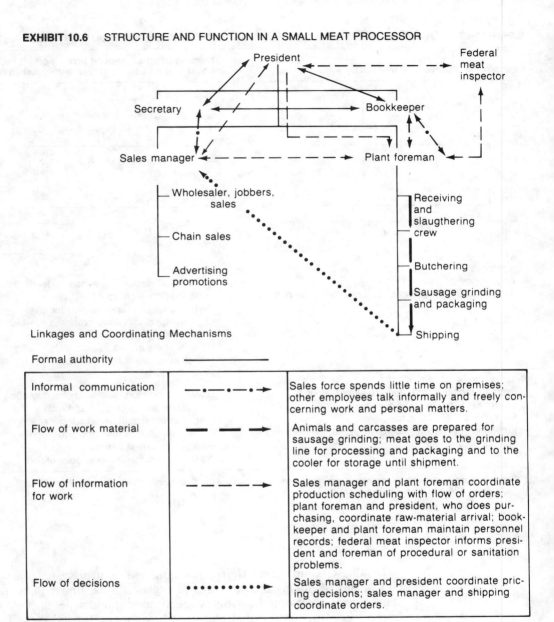

Linkages and Coordinating Mechanisms

Formal authority	────────	
Informal communication	──•──•──•─►	Sales force spends little time on premises; other employees talk informally and freely concerning work and personal matters.
Flow of work material	──── ─── ─►	Animals and carcasses are prepared for sausage grinding; meat goes to the grinding line for processing and packaging and to the cooler for storage until shipment.
Flow of information for work	─── ─── ─►	Sales manager and plant foreman coordinate production scheduling with flow of orders; plant foreman and president, who does purchasing, coordinate raw-material arrival; bookkeeper and plant foreman maintain personnel records; federal meat inspector informs president and foreman of procedural or sanitation problems.
Flow of decisions	•••••••••►	Sales manager and president coordinate pricing decisions; sales manager and shipping coordinate orders.

planning and resource allocation. These groupings produce the familiar organization charts. Exhibit 10.7 shows client, activity, and output groupings and lists the advantages and disadvantages of each. Like the aerospace firm in Exhibit 10.7, most organizations that have attained any size or have expanded beyond their original geographic scope or product line use a combination of groupings by activities, output, and clients.

EXHIBIT 10.7 ADVANTAGES AND DISADVANTAGES OF ACTIVITY, CLIENT, AND OUTPUT GROUPINGS

Grouping in a university by activity

Grouping in an aerospace firm by client (company as a whole) and by output (commercial aircraft)

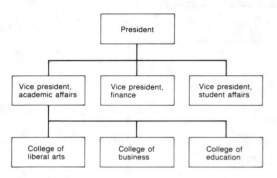

Advantages

Encourages specialization

Allows pooling of resources across different work flows

Disadvantages

Detracts attention from end product or service

Individuals focus on means, not ends

Performance difficult to measure

Problems may rise in hierarchy beyond level where they can be understood

Advantages

Contains all resources needed to deal with a work flow in primary group

Performance can be measured for unit

Unit managers can solve problems of which they have direct knowledge

More flexibility in task assignments

Can grow or shrink by adding units

Disadvantages

Less specialization, so less knowledge about more things

Less suited for specialized and routine tasks

Detracts from emphasis on specialization

Duplication of personnel and equipment wastes resources

Loss of economies of scale

Wasteful interorganizational competition

Source: Advantages and disadvantages are taken from H. Mintzberg, *The Structuring of Organizations,* Prentice-Hall, Englewood Cliffs, N.J., 1979, pp. 124–133. Used by permission.

Linking Organizational Units Planning and control systems are an important means of linking the activities of organizational units. Plans provide for standardization of output, budgets specify costs, and schedules establish time frames. Controls ensure that plans are being met. Beyond these formal linkages, individual points of contact are established by the organization to achieve coordination not provided by other means. These points of contact are known as liaison devices and should be considered if the new strategy requires substantial change. Liaison devices include the following:

• *Liaison positions.* Managers who maintain contact with managers in other groups to open lines of direct communication between groups
• *Task forces and standing committees.*

• *Integrating managers*. Managers who have formal authority over two work units for some, but not all, activities

Decision Making   The variables previously discussed do not address the issue of centralization and decentralization, which is the final concern of the strategist attempting to match strategy and structure. An organization is decentralized to the degree that decision-making authority is delegated and pushed down in the organization. This is of critical importance when the new strategy requires a quick response to customer needs or technological changes. If decision-making authority is retained at the apex of the organization, response time will be slowed. While centralization provides the best means of coordination, the strategist should consider decentralization because:

• No top manager in an organization of any size is able to comprehend all the pertinent issues or has all the knowledge required to make decisions.
• Decentralization decreases response time to environmental changes and to customers.
• Decentralization motivates creative and intelligent people and provides training for future responsibilities.

The process of matching structure to strategy is a complex one and should proceed with a thorough understanding of the historical development of the current structure, the requirements of the organization's environment and technology, and the political relationships which will be affected by any change. Example 10.7 illustrates this process with a history of structural evolution at General Motors.

IMPLEMENTATION: THE CHALLENGE

The task of strategy implementation is as difficult as it is important. Simply maintaining an awareness of all the tools of strategy implementation is an intellectual feat. Knowing how and when to use them is a skill honed by training and experience. Accepting the risks of executing a carefully conceived strategy in an organization of individuals with divergent interests and working to decrease those risks is the essence of strategic leadership.

SUMMARY

Individuals in organizations respond to a variety of signals which indicate what is expected of them. Mission, strategy, and objectives provide general and specific guidance; other important sources of information include the leadership stance of management, the choice of measures in the control system, the nature and timing of rewards, and the structural arrangements which coordinate activities.

Leadership sets the tone and instills the values of the organization. The values set for the organization by its most visible executives provide a point of reference for other organization members as they carry out their duties. The

EXAMPLE 10.7

Structural Evolution at General Motors

General Motors adopted a divisionalized structure by product line under the leadership of President and Chairman Alfred P. Sloan, Jr. Sloan's intent was to centralize planning on the corporate level while decentralizing operations so that those closest to the action could make decisions. The divisions shared parts but developed their own body styles and identities as separate models in customers' eyes. In the 1960s, GM began to add models and to specialize divisions by function. Assembly was centralized and Fisher Body continued to design bodies and produce body panels. In the 1970s, downsizing added to the complexity, and project centers were created to coordinate product development. By this time, the lines of command were muddled and the customers were confused, as all GM cars seemed to look alike.

In 1984, GM announced a massive restructuring to clear up the confusion and move the development of cars to centralized engineering and product development groups. Manufacturing would also be more centralized. The focus of the new structure is two car groups. One, Chevrolet-Pontiac-GM Canada Group, would engineer and build small cars. The other, Buick-Cadillac-Oldsmobile Group, would develop the intermediate and large cars. The car divisions would become marketing units for the two groups. The reorganization was intended to achieve the following:

- Launch new models on schedule
- Better control cost
- Control quality to compete with foreign cars
- Return to distinctive models for each car division

Clearly, at GM, the relationship between strategy and structure is a complex one, but the cost of a misfit has been high.

Source: "Can GM Solve Its Identity Crisis?" *Business Week,* January 23, 1984, pp. 32–33.

executives of the organization reflect and define strategy through their statements, interactions, and activities. The ability of executives to fulfill the leadership requirements of a particular strategy depends on their training, experience, and personality. Because these characteristics are not easily changed, a change in strategy may be accompanied by a change in leadership.

Control involves monitoring current performance and comparing performance with predetermined standards or objectives. Variance from standards alerts managers to a problem or potential problem before it becomes critical. If the control system is biased toward certain activities, employees interpret those activities as being the most important and prioritize their activities to protect themselves from unpleasant feedback. Employees pay careful attention to the control system, and it should be consistent with the requirements of the strategy. Design factors to be considered include the looseness or tightness of the controls, the time emphasis, and the type of measures used.

Information systems provide decision support by providing timely, relevant, and accessible information to decision makers. Strategies vary in informational requirements, and the systems should be adjusted to meet strategy requirements.

The way that management recognizes outstanding performance—or fails to recognize it—sends signals throughout the organization about what is desired and what it is worth to try to achieve it. The reward system should support the overall strategic direction of the firm. Rewards can be used to direct attention toward long- or short-term performance or toward some combination of the two. They may also promote or inhibit cooperation among organizational units. Because of legal and market constraints, nonmonetary rewards such as status, recognition, and attention can be more easily conveyed to support strategy.

In addition to clarifying and defining strategy through the delegation of authority and responsibility, the structure of the organization can either facilitate or inhibit strategy implementation. Structure includes all the ways that an organization divides its labor into tasks and coordinates the resulting specialized activities. This process often begins with grouping, which produces structural types, but also includes flows of work materials, control information, and decisions. Matching structure to strategy is a complex process and should proceed only with a thorough understanding of the historical development of the current structure, the requirements of the organization's environment and technology, and the political relationships which will be affected by any change.

CHAPTER 10 REVIEW QUESTIONS

1 How does executive leadership in a large organization differ from such leadership in a small organization?
2 Under what conditions would matching the skills of an executive with the requirements of a strategy be appropriate?
3 How do control systems reinforce strategy?
4 What types of rewards are available to implement strategy?
5 How does the design of a reward system for a diversified organization differ from the design of a system for an organization following a concentration strategy?
6 What are some advantages and disadvantages of functional, divisional, and matrix structures?
7 What options does the strategist have for ensuring that the organization is structured to implement a new strategy?

CHAPTER 10 DISCUSSION QUESTIONS

1 Consider two organizational leaders whose actions you are familiar with or whom you have learned about through library research. How do their actions communicate their plans for their organizations and their expectations for subordinates?
2 A small manufacturer of children's clothing is currently organized into functional (activity) groups. The president is contemplating changing to groupings by customers to

provide better service to chain store accounts (it also sells to the traditional retail department stores). What advice would you give the president concerning the merits of such a change?

3 *Business Week* annually publishes a study of top executive compensation. Secure the most current executive compensation issue from your library and try to draw some conclusions about the relationship of pay to performance in the companies surveyed.

CHAPTER 10 REFERENCES

1 R. L. Daft and N. B. Macintosh, "The Nature and Use of Formal Control Systems for Management Control and Strategy Implementation," *Journal of Management,* vol. 10, no. 1, 1984, p. 47.

2 T. J. Peters and R. H. Waterman, Jr., *In Search of Excellence,* Harper & Row, New York, 1982, pp. 279–280.

3 This section based on A. K. Gupta, "Matching Managers to Strategies: Point and Counterpoint," *Human Resource Management,* vol. 25, no. 2, Summer 1986, pp. 215–134.

4 Daft and Macintosh, op. cit., pp. 51–52.

5 G. Dalton and P. Lawrence, *Motivation and Control in Organizations,* Irwin, Homewood, Ill., 1971, p. 8.

6 C. A. O'Reilly III, "Variations in Decision Makers' Use of Information Sources: The Impact of Quality and Accessibility of Information," *Academy of Management Journal,* vol. 25, no. 4, 1982, pp. 756–771.

7 J. R. Galbraith and R. K. Kazanjian, *Strategy Implementation: Structure, Systems, and Process,* West, St. Paul, Minn., 1986, pp. 43–44.

8 H. Mintzberg, *The Structuring of Organizations,* Prentice-Hall, Englewood Cliffs, N.J., 1979, p. 2.

9 Ibid., p. 105.

10 I. C. MacMillan and P. E. Jones, "Designing Organizations to Compete," *The Journal of Business Strategy,* vol. 4, no. 4, Spring 1984, pp. 11–26.

STRATEGIC CONTROL AND EVALUATION

LEARNING OBJECTIVES

After studying this chapter, the reader should be able to:

1 Describe the evaluation and control phases of the strategic management process
2 Discuss techniques for strategic control and evaluation
3 Identify potential trouble spots in the management of strategy formulation and implementation
4 Recognize potential problems in a competitive setting which might impair the effectiveness of the organization

CHAPTER OUTLINE

SETTING UP STRATEGIC CONTROLS
Financial Controls
Nonfinancial Controls
STRATEGY EVALUATION
Consistency
Consonance
Advantage
Feasibility
McKinsey's 7-S Framework
PITFALLS OF THE STRATEGIC MANAGEMENT PROCESS
Errors Relating to the Use of Strategic Management
• Inability to Think Strategically • Inappropriate Use of Management Levels • Undue Emphasis on Form and Procedure • Isolation from the Environment • Too Much Emphasis on the Near Term • Improper Use of Planning Resources

Less Predictable Changes
- Innovations—New Products or Services • Government Regulations
- Weather • Shortages in Raw Materials • Consumer Preferences
- New Competitors or Changes in a Competitor's Abilities

SUMMARY

REVIEW QUESTIONS

DISCUSSION QUESTIONS

REFERENCES

Strategic control is concerned with tracking the strategy once it has been implemented, detecting any problem areas or potential problem areas, and making necessary adjustments. Because strategic management is heavily oriented toward the future and because the future is continually changing, adjustments are expected and do not necessarily reflect a poor strategy. The purpose of strategic control is to alert the manager to potential problems before it is too late to do something about them.

Newman and Logan use the term "steering control" to highlight some important characteristics of strategic control.[1] Ordinarily, there is a significant time span between the initial implementation of strategy and the measurement of results. In the meantime, both the environmental situation and the internal situation on which the strategy was based are developing and evolving. Strategic control must provide some means of correcting the direction on the basis of intermediate performance and new information. This is achieved by identifying the key assumptions on which the strategy is based and monitoring those assumptions through updated forecasts. When assumptions fail or alter significantly, corrective action should be taken. Also, at major milestones in the strategy implementation process, new information can be incorporated into a review of the strategy.

SETTING UP STRATEGIC CONTROLS

Careful preparation within the organization is needed to make strategic controls work.[2] The organization must be prepared to systematically and critically question the main strategic course being followed. This requires its managers to be courageous enough to voice doubts even in the face of group pressures. Managers should feel free to question long-standing operating procedures and even traditional values and norms. This type of behavior requires a management team that is not afraid of questioning the ideas of the chief executive officer (CEO). This also requires a CEO that is not afraid to be questioned. Thus, for strategic control to work at its best, a climate which encourages openness is essential.

The first step in setting up strategic controls is to identify the parts of strategy that have a reasonable likelihood of variance. This is not always easy. Past experience and a thorough analysis of both the internal and external environments normally will provide clues as to potential problem areas. Any alternate scenarios that were developed as part of the contingency planning process will also identify variables that should be monitored. For example, a construction company might identify several scenarios that are dependent on the weather and interest rates. Thus, the weather and interest rates represent variables that should be closely monitored as part of the strategic control process.

Once the variables to be watched have been identified, early warning signals should be developed for each variable. These signals should be designed to detect any meaningful changes in the variable. One useful approach to developing early warning signals is to identify a list of milestones, or major intermediate progress points, relating to the objectives being pursued. Once these milestones have been identified, they should be carefully monitored.

Financial Controls

Financial data are some of the most commonly used warning signals. Commonly used financial measures include consideration of profit, sales, return on investment (ROI), return on equity, cost figures, and trends in these and other related measures. Financial figures are periodically monitored and compared with projected or expected figures. Substantial discrepancies in any of the figures usually indicate that something unanticipated is happening.

The most frequently used tool for monitoring financial performance is the budgetary process. A budget is a statement of expected results or requirements expressed in financial or numerical terms. In essence, a budget is a plan for allocating resources. When used for control purposes, budgets have many advantages:[3]

1 The accounting information on which the system is based is readily available and familiar.

2 All aspects of the operation receive the same attention.

3 Comparison across departments and units is facilitated by the use of common units of measure.

Budgetary controls are not without drawbacks, however:

1 They are only as good as the accounting system on which they are based and do not measure intangibles or nonfinancial objectives such as market share and morale.

2 Warnings of trouble may not arrive in a timely fashion.

3 Arbitrary cost allocations to meet financial reporting requirements can be misleading.

Many different types of budgets are in use. Exhibit 11.1 summarizes some of the most common types.

Nonfinancial Controls

In addition to financial data, there are many other early warning signals that can be used to alert the strategist to potential problems. Some of the most fre-

EXHIBIT 11.1   TYPES AND PURPOSES OF BUDGETS

Type of budget	Brief description of purpose
Revenue and expense budget	Provides details for revenue and expense plans
Cash budget	Forecasts cash receipts and disbursements
Capital expenditure budget	Outlines specific expenditures for plant, equipment, machinery, inventories, and other capital items
Production, material, or time budget	Expresses physical requirements of production, or material, or the time requirements for the budget period
Balance sheet budget	Forecasts the status of assets, liabilities, and net worth at the end of the budget period

Source: Leslie W. Rue and Lloyd L. Byars, *Management: Theory and Application,* 4th ed., Irwin, Homewood, Ill., 1986, p. 307.

quently used *nonfinancial* signals are measures of productivity, measures of quality, personnel-related measures, and feedback from customers. Most organizations use a combination of financial and nonfinancial early warning signals.

Nonfinancial controls are frequently structured around objectives. If an organization has an objective that is central to its strategy, it may regularly review performance against specifically identified milestones. For example, the research and development department may have an objective to develop a particular new product by the end of the year. Performance milestones might include having a prototype for testing by March and a limited production run for customer development trials by September. If these milestones are not met, the company would need to determine why.

Frequently, organizations either monitor whatever is easiest to monitor or what they are most accustomed to monitoring. To properly implement a strategy, the organization must focus its efforts on those aspects of performance that are important to the strategy. For example, if a manufacturer chooses to follow a competitive strategy based on differentiation, its key control measures should reflect an emphasis on differentiation and not some other factor such as cost reduction.

Wickham Skinner has pointed out that many organizations monitor and control performance using definitions of performance that are not consistent with their strategy.[4] For example, because most manufacturing organizations define performance in terms of productivity, a problem often occurs when marketing and top management try to move the company in the direction of higher quality, broader product lines, and a stronger service orientation. Although these goals may make the company more profitable and competitive in the long run, in the short run they can hurt productivity. Unless the company deliberately sets out to change its understanding of performance throughout the organization, manufacturing may continue to monitor and control performance using productivity measures that tend to work against, rather than for, the company's competitive strategy.

STRATEGY EVALUATION

Early warning signals and other similar strategic controls are used to detect something specific which has gone wrong or which is about to go wrong with operations. There is no doubt that strategic controls are a very valuable and necessary part of the strategic management process. Without them, things could easily get "out of control." Example 11.1 summarizes how Toys 'R' Us has avoided mistakes in the "trendy toy" business by using a sophisticated inventory control system.

Unfortunately, one problem inherent in traditional strategic controls is that they are usually designed to monitor day-to-day operations and do not focus on the overall strategy. As emphasized above, this does not mean that such controls are not useful and even necessary, but it does suggest that they should be supplemented with information for evaluating the overall strategy.[5] Strategy evaluation, as used here, "is an attempt to look beyond the obvious facts regarding the short-term health of a business and appraise instead those more fundamental factors and trends that govern success in the chosen field of endeavor."[6] Thus strategy evaluation is concerned with appraising the overall impact and appropriateness of the strategy.

Richard Rumelt has proposed four criteria with which to evaluate a given strategy. Each of these is briefly discussed below.

Consistency

In order to be consistent, a strategy must present mutually consistent goals and policies. There are many types of inconsistency that can occur to undermine a strategy. Continuing conflicts between functional areas usually indicate strategic inconsistencies. A clear and consistent strategy should foster a

---

EXAMPLE 11.1

How Inventory Control Has Helped Toys 'R' Us

Founder and Chief Executive Officer Charles Lazarus has made Toys 'R' Us a major contender in the off-price toy market by taking full advantage of a sophisticated, centralized, computerized inventory control system. All buying and pricing decisions are made at corporate headquarters. The elaborate inventory control system used includes daily sales reports by store and item. Real sales are constantly monitored and compared with forecasts. When a significant discrepancy exists, slow items are marked down and big sellers are reordered in larger quantities. With this automated forecasting system linked to daily sales reports, Lazarus was able to move the stock of video games, at reduced prices, before the crash of that market. Their system also predicted the demand for Rubik's Cube and allowed Toys 'R' Us to capitalize on that knowledge.

climate of mutual understanding and coordination. A second type of inconsistency that can occur is between the organizational strategy and the organizational culture. As discussed in Chapter 7, the strategy must mesh with the organization's culture.

Consonance

For consonance to be present, a strategy must represent an adaptive response to the external environment and to the major changes occurring within it. The emphasis of consonance is on the match between the strategy and the major trends taking place in the environment. Consonance focuses on the major environmental trends affecting the entire industry. It can best be evaluated by developing a thorough understanding of why the organization exists and then determining the likely impact of key trends and changes on its existence.

Advantage

For a strategy to be successful, it must provide for some type of competitive advantage in the selected area of operation. Unlike consonance, advantage is concerned with specific competitive differences between a given firm and its competitors. The bottom-line question dealing with advantage is "How can this company perform better than, or in place of, the competition?" Competitive advantage can usually be evaluated in terms of three factors: (1) superior resources, (2) superior skills, and (3) superior position.

The advantages offered by superior resources and/or superior skills are obvious. A company with inferior equipment and/or personnel is not going to be able to compete effectively. Positional advantage relates to being in the "right place at the right time." Exhibit 11.2 gives several examples of positional advantages.

Feasibility

In order to be acceptable, a strategy must be feasible in terms of the organization's existing, or readily attainable, skills and resources. The financial fea-

---

EXHIBIT 11.2 EXAMPLES OF POSITIONAL ADVANTAGES: ECONOMIES OF SCALE ASSOCIATED WITH BEING LARGE

- Successful trade names such as Izod or Polo
- Ownership of special raw-material sources or long-term supply contracts
- Being located near key customers in a business involving high transportation costs
- Being a full-line producer in a market with heavy trade-up phenomena
- Having a wide reputation for providing a needed product or service trait such as reliability and dependability

Source: Richard Rumelt, "The Evaluation of Business Strategy," in William F. Glueck (ed.), *Business Policy and Strategic Management,* 3d ed., McGraw-Hill, New York, 1980, p. 363.

sibility of a strategy can be evaluated by using standard financial analyses (see the appendix, which appears after Chapter 12).

It is usually somewhat more difficult to evaluate a strategy's feasibility from a human-skills viewpoint. Rumelt has suggested three pertinent questions relating to an organization's human abilities to carry out a strategy:[7]

1 Has the organization demonstrated the problem-solving abilities and special competences required by the strategy?
2 Has the organization demonstrated the coordination and integrative skills necessary to carry out the strategy?
3 Does the strategy challenge and motivate key personnel, and is the strategy acceptable to those who must support it?

A strategy which scores high on each of the above four criteria is not guaranteed to be a success, but it certainly has advantages over one that falls short on one or more of the criteria.

McKinsey's 7-S Framework

The international consulting firm of McKinsey and Company has developed the McKinsey 7-S Framework for evaluating strategy. The underlying premise of the 7-S Framework is that the value of any given strategy depends not only on its content but equally as much on whether it can be successfully executed.[8] To quote Robert Waterman, Jr., who helped develop the 7-S Framework, "A good strategy is not synonymous with a doable one. Nor is a doable strategy synonymous with a good one. The challenge is to find a good doable strategy."[9]

The 7-S Framework is based on the concept that any strategy, in order to be successfully implemented, must fit with the culture of the organization. As shown in Exhibit 11.3, the 7-S Framework views culture as a function of seven variables: strategy, structure, systems, style, staff, skills, and shared values. Exhibit 11.4 presents definitions of the variables as they are used in the 7-S Framework. According to the 7-S Framework, a strategy is usually successful when the other S's in the framework fit, or support, the strategy. On the other hand, if a chosen strategy has run into problems during or shortly after implementation, it is often because there is a lack of fit between the strategy and one or more of the other S's. While the 7-S Framework can be a help in the strategic choice process or in the determination of why a strategy has gone awry, its major contribution is that it emphasizes that a successful strategy is dependent on many variables and many interrelationships.

PITFALLS OF THE STRATEGIC MANAGEMENT PROCESS

When strategic management is being practiced, two major categories of errors can occur. The first category includes errors resulting from the manner in which strategic management is used. Many of the errors falling into this category are avoidable and stem from a lack of understanding of the process. The

EXHIBIT 11.3 McKINSEY 7-S FRAMEWORK

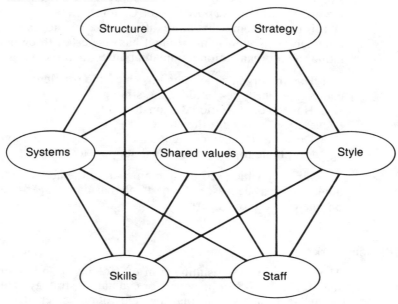

Source: Robert H. Waterman, Jr., "The Seven Elements of Strategic Fit," *Journal of Business Strategy,* Winter 1982, p. 70.

second category includes errors which result from uncertainties that are inevitably associated with the process.

Errors Relating to the Use of Strategic Management

Many of the most commonly encountered errors relating to the manner in which strategic management is used have been discussed in the previous chapters of this book. The primary purpose here is to synthesize and highlight these potential errors.[10]

Inability to Think Strategically   The ability to think in strategic terms is the first requirement of successful strategic management. Unfortunately, a person who is a good operations manager is not necessarily a good strategic thinker. Benjamin Tregoe, a management consultant who specializes in problem solving and strategic planning, has identified certain barriers that tend to inhibit effective strategic thinking.[11]

Tregoe has come up with a list of "seven assumptions that kill strategic thinking":

1 My top team is a closely knit group.
2 Our team controls our organization.
3 If it's long-term, it's strategic.

EXHIBIT 11.4   DEFINITIONS OF THE McKINSEY 7-S VARIABLES

1. *Strategy.* A coherent set of actions aimed at gaining a sustainable advantage over competition, improving position vis-à-vis customers, or allocating resources.

2. *Structure.* The organization chart and accompanying baggage that show who reports to whom and how tasks are both divided up and integrated.

3. *Systems.* The processes and flows that show how an organization gets things done from day to day. (Information systems, capital budgeting systems, manufacturing processes, quality control systems, and performance measurement systems all would be good examples.)

4. *Style.* Tangible evidence of what management considers important by the way it collectively spends time and attention and uses symbolic behavior. It is not what management says is important; it is the way management behaves.

5. *Staff.* The people in an organization. Here it is very useful to think not about individual personalities but about corporate demographics.

6. *Shared values* (or superordinate goals). The values that go beyond, but might include, simple goal statements in determining corporate destiny. To fit the concept, these values must be shared by most people in an organization.

7. *Skills.* A derivative of the rest. Skills are those capabilities that are possessed by an organization as a whole as opposed to the people in it. (The concept of corporate skill as something different from the summation of the people in it seems difficult for many to grasp; however, some organizations that hire only the best and the brightest cannot get seemingly simple things done, while others perform extraordinary feats with ordinary people.)

Source: Robert H. Waterman, Jr., "The Seven Elements of Strategic Fit," *Journal of Business Strategy,* Winter 1982, p. 71.

4 Established corporate strategy means clear divisional or overall strategy.

5 Stable organizations do not need strategy.

6 Our long-range plans tell us where we're going.

7 Our top team is bright, talented, experienced; therefore, they've got what it takes to set strategy.[12]

The above assumptions may or may not apply in a given situation. Much of top management's time is spent on operating decisions which may be presumed to be strategies, but strategy may really be set implicitly by others inside or outside the corporation. As mentioned in previous chapters, the best time to think strategically is *before* a crisis comes. Adjustments should be ongoing. The long-range plan should result from strategy, not the reverse. And just because your managers are operationally sophisticated does not mean they are brilliant strategists.

Inappropriate Use of Management Levels   The most commonly encountered problems related to the use of management time include inadequate involvement of line managers and ineffective use of top management. There are at least two major reasons for involving line managers in the strategic management process: to evoke their commitment and to have access to the valuable information they can contribute. Ineffective use of time by top management means a large portion of its time is spent focusing on details instead of on major strategic issues.

Undue Emphasis on Form and Procedure A common tendency is to become so engrossed in the planning procedures that the means of the process become confused with the purpose of the process. This type of situation occurs when people engage in the strategic process "because they have to." It is always important to keep sight of the purpose of the process. A related problem occurs when excessive reporting requirements are demanded. It is not at all unusual for the reporting requirements to mushroom over the years. For example, one company reported that the amount of routinely reported information had increased by a factor of 10 over a period of 7 years.[13] A good practice is to review each reporting requirement annually to determine whether it is still necessary.

Isolation from the Environment Keeping up with environmental changes is obviously critical to any strategic management program. The key point here is to foster an open attitude and to monitor the environment continually for any changes that might affect the organization. The following quote emphasizes the importance of environmental scanning:

> Each planning cycle requires a fresh and global look at the business, economic, regulatory, social-political, and technological environment. Without this look, management is likely to be surprised and embarrassed.[14]

There is often a tendency to view the future as merely an extrapolation from the past: "If it worked in the past, it will work in the future." Unfortunately, numerous examples exist of companies and even industries that have gone by the wayside by subscribing to this philosophy. Example 11.2 describes one such situation.

Too Much Emphasis on the Near Term As discussed in Chapter 1, strategic management is the set of managerial decisions and actions that determine the long-run direction and performance of the organization. Thus, by definition, strategic management is concerned with the long term. Emphasis on the short term often results from certain pressures applied by various groups of stakeholders. For example, investors, lenders, and stock analysts are often interested in short-term results even at the expense of the long term. Top management sets the tone and should stress the importance of long-term orientation.

Improper Use of Planning Resources Once the decision has been made to commit resources to planning, it is critical that these resources be effectively used. All too many managers have the misconception that the allocation of resources is all that is required for success. Potential misuses of resources include an inappropriately sized planning staff, unclear focus on the planning effort, and an uncoordinated planning effort.

Less Predictable Changes

Certain pitfalls are inherent in the strategic management process and are often difficult to avoid. Most problems which fall into this category stem from hard-

EXAMPLE 11.2

The Underwood Typewriter Ceases to Exist

In 1896, John Thomas Underwood launched the Underwood Corporation with his fantastic typewriter. The Underwood machine was the marvel of its time, and perhaps millions of students and office personnel became attached to that machine. Underwood ensured his own success by seeing that his typewriter was used in U.S. high schools. In that way, the name Underwood became synonymous with the typewriter. But by the end of World War II, the success was beginning to pale. The Underwood Corporation failed to diversify and keep up with the demand for new and better office products. Olivetti bought 34 percent of the company in 1956 when Underwood had been in the red for 3 years. Between 1956 and 1963 the company lost $80 million. The company's net worth was negative $8,681,000 by the end of 1963. In 1971, the name Underwood and the Underwood typewriter ceased to exist, a victim of the failure to keep up with the changing trends in the "office of the future."

Source: Adapted from "What Happened to Underwood," *Fortune,* May 1971, p. 267.

to-predict changes in the external environment. The solution is to develop early warning signals and then to respond quickly. Some of the most frequently encountered problem sources are discussed in the following paragraphs. Naturally, some of these are more applicable to certain industries than to others.

Innovations—New Products or Services It is extremely difficult, if not impossible, to predict when a competitor or someone else might introduce a new product or service. At the same time, the introduction of a new product or service can completely revolutionize an industry. For example, consider the impact of the electronic hand-held calculator on the mechanical slide rule industry. Similarly, consider the impact of the inexpensive digital watch on the watch industry (see Example 11.3).

Government Regulations Although changes in local, state, or federal laws are not always predictable, they rarely come as a total surprise. The decision of the federal government in 1969 to ban cyclamates had an adverse impact on many companies which had not anticipated the change (see Example 11.4). In 1977, the government of India asked Coca-Cola to turn over its recipe and secret ingredient 7X; the decision resulted in Coke's leaving India by the end of the year and forbidding imports from neighboring Nepal.

Weather Lengthy periods of rain, extreme temperatures, and severe storms can affect a variety of industries. Among those directly affected by weather are industries in all areas of agriculture, construction, and transportation.

EXAMPLE 11.3

The Revolution in the Watch Industry

The digital watch didn't seem to have much of a future when it hit the market at a stiff $2000 in the early seventies. Within a little over 5 years you could purchase a digital watch with a liquid crystal display for a mere $10! By 1975, when Texas Instruments introduced its $20 model, the market had been taken away from the traditional Swiss-movement watch. Gruen Industries, Inc., a 100-year-old traditional manufacturer of fine watches, was forced to file for bankruptcy. Many fledgling manufacturers of digital watches did not survive the vicious price-cutting which resulted from the economies of scale of mass production. Initial production costs were reduced by 60 percent as volume increased. The seasonality of the watch industry, which had sold 45 percent of all items during the fourth quarter, changed to a more even distribution. By 1976, 18 million digital watches were sold, about 5 times the 1975 volume. Because of the efficient production of the components by semiconductor producers, which made both high volume and low cost a reality, the digital watch had captured 40 percent of the market from traditional watches by 1978—instead of the more conservative estimate of 1985! The watch business has never been the same.

Source: Adapted from "A Digital Watch for the Mass Market," *Business Week,* December 18, 1974, p. 38; "The Great Digital Watch Shakeout," *Business Week,* May 2, 1977, p. 78; and "This Electronic Watch Has Hands," *Business World,* July 31, 1978, pp. 37–38.

Shortages in Raw Materials While many raw-material shortages are predictable, to some extent some are not. For example, at least twice in the past 10 years, the construction industry has been faced with a shortage of gypsum board (Sheetrock). The inability to get a needed raw material obviously can disrupt production and may result in the loss of customers.

Consumer Preferences Consumers are often fickle and their resulting preferences unpredictable. From year to year certain styles seem to come and go in ways that are sometimes impossible to forecast. For example, who could have predicted the Rubik's Cube craze of a few years ago? Another example was the widespread popularity of the citizens band (CB) radio in the late 1970s.

New Competitors or Changes in a Competitor's Abilities It is not uncommon for a major company to enter new fields and create viable competition almost overnight. In addition to introducing new products and services (discussed above), existing competitors may merge or acquire other companies and gain new capabilities. The acquisition of Miller Brewing Company by Philip Morris provided Miller with the financial support necessary to wage a major advertising campaign and make Miller a much more viable competitor.

EXAMPLE 11.4

Federal Ban on Cyclamates Causes Shakeup in Diet Industry

When the FDA announced the banning of cyclamates, the largest producer, Abbott Laboratories, took a beating on Wall Street. Another company especially hard hit was Royal Crown because 25 percent of its sales were in the diet cola market. Fruit canners like Del Monte were left with a season's canned fruits that could not be sold between October and January 1, 1970, deadline for getting the products off the shelves. Taken by surprise, the fledgling low-calorie industry, which had been growing at the rate of 10 percent each year, was at first abandoned by some producers. Others, like Coca-Cola, returned to the use of sugar combined with saccharin in February 1970. Because of an almost unknown 1958 amendment to the Pure Food and Drug Act, which required the removal from public sale of cancer-causing food additives and the incidence of bladder tumors in laboratory rats exposed to cyclamates, a whole industry had to retrench.

Source: Adapted from "Diet Industry Has Hungry Look," *Business Week,* October 25, 1969, pp. 41–42; and "Slim with Sugar," *The Economist,* November 1, 1969, p. 47.

Coca-Cola's entry into and departure from the wine industry is another example of a situation in which the competition changed in a very short period of time. When Coke first entered the wine business by purchasing Taylor Wine in 1976, Taylor ranked sixth in the industry in total sales. When Coke sold its Wine Spectrum (which included Taylor and several other acquisitions) in 1983, Taylor ranked second in total sales in the industry.

SUMMARY

Strategic control is concerned with tracking a strategy once it has been implemented, detecting any problem areas or potential problem areas, and making any necessary adjustments. The first step in setting up strategic controls is to identify those parts of the strategy that are most likely to vary from the plan or forecast. Once the variables to be watched have been identified, early warning signals should be developed for each of the variables. Financial data such as profit, sales, return on investment, and cost figures are some of the most commonly used early warning signals. In addition to financial figures, there are many other early warning signals that can be used. These include measures of productivity, measures of quality, personnel-related measures, and feedback from customers.

Strategy evaluation "is an attempt to look beyond the obvious facts regarding the short-term health of a business and appraise instead those more fundamental factors and trends that govern success in the chosen field of endeavor."[15] Four criteria were presented to evaluate overall strategy: (1)

consistency, (2) consonance, (3) advantage, and (4) feasibility. McKinsey's 7-S Framework views culture as a function of seven variables: strategy, structure, systems, style, staff, skills, and shared values. Many of the errors encountered in the strategic management process are avoidable and result from an inability to understand the process. These errors include (1) inability to think strategically, (2) inappropriate use of management levels, (3) undue emphasis on form and procedure, (4) isolation from the environment, (5) too much emphasis on the near term, and (6) improper use of planning resources. Certain pitfalls are inherent in the strategic management process and are often difficult to avoid. These pitfalls include (1) innovations—new products or services, (2) government regulations, (3) weather, (4) shortages in raw materials, (5) consumer preferences, and (6) new competitors or changes in a competitor's abilities.

CHAPTER 11   REVIEW QUESTIONS

1 What is the purpose of strategic control? Where does it fit in the strategic management process?
2 Describe the steps used in setting up a strategic control system. Be specific about the variables that should be monitored, and explain why they should be monitored.
3 Define "budget." List several types of budgets in use in a strategic control system. How is a budget used in a good strategic control system?
4 Many nonfinancial controls are important in an efficient strategic control system. What are some of those, and how would you use them effectively?
5 List and explain the four criteria Richard Rumelt uses to evaluate strategy. What is strategic evaluation?
6 Why is it more difficult to evaluate a strategy's feasibility in terms of human skills? Is this a necessary part of strategic control?
7 Describe the McKinsey 7-S Framework. How is it used to evaluate strategy?
8 Benjamin Tregoe has listed "seven assumptions that kill strategic thinking." Use your knowledge of the strategic management process to show how these assumptions might adversely affect top management's thinking.
9 What kinds of pitfalls might result because of unexpected changes in the strategic management process?
10 Why is it important to constantly monitor strategic decisions and their implementation and control?

CHAPTER 11   DISCUSSION QUESTIONS

1 Why types of strategic controls would be appropriate for a bank moving into regional banking, a steel manufacturer attempting a turnaround, a retail clothing store adding a women's line to its current men's line? What would these controls have in common?
2 Some people might argue that the price of an organization's stock is the best single evaluation of its strategy. What could you say to refute this argument? To support it?
3 Do you agree with Robert Waterman's contention that the challenge is to find a good *and* doable strategy? Use your knowledge of the strategic management process in your answer.

CHAPTER 11 REFERENCES

1 W. H. Newman and J. D. Logan, *Strategy, Policy, and Central Management,* South-Western, Cincinnati, 1976, pp. 505–506.

2 Parts of this paragraph are drawn from Georg Schreyogg and Horst Steinmann, "Strategic Control: A New Perspective," *Academy of Management Review,* January 1987, pp. 91–103.

3 Newman and Logan, loc. cit.

4 Wickham Skinner, "The Productivity Paradox," *Harvard Business Review,* July–August 1986, pp. 55–59.

5 Much of this section is drawn from Richard Rumelt, "The Evaluation of Business Strategy," in William F. Glueck, ed., *Business Policy and Strategic Management,* 3d ed., McGraw-Hill, New York, 1980, p. 359.

6 Ibid., p. 364.

7 Ibid., p. 369.

8 Robert H. Waterman, Jr., "The Seven Elements of Strategic Fit," *Journal of Business Strategy,* Winter 1982, pp. 69–73.

9 Ibid., p. 69.

10 Parts of this list are adapted from the following sources: Graham J. Sharman, "New Life for Formal Planning Systems," *Journal of Business Strategy,* Spring 1982, pp. 100–105; Alex R. Oliver and Joseph R. Garber, "Implementing Strategic Planning: Ten Sure Fire Ways to Do It Wrong," *Business Horizons,* March–April 1983, pp. 49–51; and Robert Lamb, "Is the Attack on Strategy Valid?" *Journal of Business Strategy,* Spring 1983, pp. 68–69.

11 Benjamin Tregoe, "Seven Assumptions that Kill Strategic Thinking," *Chief Executive,* Autumn–Winter 1981.

12 Ibid.

13 Sharman, op. cit., p. 101.

14 Oliver and Garber, op. cit., p. 51.

15 Rumelt, op. cit., p. 364.

12

INTERNATIONAL STRATEGY AND GLOBAL STRATEGIES

LEARNING OBJECTIVES

After studying this chapter, the reader should be able to:

1 Explain the reasons for the changing international environment
2 Define and describe multidomestic and global industries
3 Discuss the use of portfolio planning in international strategy formulation
4 Describe international strategy alternatives
5 Describe stages of market development and alternatives for entering a new country
6 Discuss difficulties of configuring and coordinating international activities

CHAPTER OUTLINE

THE CHANGING INTERNATIONAL ENVIRONMENT: A HISTORICAL PERSPECTIVE

THE INTERNATIONAL ENVIRONMENT: RECENT TRENDS
    Slowing Economic Growth
    Diffusion of Innovation
    Protectionism

MULTIDOMESTIC VS. GLOBAL INDUSTRIES

FORMULATING INTERNATIONAL STRATEGY
    Portfolio Planning

Since the 1970s, international trade and investment have exploded. That is not to say that international business is strictly a twentieth-century phenomenon. Products ranging from textiles and home furnishings to spices and wines have been traded across national borders for hundreds of years. However, during the latter half of the twentieth century the internationalization of markets has become more widespread, with virtually all major corporations involved in some way with markets outside their home country.

This growing trend toward international expansion has presented opportunities for some companies and substantial threats for others. Whether an opportunity or a threat, the increasing internationalization of markets is a strategic factor of such magnitude that it deserves a chapter of its own.

THE CHANGING INTERNATIONAL ENVIRONMENT —A HISTORICAL PERSPECTIVE

Why have industries become more international? There are several contributing factors.[1] First, barriers of distribution between countries have been reduced substantially by technological improvements in transportation and communication. Within the last 100 years, transatlantic communications and travel have gone from being measured in weeks and months to seconds and hours.

Second, the world demand for products has changed significantly. As recently as the 1950s and 1960s, the United States provided most of the demand for a large variety of products including automobiles, appliances, and some consumer electronics. Increasing industrialization of the rest of the world has resulted in the United States accounting for a much smaller component of world demand.

Third, institutional barriers to international trade (for example, tariffs and quotas) have declined since World War II. Formation of trade groups such as the European Community and development of the General Agreement on Tariffs and Trade (GATT) have worked to lower national barriers to trade.

Fourth, technological advances in product and process development have helped to internationalize markets. The high costs of technological advances have forced many companies to look to international markets as a way of achieving the economies of scale necessary to pay off large research and development investments.

Finally, international competition has increased and improved in quality in recent decades and has caused dramatic shake-ups in some industries. In the early 1960s, the United States produced nearly 90 percent of the color televisions made in the world. Today, Japan supplies over 50 percent of the world demand for TV sets. In 1964, the United States accounted for 23 percent of world machine tool exports and imported only 4 percent of domestic demand. Today 47 percent of domestic demand is imported, and the United States share of world exports is down to 4 percent.[2] In industry after industry, international competitors have forced a rethinking of competition in global terms.

THE INTERNATIONAL ENVIRONMENT: RECENT TRENDS

In recent years the rules of international competition have been changing significantly. Three trends are having a dramatic impact on the intensity of competition among rival nations and on the strategies they can employ when competing with each other. The three trends are (1) slowing economic growth; (2) the rapid diffusion of product, market, and technological innovation; and (3) increasingly protectionist tendencies in the United States.

Slowing Economic Growth

Generally, the decision to extend an organization's operations to other countries has two objectives: profit and stability. In terms of profit, international operations give organizations the chance to meet the increasing demand for goods and services in foreign countries. In addition, new sources of demand found in other countries may have a stabilizing effect on the organization's production processes and provide for improved economies of scale.

Ever since the oil crisis of the early 1970s, many industries have been faced with slow or negative growth and very intense competition in their home markets. As mentioned in Chapter 3, growth is ingrained in most managers as the path to success. In order to find that growth in today's economy, managers are looking outside of their traditional market areas toward international markets. The interest in international markets is no longer the casual interest that it once was. Now many businesses realize they must succeed in foreign markets if they are to survive. Exhibit 12.1 shows the 20 largest multinational corporations in the United States.

Diffusion of Innovation

The trading of goods and services across national boundaries results from the principle of comparative advantage. A country has a comparative advantage when it can produce goods and services more efficiently or cheaply than other

EXHIBIT 12.1   TWENTY LARGEST U.S. MULTINATIONAL CORPORATIONS

1986 rank	Company	Foreign revenue (millions)	Total revenue (millions)	Foreign revenue as % of total
1	Exxon	$50,337	$ 69,888	72.0%
2	Mobil	27,388*	46,025*	59.5
3	IBM	25,888	51,250	50.5
4	Ford Motor	19,926	62,716	31.8
5	General Motors	19,837	102,814	19.3
6	Texaco	15,494	31,613	49.0
7	Citicorp	10,940	23,496	46.6
8	El du Pont de Nemours	9,955†	26,907	37.0
9	Dow Chemical	5,948	11,113	53.5
10	Chevron	5,605	24,352	23.0
11	BankAmerica	4,659	12,483	37.3
12	Philip Morris	4,573	20,681	22.1
13	Procter & Gamble	4,490	15,439	29.1
14	RJR Nabisco	4,488	15,978	28.1
15	Chase Manhattan	4,356	9,460	46.0
16	ITT‡	4,180	17,437	24.0
17	Eastman Kodak	4,152	11,550	35.9
18	Coca-Cola	4,019	8,669	46.4
19	Xerox‡	3,996*	13,046*	30.6
20	Amoco	3,931*	18,478*	21.3

*Includes other income.
†Includes excise taxes.
‡Includes proportionate interest in unconsolidated subsidiaries and affiliates.
Source: "The 100 Largest U.S. Multinationals," *Forbes,* July 27, 1987, p. 152.

countries. Factors determining a country's comparative advantage have traditionally included the presence of natural resources, adequate quality and quantity of labor and capital, available technology, and the costs of these resources.

In recent years these traditional sources of comparative advantage have taken on less importance. New manufacturing and service technologies have made direct labor costs a smaller part of total product and service costs. These and other technological and marketing advances are then rapidly diffused to other countries so that any comparative advantage is short-lived. Example 12.1 describes how the Sony Corporation has suffered from rapid diffusion of its product innovations to competitors.

Protectionism

Tariffs are government-imposed taxes charged on goods imported into, or exported from, a country. A quota establishes the maximum quantity of a good that can be imported or exported during a given time period. Tariffs and quotas are generally thought of as barriers to free trade. Following World War II,

---

EXAMPLE 12.1

Sony Loses Its Advantage to Strong Competition

Competition in consumer electronics is always intense and frequently cutthroat. For many years the Sony Corporation seemed to emerge from the battles as one of the industry's superstars. Sony was the developer of such high-quality, innovative products as Trinitron TVs and Walkman tape players. After those products were introduced, it took about 2 years for competitors to come out with comparable products. Sony's reputation for quality was so superior to its competitors that they were able to use the phrase "It's a Sony" as the center of a very successful advertising campaign.

In recent years, Sony has watched its sales slip and its profits plummet. Although the high yen has been part of the problem, Sony has suffered because its competitors have narrowed or eliminated Sony's advantage in many areas. American competitors have dramatically improved the quality of their products and now respond to Sony's new products in months rather than years. To worsen problems, the South Koreans are increasingly able to take advantage of their low costs and undercut Sony in many markets.

Source: Larry Armstrong, "Sony's Challenge," *Business Week*, June 1, 1987, pp. 64–69.

---

many of these barriers to free trade were brought down. However, in recent years a new spirit of protectionism has emerged in the United States. Industries that are particularly threatened by foreign imports are calling for quotas, high tariffs, and (in some cases) requirements for local ownership of companies. Steel, textile, shoe, semiconductor, and automobile manufacturers have all lobbied for protection from foreign competition.

The major reason for the growing spirit of protectionism is the increasing foreign trade deficit in the United States. The trade deficit exceeded $160 billion in 1986, which means the value of goods and services purchased by American consumers from foreign companies exceeded by $160 billion the value of goods and services sold by American companies to foreign consumers. The trend has been particularly startling in electronics. In the United States, the total balance of trade in electronics shifted from a surplus of $7 billion in 1980 to a deficit of almost $7 billion in 1984. In the same 4 years, imports rose and exports fell in computing equipment, instruments, communications equipment, semiconductors, office machines, and consumer electronics.[3]

Although arguments for protectionism frequently claim unfair trade practices on the part of the foreign companies, the problem frequently relates to the inability of companies in the United States to acknowledge the inevitable internationalization of their markets. Example 12.2 describes how even the banking industry is an international industry.

EXAMPLE 12.2

The Japanese Banking Industry in Middle America

According to *Business Week,* "America is running on Japanese money." Involvement of the Japanese in the American banking industry has increased dramatically in just a few years. In 1981, the Japanese purchased less than $5 billion worth of U.S. government and corporate bonds and made about $80 billion in loans.

In 1986, Japan's banks and securities houses bought $55 billion in bonds from the U.S. Treasury and $10 billion in bonds from corporations in the United States. About $200 billion in loans and bond purchases were provided by Japanese banks to state and city governments and to businesses. Now the Japanese are pursuing the "middle market" of financing—loans to companies with sales in the $50 million–$150 million range.

Source: Adapted from William Glasgall and James Treece, "Japanese Capital Finds a Home in Middle America," *Business Week,* July 14, 1986, pp. 52–53.

MULTIDOMESTIC VS. GLOBAL INDUSTRIES

According to Michael Porter, the proper unit of analysis when deciding international strategy is the industry group—because it is within that industry group that competitive advantage is won or lost.[4] The patterns of international competition—and, therefore, the strategy-making environment—differ according to the characteristics of the industry group.

A *multidomestic industry* is one that is represented in more than one country. However, competition within any one country is independent of that in other countries. Factors of competition tend to occur on a country-by-country basis, and the company's operations within a country tend to be highly autonomous. An example of a company involved in a multidomestic industry is Toys 'R' Us, the giant toy retailers. Each year Toys 'R' Us opens toy stores in several foreign countries. Except for questions of the availability of funds, the decision to enter Germany is independent of a decision to build a new store in Singapore. Other examples of multidomestic industries are all forms of retailing as well as insurance and consumer finance.

At the other end of the spectrum are *global industries*. Porter defines a global industry as "an industry in which a firm's competitive position in one country is significantly affected by its position in other countries."[5] In these industries, markets are world markets and competitors may come from any nation. Examples of global industries are the semiconductor, television set, and automobile industries. The relative positions of the United States, Japan, Western Europe, and USSR in a few of the high-technology global industries are shown in Exhibit 12.2.

EXHIBIT 12.2 HOW THE UNITED STATES RANKS IN THE APPLICATION OF HIGH TECHNOLOGY

	United States	Japan	W. Europe	USSR
Biotechnology	8.9	5.7	4.9	1.8
New materials	7.7	6.3	6.0	3.8
Optoelectronics	7.8	9.5	5.7	3.6

Note: The above rankings were developed as the average of 10 rankings from industry experts in each area.
Source: Gene Bylinsky, "The High Tech Race: Who's Ahead?" *Fortune,* October 13, 1986, pp. 26–37.

FORMULATING INTERNATIONAL STRATEGY

The distinction between multidomestic and global industries has important implications for the formulation of international strategy. Since participation in a multidomestic industry involves managing several businesses that are independent, the principles of corporate portfolio planning can be applied effectively. The industries in different countries can be thought of as similar to independent strategic business units (SBUs), with the focus of the planning effort on the allocation of resources among countries.

Portfolio Planning

The portfolio planning matrices discussed in Chapter 8 are very useful for visualizing the dimensions of the separate SBUs or countries. Exhibit 12.3 shows a growth-share matrix developed by the Norton Company as a way of analyzing its portfolio of international SBUs. The circles represent a country, and the size of the circle is proportional to Norton's sales in that country. The vertical axis measures market growth rate, and the horizontal axis measures Norton's market share relative to the market share of major competitors (1.0 indicates equal market shares). As shown, all Norton's sales are in low- to moderate-growth countries.

Portfolio planning matrices may also be used to analyze problems that are unique to the international setting. Exhibit 12.4 shows a matrix developed with the dimensions of (1) political risk and (2) return on investment. Once again, a circle represents a country, and the size of the circle is proportional to sales in that country. The matrix allows managers to visualize whether the corporate portfolio is balancing profitability and risk in a way that is consistent with corporate philosophy.

Some of the issues that might be addressed during the corporate portfolio planning process are:

• Where are the high-growth countries?
• Should we enter a new country this year? If so, which one?
• Are we overcommitted in country X?
• Are we too involved in countries with high political risk?
• How much investment should we make in country Y this year? How will that decision impact funding for country Z?

EXHIBIT 12.3   GROWTH-SHARE MATRIX FOR NORTON COMPANY

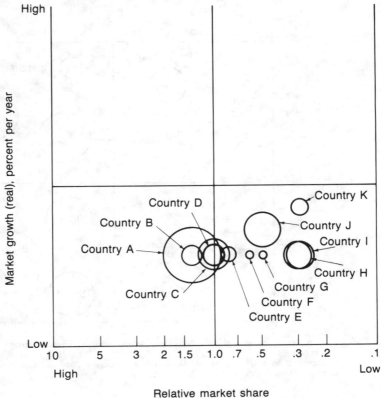

Note: Circles proportional to SBU company sales.
Source: R. Cushman, "Norton's Top-Down, Bottom-Up Planning Process," *Planning Review 7,* November 1979, p. 7. Published by Robert J. Allio & Associates, Inc., for the North American Society of Corporate Planning, copyright 1979.

Porter stresses that, in a global industry, managing activities using a portfolio approach will undermine the ability of the firm to gain a sustainable competitive advantage.[6] If the industry is truly global with a product or service sold in the world marketplace against international competition, all the activities of the firm that are related to that product and market are, in essence, operating as one SBU. Issues of allocation of resources among *independent* SBUs are not really relevant. A decision to enter, fund, or leave a country must be considered in light of the competitive situation throughout the world and the interaction among the company's investments in other countries.

EXHIBIT 12.4 POLITICAL RISK/PROFITABILITY PORTFOLIO

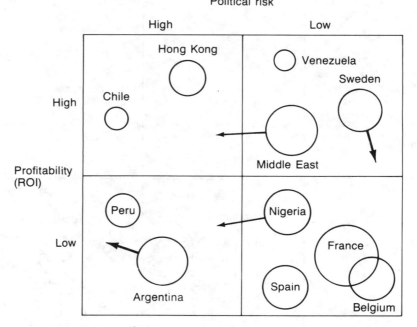

Note: Circles are proportional to SBU sales; arrows indicate projected change in SBU position in 5 years.

Source: James C. Leontiades, *Multinational Corporate Strategy*, Lexington Books, Lexington, Mass., 1985, p. 45.

Strategy Alternatives

Once management chooses to enter a new country, there are a number of generic strategy types that may be followed.[7] In very broad terms, a firm may choose to follow a skim, penetrate, dump, or explore strategy. The choice of strategy is dictated by the level of commitment the organization wants to make in the country.

Skim Strategy A skim strategy usually involves a low-risk exporting or licensing approach. The objective is to minimize investment of resources so that the rate of return is high.

Penetration Strategy A penetration strategy involves a long-term commitment to new national markets with large investments in local facilities and long-term relationships with local customers and suppliers. IBM has committed to a penetration strategy in its international efforts by building manufacturing facilities and establishing local sales groups in each of its overseas market areas.

Dump Strategy A dump strategy is used when a company wants to deal with problems of overcapacity. Excess production is sold in international markets at a low price as a way of stabilizing production and unloading costly inventories. Those companies that follow a dump strategy usually do so on a short-term basis and make little attempt to associate their company name with their efforts. Companies in the United States have followed a dump strategy in the past in areas such as household appliances, chemicals, and plastics. In recent years, the Japanese have been accused of dumping in the consumer electronics and semiconductor markets. The most important points to remember about this strategy are that it takes a very short-term view of the market opportunity in those countries where the dumping takes place. A dumping strategy may even be illegal if the price is below cost.

Explore Strategy An explore strategy involves making a limited investment in a country so that the company can acquire some experience and contacts. The objective of this strategy is to get a close look at the market to see if the company should make a larger commitment at a later time.

IMPLEMENTING INTERNATIONAL STRATEGY

Implementation of international strategy involves many decisions and actions that are unique to the international environment. One of the important implementation issues is how to go about entering a new national market. Should the entry involve a large or a small commitment of resources? Implementation also involves all the decisions required to structure or configure the existing multinational activities. Are manufacturing facilities located in each country or in one base country with distribution to other countries? Finally, implementation requires developing processes for the coordination of the myriad of activities that take place at the functional level.

Assessing the Stage of Market Development

Since countries vary widely in their level of economic development as well as tastes, a product that has been widely used for many years in one country may be a new product with limited distribution in another. As an aid in determining what some of the international implementation issues are in an industry, James Leòntiades has recommended that countries be classified according to the stage of market development for a particular product.[8] Using his procedure, each country is classified under one of five market development stages: premarket, less developed markets, take-off markets, early mass markets, and mature mass markets.

At each stage of market development there are several market characteristics that are typical. As shown in Exhibit 12.5, if a market is characterized as being in the "less developed" stage, the product will most likely be an imported, high-priced luxury item. If the product falls into the "early mass market" category, the product will probably fall into a low-price category, be

EXHIBIT 12.5   STAGES OF PRODUCT-MARKET DEVELOPMENT, WORLD AUTOMOBILE MARKETS

	Stages				
	I	**II**	**III**	**IV**	**V**
Variables	**Premarket**	**Less developed markets**	**Take-off markets**	**Early mass markets**	**Mature mass markets**
Product source	Occasional imports	Regular imports	Domestic assembly and partial manufacture imported parts	Domestic mass production	Domestic research design and mass production "new style"
Product Characteristics	Assorted types	Luxury products	Moderate-size product designed for local production and broad appeal	Utility product designed for new mass market infrequent design changes	Specialized products, frequent model change, wide range, many options
Price	No discernible trend	High-price category (low volume)	Moderate price	Low-price category (high volume)	Broad range of base prices directed at all market segments
Distribution	No company facilities	Single company appointed distributor	Multiple retail outlets serviced by local plant staff	Manufacturer sells to wholesale and retail outlets	Close coordination of factory and retail level electronic ordering
Service facilities	No company facilities	Low-volume personalized service by distributor	Local plants supply parts and training to outlets	Geared for high-volume low-cost service	Training and equipment for wide range of specialized products
Brand	Foreign brands	Foreign brands	Foreign brands produced domestically and identified with host country	Domestic brands	"Families" of domestic product brands tied in with single company brand
Advertising and promotion	None	Point of sale and personal contact	Wide use of printed mass media	Extensive use of all mass media (less emphasis on personal contact)	Research-directed use of all mass media; specialized campaigns for major market segments

Source: Adapted from James C. Leontiades, *Multinational Corporate Strategy*, Lexington Books, Lexington, Mass., 1985.

mass produced domestically, and be distributed through wholesalers and retailers. Although the market stages and the corresponding characteristics may be altered to fit the situation, use of such a matrix makes it easier to visualize the issues in pricing, distribution, advertising, promotion, and product sourcing.

Ways to Enter a New Country

There are several options available for entering a new country. *Exporting* to a new market has the advantage of low risk, yet it has the disadvantage of high transportation costs, difficulties in maintaining control, and (in some markets) high tariffs. One way to improve control is to establish *local sales branches* that sell the company's exports. Unfortunately, this alternative does not remove the problems of transportation costs and tariffs.

Another low-risk way of entering a market is to sell company technology through *licensing and franchising* agreements. This option gets around most problems of transportation costs, tariffs, and quotas but it may not provide adequate control.

A *joint venture* may be an attractive option if the company wants to make a strong commitment to a new national market but does not know the country well or does not have readily available capital. Joint ventures have become very common ways for companies in the United States to enter new markets. In fact, in the truly global industries, joint ventures are becoming increasingly common as a way for American companies to broaden their product lines and reduce production costs. The trend in the automotive industry is for joint ventures between American and Japanese automakers. Example 12.3 describes

---

EXAMPLE 12.3

American-Japanese Joint Ventures: Good or Bad?

American and Japanese companies:

General Motors–Toyota (automobiles)
Honeywell–NEC (computers)
IBM–Sanyo Seiki (robots)
General Electric–Matsushita (disc players)
Ford–Mazda (automobiles)
Boeing–Mitsubishi (airplanes)
Kodak–Canon (copiers)

According to some industry experts, joint ventures between the United States and Japan are very destructive to the United States. These ventures support an implicit Japanese strategy of keeping the better, high-paying jobs in Japan. More important, these ventures are structured so that the Japanese get manufacturing experience. It is through learning in manufacturing and incremental process improvements that sustainable competitive advantages are made. American companies participate to a limited degree in basic research and to a much greater degree in low-tech final assembly and marketing.

Proponents of the joint ventures argue that these "global strategic partnerships" are the only way for many companies to prosper in the future and that the ventures are just part of doing business in a global economy.

Source: Adapted from Robert B. Reich and Eric D. Mankin, "Joint Ventures with Japan Give Away Our Future," *Harvard Business Review*, March–April 1986, pp. 78–86.

some of the contradictory opinions about the value of American joint ventures with Japan.

All the above alternatives involve varying levels of commitment of production and marketing resources. The most serious commitment to a new national market involves *establishing local production and marketing facilities*. When compared with the other entry alternatives, this method offers improved control and avoids high transportation costs and tariff problems. However, it is riskier than the other alternatives because of the required organizational commitment and large capital investment.

The choice of an entry method should be consistent with the company's international strategy and the country's stage of market development. If the company wants to pursue a low-risk, low-commitment skim strategy, then exporting or licensing arrangements might be appropriate. An explore strategy might be implemented with local sales branches or a joint venture arrangement. A penetration strategy would most likely need an organizational commitment to local facilities.

Configuration of International Activities

A firm performs many and varied activities as it produces and sells its products or services. One of the major issues in implementing international strategy is how to structure or configure those activities in different places around the world. At one extreme, a company may perform an activity in one location and use it as a base from which to serve many other countries. At the other extreme, the company may choose to perform every activity in each country. The decision of how to configure activities is a function of the competitive strengths derived from decentralization versus centralization.

In general, a firm's activities can be divided into two groups: downstream activities and upstream activities. Downstream activities such as sales and service frequently must be physically close to the customer. In some cases, upstream activities such as purchasing, production, and research and development can benefit from being centrally located.

There are several industry characteristics that tend to support decentralization of activities. High transportation, storage, and communication costs can make it desirable to locate activities near the marketplace. In many industries, product needs differ from country to country. In those cases, manufacturing and product development may need to be located in or near the target country. This is particularly true of food products. For example, British-style bacon must be sold in Britain and North American Swiss chocolate recipes are not well received outside of North America. On the other hand, Coca-Cola does not modify its soft drink concentrates to suit various national tastes. Therefore, research and development (R&D) is not required for each market area.

There are several factors that favor centralization of activities. The most common is economies of scale. If a firm enjoys economies of scale in production, it may choose to centralize all production in order to pursue a low-cost strategy. Another factor that would encourage centralized activities is a comparative advantage in the country where the activity is performed. For example, many consumer appliance companies locate their production in low-wage areas such as Korea and Taiwan and then distribute and sell to the rest of the world.

One of the purest examples of an industry that benefits from a centralized configuration is the aircraft industry. Because of high development costs, worldwide sales are needed to make development efforts worthwhile. Also, there are significant learning-curve effects and economies of scale in production. Distribution costs are relatively low and sales are infrequent enough to not require a local sales force. For aircraft companies such as Boeing and McDonnell Douglas, it is very reasonable for all activities to be located in one area although their aircraft are sold worldwide.

Coordination of International Activities

An issue related to configuration is coordination. Coordination relates to how similar activities performed in different countries are coordinated with each other. For example, if an organization finds it necessary to maintain R&D in more than one country, how are R&D tasks allocated among locations? What is the extent of interaction among the R&D groups and how is it facilitated? Similar questions arise when production facilities are located in multiple countries. How are process technology advancements transferred? Should raw-material purchases be coordinated? If so, how? If marketing activities are located in many countries, brand names, prices, and distribution channels may need to be coordinated.

Developing and maintaining an international organization is usually very difficult. Many of the problems can be traced to the difficulty of maintaining a strong company culture in a multinational organization. Even in a small domestic organization, there is a tendency for functional areas to be in conflict with each other and for personal differences to get in the way of doing business. When these conflicts are reinforced and magnified by geography and differences in language and national background, the effects can work against organizational coordination and consistency.

To counter the tendency to become a collection of subcultures, many companies have developed special personnel programs for encouraging a wider organization view among employees. Some of the programs stress international career paths rather than the strictly national career paths that most people expect. Some companies use multinational training programs to reinforce company procedures and techniques. The informal contact among employees during the training sessions encourages a feeling of being part of one organization. Another way of encouraging the development of a common culture is to create linked information systems that keep managers and employees at even the most remote locations up to date on corporate activities. Example 12.4 describes the efforts of McDonald's Corporation to maintain a common culture among its multinational franchise owners.

VIEWING STRATEGIC MANAGEMENT AS AN OPPORTUNITY

Considerable space has been devoted in this book to extolling the merits of strategic management. Research studies have been cited and many real-life ex-

EXAMPLE 12.4

Spreading the McDonald's Culture

In recent years nearly 40 percent of all new McDonald's locations have been out-side the United States and one-fifth of the company's $11 billion in sales are from branches outside the United States. McDonald's has branches in 42 countries in-cluding France, Japan, West Germany, Singapore, Malaysia, and Mexico.

The biggest challenge that McDonald's faces in exporting its very successful way of doing business is in getting international franchise owners to enthusiasti-cally adopt the McDonald's operating strategy, including its culture and standard-ized procedures. So far, the company has met with considerable success. Ac-cording to the managing director of McDonald's Restaurants Singapore, "McDonald's sells only a system, not products," to its franchise owners. In or-der to encourage owners and operators to adhere to procedures, McDonald's sends each foreign operator to one of its four Hamburger Universities and sends company consultants around to different locations regularly. International own-ers are encouraged to visit each other to trade ideas and nurture a family feeling. The company even uses its selection procedure to reinforce its culture. Rather than looking for successful owners, McDonald's looks for "true believers" in the McDonald's system.

Source: Adapted from Madlyn Resener, Cheryl Debes, Graham Lloyd, and Rik Turner, "From Singapore to Sao Paulo, A Network of True Believers," *Business Week,* October 13, 1986, pp. 80–81.

amples have been presented to support this viewpoint. In spite of the available data and the worldwide attention that strategic management has enjoyed over the past decade, some chief executive officers and other managers maintain a negative view of strategic management. A major reason for this attitude is their lack of familiarity with the process. It is a well-established fact that managers tend to fear the unknown. Therefore, when the strategic management process is an unknown, it is naturally feared. The obvious solution to this problem is to educate managers concerning strategic management. Our goal has been to help readers understand strategic management better and, therefore, not to fear it but rather to view it as a genuine opportunity!

SUMMARY

In recent years the rules of international competition have changed. Intense, high-quality international competition has forced the rethinking of competition in domestic markets, and slowing economic growth has forced many companies in the United States to look outside the United States for new growth markets.

A multidomestic industry is one that is represented in more than one country. However, competition within any one country is independent of what is happening in other countries. Factors of competition tend to occur on a country-by-country basis, and the company's operations within a country tend to be highly autonomous. At the other end of the spectrum are global industries. In a global industry, a firm's competitive position in one country is significantly affected by its position in other countries. In these industries, markets are world markets and competitors may come from any nation.

The principles of corporate portfolio planning can be effectively applied in multidomestic industries. The efforts in different countries can be thought of as independent strategic business units. In global industries, a decision to enter, fund, or leave a country must be considered in light of the competitive situation throughout the world and the interaction among the company's investments in other countries.

Once management chooses to enter a new country, there are a number of strategy types that may be followed: skim, penetrate, dump, and explore. The choice of strategy is dictated by the level of commitment the organization wants to make in the country.

Implementation of international strategy involves many decisions and actions that are unique to the international environment. Important implementation issues are how to go about entering a new national market and how to structure or configure the existing multinational activities. Finally, implementation requires developing processes for the coordination of the myriad of activities that take place at the functional level.

CHAPTER 12 REVIEW QUESTIONS

1 Why has international competition become more intense in the last 25 years?
2 What is a multidomestic industry? A global industry?
3 Why are portfolio planning techniques appropriate for use in analyzing multidomestic industries but of limited usefulness in analyzing global industries?
4 What are the different strategies that may be followed when entering a new country?
5 There are several ways to enter a new country. What are the different ways and how do they differ?
6 What industry characteristics support a decentralized configuration of activities? A centralized configuration?
7 Why is the coordination of activities a particular problem for multinational companies? What role does corporate culture play?

CHAPTER 12 DISCUSSION QUESTIONS

1 Example 12.3 described some of the pros and cons of joint ventures between the United States and Japan. Do you think these joint ventures are throwing away America's future? Why or why not?
2 Think of some industries that are multidomestic. Do you think they will eventually become global? Why or why not?
3 Choose a corporation that has activities in many nations. Using company annual reports, 10-K reports, and periodicals, investigate how the company has configured its

organization. What procedures, if any, does the company use to encourage consistency and coordination?

CHAPTER 12 REFERENCES

1 James C. Leontiades, *Multinational Corporate Strategy,* Lexington Books, Lexington, Mass., 1985, p. 5.
2 Otis Port and J. W. Wilson, "Making Brawn Work with Brains," *Business Week,* April 20, 1987, pp. 56–60.
3 John W. Wilson, "America's High Tech Crisis," *Business Week,* March 11, 1985, pp. 58–59.
4 Michael E. Porter, "Changing Patterns of International Competition," *California Management Review,* Winter 1986, p. 11.
5 Ibid., p. 12.
6 Ibid., p. 12.
7 Leontiades, op. cit., p. 130.
8 Ibid., p. 78.

FINANCIAL ANALYSIS

Financial analysis is a comprehensive term that refers to any use of available financial data to evaluate the performance, condition, or future prospects of an organization. Many tools and techniques are available for examining an organization's performance. The most useful tools for managers are those which increase the understanding of the cause-and-effect relationships in the organization, those which identify trends, and those which allow comparisons with other organizations.

The primary sources of company financial data are the company's annual report and Form 10-K. *Form 10-K* is a financial report that is required by law to be filed annually with the Securities and Exchange Commission by all companies listed on the stock exchange. Most companies will provide a copy of their annual report upon request. Many college and public libraries maintain files of the annual reports and 10-K reports of various public companies. Industry composite data are available through a variety of sources, some of which are listed in Exhibit A.1.

Very few of the data in financial statements are significant when taken in isolation. The objective of financial analysis is to establish relationships between data items and to highlight changes and trends that may explain a company's past performance and give clues to its future performance. In general, financial analysis involves (1) converting data into ratios and percentages that indicate relationships and trends and (2) comparing the relationships and trends with standards of performance.

No one calculation gives sufficient information for evaluating the financial condition and performance of an organization. Reasonable judgments can be made only when groups of calculations are considered.

CALCULATION TECHNIQUES

Some of the most common techniques used in converting data to a useful form involve calculating (1) dollar amount and percentage changes and (2) ratios.

Dollar Amount and Percentage Changes

Dollar amount and percentage changes of particular items measure the degree of change from one year to another. Although dollar and percentage changes can be calculated for virtually every item in a financial statement, the more typical calculations include percentage changes in sales, income, current liabilities, and working capital. A sample calculation is shown in Exhibit A.2.

Working Capital Calculating the change in working capital is of particular importance when a company's financial position is being analyzed. The section of an organization's financial statement called "Sources and Application of Funds" gives information about the inflow and outflow of working capital during an accounting period. Working capital inflow is provided by net profit and depreciation. Cash is then used to pay dividends and other payables. The difference between inflows and outflows provides an increase or decrease in working capital. A growing, healthy company will usually experience growth in working capital from year to year. A trend of decreasing working capital often indicates future problems with the organization's ability to pay its debts.

EXHIBIT A.1 SOURCES OF INDUSTRY FINANCIAL DATA

- Dun & Bradstreet, *Dun's Review*
- Dun & Bradstreet, *Industry Norms and Key Business Ratios*
- Moody's Investment Service, *Quarterly Handbook*
- Robert Morris Associates, *Annual Statement Studies*
- Standard & Poor, *Standard and Poor's Industry Survey*
- Troy, Leo, *Almanac of Business and Industrial Financial Ratios*

EXHIBIT A.2 CALCULATION OF DOLLAR AND PERCENTAGE CHANGE IN SALES AND INCOME (IN $1000s)

	Year 3		Year 2		Year 1
Sales	200		150		100
Dollar change		50		50	
% change		$50 \div 150 = 33.3\%$		$50 \div 100 = 50.0\%$	
Income	25		18		10
Dollar change		7		8	
% change		$7 \div 18 = 38.9\%$		$8 \div 10 = 80.0\%$	

Ratios Ratios are of two general types: (1) common-size, or component percentage, ratios and (2) financial ratios.

Common-size ratios show the relationship between a particular financial figure and a significant total. When several figures are expressed as a percentage of the same total, the relative importance of each can be inferred. For example, each item on a balance sheet may be expressed as a percentage of total assets to show the relative importance of current and other assets and the relative levels of financing from creditors and stockholders. The calculations may be used to show a "snapshot" of the organization at a particular point in time, or calculations from more than one year may be compared to show trends. For example, research and development (R&D) expense may be expressed as a percentage of sales for several years as an indicator of organizational commitment to R&D.

Financial ratios state particular relationships from balance sheets and income statements, e.g., inventory to sales or debt to equity. The ratios are then used to analyze one firm's performance over time or to compare one firm to other similar firms or an industry composite. Although the number of ratios that may be computed from financial statements is large, there are certain ratios which are commonly used.

Financial ratios can be divided into four types: profitability, liquidity, debt, and activity ratios. Sample calculations for the hypothetical XYZ Company are made using data from Exhibits A.3 and A.4.

Profitability Ratios Profitability ratios indicate the firm's operational efficiency, or how well the firm is managed. Profits can be reported as a percentage of sales or as a percentage of investment.

Gross profit margin shows the profit of the firm relative to sales after the production cost of goods sold (COGS) is deducted:

$$\text{Gross profit margin} = \frac{\text{sales} - \text{cost of goods sold}}{\text{sales}} \times 100$$

For XYZ, the gross profit margin is:

$$\frac{\$5,980,000 - 3,340,000}{\$5,980,000} \times 100 = 44\%$$

EXHIBIT A.3   XYZ COMPANY BALANCE SHEET AS OF DECEMBER 31, 1983

	1983	1982
Assets		
Cash	$ 560,000	
Securities at cost	240,000	
Accounts receivable	845,000	
Inventory	1,340,000	$1,000,000
Total current assets	$2,985,000	
Fixed assets		
Land	$ 660,000	
Building	1,250,000	
Equipment	420,000	
Less: Depreciation	350,000	
Total fixed assets	$1,980,000	
Total assets	$4,965,000	
Liabilities		
Current liabilities		
Accounts payable	$ 730,000	
Notes payable	843,000	
Accrued taxes payable	210,000	
Accrued expenses payable	342,000	
Total current liabilities	$2,125,000	
Long-term liabilities	$1,560,000	
Stockholders' equity		
Common stock	$ 956,000	
Capital surplus	180,000	
Retained earnings	144,000	
Total stockholders' equity	$1,280,000	
Total liabilities, equity	$4,965,000	

EXHIBIT A.4   XYZ COMPANY INCOME STATEMENT FOR THE YEAR
ENDING DECEMBER 31, 1983

Net sales	$5,980,000*
Cost of goods sold	3,340,000
Depreciation	205,000
Administrative expenses	565,000
Operating profit	1,870,000
Less: Interest expense	675,000
Income before taxes	1,195,000
Less: Federal taxes	560,000
Net income	$ 635,000

*All sales are on credit.

A comparison of the gross margins of firms within an industry indicates how successfully each company has anticipated changes in the marketplace and how effective each company's marketing and pricing strategies have been.

The net profit margin is a more specific ratio of profitability than is the gross margin. Net margin shows efficiency after all expenses and income taxes have been considered:

$$\text{Net profit margin} = \frac{\text{net profit after taxes}}{\text{sales}} \times 100$$

For XYZ, this ratio is:

$$\frac{635,000}{5,980,000} \times 100 = 10.6\%$$

Net profit margin and gross profit margin are particularly useful when considered together. If gross margin falls over time, the cost of producing goods relative to sales has increased. However, if gross margin remains constant while net margin falls, the cause must be an increase in other expenses or taxes.

Profitability can also be reported in relation to investment. Return on assets (ROA) indicates the amount of assets needed to generate a dollar of income:

$$\text{ROA} = \frac{\text{net profit after taxes}}{\text{total assets}} \times 100$$

For XYZ Company, ROA is:

$$\frac{635,000}{4,965,000} \times 100 = 12.8\%$$

ROA is a useful measure when compared with industry averages, since it indicates how effectively assets are being utilized compared with similar firms.

Return on equity (ROE) reveals the rate of return on shareholders' book investment:

$$\text{ROE} = \frac{\text{net profit after taxes}}{\text{stockholders' equity}} \times 100$$

For XYZ, ROE is:

$$\frac{635,000}{1,280,000} \times 100 = 49.6\%$$

Because of the manner in which balance sheets are set up (total assets − total liabilities + equity), ROE will always be greater than ROA for any company which has a positive net worth. Different forms of this ratio are used to calculate the rate of return in terms of total common stock equity or return per share of common stock.

Liquidity Ratios Liquidity ratios are used to judge how well a business will be able to meet its short-term financial obligations. The current ratio shows the relationship between current assets and current liabilities and is an indicator of short-term cash solvency:

$$\text{Current ratio} = \frac{\text{current assets}}{\text{current liabilities}}$$

For XYZ, the current ratio is:

$$\frac{2,985,000}{2,125,000} = 1.4 \text{ times}$$

The rule of thumb is that a firm's current ratio should be 2 or more. A current ratio of less than 2 might indicate that the firm is having problems getting the cash needed to pay its debts. However, if the current ratio exceeds 2 by an amount greater than that of other firms in the same industry, the firm may be overly liquid. The 1.4 current ratio for the XYZ Company is an indicator that further investigation into the firm's liquidity is needed.

The current ratio is only a crude measure of liquidity because it does not consider the liquidity of the individual components of current assets. Inventories are the least liquid component of current assets because of the time that may be required to convert them to cash. Also, the value of inventories may reflect the accounting practices of the firm rather than the realizable value of the inventories when sold.

The quick, or acid test, ratio focuses on cash, marketable securities, and receivables in relation to current liabilities and is a somewhat more accurate indicator of liquidity:

$$\text{Quick ratio} = \frac{\text{current assets} - \text{inventories}}{\text{current liabilities}}$$

For XYZ Company, this ratio is:

$$\frac{2,985,000 - 1,340,000}{2,125,000} = .77 \text{ times}$$

The rule of thumb is that 1 or higher is a satisfactory quick ratio. Given the XYZ Company's quick ratio of .77, the company's ability to pay its short-term debts may indeed be in jeopardy unless it has a very short collection period.

Leverage, or Debt, Ratios Leverage ratios measure the magnitude of owners' and creditors' claims on the firm and indicate the firm's ability to meet long-term obligations.

The debt-to-equity ratio shows the relative commitment to creditors and owners:

$$\text{Debt-to-equity ratio} = \frac{\text{total liabilities}}{\text{stockholders' equity}} \times 100$$

For the XYZ Company, the debt-to-equity ratio is:

$$\frac{3,685,000}{1,280,000} \times 100 = 287.9\%$$

A high ratio would indicate that the firm is committed to a high level of loan repayments or that the equity has declined.

The ratio of total debt to total assets indicates the percentage of total funds which has been provided by creditors. This is important because creditors' claims must be paid before any profits can be taken out of the business by its owners.

$$\text{Total debt to total assets} = \frac{\text{total liabilities}}{\text{total assets}}$$

The debt-to-assets ratio for XYZ Company is:

$$\frac{3,685,000}{4,965,000} \times 100 = 74\%$$

Activity Ratios   Activity ratios are used to evaluate how effectively a firm is managing some of its basic operations.

Asset turnover is a rough measure of how well assets are being used to generate sales, although nothing is revealed about operating costs or the profitability of the sales. This ratio is particularly sensitive to the type of industry involved. Some firms in capital-intensive industries, such as most capital goods manufacturers, will have relatively low ratios because of hefty investment in assets. On the other hand, some retailers may be able to operate with relatively little inventory and, by leasing and renting, may have few assets of any kind. While their asset turnover would be high, their operating expenses and current liabilities would also be high.

$$\text{Asset turnover} = \frac{\text{sales}}{\text{total assets}}$$

For XYZ, the asset turnover ratio is:

$$\frac{5,980,000}{4,965,000} = 1.2 \text{ times}$$

Inventory turnover relates the cost of goods sold over the course of a year to the average inventory over the same period. This ratio shows how fast a firm moves its inventory. Although this figure varies widely by industry and even by type of merchandise, a comparison of firms with closely related lines can indicate serious problems or significant operating advantages.

$$\text{Inventory turnover} = \frac{\text{cost of goods sold}}{\text{average inventory}}$$

For XYZ, inventory turnover is:

$$\frac{3,340,000}{1,170,000} = 2.85 \text{ times}$$

Average collection period is a common calculation for showing the number of days required to collect receivables. If the collection period is longer than that of other similar firms or if it has lengthened over time, then credit policies or collection practices may be too lenient. However, it is possible that management made a decision to loosen credit policies in order to promote sales. In such a case, it would be appropriate to check sales figures and bad-debt expense.

$$\text{Average collection period} = \frac{\text{receivables} \times 365 \text{ days}}{\text{annual credit sales}}$$

For XYZ, the average collection period is:

$$\frac{845,000 \times 365}{5,980,000} = 51.6 \text{ days}$$

The collection period is close to 2 months for the XYZ Company. As indicated earlier, a very short receivables collection period would be needed to offset XYZ's relatively low liquidity. Together, the moderate collection period and the quick ratio of substantially less than 1 indicate serious problems with the company's ability to pay debt.

A modification of this collection period calculation is accounts receivable turnover.

$$\text{Accounts receivable turnover} = \frac{\text{annual credit sales}}{\text{receivables}}$$

Receivable turnover for XYZ is:

$$\frac{5,980,000}{845,000} = 7 \text{ times}$$

A high turnover, equivalent to a short collection period, is generally desirable, but it can indicate that credit policies are too strict and, as a result, that sales are being lost. Financial ratio calculations are summarized in Exhibit A.5.

Sustainable Growth Rate Calculations

Financial analysis provides information about the organization's need for cash to sustain a given growth rate. The cash flow reinvestment ratio compares the

EXHIBIT A.5   SUMMARY OF FINANCIAL RATIO CALCULATIONS

Ratio	Calculation	Purpose
Profitability ratios		
Gross profit margin	$\dfrac{\text{Sales} - \text{COGS}}{\text{Sales}} \times 100$	Indicates efficiency of operations and product pricing
Net profit margin	$\dfrac{\text{Net profit after tax}}{\text{Sales}} \times 100$	Indicates efficiency after all expenses are considered
Return on assets (ROA)	$\dfrac{\text{Net profit after tax}}{\text{Total assets}} \times 100$	Shows productivity of assets
Return on equity (ROE)	$\dfrac{\text{Net profit after tax}}{\text{Stockholders' equity}} \times 100$	Shows earnings power of equity
Liquidity ratios		
Current ratio	$\dfrac{\text{Current assets}}{\text{Current liabilities}}$	Shows short-run debt paying ability
Quick ratio	$\dfrac{\text{Current assets} - \text{inventories}}{\text{Current liabilities}}$	Shows short-term liquidity
Debt ratios		
Debt to equity	$\dfrac{\text{Total liabilities}}{\text{Stockholders' equity}}$	Indicates long-term liquidity
Total debt to total assets (debt ratio)	$\dfrac{\text{Total liabilities}}{\text{Total assets}}$	Shows percent of assets financed through borrowing
Activity ratios		
Asset turnover	$\dfrac{\text{Sales}}{\text{Total assets}}$	Shows efficiency of asset utilization
Inventory turnover	$\dfrac{\text{COGS}}{\text{Average inventory}}$	Shows management's ability to control investment in inventory
Average collection period	$\dfrac{\text{Receivables} \times 365 \text{ days}}{\text{Annual credit sales}}$	Shows effectiveness of collection and credit policies
Accounts receivable turnover	$\dfrac{\text{Annual credit sales}}{\text{Receivables}}$	Shows effectiveness of collection and credit policies

cash flow generated over a given time period with the cash flow needed to support the organization's growth solely by internal cash generation. The formula is:

$$R_{cf} = \frac{\text{after tax cash flow}}{\text{new investment needed to support additional sales}}$$

$$= \frac{\text{after tax cash flow}}{(\$ \text{ sales})(\text{annual growth rate})\left[\left(\dfrac{\text{working capital}}{\$ \text{ sales}}\right) + \left(\dfrac{\text{fixed assets}}{\$ \text{ sales}}\right)\right]}$$

When R_{cf} is greater than 1, excess cash is available; when $R_{cf} = 1$, the growth rate can be supported internally; and when it is more than 1, outside financing will be needed. Five-year averages are used for annual growth rate, working capital/$ sales, and fixed assets/$ sales.

COMPARISONS WITH STANDARDS OF PERFORMANCE

Once the financial calculations have been made, they must be compared with certain standards of performance for interpretation. The most common of these standards are (1) the historical performance of the organization and (2) the performance of other companies in the same industry. A thorough analysis would include an evaluation of performance against both sets of standards.

Historical Performance Comparisons

An organization is evaluated in light of its past performance in order to reveal underlying problems and trends that may impact the future performance of the organization. Information about sales and profit growth, gross margin fluctuations, changes in working capital, and increases and decreases in the funding of particular accounts indicates the financial health of the organization and provides clues to management's philosophy and future performance.

An evaluation of historical performance usually begins with an analysis of sales and profit growth. Analysis can involve looking at totals for several years, percentage changes between totals for any 2 years, or a calculation of the compound annual growth rate over a period of several years. Different common-size and financial ratios can also be compared for different years to show changes in profitability, liquidity, the structure of funding, and the internal control of activities.

Industry Comparisons

A comparison of an organization with other companies in the same industry also yields important information. What may seem like a poor increase in sales carries new implications in light of information that sales declined significantly for the industry as a whole. Likewise, a large investment in assets may yield a small return even in good years for some industry groups, while for others a minimal investment in assets might be required to realize the same dollar return.

POINTS TO REMEMBER

The following list summarizes some of the major points of the earlier sections of this appendix and is intended to help you guard against commonly encountered mistakes.

1 *Watch for trends.* The figures for any single year will probably reveal very little. Try to compare figures and ratios for at least a few years in order to detect any trends and to avoid being misled by one-time factors.

2 *Make comparisons with industry averages or similar firms.* For most purposes, it is totally unrealistic to compare figures of firms which are in different lines of business. Industry averages serve as a benchmark of what is typical in a particular industry. If industry averages are unavailable, use carefully selected firms that are similar in size and product line.

3 *Remember that, by definition, it takes two numbers to make a ratio.* A large ratio of net profit after taxes to equity may indicate either an unusually large numerator (profits) or an unusually small denominator (equity). The former case is desirable, but the latter suggests that the firm may be going bankrupt—or at least is carrying too much debt.

4 *Be alert for the reasons behind changes.* An apparently unfavorable figure may be explained by something that does not show up on a balance sheet or an income statement. For example, an increase in debt might be the result of expenses incurred in launching a new product. Read the company president's statement to the stockholders in the annual report for some of the reasons why particular things happen.

5 *Beware of differences in accounting methods.* Many of the individual items on an income statement or a balance sheet are subject to interpretation, depending on the accounting methods used by the firm. For example, there are many different methods for valuing inventory and determining depreciation expense.

6 *Use only audited statements.* Figures marked "preliminary" or "unaudited" may be adjusted after more complete information has become available or after an auditing firm has examined them.

CASES

APPLE COMPUTER, INC. (A)

Prepared by William E. Fulmer, Harvard University, and Russ LaGrone, University of Alabama.

In early 1983, Steven Jobs was reflecting on how much his life had changed in six years. Although he still liked to wear frayed jeans, suede boots, and a cowboy shirt and he still used a small office with only a steel desk and two chairs and had no reserved parking place, he was now chairman of the board of a company which had in 1982 broken into the *Fortune 500* with a 411 ranking and whose stock had a market value of over $1.7 billion.

In spite of his incredible success and wealth (personal worth in excess of $210 million), his life was much more complicated than it had been just a few years before. Although his company had broken the $100 million sales mark ($133.6 million) in the first fiscal quarter of 1982 and he had made good on his promise to give all 3,391 employees an extra week of vacation, he had little time to vacation himself. In fact, he had been able to take only a few days off in the last few years to go backpacking in Yosemite National Park. Except for some Japanese wood prints and a Maxfield Parrish painting, his unpretentious home was largely bare. *Time* described his home in Los Gatos as "nothing that would interest *Architectural Digest* : freshly laundered shirts lie on the floor of an unfurnished second bedroom, a love letter is magneted to the kitchen fridge, the master bedroom holds a dresser, a few framed photos (Einstein, Jobs with his buddy Governor Jerry Brown, a guru), a mattress, an Apple II."

In recent months, Apple Computer had been hit with a host of unexpected problems, ranging from counterfeit Apples to an antitrust suit to the likely resignation of its president. In addition, expected problems such as the effect of the recession on sales, increased competition (especially from IBM), and the introduction of Apple's new Lisa and MacIntosh models were serious concerns. The challenges facing Jobs were enough to keep any 28-year-old occupied.

THE PERSONAL COMPUTER[1]

The manufacture of the personal computer became possible with the development by Intel Corporation in 1971 of the microprocessor, a tiny electronic computer engraved on a silicon chip. Today it is used in an immense variety of smart machines, from microwave ovens to video games and sophisticated military weapons.

Soon after microprocessors became commercially available, electronic tinkerers in the back shops and garages in California's Silicon Valley and elsewhere began building crude personal computers. The early hand-soldered machines were inelegant, barely functional, and almost incomprehensible to anyone without a degree in electrical engineering.

By 1982 the typical personal computer consisted of a computer with a standard typewriter keyboard, at least 32,000 (32K) bytes[2] of working memory, one floppy disk drive or computer-controlled tape drive, a video monitor, and an inexpensive printer. However, peripheral products, such as color display screens, additional memory storage, and an immense variety of software, could turn even the most simple personal computer into a powerful machine. Most of the computers utilized an 8-bit[3] microprocessor, but many of the newer models used 16-bit microprocessors, and 32-bit machines were expected on the market soon.

The power of the new personal computers can be understood by comparing them to the mainframe computers of years past. The IBM 360 model 30 mainframe introduced in the early 1960s required special handling—an air-conditioned room about 18 feet square, which housed the central processing unit (CPU), the control console, a printer, and a desk for a keypunch operator. The CPU alone was 5 feet high and 6 feet wide and had to be water cooled to prevent overheating. The CPU of IBM's new desk-top Personal Computer (PC) was inscribed on a silicon chip smaller than a fingernail. The 360 model 30 could do 33,000 additions a second at full speed. The personal computer could do 700,000 a second. In 1960 dollars the model 30 had a cost of $280,000. The personal computer, fully equipped, retailed for $4,000 to $5,000.

INDUSTRY BACKGROUND

In 1981 approximately 500,000 personal computers were sold. For the first time over $1 billion of U.S. sales were achieved, with total worldwide sales eclipsing the $2 billion mark. Growth estimates for the market for the next five years ranged from 50 percent to 100 percent annually with estimates of total sales ranging anywhere from $4 billion to $15 billion by 1986.

By 1982 at least 150 firms were battling for position in the exploding market. Competitors included such companies as tiny Sinclair Electronics and giants of the business computer and electronics industries—IBM, Digital Equipment (DEC), and Hewlett-Packard (HP). The competition also included firms from Japan, Britain, and Italy (Exhibits C1.1 and C1.2). U.S. market share for 1980–82 was estimated by *Business Week* to be divided as shown in the following table:

EXHIBIT C1.1   PRODUCT COMPARISONS, 1981

Computer/ price range	Where to buy it	Primary applications	Advantages/ disadvantages
Apple II $1,330–$7,000	Computer stores	Home, schools, small business, professionals	Lots of software, but not enough power for some business uses
Apple III $4,240–$5,810	Computer stores	Professionals	Not much software
Atari 400 $399–$720	Computer, department, and electronics stores	Home	Low cost and excellent graphics, but keyboard difficult to use
Atari 800 $1,080–$2,000	Computer, department, and electronics stores	Home, schools, professionals	Excellent graphics, but cannot expand into a large system
Commodore VIC $299–$550	Computer and department stores	Home, schools	Low cost, but not much software
Commodore PET $995–$2,885	Computer stores	Home, schools	Not supported well in field
Commodore CBM $1,495–$4,000	Computer stores	Small business, professionals	Not supported well in field
Hewlett-Packard 85 $3,250–$6,000	Computer stores, direct sales	Scientific/technical, professionals	Special features for technical users, but small screen
IBM $1,565–$6,000	Computer stores, direct sales	Home, schools, small business, professionals	Good field support, but availability could be limited
Osborne Computer $1,795	Computer stores	Professionals	Portable, but small screen
Radio Shack Model 2 $3,000–$8,000	Radio Shack stores	Professionals, small business	Lots of software, but no color
Radio Shack Model 3 $699–$4,000	Radio Shack stores	Home, schools, small business, professionals	Low price, but no color
Texas Instruments 99/4 $525–$4,000	Department stores, catalogs	Home, schools	Low price, but limited software
Xerox 820 $3,195–$6,400	Computer stores, direct sales	Small business, professionals	Good support, but no color
Zenith Z89 $2,895–$9,000	Computer stores, Heath Electronic centers	Small business, professionals	Very reliable, but no color

Source: Business Week, Sept. 28, 1981, p. 80. Data from Datapro Research Corp., Future Computing, Inc., and Gnostic Concepts, Inc.

IBM Personal Computer

1. Computer	IBM Personal Computer	$1,268
2. Working memory	64K (with expansion modules)	415
3. Mass storage	160K/disk (with interface)	790
4. Video display	11½ inch B/W (with interface, 25 rows, 79 characters)	680
5. Printer	Dot matrix (with interface)	755
6. Operating system	IBM DOS	40
System total		$3,948

Software: Good selection available now, including VisiCalc and word processing, and IBM is working on developing an extensive selection.

Other comments: The IBM Personal Computer is a competitively priced unit backed by IBM's extensive service network. It is the only computer in this collection built around a 16-bit microprocessor, which allows it to process information with the speed of a minicomputer. It is available with color graphics plus the cost of a color TV monitor.

Osborne I

1. Computer	Osborne I	$1,795
2. Working memory	64K	Included
3. Mass storage	102K/disk	Included
4. Video display	5-inch B/W (24 rows, 52 characters)	Included
5. Printer	User supplied	500
6. Operating system	CP/M	Included
System total		$2,295

Software: An almost unlimited selection with CP/M operating system. The computer comes standard with software that if purchased separately would cost about $1,500.

Other comments: The Osborne I is a new portable computer that weighs about 24 pounds. Supply is limited with a four-to-six-month waiting time.

TRS-80 Model III

1. Computer	TRS-80 Model III	$2,495
2. Working memory	48K	Included
3. Mass storage	175K/disk	Included
4. Video display	12-inch B/W (16 rows, 80 characters)	Included
5. Printer	TRS Line Printer VII (dot matrix)	399
6. Operating system	TRSDOS	Included
System total		$2,894

Software: Like Apple, Radio Shack has developed extensive software for both models of the TRS-80, including VisiCalc.

Other comments: Radio Shack has the largest unit-volume market share in personal computers. The Model III's price-performance ratio is competitive with just about any personal business computer on the market, while the Model II is able to run more complex software packages.

Apple II Plus

1. Computer	Apple II Plus	$1,530
2. Working memory	48K	Included
3. Mass storage	143K/disk	645
4. Video display	12-inch B/W (24 rows, 40 characters)	320
5. Printer	Silentype (thermal)	395
6. Operating system	Apple DOS	Included
System total		$2,890

Software: While the Apple doesn't use the CP/M operating system, the company and independent publishers have developed extensive software for the Apple II Plus. VisiCalc, for instance, was first written for the Apple and is widely credited with pushing Apple Computer, Inc. into first place in dollar sales in the personal computer market.

Other comments: With 2,500 independent dealers around the world selling Apples, the machine is easy to get serviced. It is also expandable in ways its designers never dreamed of and can create good color graphics with the appropriate peripherals. (The Apple III system, which is slightly more expensive than $5,000, offers color graphics standard and is more powerful than the II Plus.)

Xerox 820-III

1. Computer	Model 820	$2,995
2. Working memory	64K	Included
3. Mass storage	81K/disk	Included
4. Video display	12-inch B/W (24 rows, 80 characters)	Included
5. Printer	User supplied	400
6. Operating system	CP/M-80	200
System total		$3,595

Software: An almost unlimited selection with CP/M operating system.

Other comments: The Model 820, a high-quality, low-priced machine, backed by Xerox's use of CP/M for the 820, in many ways made CP/M the de facto operating system for personal business computers.

NEC APC

1. Computer	PC 8012A with 8012A	$2,090
2. Working memory	64K	Included
3. Mass storage	160K/disk	1,295
4. Video display	12-inch B/W (25 rows, 80 characters)	285
5. Printer	High-speed dot matrix	795
6. Operating system	CP/M	150
System total		$4,615

Software: Almost unlimited selection with CP/M operating system.

Other comments: The NEC PC-8000 is a new system.

EXHIBIT C1.2 (*CONCLUDED*)

	1980	1982
Apple	27%	26%
IBM	—	17
Commodore	20	12
Nippon Electric	5	11
Radio Shack (Tandy)	21	10
Hewlett-Packard	9	7
Others	18	17

Source: Money, November 1982, pp. 102–115,
and *Inc.,* October 1981.

The growth of the personal computer market was not only hard to predict in total but especially difficult by segment (Exhibits C1.3 and C1.4). Although the upper-end segment, designed primarily for business application and typified by the Apple II and Apple III and IBM's PC, accounted for 90 percent of the total sales in 1981, both the home and portable segments were expected to realize tremendous growth over the next five years. The basic price of an upper-segment model was about $1,500 but additions of sophisticated peripherals frequently drove the price over $6,000. Sophistication in the upper end ranged as far as Xerox's $16,000 Star Work Stations, which featured a personal computer and an array of products tied together by a coaxial cable network.

The most significant development of 1981 in the upper-end market was the introduction of the IBM PC in August. Utilizing a 16-bit microprocessor, the IBM computer achieved third place in industry revenues within six months. Sales for the first year were

EXHIBIT C1.3

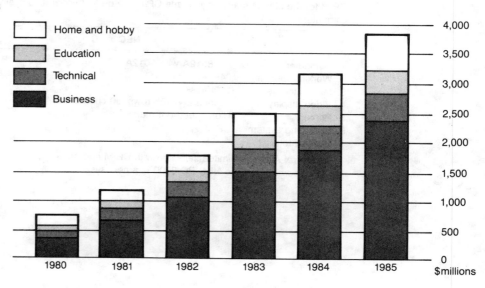

EXHIBIT C1.4   U.S. MARKET FOR PERSONAL COMPUTERS, 1981–1983

	1981	1982*	1983*
Home (less than $1,000):			
Sales (units)	235,000	1.05 million	2.05 million
Value of market	$165 million	$630 million	$1.13 billion
Leaders: Atari, Texas Instruments, and Commodore			
Professional (less than $3,000):			
Sales (units)	440,000	670,000	895,000
Values of market	$1.2 billion	$1.9 billion	$2.6 billion
Leaders: Apple, Radio Shack, IBM, Osborne, and Hewlett-Packard			
Small business (less than $10,000):			
Sales (units)	80,000	140,000	200,000
Value of market	$768 million	$1.3 billion	$1.8 billion
Leaders: Radio Shack, Apple, Vector Graphic, Cromemco, and Atlas			

*Estimates.
Source: Business Week, Oct. 25, 1982, p. 31.

150,000 units. This success prompted rumors that other IBM personal computer models would follow as early as 1983. Some industry analysts were predicting that the industry was "now in a market driven by IBM, not Apple." Even Apple executives conceded that their biggest rivals were "IBM, IBM, and IBM."

Although the home computer segment achieved sales of $120 million and 160,000 units in 1981, in 1982 all four of the segment's leaders—Atari, Tandy, Texas Instruments, and Commodore—were expected to exceed 160,000 units of sales, with total units reaching 2.2 million. Many industry experts predicted that by 1985 home computer sales alone would top the $3 billion mark, with such companies as Mattel and Coleco entering the market. The four leaders used a wide combination of price reductions, rebates, and dealer discounts to hold or increase their market shares. Tandy's price reductions lagged behind the other three, causing a serious erosion of market share.

A newer segment of the personal computer market was the portable computer, such as a hand-held or fold-up model. In 1981, 55,000 units were sold and estimates were that it would be a $1.25 billion industry by 1986. Models ranged from the $79.99 build-it-yourself portable up to a deluxe $8,150 model. The early star was the Osborne I ($1,795)—a complete system with disk memories, 2.6-inch by 3.6-inch video screen that displayed 24 lines, powerful enough to do word processing and accounting programs, and yet it could be folded up and placed under an airplane seat. Although a portable unit, the Osborne contained memory comparable to the Apple II. It took only 40 screws and 68 minutes to assemble. In 1982, approximately 130,000 Osborne units were sold.

A major problem facing the personal computer industry was how to reach the customer. Three basic approaches existed for a computer manufacturer to market its product—independent specialty chains, mass merchandisers, or the computer manufacturer's own sales force.

The specialty chains were the hottest segment of distribution. The first "mom and pop" stores opened in the mid-1970s and were primarily aimed at technicians and engineers. Little attention was given to developing skills of retailing. With the arrival of the fully assembled personal computers, requests poured in for standardized programs to fit the new computers. Many of the computer stores did not adjust to meet the new demands and, even though the market was expanding, many stores were only marginally profitable; in 1981 over 100 stores went out of business.

By the late 1970s the large specialty chains were a major force in the distribution system. In 1981 ComputerLand was the largest chain, with approximately 300 units, and was opening new stores at the rate of one a day. Each store averaged $1 million in sales. Its chief rivals included Compushop, Microage, and Computer Store. The strategy of the specialty chain was to carry a broad range of products from various manufacturers (at least four makers), price them competitively, and offer the expertise of store personnel to assist in training and in the utilization of the computers. Store owners estimated that customers needed four visits, totaling up to seven hours, before they bought.

Established mass retailers concentrated primarily on the low-priced compact machines that needed little explanation or support. Sears, J. C. Penney, and Montgomery Ward all had entered the personal computer distribution market by the early 1980s. In 1981 Sears took a broad step from long-standing policy by establishing five computer stores separate from its department stores. They stocked personal computers, copiers, word processors, and other products made by IBM, Hewlett-Packard, and Exxon. Most industry experts expected department stores ultimately to sell millions of computers, most likely for use in the home.

Discount stores such as Toys "R" Us and K-mart began to carry the Commodore home computer designed to compete with video games. Texas Instruments and Atari also tried to sell their wares through mass merchandisers.

Opening up mass merchandising channels was expected to allow other competitors to enter the personal computer competition. General Electric, RCA, and Zenith all reportedly had begun planning the introduction of a personal computer as part of a home entertainment system. AT&T had the freedom to enter the data processing field and could become a major force.

Japanese firms also would benefit from a larger distribution system. Early efforts to enter the American market by Nippon Electric, which held 40 percent of the $362 million Japanese personal computer market, and Sony were largely unsuccessful. Part of the failure was the result of a lack of understanding of the distribution system where many brands competed for shelf space in dealerships. A large system would make room for a renewed Japanese invasion. According to Mike Markkula, Apple's president, "The Japanese will continue to study what is required to succeed in the personal computer business and will invest heavily in doing these things. Over a five- to eight-year period, the Japanese will become one of the major factors in the marketplace."

Several of the established computer makers such as IBM, DEC, and Xerox used their sales force to aid in the introduction of a personal computer. The advantage of the established sales force was that it was well equipped to deal with corporations in making large batch sales. However, many independent dealers looked upon the sales forces as undermining their market.

Several manufacturers chose to establish their own stores. The success of Tandy's 6,000 Radio Shack electronic stores (with 641 computer departments) prompted such manufacturers as IBM, Xerox, and DEC to establish retail stores to sell business equipment. Some of the stores carried other manufacturers' equipment. Even Tandy had begun operating a chain devoted to computers (466 stores in 1982 and opening 12 each month) and had agreed to sell a line of home computers through independent distributors and retailers.

STEPHEN WOZNIAK

Stephen Wozniak, "Woz" to his friends, began learning about computers in the fourth grade when, with the help of his father, an electronics engineer at Lockheed Corporation's Missile and Space Company in Sunnyvale, California, he began designing logic circuits. By the eighth grade, he was building entire computers.

One of his best friends at Homestead High School in Los Altos was Steven Jobs. Pooling their talents, the two Steves built and sold so-called blue boxes, illegal electronic attachments for telephones that allowed users to make long-distance calls for free. *Time* reported that on one occasion Wozniak called the Vatican, pretending to be Henry Kissinger, and asked for Pope Paul VI. It was only after the Pontiff was summoned and a Bishop came on the line to act as translator that Vatican officials caught on to the ruse. Although he claimed never to have used the box to defraud AT&T, Woz acknowledged that he would "get on the phone all night long and try to figure out how to work my way through the labyrinth of the worldwide phone system."

After high school, Wozniak attended the University of Colorado where he became interested in minicomputers but then transferred to DeAnza College in Cupertino, where he came close to designing what he thought was the first low-cost hobby computer. After a year of designing software for a small West Coast firm, he enrolled at the University of California in Berkeley but then left in 1972 to take a design position with Hewlett-Packard in Palo Alto, California. In that job, he proposed a personal computer for HP but, according to an associate, "He couldn't get anybody to listen."

STEVEN JOBS

Time recounted Steven Jobs's background thusly:[4]

His parents, Paul and Clara Jobs, adopted Steven in February, 1955, and later moved from Mountain View on the peninsula south of San Francisco, to Los Altos after their son complained of rough times at the junior high school. "He came home one day from the seventh grade," Paul Jobs remembers, "and said if he had to go back to school there again he just wouldn't go. So we decided we'd better move."

Jobs made his way through Homestead High, recalls electronics teacher John McCollum, "as something of a loner. He always had a different way of looking at things." Solitude may, however, have bred ambition. McCollum was stunned to learn that the young loner, needing parts for class projects, picked up the phone and called Burroughs collect in Detroit and Bill Hewlett, co-founder of Hewlett-Packard, over in Palo Alto.

Hewlett wound up supplying Jobs with parts for a frequency counter, a device that measures the speed of electronic impulses. This introduced Jobs to the concept of timing, critical for understanding a computer, and furnished him with a cornerstone that, according to Wozniak, he never bothered to build on. Says Wozniak: "I doubt Steve was careful down to the last detail, which is really the key to high-level engineering." Shape, not subtlety, was more in Jobs's line, foreshadowing what one Apple manager calls the "technical ignorance he's not willing to admit." It was the practical applications of technology that excited Jobs, whether it was getting together with Wozniak to use "blue boxes" to make free long-distance calls or helping to design for the graduating class of '71 a mechanical sign that showed a huge hand making a time-honored gesture of rudeness.

Despite such spirited eruptions, Jobs was still uncertain, displaced, curious. He graduated, dropped acid for the first time ("All of a sudden the wheat field was playing Bach") and lived with his first serious girlfriend in a small wooden house along the Santa Cruz Mountains. As the summer ended, he headed for Reed College in Oregon. His father recalls what must have been a familiar litany: "He said if he didn't go there he didn't want to go anywhere." Jobs lasted only a semester but hung around the campus wandering the labyrinths of postadolescent mysticism and post-Woodstock culture. He tried pre-philosophy, meditation, the *I Ching,* LSD and the excellent vegetarian curries at the Hare Krishna house in Portland. He swore off meat about this time and took up vegetarianism "in my typically nutso way." One temporary result, say friends, was skin tinted by an excess of carotene to the color of an early sunset.

Cutting loose from Reed in 1974, Jobs journeyed back toward home and, answering a help-wanted ad in a local newspaper, landed a job at a video-game outfit called Atari, then in its second year of business. Jobs became the 40th employee of the small and idiosyncratic company founded by Nolan Bushnell and fueled by the success of Pong, the first of a long line of video recreations that turned simple games into eye-glazing national obsessions. Atari was a pretty loose place—staff brainstorming sessions were fueled with generous quantities of grass—but even there Jobs did not quite fit in. "His mind kept going a mile a minute," says Al Alcorn, Atari's chief engineer at the time. "The engineers in the lab didn't like him. They thought he was arrogant and brash. Finally, we made an agreement that he come to work late at night."

His Atari salary helped stake Jobs to a trip to India, where he met up with a Reed buddy, Don Kottke. "It was kind of an ascetic pilgrimage," says Kottke, "except we didn't know where we were going." Seeking spiritual solace and enlightenment with a shaved head and a backpack did not distract Jobs from stubbornly haggling over prices in the marketplace and dressing down a Hindu woman for apparently watering their milk. An erratic Siddhartha at best, Jobs came home in the fall of 1974 with more questions than answers. He tried primal therapy, went in search of his real parents and on a friend's farm bumped his head on one of the last vestiges of '60s idealism: communal living. "Once I spent a night sleeping under a table in the kitchen," Jobs says. "In the middle of the night everybody came in and ripped off each other's food."

Jobs turned from life science to applied technology. Wozniak and some other friends gravitated toward an outfit called the Homebrew Computer Club in 1975, and Jobs would occasionally drop by. Wozniak was the computer zealot, the kind of guy who can see a sonnet in a circuit. What Jobs saw was profit. At convocations of the Homebrew, Jobs showed scant interest in the fine points of design, but he was enthusiastic about selling the machines Wozniak was making.

"I was nowhere as good an engineer as Woz," Jobs freely admits. "He was always the better designer." No one in the neighborhood, however, could match Job's entrepreneurial flair and his instincts for the big score.

COMPANY BACKGROUND

During this period, Jobs and Wozniak met often while tinkering with various electronic devices. They began serious collaboration in 1976 when over a six-month period they designed their first machine, a circuit board, in Jobs's bedroom; built it in his parents' garage in approximately 40 hours from scrounged parts; and showed it to a local computer store owner who promptly ordered 50 boards, fully assembled and tested. Jobs's response was "hot damn, we're in business." By June they made the first shipment on the order for $666.66 per board.

Whereas Wozniak saw the new machine as a gadget to show his fellow computer buffs, Jobs saw the commercial potential of the machine and urged that they form a company to market the computer. According to Wozniak,

> Steve didn't do one circuit, design, or piece of code. He's not really been into computers and . . . has never gone through a computer manual. But it never crossed my mind to sell computers. It was Steve who said, "Let's hold them up in the air and sell a few."

By selling Jobs's Volkswagen microbus and Wozniak's Hewlett-Packard scientific calculator, they raised $1,300 and opened a makeshift product line in Jobs's parents' garage. They obtained $10,000 worth of parts on credit from several sources. According to Jobs, "They'd say, 'Well, how's 30 days net?' We said, 'Sign us up.' We didn't know what 30 days net was." They made 200 more boards and quickly sold 75. Eventually they built 600 units. Jobs, recalling a pleasant summer that he had spent working in the orchards of Oregon, named the new company Apple. According to Jobs, "One day I just told everyone that unless they came up with a better name by 5 P.M. we would go with Apple."

They quickly started designing a new machine, Apple II, that would be fully programmable. They also placed a technical article in a leading trade journal, established a distribution agreement with several computer retailers, and persuaded an attorney to provide legal services on a pay-later plan.

When demand for the personal computer, which came mainly from hobbyists, quickly outstripped their ability to produce they began looking for help. According to Jobs, "We didn't know what the hell we were doing, but we were very careful observers and learned quickly." First they called Intel Corporation and asked who did their advertisements. When told that the agency was Regis McKenna, Inc., of Palo Alto, Jobs pestered Regis McKenna to take on Apple as a client. After refusing twice, McKenna finally agreed. Again, the arrangement was a pay-later basis. All during this time and until 1977 the company's receipts were kept in a desk drawer.

For advice on how to raise money, Jobs consulted both McKenna and Nolan Bushnell of Atari. They suggested that he call Don Valentine, an investor who frequently put money into new firms. When Valentine came around to inspect the new computer, he found Jobs wearing cut-off jeans and sandals while sporting shoulder-length hair and a Ho Chi Minh beard. Valentine later asked McKenna, "Why did you send me this renegade from the human race?"

Valentine mentioned the company to Mike Markkula, a 35-year-old marketing manager at Intel. In exchange for his expertise and $250,000, he was made an equal partner. According to Jobs, "He has sensitivity and knew we were not just two guys in a garage. And the chemistry clicked." By February 1977 Markkula had helped arrange a credit line with the Bank of America and had persuaded venture capitalist Arthur Rock and Teledyne Chairman Henry Singleton to invest $57,600 and $320,000, respectively. In March 1977 Apple incorporated and moved out of the garage.

As a *Time* article reported, Jobs had a tough time making the transition:[5]

> Jobs, hyper and overwrought from the flush of such success, would occasionally burst into tears at meetings and would have to be cooled out with a slow walk around the parking lot. His personal life was also precarious. He again met the woman with whom he spent the summer in the mountains, and she became pregnant before they finally broke up anew. The baby, a girl, was born in the summer of 1978, with Jobs denying his fatherhood and refusing to pay child support. A voluntary blood test performed the following year said "the probability of paternity for Jobs, Steven . . . is 94.1%." Jobs insists that "28% of the male population of the United States could be the father." Nonetheless, the court ordered Jobs to begin paying $385 a month for child support.

As more individuals became involved in the company, the question arose, "Who wants to be president?" Neither Jobs nor Wozniak wanted the day-to-day operating job, so they chose Markkula as chairman and at his suggestion persuaded Michael Scott to join them as president. Scott, who at 33 was director of manufacturing at National Semiconductor Corporation, was willing to take a 50 percent pay cut to join Apple. At the time Jobs claimed that Scott's selection was "one of the best moves we've made." Jobs became vice chairman; Wozniak, vice president of research and development; and Markkula, vice president of marketing.

One of the first tasks of the new management team was to redesign the prototype of the Apple II. Jobs insisted that the cases for the keyboard and the video display be made of light, attractive plastic instead of metal. They also wrote clear, concise instruction manuals that made the machine easy for customers to use. The basic Apple II consisted of a typewriter keyboard, about the size of an attaché case, that plugged into any TV set and flashed information on the screen. It was designed with 136 standard integrated circuits and had a feature that included eight slots inside the Apple II into which the additional parts could be plugged. The product was assembled with semiconductors, plastic and metal parts, and certain electromechanical subassemblies purchased from independent suppliers. Most of the parts were standard, but a few (such as circuit boards) were built to Apple specifications. Certain components (power supplies and integrated circuits) were obtained from a single source, although the company believed there were other sources available. In time, Apple began to manufacture such components as disk drives and keyboards, but the company's operations consisted mainly of testing materials and components and assembling purchased parts into computer products.

Sales increased from $200,000 in 1976 to $2.7 million in 1977, and pretax profits increased from 20 percent to 30 percent. The management team concluded that Apple, in order not to be acquired or run out of business, had to grow rapidly and become one of the dominant firms in the new industry. They set high goals ($18 million sales in 1978 and $50–75 million for 1979) and hired overqualified personnel. According to one industry observer, even without Markkula, Jobs and Wozniak would have been successful. Both had "the smarts to find out what they didn't know. Many others were doing the same thing, but the others let their egos get in the way."

The rapid growth was hard to control. According to Markkula, the problem became how to "keep the racecar on the track." They did keep it on the track by managing on a consensus basis. According to Jobs, "Bascially if we have a hard decision to make, we get everyone to agree. There is a sort of balance and the chemistry works well." The management philosophy was described by Jobs as "just common sense."

By 1978 the company had grown to 150 employees and had sold 25,000 Apple IIs at prices ranging from $1,195 for the basic model to $3,000 for a model with all the trimmings such as two floppy disks, a graphics tablet, and a printer. Total sales were reported to be approximately $17.5 million. At the time Jobs was predicting, "We will sell more computers this year than IBM has in five."

In 1979 total employment had grown to 400 and sales had reached $70 million. In reflecting on the growing demand for personal computers, Jobs observed that "people are hungry for more data—from the date of Don Larson's perfect game to an instant glance at a diet program—and we're trying to satisfy that hunger."

The Apple II could be programmed by anyone familiar with BASIC, the simplistic computer language, to do income tax, balance a worksheet, record recipes, update the Christmas card list, and play chess and backgammon. Some people used their Apple II for evaluating security portfolios and doing cash flow projections. A belly dancer used her Apple to keep track of her inventory of exotic costumes and records. An oil company depended on one to operate a rig off California, and others kept track of statistics for politicians, controlled lights in theaters, and synthesized music for rock stars. The Rolling Stones used an Apple to help their official biographer store information to write the group's history. Even children were using them in elementary schools. According to Jobs, "Here comes 1984, and instead of huge monolithic computers, you have seven-year-olds playing with computers. Things aren't turning out the way people had feared."

As for Apple's role in the industry, Jobs claimed:

> We're trying to move into the big leagues in a hurry and 1979 will be our pivotal year. If we survive, we'll be the DEC of the personal computer industry. Every dollar we make we're plowing back into the company. Sure, we'll be up against the biggies, but we're defining the right product for the market. And the reason we have a chance is that it is a totally brand new market. And nobody knows how it will go.

At the time, Jobs's opinion was that if his company were to be sold, it could bring a purchase price of over $10 million.

By 1979, although there were 50 firms in the $300 million personal computer field, it was dominated by Apple, Radio Shack, and Commodore. However, Texas Instruments had just introduced a model and as many as a dozen large companies were expected to join the market for personal computers costing less than $10,000. IBM, Xerox, and Digital Equipment were all reportedly working on personal computers and some Japanese firms were preparing to enter the U.S. market.

There was no question that many of these companies were aiming to take away Apple's business. At Xerox, members of the personal computer development team referred to their machine as "the worm." Other manufacturers were elbowing in on Apple's distribution network. For example, shortly before the end of 1980 Commodore signed a deal with ComputerLand, the independent chain of retail computer stores that was selling 14 percent of all Apple computers. Apple executives publicly welcomed the new entrants, claiming that the newcomers would help expand the market for all by advertising heavily. They predicted that Apple would hit the billion-dollar mark in annual revenue by 1990 and set as their goal to be a quarter-billion-dollar company by 1982.

In May 1980 the Apple III was introduced at the National Computer Show. Jobs described it as the first microcomputer designed specifically for professional and small-business users. Priced from $4,340 to $7,800, the new product began to be shipped in November and was eventually supported by some 30-odd hardware and software products, each designed for the needs of a particular market. Actually there were two versions of the Apple III. The first was priced at about $4,400, had a 96,000-character memory, and included software. The second was a word processor costing approximately $5,400 and included such accessories as a printer. Already there were rumors of an Apple IV, expected to come out within the next 18 months.

In 1980 Apple management decided it needed to increase its recognition factor. A six-week radio campaign boosted its awareness level from 8 percent of the population to 39 percent and after six weeks of TV ads, it was known by 80 percent of those polled. By late 1980, industry observers were saying that Apple had developed an "IBM-like reputation for quality. When people think of personal computers they think of Apple."

Although Apple's growth was 100 percent in 1980, a big concern for the cofounders was the possibility of boredom. In reflecting on where the company had been and where it was headed, Jobs remarked that "we have made our mistakes but we strive for the little ones. We've never made big glaring mistakes, the kind that would be large enough to kill the company." He explained that Apple managers made 4 to 10 times as many daily decisions as most other managers make, even in the fast-paced Silicon Valley. "You can't slow that process down. There is no time to research each decision." In reflecting on business, he called it "the best-kept secret. It is incredible as a practice and a concept. Most of the bright minds I know didn't go into business. It's really sad." He felt that they were wasting their lives pursuing nonproductive pursuits.

He described the management of creative employees as a "most important problem. If we have 18 ideas and can go with only two, we will have 16 unhappy people." On the other hand, the "bean counters" in the company "go crazy" when individuals "enamored by technology" are granted funding for a pet project.

To develop an atmosphere that pampered creative employees, an incentive program was begun to develop computer literacy. Any employee demonstrating proficiency with two programs was loaned an Apple II for use at home, and after one year title was given to the employee. Jobs described this "loan-to-own" program "as part of an overall desire to institute a more humane workplace." He claimed that it gave employees "the chance to get involved in solving problems that can ultimately affect the success of the entire company."

In a 1980 memo, Mike Scott announced:

EFFECTIVE IMMEDIATELY!! NO MORE TYPEWRITERS ARE TO BE PURCHASED, LEASED, ETC., ETC. Apple is an innovative company. We must believe and lead in all areas. If word processing is so neat, then let's all use it! Goal: By 1-1-81, NO typewriters at Apple. . . . We believe the typewriter is obsolete. Let's prove it inside before we try and convince our customers.

By late 1981, there were only 20 typewriters for 2,200 employees. The Apple II was being used to compose and disseminate letters, memos, documents and reports, catalogue the more than 1,500 resumes received each month, create graphs and charts, and perform various financial, marketing, and production functions.

Another decision was to drop the term *secretary* and replace it with *area associate* to reflect the more varied responsibilities made possible by personal computers. According to Ann Bowers, vice president of human resources, ''We felt we needed a different term because 'secretary' was so loaded with connotations of typist, errand-runner, and phone answerer. We wanted to expand the area associates' functions so they could use their brains, in addition to their clerical skills.'' As a result of ''working smarter,'' Bowers felt there was greater job satisfaction and

> virtually no job turnover. Our middle-management people have more time to do what they're best at—coaching their employees instead of shuffling paper. There's also a wonderful thing that happens in terms of relationship with your support staff. I feel it when I ask my area associate to do more responsible things than just type letters.

There were, however, other motivators for employees at Apple. The private company in 1980 was 78 percent owned by the employees with the balance owned by a few outsiders. According to Jobs, ''We like it that way because it contributes to people working hard. They know that if Apple is successful, that it would change their lifestyle.'' Although only nonhourly employees owned stock in the company, management's goal was to have all the employees as shareholders. If that was to happen, management felt that the firm would have to go public, something the officers did not want. They felt that going public would cause the loss of 20 percent of the time of Apple's top officers as they would have to devote time to SEC paperwork; annual and interim reports, and appearances before and interviews with financial analysts. ''We're frustrated, and there is no solution. The problem is taking up a lot of time,'' according to Jobs.

In 1980 the company had a key employee bonus plan, a profit participation plan and a stock option plan. The bonus plan was primarily for management and provided for a bonus pool ($554,000 in fiscal 1980) determined by a formula based on annual sales and pretax profit margins. Ninety percent of the pool was available to individuals in specific job categories (70 percent was automatically awarded, and 30 percent was awarded at the discretion of the president), and 10 percent was available for award at the discretion of the president to individuals not in the specific job categories. The profit participation plan distributed up to 3 percent of pretax earnings for each calendar quarter ($379,000 in fiscal 1980) to all employees working at least 30 hours per week and who had a minimum of six months' company service, except officers and directors. The 1980 stock option plan reserved 3.2 million shares of common stock for issuance.

In a 1980 interview with *Industry Week,* Steve Wozniak explained some of the less-material rewards of working at Apple. ''We are making the emerging industry grow correctly, without getting it all screwed up. We will have the right products, at the right price, at the right time. We want to be a major contributor.''

Wozniak and Jobs were convinced that from their industry would come some of the major societal contributions of the next five years. They cited as an example the Minnesota Educational Consortium selecting the Apple II for Minnesota's schools. ''There is not one child in the elementary school system that is not affected,'' according to Jobs. Another project under way was a special outreach project in which schools in the San Francisco Bay area were visited with a van full of Apple IIs, bringing classes in programming to elementary and high school students in their classroom.

On December 12, 1980, Apple Computer went public with 4,600,000 shares of stock at $22 a share. *Fortune* reported that Arthur Rock ended up with stock worth $14 million, Henry Singleton with $26 million, Mike Markkula with $154 million, and Scott with $62 million. Jobs instantly became worth $165 million, and Wozniak became worth $88 million, plus his parents and siblings owned nearly $3 million in Apple stock, and his first wife owned $27 million. The top four officials owned 40 percent of the company.

Some observers believed that the stock market had overreacted to Apple's offering. At its opening price of $22 per share Apple was selling at 100 times its per share earnings of 24 cents for the year ending September 26. By contrast, Tandem Computers, Inc., one of the industry's hottest companies, with nearly a 100 percent earning growth rate, was selling at about 60 times earnings over the same period. Nevertheless, Apple's stock jumped to $29 per share on the first day of trading. As a result, Apple officers were already referring to IBM as "the other computer company."

1981—A PROBLEM YEAR

Although 1980 ended on a positive financial note (Exhibits C1.5, C1.6, and C1.7), bad news was to follow. In early 1981 Stephen Wozniak crashed a Beechcraft Bonanza airplane on take-off at a small California airport. Not only did it nearly kill him but he hit his head so hard that he still cannot remember the accident. After the accident, he announced his plans to leave Apple and return to Berkeley to finish his bachelor's degree in computer science. He also married for the second time and bought a mansion in the hills above Santa Cruz. Described by *Newsweek* as a "brilliant—if somewhat erratic—engineer," whose passion was designing electronic gizmos, Woz was con-

EXHIBIT C1.5   APPLE COMPUTER, INC.: CONSOLIDATED INCOME STATEMENT, 1977–1982
(\$000, Except per Share Amounts)

	1982*	1981*	1980*	1979*	1978*	1977†
Net sales	$583,061	$334,783	$117,126	$47,867	$7,856	$ 774
Cost and expenses:						
Cost of sales	288,001	170,124	66,490	27,450	3,960	403
Research and development	37,979	20,956	7,282	3,601	597	76
Marketing	119,945	55,369	12,619	4,097	1,291	162
General and administration	34,927	22,191	7,150	2,617	486	76
	480,852	268,640	93,541	37,765	6,334	717
Operating income	102,209	66,143	23,585	10,102	1,522	52
Interest, net	14,563	10,400	567	3	25	<5>
Income before taxes	116,772	76,543	24,152	10,105	1,547	57
Provision for taxes	55,466	37,123	12,454	5,032	754	10
Net income	$ 61,306	$ 39,420	$ 11,698	$ 5,073	$ 793	$ 42
Earnings per common and common equivalent share	$1.06	$.70	$.24	$.12	$.03	‡
Common and common equivalent shares used in the calculation of earnings per share	57,798	56,161	48,412	43,620	31,544	16,640

* Fiscal year end 9/30.
† Fiscal year end 1/3/77.
‡ less than $.01.
Source: Consolidated Statement of Income Apple Computer, Inc. and Prospectus 12/12/80.

EXHIBIT C1.6   APPLE COMPUTER, INC.: CONSOLIDATED BALANCE SHEETS, 1979–1982 ($000)

	1982	1981	1980	1979
Assets				
Current assets:				
Cash and temporary cash investments	$153,056	$ 72,834	$ 363	$ 563
Accounts receivable	71,478	42,330	15,814	9,178
Inventories	81,229	103,873	34,191	10,103
Other current assets	11,312	8,067	3,738	
Total current assets	317,075	227,104	54,106	19,844
Property, plant, and equipment:				
Land and buildings	7,220	4,815	243	
Machinery and equipment	26,136	14,688	3,669	404
Office furniture and equipment	13,423	6,192	1,673	322
Leasehold improvements	10,515	5,129	710	384
Total property, plant, and equipment	57,294	30,824	6,295	1,110
Accumulated depreciation and amortization	(22,811)	(8,453)	(1,516)	(210)
Net property, plant, and equipment	34,483	22,371	4,779	900
Reacquired distribution rights			5,311	
Other assets	6,229	5,363	1,154	427
Total assets	$357,787	$254,838	$65,350	$21,171
Liabilities and shareholders' equity				
Current liabilities:				
Notes payable to banks	$ 4,185	$ 10,745	$ 7,850	
Accounts payable	25,125	26,613	14,495	$ 5,411
Accrued compensation and employee benefits	11,774	7,759	2,553	1,720
Income taxes payable	15,307	8,621	8,135	1,879
Accrued advertising	8,815	3,540		
Other current liabilities	20,550	13,002	4,747	22
Total current liabilities	85,756	70,280	37,780	9,032
Noncurrent obligations under capital leases	2,052	1,909	671	203
Deferred taxes on income	12,887	5,262	951	2,255
Shareholders' equity				
Common stock, on par value, 160,000,000 shares authorized	141,070	123,317	12,348	4,298
Retained earnings	118,332	57,026	17,606	5,908
	259,402	180,343	29,954	10,206
Notes receivable from shareholders	(2,310)	(2,956)	(4,006)	(525)
Total shareholders' equity	257,092	177,387	25,948	9,681
Total liabilities and shareholders' equity	$357,787	$254,838	$65,350	$21,171

sidered Apple's "creative force." Wealthy beyond his wildest dream and the acknowledged dean of Apple's freewheeling cadre of computer crazies, he had a taste for rich men's toys but talked about going back to Apple at the bottom, as a rank-and-file engineer. His real goal would be "to fix a lot of motivational problems" in a company that had grown rapidly since the garage days. He also hoped to stage rock concerts and to that end formed a corporation, Unuson (Unite Us in Song), to promote rock concerts

EXHIBIT C1.7 APPLE COMPUTER, INC.: CONSOLIDATED STATEMENTS OF CHANGES IN FINANCIAL POSITION, 1980–1982 ($000)

	1982	1981	1980
Working capital was provided by:			
Operations:			
Net income	$ 61,306	$ 39,420	$11,698
Charges to operations not affecting working capital:			
Depreciation and amortization	16,556	8,590	1,377
Deferred taxes on income (noncurrent)	7,625	4,311	747
Total working capital provided by operations	85,487	52,321	13,822
Increases in common stock and related tax benefits, net of changes in notes receivable from shareholders	18,399	112,019	4,569
Increases in noncurrent obligations under capital leases	1,172	1,747	752
Total working capital provided	105,058	166,087	19,143
Working capital was applied to:			
Purchase of property, plant, and equipment, net of retirements	26,470	24,529	4,878
Reacquisition of distribution rights			5,401
Other	4,093	1,060	1,298
Total working capital applied	30,563	25,589	11,577
Increase in working capital	$ 74,495	$140,498	$ 7,566
Increase (decrease) in working capital by component:			
Cash and temporary cash investments	$ 80,222	$ 72,471	$(200)
Accounts receivable	29,148	26,516	6,688
Inventories	(22,644)	69,682	24,089
Other current assets	3,245	4,329	3,685
Notes payable to banks	6,560	(2,895)	(7,850)
Accounts payable	1,488	(12,118)	(9,084)
Accrued compensation and employee benefits	(4,015)	(5,206)	(1,727)
Income taxes payable	(6,686)	(486)	(4,205)
Accrued advertising and other current liabilities	(12,823)	(11,795)	(3,830)
Increase in working capital	$ 74,495	$140,498	$ 7,566

and a "new kind of unity." The for-profit corporation's goal was to eliminate what he saw as a distressing national tendency to ask, "What's in it for me?" Instead, he wanted young Americans to ask "What's in it for us?" In addition, he hoped to pursue his interest in the mechanisms of human, rather than electronic, memory. "I've got enough money to sit back in the pool and watch it all go by. But I want to be in life."

Shortly after the Apple III hit the market, observers were calling the introduction a "fiasco." The new machines were plagued by technical and mechanical problems. The following excerpt from *The Wall Street Journal*[6] indicated the extent of the problem:

> It is the first group of 1,000 or so Apple IIIs that has given the most trouble. Lawrence Shephard bought one of these in February, and though he considers himself an Apple loyalist, four failures in two months have turned him sour on the product.

Mr. Shephard planned to use his $5,000 machine to track tax accounts and store data for the agricultural economics class he teaches at the University of California at Davis. "A week after purchase, the words 'system error' lit up on the screen," Prof. Shephard recalls. He brought the computer back to the store, where a serviceman removed a loose screw and reinserted some chips.

"It worked about 10 hours before the same error reoccurred," Mr. Shephard continues. This time, the machine went back to the factory, and he got another one on loan.

Then, "within 20 hours my loaner failed, too," he says, his anger flashing as the memory returns.

Prof. Shephard soon got his original back, outfitted free of charge with new memory chips. But, "15 hours after I got it home it started to crackle and threw some jibberish on the screen."

If this sounds like the Woody Allen routine, in which the comic is driven mad by a gang of rebellious kitchen appliances, Mr. Shephard isn't laughing. "I know computers, and I've used the big ones, IBM and Burroughs machines," he says. "It isn't as if I took my Apple III home and tried to make toast on it."

Apple adopted a policy of outright exchange to placate users like Mr. Shephard. Getting the faulty machines back also helped in diagnosing the trouble. Among the problems found were: (1) Chip sockets often were too loose so that chips slipped out during shipment. This problem rendered 20 percent of the first computers dead on arrival. (2) A clock/calendar chip, purchased from National Semiconductor Corporation, turned out not to meet specifications. Apple gave customers a $50 rebate and stopped using the chip. (3) Cables to the computer keyboard were too short. (4) Connectors, the metal slots attaching the printed circuit board to the computer, had a variety of mechanical problems. In at least one case, Apple's solution gave rise to new problems. When assembly workers tightened chip sockets they had to push in the chip carriers with such force that some pins were bent. This defect was discovered only after shipment. In responding to the problems with the Apple III, the company strengthened test and inspection procedures and eased out the general manager of personal computer operations. Eventually 14,000 IIIs had to be recalled.

To some dealers the most damaging problem with the Apple III was the delay in supplying special Apple III software, especially a word processing program. This program, called the Word Painter, was originally promised for May 1981, but its scheduled availability was postponed for seven or eight months. According to Markkula, "One of our key guys on the project was in the hospital." Consequently, the Apple III was unsupported by any of the special programs that would place it beyond the Apple II.

As a result of the problems with Apple III, the company was restructured, and in March 1981 a major reorganization occurred. In the management shake-up, a top-level team of vice presidents took over the running of the company from Michael Scott, who was demoted from president to vice chairman soon after he fired 40 employees. Scott's management style was described as "decisive, but also authoritarian and insensitive." His demotion (he later resigned), according to Ann S. Bowers, "was a clear signal that we were not pleased with the way he dealt with the problems." Markkula became president and Jobs became chairman.

One Apple manager, a veteran of the semiconductor industry, described the company during this period as "Camp Run Amok." Another manager, who joined the company in 1981 when the company doubled its size to nearly 2,500 employees, observed that "there seems to be so little control and so much chaos that I can't believe the company isn't flying off into space in a thousand pieces. On the other hand it does seem to keep pulling off its plans."

Markkula has been described as "pragmatic," and his "wryly humorous approach" is seen as an "essential counterweight to Jobs's creative temperament and sometimes arrogant demeanor."

Yet Jobs's qualities, which engender a certain nervousness in the financial community, are to some degree mirrored in Apple's corporate culture and make the company attractive to bright young engineers and business school graduates. "Apple is seen as a dynamic and creative place to work, where you get a chance to make a contribution," says product manager Kristen A. Olson, who joined Apple after she got her M.B.A. in 1981.

Jobs himself characterizes the Apple corporate culture as one in which "we have what you might call an eccentric passion for what we are doing."[7]

Employees and friends describe Jobs in a variety of ways:

"He (Jobs) can con you into believing his dream," says Bill Atkinson, who by some estimates is the most gifted programmer at Apple. A company consultant, Guy Tribble, says that Jobs sets up what he calls "a reality-distortion field. He has the ability to make people around him believe in his perception of reality through a combination of very fast comeback, catch phrases and the occasional very original insight, which he throws in to keep you off balance. . . ."

As a boss, Jobs is admired for courting long chances, but adds a friend, "Something is happening to Steve that's sad and not pretty, something related to money and power and loneliness. He's less sensitive to people's feelings. He runs over them, snowballs them." Adds Jeff King, a former Apple publications manager: "He would have made an excellent King of France. . . ."

Jobs drives the staff hard, expecting long hours, high productivity, and infinite patience with his scattershot ideas. "He should be running Walt Disney," says a longtime Apple manager. "That way, every day when he's got some new idea, he can contribute to something different."

Taking care of business means, for Jobs, not just lighting fires under the staff and gladhanding the media. It also involves—crucially—keeping the lines open to the young. His planned donation of 10,000 Apples to California schools gets him goodwill, a generous tax break, and an even stronger foothold in what Hollywood likes to call "the youth market." He makes periodic campus appearances, where he is likely as not to sit, shoes off, in the lotus position atop a dormitory coffee table and engagingly field questions. Nothing too specific, mind. The students will not press for details on "Supersite," a hazy combination of Disneyland and industrial park that Jobs has been formulating. They may not even know that Jobs, an independent, has at times mulled over some vague political plans, perhaps following in the unorthodox footsteps of Jerry Brown.[8]

Although volume sales finally began for the Apple III in March 1981, the company had to turn its attention to a rumor that it had a new product under development that was intended to supplant Apple III. According to Markkula, "It's untrue. The Apple III is designed to have a 10-year life span."

Some software suppliers were growing concerned that unless Apple positioned the II against Apple III very carefully, competition was going to hurt the III. In spite of such concerns, Jobs predicted that the Apple III would outsell the new IBM machine in 1982.

Some industry sources reported, however, that they would be surprised if Apple III sales exceeded 50,000 units in 1982 while they expected IBM to sell at least 200,000, provided the company could make that many.

Another issue confronting the company was the possibility of vertical integration. The company was beginning to do more of its own software development and not just for the new products in the pipeline. Although Markkula denied these products indicated a move toward vertical integration in software, Apple was entering into a head-on competition with the independent software vendors on which it had depended for most of its business applications software. The software business was expected to grow from $400 million in 1981 to $4.2 billion in 1986, as over 100 new programs hit the market every month. By late 1982 approximately 16,000 software programs had been written exclusively for the 700,000 buyers of Apple II.

Another problem area concerned product distribution. Although Apple did acquire a wholesale distributor in 1980 to sell its machines, it depended on independent dealers. According to Markkula, "We believe that customers want stores carrying more than one personal computer, and we do not think it would be practical for Apple to own that store." He also had ruled out a direct sales force.

To develop strong ties with its retail outlets Apple used such tools as sales and product training, toll-free software hotlines manned by applications specialists, monthly newsletters, and a handsome magazine that focused on a particular application area in each issue. Also they used a co-op ad program in which dealers were reimbursed up to 3 percent of their dollar purchases.

In March of 1981 Apple scrapped its arrangement of marketing through five independent distributors, who purchased products for resale to retailers, and began to sell to the stores through its own regional support centers. Four were in existence in 1980 and three more were planned for 1981 (Exhibit C1.8). Apple's objectives were to gain tighter inventory control, enhance direct training of dealers, and gain better access to end users.

To reinforce its new strategy, Apple launched the *Apple Means Business (AMB)* program, designed to help dealers go after targeted markets. *AMB* gave dealers a series of objectives and such help as sales seminars for 6–20 prospects at a time built around a single application, and structured presentations the dealers could use, along with a kit of 172 color slides for illustrating the various applications. Dealers were taught how to organize the seminars and execute the post-meeting follow-up, and were even told how many computers they could sell in a given period of time.

In the service area, Apple trained and certified 650 dealers to provide same-day, walk-in repairs. Dealers were also trained to provide service at a profit for equipment not under warranty.

In August 1981 Apple asked its 1,100 retail dealers in the United States and Canada to sign amended contracts promising not to engage in telephone or mail-order sales. In a letter accompanying the contract Apple's vice president of sales, Jean Carter, explained that "mail-order sales are neither suited to providing the consumer education that emerging markets require, nor are they structured to providing the consumer satisfaction that has become associated with the Apple name." The company's policy was quickly challenged in court on antitrust grounds.

Apple's chief antagonist was Francis Ravel, who owned Olympic Sales Company in Los Angeles. On December 3, 1981, Mr. Ravel and his attorney asked for a temporary restraining order to block Apple from enforcing its new policy on the grounds that it constituted restraint of trade. Describing this as a temporary step, Ravel said he would

EXHIBIT C1.8 PLANT AND OFFICE FACILITIES

	Square feet	Lease expiration
Manufacturing:		
Cupertino, California (2 locations)	54,000	11/83 to 6/89
San Jose, California	35,000	5/86
Sunnyvale, California	92,000	4/86
Garden Grove, California (2 locations)	43,000	8/84 to 9/86
Newbury Park, California	6,000	8/83
Carrollton, Texas	282,000	7/85
County Cork, Ireland	83,000	Owned
Singapore	75,000	6/84
	670,000	
Distribution:		
Sunnyvale, California (2 locations)	82,000	12/82 to 6/85
Irvine, California	32,000	8/86
Charlotte, North Carolina	29,000	9/85
Carrollton, Texas	39,000	7/85
Zeiat, Netherlands	29,000	5/85
Munich, Germany	15,000	3/86
Toronto, Canada	15,000	3/86
	241,000	
Administration and research and development:		
Cupertino, California (11 locations)	166,000	12/81 to 12/90
Cupertino, California	3,000	Owned
Slough, England	7,000	12/82
	176,000	
Expansion—committed but not yet occupied:		
Cupertino, California (adm. and R&D)	99,000	12/91
Ireland (3 locations) (mfg.)	175,000	Owned
Singapore (mfg.)	58,000	6/84
	332,000	

seek a formal hearing on the issues and seek a preliminary injunction. According to Ravel, "There are about 150 (Apple claimed there were only 75) black sheep like us. All we want is to buy and sell and be left alone. Fair trade laws have been abolished. They can't tell us not to ship from our store. Hewlett-Packard wouldn't dare do that." According to Jobs, "It's not discounting that bothers us. It's the smile—or rather, the lack of it—on our customer's face when service is inadequate. What we're doing is the state-of-the-art in antitrust law. We could go all the way to the Supreme Court."

One owner of a computer store claimed that 75 percent of his company's $6 million in annual sales came from mail-order sales and that if Apple cut him off, "we'll go out of business." Even if Apple cut off its authorized dealers, it was not clear if they could stop unauthorized dealers. One such New York store expected to sell approximately 3,000 Apples in 1981. A source familiar with unauthorized dealerships said they generally get their stock from dealers who order more Apples than they can sell. A typical New York dealer's contract yielded 38 percent profit on resale if 80 or more units were bought and only 29 percent if a few were purchased. According to one West Coast store owner, "Mail-order sales have increased Apple's market share quite a bit. They're cutting off their nose to spite their face."

Apple's policy change reportedly encouraged its network of full service dealers. According to ComputerLand president, Edward Faber, it cost $150,000 to open a store with the service centers, test equipment, and the technicians that Apple required.

> If the dealer makes that kind of investment, he must get a return on the sale of the product. If the retail pricing is being watered down, by mail order discounting, then it becomes difficult. It's discouraging to do all the presale education and support of a prospective customer and then have him buy the equipment somewhere else.

As an example of the concern, 47th Street Photo in New York, with estimated annual sales of $100 million (one quarter in computer goods), was selling Apple IIs for $1,095 when the authorized dealer price was $1,330. To meet competition, some New York dealers had only an 8 percent margin.

Apple officials said that their intent was to go after big-volume mail houses but there would be no exception to its policy. ComputerLand claimed it would continue mailing to long-standing or geographically remote customers.

1982—ANOTHER PROBLEM YEAR

In early 1982 Apple executives were considering plans to cut off sales of its personal computers to ComputerLand's corporate purchasing department. ComputerLand accounted for approximately 10 percent of Apple's 1981 sales (down from 14 percent in 1980), yet Apple had become concerned about the growing competition between ComputerLand stores and its other dealers. It was considering insisting that they sign a new contract giving Apple the right to decide which ComputerLand stores could sell Apple computers.

Early reports of counterfeit Apples were written off by Apple executives as insignificant, but by early 1982 Apple's legal counsel, Albert Eisenstat, returned from an eight-day swing through Taiwan and Southeast Asia and reported finding at least a half-dozen "garage-type" operations turning out counterfeit copies of the Apple II. According to Eisenstat, "Our fear is that, if we do nothing, it might encourage larger, better-financed operations to follow suit." One example of the alleged counterfeits was a machine stamped with the Apple logo, identical down to the crescent-shaped bite, and labeled with a name similar to Apple, in identical type.

The proliferation of personal computer manufacturers in Asia began when video game sales began to slip and manufacturers with inventories of electronic parts and personnel skilled in assembling and copying electronic machines looked for new products. A local trade magazine printed the main electronic schematics for the Apple II, and before long there were 20 good-size manufacturers making microcomputers, not counting the students and retired people who assembled them to earn pocket money.

At first Apple counterfeiters passed off their machines as the real thing but soon came to realize that fake Apples could be almost as good as the real thing. Computer vendors merely showed that their machines could use Apple programming. To advertise that fact, the machines frequently had names like "Ap It," "Apcom," and even the Chinese name for "Green Apple."

Lin Hsiao-chi, general manager of a Taiwan computer company, while acknowledging that he copied the Apple II "to gain experience," said he might stop production of his Apollo II, which he sold for $400, and introduce his Apollo III at under $600. He claimed the Apollo III was not a carbon copy of the Apple III but was similar and could use the same programs.

By the end of summer observers estimated that anywhere from 2,000 to 4,500 counterfeit Apple IIs were being turned out each month in Taiwan alone. Apple distributors in the area, however, were selling only 300 to 400 authentic Apples a month. According to the general manager of an Apple regional distributor, for every genuine Apple II sold in Hong Kong, there were five fakes sold.

By August the problem had spread to other areas of the world. In New Zealand the "Orange" was one of the hottest-selling computers. In Italy, the "Lemon" was selling well. The impact could be seen in Australia, where in 1978 Apple's share of the market was 90 percent but by mid-1982 had dropped to below 30 percent.

Even in the United States at least one company was making a machine that could run all Apple II software, and by mid-1982 approximately 60 companies, mostly in the United States, had sprung up to sell Apple II attachments for replacements for many of its major parts. Even its brain could be changed so that the Apple II could act like another brand of computer. For example, a California company had begun making a plug-in that raised Apple memory above the IBM memory level. Another plug-in from a Michigan firm allowed the Apple to create financial planning models with VisiCalc, the most popular modeling program, that were several times larger than the IBM computer could handle. A Colorado firm announced an attachment that opened the Apple owner's door to IBM personal computer programs.

By 1982 Apple was under pressure to bring out new products since it was lagging behind IBM and Tandy in bringing out a 16-bit machine. Apple planned to outpace the competition by maintaining an innovative edge. Spending on research and development increased from $3.6 million in 1979 to $7.3 million in 1980 and $20.9 million in 1981. The budget for 1982 was forecast at approximately $30 million. Such expenditures were expected to pay off in new products. According to John D. Couch, general manager of Apple's personal office systems division, "We're driven by the desire to build products that combine ideas already out there at low enough cost to make them useful. We're not really a technology-driven company."

LISA

In early 1983 the company hoped to unveil a new machine, code-named Lisa, after one of Jobs's ex-girlfriends. According to Jobs, it will "reduce the time it takes a new user to get up to speed on a personal computer from 20–40 hours to 20 minutes." To provide such innovative features would take a major investment in software. More than 200 man-years of basic software development ($20 million) will have gone into Lisa when it is introduced. This compared with 25 man-years for the Apple III and 2 man-years for the Apple II.

The development of a Lisa began in 1978 when Jobs decided to go after the market of 15 million managers, professionals, and administrative assistants. He recruited 30-year-old John Couch from Hewlett-Packard, who not only agreed with Jobs that the key to success would be good software that was easy to use but also was willing to take a cut in salary from $55,000 to $40,000 and a cut in responsibilities, from 141 people to none.

Jobs and Couch had no trouble convincing others of the promise of an easy-to-use computer:

Eighteen programmers followed Couch from Hewlett-Packard. Lisa's chief engineer, Wayne Rosing, 36, came from Digital Equipment Corp. One day in 1980, Rosing was on a quick trip to California when he stopped in to see Couch on the recommendation of a friend. Within minutes he knew he wanted to work for Apple. By the next day he had a deal with Couch and phoned Digital to resign. Four colleagues from Digital joined him at Apple. Lawrence G. Tesler, 37, who was the software manager for Lisa, was formerly a computer researcher for Xerox. In December 1979 he was demonstrating some techniques in computer friendliness Xerox had developed to a troupe of Apple engineers and marketing executives led by Jobs and Couch. "I was expecting a bunch of hobbyists," Tesler recalls, "and was impressed to find people sophisticated in computer science." Tesler decided on the spot to join Apple. (Eventually more than 15 Xerox engineers joined the project.)

That day of briefings at Xerox was the turning point in Lisa's development. Although Jobs and Couch had been brainstorming about the project, occasionally while sipping brandy in the hot tub at Couch's house at Los Gatos, and company engineers had been busy building prototypes of a new machine, the critical software remained only a vague concept. The Xerox researchers demonstrated a programming language called Smalltalk that worked with a mouse.[9] Suddenly the possibilities became apparent.

Xerox has since incorporated some features of Smalltalk into a product called Star. While a technological marvel, Star has not sold well since its introduction in April 1981. Each Star computer costs $16,600 and won't work well unless hooked up to a large disk drive costing $55,000 or more. According to industry rumors, Xerox is working on a smaller, less expensive version of Star. E. David Crockett, senior vice president of Dataquest, a market research firm in Cupertino, California, says Xerox is selling about 100 to 200 Stars per month. "It's a product looking for a home," he says. In one sense, it has found a home at Apple.

The Apple group resolved to create on Lisa's screen the look and procedures of an everyday office. To do this, they have used pictures to represent certain procedures—a wastebasket for the disposal of information, a clipboard for temporary storage, a folder for filing data. But they soon discovered that even the simplest improvement demanded much more software. The mouse on Xerox's Star, for example, has two different command buttons. It took the Apple team six months to reduce their mouse's buttons from two to one.[10]

Keeping the Lisa project moving at Apple took several forms. First there were rambling late-night rap sessions between Jobs and Couch, then the installation of a 40-man team in quarters behind the Good Earth health food restaurant in Cupertino, California. Finally, in 1982, a 400-man force, many in their 20s, was established in three one-story beige- and red-tile buildings near Apple's antiseptic headquarters in Cupertino. Couch fired up the workers with what he called the "Outward Bound School of Business," stressing the virtues of originality and sweat. New workers were employed as pristine users, and psychologists tested new features for what the industry called "user friendliness."[11]

Peter Nulty in a feature article in a 1983 issue of *Fortune* magazine described some of the obstacles of developing Lisa:

The greatest mystery of all in the Lisa development was how to integrate the different computer applications, such as word processing, statistical and graphics programs, so that the user could easily swap material. Tesler says he estimated in 1980 it would take anywhere from two months to two years to accomplish that. Years was closer to the mark. By last summer, however, the programs were beginning to come together. One July afternoon, Tesler recalls, the programmers succeeded in getting all six application programs on the screen at the same time. Lisa was expertly pulling the budget report, for instance, out of the middle of the pile of documents and then putting it in full view on top.

To celebrate their achievement, the programmers broke out bottles of Stanford, a California champagne (price: $4.29 per bottle). Soon feeling giddy, some people decided to work on the next project: moving the data from within one program to another. The schedule allotted two weeks for this development, but with their champagne-induced confidence, the programmers had it working within hours. So they had a second champagne party that night—this time uncorking Korbel, which is twice as expensive as Stanford. "Since then, there have been a lot of parties," says Tesler. "But we really knew we had done well when the marketing department started paying for the bubbly."

Basically the 50-pound, $9,995 Lisa uses a graphic list of functions and data file arrays called "menus," including pictures of a file folder, a document, a wastebasket, or other familiar office tools (Exhibit C1.9). This format enables a user to select a piece of data or initiate a task without typing coded commands. It includes a 12-inch black-and-white screen with high-resolution imaging, 1 million bits of main memory storage, a profile hard disk supplying 40 million bits of data storage, electric typewriter style, expanded keyboard with a separate 10-key-pad for numerical calculations, and a mouse which can be used to select data files or functions illustrated on the screen.

Included in the Lisa system are six integrated software applications: LisaCalc, an electronic spreadsheet; LisaGraph, for plotting spreadsheet data in bar, line, pie, or other graphic formats; LisaDraw, a freehand graphics package; LisaList, an electronic file folder, and LisaProject, a project-management tool for tracking progress of industrial or financial projects. Further, it can be infinitely expanded.

Lisa systems will run BASIC, COBOL, and Pascal, and there are plans for equipment that will allow Lisa to talk to IBM mainframe computers.

Although Jobs claimed that "with Lisa's technology we have set the direction for the computer industry for the next 5 to 10 years," and that he did not "think we will have any trouble selling all the Lisas we can build," Markkula concedes, "It's going to take time to get the message of what Lisa's all about across," and Couch acknowledges, "If we had known how big Lisa would get, I'm not sure we would have begun at all. It turned out to have a $50 million start-up cost." Even Jobs acknowledges that "Lisa was just bigger than we anticipated. Scheduling is an art. Most of Lisa's software was created from scratch, and that's very hard to predict."

Although Lisa has a balky printer, a sluggish word processor, no color, is relatively slow in retrieving information, and its software can run only on Lisa machines, Apple expected more than one-third of its sales in 1983 to be to the 2,300 U.S. companies with over $120 million in annual revenues. Published estimates of first-year sales ranged from 2,000 to 50,000 units.

EXHIBIT C1.9   LISA—BUSINESS GRAPHICS AND MONITOR SCREEN

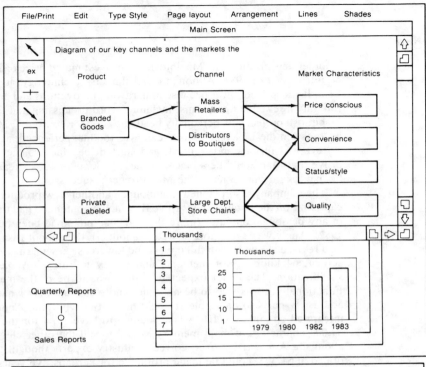

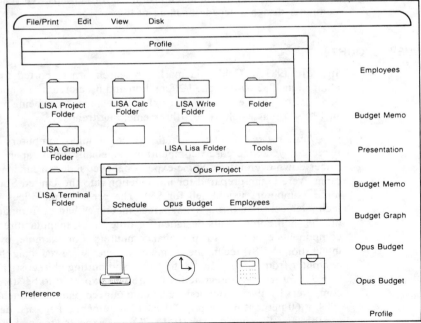

Source: Newsweek, Jan. 31, 1983, and *Fortune*, Feb. 7, 1983.

MACINTOSH

Another new product, the Macintosh, with an estimated price of $2,000 to $5,000, was to be introduced in 1983. Although using the Lisa technology, it was incompatible with Lisa. It was priced lower because of hardware innovations and because it initially would run only a few fixed programs, including word processing and financial modeling. The Macintosh project was personally headed by Jobs. Reportedly, Michael Scott refused to let Jobs run the Lisa team because he was too inexperienced; according to one insider, "Steve was furious and went off and started the Mac project. He was determined to prove that Mac could be a bigger success." Some of Jobs's team put in seven-day 90-hour weeks trying to make the Mac project a success.

The company also planned to announce another new product in 1983, Apple IIE, to capitalize on the popularity in Apple II, which it contended had the largest-installed base of any personal computer (more than 700,000 units had been purchased by the end of 1982). Apple was even more secretive about IIE than about Lisa, but it was reported to be a revised Apple II with full upper- and lowercase keyboard, video display, 80-column screen, 64 kilobytes of memory, and ability to run all Apple II programs without modification. The major expected change was to be in the manufacturing approach. Functionally it was said to be not much more capable than what a customer willing to add a few parts to an Apple II could have. But while the Apple II had 136 standard integrated circuits, the IIE was scheduled to have 11, 1 for the microprocessor, 8 for 64,000 characters of main memory, and 2 for all the other electronics. If speculation about the Apple IIE proved correct, industry experts thought that the new machine, priced at $1,395, could be made profitable for perhaps five years, giving Apple's basic computer design a decade or more of life.

1983—A NEW EPOCH?

In early 1983, a California market research firm reported that personal computers shipped in 1982 had reached 2.8 million and predicted unit shipments of 10.5 million in 1985. Also, it was estimated that 300 new machines were being prepared for introduction in 1984–85 that would reflect three emerging trends:

• *Less expensive.* Although the price of microcomputers had tended to fall 25 percent a year, increased competition, especially from Japan, was expected to push prices down even faster. Some experts believed a dozen Japanese products in the $100 range were being prepared for introduction into the United States and that ultimately home computers would sell for $50. The pressure on prices was also coming from technological breakthroughs. Whereas machines had been made chiefly with standard off-the-shelf components designed for other uses, manufacturers had begun designing components especially for personal computers. For example, by using very large-scale integration (VLSI) techniques some companies were reducing the number of chips in a computer from more than 100 to 1 or 2 and cutting chip costs by 90 percent.

• *Easier to use.* Integrated software was expected to be standard on most desk-top computers by 1985. Commodore had announced plans to launch a Lisa-like product by 1984 at 60 percent of the price. Texas Instrument's Pegasus, designed so that it could use the same files and data as IBM's PC, was expected to combine 64K bytes of memory and a 320K-byte floppy disk with the capability to respond to a limited number of spoken commands and accept certain commands in English sentences at a price of

A. C. Markkula, Jr.   President and Chief Executive Officer (age 39)

Mr. Markkula has been a director of the Company since March 1977 and has served as President and Chief Executive Officer since March 1981. In addition, he served as Chairman of the Board from May 1977 to March 1981, as Vice President—Marketing from May 1977 through June 1980, and as Executive Vice President from June 1980 to March 1981. From 1971 to December 1976, he was Marketing Manager at Intel Corporation, a manufacturer of integrated circuits.

Steven P. Jobs   Chairman of the Board and Vice President (age 26)

Mr. Jobs, a cofounder of the Company, has served as Chairman of the Board since March 1981 and as Vice President since May 1977 and has been a director since March 1977. He served as Vice Chairman of the Board from August 1979 to March 1981. Prior to March 1977 he worked as an engineer for two years with Atari, Inc., a computer games manufacturer.

Kenneth R. Zerbe   Executive Vice President—Finance and Administration (age 46)

Mr. Zerbe joined the Company in April 1979 as Vice President—Finance and Administration and served in that position until June 1980, at which time he was promoted to Executive Vice President—Finance and Administration. From April 1976 to April 1979, he was Senior Vice President of Finance and Administration for American Microsystems, Inc., a manufacturer of semiconductors. Prior to that time, he was Senior Vice President of Finance at Fisher and Porter Co., a manufacturer of electronic process instrumentation.

Ann S. Bowers   Vice President—Human Resources (age 44)

Ms. Bowers joined the Company in July 1980 as Vice President—Human Resources. From October 1976 through June 1980, she served as an independent personnel management consultant to high technology growth firms. Prior to that time she served as Director of Personnel at Intel Corporation for over six years.

Gene P. Carter   Vice President—Sales (age 47)

Mr. Carter joined the Company in August 1977 as National Sales Manager and in December 1978 was promoted to Vice President—Sales. Prior to that time he was Director of Microprocessor Marketing at National Semiconductor Corporation, a manufacturer of integrated circuits and computers.

John D. Couch   Vice President and General Manager—Personnel Office Systems (age 34)

Mr. Couch joined the Company as Product Manager in October 1978 and was promoted to Vice President in April 1979. For more than five years prior to that time he held various engineering management positions at Hewlett- Packard Company, a manufacturer of business computers, during which time he was responsible for software development for the HP-3000 family of computers.

Albert A. Eisenstat   Vice President—Secretary and General Counsel (age 51)

Mr. Eisenstat joined the Company in July 1980 as Vice President and General Counsel and has also served as Secretary of the Company since September 1980. From December 1978 to July 1980 he was Senior Vice President of Bradford National Corporation, a computer services firm serving the banking, securities, and health care industries. From December 1974 through December 1978, he was Vice President and Corporate Counsel of Tymshare, Inc., an international computer time-sharing and services company. In both of these positions, he was responsible for legal and administrative duties.

Joseph A. Graziano   Vice President—Finance and Chief Financial Officer (age 38)

Mr. Graziano joined the Company in October 1981 as Vice President—Finance and Chief Financial Officer. From 1976 to 1981, he was employed at ROLM Corporation, a manufacturer of computer-controlled telephone systems and Mil-Spec computers, where he served as Treasurer from 1979 to 1981 and Assistant Treasurer from 1976 to 1979.

Frederick M. Hoar   Vice President—Communications (age 55)

Mr. Hoar joined the Company in July 1980 as Vice President—Communications. From March 1980 until his employment with the Company, he was Vice President—Public Affairs and Communications at Syntex Corporation, a pharmaceutical company. For more than five years prior to that time he was Vice President—Communications for Fairchild Camera & Instrument Corporation, a semiconductor manufacturer.

Wilfrid J. Houde   Vice President and General Manager—Personal Computer Systems (age 44)

Mr. Houde joined the Company in January 1979 as Director—Service and Operations. In April 1980, he was promoted to Director—Service, Operations, and Distribution. In April 1981, he was promoted to General Manager—Personal Computer Systems. In June 1981, he was promoted to Vice President and General Manager—Personal Computer Systems. Prior to his employment with the Company, he was Operations Manager—Computer Support at Hewlett-Packard Company for seven years.

Thomas J. Lawrence   Vice President and General Manager—Europe (age 47)

Mr. Lawrence joined the Company in August 1980 as Managing Director—Europe. In June 1981, he was promoted to Vice President and General Manager—Europe. From 1973 to 1980 he was employed at Intel Corporation, where he served as General Manager—Europe, and Vice President of Intel International.

John Vennard   Vice President and General Manager—Peripherals (age 41)

Mr. Vennard joined the Company in June 1979 as Production Engineering Manager. In January 1979 he was promoted to General Manager—Peripherals. In June 1981 he was promoted to Vice President and General Manager—Peripherals. Prior to his employment with the Company, he held various technical management positions, including Director of Operations at National Semiconductor Corporations.

Delbert W. Yocam   Vice President and General Manager—Manufacturing (age 46)

Mr. Yocam joined the Company in November 1979 as Director of Materials. In August 1981, he was promoted to Vice President and General Manager—Manufacturing. From May 1979 to November 1979 he was Line Material Manager for Fairchild Test Systems, a division of Fairchild Camera & Instrument Corporation. From May 1978 to May 1979, he was Staff Manager—Production Control and Planning at ITT Cannon Electric. From 1976 to 1978, he was Line Material Manager at Computer Automation, Inc.

*Porter O. Crisp**   Board Member

Mr. Crisp is founding and managing partner of Venrock Associates, a limited partnership formed by the Rockefeller family to invest in technology-based enterprises. Elected to Apple's board of directors in October 1980, he also serves as a director of Crum and Forster, Eastern Airlines, Inc., Evans and Sutherland Computer Corporation, Itek Corporation, Thermo Electron Corporation, and a number of private companies.

EXHIBIT C1.10   (*CONCLUDED*)

Arthur Rock*   Board Member

Mr. Rock, one of the company's early investors, became a director of Apple in October 1980. Between 1969 and 1981 he was a general partner of Arthur Rock and Associates, venture capitalists, and for the past three years has been a limited partner of the San Francisco–based investment banking firm, Hambrecht and Quist. Mr. Rock also serves on the boards of Intel Corporation, Teledyne, Inc., and several privately held companies.

Philip S. Schlein*   Board Member

Mr. Schlein, chairman of the board and chief executive officer of Macy's California, became an Apple director in June 1979. He also serves as a director of R. H. Macy and Co., parent of Macy's California.

Henry E. Singleton*   Board Member

For 22 years, Dr. Singleton has been chairman and chief executive officer of Teledyne, Inc., a diversified manufacturing company. He became a director of Apple in October 1978.

*Board of Directors.

$2,595. VisiCorp soon was expected to introduce a program, costing less than $1,000, that would work with IBM's PC and do most of what Lisa could so. Furthermore, sales of small computers, weighing 15 pounds or less, were expected to grow more quickly during the next two years than other segments. Nippon Electric had recently unveiled a $550 computer the size of a loose-leaf binder with a flatpanel display that would run on batteries for 18 hours, yet with the computing power of an Apple II and a full-size keyboard.

• *More powerful*. Machines were being designed with 32-bit microprocessors and with the capability of being upgraded with higher- capacity memory in just five minutes without using tools.

As Steven Jobs evaluated the myriad problems facing his company in 1983, he knew that Apple needed to establish a clear direction to remain the leader in the industry. Sales of Apple II had hit a plateau of 30,000 a month in late 1982, a price war was developing, and sales of Apple III were only 3,000–3,500 per month even at the reduced $2,995 price.

Even Lisa and Macintosh raised new problems for him, not the least of which was how to introduce and market them. For example, should Lisa be sold through a small sales force, or should Apple rely on selected local dealers? How should service and support be provided? The full-service dealers were already unhappy with recently announced plans to discount Apple II and cut dealer margins in half.

The IBM challenge was growing. Not only was IBM selling 20,000 units per month and approaching 20 percent market share but it was rumored to be readying a new 16-bit machine, "Peanut," that would sell for less than $1,000, and an executive workstation, "Popcorn," that might take Lisa head-on.

As Jobs glanced through the materials on his desk, his attention was caught by an article in a major business publication, "The Coming Shakeout in Personal Computers." He could not help but wonder how his company with its young management team (Exhibit C1.10) would fare over the next few years and if a suitable replacement could be found for Mike Markkula, who for months had been talking about his plans to resign as president and take life a little easier. What Apple needs, he thought to himself, is a "heart transplant."

REFERENCES

1 Much of the material in this section is based on "To Each His Own Computer," *Newsweek*, February 22, 1982, pp. 50–56.

2 A byte refers to a character of memory. A computer with 64K (or "kilobytes") of memory can store about 64,000 characters, roughly the same as 35 typewritten pages. Computers have a set amount of working memory, i.e., directly accessible memory, but an almost unlimited amount of mass storage can be added.

3 A bit refers to a basic unit of information. Everything the computer does, whether it sends a spaceship streaking across a color video screen or takes dictation, is represented in numbers, counted out in a binary code the way people would count if endowed with only two fingers: 0, 1, 10, 11, 100, 101, and on and on. A 16-bit microprocessor can process 16 basic units of computer information at one time, compared with the 8-bit processor, which can handle only 8 units. Thus the 16-bit processor is much faster and more powerful than the 8-bit processor.

4 Jay Cocks, "The Updated Book of Jobs," *Time*, January 3, 1983, p. 26.

5 Ibid, p. 27.

6 *The Wall Street Journal*, April 15, 1981.

7 "Apple Takes on Its Biggest Test Yet," *Business Week*, January 31, 1983, p. 79.

8 Cocks, op. cit., pp. 25–27.

9 The mouse is a cigarette pack–size plastic box with a button on top and a cable connected to the computer. When the mouse is moved on the surface of a desk, an arrow moves on Lisa's TV-like monitor screen. This permits the user to juggle words or statistics around.

10 Peter Nulty, "Apple's Bid to Stay in the Big Time," *Fortune*, February 7, 1983, p. 40.

11 Philip Faflick, "The Year of the Mouse," *Time*, January 31, 1983, p. 51.

APPLE COMPUTER, INC. (C)

Prepared by Caron St. John, Clemson University.

In the fiscal year which ended September 30, 1983, Apple Computer experienced a 69% increase in sales and a 25% increase in profit over 1982. However, the positive financial performance did not tell the entire story. Most of the 1983 sales increase was a result of strong sales of the Apple II and the new enhanced version of the Apple II, the Apple IIE. The two machines that Apple Computer had targeted for the business marketplace—the Apple III and the Lisa—showed generally disappointing sales. Although Apple Computer publically attributed the problems to lengthy evaluation and purchasing cycles,[1] many industry analysts felt the failure of the Lisa was evidence that Apple was not viewed by businesspeople as a serious alternative to IBM in the business market segment.

JOHN SCULLEY

Although the failure of the Lisa was highly publicized, the biggest event for Apple in fiscal 1983 was the hiring of a new president—John Sculley. Sculley, president of domestic operations for PepsiCo, joined Apple in May 1983. At age 45 and with 16 years invested in his career with PepsiCo, Sculley seemed an unlikely candidate for the presidency of a flamboyant West Coast company. Although Sculley was sought after by Steven Jobs and Apple for his expertise in consumer marketing, he quickly learned the intricacies of the computer business.

In the statement to the stockholders in the September 1983 annual report, Jobs and Sculley addressed what they saw as the major problems facing Apple:

1. Continuing to develop innovative technology

2. Surviving the personal computer shakeout
3. Maintaining control over the rapidly growing organization

In order to address these problems, Sculley promised a new emphasis on discipline. He wanted heavy investment in R&D and marketing, with a minimal increase in staff. "We are going to sacrifice short term gains for long term health," he said.[2]

During his first 18 months as president, Sculley was involved in two successful product introductions—the Apple IIC (a compact, portable version of the Apple II) and the Macintosh. He devised an elaborate reorganization that resulted in the consolidation of five divisions into two, including the merging of the Lisa and Macintosh divisions. In order to raise money for investment, he froze hiring, cut out several unprofitable operations, and limited the profit sharing program.[3] Advertising was increased dramatically and novel promotions were developed, including the "Test Drive a Mac" campaign, which allowed potential customers to take a Macintosh home overnight.

1984–1985: A NEW STRATEGY FOR THE FUTURE

In 1984, the total U.S. market volume for personal computers in the $1,000 to $10,000 price range was $14.5 billion—almost twice the 1983 level of $7.4 billion. In the fiscal year which ended September 1984, Apple again experienced a substantial 54% increase in sales to $1.5 billion, but profits fell 16% to 64.1 million. Apple attributed the sales increase to heavy demand for the Apple IIC and the Macintosh.[4] Despite the very good sales growth, Apple lost its share in the personal computer market to IBM (see Exhibit C2.1). Apple computers were still not being purchased by businesspeople—and businesses accounted for two-thirds of the personal computer market.

At the beginning of fiscal year 1985, Jobs and Sculley announced an all-out attack on IBM's position in the personal computer business segment and the intent to promote the Macintosh as the quintessential office machine. In order to position the Macintosh, Sculley and Jobs prepared a strategy they felt would build enthusiasm for the easy-to-operate Macintosh and help establish Apple Computer as a serious threat to IBM. *Business Week* reported Apple's strategy as follows:

Introduce the Macintosh Office—In January (1985), Apple will announce a lineup of office products that will turn the Macintosh into a complete office system. Deliveries will start later in the year. The package will include a low-cost, local-area communications network that will link together all Macintosh units in an office, a high speed laser printer that will produce correspondence-quality text, and a memory device that will permit Macintoshes in an office network to share data stored in a common file.

To fit into the IBM world, Apple is promising to deliver a communications product that will allow Macintoshes in a network to exchange data with IBM computers. Apple will also sell a special device that can be plugged into an IBM PC so that it can become part of an Apple network.

Speed Mac Software Development—No matter how well designed or powerful a computer is, no one will buy it if it has no programs to run. To get outside developers going, Apple must convince them that a large number of the machines will be sold, creating a large market for their programs.

Sign Up Large Customers—The Apple national accounts team is busily wooing a flock of large corporate buyers, going so far as to fly them to its

EXHIBIT C2.1 APPLE GROWS BUT IBM GAINS

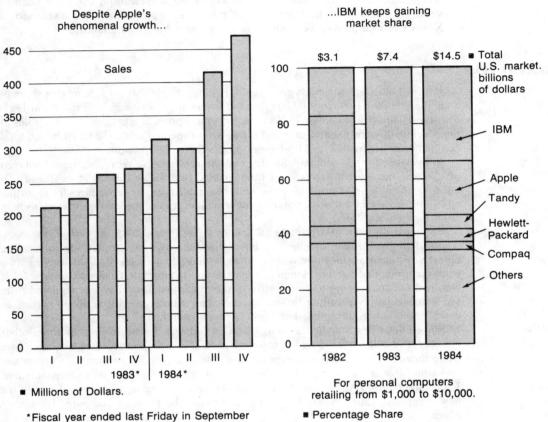

Despite Apple's phenomenal growth...

...IBM keeps gaining market share

- Millions of Dollars.

*Fiscal year ended last Friday in September

For personal computers retailing from $1,000 to $10,000.

- Percentage Share

Source: Deborah Wise and Catherine Harris, "Apple's New Crusade," *Business Week*, Nov. 26, 1984, p. 152.

Cupertino headquarters and then lay out its future product strategies. Apple has already placed a handful of Macs in more than 50 companies, including Honeywell Inc. and H. J. Heinz Co., and is counting on some of these highly visible companies to become major Mac customers.

Improve Dealer Relations—Keenly aware of how important its relations with retailers are—retail stores currently sell 80% of all personal computers—Apple in October completely replaced its network of manufacturer's representatives, who acted as the middlemen between the computer maker and its retailers, with its own 350-person sales force. The Apple force is designed to support dealers and train their salespeople. Some dealers fear that Apple's sales force will turn into a direct-selling tool, but others hope it will help Apple stop the discounting done by some retailers, which brings on price wars and lower profit margins.

Form Strategic Alliances—In 1985, Apple expects to make distribution and technology agreements with several other major companies. Such relationships would be a big plus to Apple in selling national accounts. Reports of alliances with Wang Laboratories Inc. and American Telephone & Telegraph Co. have been strongest, but none of the companies will comment. In November, Apple selected Xerox Corp. to market its products in some Latin American countries.[5]

A TURBULENT YEAR

As it turned out, 1985 was not a good year for Apple. Apple's worldwide market share of computers in the $1,000 to $10,000 range fell from a high of 19% in 1983 to 11% in 1985. Macintosh capacity utilization in 1985 was extremely poor, at less than 15%, and sales of the Macintosh were one-fourth of what had been expected since 1984.[6] Although total company sales increased to $1.9 billion, profits fell to $61 million.

In response to the problems, Sculley undertook a massive reorganization. He layed off 20% of the work force, closed three plants, and hacked away at overhead. To improve planning and control systems, Sculley established new procedures for reporting costs and reviewing proposals and he implemented a new forecasting system to help control inventory costs.

The most dramatic move made by Sculley came in mid-1985. As part of the companywide reorganization, Sculley combined the Macintosh and Apple II divisions. One objective of the reorganization was to eliminate the redundancies of two marketing, two manufacturing, and two development departments. In addition, Chairman Steven Jobs, who had maintained day-to-day control of the Macintosh division, was removed from line management. According to Sculley, Jobs had interfered with Sculley's efforts to make Apple a more disciplined and orderly organization.

Steven Jobs first fought the reorganization but was forced to give in when other members of Sculley's hand-picked top management team supported the new plan. For a while Steven Jobs seemed to accept his new role as a corporate visionary without any real control over the organization. However, a few months after the reorganization, Jobs resigned from Apple and started a new computer company. The stated goal of his new company, called Next, Inc., was to provide the ultimate computer for higher education.

When Jobs left Apple, he took several employees with him. Apple filed suit against Jobs claiming he had violated his fiduciary responsibilities as chairman and taken trade secrets. Apple and Jobs reached an out-of-court settlement in 1986 that prohibited Next, Inc., from using Apple technology and gave Apple the right to inspect the first Next product before market introduction.

1986

In 1986, Apple began to turn things around. Shipments of Macintosh computers doubled—largely because of its widespread acceptance in desktop publishing. Although only about 7% of Macintosh sales were to business, the Excel spreadsheet program developed by Microsoft Corporation allowed the Macintosh to compete directly with those IBM PCs that used Lotus 1-2-3.

Although Macintosh sales improved in 1986, Apple II sales began to slow—which resulted in no overall sales growth for the year. However, cost cutting and the improved position of the Macintosh contributed to an earnings jump of 151% to $154 million.

Apple management claims the company will continue to target the business market for future versions of the Macintosh. Several improvements are planned to address the many problems identified by the business community. In order to support the new product efforts, Apple is planning to increase its research and development budget by 30% in fiscal 1987.

Two new products already developed are the Mac Plus and the Open Mac. The Mac Plus, introduced in early 1986, is a more flexible version of the original Macintosh with double the memory and a high speed socket that allows hardware options to be connected. The Open Mac is a major new product development. While the original Mac was a closed system that was nearly impossible to customize, the intent of the Open Mac is to have an open system that is as easy to customize with new circuit cards as an IBM PC.

Over the years, one of the major objections to the Macintosh was that it was not compatible with the IBM PC. Apple has now announced that it will sell a card that will allow an Open Mac to run IBM software.

REFERENCES

1 Apple Computer, Inc., 1983 Annual Report.
2 Deborah Wise and Catherine Harris, "Apple's New Crusade," *Business Week,* Nov. 26, 1984, p. 154.
3 Ibid.
4 *The Wall Street Journal,* Oct. 19, 1984, p. 51.
5 Wise and Harris, op. cit., pp. 148–149.
6 Deborah Wise and Geoff Lewis, "Apple, Part 2: The No-Nonsense Era of John Sculley," *Business Week*, Jan. 27, 1986, pp. 96–98.

ARTISAN INDUSTRIES (C)

Prepared by Frank C. Barnes, University of North Carolina at Charlotte.

Artisan Industries was a $9-million-a-year family-run manufacturer of wooden decorative products. They were approaching their first fall sales season since last year's successful turnaround under the direction of the new 29-year-old president, Bill Meister. Last fall had begun with a year-to-date loss of $125,000 and, through Meister's actions, had ended with a $390,000 profit. This had been the first profit in several years and capped a challenging 8 months for the new president.

Meister had hired his first man while his father was still president, bringing in 27-year-old Bob Atwood from the local office of a "Big Eight" firm to begin modernizing the accounting system. On June 10th, 1976, Bob was in Bill's office for further, and he hoped final, discussion of plans for this fall season. Artisan's sales were quite seasonal and on June 10th there were about 2 more months during which production would exceed sales. Atwood, concerned with the company's limited capital, proposed a production plan to hold the inventory buildup to $1,600,000, or about twice the level shown on the last full computer listing.

The president, based on his feel for conditions after the successful 1975 season and viewing sales in the first weeks of 1976, believed total sales for this year would really beat Bob's estimate of the same as last year's and reach $9 million. But he would like to have stronger support for his opinions; a lot rested on this estimate. If sales were much beyond their plans he could expect to lose most of them and create difficulties with his customers. New customers might even be lost to the competition. Bill was also concerned with developing contingency plans for dealing effectively with the potentially oversold condition. Besides getting more production from the plants at the last minute,

---

This case was prepared as a basis for class discussion rather than to illustrate either effective or ineffective handling of an administrative situation. Used by permission.

there might be good ideas which involved the customers and salesmen. For example, if all orders couldn't be filled, should some be fully, shipped and others dropped, or should all be shipped 75–95% complete? Overall in 1975 orders had been shipped 75% complete and during the peak months this had fallen to 50%. Partial shipments might be a way to keep everyone happy. If orders are canceled should they be the ones from the small "mom and pop" stores or the large department stores? The small stores are more dependable customers, but on the other hand large department stores systematically evaluate suppliers on their order completion history. Also the department store buyers must "commit" funds when they place an order, thus their resources are idle until the order is filled. There are potential benefits from good communications, for if you inform the buyer of any delay quickly he can cancel that order and order something he can get. Such sensitivity to the customer's needs could win the company many friends and aid Meister in building a desirable reputation. On the other hand, poor communication could cause the opposite. Meister wondered if there was some way to usefully involve the salesmen, many of whom had left a sales representative organization 6 months earlier to work solely for Artisan.

After about mid-August total annual sales were limited to what had been built up in inventory beforehand and production through mid-November. Thus holding back now put a lid on total sales for the season.

If, on the other hand, the sales plan was not reached there could also be serious consequences. Last year after the fall sales period the inventory loan had been paid off for the first time since the 1960s. This had made a very favorable impression on the lending institutions and brought a reduction in the high interest rates (from 12% to 10¼%). They considered Bill a "super-star," with his youth, professional appearance, and modern ideas, and their fears for the Artisan loan were diminishing. Trouble at this time might erase all this and suggest last year was just a fluke.

If sales don't materialize, inventories could be held down by cutting back on production. But Bill believed the plants operated inefficiently during any cutbacks and such moves very likely saved nothing. He held a similar opinion of temporary second shifts. In many past years overproduction early in the year had resulted in big layoffs in December and January and in the financial drain of carrying over large inventories. Meister was highly interested in building an effective work environment for people at Artisan, where attitudes were historically poor. The people, workers, and supervision, had little exposure to "professional" managers and had much to learn. The long process had been begun but a layoff now could undermine all his effort and, he felt, lose him what little confidence and support he had been able to encourage.

The strategy for this fall was of critical importance to Bill and his hopes for Artisan and his future.

ARTISAN'S HISTORY

Artisan Industries is the product of a classic entrepreneur—W. A. (Buddy) Meister. After a variety of attempts at self-employment, such as running a dry-cleaning shop, a food shop, and an appliance store, he began to have some success making wooden toys. One try in 1950 with his father and brothers failed, leaving Buddy with an old tin building and some worn-out equipment.

During the next few years Buddy put his efforts into making a collection of 10 to 15 toys, sold via direct mail, house-to-house, on television, and on the roadside, all without a salesman. One day a visiting gummed-tape salesman offered to take on the line, and a pattern of using outside sales reps was established.

The first attempt at a trade show was a last minute entry into the regional gift show 40 miles away. Out of sympathy for Buddy, Artisan was allowed to pay the $25-a-week rent after the show. Buddy brought home $3,000 in sales but lacked the money to produce them until a friend offered a loan. The orders were produced in a dirt-floor barn. In the following months, Buddy and his wife drove off to other markets, showing the goods in their motel room.

In 1953 sales reached $15,000; then climbed to $30,000 in 1954, $60,000 in 1955, and $120,000 in 1956. Then in April the plant, or barn, burned down, destroying everything. With hardly a delay Buddy jumped into rebuilding and sales continued to double. In 1958, success allowed Artisan to move into a 30,000-square-foot building and continue using its two old buildings for finishing and shipping. Then in March of 1960 these two burned down. Again Buddy fought back and sales doubled into 1961. The rate of growth slowed to 50% in 1962.

The third and most disastrous fire occurred in February of 1963. The entire main plant was burned to the ground with the exception of the new office, which stood under a foot of water and was damaged by smoke and water. The company was in the middle of manufacturing its show orders and the only thing saved was the inventory in the paint shop. All the jigs were burned and before work could begin new jigs and patterns had to be made. "Only the plant in Spencer, built only a year before, saved us. The entire operation, with the exception of the office, was moved to Spencer, and working three shifts, we were able to keep most of the 200 employees. Many employees worked night and day for approximately six months to help us get on our feet again." Before Christmas of 1963 the company was back in full operation in the main plant.

Sales reached $4 million in 1966 and $8 million in 1971. During that 6-year span Buddy's five children reached ages to begin full-time jobs in the company. The youngest, Bill, was the last to join. Typical of the youngest, he had it best, having all the "toys" his father could provide. He attended Vanderbilt University, where he majored in Business Administration and the "good life." But his good time was at last interrupted by graduation and employment at Artisan.

Bill wanted no major role in the company but over the next 3 years found himself getting more involved. Buddy had developed no modern management systems; accounting was ineffective, sales was in the control of outside reps, manufacturing was outdated and unprofessional. The lack of order fit Buddy's style, close personal control and manipulation. As the company problems increased, family conflict intensified. Bill's older brother lost the support of his father and then of other family members and left. Bill moved up to the role of spokesman for a change.

In early 1974, though sales were booming, the financial situation at Artisan was "tight." A second shift was in operation, though production was generally inefficient. By October sales had slackened and in November, to hold inventories down, layoffs began. Accounts Receivable were worsening and the worried bankers were forcing the company to pay off some of its $2,500,000 loan. The inventory was reduced some and Accounts Payable were allowed to increase. In December the plant was closed for 3 weeks and $100,000 in cash was raised through a warehouse sale. But in the end 1974 closed with a loss of over a million dollars.

As 1975 began the sales picture looked bad. Even with the large inventory there was difficulty shipping because it contained the wrong things. But, since it tied up capital, production of salable items was limited. There were more layoffs and shutdowns in

January. Some old suppliers cut off the company's credit. In February, under the threat of the local bank calling the loan, Bill and Bob negotiated a new loan with a New York firm. This was composed of an inventory loan with a ceiling of $500,000, an Accounts Receivable loan of up to $1 million, and a long-term loan on the warehouse and real estate of approximately $350,000. The package was finalized and the funds transferred about one week prior to payment deadline with the bank. "Had we not completed the deal with the other group, there was no way we could have made the $25,000 payment" according to Bill.

As the troubles deepened in the spring, Buddy had few solutions, and worse, blocked Bill's actions. The atmosphere in the company became grim. As Bill put it:

> It became a fight between who was going to make decisions about what. Through the Spring the conflict between us continued at a heightened pace. The effect was that most people became very nervous because no one understood who was really in control. With the company in the financial condition it was then, the last thing it needed was a power struggle over who should be in charge. So, in April I went to Buddy and explained the situation that the company needed one person who was clearly in authority and in control, that one person would be better than two, and that I felt that he should leave or I should leave. He suggested that since he had gotten there first, I should leave.

Bill went to the mountains for good.

But 2 weeks later, under pressure from the lenders, Buddy stepped aside and Bill became the chief executive.

In May 1975 when Bill Meister became president, Artisan was in critical condition. Sales had fallen off dramatically, there had been little profit for 3 years, the number of employees had fallen from 600 to 370, modern management systems existed in no area of the company, and there were few qualified managers.

> When I took over, sales were running 50% off and we could not get a line of credit through our suppliers, we were on a cash basis only, inventory was still relatively high, Accounts Receivable were running over 120 days, manufacturing was without anyone in charge, and the company was sustaining a loss of approximately $10,000 a week. The general situation looked pretty hopeless.

BILL MEISTER'S FIRST YEAR AS PRESIDENT

When Bill became president in May changes began. Although Bill controlled many of the changes, others were the result of actions by his managers or outside forces. By midsummer of 1975 he had reestablished contact with a business professor he particularly respected at his Alma Mater and was in regular contact with a management professor at a local school. The small number of trained managers, their lack of experience, and the absence of cooperation among them was a serious handicap to his rebuilding effort. He hoped interaction with the professors would make up for the lack of inside managers to interact with.

Exhibit C3.1 shows the organization chart in June 1976. Buddy moved up to Chairman, but remained around the office. Bill's sister Edith and Uncle Sam helped in the sales area. Another sister, Sally, worked for Bob Atwood in accounting. A new man, Will Shire, was over production, mainly Plant One. Two long-term men, Charles Scott

EXHIBIT C3.1   ORGANIZATION CHART, ARTISAN INDUSTRIES, JUNE 1976

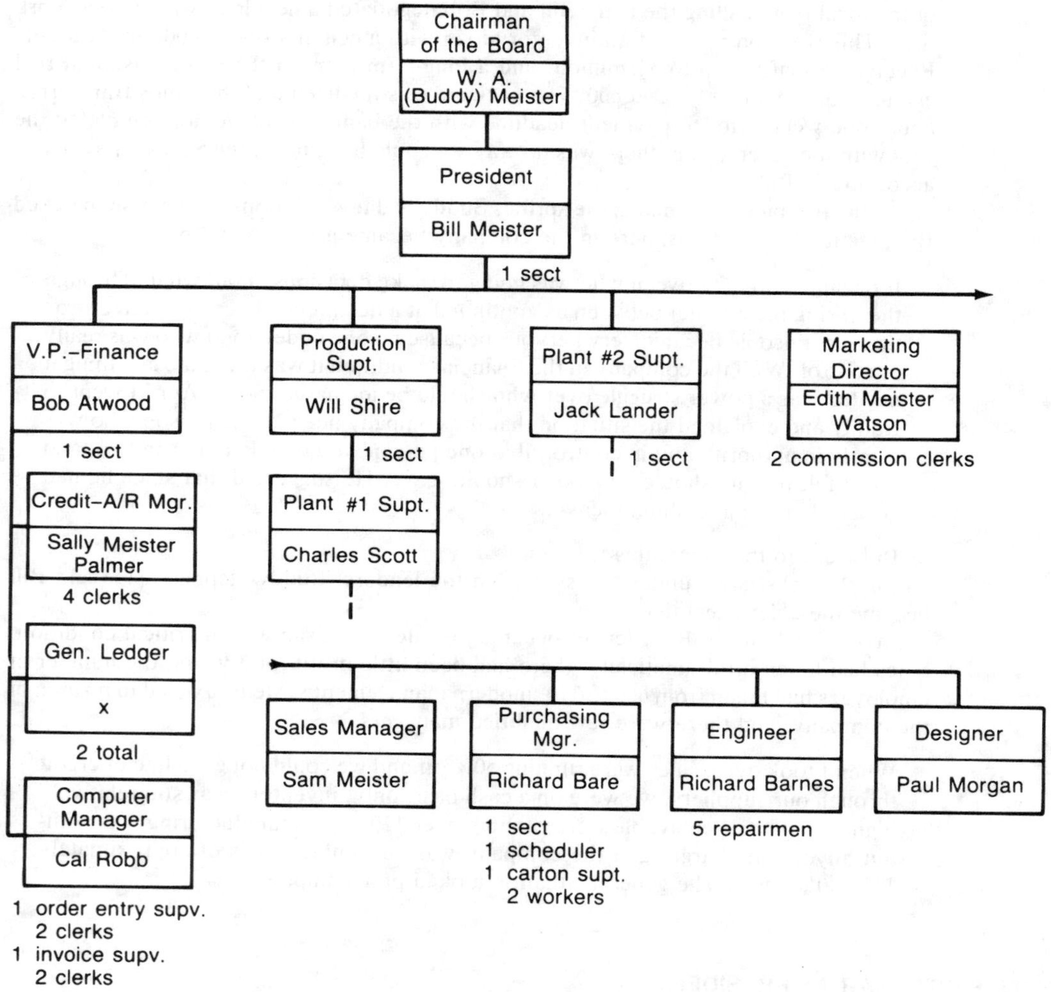

```
                        ┌─────────────────┐
                        │   Chairman      │
                        │  of the Board   │
                        ├─────────────────┤
                        │    W. A.        │
                        │ (Buddy) Meister │
                        └────────┬────────┘
                                 │
                        ┌─────────────────┐
                        │   President     │
                        ├─────────────────┤
                        │  Bill Meister   │
                        └────────┬────────┘
                              1 sect
```

V.P.–Finance	Production Supt.	Plant #2 Supt.	Marketing Director
Bob Atwood	Will Shire	Jack Lander	Edith Meister Watson
1 sect	1 sect	1 sect	2 commission clerks

Credit–A/R Mgr.	Plant #1 Supt.
Sally Meister Palmer	Charles Scott
4 clerks	

Gen. Ledger
x
2 total

Sales Manager	Purchasing Mgr.	Engineer	Designer
Sam Meister	Richard Bare	Richard Barnes	Paul Morgan
	1 sect	5 repairmen	
	1 scheduler		
	1 carton supt.		
	2 workers		

Computer Manager
Cal Robb

1 order entry supv.
2 clerks
1 invoice supv.
2 clerks

and Jack Lander, headed the plants. Two other long-term employees were in management: Cal Robb over the computer and Richard Bare over purchasing. A young man, Richard Barnes, had been hired recently for plant engineering. Paul Morgan had been with Artisan about 2 years in design.

Marketing

The company was one of four making up the wooden decorative products industry. Sales were seasonal, peaking with the Christmas period. Monthly shipments are shown

EXHIBIT C3.2   MONTHLY SHIPMENTS ($1,000)

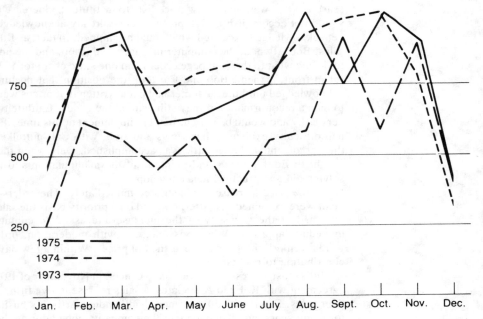

in Exhibit C3.2. Artisan's customers were some 13,000 retail shops which were serviced by outside sales representatives. Regional market shows were an important part of the marketing activity. The product line consisted of over 1,400 items and included almost anything for this consumer. The largest item was a tea cart and the smallest a clothespin-type desk paper clip. New products were continually coming up; about 100 a year were added to the line. Practically no items were ever dropped. The top 100 products averaged 5,000 units a year. The first 25 items had double the sales units of the next group. Two hundred and fifty sold over 1,000 units. The average wholesale price was $3.75. The top item sold 31,000 units last year for about $75,000 in sales. The 200th had sales over $10,000.

Marketing was the function where Bill wanted to spend most of his time. His father had left this mainly with outsiders but Bill was determined to put the company in charge of its own marketing. He attended all shows and found out firsthand what was going on. He felt the outside salesmen had let Artisan slide into making anything they could sell easily, regardless of costs and profits.

Bill hired a local young man with a good design talent, but little experience, to set up a design department. They soon came up with a new "theme" line of items which became the talk of the industry and Bill planned to try others. He engaged a New York advertising agency for a professional program of advertising in the trade journals and publicity in the newspapers. He produced an artistic catalog with color photographs rather than the dull listing used before.

There had been no price increases in quite awhile and with the recent inflation Atwood estimated the current sales prices would not yield a profit. In mid-October an immediate price increase appeared imperative if 1975 was to end with a profit. But there was great concern about the advisability of such action in the middle of the major sales season. Also, waiting on new price lists to institute the increase in an ordinary manner would not accomplish a 1975 profit; orders already acknowledged or in-house but not yet acknowledged exceeded what could be shipped. In fact, as Bill, his sister Edith from sales, Bob Atwood, the computer manager, Cal Robb, and the university professor met to decide what to do, a 30-page order from one store chain for $221,000 at the old prices sat in front of them. Bob and Cal took the position that no further orders should be acknowledged until the customer had been written that prices were increased and asked to mail a reconfirmation if they still wanted the goods. Edith felt the price increase was very risky and would be very difficult to implement at this time, if even possible. But she had difficulty explaining her views and Bob, with Cal, outtalked her. Bill listened to their arguments although little was accomplished. Only when the consultant added his weight to Edith's views and pointed out the manipulation and lack of good problem-solving did any practical ideas develop.

A 16% price increase was instituted immediately. The orders awaiting acknowledgment were examined that afternoon and on a priority basis the salesmen were called and informed of the necessity of the increase and asked to contact their customers for immediate approval. When possible, and with moderation, orders at the new prices were given priority over those at the old prices. Within a few days the new prices were contributing to profits.

Bill's most aggressive move was to cancel, in November of 1975, the company's long agreement with E. Fudd Associates, a sales representative firm. Accounting for 60% of their sales, Fudd, with 50 salesmen, had handled Artisan's business in about 20 states for many years, and had even lent the company money during the previous December. But Fudd was an old-style "character" much like Buddy—and Bill had been unable to systematically discuss market strategies or improvement ideas with him. Bill felt the 15% commission Fudd was setting could be better used at 10% directly to the salesmen and 5% in a company controlled advertising budget.

Bill had planned to deal with E. Fudd Associates after the first of the year. It would take careful action to break with Fudd and assist any reps wishing to go independent on Artisan's line. But an accidental leak had forced Bill's hand in the middle of the critical sales season. Bill did not back off but broke with Fudd immediately. Fudd countered with suits against Artisan, threats of displacing Artisan's goods with others, claims of tossing Artisan out of major regional market shows, and even withholding back, unpaid commissions on salesmen going with Artisan. Fudd spread rumors of Artisan's impending bankruptcy and sued any salesmen leaving him. Though there were bad moments, Bill held firm and in a few weeks it was over. Bill had gotten all the salesmen he wanted, was lined up for his own space in the critical shows, and the rumors were going against Fudd.

Accounting

With the hiring of Bob Atwood in the Fall of 1974 improvement in the accounting systems began, though slowly. By the spring of 1976 the outside Service Bureau had been replaced by a small in-house computer to handle order-entry and invoicing, including an inventory listing. Financial statements are shown in Exhibit C3.3.

The small computer system was delivered in January of 1976. Prior to that $85,000 to $100,000 a year had been spent for assistance from the Service Bureau. This assistance

EXHIBIT C3.3   FINANCIAL STATEMENTS

Balance sheets (in thousands)

	Five months May 31, 1976	Dec. 31, 1975	Five months May 31, 1975	Dec. 31, 1974	Dec. 31, 1973*	Dec. 31, 1972*	Dec. 31, 1971*	1970†	Sept. 30, 1969*‡	Sept. 30, 1968*‡
Assets										
Current assets:										
Cash	111	83	146	97	66	78	69		17	37
Accounts Receivable	552	608	444	693	1,191	1,286	968		911	879
Inventories:										
Finished goods	982	394	537	754	652	652	464		541	576
Work-in-process	247	247	75	136	551	444	426		367	379
Raw materials	406	348	352	604	719	547	446		390	252
Supplies	50	41	33	95	79	63	66		83	52
Total inventories	1,686	1,032	997	1,591	2,003	1,708	1,404		1,382	1,261
Other	37	36	79	256	88	1	1		219	–
Total current assets	2,386	1,759	1,666	2,637	3,349	3,073	2,442		2,529	2,177
Property and equipment	600	616	611	666	745	753	783		844	448
Other assets	143	86	54	60	731	416	610		163	139
Total	3,129	2,461	2,332	3,365	4,826	4,242	3,836		3,538	2,766
Liabilities										
Current liabilities										
Accounts Payable	168	228	329	694	543	195	411		467	166
Notes Payable	1,195	643	902	1,222	1,871	1,647	1,040		1,428	1,159
Other	448	375	204	282	131	256	275		377	329
Total current liabilities	1,811	1,246	1,435	2,198	2,545	2,098	1,726		2,272	1,654
Longer term (Adv. from stk. hldrs.)	269	367	651	705	854	593	692		252	226
Stockholders' equity	1,049	847	245	461	1,426	1,550	1,417		1,012	884

Statements of income (in thousands)

	Five months May 31, 1976	Dec. 31, 1975	Five months May 31, 1975	Dec. 31, 1974	Dec. 31, 1973*	Dec. 31, 1972*	Dec. 31, 1971*	1970†	Sept. 30, 1969*‡	Sept. 30, 1968*‡
Net sales	2,769	6,898	2,399	9,441	9,038	8,462	6,992		5,942	5,037
Less cost of goods sold	1,815	4,758	1,921	7,452	7,093	6,145	5,163		4,513	3,676
Gross profit on sales	954	2,139	478	1,988	1,945	2,316	1,828		1,428	1,361
Selling and distribution expenses	412	992	332	1,370	1,343	1,215	958		682	639
General and administrative expenses	306	586	233	897	543	549	429		340	303
Other income (expense)	47	(172)	(77)	(909)	(255)	(152)	(215)		(143)	(120)
Income (loss) before income taxes	283	389	(164)	(1,189)	(196)	399	226		263	298

* Prepared by local accountant.
† No copy in company files.
‡ Year ending September

had been primarily invoicing. After orders were manually checked for accuracy and credit, they went to the Service Bureau where a warehouse packing ticket was prepared. Then after shipment a form went back to initiate the invoice. Besides invoicing, they produced a monthly Statement of Bookings and Shippings which summarized activity by item, customer, and state. The bureau was not involved with Accounts Receivable; aging used a manual process which took 30 days and was possibly only accurate to within $25,000. In 1974 checks had been posted, taking about 3 hours per day, and then forwarded directly to the lender. This had added 3 to 4 days of work for Atwood.

The computer had caused a small management crisis for Bill. Cal Robb and Bob Atwood, neither of whom had any special knowledge or experience with computers, had selected the system they wanted with no help beyond that of computer salesmen. With only verbal arguments and several contract notebooks from the supplier, they pressured Bill for his approval. When he failed to act they saw him as foot-dragging and lacking respect for their opinions. With the counsel of the university consultant, Bill took the unpopular step of sending them back to prepare a proper proposal and timetable. In work with the vendor several serious omissions were found and corrected and all agreed the further documentation had been worthwhile. Bill approved the project.

The new system consisted of a 48K "small" computer with a 450-line-per-minute printer, two disc drives with 2 million bytes each, and seven CRTs. Monthly rental amounted to about $4,000. The software was developed in-house by Robb using basic systems supplied by the vendor at no charge. Robb was the only staff for the computer. He was 36, with a business administration degree with some concentration in accounting from a good state university. Prior to Atwood's hiring he had been controller.

By May, inventory accounting was on the computer. The inventory listings computing EOQs (economic order quantities) were available but inaccurate. Atwood believed a couple of months of debugging was necessary before computer inventory control would be possible. The data needed for the EOQ model were all old and inaccurate; lead times, prepared by a consultant years ago, were considered by all to be way off.

By June, invoicing was fully on the computer and the lender had stopped requiring the direct mailing of checks. About 3,000 invoices were prepared each month. The Accounts Receivable systems, including statements and weekly aging of delinquent accounts, were operational and about 2,500 statements were being prepared monthly. The controller felt both systems were running well and providing for good control. The computer supplier felt they had been lucky to get the system operational as quickly as they did.

Cal expected Inventory Control would be on the computer by February. In another month he would add Accounts Payable payroll, and general ledger.

Monthly preparation of financial statements had begun in January. Production costing for the statements had been based on historical indexes, but Bob reported few resulting errors. The statements were out, in typed form, 30 days after the close of the period.

Production

There were two plants, roughly identical and 5 miles apart, each with about 60,000 square feet. Kiln dry lumber, mainly high-quality Ponderosa Pine, was inventoried in truck trailers and covered sheds at the rear of the plant. The lumber width, totally random, depended on the tree, and the length was from 8 to 16 feet, in multiples of 2.

The thickness started at the lumber mill at 4, 5, or 6 "quarter" ("quarter" meaning ¼ inch, therefore 4 quarter is 1 inch). By the time it reached the plant it was about ⅛ less.

The Rough Mill foreman reviewed the batch of production orders he was given about every week and decided on the "panels" the plant would need. A panel is a sheet of wood milled to a desired thickness and with length and width at the desired dimension or some multiple. Clear panels, ones with no knots, can be made from lower-grade lumber by cutting out the defects and then glueing these smaller pieces into standard panels. Artisan did no such glueing but cut high-quality, clear lumber directly to the desired length and width. The necessary panels would be made up in the Rough Mill from lumber or from purchased glued panels. Artisan spent about as much on purchased panels as it did on raw lumber, paying about twice as much for a square foot of panel as for a square foot of lumber. Surfacers brought the wood to the desired thickness, the finished dimension plus some excess for later sanding. Rip saws cut the lumber to needed width and cut-off saws took care of the length. About 30 people worked in this area, which had about 15% of the labor cost.

The plant superintendent worked with the Machine Room foreman to decide on the sequence in which orders would be processed. Schedule due dates for each department were placed on the orders in Production Control but they followed up on the actual flow of orders only if a crisis developed. In the Machine Room 22 workers (17% of the labor cost) shaped panels to the final form. The tools included shapers, molders, routers, and borers. Patterns and jigs lowered the skill requirements, still the highest in the plant. This part of the plant was noisiest and dustiest.

In the third department, Sanding, the parts were sanded by women working mainly at individual stations. There were 24 people here. The sanded components were moved to a nearby temporary storage area on the carts which originated at Machining. It was estimated there were six to eight wooden parts in an average item. In addition there were purchased parts such as turnings and glass or metal parts. Sanding added about 19% of the direct labor to the products.

The Assembly foreman kept an eye on the arrival of all parts for an order. Assembly began when all parts were available. Eighteen people assembled the items using glue, screws, nail guns, or hammer and nails. Jigs assisted the work where possible and usually only one person worked on an order. Fourteen percent of direct labor derived from this step. Little skill was needed and dust and noise weren't a problem.

The assembled items were moved promptly to the separate Finishing area. Here they were dipped by hand into stains and sprayed with several clear coats. After oven-drying they proceeded to Packing. Most were packed individually into cartons made in the company's small plant. Finishing and Packing employed about 50 people and accounted for 34% of direct labor costs. The new 60,000 square foot Finished Goods Warehouse was 2 miles away.

The labor rates ranged from $2.30 to $5.60 per hour. The average was probably $3.00 with about a dozen people making over $4.00. Factory overhead was about 60% of direct labor. Labor costs as a percent of the wholesale selling price ran about 20%; direct material 35%. Variable costs totaled about 75%, with about another $1,800,000 in total company fixed costs. There was a three-percentage-point difference between the plants in labor costs. The capacity of the plant with 150 people working was estimated to be less than $110,000 a week. Indirect labor amounted to about 12% of plant overhead.

Most jobs did not require high skill levels. The average jobs in the Rough Mill and Machine Room, where the skilled jobs were, required no more than 5 weeks to master because the employee would usually already have advanced skills. Elsewhere a week was adequate. The managers considered the work pace quite slow.

Production Scheduling The Production Control Department began the scheduling process which is shown in Exhibit C3.4. About every week, sometimes longer, the clerk prepared a batch of production orders for each plant. Several factors determined when a batch of orders was prepared, whether the plants said they needed more work, how sales were doing, what the situation was in the warehouse, etc. The clerk examined the "Weekly Inventory Listing" for items which appeared low and the open order file to see if the items were already on a production order. He converted the information to an available supply in weeks and selected any with less than 8 weeks. If the total of orders obtained this way did not add up to an amount he had in mind, such as $60,000 to $100,000, he went back through the lists for more things to run.

A brief look at the inventory listing for December showed the first 20 items were 23% of the current inventory value. The tenth group of 20 items was 2% of inventory; the cumulative value to this point was 82%. The fortieth item had $1,800 in inventory and the two-hundredth $625.

Turning through the open order file showed almost 300 open orders, perhaps 30–50% past the due date. Several items had two or even three different production orders 2 weeks or so apart. The order size appeared to average 200 at most. One in ten was for more than 250 pieces. Only a couple were for 500 or more; the maximum was 1,000 pieces. The typical items appeared to contain about six parts and each took three to five processing steps.

The engineer was trying to estimate standards for new items as they were priced. A quick look at eight items showed a total of 1,800 minutes of set-up time for the eight and a total of 6,400 minutes per 100 units of run-time. The set-up times ranged from 100 to 250 minutes for the products but several of the parts required no set-up in some departments. Many parts required less than 30 minutes of processing in a department. The lot size on the sample items ranged from 100 to 200 units; seven were priced around $4.00 and one at $25.00.

Production Problems Bill felt production efficiency was a major problem. In talks with machinery salesmen and other visitors to the plant over recent years, Bill had come to feel the machinery was generally appropriate. But based on guesses about his competitors he felt his labor costs must be reduced. Earlier attempts to work with the plant superintendents and the various supervisors to systematically improve output had met with no success. The supervisors had been unable to identify the needs for change in the plant or to develop the programs for bringing about improvement. To help the supervisors begin to improve their operations, a weekly production meeting was begun in June 1975. At the meeting the supervisors were to examine the total dollar output and total labor cost for each plant for the past week, compare it to the labor percent goal, (16% set by Bill), and think about what could be done to improve operations for the coming week. Data on department performance were not initially available. During the first several meetings, the visiting consultant had to provide direction and ideas; the plant superintendent and his supervisors volunteered no ideas about what specifically limited the previous week's output. Bill reported that some discussion of problems began 3 or 4 months later. It was Bill's opinion that this kind of thinking and planning was not required under his father's management. The supervisors in general felt nothing was wrong in the plant, and really seemed puzzled at the thought of doing anything except continuing what they had always done.

In March of 1976, after a good deal of thought and search, Bill hired two young men for the production system. One man, Will Shire, aged 28, was hired to be general superintendent over everyone in production, and the other, Richard Barnes, aged 27,

EXHIBIT C3.4 PRODUCTION SCHEDULING SYSTEM

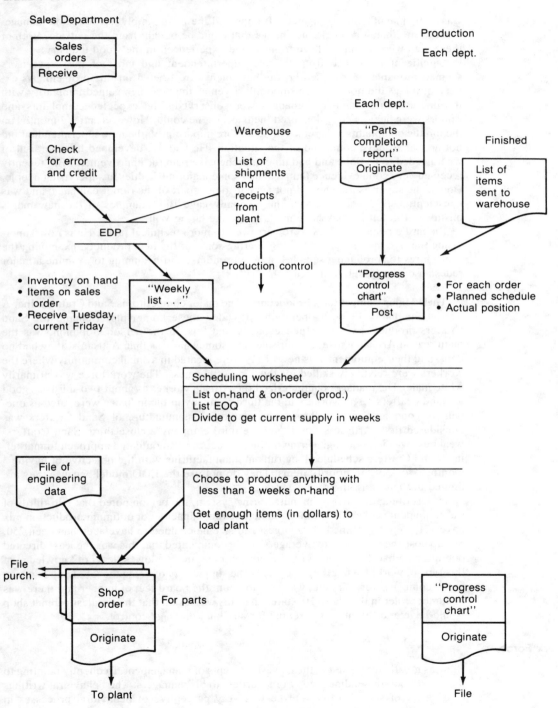

was to be manufacturing engineer. It appeared the plant simply needed good management rather than any single big change that could be bought from the outside. Both of these men were young, college trained, and experienced in the wood industry.

Significant resistance from the old superintendent and most of the supervisors seemed probable. Consequently, the new men were briefed on this problem. As expected, things did not advance smoothly. Even as the new men gained familiarity with the operation no significant changes were observed. The expected complaints and rumors were heavy and Bill ignored them as best he could. However, after 3 months on the job the complaints still persisted and, more importantly, the new superintendent did not appear to have command of the situation. He had not developed his appraisal of what needed to be done and had no comprehensive plan for improvement. Bill recently received very good evidence that Will had some major difficulties in supervising people. One of the supervisors who did not appear to be a part of the rumor campaign and was conscientiously concened about the company gave Bill examples of the new man's mistakes. Bill felt he may have made a mistake hiring Will.

Richard's responsibilities were narrowed to more technical tasks. He is now supervising the five man repair crew, engineering some of the new products, examining the procedures for producing samples of new products, and beginning to examine a major redesign of the Rough Mill area.

Their Major Competitor's Production   The major competitor is Sand Crafters, Inc. A person familiar with both operations provided these comments. Demand for Sand Crafters products exceeded their capacity and this, in the person's opinion, was the main reason Artisan existed. Their sales are somewhat less than Artisan's, they had no debt, and their equipment was new. They were located in a small community where the workers were relatively skilled for this kind of business. The work force was primarily white male. The manager characterized the Artisan worker as about two-thirds as good as Sand Crafters'. The workers in the third company in the industry were rated as one-half as good as Sand Crafters'. The quality of manufacture of Sand Crafters was considered first, Artisan second, and the third company a close third. Sand Crafters' weakness was in poor engineering of the products and an outdated approach to marketing. Sand Crafters schedules long runs in manufacturing with the objective of having 3 months' stock of top priority items. They do not use the EOQ model because they are limited in their work-in-process space.

In describing the Artisan manufacturing system, the person noted that two-thirds of the equipment is idle at any time, and that neither capacity nor optimum production mix have yet been determined. The largest run size he claimed to have seen had been 250. Set-up costs he estimated to average $30. He commented that this was the least directed operation he had ever seen, with the slowest pace and the lowest level of knowledge of this type of work. He felt they knew only the simple way of doing the job. Only one man in the company, for example, was able to count the board feet of lumber and there was no lumber ruler in the plant. He stated that this was a skill that the smallest cabinet shop would have and that it was essential for any kind of usage control.

The Work Force

Bill was greatly interested in the newest concepts of management, frequently pointing to the latest book or sending a copy of an article to his managers. The behavioral writings made a lot of sense to him and he was very perceptive of behavioral processes in meetings or situations. The participative management systems and cooperative team environments were ones Bill wanted for Artisan. However, he recognized his managers and the work force were not yet ready for this. His managers manipulated more than cooperated and the workers were neither skilled nor very productive. When he discussed the workers' desires with the supervisors he was told they wanted a retirement program and higher pay, nothing else. Bill felt this was really what the supervisors themselves wanted.

As a basis for beginning change in this area, an outside consultant conducted an employee attitude survey in May of 1976. All employees in the company were assisted in small groups in completing the written questionnaire. The questionnaire was designed (1) to find out what the employees wanted, for example, more pay, retirement plans, more or less direction, etc., (2) to gain insight into the probable impact of participative management moves, (3) to establish benchmarks of employee satisfaction so that changes over time could be monitored, (4) to develop an objective profile of the workers, and lastly (5) to look for significant differences in attitudes between the various stratifications possible.

The survey included questions developed specifically for this situation as well as a highly regarded attitude instrument, the Job Descriptive Index (JDI). Although the wording is considered simple, many of the workers did not understand such words as "stimulating," "ambitious," or "fascinating," and it became necessary to read the entire questionnaire to them.

The study showed minorities accounted for 80% of the 300 employees; white females were the largest group at 40%. The work force was 58% female, 57% white, and 39% over 45 years old. As many people have been with the company under 2 years as over 10 years—24%. The pay was only a little above the legal minimum, but many workers felt fortunate to have their jobs. There did not appear to be a "morale" crisis; the five JDI measures located the company in about the middle of the norms. The supervisory group was highest in "morale" while management was lowest. Exhibit C3.5 summarizes the JDI scores.

EXHIBIT C3.5   SUMMARY OF J.D.I. SCORES BY LEVEL
(Percentile)

Group	No. of respondents	Attitude toward:				
		Coworker	Work	Super-vision	Promo-tion	Pay
Maximum score	—	54	54	54	27	27
Total company	318	41.2	32.3	40.4	11.1	7.1
Management	7	38.0	39.4	48.0	18.7	15.9
(percentile)		(35)	(60)	(70)	(80)	(55)
Office	18	45.8	36.6	47.4	6.9	7.7
(percentile)		(60)	(50)	(65)	(50)	(25)
Supervision	13	46.8	39.2	46.1	16.1	12.2
Plant #1, hourly	141	40.4	31.6	38.4	11.7	6.6
Plant #2, hourly	101	39.8	31.3	42.6	11.0	5.9

Department: _____

		Total group					
		%		%		%	%
Sex	Male	42.2	Female	57.7			
Race	White	57.4	Black	42.5	Other	0.0	
Age	Under 25	19.8	26–35	19.5	36–45	21.4	Over 45 39.0
Years with company	Under 2	23.2	2–5	34.8	6–10	18.5	Over 10 23.5

How important would improvement in
the following things be to you?

		% of answers						
	Rank	Very little or not at all	A little	Fairly important	Very important	Extremely important	Mean	Std. dev.
Longer coffee breaks	15	33.7	20.0	16.5	18.1	11.7	2.54	1.41
More holidays	8	19.0	19.0	23.0	23.6	15.4	2.97	1.34
Guaranteed work	2	9.7	3.9	8.7	25.8	51.9	4.06	1.28
Flexibility in hours or days off	10	29.7	11.2	18.2	21.8	19.1	2.89	1.51
More overtime opportunity	17	40.8	14.1	12.4	17.3	15.4	2.52	1.53
Better insurance	6	26.0	8.9	16.1	21.7	27.3	3.15	1.55
Better working conditions	4	14.1	10.3	13.8	27.0	34.7	3.58	1.41
Retirement plan	3	12.0	6.5	9.7	18.5	53.2	3.94	1.40
Higher pay	1	3.2	5.4	8.0	19.2	64.1	4.36	1.05
Education refund	16	40.8	14.0	14.4	14.7	16.1	2.51	1.52
Treated more as an individual	7	29.6	8.1	18.2	21.5	22.5	2.99	1.54
Better way to get complaints heard	5	22.3	11.0	13.6	23.3	29.9	3.28	1.53
Better equipment	4	16.4	12.1	14.8	23.6	33.1	3.45	1.46
More direction from supervisor	14	33.8	20.0	12.5	18.4	15.4	2.62	1.48
More opportunity to learn and improve self	4	14.5	9.8	14.1	26.9	34.4	3.56	1.42
More say in how my department does things	13	37.1	14.5	13.2	18.7	16.5	2.63	1.53
More opportunity to contribute to company success	9	24.5	14.9	18.9	24.2	17.5	2.95	1.44
Better decisions by top management	12	29.8	21.4	14.9	16.2	17.8	2.71	1.48
More information on what's going on	4	16.1	9.7	12.3	29.4	32.6	3.53	1.44
Be more in charge of own self	11	53.3	10.7	16.8	19.7	19.4	2.81	1.54
Other: _____								

314

What is your opinion of the following
statements? Do you agree or disagree? (Please mark the appropriate box.)

	Strongly disagree	Disagree	No opinion	Agree	Strongly agree	Mean	Std. dev.
			% of answers				
I enjoy taking this test.	3.2	3.8	17.3	44.4	31.3	3.97	.96
My pay is fair for this kind of job.	34.4	35.3	5.4	19.9	5.0	2.26	1.26
My coworkers are good to work with.	2.9	3.5	7.3	49.4	36.9	4.14	.91
My complaints or concerns are heard by management.	12.2	18.4	17.1	39.5	12.8	3.22	1.24
Things are getting better here.	6.3	12.1	29.2	38.9	17.5	3.45	1.16
The supervisors do a poor job.	25.3	39.9	17.2	9.1	8.4	2.35	1.19
I am fortunate to have this job.	3.2	3.8	15.7	48.7	28.5	3.95	.94
Working conditions are bad here.	17.3	41.7	16.3	17.9	6.7	2.55	1.00
I benefit when the company succeeds.	12.4	24.8	16.9	31.3	14.7	3.11	1.28
I have all the chance I wish to improve my-self.	11.8	21.4	19.2	31.3	16.3	3.19	1.27
The company is well run.	6.1	18.2	38.1	36.1	11.5	3.29	1.00
Communications are poor.	13.4	27.8	25.2	21.6	12.1	2.91	1.23
I don't get enough direction from my su-pervisor.	19.6	37.5	20.2	13.1	9.6	2.56	1.22
I enjoy my work.	2.8	2.5	10.1	47.5	37.0	4.13	.90
I look for ways to improve the work I do.	1.0	2.6	8.0	51.4	37.1	4.21	.77
I need more of a chance to manage my-self.	8.3	25.2	26.5	26.5	13.4	3.11	1.17
I don't expect to be with the company long.	28.9	31.8	23.6	9.5	7.2	2.35	1.19
Morale is good here.	6.2	15.0	18.8	39.5	21.2	3.55	1.16
We all do only what it takes to get by.	32.2	39.7	10.1	12.7	5.2	2.19	1.17
I am concerned about layoffs and losing my job.	9.9	16.9	13.1	32.8	27.4	3.51	1.31
I like the way my supervisor treats me.	4.2	5.1	11.9	42.4	36.3	4.02	1.03
We need a suggestion system.	3.0	7.9	25.6	38.4	25.2	3.75	1.01
I want more opportunity for advancement.	4.02	3.7	17.4	36.1	33.5	3.86	1.10
My supervisor knows me and what I want.	5.1	15.4	18.3	40.5	20.6	3.56	1.13
We are not expected to do a very good job here.	48.2	29.1	4.2	10.2	8.3	2.01	1.30
There are too many rules.	18.1	38.2	21.0	12.6	10.0	2.58	1.21
I feel like part of a team at work.	5.7	6.7	12.4	50.3	24.8	3.52	1.06
The company and my supervisor seek my ideas.	14.2	19.4	24.6	29.1	12.6	3.06	1.25
I can influence dept. goals, methods and activities.	9.2	22.0	34.8	25.2	8.5	3.01	1.08
There is too much "family" here.	20.7	24.6	25.2	15.9	13.6	2.77	1.31
This company is good for the community.	2.2	3.5	11.1	36.3	46.8	4.22	.93

EXHIBIT C3.7   HOW IMPORTANT WOULD IMPROVEMENT IN THE FOLLOWING THINGS BE TO YOU?

	Importance			
Extreme	**Very**	**Fairly**	**Little**	**None**
Higher pay				
	Guaranteed work			
		Retirement plan		
			Better working conditions	
			Opportunity to learn/improve	
			More information	
				Better equipment
				Get complaints heard
				Better insurance
				Treated as individual
				More holidays

They were also questioned about a number of aspects of their work which could be improved. Exhibit C3.6 shows these questions. Exhibit C3.7 summarizes their views on how important improvement in the more important areas would be to them.

Employees' views of the orgnaizational climate were relatively good. They claimed to enjoy their work, looked for ways to improve it, and felt expected to do a good job. They especially felt their coworkers were good to work with and felt part of a team. They appeared to like their supervision.

Their views did not suggest need for a different manner of supervision. And they did not respond positively to the suggestion of being more in charge of themselves, did not feel strongly about having more of a say in how things were done, and didn't feel there were too many rules.

The survey revealed no critical problems, differences between groups were not extreme, and the resulting view of the worker was moderate. However, the workers were relatively unsophisticated, and there was concern they might not have accurately expressed their true feelings on the instrument.

THE MEETING WITH BOB ON JUNE 10TH

The last months of 1975 had been very good in spite of fears caused by the price increase and the changes in the sales organization and had resulted in a $390,000 profit. Bob Atwood reported that the original plan for 1976 had been for no major changes. However, there was no formal written plan. As actual sales in January and February ran well ahead of the prior year, production was allowed to stay higher than the plan. Bill believed Bob's estimate of sales at $6.5 million was very low. A quite conservative estimate, he felt, was $9 million. This level became accepted as the premise for production plannning in the first part of the year. But March and April were disappointing and May was only fair. Bill still felt the $9 milllion was reasonable. At the same time, he recognized the risks and was concerned. Bill hoped the gift shows in July would clarify the sales picture for the year.

On June 10, 1976, Bob Atwood had returned to Bill's office to press for a decision on the inventory level. He wanted Bill to pull back on plans for 1976. As sales had been slower coming in and inventories had increased more than expected, Bob had become increasingly worried. The level on the last full inventory listing prepared about 6 weeks before stood at $800,000 in wooden goods. The current level was nearer $1,100,000. From a financial perspective Bob was willing to accept a level as high as $1,600,000. But this called on limiting production now. His report dated May 13 (Exhibit C3.8) presented

EXHIBIT C3.8   ANALYSIS OF PRODUCTION LEVELS, MAY 13, 1976

| | | Sales | | | | 1976 Order receipts |
| | | Shipments | | Order receipts | | |
Month	Week	1975	1976	1975	1976	1975 Order receipts
January	1			60,428	75,517	1.25
	2			210,873	354,705	1.68
	3			176,981	247,592	1.40
	4			329,441	384,532	1.16
Total		267,000	314,000	777,723	1,062,346	1.36
February	1			215,285	143,899	.66
	2			160,996	160,932	.99
	3			230,456	238,577	1.03
	4			168,703	285,378	1.69
Total		616,000	692,000	775,440	832,786	1.06
March	1			155,339	168,217	1.08
	2			124,993	114,936	.91
	3			141,163	122,189	.86
	4			167,915	79,839	.47
Total		554,000	725,000	589,410	485,181	.82
April	1			122,692	116,221	.94
	2			135,976	120,878	.88
	3			88,148	107,590	1.21
	4			157,382	87,861	.56
Total		451,000	432,000	504,298	432,550	1.85
Year-to-date total		1,888,000	2,163,000	2,646,871	2,808,863	1.06
May	1			107,906	91,791	.85
	2			78,723	88,040	1.11
	3			89,694	114,832	1.28
	4			128,175	112,936	.88
Total		566,000	554,000	404,498	407,599	1.00
June		361,000		756,377		
July		557,000		1,057,604		
August		590,000		1,240,813		
September		922,000		1,753,880		
October		592,000		684,186		
November		896,000		322,049		
December		437,000		157,156		
Year-to-date total		6,809,000		9,023,434		

Production

	Jan.	Feb.	Mar.	Apr.	May
1975	206,899	428,899	507,589	370,221	348,151
1976	658,306	635,228	762,083	593,246	607,606

	Order receipts 1975		Projected receipts 1976	Less bad credit @ 2.4%	Credit-worthy orders	From inv. @ 9.5%
Prior	$2,646,871	× .85	$2,808,863	$ (69,496)	$2,739,367	$2,602,398
May	404,498	× .85	343,823	(8,251)	335,572	318,793
June	756,377	× .85	642,920	(15,430)	627,490	596,115
July	1,057,604	× .85	898,963	(21,575)	877,388	833,518
August	1,240,813	× .85	1,054,691	(25,312)	1,029,379	977,910
September	1,753,880	× .85	1,490,798	(35,779)	1,455,019	1,382,268
October	684,186	× .85	581,558	(13,957)	567,601	539,220
November	322,049	× .85	273,741	(6,569)	267,172	253,813
December	157,156	× .85	133,582	(3,205)	130,377	123,858
	$9,023,434		8,228,939	(199,574)	8,029,365	7,627,893

Forecasts based on production level

							Optimum
Beginning—May	$1,100,000	$1,100,000	$1,100,000	$1,100,000	$1,100,000	$1,100,000	$1,100,000
May production	720,000	670,000	620,000	570,000	520,000	470,000	600,000
May shipments	(318,793)	(318,793)	(318,793)	(318,793)	(318,793)	(318,793)	(318,793)
	1,501,207	1,451,207	1,401,207	1,351,207	1,301,207		1,381,207
June production	720,000	670,000	620,000	570,000	520,000	470,000	600,000
June shipments	(596,115)	(596,115)	(596,115)	(596,115)	(596,115)	(596,115)	(596,115)
	1,625,092	1,525,092	1,425,092	1,325,092	1,225,092		1,385,092
Jul. production	540,000	502,000	452,000	402,000	352,000	302,000	450,000
Jul. shipments	(833,518)	(833,518)	(833,518)	(833,518)	(833,518)	(833,518)	(833,518)
	1,331,574	1,193,574	1,043,574	893,574	743,574		1,001,574
Aug. production	720,000	670,000	620,000	570,000	520,000	470,000	600,000
Aug. shipments	(977,910)	(977,910)	(977,910)	(977,910)	(977,910)	(977,910)	(977,910)
	1,073,664	885,664	685,664	485,664	285,664		623,664
Sept. production	720,000	670,000	620,000	570,000	520,000	470,000	600,000
Sept. shipments	(1,382,268)	(1,382,268)	(1,382,268)	(1,382,268)	(1,382,268)	(1,382,268)	(1,362,268)
	411,396	173,396	(76,604)	(326,604)	(576,604)		(158,604)
Oct. production	720,000	670,000	620,000	570,000	520,000	470,000	600,000
Oct. shipments	(539,220)	(539,220)	(539,220)	(539,220)	(539,220)	(539,220)	(539,220)
	592,176	304,176	4,176	(295,824)	(595,824)		(97,824)
Nov. production	720,000	670,000	620,000	570,000	520,000	470,000	600,000
Nov. shipments	(253,813)	(253,813)	(253,813)	(253,813)	(253,813)	(253,813)	(253,813)
	1,058,363	720,363	370,363	20,363	(329,637)		248,363
Dec. production	540,000	502,000	452,000	402,000	352,000	302,000	450,000
Dec. shipments	(123,858)	(123,858)	(123,858)	(123,858)	(123,858)	(123,858)	(123,858)
	1,474,505	1,098,505	698,505	298,505	101,495		574,505

EXHIBIT C3.8   *(CONTINUED)*

Advantages and disadvantages

Advantages of $600,000 production level:
1. Reduces scope of operation to afford high degree of control
2. Maintains positive cash flow position for remainder of year
3. Maintains more liquid corporate position

Disadvantages of $600,000 production level:
1. More customer dissatisfaction from possible low service level
2. Probable lost sales if orders increase

Advantages of $720,000 production level:
1. High service level to accounts
2. Low probability of decrease in service if orders increase

Disadvantages of $720,000 production level:
1. Risk of inventory buildup
2. Risk of being in a "layoff" situation if orders do not increase

(Note: Funds available on inventory loan *will* support $720,000 level of production.)

Assumptions

Order volume	Order receipts for the remainder of 1976 will be 85% of order receipts for the prior year on a dollar-to-dollar basis.
Orders not creditworthy	.0374 of the dollar volume of orders will not initially clear credit. Of these, ⅔ will eventually qualify for shipment via prepayment, etc.
Service level	A 95% service level of order completion will be maintained. All orders will be shipped in month of receipt. Production from plants will be received by the Warehouse prior to orders for shipment.
Production levels	1 week of production will be lost in July and 1 week of production will be lost in December.

Possible causes of sales decrease:
1. Rejection of price increase by wholesale accounts
2. Rejection of price increase by consumer
3. Reaction to poor service level of 1975
4. Loss due to new representation

several alternative production levels for the fall. The first page of the report showed monthly shipments and order receipts for 1975 and 1976 to date and production to date in 1975 and 1976. The second page projected inventories on the basis of several production levels. He advocated a production rate of $600,000 per month.

Bob recommended they immediately cut production and make Richard Bare, the purchasing agent, production control manager with the responsibility for guiding the controlled inventory buildup. Bob felt there had been unnecessary delay in making a decision and was impatient for Bill to put this to rest.

THE ASSOCIATION FOR RETARDED CITIZENS OF GEORGIA, INC.

Prepared by William A. Jones, Jr., Georgia State University, and Victoria E. Johnson, Mercer University, Atlanta Campus.

The year was 1855. The place, Scotland's romantic, ageless Edinburg. The time was a cold, foggy twilight hour. A small, frail five-year-old boy stood with his nose pressed firmly against the windowpane of his upstairs bedroom staring intently into the street below. For twenty-five minutes a loving but gradually-growing-impatient Nanny had been gently urging him toward preparation for bedtime. And he, as small boys had been wont to do from time immemorial, was using every device at his command to postpone the inevitable. Finally, in a voice that gave full indication of her rising indignation, the Nanny called sharply: "But what in the world are you doing so long Bobby?"

"Watching old Thomas," came the matter-of-fact reply.

"But what could old Thomas possibly be doing to keep you spell-bound for all this time?" queried the now curious Nanny.

"He's punching holes in the dark," answered the wee Robert Louis Stevenson, continuing to watch with fascinated gaze as crippled old Thomas, the street's lamplighter, moved slowly down the street, lighting each lamp until the street was safe for all to pass by. It was a scene of breathtaking beauty for the small, imaginative boy whose physical world was often limited to the four walls of his bedroom.

The Association for Retarded Citizens of the United States (ARC/U.S.) uses the above passage to symbolize the efforts of the many people who attempt to meet the needs of citizens with retardation.[1] The ARC/U.S. is concerned specifically with local-, state-, and national-level efforts which will:

Used by permission.

Promote the general welfare of mentally retarded individuals of all ages everywhere, at home, in the communities, in institutions and in public, private and religious schools and to prevent mental retardation in children yet unborn.[2]

While all units of the association share this common goal, the state- and local-level units also differ from one another in many ways. Member units vary in such characteristics as age, size, experience, public acceptance, and financial resources.

THE ASSOCIATION FOR RETARDED CITIZENS OF GEORGIA, INC.

The Association for Retarded Citizens of Georgia, Inc. (ARC/Ga.) is one of these member units. It has been in existence since the mid-1950s and currently has about 5,000 members throughout the state. It was originally created for the purpose of providing services to persons with mental retardation. As the various levels of government have become more active in the provision of such services, the ARC/Ga.'s purpose has changed from services to advocacy—or as the association president stated in a presentation to a graduate-level business class ". . . from pity and charity to human rights."[3]

The mission of the ARC/Ga. is to promote productive lives for mentally retarded persons. The organization monitors legislative, judicial, and executive branch activities of both the national and state governments. It actively seeks to inform parents and others of the rights of individuals with mental retardation, and it works with anyone requesting assistance in obtaining such rights and/or services. ARC/Ga. actively lobbies for new legislation and funding for services that have been legislated but not appropriated, and it provides legal representation on behalf of its clients. The association seeks to assure that promises made by legislatures do not go awry as the cup of bureaucracy moves toward the lips of needy clients.

The constitution of the ARC/Ga., last amended on June 15, 1984, is collectively established by local units throughout the state of Georgia. These local units, the "grass roots" of the association, are nonprofit groups of parents and friends of persons with mental retardation. Units are defined in terms of geographic area, usually one or more counties. Throughout Georgia there are a total of 159 counties and a total of 50 local units of the ARC/Ga. The 50 local units are organized into 9 ARC/Ga. regions.

Officers of the association include a president, senior vice president, regional vice presidents from each of the nine regions, a secretary, and a treasurer. The board of directors includes the officers, the immediate past-president, one delegated representative of each local unit, and five board members-at-large. Governance of the association is conducted through an annual meeting. The board of directors meets quarterly and governs the association between meetings. An executive committee exercises board powers, subject to review, between board meetings.

An executive director is employed by the board to administer the association's affairs. This individual serves at the pleasure of the board and is responsible for carrying out the policies of the association in consultation with the board members. The current executive director first came to ARC/Ga. in 1980 as a temporary employee. She had earlier been a high school science teacher, obtained a master's degree in special education, and worked as a volunteer in the field of mental retardation. She became executive director in 1982 and has worked diligently since that time to improve the administrative policies and procedures of the association. To assist in her efforts, the executive director is empowered to hire a small staff, currently three individuals with training/experience in the mental retardation field, and one secretary-bookkeeper. The executive director sees time, and dollars, as her greatest current needs.

WINDS OF CHANGE IN THE NONPROFIT SECTOR

The late 1980s are bringing major change across the landscape of American nonprofit organizations. While it is far too early to tell where these changes will lead, many such organizations will clearly be quite different in the future. The driving force behind this revolution is the shifting view of government's role in society. The "answers" to societal problems that governmental programs seemed to promise in the 1960s and 1970s are in hasty retreat. Defense priorities, trade and budget deficits, and other problems have conspired to gnaw away at the federal government's support for the nonprofit sector of the economy.

The New York Times reported that the federal government cut aid to nonprofits by 20 percent between 1981 and 1984—a total of $12.5 billion.[4] The same report noted that contributions from individuals, foundations, and corporations came nowhere near making up the shortfall; and that individual nonprofits are trying a variety of approaches in seeking support. Big Bird has become big business for the Children's Television Workshop, the Red Cross has started selling first-aid kits, public television stations are moving closer to accepting advertising, and Planned Parenthood tried to market condoms until its affiliates quashed the idea.

Such alternative approaches to fund-raising have had mixed results. Aside from the organizations' mixed abilities to market, there are other difficulties. The Small Business Administration has suggested making the code that governs the tax status of nonprofits more restrictive. The Internal Revenue Service may question business ventures not considered central to the mission of a nonprofit. Efforts to engage in profit-making ventures take time and energy away from an organization's central goals. Should commercial ventures succeed, contributors may perceive such success as indicating their donations are no longer needed.

The 1986 tax law is the latest in a series of concerns for the nonprofit sector.[5] Tax reform could reduce incentives for private giving. Under the top personal tax rate, which takes effect in 1988, it will cost the contributor 72 cents to make a $1 contribution. In December of 1986, under the old tax law, the corresponding cost was 50 cents. Potentially more worrisome, according to some, is the fact that taxpayers who do not itemize will be barred from deductions for charitable gifts. One estimate is that these changes in the tax law will slash contributions by $11 billion in 1988. Coupled with Reagan administration efforts to reform federal spending patterns, tax reform could have hardly come at a worse time.

Nonprofit organizations appear to have two alternatives for survival in the current environment. They can "go into business" or they can "do fund-raising." Indications are that either route will be filled with difficulties for the forseeable future.

THE ARC/GA. STRIVES TO COPE

On July 1, 1985, attorney Patricia Smith became the president of ARC/Ga. On that day she also inherited an association budget with a deficit of $30,000. After deliberating alternative ways to reduce expenses, two members of the board of directors stepped forward and agreed to obtain personal bank loans to balance the budget. With that decision made, the board voted to approve the 1985–86 budget of $185,000. Salaries, rent, postage, and other expenses could be met—the association's survival was assured for one more year.

Formidable challenge is certainly nothing new for the ARC/Ga. Its 30-year history has consistently been filled with such "opportunity," both in terms of its programmatic goals, and in terms of survival. Currently, the basic source of income for the association is the affiliation fee that is paid by each of the 50 local units. Each local pays a formula-determined amount based on a combination of area population and buying power. Local units pay amounts ranging from $500 to $30,000 each year. Because they also have budgetary problems, locals would naturally prefer to retain these funds at the local level. A similar situation exists for the ARC/Ga. An affiliation fee must be paid to the Association of Retarded Citizens/U.S., which is $25,000 plus $6 for each member within the state of Georgia.

During 1986 the ARC/Ga. was also administering three federal grant programs. The grants, all designed to reach/educate parents of children with special education needs, totaled $220,000. Sixty-five percent of the executive director's time has been "dedicated" to these programs. While grants of this type are definite assets for the association, they do redirect some staff energy, and their future availability is uncertain at best.

A mainstay in the ARC/Ga. income stream has been supplied for a number of years by the Knights of Columbus. Each year members of this organization sell "Tootsie Roll" candies. One-half of the funds that are raised is contributed to ARC/Ga. and the other half goes to participating ARC local units. Many of the locals use these funds as the source of their affiliation fees paid to ARC/Ga.

The board also voted to try a new fund-raising approach for the first time in 1986—an auction. This event, held during February of 1986, offered a wide range of items for interested bidders. Former First Lady Roselynn Carter sent an autographed copy of her book, *First Lady From Plains*. Other items included such things as rugs, china, trips to Europe and the Bahamas, and several University of Georgia items. The well-known coach and athletic director at the University of Georgia, Vince Dooley, agreed to be the honorary chairperson for the auction. Professional auctioneers volunteered to conduct the event. Despite the lack of experience with designing and implementing auctions, and a relatively short timeframe, the event was sufficiently successful that approximately $9,000 was raised. Perhaps more significant, however, is the fact that all who participated in developing and implementing the idea agreed to continue it in future years. With added experience, and good luck, the auction will become a regular part of the activities, and income, of the association.

The most recent development of significance occurred when the Southern Bell "Pioneers," Dixie Chapter, agreed to work on behalf of the ARC/Ga. for a period of one year. The Pioneers organization, made up of active and retired Southern Bell employees, selects a different nonprofit/charitable organization each year. Some of the Pioneer members may develop continuing interest in the ARC/Ga., and extend their individual efforts over a much longer period of time.

Most of the local units in Georgia are essentially groups/clubs of parents who have children with some degree of mental retardation. Probably 90% of the local units are in this category. Five or six of the units have grown beyond this stage of development and have been able to hire one or more staff to work on issues of concern to the members of the local organization. A few local units have established business ventures in an attempt to raise funds. The Cobb County unit, as an example, has launched a thrift shop which retails used clothing and other merchandise. Such retail operations are difficult to sustain over a long period of time, primarily because they are staffed with volunteers.

One wish, possibly a dream, of ARC/Ga. President Patricia Smith is to develop a mechanism for financial support that could essentially be "franchised" to local units, as well as used by the state-level organization. The ideal franchise would generate a steady income of sufficient proportion, it would also be self-supporting, and ARC/Ga. staff and volunteers could work full-time on the association's mission.

HELP!

Dr. Thomas B. Clark
Chairman, Department of Management
Georgia State University
Atlanta, Georgia 30303-3083

Dear Dr. Clark:

The Association for Retarded Citizens of Georgia needs your help. In these days of decreasing government funds for charitable organizations, we must find creative and innovative ways to finance ourselves or cease to provide the services that we have given so freely for many years.

In our attempt to create new sources of revenue we first turned to out-and-out fund raising. This, however, is an activity which consumes inordinate amounts of time for a very speculative return and is often not cost efficient. Thus, we wish to explore other avenues of revenue production.

It has occurred to us that we need to go into business. Our current fund-raising projects will bring us in some money, but if we just turn around and spend it for our operating costs it will be gone and we will have to go through the same process each year. How much wiser it would be to invest the money in some type of business enterprise that will give us a reasonable return on our investment year after year.

But what do we invest in? How do we maximize our nonprofit status? Should we operate something ourselves or buy into someone else's operation or contract for use of our name or what? What is there a market for; how do we access the market; how do we sell our product; how do we decide the wisest avenue for us to follow?

We don't know any of these answers. Therefore, we decided to look for a university business college that would be willing to take us on as a project. Your students could benefit greatly, because this would not be a simulation—the end product would be a real business—and we would have the benefit of all of your expertise in marketing, management, tax, etc.

We have lots of ideas, but we don't know how feasible they are and we have no actual business experience. Hopefully, we sound like the kind of challenge that would add an exciting and rewarding dimension to several people's academic career. We will meet with anyone there to explore this further and we would like to get going as soon as possible. If no one is interested please let us know quickly so that we can look elsewhere.

Sincerely yours,

Pat Smith
President
The Association for Retarded
  Citizens of Georgia, Inc.

APPENDIX: Overview of the Mental Health Environment

Historically, the family bore primary responsibility for mentally ill or mentally retarded family members. Public institutions were scarce and "distracted" individuals were either tolerated or confined to cellars or attics. An increasing population, rapid urbanization, and an increase in the number of sick and dependent people necessitated a more institutionalized system of care. These early almshouses were multi-purpose, welfare institutions serving a diverse population of orphans, retarded, poor, aged, and infirm, and mentally ill.[6]

The first hospital with a ward serving only the "mentally disabled" was established in Philadelphia in 1756 by the Society of Friends. The state of Virginia established the first public institution devoted exclusively to the care of the mentally ill in 1772. Built as a matter of conscience and/or fear of the insane, the facilities provided a method for maintaining and segregating mentally disabled from the mainstream of urban activity. Because the general population viewed mental disorders as incurable, or as moral defects, state and local governments found it politically unwise to appropriate adequate resources for humane care. The bulk of traditional mental health services was provided in isolated, depersonalized, coercive contexts.

A breath of reform occurred during the early 1900s with the influence of "moral therapy." The importance of kindness, patience, and understanding in dealing with the mentally ill was emphasized. Physical and occupational therapy, a nutritional diet, and a close and trusting relationship between staff and patients were part of this approach. This model eventually succumbed, however, to an enduring belief that mental disorders were incurable. Public institutions reverted to custodial warehouses, and institutional authority over patients was virutally unlimited. Patients were denied due process and other civil rights and released at the discretion of hospital officials. Periods of hospitalization were unspecified, reviews of confinement were ignored or cursory, and commitment orders were signed without testimony.[7]

Despite the establishment of a program of public health grants by the Social Security Act of 1935, mental health needs continued to be neglected, until events of World War II altered national attitudes. The rejection of almost 2 million men for service due to mental problems prompted Congress to authorize substantial federal expenditures for the treatment, prevention, and control of mental illness.[8]

The federal government became a permanent presence in the field of mental health with the enactment of the National Mental Health Act of 1946. This statute established the National Institute of Mental Health to administer research grants, training programs, and demonstration projects, and to oversee the collection and dissemination of mental health information. Congress passed the Mental Health Study Act in 1955, establishing the Joint Commission on Mental Illness and Health to conduct a comprehensive examination of the nature and treatment of mental illness in the United States. The commission's six-year study called for more federal support for basic mental health research, and additional resources for recruitment and training of mental health professionals and support personnel.[9]

Despite these important events, actual conditions of the mentally disabled remained virtually unchanged until the mid-1960s. That decade witnessed a flourishing economy, extensive domestic program funding, a heightened public responsibility for the disadvantaged, and powerful mental health allies at the national level. Activism brought major revisions in the laissez-faire attitude of the government and in the awareness of constituent groups. Using the momentum and the successes of the broader civil rights movement, advocates, such as the national Association of Retarded Citizens and the Council for Exceptional Children, demanded constitutional guarantees.

JUDICIAL AND CONGRESSIONAL RESPONSES

The courts became a potent force in changing societal conditions of the disabled as the scope of existing laws and programs expanded. Three landmark cases which established rights in this area were: *Pennsylvania Association for Retarded Children (PARC) v. the State of Pennsylvania* (1971); *Mills v. D.C. Board of Education* (1972); and *Wyatt v. Stickney* (1971).[10] *PARC* and *Mills* both addressed the exclusion from public schools, and the lack of appropriate educational programming for certain handicapped children. *Wyatt* involved inmates at three Alabama mental hospitals. The courts in these cases supported rights of the handicapped to a free public education and to a least restrictive environment. These basic rights have been modified and extended in subsequent court decisions regarding various programs designed to meet individual needs (*Armstrong v. Kline*, 1979; *Norris v. Massachusetts Department of Education*, 1981; and *William S. v. Gill*, 1982).[11]

The legal doctrines reflected in these cases were incorporated in Congressional efforts to assure the rights of handicapped citizens. Two of the most significant are The Rehabilitation Act of 1973 and The Education for All Handicapped Children Act of 1974.[12] The Rehabilitation Act requires affirmative action in employment and prohibits discrimination because of handicapping conditions in any program receiving Federal assistance. The Education for All Handicapped Children Act guaranteed a "free appropriate education" to all handicapped children ages 3–21 in the "least restrictive environment."

The Rehabilitation Act included no program provisions or funds for policy implementation. It did, however, contain a provision for withdrawal of funding for noncompliance. On the other hand, Congress authorized generous sums for the education of children. Federal assistance was intended to defray a percentage of the state and local costs associated with educating handicapped children. Originally, this amount was to be approximately 15% of the excess expense, with a ceiling of 40% by 1982. The actual funded percentage has been significantly less. For example, in 1984, the appropriated amount of $998 billion represented an 8% reimbursement of state and local costs for educating handicapped children.[13]

NOTES

1 Dorothy G. Murray, "Punching Holes in the Dark," in *The Local Association for Retarded Citizens: A Guide for Boards, Officers, and Committee Chairmen* (Arlington, Texas: National Association for Retarded Citizens, 1978), p. ii.

2 Ibid., p. ii–1.

3 Presentation by Patricia Smith to business policy class at Georgia State University, May 1986.

4 William Meyers, "The Nonprofits Drop the 'Non'," *The New York Times*, November 24, 1985.

5 "'Tis the Season for Charities to Worry," *Business Week*, December 1, 1986, pp. 70–74.

6 D. Rothman, *The Discovery of the Asylum* (New York: Little, Brown, 1971).

7 J. Levine, *The History and Politics of Community Mental Health* (New York: Oxford University Press, 1981).

8 United States Congress House Committee on Interstate and Foreign Commerce, 79th Congress, 1945.

9 Joint Commission on Mental Health of Children; *Crisis in Child Mental Health: Challenge for the 1970's* (New York: Harper & Row, 1969).

10 *Pennsylvania Association for Retarded Children v. Pennsylvania*, 334 F. Supp. 1257 (E.D.Pa. 1971); *Mills v. Board of Education*, 348 F. Supp. 866 (D.D.C. 1972); *Wyatt v. Stickney*, 325 F. Supp. 781, 784 (M.D. Ala. 1971).

11 *Armstrong v. Kline*, 476 F. Supp. 583 (E.D. Pa., 1979); *Norris v. Massachusetts Department of Education*, 529 F. Supp. 759 (D.Mass. 1981); *William S. v. Gill*, 536 F. Supp. 505 (N.D. Ill. 1982).

12 Education of All Handicapped Children Act of 1974, P.L. 94–142, 10 U.S.C. Section 1401 et seq.; Rehabilitation Act of 1973, 19 U.S.C. Section 701 et seq.

13 Angela Evans, *Education of the Handicapped, Issue Brief* (Washington: Congressional Research Service, 1983).

CASE 5

CANADIAN CELLULOSE
COMPANY, LIMITED

Prepared by Robert W. Sexty,
Memorial University of Newfoundland.

Friday, June 29, 1973. The deal was completed at 10:53 A.M. Champagne was opened and toasts were given. Employees were treated to a smorgasbord lunch. Executives, lawyers, accountants, consultants, and politicians involved in the deal went to a special dinner at the Vancouver Club.

The deal was the takeover, by the government of British Columbia, of Columbia Cellulose Company, Limited (Colcel), a subsidiary 91.3 percent owned by Celanese Corporation of New York. A new corporation, Canadian Cellulose Company Limited (CanCel), was formed with 79 percent of the shares owned by the government.

Colcel had been operating in British Columbia for about 25 years. The company operated plants in two parts of the province: in the Northwest, sulphite and bleached kraft pulp mills at Prince Rupert and a sawmill at Terrance; and in the southern interior, a bleached kraft pulp mill and sawmill at Castlegar. The operations of the company had suffered from financial, production, and management problems. Over the years, the parent company, Celanese Corporation, had lost about $120 million in Colcel, including an operating loss of $17 million on sales of $83.5 million in 1971. Colcel had only one small profit in the 1966 to 1972 period, a large accumulated earnings deficit, a negative net worth, and a heavy load of short- and long-term debt. Highlights of Colcel's performance during the years 1968 to 1972 are included in Exhibit C5.1.

REASON FOR TAKEOVER

The British Columbia government decided to take over Colcel in 1973 for several reasons. The majority owner, Celanese, had been attempting since 1968 to sell its interest in Colcel. In 1972, Celanese received an offer to purchase the part of Colcel's

Used by permission.

EXHIBIT C5.1 CANADIAN CELLULOSE COMPANY, LIMITED, TEN-YEAR REVIEW OF FINANCIAL PERFORMANCE, 1968–1977*

	1977	1976	1975	1974	1973	1972	1971	1970	1969	1968
Earnings and financial position (millions)										
Net sales	$161.1	$177.6	$156.0	$191.5	$133.8	$118.8	$ 83.5	$ 83.5	$103.5	$ 88.2
Net earnings/loss	17.3	26.1	27.5	50.9	12.3	(8.0)	(48.8)	(3.9)	1.4	(9.5)
Working capital	57.1	65.3	65.6	52.6	13.2	(32.6)	19.5	12.0	20.6	24.4
Fixed assets	347.6	272.3	276.9	263.6	252.3	253.1	245.9	241.8	237.2	227.4
Accumulated depreciation, amortization, & depletion	(204.8)	(195.5)	(216.0)	(206.4)	(198.1)	(125.3)	(116.9)	(81.7)	(75.6)	(67.4)
Other assets	3.1	4.3	4.0	3.4	2.6	3.5	4.4	4.5	2.3	2.6
Long-term debt	79.5	41.2	47.7	54.2	60.5	71.2	117.4	103.6	102.8	105.4
Deferred income taxes	50.0	.1	.1	.1	.9	—	—	2.7	6.5	6.4
Minority interest	—	—	—	—	—	29.9	29.9	15.5	15.5	15.5
Shareholders' equity	118.5	105.1	82.7	58.9	8.6	(2.4)	5.6	54.8	59.7	59.7
Earnings per share†										
Earnings before extraordinary items	$ 1.03	$ 1.20	$ 1.25	$ 2.38	$ .58					
Net earnings	1.41	2.14	2.25	4.17	1.01					
Dividends	.32	.30½	.30	.30	.05					
Changes in financial position (millions)										
Sources: Cash flow from operations	$ 32.7	$ 37.3	$ 38.4	$ 61.9	$ 24.1	$ 2.8	$ (8.0)	$ 3.0	$ 11.9	$ 1.9
Other, including long-term debt	47.5	.1	.4	.1	42.3	1.6	35.3	13.1	2.7	17.6
Total sources	80.2	37.4	38.8	67.0	66.3	4.4	27.3	16.1	14.6	19.3
Applications of:										
Fixed assets	77.9	27.5	14.9	14.6	9.5	10.2	12.1	11.2	12.7	4.0
Dividends	3.9	3.7	3.7	.6	—	—	.5	1.0	1.5	.5
Long-term debt	6.5	6.5	6.5	7.1	7.3	46.2	7.2	9.9	4.2	4.3
Other	.1	—	.7	.3	3.7	.1	—	2.6	—	15.6
Total applications	88.4	37.7	25.8	22.6	20.5	56.5	19.8	24.7	18.4	24.4
Increase (decrease) in working capital	(8.2)	(.3)	13.0	39.4	45.8	(52.1)	7.5	(8.6)	(3.8)	(5.1)

* Comparative data for 1972 and prior is that of Columbia Cellulose Company Limited.
† Per share information is not available for 1968–1972 since the reorganization at June 29, 1973, renders comparison with Columbia Cellulose inappropriate.
Source: Company annual reports.

British Columbia operations in the Castlegar area from Weyerhaeuser Canada Limited. The proposed sale required the consent of the government, as the transfer of timber rights was necessary. The government would not consent to the transfer, as it was concerned about the future of the Province's Northwest region. It was felt that the Prince Rupert operations, being less viable and unprofitable, might be closed, creating more unemployment. The government had concluded that the takeover was necessary to encourage development in British Columbia's Northwest.

Celanese could not find a purchaser for the entire company. Prospective purchasers were discouraged by the corporation's remote location and a corporate situation that inhibited expansion.

Another consideration was the status of the minority shareholders. When the deal to assume 79 percent was announced by R. A. Williams, minister of lands, forests, and water resources, in the legislature on April 2, 1973, he stated:

> . . . The remaining 21 percent common shares of Canadian Cellulose would be distributed to Columbia Cellulose's more than 8,000 public shareholders. Thus, under this agreement, the powerless minority within the present corporation structure of these companies would be assured of their position in relation to the assets of the company. . . . This action by the government ensures the position of the minority shareholders which would have been in jeopardy had the proposed sale of the southern operations gone ahead. If, for example, the company's Castlegar operation, Celgar, had been sold to Weyerhaeuser Canada Limited last August, these shareholders would not have been able to recover any of their original investment which was some $25 million.[1]

In addition, many senior employees of Colcel and the government preferred the company be Canadian owned.

The principal features of the completed deal were:

• The preferred shareholders were to receive $1.80 per share, accrued dividend arrearages, and two common shares of CanCel for each preferred share of Columbia Cellulose. The estimated $1.5 million cost of the dividend payment was to be borne by Celanese, the parent company. Former preferred shareholders now hold 14 percent of the new company's common stock.

• Former Colcel common shareholders now hold 7 percent of the common stock.

• The government assumed the guarantee obligations for the first mortgage bonds of Columbia Cellulose and the bank debt of some of the subsidiaries, amounting to about $78 million. An annual standby fee of one-quarter of 1 percent on the outstanding balance of long-term bonds is paid by Canadian Cellulose to the Province in respect of the guarantee.

• The government made no payments to Celanese or Columbia Cellulose but acquired 79 percent of the common stock.

• Celanese was to release CanCel from its $73 million debt to the parent company.

• 9.1 million acres of land in tree farm licensed areas were returned to the Province.

The government already held equity interests in several forest industry enterprises, Kootenay Forest Products Ltd., Ocean Falls Corporation, and Plateau Mills Limited. Opposition politicians and the business community were critical of public ownership in a private-sector industry. The sceptics also feared that taxpayer money was to be invested to bail out a financially inept and unprofitable corporation.

THE COMPANY IN 1973

The reorganized management team took over on June 29. Top management, including former Colcel executives and others hired from outside, was headed by Ronald M. Gross as president and chief executive officer. Mr. Gross had been an executive vice president and secretary with Colcel. A board of directors of nine men was appointed and was comprised of:

E. Bertram Berkley, chairman and president of Tension Envelope Company of Kansas City, the second largest envelope manufacturer in the U.S.

Alan S. Gordon, chairman of Merrill Lynch Royal Securities Ltd. of Montreal and director of various companies

Ronald M. Gross, Canadian Cellulose president

Max Litvine, managing director of Compagnie Bruxelles Lambert of Brussells

Harry L. Purdy of Vancouver, former professor of commerce and business administration at the University of British Columbia

John H. Spicer of Edmonton, vice president of the Mountain Region of Canadian National Railways

Ira D. Wallach of New York, president of Gottesman-Central National Organization, a pulp marketing firm

Donald N. Watson of Vancouver, president of Pacific Western Airlines Limited

Charles C. Locke of Vancouver, partner in the law firm of Ladner Downs.

The board had been appointed by the government upon the recommendation of CanCel's management. There were no politicians or civil servants included, all members being from the private sector.

An immediate challenge faced the new management team and board. Colcel had not been considered as a serious operator in the British Columbia forest industry. Its management had been largely Americans who lacked knowledge of the British Columbia industry. Management had also become demoralized by the performance of the company and the uncertainty created by Celanese's attempts to sell. Some of Colcel's physical plant had been allowed to deteriorate during the period of uncertainty.

Top management set about immediately to make CanCel a viable enterprise. It identified several challenges and/or opportunities that had to be faced:

1 There was a need to develop a more appropriate pulp marketing strategy.

2 It was essential to improve the company's financial condition.

3 The problem of an inefficient and obsolete sulphite mill had to be resolved.

4 There had to be an improvement in the wood resource utilization.

5 A long-term environmental program had to be developed.

Studies were initiated immediately on the best use of the Prince Rupert sulphite mill, the availability of timber in the Kootenay operations, and the possible increase in capacity of the Castlegar pulp mill and sawmill operations. Gross also began long-term planning and the setting of priorities for future capital expenditures.

THE DEVELOPMENT OF STRATEGY

Faced with these challenges/opportunities, top management and the board developed a corporate strategy. The markets of the company's products, timber, sulphite pulp, and draft pulp were assessed. The decision was made that the most viable product was bleached kraft pulp. As Gross stated:

> . . . We decided to build on our principal strength, which is in bleached softwood kraft pulp. We sell this product in more than 20 countries, and concluded that it offered the most promising long-term market prospects.[2]

With this in mind, CanCel embarked on a capital development program. The program, announced in 1975, was to be in two phases. Phase I involved the conversion of the Prince Rupert sulphite mill to kraft pulp at a cost of about $100 million. Phase II, which was subject to assessment of market and financial conditions, involved the construction of a new bleached kraft mill at Castlegar at a cost of about $205 million. The rationale for this program was provided by Gross:

> . . . Expansion first at Castlegar would have been an attractive proposition, but there were disadvantages. . . . In the first place, we would still have been saddled with the situation at Prince Rupert. Secondly, the capital required for Castlegar— we estimate $205 million in 1975 dollars—is double what we will spend at Prince Rupert.
>
> We didn't want to embark on a project of that size right now because it would have been very difficult without additional equity financing. We didn't feel that the company, or the financial markets generally, were in a position to accept equity financing at present. Turning the Prince Rupert operation around will give us a stronger production and earnings base, and enable us to go ahead later with expansion at Castlegar.[3]

The decision regarding the Prince Rupert sulphite mill was complicated. The sulphite mill was obsolete and the costs of production were high, with 30 percent more wood, three times more energy and more chemicals required to produce the sulphite than in a mill using modern technology. The market for the mill's product, an acetate specialty pulp, was also declining. Attempts to produce other grades of sulphite pulp in greater demand were not successful. In addition, the mill was a polluter of the air and water, and an expenditure of approximately $80 million would have been required to alleviate the problem. The total investment of $100 million was only $20 million more than the expenditure required to meet pollution regulations on the old plant. The new mill would meet pollution regulations and allowed the company to convert production to kraft pulp for which markets were more promising.

CanCel was a nonintegrated producer of lumber and pulp. The production of its sawmills and pulp mills was not sold to another CanCel division or associated company. Management considered this an advantage as CanCel was one of a few pulp producers without an affiliation with a paper plant. There was no "captive" forward integration and thus customers were assured a pulp supply, as supplies would not be preempted by CanCel's own paper mills.

The marketing strategy for pulp became explicit. Eighty percent of the kraft pulp was sold on long-term contracts in over 20 countries. The company decided not to accept 100 percent of a customer's business, but to take no more than 10 percent of the market in any one country and supply no more than 50 percent of an individual customer's needs.

No sales were made in Canada, and the customers were not integrated enterprises in the paper industry. Sales contacts were made from the top management level of CanCel to the top management of the customer. The president participated in the corporation's marketing program and two vice presidents were involved, one handling sales in North America, the other handling sales in Europe and Japan. Efforts were made to develop close and long-term sales relationships between CanCel, the nonintegrated producer of pulp, and its customers, nonintegrated producers of paper products. The lumber products were sold in the U.S. to several nonintegrated customers by a similar strategy.

The operations of the company are decentralized by plant with a sparse corporate office organization. The corporate office was involved with long-term planning, the establishment of board policy, and the monitoring of progress. Company executives pointed with pride to the low proportion of selling and administrative costs to sales.

The performance of the company improved immediately. The price of kraft pulp increased from $175 per ton in 1973 to $460 in 1975. The company was able to take advantage of this increased demand, a profit was made in 1973, and dividends were paid in 1974. Profits were made every year from 1973 to 1977 (refer to Exhibit C5.1). Gross attributes CanCel's successful turnaround to several factors:

> . . . The company's board of directors and professional management were allowed to operate in an independent fashion without interference from government. We were able to capitalize on the very strong 1973–74 pulp market. And we switched to a long-term marketing strategy from mainly selling pulp into spot markets. Effort was also made to spread the risk around by diversifying our customer base. As a result, CanCel now sells its pulp in about 24 countries, and is not tied to one market.[4]

Sceptics, critical of the takeover, were now silent. One investment firm even recommended CanCel stock as a " . . . speculative issue for aggressive investors"[5] and predicted improved performance. Another industry analyst referred to the takeover as a " . . . pretty canny capitalist deal by the former socialist government."[6] A headline of a *The Financial Post* article read, "David Barrett's CanCel Deal Was a Good Buy."[7] A typical comment from the business press summarizes the change of attitude towards the corporation:

> . . . Three years ago when British Columbia's then-NDP government stepped in to revive the floundering Columbia Cellulose Co. Ltd., the sceptics were vocal in their criticism of the government's rescue of a chronic money-loser that was all but disowned by its American parent.
>
> Those critics are no longer heard from. In what must be one of the most dramatic turnabouts in recent corporate history, Canadian Cellulose Co. Ltd. (as it is now called) stands among the biggest and most profitable companies in the Canadian forest products industry.[8]

CHALLENGES TO MANAGEMENT

An improvement in the company's performance came soon after the reorganization. However, in the five years after the reorganization, the management had to confront a series of challenges involving economic, political, and social consequences.

Relationship to Government

Due to the fact that the major shareholder was the British Columbia government, CanCel was viewed by some as an instrument of government, that is, as a crown corporation. Politicians would frequently boast about "our company." Few people realized that CanCel was not a crown corporation but instead a separate legal entity incorporated under the British Columbia companies legislation.

In the early years of CanCel's operations, persons did attempt to communicate through politicians. For example, during a strike at the corporation's Castlegar pulp mill in 1973, the president of the Pulp and Paper Workers of Canada, Local I, sent a telegram to Resources Minister Robert Williams, complaining about what he claimed was the intransigent attitude of CanCel's management. Government tried to discourage such communications, and the corporation resisted all such attempts. Nevertheless, various announcements by the company were used politically. For example, layoffs at the Castlegar sawmill during an election campaign or announcement of planned expansions were used by different politicians depending upon their circumstances.

A serious problem for the government was the charge that it was in a conflict of interest position as owner and corporate exploiter of natural resources. Also, there was a charge that the government might use the company to provide extensive employment opportunities. The employment record of government appears to disprove this, as employment was 3,000 in 1973, rose to 3,200 in 1974, and then fell to 2,600 in 1977.

Government and management argued that relations with the government had to be, and were, at arm's length, because the policies of government in the areas of resource management, environmental control, and labor relations must apply equally to all. Despite this, Gross frequently claimed that government ownership was a handicap to the company. However, he always insisted that the company received no favored treatment and that the decision of the government to entrust responsibility for CanCel to an independent board of directors and professional management was crucial in the success of the company. In Gross's words:

> . . . We [CanCel] have received no special treatment from the government of British Columbia, none has been asked for, offered or is required. In fact, in everything, our majority ownership may even be a handicap since it frequently appears to us that the province leans over backwards to make sure that it can never be said that we receive any favoured or special treatment of any kind.[9]

Despite Gross's assurances of an independent relationship with government, he still advocated the reduction of government ownership to about 50 percent. A typical statement by Gross on this matter was:

> . . . But even though we have an independent relationship, . . . we have suggested to the government that it would be in CanCel's best long-term interests for the province to reduce its shareholding in order to obtain a wide distribution of shares.[10]

Industry View

Despite efforts to convince the sceptics of CanCel's independence, the corporation was viewed by other enterprises in the British Columbia forest industry as being in a favored position. The reputation of Colcel had to be overcome and the viability of CanCel's operations demonstrated. Executives of CanCel became more active in the industry trade associations. Having a board of directors from the private sector also helped to dispel industry misconceptions. The president conducted a highly visible public relations effort to ''tell CanCel's story'' and cited foreign examples of enterprises in similar circumstances that had been successful. Extensive and favorable coverage was given to CanCel in the Canadian financial press and forest industry trade publications. In its five years, CanCel management did much to dispel the misconceptions and to be viewed as another commercially viable enterprise in the private sector.

Industrial Relations

Soon after CanCel was formed in 1973, a series of labor difficulties plagued the company. Workers of the Prince Rupert plants became frustrated with labor negotiations and staged a wildcat strike in July. The Castlegar pulp mill workers went on a legal strike in August. Industrywide bargaining was involved, but it was speculated that CanCel was the strike target because it was run by the government. It was believed that an N.D.P. government, supported by labor, would not allow a prolonged strike and would perhaps impose a generous settlement that would set the pattern for the rest of the industry.

One of CanCel's long-standing problems had been high employee turnover especially in its northern operations. Factors contributing to the turnover included the uncertainty surrounding the corporation's future prior to the CanCel reorganization and unsatisfactory working conditions in the Prince Rupert operation. Management initiated several programs to alleviate this problem, including a housing project for employees, increased management training, and the conversion designed to make the Prince Rupert operation viable. Employee turnover dropped, but a contributing factor might also have been a shortage of jobs.

Since majority ownership of the company was held by the government, numerous requests were made for worker participation on the board of directors. However, management did not consider the approach appropriate, and none of the requests were followed through by their supporters.

Plant Closure and Layoffs

When the company decided to close the Prince Rupert sulphite pulp mill in October 1976 in order to convert it to kraft pulp production, about 300 workers were laid off. The decision met with considerable resistance. It was claimed that the layoff of the 300 workers by CanCel in the Prince Rupert area would have a ripple effect and actually result in the loss of 700 to 800 jobs in the community. The new plant would employ about 60 workers, but would not be completed until late 1978.

The mayor of Prince Rupert claimed that CanCel had a moral obligation to retain those workers losing jobs and to assist workers in finding comparable jobs. The corporation spent $2 million on a program to ease the problem. The program involved early retirements, job relocation aid, promises of hiring preferences as jobs became available, and assistance with the expense of real estate sales. CanCel also organized recruiting by Alcan and Cominco. Recruiting teams from these corporations visited Prince Rupert in the fall of 1976, but had limited success in obtaining workers. In December 1976, it was estimated that one-half of the laid off workers had found jobs.

During an election campaign, the leader of the Social Credit party, William Bennett, had promised that the mill would stay open. Bennett was elected premier and faced a dilemma. If the government, as the principal shareholder, forced CanCel to keep the mill open, it would be vulnerable to an attack from the minority shareholders who would claim that keeping the mill open was not in their best interests. However, social and political goals also confronted the government. The election promise had been made, and it was economically desirable to keep the mill open in an area of high unemployment. There appeared to be no way to satisfy the demands of both sides. The government had also considered paying a subsidy to Canadian Cellulose to keep the mill operating, but decided against it. Bennett summarized the government's actions as "We're acting as the government of the province of British Columbia, not as the shareholders."[11] Bennett eventually announced that he would not interfere with the closure. He felt that the company had acted responsibly in making the decision to close the mill as world markets for sulphite pulp were depressed, the plant was a serious polluter of the environment, and generous layoff benefits had been arranged for employees.

Environmental Pollution

As soon as CanCel began operating, the Federal Environment Department was pressuring it to clean up the air and water pollution problems at the Prince Rupert sulphite plant. The pollution problem at this mill was a contributing factor in the decision to close the mill. An investment report from Pemberton Securities Limited noted that the mill was one of the worst polluters in British Columbia and then went on to observe:

> . . . Strangely enough, the federal government through Environment Minister Jack Davis has suddenly adopted a get-tough attitude now that the provincial government holds a controlling interest in the company.
>
> Provincial Resources Minister Robert Williams, under whose jurisdiction the problem lies, has told the federal government that Canadian Cellulose cannot afford to immediately eliminate the discharge problem.[12]

In January 1977, severe pollution was caused when polychlorinated biphenyls (PCBs) were spilled at the Prince Rupert plant. The company spent $200,000 to clean up the pollution and in March 1978 was fined $24,500 under the Federal Fisheries Act.

Corporation executives claim that they have responded in the same way as any other corporation would to pollution problems. The fact is that a major shareholder of the corporation has not caused CanCel to pay more or less attention to environmental problems than any other private-sector company would in the same circumstances.

Minority Shareholder Rights

In 1974, there were about 6,500 other CanCel shareholders. By 1978, the number was 5,100. Part of this reduction is accounted for by the government's increasing its share ownership by 2 percent to 81 percent. Some shareholders claimed that the government, as a major shareholder, was in a conflict of interest situation. The government's concern for employment and development may not be in the minority shareholders' best interests. It was claimed that the dividends paid were too low, as the government was interested in retaining earnings, not dividends. It was suggested that assets of the company were undervalued and that the directors were not representing all shareholders as they were supposed to since interest of the majority and the minority shareholders were incompatible.

Business Conditions

During its five years of operation, CanCel has been faced with the usual changes in business conditions applicable to all enterprises in the forest industry. Prices of raw material increased, creating pressure on profits. The Anti-Inflation Board regulations limited the scope of management's actions in some areas. Government policies relating to the management of the province's forests had to be complied with; for example, the additional costs associated with meeting the regulations relating to road building in the logging and woods operations. Management also had to contend with the cyclical nature of the pulp prices that peaked in 1975, then reached a low again in 1978, before recovering. Foreign exchange circumstances had to be closely monitored, especially when the Canadian dollar was at a premium in relation to the American dollar. Additional social responsibility concerns surfaced at various times. In 1975 roads formerly leased by CanCel from three Indian reserves were closed as a tactic in forcing the provincial government to negotiate the Indians' land claims. Canadian Cellulose got into the housing of workers in 1974 by providing rental accommodations for single and married employees. A sit-in occurred at an associated company in Belgium, Papeferies de Gastushe, when the decision was made to liquidate the company in 1976. Canadian diplomats were asked to mediate in the workers' effort to save the company.

In the face of these circumstances, CanCel's president still insisted that the corporation had to operate on the basis of the profit motive and suggested that a 15 percent return on invested capital would be desirable in the pulp industry in order to compensate for the risks taken and the employment provided. CanCel's performance was considered to be satisfactory during the 1973 to 1977 period, in light of the difficulties faced by the company (refer to Exhibit C5.1). Earnings before a special tax credit for the 1973 fiscal year were $7.1 million; in 1974, $29 million; in 1975, $15.3 million; in 1976, $14.6 million; and in 1977, $12.6 million. In 1976, CanCel borrowed $70 million in long-term promissory notes and in 1978 arranged for $45 million in bank credit. Neither borrowing was guaranteed by the government.

THE COMPANY IN 1978

Executive, a business publication, claimed that CanCel's performance was one of the dramatic turnabouts in recent corporate history. The company had come from a nonprofitable position prior to 1973 to a state of financial stability in 1978. Operations were expanded and the corporation's position as an important world supplier of softwood pulp and lumber was established. The corporation went from a foreign owned subsidiary to a 98 percent Canadian owned enterprise. No government money was invested and dividends were paid to shareholders, including the government. The corporation appeared to have responded well to the challenges and opportunities it identified in 1973. The rescue operation had been successful.

There are several reasons to which CanCel's success could be attributed. Management and the business media believed that the British Columbia government (under NDP and Social Credit) had accepted the principle that CanCel was to be operated independently by professionals on a business basis, with a board of directors comprised of individuals from the private sector.

The ability of top management to use a strategic management approach also may have helped. Management's ability to identify markets, make large capital investment decisions, and cope with social demands with a planned instead of crisis approach was bound to have contributed to the performance of the company.

It might also be argued that the success was a result of a good sense of timing and maybe even luck. The corporation capitalized on the strong 1973 and 1974 pulp market. The decision to expand bleached kraft softwood pulp capacity was also timely, as demand increased and prices recovered.

THE FUTURE

Effective March 1, 1978, Ronald M. Gross resigned as president and chief executive officer. Donald N. Watson took over from Mr. Gross. Mr. Watson was the former chief executive of Pacific Western Airlines Limited and had been a CanCel Director since 1973 and chairman of the board since 1976. The five-year period from 1973 to 1977 appears to be a definite stage in the life of the corporation. With performance greatly improved and a new president, the year appears to be the beginning of a new stage.

In 1978, another event occurred that may be important to CanCel's future. The British Columbia Resources Investment Corporation (BCRIC), a crown corporation, was established in 1977 and began operations early in 1978. BCRIC is to be the holding company, or investment company, that would take over several major enterprises in which the British Columbia government had an investment. Included in the BCRIC portfolio would be the government's 9.8 million shares of CanCel. Two BCRIC directors are also to be on CanCel's board. It is planned that BCRIC would sell shares to the public in the near future, thus reducing government investment to 50 percent or less.

The question for top management in 1978 was how to maintain the corporation's performance and to ascertain a future course of action. Several possibilities existed for CanCel, including: further improvement in the corporation's performance with existing facilities; expansion of existing facilities and building of new plants; participation in joint ventures; diversification horizontally or vertically; and acquisition of other corporations. Management also had to decide whether to remain British Columbia based, or to expand outside the province. The reduction of government ownership will be an issue with the possibility existing for the sale of some, or all, of the shares to private-sector investors.

REFERENCES

1 Hon. R. A. Williams (Minister of Lands, Forests, and Water Resources), *Debates of the Legislative Assembly of British Columbia*, 2nd Session, 30th Parliament, April 2, 1973, p. 2004.
2 Patrick Durrant, "A Sickly Discard Learns to Stand," *Executive*, June 1976 (quotation from article).
3 Ibid.
4 Willard E. Mies, "After Major Turnaround, CanCel Begins Biggest Expansion in British Columbia," *Pulp and Paper*, October 1976.
5 "Analyst Likes CanCel Prospects," *The Vancouver Sun*, July 17, 1973 (quotation from article).
6 Mies, op. cit.
7 Brian Roger, *The Financial Port*, November 16, 1974.

8 Durrant, op. cit.

9 Jim Lyon, "Government Takeover Defended," *The Vancouver Sun,* April 24, 1974 (quotation from article).

10 Durrant, op. cit.

11 Hall Leiren, "Government Subsidy for CanCel Studies to Delay Announced Plant Closing," *The Vancouver Sun,* July 30, 1976 (quotation from article).

12 "Analyst Likes CanCel Prospects," op. cit.

CHICK-FIL-A:
THE TASTE LEADER

Prepared by Jean M. Hanebury, Salisbury State University; and
Leslie W. Rue, Georgia State University.

How many ways can a chicken breast be cooked? Truett Cathy would answer this question in one way and one way only: the *Chick-fil-A* way. Chick-fil-A is a breast of chicken sandwich garnished with a pickle and served on a fresh buttered bun. The chicken is marinated, seasoned, and pressure-fried using Mr. Cathy's own special seasonings and pressure-cooking method. Chick-fil-A is also the name of the restaurant chain that Mr. Cathy founded. In 1986, the nationwide sales reached $181.4 million, up $20 million over the previous year. Average sales of $540,000 per unit were recorded. In 1985, thirteen of the units posted sales of $1 million or more. Average operator income was more than $50,000. Chick-fil-A, Inc. posted a 12.24 percent sales increase, which outperformed the fast food industry average by more than 3 to 1. The industry average was just 4 percent in 1986. This record was achieved in an industry reaching maturity and marked by fierce competition. Company spokesperson Don Perry remarked: "Chick-fil-A is one of the nation's largest privately held restaurant chains and the dominant in-mall fast food chain." It is the fifth largest chicken chain.

THE FAST FOOD INDUSTRY

The fast food industry is a maturing industry with emphasis being placed more on market orientation: advertising, purchasing economies, menu diversification, site location, decor, and home delivery service. In 1985, new product introductions and new marketing campaigns were prevalent. In 1986, redefinition of the organization, operations, and new franchise concepts were key issues for all competitors in all segments. Fast food is a tough market. Many segments such as hamburgers face flat domestic

Used by permission.

FIGURE C6.1   ONE WAY TO BEAT THE CRUNCH
(Chains Join Forces to Reduce Fixed Costs)

"Complementary-concepts" within the host unit	Host unit
Bressler's Ice Cream ⟶	Taco John's
Mister Donut ⟶	Dairy Queen
Baskin-Robbins ⟶	Wendy's
Dreyer Ice Cream ⟶	Carl Jr's
Steve's Ice Cream ⟶	D'Angelo's
Winchell's Donuts ⟶	Circle K
Hardee's Church's Rocky Rocco's } ⟶	7-11

Source: Restaurant Business, May 1, 1986, p. 197.

sales, stiffer competition from national and regional rivals, and fickle customers. There is a real shortage of prime restaurant sites. Overseas expansion is a possible cure.

The industry is marked by increasing competition and market saturation resulting from many factors. Among these factors are physical market congestion, a host of new restaurant and menu concepts, and supermarkets offering take-out meals. New restaurant concepts are the result of these market saturation pressures. One trend is called the "dual-concept" unit, or a restaurant paired with some other business housed under the same roof. See Figure C6.1 for some examples. Wendy's is pairing with Baskin-Robbins Ice Cream Company, K-Mart, and Days Inn motels. Hardee's is testing operations with 7-Eleven convenience stores.

The fast food industry is currently dominated by six major competitors: McDonalds, Burger King, Kentucky Fried Chicken, Wendy's, Hardee's, and Pizza Hut. Many of the most successful chains are owned by large corporations (see Figure C6.2). The industry

FIGURE C6.2   RECENT ACQUISITIONS

Acquirer	Acquiree	Final disposition
Marriott	Gino's	Majority converted to Roy Rogers'; others sold
IMASCO	Burger Chef	Majority converted to Hardee's; others sold
Sizzler	Rustler (77 units)	Majority converted to Sizzlers; others sold
Denny's	Sambo's	Converted to Denny's
Vicorp	Sambo's	Converted to Village Inns
PepsiCo	Straw Hat	Converting to Pizza Hut
Marriott	Howard Johnson	Converting restaurants to Big Boy's; H.J. hotels sold
Hershey	Litchfield (23 units) Farm Shops	Converting to Friendly's
Hershey	Idlenot Family Restaurants	Converted to .Friendly's

Source: Restaurant Business, May 1, 1987, p. 197.

can be divided into the following segments: chicken, burgers/franks/roast beef, pizza, Mexican, seafood, pancakes, steak/full menu, sandwich/other. Sales growth within the various segments of the fast food industry during 1986 ranged from 30 percent in the steak segment to 140 percent in the Mexican segment. The industry average was 71 percent in 1986.

Each segment of the fast food industry is marked by keen competition and each has its own leaders. Who does not recognize the Golden Arches and what they stand for in terms of a fast, hot hamburger? McDonald's is the leader in this segment with Burger King and Wendy's a distant second and third. This segment is mature and oversaturated. Competition is characterized by menu diversification, stiff advertising competition, and customizing the decor of the unit to fit the location. Total advertising expenditures continue to outpace fast food restaurant sales as exhibited in Figure C6.3. These advertising dollars are necessary just to maintain market shares. Fast food leader McDonald's offers packaged salads and chicken nuggets as well as their successful Mc.D.L.T. Almost every type of fast food outlet carries some type of chicken product in an attempt to cater to the purported health-conscious 1980s consumer. Late-nite service has been added to some chains: Burger King, Wendy's, and Hardee's to name a few. In North Carolina, Hardee's offers 24-hour service. All competitors are concerned with shifts in the economy and share a concern with appealing to a broader customer base. These issues operating within the hamburger segment of the industry are also operating in most other segments of the market.

FIGURE C6.3 TOTAL ADVERTISING EXPENDITURES OUTPACE FAST FOOD RESTAURANT SALES

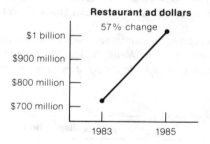

Source: Leading National Advertisers. From *Restaurant Business*, March 1, 1987, p. 2.

Franchised restaurants of all types continue to dominate the growth within the fast food industry. Figures C6.4 and C6.5 provide comparison of company-owned and franchisee-owned units from 1981 through estimates for 1986. Numbering 61,846 in 1981, fast food restaurants are expected to top 78,288 units by the end of 1986. According to *Restaurant Business* and U.S. Department of Commerce surveys, franchised restaurants will continue to be the most popular sector of franchising activity. Upscaling menus, service, and decor will be seen in all segments of the fast food market.

The number of franchised chicken restaurants grew 9.9 percent in 1985 and despite competition from just about every quarter, chicken chains are by and large profitable and growing according to the National Restaurant Association. Sales at chicken restaurants were expected to reach $5.1 billion in 1986, posting a 15.5 percent gain over 1985. The chicken segment of the industry is dominated by Kentucky Fried Chicken's (KFC's) 6,575 restaurants. The chicken competitors are ranked by systemwide sales, number of units and sales by unit in Figure C6.6. Church's seems to have become a solid number two in this segment with Popeye's, Chick-fil-A, Bojangles, and Grandy's in close pursuit. Franchising is the way that these new competitors have chosen to take advantage of the nationwide trend toward lighter food. Chicken consumption per capita in the United States is rising steadily. The National Broiler Council reported that in 1986 the average American consumed 60 pounds of chicken as compared to 50 pounds in 1980. Poultry consumption surpassed beef consumption for the first time in U.S. history in that year also. The rising consumption of chicken is a mixed blessing for those in that market segment because it has resulted in unstable and increasing wholesale chicken prices as well as competition from such giants as McDonald's and Burger King.

One of the biggest innovations in the past five years has been the introduction of chicken nuggets, a breaded, deep-fried meat product. Chick-fil-A claims to have been the originator of this product in 1982. There are now at least 20 chains with a nugget or chicken tender product including KFC and McDonald's. Chicken nuggets were introduced because the customer wanted more chicken and wanted to be able to eat it on the run. With the introduction of this product demand for other chicken items like chicken breast sandwiches has increased.

New contenders are still penetrating the chicken market with a new menu concept: marinated and open-pit charcoal broiled chicken with Mexican side dishes. These new chains are El Pollo Loco and El Pollo Flojo, based in Mexico and Phoenix, Arizona, respectively. Arby's and Mrs. Winners have added roasted chicken to their menus to appeal to the diet conscious consumer.

The fast food market, in general, is marked by a more discriminating and sophisticated customer base and ever-increasing competition. Therefore, the fast food industry will be moving in the direction of more sophisticated business management practices. Trends for the industry include:

1 Moderate industry growth with market saturation and expansion into foreign markets.
2 Consumer driven, broader, and more diverse menus.
3 New concepts in fast food like Mexican food, table service, home delivery, and dual concepts.
4 Increased focus on productivity and asset management including size and configuration of the unit.
5 Increasing emphasis on efficient procurement strategies to provide economies of

FIGURE C6.4 RESTAURANT FRANCHISING, 1985-1987
Sales ($000)

Major activity	Firms	1985			1986*			1987*		
		Total	Company-owned	Franchisee-owned	Total	Company-owned	Franchisee-owned	Total	Company-owned	Franchisee-owned
Chicken	30	$4,118,947	$1,691,050	$2,427,897	$4,488,168	$1,886,131	$2,602,037	$4,994,913	$2,082,946	$2,911,967
Hamburgers, franks, roast beef, etc.	105	23,407,433	5,862,555	17,544,878	25,609,781	6,607,980	19,001,801	28,591,880	7,357,159	21,234,721
Pizza	102	6,193,899	2,410,905	3,782,994	6,939,483	2,638,774	4,300,709	8,067,688	2,979,639	5,088,049
Mexican (taco, etc.)	36	2,400,009	1,312,760	1,087,249	2,571,079	1,417,348	1,153,731	2,881,165	1,620,012	1,261,153
Seafood	14	1,212,951	713,263	499,688	1,355,337	791,308	564,029	1,526,190	874,540	651,650
Pancakes, waffles	13	1,101,858	331,594	770,264	1,169,664	349,139	820,525	1,285,229	382,739	902,490
Steak, full menu	117	8,562,410	4,811,355	3,751,055	8,541,838	4,536,237	4,005,601	9,500,179	4,935,440	4,564,739
Sandwich and other	53	680,854	123,965	556,889	812,792	105,531	707,261	1,103,888	143,822	960,066
Total	470	$47,678,361	$17,257,447	$30,420,914	$51,488,142	$18,332,448	$33,155,694	$57,951,132	$20,376,297	$37,574,835

* Estimated by respondents.
Source: Restaurant Business, March 20, 1987, pp. 184–185.

FIGURE C6.5 RESTAURANT FRANCHISING, 1985–1987
(Number of Units)

Major activity	Firms	1985			1986*			1987*		
		Total	Company-owned	Franchisee-owned	Total	Company-owned	Franchisee-owned	Total	Company-owned	Franchisee-owned
Chicken	30	8,720	3,241	5,479	9,219	3,386	5,833	9,883	3,545	6,338
Hamburgers, franks, roast beef, etc.	105	30,563	6,666	23,897	32,039	7,250	24,789	34,537	7,848	26,689
Pizza	102	14,174	4,651	9,523	15,874	5,116	10,758	18,113	5,636	12,477
Mexican (taco, etc.)	36	4,125	1,865	2,260	4,431	1,976	2,455	4,951	2,236	2,715
Seafood	14	2,423	1,362	1,061	2,569	1,457	1,112	2,826	1,603	1,223
Pancakes, waffles	13	1,761	542	1,219	1,817	559	1,258	1,981	606	1,375
Steak, full menu	117	9,466	4,766	4,700	9,204	4,345	4,859	9,855	4,481	5,374
Sandwich and other	53	2,660	481	2,179	3,135	283	2,852	4,253	338	3,915
Total	470	73,892	23,574	50,318	78,288	24,372	53,916	86,399	26,293	60,106

* Estimated by respondents.
Source: *Restaurant Business*, March 20, 1987, pp. 184–185.

FIGURE C6.6   TOP CHICKEN CHAINS

Ranked by systemwide sales

Chain	Fiscal year ends	Systemwide sales (by fiscal year, in millions)	
		Current	Latest full
Kentucky Fried Chicken	Dec.	$3,286	3,100
Church's	Dec.	645	640
Popeyes	Oct.	399	335
Bojangles'	Dec.	212	210
Grandy's	June	204	200
Chick-Fil-A	Dec.	176	161

Ranked by number of units

Chain	Fiscal year ends	Number of units (by fiscal year)	
		Current	Last full
Kentucky Fried Chicken	Dec.	6,729	6,396
Church's	Dec.	1,585	1,549
Popeyes	Oct.	640	521
Chick-Fil-A	Dec.	350	319
Bojangles'	Dec.	307	328
Grandy's	June	180	180

Ranked by sales per unit

Chain	Fiscal year ends	Sales per unit (fiscal year, in thousands)	
		Current	Last full
Grandy's	June	$1,120	$1,160
Popeye's	Oct.	720	743
Bojangles'	Dec.	690	640
Kentucky Fried Chicken	Dec.	630	595
Chick-Fil-A	Dec.	540	520
Church's	Dec.	442	433

Source: NRN research, chain analysis. From *Nation's Restaurant News*, December 15, 1986, p. 129.

scale. The cash register as a computer will help streamline all phases of operation from menu planning through inventories.

Chick-fil-A is not included in many industry statistics because it is not a public company. But the trends within the whole fast food industry and the chicken segment in particular apply to its operations. Let's examine Chick-fil-A in light of these industry trends and statistics.

EARLY YEARS AT CHICK-FIL-A

The Chick-fil-A concept grew out of long experience in the restaurant business. Mr. Cathy opened his first restaurant on Central Avenue in Hapeville, Georgia, on the outskirts of Atlanta in 1946. The Hapeville location, originally called the Dwarf Grill, is still in operation today as the Dwarf House Restaurant. It is a popular lunch stop for all those living and working in that area. Ask anyone in Hapeville and they will tell you about the good meals served at the Dwarf House. When Mr. Cathy first went into the restaurant business hamburgers were the big seller on the menu. Those staples sold for 20 cents. Cokes and fried apple or peach pie cost only one nickel. A steak platter was the high-priced item, selling for 90 cents. For that exorbitant amount you got a seven-ounce ribeye, homemade French fries, and rolls!

A second location not far away became the original Dwarf House. This restaurant was Mr. Cathy's favorite and he was quite devastated when it burned to the ground in 1962. A new Dwarf House was built near the burned-out shell and self-service was introduced. This first attempt at innovation was not completely successful. Customers used to traditional table service often just got up and walked out when no waitress appeared to take their order. Mr. Cathy's pressing financial obligations and the initial failure of the self-service concept led him to lease the location to Atlanta's first Kentucky Fried Chicken franchise.

One of the problems Mr. Cathy faced at the Dwarf House was supplying fully cooked fried chicken to customers on the run. He experimented with boned chicken in various ways before developing his special recipe for pressure-fried chicken breast sandwiches. The seasonings are still a secret but the finished product is a tasty chicken breast cooked for 3½ minutes in peanut oil. To promote his new sandwich idea Mr. Cathy entered it in the sandwich idea contest sponsored by the National Restaurant Association in 1963. It didn't even earn honorable mention. But Mr. Cathy was undaunted. He heard that Lady Bird Johnson would be campaigning for her husband, President Lyndon Johnson, in Georgia and that she would be hosted by the U.S. Senator and Mrs. Herman Talmadge. The menu was to consist of all kinds of Southern delicacies like country ham and fried chicken. It seemed an ideal place to introduce his new concept in chicken sandwich. After taking some samples of the product to Mrs. Talmadge, Mr. Cathy earned the privilege of serving Chick-fil-A to the First Lady, Mrs. Johnson. He then faced the problem of how to prepare and deliver a flavorful meal to the location near Savannah, which was 200 miles from the Dwarf House. Cathy made an arrangement with a restaurant near Savannah to use their facilities during off hours to prepare the meal. Chick-fil-A was so good Mrs. Johnson commended Mr. Cathy in a personal letter.

Truett Cathy continued to manage his original location, which stayed open 24 hours a day and franchised the chicken sandwich to other restaurants. The cooking instructions and special seasonings were distributed to many different kinds of establishments. It was soon apparent that there was a problem with quality, however. Mr. Cathy could not count on a consistent, high-quality, good-tasting chicken breast sandwich. Some operators failed to change the oil often enough, some kept the sandwiches in warmers. Ensuring the Chick-fil-A high standard of quality was beyond Mr. Cathy's control.

These franchise frustrations led to the establishment of Chick-fil-A as a chain operation centered around the Chick-fil-A Sandwich. The first of these operations, which opened at Greenbriar Mall in Atlanta in 1967, was just a tiny "hole in the wall." It was two years before another location was opened. By the end of 1986 there were 345 Chick-fil-A restaurants in 31 states. Plans call for 30 additional Chick-fil-A outlets from coast to coast by the end of 1987. New freestanding Chick-fil-A units and a freestanding Dwarf House Restaurant opened in the Atlanta area in 1986. About 90 percent of the money it takes to finance each new unit is still generated internally!

AN EMPHASIS ON PEOPLE

Chick-fil-A is a special business entity in many ways. Its consistent record of success in the highly competitive fast food business stems from various factors which emphasize all of Chick-fil-A's people, perhaps especially its founder.

The Founder

S. Truett Cathy, founder and president, is a remarkable kind of businessman. He is always immaculately groomed and soft-spoken. He is a man who commands immediate respect. His background has shaped him to value service as much as he values good business sense. Just how unique an individual he is can be revealed by a story that is still told in Hapeville. When Mr. Cathy was not only trying to establish his first restaurant but also trying to gain recognition for his special chicken breast sandwich, he took advantage of a local feud to advertise his specialty. There were two local newspapers in the area and two local newspaper publishers. These individuals were opposed to each other on every subject from ball games to political issues. They also, of course, fought for the local share of advertising dollars. Mr. Cathy decided that he might capitalize on their quest for new advertising. He made an appointment with each after the noon rush on the same day, advising both men that he would like to discuss taking out a full-page advertisement. The one thing he failed to tell them was that he had invited them to the Dwarf House at the same time. Both men arrived and Mr. Cathy invited them to sit down at the same table and enjoy a free chicken sandwich. It was soon evident how painful it was for each of these opponents to accept. The meal was quite strained, but when they had both finished, Mr. Cathy made them an offer they could hardly resist. "If you two will shake hands and let me take a picture of it, I'll buy a full-page ad in both your papers." How could either man say no? The resulting advertisement was a blowup of the historic handshake with the following caption: "We disagree on almost everything, but we both agree this is the best chicken sandwich we have ever eaten." That ad did wonders for local business.

Truett Cathy's business acumen is something he seems to have possessed since he was born. When he was 8 years old he bought six bottles of Coke for a quarter and sold them for a nickel apiece. He soon added the *Ladies Home Journal* and the *Saturday Evening Post* to the items he had for sale. The energetic young Cathy also worked as a paperboy for *The Atlanta Journal*. When asked about his early career, Mr. Cathy responds: "The family was not very well off. This was my way of getting some spending money. My mother had to take in boarders to provide food for our table." Always independent, Mr. Cathy decided to go into business for himself when he left the Armed Service in the 1940s.

There is another part of Mr. Cathy's personality that he believes has greatly contributed to Chick-fil-A's success. That is his deep religious faith. Mr. Cathy is a Christian businessman. Chick-fil-A's corporate purpose statement as printed in the annual report and reiterated by Dan Cathy, the founder's son, reflects Mr. Cathy's way of life: "To glorify God by being faithful stewards of all that is entrusted to us. To have a positive influence on all who come into contact with Chick-fil-A." Mr. Cathy is quick to tell anyone who questions the Christian orientation of his firm that as a "business run by Christian principles . . . it is not a prerequisite that you be Christian to be a part of us. We hire people of other religious faiths and we don't see a conflict there."

What does it mean to believe in service and in helping others? Mr. Cathy's whole life is an example of this orientation. In addition to his commitment to the quality of his product and to the excellence of his company, Mr. Cathy has spent as much time as possible helping others develop their potential. He teaches a Sunday school class of 13-year-old boys and often invites one or two to his farm for the weekend. He believes in the value of hard work and before these boys can ride dirt bikes with their benefactor, they must help with the chores around the farm. He is active in many civic organizations, and many local papers carry stories about his charitable works. He is also a member of a motorcycle gang called the "Holy Rollers." Mr. Cathy still has the time and energy to personally attend the opening of *all* new Chick-fil-A units!

Other Corporate Personnel

Chick-fil-A is a privately held firm. Except for a few shares held by relatives, the company's stock is held by Truett Cathy. The founder feels that the firm can remain privately held and controlled almost indefinitely. His family has always been intimately involved in running the company, ever since he started with his first restaurant in Hapeville. Wife Jeannette, daughter Trudy, and sons Don and Dan have all at one time or another been involved in the daily business at Chick-fil-A. Dan Cathy is senior vice president for operations and Don Cathy is vice president for development. The following statement by Dan Cathy reflects their philosophy toward Chick-fil-A: "We grew up sitting around the table and listening to Dad talk about Chick-fil-A and the restaurant business. It is hard to think of an opportunity or occasion apart from Chick-fil-A. Dad's ideas and spiritual values were applied to the business. Each of us grew up with a conviction that we were going to be doing something for the business that would last a lifetime."

The executive vice president, James L. S. Collins, has a long history of service with Chick-fil-A. When Mr. Cathy first decided to build the Dwarf House he used Mr. Collins's expertise as a restaurant designer. He again got Mr. Collins to help when he was ready to open his prototype Chick-fil-A mall store at Greenbriar. He soon asked Mr. Collins to join the Chick-fil-A family and they have had a solid working relationship ever since. Industry experts said that Truett Cathy had the perfect chicken sandwich and Jimmy Collins knew how to design the perfect kitchen. This combination is still going strong.

The corporate staff is illustrated in Figure C6.7. Corporate headquarters was relocated in 1982 to 75 heavily wooded acres containing three streams and a 1½-acre lake. The 110,000-square-foot building featuring a 80-foot atrium lobby and 5-story spiral staircase cost $7.5 million. Each floor opens onto the lobby, which is topped by a clear, skylighted roof. Two glass elevators ride up the outside of the elevator shaft. Mr. Cathy wanted the building to blend into its peaceful surroundings, and it seems almost lost among the trees. It is hard to believe that a busy major highway is nearby. It is expected that about 300 employees will eventually be housed there.

FIGURE C6.7 EXECUTIVE OFFICERS AND DIRECTORS

S. Truett Cathy
President and Founder

James L. S. Collins
Executive Vice President

Dan T. Cathy
*Senior Vice President,
Operations*

Stephen G. Mason
*Director, Field Operations
Southwest/Far West Regions*

Younger D. Newton, II
*Director, Field Operations
Northeast/Midwest Regions*

Jack B. Sentell
*Senior Director
Field Operations
Southeast Region*

Costelle B. Walker
*Senior Director, Training
and Development*

Donald M. Cathy
*Vice President,
Development*

Bureon E. Ledbetter, Jr.
*Vice President, General
Counsel*

James B. McCabe
Vice President, Finance

Philip A. Barrett
Controller

Roger E. Blythe, Jr.
Director, Stores Accounting

William H. Lowder
Director, Data Processing

H. Allen Smith
Director, Tax Accounting

Perry A. Ragsdale
*Vice President, Design
and Construction*

Brian C. Ray
*Vice President, Support
Services*

C. Cleveland Kiser
*Director, Career
Development*

Nolan C. Robinson
*Senior Director,
Administration*

Huie H. Woods, Jr.
*Senior Director, Human
Resources*

Steve A. Robinson
Vice President, Marketing

William L. Baran
*Director, Research
and Development*

John W. Russell
*Director, National
Advertising*

Source: Annual Message, Chick-fil-A, 1986.

Operators

One of Chick-fil-A's most interesting characteristics is its relationship with its operators. Mr. Cathy has structured the operator relationship in a rather unusual manner. Going back to his own philosophy and his experience as a young family man trying to make a living and to have a happy family life, Mr. Cathy incorporated his realizations into the conception of how his restaurants would be organized and staffed. His son Dan puts it this way: "Dad's vision is all based on his prior restaurant experience. You can handle any other pressure if you don't have financial pressure. Consequently the Chick-fil-A system is designed to relieve our operators from financial burdens and requires the operator to invest only $5,000."

For the initial investment of $5,000, an operator is completely trained in the operations end of the business. New operators are guaranteed a minimum income of $20,000 for the first two years. After this initial period, they are guaranteed $12,000 plus 50 percent of the net profits. The parent company receives 15 percent of gross sales each year. Three and one quarter percent of sales are used in the national advertising program. All these monies are spent back in the local markets. There are three or four national advertising campaigns per year. Additionally, hundreds of thousands of pounds of chicken are given away in front of stores per year. A minimum of 3,000 pounds of chicken, usually in the form of chicken nuggets, is distributed at *each* location per year.

The successful operator must be ready and willing to invest long hours of time to make the unit a success. The units operate six days each week. It is a cardinal rule with Mr. Cathy that *no* Chick-fil-A will be open on Sunday. The only operator to violate this dictum is no longer with the company. The average operator can reasonably expect to make $50,000 after five years. In 1985, 39 operators made more than $70,000.

One of Truett Cathy's firm convictions is that he will never franchise. He feels that each of his operators can manage just one Chick-fil-A. "Absentee ownership just doesn't work." Mr. Cathy firmly asserts. Mr. Collins sees this philosophy as a key to success, "Each operator must run his own store. Taking on more than one would disturb his (the manager's) effectiveness," emphasizes Mr. Cathy. But unit managers are encouraged to make as much money as possible from their own unit. In fact, they can and do make more money each year than most of the headquarters staff.

Mr. Cathy has a very firm philosophy about the people he attracts to Chick-fil-A and how to get the right people to do the best job. Previous restaurant experience is not a governing criterion. Mr. Cathy often says,

You can train anyone to cook chicken and make cole slaw. But it is more important to carefully select the person you train because everything else follows from that initial personnel selection. We establish work habits and work attitudes. When you have high expectations, people will do their best. It's like a football team, if you pick the right players and inspire them to hard work, they will be doing their very best for the team.

What kind of person is Chick-fil-A looking for to operate their outlets? Someone with entrepreneurial spirit with a successful track record, a stable family background, and a history of community service is the prime candidate. The selection process is quite protracted. Huie Woods, senior director of human resources, reiterates the philosophy described earlier: "The boss (Mr. Cathy) insists that human resources are the most important asset that we have. If you are right at the people end of the business, you can't fail."

Most of the emphasis is on the selection end of this human resource process. All selections are made at the Atlanta headquarters. The process is as follows: A prospective operator submits a resume accompanied by a recent photo and completes an extensive application. A lot of time is spent reviewing these applications looking for people who hold mutual goals and values to those that exemplify the corporate purpose of Chick-fil-A. There were 4,096 applications in 1983 for 12 staff jobs and 26 operator positions. Every inquiry is answered except for blanket resumes obviously sent out at random. Once a good prospect is identified, he or she is invited to the Atlanta headquarters for an initial interview and battery of tests. References are also explored at this point in the selection process.

Mr. Woods reiterated both Truett and Dan Cathy's words. Chick-fil-A has a Christian orientation. "We don't look for a specific denomination as such, but the people chosen are those with high moral standards, with strong family values, ties in their local community, and demonstrated leadership ability." There is another unique Chick-fil-A policy regarding picking the right operator for each location. They seek those in the local community rather than recruiting and transferring young trainees from another part of the country.

About 10 percent of those accepted have previous fast food experience. Many have sales experience or have supervised young people in some capacity. It will become increasingly apparent as the operation is developed how much rides on making an informed choice when selecting Chick-fil-A operators. The initial investment of $5,000 is a prerequisite, but Mr. Cathy has often helped candidates finance this initial investment if they show the potential he is always seeking in those around him. It is not unusual for an employee who started out making the cole slaw at a Chick-fil-A location to eventually become an owner operator.

One such former crew member is "Jac" Borger of Paramus, New Jersey. He started as a crew member in 1974 and became an operator six months later. By 1985, the Paramus Park unit generated $1 million in sales. Borger states: "You set your own income goals, and reach them with determination and initiative." Another former crew member, Pete Burgess, finished college and expects to be making $40,000 per year at age 27. Nell Russell, with 13 years as a Chick-fil-A operator, was the first woman to reach the $1 million annual sales mark. She says: "My success has literally been a family affair. I jumped at the opportunity to operate my own restaurant as a way to support my three children. They eventually became crew members with two of them qualifying for Chick-fil-A college scholarships."

There are field consultants and regional directors of field operations that keep in contact with each location. After the first two months in a new location one of these corporate representatives will visit to offer assistance and to see how the new operator is coping with the infant business. Dan Cathy reports once the initial training and evaluation is completed successfully, there may be no further on-site visits from field representatives for two to three years. As long as all indications such as sales growth, employee turnover, and supply costs are in line, the operator and location are deemed healthy. Operator turnover runs between 4 and 5 percent per year. In 1983, turnover was 5.8 percent. The industry average for restaurant managers is between 100 and 200 percent each year!

Chick-fil-A offers their operators a special benefit package. Ongoing management training is one facet of the package. As noted in the 1986 Annual Message, "Every February Chick-fil-A invites operators and their spouses to an expense paid, five-day seminar at a luxury resort." In 1985, the seminar was held in Colorado Springs. In 1986, over 800 operators and their spouses attended the five-day seminar in Bermuda. These yearly retreats are not just all state-of-the business reports, awards ceremonies, operational workshops, and new marketing plans. "Operators and their spouses enjoy the camraderie of sharing with old and new friends."

Chick-fil-A's incentive package includes the Symbol of Success program. "Operators who increase their restaurant's sales by 40 percent or more over the previous year are awarded the use of a new Lincoln Continental Mark VII for one year." An annual increase of $200,000 is required for higher-volume units. Should the operator continue this 40 percent sales growth through another year, the car is his or hers to keep. Since its introduction in 1975, more than 100 operators have been presented with the Symbol of Success.

Sharing between corporate staff and operators is encouraged. Two house organs, the *Chick-fil-A Operator Newsletter* and *Chicken Chatter,* keep the Chick-fil-A family in touch. Operators share promotional ideas and get reports on new corporate directions. Personal milestones like new babies, marriages, and other personal or family triumphs are also shared.

Career Development Program   A one-year internship is offered to four-year college graduates between the ages of 22 to 26 who might consider becoming operators. Salary for the year is $16,000, and 75 to 80 percent of the time is spent in operating different Chick-fil-A units on an interim basis. The program is geared to introducing young people to all aspects of the operator concept. About 18–20 of these positions are offered each year. An increasing number of the interns become operators of their own Chick-fil-A units.

There are usually only one or two full-time personnel other than the operator at each location. In many instances the operator's spouse or another family member makes up the core of the staff. Other employees are called "crew members." Eighty percent of the employees are students. They are part-time employees with an average workweek of 20 hours. These crew members are another focus of Chick-fil-A's recipe for success.

Crew Members

As indicated previously, Chick-fil-A operators make all other hiring decisions. They staff their location and decide how much to pay each worker. Using tested methods developed over the years by the headquarters staff, each location trains its own crew members. Dan Cathy described the kinds of young people that Chick-fil-A operators attract.

> Lots of these youngsters are class leaders. They are the kind of young people who attract other prospective employees. It is also not unusual for brothers and sisters to follow one another into the Chick-fil-A ranks. Often younger children can't wait to follow an older sibling as a Chick-fil-A employee. We have had as many as three members of one family as crew members at the same time.

In fact this is the kind of relationship that the corporate and local managers strive to develop. It exemplifies the team and family spirit that has made Chick-fil-A a success.

Crew training is quite extensive. All new employees start in the back of the location making the fresh food from scratch each day. They are carefully cross-trained in all aspects of the operation from cutting cabbage for cole slaw to manning the counter. A friendly atmosphere is important, so the new crew members are gradually introduced to public contact. Pleasing the customer is another key to success and each Chick-fil-A team member must have that in mind. Each new employee receives an individual "Crew Member Training Program." To quote Dan Cathy,

> One of the most fulfilling aspects of operating a Chick-fil-A Unit is observing the development of business skills in crew members. For many, employment at Chick-fil-A is their first business exposure. Having the privilege of taking an active involvement in their development is a great responsibility.

Figure C6.8 lists the objectives of the Crew Member Training Program. Three training levels, I, II, III, are administered according to the individual's progression through the previous levels of training. Industrywide turnover for employees like the youngsters who serve you hamburgers at Wendy's or McDonald's is over 400 percent. Turnover at Chick-fil-A has remained in the 40 to 50 percent range. Even more impressive is the fact that in an era of scarce teenage labor, with large fast food chains like McDonald's using tray placemats as employment applications, Chick-fil-A has not experienced a similar labor shortage. Mr. Cathy says that is because of the unique benefit programs his organization offers: Chick-fil-A scholarships and the WINSHAPE Centre.

Benefits for crew members are something special at Chick-fil-A. The annual report states: "Student workers are offered special incentives to stay and grow with Chick-fil-A. Any student who works an average of 20 hours a week for a period of two years or more, while maintaining a 'C' or better grade average, receives a $1,000 scholarship to

FIGURE C6.8   CREW MEMBER TRAINING GOALS

1. Meet ongoing training needs by providing continuous training and retraining in order to fully capitalize on employee potential.

2. Systematically provide required training by breaking training into "bite-size" pieces. In other words, the program does not encourage teaching complete jobs, but centers on teaching the tasks which make up complete jobs.

3. Challenge employees to become competent in all areas of operations and reduce, if not eliminate, the need for specialists.

4. To improve profitability in the unit through more consistent and uniform implementation of cost control procedures in food portioning, waste control, and employee productivity.

5. Provide a system of recognition and incentives to motivate crew members to constantly strive for increased levels of performance and productivity.

6. Be manageable in that the operator needs not be required to devote an unreasonable amount of time administering the program.

Source: Company documents.

the college of his or her choice." More than $4 million in scholarships has been awarded since 1973. Half of this total has been given in the past four years alone.

Nineteen hundred and eighty-four marked a milestone for the Chick-fil-A crew member incentive package and perhaps for the industry. Chick-fil-A and Berry College, a four-year liberal arts institution located in Rome, Georgia, entered into a scholarship grant program. Berry is situated on 28,000 acres of forests, fields, mountains, lakes, and streams. Chick-fil-A's founder, Truett Cathy, and Berry's founder, Martha Berry, shared common goals: to incorporate religion in life; to excell in work and study; and to take pride in a job well done. This philosophy is well illustrated in the letter Martha Berry left to be opened on her death (see Figure C6.9).

Approximately 1,500 students from all over the United States and several foreign countries make up the student body. In its first year of operation, 1984, the joint grant program allowed 75 young people from Chick-fil-A restaurants nationwide to begin college at Berry. Chick-fil-A–sponsored students were housed in the Berry Academy, a former secondary school located on the main campus. This facility was renamed the WINSHAPE Centre to exemplify Truett Cathy's goal to "shape winners." To be eligible for the grant, interested students must have worked for Chick-fil-A for six months. They must apply and be accepted for admission to Berry before receiving approval from Chick-fil-A to enter the grant program. Additional opportunities for individual growth and leadership development are made available through Chick-fil-A–sponsored recreational, academic, and religious programs. Mr. Cathy in his President's Message for 1984 stated: "The time is coming when a large number of operators and staff will come from this pool of young people who work in Chick-fil-A restaurants. For instance, one new Chick-fil-A operator, age 22, has nine years of experience with the company already. He started out as a crew member at age 13 wiping tables after school." By early 1987, 20 percent of the chain's restaurant operators and 33 percent of the corporate headquarters staff were recipients of the $1,000 scholarships. And, 90 students from 19 states were enrolled in the WINSHAPE Centre at Berry.

Some new programs have been added to the WINSHAPE Centre as well. These programs are peripheral to the Chick-fil-A employee family but they are in the spirit of its founder's goals. The centre has become a foster home for needy children. Right now

FIGURE C6.9   MISS BERRY'S FINAL LETTER TO ALUMNI

The Berry Schools
Mount Berry, Georgia
July 1, 1925

To the Graduates of the Berry Schools:

When I am gone, I want you to always think of me as alive—alive beyond your farthest thoughts, and near and loving you, and growing more like God wants me to become. I want you to love the Berry Schools and stand ready to help them in every emergency. Use all of your influence to hold the Schools to the original plan, *simple living, work, prayer, the Bible being taught, Christian teachers; keeping the Schools a separate community, protecting and guarding the property and the good name of the Schools.* I feel that I shall not be separated from the Schools which have been my life and work and which I have always loved so dearly. I shall not be separated from any of the boys and girls who are my logical heirs. I shall just be closer to God, and will understand better the way in which prayer and faith can open the ways through which God can keep and guard our beloved Berry Schools.

I would like to leave an especial message to the graduates of the Berry Schools who are *giving back in service what you have gotten from the Schools.* You who are putting your lives into the work are the real dependence of the Schools and I want to ask you especially to be faithful and guard and protect the Berry Schools. My prayer is that the Schools may stand through the ages, for the honor and glory of God and for the Christian training of poor boys and girls of the mountains and country districts.

I leave with each one of you the motto which I have kept on my desk for years, "Prayer Changes Things."

Faithfully yours,

Martha Berry

Note: This letter was attached to Miss Berry's will and marked. "To be opened after Miss Berry's death."

5 are housed there and a $200,000, 5,000-square-foot house to accommodate 12 young people and two house parents is planned. Camp WINSHAPE for boys is also in operation. The camp is a summertime adventure for boys between the ages of 7 and 16. Five hundred enjoyed camp activities in the summer of 1987. The camp is dedicated to another of Mr. Cathy's mottos: "It is better to build boys than to mend men." With these campers and with his Sunday school class of 13-year-old boys, Mr. Cathy maintains an idealistic approach. He talks to the boys about the importance of making good decisions throughout life. "The three most important decisions are: Who will be my Master? What is my mission in life? and Who will be my mate?"

Careful Selection Pays Off

At this point it is important to note some statistics that relate to Mr. Cathy's emphasis on choosing the right people for each operation. Truett Cathy says it best: "When we choose our operators we look at the character of an individual and his desire to be rewarded for extra effort and ability. We want positive thinkers who are able to impart that attitude to others. We don't select an operator or member of the staff unless that person wants to be with us until one of us retires or dies." Not one of Chick-fil-A's locations has ever closed. There has been operator turnover as indicated previously but it has remained well below industry standards. Average incomes of operators are more than other managers' in the mall locations, including large chain stores. On the average, Chick-fil-A units generate more sales per square foot than any fast food tenant in malls with Chick-fil-A locations. Chick-fil-A has been recognized in many industry publications as having a friendly, positive attitude among its employees. This friendliness and positive attitude also is noted by its customers.

Mr. Cathy says, "Keep your chin up and your knees down and it is impossible to fall." His tenacious spirit and careful supervision of the selection process continues to guide Chick-fil-A to excellence. He still personally interviews each of the final employment candidates for all corporate and operator positions.

OPERATIONS

As with other aspects of the business, a firm set of guidelines organizes all phases of operation from the construction of the unit through the menu served at each location. Monthly profit and loss statements from each location are the strongest management tool used by corporate headquarters to monitor and modify the business. Each afternoon after 5 p.m. operators call into the main computer at headquarters to enter daily sales data. Personal computers are located at each unit so that analyses of sales can be done on-site.

Sales and percentage increase for 1980 through 1985 are found in Figure C6.10. About six of the 285 units didn't make a profit in 1983, but they were mostly the new locations. An increase in sales of 29 percent over 1982 was recorded in 1983. The average sales *per square foot* were over $340. In 1986, the average sales *per unit* were $540,000.

Chick-fil-A has units in 31 states. Seventy-five percent are located in Texas, Florida, North Carolina, and Georgia. New units in the Northeast are heavily concentrated in the Philadelphia area and New Jersey. Much new expansion is centered in the Southwest and California. There are also 15 mall locations in the Chicago area that are prime candidates for the Chick-fil-A concept. Expansion plans for 1986 continued to be described as "aggressive." More than 30 new mall locations were planned along with a continuation of Chick-fil-A's entry into the freestanding arena. Starting in 1985, a Dwarf House restaurant based on the original of that named was opened as a freestanding location. Two more Dwarf House restaurants were opened in the Atlanta area in 1986 as well as the first two freestanding Chick-fil-A restaurants, also in Atlanta. All Chick-fil-A and Dwarf House restaurants follow the policy of never opening on Sunday.

A Typical Chick-fil-A Unit

Most Chick-fil-A units are mall locations. The company selects all the sites. Chick-fil-A looks for enclosed malls having the following specifications:

1 50,000 square feet or more
2 Two or more anchor stores such as Sears or Penney's
3 Sixty or more in-line merchants

Regional malls have been the primary targets of Chick-fil-A's development plans.

Chick-fil-A's location strategy is quite different from the industry norm. It is very unusual for mall owners to sign long-term leases with tenants. Chick-fil-A always seeks

FIGURE C6.10   SALES AND PERCENTAGE INCREASE

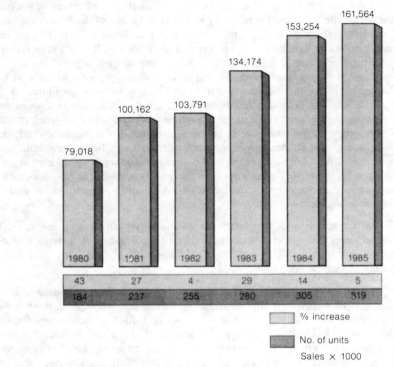

	% increase
	No. of units
	Sales × 1000

Source: Annual Message, Chick-fil-A, 1986.

and receives a 10- or 15-year lease agreement. Once the site is located, it costs about $250,000 to build and equip a typical unit. Chick-fil-A corporate headquarters handles all details of leasing, building, and equipping the location. The local operator is sought in conjunction with long-term development plans in each area. Approximately 90 percent of the annual construction budget is internally financed. Each unit is custom designed, not a clone of every other unit as in many fast food chain competitors like McDonald's or Hardee's. In the last few years, other fast food contenders have adopted a more diverse design as noted previously.

Malls usually receive a set amount of rent for each unit or 6 percent of gross sales, whichever is higher. Typically the 6 percent figure is received. Because of the returns mentioned previously, Chick-fil-A is a tenant that is vigorously sought by mall developers across the nation.

All locations are built to the specifications initially developed by Mr. Collins. Whenever possible Chick-fil-A does not locate in a food cluster part of the mall. Experience has indicated that it is more attractive to repeat customers to locate away from other fast food operations. The rationale behind the choice of mall locations is to be in a high-traffic area while keeping costs low and size small. They want to attract the shopper who wants quick food that is hot and tasty. The typical Chick-fil-A is 1,800 square feet versus the 4,000- to 5,000-square-foot typical McDonald's or Wendy's. Table service is not offered in any Chick-fil-A mall location. There is an ongoing trend in malls to cluster all fast food into what is called a "food court." With this trend, many new Chick-fil-A units are within the food court area. They still tend to be one of the best sellers in those malls.

Renegotiations of the original contracts for additional 12- to 15-year leases are not unusual. In fact Chick-fil-A has never pulled out of a mall location or failed to complete construction of a unit. As Huie Woods said, echoing the Cathys: "We are going to make it. That's why the mall developers seek us." Once the new location is equipped and staffed it usually takes about two to three years to become profitable.

Once the site selection has been made, the new operator is chosen and travels to corporate headquarters in Atlanta to undergo an extensive four-week training program. Every aspect of the business is explored, although this session only touches on personnel training. Next the new operator returns to the brand-new unit, and organizes operations. All local hires, personnel policies (including things like insurance coverage), pay scales, local sales promotions, in fact, all aspects of the business including buying supplies are up to the individual Chick-fil-A operator. Operators have no control over the following items:

1 Contracts cannot be negotiated individually with poultry suppliers. Five poultry houses supply the special seasoned and sized chicken breasts. Breast trimmings become nuggets.

2 Recipes cannot be altered.

The new freestanding Dwarf House and Chick-fil-A restaurants are alternatives planned and instituted for the time in the future when mall operations become a completely saturated market. Not only has Chick-fil-A already entered a large portion of the most desirable mall locations, but also market studies show that people's behavior and tastes are changing. The new freestanding concept, which was once a prototype model housed in an otherwise vacant area in corporate headquarters, has been developing over the past several years. A combination of waitress and self-service, an expanded menu and hours are part of that new direction. These units include both a walk-up, take-out counter and a regulation sit-down restaurant area.

The Menu

Like the many other fast food operations, Chick-fil-A started out with a limited menu centered around the Chick-fil-A sandwich. They have stuck to this limited menu more consistently than most of their competitors. All items on the menu, with the exception of french fries, are made from scratch every day. The core element is the marinated filet breast of chicken that goes into the Chick-fil-A sandwich. They are still served with a pickle on a buttered bun without condiments. The sandwich relies on the taste of the chicken itself, not some special sauce. Fresh lemonade, homemade cole slaw, and homemade lemon pie complete the original menu. Soft drinks and iced tea are also available. Chicken nuggets have been added and are an increasingly popular item. Recently they have been made larger to differentiate them from all the competition. Breast of chicken soup has also been added. Truett Cathy feels his sandwich is the model for chicken sandwiches copied by other fast food competitors. There is some feeling also that when fast food competitors like Burger King introduced a lower-quality chicken sandwich, some customers were driven away from all chicken sandwiches.

Breakfast menu items such as biscuits and eggs have been introduced at some locations. Twenty percent of McDonald's sales are now in breakfast menu items. The test market for breakfast items were the freestanding locations in downtown Houston and Atlanta. Mall locations now offer breakfast biscuits as well.

A press release from Chick-fil-A in early 1987 reiterated what has been true since 1982. Chick-fil-A sandwiches and chicken nuggets score at the top on taste and quality when compared with such fast food giants as Burger King, Wendy's, and Hardee's. Independent research conducted by Marketing & Research Counselors, Inc. concluded that consumers rank Chick-fil-A highest for overall food quality. Truett Cathy traces this success to the fact that "our menu is limted to what we do best—chicken. And our primary chicken products are made with all natural breast meat, unlike many chains which make their sandwiches and nuggets from processed white and dark meat chicken." Chicken consumption is up 100 percent since 1960, while consumption of beef has increased by a slow 22 percent. Chicken has become a major item for more than 200 food chains and frozen food retailers who are mounting a challenge in the nation's grocery stores. Despite such stiff competition, Chick-fil-A plans to continue what it does best in both mall and freestanding locations and expects to be one of the long-run survivors in a fast food industry that faces the real issue of market saturation. While the number of chain and independent restaurant failures, poor financial performances, and exits from the business have never been so marked, Chick-fil-A has a commitment to an ideal that helps it survive.

During discussions with both Truett and Dan Cathy, each returned many times to the elder Cathy's philosophy. Both feel strongly the gift and tremendous responsibility that comes along with the more conventional rewards of being a successful business. They believe in Christian stewardship. They feel a responsibility to operators, crew members, corporate personnel, and the public in general. Truett Cathy and all that he has helped to develop at Chick-fil-A seem to espouse the same ideals of service. Cathy summed it up with these words: "I am 65 and I feel as though I'm just getting into second gear. In my office I have a poster which expresses my philosophy. It shows an individual climbing a mountain with the proper attire and safety rope. The caption says: 'No goal is too high if you climb with care and confidence.'" Still, "I often wish I could divorce myself from business, and just get to know the kids in Sunday school though."

CASE **7**

CLUB MEDITERRANÉE (A)

Prepared by Jacques Horovitz, IMEDE.

Sipping a cognac and smoking one of his favorite cigars on his way back to Paris from New York on the Concorde, Serge Trigano was reviewing the new organization structure that was to be effective November 1981. In the process, he was listing the operational problems and issues that were yet to be resolved. Son of the chief executive of the "Club Med," Serge Trigano was one of the joint managing directors and he had just been promoted from director of operations to general manager of the American zone, i.e., responsible for operations and marketing for the whole American market. Having experienced a regional organization structure that was abandoned some four years ago, he wanted to make sure that this time the new structure would better fit the objectives of Club Med and allow its further development in a harmonious way.

COMPANY BACKGROUND AND HISTORY

Club Med was founded in 1950 by a group of friends led by Gérard Blitz. Initially, it was a nonprofit organization, set up for the purpose of going on vacation together in some odd place. The initial members were essentially young people who liked sports and especially the sea. The first "village," a tent village, was a camping site in the Balearic Isles. After four years of activities, Mr. Gilbert Trigano was appointed the new managing director. Mr. Gilbert Trigano came to Club Med from a family business involved in the manufacture of tents in France, a major supplier to Club Med. With this move, and in the same year, the holiday village concept was expanded beyond tent villages to straw

Note: This case was prepared as a basis for class discussion rather than to illustrate either effective or ineffective handling of an administrative situation.

hut villages, the first of which was opened in 1954. Further expanding its activities, in 1956 Club Med opened its first ski resort at Leysin, Switzerland. In 1965, its first bungalow village was opened, and in 1968 the first village started its operation in the American zone. Club Med's main activity, and still today, was to operate a vacation site for tourists who would pay a fixed sum (package) to go on vacation for a week, two weeks, or a month and for whom all the facilities were provided in the village. Club Med has always had the reputation of finding beautiful sites which were fairly new to tourists (for instance, Moroccan tourism was "discovered" by Club Med) which offered many activities, especially sports activities, to its members. (When going on vacation to any of Club Med's villages, one becomes a "member" of Club Med.) In 1981, Club Med operated ninety villages in forty different countries on five continents. In addition to its main activity, it had extended to other sectors of tourism in order to be able to offer a wider range of services. In 1976, Club Med acquired a 45% interest in an Italian company (Valtur) which had holiday villages in Italy, Greece, and Tunisia, mainly for the Italian market. In 1977, Club Med took over Club Hotel, which had built up a reputation over the last twelve years as a leader in the seasonal ownership time-sharing market. The result of this expansion had been such that in 1980 more than 770,000 people had stayed in the villages of Club Med or its Italian subsidiary, whereas they were 2,300 in 1950. Most members were French in 1950, and in 1980 only 45% were French. In addition, 110,000 people had stayed in the apartments or hotels managed by its time-sharing activity. Actually in 1980, Club Med sales were about FF 2.5 billion and its cash flow around FF 170 million. (See Appendix A for the last ten years' financial performance.) Appendixes B, C, and D show the number of people who had stayed at the holiday centers of Club Med, the number of beds it had as of 1980, and the nationality of its members. The present case focuses exclusively on the organization structure of the holiday village operations and not on the time-sharing activities of the company.

SALES AND MARKETING

In 1981, Club Med was international with vacation sites all over the world and so were its customers. They came from different continents, backgrounds, and market segments, and did not look for the same thing in the vacation package. Club Med offered different types of villages (most villages offered by Club Med are rented by the company or run under a management contract), a wide range of activities to accommodate all the people who chose to go on a package deal. The Club offered ski villages, i.e., hotels in ski resorts for those who liked to ski; straw hut villages with a very Spartan comfort on the Mediterranean, mainly for young bachelors; hotel and bungalow resort villages with all comforts open throughout the year, some with special facilities for families and young children. An average client who went to a straw hut village on the Mediterranean usually did not go to a plush village at Cap Skirring in Senegal (and the price was different too), although the same type of person might go to both.

A family with two or three children who can afford the time and money needed to travel to a relatively nearby village with a baby club was less likely to go to a village in Malaysia due to the long journey and the cost of transportation. Broadly speaking, a whole range of holiday makers were represented among the club's customers. However, there was a larger proportion of office workers, executives, and professional people and a small proportion of workers and top management. The sales and marketing of the club, which began in Europe, had expanded to include two other important markets: the American zone, including the U.S., Canada, and South America, and the Far Eastern Zone, including Japan and Australia. The club's sales network covered twenty-nine countries; sales were either direct through the club-owned offices, twenty-three of which existed at the moment (see Appendix E for countries where the club owns commercial offices as well as villages and operations), or indirect through travel agencies (in France, Havas was the main retailer). Originally, all the villages were aimed at the European market; in 1968 with the opening of its first village in America, the Club broke into the American market and opened an office in New York. Since then, the American market had grown more or less independently. Eighty percent of the beds in the villages located in the American geographical area were sold to club members in the United States and Canada. Sixty-five percent of French sales, which represent 47% of the Club's turnover, were direct by personal visits to the office, by telephone, or by letter. However, in the U.S., direct sales accounted for only 5% of the total, the remaining 95% being sold through travel agencies. These differences were partly explained by national preferences, but also by a deliberate choice on the part of the club. Until the appointment of Serge Trigano to lead the U.S. zone, all sales and marketing offices reported to a single worldwide marketing director.

THE VILLAGE

Club Med had around ninety villages and it was growing fast. In the next three years (1981–84) about twenty new villages were scheduled to open. At Club Med a village was typically either a hotel, bungalows, or huts in usually a very nice area offering vacationers a series of several activities among which were swimming, tennis, sailing, water skiing, windsurfing, archery, gymnastics, snorkeling, deep sea diving, horseback riding, applied arts, yoga, golf, boating, soccer, circuits, excursions, bike riding, and skiing. There were also usually on site a shop, a hairdresser, even some cash changing, car renting, etc., and a baby or mini club in many places. Club Med was well known for having chosen sites which were the best in any country where they were, not only from a geographical point of view, but also from an architectural point of view and the facilities provided. Exhibit C7.1 below shows the number of villages which were open during the winter or summer season by type.

Essentially, there were three types of villages: the hut villages which were the cheapest, open only during the summer season, and which started Club Med, and which were on the Mediterranean. They did not offer all the comfort that the wealthy traveler was used to (common showers). Then there were bungalows or hotels or "hard-type" villages which were more comfortable with private bathrooms. Most were still double-bedded which meant that two single men or women would have to share the same

EXHIBIT C7.1   NUMBER OF VILLAGES BY TYPE AND SEASON

	Sea				
	Huts	**Bungalows**	**Hotels**	**Mountain**	**Total**
Summer season	14	31	26	10	81
Winter season	0	19	11	23	53

Source: Club Méditerranée Trident N123/124, Winter 80–81, Summer 81.

bedroom. In a village, there were two types of people: the GMs or "gentils membres," who were the customers and came usually for one, two, three, or four weeks on a package deal to enjoy all the facilities and activities of any village; the GOs or "gentils organisateurs," who helped people make this vacation the best; there were GOs for sports, for applied arts, for excursions, for food, for the bar, as disk jockeys, as dancing instructors, for the children or babies in the mini clubs, for maintenance, for traffic, for accounting, for receptions, etc. (Although the GOs were specialized by "function," they had also to be simply "gentils organisateurs," i.e., making the GM's life easy and participating in common activities, such as arrival cocktails, shows, games, etc.) On average, there were 80 to 100 GOs per village.

There was a third category of people who were behind the scene: the service people, usually local people hired to maintain the facilities, the garden, to clean up, etc. (about 150 service people per village). They could also be promoted to GOs.

Every season, i.e., either after the summer season in September and winter season in April, or every six months, all the GOs would be moved from one village to another; that was one of the principles of the club since its inception, so that nobody would stay for more than six months in any particular site. The village chief of maintenance was an exception. He stayed one full year; if a village was closed in the winter, he remained for the painting, the repair, etc. The service people (local people) were there all the year around or for six months, if the village was only open in the summer (or winter for ski resorts). Exhibit C7.2 shows a typical organization structure of a village from the GO's point of view.

Under the chief of the village there were several coordinators: one for entertainment, responsible for all of the day and night activities (shows, music, nightclub, plays, games, etc.); the sports chief who coordinated all the sports activities in any particular village; the maintenance chief who would see to the maintenance of the village, either when there was a breakdown or just to repaint the village or keep the garden clean, grow new flowers, etc., and who was assisted by the local service people; the food and beverage chief who coordinated the cooking in the different restaurants as well as the bar. Usually there was a bazaar for miscellaneous, a garment boutique, and a hairdresser under a boutique's coordinator. There was a coordinator for the baby club (if existent) within the village to provide the children with some special activities; this coordinator was also responsible for the medical part of the village (nurses and doctor). Many times there was a doctor on site, especially when a village was far from a big town. There was a coordinator of excursions and applied arts. Its services would help the GM to go somewhere or propose accompanied excursions (one, two, three days) for those who wanted it, or try with the help of a GO to make a silk scarf or pottery. There was a coordinator of administration, accounting, and control who dealt with cash, telephone, traffic, planning and reception, basic accounting, salaries for GOs and service personnel, taxes, etc. The services of food and beverages and the maintenance were the ones who were the heavy users of local service personnel.

COMPANY ORGANIZATION STRUCTURE

Exhibit C7.3 shows the organization structure of Club Med's holiday village activity just before Serge Trigano's appointment as director of the U.S. zone. (The rest—time-sharing activities—are additional product-market subsidiaries.)

There were several joint managing directors who participated in the management committee. Essentially, the structure was a functional one with a joint managing

EXHIBIT C7.2 ORGANIZATION CHART OF A TYPICAL VILLAGE

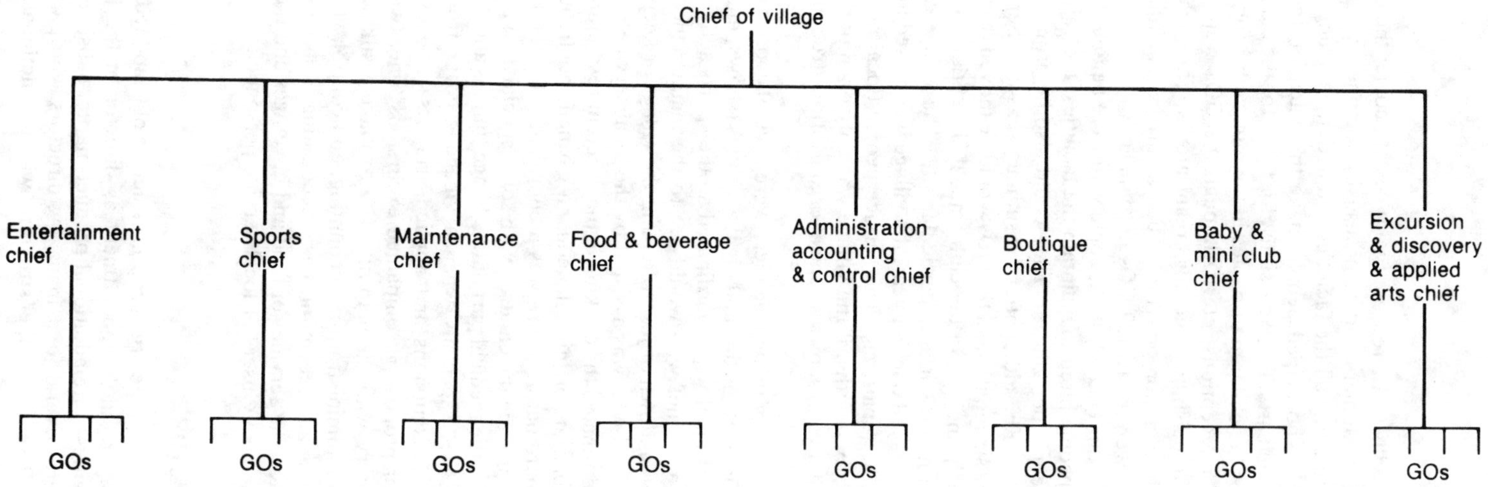

Chief of village

- Entertainment chief
  - GOs
- Sports chief
  - GOs
- Maintenance chief
  - GOs
- Food & beverage chief
  - GOs
- Administration accounting & control chief
  - GOs
- Boutique chief
  - GOs
- Baby & mini club chief
  - GOs
- Excursion & discovery & applied arts chief
  - GOs

EXHIBIT C7.3   ORGANIZATION CHART BEFORE NOVEMBER 1981*

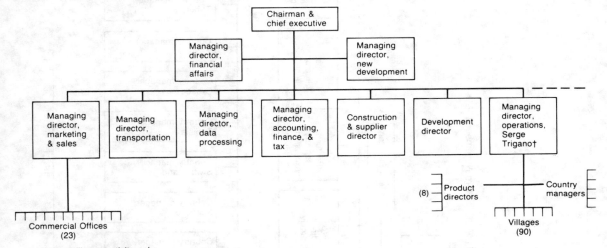

* Holiday villages activity only.
† Until his recent appointment as managing director, American zone.

director for marketing and sales, another one for operations, and several other function heads like accounting, finance, and tax. Exhibit C7.4 shows how the operations part of the organization was structured.

Essentially the structure was composed of three parts. As there was an entertainment chief in the village, there was a director of entertainment at head office—the same for sports. There were several product directors who mirrored the structure of the village. There were country managers in certain countries where the club had several villages in operation, and then there were the ninety villages. All reported to Serge Trigano.

The Role of the Product Directors

Product directors were responsible for the product policy. They made decisions with respect to the policy of Club Med in all the villages, such as the type of activities that should be in each village, and the maintenance that should be done. They recruited and trained the various GOs needed for their domain (i.e., sports GOs, entertainment GOs, administration GOs, cooks, etc.). They staffed the villages by deciding with the director of operations which chief of village would go where and how many people would go with him. They made investment proposals for each village for maintenance, new activities, extension or renovation purposes. They also assumed the task of preparing the budgets and controlling application of policies in the villages by traveling extensively as "ambassadors" of head office to the villages. Each one of them was assigned a certain number of villages. When visiting the village, he would go there representing not his particular product but Club Med's product as a whole. Also, each of them, including the director of operations, was assigned, on a rotating basis, the task of answering emergency phone

EXHIBIT C7.4. ORGANIZATION CHART—OPERATIONS JUST BEFORE THE NEW MOVE (Before November 1981)

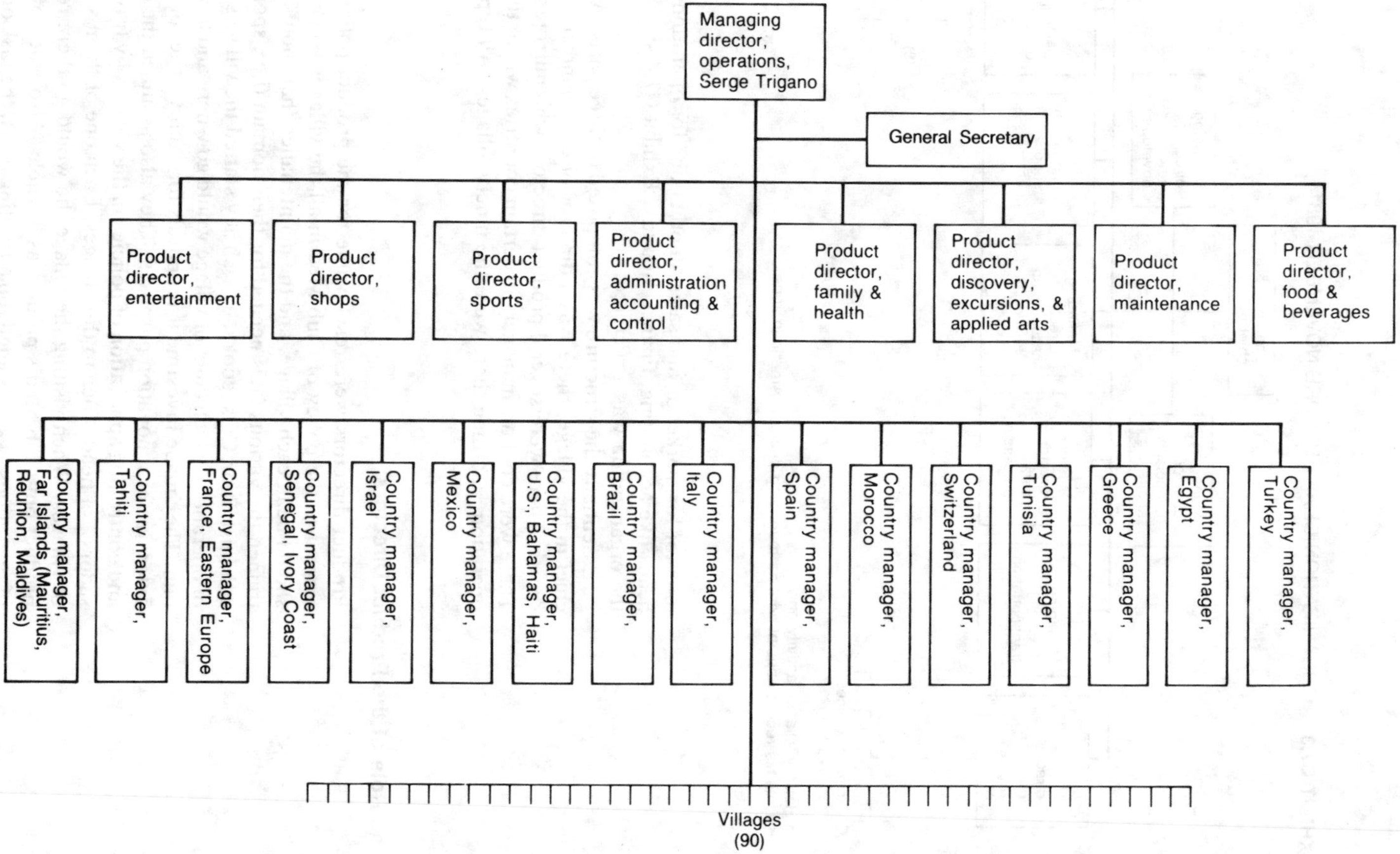

Managing director, operations, Serge Trigano

General Secretary

Product director, food & beverages
Product director, maintenance
Product director, discovery, excursions, & applied arts
Product director, family & health

Product director, administration accounting & control
Product director, sports
Product director, shops
Product director, entertainment

Country manager, Turkey
Country manager, Egypt
Country manager, Greece
Country manager, Tunisia
Country manager, Switzerland
Country manager, Morocco
Country manager, Spain

Country manager, Italy
Country manager, Brazil
Country manager, U.S., Bahamas, Haiti
Country manager, Mexico
Country manager, Israel
Country manager, Senegal, Ivory Coast
Country manager, France, Eastern Europe
Country manager, Tahiti
Country manager, Far Islands (Mauritius, Reunion, Maldives)

Villages (90)

calls from any village and making emergency decisions, or taking action if necessary. Exhibit C7.5 presents examples of product organization. In the new regional structure, the product director's role and place were questioned.

The Role of the Country Manager

Country managers were mainly the ambassadors of Club Med in the countries where Club Med had villages. Usually they were located in countries with more than one village. They would handle political relations themselves, maintaining lasting relationships with elected bodies, mayors, civil servants, regional offices, etc. They would introduce to the new team coming every six months what the country had to offer, its constraints, local mores, the local people to be invited, local artists to be invited, the traps to be avoided, the types of suppliers, the type of local events that might be of interest for the village (so that the village would not forget, for instance, national holidays, etc.). They would try to get Club Med more integrated politically and socially in the host country, in particular in less developed countries where there was a gap between the abundance and richness of the club as compared to its immediate environment. They also had an assistance role such as getting work permits for GOs and also finding suppliers; sometimes, in fact, the country manager had a buyer attached to his staff who would purchase locally for the different villages to get economies of scale. In addition, the country managers personally recruited and maintained lists of the service personnel available to Club Med. They would go and negotiate the salaries, wages, and working conditions of the service personnel with the unions so that the village was free of being involved every six months in a renegotiation. Also, they might have an economic role by helping develop local production or culture, as the club was a heavy buyer of local food and products. They could also act as a development antenna looking for new sites or receiving proposals from local investors and submitting them to the head office. They would also handle legal and tax problems when Club Med had a local legal entity as well as maintain relationships with the owners of the land, hotels, or bungalows when Club Med—as was often the case—was only renting the premises.

PROBLEMS WITH THE CURRENT STRUCTURE

The current structure had been set up about four years ago. It had also been the Club Med's structure before 1971, but in between (1971–1976) there had been a change in the operations side only which had involved setting up area managers; instead of having one director of operations, there had been five directors who had under their control several countries and villages. From 1971 to 1976, there had been no country managers and each of the area managers had had about ten or fifteen villages under his supervision. This structure was changed in 1976 because it seemed to have created several Club Meds in one. The area managers had started to try to get the best chiefs of village and people for their area. As a result, GOs were not moving around every six months from one area of the world to another as was the policy, and also area managers started giving different types of services to their customers so that, for instance, a Frenchman going to one of the zones one year and to another the next year would find a different Club Med. These reasons had led to the structure presented in Exhibit C7.4 for operations. But until now marketing had always been worldwide.

Of course, the structure used until now had created the reverse problem: it seemed to

EXHIBIT C7.5   EXAMPLES OF PRODUCT MANAGEMENT

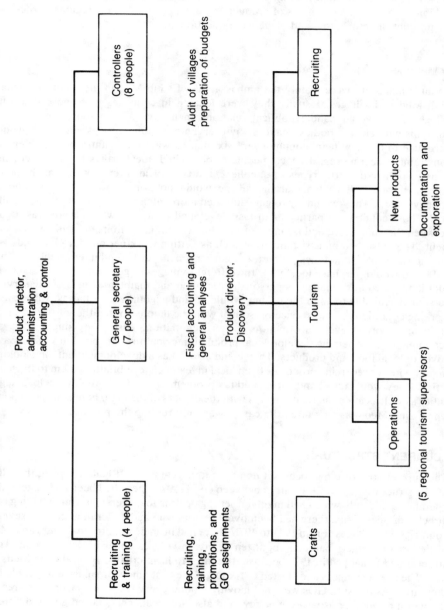

Product director,
administration
accounting & control

Recruiting
& training (4 people)

General secretary
(7 people)

Controllers
(8 people)

Recruiting,
training,
promotions, and
GO assignments

Fiscal accounting and
general analyses

Audit of villages
preparation of budgets

Product director,
Discovery

Crafts

Operations

Tourism

New products

Recruiting

(5 regional tourism supervisors)

Documentation and
exploration

EXHIBIT C7.5 *(CONTINUED)*

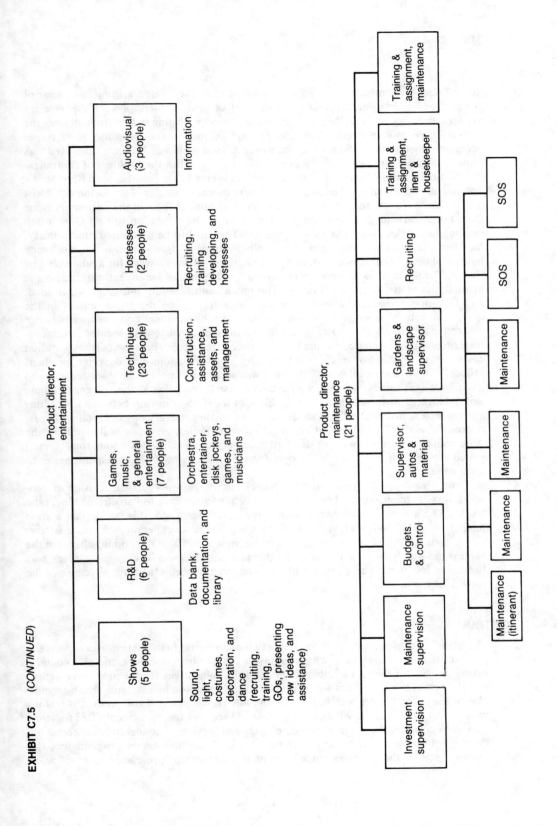

Product director, entertainment

- **Shows (5 people)**
  Sound, light, costumes, decoration, and dance (recruiting, training, GOs, presenting new ideas, and assistance)

- **R&D (6 people)**
  Data bank, documentation, and library

- **Games, music, & general entertainment (7 people)**
  Orchestra, entertainer, disk jockeys, games, and musicians

- **Technique (23 people)**
  Construction, assistance, assets, and management

- **Hostesses (2 people)**
  Recruiting, training developing, and hostesses

- **Audiovisual (3 people)**
  Information

Product director, maintenance (21 people)

- Investment supervision
- Maintenance supervision
- Budgets & control
- Supervisor, autos & material
- Gardens & landscape supervisor
- Recruiting
- Training & assignment, linen & housekeeper
- Training & assignment, maintenance

- Maintenance (itinerant)
- Maintenance
- Maintenance
- Maintenance
- SOS
- SOS
- SOS

Serge Trigano and others that it was too centralized. In fact, Serge Trigano had a span of control (which is rarely achieved in industry) of ninety chiefs of village plus eight product directors and fourteen country managers, all reporting to him from all over the world. There was an overload of information, too much detail, and too many issues being entrusted to him which would be worse as time would go by since Club Med was growing and doubling its capacity every five years. Besides the problem of centralization and information overload, another problem seemed to appear because Club Med's operations had not adapted enough to the international character of its customers. Most of the GOs were still recruited in France, whereas now 15–20% of the customers came from the American zone. France was not even the best location to find GOs, often needing to speak at least one other language. They had to be unmarried, under thirty, they had to change countries every six months, with no roots, and they had to work long hours and be accessible twenty-four hours a day, seven days a week for a relatively low salary. The feeling was that maybe one could find happier and more enthusiastic people in Australia or Brazil than in France. Too much centralization, information overload, and lack of internationalization in operations were among the big problems in the current structure. Also, there was a feeling that a closer local coordination between marketing and operations could give better results since customers seemed to concentrate on one zone (American in the U.S., European in Europe) because of transportation costs, and a coordination might lead to a better grasp of customer needs, price, product, offices, etc. For example, when Club Med was smaller and only in Europe, departure to its villages was done only once a week. As a result, reception at the village, welcome and departure, was also once a week. Lack of local coordination between operations and marketing had created arrivals and departures almost every day in certain villages, overburdening GO's smiles and organization of activities. As another illustration, the American customer was used to standard hotel services (such as bathroom, towels, etc.) which may be different than in Europe. Closer local ties might help respond better to local needs.

Centralization had also created bottlenecks in assignments and supervision of people. Every six months everybody—all GOs—was coming back to Paris from all over the world to be assigned to another village. Five or ten years ago, this was in fact a great happening that allowed everybody to discuss with the product people, see headquarters, find friends who had been in other villages, but now with 5000 GOs coming almost at the same time—and wanting to speak to the product directors—reassigning them was becoming somewhat hectic. It was likely to be even worse in the future because of the growth of the company.

PLANNING AND CONTROL

The planning cycle could be divided into two main parts: first, there was a three-year plan started two years ago, which involved the product directors and the country managers. Each product director would define his objectives for the next three years, and the action programs that would go with it, and propose investments that he would like to make for his product in each of the ninety villages. All the product directors would meet to look at the villages one by one and see how the investment fitted together as well as consider the staffing number of GOs and service personnel in broad terms for the next three years. Of course, the big chunk of the investment program was the maintenance of the facilities since 55% of the investment program concerned such maintenance programs. The rest was concerned with additions or modifications of the villages, such as new tennis courts, a new theater, restaurant, revamping a boutique, etc. The country managers were involved in that same three-year plan. First of all they would give the product directors their feelings and suggestions for investments as well as for staffing the villages. In addition, they would provide some objectives and action programs in the way they would try to handle personnel problems, political problems, economic problems, cultural and social integration, sales of Club Med in their country, and development.

Besides this three-year operational plan, there was the one-year plan which was divided into two 6-month plans. For each season a budget was prepared for each of the villages. This budget was mostly prepared by the product director for administration accounting, and it concerned the different costs, such as goods consumed, personnel charges, rents, etc. This budget was given to the chief of the village when he left with his team. In addition to this operational budget, there was an investment budget every six months in more detail than the three-year plan. This investment budget was prepared by the maintenance director under the guidance and proposal from the different product directors. It was submitted to the operations director and then went directly to the chief executive of the company. It had not been unusual before the three-year plan had been controlled that the proposals that product directors were making to the maintenance director were three times as high as what would be in fact given and allowed by the chief executive.

On the control side, there was a controller in each of the villages (administrator chief of accounting and control) as well as central controllers who would be assigned a region and would travel from one village to the other. But the local controller and his team in fact were GOs like any other ones and they were changing from one village to another every six months. There was a kind of "fact and rule book" that was left in the village so that the next team would understand the particular ways and procedures of the village. But mostly speaking, each new team would start all over again each time it was coming with a new budget and standards, rules, and procedures from central head office as well as with the help of the fact and rule book. These two tools—the three-year plan and the six-month (a season) budgets were the main planning and control tools used.

OBJECTIVES AND POLICIES

Five objectives seemed to be important to Serge Trigano when reviewing the structure.

One was that the club wanted to continue to grow and double its capacity every five years, either by adding new villages or increasing the size of the current ones.

The second objective, which had always guided Club Med, was that it would have to continue to innovate, not to be a hotel chain but to be something different as it had always been and to continue to respond to the changing needs of the customers.

A third objective stemmed from the fact that Club Med was no longer essentially French; the majority of its customers in fact did not come from France; as a result, it would have to continue to internationalize its employees, its structure, its way of thinking, training, etc.

The fourth objective was economic. Costs were increasing, but not all these costs could be passed on to the gentils membres unless the club wanted to stop its growth. One way of not passing all costs to the customer was to increase productivity by standardization, and better methods and procedures.

The fifth objective was to keep the basic philosophy of Club Med: to keep the village concept an entity protected as much as possible from the outside world, but integrated in the country in which it was; to keep the package concept for GMs; and finally the social mixing. Whatever your job, your social position, etc., at Club Med you were only recognized by two things: the color of your bathing suit and the beads you wore around your neck, which allowed you to pay for your scotch, orange juice, etc., at the bar. Part of the philosophy, in addition, was to make sure that the GO's nomadism would continue: change every season.

THE PROPOSED NEW STRUCTURE

With these objectives in mind, the new structure to be effective November 1981 had just been sketched as shown in Exhibit C7.6. The idea would be to move the operations and marketing closer together in three zones. One would be America (North & South), another Europe and Africa, and the third (in the long run when this market would be more developed) the Far East. In each area, a director would manage the operations side, i.e., the villages, and the marketing side, i.e., promotion, selling, pricing, distributing Club Med's concept. In fact, most of the American GMs were going to the American zone villages; most of the European GMs to the European zone; and most of the Asian GMs to the Asian zone. As the cost of transportation from one zone to another was increasing, people could not afford to go very far.

EXHIBIT C7.6   THE PROPOSED STRUCTURE

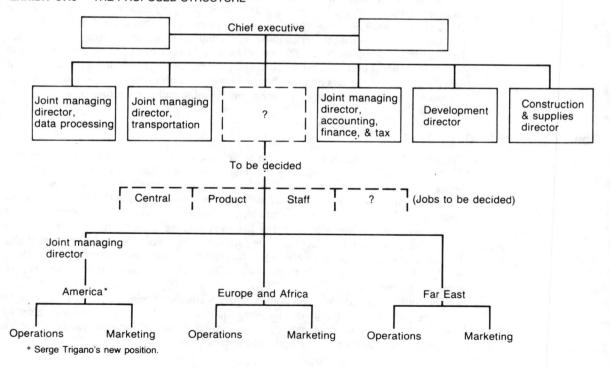

* Serge Trigano's new position.

This was the general idea and now it had to be pushed further. Among the main interesting and troublesome aspects of the new structure were the following: how to avoid with this structure that Club Med would separate into three different entities with three different types of products? Should such occurrence be avoided? It seemed that this should not be allowed; that's why the structure which had been there four years ago with five regions failed. It had transformed Club Med into five mini Club Meds, although even at that time the five area managers did not have marketing and sales responsibility. In addition to this major issue of how to preserve the unity and uniqueness of Club Med with a geographic structure, several other questions were of great importance:

- Who would decide what activities would take place in a village?
- Who would decide the investments to be made in a village?
- Who would staff a village?
- Would there be a central hiring and training of all GOs or only some of them?
- How would the geographic managers be evaluated in terms of performance?
- If they wanted to continue with the GOs and give them the right and possibility to move every six months from one part of the world to another, how would the transfer of GOs be done?
- How should the transfer of GOs be coordinated?
- Should there be some common basic procedures, like accounting, reporting, etc., and in that case, who would design and enforce those procedures?
- How could there be some coordination and allocation of resources among the three regions, who would do it, and how would it be done?

Also of importance was the problem of transition.

- What would happen to the country managers?
- What would happen to the product directors?
- What would happen to central marketing and sales?

These were some of the questions that bothered Serge Trigano on the flight to Paris from New York.

APPENDIX A FINANCIAL PERFORMANCE
(in 000 FFr)

	69/70	70/71	71/72	72/73	73/74	74/75	75/76
Sales	313,000	363,000	427,000	502,000	600,000	791,000	1,060,000
Net income	....	....	13,400	22,500	27,300	40,000	51,800
Cash flow	....	....	25,100	37,000	42,800	56,790	70,900
EPS	5.31	5.73	7.41	10.88	12.78	16.08	20.78

	76/77	77/78	78/79	79/80
	1,350,000	1,616,000	1,979,000	2,462,000
	67,870	72,135	85,900	111,600
	103,645	114,578	138,300	173,100
	20.98	23.78	28.42	36.91

APPENDIX B   GROWTH IN NUMBER OF CLUB MEMBERS

	Number of members
1950	2,300
1955	10,000
1960	45,000
1965	90,000
1970	293,000
1975	432,000
1980	770,000 (including Valtur)

APPENDIX C   NUMBER OF FACILITIES (1981)

	No. of holiday centers	No. of beds
Club Med and Valtur	102	60,400
Hotels	7	1,000
Apartment buildings	24	11,000
Total	132	72,500

APPENDIX D   MEMBERS OF CLUB MED ACCORDING TO COUNTRY OF ORIGIN (1979)*

France	301,000	43.1%
U.S.A./Canada	124,000	17.8
Belgium	41,600	6
Italy	34,400	4.9
W. Germany	34,100	4.9
Switzerland	18,500	2.6
Austria	6,800	1
Australia	18,400	26
Others	84,900	12.1
Conference & seminars	34,700	5†
	698,500	100 %

* Excluding Valtur.
† Most seminars are in France for French customers.

374

APPENDIX E   COUNTRIES OF OPERATIONS
(Before New Structure)

Country	Separate commercial office	Country manager	Country manager supervising commercial operations	Villages
Germany	x			
Switzerland	x	x		x
Turkey			x	x
Italy	x	x		x
Venezuela	x			
Belgium	x			x
Mexico			x	x
U.S.A.	x	x		
Bahamas		x ⎫ same as U.S.A.		x
Haiti		x ⎭		x
Brazil			x	x
Japan	x			
Great Britain	x			
Tunisia			x	x
Morocco		x		x
Holland	x			
Greece	x	x		x
Israel			x	x
Malaysia	x	x		x
France	x	x		
New Zealand	x			
Australia	x			x
Egypt		x		x
Singapore	x			
Canada	x			
Tahiti		x		x
South Africa	x			
Spain	x	x		x
Senegal		x same		x
Ivory Coast		x		
Mauritius		x same as Reunion		x
Sri Lanka		x same as Mauritius		x
Guadeloupe		x ⎫ same as U.S.A.		x
Martinique		x ⎭		x
Reunion Island		x		x
Dominican Republic		x same as U.S.A.		x
United Arab Emirates				x

APPENDIX F   CAPITAL STRUCTURE (1981)

Compagnie Financière group (Rothschild)	7	%
Banque de Paris et des Pays Bas	6	
REDEC group	5	
Crédit Lyonnais	7.5	
Union des Assurances de Paris	7.5	
The IFI International group	7	
The company personnel's common investment fund	5	
Subtotal	45	%
Public	55	
Total	100	%

APPENDIX G   EVOLUTION OF GMs BY NATIONALITY

	72/73	78/79
France	60.6%	47.2%
U.S.A.	7.7	17.8
Belgium	8.7	6.0
Italy	7.5	5.6
W.Germany	7.4	4.9
Switzerland	2.4	1
Others	5.7	12.2
	100 %	100 %

APPENDIX H THE CLUB GROWTH IN NUMBERS

	69/70	70/71	71/72	72/73	73/74	74/75	75/76	76/77	77/78	78/79	79/80
Objective	255,000	293,000	299,000	318,000	339,000	408,000	475,000	540,000	578,000	615,000	698,500
Villages	25	55	55	60	61	69	70	74	74	78	83
Beds	....	33,900	34,300	36,400	37,000	49,300	50,400	53,800	55,600	58,600	64,600
No. of hotel nights											
Winter	....	881,000	948,000	~1,018,000	1,044,000	1,240,000	1,628,000	1,790,000	1,940,000	2,011,000	2,250,000
Summer	....	2,651,000	2,801,000	2,850,000	2,920,000	3,210,000	3,400,000	3,550,000	3,710,000	3,970,000	4,265,000
Occupancy rates	68.07	69.52	66.81	66.76	69.63	70.70	71.19	71.65	72.87	72.88	
No. of permanent employees	793	938	950	978	977	1,035	1,157	1,132	1,192	1,286	1,297
No. of GOs in villages (summer season)											~ 6,000
No. of service personnel in villages (summer season)											~10,000
No. of employees in Paris (operations only)											250
No. of employees country management											100

COCA-COLA WINE SPECTRUM (C)

Prepared by Carol Reeves, University of Miami,
Phyllis G. Holland, Valdosta State College,
and William R. Boulton, University of Georgia.

In an effort to increase its earnings and broaden its base of business outside the field of soft drinks, the Coca-Cola Company (Coke) purchased the Taylor Wine Company (New York), Sterling Vineyards (California), and Monterey Vineyards (California) in 1977. The purchases were met with skepticism by industry insiders. Such marketing giants as Beatrice Foods, Pillsbury Company, and Jos. Schlitz Brewing had tried the wine business and each had soon withdrawn from it. The skepticism quickly turned to animosity, however, when Coke introduced a controversial comparative advertising campaign in 1978. Sales skyrocketed, and Coke's gamble seemed to be paying off handsomely. By 1983, Coke's wine unit, the Wine Spectrum, had grown from the sixth largest American winery to the third largest. However, in September of 1983, citing the need to "concentrate our resources in the areas of our business where returns are highest," Roberto Goizueta, chairman and chief executive officer of Coca-Cola, announced that Jos. E. Seagram & Sons, Inc., would purchase the Wine Spectrum. After 6 years and a number of successes, why the sudden withdrawal? This case will examine the rationale for entering the wine business, the impact of Coca-Cola's participation, and the circumstances surrounding Coke's withdrawal.

THE CREATION OF THE WINE SPECTRUM

During the 1970s wine consumption was increasing in both absolute amounts and per capita. In 1977, 6% more wine entered distribution channels than in 1976, and the same advance was predicted for 1978. Wine consumption was 400 million gallons in 1977, or 1.85 gallons per capita, as compared with 1.7 gallons per capita in 1976.

Demographic trends indicated a healthy future for the wine industry. The typical wine drinker is 25–54 years old, is well educated, has a good income, and lives in or near a large city. The percentage of the American population fitting this description would steadily increase as the "babyboom" generation matured. In contrast, the heaviest carbonated beverage drinkers are 10–24 years old, a declining segment of the population.

Coke had been exploring new profit and growth opportunities within its area of expertise, the food and beverage industry. The wine industry, and the Taylor Wine Co. in particular, seemed to fit its needs. Wine consumption, in both absolute and per capita amounts, was increasing. Although there were many differences between the wine and soft drink industries, Coke felt that its expertise in the beverage industry could be successfully adapted to the wine industry.

On August 6, 1976, Lincoln First Bank of Rochester, New York, put out a preliminary prospectus for the sale of 603,000 of the 900,000 shares of Taylor Wine Company stock that it held for trust customers. The motive behind the sale was to raise cash for the trusts involved. Taylor was informed of the proceedings because 10% of the outstanding stock was involved. Several companies responded to the prospectus, including Coca-Cola, PepsiCo, Beatrice Foods, and Norton-Simon, as well as five private investors headed by Marne Obernauer (a former Taylor director and owner of Great Western before it was purchased by Taylor). Coca-Cola was interested in more than the 603,000 shares, so when they and the bank reached an agreement, the secondary offer was withdrawn and Coca-Cola entered into merger talks directly with Taylor, which had suffered in the cyclical turns of the decade.

Conditions in the Wine Industry

In 1972, wine prices were rising dramatically and there was great interest in entering the industry. More acreage was planted in 1971, 1972, and 1973 than the total of all previous plantings. In addition, speculators observed that foreign wines selling for $25 per case in the 1950s were selling for $500 to $1,000 per case, and they began to put bottles in storage. The 1972 vintage was bad and did not sell well, and the 1973 harvest was the largest in history. The increased supply led to a decline in prices, which accelerated when the speculators put the hoarded wine on the market. By the time the first wine from the new plantings hit the market in 1974, inventories were at an all-time high. The oversupply was further increased by another large harvest in 1975.

In 1972, the average return to a California grower per ton of grapes crushed was $217. The return dropped to $131 in 1974, and to $100 in 1975. By 1976, conditions were improving. Inventories were slowly being worked off, and more grape vines were taken up than planted. Producers were still cautious even though prices began to rise.

The Taylor Wine Company

Taylor had been a leading domestic producer of premium still and sparkling wines, which were marketed under the "Taylor" and "Great Western" labels. The record of Taylor from 1972 to 1976 reflected the cyclical swings in the industry during that period (see Exhibit C8.1 for financial data). In 1973, record sales of $51 million reflected an 18% increase over 1972, with profits up 25% to $6.8 million, or $1.57 per share. In 1974, sales increased to $56 million, while profits increased to $6.9 million, or $1.58 per share.

EXHIBIT C8.1 10-YEAR FINANCIAL SUMMARY, TAYLOR WINE, 1967–1976

Financial position, year-end June 30	1976	1975*	1974	1973	1972	1971	1970	1969	1968	1967
Total assets	$74,839	$68,549	$58,129	$54,787	$50,081	$42,808	$35,247	$29,992	$27,210	$25,100
Current assets	47,475	41,354	33,566	31,686	29,275	23,855	20,176	16,694	14,982	13,556
Total investment in plant and equipment at cost	45,310	42,929	38,170	34,986	30,952	27,541	22,300	19,472	17,328	15,816
Additions to plant and equipment for the year at cost	2,509	4,850	3,472	4,373	3,619	5,498	2,967	2,261	1,755	2,155
Depreciation provision accumulated	18,849	16,596	14,390	12,635	10,884	9,219	7,829	6,712	5,625	4,759
Total liabilities	15,326	11,982	4,343	5,444	5,408	12,215	7,959	5,339	5,202	5,340
Portion of notes payable due after 1 year	6,000	37	63	32	224	397	555	722	809	1,058
Working capital	39,053	30,285	30,114	27,058	24,840	21,050	13,452	12,706	11,235	9,778
Current ratio	$64 to 1	3.74 to 1	9.72 to 1	6.85 to 1	6.60 to 1	8.51 to 1	3.00 to 1	4.19 to 1	4.00 to 1	3.59 to 1
Shareholders' equity	59,513	56,567	53,786	49,343	44,674	30,593	27,287	24,653	22,008	19,735
Shareholders' equity per share†	13.67	12.99	12.35	11.33	10.52	7.67	6.84	6.18	5.51	4.94
Retained earnings	40,876	37,930	35,149	30,706	26,036	22,611	21,990	19,355	16,710	14,437
Retained earnings per share†	9.39	8.71	8.07	7.05	6.13	5.67	5.51	4.85	4.19	3.62
Earnings operations, year-end June 30										
Net sales	$59,617	$57,604	$56,421	$51,050	$43,201	$40,839	$34,688	$32,126	$27,206	$25,992
Gross profit	24,755	23,244	25,192	24,902	21,412	20,376	18,414	16,893	14,725	13,803
Interest on debt	922	707	79	75	274	610	292	147	140	151
Income before taxes on income	11,485	10,611	13,831	13,863	10,998	10,080	9,113	9,089	7,624	7,185
Taxes on income	5,839	5,218	6,950	7,017	5,526	5,072	4,882	4,981	4,020	3,621
Net income	5,646	5,393	6,881	6,847	5,471	5,009	4,231	4,108	3,604	3,565
Income taxes as a percent of pretax income	50.84%	49.18%	50.25%	50.61%	50.25%	50.31%	53.7%	54.80%	52.73%	50.39%
Net income per share†	1.30	1.24	1.58	1.57	1.29	1.26	1.06	1.03	.90	.89
Net income as a percent of average shareholders' equity	9.73%	9.77%	13.35%	14.56%	14.54%	17.31%	16.29%	17.61%	17.27%	19.26%
Dividends	2,699	2,612	2,438	2,177	2,046	1,703	1,596	1,463	1,330	1,117
Dividends per share†	.62	.60	.56	.50	.48	.43	.40	.37	.33	.28
Depreciation and amortization	2,360	2,287	2,019	1,996	1,850	1,555	1,288	1,233	1,109	979
Working capital provided by operations	8,023	7,676	8,948	8,936	7,275	6,533	5,577	5,422	4,813	4,580

* In 1975 the company adopted the last-in, first-out method of pricing inventories.
† All per share amounts give effect for all years for the 3-for-1 stock split in August 1971.
Source: Annual report, The Taylor Wine Company, 1976.

Results worsened as Taylor reported sales and profits of $57.6 million and $5.4 million, or $1.24 per share, in 1975 and $59.6 million and $5.6 million, or $1.30 per share, in 1976. Taylor stated in its 1976 annual report that the company had "successfully weathered the recession of the past two years and [was] in a strong position to take advantage of the recovery the wine industry appear[ed] to be experiencing."

After the Taylor board's approval of the proposed merger, Taylor's president, Joseph Swarthout, explained to the shareholders in the December 2, 1976, prospectus:

> The U.S. wine market has never been more competitive. As I stated at our Annual Shareholders' Meeting in September, our major competitors are stronger than ever. In several cases they have significantly stronger financial backing than we have. Under these conditions, it becomes increasingly difficult to improve, or even maintain, our share-of-market. . . . It is now my firm belief that the Taylor Wine Company would enjoy substantially greater opportunities for success in the future through the financial strength and diversity of the Coca-Cola Company.

Exhibit C8.2 compares balance sheets of Taylor and Coca-Cola just before the merger.

Under the terms of the merger agreement approved by stockholders of both companies in January 1977, all outstanding shares of Taylor stock were converted into shares of common stock of Coca-Cola at the rate of one share of Coca-Cola stock for each 3.75 shares of Taylor stock. No changes in Taylor management were planned, and the company was to operate as a wholly owned subsidiary of Coca-Cola with Coca-Cola officials on its board of directors. Exhibit C8.3 shows the stock price movements for Coca-Cola and Taylor.

Analysts seemed to agree that the Taylor acquisition was a bargain for Coca-Cola. By maintaining premium prices while others were cutting prices, Taylor had maintained its profitability and its record of increasing dividends. Although not investing heavily in such capital projects as a bottle factory, the company had kept its facilities up to date and in good shape. The slipping market share and lack of national image for Taylor were the kind of problems that Coca-Cola's $387 million in cash could solve. Taylor was not in debt, was profitable, and had the nation's best-known label and widest distribution system after Gallo. The crucial property needed to capitalize on the predicted wine boom had been acquired, and two more acquisitions completed the Wine Spectrum Division.

Sterling Vineyards

To secure a place at the top end of the wine business, Coke purchased Sterling Vineyards in July 1977. Sterling was the 100th largest winery in the U.S., with a capacity of 60,000 cases per year. Albert Killeen, the man Coke selected to head the Wine Spectrum, explained the reasoning behind the Sterling purchase:

> They produce superb wines. They are recognized here and abroad as producing wines of exceptional quality and distinction. The winery itself is one of the most beautiful in the world. By acquiring Sterling and, with it, a Napa Valley appellation, and giving the winery the necessary resources to produce only estate bottled vintage varietals, two whites and two reds, the wine world would know that Coca-Cola was committed to quality and the finest tradition of wine-making.

EXHIBIT C8.2   THE COCA-COLA COMPANY AND SUBSIDIARIES AND THE TAYLOR WINE COMPANY, INC.,
PRO FORMA COMBINED CONDENSED BALANCE SHEET AS OF JUNE 30, 1976
Unaudited (in $1000s)

	Coca-Cola	Taylor	Adjustment note	Pro forma combined
Assets				
Current assets:				
Cash	$ 78,571	$ 1,175		79,744
Marketable securities	229,795			299,795
Trade accounts receivable—net	250,947	4,356		255,303
Inventories	374,920	41,766		416,686
Prepaid expenses	28,467	180		28,647
Total current assets	962,695	47,475		1,010,175
Property, plant, and equip.—net	647,684	26,462		674,146
Other assets	209,641	902		210,543
Total	$1,820,023	$74,839		$1,894,862
Liabilities and stockholders' equity				
Current liabilities:				
Notes payable including current maturities of long-term debt	$ 24,891	$ 3,037		$ 27,928
Accounts payable and accrued accounts	337,129	3,656		340,785
Accrued taxes	121,763	1,729		123,492
Total current liabilities	483,783	8,422		492,205
Long-term liabilities and deferred taxes	44,092	6,904		50,996
Stockholders' equity:				
Common stock—no par value, the Coca-Cola Co.	60,485		$ 1,175	
Common stock—$2 par value, The Taylor Wine Co., Inc.		8,707	(8,707)	
Capital surplus	87,938	9,930	7,534	105,402
Earned surplus	1,159,090	40,876		1,199,466
Treasury shares	(15,363)			(15,365)
Total stockholders' equity	1,292,148	59,515		1,351,661
Total	$1,820;023	$74,839		$1,894,862

Note: The pro forma adjustment reflects the issuance of 1,161,000 common shares of the Coca-Cola Company upon conversion of each of the presently issued common shares of Taylor for .267 common shares of the Coca-Cola Company pursuant to the terms of the merger.

Wines from Sterling give the Wine Spectrum an entry to the finest restaurants, clubs, hotels, and wine merchants in the United States and abroad. Sterling is the Wine Spectrum's crown jewel.[1]

Monterey Vineyards

The purchase of Monterey Vineyards, located near Gonzales, California, was announced by Coca-Cola in November 1977. Monterey owned no vineyards but had a

EXHIBIT C8.3   COMPARATIVE STOCK PRICES

	Taylor common stock		Coca-Cola common stock	
	High bid price	Low bid price	High sale price	Low sale price
1974				
First quarter	$38.25	$23.75	$127.75	$109.50
Second quarter	24.25	16.50	118.375	98.375
Third quarter	17.75	12.25	109.00	48.00
Fourth quarter	13.75	9.25	68.75	44.625
1975				
First quarter	20.875	10.125	81.50	53.25
Second quarter	19.50	16.00	93.50	72.75
Third quarter	18.375	11.0	92.00	69.625
Fourth quarter	15.375	10.75	89.75	69.875
1976				
First quarter	17.50	13.50	94.25	82.00
Second quarter	15.50	12.25	89.00	77.625
Third quarter	19.375	12.875	89.625	82.875
Fourth quarter, November 20, 1976	20.75	16.875	86.25	76.25

Note: The Coca-Cola Company announced that it had entered into merger negotiations with Taylor on September 8, 1976, and preliminary agreement on the exchange rate was announced on October 14, 1976.

production capacity of 7 million cases and storage capacity of 2.2 million gallons. It produced eight varietals and one blend.

Killeen felt Monterey Vineyards gave Spectrum

a modern, flexible winery only completed in '75, set in the heart of what I believe is destined to be one of California's and this nation's most prestigious vineyard areas. This vineyard's unique soil and climatic conditions yield grapes of the highest wine-making quality and I speak of grapes for white wines, Chardonnay, Chenin Blanc, Sauvignon Blanc, Johannisberg-Riesling, and Gewürztraminer, grapes vital for sustained, expanding growth, as white wines continue to grow and gain in popularity.[2]

Killeen assessed the components of the Wine Spectrum as follows:

Taylor is the keystone of the Company's wine business because of its reputation for quality, its strong distribution system and its fine sales organization. The Sterling and Monterey wineries add geographic balance as well as new brands of varietal wines to our product mix. We now have really the best of both worlds— the distinguished tradition of wine making from the Finger Lakes region of New York State, known for its fine champagne and sherries, and the fresh and exuber-ant ambience of the California growing regions, known for their table wines. Even the two California wineries were carefully chosen to balance one another. One is in a region that produces a very fine Cabernet Sauvignon grape, for example; the other, in a much cooler region, fosters some of the best Johannisberg Riesling and Gruner Sylvaner grapes available anywhere. So our combination of vineyards puts us in a prime position for taking advantage of opportunities to produce a wide variety of high-quality American-grown wines for optimum acceptance among American consumers and consumers around the world.[3]

Coke's master plan included acquiring grapes and wineries on the West Coast to complement its Taylor purchase. The acquisitions had to be made very quickly, "before competition or the industry saw the real thrust of our ambitions."[4] Marrying Taylor's eastern label with the western fruit of Monterey and Sterling Vineyards, Coke introduced Taylor California Cellars wine in 1978. A complete, integrated marketing plan for Taylor California Cellars, which included four wines and three package sizes, was ready only 17 months after the Taylor purchase and 7 months after the Monterey Vineyard purchase completed the Wine Spectrum.

THE WINE SPECTRUM'S ACTIVITIES AND IMPACT ON THE INDUSTRY

Coca-Cola's presence was felt immediately and continuously during its 6½ year stay in the wine industry. Its marketing and advertising practices infuriated the staid and traditional wineries and forced established companies to scramble just to hold onto the business they had. Spectrum's competitors were not the only ones who were forced to contend with Coke's considerable muscle. The alcohol and beverage industry is highly regulated on both the state and the federal levels. In its first 5 years, Spectrum went to court three times to fight agencies which disputed its marketing plans, and it won each time. As Lewis Bromberg, a consultant to the industry for decades, put it, "Coke has had more impact on the industry than anything since Prohibition."[5]

Coca-Cola is known for its marketing strength, and it immediately capitalized on its expertise in this area. Rather than buying vineyards or facilities, Coke used its resources to market the Wine Spectrum products. Coke believed it could build sales and market share by "demystifying" wine and creating products to suit consumers' desires. Rick Theis, director of public relations for the Wine Spectrum, claimed, "We take credit for single-handedly changing the industry from product-driven marketing to consumer-driven marketing."[6] Coke had ambitious plans and goals for its wine unit. The only way to achieve them was to develop desired products, promote them effectively, create wide distribution networks, and price the products to fit the needs of its target market.

Product Development

To capitalize on the rapidly growing table wine market, which rose from 50% of total sales in 1970 to 75% in 1975, Taylor California Cellars (TCC) was introduced by the Wine Spectrum in 1978. TCC wines were specially contracted and blended California wines which used Taylor's New York name and wide distribution network. TCC was met with skepticism by the California wine community. In what would become a familiar pattern for most of Spectrum's innovations, the skepticism turned to animosity, then to a grudging admiration, to emulation, and finally to head-to-head competition.

The Taylor California Cellars line consisted of four premium generic wines—chablis, rhine, rosé, and burgundy. Spurred by a controversial comparative advertising campaign, TCC quickly surpassed the most optimistic projections for its success. Wine Spectrum executives hoped a half-million cases could be sold in the 4 months after Taylor's introduction in September 1978. The sales goal for 1979 was 1.5 million cases, and for 1980, 3 million cases. The first two goals were met and the 1980 goal was easily exceeded, with sales totaling 3.8 million cases. The TCC product generated more than $100 million in retail sales in its second full year of production. Killeen felt, and many agreed with him, that Taylor California Cellars was the most successful new wine product introduced in the 1970s.[7]

In 1981, the Wine Spectrum sought to further expand its market by introducing "light," or lower-calorie, wines. The health and fitness trend in the country was continuing, and low-calorie products had been very successful in the beverage industry. From 1975 to 1982, light-beer consumption increased by 800%, while total market increase was only 19%. By 1981, low-calorie soft drinks accounted for 17.5% of the market and sales continued to rise.[8] Perhaps the most promising aspect of these trends was that the low-calorie products weren't cannibalizing existing products but rather were bringing new consumers to the beer and soft drink markets.

One of the biggest hurdles the Wine Spectrum had to overcome before it could market a light wine was approval of the "light" designation on its labels. Historically, "light" had been used to describe dessert wines, which contained greater than 14% alcohol but less than their full normal amount of liquor. When the Bureau of Alcohol, Tobacco, and Firearms (BATF) refused to approve the "light" label for Taylor California Cellars Light Chablis, Spectrum took the bureau to court. Spectrum won the case and the right to call its low-calorie wines light.

Taylor California Cellars Light Chablis was positioned as a wine for "other occasions," rather than as a table wine (see Exhibit C8.4). It was targeted to those who drank soft drinks, Lambrusco, beer, or spirits. To produce wines with a lower alcohol content and fewer calories, grapes must be picked before they are fully ripe. This results in a wine that is less tasty than normal and that few regular wine drinkers would consider palatable. But the Wine Spectrum and other wineries were more concerned with attracting new wine drinkers than in convincing current drinkers to switch.

The advertising campaign for Taylor's Light Chablis, Light Rhine, and Light Rosé focused on the reduced calorie content of the products. Light Chablis had only 53 calories per 100 milliliters serving, 25% fewer calories than regular Taylor wines. A

EXHIBIT C8.4   TAYLOR CALIFORNIA "LIGHT" LABEL

TAYLOR CALIFORNIA CELLARS LIGHT CHABLIS is a new dimension in wine. It is low in alcohol (9.4%) and contains 25% fewer calories than our regular Chablis.

Average analysis per 100 ml. serving:

Calories	57
Carbohydrates	0.2 grams
Protein	0.0 grams*
Fat	0.0 grams*

* Same as our regular Chablis.

Our smooth and gentle Light Chablis is perfect after sports such as tennis or skiing, and for other occasions that call for a refreshing drink. Serve it chilled or on the rocks.

Source: David Drum, "Marketing Wine Keeps Growing at Taylor Cal," *Advertising Age,* July 27, 1984, p. S-40.

distinctive label was developed for the family of light wines, and it was "incorporated into a complete set of point-of-sale materials . . . which include dramatic risers, cut-case cards, shelf danglers, cold box stickers, shelf strips, table tents, menu clip-ons, polar motion light boxes, and informative consumer brochures, all of which emphasize the message of 25% fewer calories than regular Taylor California Cellars."[9]

The initial consumer reaction to light wine was very favorable, and several wineries, including Los Hermanos, Sebastiani, and Geyser Peak, brought out light wines in 1981. Gallo believed the technology needed to produce a quality light wine was not yet available and chose to concentrate its resources on established products. Light-wine producers thought sales would soar and projected that light wines would account for 15% of the wine market by 1990. Because light wines were targeted toward non-wine drinkers, the wineries felt light wines presented a golden opportunity to increase their sales and market share.

Italian wineries had identified "chillability" as a key ingredient in the American consumer's beverage tastes in the mid-1970s. They marketed their fizzy, fruity Lambruscos as wines that went "nice on ice" and watched their U.S. sales grow from 4 million gallons in 1970 to 59.8 million gallons in 1981. The Wine Spectrum felt it could further expand its market by capitalizing on the booming popularity of Lambrusco wine. Not only would a Lambrusco-type wine expand Spectrum's market, it would also allow them to deplete excess red-grape inventory and produce wine at the severely under-utilized Hammondsport (New York) winery. The resultant product was Lake Country Soft, a light, fruity, slightly carbonated red wine which was introduced in 1981 to mixed reviews. Wine makers hoped that "soft" wines, like Lake Country Soft, would capture 10% of the wine market by 1990.

In addition to introducing new wine products, the Wine Spectrum was in the fore-front of packaging innovations. Taylor wines in 6.3-ounce aluminum cans were test-marketed on United and Delta Airlines. Officials felt initial negative reactions would be overcome when consumers realized how convenient wine in six-pack containers would be. Spectrum also began testing wine sold in single-serving plastic bottles and 1.8-liter "bag-in-a-box" packages. Although single-serving containers and bag-in-a-box pack-ages were new in the U.S., they had been accepted in other countries for years. In Australia, bag-in-a-box packages accounted for 40% of all wine sold. The bag-in-a-box packages looked particularly promising because of the ease with which restaurants could use them. The wine could be pumped to the bar from the cellar and dispensed in the same manner as beer—or Coke. Coke had the expertise and distribution network needed for the "on-premise" marketing which had been overlooked by most other wineries.

Spectrum executives saw the wine market as highly segmented, with room for a variety of products in various types and sizes of containers. They wanted to create products which would fit individual lifestyles and tastes. Rather than following the traditional wine marketing approach, which portrayed wine as a drink for the elite, Coke presented wine as a drink for anyone, at any time. Coke's highly controversial and very successful advertising campaign was the key to this marketing approach.

Advertising

Coke's entry into the wine industry had more impact on traditional advertising practices than on any other area. Coke felt that instant recognition of Taylor California Cellars was crucial and decided to introduce the wines with a controversial and previously unheard of comparative advertising campaign. There was some question about whether comparative advertising was allowed under federal regulations, so Spectrum officials sought approval of the campaign from the BATF before the commercials were aired. The BATF would neither approve nor prohibit the ads and decided to wait until the ads had been aired to rule whether they were misleading, and therefore prohibited. Spectrum went to court to gain approval, but the court ordered that there were no grounds for suit because the ad had not been ordered stopped. According to Albert Killeen:

> For Taylor California Cellars the meter was running, and fast. Initial production costs alone of this advertising campaign . . . were $300,000 and we were committed to a TV expenditure of some $2 million. . . . The government's attorneys admitted in open court that at that time they could see nothing in the ads which would cause the Bureau to commence an enforcement proceeding. Since we knew our taste-test procedures met the most rigorous standards, and standing firm in our belief that our wines were indeed better, we went on the air with our comparative taste-test commercials.[10]

The ads were first aired in September 1978. They claimed that a panel of 27 knowledgeable wine testers preferred Taylor California Cellars to Almaden, Inglenook, and Sebastiani wines. Each of TCC's generic wines—Chablis, Rosé, Rhine, and Burgundy—was tested. The Rosé, Rhine, and Burgundy were judged superior to their competitors, and the Chablis finished a close second. Industry reaction was swift and emotional. One anonymous competitor accused Taylor of "ushering in an era of laundry bleach and detergent advertising into the wine industry" with mass merchandising methods which "are wholly inappropriate to the wine business."[11] The marketing director of Sonoma Vineyards said the approach would

> shoot the camaraderie of the industry all to hell. I can walk into any winery in the state and be shown the entire process used for wine and ask how they got a particular characteristic I liked in their wine. But if I ran ads saying that my wine is better than theirs, they'd lock the doors on me.[12]

Another competitor accused Coca-Cola of transferring the Pepsi Challenge to wine.

Marvin Shanken, editor of *Impact*, the wine industry newsletter, assessed the situation for the industry as follows:

> The implications of Taylor's move are vast and far-reaching because they are likely to force Almaden, Inglenook, Paul Masson, and Gallo to substantially increase their ad budgets—particularly in broadcast—in order to defend their market position.
>
> Until now, California vintners have really looked down their noses at wineries outside of California. Taylor is now demonstrating that it is not a weak sister. With a flow of quality wine coming from Monterey Vineyards, coupled with Sterling Vineyards' giving Coca-Cola access to specialty retail outlets and fine restaurants, there's no way California vintners can stop Taylor from becoming a major force in this business. Only the consumer can do that.[13]

The BATF had received three complaints about the ads by mid-October, and another was being considered. Eight specific questions regarding the ads were soon raised by the BATF, and Wine Spectrum officials were advised that their license was at risk if they didn't respond by a certain date. According to Killeen:

Our response to the eight questions raised by the BATF was factual, hard-hitting, meticulously documented, and explosive as a hand grenade. I'm sure that BATF realized if they played around with our response, the package could explode in their face. Furthermore, we saw to it that every responsible journal had a copy of our response in their possession.[14]

The advertising campaign was approved, and a new era of wine advertising was beginning. By 1981, most wine makers had inserted comparative ads into their marketing strategy. Even Gallo began using wine experts to endorse its products. Spectrum executives felt a certain amount of satisfaction when other wineries followed their advertising lead. Pierre Ferrari, brand manager of Taylor California Cellars, said: "The very copying they've done recognizes our concept and our ideas as superior. . . . This is clearly plagiarism on their part and, to us, this indicates they've yielded their primacy in the wine business."[15]

Production and Distribution

Rather than investing in vineyards or crushing grapes from scratch, Spectrum executives initially concentrated their resources on product development and advertising. They continued the Taylor Company's practice of purchasing 90% of their grapes from independent growers. They also contracted for underutilized facilities to ferment and store young wine. By the time Taylor California Cellars had become an established product, the Wine Spectrum was ready to invest more in its facilities. Coke's $34 million investment in its state-of-the-art plant at Gonzales was its largest investment in a production facility in its history. Some of the wine bottled in the plant was shipped to the Hammondsport facility to be bottled as Taylor California for Eastern distribution. Although Spectrum continued to use a four-tier distribution system (growers, wineries, distributors, retailers), it was beginning to consolidate the process, reducing its dependency on outsiders.

The first objective for the Wine Spectrum was to build a strong production and distribution base on both coasts. Toward this end, it hired one of Gallo's top salespeople, built on Taylor's already strong distribution network, and began offering a vast array of point-of-sale materials to retailers. Claiming it was the first in the wine field to match space needs with profit requirements, Spectrum offered computerized shelf-alignment studies to help retailers allot space for all products.

Albert Killeen has predicted there will be a revolution in the marketing of wine, with distributors becoming much more important. Although there has been talk of central warehousing and direct sales from manufacturer to chains, Killeen feels if distributors develop the expertise to effectively distribute wine, the present distribution system will remain basically intact. However, he feels more emphasis will be placed on differentiating among the major wine purchasers. He has separated the purchasers into three groups—food stores and large chains; liquor stores; and hotels, restaurants, and clubs. He feels that each of these requires a separate and distinct marketing approach and that distributors will have to tailor their services to fit the needs of each.

In addition to building a strong domestic distribution network, Spectrum sought to capitalize on export potential. It set up export channels in Britain, Japan, and the Caribbean, "where grape-based wine is not indigenous and there is a chance to build a market presence."[16] American wines have traditionally been considered inferior in

Sterling Vineyards
(Napa Valley, California)

Chardonnay	Cabernet Sauvignon
Sauvignon Blanc	Reserve Cabernet Sauvignon
Cabernet Blanc	Merlot

The Monterey Vineyard
(Upper Monterey, California)

Chardonnay
Pinot Blanc
Fume Blanc
Chenin Blanc
Johannisberg Riesling
Gewürztraminer
Rose of Cabernet Sauvignon
Classic California Dry White
Classic California Red
Classic California Rosé
Special signatures wines:
  Thanksgiving Harvest
    Johannisberg Riesling
    Botrytis Sauvignon Blanc

Taylor California Cellars
(Gonzales, California)

Chablis
Rhine
Rosé
Burgundy
Chardonnay
Sauvignon Blanc
French Colombard
Chenin Blanc
Johannisberg Riesling
Cabernet Sauvignon
Zinfandel
Dry White
Dry Red
Light Chablis
Light Rhine
Light Rosé

Great Western
(Hammondsport, New York)

Special selections:
  Verdelet
  Aurora Blanc
  Vidal Ice Wine
Natural Champagne
Brut Champagne
Extra Dry Champagne
Pink Champagne
Cold Duck
Sparkling Burgundy
Cooking Sherry
Solera Sherry
Solera Dry Sherry
Solera Cream Sherry
Port
Tawny Port
Chablis
Rhine
Rosé
Burgundy
Aurora
Seyval Blanc
Delaware
Diamond
Dutchess
Rose of Isabella
Pink Catawba
Sweet Vermouth

Taylor
(Hammondsport, New York)

Brut Champagne
Extra Dry Champagne
Pink Champagne
Sparkling Burgundy
Cold Duck
Lake Country Chablis
Lake Country White
Lake Country Gold
Lake Country Pink
Lake Country Red
Lake Country Soft White
Lake Country Soft Pink
Lake Country Soft Red
Extra Dry Vermouth
Sweet Vermouth
Chablis
Rhine
Sauterne
Rosé
Pink Catawba
Burgundy
Sangria
Cooking Sherry
Dry Sherry
Golden Sherry
Cream Sherry
Empire Cream Sherry

Europe, but Spectrum hoped to convince foreigners that American wines had come of age and were no longer the weak sister they had been. There were formidable export barriers which had to be overcome, however, and few believed *any* American winery could successfully exploit foreign markets, especially European markets. The greatest trade barriers in the European Economic Community (EEC) are on agricultural products. Even if these could be overcome, other factors made the outlook for exports bleak. Because American wineries have not already penetrated the European market to a significant degree, it will be difficult for them to expand the limited role they play.

Although American wineries decry foreign barriers, some of the greatest problems they face in this country are federal, state, and local regulations. Regulations are often confusing and inconsistent. Wine and liquor sales are restricted to state-owned stores in 16 states. Only 20 states allow grocery stores to sell wine. To prevent large chain stores from selling wine in all their outlets, 12 states and the District of Columbia restrict the number of table wine licenses a retailer may possess. Thirty-two states have "dry" localities, and 43 states have local or state blue laws which prohibit the sale of alcohol on Sunday.

Pricing

Wines are segmented by price as popular (mass market), premium (better quality), or super-premium (aged classics). Taylor California Cellars is priced slightly higher than premium wines, but officials felt its superior taste justified the price. Sterling Vineyards' estate-bottled wines fall in the super-premium category. To exploit the growing consumer demand for economy-priced wine, Spectrum introduced Vivante in four Eastern states in mid-1983. A Wine Spectrum official estimated economy-priced wines had grown 12% in 1982 and represented 25% of U.S. wine sales.[17] Exhibit C8.5 on page 389 lists Wine Spectrum products.

Results

The Wine Spectrum, spurred by the comparative advertising campaign and led by its Taylor California Cellars line, was a remarkable success. Sales of Taylor California Cellars increased from a half-million cases in 1978 to 8.5 million cases in 1982.[18] Total sales for the Wine Spectrum rose from 14 million gallons in 1978 to 31.6 million gallons in 1982. Even when industry-wide sales slowed, Spectrum continued to show improvements. Sales increased over 20% in 1981, while the rest of the industry experienced a 7% growth. In 1982, Spectrum's sales rose 16.6%, the greatest increase by the top-15 wineries. Furthermore, 10 of the 15 either showed no increase or lost sales. (See Exhibit C8.6.)

Spectrum entered the wine industry with a 3% market share, making it the sixth largest winery. By the end of 1982, Spectrum claimed a 5.8% market share, was the third largest winery, and was quickly closing in on the United Vintners' second-place ranking. When it entered the wine business, Spectrum was selling 11 million gallons a year, compared with Vintners' 59 million gallons. In 1982, Spectrum sold 31.6 million gallons; Vintners sold 47.5 million gallons.[19]

The Wine Spectrum's competitors didn't give up their sales and market share without a fight. However, with the exclusion of Gallo, their efforts had little effect.

THE WINE INDUSTRY: COMPETITORS

Gallo

For years, Gallo has accounted for approximately one-quarter of the wine sold in the U.S., more than its next four competitors combined. Gallo enjoys economies of scale at every stage of the wine-making process. Fifteen-year contracts with growers ensure a steady supply of grapes. The Gallos own their own glass manufacturing plant, delivery fleet, and wholesaling network that distributes more than 10% of their products. Gallo's technical expertise is legendary: many consider its technical staff equal to the famed enology department of the University of California at Davis. And no one has been able to beat Gallo at the game of promotions, trade discounts, advertising, and distribution.

Gallo is a private, family-owned business that is solely concerned with the wine-making business. There is no pressure from outsiders for short-term profits, enabling Gallo to go years with depressed margins. If trade discounts are required to meet a competitor's challenge, Gallo can easily offer them. The Gallo brothers, Ernest and Julio, are secretive to the point of reclusiveness, but they are reportedly debt-free, with yearly dollar volume sales of $650–$700 million and a family fortune estimated at between $700 million and $1.2 billion.[20]

In 1977, the Gallos signed a consent decree with the Federal Trade Commission to stop "exclusionary marketing practices." At that time, Gallo controlled 29% of the market and was twice as large as its nearest competitor, United Vintners.[21] By 1982, Gallo still controlled 25% of the market but was almost three times as large as United Vintners.[22] Out of the fear that increased market share could bring a divestiture order from the FTC, the company concentrated its resources on increasing the quality, and thus the price, of its wines. Gallo's competitors have already conceded the low-priced segment of the market to Gallo's Carlo Rossi jug wine and low-priced imports. By applying the same economies of scale to the high-return premium wine market, Gallo could further erode its competitors' market share. Antitrust pressures have ebbed under the Reagan administration, and Gallo has applied to overturn the consent decree, prompting anger and fear from competitors. According to Ernest's nephew, "They [Ernest, 72, and Julio, 71] want to go out being known as the greatest wine makers, as well as the greatest wine marketers."[23]

Although Gallo had less to fear from Coke's entry into the wine industry than did smaller competitors, Ernest and Julio did not react complacently. They increased their advertising budget to $27 million and, although not challenged directly in Coke's comparative ads, began using wine celebrities to tout their wine. After Coca-Cola won a court battle to offer rebates in California, Gallo began offering rebates. Gallo did not introduce a light wine, because it didn't feel the technology was available to introduce one of acceptable quality. Given the flat sales growth of light wines recently, it is doubtful this will have an adverse effect on Gallo's market share in the near future.

When Coke entered the wine industry in 1977, Gallo controlled 29% of the market. Even though it was operating under a consent decree, Gallo still controlled 27.7% of the market when Coke left in 1983. The Wine Spectrum's gains came at the expense of other wineries, not at the expense of Gallo. Emanual Goldman, a partner in Montgomery Securities of San Francisco, said the real reason Coke got out of the wine business was the competition from Gallo. Coke knew wine was a low-return business when it bought Taylor, but it didn't expect Gallo's response. "They did everything Coke did in spades . . . from advertising to merchandising to price promotion."[24] If Gallo was to be challenged, someone other than Coke would have to do it.

EXHIBIT C8.6 U.S. WINERIES: SALES AND MARKET SHARES, 6 LARGEST WINERIES (1976–1982) AND TOP-32 WINERIES (1980–1982)

Winery	1976 Sales*	1976 Share	1978 Sales*	1978 Share	1980 Sales*	1980 Share	1982 Sales*	1982 Share	Rank 1976	Rank 1982
E. & J.Gallo	102	27%	102.0	24.6%	119.0	23.3%	135.2	24.7%	1	1
United Vintners	59	15	56.0	13.1	51.1	10.1	47.5	8.7	2	2
Almaden	19	5	26	6.0	31.7	6.2	28.4	5.2	4	4
Wine Spectrum	11	3	14	3.3	22.2	4.3	31.6	5.8	6	3
Wine Group	22	6	22	5.1	18.2	3.6	15.7	2.9	3	7
Paul Masson	10	3	14	3.2	16.3	3.2	15.9	2.9	5	6
Canadaigua					13.6	2.7	17.6	3.2		5
Monarch					12.4	...	12.6	2.3		8
Guild					12.3	2.4	10.9	2.0		9
Sebastiani					10.0	2.0	7.2	1.3		10
Beringer					3.3	0.6	4.1	0.8		11
Gibson					4.5	0.9	3.9	0.7		12
Christian Bros.					5.0	1.0	3.7	0.7		13
C. Mondavi					5.0	1.0	3.5	0.6		14
Bronco					3.4	0.7	3.3	0.6		15
Lamont					3.2	0.6	3.0	0.5		16
Delicato					2.0	0.4	2.6	0.5		17
Mogen David					5.0	1.0	2.5	0.5		18
Guimarra					2.2	0.4	2.2	0.4		19

					Rank
Welbel	1.6	0.3	1.8	0.3	20
F. Korbel	0.9	0.2	1.5	0.3	21
Wente	1.7	0.3	1.3	0.2	22
Robert Mondavi	1.3	0.3	1.3	0.3	22
East-Side	1.4	0.3	1.1	0.2	23
Sonoma	1.4	0.3	1.1	0.2	23
Mirassou	0.8	0.2	0.8	0.1	24
San Martin	0.6	0.1	0.7	0.1	25
Brookside	1.8	0.2	0.6	0.1	26
Louis Martini	0.7	0.1	0.6	0.1	26
California Growers	1.2	0.2	0.5	0.1	27
M&H	0.3	…	0.5	0.1	27
Pacific Land & Viticulture†	0.2	…	0.1	…	28
Perelli-Minetti	1.2	0.2	‡	‡	28
Subtotal	353.2	69.0	363.3	66.4	
Other Domestic	54.3	10.6	62.6	11.4	
Total Domestic	410.1	80.1	425.9	77.8	
Imports	102.1	19.1	121.6	22.2	
Total	512.2	100.0	547.5	100.0	

* In millions of gallons.
† Formerly Concannon.
‡ Now part of Sierra Wine Co.
Source: Compiled from "Creating a Mass Market for Wine," *Business Week*, Mar. 15, 1982, p. 110, and John C. Maxwell, Jr., and Mary B. English, "Wine Imports Up, Domestics Drop, 1982 Data Show," *Advertising Age*, Aug. 15, 1983, p. 67.

Imports

The increasing strength of imported wines further complicated Coke's efforts to gain an acceptable return on its investment in the Wine Spectrum. The imports' share of the domestic market rose from 5% after World War II to 13% in 1975, and it now represents 25% of wine sales in the U.S. The continuing strength of the imports can be attributed to several factors:

1 As the dollar becomes stronger, the price of imports declines. The French franc has declined over 60% against the dollar since 1981. This has made good French wines very affordable for the American consumer. The price of vintage Bordeaux wines has dropped from $25 to $10 and other French wines have shown similar decreases.

2 The wine industry commands considerable clout in Europe and few politicians are willing to antagonize this group. European governments have erected trade barriers to reduce imports and also subsidize their wine industries, aiding their competitive position.

3 European wineries have faced record harvests and declining consumption at home, making exports critical to financial success.[25]

The most successful exporters have been the Italians. United States sales of Italian wine grew from 4 million gallons in 1979 to 59.8 million gallons in 1981. Six of the top-ten imports are from Italy, and they now account for 61% of total imports. Villa Banfi, importer of Riunite, considers any liquid to be a competitor and has positioned itself accordingly. The low-alcohol, effervescent, chillable lambruscos are preferred by many Americans. It was not until the introduction of "soft" wines, such as Taylor Lake Country Soft, in the early 1980s that American wineries began actively competing with the Italians for this segment of the market.

Exporters did not have to lower their prices to compete with American wines; American wineries did not enjoy the same situation. The low-priced imports would have undoubtedly captured an even greater share of the domestic market had American wineries not cut their prices to meet the competition. Spectrum had no choice if it wanted to maintain and increase its market share; prices had to be cut and immediate profits sacrificed.

Other Wineries

The wineries most affected by Coke's presence were those which vied for national distribution but which lacked Gallo's muscle. The vintage wines of small estate wineries seldom competed with the Wine Spectrum's products, and Gallo was in a class by itself. Spectrum lost little time before going head-to-head with its closest competitors.

Competitors responded quickly. In 1980, United Vintners (Inglenook) increased its advertising budget from $14 million to $20 million; Almaden expenditures rose from $6 to $10 million; and Paul Masson increased its expenditures to $17 million.[26] Spectrum's spending far outpaced all of these. It spent approximately $30 million to promote Taylor California Cellars; promotional spending by the entire industry was barely double that in 1977.[27] The tone of the ads also changed, with hard-hitting, comparative ads being used much more frequently.

Competitors also responded by introducing new products. Geyser Peak Winery, under its Summit label, was the first to introduce wine in cans. The 18-liter bag-in-a-box concept was pioneered by Geyser and Almaden. Summit's 4-liter Wine-in-a-Box, which is convenient for home refrigerator use, was the first to be accepted by consumers.

The most competitive area of new product offerings has been light wines. In addition to Spectrum, at least four wineries, including Beringer Vineyards (Los Hermanos Light), Sebastiani (Light Country White), Geyser Peak Wineries, and Paul Masson, had introduced light wines by mid-1981.[28] Given the nation's emphasis on health and fitness and the success of other low-calorie products, the wineries expected great growth in this area and treated their new products accordingly. Sam Sebastiani introduced his light wine in Atlanta to gain free publicity and to retaliate against Coke for making his wine the butt of the comparative advertising campaign. Paul Masson used $6.5 million of its $17 million advertising budget to introduce its light wine. The initial optimism about light wine's potential soon wavered, however. Light wines represented only 1–3% of wine sales in 1982, and only two brands, Masson and Taylor, had shown real strength.[29]

THE WINE CYCLE TURNS

Wine experts had considered the wine industry to be immune from economic downturns, but they discovered during the 1982 recession that wine is a price-elastic commodity. Exhibit C8.7 shows consumption variations. Declining consumption coincided with record harvests here and abroad and with a strengthened U.S. dollar, which made imports more affordable than ever.

Encouraged by reports projecting high growth rates, many individuals and firms decided to enter the wine industry in the 1970s. The number of wineries in the United States jumped from 413 in 1970 to over 900 in 1982.[30] Those already in the industry added acreage and facilities. Farmers in California planted 163,000 acres of wine grapes in the 1970s, bringing total wine-grape acreage to 343,000. The new plantings reached full maturity in the early 1980s, and immense harvests resulted. In 1982, the 3.1-million-ton grape crush, up 29% from 1981, broke all records. Between 1981 and 1982, wine inventories increased 16% to 685 million gallons.[31] U.S. wine shipments totaled 510 million gallons in 1981, and producers were now faced with the dilemma of pushing an extra 100 million gallons through the pipeline before the large 1983 crush began.[32]

To further compound the problem, European wineries were also experiencing declining consumption and record harvests. Their 1-billion-gallon surplus dwarfed the surplus in the U.S. The natural outlet for the excess inventory was the United States, where a strong dollar, low import duties, and excited wine drinkers awaited the cheap imports.

EXHIBIT C8.7   THE CHANGING WINE MARKET, 1980–1983

	1980	1981	1982	1983
Total gallons	453,819	460,016	496,016	508,109
% change from prior year	. . . .	1.3	7.8	2.4
% table wines	70%	81%	80%	80%
Gallons per adult	3.0	3.0	3.0	2.1
Wholesale value	$2,828,663	$3,239,106	$3,495,183	$3,638,012
% change from prior year		14.5%	7.9%	4.1%

Source: *Beverage World*, May 1982.

The sale of imports increased 6.4% in 1982. In contrast, sales of domestic wine rose only 1.3% and exports decreased 16%. An exasperated United Vintners official claimed the Europeans "smell blood and see a way of exporting some of their unemployment."[33]

U.S. wine makers reacted to the competition by making drastic price cuts and offering unprecedented promotions. Gallo increased its trade allowance to wholesalers from 50¢ to up to $4 per case, and other wineries followed suit. Even with the discounts, sales remained flat. What had been a non-zero-sum game, where everyone could enjoy growth, had become a zero-sum game: any sale increases would come at the expense of a competitor. Marvin Shanken, a noted wine expert, described the situation as "Vietnam in the aisles of U.S. food stores."[34]

The Wine Spectrum responded to the downturn in sales and competitors' price cuts by offering a new economy-priced product, Vivante. Sales were flat and Coke soon had to offer large discounts on an item which already had a low profit margin. Sales of Taylor California Light also slowed, and Spectrum began offering $3 rebates on bottles selling for $2.99.

To reduce expenses, Spectrum lowered its advertising budget from $30 million in 1981 to $15 million in 1982 and to $5 million in 1983. Workers were laid off. Although Coke claimed its unit was profitable in 1982 and marginally profitable in 1983, questions were raised about how long Coke would and should stay in the business.

DIVESTMENT

Due to cheap imports and an extremely competitive battle among U.S. wine producers to retain market share, profits in the wine industry became almost nonexistent in 1982 and 1983. It was estimated that the Wine Spectrum earned only $6 million on $220 million in sales in 1982, a return on sales of 2.7%.[35] Pretax operating profits for soft drink concentrates are normally greater than 20%; for wine the figure was 5%.[36] During the first 6 months of 1983, Spectrum's shipments declined for the first time. Rumors began circulating that Coke, feeling pressure from Wall Street, might be willing to part with its wine unit.

In 1981, Jos. E. Seagram & Sons hired former Bendix executive Mary Cunningham to head its strategic planning in wine. Cunningham was very optimistic about the wine industry's future and recommended that Seagram greatly expand its wine operations. The distilled spirits industry was losing sales, due in part to increased wine consumption in this country, and Cunningham felt some of Seagram's cash flow could be more profitably used in Seagram's wine operation. In early 1982, three Seagram subsidiaries, Brown Vintners, Gold Seal Vineyards, and Paul Masson Vineyards, were consolidated to form a new subsidiary, Seagram Wine Companies. Seagram wanted to expand its wine operations so that it could enjoy the economies of scale it felt were crucial for success in the wine business. The simplest way to accomplish this in the short run would be to acquire another wine company.

Seagram made a formal offer to Coke for the Wine Spectrum on September 19, 1983. Moving swiftly, the two companies announced that an agreement had been reached on September 26, and the Boards of Directors approved the sale on November 6. Coke had invested $200 million in the Wine Spectrum since 1977, and Seagram purchased the unit for a little over that amount. Industry analysts attributed Coke's decision to sell its wine unit to two major factors: (1) unrealistic goals which had proved impossible to achieve and (2) the Gallo brothers, who made it clear to Coke, through price cuts and promo-

EXHIBIT C8.8 SALES AND SHARE OF THE 6 LARGEST U.S. WINERIES, 1983

Winery	1983 Shipments*	Share
E. & J. Gallo	148.3	27.7%
Seagram (includes the Wine Spectrum)	59.9	11.2
Heublin (Inglenook)	34.5	6.5
Villa Bonfi (Riunite)	32.1	6.0
Almaden	28.0	5.2
The Wine Group (Franzia, Mogen David)	22.1	4.1

* Millions of gallons through October 1983.
Source: Ruth Stroud, "Seagram Zeroes in on Gallo," *Advertising Age,* Oct. 3, 1983, p. 3.

tions, that they would make it very difficult and expensive for Spectrum to succeed in the industry.

Most analysts felt both companies had made a wise decision. Low returns were unacceptable to Coke, but Seagram had a longer-term approach to the business and could afford to weather what was probably a temporary downturn in order to reap long-term profits. Projections were that wine consumption would increase at least through the 1980s. The deal increased Seagram's market share to 11.2%, second only to Gallo (see Exhibit C8.8). Michael P. H. Cliff, president of Seagram Wine Company, stated: "We believe you can make money in this business in two ways: Remain a small boutique winery, or become large and achieve economies of scale—and this is what we're doing."[37]

Seagram officials felt Spectrum's products complemented, rather than competed with, their existing lines—Paul Masson, Gold Seal, and Barton & Gueistier Wines of France. Seagram now had a product for any budget, no matter how large or small, and any palate, no matter how refined. Additionally, Masson Light and Taylor California Cellars Light were the only two successful light wines, and Seagram seemed certain to take control of this segment of the market. Officials felt the two lights wouldn't compete, since TCC Light was targeted to diet-conscious women over 35, while Masson Light was targeted to a more unisex, athletic audience. Seagram established the Seagram Wine Group to operate the Wine Spectrum and Seagram Wine Company and felt it now had the capability to be a major force in the wine industry.

Seagram's greatest problem in the near future is likely to be the one that led to Coke's exit: Gallo. While under a consent decree, Gallo focused its efforts on improving its image and its products. Its varietals and vintage wines are now being more readily accepted in the wine community. These wines have a higher profit margin than Gallo's generic jug wines, and Gallo is ready to capitalize on its investment in this area. The antiregulatory philosophy of the Reagan administration should remove the only barrier Gallo had to increasing its share of the market. Seagram has the capital it needs to successfully expand and improve its wine operations. Whether it can do this at the expense of Gallo remains to be seen.

REFERENCES

1 "The House that Killeen Built: Exclusive Interview," *Impact,* Mar. 15, 1982, p. 5.
2 Ibid.

3 *Refresher USA,* vol. 4, 1977, p. 15.
4 "House that Killeen Built."
5 Gilbert T. Sewall, "Trouble for California Winemakers," *Fortune,* Apr. 8, 1983, p. 57.
6 David Clark Scott, "How Spirits Industry Takes Advantage of Changing Tastes," *Christian Science Monitor,* July 29, 1983, p. 10.
7 "Taylor Introduces Its Light Wine Campaign," *Beverage Industry,* Mar. 26, 1982, p. 31.
8 Bruce M. Galphin, "Wine Battle Is Uncorked Here," *The Atlanta Constitution,* June 29, 1981, p. B3.
9 "Taylor Introduces Its Light Wine Campaign."
10 "House that Killeen Built," p. 11.
11 "Competitor Rips Taylor Ads," *Advertising Age,* Oct. 9, 1978, pp. 1, 117.
12 Ibid.
13 Ibid.
14 "House that Killeen Built," p. 12.
15 David Drum, "Marketing Wine Keeps Growing at Taylor Cal," *Advertising Age,* July 27, 1981, p. S-40.
16 "Creating a Mass Market for Wine," *Business Week,* Mar. 15, 1982, p. 118.
17 Ruth Stroud, "Coke Wine Unit Adds Price Line," *Advertising Age,* June 6, 1983, p. 2.
18 John C. Maxwell, Jr., and Mary B. English, "Wine Imports Up, Domestics Drop, 1982 Data Show," *Advertising Age,* Aug. 15, 1983, p. 67.
19 Ibid.
20 Sewall, op. cit., pp. 56–57.
21 "Creating a Mass Market for Wine," p. 114.
22 Maxwell, loc. cit.
23 "Creating a Mass Market for Wine," p. 108.
24 Daniel Cuff, "Coca-Cola without Wine," *New York Times,* Sept. 28, 1983, p. D-12.
25 Maxwell, loc. cit.
26 "Creating a Mass Market for Wine."
27 Mitchell J. Shields, "Coke and Wine Are It," *Advertising Age,* June 6, 1983, p. 16.
28 Craig Goldwyn, "Four Who Buck Convention with Savvy and Style," *Advertising Age,* Jan. 10, 1983, p. M-9.
29 Stroud, op. cit., p. 62.
30 Sewall, op. cit., p. 54.
31 "The Wine Wars Get Hotter," *Business Week,* Apr. 11, 1983, p. 65.
32 Ibid.
33 Ibid., p. 61.
34 "Why Coca-Cola and Wine Didn't Mix," *Business Week,* Oct. 10, 1983.
35 Thomas Oliver, "Coke Is Selling Its Wine Unit," *The Atlanta Constitution,* Sept. 27, 1983, p. D-1.
36 Why Coca-Cola and Wine Didn't Mix," p. 30.
37 Ruth Stroud, "Masson Ads Stress Low Alcohol, Calories," *Advertising Age,* Apr. 9, 1984, p. 6.

COMMODORE INTERNATIONAL, LTD.

Prepared by Mike Crone and Craig Hethcox,
Georgia State University.

As recently as 1981, the total market for microcomputers in the United States was near $500 million, with forecasts showing a near doubling every year through 1986. With those kinds of projections, the market offered what appeared to be the best single opportunity seen by the electronics industry in recent years. Entrepreneurs and venture capitalists felt the same enthusiasm. Many fortunes were made in the early computer industry. Microcomputers presented a potential chance of a lifetime to entrepreneurs and venture capitalists, and in the early eighties, such individuals wanted to talk to anyone with a good computer story. But the market changed significantly by 1984. A firm with zero market share in 1980 had suddenly become the market leader and supposed dictator—IBM. This sent the competition flurrying. Apple Computer has reorganized, and Commodore has developed executive software and has purchased a firm in preparation for real competition. Other companies are attempting to solidify and even save their market position.

Watching the microcomputer industry has been like watching a swarm of airplanes trying to land at the same airport simultaneously, according to observers. You know there is going to be a crash, but when—and how bad? Some say that the market leaders have supplied the answer to that question.[1] Price cuts offered by IBM in June 1984, and again in October 1984, on its desktop computer set the stage for a series of failures in an overcrowded and increasingly strained industry. The price cuts were sharper than expected and hit directly at the IBM impersonators, or the compatible manufacturers, as well as at other makers. The compatible manufacturers, those that provide certain hardware and software products which can be used interchangeably with IBM products, account for over 30 companies and close to two-thirds of sales in a $20 billion industry. Additionally, many manufacturers' production lines have caught up with present demand. So, with lower-priced models and a plentiful supply on behalf of IBM, Commodore, Apple, and others, perhaps the moment of market truth has arrived.

Some experts surmise that the buildup by Commodore, the reorganization of Apple, and the price-cutting by IBM are only typical strategies employed by those firms in an attempt to strengthen themselves internally. However, other analysts argue that the industries are bracing for a shakeout, a fallout, a massive going-out-of-business sale.[2]

One story is told of a venture capitalist looking for a small microcomputer company to buy. He found ten of them at near giveaway prices. He spoke to another speculator who was also looking for such a firm to purchase. After comparing notes, they discovered that the ten available companies on each of their lists were completely different. Still another story concerns the company that couldn't go out of business because there would not be enough assets left to pay legal fees.[3]

The shakeout has been a long time coming, according to the Gartner Group, a Connecticut-based market research firm. Gartner states that microcomputers are commodities and that the market could not possibly support all the new or old firms entering the business. The marketplace did not need 90 microcomputer manufacturers, but the market does indeed have that many competitors. The Gartner Group predicts that a dozen firms will survive the crash of the market.[4]

How does the remainder of the history of the microcomputer industry read? There is likely to be fierce competition, unique strategies, and mergers. The larger firms are already jockeying for position. And there will be several withdrawals from the marketplace. No silence equals that of a large company retreating.[5]

Commodore International, in the thick of the battle, is a manufacturer of microcomputers and related peripheral products and accessories, including the following: *systems,* for home, business, and educational use, and portable systems; *software,* including programs in recreation and lifestyle, business and productivity, education and home learning, and programming aids categories; *semiconductors;* and *office equipment and consumer electronics.*

As of fiscal 1983, Standard & Poor's reported the following sales makeup for the company:

% Sales	Category
45	Home computers
23	Business and educational systems
19	Peripheral equipment and accessories
9	Software and publications
3	Office equipment
1	Semiconductor components

As shown in Table C9.1, 26.5% of total worldwide sales were outside the United States.

Commodore's growth over the past decade has been nothing short of phenomenal. When predicting the survivors of the expected market shakeout, the press has often touted Commodore as a "dark horse" or as a doubtful investment. Commodore has nonetheless managed a compound growth rate of 42% in its stock price and earnings since 1972. By contrast, the computer industry average growth rate over the same period of time was approximately 12%, with the industry giant, IBM, averaging 14%. An investor who invested in 100 shares of Commodore stock in 1977 (at under $2 per share)

TABLE C9.1   SALES INCREASES BY REGION, 1982–1984: NET SALES
(Millions)

	1984	% Change	1983	% Change	1982
North America	$ 761.2	52	$500.6	187	$174.3
Europe	463.6	198	155.6	47	106.0
Australia-Asia	42.4	70	25.0	3	24.2
	$1267.2	86	$681.2	124	$304.5

would now own $70,000 worth of stock. Commodore has seen five stock splits in as many years, splitting 3 for 2 and 3 for 1 in 1980 alone. Growth in revenues and profits has enjoyed an even healthier pace than stock prices. In recent years sales and profits have doubled each year. (For financial information, see Table C9.2.)

TABLE C9.2   FIVE-YEAR COMPARISON OF SELECTED FINANCIAL DATA FOR COMMODORE INTERNATIONAL LIMITED AND SUBSIDIARIES
(000s Omitted Except for per Share Amounts)

	1984	1983	1982	1981	1980
Year ended 30 June					
Net sales	$1,267,200	$681,200	$304,500	$186,500	$125,600
Gross profit	$ 466,880	$320,800	$145,400	$ 82,800	$ 50,600
Operating expenses	221,900	199,900	88,400	48,100	29,100
Interest expense net	20,400	8,000	6,200	3,900	3,200
	242,000	207,900	94,600	52,000	32,300
Income before income taxes and extraordinary item	224,500	112,900	50,800	30,800	18,300
Provision for income taxes (net of reversal of $1700 in 1980 for U.K. taxes)	80,700	24,900	10,200	5,900	2,100
Income before extraordinary item	143,800	88,000	40,600	24,900	16,200
Extraordinary item*	—	3,700	3,700	500	700
Net income	143,800	91,700	44,300	25,400	16,900
Earnings per share†					
Income before extraordinary item†	$ 4.66	$ 2.86	$ 1.32	$ .81	$ .52
Extraordinary item*	—	.12	.12	.01	.02
Net income	$ 4.66	$ 2.98	$ 1.44	$ .82	$ .54
Weighted average shares†	30,359	30,809	30,800	30,920	31,186
Financial position: 30 June					
Current assets	$ 574,400	$532,700	$182,300	$111,700	$ 67,100
Current liabilities	269,900	327,900	83,200	50,200	29,100
Working capital	304,500	204,800	99,100	61,500	38,000
Total assets	679,000	614,600	235,400	145,100	88,900
Long-term debt	77,300	92,000	44,400	32,000	24,300
Shareholders' equity	324,400	190,700	105,900	61,600	35,500

* Tax benefit of net operating loss carried forward.
† Earnings per share and weighted average shares for fiscal years 1980 through 1982 reflect all stock splits.
Source: Annual report, Commodore International, Ltd., 1984.

COMMODORE AND JACK TRAMIEL

Beginnings

behavior.

Commodore was founded in 1958 by Jack Tramiel, the survivor of a nazi concentration camp in World War II, as a marketing company to sell typewriters and other business machines. In 1970 Tramiel was joined by Irving Gould, a Canadian financier, who helped the then-failing company with an infusion of capital, thus becoming chairman and controlling shareholder. In the early 1970s Commodore, led by Gould and Tramiel, jumped into the calculator market. *Forbes* described their actions:

> Once Gould put his money in, however, he took firm control of the finances, selling off assets and reducing debt. Having sold Commodore's adding machine manufacturing plant, Tramiel and Gould took their adding machine design to Japan and got Ricoh to manufacture it for them. That's when Tramiel showed his mettle. He got his first look at an electronic calculator. Sensing that it would soon spell the doom of the electromechanical adding machines, he quickly signed up Casio and others to manufacture electronic calculators to be sold in the United States under the Commodore name, thus getting into the market as it began to take off. In 1969 Commodore began to manufacture calculators itself, using semiconductor chips made by Texas Instruments, among others. Sales grew rapidly and Commodore was on its way again.[6]

> However, in 1974 Commodore got caught with a large inventory of calculator chips when prices of these chips were falling dramatically. This turned out to be a blessing in disguise. When Tramiel decided to integrate backward to survive, he bought MOS Technology, a failing manufacturer of calculator chips, for $800,000 (the replacement cost of this company today is on the order of $300 million). MOS was the maker of the 6502 microprocessor, which was to become the brain of many small computers, including all those made by Apple and Atari.

The Pet

strategy

It was about this time that Tramiel and Gould came to some critical conclusions about Commodore's markets. One conclusion was that the market for electronic calculators and watches was saturated, and the second was that the microcomputer market for personal and small business computers was about to explode. "We decided to put our money into computer systems," said Gould. So in 1977 Commodore bought out the Pet computer for $3 million and launched the first microcomputer system for under $1000. Another personal computer, the Apple, was introduced the same year. The Pet was an instant success and Commodore's earnings jumped from 50 cents per share to $1.14 in 1978 and then to $1.86 in 1979. *Forbes* offered the following analysis:

strength

> Although the Pet was well received, Tramiel made some marketing mistakes, including pricing the machine too low. In the early days of small computers, he lost control of the U.S. market to Apple and Radio Shack, both of which used MOS-designed chips. But Commodore did better in Europe, where it had a ready-made distribution system from its adding machine days. Priced at $1,295 in Europe—vs. the $795 price in the U.S.—the Pet had sufficient margins to be supported aggressively. Commodore dominates the European market today with more than 50% of the market in many countries.[7]

Commodore's international sales were strong because of its excellent distribution network of dealers which had been established earlier. It had established strict rules governing territories and the number of dealers in a given area, thus ensuring that even the smallest dealer could sell three or four systems a month and that the largest dealers could sell as many as 100. When a "gray" market developed for Commodore computers, in which unauthorized dealers were buying machines in the U.S. and reselling them in Europe for less than the going dealer rate, Commodore simply lowered its European prices to protect the dealers there. The payoff—excellent dealer loyalty.

The VIC-20

In 1980 Pet sales in the European market were booming, but U.S. sales lagged dangerously behind Apple and Tandy, so Commodore introduced the VIC-20 computer and a new strategy. Specifically, it was seeking market share in the U.S., and it pursued this goal by following an aggressive pricing strategy (buoyed by extensive vertical integration) and by selling through mass merchandisers. The VIC computer was the first of its kind to be sold for under $300 (it now sells for under $100); thus Commodore redefined the market segment for "home computers" and opened the door to many potential buyers. ("Home computers" had previously been defined by some as those computers costing less than $1000.) Although the so-called "early adopters" of the personal computer—characterized as computer aficionados—were attracted to the highly stylized specialty stores where semiexpert salespeople could speak to them in "computerese," the masses of consumers—judged correctly by Tramiel—would be attracted by a relatively inexpensive chance to purchase a bit of "high tech" in a store where they didn't feel out of place. Commodore sold its VIC-20's through more than 10,000 mass merchandise retail outlets such as K-Mart and Sears. The peripherals and software which were marketed along with the computer were targeted for an audience whose primary interest was playing games.

The Developing Strategy

1980 was a milestone year for Commodore International. Not only did it penetrate and suitably develop the low-priced home computer segment of the market with the VIC, but it also produced an encore with the introduction of the Commodore 64 computer—a more powerful unit capable of going head-to-head with the popular Apple II for about half the price. It was becoming obvious to the major competitors (Apple, Radio Shack, etc.) that Commodore was trying to penetrate other segments of the microcomputer market. *Datamation* reported:

Commodore has set ambitious objectives to increase penetration of this market. These efforts were initiated in 1980 by eliminating independent distributors and establishing seven regional distribution centers that will also be dealer support centers. Commodore focused initially on the northeast corridor, running trade shows in Philadelphia and Boston. These trade shows were modeled on the company's successful shows in the United Kingdom. In addition, Commodore, for the first time, is running a national advertising campaign. Gains in the educational market were also noteworthy. . . . Commodore is very active in introducing its new products. In addition to the VIC-20, it introduced several peripheral products, including disk drives and printers. Commodore also introduced a point-of-sale (POS) system designed around the 6502 microprocessor. Priced under $3,000, the product will be sold through dealers to grocery stores and later to general merchandisers.[8]

Also in 1980, CI opened a new German plant to help meet the rising demand in Europe.

In the Giant's Shadow

As 1981 dawned, Wall Street analysts were decrying the coming shakeout in the PC market. Industry watchers seemed to be spending more time making predictions about the hopefuls in the race than reporting the technological advances that were making the race possible. The major cause of the considerable uncertainty experienced in the industry was the popular assumption that the computer industry giant, IBM Corporation (sales approaching $30 billion), would enter the market for small computers. It seemed imminent. One *Time* reporter put it this way:

> The industry is anxiously awaiting the entry of International Business Machines. Thus far, the Aronk, N.Y., behemoth has shunned the personal computer market; its smallest model costs about $10,000. But sales of big main-frame computers are not growing as fast as those of the small machines, and experts believe that IBM will not ignore the potential profits in the new market. Says William D. Barton, president of the Datel computer store in Manhattan: "IBM's entry into the field is imminent." IBM has not yet announced any plans to market the small machines, but late last year it opened its first retail stores in Baltimore and Philadelphia. These may be the beginning of a network that will eventually provide outlets for the new smaller models.[9]

In the latter part of the year IBM unveiled its new "PC" at the Waldorf-Astoria Hotel in New York City. Over 160 reporters attended this event. In a little over a year after the entry of the PC, IBM sales of the PC surpassed Apple Computer's sales and left Commodore in fourth place. As a symbol of the computer giant's ability to move quickly in a fast-paced business, one IBM executive keeps a mammoth mock-up in his office of a pink elephant wearing tap shoes. The elephant had learned to dance. Apple Computer president A. C. "Mike" Markkula declared that his three biggest rivals were "IBM, IBM, and IBM." By 1982, more software houses and programmers were writing software for the IBM PC than for any other small computer, and since users were becoming more sophisticated, this undoubtedly helped sales.

Master of the Home

In spite of IBM's presence, Commodore continued to make major strides in the home market (a market that IBM vowed not to be interested in) and by the close of 1981 had leapfrogged the competition, tallying approximately a 25% share. And in 1984, when price wars broke out among the contenders for the home market, Commodore handily won 60% of the market, with Texas Instruments and Timex-Sinclair dropping out.

In spite of market share gains, Commodore stock prices and earnings took a nosedive in the first two quarters of 1984, and again the "gurus" of Wall Street were anxious to discuss the "coming shakeout" and Commodore's prospect for weathering the storm.

But the computer industry as a whole (IBM included) saw prices and earnings slide during this same time, and certainly a plausible reason was the "cooling off" period following the initial economic recovery surge. An upswing for most computer firms, including Commodore, occurred during the third quarter and is evidence that indeed this may have been the case. Saturation of the home computer market is one reason cited for the decline, but it is estimated that only 6% of all U.S. households own computers. By comparison, 20–25% of all households owned video games when that industry peaked. Other possibilities for the slower-than-usual growth are:

1. Growth in sales in 1983 may have unduly raised expectations for 1984.
2. The business is more seasonal than anyone thought.
3. The home computer industry was simply short of product after losing three competitors during the last year.

MANAGEMENT CHANGES: COMMODORE AFTER TRAMIEL

In addition to facing industry uncertainty, Commodore has been plagued by organizational instability. Some attribute the reason for this instability to Jack Tramiel, who, to be sure, has been a fiery person. An aggressive entrepreneur, Tramiel has used unpopular tactics in dealing with his competitors and employees alike. Peter Nulty of *Fortune* writes:

> The former typewriter repairman stomped all over the toes of suppliers, customers, and subordinates, but he built Commodore into the lord of home computers; its annual sales have grown sevenfold in only three years to over $1.2 billion. . . .
>
> Tramiel's harangues became so famous and feared at Commodore that the company named in his honor a video game in which a warrior defeats his enemies by jumping on their heads before they jump on his. The title: Jack Attack.[10]

In January of 1984, after an extraordinary meeting of Commodore's board, Jack Tramiel's resignation was announced. Of course, there was speculation about whether it was voluntary, since Tramiel owned 7% of a very profitable company and had just announced plans for new products. Some observers feel that Commodore chairman Gould simply could not tolerate the uncertainty of Tramiel's abrasive management style, regardless of its results. *Business Week* reported:

> For all his business brilliance, however, Tramiel's dominant personality led to constant management turnover. The 55 year old survivor of a World War II German concentration camp "ran Commodore like a dictatorship," says Alan H. Friedman, a former finance director of Commodore who left last April after two years. According to Ralph D. Seligman, a director and attorney based in Nassau, the Bahamas, where Commodore has its corporate headquarters, "all sorts of heads have rolled at Commodore" because of Tramiel's nature.
>
> But turmoil did not keep Tramiel from establishing a low-cost vertically integrated manufacturing operation that allowed him to transfer his cutthroat management style to the cutthroat home computer market. In a blitz of price reductions that started in early 1983, Commodore's profits soared, and it won a 38% share. Meanwhile, some of its competitors—namely Texas Instruments, Atari, and Mattel—suffered crippling losses. Gould characterized Tramiel as a man with "a certain style that can take a company to $1 billion but can't take it to $10 billion."[11]

Tramiel will be a tough act to follow. "Jack was a terrific marketer and a terrific purchasing guy, exciting, thrilling, frustrating, and devastating," says James Finke, who left Commodore in 1982 after 18 months as president and chief operating officer, following a clash with Tramiel.

Gould chose Marshall Smith, president of Thyssen-Bournemizza, the U.S. subsidiary of the Netherlands company by the same name, to replace Tramiel. According to Gould, Smith has "fantastic managerial experience . . . and will bring a great deal of professionalism to Commodore. According to *Business Week,* there will be fences to mend:

— new strategies for future

First he will have to strengthen Commodore's management and mend relationships with many of the company's computer dealers, who are angry at the way the company shifted its distribution channels from them to mass merchants. A number of lawsuits are pending, and Commodore is involved in countersuits. A newly formed Coordinating Committee for Commodore Lawsuits, in Hollywood, CA, sent out a letter on December 14 asking if dealers needed legal help.

Some say that Tramiel himself was the major problem. "Now that Tramiel is out, there may be a chance to work out the difficulties," says William Harris, president of Desks Inc., a Santa Ana ex-Commodore dealer who is sueing Commodore for its trade practices.[12]

TRAMIEL'S LEGACY: COMMODORE INTERNATIONAL IN 1984 PRODUCTS

Commodore's current best-seller in the U.S. is the C-64 (Commodore 64), an 8-bit machine built around MOS Tech's 6502 microprocessor. It has 64K bytes of RAM (read-write memory), a full typewriter keyboard, and various ports for accessories (disk drive, printer, joysticks, etc.); plugs into a television or monitor; and currently sells for under $200. The older VIC-20, a less powerful machine, sells for under $100 and is still accounting for a major portion of Commodore's European sales. The European market lags behind the U.S. market by approximately two years, so demand in Europe will continue even on machines which are obsolete in the U.S. The target market for these two machines is primarily the home, although some small businesses have purchased the C-64. Commodore has also introduced a business-oriented machine, the CMB 8032, which retails for $1495, but it has not competed favorably with comparably priced machines from IBM, Tandy, and Apple. Three new machines were introduced in 1984: the Executive-64, a portable upgrade of the C-64; the PLUS-4, a machine similar in power to the C-64 but including on-board programs (read only memory) for word processing, data-base management, spreadsheet analysis, and graphics; and the C-16, a new low-end computer advertised "for beginners" at under $100. Another machine which is portable and uses a 16-bit microprocessor, and which will be compatible with the IBM PC at "half the price," is to be initially introduced in Europe. According to *Fortune:* [10]

It's expected to undersell the PC portable and the Compaq. Barbara Isgur, a computer analyst at the securities firm of Paine Webber, thinks this could be the next big coup for Commodore.

↖ sudden action to obtain power.

Another product which is aimed at the high end of the market is a business computer using an operating system invented by AT&T. Called Unix, the system is especially adept at linking up computers in a network.

In addition to introducing new computers, Commodore has added several peripherals to its line, making available to those consumers who desire to do more such products as disk drives, cassette storage, monitors, printers, and special ROM cartridges.

Until 1983 Commodore apparently didn't worry too much about producing its own software, arguing that establishing an "installed base" of computers was more important and that software writers would recognize the demand and meet it. So far, this has been the case. But now the firm recognizes that software support will be increasingly important to future revenues in two ways: First, the immense base of installed machines (over 1 million) represents a substantial software demand and potential revenue source all its own. Second, for a company to compete in the higher end of the market, software needs to be available and sometimes even bundled (as with the PLUS-4) to the machine. As a result, Commodore has taken major steps toward becoming a force in the software segment of the market, even going so far as to fire Sigmund Hartman, president of the software division, because he didn't reach his overambitious goal of $500,000 in software sales for 1984.

PRODUCTION CAPABILITIES

Commodore's vertical integration allows it to react quickly to market changes and to do so at minimum cost. Through MOS Tech Inc. (a $300 million asset) it produces its own microprocessors and associated circuit chips. It has production plants strategically located across the U.S., Canada, the United Kingdom, Germany, Japan, and Hong Kong, as well as a major operation in Taiwan. It uses foreign labor for the labor-intensive parts of production and has signed agreements with Mitsumi of Japan to produce disk drives. Commodore also signed an agreement with Intel (as did IBM) to allow it to produce the 8088 microprocessor—a move that will allow it to produce a 16-bit micro without being dependent on suppliers. Most recently, the company has acquired Amiga Corporation, a small Silicon Valley company, which has developed an inexpensive microcomputer designed to compete with Apple's latest entries.

DISTRIBUTION CHANNELS

Here lies Commodore's possible Achilles' heel. In the aftermath of Jack Tramiel's blitzkrieg-style dictatorship over Commodore and its sales force, many independent dealers have left the fold and some have even brought lawsuits, claiming unfair trade practices. Under Tramiel's directive most of the sales force was fired, independent dealers were ignored, and the company turned to mass merchandisers to market its machines. Although the tactic worked very well, the door to a strong U.S. independent dealer network was shut. This network may be needed in the future if Commodore plans to grab any more of the business market. For now, Commodore continues its main marketing through Sears, K-Mart, Toys "R" Us, and others. Displays of its merchandise at these stores were upgraded considerably for the 1984 holiday season. The European dealer network is still quite sound and a key factor in future success overseas. In 1984 there were 35,000 distributors worldwide, compared with 3,000 in 1981. It also appears that Commodore plans to use this network to test the acceptance of some products before their introduction into the U.S.

ADVERTISING AND PROMOTION STRATEGY

Major media advertising has recently become fairly seasonal in apparent recognition of the seasonality of sales. Computers seem to sell best between September when school starts, and the Christmas holidays. Magazine advertising (other than the holiday blitz) is spread over the year. Commodore enjoys, due again to the large "installed base," quite a bit of free publicity from a large, loyal user-group network (which the company supports through the computer information network, CIN) that is linked by an arrangement with a national telecommunications network (Compuserve). Commodore also receives free publicity from several column writers in hobbyist magazines like *Microcomputing.*

Current advertising has revealed four distinct themes relevant to Commodore's strategy:

Theme 1. Commodore is the leader in the number of computers sold and installed. (Ads compare to those of IBM and Apple.)

Theme 2. Commodore is the value leader—the most machine for the money. (Ads compare to those of IBM and Apple.)

Theme 3. Commodore has multiple uses in the home—more than just for playing games—and is used by all family members of any age.

Theme 4. Commodore is committed to education and to providing quality tools for the disadvantaged masses.

Commodore's major pitch is still to the masses of consumers in the home market—no attempt is made to woo the small-business market. The latest products are aimed at both the high end and the low end of the market. The market niche that opened last year as the price wars caused prices to drop in the home market, while prices remained unchanged in the high end of the market, is being attacked by the new PLUS- 4, which retails at just under $300. The C-16 ($100) allows a relatively inexpensive start for latecomers to the market and causes the C-64 (along with its past buyers) to move up in status if not in price.

THE FUTURE

Significant events in the development of technology and trends in the world markets will determine Commodore's future. As happened in the calculator and watch industries, component prices are predicted to fall drastically as their densities increase. This will mean significant advances in the power of computers, in their size, and in their usefulness. In turn, this will put the power of computing in more and more hands—hands that couldn't afford this technology in the past. A revolution akin to the industrial revolution is being predicted by the technical journals. The business market is just beginning to take off and will constitute the bulk of sales dollars through the end of this decade. Since the major large-computer manufacturers have jumped into the market, small machines have grown in credibility with businesses. It is predicted that the world market will be the fastest-growing market by the end of the decade and will contribute the largest share of sales as more and more countries come to rely on the usefulness of computers and are able to purchase them.

Major competition will come from IBM, of course, with Apple and Tandy close behind, but none of these competitors has shown the desire to compete in the same price range or to use the same mass merchandising channels as Commodore. Thus, when the predicted fall in component prices occurs in the near future, Commodore will have the added edge it needs to defend its territory. Commodore has the strongest hold on the

TABLE C9.3 PC REVENUES OF LEADING PC COMPANIES (1983)

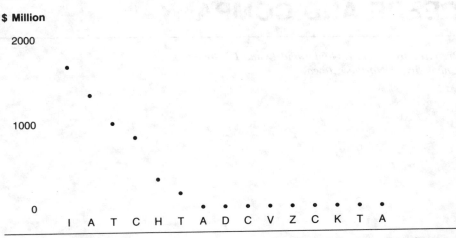

Note: I = IBM; A = Apple; T = Tandy; C = Commodore; H = Hewlett-Packard; T = Texas Instruments; A = Atari; D = DEC; C = Convergent; V = Victor; Z = Zenith; C = Compaq; K = Kaypro; T = Televideo; A = Altos

world market at present and stands to benefit more than the other companies if this market explodes in the latter part of the decade as predicted. The only stone left unturned is consideration of Japanese companies as contenders. They have been preparing to enter this market for some time now and, in their characteristic style, have used Europe and Australia as test markets for their products. Quite a few peripherals have already been marketed in the U.S., and Sanyo introduced its entry into the personal computer market early in 1984. This machine is just as powerful as the IBM PC for a third of the cost. Commodore still has some advantages in terms of chip technology and marketing ability, but the Japanese companies are coming fast and should not be underestimated. Some predict that they will not stop until they have 50% of the U.S. market. Table C9.3 shows revenues for major competitors in the industry.

REFERENCES

1 T. P. Murphy, "May Day, May Day!" *Forbes,* July 16, 1984, p. 174.
2 D. Myers, "Price Cutting Causes Shakeout," *Fortune,* July 1984, p. 107.
3 W. F. Alber, "Desktops Show Fastest Growth," *Fortune,* June 1983, p. 60.
4 Ibid.
5 Ibid.
6 S. H. Chakravarty, "Albatross," *Forbes,* Jan. 13, 1983, p. 47.
7 Ibid.
8 *Datamation,* June 1981, p. 147.
9 "Small Computer Shootout," *Time,* Mar. 2, 1981, p. 69.
10 "Cool Heads Are Trying to Keep Commodore Hot," *Fortune,* July 23, 1984, pp. 36–40.
11 "Following a Tough Act . . ." *Business Week,* Jan. 30, 1984. p. 30.
12 Ibid.

DEERE AND COMPANY

Prepared by Peter G. Goulet and Lynda L. Goulet,
University of Northern Iowa.

The past year [1982] has proved another disappointment to farmers. . . . farmers experienced the third year in a row of depressed farm income and, more recently, declining asset values. . . . [There is] the prospect of modest improvement in farm income in 1983 . . . (M. Duncan and M. Drabenstott, "Outlook for Agriculture: Is the Recovery on the Way?" *Economic Review: Kansas City Federal Reserve Bank*, December 1982, pp. 16–17.)

Prospects for a North American farm equipment recovery are clouded. . . . (Deere and Company Annual Report, 1982.)

Now as the U.S. is about to propel the world into an economic recovery, it is becoming abundantly clear that the rebound will bypass agriculture. . . . Sales prospects are grim for farm suppliers. ("Why Recovery May Skip the Farm Belt," *Business Week*, Mar. 21, 1983, pp. 106–114.)

The U.S. Farm sector began its climb back to health in 1983. . . . Farm income will likely post future gains in 1984. ("Better Times Ahead for Agriculture," M. Duncan and M. Drabenstott, *Economic Review: Kansas City Federal Reserve Bank*, December 1983, pp. 22–35.)

No one can predict with assurance at this time whether the recovery in the world economy will endure long enough to restore equipment demand to levels experienced in the 1970's. (Deere and Company Annual Report, 1983.)

U.S. Agriculture began 1984 with renewed hopes for a stronger farm recovery, and the record will show farm income did rebound sharply. But . . . farm liquidations and declining asset values are visible symptoms of ongoing adjustments to market forces. (M. Drabenstott and M. Duncan, "Another Troubled Year for American Agriculture," *Economic Review: Kansas City Federal Reserve Bank*, December 1984, pp. 30–43.)

Once again, I must report to you that Deere & Company has completed a very difficult year. . . . Although 1985 will be another challenging year, we are determined to make it a year of constructive progress. (Deere and Company Annual Report, 1984.)

The big question for the battered farm machinery makers is no longer when the recovery will arrive but whether it ever will. (F. Rice, "Cruel Days in Tractorville," Oct. 29, 1984, pp. 30–36.

. . . in 1985 . . . Farm income dropped and farmland values fell further. *Another difficult year lies ahead in 1986* [emphasis added]. (M. Drabenstott, *Economic Review: Kansas City Federal Reserve Bank*, December 1985, pp. 35–49.)

The economic environment surrounding our industries remains difficult and uncertain. . . . Nonetheless, we are determined to make the most of these challenging times. (Deere and Company Annual Report, 1985.)

Like Tantalus in Dante's *Divine Comedy*, farm equipment makers have spent the years since 1981 pushing their rock up the hill only to see it poised to roll back over them. Even the largest and most efficient of these manufacturers, Deere and Company, has failed to generate an operating profit since 1981. The other large equipment maker, International Harvester (now Navistar), has maintained its identity only by selling its IH farm equipment business to Tenneco. White Farm Equipment and Massey-Ferguson (now Varity) have also suffered the ravages of bankruptcy.

BACKGROUND AND OPERATIONS[1]

Deere and Company, like its other large counterpart, International Harvester, began as the result of an invention. John Deere, a blacksmith originally from Vermont, developed one of the first plows which could effectively turn the sticky, rich, black soil of the giant prairies of the midwestern U.S. In 1868, John Deere formed his company to make and distribute these plows. The distribution system and the founder's philosophy of emphasizing service and quality was developed in these early years and were critical factors in the firm's continued growth and success.

The next major turning point for the firm came in 1911, when six noncompeting farm equipment companies were consolidated into the company to form a full-line manufacturer of farm equipment. In 1918, this expansion continued with the purchase of the Waterloo Gasoline Engine Company, based in Waterloo, Iowa. This purchase brought the company into the mainstream of the conversion from animal to machine power on the farm.

Deere and Company has, for most of its existence, had unusually stable leadership, having only two CEOs during the period 1928–1982. During this period the firm became the leading manufacturer of farm equipment in the world, developed its extensive and valuable dealer network, became a major supplier of construction machinery, and established facilities or affiliates throughout the world.

PRODUCT LINES

The main engine of agriculture is the tractor. By standard industry practice farm tractors are categorized in four major subgroups: utility tractors under 40 h.p. and from 40 to 100 h.p., row crop tractors over 100 h.p., and large four-wheel-drive tractors. Though Deere supplies tractors in all these categories, the majority of its sales come in the two groups of large machines. In recent years, the vast majority of the output in the smaller categories, those under 100 h.p., has been manufactured overseas and imported to the U.S. By 1985, 100% of the under 40 h.p. utility tractors were made offshore, with 89% of Japanese origin. Further, 95% of the 40 to 100 h.p. models came from Europe (70%) or Japan (25%).[2]

Farm implements drawn behind tractors make up several equipment categories. These include: soil preparation, tillage, and planting equipment (often combined for low-tillage applications); harvesting machinery; and crop handling equipment. In addition, some harvesting and crop handling functions are combined in self-propelled machines called "combines." Self-propelled combines can be used to harvest corn, soybeans, cotton, tomatoes, grapes, and wheat. There are literally hundreds of items in these categories, each suited for particular soil conditions and crop needs. Deere and the other large full-line supplier, the Case-International Harvester Division of Tenneco, sell most, if not all, of the implement types in these categories. Other producers provide a selected subset of these items.

Another important line of products manufactured and sold by Deere and Company is industrial equipment. This includes machines involved in earth moving, forestry, and construction. Typical products include: bulldozers, backhoes, loaders, graders, scrapers, excavating equipment, and tree harvesting and log handling equipment. Though Deere does not provide as broad a line of construction equipment as its large competitors such as Caterpillar, it has entered the market in a variety of segments and sold nearly a billion dollars worth of these products in 1985.

The fastest-growing product line for Deere in the 1980s is the lawn garden implement line. The company makes and sells a variety of small lawn and garden tractors, mowing implements, snow blowers, riding mowers, and other outdoor power equipment. Some estimates place the size of the lawn and garden equipment market at $3 billion in 1985, growing at roughly 6.8% annually since 1976. The outdoor power products line is complemented by a number of minor items manufactured for the firm by others, including tools, clothing, and accessories.

In addition to those products the firm sells which are designed for end-users, the firm has begun to use its facilities and engineering expertise to develop a growing line of components and other products for other producers of heavy equipment and vehicles. These products are called OEM components and include such items as castings, shock absorbers, steering gear, and so forth. Also, in 1984, Deere bought the U.S. rights to the manufacture and sale of the rotary engine from Curtiss-Wright Corporation. This engine has a number of possible applications in products both related and unrelated to Deere's current business.

Finally, another source of income for Deere, as for many firms making durable goods, is its financial subsidiary. Besides providing equipment financing for its dealers and loans to farmers, the firm also has an insurance division. These operations, currently holding around $3.7 billion in assets, have often helped offset operating losses in the 1980s, providing the firm's profits in several of those years.

FACILITIES AND OPERATIONS

Deere and Company has 12 factories in the U.S. and Canada, with a total of more than 33 million square feet. In addition, the firm also owns and operates tractor manufacturing plants in Mexico, Germany, and Spain; farm implement facilities in France, Germany, and South Africa; and an engine factory in Spain. Other facilities and affiliated companies are operated in South America and Australia.

Since 1976, the firm has spent about $2 billion expanding or upgrading its facilities. Much of this capital investment was intended to make Deere the technological leader in its industry. According to some analysts, the operations in Blackhawk County, Iowa, include some of the most modern and efficient manufacturing plants to be found anywhere in the world. In the Waterloo tractor factory ten minicomputers direct the facility's many functions including materials management, scheduling, painting, and various other manufacturing operations. Rubbish is even recycled to provide energy for the computer-controlled environment of the plant.

The Waterloo engine manufacturing facility is also highly automated, its heart being a 900-foot-long automatic engine-block machining line. This plant will be instrumental in a new joint venture planned with the Detroit-Allison Division of GM. Under this planned venture Deere will help develop and produce diesel engines for the leading automaker.

Although Deere uses parts from a number of outside suppliers, it is a highly integrated manufacturer, making its own engines, hydraulic components, transmissions, castings, and other components such as steering mechanisms. The expertise developed by the firm through this integration provides the firm with a number of possible original equipment (OEM) products which could become an increasing source of sales for the firm in the latter half of the 1980s and beyond.

In addition to its manufacturing facilities, the company maintains major research and development facilities in Waterloo (Product Engineering Center) and Moline, Illinois (Combine Research Center). These facilities have been expanded at a cost of over $40 million since 1980, greatly increasing the firm's ability to develop the technologies it needs to maintain its position of industry leadership. The firm has also worked with N.A.S.A. to develop improved metal alloys. The acquisition of the rotary engine technology is intended to provide the firm with opportunities for a variety of product applications and improvements, including a new generation, fuel-efficient aircraft engine. The diesel engine venture is also intended to advance the state of the art in this area, putting Deere in a position to be a leading designer and builder of a variety of engines.

Though Deere possesses some of the finest facilities of any industrial firm in America, it has been unable to utilize them to the fullest extent in the mid-1980s. The entire agricultural equipment industry has been operating with excess capacity throughout the decade. Standard & Poor's estimates that since 1979, the industry has cut production capacity by 50%.[3] In that year the industry had its sales peak and still operated at only 70–75% of capacity. In spite of the capacity contraction, operating rates stood at only about 30% in 1985. By mid-1986, S&P expects capacity to be cut an additional 15–20%, raising operating rates somewhat.

MARKETING AND DISTRIBUTION

Even the most efficient manufacturer of a durable good such as farm equipment cannot hope to control a significant portion of the market without a strong dealer network. The customer needs to have ready access to the product, the means to finance it, and the ability to have it repaired. It is especially critical for field crop farmers to have access to emergency repairs when the narrow "windows" for certain operations such as planting and harvesting are open. Over the years, Deere has taken great pains to develop its dealer network into the strongest in the industry.

Regardless of its strength the dealer network has been under great stress. Slow sales at the retail level have left the dealers scrambling for income to stay in business. Because of the high value of farm equipment—large tractors and combines often sell for more than $100,000—it is difficult for equipment dealers to finance their inventories, often running to several million dollars. From 1980–1985 the National Farm and Power Equipment Association reports that it has lost 20% of its members.[4] Most of the approximately 3500 Deere dealers who remain are hanging on through a combination of service and parts sales and interest concessions from the company.

Since 1979, Deere has seen accounts receivable grow from $1.4 to $2.75 billion while sales of equipment have gone from $5 billion down to $4.1 billion. In 1984 and 1985 Deere made special interest and payment concessions on as much as $600 million of its receivables. This cost the firm as much as $50 million in lost interest income in 1985. Further, up to 23 months of interest-free credit can be obtained under the current "normal" credit arrangements available from the company. As of October, 1985, 15% of the firm's outstanding receivables were not due for over one year. It is clear that Deere is spending a great deal of its resources to support its dealers, giving some indication of how critical they are to the firm's success. The firm's marketing policy manual says, "Our dealers are our greatest assets. . . . If they do not succeed, any success we have is bound to be short-lived."

Historically, the typical Deere dealer has generated annual revenues of about $3 million. About 380 dealers sell only industrial equipment, with revenues of $10 million being achieved by some of these dealers. Overseas sales are generated through sales branches in Europe, South America, Australia, South Africa, and Mexico. These branches supply 1300 overseas retail dealers. Four export branches supply products to over 100 countries through 160 distributors.

The financial function of the dealer network is supported by the John Deere Credit Company, which also helps finance retail sales of farm and industrial equipment. However, a great portion of the retail sales is supported by outside lenders. Through its purchase of Farm Plan in 1984, Deere Credit will also supply credit services to farmers for the purchase of seed, feed, planting supplies, and other needs.

The company's image is fostered by specialized forms of advertising. The company publishes technical support material and a farm magazine called the *Furrow*. The *Furrow*, published worldwide in 10 languages and 27 editions, is estimated to have a circulation of 2 million readers. The company's marketing philosophy is perhaps best embodied by the following comments of the advertising planning manager: "We decided to position our tractors in the customers' minds as the most productive tractors on the market. Perhaps, just as important, our competitors in their advertising had left this position open to us."

It is hard to gauge Deere's market success precisely. Market share figures for various products are not generally published. However, it is estimated that Deere has over 40% of the North American market, which makes it the leading supplier. As late as 1984, it

TABLE C10.1   AGRICULTURAL EQUIPMENT MARKET SHARES, 1984

Firm	World share
Deere & Co.	32.4%
Case-IH	19.8*
Ford-New Holland	15.0*
Massey-Ferguson	11.1
Kubota	9.0
Fiat	8.7
Allis-Chalmers	4.0

* Estimated by the authors based on subsequent mergers.
  Note: The Case-IH share for 1985 and beyond is lower because of subsequent capacity reductions and product rationalization, making Ford number 2.
  Source: Wertheim & Co.

was estimated that Deere led worldwide sales with 32.4%, with the rest of the firms having the estimated shares shown in Table C10.1.[5]

AGRICULTURAL ENVIRONMENT

Agriculture is perhaps the oldest organized activity in which humankind participates. It is responsible not only for the production of food, but also for the fiber from which clothing and industrial goods are made. Though there are very few places on the globe where agriculture is not practiced in some form, the effort differs greatly, depending on climate, culture, resources, and other important variables. One important factor varies little across much of the agricultural sector, however—the role of the markets for these goods. Even planned economies with state-managed distribution systems participate in the world markets for agricultural commodities.

Role of Commodity Markets

Agriculture is a highly fragmented activity with large numbers of producers, each wishing to market their largely undifferentiated products. The number of buyers of agricultural commodities is also large. When a market has these characteristics, the prices in the market tend to be volatile; they cannot be controlled by individual buyers or sellers. This situation is further exacerbated by the fact that it is relatively easy for new producers to enter the market.

Many of the critical inputs to agriculture, especially in more developed economies, are not commodities. The chemicals and mechanical implements used in planting, cultivating, and harvesting are produced and sold by concentrated groups of manufacturers with sufficient bargaining power to control prices. Even the critical inputs of land and money, though traded in competitive markets, result in fixed costs which must be met regardless of the quantity of output produced by the farmer or the price at which it may be sold.

As a result of this market structure agricultural producers face output prices that vary greatly, while inputs like chemicals, tractors, and land become more and more expensive. This leaves the farmer with very few options for protecting or improving profits.

Any individual farmer cannot control the number of producers, what they choose to plant, or how much they produce. This means that each farmer must employ an approach that is essentially a self-sufficient solution to the problem. One option is to produce a crop in short supply which could be sold at a premium price. The main difficulty with such a strategy in the long run is that every other farmer is trying to do the same thing, given suitable climate and land, reducing the time available to exploit the advantage.

The most obvious option for any particular farm producer is to simply produce more output per unit of input than the competitors, thus raising productivity. Since so many of the costs of farming are fixed in relation to the farm operation as a unit, or per acre, for example, the more output per acre the farmer produces, the lower the cost per unit of crop produced. This strategy, too, has long-run ramifications. The more farmers generally increase productivity, the more they produce relative to effective world demand, with the result that commodity prices, in general, tend to trend lower.

Though Deere's agricultural equipment products are directed primarily at the production of coarse grains such as wheat, corn, and soybeans and this context is of the most immediate impact on the firm, all mechanized farmers face the general environmental structure described above. Domestically agriculture produces output in four main segments: coarse grains, livestock, fruits and vegetables, and fibers. The main impact on Deere is in the first segment, though grain production is also indirectly linked to livestock production and market behavior.

Impact of Environmental Trends

The drive to increase productivity initially created a strong demand for more effective tools needed to accomplish the task. Though the entire post–WW II period has been characterized by increasing farm productivity, in the decade of the 1970s especially, a number of forces combined to drive the demand for increasingly expensive and productive farm implements to record levels. Technological advances, dramatic rises in the rate of increase in the prices of all farm inputs, and the ready availability of cash supported by increases in land values all encouraged the trend toward increased equipment purchases. In addition to using improved equipment, farmers can also improve productivity through the use of improved chemical and cultivation techniques. Innovations in biotechnology have also begun to contribute to productivity gains, with even more promised for the future.

The movement toward the use of chemicals and capital equipment to increase productivity was well on its way when the activities of OPEC began to influence the environment. The rising price of oil had an impact in two vital areas. Most farm chemicals, including fertilizer, are produced from inputs based on petroleum or natural gas. This caused a rise in the cost of these important aids to productivity improvement. Oil price increases also caused all fuels to rise in price, making the operation of farm equipment more expensive. Farmers in developed countries, especially, began to trade in old equipment for newer, more efficient tractors and harvesters.

Rising fuel prices had an even greater impact outside the agricultural sector. Higher prices for oil and its derivatives dramatically changed world capital flows and forced many developed nations to scramble for exports that could be exchanged for oil. The most efficient food-producing nations naturally tried to raise exports of farm products to pay for their much needed oil. Rising fuel prices also helped touch off a general inflation across all sectors of the major developed economies, making it that much more imperative for farmers to increase productivity to offset generally rising input costs. Finally, interest rates also rose dramatically as a result of the general inflation, eventually making the purchase of expensive agricultural inputs such as equipment and land more risky.

Land values in the 1970s proved to be something of a paradox. Prices rose steadily, helping add value to an important source of wealth for farmers. Land is the critical foundation for the collateral farmers need for seasonal borrowing. However, rising land prices, combined with rising interest rates and increasing equipment purchases, greatly increased the amount of cash flow needed by farmers who purchased land during the last decade. Early in the decade price increases in farm commodities supported the increased cash flow requirements of farmers and encouraged expansion. The size of the typical farm in the U.S. increased, reflecting consolidation and land purchases. Farmers who did not expand during the period have not been affected by these land-associated costs. (See Tables C10.2 and C10.3 for summary data reflecting these trends.)

Eventually, rising productivity and a recession, induced in part by monetary policy designed to reduce inflation and interest rates, put an end to the inflationary prosperity. Farmers were left with shrinking land values and high fixed costs. Productivity improvements raised production quantities above demand, causing surpluses and falling prices for crops. The resulting spiral put tremendous pressure on the agricultural sector. The more cash the farmers needed, the more they had to try to produce. The more they produced, the lower farm prices became. Evidence of this set of interlocking trends can be seen in Tables C10.2, C10.3, and C10.4. Note especially the behavior of interest rates, land values, farm debt as a proportion of farm assets, commodity prices, and general inflation.

TABLE C10.2   SELECTED FARM PRODUCTION DATA FOR INDEX 1977 = 100
(All but index = mil. metric tons)

			Less:			
(2.1)	(2.2)	(2.3) Plus:	(2.4)	(2.5)	(2.6)	(2.7) Index of farm productivity
Year	Starting stocks	prod. + imports*	Domestic use	Exports	Ending stocks	
1976	43.3	257.0	153.6	78.1	68.6	98.0
1977	68.6	264.8	161.7	88.4	83.3	100.0
1978	83.3	275.0	179.7	94.5	84.1	101.0
1979	84.1	301.2	184.6	111.2	89.5	105.0
1980	89.5	268.2	171.0	114.9	71.8	101.0
1981	71.8	328.8	178.6	110.8	111.2	116.0
1982	111.2	331.4	193.1	96.3	153.2	116.0
1983	153.2	206.9	183.0	97.7	79.4	98.0
1984	79.4	313.7	197.0	97.3	98.8	115.0
1985	98.8	345.7	300.8	62.8	80.9	127.0

* Import amounts in all years less than 1.0 mil. metric tons.
Source: U.S. Department of Agriculture.

TABLE C10.3   SELECTED FARM FINANCIAL DATA

(3.1) Year	(3.2) Net farm income (bil. $)	(3.3) Dir. gov. payments (bil. $)	(3.4) Value of ld. & bld. 1977 = 100	(3.5) All farm debt (bil. $)	(3.6) Debt / assets (%)	(3.7) Ave. farm size (acres)
1976	$20.1	$0.7	86.0	$ 91.5	15.9%	422.0
1977	19.8	1.8	100.0	103.9	15.6	427.0
1978	27.7	3.0	109.0	122.7	16.7	429.0
1979	32.3	1.4	125.0	140.8	16.1	428.0
1980	21.2	1.3	145.0	165.8	16.5	427.0
1981	31.0	1.9	158.0	182.0	18.2	425.0
1982	22.3	3.5	157.0	201.7	20.1	428.0
1983	17.8	9.3	148.0	216.3	20.4	432.0
1984	34.5	8.4	146.0	212.6	22.2	437.0
1985	27.0	9.0	134.3	212.1	23.7	440.0

Source: U.S. Department of Agriculture.

TABLE C10.4   CRITICAL PRICE LEVELS INDEX #'s—1977 = 100

(4.1) Year	(4.2) CPI	(4.3) All farm inputs	(4.4) All farm receipts	(4.5) Agricul. equip.	(4.6) Land prices	(4.7) Interest paid
1976	93.9	95.0	102.0	92.5	86.0	88.0
1977	100.0	100.0	100.0	100.0	100.0	100.0
1978	107.7	108.0	115.0	107.7	109.0	117.0
1979	119.8	123.0	132.0	117.3	125.0	143.0
1980	136.0	138.0	134.0	131.0	145.0	174.0
1981	150.1	150.0	139.0	145.7	158.0	211.0
1982	159.3	157.0	133.0	157.2	157.0	241.0
1983	164.4	160.0	134.0	164.9	148.0	250.0
1984	171.4	163.0	142.0	169.8	146.0	251.0
1985	179.6	163.0	128.0	170.5	134.3	250.0

Source: U.S. Department of Agriculture, Bureau of Labor Statistics.

Other Agricultural Environment Issues

The attempts by farmers to improve productivity are not solely responsible for crop surpluses and falling prices. Government intervention and high exit barriers are also key culprits. Overproduction produces "carryover" stocks which depress prices, often to levels below the unit cost of production. Even the presence of a billion hungry people around the globe does little to reduce this problem. Most of these potential customers cannot afford to buy what they need. The critical political importance of food to all nations is a key factor encouraging the intervention of many governments in the agricultural marketplace. The magnitude of the overproduction issue is illustrated in Table C10.2.

In the developed nations farmers producing surpluses have had sufficient political clout to force their governments to subsidize overproduction, eliminating the negative market action that would normally force many producers from the industry. One style of program encourages reduced planting, while paying the farmers not to produce. Another typical program involves government purchases of surplus stocks, increasing prices, and reducing farmer-owned carryovers. Once in possession of this surplus food, the government is free to sell it or give it away as foreign aid. Such programs are not limited to U.S. farming. Nations in the European Economic Community (Common Market) also provide heavy subsidies to farmers in every sector.

Farming is a key source of trade receipts for many countries. Increased production in Brazil, Canada, Australia, Argentina, and other nations has served to improve the trade positions of all these countries. Though this increased activity has been helpful to equipment and other farm sector suppliers, the rise in world output has generally depressed world farm commodity prices. Outside the U.S. productivity is not as high as it is here but labor and land costs are lower. This leaves the U.S. with a number of tough competitors worldwide. Further, the governments of these competitor countries are not committed to the political issues which have recently plagued U.S. farmers in the form of trade embargoes to the U.S.S.R. and South Africa, for example.

In the U.S. government intervention has also taken place in the credit markets, through the manipulation of Federal lands—especially forestland, with insurance programs, and through numerous other less ambitious programs. Though the Reagan administration has vowed to reduce government intervention in farming, the political forces in the Congress, especially the Senate, and the depth of the farm recession in the 1980s will make such a withdrawal difficult. Farm payments in 1986 reached record levels and the 1987 federal budget asking for agriculture exceeded $50 billion.

Normally when a particular business entity is unable to meet its obligations it should be forced to leave its industry. It is generally agreed that farm capacity in the U.S. is 25–30% higher than it should be. However, who should leave? Two farmers producing identical crops with identical productivity levels could find themselves in very different financial positions depending on when they purchased their land. It is difficult for any farmer whose troubles seem to stem from timing to feel it is fair to be forced out of business. Food production and land ownership are also emotional issues in our society—supported by much mythology and historic cultural connections. Finally, realistically, the disposal of 25–30% of our farm assets is probably impossible in the short run. All these exit barriers encourage political pressure and farm surpluses.

Finally, productivity improvement is not a strategy with unlimited capability. There is a point at which the scale economies deriving from larger farm sizes and more powerful equipment no longer have a significant impact. As tractors become larger they become more difficult to use on hilly ground. They also tend to compact the soil, making it more difficult to cultivate. High-yield agriculture based on heavy equipment works best on wide-open ground, which subjects the farm to erosion. The loss of vital topsoil through erosion by wind and water has become a critical issue in agriculture.

To avoid loss of soil by erosion and to save fuel some farmers have begun to utilize reduced-tillage farming techniques. Reduced-tillage methods eliminate post-harvest plowing and disking operations, leaving crop residue to hold loose soil. In its most efficient form, reduced-tillage planting takes place in only one or two passes through the field. Seeds are planted in crop residue, with the soil being loosened by chisel plows mounted with the planting equipment. Weeds and pests are controlled by the heavy use of chemicals, sometimes applied with the seeds. However, the multiple operations of reduced tillage require more technologically complex tractors. The cost of the equipment required for reduced-tillage farming has reduced the rate of diffusion, despite its

TABLE C10.5 CURRENT AND CONSTANT DOLLAR SALES, AGRICULTURAL EQUIPMENT

		Industry			Deere		
(5.1) Year †	(5.2) Equip. expen.‡ bil. $	(5.3) Price index '77 = 100 (4.5)	(5.4) Expen. index '77 = 100 (from 5.2)	(5.5) Real expen. '77 = 100 (5.4/5.3)	(5.6) Ag. eq. sales* bil. $	(5.7) Sales index '77 = 100 (from 5.6)	(5.8) Real sales '77 = 100 (5.7/5.3)
1976	$ 8.05	92.5	95.4	103.1	$2.68	91.4	98.8
1977	$ 8.43	100.0	100.0	100.0	$2.93	100.0	100.0
1978	$10.44	107.7	123.8	115.0	$3.30	112.4	104.3
1979	$11.75	117.3	139.3	118.8	$3.94	134.2	114.4
1980	$10.64	131.0	126.2	96.3	$4.49	153.0	116.8
1981	$10.22	145.7	121.2	83.2	$4.67	159.0	109.1
1982	$ 7.98	157.2	94.6	60.2	$4.03	137.5	87.4
1983	$ 7.58	164.9	89.8	54.5	$3.31	113.0	68.5
1984	$ 7.28	169.8	86.3	50.8	$3.51	119.5	70.4
1985	$ 7.25	170.5	86.0	50.4	$3.12	106.3	62.3

* Excludes industrial equipment.
† Reference to columns used in calculations.
‡ Equipment expenditure data represent USDA figures for actual equipment purchases.
Source: Agriculture Department, Deere and Company Annual Reports.

multiple benefits. Yields are also lower with reduced tillage, offsetting some of the cost savings from the smaller number of operations required.

CONSTRUCTION AND CONSUMER ENVIRONMENTS

Though Deere and Company was founded as a producer of agricultural equipment, and though this is still the firm's primary activity, declines in the market for these products have forced the firm to increasingly rely on other markets. The fastest-growing segment of the business is the consumer and industrial market for lawn and garden implements and tractors. It has been estimated that lawn tractors and implements made up $650 million of Deere's sales in 1985. (These data are apparently included in the agricultural product line data shown in Tables C10.6 and C10.7.)[6]

The demand for these consumer product lines is directly affected primarily by levels of personal disposable income and construction of single-family housing.[7] Because the engine component makes up 50–70% of the value of the typical unit of outdoor power equipment, engine producers are important contributors to the industry. Domestic small gasoline engine production for these applications is dominated by two firms, Briggs and Stratton and Tecumseh. Kawasaki, Honda, and other Japanese firms are also involved, both in engines and equipment production. Kawasaki provides engines for some Deere lawn tractors, for example.

Construction Equipment

The production of construction equipment resembles the agricultural equipment market in many ways. It is cyclical, heavily dependent on dealer networks and the availability

TABLE C10.6 DEERE AND COMPANY INCOME STATEMENTS FOR SELECTED YEARS ENDING OCTOBER 31
(Millions)

Item	1976	%	1981	%	1984	%	1985	%	Ave. grow. per year
Farm equip.	$ 2,682	85.6	$ 4,665	85.6	$ 3,505	79.7	$ 3,118	76.8	1.7%
Indus. equip.	452	14.4	782	14.4	894	20.3	943	23.2	8.5
Net sales	3,134	100.0	5,447	100.0	4,399	100.0	4,061	100.0	2.9
− Cost of sales	2,316	73.9	4,274	78.5	3,598	81.8	3,355	82.6	4.2
Gross profit	818	26.1	1,173	21.5	801	18.2	706	17.4	−1.6
Less									
G & A expen.	316	10.1	515	9.5	501	11.4	508	12.5	5.4
Other op. exp.	47	1.5	142	2.6	42	1.0	54	1.3	1.5
Depreciation	66	2.1	177	3.3	192	4.4	184	4.5	12.2
Total op. exp.	429	13.7	834	15.3	735	16.7	746	18.4	6.4
Op. profit	389	12.4	338	6.2	66	1.5	−40	−1.0	N/A
+ Other income	75	2.4	265	4.9	237	5.4	206	5.1	11.8
− Int. & other	57	1.8	232	4.3	235	5.3	199	4.9	15.0
Income bef. tax	408	13.0	371	6.8	69	1.6	−34	−0.8	N/A
− Income tax	165	5.3	120	2.2	−36	−0.8	−65	−1.6	N/A
Net income	$ 242	7.7	$ 251	4.6	$ 105	2.4	$ 31	0.8	−20.4
Dividends	$ 62		$ 133		$ 68		$ 68		1.0
% of net inc.		25.6%		53.0%		64.8%		218.0%	
Curr. cash flow	$ 308	9.8	$ 428	7.9	$ 296	6.7	$ 215	5.3	−3.9
# of Comm. sh's	60		66		68		68		
EPS	$ 4.05		$ 3.79		$ 1.54		$ 0.46		−21.5
Capital invest.	$ 126		$ 303		$ 89		$ 144		−3.4
# Employees (act.)	55,242		60,857		43,011		40,509		
Sales/employee (act.)	$56,728		$89,500		$102,280		$100,240		

Source: Deere and Company Annual Reports.

421

TABLE C10.7 DEERE AND COMPANY BALANCE SHEET AS OF OCTOBER 31
(Millions)

Year	1976	%	1981	%	1984	%	1985	%	Ave. grow. per year
Assets									
Current assets:									
Cash	$ 173	5.9	$ 68	1.2	$ 41	0.7	$ 88	1.6	-7.3%
Acct's rec.	1,048	35.6	2,374	41.8	2,847	50.0	2,749	50.3	11.3
Inventory	623	21.2	872	15.3	540	9.5	447	8.2	-3.6
Other	253	8.6	250	4.4	246	4.3	150	2.7	-5.6
Total C/A	2,096	71.2	3,564	62.7	3,675	64.5	3,435	62.9	5.6
Fixed assets:									
Plant & equ't.	1,066	36.2	2,446	43.0	2,484	43.6	2,629	48.1	10.6
- Accum. deprec.	495	-16.8	1,038	-18.3	1,452	-25.5	1,613	-29.5	14.0
Other F/A net	277	9.4	711	12.5	990	17.4	1,012	18.5	15.5
Total F/A	848	28.8	2,119	37.3	2,023	35.5	2,028	37.1	10.2
Total assets	$2,944	100.0	$5,684	100.0	$5,697	100.0	$5,462	100.0	7.1%
Liabilities and owner's equity									
Current liabil.:									
Acct's pay.	$ 646	21.9	$1,320	23.2	$1,143	20.1	$1,044	19.1	5.5%
Notes pay.	112	3.8	679	11.9	568	10.0	521	9.5	18.7
Curr. pay. LTD	23	0.8	15	0.3	158	2.8	16	0.3	-3.6
Taxes pay.	238	8.1	291	5.1	350	6.1	333	6.1	3.8
Total C/L	1,018	34.6	2,304	40.5	2,219	38.9	1,914	35.0	7.3
Long-term debt									
Bonds & notes	539	18.3	760	13.4	1,080	19.0	1,239	22.7	9.7
Def'd. taxes	17	0.6	170	3.0	108	1.9	51	0.9	13.2
Total LTD	555	18.9	930	16.4	1,188	20.8	1,290	23.6	9.8
Equity									
Common stock	214	7.3	482	8.5	490	8.6	491	9.0	9.7
Retain. earn.	1,157	39.3	1,967	34.6	1,801	31.6	1,767	32.4	4.8
Total equity	1,371	46.6	2,450	43.1	2,291	40.2	2,259	41.4	5.7
Total L. & O.E.	$2,944	100.0	$5,684	100.0	$5,697	100.0	$5,462	100.0	7.1%

Source: Deere and Company Annual Reports.

of financing, and influenced heavily by development in power-train technology. The structure and dynamics of the industry, however, are much different. Customers of this industry are primarily contractors, industrial buyers, and specialized users, such as mining and logging companies, for example, whose demand derives from a variety of forces. A major segment of the market is involved with lift trucks and other heavy material handling equipment. Further, 40% of the value of shipments in the industry is exported. As in the agricultural equipment market, overseas producers are growing and overcapacity generally plagues the industry. Also, as in the agricultural market, many domestic suppliers are importing components or moving the production of some small equipment offshore.

Deere and Company is a relative newcomer in the construction equipment market. Caterpillar Tractor Company is the world's leading producer of construction equipment, followed by Komatsu in Japan. Other firms are important producers, specializing in a narrow segment of the market. Clark Equipment is a major producer of material handling equipment, while Joy Manufacturing dominates underground mining equipment production, with Bucyrus-Erie and Koehring being important producers of surface mining equipment and cranes, respectively. Overall, with $943 million of sales in 1985, Deere appears to have about 6% of the total market.[8] Six U.S. producers account for roughly three-quarters of the value of worldwide shipments and 69% of U.S. exports. The total number of U.S. producers is about 700.

AGRICULTURAL EQUIPMENT INDUSTRY

During the 1980s the agricultural equipment industry has undergone considerable consolidation with the result that only two producers of farm tractors remain in the U.S., Deere and Tenneco's J.I. Case-International Harvester unit. Massey-Ferguson (Varity), reorganizing after bankruptcy, has closed all U.S. production. IH tractor production has been absorbed by Case, eliminating much of the firm's capacity and overlapping product lines. White has been unable to reopen after entering reorganization. Allis-Chalmers has sold the bulk of its assets to Klockner-Humboldt-Deutz of West Germany. Ford has moved its tractor production overseas after purchasing Sperry–New Holland in 1985.

Unit tractors sales under 100 h.p. make up about 80–85% of the total, while accounting for only 50% of the tractor revenues of the industry. The $1.5 billion trade surplus in farm equipment experienced in 1981 largely disappeared by 1986, because of flagging demand and the transfer of most small tractor production overseas. Tractors account for roughly half of all international trade in farm machinery, with harvesters and implements accounting for the remainder.

One factor influencing the change in trade patterns has been the loss of the traditional technological advantage enjoyed by U.S. firms. European tractors now embody many features not yet found on U.S. models. Further, where European and Japanese firms (Kubota is the primary Japanese producer) have traditionally limited production to small (under 100 h.p.) units, European producers are now producing many of the larger models as well.

Though tractors are the biggest single revenue source for the farm equipment industry and few producers remain, there are hundreds of niche market firms producing a variety of specialized equipment lines. These small firms have not escaped the problems of the industry and several such as Hesston and Steiger have been acquired or forced into bankruptcy.

Tenneco

Tenneco entered the farm equipment business in 1967 when it acquired J.I. Case. The current chief executive of Tenneco, Jim Ketelsen, started as president of the Case subsidiary just after the acquisition. With the IH acquisition in late 1984, Tenneco became the third largest producer in the industry, broadened its product line, and strengthened its dealer network. As a result of the Tenneco acquisition 30–40% of total U.S. tractor production capacity was eliminated and Ford was bumped up to second place in the market in terms of sales (though Ford no longer produces tractors in the U.S.).

RECENT DEVELOPMENTS AND STRATEGY

Deere and Company has become the leader in the farm equipment industry in recent years because it has recognized a number of important requirements of the environment. Recognizing that the key to selling its products is close contact with the customer, the firm has consistently supported its strong dealer network. This group not only sells the product but is also responsible for the service that maintains the firm's reputation for quality.

Deere has also recognized that to keep the goodwill of the customer an equipment maker must make a product that will do the work it was designed to do without breaking down. Weather conditions are very important to the farmer, especially when the growing season is limited. There are only a few days when fields are dry enough for field work in the spring, for example. If the farmer does not complete needed soil preparation and planting in those days, the very least that will happen is that yields will be significantly reduced. At worst, the farmer may not be able to plant any profitable crop. An equipment breakdown in one of the critical periods could cause serious delays and a great deal of ill will for the company.

In the last 15 years a number of changes have taken place in farming. These changes became especially pronounced after oil prices and general price levels began to squeeze the farmers' profits and farmers began to recognize the importance of productivity. To improve per-acre yields in relation to costs it became essential to have equipment which could plant and harvest to very critical tolerances. An error of even a foot in the width of a row during planting process multiplies over a large field to such a degree that hundreds or even thousands of dollars in revenue can be lost. Many farmers and industry leaders also feel that the larger the farm, the lower the average production cost of the crop. Large farms require more powerful, sophisticated equipment.

In this context Deere made a strong commitment to the production of large, powerful, sophisticated tractors and implements. George Stickler of Deere's Technical Center has said, "We've never found a way to refute the economies of scale of larger farms. . . . I think the whole idea about going back to the old ways of agriculture is just a lot of baloney."[9] Accordingly, in recent years over 50% of Deere's farm equipment sales come from high horsepower row-crop and four-wheel-drive tractors and combines serving primarily coarse grain farmers.

Not all the most efficient and prosperous farms are large, however. A recent Agriculture Department report says that though only one out of every 250 farms (0.4% of the total number) has revenues over $1 million, these "super" farms account for more than 20% of total farm revenue. In spite of this monopoly on revenues, however, one-third of these farms are less than the average size. In fact, 10% of the richest farms have fewer than 50 acres.[10] Obviously, these relatively small superfarms are not generating that much revenue from planting soybeans. Rather, they are involved in high-revenue, specialty outputs such as vegetables and herbs; costly nuts such as pistachios and cashews; and exotic livestock such as buffalo and deer.

As the agricultural equipment industry has become more and more mature in recent years Deere has also seen the need to improve the productivity of its manufacturing operations. The massive capital investments of the last decade have created increased capacity and helped the firm become a leader in industry productivity. Sales per employee for the firm have nearly doubled from about $56,700 in 1976, to just over $100,000 in 1985. Labor costs have also been reduced as a result of these kinds of improvements. For example, at 4% of unit cost, labor costs on the firm's latest industrial equipment product line are proportionally only half of what they were in the mid-1970s.

These productivity improvements are not achieved without cost, however. Reducing labor costs through the use of capital equipment creates fixed costs, which tend to raise a firm's breakeven point. Sales declines such as those which have been experienced by Deere can cause great losses or force huge price increases. To avoid both these undesirable outcomes a firm must develop more efficient schedules, reduce waste, reduce white collar personnel, and otherwise operate with the minimum possible cost. Throughout the slump in agricultural equipment sales Deere has worked hard to control costs and drive down its breakeven point. In fact, the manager of the firm's Component Works—the division that produces major component parts for the firm—has set a goal of reducing the breakeven point of the division by 33% in 1986, to an astonishing 22% of capacity.[11] There are limits to such activities, however. In the long run the firm may have to consolidate its facilities, closing some of its older plants as Case-IH has done, to reduce fixed costs.

Financial Results

The results of Deere's strategies in the last decade have been mixed at best. Until the deterioration of the farm situation in the 1980s the firm had achieved steady growth in sales, averaging 11.7% per year from 1976 through 1981. Since then sales have declined an average of 7.1% per year. Profits have not displayed such a clear trend. From 1976–1981 profits grew at only 0.75% per year, declining at the rate of 41% a year since then. Financial results for selected years are shown in Tables C10.6 and C10.7. A context for these financial results is provided by Table C10.5, highlighting the influence of price inflation on the sales growth for both the firm and the industry as a whole.

A significant part of the assets and income controlled by Deere and Company is not shown in the company's regular financial statements. The firm's two large financial subsidiaries and its interest in its partially owned foreign affiliates are reported only in the notes to the financial statements. These data are shown in Tables C10.8 and C10.9. The total income from the two finance subsidiaries is about half of the "other income" shown on the income statement for 1985 (Table C10.6), for example.

Table C10.10 reports the sales, operating income, and identifiable assets reported for each of the firm's two major segments of business, agricultural equipment and industrial equipment. (The sum of the operating income figures in Table C10.10 and those in Table C10.6 do not match because the latter has been recast to a more conventional form to better reflect company operations as separated from the impact of the affiliates.)

TABLE C10.8 DEERE AND COMPANY FINANCIAL RESULTS—NONCONSOLIDATED SUBSIDIARIES, SELECTED YEARS ENDING OCTOBER 31
(Millions)

Income statements

	Retail finance subsidiary				Insurance subsidiary		
	1985	1984	1981		1985	1984	1981
Net revenues	$ 335.4	$ 333.9	$ 360.0	Net revenues	$260.2	$250.5	$266.0
Less: Expenses				Less: Expenses			
Gen. & admin.	28.4	19.1	2.0	Gen. & admin.	35.1	31.9	35.5
Deprec.	10.2	12.4		Claim costs	192.1	188.5	203.3
Insurance	24.2	22.8	12.1				
Operating inc.	272.6	279.6	345.9	Operating inc.	33.0	30.1	27.2
− Interest	172.5	183.0	238.3	− Interest			
Inc. before tax	100.1	96.6	107.6	Inc. before tax	33.0	30.1	27.2
− Inc. tax	40.1	39.3	49.9	− Inc. tax	7.1	4.6	
Net income	$ 60.0	$ 57.3	$ 57.7	Net income	$ 25.9	$ 25.5	$ 27.2

Balance sheets

Assets				Assets			
Retail n./rec.	$2,623.5	$2,586.6	$2,300.9	Cash	$ 39.9	$ 45.1	$ 59.2
Lease invest.	442.8	396.8		Secur. invest.	410.6	365.5	213.1
Deferred assets	1.0	5.1					
Other assets	94.1	32.4	53.3	Other assets	70.8	70.8	17.4
Total assets	$3,161.4	$3,020.9	$2,354.2		$521.3	$481.4	$289.7
Liabilities							
Notes payable	$1,287.9	$1,344.5	$1,133.4	Policy reserves	$218.0	$199.1	$ 87.7
Due JD & Co.	76.1	155.7	232.6	Unearned prem.	56.7	50.1	46.7
Other	370.4	387.8	280.3	Other	32.5	32.8	23.2
Long-term debt	817.6	559.4	324.6				
Total liabil.	2,552.0	2,447.4	1,970.9	Total liabil.	307.2	282.0	157.6
Owner's equity	609.4	573.5	383.3	Owner's equity	214.1	199.4	132.1
	$3,161.4	$3,020.9	$2,354.2		$521.3	$481.4	$289.7

Source: Deere and Company Annual Reports.

Reorganization

In the years since 1980, Deere and Company has undergone at least two major periods of reorganization. In the early part of the decade the firm undertook a major physical reorganization of its Blackhawk County, Iowa, facilities. The completion of the Engine Works and Waterloo Tractor Works facilities in 1980 added a large chunk of capacity and permitted the firm to consolidate much of its internal supply operation in the former tractor assembly facilities. This new consolidated supply operation was designated as the Component Works. There are four major operations consolidated in the Component

TABLE C10.9   AFFILIATES—DEERE AND COMPANY, FINANCIAL RESULTS, SELECTED YEARS ENDING OCTOBER 31 (Millions)

Position in affiliated companies:

	1985	1984
Net revenues −	$407.7	$307.2
expenses	377.6	311.7
Net inc. (loss)	$ 30.1	$(4.5)
Deere's share	9.3	0.8
Total assets −	$277.2	$245.9
liabilities	147.8	146.5
Net assets	$129.4	$ 99.4
Deere's share	43.3	35.6

Source: Deere and Company Annual Reports.

TABLE C10.10   DEERE AND COMPANY SEGMENT SALES FOR SELECTED YEARS ENDING OCTOBER 31 (Millions)

	1985	1984	1981
Sales:			
Ag. equipment	$3,118	$3,505	$4,665
Indus. equip.	943	894	782
	4,061	4,399	5,447
Operating income and equity investments:			
Ag. equipment	$ 65	$ 181	$ 560
Indus. equip.	22	5	(38)
	87	186	522
Identifiable assets:			
Ag. equipment	$3,625	$3,838	$3,868
Indus. equip.	732	726	890
Corporate	1,105	1,133	926
	$5,462	$5,697	$5,684

Source: Deere and Company Annual Reports.

Works: the foundry, hydraulics production, drive train production, and a miscellaneous group to make gears and other machined parts. The total Component Works operation occupies 6.5 million square feet, producing 70% of the finished parts used in the firm's tractors.

More recently, the Component Works was again reorganized to implement a concept the firm calls the "focused factory." Under this notion the four operational component units were given operational autonomy within the overall divisional structure, becoming "factories within a factory." The purpose of this action was to focus the energy of the four group managers on a narrower product line. It is intended that through this focus flexibility and efficiency could be developed in management and engineering. Management feels this change will enhance skill development consistent with its need to produce high-quality, complex components at a lower cost.

The primary purpose of the "factory within a factory" structure is designed to facilitate flexibility, problem-solving, communication, and a number of related management processes. In addition, however, it also facilitates the development of saleable products which can be used to fill excess capacity in the various components divisions, thus reducing the cost burden on the parent organization.

New Ventures

Though exact capacity utilization figures are not available, in 1985 the firm certainly operated far below its capacity. As a result of this continued difficulty the firm has sought to identify a number of areas in which to diversify to create additional revenues.

• *Chinese sale:* In 1984, Deere signed a $25 million contract with China to provide a limited number of products and the technology to develop several models of tractors. Presumably, as the technological development continues the firm will play a further role in the process, generating additional revenues.

• *Rotary engine:* Also in 1984, Curtiss-Wright sold its patents and other interests in the rotary engine technology to Deere. Subsequent development of this technology is being directed toward a number of possible products. The chief focus, however, is on the joint development of a rotary aircraft engine under a contract with Avco-Lycoming. The agreement with Avco gives that firm world rights to aircraft uses of the engine in exchange for royalties. Deere is then free to develop other uses for the engine. As much as $50 million in research money may be allocated to the development of this engine in the near future.

• *Purchase of Farm Plan:* In July 1984, Deere took another step in the diversification of its financing unit with the acquisition of a Wisconsin-based financial services firm called Farm Plan. This firm joins with local banks in 23 states to make loans to farmers for the purchase of equipment, seed, fertilizer, feed, and other necessary inputs. This gives Deere a range of financial services to aid the farmer in addition to its current retail equipment financing and its insurance.

• *Articulated truck:* In early 1985, Deere announced the introduction of a new heavy dump truck based on a number of components supplied by various divisions of the firm. The engine, transmission, other power train parts, steering, hydraulic components, and other key parts are made by the Engine and Component Works divisions of the firm. The truck itself is built by Kress Corporation.

• *Diesel engine development:* Deere is in the process of developing a number of outlets for its sophisticated diesel engine technology. In 1986 it began to set up a joint venture with GM's Allison Division involving the joint development of a line of diesel engines for a wide range of powered vehicles. Deere is expected to contribute manufacturing and engineering facilities in Waterloo, Dubuque, and France, involving about 1500 employees. GM is expected to contribute its Detroit Diesel Allison Division with about 4500 employees. The new venture will produce a broad range of engines. Annual sales for the venture have been estimated at $1.5–2 billion.[12]

• *Other engine developments:* The company has also begun to bid actively for contracts for military applications of its engines. A new program to be undertaken in 1986 is aimed at "seeding" engines to key customers in the replacement diesel engine market, with 1987 to be the first year for a primary thrust into this market segment. Ultimately, the firm has a goal of 40,000–50,000 extra diesel engines annually.

• *Engine blocks:* In addition to producing complete engines for the original equipment (OEM) and replacement markets, Deere is also beginning the production of engine parts for other firms. In 1986, the firm will begin significant production of engine blocks for the Pontiac Division of GM. The ultimate goal of this product line is 50,000–70,000 tons of outside foundry business per year, with the initial contract placed at 18,000 tons.[13]

• *Motor home chassis:* Another major project for the firm in 1986, is the production of chassis for motor homes. The amount of production expected under this agreement with Winnebago is unknown, though it has been estimated that production could be in the range of 2000–3000 units. This project could also pave the way for the production of similar products such as truck chassis.

FUTURE GOALS AND DIRECTIONS

Since 1984, Deere has made an initial broad commitment to diversify its activities into a number of OEM products in order to utilize its excess capacity and expertise. In addition, many of these projects could foster the development of even more expertise, leading to a further strengthening of the firm's position in a variety of heavy equipment market segments. The management of the Component Works has set a goal of having $100 million in OEM sales by 1991. Though precise figures are not available, the fastest-growing division of the firm in 1986 is the home lawn care and lawn tractor line, marketed with full exploitation of the company logo and color scheme to carry the firm's quality image into this market segment. In 1986, the marketing effort for these products has been increased and includes a significant price cut in the marketing mix.

The exact future of Deere's main business is still subject to question. In late 1984, CEO Hansen said he expected to see significant growth back to the historical sales

TABLE C10.11   HISTORICAL PRICE BEHAVIOR, DEERE AND COMPANY COMMON STOCK

	Price range			Price earnings ratio	
Year	High	Low	EPS	High	Low
1978	37	22½	$4.38	8.45x	5.14x
1979	41½	31¾	5.12	8.11	6.20
1980	49¾	28½	3.72	13.37	7.66
1981	49¾	32⅛	3.79	13.13	8.48
1982	36⅞	22	.78	47.27	28.21
1983	42⅜	28½	.34	124.62	83.82
1984	40⅜	24⅝	1.54	26.22	16.00
1985	33⅛	24¼	.46	72.00	52.71
1986	35⅛	27¼	.60*	†	†

* Consensus estimate.
† P/E in early 1986 based on last full year's earnings = 75x.

levels—though he doesn't say when. Others disagree, saying that sales may never rise to more than 10–15% above the levels achieved in 1984–1985.[14] In spite of the problems in the industry and the sliding sales and profits in the firm, however, Deere's common stock was selling for around 70 times current earnings in March 1986! Such a high multiple might offer the firm a golden opportunity for making acquisitions designed for further diversification. At the very least such a multiple would seem to show a high degree of investor confidence in the firm's future. Table C10.11 on page 429 shows the historical price behavior of the firm's stock, as well as accompanying data on EPS.

REFERENCES

1 The authors wish to thank Ashwani Bansal of Deere and Company for his help in the preparation of this section of the case.

2 *Industry Surveys, Steel and Heavy Machinery,* Standard & Poor's Corporation, Feb. 13, 1986, p. S40.

3 Ibid., p. S41.

4 M. Thompson, "Implement Dealers Find Tough Going," *Waterloo Courier,* Feb. 16, 1986, p. G7.

5 J. Risen, "Dominent Deere Views Case-International Harvester Combination," *Waterloo Courier,* Dec. 2, 1984, p. A12; T. Petzinger, Jr., and B. Morris, "Tenneco to Buy Farm-Gear Unit from Harvester," *The Wall Street Journal,* Nov. 27, 1984, p. 2.

6 J. Flint, "Root, hog! Or die," *Forbes,* Nov. 4, 1985, pp. 170–178.

7 Department of Commerce, *1986 U.S. Industrial Outlook,* Government Printing Office, 1986, pp. 47.8–47.10.

8 *Industry Surveys,* op. cit., pp. S42–S45.

9 A. Anderson, Jr., "Future Farming," *Omni,* June 1979, pp. 90–94ff.

10 D. Kendall, "'Superfarm' Numbers Have Grown Rapidly in Past Decade," *Waterloo Courier,* Feb. 16, 1986.

11 E. Adcock, "Testing, 'Seeding' of Diesels for OEM Business Begins in '86," *Waterloo Courier,* Jan. 19, 1986, p. I1.

12 E. Adcock, "Deere, GM Plan to Form Diesel Engine Firm," *Waterloo Courier,* July 1, 1986, p. 1.

13 Flint, op. cit.

14 F. Rice, "Cruel Days in Tractorville," *Fortune,* Oct. 29, 1984, pp. 30–36.

DELOREAN MOTOR COMPANY

Prepared by Caron St. John,
Clemson University.

DeLorean Motor Company began in 1975 as John Z. DeLorean's vision to build an innovative, socially responsible automobile and ended seven years later in the wake of escalating expenses, unexpected quality problems, canceled orders, and rumors of mismanagement. During those years practically all facets of the organization were directly affected by the genius as well as the idiosyncrasies of John DeLorean.

JOHN DELOREAN

John DeLorean grew up in Detroit during the 1930s, the son of an automobile assembly-plant worker. During his childhood he developed a fascination with the auto industry that would eventually lead to a successful career with the major American automobile manufacturers.

After attending the Chrysler Institute, DeLorean briefly joined Chrysler as an engineer. He then spent four years with Packard Motor Company. In 1956, DeLorean joined the engineering staff of General Motors' (GM's) Pontiac Division. During his thirteen years with Pontiac, including four as head of the Pontiac Motor Division, DeLorean's creative and innovative ideas contributed to product developments which allowed Pontiac to set sales records that held for more than a decade. He was involved in the development of the GTO—one of the first high-powered street cars, and the "wide track" design and marketing concept.

In 1969, at age 44, he was the youngest general manager ever named to head the Chevrolet Motor Division. In August 1972, he was named group executive of General Motors North American Car and Truck Division and was rumored to be a future president of General Motors. Less than eight months later, however, on April 2, 1973, he resigned. The circumstances leading to his resignation are not clear. GM officials have stated off the record that DeLorean was forced out as a result of internal investigations.[1] DeLorean has always maintained he became disillusioned with GM and left of his own accord.

According to DeLorean, the structured committee style of management used by GM bred conformity and a form of team loyalty that discouraged creative thinking and open communications. He perceived a lack of social involvement by GM, with little regard for the unemployed or disadvantaged, and a lack of concern for product safety. He felt the entire auto industry was moving away from the design and development of new automobiles. R&D was being replaced with a marketing concept designed to convince consumers to buy a new car every three years. "It's immoral to build a car that rusts away and disappears after seven years," he proclaimed.[2]

Shortly after resigning from GM, DeLorean began to promote his idea of building an "ethical" car. He wanted the project to be the embodiment of his personal ego, dreams, and values and to show the rest of the auto industry how to build a safe, economical, long lasting, socially responsible automobile.[3] Also, he wanted to provide employment for the disadvantaged. He promised he would locate his plant in an area where unemployment was high. Finally, he wanted his car company to be an inspiration for the American entrepreneurial spirit, and he stated: "What made this country was people who believed in something and went out and did it. But the magnitude of business today makes that tough. I'd like to show that a bunch of little guys can still make it."[4]

Walter Chrysler, back in 1924, had been the last American car maker to successfully enter the American market. Numerous attempts over the last fifty years had failed. Many people felt DeLorean would succeed. His knowledge of the industry, spectacular success at GM, access to the right people, and flare for generating publicity would allow him to be more than one more failure in a long line of failures. As DeLorean explained to *Motor Trend:*

> I don't think that since Walter Chrysler . . . you've really had anybody who's been professional about it, from the standpoint of having a background in the business. . . . Walter Chrysler was general manager of Buick when he decided to go off and start his own motor company. He really knew the business, and he hired some of the finest technical people of that day. . . . I think that we have, and are assembling, an extremely competent and professional organization of people.[5]

PRODUCT DEFINITION

In 1973, while addressing a meeting of the Texas Christian University Management Alumni Association, DeLorean told his audience that he had designed a couple of little cars—a two-seater sports car and a minicommuter car with a foreign engine. At that point DeLorean's fascination seemed to be with the commuter car. The commuter would run on gasoline and, eventually, on hydrogen. However, DeLorean quickly lost interest in the commuter.

According to Bob McClean, a thirty-five-year veteran of General Motors who joined DeLorean in January of 1974, "It was always the sports car. From the moment John DeLorean left GM, he was determined to build his own sports car."[6] DeLorean had to start out with a limited-production, high-priced car. There was no way DeLorean could produce the hundreds of thousands of moderately priced cars that were the mainstay of the Big Three's output. He needed to focus on a market requiring tens of thousands of cars.

In 1974, DeLorean envisioned the major competition for his sports car as the Corvette. Selling at a rate of 50,000 per year, the Corvette sold for around $12,000. Projected sales for the DeLorean sports car were 20,000 per year at a selling price of approximately $13,500. The market competition, according to DeLorean officials, ranged from the Corvette to the Porsche.[7] Potential customers would be from two major groups—young, affluent professionals and middle-aged professionals who had reached the point where they could afford a luxury sports car.

DESIGN

One of the early design decisions concerned whether to use fiberglass for the shell of the car. Although fiberglass was lighter and cheaper to produce than steel, it required several safety measures, including a steel skeleton and backbone to counter the tendency to disintegrate on impact. DeLorean learned about a new plastic material that was stronger than steel and half the weight. The process was called elastic reservoir molding (ERM) and it involved placing fiberglass cloth on either side of open-celled foam filled with epoxy resin. The advantages of the ERM product were (1) low weight, which meant better fuel efficiency and ability to use a smaller engine; (2) strength, so safety was not sacrificed; and (3) elimination of the costly machining of metal.

The one problem with the ERM product was that it could not be painted. Since the plastic had to be covered with a thin metal coat, DeLorean chose stainless steel—the most durable material available.

DeLorean wanted gull-wing doors similar to those of the 1954 Mercedes Benz 300SL and a rear-engine design that allowed use of the front end as a crash space. DeLorean also thought the rear engine was "a little bit sexier" than the conventional engines.[8]

In October of 1974, DeLorean hired Bill Collins, an engineering "star," away from GM. Collins was charged with developing DeLorean's ideas further. Research and development continued through most of 1975, with much of the research funded by a $500,000 grant from Allstate Insurance Corporation. In exchange, DeLorean agreed to build three "safety car" prototypes.

After the initial dimensions and descriptions for the automobile were established, including air bags and other safety features, a contract for final styling and production of a mockup was given to Giorgetto Giugiaro of Ital Design of Turin, Italy, and a contract for actual development of the car was given to Lotus Cars, Ltd., of England. John DeLorean continued limited involvement in the design and development by reviewing and rejecting some proposals which did not meet his original idea, including Lotus's suggestions that the gull-wing doors, stainless steel outer skin, and rear engine be eliminated.

However, many changes were made by Lotus. The ERM technology was dropped in favor of the Lotus VARI plastic. DeLorean engineers, headed by Collins, felt the ERM process was not given a chance. "From the moment John signed with Lotus he gave up on ERM."[9] The Lotus team, headed by Colin Spooner, chose the proven Lotus technology, which created a new array of problems. The Lotus plastic underbody required a steel backbone which added weight. DeLorean, in keeping with his commitment to use metal parts that would not corrode, required that the backbone be dipped in epoxy. According to Spooner, the coating was too thick and added even more weight.

The stainless steel outer skin presented another problem. It was originally chosen because the ERM body could not be painted and needed a metal coat. However, the Lotus plastic body could be painted. The Lotus engineers complained that the metal coat was redundant and heavy. DeLorean insisted that the stainless steel coat be retained.

The Lotus engineers made many decisions based on principles used in making hand-tooled cars. According to DeLorean engineers, many of whom were from GM: "In production cars you never can duplicate the dimensions that finely. You normally design adjustment in so you can cope with that imperfection."[10] An example was the front-end suspension, which eventually prompted three recalls of DeLoreans. Lotus engineers refused to allow adjustable caster and camber. "John [DeLorean] did not want to argue with [Lotus engineers] on issues like suspensions," said Michael Loasby, DeLorean's chief engineer. "He just didn't have time for the details of the project. But attention to detail is everything."[11]

FINANCING

By the end of 1975 the car was far enough along for DeLorean to begin seeking backers. In October 1975, the DeLorean Motor Company filed with the state of Michigan for incorporation.

Finding investors turned out to be more difficult than expected. DeLorean told *Business Week:*

> When you work for GM and you want to build a new foundry in Tonawanda, N.Y., and you need $600 million, you fill out a form and send it away. You might get a phone call or two or you might not. Then within a few months this document comes back with 100 signatures on it which says go spend the $600 million. Unfortunately, that was all I knew about raising money.[12] During 1976 and 1977 the company was constantly scrambling for money to stay afloat.

DeLorean estimated that he would need over $90 million to bring his car on the market.[13] Turning to various government bodies, he sought low-cost loans and outright grants in exchange for the jobs his venture would provide. Under consideration, at one time or another, were sites in Detroit, Texas, Pennsylvania, Maine, Virginia, Alabama, Kansas, Brazil, Spain, France, Portugal, Puerto Rico, the Republic of Ireland, Northern Ireland, and virtually any other area of the world with high unemployment and a willingness to loan or give money.

Serious talks began with Puerto Rico in 1977. The production site was the old, abandoned Ramey U.S. Air Force base. With landing strips and hangars waiting for renovation, DeLorean was enthusiastic about the site. The United States Economic Development Administration and the Farmers' Home Administration guaranteed $40 million in loans, and the Puerto Rican government promised another $17.7 million in loans. In addition, the Puerto Rican government added a $3 million grant to help train the projected 2,000 workers. During the negotiations, however, uncertainty of who had title to the land and a concern about frequent power brownouts became stumbling blocks.

The Republic of Ireland, with a site in Limerick near an airport, proposed the next serious bid. Ireland wanted DeLorean to purchase the land at a much higher price than the assessed value of the property. Overpaying for a factory was the last thing the fledgling company could afford to do, so the Ireland deal collapsed.

A friend of DeLorean's at General Motors called to mention that GM was building a seatbelt factory near Belfast and that DeLorean should give the area serious consideration.[14] Talks with the British government went well. In July 1978, within forty-five days after the bid was submitted, a deal was made. The agreement was for a site near Belfast in Dunmurry, an area that was something of a neutral zone between the warring Catholics and Protestants. Unemployment in the area was a staggering 30%. The Northern Ireland Development Agency and the United Kingdom Department of Commerce promised to guarantee over $113 million in loans and grants in exchange for the over 2,000 jobs DeLorean's venture would bring.[15]

A 72-acre plant was leased in Dunmurry with an existing 50,000-square-foot building to be used as administrative offices and a training center.[16] Two major and ten auxiliary buildings were constructed for production operations. The buildings contained equipment for mold fabrication, body molding, several assembly lines, and maintenance capabilities. Production in the plant could accommodate a maximum of 30,000 cars annually.

PROBLEMS BEGIN TO SURFACE

Complaints about John DeLorean's lack of serious involvement in the sports car project started during the design stage. Reportedly, DeLorean "would wander into your office in his shirt-sleeves, very friendly, but no help at all."[17] The daily operations of the car company seemed to be of little interest to him.

DeLorean spent much of his time on private business ventures. He became very involved in a plan for a government-sponsored mass transit vehicle called *Transbus* and actually sought investors for the Transbus venture at the same time as he was trying to find investors for his sports car company. In 1979, DeLorean discussed producing miniature replicas of antique cars with Mattel. He also tried nonmechanical ventures such as boat chartering, shipping, auto leasing, an offshore oil company, and various real estate developments.

Employees, many of whom had joined the company because of DeLorean's charismatic leadership and commitment to the "ethical" car, became discouraged as DeLorean seemed to lose interest in his dream. No cost controls were established and money was spent frivolously. DeLorean was drawing large salaries from all his ventures and was known for requesting large transfers of money between divisions.

Production Problems

The plant was completed in late 1980, and production began in January 1981. The cars were much more difficult to build than anticipated. Parts that looked fine in engineering drawings proved to be inadequate in one way or another when the time came to screw them on the chassis. An objective of 50 man-hours of assembly time per car turned out to be 140 man-hours per car.

In January 1979, DeLorean told *Newsweek* his car would get 32 miles per gallon on the highway, accelerate from 0 to 60 miles per hour in under 8 seconds, and be driven for twenty to twenty-five years. He estimated the price at $15,000.[18]

When the first car rolled off the assembly line in January 1981, it weighed over 900 pounds more than early projections. According to *Road & Track*, acceleration from 0 to 60 miles per hour took over 10 seconds. The car was given a standard one-year, 12,000-mile warranty and was priced at over $25,000—considerably more than the Corvette, the major competition.

Even so, the DeLorean had a certain mystique—created by John DeLorean, the press, and the years of suspenseful waiting for the first car. Although the first cars arrived in the U.S. in June of 1981, dealers did not have a reasonable inventory until September. The first-month sales figures reflected initial acceptance—550 cars were sold in September. In October, sales climbed to 650; in November, they hit 750; but sales dropped back to 650 in December. In that last quarter of 1981, DeLorean outsold the Porsche 911SC, the Porsche 924, and the Porsche Turbo 924 and was close to the sales figures of the Mercedes 380SL.[19] However, November was to be the peak sales month. The DeLorean was soon plagued with a reputation for quality problems that quickly spread to potential buyers.

Quality Problems

Speedometers did not work. Tachometers did not work. Signal lights, windshield wipers, and fuel gauges frequently failed. In some cases the roofs leaked and the windows would either stick in the upright position or fall out of the channels. In other cases, the gull-wing doors jammed.

DeLorean established Quality Assurance Centers near the ports of entry at Wilmington, Delaware, and Long Beach, California. The centers were to make sure the fit and finish of each car was up to DeLorean standards and that the car worked as it should. Because of all the problems, many cars had to be completely reassembled. The Quality Assurance Centers could not correct everything, though. Doors still jammed. Alternators that were understrength caused problems with the electrical systems. The cooling systems leaked.

In November of 1981, the month when DeLorean sales peaked, a recall of all DeLoreans was announced: a nut holding the front-wheel ball joints together could back off and allow the front wheel to fall off. In December, a second recall was issued. Throttle cables could possibly freeze.

Sales declined to 586 in January. In February, sales dropped precipitously to 223. Beyond February, sales are unreported.

Although the quality problems, recalls, and a prevalent rumor that all DeLoreans were sold out for two years played a role, other factors contributed to the declining sales. A national economy that was slowing rapidly, a traditionally slow winter sales period, and the worst winter in fifty years in the United States also figured prominently in the sales decline. With minimal sales and the escalating cost of dealing with the quality problems, DeLorean's cash flow dropped to a dangerously low level.

COLLAPSE

Perhaps the biggest blow, however, came as a result of the extensive press coverage that had been such a plus in the early years. Headlines appeared containing the one word that stops the potential buyer cold: bankruptcy. Few customers were willing to take a chance on a foundering company, so sales virtually ceased. Creditors, who had wanted DeLorean to do well so that they would be paid, began to worry about the money DeLorean owed them.

Needing more financing to hold the company together, DeLorean searched for investors. Most potential backers became uninterested once the amount needed—$30 to $50 million—was learned. DeLorean approached the British government for more money and was refused. On February 19, 1982, the British government declared the DeLorean Motor Company, Ltd., in receivership.

In March 1982, John DeLorean fired Dick Brown, vice president of DeLorean Motor Company in charge of United States operations. Brown called the Bank of America to inform them of the change (Brown had arranged a $20 million loan with the Bank of America), and four days later the bank called in the loan. Several days of conflict between the Bank of America security guards and DeLorean-hired "muscle men" over the DeLorean cars parked on the lot followed. On March 9, the Bank of America obtained a court injunction to prevent the sale of any DeLorean car and sued to gain possession of almost 2,000 cars as collateral for the approximately $18 million owed. The DeLorean Motor Company claimed it was not in default of the loan.

DeLorean needed help badly. Several possibilities existed. Budget-Rent-A-Car offered to buy 1,000 cars, rent them for $60 per day, and then sell the cars back to the dealers in the fall once DeLorean had recovered. Although the deal would pay off the Bank of America debt, freeing cars to be sold, the main disadvantage was that in the fall 1,000 used cars would be dumped on the market—dampening new-car sales.

Consolidated International, Inc., a liquidation firm, agreed to buy 1,374 cars at $12,500 each to help pay off most of the Bank of America loan. If the DeLorean Motor Company (DMC) was successful, the cars could be bought back at $13,500. If DMC failed, Consolidated would be in the DeLorean business. The deal provided DMC with some breathing room and the restraining order was lifted.

With luck, a discounted price, and good weather DeLorean hoped to sell all the cars at the Quality Assurance Centers. In May, cars slowly began to move to the dealers once more. Meanwhile, with layoffs increasing, production at DMC in Dunmurry was down to thirty-five cars per week. At the end of May 1982, the plant closed. Approximately 8,000 DeLoreans had been built.

Still needing approximately $30 million to save the business, DeLorean pursued investors. Meanwhile, the British government was attempting to line up private financial help. Several deals were proposed, but none were accepted by both DeLorean and the British government. Finally, the British seemed to find a group willing to invest around $100 million. As a show of good faith, DeLorean was to add $20 million. The deadline to complete the deal was October 18, 1982.

On October 19, 1982, John DeLorean was arrested and charged with conspiracy to possess and distribute cocaine, possession and distribution of cocaine, and interstate travel to promote narcotics. On October 25, the DeLorean Motor Company filed for Chapter 11 bankruptcy. On October 29, DeLorean was free on bail, secured with real estate holdings.

Consolidated International, Inc., in return for the $9 million DMC owed, took over the remaining cars in the U.S., plus the inventory of parts and much of the company's furniture. Consolidated bought the rights to sell the cars already built and still in Northern Ireland and planned to sell the cars through the existing dealer network.

In August of 1984, John DeLorean was acquitted of all drug charges. However, his troubles were not all over. On September 20, 1985, DeLorean was indicted by a federal grand jury on 15 counts of racketeering, mail and wire fraud, income tax evasion, and interstate transportation of stolen property. The contention of the prosecution was that DeLorean had defrauded investors of more than $8.5 million.

REFERENCES

1 Hillel Levin, *Grand Delusion—The Cosmic Career of John DeLorean*, Viking, New York, 1983, p. 71.
2 "The DeLorean, Live a Dream," *The Wall Street Journal,* May 22, 1981, p. 1.
3 "John DeLorean Says He'll Show Industry How to Build Cars," *The Wall Street Journal,* Jan. 12, 1979, p. 1.
4 Ibid.
5 Levin, op. cit., p. 165.
6 Ibid., p. 159.
7 "How DeLorean's Dream Wound Up in Belfast," *Business Week,* Aug. 28, 1978, p. 59.
8 "Introducing the 1979 DeLorean," *Motor Trend,* September 1977, pp. 44–48.
9 Levin, op. cit., p. 266.
10 Ibid., p. 267.
11 Ibid.
12 Ibid., p. 170.
13 Ibid., p. 183.
14 John Hilton, "The Decline and Fall of the DeLorean Dream," *Car and Driver,* July 1982, p. 67.
15 Ivan Fallon and James Srodes, *Dream Maker: The Rise and Fall of John Z. DeLorean,* Putnam, New York, 1983, p. 84.
16 U.S. Securities and Exchange Commission, *DeLorean Motor Company, Form 10-K for 11/30/80,* GPO, Washington, 1980, p. 4.
17 Levin, op. cit., p. 235.
18 Ibid., p. 263.
19 Mike Knepper, "DeLorean: A View from the Bunker," *Motor Trend,* July 1982, p. 102.

D'LITES OF AMERICA

Prepared by Faramarz Parsa, West Georgia College,
and Leslie W. Rue, Georgia State University.

During the next 24 hours, 6 out of 10 Americans will eat a fast-food meal. At stand-up counters and drive-thru windows, orders for fast-food items will be placed, filled, paid for, and consumed by more than 35 million people.

D'Lites of America, a health-oriented fast-food chain, is one of the more recent entrants into the industry. The first D'Lites of America restaurant was opened in Atlanta on December 10, 1981.

Less than two years later, five D'Lites of America were in operation, and more than 500 additional units were under development. By 1990, the company planned to have 1,000 D'Lites of America outlets, coast to coast.

FAST-FOOD INDUSTRY

From the small eateries and roadside stops of the past, the fast-food industry has become a giant one, worth more than $38 billion in 1983.

The reasons for the success of fast-food chains are clear. Consistency in the quality of food and service, convenient and well maintained locations, and reasonable prices have combined to make fast food an integral part of the American lifestyle.

Restaurant chains have long been a part of the American scene, with such companies as Nedick's, Chock Full O'Nuts, Stouffer's, and Howard Johnson's as some of the original entrants. McDonald's was the first restaurant chain to standardize physical layout, menu, price, and preparation on a national scale. Over 200 national fast-food franchises have developed since McDonald's originated the fast-food industry. McDonald's, Burger King, and Wendy's currently retain the position of the "Big 3."

With the exception of the advent of the "drive-thru window" by Wendy's in 1969, there have been few landmark innovations in the fast-food industry. The primary emphasis of the industry has been on marketing strategy.

The future of the industry is interesting. A diversity in strategy is becoming apparent among the established fast-food chains. Confronted with the conventional wisdom that the industry is maturing and that changing demographics (an aging baby boom generation) are shifting demand away from traditional fast foods, many chains are trying to develop "upscale" growth vehicles, usually full-service operations that offer liquor. Others are working to fine-tune their "old" concepts to suit the consumers of the eighties. Although "mature" is the adjective experts use to describe today's fast-food marketplace, it appears that each company is pursuing a different strategy to capitalize on its target market segment. Continuing increases in advertising budgets and comparison advertising are both telltale signs that the market is indeed in the mature stage of its life cycle.

The demographics of the consumers can be summarized in a survey performed by R. H. Bruskin Associated of New Brunswick, New Jersey. The study, based on a sample of 1,000 adults across the country, looked into different aspects of consumer habits related to fast-food usage. Initially, Bruskin discovered that the younger the adult, the greater the frequency of visits to a fast-food restaurant. In an average month, adults between the ages of 18 and 24 will have eaten at a fast-food restaurant 8.1 times, compared with roughly 3 times a month for adults over the age of 50. In addition, men outspent women in paying for their meals. The average adult fast-food meal ticket is $3.78. Exhibit C12.1 shows the results of the survey.

Other interesting demographics revealed are that families with nonworking mothers tend to eat at fast-food restaurants less frequently than families with working mothers, 89% vs. 96%. With the exception of the past recessionary period, the percentage of the population eating away from home has risen from year to year, as has the percentage of women in the labor force.

The restaurant industry will face major challenges over the next few years. Customers are growing up, their demands are increasing for more sophisticated dining experiences, and market concentration is making competition very keen.

The trend expected to have the greatest impact is the maturing of the baby boom generation. The current group of 25- to 44-year-olds is better-educated, more sophisticated, and more affluent than previous generations. As a result, they are demanding more from a dining experience and, thus, the need for greater food quality, dollar value, and menu variety will likely increase.

EXHIBIT C12.1 SURVEY OF FAST-FOOD CONSUMERS

Age group	Frequency of eating at fast-food restaurant	Amount spent on meal	Men	Women
18–24	8.1	Less than $2.50	19%	31%
25–34	5.1	$2.51–$3.00	28%	28%
35–49	4.3	$3.01–$4.00	25%	19%
50–64	2.9	More than $4.00	27%	18%
65+	2.8	Don't know	1%	4%

Source: Advertising Age, Nov. 21, 1983.

Nutrition, exercise, and weight-loss programs are particularly important to this fast-growing population segment. The emphasis has switched to healthier foods and more nutritious entrees, including lighter chicken and fish dishes. Less salt and more fresh fruits and vegetables are becoming more important. Restaurants, which have adapted thus far to changing eating habits, will have to remain responsive.

Competitive Environment

The competition in the fast-food industry is tough and getting tougher. Due to the relative ease of entry (i.e., fairly low capital requirement to acquire a franchise, strong franchise sales support, etc.) many newcomers see an unfilled market niche and venture to exploit it. However, the top-10-fast-food companies remained unchanged in rank in 1982 vis-à-vis 1981. Altogether, the 10 accounted for $17.5 billion in 1982, the equivalent of 52.2% of total industry sales of $33.6 billion. McDonald's (still No. 1), Burger King, and Kentucky Fried Chicken each lost minor market share, while Wendy's recorded a slight gain. With 47.6% of total sales, the hamburger-oriented restaurant category of the fast-food industry continued as the No. 1 segment; steak and full menu restaurants took second place with 21% of total industry sales; pizza and chicken restaurants commanded third and fourth places, respectively, with 10.7% and 9.8% of total industry sales. The Mexican food restaurant group registered the largest year-to-year percentage gain in terms of sales—up 22%. Exhibits C12.2 and C12.3 give a breakdown of the top-10-fast-food companies by annual sales and the U.S. fast-food industry by product group.

Perhaps the main device for attracting customers is the menu. The menu is unquestionably a key variable for success in the industry as stated by many fast-food industry analysts. Salad bars are not the only new items designed to reach different market segments. Chains are trying to broaden their business by offering meals and items that traditionally have not been a part of their menus. These include finger foods (McDonald's Chicken McNuggets), lunches (the Personal Pan Pizza at Pizza Hut),

EXHIBIT C12.2   TOP-10-FAST-FOOD COMPANIES BY ANNUAL SALES ($ MILLION) AND MARKET SHARE

Company	Domestic sales (1982)	United States 1982, %	1981, %
McDonald's	6,362.0	18.9	19.2
Burger King	2,191.4	6.5	6.6
Kentucky Fried Chicken	1,700.0	5.1	5.3
Wendy's Int'l.	1,632.0	4.9	4.7
Pizza Hut	1,329.0	3.9	3.8
American Dairy Queen	1,200.2	3.6	3.4
Hardee's	1,167.0	3.5	3.3
Denny's	740.0	2.2	2.2
Red Lobster	625.0	1.9	1.8
Arby's	575.0	1.7	1.8
Total top 10	17,521.6	52.2	52.1
Total industry	33,592.0	100	100

Source: Advertising Age, Nov. 21, 1983.

EXHIBIT C12.3 TOP-10-FAST-FOOD COMPANIES BY PRODUCT GROUP

Companies	No. of co.	1982	% of mkt.	1983E	% of mkt.	1982–1983 % change
Hamburger, franks, roast beef, etc.	107	$15,990M	47.6	$18,100M	47.2	14.2
Steak, full menu	109	7,043M	21.0	7,849M	20.5	11.4
Pizza	94	3,605M	10.0	4,159M	10.8	15.4
Chicken	30	3,308M	9.8	3,958M	10.3	19.7
Mexican	33	1,305M	3.9	1,576M	4.1	20.7
Seafood	13	1,027M	3.1	1,211M	3.2	17.9
Pancake, waffle	15	916M	2.7	1,006M	2.6	10.6
Sandwich, other	39	398M	1.9	518M	1.3	31.6
Total	440	33,592M	100	38,383M	100	14.3

Source: Lehman Bros. Kuhn Loeb research based on Commerce Dept. data.

breakfast at steakhouses, Mexican food eateries, and menu extenders (Wendy's recently introduced stuffed baked potatoes in a variety of styles).

Overall, much of the industry has responded to various consumer and competitive trends by expanding menus. The hamburger chains, which were experiencing difficulties in 1982, by 1985 offered croissants and other items for breakfast, hot sandwiches, and dinner in a box. In addition, quality is said to have vastly improved. Exhibit C12.4 summarizes the menu development of five popular fast-food chains for three selected time periods.

BACKGROUND

D'Lites of America officially opened its first restaurant in December of 1981. The founder of the fast-food chain is Doug Sheley, who now serves as chairman of the organization. Through his insight and hard work, the chain was formed on his personal ideas.

Sheley's background for this unique concept is well founded. Being a former football player and then manager/owner of several health and fitness centers, he then became owner of 18 Wendy's franchises in eastern Tennessee. During this time people were asking him questions concerning calories and sodium in the food Wendy's served. These questions spurred Sheley into considering the healthfulness and nutrition in fast food.

As a result of Sheley's investigation, he decided to sell his Wendy's franchises, develop his ideas, and form a new company called D'Lites of America. Sheley explained, "Much of my concept came from my lifestyle; I noticed that a lot of my generation was exercising like I was and no one was giving them convenience food compatible with this lifestyle." Coining Miller Beer's "Lite" and the first letter of his name, "D," gives the name orientation of the franchise.

The company develops, owns, operates, and franchises D'Lites of America fast-service restaurants, which emphasize nutrition and offer a selection of "lite" products having fewer calories than comparable foods offered by traditional fast-service restaurants. As of July 31, 1984, the company operated 6 restaurants in the metropolitan Atlanta area. The company expects to open an additional 6 to 10 company-operated D'Lites of America restaurants in fiscal 1985, and it is engaged in various stages of construction, land acquisition, or negotiation for these restaurants. As of July 31, 1984,

EXHIBIT C12.4   MENU DEVELOPMENT OF FIVE FAST-FOOD COMPANIES

Arby's:

1973   Regular roast beef, junior roast beef, super roast beef, Swiss King, hot ham and cheese, turkey deluxe, club sandwich, potato cakes, turnovers, shakes, soft drinks

1978   In addition to the above menu: beef and cheese (American), beef & cheddar, fries, turnovers

1983   In addition to the above menu: King roast beef, bacon & cheddar, beef & swiss, Arby-Q, deli sandwiches (ham & cheese, roast beef deluxe, french dip, chicken, submarine, turkey deluxe, club sandwich), salad bar, Chipwich

Jack in the Box:

1973   Burger, Bonus Jack, Jumbo Jack, Jack Steak sandwich, Moby Jack, Breakfast Jack, taco, fries, onion rings, apple turnover, shakes, soft drinks

1978   In addition to the above menu: Double Jumbo Jack, burrito, super taco, Omelette Rancho, breakfast menu, lemon turnovers

1983   Burgers, Jumbo Jack, Moby Jack, taco, super taco, Chicken Supreme, Ham Cheese Supreme, Beef & Cheese Supreme, Bacon Cheese Burger supreme, taco salad, chicken salad, shrimp salad, chef salad, steak dinner, shrimp dinner, chicken dinner, regular nachos, Supreme Nachos, ham crescent, bacon crescent, sausage crescent, Supreme Crescent, pancakes, scrambled eggs, Breakfast Jack, fries, onion rings, apple turnover, shakes, soft drinks

Burger King:

1973   Hamburgers, double burger, Whopper, Double Whopper, Whopper Jr., Double Whopper Jr., Yumbo, Whaler, fries, onion rings, shakes, soft drinks

1978   In addition to the above menu: steak sandwich, Whaler, sundaes, Ice Burger

1983   In addition to the above menu: bacon double cheese burger, specialty sandwiches on french rolls (chicken, fish filet, ham & cheese, veal parmigiana), salad bar (platter or pita sandwich), breakfast menu

McDonald's:

1973   Burger, Big Mac, Quarter Pounder, Filet O'Fish, fries, Egg McMuffin, turnovers, shakes, soft drinks

1978   In addition to the above menu: chopped beefsteak, soft serve ice cream (cone and sundaes), breakfast menu

1983   In addition to the above menu: McChicken sandwich, Chicken McNuggets (three sizes), McRib sandwich

Wendy's:

1973   Burgers (single, double, triple), chili, fries, Frosty, soft drinks

1978   Kidsnack only addition to the menu since 1973

1983   In addition to the above menu: bacon and cheese burger, chicken sandwich, Garden Spot salad bar, taco salad, hot stuffed baked potatoes (seven different varieties)

Source: Advertising Age, Nov. 21, 1983.

franchisees operated 15 D'Lites of America restaurants located in Florida, Georgia, Louisiana, Missouri, North Carolina, South Carolina, Tennessee, and Virginia. The company expects to open between 35 and 45 additional restaurants during fiscal 1985.

MISSION

The concept of D'Lites is a very visible and identifiable one. D'Lites' mission simply stated is "to be a major contending force in the fast-food restaurant industry by offering light (low-calorie), nutritious food emphasizing quality, service, and cleanliness." This reflects Doug Sheley's personal objectives and his dominating influence over the organization. He views D'Lites as being in the restaurant industry, while his major competitors are in the burger industry.

OBJECTIVES

Extending from D'Lites' mission are its long-range objectives:

1 *Growth*. Establish 300 restaurants within 4 years and 1,000 within 10 years. A ratio of 20% company and 80% franchised is used as a target for ownership. Quality will not be lowered to reach these goals if they prove not to be possible.

2 *Sales*. Each restaurant must realize $1 million or greater in sales per year. Selection of properly evaluated sites will ensure this aim.

3 *Quality*. A high level of cleanliness, service, and consistency of product is expected. Quality will be evaluated by a field supervisor out of operations and then eventually through a field marketing manager.

D'LITES' OPERATING STRATEGIES

The main theme keying D'Lites' early success has been that "the idea sells itself." The recent rage for light food products and healthfulness allowed Doug Sheley to take the idea a step further. Fast food, which has become a mainstay of American life, is renowned for its poor nutrition. The newness and timing of D'Lites has allowed the company to adapt to the environment without having to shed a previous unhealthful image.

The following strategies are the result of D'Lites' objectives and mission.

Menu

The D'Lites menu reflects the main image of the firm's concept. The lite fast-food menu has several major criteria: (1) Traditional taste cannot be compromised; (2) every item has to be competitively priced; (3) extending from this is customer choice or customizing of sandwiches and desserts; (4) above all, the food items must be lower in calories and more nutritious.

Proving that D'Lites' food is lighter and healthier is the aim. For example, a typical fast-food order at a major chain could consist of a quarter pound cheeseburger, french fries, and soft drink. These items total over 1,000 calories. Compared with D'Lites' meal of a cheeseburger on a multigrain bun, baked potato, and sugar-free drink, the consumer saves over 500 calories. The calorie comparison of D'Lites to other standard fast foods shows D'Lites to be 150 to 200 calories lower per item, and about 400 to 500 calories lower per meal.

Coupled with lower calories is the criterion that traditional taste cannot be altered. The reason for this is to avoid the diet or health food image. Instead, the strategy is to imagine D'Lites as having great-tasting food that also has fewer calories.

The latter aim is accomplished through leaner beef and ham, low-calorie frozen yogurt instead of ice cream, vegetable oil for frying fries, and only lightly breaded chicken and fish. The food is still "fast food" except that unnecessary calories are taken out.

The third criterion of menu diversity is related to the anti–health food image. Leaving in the fast-food staples—hamburgers, french fries, etc.—gives even the non–health food consumer an option. The ability to be a fast-food restaurant to all customers is a driving theme. Family orientation is preserved this way by letting the diet-conscious eat with nondiet family members.

A reasonable price criterion is designed to keep D'Lites in the same price ranges as its competitors. An average meal at D'Lites does cost slightly more than the industry average. A slightly higher cost does, however, relate to the target market of an upper-end consumer with the ability to pay for extra quality and more healthful food.

D'Lites' menu strategy is not health food but less fattening and more nutritious versions of traditional fast-food items. The preparation to keep the calories lower has given D'Lites patent rights to several food processing techniques.

Future Menu Strategies

Future expansion of D'Lites' menu will concentrate on introducing breakfast and dinner items. Presently, wine and beer are served in the restaurants to increase dinner traffic.

Traditionally, the fast-food industry has not penetrated into the dinner market, and McDonald's has a strong hold in breakfast fast food. To counter this present situation, D'Lites plans to offer the following items at some point in the future:

Breakfast. Multigrain biscuit, pita bread egg sandwich, fruit cup, lite pancakes and syrup, leaner sausage and ham, and fresh juices

Dinner. Chicken parmigiana with low-fat cheese, hamburger Wellington, croissant stuffed with ground beef and mushroom sauce, and baked chicken and fish

The purpose of this meal expansion is to reach the growing breakfast market and to attract new customers (not just health food eaters) who have never eaten at a fast-food restaurant. Presently, D'Lites' dinner sales constitute 45% of total sales. This is significantly above the industry average.

Building Design

Corresponding to a nontraditional fast-food image, the interior and exterior of all D'Lites restaurants are a contrast to the industry. This strategy again is based upon consumer research. The existing D'Lites restaurants are all free-standing and contain approximately 3,400 square feet and approximately 112 seats.

The building itself is an unusual shape, emphasizing contoured corners and natural lighting from atrium glass windows. Natural blond wood construction and careful landscaping reinforces the theme of brightness.

Similarly, interior design includes wooden tables and padded chairs. Hanging baskets assist in giving D'Lites a greenhouse effect. Finishing the lightness theme is a high-lighted salad bar surrounded by brass and etched glass. As a result of top management's experience at Wendy's, the job station preparation and ordering areas are similar to those of Wendy's. Following typical industry practice, all D'Lites' restaurants have a standard drive-thru service. Exhibit C12.5 provides an exterior and an interior view of a D'Lites restaurant.

EXHIBIT C12.5   EXTERIOR AND INTERIOR VIEW OF D'LITES RESTAURANT

Research and Development

The overall strategy of R&D is to keep ahead of the competition's movement into the lite food concept. Research and development for D'Lites consists of two main areas: (1) food products and (2) market studies. The present size of the company forces research and development to be handled by the vice-president of marketing.

Food Development   The first food product innovation was developed before the first D'Lites opened. D'Lites' multigrain hamburger bun was the result of a $7,500 grant to the University of Tennessee and is a high-fiber, lower-calorie bun.

The strategy of out-of-house product development continues today. Typically a need for a new menu item is perceived and suppliers are approached regarding the production of a low-calorie, more nutritious version of a desired food. This allows the risk taking and expense to be shifted to the suppliers and soliciting innovators.

Many innovators offer their own variations directly to the company. One problem with this approach is that conflicts can arise in maintaining the secrecy of the product while allowing D'Lites to inspect the product.

Market Research   Market research is concerned with two main areas: test marketing of new food offerings and consumer research for particular markets. These areas are related to customer desires and affect one another.

Test marketing of new products is extensive. The company-owned stores are used as test markets. Product results are monitored daily and tested for specific time periods. Considerable expense is continually incurred on consumer research.

The demographics of Atlanta provide a large test and target market of 25- to 45-year-olds, with annual salaries over $25,000. Future test markets for D'Lites will include Denver and possibly Cincinnati. Like Atlanta, these cities were chosen for the demographics and customer type.

Advertising and Promotions

The key marketing strategy is to communicate the correct image of the restaurant and sell people on the idea. Based upon Miller Lite's beer slogan, D'Lites' main slogan is "More of a good thing. And less." D'Lites' advertising strategy uses three main devices—public relations, radio, and print. The largest concentration of effort is in public relations due to the small advertising budget. The 1984 budget is estimated at around $600,000—well below industry levels. The public relations firm of Pringle/Dixon/Pringle, who received a national award for its 1983 D'Lites' campaign, handles all media coverage.

The tactic of promoting D'Lites effectively through nonpaid media is the unique story and concept of D'Lites. The measurable objective is to get an article about D'Lites in the news each week in various sources such as national and local television, newspapers, and magazines, stressing the idea that D'Lites' imagery is played to its fullest.

Print advertising is used irregularly and is not a mainstay of the overall strategy. Included in this area is limited billboarding, direct-mail coupons, and some print ads. Presently, resources do not exist to exploit these sources heavily, nor is there a real desire by the company to use them.

Radio is a new media source for D'Lites. The jingles used on the radio revolve around communicating the quality of food and nutrition D'Lites offers. One of the two company slogans, "Just What America Needs," came from a radio campaign emphasizing lifestyle changes and the need for low-calorie, nutritious fast food.

Two other less publicly noticeable ventures exist as a means of promotion: (1) the sponsorship of an Atlanta Tennis and Golf Tournament and (2) point-of-sale tactics such as the calorie counter menu next to cash registers and the stand-up cards on restaurant tables.

VIEW OF COMPETITION

The restaurant business is highly competitive and is often affected by changes in taste and eating habits of the public, economic conditions, and traffic patterns.

D'Lites competes for restaurant locations, management personnel and other employees, franchises, and customers against a large number of national and regional restaurant chains. Many of the competitors operate with more established products and greater financial resources than D'Lites. Nevertheless, management believes that D'Lites presently enjoys the competitive advantage of being the first to use the lite-nutritious concept.

Sheley has said openly that the greatest competitive threats are from proven hamburger and/or chicken restaurants. Competing chains can offer nutritious additions to their menus, such as baked potatoes, salad bars, and chicken sandwiches.

ORGANIZATION

Structure

D'Lites' administrative structure is divided through departmentalization. Each functional area is headed by a vice president who reports to the president, Jeff Miller. Development of organizational structure and staffing has been based entirely on expected need. Presently the following departments exist.

Operations. Internal operations of each restaurant that is company-owned

Franchising. Receiving applications, legal aspects, sales and management, and site acquisition

Franchise operations. Operating manual, preoperating menu, SWAT team, and control of quality

Advertising and public relations. Promotions such as the tennis tournament, in-house direct-mail coupons, billboards, print media, radio, golf tournament, Promo kits, articles on D'Lites, work with public relations firm Pringle/Dixon/Pringle

Marketing. Pricing structures, developing franchise marketing, R&D on new products, and market research

Information systems. Computer system installation programming

Accounting and control. Generation of all company and restaurant accounting statements and company payroll

Training. Instructing hourly employees, managers, supervisors on procedures, policies, and value system

Purchasing. Dealing with suppliers

Human resources. All personnel relationships, hiring, interviewing—mainly managers and hourly employees

EXHIBIT C12.6   D'LITES ORGANIZATION STRUCTURE

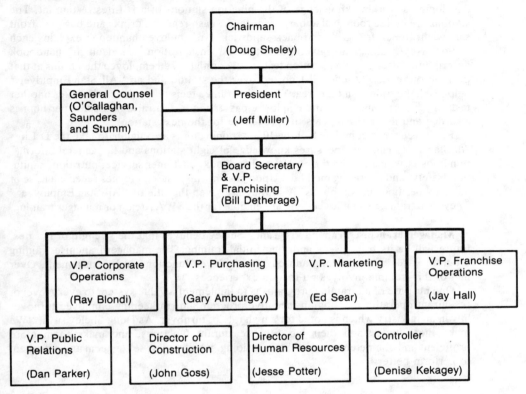

As of July 18, 1984, the company employed approximately 350 people, including 40 administrative, 40 managerial, and 270 restaurant employees, of whom 200 were part-time. Exhibit C12.6 depicts the organization structure as of July 31, 1984.

Board of Directors   The board of directors consists of 10 chairs for the venture capital firms, President Jeff Miller, and Chairman Doug Sheley. Its primary function is to monitor company decisions and to provide a sounding board for Chairman Doug Sheley. An active role is taken by all board members and it meets at least once a month.

Training Program

Because of Doug Sheley's concern for quality management, training programs have been devised for hourly employees, managers, and franchisees. The emphasis is on developing highly efficient motivated labor in what can quickly become mundane tasks in a fast-food operation.

"**All Star**" **Training Program**   This program is for hourly employees and is aimed at developing a working knowledge of the nine job stations of a D'Lites restaurant. The stations are dining room, salad bar, order taker, cash register, drinks and bagging, front sandwich, french fry, grill, and back sandwich. An employee handbook explains each station. New trainees are given a written test on a station, based on the handbook description. After passing a written test at 80% or higher, an employee then trains at that position on-the-job. A checklist posted over the station and an "All Star Employee" help teach the trainee in that area. When the trainee feels ready, he or she takes another test on job performance. If the employee passes the test, a raise of 5 cents per hour is awarded and he or she repeats the procedure for the next station.

Employees who complete 8 of the 10 job training units are eligible to take the D'Lites All Star Test. This test measures knowledge of eight stations and the general information booklet which covers the employee handbook, customer service, nutrition, sanitation, safety, and operating methods. Upon passing this test, employees receive a raise of 40 cents per hour plus a bonus. Also they are given the title of "All Star Employee." They then train new employees and are eligible for the SWAT team or manager training.

Manager/Franchise Training Program   Sheley believes that the strength of D'Lites' future will be its franchisees and their initial training. The manager/franchise training program is seven weeks long and covers employee functions and management. Over half of this training involves on-the-job experiences.

One purpose of all training programs is to implement a value system to every level of restaurant operations. Using an incentive program aids in keeping employee turnover low in an industry which is noted for a high rate of turnover. As Doug Sheley says, "We make them understand their jobs, the restaurant functions, and make them more proficient and competent at what they are doing, which builds self-esteem and gets them to perform better."

Corporate Culture

The general feeling of staff and employees of D'Lites is one of upbeatness and opportunity. As exemplified by the training program, everyone in the organization is being given a chance to grow with the company. Internal promotion supplements this feeling. Growth naturally will necessitate outside hiring for key positions such as research and development. Employees do feel the opportunity to demonstrate performance and to be recognized.

Doug Sheley himself is the basis for much of D'Lites' optimism. His enthusiasm bolsters team spirit. Sheley has been known to work in company restaurants during peak periods. He stresses involvement, saying, "I want to be sure that I lead through exemplification rather than dictation. I try to set an example in everything I do." This competitive spirit runs through all levels of the organization.

CONTROLS

With the emphasis on departmentalization, any changes distinct to one area are resolved by the vice president of that area. Included in this are procedural, employee, and reporting changes. Each vice president must establish his own policies beyond company standards.

Policies or procedures affecting the whole company or another department must go before a review board. The board usually consists of Chairman Doug Sheley and all vice presidents affected by the proposed change. A typical example is the "product board," which reviews all new product and equipment proposals. The product board includes Chairman Sheley and members from operations, marketing, and advertising. First, a decision is made as to whether or not the product or equipment fits the D'Lites' concept. If it does, then all possible problems concerning introduction must be worked through. Once the product board feels comfortable with all angles of the proposal, it then goes to the board of directors. There, a final decision is made on the proposal after a review presentation. The board meets at least once a month to review all areas of the firm.

Franchising

Franchising is the most important area for initially controlling D'Lites' growth and high quality standards. Since the first D'Lites opened in December 1981, over 5,000 applications have been received requesting franchise ownership. This includes requests from 24 countries including the first international franchise in São Paulo, Brazil. Presently, D'Lites is not accepting franchise applications.

Franchise Procedure

1 *Application approval.* Every applicant must complete a detailed application form. Information from this form determines the applicant's ability to meet the franchising board for a personal evaluation.

2 *Franchise approval.* The franchise board conducts personal interviews and bases its selection on qualifications: (1) personal integrity congruent with D'Lites' image; (2) financial adequacy; (3) franchise fast-food experience. Franchises are sold by territory with a minimum purchase of four per area. Associated costs with purchases are $25,000 per franchise unit and $750,000 approximate start-up cost for each. Many entrepreneurs outside the fast-food business have requested franchises. A qualified operating partner must then be found in order to expedite a franchise request. The main reason for this qualification is the difficult time constraint in training someone in fast-food operations.

3 *Site approval.* Franchisees must select their own sites for their territory and make real estate purchases. A site inspector from D'Lites completes a preliminary market search before the land is purchased. Frequently site acceptance is a major control factor in ensuring the goal of at least $1 million annual sales.

After acceptance of a site, all zoning, public utilities, and legal procedures must be completed by the franchisee. A franchise administrator oversees this period, giving legal advice and interfacing with state and federal officials.

4 *Construction and operations.* Construction of D'Lites restaurants must conform to the patented design and standard decor. A pre-opening manual describes all details of setting up a D'Lites' operation. Suppliers must be contacted for purchasing and meet food specifications crucial to the company concept.

Two weeks prior to opening, a traveling training team, called the SWAT team, arrives to instruct hourly employees and demonstrate a proper operating system. This support group remains until at least one week after opening.

5 *Franchise supervision.* Chairman Doug Sheley stresses the importance of quality franchise ownership and initial restaurant establishment. The chairman is quoted as saying, "When I think of the future of this company I think of the strength of the franchisees."

A regional franchise supervisor oversees all restaurants in a given region. Operations are the focus of the regional supervisor. Product preparation, service, and efficiency must be closely observed. D'Lites' motto of quality-service-cleanliness must be upheld. Additionally, each franchisee must submit weekly sales and marketing reports as well as quarterly accounting statements.

In the future, field marketing managers will inspect restaurants. Their role will be to act as problem shooters for all areas of a restaurant. Field marketing managers will also be responsible for seeing that all problems are rectified as soon as possible.

Account Control System

Presently, the focus of accounting for each restaurant is to monitor costs and deviations from expected standards. Each restaurant generates weekly and daily expense forms. A quarterly list of financial statements is also developed for each unit. Deviations in earnings and costs are scrutinized carefully by the corporate staff.

The information system used by D'Lites restaurants is still in the developing stages. In the future, customized programs will allow quick monitoring under the system known as ROSS. A part of this is advanced cashier equipment which keeps track of sales and instantly classifies sales data into usable forms. Other future improvements will include personal computers for daily relaying of information to the company's mainframe facility in Atlanta.

Financing

The initial financing of D'Lites was a personal investment from founder Doug Sheley. His start-up cost in developing the first restaurant, market research, and food was $800,000. Financial growth of the company in the first year came from selling franchise rights and operating profits.

Publicity of the chain and interest in it grew until several large investors were attracted. The first large funding came in March 1983. Five venture capital firms contributed $2.5 million for 30% control of the privately held stock. The investors were William Blair venture partners of Chicago; Crescent Fund Ltd. of Atlanta; Continental Illinois Venture Corp. of Dallas; and Northwest Growth Fund, Inc., of Minneapolis.

Selling of ownership gave D'Lites the flexibility to control franchising and monitor growth easier. This action allowed the company to take a more national, rather than regional, scope, and, therefore, attracted more large investors.

Another $26.25 million in financing was received from two investors in August 1983. These groups bought an additional 300 franchises and laid the groundwork for the 1,000-store goal previously set.

Going Public

In August 1984 D'Lites of America, Inc., filed with the Securities and Exchange Commission an initial offering of 1.2 million common shares. This represented 26% of the company's stock expected to be offered to the public at $6.50 to $8.50 a share. With the $8 million or so raised from the issue D'Lites planned to go on an expansion spree.

EXHIBIT C12.7   D'LITES' STOCK PRICE

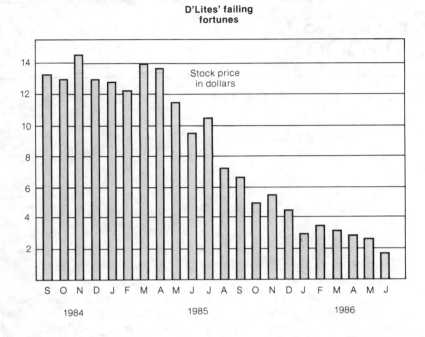

D'Lites' failing
fortunes

D'Lites boosted its original offering to 1.5 million common shares at $9.50 each through underwriters led by William Blair and Co. The company was also authorized to issue up to 1 million shares of preferred stock, $10.00 par value.

On December 11, 1984, the listed stock price of D'Lites of America traded in the over-the-counter market was 13⅝.

D'LITES' FATE

In early 1985, the stock price of D'Lites peaked at $15.50. Athletes including Herschel Walker and Joe Montana signed on for franchises. Units opened in North Carolina, South Carolina, Louisiana, Tennessee, Virginia, Ohio, Kentucky, California, Texas, and many other states.

By spring of 1985, however, problems were beginning to become evident. Per-store profits were dropping, franchisees were not opening new units as scheduled, and the stock price took a steady slide from $14 in March 1985 to under 50 cents in late 1986 (see Exhibit C12.7). By September 1986, both Sheley and Miller had been forced out in favor of Jefferson McMahon, a former Arby's president. McMahon proceeded to make large cuts in the corporate staff and closed unprofitable units. McMahon's strategy was to resurrect the chain by first making the Atlanta units healthy. In August of 1986, D'Lites filed for bankruptcy under Chapter 11. A Chicago investment company then infused $500,000 into the organization in exchange for an option for 60% of the stock. After this last desperate effort failed, the company announced the sale of 9 of its remaining 10 company-owned stores to Hardee's Food Systems Inc. for $1 million, ending a noble experiment to market lower-calorie, more nutritious fast food.

FREDERICK'S OF HOLLYWOOD

Prepared by Jean Hanebury, Salisbury State University.

Frederick's of Hollywood, established in 1946, is an innovative firm that specializes in marketing intimate apparel and related products. For over 30 years, Frederick's of Hollywood has been synonymous with provocative clothing. Products have been distributed through retail outlets in major malls, one freestanding location, and a mail-order operation. Founder Frederick Mellinger has been operating successfully within a low-growth, at times stagnant, retail apparel industry since first opening his own business.

STATISTICS AND TRENDS WITHIN THE APPAREL INDUSTRY

In 1982, retail sales of apparel were an estimated $118.3 billion, a very small increase from $114.4 billion in 1981. Even though disposable personal income increased by 7.1% during that period, a smaller and smaller percentage of income was spent on personal wardrobes. Industry watchers and other analysts still project a gradual recovery for the industry, with growth in sales for 1983 forecast at about 1.2% during the first quarter. A modest growth of 10% was projected for the full year, though apparel companies listed on the stock market have posted single-digit to triple-digit jumps in earnings to date. Because of the impact of the uncertain economic trends in the early eighties, inventories have been kept even lower than usual. Staple sellers like Levi's jeans have fallen off because of stiff competition, and many segments of the apparel industry are seeking new products and markets. The women's apparel industry is indeed changeable. Styles change for each season and consumer tastes are fickle. There are few constants except change in the volatile world of fashion.

The year 1982 saw a record number of bankruptcies in the apparel industry. It is an industry that is characteristically labor-intensive, and one that an entrepreneur can

FIGURE C13.1   SALES INCREASE BY TYPE OF STORE
(Percent Change)

| Year | Women's accessories and intimate apparel | |
	Dept. stores	Specialty stores
1981	8.5	7.5
1980	1.5	4.7
1979	6.5	7.4
1978	6.7	10.1
1977	6.3	4.3

Source: Prepared by caseworker based on data from National Retail Merchants Association.

break into with little capital investment. Backing can be obtained from suppliers, and the enterprising apparel entrepreneur can operate with little more than a desk and a telephone, contracting patterns for production and matching these with prospective clients' orders. This ease of entry contributes to the industry's high attrition rate.

Means of production are just catching up to the twentieth century in the industry. Garments are produced with techniques that are still largely tied to the technology of the sewing machine. Many garments are produced in the Far East, where the means of production may be needle and thread with cheap, plentiful labor. There is an indication, however, that productivity has been increasing through the introduction of computerized stitching machines and other state-of-the-art technology. *Industry Week* recently noted that productivity within the apparel industry is increasing by 4%, compared with 2.8% for all manufacturing industries.

Figure C13.1 presents the percentage change by apparel division for sales increases from 1977 through 1981. The division of women's accessories and intimate apparel is marked for moderate growth throughout the present decade. Increased competition from discount outlets and proliferating catalog-sales operations are other trends affecting the industry as a whole. Within this challenging industry, Frederick's of Hollywood has carved out a unique niche.

FREDERICK'S OF HOLLYWOOD

Frederick Mellinger's parents immigrated to the United States from Hungary in order to give their children an opportunity to succeed in business. While still in high school, Frederick worked as a stock boy for a women's apparel mail-order house in New York City. He was criticized as an "oversexed punk" by his boss when he suggested that nonpractical or sexy underwear be included in the company's mail-order catalog. Mellinger went to work for another mail-order firm, Aldens, after high school graduation. He began as a gofer, running errands for anyone in the office, but after only two years he became the head buyer for intimate apparel. At the same time he was taking night courses in merchandising and buying at a New York City college.

Even when World War II interrupted his budding career, Mellinger continued to plan for his future in the intimate-apparel industry. He did not fail to note trends, and he used his tour of duty in Europe to conduct informal marketing research with soldiers. He noted that the men were all impressed and intrigued by the pure silk and lace underwear that European women favored.

Upon his return to New York, Mellinger rented a loft and opened his own mail-order firm with only $100 in capital. His original catalog included line drawings and merchandise he obtained on consignment. He placed ads in women's and detective magazines. Calling his new firm Frederick's of Fifth Avenue, Mellinger was instantly successful. He was able to reinvest his earnings into the business and move to California after only two years.

A BRIEF RETAIL HISTORY

After moving to California, Frederick Mellinger operated his growing mail-order business from a rented storefront. He pioneered romantic fashions, including black lingerie and lacy, abbreviated garments. By 1952, Mellinger was ready to open his first retail store on Hollywood Boulevard in Los Angeles, California. By 1983, there were 144 boutiques in 34 states and a catalog with more than a million subscribers. With one exception, the Hollywood store, Frederick's retail outlets are located in shopping malls. Private Moments, a second group of stores, is designed to appeal to an upscale clientele. At present, there are four of these retail outlets targeted at the more conservative woman. They carry a line of brand-name merchandise. All Private Moments outlets are located in Southern California. Currently, Frederick's engages in three distinct businesses: Frederick's of Hollywood retail stores, Frederick's mail-order catalog, and Private Moments retail stores.

Merchandise

Merchandise includes lingerie, dresses, sportswear, and foundation garments at moderate to high prices. Sexual paraphernalia, books, and costumes for men and women are included in the catalogs and retail outlets. According to the Frederick's of Hollywood annual report, "Pride of craftsmanship in clothing design, quality materials and fine tailoring characterize the Frederick's look." The company specializes in ultrafeminine, glamourous fashions and accessories. Only 25% of the items available through Frederick's of Hollywood are designed by the company. Frederick's does not manufacture any of its merchandise. Suppliers number several hundred and are located in various parts of the United States and abroad. No one supplier provides a major portion of the goods sold. Mellinger has framed his career on bringing shocking fashions to the world. Typical headings on the pages of a recent catalog announce the following: "Make waves . . . make magic!" "Luscious Lace!" The emphasis is definitely on pleasing your man and "bare as you dare."

Frederick's provides items that may not be currently in vogue, like jumpsuits and miniskirts, but that still have a loyal customer base. The company carries a line of clothing and accessories that are considered sexy although they may no longer be in style. The men's wear line follows the same style as that established in the women's wear line. Typical headings for pages of the men's line catalog read: "You deserve R-e-a-l Silk!" and "Sexy fish-net briefs." Mellinger has successfully taken advantage of the sexual revolution and changing attitudes toward sex. Sex manuals have been added to catalog offerings. The Hollywood image and the sexual fantasy aspect are an explicit part of the corporate identity. The merchandise serves to emphasize Frederick's expressly stated mission: "To operate as a national retailer and mail order company which sells fantasy in the guise of lingerie, outer wear and foundation garments, and paraphernalia to customers who wish to be sexually active."

FREDERICK'S PHILOSOPHY

Frederick Mellinger likes to sum up his success in these words: "You see fashion changes. But sex is always in style. I don't carry anything—no matter how fashionable—that doesn't make women look sexy. I sell a look!"

The principal business of the company is specialty retailing, operating a chain of women's boutiques and a national mail-order business. According to Frederick, every woman is a potential customer whether she is single, married, old, or young. The goal of Frederick's is to cater to a woman's desire to be sexy and beautiful. There is a mystique about the image of Hollywood that makes people think they can become movie stars by adorning themselves with items that have the "Hollywood name or image." Frederick's merchandise is designed to be uniquely glamorous, appealing to the startlingly unconventional and daring. Mellinger firmly believes that most women dress to please men. To support this contention, he has a file cabinet of letters thanking him for everything from a thrilling evening to a rescued marriage.

Management Philosophy

Several tenets underlie the management philosophy at Frederick's of Hollywood. There is a stringent policy of guaranteeing customer satisfaction, supplying excellent customer service, and providing high-quality merchandise.

CORPORATE PERSONNEL

Frederick's of Hollywood began as a one-man operation. Mellinger holds 59% of the stock in this family-held corporation. Another 950 shares have been distributed to other stockholders. Frederick Mellinger is listed as chairman of the board and CEO for the corporation and is also listed as chairman of the Frederick's of Hollywood stores and Private Moments, Inc. He is chairman of the executive committee in charge of long-range planning for all operations. At 69, Mellinger is also in demand for various public relations activities to promote the Frederick's of Hollywood image.

The only top subsidiary office Mellinger does not hold is head of the mail-order division. Joseph A. Nussbaum, age 70, was made head of this division in 1982 after 20 years with the corporation. The corporation is a highly centralized entity organized under mail-order and retail divisions with Frederick Mellinger firmly in charge.

OPERATIONS

The corporate office and Mellinger make virtually all decisions involving merchandise selection, pricing, inventory markdowns, new retail outlets, etc. Very little discretion is left for the store managers and field supervisory personnel. There are 14 field supervisors, who are each assigned a regional group of stores. The supervisor for the Atlanta

FIGURE C13.2   FREDERICK'S OF HOLLYWOOD, INC. AND SUBSIDIARIES CONSOLIDATED BALANCE SHEET

	1982	1981
Assets		
Current assets:		
Cash and equivalents	$ 3,947,000	$ 4,638,000
Accounts receivable	286,000	185,000
Marketable securities—preferred stock	211,000	194,000
Merchandise inventories	4,333,000	4,115,000
Prepaid expenses	882,000	827,000
Total current assets	9,659,000	9,959,000
Property and equipment, at cost:		
Land	504,000	504,000
Buildings and improvements	3,469,000	3,328,000
Fixtures and equipment	3,715,000	3,357,000
Leasehold improvements	3,584,000	3,001,000
	11,272,000	10,190,000
Less accumulated depreciation and amortization	3,295,000	2,949,000
Net property and equipment	7,977,000	7,241,000
Other assets	111,000	68,000
	$17,747,000	$17,268,000
Liabilities and stockholders' equity		
Current liabilities:		
Accounts payable	$ 2,292,000	$ 2,630,000
Current installment of long-term debt	190,000	95,000
Accrued payroll	232,000	128,000
Accrued profit sharing and bonus	225,000	335,000
Other accrued expenses	294,000	325,000
Income taxes	146,000	253,000
Total current liabilities	3,379,000	3,766,000
Long-term debt	1,614,000	1,804,000
Deferred income taxes	275,000	127,000
Stockholders' equity:		
Capital stock of $1 par value. Authorized 2,000,000 shares; issued 1,571,000 shares (1,417,000 shares in 1981)	1,571,000	1,417,000
Additional paid-in capital	1,294,000	143,000
Retained earnings	9,614,000	10,011,000
Total stockholders' equity	12,479,000	11,571,000
Commitments		
	$17,747,000	$17,268,000

Source: Annual Report.

area, May Margarali, indicated that these positions primarily involve supervising personnel and acting as a corporate watchdog to make sure daily sales are reported directly to corporate headquarters. The field supervisors report directly to the director of stores, who reports directly to Robert Hansen, president of the retail subsidiary. Figures C13.2 through C13.7 provide financial data from the latest annual report.

FIGURE C13.3   FREDERICK'S OF HOLLYWOOD, INC. AND SUBSIDIARIES CONSOLIDATED STATEMENT OF EARNINGS

	1982	1981	1980
Net sales	$41,552,000	$39,300,000	$32,614,000
Cost and expenses:			
Cost of goods sold, buying and occupancy costs	22,355,000	20,426,000	17,304,000
Selling, general and administrative expenses	16,904,000	15,336,000	12,514,000
	39,259,000	35,762,000	29,818,000
Operating profit	2,293,000	3,538,000	2,796,000
Other income (expense):			
Interest income—net	231,000	415,000	440,000
Miscellaneous	288,000	223,000	22,000
	519,000	638,000	462,000
Earnings before income taxes	2,812,000	4,176,000	3,258,000
Income taxes	1,349,000	1,945,000	1,557,000
Net earnings	$ 1,463,000	$ 2,231,000	$ 1,701,000
Net earnings per share	$.93	$1.44	$1.10

Source: Annual Report.

FIGURE C13.4   FREDERICK'S OF HOLLYWOOD, INC. AND SUBSIDIARIES CONSOLIDATED STATEMENT OF STOCKHOLDERS' EQUITY

	Common stock		Additional paid-in capital	Retained earnings
	Shares	Amount		
Balance at August 31, 1979	$1,403,000	$1,403,000	$ 95,000	$ 7,123,000
Exercise of stock options	8,000	8,000	16,000	
Net earnings	. . .	. . .	. . .	1,701,000
Cash dividends	. . .	. . .	. . .	(493,000)
Balance at August 29, 1980	1,411,000	1,411,000	111,000	8,331,000
Exercise of stock options	6,000	6,000	32,000	
Net earnings	. . .	. . .	. . .	2,231,000
Cash dividends	. . .	. . .	. . .	(551,000)
Balance at August 28, 1981	1,417,000	1,417,000	143,000	10,011,000
Exercise of stock options	12,000	12,000	31,000	
Net earnings	. . .	. . .	. . .	1,463,000
Cash dividends	. . .	. . .	. . .	(598,000)
Stock dividend	142,000	142,000	1,120,000	(1,262,000)
Balance at September 3, 1982	$1,571,000	$1,571,000	$1,194,000	$ 9,614,000

Source: Annual Report.

FIGURE C13.5 FREDERICK'S OF HOLLYWOOD, INC. AND SUBSIDIARIES CONSOLIDATED STATEMENT OF CHANGES IN FINANCIAL POSITION

	1982	1981	1980
Working capital provided:			
Net earnings	$1,463,000	$2,231,000	$1,701,000
Items which do not use working capital:			
Depreciation and amortization of property and equipment	874,000	664,000	476,000
Deferred income taxes	148,000	1,000	(10,000)
Working capital provided by operations	2,485,000	2,896,000	2,167,000
Issuance of purchase money promissory note	. . .	1,899,000	
Proceeds from the exercise of stock options	42,000	38,000	24,000
Total working capital provided	2,527,000	4,833,000	2,191,000
Working capital used:			
Cash dividends declared	598,000	551,000	493,000
Net additions to property and equipment	1,610,000	2,063,000	654,000
Purchase of office building	. . .	2,675,000	
Decrease in long-term debt	190,000		
Other (net)	42,000	66,000	35,000
Total working capital used	2,440,000	5,355,000	1,182,000
Increase (decrease) in working capital	$ 87,000	$ (552,000)	$1,009,000
Changes in components of working capital:			
Increase (decrease) in current assets:			
Cash and equivalents	$ (691,000)	$ (219,000)	$ 702,000
Accounts receivable	101,000	(16,000)	(1,000)
Marketable securities—preferred stock	17,000	(47,000)	(58,000)
Merchandise inventories	218,000	687,000	616,000
Prepaid expenses	55,000	(97,000)	88,000
	(300,000)	308,000	1,347,000
Increase (decrease) in current liabilities:			
Current installment of long-term debt	95,000	95,000	
Accounts payable and accrued expenses	(375,000)	1,001,000	(61,000)
Income taxes	(107,000)	(266,000)	399,000
	(387,000)	830,000	338,000
Increase (decrease) in working capital	$ 87,000	$ (522,000)	$1,009,000

Source: Annual Report.

Retail Operations

Nearly two-thirds of Frederick's revenues are derived from the corporation's retail stores located throughout the United States. With the exception of the 5,100-square-foot Hollywood Boulevard store, Frederick's of Hollywood operates from small boutiques ranging from 900 to 1,500 square feet. Retail outlets are decorated in hot colors of pink and purple to evoke the desired Hollywood image. Merchandise is attractively and provocatively displayed. Each outlet is strategically located in heavy-traffic shopping

FIGURE C13.6 FREDERICK'S OF HOLLYWOOD, INC. AND SUBSIDIARIES FIVE-YEAR FINANCIAL SUMMARY
(Not Covered by Accounts Report)*

	1982	1981	1980	1979	1978
Operating results:					
Net sales	$41,552	$39,300	$32,614	$27,941	$25,654
Gross profit	19,197	18,874	15,310	12,665	11,464
Earnings before income taxes	2,812	4,176	3,258	1,971	1,656
Net earnings	1,463	2,231	1,701	1,027	881
Earnings per share†	.93	1.44	1.10	.67	.58
Cash dividends per share†	.38	.35	.32	.29	.29
Weighted average shares outstanding†	1,565	1,554	1,549	1,540	1,529
Financial position at year-end:					
Working capital	6,280	6,193	6,715	5,706	5,112
Total assets	17,747	17,268	12,915	11,355	10,385
Long-term debt	1,614	1,804	—	—	—
Stockholders' equity	12,479	11,571	9,853	8,621	8,018
Equity per share†	7.97	7.45	6.36	5.60	5.24
Financial ratios:					
Net earnings as a percent of sales	3.5%	5.7%	5.2%	3.7%	3.4%
Return on average stockholders' equity	12.2%	20.8%	18.4%	12.3%	11.3%
Current ratio	2.9	2.6	3.3	3.2	3.3

* In thousands except percentage and per share data.
† Adjusted to reflect the 10% stock dividend distributed March 29, 1982.
Source: Annual Report.

FIGURE C13.7 COMMON STOCK OF FREDERICK'S OF HOLLYWOOD, INC.*

	1982	1981	1980
Market price ranges†			
First quarter	$ 9¾–7½	$ 6¾–5¼	$3¾–2⅞
Second quarter	13 –8⅝	6⅛–5⅜	5½–3½
Third quarter	9 –6⅝	8½–5⅝	4⅞–3⅜
Fourth quarter	6½–4⅞	12½–7	5⅜–4⅝
Dividends‡			
First quarter	$.09	$.08	$.08
Second quarter	.09	.09	.08
Third quarter	.10	.09	.08
Fourth quarter	.10	.09	.08

* Traded on the American Stock Exchange. Ticker symbol: FHO.
 † Sets forth the closing high and low market prices per share on the American Stock Exchange of the company's common stock since December 1, 1981. Until November 30, 1981, the common stock was traded in the over-the-counter market, and the respective high and low market prices included are based on the bid prices.
 ‡ Set forth quarterly cash dividends per share of common stock for the past three years.
Source: Annual Report.

centers. Leases are usually negotiated for a ten-year period and are renewable. Frederick's must pay a base rental fee plus a percentage of sales for each store. Because retail outlets are kept small, the inventory turnover rate is high. Eighty percent of the stores reach the break-even point within six to eight weeks of opening. The total cost of opening a Frederick's of Hollywood outlet is about $50,000. Approximately $20,000 represents the cost of the merchandise and about $30,000 is preopening setup costs. There is only a 15% overlap of retail and mail-order merchandise. About 50% of the retail outlets are devoted to outer garments like dresses and costumes, while only 20% of the catalog offerings are outerwear.

Retail stores are managed by company-trained female managers and are operated by only three or four people. Frederick's seeks attractive, mature women as retail store managers. These individuals are believed to have more experience in assisting customers with fitting apparel and selecting the proper purchase.

Mail-Order Operations

Mail-order sales are generated through catalogs that are distributed internationally 11 times a year. Each catalog contains about 72 pages of merchandise. The catalogs are not sophisticated, containing low-quality photographs of live models and varicolored line drawings which parallel Frederick's original mail-order catalog. Approximately 21% of catalog recipients place an order. The average order is $54. The catalogs convey a definite sexual orientation and invoke Frederick's "total look" philosophy. The layout and offerings through the mail-order outlet have changed little in the last 35 years. All mail orders are filled at the corporation's Hollywood warehouse.

The mailing list is generated internally. Approximately 12 to 14% of the list is subscriptions, resulting in $700,000 in revenue which defrays some of the production costs. In order to update the mailing list, the 1984 catalog offered a free gift to anyone who would send in a friend's name to add to the list. In 1983, the list was cut by 4% in an attempt to narrow the target market to those who actually made mail-order purchases. Frederick's does not provide copies of its catalog to retail store customers. Mail orders still account for about 37% of Frederick's business.

Private Moments Operations

The new upscale retail operation, Private Moments, is just getting started. These stores merchandise designer names. They have twice the space of the Frederick's of Hollywood outlets and are decorated in more subdued colors like pewter and earth tones. The garish Hollywood image is not part of the new decor. A catalog that carried the new, higher-priced merchandise offered through Private Moments retail stores resulted in a $713,000 operating loss. No follow-up has been conducted by the corporation to discern why the upscale catalog failed. There is conjecture, however, that the failure was the result of a poorly conceived mailing list.

Linking Operations

Increased operating costs have affected all three of Frederick's retail vehicles. Although operations for Frederick's and Private Moments are separate, especially in terms of public identity, both retail operations have been facing increasing long-term lease costs.

Increasing real estate taxes and a higher percentage of sales charges must be covered. Escalating cost of goods sold and increasing labor costs affect all three operations.

MARKETING

Frederick's has a 38-year-old, worldwide reputation for its pioneering efforts in the development and sale of intimate apparel. Approximately $4,393,000 is spent each year on advertising. All ad campaigns are handled by an in-house agency. Retail ads are placed in Sunday papers, and catalog ads are still placed in selected women's magazines such as *Cosmopolitan* and *Family Circle*. Ads are small and black-and-white. At present, these ads appear in about 60 national women's and men's magazines with a monthly readership of over 20 million. Public relations are free-lanced to a one-person operation.

Retail promotions are limited to fashion shows held in the malls several times each year. The corporate office handles all arrangements for these periodic shows. Mail-order promotions are held twice a year through two sales catalogs sent to the people on the Frederick's mailing list. In addition, the catalogs operate as test marketing devices for products that may be introduced to one or more Frederick's retail outlets.

Mellinger himself is an advertising asset in constant demand by the media. He often shows off his scandalous fashions to audiences on *Phil Donahue, Mike Douglas, Hour Magazine,* and regional television talk shows. Mellinger has also received a great deal of free publicity from articles in major newspapers and magazines. The result is that the public associates sexy clothing with Frederick's of Hollywood.

Frederick's customers include an increasing spectrum of people from all walks of life. When Frederick's first made its apparel available, much of the trade was from show girls, etc., who no longer had to have their costumes custom-made. By the 1970s, young adults, older individuals, and women and men from all walks of life had become Frederick's market. Over 65% of Frederick's customers are married. The primary target market consists of married women with household incomes of $25,000 or less a year. Therefore, customers' family incomes run 25% below average.

FINANCE

For the year ending December 31, 1983, Frederick's reported earnings of $1,039,000, a decrease of 28.98% from 1982. Net sales are increasing due mainly to the opening of new stores. For the last several years, however, at least four stores a year have been closed because of nonrenewal of leases or financial losses. In 1982, the average sales per store were $216,882, compared with the 1983 figure of $222,381. The industry average of sales growth was 3.3%. Liquid assets have decreased, while merchandise inventories have increased. And while earnings per share have been steadily declining, cash dividends have been steadily increasing. Selling and administrative expenses have also been increasing over the last several years. Since the corporation is so closely held, the average price per share of stock fluctuates very little.

COMPETITION

Competition within the intimate-apparel industry, although not yet intense, is growing steadily. The intimate-apparel market is now a $6 billion business. New firms are springing up almost overnight to threaten Frederick's market share. Each year there are more and more mail-order houses offering lines of lingerie. Large department stores carry many more lines of intimate apparel and now carry some of the more exciting items that were a Frederick's exclusive in the past. Hard-core pornography catalogs are carrying items that make Frederick's appear tame. Discount outlets carry intimate apparel too.

Department Stores

At one time, department stores did not carry a large line of intimate apparel. Any woman who wanted to purchase unusual lingerie had to look to Frederick's to supply the desired merchandise. Today exotic underwear is carried in large department stores in ever-increasing quantities, styles, colors, and varieties.

Specialty Stores

Specialty lingerie stores are finding their way into shopping centers all over the United States. They carry merchandise such as matching ensemble pieces which department stores may not carry. The lingerie specialty shops have limited merchandise but are another alternative for today's shopper. Most of these shops cater to the high end of the market and do not attempt to promote the "sexual fantasy" image espoused by Frederick Mellinger.

Victoria's Secret

Frederick Mellinger is not the only entrepreneur who had the idea of turning the sale of intimate apparel into a profitable business. A retail firm that is providing Frederick's with stiff competition is Roy Raymond's Victoria's Secret. Raymond knew that he, like most men, was uncomfortable shopping for women's intimate apparel in a department store. Raymond saw this feeling of intimidation as a business opportunity. His first endeavor was a boutique patterned after Victorian salons. Hand-picked saleswomen were trained to help men select sizes and colors when making lingerie purchases. The basic philosophy of Victoria's Secret is romanticism. The merchandise offered is not seen as blatantly erotic apparel but as high-quality, pretty underthings that a man can feel comfortable purchasing for his "lady love." Although Victoria's Secret is still not in the same league as Frederick's of Hollywood, sales have doubled annually since the first outlet began operation in 1978. The company has generated $7.4 million in annual sales with only four retail outlets and a mailing list of 60,000.

DIVERSIFICATION EFFORTS AND FUTURE DIRECTIONS

Frederick's has stuck close to the catalog and retail lines of fashion that launched its success in 1946. There have been two unsuccessful attempts at diversification; one was a line of cosmetics which was an immediate disaster. The diversification marked by the Private Moments retail outlets is an attempt to change the basic image to reach a different market. Along with that new venture, Frederick Mellinger tried a new catalog concept, discussed earlier, which was a financial disaster. Several new Private Moments stores are planned for the coming year. Although sales have been increasing at the four units now in operation, none has yet operated at a profit.

An Interview with Mellinger

Early in 1983 a telephone interview was conducted with Mellinger to try to assess new directions in which Frederick's of Hollywood could maintain its record of success and begin to grow again. Mellinger countered most questions with the response that it would be unfair to stockholders to talk about future plans, as it would jeopardize stockholder confidentiality. At the same time, Frederick Mellinger firmly asserted that Frederick's of Hollywood had no competitors. "We are different, we have different plans and strategies," he said. He stated that the catalog will continue to expand and that "we are consistent in our goals and constantly looking for new growth and innovation; we are not a follower. We are a non-static organization."

Frederick's of Hollywood sells fantasy. Mellinger is quick to state that sex will never go out of style and that there will always be a place for the garments Frederick's offers. At the same time, Frederick's of Hollywood is selling a Hollywood image that may no longer be in style. The ideal Frederick's woman is reminiscent of Jayne Mansfield or Marilyn Monroe. The Hollywood image of the eighties is of a much more active and more independent woman with a very different figure. It is still possible that Frederick's of Hollywood, the corporation, could follow the Hollywood image of the past into a shadow of its former self if it fails to adapt to fashion's ever-changing environment and the stiff, business-oriented competition that marks the apparel industry of the eighties.

GERBER PRODUCTS COMPANY

Prepared by Nabil A. Ibrahim, Augusta College.

BACKGROUND OF THE FIRM

The story of Gerber baby foods dates back to suppertime one Sunday in the summer of 1927. Mrs. Daniel Gerber, frustrated with the task of straining vegetables for her first baby, asked her husband why the baby's food could not be strained at the family cannery in Fremont, Michigan.

Her husband and Frank Gerber, her father-in-law, consented to this innovative idea and began preparations for mass production of the first canned baby foods. This was a new idea since, at the time, most babies were given solely a liquid diet until they were one year old. So, if they were to begin manufacturing baby foods, they would be challenging long-held traditions of baby care with no idea of their potential market capabilities.

Frank Gerber ordered thorough tests of the market possibilities and of the products themselves. Experimental batches were tested on Daniel's daughter as well as other babies with great success. After a great deal of research and careful studies made by both pediatricians and infant clinics, the company launched a large-scale advertising campaign in *Good Housekeeping, Children* (later *Parents*) *Magazine*, the *Journal of the American Medical Association* and other periodicals about the new product line being put on the market in the fall of 1928.

Their task entailed not just advertising the product line, but also convincing parents to adopt new feeding concepts for their children. The product line introduced five strained baby foods: vegetable soups, carrots, peas, prunes, and spinach.

Existing baby foods were sold through pharmacies on prescription and were priced at 35 cents a can. Gerber proposed to sell theirs at 15 cents a can through grocery stores to reach a larger market. To identify the product and to reassure mothers, the "Gerber Baby" symbol was adopted as their logo. This logo soon became famous in many countries around the world.

The sale of Gerber baby foods was first handled through food brokers. They called upon doctors, leaving samples for infant patients, visited homes to tell mothers about Gerber baby foods and to leave samples, and called upon grocery stores in key markets. In the first year sales were $345,000 which was much greater than had been expected. Despite the onset of the Great Depression, Gerber expanded its baby foods output and added new lines.

As sales flourished, a sales office outside of Fremont was established in New York City. In the early 1930s, Gerber was introduced in the Canadian market. Meanwhile, the firm employed scientists in special laboratories, helped farmers improve their crops, published child care pamphlets, and issued classroom guides for home economics and nutrition.

In 1955 the corporate name was changed from Gerber's to Gerber. In 1956, the company was listed on the New York Stock Exchange for the first time. During the 1960s Gerber expanded into many foreign countries. Nonfood baby products were added to the firm's line, which included plastic panties, lotions, toys, and vaporizers. A vinyl baby pants and bibs manufacturer was acquired. By the end of 1969, Gerber offered approximately 80 food products, many baby needs manufactured by divisions and subsidiaries, and mail order insurance policies for young families.

By 1973, Gerber sales were $278 million, and it had become the world's largest supplier of baby foods. Its growth had been achieved partially through expansion and partially through acquisition.

Today, baby food is prepared in four plants in the U.S.: Fremont, Michigan; Oakland, California; Asheville, North Carolina; and Fort Smith, Arkansas. Also, plants are located in Costa Rica and Canada. Gerber offers a variety of approximately 150 foods, in addition to a large variety of merchandise and services for babies and young children. Gerber baby foods are available in 160 countries around the world. Labels are printed in 10 languages. Net sales for 1986 reached $967,865,000. Nonfood products are manufactured at 32 plants in the U.S., 1 in Canada, and 1 in Haiti.

MISSION

For over 50 years, Gerber Products Company has operated under the slogan "Babies Are Our Business." (Figure C14.1a–c). The overwhelming majority of its manufacturing and selling activities are those which are geared toward preschool children. It is proud of having earned the consumers' trust over the years.

The corporate objective is to provide high quality products and services at reasonable prices for families with infants and small children. The Gerber baby, the company claims, is the second most recognized corporate image in the world, after the Coca Cola logo. Other objectives include:

To strive in all things and with all people, to do the best they can and make our best better.

To observe and maintain the confidence of those who buy and use our products and services.

To maintain an organization of which all employees may be proud, and upon which they can depend for fair and consistent management and sound business decisions.

To serve actively as good corporate citizens in all communities where we live and work.

FIGURE C14.1*a*   THE "GERBER BABY"

THIS BABY MEANS BUSINESS

No one in the industry knows babies better than Gerber. For over 50 years we've dedicated ourselves to providing quality products for families with infants and small children. The Gerber baby is a symbol for quality and is recognized and trusted by more parents than any other trademark in baby products.

Source: Company documents.

Gerber Products Company
Corporate Mission

The people and resources of Gerber Products Company and its affiliated companies are dedicated to providing quality products and services at reasonable prices, and to meeting the needs of our customers in a responsible and responsive manner as we have for more than three generations.

Corporate Management will provide strategic planning and direction to:

◊ *maintain our position of leadership in the marketplace*

◊ *maintain our recognition as an authority in the field of infant health, nutrition, and care*

◊ *grow through aggressive consumer marketing and sound diversification and acquisitions*

◊ *protect and increase the value of our shareholders' investments.*

We strive to meet our social responsibilities and to improve the quality of life for our customers, our communities, our shareholders, and our employees.

Our reputation, established on honesty and quality, is a heritage we treasure and must continue to earn every day. We commit ourselves and pledge our resources to the continued quest for excellence so that future generations may also recognize and rely upon the integrity of Gerber Products Company.

Source: Company documents.

FIGURE C14.1c FULFILLING CORPORATE MISSION

Fulfilling Our Mission

- Maintain our position of leadership in the marketplace
  - Gerber baby food brand share was 67% of the domestic market at the close of FY 1987 with distribution in 97% of the nation's supermarkets.
  - Gerber is a major factor in all channels of distribution for infants and childrens apparel.
  - Gerber introduced more new furniture products during the year than any other childrens furniture company.
  - Gerber has the largest sales force dedicated exclusively to selling baby food and a broad line of general merchandise products for parents with young children.
  - Gerber First Foods fruits and vegetables introduced in October, 1986, captured an unprecendented 9% of the strained baby food market by the end of FY 1987.
- Maintain our recognition as an authority in the field of infant health, nutrition, and care
  - More than 8.5 million consumers benefited during the year from Gerber educational film showings and printed materials distributed through pediatricians, other healthcare professionals, and direct mail.
  - The Company and The Gerber Companies Foundation contributed $500,000 during the year to agencies or research studies devoted to child nutrition, health, or care.
  - The Gerber Research Center is the world's largest, private research facility dedicated to infant nutrition.
- Grow through aggressive consumer marketing and sound diversification and acquisitions
  - Television, direct response, and print advertising carried Gerber messages at least 24 times during the year to every target household.
  - A 10-year sales growth rate of 9%, achieved internally and through acquisitions, broadened the Gerber profile from primarily baby food to a broad range of products and services for families with children, including apparel, furniture, pre-school care centers, and insurance.
- Protect and increase the value of our shareholders' investments
  - The five-year return on Gerber stock is 33.9%, compared to 26.5% for the S & P 500.
  - The Company has paid 167 consecutive quarterly dividends.

Source: Company documents.

In its literature, the company asserts that

> No one in the industry knows babies better than Gerber. For over 50 years we've dedicated ourselves to providing quality products for families with infants and small children. The Gerber baby is a symbol for quality and is recognized and trusted by more parents than any other trademark in baby products.

Gerber emphasizes employee pride, plant cleanliness, and excellent quality control standards. Field representatives inspect seeds and take soil samples before contracting with local farmers and growers for their produce. Fresh produce is thoroughly washed and closely inspected before being conveyed from the preparation area to the kitchen. Each ingredient that goes into baby food is checked for impurity and conformity. The food products are tested for texture consistency, taste and color.

THE INDUSTRY AND COMPETITION

The whole spectrum of baby products forms a multibillion-dollar group of industries. Gerber Products Company is involved in every aspect of this group, with its traditional and primary thrust in the manufacturing and selling of baby food. In the United States, approximately $14 billion is spent on infant products during the baby's first year. A significant portion of this amount is spent on baby food.

Approximately 85% of the baby food market is controlled by only three national brands—Gerber, Heinz, and Beech-Nut. The remaining 15% is split up among several local or regional companies. As shown in Figure C14.2 Gerber has been losing some of its brand share to its competition. Figure C14.3 shows the market share of each of the three major brands in each baby food category. Although the competition was aided by a glass scare (suspected tampering) in late 1985 and early 1986, the task of holding this share has not been easy due to fierce competitive tactics.

Beech-Nut

The second largest firm in the baby food industry is Beech-Nut, which is owned by Nestlē's of Switzerland. The size and wealth of the parent company has helped Beech-Nut fight the entry barriers that were set up by Gerber.

Beech-Nut produces a line of food named "Stages." Stages is designed to meet the needs of babies at different stages of their development. Like Gerber, their food is primarily served in ready-to-serve glass jars. With the Stages line, Beech-Nut seeks a competitive advantage by selling a premium baby food at a premium price. Their pricing strategy is based on statistics which show that parents tend to be well-informed about the nutritional needs of their children and less sensitive to price.

FIGURE C14.2   BABY FOOD MARKET SHARES: 1984, 1986

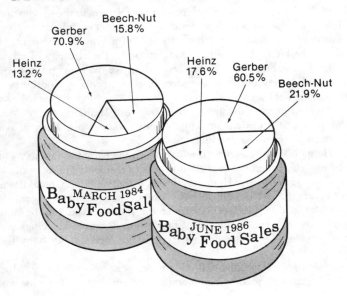

FIGURE C14.3   1986 NATIONAL BRAND SHARES (DOZENS)

Baby food categories	Gerber %	Heinz %		Beech-Nut %
		Wet	Dry	
Strained	53.1	18.4	7.1	21.4
Junior	71.8	7.8	—	20.4
Juices	64.5	11.0	—	24.5
Meats	85.5	5.8	—	8.7
High meat dinners	97.8	2.2	—	—
Cereals	81.5	3.5	.6	13.6
Toddler food	76.9	—	—	23.1
Total	61.4	13.8	3.9	20.9

Source: Company documents.

Beech-Nut was the first to drop salt and modified starches completely from the ingredients of the products. It has recently begun to place brand name products such as Chiquita Bananas and Golden Delicious Apples into its line.

To break through the noise barrier of Gerber's advertising, Beech-Nut spends over $20 million per year on its own advertising. It focuses on an upscale audience—its prime target market. It has also begun to advertise, via television, to the Hispanic community. In addition, mail-out coupons and the print media are used. The latter includes helpful baby care tips to expectant or new mothers.

Heinz

Heinz, on the other hand, competes by appealing to those who are more price sensitive. Heinz manufactures both jar food and an instant or dehydrated food. Heavy emphasis is placed on the latter, which is viewed as a type of competitive advantage. Another advantage Heinz has over its competitors is the strategy of growing its own products.

Basically, however, Gerber and Heinz use the same production methods and quality standards. They both use the stem-injection process to preserve the vitamins without using chemical preservatives.

To help grocers display more baby food, Heinz has developed a plastic bin system that permits the upright stacking of baby food in slots. Thus all available shelf space can be used to show the product.

Heinz is known as the "low-baller" in the baby food industry and has been known to sell its dehydrated products below cost to gain entry into the market. Being a multidivisional food company, Heinz carries a cost advantage. One of the main threats to Gerber is the fact that Heinz sells its baby food to the grocer at a lower price than Gerber. Heinz operates at this price level because the retailer makes more money, is willing to offer generous shelf space, and, most important, passes this savings on to the customer. This cost-saving image appeals to parents who want quality baby food at a slightly lower price.

Heinz spends around $20 million per year on advertising. Much of this money goes into 15- and 30-second commercials for network prime time and daytime television.

Also, it runs full page advertisements in baby care magazines and has a limited number of Hispanic-oriented commercials. In addition to these forms of advertising, Heinz gives free samples of its instant products to hospitals for distribution among new mothers.

Gerber

Since it was the first company to enter into the baby food market, Gerber has established a reputation of being trustworthy. In addition, most smaller competitors never stood a chance to compete against this industry leader in major outlets. Its baby food line is so large it creates a "billboard effect" in supermarkets.

Since Gerber also sells baby products other than food and has the only direct retail sales force in the industry, the company has a distinct advantage when fighting for shelf space. Also, Gerber uses its advanced marketing programs to gain partial control over its distributors. The company considers itself a partner with supermarkets and designs plans to help stores increase their product turnover. In addition, it gives supermarket managers information which can help them better serve their customers.

Nationally, Gerber leads with approximately 60% market share. Yet in certain areas such as Ohio and Kentucky Gerber ranks third in sales.

THE ENVIRONMENT

A major factor in the industry's environment is the suppliers of raw materials. Gerber, Heinz, and Beech-Nut all purchase their raw produce and meats from independent farmers. These farmers are usually located in the area of the production facilities. The suppliers' products must meet the challenge of passing several rigorous quality inspections before, during, and after the growing process. The baby food firms generally have the upper hand with regard to ease of change in suppliers, due to the large number of suppliers usually available to them. In times of drought or flood, however, prices may rise very steeply.

The force exerted by purchasers serves as another factor that shapes the baby food industry. Two important aspects about the baby food market are that the buyer is not the consumer, and that the market is constantly changing as consumers outgrow their need for the products. Based on demographics, the United States baby food market is limited to one household in twelve. The industry's performance centers around adequate forecasting of birth rates. In recent years, Gerber overestimated United States birth rates, and as a result, it overproduced. Currently, the birthrate in the United States is expected to increase 1% annually until the year 1990.

Instant baby food is a major threat confronting Gerber. It is a new product that offers convenience and savings to parents. It requires liquid to be added and allows the parent to prepare just the desired amount without having to refrigerate any leftovers. In August of 1984, both Gerber and Heinz introduced instant baby food, but problems arose and both companies returned their products to the drawing board. Heinz reintroduced the instant baby food but Gerber has not brought the product back. While Gerber and Beech-Nut continue to sell jarred baby food, Heinz continues to expand its variety of instant baby food. Since 1985, Heinz dry products have carved a comfortable niche due to the product's unique characteristics.

Heinz introduced 18 instant products in 1986, and now sells 45 varieties of dry baby food. Although Heinz has captured 10–15% of the entire market with its instant baby food, Gerber has shown no interest in competing. One plausible explanation is that, with its huge market share, Gerber would risk cannibalizing its own sales with even a minimally successful line of instant baby food.

In 1986 glass was reportedly found in Gerber products. Over 200 incidents occurred in at least 30 states. These incidents, however, share no common product, distribution outlet, or manufacturing plant. This caused Gerber's market share to drop 16%, some of which has been gained back. At that time, the FDA inspected 44,000 jars and found no health hazzard. In addition to this, Gerber had installed two years earlier plastic conveyor lines to help prevent glass breakage, product loss, and contamination of their product. Despite these precautions and efforts to reassure the public, this incident cost Gerber over $30 million in sales. Similar incidents had occurred in 1984—the company responded by voluntarily recalling 550,000 bottles of juice. Baby food sales declined 5.7% from $96.9 million in the third quarter of 1983 to $91.3 million in the same 1984 period. Clearly, the possibility of tampering will probably continue to be one of the company's major threats.

With respect to the international market, Gerber failed to enter into the European market at an earlier stage of the industry's development. Recently, however, high levels of income in Europe and elsewhere would appear to make penetration into these markets highly profitable. Nestlé's leads sales in France, Sweden, West Germany, and Japan. Heinz leads in both Canada and the United Kingdom. Morever, the Stages concept of Beech-Nut and the dehydrated concept of Heinz both were first introduced in Europe.

Gerber is attempting to gain ground by opening a plant in Egypt, and it might open one in China, where Heinz has already set up production. In addition, Gerber markets special products that are suitable to different cultures. For example, in Australia it markets strained lamb brains and in Japan strained sushi. In the United States it is manufacturing new products such as strained mango, papaya, guava, and a tropical fruit medley for sale to the Hispanic communities.

Concerning the possibility of new firms entering the market, it is extremely difficult for new entrants to compete against Gerber's long-established quality image and the economies of scale it has achieved in baby food production. Entering this industry requires high capital resources of large investments in machinery and equipment for baby food processing. Competing requires experience and good knowledge of government regulations on content, sanitation, and processing.

When considering the type of distribution channels used by the baby food industry, one finds that Gerber, Heinz, and Beech-Nut operate in basically the same manner. For example, Gerber products are sold only in carload or truckload lots directly to grocery wholesalers and supermarkets to minimize the high cost of shipping. This benefits both the baby food firms and the grocers.

POPULATION TRENDS

In the baby food industry, record sales have been achieved during the past few years. There are four major trends that are largely responsible for these increases:

1 *The rising birthrate.* Since bottoming out in 1975 at 3.2 million, the birth rate has been continually rising throughout the 1980s. Figure C14.4 shows population projections through the year 1995. The number and rate of births by state (1970–1985) are shown in Figure C14.5.

FIGURE C14.4 CHILDREN AGED 0 TO 17, 1985 TO 1995*

(In thousands)	1985	1990	1995
Under 1	3,675	3,698	3,477
1	3,609	3,691	3,497
2	3,552	3,704	3,552
3	3,551	3,707	3,607
4	3,566	3,700	3,660
5	3,546	3,682	3,705
1–5	17,825	18,484	18,022
6	3,415	3,656	3,738
7	3,311	3,606	3,757
8	3,346	3,607	3,763
9	3,097	3,624	3,758
10	3,242	3,605	3,741
11	3,243	3,475	3,716
12	3,299	3,373	3,668
13	3,494	3,409	3,670
6–13	26,446	28,356	29,811
14	3,830	3,161	3,688
15	3,764	3,307	3,669
16	3,696	3,306	3,538
17	3,615	3,362	3,435
14–17	14,905	13,136	14,330
All children aged 0–17	62,851	63,673	65,640

6–13 YEARS OLD

<6 YEARS OLD

14–17 YEARS OLD

Preschoolers should remain fairly constant during the next ten years while primary-school-aged children increase by over 3 million.
Source: U.S. Bureau of the Census.

FIGURE C14.5 LIVE BIRTHS—NUMBER AND RATE, BY STATE: 1970 TO 1985
(Registered Births. Excludes Births to Nonresidents of the United States)

Region, division, and state	Number (1,000)								Rate per 1,000 population†							
	By state of residence						By state of occurrence		By state of residence						By state of occurrence	
	1970	1975	1980	1982	1983	1984	1984*	1985*	1970	1975	1980	1982	1983	1984	1984*	1985*
U.S.	3,731	3,144	3,612	3,681	3,639	3,669	3,697‡	3,749‡	18.4	14.6	15.9	15.9	15.5	15.5	15.7‡	15.7‡
Region:																
Northeast	831	625	656	675	674	682	677	695	16.9	12.6	13.4	13.7	13.6	13.7	13.6	13.9
Midwest	1,038	855	956	928	900	901	900	902	18.4	14.8	16.2	15.8	15.3	15.3	15.2	15.2
South	1,208	1,062	1,232	1,270	1,256	1,267	1,274	1,308	19.2	15.3	16.4	16.2	15.8	15.7	15.8	16.0
West	654	602	768	807	809	819	830	855	18.8	15.6	17.8	17.9	17.6	17.5	17.7	17.9
New England	200	148	162	168	168	172	168	173	16.9	12.2	13.1	13.5	13.5	13.7	13.4	13.7
Maine	18	15	16	17	17	17	17	16	17.9	14.2	14.6	14.7	14.6	14.5	14.3	13.9
New Hampshire	13	11	14	14	14	14	13	16	17.9	13.3	14.9	14.9	14.4	14.6	12.9	15.8
Vermont	8	7	8	8	8	8	7	8	18.8	14.1	15.4	15.4	15.2	15.1	14.0	14.8
Massachusetts	95	68	73	76	76	78	79	83	16.6	11.9	12.7	13.2	13.2	13.5	13.7	14.2
Rhode Island	16	11	12	13	13	13	13	14	16.5	11.3	12.9	13.1	13.2	13.2	13.7	14.0
Connecticut	50	36	39	40	41	42	39	37	16.7	11.6	12.5	12.9	13.1	13.4	12.4	11.6
Middle Atlantic	630	477	495	508	506	509	508	522	16.9	12.8	13.4	13.8	13.7	13.7	13.7	14.0
New York	318	236	239	247	249	251	251	256	17.4	13.1	13.6	14.1	14.1	14.1	14.1	14.4
New Jersey	120	92	97	99	99	101	97	103	16.8	12.5	13.2	13.3	13.3	13.5	13.0	13.7
Pennsylvania	193	149	159	162	158	157	160	162	16.3	12.5	13.4	13.6	13.3	13.2	13.5	13.7
East North Central	754	610	668	645	624	627	623	627	18.7	14.8	16.0	15.5	15.0	15.1	15.0	15.0
Ohio	200	159	169	165	159	159	160	161	18.7	14.7	15.7	15.3	14.8	14.8	14.9	15.0
Indiana	99	82	88	84	81	80	79	81	19.1	15.4	16.1	15.3	14.8	14.6	14.4	14.7
Illinois	205	169	190	184	179	179	176	178	18.5	15.0	16.6	16.0	15.6	15.6	15.3	15.4
Michigan	172	134	146	138	133	136	135	134	19.4	14.7	15.7	15.2	14.7	15.0	14.9	14.8
Wisconsin	78	65	75	74	73	73	73	73	17.6	14.3	15.9	15.7	15.3	15.4	15.3	15.3
West North Central	284	246	288	283	276	274	277	275	17.4	14.7	16.8	16.3	15.8	15.7	15.8	15.7
Minnesota	68	56	68	68	66	67	66	66	18.0	14.4	16.6	16.6	15.8	16.0	15.8	15.8
Iowa	48	41	48	45	43	42	43	42	17.1	14.4	16.4	15.4	14.9	14.6	14.7	14.6
Missouri	81	69	79	77	76	75	79	77	17.3	14.3	16.1	15.5	15.2	14.9	15.7	15.3
North Dakota	11	11	12	13	12	12	13	13	17.6	16.6	18.4	18.8	18.2	17.2	18.5	18.6
South Dakota	12	11	13	13	13	12	12	12	17.0	16.5	19.2	18.5	17.9	17.7	17.6	17.3
Nebraska	26	24	27	27	26	26	26	26	17.3	15.4	17.4	17.0	16.4	16.3	16.5	16.0
Kansas	38	34	41	41	40	40	39	39	17.0	14.9	17.2	17.0	16.7	16.4	15.8	15.9

South Atlantic	574	482	547	563	563	576	574	602	18.7	14.0	14.8	14.7	14.5	14.6	14.5	15.0
Delaware	11	8	9	9	9	9	9	10	19.2	14.0	15.8	15.3	15.2	15.1	15.5	15.8
Maryland	69	53	60	64	64	65	59	60	17.6	12.7	14.2	14.9	14.9	15.0	13.5	13.7
District of Columbia	15	10	9	9	9	10	19	21	20.1	13.7	14.7	14.9	15.0	15.5	30.6	32.8
Virginia	86	70	78	81	81	83	79	83	18.6	13.9	14.7	14.8	14.5	14.7	14.1	14.6
West Virginia	31	28	29	27	26	25	25	26	17.8	15.3	15.1	13.9	13.2	12.6	12.8	13.2
North Carolina	98	81	84	86	84	86	87	90	19.3	14.6	14.4	14.3	13.8	14.0	14.1	14.4
South Carolina	52	47	52	52	51	51	48	49	20.1	16.1	16.6	16.0	15.6	15.3	14.6	14.7
Georgia	97	80	92	90	90	92	92	100	21.1	15.8	16.9	16.0	15.7	15.8	15.7	16.7
Florida	115	106	132	145	149	155	155	164	16.9	12.4	13.5	13.8	13.9	14.1	14.0	14.4
East South Central	248	219	240	230	223	221	224	223	19.4	15.9	16.4	15.5	15.0	14.7	14.9	14.8
Kentucky	60	55	60	57	55	53	52	52	18.7	15.8	16.3	15.4	14.7	14.3	14.0	13.9
Tennessee	72	62	69	67	65	65	70	71	18.4	14.6	15.1	14.4	14.0	13.8	14.9	14.8
Alabama	67	58	64	60	59	59	59	59	19.4	15.8	16.3	15.3	14.9	14.8	14.7	14.6
Mississippi	49	44	48	46	44	44	43	42	22.1	18.3	19.0	17.9	17.0	16.9	16.4	16.2
West South Central	386	361	445	477	470	470	476	483	20.0	16.9	18.7	18.9	18.2	17.9	18.2	18.2
Arkansas	35	34	37	35	35	35	33	35	18.5	16.0	16.3	15.3	15.1	14.9	14.2	14.9
Louisiana	74	68	82	85	83	81	83	81	20.4	17.5	19.5	19.3	18.6	18.3	18.6	18.1
Oklahoma	45	43	52	59	57	54	53	52	17.5	15.4	17.2	18.2	17.2	16.5	16.1	15.7
Texas	231	216	274	298	295	299	306	315	20.6	17.2	19.2	19.4	18.7	18.6	19.0	19.2
Mountain	172	177	226	237	233	232	230	236	20.7	17.9	19.9	19.6	18.9	18.4	18.3	18.5
Montana	13	12	14	15	14	14	14	13	18.2	16.1	18.1	18.1	17.3	17.2	16.8	16.0
Idaho	14	16	20	20	19	18	17	17	20.3	19.5	21.4	20.1	19.0	18.0	17.1	17.4
Wyoming	7	7	11	11	10	10	9	9	19.6	18.3	22.5	21.7	19.9	19.0	17.6	17.4
Colorado	42	40	50	55	55	54	54	55	18.8	15.5	17.2	17.8	17.4	17.0	17.1	17.1
New Mexico	22	21	26	28	28	27	26	29	21.8	18.1	20.0	20.3	19.7	19.2	18.4	19.9
Arizona	38	40	50	53	54	55	55	59	21.3	17.3	18.4	18.2	18.1	17.9	17.8	18.5
Utah	27	32	42	42	39	38	40	38	25.5	25.7	28.6	26.4	24.4	23.6	24.4	23.4
Nevada	10	9	13	15	14	15	15	15	19.6	14.6	16.6	16.6	16.0	16.1	16.7	16.4
Pacific	483	425	542	570	576	587	599	618	18.2	14.8	17.0	17.2	17.1	17.1	17.4	17.6
Washington	61	51	68	69	69	69	74	76	17.8	14.0	16.4	16.3	16.0	15.8	16.9	17.3
Oregon	35	33	43	41	40	40	40	40	16.8	14.4	16.4	15.4	15.0	14.8	14.8	15.1
California	363	317	403	430	436	448	455	471	18.2	14.7	17.0	17.4	17.3	17.4	17.6	17.9
Alaska	8	7	10	11	12	12	12	13	25.1	20.7	23.7	25.4	24.9	24.7	24.3	24.1
Hawaii	16	16	18	19	19	19	19	18	21.4	17.8	18.8	18.8	18.8	18.0	18.0	17.3

* Provisional

† Based on population (excluding Armed Forces abroad) enumerated as of Apr. 1 for 1970 and 1980, and estimated as of July 1 for other years.

‡ U.S. totals are based on monthly receipts corrected for observed differences between provisional and final monthly figures. State figures have not been corrected in this manner.

Source: U.S. National Center for Health Statistics, Vital Statistics of the United States, annual; and Monthly Vital Statistics Report.

2 *An increase in the number of working mothers.* Many more women are returning to the work force after having a child. As a result, the baby food industry has been strengthened by the need for manufactured food. Manufactured baby food offers an easier and quicker way for the working mothers to feed their children, while still being assured the food is nutritionally appropriate for the children. In addition, working mothers are usually an indication of two-income families. These families are known to spend up to 10% more per shopping trip. Figure C14.6 shows the age and labor force status of women who had a child for selected years during the period 1976–1985.

3 *Better-educated mothers.* Mothers today are generally better-educated than their counterparts 20 years ago. These mothers tend to take more time to shop for their children's needs and to be more willing to spend money on premium products. The social and economic characteristics of women who had a child in 1985 are shown in Figure C14.7.

4 *An increase in the number of first-born children.* In recent years, the number of first born children has been steadily increasing. This is primarily due to the decrease in the size of the family and the increase in the number of career women who are starting their families at a later age than in years past. Parents and grandparents make the majority of their expensive one-time-only purchases such as cribs, playpens, and car seats when the first child arrives in a household. This is particularly important for Gerber since, as a result of diversification, food sales account for roughly 50% of its revenues, while nonfood sales include such items as vaporizers, humidifiers, furniture, and feeding accessories.

THE PRODUCT

Baby foods are the product for which Gerber is best known. Gerber offers 165 foods, including cereals, vegetables, fruits, desserts, juices, and "main dish" combinations. New products introduced by Gerber since 1980 account for 15.8% of the total Gerber food line. In addition, Gerber is the only company in the industry that offers a line of baked goods. Its baby foods are available in 98% of the major supermarkets in the United States and new food items are continually developed in its plants.

In 1960, Gerber extended its product line to nonfood items. The apparel group began with a vinyl baby pants and bib manufacturing company. Today, the apparel group consists of four companies which manufacture and market underwear, playwear, hosiery, outerwear, and knit and woven sleepwear in sizes ranging from newborn through preteens. These four companies are Buster Brown Apparel, Bates Nitewear, Moyer, and Weather Tamer. Also, in the apparel group is G & M Finishing and Babywear, which supplies dyed and finished knit cloth to Moyer.

Of the top sellers in baby clothes is a line of clothes called "Onesies." Moyer produces this line of one-piece fashion underwear; it appears to be the most popular new item in children's clothing introduced in recent years. An extension of the "Onesies," called the "Twosies," was later introduced.

In addition to children's apparel, Gerber has a furniture division. The five companies in this group are Bilt-Rite, Century, Nursery originals, Okla Homer Smith, and Woolten. The products they offer include chests, cribs, crib lamps, playpens, car seats, wall hangings, vaporizers, humidifiers, mattresses, and dressing tables. Other products offered are generally baby items such as pacifiers, toys, nursers, bottles, and foam-filled animals.

FIGURE C14.6   WOMEN WHO HAVE HAD A CHILD, BY AGE AND LABOR FORCE STATUS—SELECTED YEARS 1976—1985

	Total, 18 to 44 years old				18 to 29 years old				30 to 44 years old			
	All women, percent in labor force	Women who have had a child in the last year	In the labor force		All women, percent in labor force	Women who have had a child in the last year	In the labor force		All women, percent in labor force	Women who have had a child in the last year	In the labor force	
Year		Number (1,000)	Number (1,000)	Per-cent		Number (1,000)	Number (1,000)	Per-cent		Number (1,000)	Number (1,000)	Per-cent
1976	59.7	2,797	865	30.9	(NA)	2,220	706	31.8	(NA)	577	159	27.6
1980	66.1	3,247	1,233	38.0	68.3	2,476	947	38.2	63.7	770	287	37.3
1981	67.2	3,381	1,411	41.7	68.9	2,499	1,004	40.2	65.5	881	407	46.2
1982	68.3	3,433	1,508	43.9	69.7	2,445	1,040	42.5	66.7	988	469	47.5
1983	69.1	3,625	1,563	43.1	70.6	2,682	1,138	42.4	67.6	942	425	45.1
1984	70.2	3,311	1,547	46.7	71.5	2,375	1,058	44.5	68.9	936	489	52.2
1985	70.8	3,497	1,691	48.4	71.3	2,512	1,204	47.9	70.3	984	488	49.6

NA: Not available
Source: U.S. Bureau of the Census, Current Population Reports, series P-20, No. 406.

FIGURE C14.7 SOCIAL AND ECONOMIC CHARACTERISTICS OF WOMEN, 18–44 YEARS OLD, WHO HAVE HAD A CHILD IN 1985

Characteristic	Total, 18 to 44 years old			18 to 29 years old			30 to 44 years old		
		Women who have had a child in the last year			Women who have had a child in the last year			Women who have had a child in the last year	
	Number of women (1,000)	Total births per 1,000 women	First births per 1,000 women	Number of women (1,000)	Total births per 1,000 women	First births per 1,000 women	Number of women (1,000)	Total births per 1,000 women	First births per 1,000 women
Total*	**50,951**	**68.6**	**27.1**	**24,788**	**101.4**	**47.1**	**26,163**	**37.6**	**8.0**
White	42,782	66.9	27.2	20,581	99.9	47.6	22,202	36.4	8.3
Black	6,523	76.4	27.1	3,433	110.8	47.1	3,090	38.1	4.9
Spanish origin†	3,816	107.3	33.1	2,023	153.6	55.6	1,793	55.2	7.8
Married, spouse present	29,118	92.0	34.8	10,634	169.4	76.8	18,484	47.5	10.6
Married, spouse absent‡	2,216	86.8	24.8	982	164.6	55.4	1,234	24.9	.5
Widowed or divorced	5,199	27.5	7.7	1,312	81.0	28.1	3,888	9.5	.9
Single	14,417	33.4	18.8	11,860	37.4	21.9	2,557	15.1	4.1
Labor force status: In labor force	36,075	46.9	21.6	17,685	68.1	36.7	18,390	26.5	7.1
Employed	33,034	43.5	19.9	15,772	62.0	33.9	17,262	26.6	7.1
Unemployed	3,041	83.5	40.0	1,913	118.3	59.5	1,128	24.5	7.1
Not in labor force	14,876	121.4	40.2	7,103	184.2	73.0	7,773	63.9	10.2
Family income: Under $10,000	8,726	93.6	34.0	5,184	132.9	53.5	3,542	36.0	5.5
$10,000–$14,999	5,858	76.9	30.5	3,291	110.3	52.3	2,567	34.1	2.7
$15,000–$19,999	5,702	69.6	29.8	2,973	108.1	55.3	2,730	27.7	2.1
$20,000–$24,999	5,457	67.5	22.1	2,629	97.5	39.9	2,828	39.6	5.5
$25,000–$29,999	4,703	70.0	28.9	2,185	110.8	53.1	2,518	34.6	7.8
$30,000–$34,999	4,606	83.0	31.6	2,014	118.8	54.1	2,592	55.2	14.1
$35,000 and over	13,801	46.0	20.3	5,584	59.6	34.1	8,217	36.7	11.0
Years of school completed:									
Not a high school graduate	7,877	96.2	28.3	4,028	155.7	52.5	3,850	38.0	3.0
High school, 4 years	22,117	68.3	29.2	10,972	109.6	53.9	11,145	27.6	5.0
College, 1–3 years	11,594	57.6	24.7	6,134	75.7	39.8	5,460	37.2	7.6
College, 4 years	6,238	61.3	22.7	2,885	61.6	31.2	3,354	61.0	15.5
College, 5 or more years	3,124	52.3	26.0	768	53.3	40.6	2,355	52.0	21.3

* Includes women of other races and women with family income not reported, not shown separately.

† Persons of Spanish origin may be of any race.

‡ Includes separated women.

Source: U.S. Bureau of the Census, *Current Population Reports*, series P-20, No. 406.

Food products are the largest source of Gerber's total operating income. However, the children's apparel and baby furniture groups are steadily increasing their contribution to Gerber's income. These divisions are providing approximately one quarter of the total operating income.

PROMOTION

In 1928, Gerber baby foods were launched with an extensive advertising campaign in magazines such as *Good Housekeeping, Child Life* and *Parents*. At the onset of the company's formation, the Gerber Baby trademark was adopted. This trademark is a charcoal sketch that was so appealing and well received that the artist's unfinished rendering became a world-famous trademark.

In 1936, Gerber offered a Gerber baby doll through a special incentive program of three Gerber baby food labels and 10¢. Also, in the early 1930s, Austin Automobiles toured the U.S. promoting Gerber baby foods. In addition, banners were used for advertising. In every type of promotion, the Gerber baby trademark was used and is still used today.

During World War II, when people could buy very little without ration stamps, Gerber used food displays that emphasized their lack of requirement for ration stamps. These displays were an incentive for consumers to buy and gave Gerber a favorable image to the public.

In 1948, the slogan ''Babies Are Our Business'' came into being. It became one of the best known mottos in many countries as it was later translated into several languages. Today, this motto is still prevalent in advertising and in consumers' minds.

In the 1950s, Gerber was the first baby food company to use television advertising. Many well-known personalities such as Perry Como, Kate Smith, Captain Kangaroo, and John Glenn were among Gerber's spokespersons.

Today, Gerber's main thrust in promotion is in direct mail advertising and sampling. Through its marketing research division, Gerber purchases various lists from hospitals of families with new infants. Over 2.8 million new parents are mailed packets one or more times a year with coupons redeemable at supermarkets. The mail sent to the parents includes information on company products and booklets on infant care. Through hospital kits or mailings, the company reaches 90% of parents with babies.

In addition to direct mail advertising, Gerber continues to utilize print media advertising. Young family magazines are the vehicles—they include *American Baby, Baby Talk, Working Mother,* and *Parents.* This type of advertising is targeted to reach 89% of all expectant and new mothers 12.8 times a year. Its purpose is to reinforce the reasons why Gerber is the leading brand. The advertising is persuasive and informative and attempts to build brand confidence. It includes a toll-free number to aid the consumer.

Gerber is very selective in its use of television advertising. It purchases network spots year round to attempt to reach only a select young parent audience.

Gerber was the first company to launch a National Charity Coupon Redemption Program. Each Gerber coupon redeemed with a charity designated (March of Dimes, ChildHelp or Special Olympics) pledges Gerber to a 5¢ donation to one of these charities. In addition, Gerber distributes over 5 million free booklets annually on infant care and feeding.

With respect to retail stores, Gerber utilizes its sales offices. It has over 600 people who offer retail stores merchandising advice (Figure C14.8). It is also promoting expansion of nonfood items.

FIGURE C14.8   GERBER'S CONSUMER PROFILE

CONSUMER PROFILE

Today's Parents

- *Older — Over 55% of babies born are to women 25 years of age or older.*

- *Better Educated — 78% of mothers having a baby have high school or higher educations.*

- *More Affluent — 27.1% of families with women 18-44 years old have incomes in excess of $37,000.*

- *Employed — 48.4% of women having a baby in 1985 were in the labor force. These parents spend 10% more per shopping than other customers.*

Shopping Habits

- *53% of mothers with babies make weekly trips to the supermarket. 15% shop 2-3 times per week.*

- *Young parents demand quality and convenience.*

- *They are extremely brand conscious and have high brand loyalty.*

- *Prefer a full line and good selection of baby foods including Strained, Junior, Cereals, Juices and Meat items.*

- *Like Baby Needs located with baby foods and tend to shop stores offering a complete department with a variety of merchandise.*

Source: Company documents.

482

To accomplish these goals, Gerber has recently doubled its advertising budget to around $36 million per year. It is also considering the aiming of its advertising at grandmothers and aunts as potential influence groups.

FINANCIAL POSITION

Although the 1987 fiscal year showed record high sales of $917,320,000, net earnings from continuing operations declined 16 percent to $37,147,000. (See Figures C14-9 through C14-10 for financial information.) In 1987 the company made continual progress in recovering its position in baby food. At the end of April, Gerber's baby food brand share stood at 67 percent. This recovery was not without cost, however; advertising and promotional expenditures for baby food were increased $12 million during the year. While that increase was essential to the recovery, it certainly had an impact on earnings. Gerber plans to continue this higher level of advertising and promotion during fiscal 1988, directed toward greater consumer awareness and response.

FIGURE C14.9   GERBER PRODUCTS COMPANY AND SUBSIDIARIES
CONSOLIDATED STATEMENTS OF OPERATIONS
(In Thousands of Dollars)

	Year ended March 31		
	1987	1986	1985
Net sales	$917,320	$839,437	$795,633
Interest, royalties and other income	4,113	4,017	7,156
Share of earnings of unconsolidated companies	1,172	1,690	2,541
Total income	922,605	845,144	805,330
Deductions from income:			
Cost of products sold	602,938	538,461	508,466
Marketing, distribution, administrative and general expenses	235,209	209,752	191,367
Provision for plant closing costs		8,100	
Interest expense	16,719	10,852	10,314
	854,866	767,165	710,147
Earnings from continuing operations before income taxes	67,739	77,979	95,183
Income taxes	30,592	33,949	42,380
Earnings from continuing operations	37,147	44,030	52,803
Discontinued operations			
Earnings (loss) from operations, net of applicable income taxes	(786)	1,465	3,584
Loss on disposal, including provision for income taxes	(7,900)		
Earnings (loss) from discontinued operations	(8,686)	1,465	3,584
Net earnings	$ 28,461	$ 45,495	$ 56,387
Earnings (loss) per share:			
From continuing operations	$1.85	$2.16	$2.59
From discontinued operations	(.43)	.07	.18
Net earnings per share	$1.42	$2.23	$2.77

Source: Annual Report, Gerber Products Company, 1987.

FIGURE C14.10 GERBER PRODUCTS COMPANY AND SUBSIDIARIES
CONSOLIDATED STATEMENTS OF FINANCIAL POSITION
(In Thousands of Dollars)

	March 31	
	1987	1986
Assets		
Current Assets		
Cash	$ 9,999	$ 8,648
Short-term investments	707	10,693
Trade accounts receivable, less allowances (1987—$3,629; 1986—$2,807)	114,315	87,532
Inventories		
Finished products	91,516	80,296
Raw materials and supplies	100,659	71,773
	192,175	152,069
Current assets of discontinued operations	13,473	14,339
Prepaid expenses and other	6,862	16,689
Total current assets	337,531	289,970
Other Assets		
Investment in unconsolidated companies	43,174	30,852
Miscellaneous receivables, prepayments and other accounts	35,892	26,271
Intangible assets, less amortization (1987—$10,059; 1986—$8,586)	26,456	30,960
Other assets of discontinued operations	6,042	5,543
	111,564	93,626
Land, buildings and equipment—Note G		
Land	11,789	8,848
Buildings	110,184	93,375
Machinery and equipment	209,904	176,952
Construction in progress	28,804	15,996
Allowances for depreciation (deduct)	(127,802)	(116,213)
	232,879	178,958
Fixed assets of discontinued operations (net)	34,858	38,636
	267,737	217,594
	$716,832	$601,190

	March 31	
	1987	**1986**
Liabilities and shareowners' equity		
Current Liabilities		
Short-term borrowings	$ 40,429	$ 9,950
Trade accounts payable	50,801	40,910
Salaries, wages and other compensation	20,701	16,541
Local taxes, interest and other expenses	23,325	16,878
Income taxes	2,520	512
Current liabilities of discontinued operations and provision for estimated loss on disposal	23,465	15,072
Deferred income taxes		3,661
Current maturities of long-term debt	2,012	3,669
Total current liabilities	163,253	107,193
Long-term debt, less current maturities	176,227	82,518
Deferred income taxes	45,186	30,884
Plant closing expenses		2,875
Noncurrent liabilities of discontinued operations	3,378	3,220
Shareowners' equity		
Common stock, par value $2.50 a share—authorized 50,000,000 shares; issued:		
20,826,861 shares	52,067	52,067
Additional paid-in capital	3,155	3,639
Retained earnings	324,444	322,558
Foreign currency translation adjustments (deduct)	(1,726)	(834)
Cost of common stock in treasury (deduct): (1987—1,142,263 shares;		
1986—248,130 shares)	(49,152)	(2,930)
	328,788	374,500
	$716,832	$601,190

Source: Annual Report, Gerber Products Company, 1987.

FIGURE C14.11 GERBER PRODUCTS COMPANY AND SUBSIDIARIES
CONSOLIDATED STATEMENTS OF SHAREOWNERS' EQUITY
(In Thousands of Dollars)

	Common stock	Additional paid-in capital	Retained earnings	Foreign currency translation adjustments	Cost of common stock in treasury
Balances at April 1, 1984	$34,465	$15,198	$274,367	$ (336)	$ (2,206)
Net earnings for the year			56,387		
Cash dividends of $1.16 per share			(23,566)		
Repurchase of 250,000 shares for treasury					(5,825)
Issuance of 101,472 shares of treasury stock upon exercise of stock options		30	(335)		2,074
Issuance of 6,890,714 shares in connection with 3 for 2 stock split	17,227	(15,228)	(2,060)		
Foreign currency translation adjustments for the year				(308)	
Balances at March 31, 1985	51,692		304,793	(644)	(5,957)
Net earnings for the year			45,495		
Cash dividends of $1.32 per share			(26,942)		
Issuance of 150,000 shares in connection with conversion of debt	375	3,125			
Issuance of 129,938 shares of treasury stock upon exercise of stock options—Note J		514	(788)		3,027
Foreign currency translation adjustments for the year				(190)	
Balances at March 31, 1986	52,067	3,639	322,558	(834)	(2,930)
Cumulative foreign currency translation adjustment at April 1, 1986				(1,068)	
Net earnings for the year			28,461		
Cash dividends of $1.32 per share			(26,575)		
Repurchase of 985,000 shares for treasury					(49,378)
Issuance of 72,040 shares of treasury stock upon exercise of stock options		(369)			2,212
Issuance of 18,827 shares of treasury stock to employee stock ownership plan		(115)			944
Foreign currency translation adjustments for the year				176	
Balances at March 31, 1987	$52,067	$ 3,155	$324,444	$ (1,726)	$(49,152)

Note: ( ) Denotes deduction.
Source: Annual Report, Gerber Products Company, 1987.

FIGURE C14.12 GERBER PRODUCTS COMPANY AND SUBSIDIARIES
CONSOLIDATED STATEMENTS OF CHANGES IN FINANCIAL POSITION
(In Thousands of Dollars)

	Year Ended March 31		
	1987	**1986**	**1985**
Cash from operations			
Earnings from continuing operations	$ 37,147	$ 44,030	$ 52,803
Items not currently affecting cash:			
Depreciation and amortization	24,018	20,357	18,633
Deferred income taxes	9,420	3,394	2,754
Share of earnings of unconsolidated companies	(1,172)	(1,690)	(2,541)
Accrued plant closing costs		4,642	
Other	(825)	1,800	1,800
Total from continuing operations	68,588	72,533	73,449
Changes in certain working capital items			
Trade accounts receivable	$(14,925)	$ 7,269	$ (4,899)
Inventories	(12,012)	(5,843)	(18,413)
Prepaid expenses and other	9,827	(2,667)	(14,022)
Trade accounts payable	8,305	(4,806)	1,319
Due to unconsolidated subsidiary		(8,600)	8,600
Other current liabilities	9,843	(4,122)	(107)
	1,038	(18,769)	(27,527)
Total from continuing operations after changes in working capital	69,626	53,764	45,922
Cash from discontinued operations			
Earnings (loss) from discontinued operations	(8,686)	1,465	3,584
Items not currently affecting cash:			
Depreciation and amortization	6,519	6,318	4,396
Deferred income taxes	223	919	929
Decrease (increase) in net current assets of discontinued operations	9,283	2,502	(2,291)
Total from discontinued operations	7,339	11,204	6,618
Total from operations	76,965	64,968	52,540
Financing activities			
Proceeds from long-term borrowings	102,500	11,000	10,093
Realization of purchased tax benefits	1,221	4,736	5,273
Payment of long-term debt	(10,448)	(8,919)	(10,379)
Repayment of short-term debt of acquired companies		(5,318)	
Other increase (decrease) in short-term borrowings	30,479	9,950	(361)
Repurchase of shares for treasury	(49,378)		(5,825)
Issuance of common stock		3,500	
Cash dividends	(26,575)	(26,942)	(23,566)
Issuance of shares under stock option and employee stock ownership plans	2,672	2,754	1,769
Financing activities of discontinued operations	(89)	(197)	(943)
	50,382	(9,436)	(23,939)

FIGURE C14.12 (*CONTINUED*)

	Year Ended March 31		
	1987	**1986**	**1985**
Investing activities			
Purchased companies:			
Net current assets acquired, excluding cash	(35,594)	(2,347)	(5,318)
Land, buildings and equipment	(23,485)	(7,619)	(8,372)
Intangible assets	(575)	(7,274)	(10,087)
Long-term liabilities assumed		3,698	2,538
Other—net	(908)	(779)	(2,853)
	(60,562)	(14,321)	(24,092)
Investment in net noncurrent assets (principally land, buildings and equipment) of discontinued operations	(3,240)	(9,959)	(12,769)
Other additions to land, buildings and equipment	(61,115)	(44,735)	(32,722)
Disposals of land, buildings and equipment	8,571	4,755	5,943
Decrease (increase) in investment in unconsolidated subsidiaries	(11,150)	1,533	(4,041)
Other—net	(8,486)	4,899	(9,366)
	(135,982)	(57,828)	(77,047)
Decrease in cash and short-term investments	(8,635)	(2,296)	(48,446)
Cash and short-term investments at beginning of year	19,341	21,637	70,083
Cash and short-term investments at end of year	$ 10,706	$ 19,341	$ 21,637

Note: ( ) Denotes use of cash and short-term investments.
Source: Annual Report, Gerber Products Company, 1987.

FIGURE C14.13   GERBER PRODUCTS COMPANY AND SUBSIDIARIES
10-YEAR REVIEW
(In Millions of Dollars)

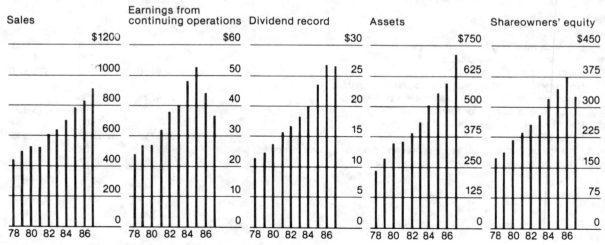

Source: Annual Report, Gerber Products Company, 1987.

488

In the 1987 fiscal year, the apparel group's net sales increased to $248,457,000 from $175,030,000 for the previous year. Operating income rose to $18,642,000 from $18,608,000 for fiscal year 1986. The second-quarter acquisition of the children's wear, cloth diaper, and bedding products line sold under the Curity brand by Soft Care Apparel, Inc., a Gerber subsidiary, completed the initial phase of Gerber's plan to be a major factor in the $14 billion childrens apparel market.

The furniture group's net sales in fiscal year 1987 increased to $107,803,000 compared with $105,446,000 for the previous year. Operating income for the year declined to $4,767,000 versus $5,522,000 for fiscal year 1986 as a result of expenses relating to restructuring and productivity improvement efforts.

GLOBAL MARINE, INC.

Prepared James W. Clinton, University of Northern California.

"You would not want to stay in this business if you expected the price of oil to drop," asserted David Herasimchuk, vice president for market development, Global Marine, Inc. Saudi Arabia's decision in the fall of 1985 to increase crude oil production caused oil prices to drop dramatically and led to widespread unprofitability and disarray within the international offshore oil and gas drilling industry. However, optimism is endemic to the industry, and most independent offshore oil and gas drilling contractors at the beginning of 1986 believed the worst was over.

CORPORATE ORGANIZATION

Global Marine, Inc. (GMI), a member of the international offshore oil and gas drilling industry, has three subsidiaries: Global Marine Drilling Company, Challenger Minerals, Inc., and Applied Drilling Technology. The corporate headquarters and the headquarters of subsidiaries are located in Houston, Texas. The corporate organization of Global Marine, Inc., is shown in Figure C15.1.

THE 1977 SEVEN-YEAR STRATEGIC PLAN

C. Russell Luigs became CEO of Global Marine, Inc. (GMI) in 1977. GMI's offshore drilling capability at that time was limited entirely to eight oceangoing drill ships that

FIGURE C15.1   ORGANIZATION CHART, GLOBAL MARINE, INC., 1986

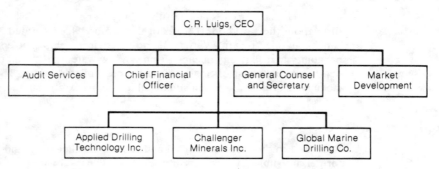

were becoming technologically obsolete. The choice facing Luigs and GMI was either to maintain an existing conservative philosophy of bidding for drilling contracts with obsolete and, therefore, inferior equipment, or take the high-risk option and develop a worldwide capability to drill in any offshore environmental conditions and be a major factor in the industry. Russ Luigs, with the consent and encouragement of the board, embarked upon the high-risk alternative. Global Marine's expansion strategy for the 1980s locked the company into large capital commitments with high penalties if rig construction contracts were canceled.

GMI diversified at first into semisubmersibles and then into jackups (see next section for a description of drilling equipment). GMI's 1981 budget provided for an inventory of 52 offshore drilling rigs. In 1981, however, David Herasimchuk, GMI's director of market development, noted that: (1) rigs were being delivered to contractors at three times the rate of 1978, (2) shipyards were able to deliver two jackups a month, and (3) delivery rates of jackups implied a 27% increase in jackups for 1981 and a 29% increase in jackup inventories in 1982. Herasimchuk concluded that any change in year-to-year demand of less than 25% could create a serious oversupply of jackup rigs and reduce day rates charged for offshore drilling as much as 50%. At the time, however, there was a lack of unanimity within the industry concerning the outlook for offshore oil drilling since industry rig utilization rates averaged above 95% between mid-1979 and mid-1982, and within the industry the rule is that new rig construction is justified when the utilization rate is above 95%.

(Note: Construction lead times for jackups normally were about 2 years and as little as 18 months. At the height of the rig construction boom in 1981, lead times were 3 years. By adding together existing inventories of offshore drilling rigs and anticipated additions to inventory, the supply of rigs is known. Industry analysts can then forecast what demand is necessry for day rates to stay within a profitable range.)

In April 1982, GMI's management concluded that the industry's expansion plans were overly ambitious and reduced the company's offshore drilling rig construction program by about one-third, setting a target of 35 rigs. GMI decided also not to order any more 250-foot jackups and to order a 300-foot jackup only if the company had a firm contract for its use. GMI thus canceled delivery of all jackups that it was possible to cancel, and deferred delivery of some jackups until 1984, anticipating that the industry cycle would peak once again, as it had in the past, at a later date.

GLOBAL MARINE DRILLING COMPANY (GMDC)

GMDC, Global Marine's largest subsidiary, is engaged in offshore oil drilling operations throughout the world. GMDC, as of the end of 1985, operated 34 offshore drilling rigs capable of operating in a variety of marine environments. The entire fleet possessed the capability to drill in any ocean—from shallow water in the Gulf of Mexico to 2,500-foot depths off the coast of Spain to the ice caps of the Arctic. The fleet consisted of 21 jackups, 7 drill ships, 5 semisubmersibles, and 1 Arctic submersible.

Drilling Equipment

Rigs used to drill offshore for oil and gas are sturdier than land-based rigs because the former are subject to greater stresses. GMDC uses a variety of rigs in offshore drilling operations. The most frequently used rigs (and the sequence in which they generally are utilized) are: (1) jackup rigs, (2) drill ships, (3) semisubmersibles, and (4) fixed platforms.

Jackups   The jackup rig is so named because of steel legs located at the three corners of the rig that are extended (jacked) down to the ocean floor to provide a stable drilling platform or raised up above the main platform of the rig to allow the rig to be towed to another drilling site. Jackups generally drill in water depths of 15 to 375 feet and can drill to a depth of up to 25,000 feet. Jackups are used both for exploration and field development drilling.

Some jackups are cantilevered so that they can drill over a fixed ocean platform without putting weight on the platform—thus permitting the fixed platform to be lighter and, therefore, less costly.

Drill Ships   Drill ships are oceangoing vessels which, unlike most jackups and semisubmersibles, do not require towing. Drill ships typically operate in water depths up to 1500 feet and can drill to a depth of about 25,000 feet. Drill ships are self-contained rigs configured to the shape of a ship. Drill ships are used for deepwater exploration in moderate environments and in remote areas. They possess the advantage of mobility and are able to carry large loads necessary for remote drilling operations.

Most moored ships and semisubmersibles are limited to drilling in water depths between 600 and 1500 feet. Dynamically positioned ships and semisubmersibles operating without a mooring system are generally capable of drilling in water depths of 3,000 to 6,000 feet.

Semisubmersibles   Semisubmersible ocean drilling rigs are mobile and float in the water on very large pontoons submerged below the ocean surface to provide stability to the platform floating on the pontoons above the water. Semisubmersibles drill in water depths up to about 1500 feet and can drill to a depth of 25,000 feet. Semisubmersible rigs operate in most of the same areas in which drill ships are used and are preferable for deep water drilling in more hostile seas.

Fixed platforms   If an offshore operator drills a successful exploratory well, a platform rig may next be used to drill additional, developmental wells in the oil field. The platform can only be justified economically, however, if the oil field is large.

GMDC Drill Rig Inventory and Utilization

GMDC owns all its rigs now in service except for one jackup rig, the Glomar Main Pass II, and the Concrete Island Drilling System (CIDS), which are under long-term lease. All rigs owned by GMDC are subject to mortgages except for the Glomar Platform I, the Glomar Biscay I, and the Glomar Adriatic VIII.

The average age of GMDC's fleet of rigs is 6 years, compared to an industry average of 9 years. GMDC operates a modern rig training and drilling simulation center in Houston, Texas. Drilling crews receive periodic refresher training as part of the company's objective of developing the most highly skilled crews in the industry.

Global Marine recognized in 1982 that offshore oil and gas drilling was below earlier forecasts. The company, as a result, delayed delivery of three semisubmersible rigs and one drill ship and canceled orders for four jackup rigs. The company also agreed to reduce drilling rates charged customers if customers agreed either to use Global Marine rigs in the future or extend existing drilling contracts.

During 1985 the company concluded 71 drilling contracts and contract extensions. As of January 1, 1986, drilling contracts for 31 of the company's 34 rigs were due to expire during 1986. For 1987, rigs were presently contracted for drilling for only 3% of their availability. Utilization rates of the company's rigs for the last 8 years and the rate estimated for 1986 are shown below. Utilization rate is computed by dividing number of days a rig earned revenues by total days the rig was available for work.

	1986	1985	1984	1983	1982	1981	1980	1979	1978
Rigs in fleet at end of year	32	34	35	32	28	28	18	14	11
% Utilization	30%	91	92	92	93	100	100	98	91

Arctic Exploration

Global Marine also designs and develops the latest in state of the art offshore oil drilling technology and other oil service equipment. The company has developed a new concept to replace arctic drilling platforms used only one time. There is great interest in a mobile drilling platform for Arctic operations because a $140 million dryhole in the Arctic involved a platform costing about $85 million which had to be abandoned since it was permanently constructed on the drilling site. This costly approach was labeled the "gravel island" concept. Global Marine's concept involves the use of a concrete and steel island capable of operating in water depths 35 to 52 feet with a maximum drilling depth of 25,000 feet. The island can be ballasted (temporarily seated on the ocean floor), deballasted (prepared for towing), moved, and used again.

Global's portable island, labeled the Concrete Island Drilling System (CIDS), was first used by Exxon in November 1984 to explore an area near Prudhoe Bay. CIDS is 300 by 300 feet, and was constructed in Japan. CIDS is intended to replace gravel islands constructed in shallow waters in the Arctic that cannot be moved. The company presently is researching a more advanced concept that can operate in deeper Arctic waters. Approximately twenty United States and Canadian oil companies are potential customers for Global Marine's Arctic drilling equipment.

THE OFFSHORE OIL AND GAS DRILLING INDUSTRY

Current Situation

At the beginning of 1986, international oil and gas drilling contractors were engaged in offshore drilling operations around the world in the North Sea, the Mediterrannean Sea, Southeast Asia, South America, and the Gulf of Mexico. Contractors were experiencing reduced demand for their offshore drilling rigs and profit margins were narrowing or nonexistent. The entire industry was exceedingly competitive.

Offshore, a publication about the offshore oil and gas industry, reported in June 1985 that worldwide rig usage showed 550 rigs of a total 742 were working, 8 were en route to drill sites, and 184 were idle. This compared to 1984 figures of 539 working, 170 idle, and 8 en route. In addition to these 742 mobile offshore drilling rigs, approximately one hundred other drilling rigs were located in Eastern bloc communist countries or positioned in Lake Maracaibo, Venezuela (an unusually placid body of water not subject to stresses encountered in the open sea).

Most offshore oil and gas drilling rigs are owned by independent contractors. Some foreign governments that control nationalized oil companies operate their own rigs, and several major international oil companies maintain equity positions in offshore drilling rigs to influence rig design related to specialized needs.

Historical Background

The offshore oil and gas drilling service industry was born out of the desire by international oil companies to concentrate on those areas they knew best and expected the greatest profit—purchase or lease of oil and gas properties, transporting, refining, and marketing of petroleum and petroleum by-products. Independent offshore drilling contractors provided and operated drilling rigs at locations selected by the international oil companies' own geologists. Contractors absorbed the risk of low rig utilization in exchange for rates that returned a satisfactory profit—when and if most drilling rigs were under contract.

Post–World War II   Since the end of World War II, the offshore oil drilling industry has experienced a succession of boom and bust cycles that led contractors to conclude that if demand for rigs was depressed, recovery and future prosperity were not far off. The fortunes of the offshore oil and gas industry are inextricably tied to the international oil and gas industry. When demand for oil and gas is high, and prices paid for oil and gas are similarly high, the world's major oil companies exert strong demand for offshore mobile drilling rigs. The reverse is also true—low oil and gas demand coupled with low prices reduces the demand for drilling rigs.

1970–1979   Some major oil producers anticipated a constant increase in oil prices because of expected steady growth in consumer demand. Natural gas was in short supply during the 1970s, culminating in 1978 in widespread media publicity about aged widows freezing to death because they were unable to pay large utility heating bills. This unacceptable human suffering led the federal government to halt construction of new utility plants using natural gas and effectively limit new construction to nuclear and electricity-generating facilities.

1979–1981 Between 1979 and 1981, demand for offshore drilling rigs drove daily rental rates (day rates) up to record levels and encouraged substantial increases in construction of new drilling rigs.

1983

Declining Demand for Natural Gas A combination of factors led to a major decline in demand for natural gas in 1983. In addition to federal restrictions on natural gas utility plants, the United States experienced a recession. American consumers also proved more adept at conserving gas and oil than anticipated. Meanwhile, the United States was shifting from a production to a service economy, requiring less energy per employee, and the traditionally high consumers of energy, "the smokestack industries," were depressed as a result of increased low-priced foreign competition.

Gas pipeline companies had commonly committed themselves to 15- to 20-year long-term contracts for gas deliveries when both demand and prices were high, and demand was expected to increase steadily. The decline in demand for gas forced many pipeline companies to renege on long-term contracts because they could not sell the gas at the prices or volumes at which they had agreed to buy. Many of these canceled contracts are still under litigation.

Expanded Availability of Federal Offshore Leases James Watt, secretary of the interior, further complicated the nature of the natural gas industry and its economics. Secretary Watt eliminated the previous practice of major oil and gas companies proposing certain tracts of acreage for drilling and negotiating a price directly with the government. Secretary Watt introduced an areawide leasing system in 1983 that opened offshore areas to competitive bidding. Watt's more liberal attitude toward the development of America's energy resources produced a fivefold increase in acreage leased for a 5-year period for oil and gas exploration.

New Drilling Rig Construction Addition of new rigs to the worldwide inventory lowered utilization rates for mobile offshore drilling units from approximately 100 percent in 1981 to a low of 74 percent in August 1983. At the same time, day rates declined as much as 75 percent.

Buying versus Exploring for Oil and Gas Reserves Oil and gas exploration in the United States, both on and offshore, declined 23% during 1983. Forty percent of oil companies surveyed in 1983 increased reserves by acquiring producing oil and gas properties or companies, reflecting a belief that oil obtained through purchase was cheaper than oil obtained through exploration and development.

1983–1984 Offshore oil and gas drilling rose late in 1983 and the signals were that a recovery was under way. However, at about this time, T. Boone Pickens, president of Mesa Petroleum, threatened takeover of several oil companies. Other major oil companies followed his lead and several giant mergers took place. Many oil companies became apprehensive that they too might be takeover targets. Their managements acted to avoid takeover by increasing financial leverage, thus becoming less attractive to raiders, but also reducing funds available for oil and gas exploration and drilling. To placate shareholders considering sale of their stock to unfriendly raiders, managements increased cash flow to shareholders through formation of royalty trusts, further curtailing drilling plans.

1985 By February 1985, utilization rates for all types of offshore drilling rigs had risen to 84 percent. Along with the increase in utilization rates, day rates also rose by about 50 percent during the same period. Major oil companies, however, reduced worldwide exploration so that offshore rig utilization declined steadily through the year to 81% at year-end. Rig utilization in the Gulf of Mexico declined even further to 75%, as of January 1, 1986. The decline in rig utilization caused a concurrent decrease in day rates.

Despite the declining demand for offshore drilling rigs, as of May 1985, there were a total of 53 new offshore drilling units under construction worldwide: 18 jackups, 32 semisubmersibles, 2 drill ships, and 1 submersible. (The characteristics of these rigs were discussed previously under the subheading "Drilling Equipment.")

In December 1985, George Gaspar, an oil and gas industry analyst, forecast oil prices in 1986 to decline $1 to $2 a barrel from 1985's average price of $27.50 per barrel. Oil prices were forecast to continue to fall $1 to $2 a barrel through 1988 before reversing direction.

A positive factor for the domestic offshore drilling industry was that about 2,000 leases of offshore drilling tracts bought by oil companies for $6.4 billion are due to expire between 1986 and 1988. The oil companies must drill before the leases expire or lose the leases.

INFLUENCES ON OIL AND GAS EXPLORATION AND PRODUCTION

Oil and gas exploration and production are influenced by a variety of factors that include: (1) governmental regulation of production, (2) availability of government off-shore lands for drilling, (3) prices for competitive fuels, (4) seasonal variations in demand, (5) investment tax credits and other regulations that either encourage or discourage oil exploration and production, (6) attempts by the Organization of Petroleum Exporting Countries (OPEC) to administer prices and establish a single world-wide price, and (7) efforts by individual nations to increase market share of total oil production, regardless of price.

Oil supply. The world supply of oil is generated by OPEC and non-OPEC countries. OPEC is an international cartel that attempts to control supply, and thus the price of oil. However, OPEC's members squabble among themselves concerning their fair share of oil production and some secretly sell more than their allotted share, thus increasing supply and tending to reduce the price of oil. As non-OPEC countries compete to sell their supply and acquire larger market share, OPEC becomes less influential. Up to 90% of the increase in non-OPEC oil production since 1978 is derived from offshore wells. Offshore oil production represents 28% of total world production. Non-OPEC oil production was two-thirds of worldwide oil production in 1985, compared to only one-third of worldwide production in 1975. If both OPEC and non-OPEC countries reduce supply, however, prices will rise and offshore drilling outside of the Persian Gulf becomes attractive. Low-priced oil makes many offshore drilling areas uneconomical to drill.

Oil demand. Demand for oil is related to price and alternative forms of energy, the price of these alternatives, and the latter's compatibility with environmental laws and regulations. Oil is the more popular energy alternative since it burns cleaner than coal. When consumers conserve use of petroleum, demand for oil routinely declines.

Supply of drilling rigs. The number of offshore drilling rigs available in the industry and their ability to drill in the specific environment for which needed is a major factor affecting day rates for offshore rigs. When demand for drilling rigs falls below the supply of rigs, day rates fall rapidly and drilling contractors compete to keep their rigs busy.

The cost of money. The offshore drilling industry is capital intensive because of the high cost of drilling rigs. If drilling contractors borrow money at high interest rates, they are committed to long-term debt repayment of interest and principal, possible only if owned drilling rigs are leased to achieve high utilization rates. When day rates decline, contractors are squeezed and profitability is difficult. The more modern the drilling fleet, the higher the company's fixed payments and the greater its vulnerability to a decline in day rates.

Foreign tax rates. Offshore oil exploration budgets of the major oil companies typically followed increases in oil prices. Higher oil prices, however, led foreign governments hosting drilling rigs to raise taxes on recovered oil and several years thereafter, oil exploration decreased.

The federal debt. Some industry analysts suggest that the ballooning size of the federal debt soon would lead to a new tax on oil, lead to additional consumer conservation, and reduce the need for offshore oil exploration.

Costs of exploration vary. Exploration, drilling, and development costs for offshore oil vary widely throughout the world. In the Persian Gulf, the total cost to find and develop a barrel of oil was $1 a barrel in 1984. United States major oil companies at other foreign offshore locations incurred a $7-a-barrel cost, up to and including development of the drill site location. In the continental United States, onshore drilling costs were $12 a barrel. Offshore drilling in the North Sea near the United Kingdom was $14 a barrel. Additional costs depend upon the tax structure of the country or state in which the drilling takes place. One industry expert estimates that a drop from $30 to $20 a barrel would decrease the number of drillable offshore prospects by about 25%.

RISKS AND ENVIRONMENTAL HAZARDS

Offshore drillers experience hazards and difficulties their land-based competitors do not have to contend with. Offshore oil spills near resort areas can inflict substantial damage upon beaches, the tourist trade, and sea life, and cause major environmental harm. The spill of oil from a well being drilled from an offshore drilling platform in the Santa Barbara Channel off the California coast in 1969 led to a 10-year moratorium on all drilling off the California coast and stricter state regulation of subsequent offshore drilling operations. Owners and operators of offshore facilities on the Outer Continental Shelf of North America, moreover, are liable for damages and for the cost of removing oil spills for which they are responsible.

Since 1970, only one oil spill has released more than 10,000 barrels of oil into the environment. That spill was the result of a ship's anchor being dragged across a seabed and rupturing an oil pipeline. Between 1975 and 1982, the U.S. Department of the Interior reports that total oil spillage related to offshore drilling in federally leased waters amounted to about 17,000 barrels of oil—only 0.07 of 1% of total oil produced.

When drilling for oil, "mud" is pumped to the bottom of the well bore to raise rock chips cut by the drill bit up from the well and control well pressure and avoid "blowouts." Mud is a mixture of clay, barite, water, and several concentrated chemicals. Most mud does not pose a threat to the environment. According to the National Academy of Sciences, natural seepage from the earth accounts for 15 percent of the oil that reaches the world's water surfaces. Runoff from industry onshore generates additional oil pollution. In contrast, offshore drilling operations in U.S. waters account for 5/100 of 1 percent of oil pollution of the world's oceans.

Drilling for oil and gas involves the hazard of a blowout, an uncontrolled high-pressure flow of oil or gas from a well bore, that can catch fire and destroy a rig.

Offshore rigs are also susceptible to collisions while being towed or positioned for drilling. Rigs under tow have sometimes run aground and some rigs have been destroyed or severely damaged by hurricanes, storms, tidal waves, and typhoons.

Global Marine, Inc., experienced a major maritime disaster on October 25, 1983, when its drill ship, the *Glomar Java Sea,* capsized and sank during Typhoon Lex in the South China Sea. All 81 persons aboard the drill ship are presumed dead. The *Glomar Java Sea* was valued at $35 million. The National Transporation Safety Board (NTSB) determined that the ship sank due to a structural failure. The NTSB also stated:

> Contributing to the structural failure was the decision that the drillship would remain anchored with all nine achors, which subjected the vessel to the full force of the storm. Contributing to the large loss of life was the failure of the master and Atlantic Richfield Company and Global Marine management personnel to remove nonessential personnel from the *Glomar Java Sea.*

Oil drilling contractors who operate in foreign locations encounter additional risks that include: (1) expropriation, (2) nationalization, (3) foreign exchange restrictions, (4) foreign taxation, (5) changing political conditions, (6) foreign and domestic monetary policies, and (7) foreign government regulations that give preferential treatment to local contractors or require foreign contractors to employ local citizens or purchase supplies locally.

CHALLENGER MINERALS, INC. (CMI)

Global Marine's second major subsidiary, CMI, is engaged in both onshore and offshore oil and gas exploration. The company's primary exploration and development areas are in the Gulf of Mexico and onshore within four states in the U.S.

A CMI customer for natural gas has refused delivery of a minimum quantity of gas previously contracted for. Gas intended for such delivery is produced at CMI's Weatherford properties in Oklahoma. The Weatherford properties were the source of slightly over one-half of CMI's oil and gas revenues for 1984. Because of this customer's refusal to accept delivery, CMI has been forced to reduce or close down approximately one-half of the company's current production capacity. Global Marine has filed suit against Southern Natural Gas Company (SONAT) for failure to honor its gas purchase contract and is attempting to require SONAT to accept delivery of such gas. CMI is claiming damages of about $99 million.

Another major CMI customer also has refused to accept future delivery of gas previously contracted for. During 1984, CMI evaluated 17 of the company's leased drilling areas and determined that declining oil prices and a reduction in the properties' production potential lowered the properties' value. Consequently, CMI charged $73 million against 1984 income. In 1983, CMI made a similar charge of $26.9 million.

APPLIED DRILLING TECHNOLOGY, INC. (ADTI)

ADTI, Global Marine's third major subsidiary, provides offshore turnkey drilling services; that is, ADTI guarantees a customer a specified fixed cost for drilling a well that includes all supervision and management, necessary equipment, material and personnel. ADTI drilled four turnkey wells in 1985 compared to ten drilled during 1984, and has completed a total of 41 turnkey wells since 1980. Through 1984, ADTI performed 75% of all offshore turnkey drilling in the Gulf of Mexico.

MARKETING

Global Marine maintains sales offices at nine overseas locations: Aberdeen, Scotland; Anchorage, Alaska; Cairo, Egypt; Calgary, Alberta; Jakarta, Indonesia; London, England; Port Gentil, Gabon (west-central Africa); Singapore, and Siracusa, Sicily. Global Marine also operates offices in Bakersfield and Los Angeles, California, and Lafayette and New Orleans, Louisiana.

GMI's potential customers are relatively few, numbering about 57 major oil and gas companies, and include affiliates of major oil companies. Customer buying decisions vary from total control at the company's headquarters to delegated decision making in the field. In between, the field manager makes his recommendation to headquarters and usually his choice is confirmed.

GMI's field representatives are expected to develop a relationship with each potential customer, assuring them that GMI is capable of performing a wide range of drilling requirements, and thus establish customer trust and confidence in GMI. Since many of the drilling contractors have similar capabilities, the difference between winning and losing a contract can depend upon the nature of the relationship between GMI's representatives and their customer contacts.

GMI develops a profile of each customer, noting customer concerns and preferences, which are incorporated within the bid the company makes to secure a drilling contract. GMI develops similar information about competitors, accumulating information about what they paid for their rigs, the length of existing contracts, availability of rigs for bidding, and what competitors bid on contracts either awarded or lost.

Bidding on contracts varies among competitors; some bid low to keep their rigs busy; others insist upon a minimum return on investment and will not contract for less; still others bid to maintain a target market share. Some bidders, prior to 1985, might even bid at a higher than expected price, anticipating the low bidders to drop out because of other jobs.

The first step toward obtaining a contract is to get on the qualified bidders list maintained by customers. Usually each company identifies about a dozen or so drilling contractors as qualified to drill for offshore oil and gas.

FINANCE

Global Marine lost $220 million in 1985 on revenues of $360.7 million, compared to a loss of $91.2 million in 1984 on revenues of $385.8 (see Table C15.1). Contributing to the 1985 loss was a charge of $102 million, made because of a lowered revaluation of the company's oil and gas properties—associated with a major decline in oil and gas prices (see Table C15.2). The previous 6 years, Global Marine earned a profit.

To conserve cash, Global Marine reduced 1985 capital expenditures to $36 million, a decline of $348 million from the previous year's $384 million capital expenditures.

Global Marine suspended dividend payments on both common and preferred stock in May 1985. On July 1, 1985, Global Marine suspended interest and principal payments (which amounted to approximately $240 million per year) on substantially all long-term debt and is, therefore, in default on most of its long-term debt. As a result, debt formerly identified as long-term has been reclassified as current debt.

Between 1980 and 1983, Global Marine spent approximately $1.3 billion on capital expenditures. Expenditures were financed from a variety of sources, which were: (1) current operations, (2) two stock issues that raised $178 million, (3) a convertible subordinated debenture issue of $100 million, (4) two subordinated debenture issues of

TABLE C15.1 GLOBAL MARINE CONSOLIDATED STATEMENT OF CHANGES IN
FINANCIAL POSITION
($ millions)

	1985	1984	1983
Cash from operations			
Net income (loss)	$(220.0)	$ (91.2)	$ 49.3
Noncash charges	192.2	111.5	109.2
Cash from operations	(27.8)	20.3	158.5
Changes in working capital*			
Accounts receivable	5.2	(13.3)	26.7
Materials and supplies	1.5	12.9	(5.7)
Other current assets	1.9	(0.3)	(3.1)
Current maturity of L-T debt	—	—	—
Accounts payable	(18.0)	12.4	(8.2)
Accrued liabilities	56.0	1.4	16.9
Change in working capital	46.6	10.1	26.6
Net cash from operations	18.8	33.4	185.1
Cash required to expand operations			
Capital expenditures	(35.9)	(384.0)	(332.1)
Disposal of properties	4.6	3.3	23.2
Equity investment	—	—	(17.5)
Other, net	(12.3)	.1	(8.2)
Total	(43.6)	(380.6)	(334.6)
Cash before financing	(24.8)	(347.2)	(149.5)
Financing activities			
Long-term borrowing	7.3	241.6	393.6
Reduction in long-term debt	(63.8)	(110.5)	(130.3)
Sale-leaseback of drilling rig	—	77.8	—
Preferred/common stock dividends	(6.6)	(23.9)	(8.6)
Sale of preferred stock	—	—	107.6
Other	(3.4)	4.5	79.3
Cash from financing	(66.5)	$189.5	441.6
Increase (decrease) in cash	(91.3)	$(157.7)	$292.1

* Excludes cash, short-term investments, and current maturities of long-term debt.

$201 million, (5) $361 million received from subsidized or government-guaranteed financing in support of shipyard deliveries, (6) a special lease transaction, (7) $168 million from the sale of tax benefits, (8) secured and unsecured loans from banks, and (9) $100 million from United States Title XI government-guaranteed bonds secured by three of the company's previously unencumbered drilling rigs (see Table C15.3 for a summary of key 1981 to 1985 data).

Some Global Marine creditors require their approval before the company can borrow additional funds. Another creditor restriction requires the company to maintain a minimum of $428.7 million in shareholders' equity.

TABLE C15.2   GLOBAL MARINE CONSOLIDATED BALANCE SHEET, 1983–1985
($ millions)

	As of December 31		
	1985	**1984**	**1983**
Assets			
Cash	$ 11.1	$ 4.3	$ 3.3
Short-term investments	78.7	176.8	335.5
Accounts receivable	59.5	64.7	51.4
Materials and supplies	24.3	25.8	38.7
Prepaid expenses	10.6	4.9	6.9
Deferred income taxes	—	7.6	5.3
Total current assets	$ 184.2	$ 284.1	$ 441.1
Rigs and drilling equipment (less accumulated depreciation)	$1,260.3	$1,324.6	972.0
Rigs under construction	—	—	80.3
Oil and gas properties			
Subject to amortization	90.2	168.7	222.5
Not subject to amortization	—	15.1	85.7
Net properties	1,350.5	1,508.4	1,360.5
Other assets	38.3	54.3	42.5
Total assets	$1,573.0	1,846.8	1,844.1
Liabilities			
Current maturity of long-term debt	—	$ 97.8	83.5
Accounts payable	30.6	48.6	36.2
Accrued liabilities	30.2	71.5	70.1
Long-term debt reclassified due to default	1,087.7	—	—
Related accrued interest	97.3	—	—
Total current liabilities	$1,245.8	$ 217.9	189.8
Long-term debt	—	$1,035.0	902.9
Other long-term liabilities	25.5	22.6	18.7
Deferred income taxes	—	21.6	76.2
Deferred credits	11.1	34.6	28.3
Total long-term debt	$ 36.6	$1,113.8	$1,026.1
Shareholders' equity			
Cumulative convertible pfd. stock	$ 115.0	$ 115.0	115.0
Common stock	4.1	4.0	3.9
Additional paid-in capital	211.8	209.8	207.9
Retained earnings	(40.3)	186.3	301.4
Total shareholders' equity	$ 290.6	$ 515.1	628.2
Total liabilities and equity	$1,573.0	$1,846.8	$1,844.1

TABLE C15.3   GLOBAL MARINE FIVE-YEAR REVIEW, 1981–1985

	Year ended, $ millions				
	1985	1984	1983	1982	1981
	Summary of Operations				
Revenues:					
Marine drilling	$360.7	$385.8	$421.2	$421.0	$324.2
Oil and gas	17.9	20.6	22.3	24.4	16.3
Other energy services	—	.2	3.5	10.3	11.9
Total revenues	$378.6	$406.6	$447.0	$455.7	$352.4
Net income (loss)	(220.0)	(91.2)	49.3	85.0	79.8
Shareholders' equity ($ millions)	290.6	$515.0	$628.0	$476.0	$394.0
Net income (loss) per common	($7.27)	($3.35)	$1.52	$2.71	$2.61
Dividends paid per common share	$.06	$.24	.24	.23	.175

The company's ability to pay maturing debt obligations depends largely upon the extent to which rigs are contracted out and the rates obtained for these contracts. Because most of the company's drilling contracts are short-term in nature, annual cash flow is difficult to project. The decline in Global Marine's 1985 drilling revenues was attributed to lower rates at which the company's drilling rigs were leased to customers under new contracts.

Global Marine currently has 68 claims, totaling $208.5 million, pending in connection with the loss of the *Glomar Java Sea* (discussed earlier under industry hazards). Five other claims have been settled by Global Marine. An additional five lawsuits have been filed against the company, seeking $240 million in damages. Global Marine is confident that existing insurance covers pending lawsuits and claims against the company.

COMPETITIVE FINANCIAL PERFORMANCE

The financial performance of major competitors in the offshore drilling industry for the period 1980 to 1985 appears in Table C15.4.

Mr. David Herasimchuk of Global Marine offered the following comments about several offshore drilling contractors:

Rowan Drilling Company and the Offshore Drilling and Exploration Company (ODECO) are financially conservative. Rowan finances capital investments primarily from operations.

Atwood Oceanics, 41% of which is owned by Helmerich and Payne, is conservatively managed and does not order offshore drilling rigs constructed on speculation. The company has equipment that tends to be obsolete. The company's financial condition, however, is excellent. Atwood has accumulated cash while using older rigs and invested profits in major oil companies—its customers—rather than purchase high technology offshore drilling equipment.

TABLE C15.4 FINANCIAL PERFORMANCE, SELECTED OFFSHORE DRILLING CONTRACTORS, 1981–1985

	1985	1984	1983	1982	1981
Global Marine, Inc.*					
Revenues (mil.)	$378.6	406.6	447.0	455.7	352.4
Net income (mil.)	(220.0)	(94.9)	49.3	85.0	79.8
Book value: Common	$ 5.34	12.86	16.13	15.15	12.81
Ocean Drilling and Exploration Company (ODECO)*					
Revenues	$633.8	698.6	811.7	979.6	892.2
Net income	33.7	65.8	119.4	191.9	175.0
Book value: Common	$ 16.30	16.34	16.31	15.05	12.09
Reading & Bates Corporation*					
Revenues	$236.7	329.2	431.1	516.8	530.5
Net income	(83.2)	18.7	38.2	73.3	93.4
Book value: Common	7.87	15.36	15.21	14.80	13.07
Rowan Companies, Inc.*					
Revenues	$272.5	198.4	206.5	400.4	369.0
Net income	3.8	4.2	21.9	119.4	111.8
Book value: Common	$ 10.61	10.66	10.66	10.54	8.23
Zapata Corporation*					
Revenues	$288.7	421.3	443.0	537.1	413.0
Net income	(63.9)	26.1	52.5	103.9	81.7
Book value: Common	$ 19.05	23.21	22.65	20.90	18.30
Helmerich and Payne					
Revenues	$192.0	192.6	208.1	338.2	287.6
Net income	18.5	21.4	47.8	75.7	75.3
Book value: Common	$ 17.01	16.63	16.12	14.54	12.04

* Source: *Value Line,* June 13, 1986, pp. 1868–1878.

MANAGEMENT

Corporate Officers

C. Russell Luigs, 52, is chairman of the board, president, and chief executive officer. Luigs was elected president and chief executive officer in May 1977. He has served as chairman since 1982. Luigs previously was president and a director of U.S. Industries, a diversified manufacturing and service company, from 1974 to 1976.

Jerry C. Martin, 53, senior vice president and chief financial officer, joined Global Marine in 1979 and was elected to his present position in May 1985. Other officers include:

James T. Goodwyn, Jr., 57, president, Challenger Minerals, Inc. (joined Global Marine in February, 1985)

Gary L. Kott, 43, president, Global Marine Drilling Company (joined Global Marine in 1978 and appointed to present position in 1979)

Thomas E. Short, 57, president, Applied Drilling Technology, Inc. (1979)

Robert E. Sleet, 39, vice president and treasurer (joined Global Marine in April, 1985)

David A. Herasimchuk, 43, vice president, market development (August, 1980)

John G. Ryan, 33, senior vice president, secretary and general counsel

James C. Schmitz, 37, vice president, Tax and Government Affairs

Board of Directors

The board of directors includes Chairman Luigs and:

Retired (1985) Senior Vice President William R. Thomas

Donald B. Brown, 58, an oil and gas consultant (elected to the board in 1982)

Edward J. Campbell, 56, president and chief executive officer, Newport News Shipbuilding, a Tenneco subsidiary (elected in 1981)

Hubert Faure, 65, senior executive vice president, United Technologies Corporation (elected in 1984)

John M. Galvin, 52, senior vice president, Aetna Life and Casualty (joined the board in 1979)

Warren F. Kane, 61, private consultant and recently retired president of Baker Drilling Equipment Company, a subsidiary of Baker International Corporation (elected in 1982)

Lynn L. Leigh, 59, chairman, president, and chief executive officer, Summit Oilfield Corporation (elected to the board in 1981)

William C. Walker, consultant to the petroleum industry (1985)

Antitakeover Action in 1985

The board of directors was concerned in 1985 about the possibility that Global Marine was vulnerable to takeover by a larger company. Therefore, several antitakeover provisions were proposed for inclusion in the company's certificate of incorporation. These proposals would: (1) divide the board of directors into three classes serving staggered 3-year terms; (2) allow board size to range from a minimum of 3 to a maximum of 15 directors; (3) require stockholder actions be initiated only at a stockholders' meeting to which all stockholders were invited; (4) permit incumbent directors to fill any vacancies on the board; (5) increase the stockholder vote required to change, amend, or replace company bylaws from a majority to 80% of the stock available for voting.

REEVALUATING GMI's FUTURE DIRECTIONS

Russ Luigs joined Global Marine in 1977 and shortly thereafter introduced a 7-year plan intended to place the company in a position of preeminence within the industry. During most of those years, Global Marine experienced profitability and record growth in assets and revenues. 1985 was a watershed year for Global Marine, however. The company's

$1 billion investment in state of the art technology had indeed brought Global Marine to a leadership position among offshore oil and gas drilling contractors but cash flow was insufficient to pay off the company's indebtedness.

Luigs might well reflect on those factors critical to success and survival in the offshore drilling industry. He had driven Global Marine to the cutting edge of offshore drilling technology and assembled a fleet of rigs capable of meeting any customer's needs, no mattter what the environment. His organization personified the concept, "The Customer is King."

In an industry renowned for risks, Russ Luigs had taken no more than a conventional approach and pursued a strategic course of action that he, his board of directors, and his creditors did not perceive as excessively risky. Was the price of industry leadership too high? Should he and could he have acted differently? What basis was there to indicate that an alternative course of action would have led to a more favorable set of circumstances?

Global Marine, Inc., as of January 1, 1986, had no 7-year strategic plan for the future. The company's primary objective was survival, as stated by Mr. Luigs in the company's 1985 Annual Report. Although hindsight indicated that the company could have pursued less ambitious objectives, Global Marine's current concerns were what actions and circumstance might combine to preserve the company as an independent entity in the international offshore oil and gas drilling industry.

HARLEY-DAVIDSON

Prepared by Nabil A. Ibrahim, Augusta College.

The unique form of transportation known as the motorcycle has been an integral part of American life now for nearly a century. Sadly, only one American motorcycle manufacturing concern, Harley-Davidson, whose corporate logo reflects the American ideals of strength, freedom, and patriotism in a majestic bald eagle poised for flight, continues to produce American-made motorcycles. Harley-Davidson competes alone against a vast array of Japanese and European-built motorcycles which have captured a large share of Harley-Davidson's domain: large, powerful sport and cruising motorcycles. Undaunted and refusing to relinquish its hold on its proud heritage, the company which began at the turn of the century with its namesakes William A. Davidson, Walter C. Davidson, Arthur Davidson, and William S. Harley carries on today as the producer of what many people consider the finest motorcycles ever made.

BEGINNINGS

Bicycles were, of course, the immediate predecessor of the motorcycle. By the close of the 19th century, bicycle racing had become quite a celebrated sport, and the first experimental "motor bicycles" had appeared in Europe. Although the early models usually used steam power, there had been some tinkering with the idea of a power-driven, two-wheeled vehicle in America prior to the turn of the century, but the first commercially produced motorcycle in the United States did not appear until 1901.

It was not long after this that two young childhood friends and bicycle enthusiasts from Milwaukee, Wisconsin—William Harley and Arthur Davidson—turned their inquisitive minds to the development of a motor-powered bicycle of their own. By the

Used by permission.

spring of 1903 the first prototype model was completed. It was capable of speeds of almost 25 miles per hour.

Realizing the limits of simply attaching a small motor to a bicycle frame, the two original entrepreneurs designed a whole new bicycle from the ground up with a frame made of heavy-gauge tubing, a lengthened wheel base, and the now-standard two-stroke DeDion gasoline engine. This became the first commercial Harley-Davidson motorcycle.

William and Arthur were now joined by the remaining Davidson brothers, William and Walter. Erecting a 10 × 15 wooden shed in the backyard of the family home and painting "Harley-Davidson Motor Co." on the door, these four young men quietly heralded a new chapter in American transportation history.

Enlisting the aid of an uncle, James McLay, who possessed the necessary capital, the four young visionaries built the first major production facility at the corner of 27th and Chestnut streets in the industrial sector of Milwaukee. By 1906, production was approaching 50 machines a year, all quickly snapped up by Milwaukee residents. As the first mass-produced inexpensive automobile was not yet available, motorcycles were an attractive substitute. On September 22, 1907, the Harley-Davidson Motor Company of Milwaukee was legally incorporated and entered the growing field of American motorcycle producers.

By spring 1908, factory floor space had increased to 5000 square feet and production had reached 456 machines a year, produced by some 36 employees. Early on, retailing was established through bicycle dealerships which by then were selling Harley-Davidsons all through the Eastern United States. The industry was somewhat crowded, with about 33 different manufacturers. Only several were considered at high enough quality to really compete with Harley-Davidson, the most notable being Indian, Excelsior, Pope, Iver Johnson, Merkel, Reading Standard, and Wagner. A major marketing achievement occurred in 1909 when Arthur Davidson demonstrated his machine to a convention of rural free delivery mail carriers, who promptly switched in large numbers from their Wagners to Harley-Davidsons. By the mid-teens there were many American companies manufacturing motorcycles, but the "Big Three" were Indian, Excelsior, and, in third place, Harley-Davidson.

Motorcycle racing had become serious sport before the end of the first decade of the 20th century and Walter Davidson immediately realized what an advertising campaign it could potentially be. Entering himself in the 1908 endurance run, sponsored by the infant Federation of American Motorcyclists, and against 84 other riders, he finished the grueling 24-hour course with a perfect score of 1000.

Europe was already in the throes of World War I and almost all motorcycle production there had been diverted to military use. While it was not immediately apparent, a subtle difference in motorcycle design had been taking place between the European and American machines. Because the United States was still a growing, developing country (when Harley-Davidson was founded there were only 45 states), the American-made motorcycle required greater durability and more power than was necessary for European machines. American roads—where they existed—were mostly unpaved; distances were farther. Frequently riders resorted to using railroad tracks, bumping along on the ties, in preference to the morass of muddy roads. As a result, the motorcycle that evolved was better suited to wartime duties than the usually smaller, lighter, and more fragile European machine.

In America there was a bewildering variety of motorcycle brands and sizes available and the number of features offered was enormous. Within a brand (and sometimes between brands) there was a great deal of parts interchangeability. By 1915 such "de luxe" accessories as optional electric lighting, luggage carriers, footboards, and rear stand were being offered with Harley-Davidson motorcycles.

America entered World War I in April of 1917 and the motorcycle industry switched immediately to military production. The war provided a huge market for motorcycles equipped with sidecars for use by the allied forces. Cycles already had seen some warlike duty at the Mexican border when Pancho Villa had attempted a token invasion of New Mexico (which had only recently become a state). Impressed with the performance of motorcycles at that time—often cycles could "get through" when larger, four-wheeled vehicles could not—the government placed large orders with the Milwaukee-based Harley-Davidson.

By 1917–1918, half of Harley-Davidson's production went into government service. The "Big Three" motorcycle producers supplied to the war effort 41,000 Indians, 15,000 Harley-Davidsons, and 2,600 Excelsiors.

At the close of World War I, Harley-Davidson and Indian were producing 35,000 motorcycles a year; Excelsior followed with 25,000. With the original factory greatly enlarged and now located on Juneau Avenue, Harley-Davidson was rapidly gaining on the long-standing first-ranked producer, Indian.

The 1920s saw a decline in popularity of the motorcycle, as affordable automobiles had at last become a reality. While domestic demand declined, overseas interest picked up and by 1927, 50% of all American-made motorcycles made their way to Europe. By this time, Harley-Davidson's top of the line was the 74 Cruising J-model, constituting the backbone of Harley-Davidson as the industry leader.

With the arrival of the Great Depression, Excelsior folded and a vicious competitive battle developed between Harley-Davidson and Indian, which had been saved from financial ruin when it was acquired by E. Paul du Pont. During this period, the American law enforcement community became an important market for Harley-Davidson, as it still is today. By 1935, sales were reviving, with Harley-Davidson producing a little over 10,000 units for the year.

The close of the depression was marked by two bitter events: unionization of Harley-Davidson's workers and the death of William Davidson. While Harley-Davidson had never employed "sweat shop" labor, pro-union sentiment was strong. In 1936, the employees joined the United Auto Workers Union. Shortly thereafter, Harley-Davidson suffered a second blow in the death of William Davidson. Nevertheless, year-end production for 1937 reached 11,674 units, an increase over 1936 of nearly 3,000 machines. Over 50% of this output was sold overseas.

The 1930s saw the concentration of Harley-Davidson production in two main motorcycle types which would be the mainstay of the line for the next three decades. The 61E "Big Twin" was perfected despite initial faults, and the 45 Model, although less in demand than the Big Twin, still saw much service as a utility vehicle fitted with a sidecar.

The Harley-Davidson Big Twin had reached a level of reliability equal to current automobiles and, capable of carrying an extra passenger on a buddy seat, it was a machine in which a rider could plan with certainty to travel across the United States with only minor maintenance.

By 1940, because of wartime production for the government, the main Juneau Avenue production facility was expanded and put into round-the-clock production. Shortly afterward, the company lost another original founder, President Walter Davidson. He was succeeded in the leadership of Harley-Davidson by his son, William Davidson. A third founder, William Harley, died in 1943.

Harley-Davidson's cumulative war production had been stupendous, rolling out 88,000 machines before the cancelation of the government contracts. A side effect of the war effort was increased awareness of the Harley-Davidson motorcycle by thousands of GIs who learned to ride on Army motorcycles. This eventually translated into more sales in the domestic market after the war.

THE POSTWAR ERA

Although the war had increased awareness of motorcycling, the early postwar period saw the beginning of serious inroads by imported motorcycles into the American market. Most of these early imports were British and, by the end of 1946, over 10,000 had been sold. The foreign middle-weight models had no counterpart coming from the American motorcycle industry. Although, an import tariff of 8% was levied in the United States, exported Harley-Davidsons felt the weight of a 33% to 50% tariff.

The postwar era also saw the rise of the now notorious "outlaw" motorcycle riders and gangs. While these so-called outlaw motorcyclists became the focus of national attention, they did not represent a significant percentage of American motorcycling enthusiasts and Harley-Davidson dealerships refused to deal with them in the servicing of their machines.

Arthur Davidson, the last of the founders, died in the early 1950s. The decade also ushered in the first significant threat to the company from imports.

But despite the imports, Harley-Davidson managed to continue to sell all it produced. A new introduction, the Harley-Davidson 125, a smaller machine designed to compete against the imports, sold 10,000 in its first year of production. However, as an ominous note of things to come, a November 1959 issue of *Cycle Magazine* featured an advertisement introducing the Honda; a small machine, 50 cc, it featured electric starting. The first advertising line read "You meet the nicest people on a Honda."

The mid-1960s brought Harley-Davidson to a precarious position—it claimed only 6% of the market, although sales were at a record high amount of $31 million. At this time it was decided to offer stock to the public, a first time ever infusion of outside capital. Control of the corporation remained in the hands of the surviving members of the Harley and Davidson families, who held a majority of the tendered stock.

Despite the injection of capital, Harley-Davidson continued on shaky financial ground through the mid-1960s, and in 1967 it was decided to put the company up for sale to a conglomerate, although the Harley-Davidson top management called it a "merger." American Machine and Foundry (AMF) acquired Harley-Davidson for an exchange of AMF stock valued at $210 million. Harley-Davidson management and most of its staff were retained.

The acquisition of Harley-Davidson by AMF brought about a harsh reappraisal of Harley-Davidson's problems. While the four founders had run the company well in the early years and managed to survive the Great Depression, their deaths and replacement by their descendants was not the best thing for the company. Control was spread out among too many Harleys and Davidsons, some of whom lacked the ability to be in upper-level management. Harley-Davidson's production facilities were incredibly outdated and badly in need of modernization and retooling. The problem of Harley-Davidson's management was not addressed during this period, but critical renovation and retooling of the production facilities was accomplished. The product line was also expanded somewhat with the introduction in 1970 of the "Superglide."

A new approach to marketing was developed in 1970. The once shunned custom motorcycle enthusiasts were now being sought. At this time a new logo was also introduced: a broad-ribboned number "1," carrying a symbol of the American flag together with the slogan "The All American Freedom Machine."

In addition to the retooling of the Milwaukee facilities, AMF opened another production outlet in York, Pennsylvania.

With an expanded product line and new facilities, 1973 was a record year for the industry and for Harley-Davidson. It was generally believed the greatly increased demand was primarily due to the baby boomers who were maturing into driving and motorcycling age.

The increased output and transition from more traditional, craftsmanlike production to modern assembly-line techniques brought on a sharp rise in quality control problems. Riders began to discern a distinct difference between Milwaukee and York machines, mainly because about half the York-made machines were defective in some respect. The problem was further complicated by AMF's policy of reimbursing dealers for shop time necessary to bring defective machines up to running standards only if they could prove the defect had occurred in the factory. These various problems coupled with AMF's huge capital infusion into Harley-Davidson that had yet to show a substantial return caused AMF's management to begin considering getting rid of Harley-Davidson.

THE EARLY 1980s

Signaling the end of an era, in 1981 Harley-Davidson's top management, led by Vaughn Beals, took the company private again by separating it from the AMF conglomerate in exchange for $80 million. The company immediately began an aggressive advertising campaign which included such slogans as . . . "motorcycles by the people, for the people," and stressed an almost patriotic theme to encourage the public to support this veteran American industry. They instantly began in a new direction for the reorganized company through marketing and more dealer cooperation in updating present products and developing additional models.

A newly formulated mission statement described Harley-Davidson as a company which "designs, manufactures and sells heavyweight touring and custom motorcycles and a broad range of related products. The Company is the only American manufacturer of motorcycles. In addition, the Company manufactures other products for the defense industry including metal bomb casings and liquid fuel rocket engines."

The most pressing problem to be solved was quality control, which was hurting dealer-factory relationships. There were still warranty claims, ranging from $5,000 to $30,000 for a 1-year period, which were still unresolved.

During the first months of 1982, the company began an aggressive legal campaign designed to do away with the large number of unfranchised garages and repair shops across the country for their unauthorized use of Harley-Davidson trademarks and logos. There were estimated to be approximately 3,000 of these types of operation. Also during 1982, the country was experiencing an economic recession and motorcycles were among the first to be affected. In Japan, however, production increased at a very rapid pace due to an industrial system which fostered good labor-management relations. In order to protect this relationship, Japanese management maintained high production and would take a reduction in profits in order to do so. This resulted in a surplus of goods now being "dumped" at very low prices in the world market. Motorcycles were among these goods, of which United States buyers purchased approximately 800,000 units during 1981.

The effect was drastic for the sales of domestic motorcycles. Many of these importers were ordered to clear their surplus stock by any means. Many dealers were already swamped with excess inventories and were selling the products at very low prices. Harley-Davidson, having never been very competitively priced, was hurt.

With a month-long plant shutdown occurring in 1982 to reduce inventories and falling sales throughout the country, Harley-Davidson was now faced with a severe cash flow problem. Many dealers who were loaded up with machines which were taking up floor space and were eating up interest were now offering models at prices near their own factory cost.

It was at this time that Vaughn Beals, president of Harley-Davidson, announced that the country's oldest motorcycle manufacturer faced bankruptcy. He began to cut company operations by eliminating nearly 200 clerical jobs, and in the spring of 1982 he laid off 3,800 employees. Meanwhile, many dealers were complaining of quality control problems and were deluging the factory with warranty demands.

THE 1983 TARIFF

Despite several drastic cost-saving efforts, the company was still teetering on the edge of disaster. In September 1982, Harley-Davidson took its complaints before the Federal Trade Commission (FTC), claiming the Japanese were dumping large motorcycles in the United States at very cheap prices and were threatening Harley-Davidson with bankruptcy.

In April 1983, President Ronald Reagan took the advice of the FTC and raised the tariffs and imposed quotas for 5 years on motorcycles over 700 cc in displacement. This was said to be the most aggressive trade restraint ever taken by the United States.

In some instances, the large motorcycle importers were not hurt a great deal. For instance, Honda was currently shipping parts into the United States and was then assembling the machines here. This allowed them to get around the strict import tariffs. Another way the Japanese avoided the tariff was by replacing many of their 750 cc models with engines with 690 to 699 cc engines. In addition, the tariff contained a provision where during the 5-year tariff period, the rates would be declining annually.

Harley-Davidson took another bold step on July 8, 1986, by going from a private to a public company. It was on this date the company completed a public offering of 2 million shares of common stock and $70 million of unsecured subordinated debentures. A portion of these funds was used to repay outstanding loan balances and to purchase warrants which would allow the company to acquire its common stock which was held by its creditors. The remainder of the funds were used for capital expenditures and for additional working capital.

A significant move was made by Harley-Davidson in December 1986 when it acquired the Holiday Rambler Corporation. (See appendix for product line.) As part of a new diversification strategy, Holiday Rambler was seen as an excellent opportunity because both companies are manufacturing-intensive and both produce leading recreational vehicles. They both are companies that sold products to very committed groups of people whose lifestyles are heavily influenced by their recreational activities. One final reason for this acquisition was to diversify into an industry that is without Japanese competition.

ASSUMING A COMPETITIVE POSTURE

In order to successfully compete with imported motorcycles, the company undertook significant engineering programs that would make dramatic improvements in its V-twin engine designs and, at the same time, would result in markedly lowered production

FIGURE C16.1 HARLEY-DAVIDSON'S U.S. MARKET SHARE
Super Heavyweight Motorcycles (850cc +)

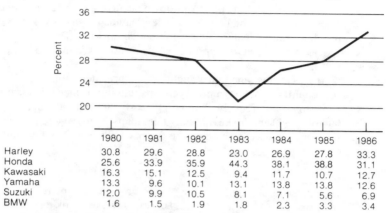

	1980	1981	1982	1983	1984	1985	1986
Harley	30.8	29.6	28.8	23.0	26.9	27.8	33.3
Honda	25.6	33.9	35.9	44.3	38.1	38.8	31.1
Kawasaki	16.3	15.1	12.5	9.4	11.7	10.7	12.7
Yamaha	13.3	9.6	10.1	13.1	13.8	13.8	12.6
Suzuki	12.0	9.9	10.5	8.1	7.1	5.6	6.9
BMW	1.6	1.5	1.9	1.8	2.3	3.3	3.4

Source: Harley-Davidson, Inc., Annual Report, 1986.

costs. In addition, the company substantially broadened its product line—offering 16 heavyweight models as compared with only three models in 1976. Also, Harley-Davidson reorganized its plant under a system that borrowed heavily from the Japanese style of management. The system which stressed worker involvement in the manufacturing process, just-in-time manufacturing, and statistical control of operations became a model for many other companies. An extensive quality control campaign was also introduced.

As a result, the company raised the percentage of motorcycles leaving its production lines without defects from about 50% to more than 98%, and there was a sharp drop in the number of warranty claims and consumer complaints. In one year, the company was able to lower its break-even point by one-third, from 53,000 to 35,000 units annually.

As Figure C16.1 shows, by 1986, Harley-Davidson's share of the U.S. market for heavyweight motorcycles moved up to 33%—it had dipped from 42% in 1976 to 23% in 1983. For all types of motorcycles, the company's share increased from 12.5% in 1983 to 19.4% in 1986.

The company also began a program to assist dealers in remodeling their dealerships. Each new store was designed to improve traffic flow as well as increase their appeal to a much larger number of people.

The company should see an even greater increase in sales due to a brilliant marketing move in their motorcycle sector. In early 1987, the company introduced a "Ride Free" program whereby the purchaser of an 883 Sportster model is guaranteed a trade-in value of $3,995 (the original price) on the purchase of a larger motorcycle. Harley-Davidson's competitors would probably find it difficult to follow suit because they have not had as high a resale value on their products as Harley-Davidson has.

In March 1987 the company concluded that its competitive position had improved so much that it asked President Reagan to end its tariff and quota protection a year early. Indeed, Harley's motorcycle business was profitable in 1986 for the first time since the company's managers bought it from AMF in 1981. Vaughn Beals was quoted saying: "We're profitable again. We're capitalized. We're diversified. We don't need any more help." A few weeks later, the company announced that, for the first quarter in 1987, it had sales of $162 million and a net income of $5.2 million. These compared with $70 million in sales for the first quarter in 1986 and a net loss of $0.16 million.

FINANCIAL HIGHLIGHTS

The increase in liability expense is a factor that is affecting almost every aspect of business today, especially due to the large monetary awards which juries are awarding plaintiffs in the case of product liabilities against the manufacturer. Not surprisingly, then, Harley-Davidson's product liability insurance limits and their coverages have been adversely affected and the cost for obtaining this type of insurance has increased.

Accidents involving personal injuries and property damage occur in the use of motorcycles. Harley-Davidson is currently a defendant in a number of lawsuits involving product liability claims; some of these cases involve substantial sums and some involve claims for punitive and exemplary damages. When the company was acquired from AMF in 1981, an agreement was reached whereby AMF would indemnify the company against all losses and liabilities in connection with all motorcycle product liability claims arising out of accidents prior to June 10, 1981 (the acquisition date), with respect to products sold prior to this date. In an effort to curb these lawsuits, the company investigates all motorcycle accidents which involve serious injuries and fatalities and conducts frequent safety reviews on their products. It is believed these reviews were responsible for a reduction in product liability claims of nearly 35% from June 1981 to April 1986.

In 1986, sales to the Defense Department were lower than in previous years due to a decrease in demand from the government for production of 500-pound metal bomb casings.

In addition, the company had been providing wiring harnesses to a major computer manufacturer. However, in February 1986, the manufacturer discontinued the use of these harnesses. Prior to 1986, this sector had contributed very well to Harley-Davidson's income with revenues of $3.9 million in 1983, $9.9 million in 1984, and $7.5 million in 1985. The company is currently working out contracts with this same computer manufacturer to provide manufacturing engineering for computer peripheral equipment. This should prove to be additional revenue in the near future.

The consolidated financial statements (Figures C16.2 and C16.3) do not reflect the operations of the Holiday Rambler Corporation (acquired in December 1986). However, based on the Proforma statements (Figures C16.4 and C16.5) we can see just how much this acquisition will mean to Harley-Davidson. It will mean additional sales of approximately $289 million or an increase of nearly $3.6 million in additional net income. One drawback is that the additional revenues will not increase their net margin, which is around 1.5%. Holiday Rambler's major competitor is Airstream, considered to be the top of the line in this category of motor homes, travel trailers, and related products. However, since Airstream is priced much higher than Holiday Rambler, there should be enough market share for both.

CONCLUSION

The biggest setbacks to motorcycle sales are the danger and image motorcycles have. Rather than seeing them as an economical mode of transportation, many people associate motorcycles with gangs and "bad elements." Thus, while the name Harley-David-

FIGURE C16.2   HARLEY-DAVIDSON, INC. CONSOLIDATED BALANCE SHEET
(In Thousands)

	December 31	
	1986	**1985**
Assets		
Current assets:		
Cash	$ 7,354	$ 9,070
Temporary investments	20,500	4,400
Accounts receivable net of allowance for doubtful accounts	36,462	27,313
Inventories	78,630	28,868
Prepaid expenses	5,812	3,241
Total current assets	148,758	72,892
Property, plant, and equipment at cost, less accumulated depreciation and amortization	90,932	38,727
Deferred financing costs	3,340	2,392
Intangible assets	82,114	—
Other assets	2,052	81
	$327,196	$114,092
Liabilities and stockholders' equity		
Current liabilities:		
Notes payable	$ 14,067	$ —
Current maturities of long-term debt	4,023	2,875
Accounts payable	29,587	27,521
Accrued expenses and other liabilities	61,144	26,251
Total current liabilities	108,821	56,647
Long-term debt less current maturities	191,594	51,504
Long-term pension liability	622	1,319
Commitments and contingencies		
Stockholders' equity		
Common stock, 6,200,000 issued in 1986 and 4,200,000 in 1985	62	42
Class B common stock, no shares issued	—	—
Additional paid-in capital	26,657	10,258
Deficit	(717)	(5,588)
Cumulative foreign currency translation adjustment	287	40
	26,289	4,752
Less treasury stock (520,000 shares) at cost	(130)	(130)
Total stockholders' equity	26,159	4,622
	$327,196	$114,092

Source: Harley-Davidson, Inc., Annual Report, 1986.

FIGURE C16.3   HARLEY-DAVIDSON, INC. CONSOLIDATED STATEMENT OF INCOME
(In Thousands, Except per Share Amounts)

	Year ended December 31		
	1986	1985	1984
Net sales	$295,322	$287,476	$293,825
Operating costs and expenses:			
Cost of goods sold	219,167	217,222	220,040
Selling and administrative expenses	51,060	47,162	47,662
Engineering research and development expenses	8,999	10,179	10,591
	279,226	274,563	278,293
Income from operations	16,096	12,913	15,532
Interest income	1,138	—	—
Interest expense	(9,511)	(9,412)	(11,256)
Other expense–net	(388)	(338)	(311)
Income before provision for income taxes, extraordinary items, and cumulative effect of change in accounting principle	7,335	3,163	3,965
Provision for income taxes	3,028	526	1,077
Income before extraordinary items and cumulative effect of change in accounting principle	4,307	2,637	2,888
Gain (loss) on refinancing net of taxes	(847)	2,876	—
Benefit from utilization of loss carryforward	1,411	4,442	2,718
Cumulative effect of change in accounting principle	—	—	860
Net income	$ 4,871	$ 9,955	$ 6,466
Per common share			
Income before extraordinary items and cumulative effect of change in accounting principle	$ .82	$ .72	$ .79
Extraordinary items	.11	1.99	.74
Cumulative effect of change in accounting principle	—	—	.23
Net income	$ .93	$ 2.71	$ 1.76

Source: Harley-Davidson, Inc., Annual Report, 1986.

FIGURE C16.4 CONSOLIDATED PRO FORMA REVENUE MIX

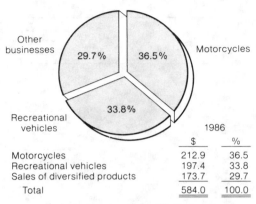

	$	%
Motorcycles	212.9	36.5
Recreational vehicles	197.4	33.8
Sales of diversified products	173.7	29.7
Total	584.0	100.0

Source: Harley-Davidson, Inc., Annual Report, 1986.

FIGURE C16.5 COMPARISON OF 1986 PRO FORMA FINANCIALS INCLUDING HOLIDAY RAMBLER, WITH THOSE REPORTED IN 1986 EXCLUDING HOLIDAY RAMBLER
(In $ Millions)

	1986	
	Pro forma	Reported
Net sales	$584.0	$295.3
Net income before extraordinary items	$ 7.9	$ 4.3
Earnings per share, before extraordinary items	$ 1.34	$ 0.82

Source: Harley-Davidson, Inc., Annual Report, 1986.

son evokes nostalgic images of a company and a machine with a certain mystique, the thought of a Harley-Davidson rider is not nearly so pleasant. The company, however, estimates that "outlaws" represent far less than 1% of all motorcycle riders. On the other hand, the danger element seems to be somewhat justified. In 1979, for example, when there were about 5 million motorcycles in the United States, almost 5,000 people died in motorcycle accidents.

More recently, however, it appears that there is a "new" Harley-Davidson rider that has evolved with the "new" Harley-Davidson. The Harley rider is generally more educated, has a higher income, and is more likely to be a professional or a manager than the owners of Japanese motorcycles. The comparative figures show that Harley-Davidson is becoming the choice of middle-and upper-income motorcycle enthusiasts (Figure C16.6).

FIGURE C16.6 A COMPARISON OF THE FIVE MAJOR MOTORCYCLE MANUFACTURERS ALONG
SEVERAL DEMOGRAPHIC DIMENSIONS

Factor	Honda	Kawasaki	Suzuki	Yamaha	Harley
Men vs. Women	75–25	72–28	90–10	78–22	96–4
Age					
18–24	21.4	27.7	25.8	22.4	12.0
25–34	32.6	20.1	30.2	45.6	42.0
35–44	26.3	26.9	20.7	19.4	24.0
45–54	13.9	15.9	17.0	7.1	14.0
55 +	5.8	9.4	6.4	5.5	7.0
18–34	54.0	47.8	56.0	68.0	54.0
18–44	80.3	74.7	76.7	87.4	78.0
25–44	58.9	47.0	50.9	65.0	68.0
Education					
Some College +	38.9	34.2	36.6	36.5	44.0
High School	42.7	35.6	50.7	44.6	43.0
Less than High School	18.4	30.2	12.6	18.9	11.0
Employment					
Professional/technical	8.8	11.2	9.9	14.3	17.0
Manager/administrator	9.3	7.8	6.8	10.1	13.0
Craftsmen/foreman	19.8	17.6	18.7	41.1	27.0
Other employed	31.6	22.0	39.1	25.7	
Income					
Greater than $35,000	11.2	5.4	20.4	11.6	28.3
Greater than $25,000	12.8	12.4	13.2	14.5	35.1
$15,000–$24,999	30.8	44.6	33.9	25.1	24.0
Less than $14,999	19.0	17.5	7.4	22.4	14.0
Region					
Northeast	13.0	8.9	20.0	14.6	19.0
North central	36.1	39.6	32.7	37.8	39.0
South	20.1	25.0	24.9	16.4	26.0
West	30.7	26.4	22.4	31.2	16.0
Marital status					
Single	21.2	23.5	25.4	27.4	23.0
Married	73.1	65.9	66.1	64.8	58.0
Divorced	5.7	10.6	8.4	7.8	15.0
Parents	53.3	41.1	40.3	51.6	
Household size					
1 Person	5.7	6.1	4.3	6.8	6.1
2 Persons	19.8	26.5	30.3	25.2	24.0
3 or 4 persons	52.5	50.4	46.9	38.5	49.0
5 or more persons	22.0	16.9	18.5	29.5	20.9

Source: Mediamark Research, Inc., Spring 1982.

APPENDIX: Divisions

    I Harley-Davidson Motorcycles—manufactures motorcycles from 883 cc to 1340 cc.

  II Holiday Rambler—manufacturer of premium motor homes, travel trailers, specialized commercial vehicles, and a diverse range of related products.

    A Holiday House—builds three models of park trailers from 320 to 400 square feet.

    B Aviator—van conversion, redesigns interiors and exteriors of full-size vans and mini-vans. Also customizes other recreational vehicles.

    C Nappanee Wood Products—manufacturers of custom wood cabinetry primarily for Holiday Rambler recreational vehicles.

    D Creative Dimensions—produces a full line of contemporary office and drafting furniture.

    E B & B Molders—designs and manufactures custom and standard tooling and injection molded plastic pieces.

 III Defense and other businesses

Department of Defense—manufactures 500-pound metal bomb casings and liquid fuel rockets.

IOWA BEEF
PROCESSORS, INC. (A)

Prepared by Phyllis G. Holland, Valdosta State College.

Iowa Beef Processors, Inc. (IBP) celebrated the twentieth anniversary of its founding in 1981. The founders, Currier J. Holman and Andrew Anderson, borrowed $300,000 from the Small Business Administration and sold stock to local farmers to finance a beef slaughtering operation. Located in Denison, Iowa, the plant was close to the farms and feedlots of the midwest and designed to operate with unskilled labor. Cattle were brought to slaughter before they began to lose weight ("shrink") as they were transported to distant slaughterhouses. This increased the yield and provided more beef for its dollars to Iowa Beef. The assembly-line operations at IBP lowered labor costs so IBP's early success was based on controlling "shrink" and costs.

In operation for only 7 months of 1961, IBP generated sales of about $35 million and earnings after taxes and bonuses of $232,382. Earnings increased 100% each of the next 2 years and have continued to grow. In 1980, the company earned $53.1 million on sales of $4.6 billion. These earnings represented better than an 18% return on capital and 22.3% on stockholders' equity. This was the eleventh consecutive year of increased earnings. For the previous decade, sales had grown at an annual compound rate of 23.6% while earnings growth for the same period was 25.5%.

IBP's growth has come at the expense of older meat packers who were saddled with inefficient and labor-intensive operations. By performing more of the butchering operations at the slaughterhouse, IBP perfected the shipping of packaged beef cuts in boxes to customers. Efficient operations, lower labor costs, better use of by-products, and lower transportation costs for boxed beef as opposed to carcasses gave IBP a cost advantage which has made IBP the nation's largest meat packer.

Note: This case was prepared as the basis for class discussion rather than to illustrate either effective or ineffective handling of an administrative situation. Copyright © 1982. Used by permission.

Having established dominance in beef processing, IBP managers had begun to evaluate opportunities for long-term growth. The pork segment of the red meat industry had generated the most support. The major question to be answered was whether or not IBP's unquestionably successful strategy in beef would work as well in the pork industry.

The other issue which management of IBP faced in its twentieth anniversary year was quickly resolved. Occidental Petroleum purchased IBP in a stock swap valued at $800 million. Negotiations were initiated by IBP's largest stockholder in June of 1981 and the merger was approved by stockholders of both companies in August. The rationale for the merger as well as the possible long-term effects on IBP were the subject of much inconclusive debate among observers.

This case will provide information on the beef and pork sectors of the red meat industry, strategy and operations of IBP, and the terms of the merger.

THE BEEF INDUSTRY

The provision of beef for American tables begins in the Plains areas where breeding cows and calves are pastured.

Calves are sold or moved to better pastures when they reach 6 to 8 months of age and at about 1 to 1½ years are ready for drylot feeding. The purpose of drylot feeding is to produce USDA Choice and USDA Prime carcasses.[1] Physical activity of the animals is restricted and feed mixtures are calculated to produce the maximum weight gain per dollar of feed. Growth hormones are typically used. At the conclusion of the feeding period (3 months is considered the minimum time period to produce USDA Choice) the cattle are shipped to major livestock centers for sale or sold in the "country" to buyers

EXHIBIT C17.1   SELECTED EXPENSES OF CORN BELT CATTLE FEEDING

Expenses	$ per head		
Purchased during **Marketed during**	**July '75** **Jan. '76**	**July '80** **Jan. '81**	**July '81** **Jan. '82**
600-lb feeder steer	208.20	439.92	375.32
Transportation to feedlot (400 miles)	5.28	5.26	5.28
Corn (45 bu.)	122.40	122.85	141.75
Silage (1.7 tons)	35.12	36.47	42.84
30% soy protein supplement (270 lbs)	22.82	31.55	35.78
Hay (400 lbs)	8.70	9.45	11.45
Labor (4 hours)	8.76	12.92	14.80
Vet medicine	2.99	4.47	4.87
Interest on purchase (6 months)	10.41	30.75	34.66
Power equip., fuel, shelter, depr.	13.94	20.87	22.73
Death loss (1% of purchase)	2.08	4.40	3.79
Transportation (100 miles)	2.31	2.31	2.31
Marketing expenses	3.35	3.35	3.35
Miscellaneous & indirect costs	10.41	15.48	17.23
Total	456.77	740.11	720.16

Source: Federal Livestock Marketing Survey.

EXHIBIT C17.2   COMMERCIAL CATTLE SLAUGHTER (1971–1980)

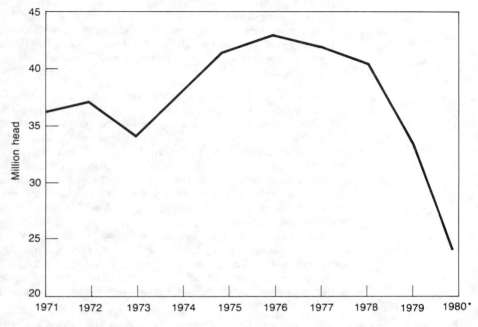

*First three quarters

Source: Federal Livestock Marketing Survey.

representing packers. Country sales accounted for about 60% of such sales in the late 70s as the industry moved toward decentralization.

The supply of feeder cattle depends on such factors as the weather, the price of grain, and the management of breeding and feeding operations. Exhibit C17.1 shows the breakdown of expenses for fed cattle while Exhibit C17.2 indicates the fluctuations in the number of cattle slaughtered during the 70s.

Slaughter and Processing

The killing of cattle is done according to a procedure established by the Humane Society to insure humane treatment. The carcass is drained of blood and various organs and other parts are removed. The hide is also removed. The remaining carcass is stored in large coolers until it is ready for shipment or further processing. This process is frequently referred to as a "kill and chill" operation.

Further processing of carcasses results in products and by-products which include:

Meat, fresh and frozen
Meat, canned and cooked
Hides and skins for leather
Edible fats, and inedible fats for soap

> Bones for buttons, knife handles, and bone meal
> Blood meal and fertilizer
> Glycerin with industrial uses
> Hair for brushes, felt, rugs, upholstering, and baseball gloves
> Intestines for sausage casing, violin strings, and surgical ligatures
> Gelatin, glue, sandpaper, pet food, and neat's foot oil
> Pharmaceuticals

The by-products of slaughter are called the "drop." Dressed beef is usually sold for less total dollars than the initial total dollar cost of the live animal. The "drop" makes up the difference and provides the profits. And profit margins are small, usually under 1%.

Traditionally, packers supplied carcass beef to local butchers for further processing in a complex distribution system. In the mid-60s, boxed beef was introduced and by 1981, more than half the nation's meat was supplied to retailers in boxed form. The transition from carcass to boxed beef has had a profound—some say revolutionary—effect on the structure of the industry. Exhibit C17.3 compares the two systems on some important dimensions. The channel of boxed beef is significantly shorter than for the traditional carcass method.

Although boxed beef was introduced by some retail grocery chains, its most vigorous and successful proponents have been newcomers to the industry—IBP and MBPXL, formerly Missouri Beef Packers and now a subsidiary of Cargill. The newcomers set up operations in new, efficient plants in rural areas close to the supply of beef. Plants were designed to eliminate the need for costly union labor. The older packers were saddled

EXHIBIT C17.3   PRODUCTION AND DISTRIBUTION OF CARCASS BEEF (TRADITIONAL) COMPARED WITH PRODUCTION AND DISTRIBUTION OF BOXED BEEF

	Traditional	Boxed
Steps		
Slaughter	Live cattle are killed; carcass is bled; hide, vital organs, other by-products are removed; carcass is chilled in cooler.	Slaughtering, breaking, and boning performed by processor. Beef is trimmed and boxed ready for final sales or fabrication.
Breaking	"Breaker" buys carcasses for breaking into primal cuts (rounds, chucks, ribs and loins).	
Boning	"Boner" buys cuts for boning and some processing.	
Processing and fabricating	Chain, food service supply house, or other processor buys meat to prepare for final sale. Fresh meat is further trimmed and packaged or meat is processed into portions and frozen or partially cooked and frozen.	Meat prepared in individual portions; usually involves cooking and/or freezing.
Labor	Each step requires skilled labor (butcher) paid by union scale.	Facilities and process designed for unskilled labor; high capital investment.
Location of facilities	Slaughterhouses located for convenience or shipping live cattle by rail, usually in urban centers.	Located for minimal shipping of live animals; truck access to markets.
Shrink	Live cattle subject to shrink in transport to slaughterhouse; carcass subject to further shrink in transport.	Minimal shrink of live cattle; no shrink of cuts when packaged and shipped.
Drop	By-products collected at every stage.	All by-products collected before boxing.

EXHIBIT C17.4   ACQUISITIONS AND DIVESTITURES OF LARGE MEAT PACKERS (1967–1981)

Packer	Acquired by	1981 Status
Wilson and Co.	LTV in 1967 for $81 million	Parent spinning off by offering 1 share of Wilson for 10 of LTV
Armour and Co.	Greyhound in 1970 for $400 million	Restructuring organization and management
Cudahy Co.	General Host in 1971 for $70 million	Negotiating agreement to sell to current management
Swift	Esmark in 1972	Divested fresh meat segment (now SIPCO) to public and concentrated on branded products
Oscar Mayer	General Foods in 1981	Being restructured to stress food service and branded products
MBPXL (originally Missouri Beef)	Cargill	Slaughter and pack boxed beef

with 50-year-old multistory plants in central locations. They employed skilled butchers to perform breaking and processing operations. Their operations were inherently more costly and their yields were lower because of these factors. Exhibit C17.4 traces the recent history of some of the major traditional meat packers. All the former giants in the industry have been purchased by conglomerates and are undergoing significant changes.

Price

Beef processing is essentially a commodity business. Much fresh meat sold is unbranded so meat packers have had little control over selling price. In addition, the price of cattle fluctuates according to supply, which in turn is dependent on the price and availability of feed grain and on the weather. What the packer does control is the cost of processing and this, along with volume, is the key to profitability in the industry.

Federal Regulation

Federal regulation of the meat industry began in 1906 with the Meat Inspection Act. This legislation requires inspection of live animals before slaughter and of the carcass to insure that no diseased animals are used for food. There are around 70 known diseases that are transmittable from animal to humans. Federal meat inspectors also check for clean and sanitary handling and/or preparation of food, for adulteration of meat, and for proper labeling of meat and meat products. Meat is stamped by inspectors for identification purposes.

The Wholesome Meat Act of 1967 had the effect of extending the regulations under which the large national meat packers operated to smaller meat packers. The smaller operations had been subject to inspection by local authorities and were eligible to obtain a certificate of exemption from federal inspection for interstate shipping if their operations satisfied local inspectors. This eligibility was discontinued by the act and these packers were given until the end of 1970 to reach compliance. Many marginal firms failed to comply and discontinued operations.

The Federal Grading Service was instituted in 1927 and grading is done by employees of the U.S. Department of Agriculture. Use of this service is voluntary and a little over half of all beef is graded. Since 1964, federal law requires that packers pay for cattle within 48 hours of purchase. Packers, on the other hand, generally wait at least 2 weeks for payment from their own accounts.

The cost of federal inspection per animal was estimated at $1.24 in 1978 and the cost of grading in that year was $20 per hour. The 48-hour payment requirement requires extra working capital.

Individual meat packers and the industry as a whole have periodically received scrutiny from a variety of government bodies including Congress, the Justice Department, the USDA, and state and local investigators. Charges have included price-fixing, monopolistic practices, and conspiracy.[2]

The industry uses large quantities of water and produces significant waste in spite of the practice of "using everything but the squeal" and thus is subject to regulation by the Environmental Protection Agency.

Industry Outlook

The per capita consumption of beef is declining (see Exhibit C17.5) as demand has shifted to poultry, pork, and fish. Polls indicated that 20% of beef eaters were concerned about their health but only 9% reduced consumption because of that concern. On the other hand, 73% objected to the price of beef. A farm management specialist described the industry outlook for beef producers compared to other sectors of the meat industry.

EXHIBIT C17.5   PER CAPITA CONSUMPTION OF BEEF AND PORK (1973–1980)

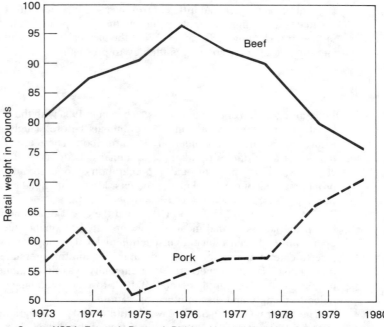

Source: USDA, Economic Research Division, Livestock and Meat Situation and Outlook.

All these people (pork and chicken producers) have done a good job of promotion. And they have better feed converters in chickens and hogs. A chicken will have a pound of gain for 2½ pounds of feed. A hog will make the same gain with 4½ pounds of feed while it takes 8 pounds to add a pound of weight to a steer.

The one big advantage the cattle raiser has, and perhaps the only one is that he can grow cattle on land unfit for cultivation. This is not true for poultry and hogs, because they must be confined to smaller areas and given some kind of prepared farm-grown feed from infancy.

Getting people to eat more beef is a serious problem and it may get worse before it improves. Back in 1975 we were consuming 130 pounds of beef per person in the U.S. By 1981, it was projected at 105 pounds, and indications are that before long it may drop below 100 pounds per person.

I don't think this is because people no longer prefer beef. Rather it is a matter of economics. Eventually people may get tired of eating pork, fish, and poultry and return to beef, but it doesn't seem likely within the near future.[3]

Vertical Integration

Vertical integration has been suggested and attempted as a means of smoothing out the fluctuations in price and supply of cattle. One proposal is for packers to forward contract with producers to assure a constant supply of finished cattle of the desired grade. Feeders and packers could also form cooperatives to make the supply and quality more consistent. Another proposal is for three-way cooperatives of producer-feeders, packers, and retailers—presumably chain stores. The feeder would charge a cost-plus management fee. The feeder would charge a cost-plus per head fee for slaughter and/or fabrication. The retailer would be assured a supply of beef of the desired quality and quantity.

Capacity Utilization

Increased capacity utilization is another concern of the industry which is operating at an estimated 70–75% capacity. Modernization and double shifts are offered as options to increase utilization.

Boxed Beef and Packaging

The boxed beef concept was intended to improve efficiency in the distribution of beef by breaking the carcass at the slaughterhouse rather than locally. Less waste fat and bone were shipped and retailers could choose the cuts they wanted. Meat marketing researchers at Michigan State University say that 65–70% of beef sold to retail stores in 1981 was boxed beef and the figure is expected to rise to 80% by 1985. "The trend is for the processor to do more of the work in some way," according to a chain store executive. "There may even come a time when there is no cutting at the store level at all."

The National Livestock and Meat Board listed the following packaging systems that rely on the boxed beef concept:

- A Detroit, Michigan, supermarket chain is test-marketing retail cuts that have been centrally cut and packaged in transparent, vacuum-sealed packages. The package allows 100% visibility, and extends marketing life to 15 days at 28–32 degrees F.

• About 91% of the U.S. meat merchandisers now offer a "family pack" of meat cuts, and 79% see greater use of them in the future.

• Some retailers are offering wholesale subprimal meat cuts in bags directly to the consumer, saving consumers 20 to 30 cents per pound.[4]

A continuing packaging concern is the development of packaging systems which will not discolor red meat.

THE PORK INDUSTRY

Pork is a $20 billion industry. Per capita consumption is shown in Exhibit C17.5. Hogs are bred to yield over 50% of the carcass weight in trimmed hams, loins, picnics, and Boston butts. The process of breeding, feeding, and selling hogs is very similar to that of beef cattle with the exception that hogs cannot be initially pastured as cattle can.

Hogs yield a variety of products which include:

Meat, fresh and frozen
Meat, smoked, cured, canned, and cooked
Sausage and variety meats
Hides and skins for leather
Edible fats (lard) and inedible fats
Pork fat by-product used for truck tires, insecticides, and germicides
Hair for brushes, felt, rugs, upholstering
Gelatin
Pharmaceuticals

Volume can be an important factor in the production of by-products. The pancreas of about 100,000 hogs must be saved to produce one pound of dry insulin, for example.

Characteristics

Although some have compared the pork industry of the 80s to the beef industry of the 60s citing old plants, high labor costs, and locations far from current hog-growing regions, others disagree. Pork, they point out, is less labor intensive than beef and some pork slaughterhouses have already adopted the boxed beef concept. Furthermore, more pork is sold branded. While most beef is sold as a commodity, an estimated 50–75% of the hog is processed into products such as bacon, hot dogs, and cured hams and sold under brand names which are frequently heavily advertised.

Local processors are more significant in pork because of their ability to match their products to regional tastes. These brands are also well-advertised in their areas and may outsell national brands. These processors may or may not also slaughter; many found that their slaughtering facilities could not be brought up to the national standards as required by the Wholesome Meat Act of 1967 and were forced to stop slaughtering operations and become customers of former competitors. The number of pork-processing plants in the U.S. dropped 15% from 1974 to 1978, while the number of hogs slaughtered remained constant.

The pork industry is unionized, with the bulk of its workers organized by the United Food and Commercial Workers Union. The industry is governed by nationwide master agreements with the UFCW which have a common expiration date.

Government Regulation

Pork slaughter and processing is regulated by the federal government under the Meat Inspection Act and the Wholesome Meat Act to insure slaughtered animals are free from disease and that meat is handled properly, unadulterated, and accurately labeled. Grade standards were established in 1952 and are based on yield and quality of meat. There are three grades, Choice, Medium, and Cull, with three further divisions within the Choice grade.

GOALS AND OBJECTIVES OF IBP

In 1968, IBP management identified four phases of development for the company. These four phases represent the general direction the company followed in the ensuing years. Phase 1 was slaughter; Phase 2 was breaking and fabricating; Phase 3 was variety meats; and Phase 4 was portion cutting, cooked and frozen foods. Management has indicated that it would consider the company "mature" when it has entered the portion control segment of the meat industry.

As the company seeks extension of operations in meat processing, management has reiterated that the means of accomplishing growth should be primarily internal. A 1978 statement emphasizes this philosophy and includes other goals and objectives:

> We seek to render values and to provide ourselves and our shareholders with controlled growth and a return on their investment consistent with reasonable risks; to serve real needs and to help feed a hungry world; to be a responsible member of our society; to provide the best of markets to our producers, the finest products to our customers, and excel in our service to both; and finally, to provide a part of the jobs that are so necessary to the economic health of our home communities.[5]

IBP executives have stated their aims in even more simple language: "We are only out to be the lowest cost producer in the industry."

SLAUGHTER OPERATIONS

IBP's original name, Iowa Beef Packers, reflected the emphasis on slaughter operations (Phase 1) in the early years of the company. The old, established meat packers had located their facilities based on the system of rail transportation which brought cattle to stockyard towns—Chicago, Des Moines, Los Angeles, Omaha, among others. As a newcomer to the industry IBP was free to build in new locations which were close to the large feedlots and still accessible to the nation's large markets by the interstate highway system and trucks.

IBP's cattle buyers were sent to local feedlots in radio-equipped cars to buy directly from the farmers while coordinating their buying with the needs of the plant. The price paid the farmer was roughly the same offered in Chicago or Kansas City but saved them transportation, yard costs, and commissions. On the IBP side, the yield was better because the cattle were slaughtered before the "shrink" could begin. According to IBP President Robert Peterson, "If you lose even a pound, not 10 pounds, but a pound—on today's (1981) market, that's $1 a head, and when we make only $5 or $6 a head out of the entire system, you've got to be careful."

In addition to using new criteria for choosing plant location, the founders of Iowa Beef Processors also approached the actual slaughtering operations differently with large, single-story plants in which cattle were stunned, lifted by one hoof onto a moving chain, killed, halved, and quartered, all on a moving line. The processing was done, not by skilled butchers, but by a succession of relatively unskilled workers performing a number of elementary tasks—removing the hoofs or tail, slitting open the abdomen or halving a carcass, making a single cut with an electric saw.

The first plant Holman designed had a kill cost of $10 a head, vs. $15 to $20 for conventional plants. Although absolute costs have risen, the advantage has been maintained. Slaughter on the assembly line is labor-intensive but by breaking the work down into its simplest elements, IBP was able to replace the highly skilled and high-cost packinghouse butcher with relatively low-cost assembly-line labor. So labor made part of the difference in cost. The rest came from the economies of scale offered by plants capable of killing 300,000 or 500,000 or a million cattle a year. IBP diligently pursued these scale economies.

Some of the most notable economies come from making more efficient use of the drop—the by-products of the meat packing process—tongues, liver, hearts for the export market, ingredients for sausage and pet food. Urban butchers shipped fat to tallow makers for shortening, bone to glue factories. But IBP with its large-scale plant could collect these products for conversion into edible animal feeds, gather the glands for use in pharmaceuticals, prepare the hides for tanning, even collect the gallstones for aphrodisiacs. "Our drop can get as high as $50 a head," Peterson says, "and our kill costs are less than that." A lot less, in fact—less than $20 a head. IBP slaughters about 6 million cattle a year.[6]

BREAKING AND FABRICATING OPERATIONS

In 1967, Iowa Beef moved into the second phase of its development program with the addition of breaking and fabricating to its operations and utilization of the boxed beef concept. While IBP did not originate the idea of boxed beef, the name of the company has become virtually synonymous with the concept because of their persistent promotion of boxed beef and their ultimate success. The development of the concept and the problems which the company encountered in gaining entrance into major markets are reported in the following excerpt from an article which appeared in the June 22, 1981, issue of *Forbes:*

The usual procedure (for processing beef) involved shipping carcasses in halves or quarters to the wholesaler, food chain or retail butcher, who then broke the carcass down into the various primal and subprimal cuts—loins, ribs, rounds and chucks; top sirloin, strip and tenderloin. IBP was prepared to do that itself, to take out the unneeded fat and bone, as well as to wrap the primal cuts in cryovac film, box them and ship them to market. Putting the beef in a vacuum-packed plastic bag not only added 21 days to the normal 3-to-7 day shelf life of the carcass, it also sharply reduced the shrink that refrigeration exposed the carcasses to, and it expanded the beef packers' marketing area.

In boxed beef, a concept pioneered by Safeway and Armour, IBP found it necessary to reorganize the market, and that took some doing. The only market big enough to absorb the output of the great new plant Holman built at Dakota City, Nebraska was metropolitan New York, which consumes maybe a quarter of the nation's meat production. Though IBP's executives may have been barefoot boys from the cornfields of Iowa, they weren't born yesterday, and they could hardly have been unaware that getting boxed beef into the New York market was going to take some heavy payoffs in the right places. As one IBP executive admitted later, "It was a common practice that people paid off other people to do business in New York City."

For IBP's boxed beef to prevail, the supermarkets were going to have to scrap their traditional butchering methods and the unions were going to have to accept the fact that a lot of their member butchers would lose their jobs. The situation was especially touchy insofar as the union that controlled the New York market, the Amalgamated Meat Cutters—now the UFCW—was also the union that had just organized IBP's new Dakota City plant and gone out on strike. When that happened, the New York meatcutters had an excuse to lend their support and banned boxed beef from the New York market.

IBP was prepared to make a deal with New York mob associate Moe Steinman, a labor consultant who had influence both with the local meatcutters union and the beef-buyers of most of the New York supermarkets. If the Dakota City strike went on, the IBP could not find a market for its beef; the company's very existence would be endangered. In April, 1970 Steinman brought Holman together with union officials in New York, and the problem was solved. Holman was told, as he later confided to *Forbes,* that IBP could get the beef into New York if it agreed to settle the strike in Dakota City. The strike ended. IBP agreed to suspend a $4.5 million damage suit against the union and the union agreed to suspend its boycott of IBP's boxed beef.

But the mediation had its price. Soon thereafter Steinman set up a sales agency known as C.P.Sales, into which IBP paid a cent on average for every pound of beef it sold in New York. The courts concluded that those funds were intended to bribe both union executives and supermarket buyers to let IBP's beef into New York City and found both Holman and IBP guilty of conspiracy to bribe union and supermarket officials.

Although Holman and the company were found guilty, Mr. Holman was granted an unconditional discharge and the company was fined $7,000. The charges were appealed but the conviction upheld. Federal charges resulting from the investigation were dropped. In the aftermath of the investigation, rumors of mob involvement persisted as reported in the 1975 *Annual Report.*

Mr. Bodenstein has managed on a contract basis IBP's most successful sales agency, C.P. Sales, Inc., serving the New York City area, and was the logical choice (for Group Vice President of) the Processing Division and its marketing reorganization program. The drawback was that his wife's father had been convicted of admitted bribery in the meat business prior to 1970 and was alleged to have underworld connections. The press played up the association. We believe that Mr. Bodenstein was victimized and is not guilty of any wrongdoing. Nevertheless, inferences made led the New York Stock Exchange to temporarily halt trading in IBP stock for five days, and some members of Congress spoke out. The Board of Directors felt obliged to authorize a full-page statement of the Company's position in the Midwest newspapers and the *Wall Street Journal* on December 1 and 2. The lesson learned by IBP from this encounter with misperceptions, on the part of several important audiences, is that better anticipation of likely public reaction, however baseless in fact, must be given greater consideration in decision-making. Public opinion ran the gamut—from fears that outside forces were taking over IBP to alarms that we were unwisely trying to manipulate such forces—all somewhat baffling to Midwestern naivete and to our native self-reliant sense. One IBP Vice President said that the Bodenstein appointment was "the wrongest right decision" we have made.

With New York penetrated by boxed beef, the company turned its marketing attention to cities within the Chicago/Houston/Denver triangle. Although labor contracts between meat cutters' locals and retailers slowed the entry of boxed beef, they were opened up, one by one. By 1981, only St. Louis remained closed to boxed beef. The only other really large market remaining was Los Angeles (second to New York in beef consumption and supplied by local packers). By 1981, demand for boxed beef exceeded IBP's capacity to supply and it was estimated that well over half of all beef moved in boxes with 40% of those boxes originating in IBP plants. Boxed beef's share of the market by 1983 was expected to exceed 80%.

IBP's attack on what is called the "closed cities" depended on price and service as well as dealings with the unions. Cost advantages in the factory could be translated into lower prices for the retailer. The company claimed to be able to process and deliver boxed beef to a retail store for $23 to $36 a head less than the retailer could buy and process the carcass for himself. The company also emphasized service centers as part of their sales efforts.

Chains are also turning to boxed beef. Some of the converts include Grand Union, Stop and Shop, Safeway, and Albertson's. Of the large chains, only Kroger and Winn-Dixie are committed to carcass beef with their own multimillion-dollar breaking facilities. It would be difficult for chains to return to doing their own slaughtering and breaking once they stop because of the increasing capital investments required to obtain the efficiency and volume of an IBP plant. Packers who once sold carcass beef to chains are also unable to build their own breaking facilities and are either going out of business or selling premium carcasses to other breakers and boxers. Dubuque Packing, a large slaughterer, is becoming an important IBP supplier.

IBP's real competition is the packers who are also providing boxed beef to meet the demand which IBP has generated but since 1976 has not been able to meet. MBPXL (a subsidiary of Cargill), Swift Independent, and Spencer Beef (subsidiary of the Land O Lakes farm cooperative) are following similar strategies to that of IBP with success.

CURRENT OPERATIONS

Scope and Capacity

IBP operates beef slaughter, beef processing, and pork slaughter plants (see Exhibit C17.6: Plant locations and principal activities). All of the production of the pork plant

EXHIBIT C17.6   PLANT LOCATIONS AND PRINCIPAL ACTIVITIES

Plant	Activities
Amarillo, Texas	Slaughter; breaking and fabricating; hide treatment; metal fabrication
Boise, Idaho	Slaughter
Dakota City, Nebraska	Slaughter; breaking and fabricating, hide treatment, executive and administrative offices
Denison, Iowa	Slaughter; hide treatment; confined feedlot
Emporia, Kansas	Slaughter; breaking and fabricating; hide treatment
Finney County, Kansas	Slaughter; breaking and fabricating; hide treatment
Fort Dodge, Iowa	Slaughter
Irvington, Iowa	Farming
Duverne, Minnesota	Kosher slaughter
Madison, Nebraska	Pork slaughter and processing
Pasco, Washington	Slaughter; breaking and fabricating; tallow refining; hide treatment
Salix, Iowa	Farming
Sioux City, Iowa	Ground beef and related products (not operating in 1980); aviation
West Point, Nebraska	Slaughter

was sold to Armour in 1981. Plant activities are described in detail in the prospectus prepared in connection with the Occidental Petroleum IBP merger proposal:

IBP's slaughter plants reduce cattle to dressed carcass form and process certain by-products. After stunning, the cattle move by conveyor systems through the plants until, in the form of dressed carcasses, they are placed in coolers, graded by the United States Department of Agriculture, and held for shipment or further processing.

IBP's processing plants at Dakota City, Emporia, Finney County, Amarillo and Pasco conduct breaking and fabricating operations to reduce dressed carcasses to bone-in or bone-less primal and subprimal cuts of beef. In these plants, production employees work at either side of fabricating tables having conveyor tops. The primal and subprimal cuts are channeled along the production lines, cut and trimmed to specifications, packaged in plastic film, boxed, and moved by a complex of continuous conveyors to cooled inventory storage areas where they are held to await loading for delivery. IBP's production process requires a minimum of production handling and eliminates the shipping of surplus fat and bone. In both the slaughter and processing plants, each employee is assigned specified tasks, which facilitates the training and use of unskilled labor, promotes a high degree of work proficiency, and thus enhances production capacity.

The approximate capacity of all the IBP's beef slaughter plants is 21,400 head of cattle per day. The approximate capacity of all of IBP's beef processing plants is 16,800 head per day. IBP sells to others carcasses not meeting the specifications of its processing plants and when necessary, purchases carcasses from others for its processing plants. The processing division currently purchases approximately 8% of the beef carcasses used in its operations from outside sources. These purchases are subject to significant fluctuations resulting from live cattle supplies, customer demand and the quality of slaughtered cattle. Through the first six months of fiscal 1981, IBP's various slaughter facilities operated at approximately

88% of capacity and the processing facilities operated at approximately 89% of capacity.

By-products are handled in bulk with the exception of butcher products, sausage, pet food, and pharmaceutical commodities which are trimmed, boxed, and frozen in small lots. Facilities for curing hides are located in six plants and use modern, automated equipment for brine curing.

Supplies

The cattle supply is a variable which is given to uncertainty as an agricultural commodity. IBP does not enter long-term cattle buying agreements, preferring the vicissitudes of the open market to the fluctuations of the cattle futures market. Cattle costs are always close to current market levels.

Most of IBP's cattle are purchased from farmers and feeders in Kansas, Iowa, Texas, Nebraska, Colorado, Oklahoma, Washington, South Dakota, Minnesota, Idaho, and Oregon. Cattle are purchased for immediate slaughter and the company has no facilities for holding cattle over an extended period of time. Coordination of cattle purchases and production schedules of plants is achieved by radio communication between buyers and production schedulers. Generally purchases are sufficient for operations of a week or less.

Long-term difficulties with this system are described in the prospectus:

> Cattle supplies or prices may be adversely affected if a lack of moisture in major grain-producing areas increases the cost of feeding operations. Permanent or long-term water shortages could make operation of certain plants less economical. However, IBP believes it has located its plants in areas least likely to be adversely affected by water shortages.

The exception to IBP's policy of not entering into long-term cattle buying agreements was their agreement with a marketing cooperative which operated feedyards that provide cattle for slaughter and processing in the Northwest. This agreement was investigated by the Justice Department and ended on June 22, 1982, after 5 years.

Products

IBP's principal product categories are carcasses; broken, fabricated, and other processed products; and by-products and pork. Exhibit C17.7 (percentage of sales revenue

EXHIBIT C17.7   PERCENTAGE OF SALES REVENUES BY PRODUCTS

	Percent of sales during fiscal year				
Product	**1976**	**1977**	**1978**	**1979**	**1980**
Carcasses	22%	27%	22%	20%	20%
Broken, fabricated, and other products	67	60	66	66	69
By-products and pork	11	13	12	14	11
	100%	100%	100%	100%	100%

by principal product category) indicates how sales are distributed among these products.

Customers

The merger prospectus described IBP's customers as follows:

> IBP currently has approximately 3,000 active customers which include grocery chains, meat distributors, wholesalers, purveyors, and restaurant and hotel chains. Approximately 2,200 customers purchase broken and fabricated cuts of beef which are boxed and shipped in vacuum packages from the Amarillo, Dakota City, Emporia, Finney County, and Pasco plants. Purchasers of carcass beef shipped from all slaughtering units total approximately 200 accounts.
>
> Approximately 45% of all sales are made directly by IBP's employees. Approximately 53% of all sales are made through offers to buy from customers solicited by nine IBP Service Centers located in Atlanta, Boston, Chicago, Columbus (Ohio), Dallas, Fairfax (Virginia), Los Angeles, Lyndhurst (New Jersey), and Vancouver (Washington). The balance of about 2% is sold through brokers. Normally, IBP's largest single customer accounts for less than 4% of its total sales volume. Approximately 88% of sales are on open account and the balance on secured terms.
>
> IBP operates a training program for customers and prospective customers at its Center for Modern Meat Management at Dakota City. In addition to the Center's programs, IBP and the service centers each maintain a staff of field consultants who service customers using IBP boxed beef.

Facilities

One of the original founders of IBP, Mr. Andrew Anderson, had as his major responsibility the construction of the facilities. Until 1970, this was accomplished in-house with planning, design, and actual construction performed by IBP's Construction Division. During that time, 44 separate patent claims were allowed on breaking and fabrication facilities. Plant construction crews became an important source of employees according to the 1980 *Annual Report:*

> That first plant at Denison was built by a crew of young farmers who wanted the construction work because farm income was declining. When the plant was completed, many of the young farmers stayed on as production workers or in supervisory capacities. To this day construction crews at new IBP plants are given the first opportunity at production jobs when the project is finished because they have first hand knowledge of how the equipment has been set up and how it should operate. A number of present IBP production management personnel, including several plant managers, started their careers at the company as members of a plant construction crew.

The construction division continued to design and supervise the construction of plants after Mr. Anderson's retirement in 1970. IBP management feels that this practice has decreased shakedown periods and start-up costs. The division is also responsible for renovation, expansion, and updating of existing facilities with the goal of remaining the low-cost producer in the meat industry. A sampling of such projects in 1980 included installation of a new processing floor and material handling system in the Dakota City plant, a new waste treatment system for the Pasco, Washington,plant, and "a major improvement in the processing of edible oil."

The division supervised construction of the world's largest slaughter plant in Finney County, Kansas. The following information provides some perspective on the size of the operation:

> Its refrigeration capacity is approximately 6,000 tons. That would air condition almost 1,500 private homes the year round. About 1,140 miles of copper wiring are contained in the plant. That's enough to completely wire 3,000 homes.
>
> The total electrical capacity compares to that of a city with a population of 9,000. If the 50,000 yards of prestressed concrete in the plant were used to construct a 3 inch thick, 3 foot sidewalk, that walk would stretch 4,328 city blocks.

When processing at capacity, the plant will be capable of slaughtering and processing 1.2 million head of cattle a year. The $100 million facility is expected to be in full operation by 1984.

Financial Performance and Policies

Exhibits C17.8 and C17.9 contain financial information for the company.

Financial policy has been conservative, with most growth generated through retained earnings. The 1975 *Annual Report* explained the rationale for this and the evolution of IBP's dividend policy:

> We tend to think of growth in terms of physical expansion or what is needed to furnish the means of performance growth in a later day. Capital resources are the key at a time of severe national shortage. In a recent study by the New York Stock Exchange, it was estimated that America faces a capital shortfall of $650 billion over the next decade. In choosing among the equity market, long-term debt, and retained earnings, we have historically favored the latter as the most prudent and feasible source of capital, partly because our debt/equity ratio as reported in *Forbes* rose to 0.8 compared with an all-industry average of 0.4. We have resisted pressures to compromise growth, because we believe such policy to be in the best long-term interest of shareowners who have invested in our success.
>
> It is appreciated, of course, that the wants of stockholders vary, with some preferring a spendable return sooner rather than later.
>
> . . . To make a meaningful beginning, the Board of Directors on January 17, 1976 decided to adopt a cash dividend policy of approximately 7.5 percent of after-tax earnings, payable semiannually. The actual declaration—exact amounts—and timing of payment will be determined by the Board and announced at the annual meeting of shareholders on March 13, 1976, at Sioux City, Iowa.

The dividend payout record of IBP is shown in Exhibit C17.8.

Accounting Policy

The company has supplied information of financial results on current cost and equivalent dollar bases since 1976. Also to better state performance the company adopted the LIFO (changing from FIFO) method of accounting for inventories in 1977.

EXHIBIT C17.8 TEN-YEAR SUMMARY OF OPERATIONS
(Amounts in Thousands Except per Share Data)

	1980	1979	1978	1977	1976	1975	1974	1973	1972	1971
	For the fiscal year									
Net sales	$4,639,454	$4,216,370	$2,968,099	$2,023,765	$2,077,158	$1,805,340	$1,537,198	$1,422,271	$1,244,595	$979,718
Cost of products sold	4,506,150	4,105,533	2,872,214	1,937,823	1,990,176	1,735,592	1,483,262	1,377,686	1,212,206	956,239
Selling, general and administrative expense	42,924	34,326	31,864	27,787	24,374	22,992	19,820	16,442	12,832	11,641
Interest income (expense)—net	3,724	(2,038)	(3,138)	(3,281)	(3,666)	(3,740)	(2,906)	(4,468)	(5,612)	(5,526)
Earnings before income taxes	94,104	74,473	60,883	54,874	58,942	43,016	31,210	23,675	13,945	6,312
Income taxes	40,940	31,726	27,296	24,909	30,164	19,779	14,672	11,427	6,578	2,539
Net earnings	53,164	42,747	33,587*	29,965	28,778	23,237	16,538	12,248	7,367	3,773
Average common and common equivalent shares outstanding	10,289	9,995	9,722	9,528	9,320	8,718	8,532	8,262	8,025	7,821
Net earnings per common and common equivalent share	5.17	4.28	3.46*	3.14	3.09	2.68	1.98	1.51	.92	.48
Cash dividends paid per common share	.60	.52	.26	.25	.20					
Earnings on beginning common stockholders' equity	22.3%	21.8%	20.7%	22.3%	26.8%	29.9%	27.0%	25.0%	18.3%	10.4%
	At year end									
Common stockholders' equity	$290,480	$238,831	$196,095	$162,631	$134,292	$107,557	$ 77,617	$ 61,180	$ 48,926	$ 40,174
Property, plant and equipment, at cost	280,884	208,998	187,522	166,270	141,695	122,600	99,839	77,786	73,823	68,803
Total assets	509,492	416,789	354,778	277,527	253,437	229,684	189,246	152,913	160,726	130,370
Working capital	164,598	173,412	142,535	107,538	89,502	79,823	69,152	40,968	28,428	22,762
Current ratio	2.2 to 1	2.9 to 1	3.0 to 1	3.6 to 1	2.7 to 1	2.6 to 1	2.8 to 1	1.8 to 1	1.4 to 1	1.5 to 1

* Effective October 30, 1977, the company adopted the last-in, first-out (LIFO) method of valuing product and certain supplies inventories, the effect of which was to reduce net earnings for the year 1978 by $5,924,000 ($.61 per share) from amounts which would otherwise have been reported. The net earnings for 1977 and prior years are not comparable to those of any subsequent year as a result of this change.

535

EXHIBIT C17.9   CONSOLIDATED BALANCE SHEETS

	November 1, 1980	November 3, 1979
Assets		
Current assets:		
Cash	$ 23,334,000	$ 27,138,000
Marketable debt securities at cost	4,000,000	
Accounts receivable, net	170,941,000	155,107,000
Inventories	97,113,000	80,164,000
Deferred tax benefit	3,419,000	3,557,000
Prepaid expenses	1,891,000	1,135,000
Total current assets	300,698,000	267,101,000
Property, plant and equipment, at cost		
Land and land improvements	22,058,000	17,051,000
Buildings and stockyards	62,665,000	56,188,000
Equipment	140,462,000	128,166,000
	225,185,000	201,405,000
Less accumulated depreciation	74,228,000	62,085,000
	150,957,000	139,320,000
Construction in progress	55,699,000	7,593,000
	206,656,000	146,913,000
Other assets	2,138,000	2,775,000
	$509,492,000	$416,789,000
Liabilities and stockholders' equity		
Current liabilities:		
Note payable	$ 15,000,000	$ 20,000,000
Accounts payable and accrued expenses	102,501,000	60,182,000
Federal and state income taxes	15,096,000	10,559,000
Current maturities on long-term obligations	3,503,000	2,948,000
Total current liabilities	136,100,000	93,689,000
Deferred income taxes	20,535,000	17,410,000
Long-term debt and capital lease obligations	61,300,000	66,859,000
Other liabilities	1,077,000	
Commitments and contingencies		
Stockholders' equity		
Common stock, par value $1.50 a share:		
Authorized—24,000,000 shares		
Issued—9,905,189	14,858,000	14,537,000
Additional paid-in capital	22,000,000	18,221,000
Retained earnings	253,622,000	206,369,000
	290,480,000	239,127,000
Less common stock in treasury, at cost—16 shares	. . .	296,000
Stockholders' equity, net shares outstanding—9,905,173	290,480,000	238,831,000
	$509,492,000	$416,789,000

Management, Organization, and Administration

IBP recruits many (but not all) of its top management internally. The CEO in 1981 began his career with IBP as a cattle buyer when the company opened in 1961. Pertinent information concerning top management is contained in Exhibit C17.10.

The company is organized along functional lines with divisions of Processing, Physical Distribution, Administration, Finance, Custom Products, Research and Engineering, and a Carcass Division. The current organization is the result of a reorganization in the early 70s to better prepare the company to manage its increased size and more complex activities.

Employees and Labor Relations

Approximately 8,750 plant and production workers were employed by IBP in 1981. In addition, there were 80 cattle buyers, a sales staff of 100, and 2,500 other management and management support personnel. Hourly workers are usually locally recruited and trained by IBP. Because of the design of the jobs, less skill is involved than required for traditional breaking and meat processing. Consequently IBP's wage rates have been lower than the other meat packers who have employed skilled butchers under union master agreements which set wages industrywide. In 1981, John Morrell and Company paid $10.02 an hour at its Sioux Falls, South Dakota, beef plant while the comparable wage at the Dakota City plant of IBP was $8.20. Fringe benefits for the unionized plant were also greater than for IBP employees. Armour reported its average labor costs were 40% to 60% higher than IBP and others. The higher labor costs also prevented older companies from entering the market with boxed beef according to Swift President John Copeland, "When you're at a noncompetitive cost," he said, "the more you do to the animal, the more noncompetitive you get."

IBP has achieved its low labor costs at a price that was sometimes high. Seven strikes stopped work in various IBP plants between 1970 and 1980. Some of these involved violence ranging from sabotage to shootings, and several stretched into months of decreased production which were reflected in financial performance drops. IBP executives expressed their determination to maintain the unskilled status and thus the lower wages of their operations. It was reported that founder and former CEO Currier Holman expressed a readiness to have one out of every three plants out on strike at any given time. Current CEO Peterson says

EXHIBIT C17.10   IBP TOP MANAGEMENT

Name	Age*	Office	Background
Robert L. Peterson	48	Co-Chairman of Board, President and CEO	Group Vice President at IBP, President and Chief Operating Officer.
Dale C. Tinstman	62	Co-Chairman of Board, Chief Financial Officer	Financial consultant to IBP, President and Chief Operating Officer
Perry V. Haines	37	Executive Vice President	Group Vice President at IBP

* As of May 1981.

People who blame the labor unions for this nation's sliding productivity are barking up the wrong tree. Put the blame where it really belongs—on management, which has by default forfeited its right to manage.

Of eleven plants operated by the company in 1981, six were not organized by any union. The organization and contract expiration date of the remaining five are listed below:

1 Madison, Nebraska (United
  Food and Commercial
  Workers, Int'l AFL-CIO)   February, 1982
2 Dakota City, Nebraska (UFCW)   May, 1982
3 Fort Dodge, Iowa (UFCW)   October, 1982
4 Pasco, Washington (Teamsters)   November, 1982
5 Amarillo, Texas (Teamsters)   March, 1985

The United Food and Commercial Workers were formerly the Amalgamated Meatcutters Union and the Retail Food Workers Union. The new group represents 80% of the industry's 158,000 employees.

Legal Proceedings

IBP has been the subject of investigations and legal proceedings throughout its history. A list of these proceedings and their status as of 1981 is presented in Exhibit C17.11.

Whether IBP's alleged mob connections, chronic labor problems, or conservative dividend policy or some combination of these factors was responsible for sluggish stock market performance can be debated. IBP management noted stock prices not in keeping with the company's earnings record in 1975 as did a market analyst for Mid-America, Inc., writing in 1980:

EXHIBIT C17.11   IBP INVOLVEMENT IN LEGAL ACTIONS (1981)

Action	Status	IBP position
Price-fixing by IBP and others alleged by a group of cattle producers.	Several suits against IBP and other defendants consolidated; damages requested for triple amount of actual damages.	"Without factual foundation"
IBP and union involved in suits and countersuits; IBP claims harassment by false suits and union claiming interference with employment among other things.	Cases were consolidated; IBP seeks $15 million in damages; union and others seeking total of $35 million.	"Suits totally without merit"
Jury in New York found IBP guilty of price-fixing but could not determine injury to plaintiff (a supermarket chain).	Possibility of retrial to determine damages.	"No violation if no damage" but "any resulting damage verdict will not be material"
Various suits totaling $3 million concerning cattle-buying practices of IBP dating from 1974.	Two-thirds have been settled.	

IBP shares, currently selling at 4.9 times our 1980 earnings estimate and at a slight discount to book value, are undervalued in our opinion. Purchase is recommended.[7]

One of the major effects of the merger with Occidental Petroleum was short-term gains for the stockholders. IBP stockholders received 1.3 shares of OP common and .4 shares of OP voting nonconvertible preferred for each IBP share. The value of the offer was roughly $77 per share. The last IBP price before the merger offer was announced was $58.50 per share.

MERGER WITH OCCIDENTAL PETROLEUM

David H. Murdock, a Los Angeles developer and investor and the largest single IBP stockholder with 19% of the outstanding stock, served as a go-between in the negotiations between Occidental Petroleum and IBP. The merger was friendly although two Board members expressed reservations about the price and the desirability of losing independence. Both were outside directors. *Fortune* calculated the gains of Murdock and three officers as follows.[8]

	Gain ($ million)	Value of holdings ($ million)
David H. Murdock	35.2	146.6
Robert L. Peterson	3.0	12.7
Dale C. Tinstman	1.2	4.9
Perry V. Haines	1.4	5.8

Peterson and Haines also received employment contracts for 10 years and 5 years, respectively, and significant raises. Peterson's salary increased from $124,583 to $250,000 with bonuses of up to 80% of salary in cash and stock. Haines's salary went from $65,974 to $200,000 with a similar bonus arrangement. Peterson's bonus for the year ended in 1980 had been $200,000 while Haines had earned $93,400.

The merger made Mr. Murdock the largest single stockholder in Occidental with 2.8% of the stock. The next largest stockholder, Chairman of the Board Armand Hammer, owns 1.2%.

Occidental is a diversified energy and natural resources and chemical concern and was ranked as the thirteenth largest energy company in 1980. OP revenues in 1980 were $12.5 billion compared with $4.6 billion for IBP (see Exhibits C17.12 and C17.13 for other financial data). Its earnings base in 1981 was concentrated in foreign sources such as Libya and Peru. OP brought to the merger enough investment tax credits to shelter 2 years of IBP income. OP's President A. Robert Abboud explained the strategic background of the merger offer:

Our strategy for the 1990s is to be prominent in the food area. We're going to be running into a food scarcity situation in the 1990s in the same way that we have an energy shortage in the 1980s. We will continue to build in this area.[9]

The merger was not expected to change IBP's operations which were to continue to be autonomous. Most analysts agreed that the short-term gains for IBP stockholders were the most significant foreseeable results of the deal.

EXHIBIT C7.12 OCCIDENTAL PETROLEUM CORPORATION CONSOLIDATED STATEMENTS OF OPERATIONS
FOR THE YEARS ENDED DECEMBER 31
(In Thousands)

	1980	1979	1978
Revenues:			
Net sales	$12,476,125	$9,554,795	$6,252,574
Interest and other income	110,995	75,763	61,566
Equity in net income of unconsolidated subsidiaries and affiliates	15,577	7,689	1,483
Gain on futures contracts	123,615		
	12,726,312	9,638,247	6,315,623
Costs and other deductions:			
Cost of sales	9,057,175	6,862,503	4,668,169
Selling, general and administrative and other operating expenses	832,816	723,656	562,776
(Gain) change related to European refining investments	.....	(31,400)	122,100
Interest and debt expense, net	129,438	137,826	112,749
Minority interest in net income of subsidiaries and partnerships	11,644	11,564	8,757
	10,031,073	7,704,149	5,474,551
Income before taxes	2,695,239	1,934,098	841,072
Provision for domestic and foreign income, franchise and other taxes	1,984,454	1,372,452	834,372
Net income	$ 710,785	$ 561,646	$ 6,700
Earnings (loss) per common share	$ 8.82	$ 7.30	$ (.39)
Full diluted earnings per share	$ 8.31	$ 6.66	$ .....†

† Not applicable as the effect of the calculation is antidilutive.

THE FUTURE OF IBP

IBP's growth has been based on taking market share from competitors rather than developing new markets. Complaints of monopoly have been heard and Rep. Neal Smith (D-Iowa) has unsuccessfully introduced legislation to limit a meat packer's share of the market to 25%. Whether growth in meat packing is limited by legislation or by competition, other avenues of growth will be needed to maintain current growth rates. Some possibilities which have been explored include applying the IBP system to pork slaughter and processing, increasing exports, and adding portion control products.

Pork

IBP's involvement in pork at the time of the merger was limited to one plant which operated as a custom slaughter facility for Armour. While inefficiencies exist in pork slaughter and processing, the gap between current costs and possible efficiencies may not be as great in pork as it was in beef when IBP entered the industry. Another difference is the absence of large-scale hog-feeding operations comparable to beef feedlots. There are, however, thousands of small farms in Iowa, Illinois, and Minnesota which could supply a massive centrally located plant. Peterson has said, "We'll come big (in pork) with a couple of hundred million dollar plants."

If IBP continues the pattern of taking a new position in an old market rather than developing a new market, several approaches are possible. One would be to follow the

EXHIBIT C17.13   OCCIDENTAL PETROLEUM CORPORATION CONSOLIDATED BALANCE SHEETS (DECEMBER 31)

	1980	1979
Assets		
Current assets:		
Cash	$ 274,615	$ 246,498
Receivables—		
Trade, net	1,481,098	1,265,121
Other	17,094	33,879
Inventories	629,595	496,511
Prepaid expenses and other	34,323	28,158
Total current assets	2,433,725	2,070,167
Long-term receivables, net	31,013	27,043
Investment in, net of advances from, Occidental Land, Inc.	41,050	63,467
Investments in and advances to, net of advances from, subsidiaries and affiliates	56,942	49,754
Property, plant, and equipment, at cost, net	3,931,417	3,182,475
Other assets:		
Deferred financing costs, net of amortization	19,736	27,710
Capital project expenditures	2,806	68,800
Other	113,200	70,914
	135,742	167,424
	$6,629,889	$5,560,330
Liabilities and equity		
Current liabilities:		
Current maturities of senior funded debt and capital lease liability	$ 131,396	$ 79,560
Notes payable to banks	51,547	62,995
Accounts payable	1,007,381	904,957
Accrued liabilities	392,455	305,602
Domestic and foreign income, franchise and other taxes	549,957	477,910
Dividends payable	43,854	27,099
Total current liabilities	2,176,590	1,858,123
Senior funded debt, net of current maturities	925,422	1,044,074
Capital lease liability, net of current portion	76,482	51,905
Deferred credits and other liabilities:		
Deferred and other domestic and foreign income taxes	511,319	292,052
Revenue from sale of future production	165,280	170,000
Coal workers compensation reserve, net of current portion	109,617	102,265
Other	267,978	206,993
	1,054,194	771,310
Minority equity in subsidiaries and partnerships	117,190	133,066
Redeemable preferred stocks, $1.00 par value	225,734	238,690
Nonredeemable preferred stocks, common shares, and other shareholders' equity:		
Nonredeemable preferred stocks, $1.00 par value: stated at liquidation value	103,273	213,331
Common shares, $20 par value: authorized 100 million shares; issued 79,765,778 shares in 1980 and 72,775,613 shares in 1979 (including treasury shares of 141,446 in 1980 and 450,454 in 1979)	15,954	14,555
Other shareholders' equity—		
Additional paid-in capital (net of amounts applicable to preferred stocks)	605,260	442,057
Retained earnings	1,332,679	802,418
Treasury shares, at cost	(2,889)	(9,199)
	2,054,277	1,463,162
	$6,629,889	$5,560,330

boxed beef concept while the other would involve more emphasis on processing and branding. Most pork plants produce 60% processed meats (hams, bacon, sausage, etc.) and 30% fresh pork. IBP could produce mainly fresh pork and sell most of its output to pork producers currently slaughtering in-house for further processing. Production efficiencies and economies of scale would presumably make it possible for IBP to supply fresh pork to processors more cheaply than they could slaughter for themselves. A second possible approach would be to strive for brand identification for pork products processed by IBP. Margins for processed pork are three times that of fresh pork, but in this segment, there are many well-established brands already.

Late in 1981, the company was investigating possible sites for construction of a pork-processing plant. Of four sites under consideration, the smallest number of hogs marketed within 150 mile radius of a site was 7.4 million while the largest number for a site was 17.4 million.

Export

Most of IBP's exports have been by-products and hides. Between 1976 and 1980, the company exported 1.3 billion pounds of various meat products, generating a sales volume of over $745 million. In 1980, IBP began selling boxed beef in Europe and Japan.

Shortly after the merger, Dr. Hammer of Occidental Petroleum announced that arrangements were in progress for an exchange of technical information in the field of meat processing with the possibility of construction of a processing plant in the Soviet Union.

Portion Control

IBP's primary competitor in boxed beef, MBPXL, has already moved into the marketing of prepackaged retail-style cuts of beef, steaks, and roasts. IBP considers these products to be phase 4 of its development but does not foresee their addition to the product line before the end of the 80s.

IBP entered the 80s as the largest, most successful meat packer in the United States. The challenges of the decade will require determining how and where its resources can be utilized to maintain its position.

REFERENCES

1 Other grades in descending order of quality are USDA Good and Ungraded. Lower grades have different cooking requirements for producing a tender, flavorful result. Three other grades, Utility, Cutter, and Canner, are used in processed meat products and rarely sold in retail stores.

2 A widely distributed industry handbook contains a chapter on "Commercial Bribery" in which various forms of kickbacks are described and the legal and ethical implications of doing business on such a basis are explained.

3 Jess F. Blair, "Another tough year predicted for cattlemen in 1982." *Feedstuffs* 53 (November 24, 1981).

4 "Retail packaging will direct industry future: Meat Board." *Feedstuffs* 53 (July 13, 1981):5.

5 Iowa Beef Processors. *Annual Report,* 1978.

6 Iowa Beef Processors. *Annual Report,* 1978.

7 "Iowa Beef Processors, Inc." *Wall St. Transcript* (April 21, 1980):57569.

8 Alexander Stuart: "Meatpackers in stampede." *Fortune* (June 29, 1981):68.

9 "Occidental plans to buy Iowa Beef for $800 million." *Wall St. Journal* (June 2, 1981):2.

18

IBP (B) AND MEAT PACKING IN THE 1980s

Prepared by Phyllis G. Holland, Valdosta State College.

From the National Cattlemen's Association convention in New Orleans, to the feature pages of *Hog Farm Management*, to executive offices of poultry firms, the same question was asked in the winter of 1983–1984: "What is happening in the meat packing industry?" As raw materials suppliers to the meat packers, the cattlemen, hog farmers, and poultry producers were concerned about the demand and consumption patterns for various types of meat, the changing structure of the meat packing industry, and specific plans of leading companies like IBP, Inc.[1]

MEAT CONSUMPTION

While consumption of red meat (beef and pork) in 1984 was close to the all-time high, Exhibit C18.1 indicates that the trend toward increased consumption for most of this country was being reversed. Exhibit C18.2 reports the results of a study by Oscar Mayer of changes in consumption habits. Exhibit C18.3 from the same study reports consumers' reactions to pork specifically. These changes reflect in part health concerns of consumers. Red meat is generally viewed as high in fat (although hogs are bred to be 50% leaner than 25 years ago) and cholesterol. Red meat is also more expensive than lower-calorie white meats, and the gap is widening. In the 1950s, a pound of poultry cost about 80% as much as a pound of beef. By 1980, poultry cost about 30% of the cost of beef. In the 1960s, poultry cost 75% as much as pork; by 1980, it cost 50% as much as pork.

Companies like IBP, Inc. and Excel (subsidiary of Cargill, formerly known as MBPXL) have increased efficiency in meat packing by cutting processing costs, but they are limited in the ability to cut raw materials costs by the commodity nature of the

Used by permission.

FOOD CONSUMPTION IN THE UNITED STATES (1981–1984)

	Pounds per person			
	1981	**1982**	**1983**	**1984***
Animal products	582	574	584	578
Red meat†	157	151	155	149
Beef and veal	79	79	80	76
Pork	65	59	62	60
Other	13	13	14	13
Poultry	63	64	65	66
Eggs	34	33	34	33
Dairy products	304	302	305	305
Other	24	24	24	25
Crop products (Vegetables, sugar, grain, etc.)	814	811	814	819
Total	1,396	1,385	1,398	1,397

* Estimated.
† Red meat consumption was 122 pounds per person in 1922, 134 pounds per person in 1940, and 157 pounds per person in 1980.
Source: Economic Research Service, USDA, *Agricultural Outlook*, December 1983.

EXHIBIT C18.2 MEAT USAGE IN 1982*

	Turkey	**Chicken**	**Fish**	**Beef**	**Pork**
Eating more	28%	45%	23%	15%	18%
About the same	57	51	55	52	48
Eating less	15	4	22	33	34
Change	+13	+41	+ 1	−18	−16

* Responses to question: "How does your family's meat consumption compare to five years ago?"
Source: The National Provisioner, Feb. 4, 1984, p. 10. Based on 1,000 U.S. households.

EXHIBIT C18.3 CONSUMER REACTIONS TO PORK*

	1983	**1982**	**1981**
Preservatives	13%	14%	13%
Freshness	12	11	8
Costs too much	9	9	11
Additives	8	9	9
Salt	7	7	5
Fat/cholesterol	6	6	6
Taste	4	5	5
Not good for you	1	2	2
Nothing to change	27	26	27

* Responses to question: "Which phrases describe your feelings about pork?"
Source: The National Provisioner, Feb. 4, 1984, p. 10. Based on 1,000 U.S. households.

business and by some inherent inefficiencies of red meat animals as breeders and food processors. The situation was exacerbated in 1983 by drought and a government program (Payment In Kind) which was intended to reduce grain stockpiles but also resulted in high feed costs. *Forbes* described the commodity cycle:

> When feed prices are low, costs decline and herd sizes increase. This sends more cattle to market, which reduces prices. Reduced prices spark consumption, which in turn starts pushing prices back up as demand equals supply. Farmers then increase their herds, and the process begins again. Because it takes at least two years for a cow to grow to market size, the production curve is seldom smooth. Now [January, 1984], there is an oversupply of red meat at high prices. But the PIK program is also driving up grain costs. So packers of fresh meat are in a squeeze. "Our costs are rising while prices are dropping," said John Copeland, chairman of Swift Independent Packing Corporation.
>
> Beefpackers, of course, don't operate in isolation. At some point consumers get their fill of expensive steaks, and demand shifts to pork and chicken. "With enough time, high grain prices are better for chicken than they are for other meats," explained Don Tyson of Tyson Foods.
>
> That's because chickens require less feed. Thanks to breeding, better controlled chicken farming and computer-formulated feeds, broilers grow to a bigger market weight faster (eight weeks) than they did 20 years ago. Result: It takes only two pounds of feed to produce one pound of chicken, half the conversion ratio of the fifties.
>
> Beef and pork producers are not so lucky, and progress is slow because of longer breeding cycles. Three-and-a-half pounds of feed go into a pound of pork and seven pounds into a pound of good steak on the hoof. Thus every penny rise in the price of feed widens the cost advantage of chicken and pork over beef.[2]

In the view of one pessimistic observer, beef "may be at or past a ceiling on total per capita meat supplies which can be marketed at a profit to producers."[3] Others are more optimistic, citing the development of "light" beef, the continuing domination by beef of the away-from-home market, and industrywide advertising efforts as hopes of stabilizing consumption patterns. The proportion of red meat currently exported is about 1%. "The potential [for export] is enormous," according to Kenneth Monfort, President of Monfort of Colorado. "We have to find places affluent enough to eat meat, but which don't have their own production."[4] Japan and Europe fit the bill but trade restrictions have limited exploitation of foreign markets.

While breeders expressed their concern about the shifts in ultimate demand for their products, they were also watching carefully the changing fortunes of their immediate customers, the packers.

EVOLUTION OF AN INDUSTRY

It is difficult to imagine that the "Big Four" meat packers, Swift, Wilson, Armour, and Cudahy, were once a target for those who attacked monopolistic practices of big business earlier in the century. The Big Four were tamed in the '30s and '40s and had been swallowed up in the '60s and '70s by conglomerates. The fresh meat market was large (approximately $50 billion in 1984), which made it attractive to companies seeking growth, but the new owners found the opportunities evaporating because of net margins of less than 1% and vulnerability to agricultural cycles. For the former Big Four, another kind of cycle began. As subsidiaries competing for resources with other subsidiaries, the meat packers couldn't meet the return on investment criteria for capital allocation set up by their corporate owners and did not receive new capital. Their facilities became obsolete and, according to many observers, their management lethargic. The unions were able to negotiate industrywide master contracts which further sliced margins.

EXHIBIT C18.4   STATUS OF MAJOR COMPETITORS IN MEAT PACKING

Company	Sales* (in billions)		Ownership	Current status
	1983	1982		
IBP, Inc.	$6	$5	Wholly owned by Occidental Petroleum	Expanding into pork production after building world's largest beef slaughtering facility.
Excel (formerly MBPXL)	NA	NA	Owned by Cargill, an agricultural conglomerate	Planned acquisition of Land O Lakes Spencer Beef subsidiary blocked by courts; acquired only one of the three plants instead.
SIPCO (Swift Independent Packing Company)	2.5	1.8	Spun off to public by Esmark, which retained 35% ownership and assumed $135 million pension liability & provided $35 million working capital	Closed and subsequently reopened two plants, cutting labor costs in plants by 50%; planning expansion of pork slaughtering by acquisition of three plants with combined revenue of $500 million.
Armour	2.4	2.5	Closed by owner Greyhound in hopes of sale without burden of master contract	ConAgra has purchased some of the closed plants.
Wilson	2.2	2.2	LTV spun off Wilson Foods to stockholders, absorbing $23 million in plant closing costs	In Chapter 11 reorganization; high labor costs cited as reason for losses.
Hormel	1.4	1.4	Public	$225 million in capital improvements in recent years, including new plant; inefficient plant closed.
Monfort of Colorado	.995	.820	75% family	Vertically integrated into cattle feeding; labor costs have been a problem in older of two plants.
Dubuque Packing Company	.800	1.85	Sold meat plants to executives for $30.5 million	Reopened as FDL Foods, Inc., with $4/hour reduction in wages and work rules.
Morrell	NA	1.2	United Brands	5 of company's 7 slaughter plants have been closed; turnaround may be underway with subcontracting of slaughtering.
Rath	NA (455 million in 1981)	NA	Employee-owned	Bankrupt.
Bar S Foods	NA	NA	Spun off from General Foods' Cudahy Co. in leveraged buy-out by officers	Operating.

Into this situation came the "new" packers led by IBP. The IBP approach was based on new packing locations close to feedlots, large, modern, efficient plants, a new distribution system called boxed beef, and either nonunion labor or a policy of tough negotiations with unions to maintain low labor costs. Other companies followed IBP's lead and the lessons of freedom from conglomerate decision making and cost control were not lost on the Big Four. Exhibit C18.4 on page 547 summarizes the important changes in the affiliation and approach of industry competitors.

IBP's performance was spectacular in sales growth as well as earnings (see Iowa Beef case) and the industry experienced some dramatic changes. The number of packing plants has declined since 1971 (see Exhibit C18.5), with the decline centered in plants slaughtering less than 50,000 heads annually. The 28 large plants slaughtered more than half of the 1980 slaughter. Four-firm concentration ratios are shown in Exhibits C18.5, C18.6, and C18.7. In terms of profitability, the upper-quartile after-tax return on equity for the industry moved from 11.4 to 17.6 during the period, indicating a greater spread in profit performance. This payoff has generated conglomerate interest in the "new"

EXHIBIT C18.5   COMPARISON OF NUMBERS OF COWS AND BULLS SLAUGHTERED ANNUALLY BY REGION AND SIZE GROUP (1971, 1976, 1981)

| Region | Year | Number of plants: slaughter per year | | | |
		Less than 5,000	5,000– 49,999	50,000 & More	Total
North Atlantic	1971	62	39	0	101
	1976	50	28	5	83
	1981	59	19	2	80
East North Central	1971	118	24	6	148
	1976	83	28	10	121
	1981	64	14	6	84
West North Central	1971	62	42	9	113
	1976	44	37	18	99
	1981	40	25	13	78
South Atlantic	1971	67	16	1	84
	1976	50	26	4	80
	1981	44	13	3	60
South Central	1971	60	30	2	92
	1976	43	31	8	82
	1981	36	13	2	51
Southern Plains	1971	70	28	3	101
	1976	62	33	10	105
	1981	53	23	4	80
Mountain	1971	53	17	1	71
	1976	43	21	4	68
	1981	35	14	2	51
Pacific	1971	59	30	0	89
	1976	44	34	1	79
	1981	28	18	5	51

Source: Packers and Stockyards Administration. Includes plants reporting to P&SA.

EXHIBIT C18.6   PERCENTAGE OF TOTAL SLAUGHTER OF COWS AND BULLS ACCOUNTED FOR BY TOP FOUR FIRMS (1971, 1976, 1981)

State	1971	1976	1981	Change 1971–1976	Change 1976–1981
CA	42.8	35.1	56.5	−7.7	21.4
FL	80.0	72.9	86.7	−7.1	13.8
GA	82.7	72.7	97.1	−10.0	24.4
IA	71.8	82.7	97.3	10.9	14.6
KY	88.9	90.5	97.9	1.6	7.4
MI	79.2	78.5	87.9	−.7	9.4
MN	74.7	84.2	90.8	9.5	6.6
MS	86.7	81.6	97.3	−5.1	15.7
NE	69.5	71.4	81.8	1.9	10.4
NY	41.0	64.2	66.1	23.2	1.9
OK	69.4	60.8	78.5	−8.6	17.7
PA	37.6	62.5	77.0	24.9	14.5
SD	100.0	93.2	92.8	−6.8	−.4
TN	59.1	59.4	85.3	.3	25.9
TX	40.8	36.8	42.6	−4.0	5.8
WI	73.5	67.8	89.7	−5.7	21.9
Simple average	68.6	69.6	82.8	1.0	13.1

Source: Packers and Stockyards Administration. Includes plants reporting to P&SA.

EXHIBIT C18.7   FOUR-FIRM CONCENTRATION RATIO (1969–1981)

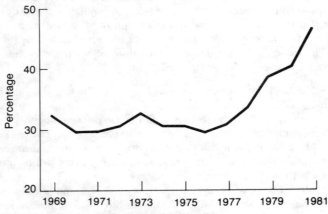

Source: Packers and Stockyards Administration.

packers as indicated by the acquisition of IBP, Inc. (by Occidental Petroleum) and Excel (by Cargill).

While these shifts in beef packing were occurring, hog packing experienced only minor changes in ownership and plant location. In the late 1970s and early 1980s, the pace of change began to accelerate. IBP entered the industry with plans to create the same kinds of efficiencies in pork that had been so successful in beef. Other competitors have fought to cut costs with varying degrees of success.

One result of the changes in beef has been opposition of smaller operators to the large producers. For the first time since the early part of the century, the words "monopoly" and "concentration" have become a rallying cry. Monfort of Colorado's legal efforts to stop the purchase of Spencer Beef by Excel were explained by Kenneth Monfort in an article by Warren Kester:

"The theory of our lawsuit was very clear. As they expand those plants and put in boxed beef facilities and double shifts, we would end up with two packers in our industry with something like 70 to 80 percent of the boxed beef market. We thought that concentration was too much."

Monfort doesn't believe such concentration would cause collusion, however. "On the contrary," he said, "We thought there would be a very tough aggressive fight for market share that would eventually chase many of the smaller packers— even this one—out of business. Once we were out of business, the largest survivors could then go back to increasing their margins."

Monfort said he used to view competition in the packing industry as a fair fight—survival of the fittest. But things have changed, he claimed, when two giant companies with the wherewithal to do with the beef market whatever they decided to do acquired the two largest packing companies. He was referring to Occidental's acquisition of IBP, the nation's largest packer, and Cargill's purchase of Excel.[5]

Some have urged cattlemen to support the strengthening of antitrust legislation, to support administrative or civil lawsuits where there is evidence of anticompetitive practices, and to support legislation such as the Smith proposal to limit the size of packers. This legislation would put a cap on market share for individual packers. Others maintain that there is no evidence of noncompetitive behavior. One observer has pointed out that meat packers have not done well as subsidiaries of other organizations and that there may be some surprises with the Big Four finally independent again and the "new" packers under conglomerate ownership.

There are also some definite predictions about the evolution of pork. One industry observer made the following predictions:

• Most old-time pork packers will be out of the hog slaughtering business by the end of the 1980s.
• New firms or organizations will be slaughtering hogs.
• Few master labor contracts will survive, and the cost of labor will decrease.
• More automation will occur in pork slaughtering and processing.
• Rather than large firms, most slaughtering firms will own only one or two plants.
• Plants will be larger.
• More plants will only slaughter, with processing at other sites.
• The major pork brands will survive but will buy meat and process only.[6]

Clearly, IBP intends to be the moving force behind several of these trends.

IBP

Acknowledged as the number one U.S. meat packer for several years, IBP was ranked number five in sales of all food processors in 1983. This ranking compared with number six in 1982. While all packers suffered lower margins in 1983, IBP continued to set the industry standards in profitability. See Exhibit C18.8 for comparative performance data.

While IBP's activities in beef have included the acquisition and renovation of a plant in Joslin, Illinois, in 1982 and several suspensions and one closing in 1983 because of capacity problems, most of the excitement was in the new pork business.

IBP's entry into pork processing came with the acquisition of a facility in Storm Lake, Iowa, in 1982. It underwent extensive renovation and opened the following September with one shift operating. With the addition of a second shift in 1983, capacity increased to 3 million hogs per year. Meanwhile, the company announced that it would build the nation's largest hog slaughtering facility, setting off competition for the site among several towns in the midwest. The field was narrowed to Sheffield, Illinois, and Stanwood, Iowa, both small towns with depressed agricultural economies. After stiff competition, marked by significant concessions to IBP by both sides, Stanwood was chosen to receive the plant. Reasons given were the location in the heart of hog raising country, the cost advantage from a federal grant Stanwood had agreed to apply for, and the "uncertain" corporate tax situation in Illinois (Illinois would tax on the basis of Occidental Petroleum's worldwide earnings, although a proposed change would have based the tax only on IBP's nationwide operations).

The federal grant for which Stanwood had agreed to apply (and upon the receipt of which the site selection was contingent) was to finance a pipeline from a nearby river to the proposed plant. The grant was for $10 million, although some claimed that the cost of the pipeline would only be about a third of that amount. The request was rejected in January of 1983 but IBP continued its plans to build. The plant will have a capacity of 4 million hogs per year and will cost $45 million. When this plant is completed, IBP's hog slaughtering capacity will be approximately 7 million hogs per year. Some competitors have complained that such plans will add new capacity to an industry where there is already considerable excess.

By early 1984, there were several indications that IBP was interested in acquiring existing capacity rather than creating any more new capacity. Occidental Petroleum offered $162 million ($95 million plus assumption of $67 million in notes, debentures, and lease obligations) for troubled Wilson Foods. The offer, which was not accepted, provoked a storm of criticism. Competitors predicted the purchase would mean further

EXHIBIT C18.8   PERFORMANCE DATA FOR SELECTED MEAT PACKERS, 1982

Company	Revenues (millions)	Net income (millions)	Return on sales	Return on stockholders' equity
IBP	$4,900*	$49*	1.0%*	NA
Swift Independent	$2,488	$25	1.0%	26.1%
Wilson Foods	$2,233	$17	0.7%	20.0%
Geo. A. Hormel	$1,427	$28	2.0%	11.4%
Monfort of Colorado	$ 996	$19	1.9%	34.5%

* Estimate.
Source: Fortune, May 2, 1983.

slashing of labor costs and speed the shakeout in pork packing. The combination would also increase IBP's domination of both suppliers and customers, critics maintained. Possible antitrust violations from such a merger also caused concern.

Another possible acquisition candidate was John Morrell and Company, the nation's third largest pork packer and a subsidiary of United Brands. Acquisition and rehabilitation of existing facilities would, if pursued, constitute a departure from IBP's successful practice of building facilities and then hiring the construction workers as employees in the finished plant. Acquisition of existing facilities would involve union workers as well.

The relationship between IBP and the Food and Commercial Workers Union (FCWU), which claims to represent 85% of the 130,000 U.S. meat packing workers, has been marked by strife since IBP entered the industry in 1961. IBP rejected the union's master contract, which set industrywide wages, and hired and trained local workers for less skilled jobs created by the new processing techniques. The resultant lower wages helped IBP gain a strong foothold in an industry saddled with expensive wage and benefit contracts.

IBP's gains in labor costs have not come without a price. Several strikes have resulted in lengthy work stoppages and violence.[7] The most recent strike at the Dakota City plant was marked by violence after 2,000 union members walked out on June 7, 1982. The workers had overwhelmingly rejected IBP's offer of a 4-year freeze of the $9.27 per hour average wage for slaughterhouse workers and the $8.97 per hour average for processing employees. The company had also demanded a clause that would allow it to reduce wages if any other local of the union signed a contract at a lower wage rate. The violence escalated when IBP reopened the plant in July with 1,400 workers, several hundred of whom were union members.

The walkout ended in October without an agreed upon contract. In July 1983, Local 222 accepted a 42-month agreement that cut wages by $1.07 per hour. IBP claimed the cuts were necessary to ensure profitability, especially given the fact that other meat packers had recently won wage concessions or freezes from their workers. The union contended IBP was trying to destroy it and vowed to regain concessions at future contract talks.

The meat packing industry in the mid-1980s had come a long way from its beginnings when salt was the only preservative and barrels the principal means of transport. The most recent changes were begun by IBP in the 1960s. Cattlemen, hog farmers, and poultry producers who watched and depended on the industry could only agree on the fact that these effects had not yet been completely felt.

NOTES

1 Iowa Beef Processors, Inc., became IBP, Inc., in 1982, a year after its acquisition by Occidental Petroleum. For details of IBP's rise to leadership in the beef industry see the case "Iowa Beef Processors, Inc."
2 Jeff Blysbal, "Food Processors," *Forbes,* Jan. 2, 1984, pp. 206–207.
3 "Beef Consumption Patterns," *Beef Digest,* July 1981, p. 12.
4 Blysbal, op. cit., p. 207.
5 Warren Kester, "Are We Heading for Monopoly in the Beef Packing Business?" *Beef,* March 1984, pp. 86–94.
6 J. Marvin Skadberg, "Who Will Slaughter the Hogs?" *Hog Term Management,* February 1984, p. 54.

7 There were nine strikes, several marked by violence, against IBP between 1969 and 1982. One of the most violent strikes occurred in 1969 at the Dakota City plant, where a company executive's home was burned and a 16-year-old girl was fatally shot. IBP executives, determined to hold down production costs, have refused to grant major concessions to the labor union, causing what is at best a strained relationship between them.

JAMES RIVER CORPORATION OF VIRGINIA

Prepared by Alan Bauerschmidt, University of South Carolina,
and Patricia McDougall, Georgia State University.

On Friday, October 21, 1983, Paul A. Engelmeyer, a staff reporter for the *Wall Street Journal*, reported that Brenton S. Halsey, the chairman and chief executive officer of the James River Corporation, had indicated that the primary goal of the company in the coming years would be consolidation and internal growth. This announcement heralded a change in the corporate strategy of the firm. The revenues of the James River Corporation had grown in a spectacular fashion over the last few years, largely as a result of an aggressive acquisition strategy. Judd Alexander, an executive vice president of the company, observed that if the rate of growth in revenue were to be maintained the firm would have to buy General Motors. And, Mr. Halsey conceded that the current pace of growth would be hard to match in the future, as there are few billion-dollar acquisitions around.

The article in the *Wall Street Journal* went on to discuss other problems associated with the past acquisition strategy of this well-respected paper manufacturing firm. These problems included the substantial debt of the firm and a rise in the price of pulp, which serves as a principal raw material of the firm. Finally, Mr. Alexander was quoted as expressing belief that the environment of the firm had changed because of the present size of the firm, leading him to conclude (as quoted by Mr. Engelmeyer), "You rarely see someone who can start a company and then manage it when it becomes this big."

The shares of the corporation closed that week at 33¾, down 3½ from the previous week, in fairly active trading on the New York Stock Exchange. The Dow-Jones average of the leading industrials traded on the New York Stock Exchange was off 1.16 percent that same week. The shares of James River fell a further 3⅜ during heightened trading the following week, to close at 30⅜. This was paralleled by a further drop in the Dow-Jones average of 2.03 percent. After a smaller drop of ⅝ in the week ending

November 4, 1983, shares in the company began a recovery that brought their value back to 37¼ by Friday, December 2, 1983. During the same period the Dow-Jones index rose to its original level. It should be noted that the James River Corporation reported earnings of $1.65 per share for the first half of the fiscal year, during the week of November 15. Earnings for the similar period in the previous year were $1.37.

HISTORY OF THE CORPORATION

The James River Corporation was founded in 1969 by Mr. Halsey and Robert C. Williams through a leveraged buy-out of a paper mill operated by the Ethyl Corporation. The latter firm was formed as a joint venture of General Motors and Standard Oil of New Jersey to produce a lead additive that would give gasoline a no-knock characteristic. Ethyl later became a public corporation and was acquired by the much smaller Albemarle Paper Company in the early 1960s. The assets of Albemarle became the foundation of the specialty paper operation of the Ethyl Corporation. The merger of these two firms was largely a financial maneuver, rather than an integration of operations.

At the time of the buy-out Mr. Halsey ran a small paper bag factory for the Ethyl Corporation, while Mr. Williams had responsibility for a papermaking R&D department of the corporation. When the managers of Ethyl decided to get rid of the assets of the company in the paper industry, Halsey and Williams borrowed the funds necessary to pay the corporation $1,500,000 for the single-machine mill on the James River in Richmond. The mill was a part of the original assets of the Albemarle Paper Company, and it was involved in the production of unbleached kraft paper that sold for $400 a ton and generated revenues of about $4,500,000. Halsey and Williams, with their backgrounds in engineering and intimate knowledge of the paper industry, converted the mill to produce papers for automotive oil filters that sold for $800 a ton.

The strategy revealed at this early point in the life of the firm has guided its growth over the past 14 years. Halsey and Williams have sought to identify and acquire paper mills and converting plants that require no more than 50 cents of investment per dollar of sales. They then transform the mill from the production of commodity paper products to specialty papers that yield a higher revenue. This requires intimate knowledge of the paper production process and today the company prides itself that the top 50 executives of the firm are so technically knowledgeable that each could operate a paper machine if required.

The spectacular growth of James River began with the acquisition of the Pepperell Paper Company in April of 1971. An 80 percent ownership of the 75-tons-per-day paper mill in East Pepperell, Massachusetts, was purchased from the St. Regis Corporation. This acquisition permitted James River to broaden its involvement in the manufacture of specialty papers. Today the mill produces paper stock that provides the base for masking tape and packaging papers for food products, as well as other grades of converting paper.

In May 1972, James River acquired a mill in Fitchburg, Massachusetts, with a capacity of 52 tons from the Weyerhaeuser Corporation. This mill is operated as a subsidiary, producing a wide variety of special industrial converting papers and other paper products.

A most notable event occurred in 1973, when it was decided to transform the privately held firm into a public corporation. This was accomplished by the sale of

205,000 of the $.10 par value shares of the firm in a public offering accomplished on March 16, at $12.00 per share. The firm retained 515,870 of the 2,000,000 shares authorized on October 29, 1972, as treasury stock, with 2,000 of these earmarked for stock options. The other 1,064,130 shares were distributed to principals associated with the founding of the company.

On October 1, 1974, the firm acquired the Peninsular Paper Company, a small independent producer of text and cover paper in Ypsilanti, Michigan. The acquisition entailed $1,136,006 in notes and 35,018 common shares, plus an additional contingent amount of $200,000. Peninsular is also operated as a subsidiary of the James River Corporation and has a capacity of 50 tons of paper per day.

The capacity of the three acquired mills, plus the mill on the James River, totaled only 199 tons of paper products per day, so the company at this point in time was still relatively small, although it manufactured a variety of specialty papers and was already geographically dispersed in its activities. In 1975, the firm more than doubled this capacity by acquiring five additional paper machines and more than doubling its work force from 598 to 1240 employees.

On September 19 the company paid the Weyerhaeuser Corporation $20,433,000 in cash, notes, and preferred stock for the facilities of Weyerhaeuser-Massachusetts, which contained the five machines. These operations form the hub of the Industrial Products Group of the James River Corporation, and the plant is operated as a subsidiary under the name of James River–Massachusetts. The products of the plant include various types of coated stock such as release backing papers and reprographic papers, with a daily capacity of 238 tons. Two series of preferred stock were developed to consummate the purchase: the first had an 8 percent yield and was convertible into 125,000 shares of common stock; the second series was participating in nature and entitled the holders to 60 percent of the earnings after taxes of the James River–Massachusetts Corporation above $1,000,000.

On January 1, 1977, the firm acquired the privately held Curtis Paper Company. This company operated a mill in Newark, Delaware, and the James River Corporation continues this operation as the Curtis Division, producing 22 tons of bend, text, and cover papers. Later in January—on the 10th of the month—the company acquired the Rochester Paper Company from the Household Finance Company. This acquisition included a mill with a 40-tons-per-day capacity in Adams, Massachusetts, and a mill in Rochester, Michigan, with an 18-ton capacity. Each plant produces a variety of specialty paper products including industrial filters. The James River–Rochester Division is operated as a part of the Filtration Products Group, while the Adams Division is part of the Printing/Packaging Group. During the period in which these two sets of acquisitions were being accomplished the James River Corporation assumed a $15,000,000 note payable quarterly from 1979 to 1991, at 10.25 percent interest. The terms of the note stipulated that the firm must maintain working capital of $15,000,000 and demonstrate certain financial ratios in respect to funded debt. This indebtedness was liquidated during 1982.

During 1977, the company also acquired the Riegal Products Corporation from Southwest Forest Industries. This acquisition included four mills in the western portion of New Jersey which produce a wide variety of specialty papers including inner liners for food packaging. One of these mills with a 15-ton capacity is now idle, while the other three are operated as the Riegal Division of James River; these mills have a capacity of 38, 200, and 75 tons daily, and, therefore, represented the largest acquisition of James

River up to that point in time. A portion of the financing of this acquisition included the issue of a third series of participating preferred shares entitled to $4.00 per annum plus dividends on the earnings of the Riegal Products Division above $3,600,000.

On January 30, 1978, the firm acquired the Otis plant of the International Paper Company in Jay, Maine. This plant is now operated as a subsidiary of the James River Corporation, producing coated, conductive, and carbonless specialty papers. The plant has a capacity of 135 tons daily.

During the period of the Otis and Riegal acquisition the firm issued an unsecured senior obligation in the amount of $12,000,000 due during the period 1982–1997 and paying 8.75 percent interest. It also released 40,000 nonparticipating preferred shares in a new series paying $8.75 in dividends.

The firm acquired what has become the James River Graphics Company for approximately $34,800,000 from the Scott Paper Company during December of 1978. This converting operation in South Hadley, Massachusetts, was the firm's first venture into coated film, and the firm uses 12 coating lines of up to 62 inches to produce photographic and reproduction paper, leatherettes, metallic-coated, embossed, decorative, and electrographic papers, along with other products of a coated or moistureproof variety.

The year 1979 provided no new acquisitions by the company and no increase in indebtedness. However, the company increased the number of common shares authorized from 3,000,000 to 10,000,000, and reported that 2,393,898 shares were outstanding (the company has earlier authorized a 3 for 2 split of the common stock). A portion of the new shares—187,000—were issued in conversion of the first series of preferred stock. The second series of preferred stock was repurchased by the company during May.

During June of 1979, the company did reach an agreement to purchase the assets of the Howard Paper Company of Dayton, Ohio, for $7,500,000, but the agreement was never consummated. Howard remains a privately held firm that operates two mills producing coated specialty papers. The mills have a total capacity of 275 tons of paper products per day, and the James River Corporation was prepared to pay $3,700,000 in cash and 165,000 shares of common stock for the firm, while refinancing $2,000,000 of the indebtedness of Howard Paper.

Up to this point in time, James River remained a specialty paper manufacturer which purchased the necessary pulp required as a raw material for its operations. In December of 1980, the firm acquired the Brown Company for $260,000,000 from Gulf & Western; Brown was involved in the production of specialty papers but it also had a pulp mill in New Hampshire. This served to vertically integrate the firm back to the required raw material. The Brown Company also had a towel and tissue operation, a folding carton operation, and a food service operation. Some of these varied activities form the Berlin/Gorham Group of the corporation, headquartered in Berlin, New Hampshire. The pulp mill in Berlin has a daily production of 100 tons of unbleached kraft and 700 tons of bleached kraft; 300 tons of the latter is market pulp. The Gorham plant produces 350 tons of bag and sack paper, creped kraft, and other forms of paper stock. This plant also produces 150 tons of sanitary tissue and interfolded and rolled towels. With this acquisition the *number* of employees of the James River Corporation reached 3,802.

In May of 1981 the firm acquired certain assets of Minerva, Inc., for $3,700,000, and in July 1982 the firm acquired the Dixie/Northern assets of the American Can Company for $480,000,000 in cash and preferred stock for $212,930,000 in working capital and $267,400,000 of other property, gaining a tissue business having a revenue of

$600,000,000 and the revenues of the Dixie cup and folding carton operation. The transaction was financed by $372,489,000 of debt, of which $100,000,000 was taken by American Can in the form of a subordinate issue convertible into 5,000,000 shares of James River Corporation common stock. The remainder of the purchase price was obtained from the assumption of $18,841,000 in other long-term debt and liabilities, the sale of $50,000,000 worth of James River common to American Can, and an issue of $39,000,000 in preferred stock to American Can that can be converted to 866,667 shares of common stock.

A major attraction leading to this acquisition was the pulp capacity of the Naheola Mill in Pennington, Alabama, which had a daily output of 1,000 tons of kraft pulp. The Halsey, Oregon, plant produces an additional 350 tons of pulp, of which 125 tons is market pulp. The Ashland and Green Bay, Wisconsin, mills are smaller operations in respect to pulp production, but the former mill produces 51 tons of creped paper based on 50 tons of pulp and the latter produces 410 tons of sanitary tissue, toweling, and converted products while having a capacity of 150 tons of pulp. James River merged the folding carton business obtained through the acquisition of Dixie with the elements obtained from the earlier Brown acquisition to create the Folding Carton Division of the Paperboard Packaging Group. The ranks of the firm grew to 17,700 employees upon completion of this acquisition that added 9,500 individuals.

On October 1, 1983, the James River Corporation concluded the $43,500,000 purchase of the H. P. Smith Paper Company from Phillips Petroleum for cash. The converting plants located in Chicago and Iowa City produce 100 tons of polyethylene-coated paper, board, and oiled papers producing sales of $51,000,000 in the previous year. This acquisition broadened the line of release papers used by industry and food packages and is operated as the KVP Group.

During 1983, James River acquired four mills from the Diamond International Corporation for $75,000,000. The latter firm was acquired by Sir James Goldsmith in 1982, and it was his decision to sell off the pulp and papermaking properties of the firm to the James River Corporation. These acquisitions include a mill in Old Town, Maine, that produces 160 tons per day of tissue and toweling, along with 600 tons of bleached hardwood and softwood kraft pulp. The managers of James River intend to organize a Penobscot division to operate this mill using personnel who performed this activity for the Diamond International Corporation.

The other three acquired mills will be organized as the Groveton Group and include the four-machine paper mill at Groveton, New Hampshire, that produces 300 tons per day of printing paper and 50 tons of facial and toilet tissue. The group will also encompass a mill at Hyde Park, Massachusetts, which produces 200 tons of printing papers daily on two paper machines and a 45-tons-per-day mill at Gouverneur, New York, that produces tissue and napkin paper on a single paper machine.

James River issued 522,057 shares of common stock with a current market value of $19,800,000, and privately placed 760,000 shares of preferred stock with a liquidation value of $76,000,000 to complete the purchase of the mills from Diamond International.

Early in 1984, James River announced that it acquired one quarter of the outstanding shares of A. B. Papers PLC of St. Andrews, Scotland, and will offer to purchase the remaining shares for a total acquisition cost of $7,750,000. The Scottish firm makes printing and specialty papers, and it owns a converting plant in Glasgow that makes heat-seal paper and particle-gum paper used for labels. A. B. Papers reported sales of $27,000,000 for the fiscal year ending on March 31, 1983, and pretax profits of $778,000. This will be the first foreign acquisition by the corporation.

NATURE OF THE PAPER INDUSTRY

The James River Corporation is a part of the eleventh largest manufacturing industry in the U.S. in volume of sales. The paper and allied products industry accounts for 3.6 percent of the value of all manufacturing in the country, and the value of shipments was $79 billion in 1982, down slightly from the peak shipments of $80.2 billion in 1981. The industry is estimated to have produced 59.8 million short tons of paper and paperboard in 1982, operating at an estimated 85.7 percent of practical maximum capacity. Elements of the industry produced 52.3 million short tons of wood pulp in 1982, of which 5.9 million short tons was marketed as pulp. The industry exported 3.5 million short tons of wood pulp in 1982, and in turn, 3.6 million tons were imported. Exports of paper and paperboard products totaled 4.3 million short tons in 1982, while imports of the same products equaled 7.9 million tons. Imports of newsprint made up 6.6 million tons of the total, while only .3 million tons were exported. The bulk of newsprint imports were from Canada. The major exports from the U.S. were in the form of linerboard and other paperboard products.

The U.S. paper and allied products industry consists of 394 companies producing paper in 655 mills and pulp in 390 mills. In addition there are 4,500 establishments involved in the transformation of the paper and pulp produced in the mills. Some of these converting establishments belong to the 394 companies operating mills, while other establishments belong to companies without mill facilities. Approximately 43.3 percent of the products of the industry are used in packaging, 31.4 percent in printing and publishing, 9.0 percent for stationery and converting, 8.7 percent in building and construction, 5.5 percent as disposable sanitary products, and 2.1 percent as industrial products.

The most distinguishing characteristic of the paper industry is its high level of capital investment. The paper and paperboard mill segment of the industry has approximately one dollar of gross fixed assets for every dollar of shipments. The paper converting segment of the industry is less capital-intensive, with $3.71 in shipments for each dollar of gross fixed assets, while the paperboard converting segment has $2.84 in shipments for each dollar of gross fixed assets. Taken together, the overall industry has shipments of $1.70 per dollar of gross fixed assets.

Papermaking is one of the oldest manufacturing technologies and technological change is relatively infrequent, although firms continue to make innovations in their production processes and the products they offer for sale. In 1980, the industry made capital expenditures of $5.2 billion, representing 17.6 percent of the value-added by paper manufacturing in that year. The overall manufacturing industries had capital expenditures of 9.1 percent in this same year. Another way to appreciate the unusual character of the paper industry in this respect is to observe that the paper and allied products industry made up 3.84 percent of the value-added by manufacturing in 1980, but it accounted for 7.40 percent of the capital expenditures of all manufacturing firms. It is estimated that the amount of capital expenditures made by the paper industry fell by 1.2 percent in 1981, and a further 6.5 percent in 1982.

Modern papermaking dates from the close of the 18th century when the paper machine of today was first developed, replacing the hand molding technique that dated back into antiquity. Paper is formed from pulp on an endless woven-wire cloth that drains and advances the forming paper through a succession of phases depending upon the type and quality of paper to be manufactured. The paper is dried, coated, and calendered as necessary. In this continuous process the web of formed paper is drawn onto a reel, where it is available for shipment or further processing. As mentioned above, various innovations are constantly being developed by equipment and raw material suppliers; however, the basic techniques of the fourdrinier and cylinder-type papermaking machines have been in existence for almost 200 years. This stability of the fundamental technology permits extended years of usefulness of the equipment found in paper and paperboard mills. Some paper machines in America and Europe have been in service for up to a hundred years, although to see such continuous use they have been remodeled again and again to incorporate advancements. The trend of these advancements is in the figures-of-merit associated with greater rates of operating speeds and consistent quality of the web of paper being formed by the machine. The trend in newly installed machines incorporates these figures-of-merit and greater width of paper formation.

The use of wood pulp in the manufacture of paper is of somewhat later origin than the papermaking machine. The wood grinding machine that permitted cheap groundwood papers to be produced was developed in Europe around 1840; however, the acceptance of this new technology took some time, and the availability of rags continued to constrain production of paper on both continents. The first sales of groundwood pulp to papermakers in the U.S. took place in 1867, at a price of eight cents per pound. The price soon dropped to four or 5 cents, and when it eventually fell to a penny a pound it reduced the price of newsprint from 14 cents in 1869, to 2 cents in 1897. This innovation in the raw materials for paper production had a revolutionary impact upon the newspaper industry, where it made the high-speed rotary printing press and the modern newspaper and magazine industries possible.

The use of wood pulp in the manufacture of the various grades and types of papers eventually followed. New uses for paper were developed as the chronic shortage of rags for pulp making disappeared. These new uses required more durable grades of paper than newsprint at a cost intermediate between rag and groundwood. Such paper stocks required the purification of the wood fiber in a chemical process, and the first of these processes that were developed used caustic soda. Today, chemimechanical and semichemical processes have improved pulp yields that original chemical methods did not allow. Much of the prepared paperboard now produced in the U.S. is made from the southern pine, which was considered unsuitable for papermaking before adaptation of the kraft sulfate process in the 1930s.

Few firms manufacture pulp to the exclusion of papermaking itself, and few papermaking firms are without pulp making capability in the U.S. It is estimated that 85 percent of the pulp produced in the U.S. is consumed captively at the same location where it is produced. The remaining quantity is shipped as market pulp to other papermaking locations of the same firm, or it is sold domestically and in foreign markets. Imports of pulp to the U.S. exceed exports, and Canada supplies 95 percent of these imports as well as being an active exporter to the rest of the developed nations. In Europe and Japan a great deal of the pulp requirement is met by recycling used paper.

Paper products include unbleached kraft paper which is a brown, somewhat coarse stiff paper used to produce heavy packaging, bags, and sack. Bleached kraft paper is a fine-textured paper manufactured from either softwoods or hardwoods and used to produce fine writing and printing papers and paperboard for packaging; the better papers are produced from softwoods. Newsprint and groundwood printing papers are course-textured papers of low strength and limited durability which tend to yellow with age. Corrugated medium is a course, low-strength paper obtained from the chemical processing of hardwoods and used in corrugated boxes as dividers and stiffeners between the paperboard liners. Linerboard is a stiff, durable, thick paper made primarily from unbleached kraft paper and used to manufacture heavy-duty shipping containers and corrugated boxes. Paperboard is a stiff paper of moderate thickness made from bleached kraft pulp to produce milk cartons, folding boxes, and individual packaging. Coated paper is a printing paper that has been treated with material such as kaolin to improve printability and photo reproduction and then used in the printing of magazines, annual reports, and books. Specialty papers are a diverse group of products ranging from thin filter papers to stiff card stock and used in such products as cigarettes;

FIGURE C19.1   LEADING U.S. PAPER FIRMS

Rank in paper business	Company	1982 Revenue from paper business ($ billion)	1982 Total revenue ($ billion)	Paper as percent of total
1	International Paper	3.379	4.015	84
2	Kimberly-Clark	2.870	2.946	97
3	Champion International	2.383	3.737	64
4	St. Regis	2.207	2.556	86
5	Scott Paper	2.117	2.293	92
6	Weyerhaeuser	2.099	4.186	50
7	Boise Cascade	2.068	2.912	71
8	Mead	2.040	2.667	76
9	Mobil	1.951	64.137	3
10	James River	1.875	1.900*	99
11	Crown Zellerbach	1.831	2.958	62
12	Georgia-Pacific	1.658	5.402	31
13	Westvaco	1.301	1.450	90
14	Union Camp	1.166	1.526	76
15	Great Northern Nekoosa	1.030	1.430	72
16	Continental Group	.979	4.979†	20
17	Time, Inc.	.922	3.564‡	26
18	Hammermill Paper	.760	1.396	54
19	Owens-Illinois	.679	3.553	19
20	Procter & Gamble	.669	11.994	6
21	Maryland Cup	.656	.656¶	100
22	Willamette Industries	.641	.929	69
23	Potlatch	.640	.820	78
24	Fort Howard Paper	.537	.537¶	100
25	Consolidated Papers	.483	.530	91
26	Sonoco Products	.473	.542	87
27	Bemis	.456	.681	67
28	Stone Container	.410	.427§	96
29	Dennison Manufacturing	.346	.577	60
30	Longview Fibre	.326	.371	88

* Reflects the 1982 acquisition of the American Can properties.
† Prior to the 1983 sale of assets that generated $ .480 billion of paper and allied products revenue.
‡ Prior to the 1983 divestiture of Temple-Inland.
§ Prior to Stone Container's 1983 acquisition of assets sold by Continental Group.
¶ These two firms merged in 1983.

filter papers, bonded papers (with cotton fibers), index cards, tags, file folders, and postcards. Tissue paper is a thin, soft, absorbent paper manufactured primarily from chemical groundwood pulps and used to manufacture toweling, tissues, and hygienic products. In all, several thousand different kinds of paper and paperboard can be manufactured.

Figure C19.1 on page 561 lists 30 firms that obtain a substantial portion of their revenues from the sale of such paper products. Various adjustments to the order of the listing could be made to reflect various circumstances, so this listing should not be taken to represent the leading paper manufacturers. Some of the firms such as Crown Zellerbach, Great Northern Nekoosa, Hammermill, Mead, and Scott Paper earn substantial portions of their revenue from the distribution of paper products, rather than from the

FIGURE C19.2   PROPORTION OF TOTAL REVENUES GENERATED BY FOREIGN OPERATIONS IN 1982

Company	Percent
International Paper	7
Kimberly-Clark	34
Champion International	13
St. Regis	13
Scott Paper	Nil*
Weyerhaeuser	22
Boise Cascade	9
Mead	Nil
Mobil	61†
James River	Nil
Crown Zellerbach	16
Georgia-Pacific	Unstated
Westvaco	26
Union Camp	10
Great Northern Nekoosa	Unstated
Continental Group	10
Time, Inc.	25
Hammermill Paper	Nil
Owens-Illinois	20
Procter & Gamble	29
Maryland Cup	Nil
Willamette Industries	Nil
Potlatch	11
Fort Howard Paper	Nil
Consolidated Papers	1
Sonoco Products	24
Bemis	14
Stone Container	7
Dennison Manufacturing	19
Longview Fibre	Nil

* Foreign subsidiary operations generate additional revenues of $11.4 billion, but this is considered as an investment return.

† Nil in respect to paper and allied products.

manufacture of such products. The Hammermill Paper Company, for example, has integrated its downstream activities to the extent that 45 percent of its revenues are attributed to wholesale distribution and only 15 percent of the products being distributed are manufactured by the company. The list could also be modified to reflect the fact that in some cases large portions of the revenues of firms are generated by foreign operations rather than the domestic manufacture and sale of paper and allied products. Figure C19.2 indicates the proportion of the total revenue of firms that resulted from foreign operations in 1982.

Other measures that might be taken into account in an assessment of the industry could include the relative degree to which firms in the industry have integrated backward to gain ownership or control of forestland that ultimately provides the raw material for the production of paper and paperboard products. Figure C19.3 provides the best information available on the amount of acreage controlled by the firms previously listed.

FIGURE C19.3 ACREAGE OF FORESTLAND OWNED OR CONTROLLED BY MAJOR U.S. PAPER FIRMS

Company	Acreage
International Paper	7,000,000
Kimberly-Clark	2,000,000
Champion International	3,300,000
St. Regis	5,870,000
Scott Paper	3,300,000
Weyerhaeuser	15,000,000
Boise Cascade	7,584,000
Mead	1,702,000
Mobil	1,046,000
James River	1,500,000
Crown Zellerbach	3,311,000
Georgia-Pacific	7,680,000
Westvaco	1,366,000
Union Camp	1,700,000
Great Northern Nekoosa	2,759,000
Continental Group	1,500,000
Time, Inc.	2,000,000
Hammermill Paper	435,000
Owens-Illinois	1,100,000
Proctor & Gamble	Unreported
Maryland Cup	Nil
Willamette Industries	558,000
Potlatch	1,400,000
Fort Howard Paper	Nil *
Consolidated Papers	667,241
Sonoco Products	265,000*
Bemis	Nil
Stone Container	475,000
Dennison Manufacturing	Nil
Longview Fibre	503,000

* Both Fort Howard Paper and Sonoco use extensive amounts of recycled wastepaper.

FIGURE C19.4 REVENUE PER TON OF PRODUCT

Company	Tons of pulp paper, and paper products	Dollar revenue per ton
International Paper	5,010,000	674.
Weyerhaeuser	3,695,000	568.
Boise Cascade	1,986,000	1041.
Mead	3,562,000	573.
James River	1,400,000	1339.
Georgia-Pacific	3,000,000	553.
Westvaco	1,993,000	653.
Union Camp	2,196,000	531.
Great Northern Nekoosa	2,243,000	459.
Willamette	1,750,000	366.
Potlatch	587,000	1090.
Consolidated Paper	631,000	765.
Stone Container	785,000	522.
Longview Fibre	599,000	544.

A few of the firms report tons of output, and from this a rough gauge can be obtained of the value of the product produced by the various companies. The revenue received per ton of output is shown for these firms in Figure C19.4.

This illustrates the heterogeneous nature of the paper and allied products industry. Firms operate in various product sectors of the industry and thus add different values to the products produced. A firm such as ITT Rayonier, which is not included in Figure C19.1, produces and markets pulp to the exclusion of any further process. All the firms in Figure C19.1 go at least one further step to manufacture paper or form products from the pulp they manufacture or purchase. Some of these papers may be the final product produced—newsprint produced from groundwood pulp would be an example of such a final product. Other papers may be shipped in the rolls for further processing or converted in some fashion in the plant in which the paper was formed from pulp. Firms which purchase paper for further processing into paper products are labeled converters, but the papermaking firms generally are integrated forward into portions of the converting segment of the industry, even if they continue to be considered as papermakers.[1]

The converting of paper is broadly divided into the making of boxes and other containers and the manufacture of other paper products. The latter category of converting is divided into the coating and glazing of paper and the production of envelopes, bags, die-cut paper and board, pressed and molded pulp goods, sanitary paper products, stationery products, and a host of miscellaneous products such as confetti, crepe paper, doilies, gift wrappers, paper tags, and telegraph tape. There is also a segment of the

[1] The case writers have detected subtle class distinctions among firms in the paper industry in respect to backward and forward integration. Generally, the closer the firm is to the trees the greater the majesty of the firm. This is sometimes rationalized by the notion that the value of paper products devolves from the trees and ultimately any profit generated in papermaking will accrue to the owner of the trees. This conflicts with the other notion that profit has historically been captured by distributors.

paper industry that is concerned with the conversion of pulp into building paper and board.

THE JAMES RIVER CORPORATION POSITION IN THE INDUSTRY

The James River Corporation has established positions in both the papermaking and converting portions of the industry. The firm is sufficiently integrated to produce the bulk of the paper and paperboard necessary for its converting operation, while still meeting its desired output of direct paper products. The firm purchases 600,000 tons of pulp to supplement the 700,000 tons of pulp it manufactures. Some 1,200,000 tons of paper and paperboard are manufactured from this pulp, while 100,000 tons of pulp is sold. Over 360,000 tons of the paper and paperboard produced by the firm is in the form of specialty and communications papers. Another 435,000 tons of paper is produced in the form of towel and sanitary tissues. Some 15,000 tons of paper is purchased to meet the additional requirements of the sanitary paper products segment of the business. The remaining 405,000 tons of paperboard produced by the company's mills is supplemented with 190,000 tons of purchased paperboard to produce Dixie cups, for packaging, and to make sales of 150,000 tons of paperboard in the marketplace.

James River considers itself to be the leading firm in the specialty paper products field, with revenues of $485,000,000 generated by this activity in 1982. These products include special paper required by industrial users as well as various forms of communication papers. They include such products as abrasive backings, absorbent papers, antitarnish papers, asphalted papers, battery paper and board, car liner, electrosensitive chart paper, cigarette tipping, duplicator paper, electrical board, electrical cable paper, filter paper, flameproof paper, fluorescent papers, foil backing, gasket stock, gumming paper, impregnated papers, laminating stock, lamp shade paper, latex-treated board and paper, leatherette papers, linen paper, map paper, mimeograph paper, opaque paper, parchment, photomount stock, poly-coated papers, postcard, poster paper, pyroxylin-coated paper, register paper, reproduction base paper, stencil board and paper, synthetic fiber papers, tag board, tag stock, text papers, tracing paper, twising paper, tympan paper, vellum, vulcanizing paper, wrapping papers, and writing papers. These items and others are produced by the six groups which make up the specialty sector of the firm.

The wide nature of the product line of the specialty sector insures a diverse band of competitors. The number of these competitors is almost as numerous as the products produced. Some firms such as the Dexter Corporation and W. R. Grace specialize in a few limited products produced by James River. Other firms such as Kimberly-Clark, Union Camp, Georgia Pacific, and Hammermill have broad lines of products which include many that are manufactured by James River. No firm has a line of products in the specialty category that matches those of the James River Corporation. The Domtar Corporation of Canada has the same broad line of products and many items that are identical in their nature; however, Domtar sells 71 percent of its product domestically and cannot be considered a direct U.S. competitor. There are a number of smaller firms that specialize in products produced by segments of the specialty and communications sectors of the industry; firms such as Hollingsworth and Vose, Howard Paper Mills, the Merrimac Paper Company, Monadnock Paper Mills, and the Mosinee Paper Company. The Mosinee Paper Company manufactures an approximate third of the specialty product line of James River, and it recently acquired the Sorg Paper Company to provide it with a position in two-thirds of the products produced by James River. Before the acquisition of Sorg Paper, Mosinee Paper had revenues of $85,000,000 and an operating income of 12.7 percent.

The specialty and communication papers segment of the industry is generally considered to be mature, with growth largely predicated upon growth in GNP. The James River Corporation believes it is the leading firm in this segment, with a 20 percent share of the market. One sector of the specialty paper market is in a contrasting circumstance to the other segments in respect to growth. Even with the direct threat of substitute plastic products, food industry papers and wraps produced by the KVP group of the James River Corporation have made substantial gains in the last few years, and such gains have defied the most recent recession. Some of the large paper companies such as Georgia-Pacific, Scott, and St. Regis produce the wet-waxed, dry-waxed, wax-laminated products and other release papers used by the food industry, but the risks of substitute products has made this a fertile field for somewhat marginal converters as well as smaller paper companies such as Badger Paper Mills, Bell Fibre Products, and the Mosinee Paper Company.

This same phenomenon of extraordinary growth extends into another line of the James River Corporation business. The paperboard packaging group of the Dixie/Northern sector produces folding boxes for the wet and dry food market. James River estimates that it has 10 percent of the U.S. market, and thus generated revenues of $370,000,000 for the company in 1982. Some 80 percent of sales of folding cartons by the company is to the food industry, while the rest of the folding carton industry has only 32 percent of sales in this category of carton. Competitors to James River's leading position in this market include the Container Corporation of America owned by the Mobil Corporation, and the Folding Carton and Label Division of International Paper. A number of other large paper companies have positions in the sanitary folding box business, but none of these come close to matching the commanding position gained by James River through its acquisitions from the American Can Company.

James River also ranks itself as first in the disposable food and beverage service product business, with 1982 revenues of $460,000,000. The firm estimates that the Dixie Products Group holds 14 percent of the market—a position just ahead of the Maryland Cup operation of the merged Fort Howard Paper Company. Other competing firms are the Solo Cup Company, Lily-Tulip (a spin-off of Owens-Illinois) and the Continental Group.

The final segment of involvement by the James River Corporation in the paper industry is in the market-driven sanitary tissue paper business. The company had revenues of $560,000,000 from this business in 1982, and it believes it ranks third or fourth in respect to bathroom tissue, towels, and napkins. It produces toilet tissues with the "Aurora," "Northern," and "Soft Touch" labels. Scott Paper Company is the leading supplier of toilet tissue, with its "Scott," "Lady Scott," and "Waldorf" brands. Kimberly-Clark follows Scott's 23 percent share of the tissue market with a 17.4 percent share, merchandizing the "Kleenex" and "Delsey" brands. Procter & Gamble holds the third position in the market, with a 14.4 percent share for its "Charmin" and "White Cloud" toilet tissues. James River estimates it holds 12 percent of the combined market, but a 10 percent share of the toilet tissue market may be a realistic estimate.

The over 60 percent of the sanitary paper product market held by these four firms is the most concentrated segment of the entire paper industry. Other firms that compete in this market include Crown Zellerbach, Fort Howard Paper, Marcal Paper Mills, Pope &

Talbot, Potlatch, and Statler Tissue Company. The tissue and toweling products that make up the largest part of the segment, along with feminine hygiene products, are noted for their noncommodity nature. These products are heavily advertised to reinforce their differentiated characteristics in the mind of the consumer. The industry uses some of the most sophisticated technology in papermaking to improve such tissue product attributes as absorbency, softness, and strength by using relatively new multilayering and air-lay forming techniques. The value of shipments by the industry is expected to grow by 3 percent in 1983; however, most of the real growth will be in disposable diapers and feminine hygiene products. Growth in sales of toweling, facial tissues, and napkins, along with toilet tissues has been relatively flat in the past few years, and these trends are expected to continue.

MISSION, OBJECTIVES, AND STRATEGY OF THE JAMES RIVER CORPORATION

Bob Williams, who serves as the president and chief operating officer of the corporation, has expressed his belief that the firm will continue its past pattern of growth (see Appendixes A through D for financial performance) and attain annual revenues of $3 billion by 1990. Part of this growth will result from an improved economy that will increase demand for products produced by the company. The firm also intends to increase the capacity of the present plant and introduce certain new products that will result in growth in revenues.

Both Mr. Halsey and Mr. Williams expect a compounded real growth in earnings per share of 15 percent, with a return on equity of 20 percent, and a reduction of debt to 45 percent of total capital. These expectations are predicated on improved operations that will result from capital investments of $800,000,000. This amount will be generated by internal cash flow and the investments will serve to both continue and extend the efficient operations of the company. In addition, the firm intends to enhance the profitable operation of the company by continued improvement in the management of operations. This will be similar to the consolidation of operations that followed the Dixie/Northern acquisition and eliminated 200 staff positions.

The record of acquisitions made by the corporation reveals the commitment of the firm to the paper business. Diversification has been concentrated in its direction toward broadened product lines. It has also led to a degree of vertical integration that is common to the various lines of business in which the firm is involved. In most cases the acquisitions made by the firm have involved to some degree their turnaround into profitable components of the firm. Mr. Halsey and Mr. Williams are depicted as having the ability to size up a candidate for acquisition in respect to potential for turnaround and incorporation into the James River portfolio. Acquired firms which extend the product line are encouraged to make a recovery as a distinct divisional entity of the corporation, with corporate resources and expertise provided as necessary. Acquired firms which have components that are similar to those already in the framework of the corporation are integrated as quickly as possible to achieve potential economies in operation. The two top executives of the corporation were described by *Fortune* magazine as involved in the reformation of some acquisitions even before the sale was final, indicating that each acquisition was the result of extensive planning and not simple opportunism.

The common thread running through the various acquisitions accomplished by the two executives is their focus on products with high value-added. They avoided acquiring plants or firms that were committed to production of commodity-type paper products and depended upon high-volume output. When the firm was limited to the business of industrial and communications papers, Halsey and Williams sought out special market niches. Even after the acquisition of the papermaking assets of American Can they remain focused on noncommodity products, although this acquisition has lead the firm away from lower-volume production and protected niches in the marketplace.

James River attempts to provide products of above-average quality in each of its markets and will never market a product of below-average quality. It will also attempt to produce its above-average-quality products at a cost which is below the industry average, but it will not avoid producing a product at a higher than industry average cost if this is what is required to produce a high-quality product that has active demand and a willingness on the part of customers to pay for such superior quality. It is surprising that the larger firms in the paper industry have not attempted to emulate this philosophical foundation to James River's business strategies.

The executives of the firm believe the company inherited considerable consumer marketing strength in the sanitary paper field when it acquired the operations of American Can. They consider themselves second only to Proctor & Gamble in this regard. The firm also gained an away-from-home sales and marketing organization from Dixie-Marathon that has enhanced institutional sales of both food service and sanitary paper products. James River sees itself as on a par with Scott Paper and only second to Proctor & Gamble in respect to the highly valued performance characteristic of tissue softness at below-average cost of production. Because of the quality of the institutional tissue products sold by James River the executives consider themselves equal to Scott Paper and superior to the lowest-cost producer, Fort Howard. Both the latter and Georgia-Pacific cannot compete in the premium tissue market.

James River considers its strength in the specialty and communications papers fields to revolve about its technical ability, as well as its product development and marketing skill. The firm operates a research center in South Hadley, Massachusetts, and the wide range of products is supported by an extensive and decentralized technical organization. The firm has production flexibility resulting from the large number of diverse types of paper machines in its various mills. Unlike the many small competitors to James River, the firm has countervailing power to that held by suppliers, and the backward integration of the firm is unusual in this segment of the industry.

Perhaps one of the greatest strengths held by James River in its disposable food and beverage service product business is the Dixie brand name. The firm also has a broad product line that permits production and marketing efficiencies and lower costs. In addition, the firm has a nationwide distribution system, and as already mentioned, they have integrated the institutional sale of towel, tissue, and food service products. The firm manufactures its own bleached paperboard used in the manufacture of the food service products.

This level of integration also extends to the paperboard packaging business of the firm. The firm operates a technical center in Neenah, Wisconsin, to serve its various plants and customers that are widely distributed across the country to best serve the food packaging industry. One of the criteria for success in this line of business is the ability to produce an attractive package, and the firm has graphic capabilities to match demanding customer needs.

ORGANIZATIONAL STRUCTURE

The corporate level structure of the James River Corporation is depicted in Figure C19.5. Figure C19.6 reflects the organization structure of the Dixie/Northern sector of the corporation that integrates activities acquired in the American Can and Brown

FIGURE C19.5

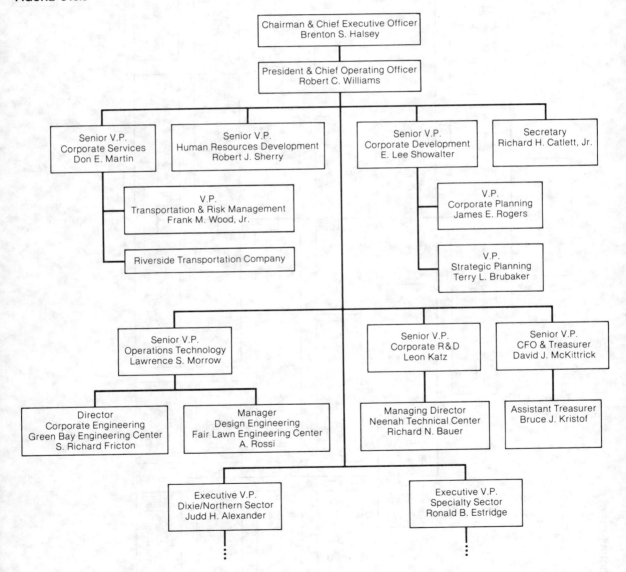

FIGURE C19.6

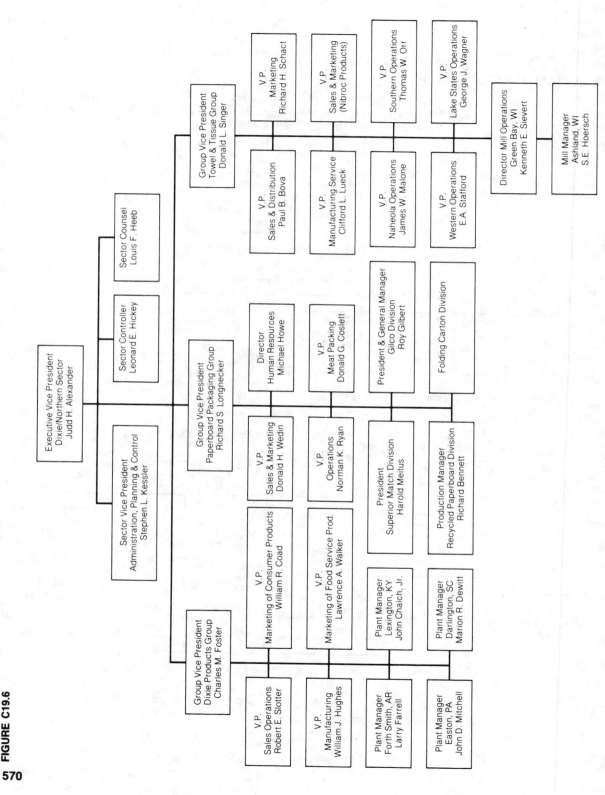

FIGURE C19.7

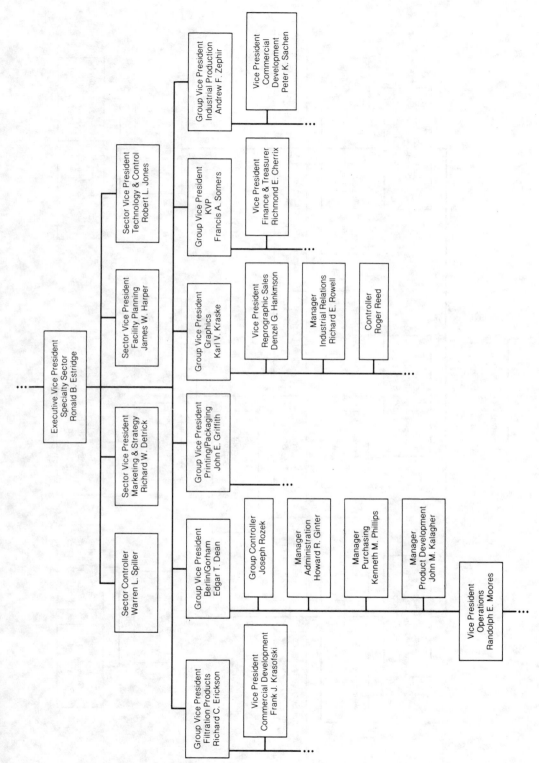

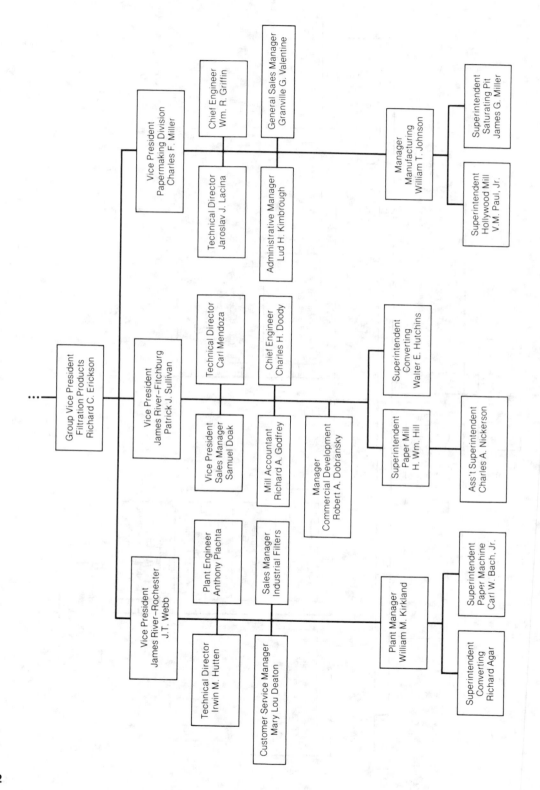

FIGURE C19.9

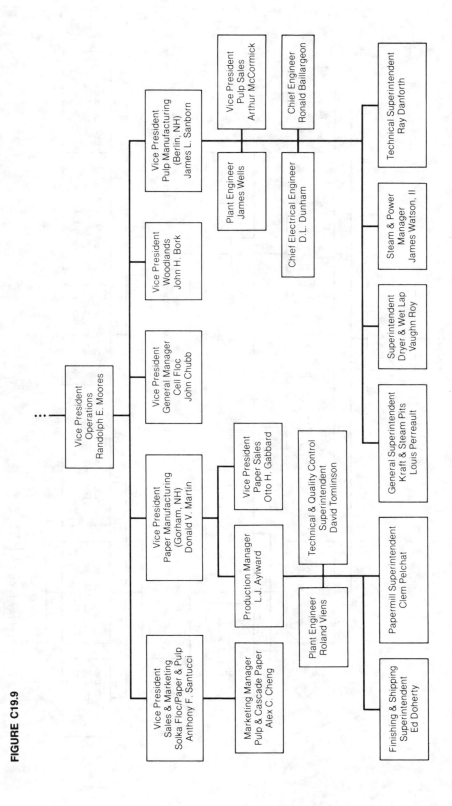

FIGURE C19.10

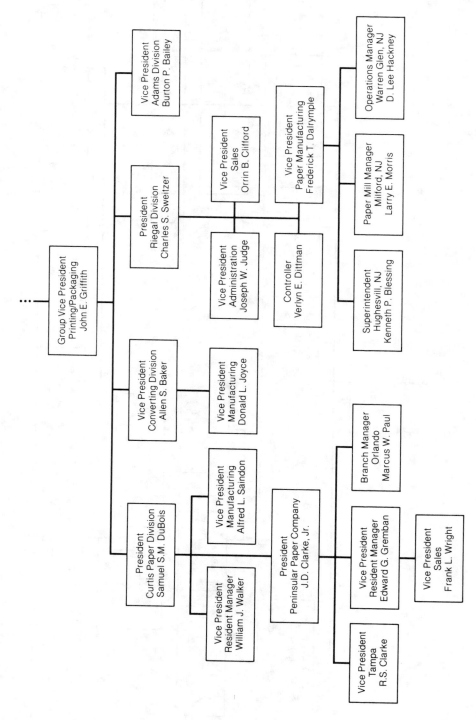

FIGURE C19.11

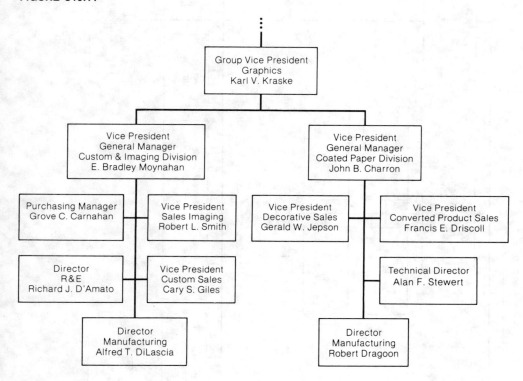

FIGURE C19.12

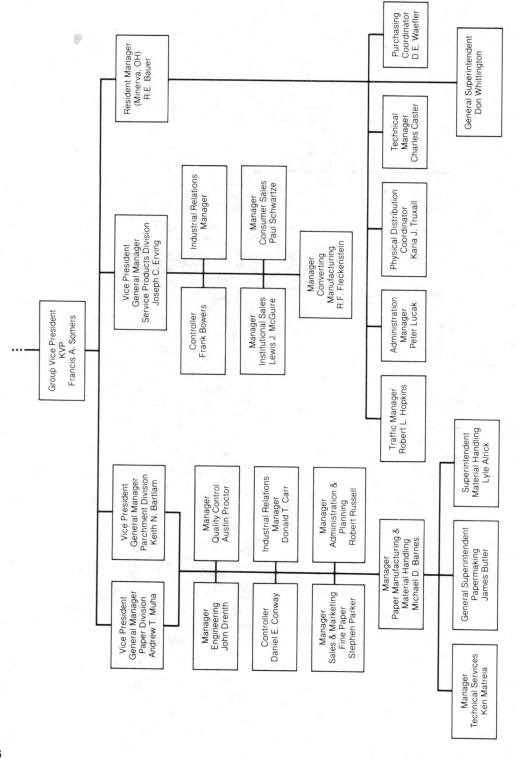

FIGURE C19.13

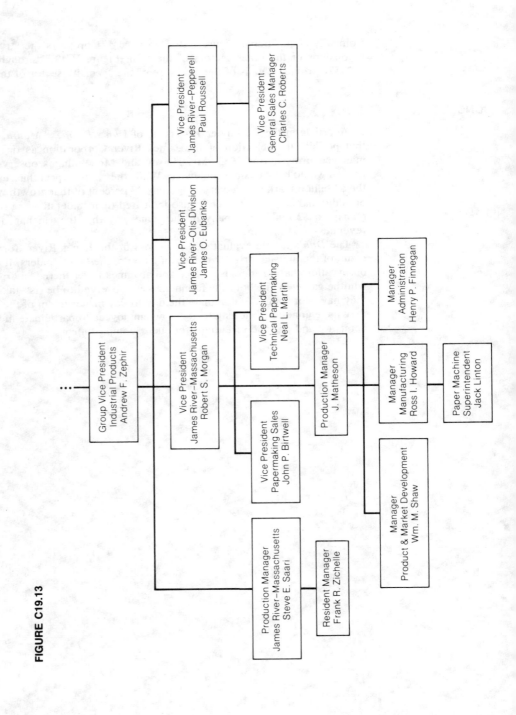

Company acquisitions. Figure C19.7 on page 571 presents the structure and interrelationships of the other sectors of the firm. Figures C19.8 through C19.13 on pages 572–577 provide details of the structure of the specialty sector of the company.

CONCLUSION

In an article in the December 1983 issue of *Dun's Business Month*, which announced that periodical's selection of the James River Corporation as one of the five best-managed firms during 1983, Mr. Halsey and Mr. Williams observed that the firm's growth would have to slow somewhat. While they both expect that revenues would pass the $3 billion mark before very long, only 20 percent of that growth would be the result of additional acquisitions. They also indicated their understanding that they could not manage a $2 billion company in the same way that they managed a firm with total revenues of $4 million.

The *Dun's* article evaluated the success of the James River Corporation to be the result of the unusual drive and determination of the two founders. It quoted Williams's observation that business is a game and at James River there is a driving motivation to win the game. While both the founders were observed to be risk-taking entrepreneurs, they have not sought to dominate the day-to-day management of the firm; they believe they have gone to great lengths to allow employees to participate in the success of the company and provide incentives for such acomplishments.

APPENDIX A
James River Corporation of Virginia
Consolidated Balance Sheet
(In Thousands of Dollars)

	1982	1981	1980	1979	1978	1977	1976	1975	1974	1973	1972
Assets											
Cash & equivalents	25,924	5,703	6,409	18,297	8,286	8,654	3,238	2,682	3,452	2,838	1,156
Accounts receivable	84,222	80,525	39,466	38,706	23,522	12,194	9,400	2,714	3,634	2,648	1,324
Inventories	103,163	107,488	46,010	43,321	27,540	14,594	11,176	4,563	3,085	2,529	1,707
Income tax refund	5,457	—	—	—	—	—	153	291	—	—	—
Prepayments	2,465	3,239	2,732	2,527	1,828	1,327	785	279	172	29	40
Total current assets	221,231	196,955	94,617	102,851	61,178	36,770	24,752	10,482	10,323	8,044	4,227
Constr. funds held by trustee	—	—	—	—	—	—	—	—	2,371	—	—
Net property, etc.	253,352	237,846	71,379	64,778	41,608	25,683	22,468	11,162	5,920	4,750	1,663
Deferred charges & other assets	3,532	3,987	2,594	2,108	1,226	797	346	231	122	35	74
Total assets	478,116	438,788	168,590	169,738	104,013	63,251	47,566	21,875	18,736	12,829	5,964
Liabilities											
Notes payable	—	3,284	1,988	1,585	774	—	4,216	850	200	200	—
Current debt mat	15,558	—	—	—	—	463	1,615	590	811	366	267
Accounts payable & accrs. lia.	86,484	84,053	31,290	34,440	21,791	10,118	7,484	2,312	3,140	2,173	1,116
Income taxes	—	1,312	—	8,024	1,915	734	—	—	655	391	110
Total current liabilities	102,042	88,649	33,277	44,048	24,479	11,316	13,315	3,552	4,806	3,130	1,493
Long-term debt	147,363	137,740	49,939	51,137	36,722	22,247	14,666	8,528	6,826	4,321	2,435
Minority interest	—	—	511	422	304	265	239	184	130	67	82
Deferred income tax	19,944	12,486	7,265	5,146	3,867	2,777	1,555	636	329	138	97
Provision for pension costs	38,790	43,782	730	638	538	404	406	372	67	42	43
Common stock p. $0.10	844	841	430	426	141	140	103	99	95	95	32
Redeem. preferred stock	—	—	—	—	—	150	150	—	—	—	—
A $8 CV. p.f.d. ($10)	—	—	—	—	1,500	500	500	—	—	—	—
B pfd. ($10)	—	—	—	5,000	5,000	—	—	—	—	—	—
C pfd. ($10)	1,724	1,724	1,724	1,970	2,457	—	—	—	—	—	—
D $8.75 pfd. ($10)	4,000	4,000	4,000	4,000	4,000	—	—	—	—	—	—
E $8.75 pfd. ($10)	4,300	4,300	4,300	4,300	—	—	—	—	—	—	—
F $6 CV. pfd. ($10)	—	—	5,000	5,000	—	—	—	—	—	—	—
Sr. G. CV. pfd. stk. ($10)	45,787	45,790	—	—	—	—	—	—	—	—	—
Additional paid-in capital	46,988	46,832	20,544	20,310	9,631	15,414	9,685	3,723	3,324	3,316	892
Retained earnings	66,333	52,643	40,869	27,341	15,372	10,034	6,947	4,781	3,159	1,720	890
Total liabilities	478,116	438,788	168,590	169,738	104,013	63,251	47,566	21,875	18,736	12,829	5,964

APPENDIX B
James River Corporation of Virginia
Consolidated Statement of Income
(In Thousands of Dollars Except per Share Data)

	1982	1981	1980	1979	1978	1977	1976	1975	1974	1973	1972
Net sales	772,682	561,318	373,946	297,940	181,922	98,607	70,576	41,848	34,279	24,454	14,884
Other income	2,791	2,118	2,701	1,278	452	601	265	314	256	87	53
Total revenues	775,473	563,436	376,647	299,218	182,374	99,208	70,841	42,162	34,535	24,541	14,937
Cost of goods sold	658,199	477,787	312,961	245,198	155,732	84,524	60,666	35,717	28,906	20,947	12,785
Selling & adm. expenses	66,418	43,784	28,116	21,247	11,742	5,874	4,015	2,711	2,172	1,614	1,121
Interest	16,574	9,842	4,680	4,131	2,831	2,125	1,431	543	401	366	180
	741,191	531,413	357,757	270,576	170,305	92,523	66,112	38,971	31,479	22,927	14,086
Income before income tax exp. & extraordinary charge	34,282	32,023	30,890	28,642	12,069	6,685	4,729	3,191	3,056	1,614	851
Income tax expense	11,929	10,667	14,231	13,933	5,850	3,208	2,341	1,431	1,521	760	393
Income before extraordinary charge	22,353	21,356	16,659	14,709	6,219	3,477	2,388	1,760	1,535	854	458
Extraordinary charge		3,475									
Net income	22,353	17,882	16,659	14,709	6,219	3,477	2,388	1,760	1,535	854	458
Income before extraordinary charge applicable to common shares	17,061	18,006	15,415	12,903	5,718	3,350	2,318	1,760	1,535	854	458
Income before extraordinary charge per common share & com. share equivalent											
Primary	$1.95	$2.29	$2.16	$2.17	$1.15	$.73	$.65	$.51	$.46	$.31	$.20
Fully diluted	$1.92	$2.21	$2.16	$2.09	$1.06	$.67	$.61	$.51	$.45	$.31	$.20
Cash dividends per common share	$.40	$.32	$.30	$.15	$.08	$.05	$.05	$.04	$.03		
Number of common shares & common share equivalents											
Primary	8,751,138	7,971,977	7,263,468	6,004,092	4,953,450	4,613,180	3,582,233	3,433,571	3,352,547	2,730,551	2,307,744
Fully diluted	11,248,599	9,287,168	7,267,676	6,231,210	5,486,606	5,038,538	3,952,673	3,440,469	3,364,028	2,738,337	2,309,057

APPENDIX C
James River Corporation of Virginia
Selected Financial Data

	1982	1981	1980	1979	1978	1977	1976	1975	1974	1973	1972
Return on net sales	2.9%	3.8%	4.5%	4.9%	3.4%	3.5%	3.4%	4.2%	4.5%	3.5%	3.1%
Return on average common equity	21.7%	22.6%	28.0%	35.0%	25.5%	21.9%	23.8%	23.2%	26.2%	24.6%	35.2%
Return on average investment	4.9%	5.9%	9.8%	10.7%	7.4%	6.3%	6.9%	8.7%	9.7%	9.5%	10.1%
Current assets to current liabilities	2.17	2.22	2.84	2.34	2.50	3.25	1.86	2.95	2.15	2.57	2.83
Capital expenditures, excluding acquisitions (in thousands)	$42,103	$21,280	$11,113	$9,377	$4,714	$2,627	$1,350	$3,697	$1,581	$1,501	$732
Equity per common share outstanding	$ 13.03	$ 11.43	$ 9.58	$ 7.53	$ 5.27	$ 4.17	$ 3.15	$ 2.57	$ 2.05	$ 1.60	$ 1.12
Common shares outstanding	8,443,408	8,411,760	6,455,276	6,382,619	4,774,691	4,736,357	3,461,370	3,344,426	3,216,707	3,203,291	1,620,000
Price range of common stock	13⅜–23¼	10¾–20½	9⅝–17⅝	6⅝–14⅞	3⅞–6¾	3⅞–7	3⅛–6⅜	2⅜–4	2½–3⅝	3⅛–3⅝	N.A.
Average weekly trading volume, shares	33,850	55,287	59,031	50,157	29,019	28,790	8,826	6,075	8,438	25,988	N.A.

APPENDIX D
James River Corporation of Virginia
Consolidated Statement of Changes in Financial Position
(In Thousands of Dollars)

	1982	1981	1980	1979	1978	1977	1976	1975	1974	1973	1972
Sources of working capital											
Operations:											
Income before extraordinary change	22,353	21,356	16,659	14,709	6,219	3,477	2,388	1,760	1,535	889	458
Charges (credits) to income not affecting working capital:											
Depreciation & cost of timber harvested	14,305	9,286	4,289	3,300	1,911	1,343	997	530	409	337	—
Deferred income taxes	7,458	5,221	2,119	1,279	1,090	1,222	937	240	170	41	67
Amortization & other	221	156	175	243	182	118	48	140	164	63	265
Working capital from operations excluding extraordinary change	44,337	36,019	23,242	19,530	9,402	6,160	4,370	2,671	2,279	1,329	790
Extraordinary charge	—	(3,475)	—	—	—	—	—	—	—	(35)	—
Issued or assumed in connection with acquisition:											
Common stock	—	21,437	—	8,812	—	—	—	394	—	—	—
Preferred stock	—	45,790	—	9,265	6,394	—	5,000	—	—	—	—
Long-term debt	—	90,491	—	16,000	14,500	1,500	—	1,136	—	2,042	1,050
Other long-term liabilities	—	43,857	—	—	—	—	—	300	3,050	1,005	—
Working capital from acquisition	—	47,582	—	17,446	10,601	4,049	2,880	772	—	20	—
Increase in long-term debt	25,000	10,800	800	—	—	15,040	267	—	—	—	—
Issuance of common stock on conversion of preferred stock and exercise of options	159	5,262	238	2,187	132	5,767	141	9	9	—	—
Other, net	7,534	3,479	(257)	—	—	—	1,500	—	300	2,522	861
Total sources	77,030	301,243	24,024	73,239	41,029	32,516	14,158	5,281	5,637	6,884	2,701

Applications of working capital

Additions to property, plant, & equipment	42,103	21,280	11,113	9,377	4,714	2,627	1,350	3,697	1,581	3,424	836
Reduction of long-term debt	15,376	14,915	1,998	1,585	693	9,024	1,436	794	925	1,260	267
Assets acquired from acquisition	—	206,975	—	35,022	23,063	5,987	6,519	1,576	—	—	—
Common stock cash dividends	3,372	2,344	1,887	831	380	263	152	—	—	—	—
Preferred stock cash dividends	5,291	3,763	1,244	1,908	501	127	70	—	—	—	—
Conversion of preferred stock	3	5,000	—	1,500	—	—	—	—	—	—	—
Redemption of preferred stock	—	—	5,246	488	—	—	—	—	—	—	—
Other, net	—	—	—	422	433	470	124	(2,198)	2,527	20	—
Increase in working capital	10,884	46,965	2,537	22,105	11,244	14,017	4,507	1,412	604	2,180	1,597
Total applications	77,030	301,243	24,024	73,239	41,029	32,516	14,158	5,281	5,637	6,884	2,701

Analysis of changes in working capital

Increase (decrease) in current assets:

Cash & short-term securities	20,221	(707)	(11,888)	10,011	(368)	5,417	576	(790)	614	1,682	701
Accounts receivable	3,697	41,058	761	15,183	11,328	2,794	6,686	(920)	986	1,324	652
Inventories	(4,325)	61,479	2,688	15,780	12,947	3,418	6,640	1,471	536	822	846
Recoverable income taxes	5,457	—	—	—	—	—	(138)	291	—	—	—
Prepaid expenses	(774)	507	205	698	501	543	506	107	143	(11)	32
Total	24,277	102,337	(8,234)	41,674	24,407	12,172	14,270	158	2,280	3,817	2,232

Increase (decrease) in current liabilities

Accounts payable & accrued liabilities	2,431	52,763	(3,150)	12,649	11,672	2,634	5,172	(828)	967	1,057	529
Long-term debt, current portion; & collateralized notes payable	12,273	1,297	403	811	311	(5,367)	4,591	229	444	299	155
Income taxes	(1,312)	1,312	(8,024)	6,109	1,180	888	—	(655)	265	280	(50)
Total	13,393	55,372	(10,771)	19,569	13,163	(1,845)	9,763	(1,254)	1,676	1,637	635
Increase in working capital	10,884	46,965	2,537	22,105	11,244	14,017	4,507	1,412	604	2,180	1,597

KING SALMON CHARTERS

*Prepared by Martin Keith Marsh, California State University at
Bakersfield, and Susan Swanson, KATA/KFMI, Arcata,
California.*

If you want an exciting fishing experience on California's rugged, scenic north coast, dial 442-FISH. That's the phone number for King Salmon Charters, Dennis Pecaut, proprietor, operating out of the King Salmon fishing resort on busy Humboldt Bay.

Dennis Pecaut, retired from the California State Highway Patrol (CHP), had previously served in both the U.S. Navy and the merchant marine. He developed a love for the sea and boats. He had always owned sport-fishing boats and had obtained a commercial fishing license while still active in the CHP. His interest in entrepreneurial ventures was demonstrated early—he operated a successful driving school for 18 or 19 years while he was still with the CHP. (He retained the Eureka, California, branch until November 1983, in the meantime having turned over another successful branch in Redding to his son.) When he retired, Dennis sought additional sources of income as well as personal autonomy, so he invested in apartments and a tavern. Although all these investments were profitable, none provided the intrinsic satisfaction that he was seeking. So he sold the apartments and tavern (successively) and purchased a fishing boat.

After selling the tavern, Dennis obtained an Ocean Operator's license from the U.S. Coast Guard (USCG) in San Francisco with the idea of operating a charter boat service. To obtain the license, he had to demonstrate his boating expertise (required—a motor boat operator's license and 2 years' experience working aboard boats, with evidence in the form of two letters verifying that experience). He was required to pass a physical exam and a written test covering such subjects as boat operations on inland and international waters, safety, first aid, fire fighting, oil pollution control, gasoline and diesel engines, weather, and navigation.

Note: This case was written for the purpose of class study and discussion, rather than to illustrate either effective or ineffective business management. Used by permission.

Dennis's license, based on his unique experience, authorizes him to operate a boat of up to 75 tons gross and to carry as many passengers as the specific vessel is licensed for. His license specifies a geographic area within which he can operate, Point St. George (near Crescent City) to Cape Mendocino and out to 100 miles from shore. Dennis must also pass a recertifying exam every 5 years.

He found the *Moku* (a Hawaiian word for "boat") at Newport, Oregon, in November 1979. The 36-foot boat, with fiberglass hull and single-screw, diesel-powered engine, cost him $45,000. She was 9 years old at the time; the radar wasn't working, the loran (direction finder) was obsolete, and there wasn't much gear on board. Because of the weather, it took Dennis 60 days to sail down the coast to Eureka. He worked on into the spring of 1980, installing new electronics (radar, auto pilot, updated loran, VHF radio, CB radio, fathometer, and fishfinder). Finally, the *Moku* was ready for her USCG inspection, and she passed with flying colors! The USCG "stability" test demonstrated that *Moku* could safely carry 20 passengers and a crew of 2. Exhibit C20.1 is a recent photograph of the boat as it passed over the bar at the entrance to Humboldt Bay on a sport-fishing voyage.

To date King Salmon Charters has experienced financial hard times, as illustrated by Exhibit C20.2, financial statements based on Dennis's reports to the Internal Revenue Service (IRS) of profit or loss from business or profession (IRS Schedule C, Form 1040) for the years 1980 to 1983. Exhibit C20.3 provides details from the firm's report of depreciation expenses for 1983 (IRS Schedule C-2). Dennis is obviously concerned

EXHIBIT C20.1   THE *MOKU* PASSING OVER THE BAR

Source: Jennie Marsh Jackson.

EXHIBIT C20.2 FINANCIAL STATEMENTS, 1980–1983

	1980	**1981**	**1982**	**1983**
Gross receipts:	$18,157	$21,530	$23,687	$32,523
Less returns & allowances	0	0	360	255
Less cost of operations	2,524	0	6,087	0
Gross income	15,633	21,530	17,240	32,268
Deductions:				
Advertising	1,123	494	785	120
Transportation	0	0	0	289
Depreciation	12,013	14,235	11,928	11,193
Dues & publications	0	68	0	107
Freight	0	37	0	49
Insurance	0	4,236	3,744	3,065
Interest	45	785	925	410
Office expense & postage	26	449	471	816
Rent	1,276	2,730	4,335	1,650
Repairs	3,591	275	2,056	3,974
Supplies	293	6,631	2,811	1,727
Taxes	10	27	0	150
Utilities & telephone	394	1,107	1,266	1,348
Travel & entertainment	45	17	0	426
Wages	0	0	0	2,906
Accounting	350	0	0	292
Fuel	3,193	2,688	2,842	2,034
Licenses	185	338	286	523
Miscellaneous	291	200	0	731
Bait	174	317	169	260
Tackle	5,054	0	0	0
Printing	0	285	0	0
Total deductions	28,039	34,919	31,618	32,070
Net profit (or loss)	(12,406)	(13,389)	(14,378)	198

about his prospects for ever turning a profit on the operation. The following section provides insights about the product and marketing policies of King Salmon Charters.

PRODUCT AND MARKET POLICIES

It is appropriate to think about King Salmon Charters as being a multi-product (or multiservice) business. Basically, the firm provides sport-fishing opportunities to tourists as well as Humboldt County fishing enthusiasts, including salmon fishing and bottom fishing. But King Salmon Charters is also involved in commercial fishing and other charter boat activities as well.

Salmon Fishing

The primary sport-fishing attraction is salmon fishing, which is best around Humboldt Bay during the height of the summer tourist season. Perhaps 70 percent of Dennis's

EXHIBIT C20.3   RECORD OF DEPRECIATION, 1983

Class of property and description	Cost	Expense deduction
Section A. Election to expense recovery property		
3 Year—VCR equipment	1,009	1,009

Class of property and description	Date placed in service	Cost	Recovery period	Method	%	Current year depreciation
Section B. Depreciation of recovery property						
3 Year						
Welding equip.	1/81	232	5	SL	20	46
New engine	6/81	8,488	5	SL	20	1,698
Sanitation device	6/81	726	5	SL	20	145
Scanner	6/81	320	5	SL	20	64
Chromoscope	6/81	2,995	5	SL	20	599
Scales	11/81	325	5	SL	20	65
VHF radio	7/82	316	5	SL	20	63
Loran	7/82	1,195	5	SL	20	239
Crab rings	7/82	600	5	SL	20	120

Description of property	Date acquired	Cost or other basis	Prior depreciation	Method	Life in years	Current year depreciation
Section C. Depreciation of nonrecovery property						
CB radio	7/78	160	80	SL	3	0
Boat	12/79	45,000	17,712	150	10	4,094
CB radio	6/79	356	356	RL	3	0
Pickup 7760, 1–3 persons	4/79	5,176	4,417	RL	5	607
Radar	3/80	3,195	1,952	DDB	7	356
Trolling & mast loran	4/80	9,998	5,990	DDB	7	1,146
Crab pots	11/80	3,415	3,077	RL	3	338
Crab block	11/80	3,895	2,003	DDB	7	540
VHF radio	6/80	425	399	RL	3	26
Freezer (used)	5/80	100	92	RL	3	8
Freezer (used)	12/80	132	102	RL	3	30
Total depreciation						$11,193

customers want to go salmon fishing. He claims that salmon are the most sought after sport fish in the world. Although the salmon season varies from year to year, typically it opens on the Saturday nearest February 15th of each year and closes on the Sunday nearest October 15th. The limit is two fish per person; one fish must be at least 22 inches in length, and the second fish must be at least 20 inches.[1]

Salmon are taken by trolling; that is, the lure or bait is trailed along behind the boat at a very low speed. Because many customers are getting their first experiences at deep sea fishing, and because of the technology involved, the operation is highly structured. To describe the situation in Dennis's words:

Ninety percent of the people don't know how to bait the hook and don't know how to fish. You have a boat 36 feet long and twelve people fishing. . . . For the sake of organization, so that everybody doesn't get their lines tangled up, and everybody won't go off in a different direction with their own methods of fishing, you [Dennis or his deckhand] have to set the lines out and you have to set certain weights on certain pole positions around the boat. . . . The amount of line you put out, how deep you fish, . . . what type of gear you have on, etc., all this has to be organized, otherwise you would have a big mess.

Dennis furnishes rod, reel, and rigging. The typical summer day of salmon trolling begins at first light, perhaps 6:00 or 7:00 A.M. Customers check in with Dennis, pay their fee of $35 (or the balance due over and above a 50 percent deposit required for people Dennis doesn't know), and board the boat. They position themselves on outward-facing seats as Dennis pilots the craft through the King Salmon channel and across the bay to its Pacific Ocean entrance. In the meantime the single deckhand places a pole in a pole-holder for each customer, rigs up the lines with an anchovy or a lure and (usually) a device called a "Deep Six," designed to keep a line underwater until a fish strikes. (Sometimes a sinker of up to 30 ounces is used.) Each customer watches his or her own pole. When a pole jiggles, someone cries out "Fish on," the signal for Dennis to take the boat out of gear while the excited customer reels in (or loses) his fish. The deckhand grabs the boat net and helps the fisherman land his catch. Once a fish is landed, a plastic, numbered tag is attached to the fish, and a duplicate of the tag is handed to the customer so that he can identify his fish at the end of the day. The fish is then tossed into a centrally located ice bin for safe-keeping.

Although silver (coho) salmon are said to range in size up to 3 feet in length and 30 pounds in weight, a typical silver weighs 6 to 8 pounds.[2] Cohos are very silver in color and are smaller and more slender than King salmon. Also, cohos are caught closer to the surface. King (chinook) salmon can be identified by their green or bluish-black backs and dark jaws. The typical catch is 8 to 20 pounds, but the King ranges in size up to 5 feet in length and 125 pounds in weight.[3] Once in a while other species of fish, such as snapper or rock cod, will strike a trolled bait or lure, but this doesn't happen very often. The real joy is latching onto the game and valuable salmon ($5 or $6 a pound is a reasonable retail price). So when Dennis has his full complement of fishermen and everyone limits out, it's a very happy occasion! There are, however, the rare trips when no one catches anything, but that's the reality of fishing!

Dennis doesn't coddle his customers. Even though a typical fishing trip lasts 5 or 6 hours, he doesn't provide refreshments or coffee. Passengers can bring their own ice chests and lunches; Dennis provides the fishing. (Many charter boats in Southern California sell refreshments at profitable prices; they don't *allow* their patrons to bring their own goodies!) There is a head (toilet) on board, but seasick passengers are discouraged from using it. Dennis explains why:

I have a little sign on the door to the head, "Seasick Passengers Must Stand at the Rail." They have a tendency to go into the head . . . and they usually wind up messing the whole place up. They have a tendency to want to curl up in little balls on the floor and hide out for the rest of the trip. That means no one else can get in there. We try to encourage them to stand outside in the fresh air. . . . They can see the horizon, or another boat in the distance, which helps stabilize them a little bit.

As an old salt, Dennis has learned to be tough when seasick passengers ask to be taken back to port. He has to consider the other passengers, who have paid their money to go fishing.

Bottom Fishing

Some customers are interested in catching fish, period, and opt for a day of bottom fishing. The ocean bottom immediately off Humboldt Bay is mud and sand and virtually flat, with only a very gradual slope out in deeper water. Such water is ideal for salmon trolling, but not ideal for the nonmigratory fish associated with "still" fishing, more popularly known as "bottom" fishing. Therefore, most bottom fishing is done off Cape Mendocino, where the bottom is rocky and nutrients are plentiful. Because of the extra sailing required to get to the fishing ground (20 to 30 miles), Dennis charges an additional $5 a head to go down there.

Both the fish and the fishing are different. Among the bottom fish caught from the *Moku* are red and black snapper; numerous varieties of rock cod (often referred to simply as rockfish), including black, orange, vermillion, and china reds; lingcod; cabezon; calcod; boccachi; greenling; and others. While the bottom fish are not as exciting as salmon, customers seldom go home without fish, and they are more likely to feel that they got their money's worth, according to Dennis.

The general limit for "fin fish" is 20, "in combination of all species with not more than 10 of any one species, except as otherwise provided."[4] The exceptions include rockfish (a limit of 15, all of which may be of the same species) and lingcod (limit of 5, minimum size—22 inches in length).[5] The log of the *Moku* reveals the degree of success of some of Dennis's better bottom-fishing trips—September 5, 1980, 7 lingcod and 120 rockfish; May 24, 1981, 2 lingcod and 150 rockfish; June 16, 1981, 2 salmon, 1 lingcod, and 90 rockfish.

Besides their abundance, rockfish are sometimes quite large and range in length up to 30 inches.[6] More typical, however, are fish around 15 to 20 inches, averaging 3 pounds in weight. Where a single 10-pound salmon might be worth $50 or $60 at retail, though, a limit of rockfish retailing at about $1.75 to $2.25 a pound (filleted) is worth $35 to $45. But, as Dennis puts it, "For pure delight of fishing, it is more fun to go bottom fishing!"

The same types of sport rods and reels used for salmon are used for bottom fish. But here there is no need for the "Deep-Six." In bottom fishing the boat drifts and the customers fish straight down. A 1-pound sinker is attached to the end of the line, or maybe a 2-pounder if the boat is drifting too fast with wind or current. Three to five hooks are attached to a single leader, and although anchovies are sometimes used, Dennis prefers lures or jigs for rockfish. It is not unusual for customers to have more than one fish on the line at a time.

The fishfinder is especially valuable for bottom fishing. As Dennis says, "If there are any fish in the area, I can find them." The big problem with bottom fishing is the loss of gear. The floor of the ocean in productive locations is rocky, with considerable seaweed and other vegetation growing in profusion. Since the boat is always drifting to some extent, it is easy to snag up on something and lose hooks, line, and sinker. Dennis estimates that he has "about $2.00 invested in the terminal gear for each fishing pole." His solution to the problem is to charge customers for each setup that they lose. (But down south, customers are required to rent pole, reel, and terminal gear, and they may even have to pay for bait, snacks, and drinks as well.)

Commercial Fishing

The *Moku* is licensed for commercial fishing as well as for commercial passenger (party boat) fishing. The "catch-22" is that Dennis cannot take salmon for commercial purposes with the *Moku* on the same day that he takes sport-fishing customers out on the boat.[7]

Commercial fishing for salmon in California is strictly hook and line trolling, although gill netting is still permissible in Washington and Alaska. Instead of trolling with poles, the fishing lines are attached to long outriggers, or booms extended horizontally from the deck. (In the photograph, Exhibit C20.1, the booms are secured vertically, because the boat is on a sport-fishing trip.)

Boats may have from two to eight wire lines in the water, each with a heavy lead ball on the end; for very deep trolling the weights may be as much as 50 or 60 pounds. Since lighter weights allow the lines to be carried shallower and farther back toward the stern of the boat, the probability of tangling is reduced by varying the weight of the lead balls.

Integral to the wire lines are sets of two welded beads, or "stops," every 2 fathoms apart (in some cases, 3 fathoms). The two stops are about 6 inches apart. Attached to the main wire line between the stops is a 2- or 3-fathom monofilament leader (which is the true fishing line). The stops are designed to keep the fishing lines from moving up and down the main wire line. At the end of the leader is the bait (herring or anchovies) or lures (spoons, or "hootchies," of varying colors). Hootchies are lures designed to resemble small squid or octopi. Sometimes "flashers" are attached ahead of the bait or lure to help attract fish.

If a boat has six wire lines in the water—three suspended from each boom—each with ten "spreads" (the term for the monofilament baited lines), there would be 60 trolled lines fished at one time. With this setup, the boat trolls slowly through the fishing grounds. Lines are retrieved periodically, depending upon how well the fish are hitting.

Dennis generated $4,564 in revenue through commercial fishing in 1981, of which $1,398 was from trolling and bottom fishing and $3,166 from crabbing. The peak months for trolling and bottom fishing were August, September, and October, with revenues of $380, $229, and $632, respectively. The peak period for crabbing was December, when Dennis caught $3,102 worth of crab.

Crabbing can be an expensive proposition, at least to get started. The *Moku* was overhauled in December 1980 to fit it out for crabbing. The overhaul cost Dennis approximately $12,000, including installing a hydraulic "puller" system—winch, hoses, etc.—for setting out and retrieving the traps. Dennis purchased about 60 traps and traded some sport-fishing gear for another 13. Altogether, the investment for traps came to perhaps $100 per trap, including lines, buoys, etc.

Northern California crabbers take mostly Dungeness crabs, according to Browning.[8] Only males can be taken, with a minimum size of 6.25 inches but ranging up to 10 inches. Females are smaller—6 inches across the carapace at most. The traps are made of steel rods and wire mesh. They are shaped like drums and are designed in such a manner as to allow the smaller crabs to escape. The traps are baited with clams, squid, or herring and set out in strings. Each trap has a line and a small plastic or foam buoy attached to enable the crabber to recover the catch and/or to rebait.

Traps are often lost; the buoys get chopped off by other boats. But sometimes another fisherman will find the lost traps and return them, since the buoys are color-coded for identification. Sometimes a crabber finds someone else's traps tangled up in his own. But there's a lot of cooperation among the professionals. As Dennis puts it:

Most of the time, when the season is open, if you find something like that [competitors' traps] you have a rough idea whose they might be, and you call them and tell them that you have their traps, and they come and pick them up. In fact, if I don't know who they belong to, I usually stack them up on the dock by the boat, and I spread the word around that I have a half dozen traps down there. . . . The people come by and look at them, and if the traps are theirs, they take them.

Dennis started out with 73 wire mesh traps in 1980, lost a number of them, and finally sold the remainder just before the 1982 season for $50 each. In that year he converted to lightweight ring nets, which do not require the heavy hydraulic puller installation, but which are retrieved with a light, relatively inexpensive hoist that Dennis installed. He bought 25 of the ring nets at $25 each. A disadvantage of the ring nets is that they must be retrieved shortly after dropping, since the crabs can easily escape.

Other Activities

Perusal of the logbook of the *Moku* reveals that Dennis also earns revenues from activities other than fishing. On occasion he has provided taxi service for Russian and other commercial fishing vessels operating off the coast of California. In 1981 this taxi service generated $925 in revenues. The *Moku* is sometimes chartered out to whale-watching groups, especially groups from the College of the Redwoods and Humboldt State University (HSU). In 1981 whale watching contributed $680 in revenues. Dennis has also taken HSU oceanography faculty and students out on research expeditions. The relative contribution of various activities in which the *Moku* engages can be seen in Exhibit C20.4.

The detail of Exhibit C20.4 appears more accurate than it really is. For instance, when the salmon trolling is slow, Dennis often switches to bottom fishing. Or, as occurred in September 1983, a fishing trip was combined with a paid-for mission to scatter ashes at sea. Although Dennis maintains excellent records, the case writers experienced some difficulty in precisely attributing revenues to the categories shown in Exhibit C20.4.

Not all the *Moku*'s voyages are profit makers. The boat's logbook shows, for example, that on October 26, 1980, Dennis took 14 passengers of a senior citizen group on a cruise. (The cruise was arranged by two HSU students for a class project.) The group toured the Humboldt Bay and did some bottom fishing inside the bay off the North Jetty, all at no charge.

THE COMPETITION

The competition in sport fishing on Humboldt Bay consists of Jim Walters and Captain Ole Skauge. Jim owns a 50-foot party boat called the *Sailfish*, which is also moored at the King Salmon resort. Jim advertises in the Yellow Pages:

One of the newest and fastest boats on the north coast. Owned and operated by Jim Walters. A dedicated skipper who takes you where the fish are.

Jim Walters charges $35 per person for salmon fishing, which includes pole and bait. The trip takes about 6 hours. Because bottom fishing takes an additional 2 hours, Jim discourages it, at least during the salmon season. Dennis and Jim are good friends. They

EXHIBIT C20.4   REVENUES BY ACTIVITY

	Sport fishing		Commercial				Nature cruises		
	Salmon	**Bottom**	**Salmon**	**Bottom**	**Crab**	**Taxi**	**Whales**	**Birds**	**Subtotal**
1982									
Jan.	0	0	0	0	515	0	0	0	515
Feb.	0	150	0	0	300	0	0	0	450
Mar.	0	0	0	0	308	50	285	0	643
Apr.	0	100	0	0	0	0	240	0	340
May	945	280	477	0	0	0	0	0	1,702
June	3,355	0	26	0	0	500	0	0	3,881
July	8,590	400	42	0	0	0	0	0	9,032
Aug.	5,028	857	63	78	0	0	0	0	6,026
Sep.	910	785	0	849	0	862	0	0	3,406
Oct.	0	285	0	293	0	0	0	0	578
Nov.	0	0	0	0	0	0	0	0	0
Dec.	0	0	0	0	524	0	0	0	524
Total	$18,828	$2,857	$608	$1,220	$1,647	$1,412	$525	$0	$27,097
1983									
Jan.	0	0	0	0	64	0	280	0	344
Feb.	0	0	0	0	0	0	0	0	0
Mar.	0	0	105	0	0	0	0	0	105
Apr.	0	0	0	0	0	0	150	0	150
May	875	379	0	0	0	0	200	0	1,454
June	5,393	0	124	177	0	150	0	0	5,844
July	12,735	0	167	0	0	0	0	0	12,902
Aug.	5,290	0	173	120	0	0	0	0	5,583
Sep.	3,185	91	0	0	0	0	0	525	3,801
Oct.	1,330	385	0	0	0	0	0	0	1,715
Nov.	0	0	0	0	0	225	0	0	225
Dec.	0	0	0	0	0	400	0	0	400
Total	$28,563	$1,100	$569	$297	$64	$775	$630	$525	$32,523

send business to one another when they have full boats. They also communicate by radio and share information about where the "hot spots" are, what kind of bait or lures the fish are hitting, etc.

Skauge's boat, *Becky,* is berthed right next to the King Salmon Charters dock. Captain Ole, as he is known, is an "old salt" (according to Dennis) who has "probably been in the business 33 years in various forms," and who "has fished a number of ports up and down the coast." The *Becky* is a small boat that fishes perhaps five to six persons at a time. Salmon trolling on the *Becky* costs $25 per person.

There are two party boats that operate out of Trinidad Bay (see Exhibit C20.5 for map). According to Dennis, "One fellow has a 6 passenger boat and his father has a 14 passenger boat. . . . The old timer up there wants to retire, and is trying to sell out." But there are serious disadvantages to operating out of Trinidad. In Dennis's words:

They do not have access to the ocean, except for the three months that the pier is open up there, June, July, and August. There are no docks to tie up to up there;

EXHIBIT C20.5 MAP OF THE NORTH COAST AREA

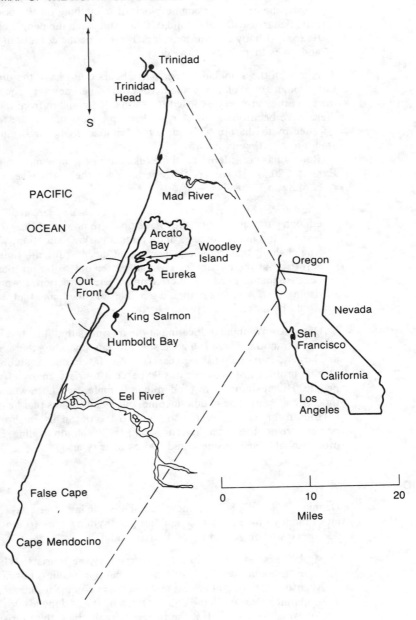

everything is mooraged out in the sheltered area from Trinidad Head. In other words, they put a big engine block or something on the bottom out there and a rope tied to it with some kind of float, and when the people come in to tie up, they tie to their buoy or their mooring. Then someone comes out in a small motorboat and takes them back to the dock.

Although the Trinidad harbor party boats don't have the disadvantage of having to sail through Humboldt Bay and across the sometimes very rough bar at the entrance to the Bay, they are very exposed to storms that come in from the southwest. In the past there have been boats sunk or washed up on the beach due to the limited protection afforded by the harbor. Of course the Trinidad boats can begin fishing almost immediately after getting under way.

Dennis has considered berthing his boat at the new marina on Woodley Island (see Exhibit C20.5). However, the operators of the marina seemed to discourage him. According to Dennis:

They were not interested in having party boats up there at all. They do not provide enough parking for what they have up there now, and they felt party boats would bring in too many vehicles and create a parking situation, which I don't think is true. I think there is adequate parking, at least for the time being. I was really surprised at their attitude. I would prefer not to be up there in the first place, because that is an additional five miles, each direction, for me to travel when I go fishing. . . . An extra hour and ten miles of travel, and fuel, etc., to go up there. It would be more expensive.

One real advantage of locating at the marina is that it is developing into an important tourist attraction. There is a good seafood cafe operating there now, and pleasure boats and larger commercial fishing vessels attract fascinated landlubbers from interior states. Dennis profiles his customers as 90 percent tourists, many of whom are sent by local people. His customers are predominantly male, but more women are going out all the time. Most seem to be middle-income, but Dennis notes that he gets a few lower-income persons from the midwest who want to try ocean fishing for the first time. Eighty percent are novices, or at least unfamiliar with salmon trolling. He sees a lot of doctors, professionals, businessmen, and white-collar types.

PROMOTION

Dennis is not really sold on the value of advertising. As he says, "I think you can put a lot of money down a big hole and not get anything back from it." What advertising he does seems to be geared to the tourist trade:

My business is predominantly governed by the tourists. When the tourists start running, about the middle of May, we get our heaviest business—June, July, and August. Then we still have a few stragglers coming to the area in September, and sometimes clear up to the end of October. It just depends upon how the fishing is. The word gets around; if the fishing is really bad, the tourists hear about it too. They just die off. Word gets around; they hear reports on the radio and they stop at the various ports coming up the coast and down the coast.

King Salmon Charters is listed in the Yellow Pages under the heading "Fishing Parties." The 3½- by 2½-inch ad is shown in Exhibit C20.6.

EXHIBIT C20.6   YELLOW PAGES ADVERTISEMENT

Further, Dennis has brochures and business cards printed up, which he distributes at motels, campgrounds, and other tourist gathering places in the community. He also leaves material at the Chamber of Commerce in Eureka (Dennis is a member of the Chamber). His lack of confidence in other forms of advertising is expressed below:

> I find that local advertising in the newspaper is not too effective. I suppose it would be helpful to some extent, but I don't feel that TV and radio would be cost effective, because the local people know we are here. As for the tourists coming in, chances are that most of them are not going to be sitting around and watching TV, though they might be listening to the radio. But, we have 4 or 5 radio stations here; it would just be too costly in my estimation to advertise on all of them.
>
> There is a fellow in town, an advertising agency that does have what they call "Fishphone," a fish information number with prerecorded messages about all the fishing in the area. He advertises on the radio, and if people happen to hear that, they get the number and call. By advertising through him I can get on his message. Then he calls me up, in turn, for information, as he does for river fishing, freshwater fishing, hunting, and various other activities.

Fishphone combines information about north coast fishing, and related weather conditions with advertisements for restaurants, resorts, and the like. The owner gets his information from charter boat operators like Dennis, sporting goods stores, and other interested sportsmen. But Dennis believes that the best advertising is word of mouth. As he says, "If you treat people right, word gets around."

PRICING, COSTS, AND OPERATIONS

Dennis seemingly prices to meet the competition, although he is sensitive to his costs of operation. He knows, for example, that the *Moku* consumes, on the average, 2.09 gallons of diesel fuel per hour. This stems from estimated fuel consumption rates of 6 to 8 gallons per hour at top cruising speed and 1 to 1.5 gallons per hour when trolling. In 1980 Dennis estimates his fuel cost him between $1.15 and $1.20 per gallon. He gets a discount by buying 360 gallons of fuel at a time.

Obviously, his costs vary depending upon what type of fishing he is doing. When he goes bottom fishing, for example, it requires 2 to 2½ hours of cruising to get down to Cape Mendocino. While bottom fishing, his engine must be idling to (1) keep it warm and ready to compensate for wind and current; (2) operate the electrical appliances—radios, fishfinder, etc.; and (3) keep the batteries charged up. So a bottom-fishing trip will require between 35 and 40 gallons of fuel.

On the other hand, trolling requires only 45 minutes to an hour to get to the fishing locations (at cruising speeds). So fuel consumption is at the lower rate of 1 to 1.5 gallons per hour for perhaps 4 hours. For a 6-hour trip, then, fuel consumption ought to range between 13 and 23 gallons.

Dennis believes that he is well justified in pricing bottom fishing at $40 per person versus only $35 per person for trolling. Regardless of the type of trip, trolling or bottom fishing, his break-even rule of thumb is that he won't go out with less than six paying passengers. In addition to fuel, other direct costs that vary with the number of cruises of the *Moku* include the cost of the crew (usually one crewman who gets 10 percent of the revenue from the trip) and the cost of bait.

Dennis can depend upon certain fixed costs associated with the charter boat operations. For instance, he is required by Coast Guard regulation to have the boat's bottom scraped at least every 18 months. Dennis's policy is to have it done annually. He estimates the cost of this operation at $600 per year. The work has been done at Johnny's boat landing at King Salmon, where the charge is $2 per running foot ($72 for the 36-foot *Moku*) to pull a boat out of the water and put it back in. Demurrage over and above 2 days (the day the boat is pulled out of the water and the day the boat is put back in) is charged at $50 per day. In addition, labor is charged at a rate of $22 per hour to knock the barnacles off with a high-pressure cleaning machine, to paint, etc., while the boat is on the ways. One year the cost went up to $1,200 because the engine was replaced and other equipment was installed.

A new "marine lift" service has been inaugurated recently at Field's Landing, just down the Bay from King Salmon, and Dennis is looking into this as a potential cost saver. This new service is provided by equipment which picks a boat out of the water on a large sling and sets it down in a location where the owner can work on it himself or herself.

GOVERNMENT REGULATION

King Salmon Charters must deal with considerable government regulation. In addition to paying federal and state taxes, Dennis is directly confronted on nearly a daily basis by the U.S. Coast Guard and agents of the California State Fish and Game Department. Another federal agency that has a significant impact, indirectly, on King Salmon Charters is the Pacific Fisheries Management Council, a working regional committee of the Department of Commerce.

The Fish and Game Department is responsible to the citizens of California for upholding the laws governing fishing in state waters, including ocean waters 3 miles from shore. The department has jurisdiction over party boat fishing. According to Mike Maschmeier, local game warden, the department maintains good relations with both commercial and party boat fishermen around Humboldt Bay.[9] Since there are only two marine wardens and one lieutenant posted locally for enforcement of fishing laws, fishermen are not scrutinized very closely. The wardens check out boats to ensure that size and limit regulations are complied with, that fishermen are licensed, etc. If a boat checks out once or twice, and if the operator seems honest, then he is not inspected very frequently. The wardens place operational priority on commercial fishing.

There is one problem involving party boat operators that concerns Mike. The 3-mile radius just outside the mouth of Humboldt Bay ("out front" in Dennis's jargon) is closed to commercial fishing. Party boats (sport fishing) are allowed to fish in this area, but only with sport poles or not more than a 4-pound weight on a down-rigger cranking system. Party boats have, on occasion, sport-fished in the restricted area with a weight heavier than 4 pounds, sometimes up to 20 pounds. This is illegal, as fishing with a weight heavier than 4 pounds is defined as commercial fishing. According to Mike, the party boat skipper typically conducts a lottery and distributes the fish caught by this method to those customers who didn't catch any salmon that day. At the present time the wardens are not doing anything about this situation, but they are considering cracking down on the practice in the future.

The U.S. Coast Guard licenses party boat operators. According to Lieutenant Gould (USCG), each operator must (1) certify that he has successfully operated oceangoing boats in the past, (2) pass a physical exam, and (3) pass a battery of tests that demonstrate his competence. Also, the party boat must be inspected every year. Boat inspections consist of inspection of fire-fighting equipment, life float, life preservers, radio beacons (emergency position indicators), and all other equipment on board. If the boat and its equipment fail to meet operating standards, the license is revoked until deficiencies are corrected.[10] Lt. Gould believes that the Coast Guard maintains good working relationships with the party boat operators and commercial fishermen on Humboldt Bay. He also indicates that the *Moku* has a good safety record. An indication of the degree of cooperation between the USCG and local fishermen is the following note extracted from the logbook of the *Moku*, dated July 21, 1981:

> Radio log note: 1330 hrs. I called CG motor lifeboat 44396 who was about two miles N of Table Bluff searching for survivors of overturned boat to report a May Day. Switch to Ch. 22. I just watched a boat about 18' to 20' white in color with two POB (persons on board) capsize in first breaker line just a little north of Table Bluff, two people in water with red lifejackets on. I will stand by & keep them in sight. I can't go in after them without jeopardizing my own passengers due to 12' to 14' swells. 1345 CG lifeboat 44396 arrived on scene & rescued both persons from inside first breaker line. The capsized boat was left adrift in surf. CG boat returning to station with both survivors. END MAY DAY. s. D. Pecaut.

The Pacific Fisheries Management Council (PFMC) makes recommendations to the Department of Commerce concerning the management of the north coast fisheries. The council's recommendations have, in recent years, included shortened seasons, mid-season closures, imposed quotas on commercial takes, etc. For instance, the PFMC secured a 6-week closure of the salmon-fishing season off the northwest coast of California from June 1, 1980, to July 15, 1980. The rationale for the closure was the very light run of salmon measured by Fish and Game researchers on the Klammath River the previous fall. For 1984, fishermen were looking at a 2-week closure in June from the 16th to the 30th. Also, the PFMC plans to prohibit the taking of silver (coho) salmon by commercial fishermen and to limit all fishermen, commercial and sport, to the use of barbless hooks.

Dwindling salmon resources on the west coast have been variously attributed to (depending upon whom you consult):

1 Damaging of coastal rivers, spawning grounds of both coho and chinook salmon

2 Accumulations of silt and debris in the spawning areas as a result of poor timber harvesting practices

3 Gill netting of salmon by Native American tribes authorized under special federal agreements

4 Excessive catches by sportsmen congregating en masse at the mouths of streams during the salmon runs

5 Overprotection of seals and other predators that feast on salmon during the runs

6 Overfishing by commercial fishermen along the coastal waterways.

In 1983 the situation was compounded by the return of a recurrent weather-related phenomenon called "El Nino," a warm-water condition which tends to deplete the resource.[11] The PFMC has the impossible task of reconciling the divergent interests of the concerned parties and managing the resources on behalf of the public for the long run.

OPPORTUNITIES?

Dennis and one of the case writers discussed the prospects for capitalizing on opportunities to increase revenues outside of sport and commercial fishing. For instance, in Southern California whale watching is big business.

Whale Watching

Fascination with the 50-foot, 40-ton California gray whales is creating a growing market for an increasingly environmentally concerned, science-oriented public. Whale-watching cruises on boats with capacities ranging from 20 to over 500 passengers sail out of Marina del Rey, Newport Beach, San Pedro, Long Beach, and Redondo Beach in Southern California.[12] Charters also operate out of Half Moon Bay, Bodega Bay, and Fort Bragg along the north coast.[13] Prices range from $4.25 for both children and adults on weekdays to a flat $18 per person regardless of age group or day of the week. Prices are usually higher on weekends; typical charges are $7 for adults and $4.50 for children on weekdays and $8 for adults and $5 for children on weekends. (Most operators offer special group rates.) The cruises tend to last for 2 to 3 hours.[14] Nonprofit organizations are also getting into the act, according to De Andreis, but their prices run higher.

For Dennis, the initiative for whale-watching charters comes from the customer. Someone will contact him with a request to take a group out, though in the past the groups have been predominantly educational institutions. According to Dennis, the season on the northern coast is November and December, when the migrating California gray whales pass close to shore on their trip to the warm-water Baja California breeding grounds, and March and April, when they return to their feeding grounds in the Bering Sea. An estimated 12,000 grays make the annual round trip.[15]

Dennis's cruises last year involved a 4- to 5-hour trip 2 or 3 miles from shore in the direction of Trinidad Head. The fee was $15 per person.[16] Dennis told the case writers that he has seen whales every time he has taken a party out, but he does not appear convinced that there is much of a local market for the activity, since the action occurs during the tourist off-season. The slow cruising speed appropriate for whale watching results in fuel consumption of perhaps 4 to 4.5 gallons per hour.

Special Humboldt Bay Cruises

There are other opportunities to increase revenues by promoting special Humboldt Bay cruises. For example, since 1979 the Humboldt chapter of the Commercial Fishermen's Wives organization has been holding an annual "Blessing of the Fleet" ceremony, with the proceeds going to a "disaster fund" to aid families of fishermen lost at sea or otherwise involved in personal tragedy. Decorated fishing boats sail past the Woodley Island Marina, where they are blessed by local ministers and priests as they pass. The colorful ceremony is attracting more and more tourists and pleasure boats, and the community is interested in promoting the event.[17] However, Dennis expresses a reluctance to attempt to exploit the revenue potential of the event. In the past he has invited personal friends to join him on the *Moku* during the blessing. He "wouldn't feel right" trying to profit from the event. (Besides, Dennis has won prizes for having the best-decorated boat in the fleet parade—second place in 1982 and first place in 1983 and 1984.)

Another example of a potential opportunity for a special Humboldt Bay cruise is the annual "Coors World Championship Great Arcata to Ferndale Cross Country Kinetic Sculpture Race" (sponsored by the Adolph Coors Company since 1982). Participants propel people-powered vehicles of unique design (presumably possessing aesthetic attributes) over a "three-day, 36-mile test of man and machine."[18] Hundreds of people crowd the course over the 3-day grind to enjoy the frolics of judges and contestants as the strange vehicles and crews negotiate hills, sand dunes, bay crossing, etc., in their quixotic quests for glory. The first day of the race is "through the Arcata Bottoms and over the sand dunes, climaxed by the infamous Dead Man's Drop, a steep incline of soft sand that usually takes its toll by causing a variety of broken parts on the machines."[19] A "spirit of cheating . . . goes along with the sculpture race."[20]

It is the crossing of Humboldt Bay and the Eel River on the second day of the race that provides an opportunity for Dennis to exploit the promotional event to the profit of King Salmon Charters. The more or less amphibious contraptions are required to cross the Bay under their own power, or rather, under the power of their occupants. The most exciting moment of the race is the launching of the vehicles onto the waters of the Bay at Field's Landing, and the subsequent navigation of the obstacle by the more fortunate participants. Boats of sightseers crowd the area, indicating high potential demand for charter boat service.

The log of the *Moku* for April 18, 1981, indicates that Dennis "took 8 friends on bay cruise to watch Kinetic Sculpture Race at Field's Landing (2½ hours)." For such an event the full 20-passenger capacity of the boat could be utilized. To date, Dennis has not perceived such events as opportunities, preferring to concentrate on commercial and sport fishing.

Two fishing-related opportunities are being considered by Dennis. Since he now uses ring nets for commercial crabbing, and retrieves his catch on the same voyage that he drops his nets, he could charter his boat to people interested in sport crabbing. Also, Humboldt Bay abounds in sharks—cow sharks, sand sharks, and leopard sharks. The former grow to be 8 to 10 feet in length and weigh up to 300 pounds. Sand sharks range in size up to 3 to 4 feet in length; leopard sharks are smaller. A small Eureka firm has begun to produce shark jerky for commercial distribution, attracting the interest of the local public. Perhaps shark-fishing trips would help fill up the slack during the off-seasons for salmon and crab.

PROBLEMS

In answer to the case writers' question, "What is your major problem?" Dennis responded, "To stay in business." He realizes that he is just getting started, but the end-of-year financial statements do cause him considerable concern. However, Dennis became more animated when he talked about the "no show" problem. According to Dennis:

> People would call up, and since I didn't have anyone sitting at the office taking the reservations, the phone would ring here at the house . . . 8 o'clock at night . . . and say they wanted to go fishing tomorrow morning. They'd be calling from some motel here in town, or maybe even from Garberville. I didn't want to get up and go down there and meet them to take a deposit, and I didn't have anyone down there to take a deposit. So the next morning they overslept or changed their mind. For whatever reason, they didn't show up.

In spite of the difficulties, Dennis is optimistic about the future. He loves the autonomy connected with owning his own business; he likes the salt air in his face; and, especially, he thrills to the shout of "Fish on."

REFERENCES

1 Mike Maschmeier, personal interview, Feb. 3, 1982
2 Peter Howorth, *Foraging along the California Coast*, Santa Barbara, Capra Press and Ross/Erikson, 1977.
3 Ibid.
4 California Dept. of Fish and Game, California Sport Fishing Regulations, 1981.
5 Ibid.
6 Daniel W. Gotshall, *Pacific Coast Inshore Fishes*, Los Osos, Calif., Sea Challengers, 1981.
7 California Dept. of Fish and Game, Fish and Game Code, Art. 6, Sec. 8235, 1974.
8 Robert J. Browning, *Fisheries of the North Pacific: History, Species, Gear, and Processes*, Anchorage, Alaska, Alaska Northwest, 1974.
9 Maschmeier, op. cit.
10 Eric Gould, personal interview, May 25, 1982.
11 *Times Standard*, "PFMC Chief Softens Stance: Says '84 Coho Season Unlikely, but not Impossible," June 19, 1984.
12 Michelle Berkey, "Thar' She Blows: Some Tips on Whale Watching," *Times Standard*, Feb. 28, 1982, pp. C4–C5.
13 Yvette De Andreis, "Around the Bay: Whale Watching," *San Francisco*, vol. 24, no. 1, 1982, p. 13; and Debra Webster, "Patricks Point Spot to See Migratory Whales," *Times Standard*, Jan. 24, 1982.
14 Berkey, op. cit.
15 Webster, op. cit.
16 Ibid.
17 Ibid.
18 *The Union*, "Foul Weather Failed to Slow Kinetics Racers," Apr. 15, 1982.
19 *The Union*, op. cit.
20 George Cox, "Offizziating Is No Easy Task," *The Union*, Apr. 15, 1982.

KMART

Prepared by Donna Bush and Joe Thomas, Middle Tennessee State University.

S.S. Kresge "five and ten cent stores" were founded by S.S. Kresge in 1897. On April 15, 1912, the company became S.S. Kresge Company of Delaware. In Michigan, 1966, the company incorporated as S.S. Kresge Company. The "Kmart" name was adopted on May 17, 1977. Kmart is the country's second largest retailer, operating a portfolio of retailing businesses. Headquartered in Troy, Michigan, the firm had sales of $22.4 billion and income from continuing retail operations of $756 million for its fiscal year ending in 1986.

On January 23, 1974, Kmart Corporation operated 2,400 retail stores; 2,215 were in the United States and 185 were in Canada. At the end of 1985, Kmart operated a total of 3,848 retail stores. Of these stores, 2,332 were general-merchandise stores consisting of Kmart discount department stores, Kresge variety stores, and Jupiter limited-line discount stores. The remaining stores are part of the Specialty Retailing Group, consisting of Pay Less Drug Stores Northwest, Inc., Walden Book Company, Inc., Builders Square, Inc., Designer Depot, Bargain Harold's Discount Limited, Big Top, Furr's Cafeterias, Inc., and Bishop Buffets, Inc.

STORE IMAGE

Kmart began a move in 1983 to upgrade the image and profitability of Kmart. Through advertising, remodeling, and upgrading of merchandise, Kmart has attempted to increase the intrinsic quality of Kmart merchandise. Moving to what Kmart calls the "look of the '80s" entailed a fine-tuning of merchandise. Designer label and brand name

This case is intended for use as a basis for class discussion. Presented and accepted by the refereed Midwest Case Writers Association Workshop, 1986. All rights reserved to the authors and to the Midwest Case Writers Association. Used by permission.

merchandise were added and the quality of private label merchandise was enhanced. The intent is to offer shoppers an expanded market basket of merchandise which will also expand Kmart's profit margin.

To promote the upgraded image, Kmart raised its advertising budget for 1984, the first full year of the program, to $480 million. This increase represented an 18% increase over 1983's advertising budget and about 3% of 1984 sales. Some Kmart divisions spent a larger percent of sales on advertising. For example, Glen Shanks, director of Designer Depot, Kmart's 30-store, off-price apparel chain, stated that Designer Depot spent 6% of sales on advertising. Other divisions such as Garment Rack and Kmart Auto Parts Center spent at similar levels.

Capital expenditures were not neglected either. In 1984 Kmart spent $430 million on capital improvements and $130 million to remodel Kmart stores.

Kmart's store of the future will reflect a shift to designer labels, brand name merchandise, and upscale private labels. Over 900 Kmart stores will be affected by this upward shift. The ultimate prototype will be a combination of 8,500-square-feet or 40,000-square-feet stores. Fashion fixtures are in and bargain tables are out as departments, such as the Home Care Center, Kitchen Korner, Bed and Bath Shop, Nutrition and Health Care Center, and Home Electronics Center, take on a store-within-a-store status. Cherry-picked assortments are displayed with fashionable, department store techniques to compete with specialty and department stores.

In the remodeled units, multitiered glass cases house upscale giftware in the front of the stores. Apparel and electronic departments have been carpeted and mass merchandise pipe fixtures have been replaced with waterfall and cube fixtures. Finger racks and freestanding walls provide a backdrop, highlighted by graphics in some cases, for Kmart's private label merchandise. A neon stripe outlines the electronic department. A partial race track pattern with outlined aisles has been installed to improve the flow of traffic.

Kmart's goal is to increase sales—not to diversify revenues to any large extent. Managers are expected to assess consumer demand and then invest corporate resources to improve market share in *each* of the several hundred merchandise categories sold. Kmart's strategy calls for improving productivity by achieving higher turnover and greater sales per square foot. While the annual turnover rate for Kmart is presently 4.25 annually, the corporate target is 5.5 in the five-year plan.

The corporate thinking at Kmart relies heavily on good communications in a human chain that runs from store manager to district manager to regional manager. While 80% of Kmart's merchandise is standardized on a national basis, store managers are free to fine-tune 10% to 20% of the mix in an effort to appeal directly to local markets.

The Kmart customer is the person who works and lives near the store. Even though Kmart is upgrading, it still plans to remain within its customers' price range. For example, Kmart will sell cardigans in the $17 to $24 range. In the past Kmart would have sold the cardigans for $15 to $17. The objective behind upgrading is to expand the upper end of its market. The tactic is to add on at the top of the line, not to abandon the lower end. Kmart officials feel that the people who bought in the middle will step up while lower-priced merchandise will still be available for the customer who buys in the lower price range.

In order to win customers over to the more ego-intensive items, Kmart advertising themes have changed from loss leaders in print advertising to higher-ticketed groups of upscaled merchandise. In television advertising, for example, Kmart is moving away from advertising individual items to promoting the Kmart name and a more positive store image. Kmart bought a $10 million television campaign tied to the 1984 Olympic Games.

Bernard Fauber, Kmart's chairman, has called for 5% to 6% annual sales increases over the next four years, with sales per square foot reaching $200 by 1988, even though the chain is no longer in the expansion mode. Kmart only built 71 new stores in 1983, compared to a five-year average of 178 units per year. Sales per square foot have already topped $200 in the specialty departments such as the Kitchen Korner, the Home Care Center, Home Electronics Center, Cameras, and Jewelry. These departments have undergone expensive remodeling and remerchandising. Larry Paukin, chairman and CEO of Kmart Apparel, claims that the remodeling and remerchandising have raised sales in his department by 40%.

Kmart is facing increased competition as more and more retailers like Wal-Mart are moving into its territories. Some financial experts feel that lower-cost retailers such as Wal-Mart are better able to weather cyclical dips in consumer demand. Industry research done by the University of Oklahoma showed before-tax profits per square foot of selling area at other discounters to be considerably higher than those earned by Kmart. For example, Target earned $12.09 versus $10.99 at Wal-Mart and $6.90 at Kmart.

Kmart has also expanded its in-store home improvement product offerings and reorganized them into mini–home center modules. Kmart was guided by customer surveys and market research. The research found that people are getting more involved in do-it-yourself activities and that they want to go to one place to purchase all the products needed to complete the project. In particular, Kmart brought together hardware, plumbing, and other products that previously might have been located in different departments. Inventories of building materials—roofing, insulation, and dimensional lumber, for example—were expanded, and, in many cases, relocated from storage areas. In combination, these moves essentially turned the home improvement modules into 8,000- to 12,000-square-feet mini–home centers within the Kmart store.

At Sears, officials say they probably will not parallel the moves made at Kmart because it is limited in how extensively it can tie in with do-it-yourself consumer trends. However, Sears has done some rearranging and remerchandising in this area. In contrast, J.C. Penney Company has backed away from the home improvement market. J.C. Penney has eliminated those product lines in order to provide additional space for more fashionable lines of merchandise, which its research showed is what customers would expect to find in department stores in regional shopping malls. This is where most J.C. Penney stores are located.

HOME CENTERS OF AMERICA

In August 1984, Kmart paid $90 million for Home Centers of America, a nine-store Texas chain of home improvement stores based in San Antonio. These stores, located primarily in Texas and Illinois, operate under the name of Builders Square. Kmart hopes this acquisition will enable it to become a dominant factor in the home improvement market by the end of 1986. Kmart also hopes to increase overall corporate sales 5% through its Builders Square acquisition.

Kmart Chairman Bernard Fauber reorganized top management by grouping Builders Square into a separate specialty operating division. The 80,000- to 100,000-square-foot "retail warehouse home improvement stores" will cater to a different market than

Kmart's in-house home centers. The Kmart in-house centers cater to the one-day or weekender projects, whereas Builders Square stores will feature products for more extensive, more elaborate projects. Builders Square stores will provide expertise and special guidance for customers. Kmart intends to initiate special training programs to enable employees to provide this kind of service.

In October 1984, Kmart opened in Chicago its first three Builders Square stores outside of Texas. It also turned a redundant Kmart store in Tulsa into a Builders Square. Kmart eventually plans to convert 10% of all existing Kmart stores into Builders Square stores. Detroit and Cleveland are next on Kmart's list for new sites. Kmart had 30 Builders Square warehouses open by the end of 1985 and planned to open 50 new units in 1986. Plans are to eventually operate a minimum of 125 Builders Square stores.

The Builders Square outlets in Chicago are 80,000 to 100,000 square feet—typically two to three times larger than local competitors. Each store carries around 35,000 items in stock worth $2.5 million. These items range from sink elbows to snow cats, and from $2'' \times 4''$ lumber to T-squares. Having a high level of specialist staffing means those stocks will have to be turned over eight times a year to break even. The average building-materials business in the U.S. turns its stock four times per year.

To move stock quickly, Kmart sells around 10% of its stock at near cost. Since Kmart purchases in large quantities, it can keep those costs low. Competitors already moan that Builders Square can sell drywall panels, for example, at a lower price than they can buy it. The rest of Builders Square stock is sold at above-average markups for the industry. Builders Square stores have caused a price war in Chicago. For example, Gee Lumber, Courtesy, Handy Andy, Forest City, and other regional chains are cutting prices and plugging lines of housewares and motor accessories that Builders Square stores do not carry. However, a serious problem confronts Kmart in that the Builders Square warehouse needs a market area of 70,000 households. While Kmart managers state that there is the potential for 400 stores the size of Builders Square, industry authorities argue that there are only 72 cities in the U.S. large enough to provide the needed market size.

The home improvement industry is growing so rapidly (19% a year in unit sales since 1974) that major companies such as Payless Cashways and the Atlanta-based regional chain Home Depot (the leader) are buying smaller, weaker companies like the Texas-based Bowater chain, which sold out to Home Depot in December 1984. Home Depot's chairman, Bernard Marcus, plans to tackle Kmart head on by opening four stores in Houston and four to six in Detroit. Detroit is close to Kmart headquarters in nearby Troy.

OTHER SUBSIDIARIES AND ACQUISITIONS

Kmart's largest diversification to date has been the $509 million acquisition of Pay Less Drug Stores in 1985. At the end of 1985, Pay Less operated 183 stores in Oregon, Washington, California, Idaho, and Nevada, with 41 additional units scheduled for opening in 1986. Kmart management sees drugstores as replacements for the variety stores for many frequently made small purchases. Stores of 25,000 square feet or more are required to provide the variety needed to meet such customer needs. Pay Less is one of the leaders in the large variety-drugstore format, with stores ranging in size from 25,000 to 80,000 square feet.

In 1984, Kmart paid $294 million for Waldenbooks. This purchase price was 24 times fiscal 1983 earnings. Waldenbooks is the nation's largest bookstore chain and had sales of $417.8 million in the year ended January 28, 1984. Waldenbooks stores maintain a wide variety of titles and can quickly obtain any title not carried in stock through their Quicktrac special order system. Waldenbooks has also developed marketing niches through book clubs emphasizing mystery, romance, science fiction, and children's books. Besides books, video and audio tapes and computer software are also sold through Waldenbooks. Though all Kmart stores also sell books, Kmart has no plans to integrate Waldenbooks and its own bookselling operations. Kmart plans to appoint someone to act as a liaison between the two companies.

It should be noted that Kmart's only internally developed subsidiary is Designer Depot. Initially, Designer Depots were directed to the higher end of the price spectrum. Designer Depot has now moved back to more midrange-priced merchandise, contributing to what Kmart managers feel is an "increased consumer perception of value." Designer Depot's refusal to sell seconds and irregulars also gives them a distinct, but unprofitable, niche within the off-price apparel field. After several years in the developmental phase, Kmart feels that this subsidiary is now positioned to begin contributing to corporate profits.

Kmart expects its new specialized retailing group (consisting of Pay Less Drug Stores, Waldenbooks, Home Centers of America, Furr's and Bishop's cafeteria chains, Bargain Harold's, Big Top, Designer Depots, Garment Rack, and Accent) to ring up more than a fifth of total company sales by 1987 or 1988. This group does not include financial and insurance services or Kmart Trading Services.

Kmart's strategy is to buy or develop hot new retailing concepts and expand them rapidly for market dominance. Frederick Stevens, executive vice president of specialized retailing, states that Kmart is looking for domination of the retail market by providing quality value to the customer. Kmart is still seeking more emerging specialty retailing companies. Kmart will not rule out any type of company as a possible acquisition target except for grocery stores and drugstores.

TABLE C21.1 KMART EXPANSION ACTIVITIES

	1983	1984			1985		
		Acquired	Opened	Closed	Acquired	Opened	Closed
Kmart							
U.S.	2041		21	7		18	11
Canada	119		2	3			
Kresge/Jupiter							
U.S.	144			24			24
Canada	58						2
Waldenbooks		860	41	3		68	11
Builders Square		9	6			15	
Pay Less					171	12	
Designer Depot	30		22			21	
Bargain Harold's					56	17	
Big Top	8		42	1		11	5
Other	147		29	7		2	10
Total	2547	869	149	45	227	164	63

Managers of newly acquired companies are usually retained, with only a single parent company executive placed as a liaison. The managers even select their own ad agencies.

Table C21.1 on page 605 shows the expansion of Kmart's operations in the U.S. and Canada for 1984 and 1985. Waldenbooks, with 955 outlets, will be expanded at the rate of 70 to 80 stores annually for the next five years. Home Centers of America (Builders Square) nearly doubled its size to 15 stores in 1984 and did double the number of stores to a total of 30 stores in 1985. Designer Depots added 21 outlets in 1985 although it continues to lose money. The cafeteria operations will add a net of 6 restaurants in 1985 to Bishop's current 31 and Furr's 124 restaurants. Kmart has also dabbled in two experimental pizza-video parlors, closing them after 18 months.

Kmart's turn to diversification for growth comes as top competitor, Sears, is re-emphasizing general merchandising and cutting back its fledgling overseas trading operations. Wal-Mart, another leading discounter, is moving to "deep" discounting and has achieved much of its growth serving small markets that Kmart has abandoned as too small.

INTERNATIONAL OPERATIONS

Kmart has operated in a number of international markets including Mexico, Canada, Europe, and the Far East. Due to a variety of cultural, business, and economic conditions, not all these operations have been successful. In September 1981, Kmart acquired a 44% interest in a joint venture with the Gentor Group of Monterrey, Mexico, to operate a retail subsidiary in Mexico. Losses for the operation exceeded $31 million through 1985. A formal plan was announced in January 1986 to discontinue these operations due to "prevailing business and economic conditions in Mexico [which] combined with the reduced value of the Mexican peso, adversely affected the joint venture's earnings and cash flow potential." The exact size of the loss is not yet known for certain, but include a bank loan of $12 million and $100 million of 16.75% notes unconditionally guaranteed by Kmart Corporation.

Kmart operates its overseas markets differently than marketing activities in the U.S. For instance, Kmart has no stores located overseas. Kmart brand merchandise is sold primarily through other retailers.

Overseas operations are handled through Kmart Trading Services (KTS), which was formed in 1982 to promote sales of U.S. goods in overseas markets and which is separate from and in balance with Kmart's large import operations. One of KTS' biggest successes has been increasing trade between the Far East and Europe. KTS also is importing foreign goods to the U.S., especially components and materials for Kmart's U.S. vendors. In general, Kmart labels merchandise from the U.S. and elsewhere with a Kmart brand name. Kmart has a $300,000 ad campaign in Taiwan as a test aimed at developing awareness of Kmart brand goods. KTS was formed after 1981 legislation was passed to encourage exports. KTS resembles Sears' World Trade service which was also formed in 1982.

FINANCIAL SERVICES

Kmart is letting Sears, Roebuck and Company and other retailers take the lead in offering financial services, and plans to overtake them later. This is consistent with

Kmart's diversification strategy of looking for retailing trends that can be rolled out quickly. Jon Hartman, corporate financial management analyst, states that this strategy is much like a runner holding back until the end of the race before sprinting past front-running opponents.

Kmart will test several in-store financial service programs, looking for successful formulas that can be adopted quickly. Kmart is considering full-service branch banking, real estate services, consumer lending, and discount brokerage services. Kmart intends to test different ideas in different regions of the country. For example, the company plans to sell an insurance program in 100 Florida and Texas stores. Kmart feels that success in retailing depends on knowing the makeup of local markets.

Advertising for the pilot programs will be handled through the agencies of the financial companies Kmart joins forces with. However, Kmart's marketing and advertising departments will oversee ad strategy of all pilot programs to ensure compatibility.

Kmart intends to lease floor space to the financial services marketers, for a combination of a flat fee and a percentage of sales volume. (A similar arrangement has been made for the leasing of Kmart footwear departments to Meldisco, a subsidiary of Melville Corporation.) Kmart feels that sales from its financial services must be at least $200 a square foot by the end of calendar 1986 to justify the floor space devoted to the new venture. Leasing departments is unlike Sears' full integration of its Financial Network.

MANAGEMENT (PERSONNEL)

Most of the candidates in Kmart's manager training program are college recruits. Kmart has an annual training budget of $20 million. The management trainees start at $15,500 and eventually make up 70% of the chain's store managers—the remainder advance from the stores. Of the 2,047 store managers employed by Kmart, 121 are female. There are no female district or regional managers. Average store managers make about $46,000 a year; however, some make over $100,000 while the low end of the scale is $32,000.

Robert A. Dewar, chairman of the finance and executive committees, says Kmart has found it difficult to bring MBAs into a structured store operations program. Therefore, Kmart prefers to provide the opportunity for MBA training, often at night, to those who have already joined the company. When MBAs are brought into the organization, they are placed in staff functions, not in line jobs. Mr. Dewar also says that Kmart hires people regardless of their college education—or lack of it. According to Mr. Dewar "Kmart rewards initiative, imagination and hard work."

Kmart believes strongly in promoting from within. Kmart management feels this builds loyalty. The majority of Kmart's senior executives in merchandising and operations advanced through the store's training programs. Kmart wants the people who work for it to know that if they perform, they will be given the opportunity to grow with the company.

In the last five years, Kmart has added 4,000 people to the payroll. Five years ago the mix of full-time to part-time employees at the store level was 80 to 20, respectively. The mix has changed to a 55/45% mix. Increasing the portion of part-time employees reduces the cost of benefits for the company and accounts for the corporate goal of 40% full-time and 60% part-time employees. Kmart also limits other benefits employees receive. Kmart store employees do not receive a discount. For the most part Kmart is nonunion, with the exception of some of its warehousing and distribution operations. Payroll represents 15.5% of sales.

TABLE C21.2   CONSOLIDATED STATEMENTS OF CHANGES IN FINANCIAL POSITION
(Dollar Amounts in Millions)

	Fiscal year ended		
Cash provided by (used for)	January 29, 1986	January 30, 1985	January 25, 1984
Continuing retail operations			
Income from continuing retail operations	$ 471	$ 499	$ 493
Noncash charges (credits) to earnings:			
Depreciation and amortization	360	303	265
Deferred income taxes	92	16	21
Undistributed equity income	(23)	(16)	(17)
Increase in other long-term liabilities	46	36	34
Other—net	20	9	1
Total	966	847	797
Cash provided by (used for) current assets and current liabilities:			
(Increase) decrease in inventories	387	(792)	(285)
Inventories of acquired companies	(336)	(214)	(1)
Increase (decrease) in accounts payable	(9)	200	204
Other—net	215	(122)	106
Net cash provided by (used for) continuing retail operations	1,223	(81)	821
Discontinued operations			
Loss from discontinued operations	(250)	—	(1)
Noncash provision for discontinued operations	229	—	—
Total from discontinued operations	(21)	—	(1)
Financing			
Increase in long-term debt and notes payable	563	646	123
Reduction in long-term debt and notes payable	(310)	(17)	(10)
Obligations incurred under capital leases	18	44	79
Reduction in capital lease obligations	(77)	(77)	(76)
Common stock issued	31	21	23
Purchase of treasury stock	—	(51)	—
Net cash provided by financing	225	566	139
Dividends paid	(171)	(151)	(132)
Investments			
Additions to owned and leased property	(561)	(646)	(406)
Owned property of acquired companies	(156)	(94)	(10)
Proceeds from the sale of property	40	62	91
Increased investment in affiliated retail companies	(107)	(3)	(15)
Other assets and deferred charges of acquired companies	(317)	(151)	—
Other—net	(20)	(38)	(13)
Net cash used for investments	(1,121)	(870)	(353)
Net increase (decrease) in cash	$ 135	$(536)	$ 474

FINANCIAL

Selected financial information concerning the recent performance of Kmart for fiscal 1984, 1985, and 1986 is provided in Tables C21.2, C21.3, and C21.4.

TABLE C21.3 CONSOLIDATED STATEMENTS OF INCOME
(Dollar Amounts in Millions, Except Per-Share Data)

	Fiscal year ended		
	January 29, 1986	January 30, 1985	January 25, 1984
Sales	$22,420	$21,096	$18,598
Licensee fees and rental income	225	207	191
Equity in income of affiliated retail companies	76	65	57
Interest income	24	40	38
	22,745	21,408	18,884
Cost of merchandise sold (including buying and occupancy costs)	16,181	15,260	13,447
Selling, general and administrative expenses	4,845	4,428	3,880
Advertising	567	554	425
Interest expense:			
Debt	205	147	84
Capital lease obligations	191	193	189
	21,989	20,582	18,025
Income from continuing retail operations before income taxes	756	826	859
Income taxes	285	327	366
Income from continuing retail operations	471	499	493
Discontinued operations	(250)	—	(1)
Net income for the year	$ 221	$ 499	$ 492
Earnings per common and common equivalent share:			
Continuing retail operations	$3.63	$3.84	$3.81
Discontinued operations	(1.90)	—	(.01)
Net income	$1.73	$3.84	$3.80

TABLE C21.4   CONSOLIDATED BALANCE SHEETS
(Dollar Amounts in Millions)

	January 29, 1986	January 30, 1985
Assets		
Current assets:		
Cash (includes temporary investments of $352 and $294, respectively)	$ 627	$ 492
Merchandise inventories	4,537	4,588
Accounts receivable and other current assets	363	231
Total current assets	5,527	5,311
Investments in affiliated retail companies	293	188
Property and equipment—net	3,644	3,339
Other assets and deferred charges	527	220
Investments in discontinued operations	—	204
	$9,991	$9,262
Liabilities and shareholders' equity		
Current liabilities:		
Long-term debt due within one year	$ 15	$ 2
Capital lease obligations due within one year	76	74
Notes payable	127	235
Accounts payable—trade	1,908	1,917
Accrued payrolls and other liabilities	548	362
Taxes other than income taxes	218	200
Income taxes	198	99
Total current liabilities	3,090	2,889
Capital lease obligations	1,713	1,780
Long-term debt	1,456	1,107
Other long-term liabilities	345	163
Deferred income taxes	114	89
Shareholders' equity	3,273	3,234
	$9,991	$9,262

THE LINCOLN ELECTRIC COMPANY, 1984

Prepared by Arthur D. Sharplin, McNeese State University.

The Lincoln Electric Company is the world's largest manufacturer of welding machines and electrodes. Lincoln employs 2400 workers in two U.S. factories near Cleveland and approximately 600 in three factories located in other countries. This does not include the field sales force of more than 200 persons. It has been estimated that Lincoln's market share (for arc-welding equipment and supplies) is more than 40%.

The Lincoln incentive management plan has been well known for many years. Many college management texts make reference to the Lincoln plan as a model for achieving high worker productivity. Certainly Lincoln has been a successful company according to the usual measures of success.

James F. Lincoln died in 1965 and there was some concern, even among employees, that the Lincoln system would fall into disarray, that profits would decline, and that year-end bonuses might be discontinued. Quite the contrary, 18 years after Lincoln's death, the company appears stronger than ever. Each year, except the recession years 1982 and 1983, has seen higher profits and bonuses. Employee morale and productivity remain high. Employee turnover is almost nonexistent except for retirements. Lincoln's market share is stable. Consistently high dividends continue on Lincoln's stock.

A HISTORICAL SKETCH

In 1895, after being "frozen out" of the depression-ravaged Elliott-Lincoln Company, a maker of Lincoln-designed electric motors, John C. Lincoln took out his second patent

Note: The research and written case information were presented at a case research symposium and were evaluated by the Case Research Association's editorial board. This case was prepared as a basis for class discussion.

Distributed by the Case Research Association. All rights reserved to the author and the Case Research Association. Used by permission.

and began to manufacture his improved motor. He opened his new business, unincorporated, with $200 he had earned redesigning a motor for young Herbert Henry Dow, who later founded the Dow Chemical Company.

Started during an economic depression and cursed by a major fire after only one year in business, Lincoln's company grew, but hardly prospered, through its first quarter century. In 1906, John C. Lincoln incorporated his company and moved from his one-room, fourth-floor factory to a new three-story building he erected in east Cleveland. In his new factory, he expanded his work force to 30 and sales grew to over $50,000 a year. John Lincoln preferred being an engineer and inventor rather than a manager, though, and it was to be left to another Lincoln to manage the company through its years of success.

In 1907, after a bout with typhoid fever forced him from Ohio State University in his senior year, James F. Lincoln, John's younger brother, joined the fledgling company. In 1914 he became the active head of the firm, with the titles of general manager and vice president. John Lincoln, while he remained president of the company for some years, became more involved in other business ventures and in his work as an inventor.

One of James Lincoln's early actions as head of the firm was to ask the employees to elect representatives to a committee which would advise him on company operations. The advisory board has met with the chief executive officer twice monthly since that time. This was only the first of a series of innovative personnel policies which have, over the years, distinguished Lincoln Electric from its contemporaries.

The first year the advisory board was in existence, working hours were reduced from 55 per week, then standard, to 50 hours a week. In 1915, the company gave each employee a paid-up life insurance policy. A welding school, which continues today, was begun in 1917. In 1918, an employee bonus plan was attempted. It was not continued, but the idea was to resurface and become the backbone of the Lincoln Management System.

The Lincoln Electric Employees' Association was formed in 1919 to provide health benefits and social activities. This organization continues today and has assumed several additional functions over the years. In 1923, a piecework pay system was in effect, employees got two-week paid vacations each year, and wages were adjusted for changes in the Consumer Price Index. Approximately 30% of Lincoln's stock was set aside for key employees in 1914 when James F. Lincoln became general manager and a stock purchase plan for all employees was begun in 1925.

The board of directors voted to start a suggestion system in 1929. The program is still in effect, but cash awards, a part of the early program, were discontinued several years ago. Now, suggestions are rewarded by additional "points," which affect year-end bonuses.

The legendary Lincoln bonus plan was proposed by the Advisory Board and accepted on a trial basis by James Lincoln in 1934. The first annual bonus amounted to about 25% of wages. There has been a bonus every year since then. The bonus plan has been a cornerstone of the Lincoln Management System and recent bonuses have approximated annual wages.

By 1944, Lincoln employees enjoyed a pension plan, a policy of promotion from within, and continuous employment. Base pay rates were determined by formal job evaluation and a merit rating system was in effect.

In the prologue of James F. Lincoln's last book, Charles G. Herbruck writes regarding the foregoing personnel innovations,

They were not to buy good behavior. They were not efforts to increase profits. They were not antidotes to labor difficulties. They did not constitute a "do-gooder" program. They were expression of mutual respect for each person's importance to the job to be done. All of them reflect the leadership of James Lincoln, under whom they were nurtured and propagated.[1]

By the start of World War II, Lincoln Electric was the world's largest manufacturer of arc-welding products. Sales of about $4 million in 1934 had grown to $24 million by 1941. Productivity per employee more than doubled during the same period.

During the War, Lincoln Electric prospered as never before. Despite challenges to Lincoln's profitability by the Navy's Price Review Board and to the tax deductibility of employee bonuses by the Internal Revenue Service, the company increased its profits and paid huge bonuses.

Certainly since 1935 and probably for several years before that, Lincoln productivity has been well above the average for similar companies. Lincoln claims levels of productivity more than twice those for other manufacturers from 1945 onward. Information available from outside sources tends to support these claims.

COMPANY PHILOSOPHY

James F. Lincoln was the son of a Congregational minister, and Christian principles were at the center of his business philosophy. The confidence that he had in the efficacy of Christ's teachings is illustrated by the following remark taken from one of his books:

> The Christian ethic should control our acts. If it did control our acts, the savings in cost of distribution would be tremendous. Advertising would be a contact of the expert consultant with the customer, in order to give the customer the best product available when all of the customer's needs are considered. Competition then would be in improving the quality of products and increasing efficiency in producing and distributing them; not in deception, as is now too customary. Pricing would reflect efficiency of production; it would not be a selling dodge that the customer may well be sorry he accepted. It would be proper for all concerned and rewarding for the ability used in producing the product.[2]

There is no indication that Lincoln attempted to evangelize his employees or customers—or the general public for that matter. The current board chairman, Mr. Irrgang, and the president, Mr. Willis, do not even mention the Christian gospel in their recent speeches and interviews. The company motto, "The actual is limited, the possible is immense," is prominently displayed, but there is no display of religious slogans, and there is no company chapel.

Attitude toward the Customer

James Lincoln saw the customer's needs as the *raison d'etre* for every company. "When any company has achieved success so that it is attractive as an investment," he wrote, "all money usually needed for expansion is supplied by the customer in retained earnings. It is obvious that the customer's interests, not the stockholder's, should come first."[3] In 1947 he said, "Care should be taken . . . not to rivet attention on profit. Between 'How much do I get?' and 'How do I make this better, cheaper, more useful?'

the difference is fundamental and decisive."[4] Mr. Willis still ranks the customer as Lincoln's most important constituency. This is reflected in Lincoln's policy to "at all times price on the basis of cost and at all times keep pressure on our cost. . . ."[5] Lincoln's goal, often stated, is "to build a better and better product at a lower and lower price."[6] "It is obvious," James Lincoln said, "that the customer's interests should be the first goal of industry."[7]

Attitude toward Stockholders

Stockholders are given last priority at Lincoln. This is a continuation of James Lincoln's philosophy: "The last group to be considered is the stockholders who own stock because they think it will be more profitable than investing money in any other way."[8] Concerning division of the largess produced by incentive management, Lincoln writes, "The absentee stockholder also will get his share, even if undeserved, out of the greatly increased profit that the efficiency produces."[9]

Attitude toward Unionism

There has never been a serious effort to organize Lincoln employees. While James Lincoln criticized the labor movement for "selfishly attempting to better its position at the expense of the people it must serve,"[10] he still had kind words for union members. He excused abuses of union power as "the natural reactions of human beings to the abuses to which management has subjected them."[11] Lincoln's ideas of the correct relationship between workers and managers is shown by this comment: "Labor and management are properly not warring camps; they are parts of one organization in which they must and should cooperate fully and happily."[12]

Beliefs and Assumptions about Employees

If fulfilling customer needs is the desired goal of business, then employee performance and productivity are the means by which this goal can best be achieved. It is the Lincoln attitude toward employees, reflected in the following quotations, which is credited by many with creating the record of success the company has experienced:

> The greatest fear of the worker, which is the same as the greatest fear of the industrialist in operating a company, is the lack of income. . . . The industrial manager is very conscious of his company's need of uninterrupted income. He is completely oblivious, evidently, of the fact that the worker has the same need.[13]

> He is just as eager as any manager is to be part of a team that is properly organized and working for the advancement of our economy. . . . He has no desire to make profits for those who do not hold up their end in production, as is true of absentee stockholders and inactive people in the company.[14]

> If money is to be used as an incentive, the program must provide that what is paid to the worker is what he has earned. The earnings of each must be in accordance with accomplishment.[15]

> Status is of great importance in all human relationships. The greatest incentive

that money has, usually, is that it is a symbol of success. . . . The resulting status is the real incentive. . . . Money alone can be an incentive to the miser only.[16]

There must be complete honesty and understanding between the hourly worker and management if high efficiency is to be obtained.[17]

LINCOLN'S BUSINESS

Arc-welding has been the standard joining method in the shipbuilding industry for decades. It is the predominant way of joining steel in the construction industry. Most industrial plants have their own welding shops for maintenance and construction. Manufacturers of tractors and all kinds of heavy equipment use arc-welding extensively in the manufacturing process. Many hobbyists have their own welding machines and use them for making metal items such as patio furniture and barbeque pits. The popularity of welded sculpture as an art form is growing.

While advances in welding technology have been frequent, arc-welding products, in the main, have hardly changed except for Lincoln's Innershield process. This process, utilizing a self-shielded, flux-cored electrode, has established new cost saving opportunities for construction and equipment fabrication. The most popular Lincoln electrode, the Fleetweld 5P, has been virtually the same since the 1930s. The most popular engine-driven welder in the world, the Lincoln SA-200, has been a gray-colored assembly including a four-cylinder continental "Red Seal" engine and a 200-ampere direct-current generator with two current-control knobs for at least three decades. A 1980 model SA-200 even weighs almost the same as the 1950 model, and it certainly is little changed in appearance.

Lincoln and its competitors now market a wide range of general purpose and specialty electrodes for welding mild steel, aluminum, cast iron, and stainless and special steels. Most of these electrodes are designed to meet the standards of the American Welding Society, a trade association. They are thus essentially the same as to size and composition from one manufacturer to any other. Every electrode manufacturer has a limited number of unique products, but these typically constitute only a small percentage of total sales.

Lincoln's research and development expenditures have recently been less than 1½ percent of sales. There is evidence that others spend several times as much as a percentage of sales.

Lincoln's share of the arc-welding products market appears to have been about 40% for many years, and the welding products market has grown somewhat faster than the level of industry in general. The market is highly price-competitive, with variations in prices of standard products normally amounting to only a percent or two. Lincoln's products are sold directly by its engineering-oriented sales force and indirectly through its distributor organization. Advertising expenditures amount to less than one-fourth of 1 percent of sales, one-third as much as a major Lincoln competitor with whom the case writer checked.

The other major welding process, flame-welding, has not been competitive with arc-welding since the 1930s. However, plasma-arc-welding, a relatively new process which uses a conducting stream of super heated gas (plasma) to confine the welding current to a small area, has made some inroads, especially in metal tubing manufacturing, in recent years. Major advances in technology which will produce an alternative superior to arc-welding within the next decade or so appear unlikely. Also, it seems likely that changes in the machines and techniques used in arc-welding will be evolutionary rather than revolutionary.

Products

The company is primarily engaged in the manufacture and sale of arc-welding products—electric welding machines and metal electrodes. Lincoln also produces electric motors ranging from ½ horsepower to 200 horsepower. Motors constitute about 8 to 10% of total sales.

The electric welding machines, some consisting of a transformer or motor and generator arrangement powered by commercial electricity and others consisting of an internal combustion engine and generator, are designed to produce from 30 to 1000 amperes of electrical power. This electrical current is used to melt a consumable metal electrode, with the molten metal being transferred in a super hot spray to the metal joint being welded. Very high temperatures and hot sparks are produced, and operators usually must wear special eye and face protection and leather gloves, often along with leather aprons and sleeves.

Welding electrodes are of two basic types: (1) Coated "stick" electrodes, usually 14 inches long and smaller than a pencil in diameter, which are held in a special insulated holder by the operator, who must manipulate the electrode in order to maintain a proper arc-width and pattern of deposition of the metal being transferred. Stick electrodes are packaged in 6- to 50-pound boxes. (2) Coiled wire, ranging in diameter from 0.035 to 0.219 inch, which is designed to be fed continuously to the welding arc through a "gun" held by the operator or positioned by automatic positioning equipment. The wire is packaged in coils, reels, and drums weighing from 14 to 1000 pounds.

MANUFACTURING OPERATIONS

Plant Locations

The main plant is in Euclid, Ohio, a suburb on Cleveland's east side. The layout of this plant is shown in Figure C22.1. There are no warehouses. Materials flow from the half-mile-long dock on the north side of the plant through the production lines to a very limited storage and loading area on the south side. Materials used on each workstation are stored as close as possible to the workstation. The administrative offices, near the center of the factory, are entirely functional. Not even the president's office is carpeted. A corridor below the main level provides access to the factory floor from the main entrance near the center of the plant. A new plant, just opened in Mentor, Ohio, houses some of the electrode production operations, which were moved from the main plant.

Manufacturing Processes

Electrode manufacturing is highly capital-intensive. Metal rods purchased from steel producers are drawn or extruded down to smaller diameters, cut to length and coated with pressed-powder "flux" for stick electrodes or plated with copper (for conductivity), and spun into coils or spools for wire. Some of Lincoln's wire, called "Innershield," is hollow and filled with a material similar to that used to coat stick electrodes. Lincoln is highly secretive about its electrode production processes, and the case writer was not given access to the details of those processes.

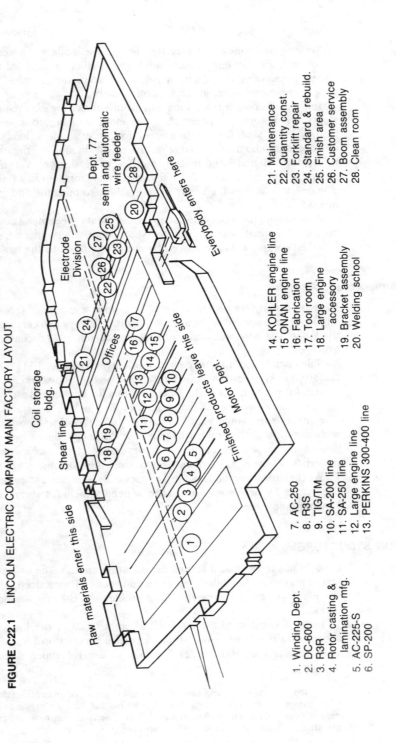

FIGURE C22.1 LINCOLN ELECTRIC COMPANY MAIN FACTORY LAYOUT

Raw materials enter this side

Coil storage bldg.

Shear line

Offices

Electrode Division

Dept. 77 semi and automatic wire feeder

Everybody enters here

Finished products leave this side

Motor Dept.

1. Winding Dept.
2. DC-600
3. R3R
4. Rotor casting & lamination mfg.
5. AC-225-S
6. SP-200
7. AC-250
8. R3S
9. TIG/TM
10. SA-200 line
11. SA-250 line
12. Large engine line
13. PERKINS 300-400 line
14. KOHLER engine line
15. ONAN engine line
16. Fabrication
17. Tool room
18. Large engine accessory
19. Bracket assembly
20. Welding school
21. Maintenance
22. Quantity const.
23. Forklift repair
24. Standard & rebuild.
25. Finish area
26. Customer service
27. Boom assembly
28. Clean room

Welding machines and electric motors are made on a series of assembly lines. Gasoline and diesel engines are purchased partially assembled but practically all other components are made from basic industrial products, e.g., steel bars and sheets and bar copper conductor wire, in the Lincoln factory.

Individual components, such as gasoline tanks for engine-driven welders and steel shafts for motors and generators, are made by numerous small "factories within a factory." The shaft for a certain generator, for example, is made from a raw steel bar by one operator who uses five large machines, all running continuously. A saw cuts the bar to length, a digital lathe machines different sections to varying diameters, a special milling machine cuts a slot for a keyway, and so forth, until a finished shaft is produced. The operator moves the shafts from machine to machine and makes necessary adjustments.

Another operator punches, shapes, and paints sheet metal cowling parts. One assembles steel laminations onto a rotor shaft, then winds, insulates, and tests the rotors. Finished components are moved by crane operators to the nearby assembly lines.

Worker Performance and Attitudes

Exceptional worker performance at Lincoln is a matter of record. The typical Lincoln employee earns about twice as much as other factory workers in the Cleveland area. Yet the labor cost per sales dollar at Lincoln, currently 23.5 cents, is well below industry averages.

Sales per Lincoln factory employee currently exceed $157,000. An observer at the factory quickly sees why this figure is so high. Each worker is proceeding busily and thoughtfully about his task. There is no idle chatter. Most workers take no coffee breaks. Many operate several machines and make a substantial component unaided. The supervisors, some with as many as 100 subordinates, are busy with planning and recordkeeping duties and hardly glance at the people they supervise. The manufacturing procedures appear efficient—no unnecessary steps, no wasted motions, no wasted materials. Finished components move smoothly to subsequent workstations.

Worker turnover at Lincoln is practically nonexistent except for retirements and departures by new employees. The appendix includes summaries of interviews with Lincoln employees.

ORGANIZATION STRUCTURE

Lincoln has never had a formal organization chart.* The objective of this policy is to insure maximum flexibility. An open door policy is practiced throughout the company, and personnel are encouraged to take problems to the persons most capable of resolving them.

Perhaps because of the quality and enthusiasm of the Lincoln work force, routine supervision is almost nonexistent. A typical production foreman, for example, supervises as many as 100 workers, a span of control which does not allow more than

---

* Once, Harvard Business School researchers prepared an organization chart reflecting implied relationships. The chart became available within the Lincoln organization, and present Lincoln management feels that it had a disruptive effect. Therefore, the case writer was asked not to include any kind of organization chart in this report.

infrequent worker-supervisor interaction. Position titles and traditional flows of authority do imply something of an organizational structure, however. For example, the vice president, Sales, and the vice president, Electrode Division, report to the president, as do various staff assistants such as the personnel director and the director of purchasing. Using such implied relationships, it has been determined that production workers have two or, at most, three levels of supervision between themselves and the president.

PERSONNEL POLICIES

Recruitment and Selection

Every job opening at Lincoln is advertised internally on company bulletin boards and any employee can apply for any job so advertised. External hiring is done only for entry-level positions. Selection for these jobs is done on the basis of personal interviews—there is no aptitude or psychological testing. Not even a high school diploma is required except for engineering and sales positions, which are filled by graduate engineers. A committee consisting of vice presidents and superintendents interviews candidates initially cleared by the personnel department. Final selection is made by the supervisor who has a job opening. Out of over 3500 applicants interviewed by the personnel department during a recent period fewer than 300 were hired.

Job Security

In 1958 Lincoln formalized its lifetime employment policy, which had already been in effect for many years. There have been no layoffs at Lincoln since World War II. Since 1958, every Lincoln worker with over one year's longevity has been guaranteed at least 30 hours per week, 49 weeks per year.

The policy has never been so severely tested as during the 1981–83 recession. As a manufacturer of capital goods, Lincoln's business is highly cyclical. In previous recessions Lincoln has been able to avoid major sales declines. Nineteen eighty-two sales, however, were about one-third below those of 1981. Few companies could withstand such a sales decline and remain profitable. Yet, Lincoln not only earned profits, but no employee has been laid off, the usual year-end incentive bonuses were paid (averaging $15,600 per worker for 1982), and common shareholders continue to receive about the normal dividend (around $8 per share).

Performance Evaluations

Each supervisor formally evaluates his subordinates twice a year using the cards shown in Figure C22.2. The employee performance criteria, "quality," "dependability," "ideas and cooperation," and "output," are considered to be independent of each other. Marks on the cards are converted to numerical scores which are forced to average 100 for each evaluating supervisor. Individual merit-rating scores normally range from 80 to 110. Any score over 110 requires a special letter to top management. These scores (over 110) are not considered in computing the required 100-point average for each evaluating supervisor. Suggestions for improvements often result in recommendations for exceptionally high performance scores. Supervisors discuss individual performance marks with the employees concerned. Each warranty claim on a Lincoln product is

Increasing Quality ⇨

QUALITY

This card rates the QUALITY of work you do.
It also reflects your success in eliminating errors and in reducing scrap and waste.

This rating has been done jointly by your department head and the Production Control Department in the shop and with other department heads in the office and engineering.

Increasing Dependability ⇨

DEPENDABILITY

This card rates how well your supervisors have been able to depend upon you to do those things that have been expected of you without supervision.

It also rates your ability to supervise yourself including your work safety performance, your orderliness, care of equipment, and the effective use you make of your skills.

This rating has been done by your department head.

Increasing Ideas & Cooperation ⇨

IDEAS & COOPERATION

This card rates your Cooperation, Ideas and Initiative.

New ideas and new methods are important to your company in our continuing effort to reduce costs, increase output, improve quality, work safely, and improve our relationship with our customers. This card credits you for your ideas and initiative used to help in this direction.

It also rates your cooperation—how to work with others as a team. Such factors as your attitude towards supervision, co-workers, and the company; your efforts to share your expert knowledge with others; and your cooperation in installing new methods smoothly, are considered here.

Increasing Output ⇨

OUTPUT

This card rates HOW MUCH PRODUCTIVE WORK you actually turn out.

It also reflects your willingness not to hold back and recognizes your attendance record.

This rating has been done jointly by your department head and the Production Control Department in the shop and with other department heads in the office and engineering.

traced to the individual employee whose work caused the defect. The employee's performance score may be reduced by one point, or the worker may be required to repay the cost of servicing the warranty claim by working without pay.

Compensation

Basic wage levels for jobs at Lincoln are determined by a wage survey of similar jobs in the Cleveland area. These rates are adjusted quarterly in accordance with changes in the Cleveland Area Consumer Price Index. Insofar as possible, base wage rates are translated into piece rates. Practically all production workers and many others—for example, some forklift operators—are paid by piece rate. Once established, piece rates are never changed unless a substantive change in the way a job is done results from a source other than the worker doing the job. In December of each year, a portion of annual profits is distributed to employees as bonuses. Incentive bonuses since 1934 have averaged about the same as annual wages and somewhat more than after-tax profits. The average bonus for 1981 was about $21,000. Bonuses averaged $15,500 and $10,400, respectively, for the recession years 1982 and 1983. Individual bonuses are proportional to merit-rating scores. For example, assume incentive bonuses for the company total 110% of wages paid. A person whose performance score is 95 will receive a bonus of 1.045 (1.10 × 0.95) times annual wages.

Work Assignment

Management has authority to transfer workers and to switch between overtime and short time as required. Supervisors have undisputed authority to assign specific parts to individual workmen, who may have their own preferences due to variations in piece rates.

Employee Participation in Decision Making

When a manager speaks of participative management, he usually thinks of a relaxed, nonauthoritarian atmosphere. This is not the case at Lincoln. Formal authority is quite strong. "We're very authoritarian around here," says Mr. Willis. James F. Lincoln placed a good deal of stress on protecting management's authority. "Management in all successful departments of industry must have complete power," he said. " . . . Management is the coach who must be obeyed. The men, however, are the players who alone can win the game."[18] Despite this attitude, there are several ways in which employees participate in management at Lincoln.

Richard Sabo, manager of public relations, relates job enlargement to participation. "The most important participative technique that we use is giving more responsibility to employees." Mr. Sabo says, "We give a high school graduate more responsibility than other companies give their foremen." Lincoln puts limits on the degree of participation which is allowed, however. In Mr. Sabo's words,

> When you use "participation," put quotes around it. Because we believe that each person should participate only in those decisions he is most knowledgeable about. I don't think production employees should control the decisions of Bill

Irrgang. They don't know as much as he does about the decisions he is involved in.

The advisory board, elected by the workers, meets with the chairman and the president every two weeks to discuss ways of improving operations. This board has been in existence since 1914 and has contributed to many innovations. The incentive bonuses, for example, were first recommended by this committee. Every Lincoln employee has access to advisory board members, and answers to all advisory board suggestions are promised by the following meeting. Both Mr. Irrgang and Mr. Willis are quick to point out, though, that the advisory board only recommends actions. "They do not have direct authority," Mr. Irrgang says, "and when they bring up something that management thinks is not to the benefit of the company, it will be rejected."[19]

A suggestion program was instituted in 1929. At first, employees were awarded one-half of the first year's savings attributable to their suggestions. Now, however, the value of suggestions is reflected in performance evaluation scores, which determine individual incentive bonus amounts.

Training and Education

Production workers are given a short period of on-the-job training and then placed on a piecework pay system. Lincoln does not pay for off-site education. The idea behind this latter policy is that everyone cannot take advantage of such a program, and it is unfair to expend company funds for an advantage to which there is unequal access. Sales personnel are given on-the-job training in the plant followed by a period of work and training at one of the regional sales offices.

Fringe Benefits and Executive Perquisites

A medical plan and a company-paid retirement program have been in effect for many years. A plant cafeteria, operated on a break-even basis, serves meals at about 60% of usual costs. An employee association, to which the company does not contribute, provides disability insurance and social and athletic activities. An employee stock ownership program, instituted in about 1925, and regular stock purchases have resulted in employee ownership of about 50% of Lincoln's stock.

As to executive perquisites, there are none—crowded, austere offices, no executive washrooms or lunchrooms, and no reserved parking spaces. Even the company president pays for his own meals and eats in the cafeteria.

FINANCIAL POLICIES

James F. Lincoln felt strongly that financing for company growth should come from within the company—through initial cash investment by the founders, through retention of earnings, and through stock purchases by those who work in the business. He saw the following advantages of this approach:[20]

1 Ownership of stock by employees strengthens team spirit. "If they are mutually anxious to make it succeed, the future of the company is bright."

2 Ownership of stock provides individual incentive because employees feel that they will benefit from company profitability.

3 "Ownership is educational." Owners-employees "will know how profits are made and lost; how success is won and lost. . . . There are few socialists in the list of stockholders of the nation's industries."

4 "Capital available from within controls expansion." Unwarranted expansion will not occur, Lincoln believed, under his financing plan.

5 "The greatest advantage would be the development of the individual worker. Under the incentive of ownership, he would become a greater man."

6 "Stock ownership is one of the steps that can be taken that will make the worker feel that there is less of a gulf between him and the boss. . . . Stock ownership will help the worker to recognize his responsibility in the game and the importance of victory."

Lincoln Electric Company uses a minimum of debt in its capital structure. There is no borrowing at all, with the debt being limited to current payables. Even the new $20 million plant in Mentor, Ohio, was financed totally from earnings.

The unusual pricing policy at Lincoln is succinctly stated by President Willis: "At all times price on the basis of cost and at all times keep pressure on our cost." This policy resulted in Lincoln's price for the most popular welding electrode then in use going from 16 cents a pound in 1929 to 4.7 cents in 1938. More recently, the SA-200 Welder, Lincoln's largest selling portable machine, decreased in price from 1958 through 1965. According to Dr. C. Jackson Grayson of the American Productivity Center in Houston, Texas, Lincoln's prices in general have increased only one-fifth as fast as the Consumer Price Index from 1934 to about 1970. This has resulted in a welding products market in which Lincoln is the undisputed price leader for the products it manufactures. Not even the major Japanese manufacturers, such as Nippon Steel for welding electrodes and Asaka Transformer for welding machines, have been able to penetrate this market.

Huge cash balances are accumulated each year preparatory to paying the year-end bonuses. The bonuses totaled $55,718,000 for 1981 and about $41,000,000 for 1982. This money is invested in short-term U.S. government securities until needed. Financial statements are shown in Figures C22.3 and C22.4.

HOW WELL DOES LINCOLN SERVE ITS PUBLIC?

Lincoln Electric differs from most other companies in the importance it assigns to each of the groups it serves. Mr. Willis identifies these groups, in the order of priority Lincoln ascribes to them, as (1) customers, (2) employees, and (3) stockholders.

Certainly Lincoln customers have fared well over the years. Lincoln prices for welding machines and welding electrodes are acknowledged to be the lowest in the marketplace. Lincoln quality has consistently been so high that Lincoln "Fleetweld" electrodes and Lincoln SA-200 welders have been the standard in the pipeline and refinery construction industry, where price is hardly a criterion, for decades. The cost of field failures for Lincoln products was an amazing .004% in 1979. A Lincoln distributor in Monroe, Louisiana, says that he has sold several hundred of the popular AC-225 welders, and, though the machine is warranted for one year, he has never handled a warranty claim.

Perhaps best-served of all Lincoln constituencies have been the employees. Not the least of their benefits, of course, are the year-end bonuses, which effectively double an

FIGURE C22.3 LINCOLN ELECTRIC COMPANY BALANCE SHEETS
(Dollar Amounts in Thousands)

	1980	1981	1982
Assets			
Cash	$ 1,307	$ 3,603	$ 1,318
Gov't. securities & certificates of deposit	46,503	62,671	72,485
Notes and accounts receivable	42,424	41,521	26,239
Inventories (LIFO basis)	35,533	45,541	38,157
Deferred taxes and prepared expenses	2,749	3,658	4,635
	$128,516	$156,994	$142,834
Other intangible assets	$ 19,723	$ 21,424	$ 22,115
Investment in foreign subsidiaries	$ 4,695	$ 4,695	$ 7,696
	$ 24,418	$ 26,119	$ 29,812
Property, plant, & equipment:			
Land	$ 913	$ 928	$ 925
Buildings*	22,982	24,696	23,330
Machinery, tools, & equipment*	25,339	27,104	26,949
	$ 49,234	$ 52,728	$ 51,204
Total assets	$202,168	$235,841	$223,850
Liabilities			
Accounts payable	$ 15,608	$ 14,868	$ 11,936
Accrued wages	1,504	4,940	3,633
Taxes, including income taxes	5,622	14,755	5,233
Dividends payable	5,800	7,070	6,957
	$ 28,534	$ 41,633	$ 27,759
Deferred taxes & other long-term liabilities	$ 3,807	$ 4,557	$ 5,870
Shareholders' equity:			
Common capital stock, stated value	$ 276	$ 272	$ 268
Additional paid-in capital	2,641	501	1,862
Retained earnings	166,910	188,878	188,392
Equity adjustment from foreign currency translation			(301)
	$169,827	$189,651	$190,221
Total liabilities and shareholders' equity	$202,168	$235,841	$223,850

* After depreciation.

already average compensation level. The foregoing description of the personnel program and the comments in the appendix further illustrate the desirability of a Lincoln job.

While stockholders were relegated to an inferior status by James F. Lincoln, they have done very well indeed. Recent dividends have exceeded $7 a share and earnings per share have exceeded $20. In January 1980, the price of restricted stock committed by Lincoln to employees was $117 a share. By February 4, 1983, the stated value, at which Lincoln will repurchase the stock if tendered, was $166. A check with the New York office of Merrill, Lynch, Pierce, Fenner and Smith on February 4, 1983, revealed an estimated price on Lincoln stock of $240 a share, with none being offered for sale.

FIGURE C22.4 LINCOLN ELECTRIC COMPANY INCOME STATEMENTS
(Dollar Amounts in Thousands)

	1980	1981	1982
Income:			
Net sales	$387,374	$450,387	$310,862
Other income	13,817	18,454	18,049
	$401,191	$468,841	$328,911
Costs and expenses:			
Cost of products sold	$260,671	$293,332	$212,674
Selling, administrative, freight, other, and general expenses	37,753	42,656	37,128
Year-end incentive bonus	43,249	55,718	36,870
Payroll taxes related to bonus	1,251	1,544	1,847
Pension expense	6,810	6,874	5,888
	$349,734	$400,124	$294,407
Income before income taxes:	$ 51,457	$ 68,717	$ 34,504
Provision for income taxes:			
Federal	$ 20,300	$ 27,400	$ 13,227
State & local	3,072	3,885	2,497
	$ 23,372	$ 31,285	$ 15,724
Net income	$ 28,085	$ 37,432	$ 18,780
Employees (eligible for bonus)	2,637	2,684	2,634

Technically, this price applies only to the unrestricted stock owned by the Lincoln family, a few other major holders, and employees who have purchased it on the open market, but it gives some idea of the value of Lincoln stock in general. The risk associated with Lincoln stock, a major determinant of stock value, is minimal because of the absence of debt in Lincoln's capital structure, because of an extremely stable earnings record, and because of Lincoln's practice of purchasing the restricted stock whenever employees offer it for sale.

It is easy to believe that the reason for Lincoln's success is the excellent attitude of Lincoln employees and their willingness to work harder, faster, and more intelligently than other industrial workers. However, Mr. Richard Sabo, manager of publicity and educational services at Lincoln, suggests that appropriate credit be given to Lincoln executives, whom he credits with carrying out the following policies:

1 Management has limited research, development, and manufacturing to a standard product line designed to meet the major needs of the welding industry.

2 New products must be reviewed by manufacturing and all production costs verified before being approved by management.

3 Purchasing is challenged to not only procure materials at the lowest cost, but also to work closely with engineering and manufacturing to assure that the latest innovations are implemented.

4 Manufacturing supervision and all personnel are held accountable for reduction of scrap, energy conservation, and maintenance of product quality.

5 Production control, material handling, and methods engineering are closely supervised by top management.

6 Material and finished goods inventory control, accurate cost accounting, and attention to sales cost, credit, and other financial areas have constantly reduced overhead and led to excellent profitability.

7 Management has made cost reduction a way of life at Lincoln, and definite programs are established in many areas, including traffic and shipping, where tremendous savings can result.

8 Management has established a sales department that is technically trained to reduce customer welding costs. This sales technique and other real customer services have eliminated nonessential frills and resulted in long-term benefits to all concerned.

9 Management has encouraged education, technical publishing, and long-range programs that have resulted in industry growth, thereby assuring market potential for the Lincoln Electric Company.

APPENDIX: The Lincoln Electric Company, 1984

EMPLOYEE INTERVIEWS

During the late summer of 1980, the author conducted numerous interviews with Lincoln employees. Typical questions and answers from those interviews are presented below. In order to maintain each employee's personal privacy, the names used for the interviewees are fictitious.

I

Interview with Betty Stewart, a 52-year-old high school graduate, who had been with Lincoln 13 years and who was working as a cost accounting clerk at the time of the interview.

Q: What jobs have you held here besides the one you have now?
A: I worked in payroll for a while, and then this job came open and I took it.
Q: How much money did you make last year, including your bonus?
A: I would say roughly around $20,000, but I was off for back surgery for a while.
Q: You weren't paid while you were off for back surgery?
A: No.
Q: Did the Employees Association help out?
A: Yes. The company doesn't furnish that, though. We pay $6 a month into the Employee Association. I think my check from them was $105 a week.
Q: How was your performance rating last year?
A: It was around 100 points, but I lost some points for attendance with my back problem.
Q: How did you get your job at Lincoln?
A: I was bored silly where I was working, and I had heard that Lincoln kept their people busy. So I applied and got the job the next day.
Q: Do you think you make more money than similar workers in Cleveland?
A: I know I do.
Q: What have you done with your money?
A: We have purchased a better home. Also, my son is going to the University of Chicago, which costs $10,000 a year. I buy the Lincoln stock which is offered each year, and I have a little bit of gold.

Q: Have you ever visited with any of the senior executives, like Mr. Willis or Mr. Irrgang?

A: I have known Mr. Willis for a long time.

Q: Does he call you by name?

A: Yes. In fact he was very instrumental in my going to the doctor that I am going to with my back. He knows the director of the clinic.

Q: Do you know Mr. Irrgang?

A: I know him to speak to him, and he always speaks, always. But I have known Mr. Willis for a good many years. When I did Plant Two accounting I did not understand how the plant operated. Of course you are not allowed in Plant Two, because that's the Electrode Division. I told my boss about the problem one day and the next thing I knew Mr. Willis came by and said, "Come on, Betty, we're going to Plant Two." He spent an hour and a half showing me the plant.

Q: Do you think Lincoln employees produce more than those in other companies?

A: I think with the incentive program the way it is, if you want to work and achieve, then you will do it. If you don't want to work and achieve, you will not do it no matter where you are. Just because you are merit rated and have a bonus, if you really don't want to work hard, then you're not going to. You will accept your ninety points or ninety-two or eighty-five because, even with that, you make more money than people on the outside.

Q: Do you think Lincoln employees will ever join a union?

A: I don't know why they would.

Q: What is the most important advantage of working for Lincoln Electric?

A: You have an incentive, and you can push and get something for pushing. That's not true in a lot of companies.

Q: So you say that money is a very major advantage?

A: Money is a major advantage, but it's not just the money. It's the fact that having the incentive, you do wish to work a little harder. I'm sure that there are a lot of men here who, if they worked some other place, would not work as hard as they do here. Not that they are overworked—I don't mean that—but I'm sure they wouldn't push.

Q: Is there anything that you would like to add?

A: I do like working here. I am better off being pushed mentally. In another company if you pushed too hard you would feel a little bit of pressure, and someone might say, "Hey, slow down; don't try so hard." But here you are encouraged, not discouraged.

II

Interview with Ed Sanderson, a 23-year-old high school graduate, who had been with Lincoln four years and who was a machine operator in the Electrode Division at the time of the interview.

Q: How did you happen to get this job?

A: My wife was pregnant, and I was making three bucks an hour and one day I came here and applied. That was it. I kept calling to let them know I was still interested.

Q: Roughly what were your earnings last year including your bonus?

A: $37,000.

Q: What have you done with your money since you have been here?

A: Well, we've lived pretty well and we bought a condominium.

Q: Have you paid for the condominium?

A: No, but I could.

Q: Have you bought your Lincoln stock this year?

A: No, I haven't bought any Lincoln stock yet.

Q: Do you get the feeling that the executives here are pretty well thought of?

A: I think they are. To get where they are today, they had to really work.

Q: Wouldn't that be true anywhere?

A: I think more so here because seniority really doesn't mean anything. If you work with a guy who has twenty years here, and you have two months and you're doing a better job, you will get advanced before he will.

Q: Are you paid on a piece rate basis?

A: My gang does. There are nine of us who make the bare electrode, and the whole group gets paid based on how much electrode we make.

Q: Do you think you work harder than workers in other factories in the Cleveland area?

A: Yes, I would say I probably work harder.

Q: Do you think it hurts anybody?

A: No, a little hard work never hurts anybody.

Q: If you could choose, do you think you would be as happy earning a little less money and being able to slow down a little?

A: No, it doesn't bother me. If it bothered me, I wouldn't do it.

Q: What would you say is the biggest disadvantage of working at Lincoln, as opposed to working somewhere else?

A: Probably having to work shift work.

Q: Why do you think Lincoln employees produce more than workers in other plants?

A: That's the way the company is set up. The more you put out, the more you're going to make.

Q: Do you think it's the piece rate and bonus together?

A: I don't think people would work here if they didn't know that they would be rewarded at the end of the year.

Q: Do you think Lincoln employees will ever join a union?

A: No.

Q: What are the major advantages of working for Lincoln?

A: Money.

Q: Are there any other advantages?

A: Yes, we don't have a union shop. I don't think I could work in a union shop.

Q: Do you think you are a career man with Lincoln at this time?

A: Yes.

III

Interview with Roger Lewis, a 23-year-old Purdue graduate in mechanical engineering, who had been in the Lincoln sales program for 15 months and who was working in the Cleveland sales office at the time of the interview.

Q: How did you get your job at Lincoln?

A: I saw that Lincoln was interviewing on campus at Purdue, and I went by. I later came to Cleveland for a plant tour and was offered a job.

Q: Do you know any of the senior executives? Would they know you by name?

A: Yes, I know all of them—Mr. Irrgang, Mr. Willis, Mr. Manross.

Q: Do you think Lincoln salesmen work harder than those in other companies?

A: Yes. I don't think there are many salesmen for other companies who are putting in fifty- to sixty-hour weeks. Everybody here works harder. You can go out in the plant, or you can go upstairs, and there's nobody sitting around.

Q: Do you see any real disadvantages of working at Lincoln?

A: I don't know if it's a disadvantage but Lincoln is a spartan company, a very thrifty company. I like that. The sales offices are functional, not fancy.

Q: Why do you think Lincoln employees have such high productivity?

A: Piecework has a lot to do with it. Lincoln is smaller than many plants, too; you can stand in one place and see the materials come in one side and the product go out the other. You feel a part of the company. The chance to get ahead is important, too. They have a strict policy of promoting from within, so you know you have a chance. I think in a lot of other places you may not get as fair a shake as you do here. The sales offices are on a smaller scale, too. I like that. I tell someone that we have two people in the Baltimore office, and they say "You've got to be kidding." It's smaller and more personal. Pay is the most important thing. I have heard that this is the highest paying factory in the world.

IV

Interview with Jimmy Roberts, a 47-year-old high school graduate, who had been with Lincoln 17 years and who was working as a multiple-drill press operator at the time of the interview.

Q: What jobs have you had at Lincoln?

A: I started out cleaning the men's locker room in 1963. After about a year I got a job in the flux department, where we make the coating for welding rods. I worked there for seven or eight years and then got my present job.

Q: Do you make one particular part?

A: No, there are a variety of parts I make—at least twenty-five.

Q: Each one has a different piece rate attached to it?

A: Yes.

Q: Are some piece rates better than others?

A: Yes.

Q: How do you determine which ones you are going to do?

A: You don't. Your supervisor assigns them.

Q: How much money did you make last year?

A: $47,000.

Q: Have you ever received any kind of award or citation?

A: No.

Q: Was your rating over 110?

A: Yes. For the past five years, probably, I made over 110 points.

Q: Is there any attempt to let others know . . . ?

A: The kind of points I get? No.

Q: Do you know what they are making?

A: No. There are some who might not be too happy with their points and they might make it known. The majority, though, do not make it a point of telling other employees.

Q: Would you be just as happy earning a little less money and working a little slower?

A: I don't think I would—not at this point. I have done piecework all these years, and the fast pace doesn't really bother me.

Q: Why do you think Lincoln productivity is so high?

A: The incentive thing—the bonus distribution. I think that would be the main reason. The pay check you get every two weeks is important too.

Q: Do you think Lincoln employees would ever join a union?

A: I don't think so. I have never heard anyone mention it.

Q: What is the most important advantage of working here?

A: Amount of money you make. I don't think I could make this type of money anywhere else, especially with only a high school education.

Q: As a black person, do you feel that Lincoln discriminates in any way against blacks?

A: No. I don't think any more so than any other job. Naturally, there is a certain amount of discrimination, regardless of where you are.

V

Interview with Joe Trahan, a 58-year-old high school graduate, who had been with Lincoln 39 years and who was employed as a working supervisor in the tool room at the time of the interview.

Q: Roughly what was your pay last year?

A: Over $50,000; salary, bonus, stock dividends.

Q: How much was your bonus?

A: About $23,000.

Q: Have you ever gotten a special award of any kind?

A: Not really.

Q: What have you done with your money?

A: My house is paid for—and my two cars. I also have some bonds and the Lincoln stock.

Q: What do you think of the executives at Lincoln?

A: They're really top notch.

Q: What is the major disadvantage of working at Lincoln Electric?

A: I don't know of any disadvantage at all.

Q: Do you think you produce more than most people in similar jobs with other companies?

A: I do believe that.

Q: Why is that? Why do you believe that?

A: We are on the incentive system. Everything we do, we try to improve to make a better product with a minimum of outlay. We try to improve the bonus.

Q: Would you be just as happy making a little less money and not working quite so hard?

A: I don't think so.

Q: You know that Lincoln productivity is higher than that at most other plants. Why is that?

A: Money.

Q: Do you think Lincoln employees would ever join a union?

A: I don't think they would ever consider it.

Q: What is the most important advantage of working at Lincoln?

A: Compensation.

Q: Tell me something about Mr. James Lincoln, who died in 1965.

A: You are talking about Jimmy Sr. He always strolled through the shop in his shirt sleeves. Big fellow. Always looked distinguished. Gray hair. Friendly sort of guy. I was a member of the advisory board one year. He was there each time.

Q: Did he strike you as really caring?

A: I think he always cared for people.

Q: Did you get any sensation of a religious nature from him?

A: No, not really.

Q: And religion is not part of the program now?

A: No.

Q: Do you think Mr. Lincoln was a very intelligent man, or was he just a nice guy?

A: I would say he was pretty well educated. A great talker—always right off the top of his head. He knew what he was talking about all the time.

Q: When were bonuses for beneficial suggestions done away with?

A: About fifteen years ago.

Q: Did that hurt very much?

A: I don't think so, because suggestions are still rewarded through the merit-rating system.

Q: Is there anything you would like to add?

A: It's a good place to work. The union kind of ties other places down. At other places, electricians only do electrical work, carpenters only do carpenter work. At Lincoln Electric we all pitch in and do whatever needs to be done.

Q: So a major advantage is not having a union?

A: That's right.

REFERENCES

1 James F. Lincoln, *A New Approach to Industrial Economics* (New York: The Devin Adair Co., 1961), p. 11.

2 Ibid., p. 64.

3 Ibid., p. 119.

4 "You Can't Tell What a Man Can Do—Until He Has the Chance," *Reader's Digest,* January 1947, p. 94.

5 George E. Willis's letter to author of 7 September 1978.

6 Lincoln, 1961, p. 47.

7 Ibid., p. 117.

8 Ibid., p. 38.

9 Ibid., p. 122.

10 Ibid., p. 18.

11 Ibid., p. 76.

12 Ibid., p. 72.

13 Ibid., p. 36.

14 Ibid., p. 75.

15 Ibid., p. 98.

16 Ibid., p. 92.

17 Ibid., p. 39.

18 Lincoln, *Incentive Management* (Cleveland, Ohio: The Lincoln Electric Company, 1951), p. 228.

19 "Incentive Management in Action," *Assembly Engineering,* March 1967, p. 18.

20 Lincoln, 1961, pp. 220–228.

MARRIOTT CORPORATION

Prepared by Jeffrey M. Wachtel, University of Nevada, Reno.

He must have been there at least once that year . . . New York, Times Square, in the heart of the theater district, as the enormous hotel (1877 room), equipped with a full-scale Broadway theater climbed up to the heights of the world's most famous skyline. He must have been there because J. W. "Bill" Marriott, Jr., visited every one of the rapidly expanding Marriott Corporation's hotels each year, spending one-third of his time in the air traveling 150,000 miles per year. He had also been to Atlanta to see the new 1674-room Marriott Marquis soar into the "New York of the South's" skyline and to visit his more modest Courtyard-by-Marriott prototype to see if it warranted nation-wide expansion in a "head to head" competition with Holiday Inn. Indeed, Mr. Marriott had made three visits to the Courtyard, changing details during construction with the gut instincts and clear business sense that had enabled him to increase annual sales six times to $2.54 billion, increase earnings five times to $94.3 million, and maintain an average earnings growth rate of 17.3%. Yes, the Marriott Corporation was highly successful, but in February of 1984 it faced some real challenges for which it was making strategic plans.

In 1984, competition in the hospitality and travel industry (a "fragmented industry") was increasing. Many cities were overbuilt, and other chains were competing for the few cities left. Marriott, like the others, was running out of cities which lacked its "luxury market" hotels. Holiday Inns' Crown Plazas (new luxury hotels) and Ramada's Renaissance hotels were examples of middle of the road chains which had entered the upscale market. Even Howard Johnson's was opening a new chain of luxury hotels. Add to that the fact that Hyatt was building new hotels and Hilton, Sheraton, and Dunfey's, among others, were refurbishing existing properties, and one saw the magnitude of competi-

Note: This case was prepared as a basis for class discussion rather than to illustrate either effective or ineffective handling of an administrative situation. Copyright © 1985. Used by permission.

tion. Other chains were doing well also. Four Seasons hotels were ultraluxury hotels. Westin had always done well, managing very large "mega" hotels like the Los Angeles Bonaventure and the Peachtree Plaza (Atlanta). In addition, foreign hotel companies such as Meridian and Trust House Forte, having learned the principles of American hotel management, were now expanding into the United States.

Thus, Bill Marriott, Jr., and his executive team had made a risky decision to build in the heart of one of the world's most expensive cities in the famous and infamous neighborhood called Times Square. Even one of New York's more daring developers had said, "To build a major convention hotel in that cesspool over there, even with the convention center going up a few blocks away, is crazy."[1]

This hotel was also to be a departure from Marriott's architecturally traditional hotels. This hotel, designed by Atlanta architect John Portman, master of the modern atrium hotel, was to have "the biggest Portman neckbender yet"—a mammoth 48-story bejungled atrium in which luminous glass elevators would bob up and down kinetically between the lobby and Manhattan's first revolving sky-view restaurant.[2] J. W. Marriott, Jr., prior to making this deal, which included the $250 million Marriott Marquis, Atlanta, had been quoted as saying, "Marriott isn't at the top of the scale in luxury or price. We offer a consistently high-quality product at a fair price; we are not flashy."[3] In 1984, it seemed as though this was about to change, as it appeared that the new hotel would require room rates of $186 per night in order to follow an industry standard of $1 per $1000 construction costs. The move to build the two new Marquis hotels in prime downtown locations was also somewhat of a departure for the hotel division's location strategy, which had predominantly seen hotels built near airports and suburban office-complex locations, moving heavily into downtown areas only when the major companies were flocking to Atlantic City to enter the gambling hotel business. *Fortune* magazine claimed that the Marquis was an effort to build the chain's image through Portman's architecture, which would "spread a halo over the chain."[4]

Simultaneously, the Courtyard concept was an attempt to go after the largest part of the lodging market, the moderate-price segment, of which Holiday Inns had the largest share (see Figure C23.1). Five Courtyards have been opened in the Atlanta, Augusta, and Columbus, Georgia, areas where there were many competing Holiday Inns and Days Inns (see Figure C23.2). In fact, Days Inns has its headquarters in Atlanta and there were 14 Holiday Inns in that city. The Courtyard by Marriott is priced from $25 to $55. It has a lobby which also serves as the restaurant and lounge; rooms are spacious and situated around a pool in the courtyard. It will have only a couple of meeting rooms. The Courtyards will be scattered around metropolitan areas in real estate areas that are less expensive than downtown locations. At a cost of $6 million per 125-room property, Stan Bruns, general manager, Atlanta Marriott, pointed out that for the price of one New York or Atlanta Marquis hotel, many Courtyards could be built. In the beginning of 1984, Marriott was unsure whether the development costs for the Courtyard would be worth it and much hope was placed on developments in Atlanta. There were also other challenges in Marriott's other divisions.

EARLY BEGINNINGS AND MILESTONES

The Marriott Corporation started the day Lindberg was flying the Atlantic, May 20, 1927, as a nine-seat Washington, D.C., A & W Root Beer stand. It was opened by offering the first glass of root beer free to the first customer. It is not competely clear

A Little Bit Of Home On The Road. Just $45 A Night Weekdays And Only $35 A Night Weekends.

As the culmination of years of intensive research into the wants and needs of today's pleasure traveller, Courtyard by Marriott is a new and innovative hotel concept featuring a consistently superior lodging experience at an affordable price. A "human scaled" hotel where special weekend rates, and a little extra effort and personality in attending to often overlooked details, go a long way in making your stay as comfortable as possible. And as convenient as possible to family, friends, shopping, and popular attractions.

Designed For Comfort, Inside And Out.

As you look around Courtyard, you will immediately notice our attention to detail and the pleasant little differences which will truly make you feel a little bit more at home. Outside, note the extent and care of the landscaping, and the terraced courtyard and pool around which the hotel is focused. Note as well the exclusively residential scale and feeling of our architecture, both inside and out.

For example, inside there is no lobby in the traditional sense—it's more of an oversized living room, from which our intimate, 60-seat, three-meal-a-day restaurant and lounge are a natural extension, not a distraction. Off this entrance area, Courtyard offers a hydrotherapy pool and a fully equipped game room for a continuation of your family's relaxation. There's even a guest laundry room provided for your convenience.

And the longer you sit, relax, and experience this "common area," the more you may notice the personal attention Courtyard guests receive from our highly-trained employees—employees who welcome your business and truly enjoy making you feel at home.

True Overnight Living Space With Room To Roam.

As you glance around your room at Courtyard, the attractive, up-to-date decor and spacious room layout are instantly impressive. King-sized and double beds, a balcony or patio, and a distinct relaxation and conversation area with a love seat which converts to a bed for more sleeping area.

If a late-night or early morning cup of coffee is your cup-o-tea, there's a boiling water faucet in each room to oblige. Cable TV and in-room movies are provided free of charge. And every room insures your safety and security with two exits, sprinklers, smoke detectors, and state-of-the-art double locking mechanisms on each door.

In addition to more than 108 guest rooms, Courtyard features 20 suites for entertaining, extended visits, or simply when more space is needed. Priced at just $65 a night on weekdays, and at the special rate of only $55 on weekends.

We're On The Road With You.

Starting in October, you will begin to see Courtyard by Marriott hotels springing up in convenient suburban locations. The first two Courtyards will open in Atlanta in early October, with easy access to and from all major highways at I-75 and Windy Hill Road, and at Peachtree-Dunwoody at I-285. In January of 1984, a third Courtyard will open on La Vista Road at I-285, also in Atlanta. And in early 1984, look for two more Courtyards in Georgia, one in Columbus and one in Augusta.

Courtyard by Marriott. Stop by starting in October. We look forward to welcoming you, and to treating you to a little bit of home on the road.

We Know What It's Like To Be On The Road.

For more information, contact Duane Quintana at 404-955-6608. For toll-free reservations, call 1-800-321-2211, or, in Atlanta, dial 955-6222.

Atlanta Area Office   1950 Windy Hill Road, Suite 300   Atlanta, Georgia 30339   404-955-6608

FIGURE C23.2   LOCATION OF FIVE MARRIOTT COURTYARDS

which event has impacted more people. Lindberg paved the way for aviation, from which Marriott In-Flight Kitchens has prospered in serving passengers of over 120 airlines. Many years later, when Charles Lindberg and J. W. Marriott, Sr., met at a White House reception, Marriott remarked, "You and I went into business on the same day back there in May, 1927."[5]

From 1927 to 1957, J. W. Marriott, Sr., led the company's expansion as a food service company. Since root beer sold well only in the summer, an overnight conversion in the company's first year yielded the Hot Shoppe concept, which was to be so successful. It was at the old Hoover Airport Hot Shoppe (Number 8) that passengers began buying sandwiches for flights in 1937. In his typical style, reacting to the environment and recognizing opportunities, Bill Marriott, Sr., called on Eastern Air Transport and began serving 22 flights daily. In 1940, the Hot Shoppe concept achieved great popularity. In 1948, Hot Shoppes opened its first hotel cafeteria, and in 1948, Bill Marriott, Sr., was elected president of the National Restaurant Association.[6] In 1955, the company entered food service management in hospitals, and in 1957, the first hotel was opened—Twin Bridges Marriott Hotel. In 1966, the company went international by engaging in airline catering overseas.

It was Bill Marriott, Jr., who was in charge of pulling together the opening of the Twin Bridges Marriott Hotel; a year after the opening, at the age of 26, he became executive vice president in charge of the Motor Hotel Program. The next years were to be hotel years as Bill, Jr., built up the hotel division to 43% of sales and 53% of operating income in 1982 (see Figure C23.3). Much of this expansion was related to the expansion

	1962	1972	1982	10-year compound annual growth rate
Sales ($ million)	71.50	423	2,541	19.5
Net income ($ million)	2.30	13.80	94.30	20.4

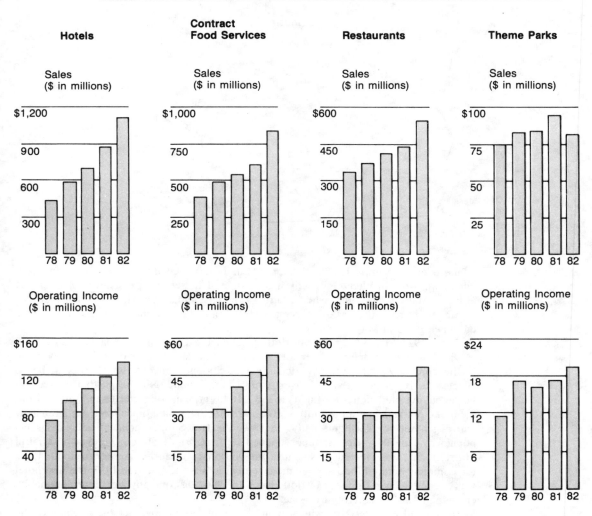

of air travel, as hotels were built near every major airport until the airport hotel market had reached saturation. The hotel division remains the company's fastest-growing division.

OPERATIONS OF THE MARRIOTT CORPORATION

Marriott's most visible business is its hotels; indeed, it was the hotels that first carried the founder's name to the public. Recently, a new hotel went further, adding the J. W. before the Marriott name, ostensibly in honor of J. Willard Marriott, Sr. As has already been indicated, the Marriott Corporation is a $2.54 billion per year diversified multinational corporation. In 1984, the company structured itself into:

1 Hotel group
   a. Owned
   b. Management contract or lease agreements
   c. Franchise-operated
2 Contract food services
   a. Airline catering
   b. Terminal and highway restaurants
   c. Food service management
3 Restaurants
   a. Fast food restaurants (Roy Rogers, Jr., Hot Shoppes)
   b. Coffee shops (Big Boy's)
   c. Specialty restaurants (Charlie Brown's, Casa Maria, Joshua Tree, etc.)
   d. Service restaurants and cafeterias (Hot Shoppes)
   e. Franchised operations (Big Boy's)
4 Theme parks—Great America
   a. Gift and craft shops
   b. Restaurants
   c. Games
5 Cruise ships—Oceanic Sun Line
6 Architecture and construction division

THE HOTEL GROUP

At the end of 1982, Marriott had 118 hotels in 81 cities with a total of 49,432 guest rooms, an increase of 22% from the previous year. During 1983 some 4400 hotel rooms were scheduled to be added in such places as Fort Lauderdale (650 rooms), Newark International Airport (414 rooms), Torrence and La Jolla, California, and London.

Marriott, like other companies, had made a change in the ownership structure of the hotel group during the mid-70s. It had sold many of its hotels and taken back management contracts. Management contracts gave the company control of operations. Typically, Marriott would earn 3% of gross revenues plus 20 to 30% of gross operating profits, depending on performance. The 3% usually covered hotel group costs, and the 20 to 30% "is all profit" claimed Gary Wilson, executive vice president, Finance and Development. Mr. Wilson further stated, "As long as we can produce hotels and lay them off on institutions we can generate infinite fees with minimal investments."[7] However, in 1981, interest rates began to rise, and insurance companies ran out of investment funds as policyholders began borrowing against their policies. Creatively, Marriott devised a plan to "sell 11 hotels to a limited partnership group that put up $18 million and borrowed $365 million more from several banks . . . there are plans for several more syndications, worth over $1 billion, within the next year."[8]

The structure of the hotel group at the end of 1982 was as follows:

	Hotels	Rooms
Company-operated	20	8,901
Management contract or leased	72	32,225
Total company-operated	92	41,126
Franchise-operated	26	8,306
Total systemwide	118	49,432

Marriott operates primarily 300- to 500-room hotels, in downtown, suburban, and airport locations, catering to business travelers and meeting groups. Eighty percent of the hotels fall in the above category, and about 20% are resorts. The hotels typically contain swimming pools, gift shops, convention and banquet facilities, a variety of restaurants and lounges, parking facilities, and sports facilities such as tennis courts and golf courses. The restaurants and other facilities contributed 48% of hotel group sales in 1982, with the remainder of sales derived from room rentals. In the industry, approximately 75% of every room-rental dollar is profit, while 17% of the food-and-beverage-sale dollar is profit. In 1982, Marriott also operated nine foreign hotels, one of which it owned. In 1982, two managed hotels in Saudi Arabia were taken over by the government, and in the same year the Europa Hotel in London was acquired. (See Figure C23.4.)

The 1982 disclosure report contains the following statement:

> The company continues to expand its operations through both the ownership and management of new hotels. The mix of owned and managed/leased hotels is controlled based on a continued assessment of changing market conditions and alternative investment opportunities other than hotels. Over 100 hotels are now in various stages of development. During 1983, approximately 4,400 company operated hotel rooms are scheduled to be added of which 3,700 will come from 10 new hotels and the remainder resulting from expansion at existing locations. Hotel room growth is expected to continue at about a 20% compound annual rate through the mid-1980s, with over 75% of the new rooms operated under lease or management agreements.

Franchised Operations

The franchise program is modest compared with that of other hotel companies. At Holiday Inns, for example, a new franchise opened once a week during its expansion period. And, indeed, television commercials in 1984 were still claiming that a new hotel opened every 7 days. Most of Marriott's expansion has been through franchise agreements. In 1983, only two Marriott franchises were to open. Franchisees paid an initial fee and then 5% of room sales.

FIGURE C23.4 MARRIOTT LOCATIONS

MARRIOT HOTELS
United States

Alabama
Point Clear
  Grand Hotel

Arizona
Scottsdale
  Camelback Inn
  Mountain Shadows Resort
Tucson

California
Anaheim
Irvine
Los Angeles
  Airport
  Marina del Rey
Newport Beach
Rancho Mirage
  Rancho Las Palmas Resort
San Francisco Bay
  Berkeley Marina
Santa Barbara
  Biltmore
Santa Clara

Colorado
Denver
  City Center
  Southeast
Vail
  Mark Resort

Connecticut
Hartford/Farmington
Stamford

Florida
Fort Lauderdale
Key West
  Casa Marina Resort
Marco Island
  Marco Beach Resort
Miami
  Airport
  Biscayne Bay
Orlando
  Orlando Inn
  Orlando Airport
Tampa
  Airport
  Westshore

Georgia
Atlanta
  Airport

Downtown
Interstate North
Perimeter Center

Hawaii
Maui Resort

Illinois
Chicago area
  Downtown
  Oak Brook
  O'Hare
  Schaumburg
  Lincolnshire Resort

Indiana
Fort Wayne
Indianapolis
South Bend

Iowa
Des Moines

Kentucky
Lexington
  Griffin Gate Resort
Louisville/Clarksville

Louisiana
New Orleans

Maryland
Baltimore
  Hunt Valley Inn

Massachusetts
Boston
  Burlington
  Long Wharf
  Newton
Springfield
Worcester

Michigan
Ann Arbor
Grand Rapids

Minnesota
Minneapolis

Missouri
Kansas City
Osage Beach
  Tan-Tar-A Resort
St. Louis
  Airport
  Pavilion

Nebraska
Omaha

New Jersey
Saddle Brook
Somerset

New Mexico
Albuquerque

New York
Buffalo
New York City area
  Essex House
  LaGuardia
  Nassau, Long Island
  Westchester
Rochester
  Airport
  Thruway
Syracuse

North Carolina
Charlotte
Greensboro
Raleigh

Ohio
Cincinnati
Cleveland
  Airport
  East
Columbus
  East
  North
Dayton

Oklahoma
Tulsa

Oregon
Portland

Pennsylvania
Harrisburg
Philadelphia
  Airport
  City Line
Pittsburgh
  Greentree
  Monroeville

Rhode Island
Providence

South Carolina
Charleston
Columbia
Hilton Head Resort

Tennessee
Nashville

Texas
Austin
Dallas
  Airport
  Market Center
  Park Central
  Quorum
El Paso
Galveston
  Hotel Galvez
Houston
  Airport
  Astrodome
  Brookhollow
  Galleria
  Greenspoint
San Antonio
  Downtown
  North

Utah
Salt Lake City

Virginia
Blacksburg

Washington
Seattle
  Sea-Tac Airport

Washington, D.C. area
  Bethesda
  Crystal City
  Crystal Gateway
  Dulles
  Gaithersburg
  Key Bridge
  Twin Bridges
  Tysons Corner
  Washington, D.C.

West Virginia
Charleston‾

Wisconsin
Milwaukee

International

Egypt
Cairo

Greece
Athens

Jordan
Amman

Kuwait
Kuwait City

639

FIGURE C23.4   MARRIOTT LOCATIONS (*CONTINUED*)

Mexico	Epcot Resort '86	*Virginia*	*Florida*
Acapulco	Fort Lauderdale	Richmond '84	Fort Lauderdale (2)
Paraiso	Beach Resort '85	Roanoke '84	Miami (5)
The Netherlands	*Georgia*	*Washington, D.C.*	Orlando
Amsterdam	Atlanta	National Place '84	Tampa
Panama	Marriott Marquis '85		West Palm Beach
Panama City	*Kansas*	**CONTRACT FOOD**	*Georgia*
Saudi Arabia	Overland Park '84	**SERVICES**	Atlanta (2)
Dhahran	*Massachusetts*	**Airline Catering**	*Hawaii*
Jeddah	Boston	**U.S. Flight Kitchens**	Hilo
Riyadh	Copley Place '84	*Alaska*	Honolulu
Khurais	*New Jersey*	Anchorage	*Illinois*
Riyadh	Newark Airport '84	*Arizona*	Chicago (2)
West Indies	*New York*	Phoenix	*Louisiana*
Barbados	New York City	*California*	New Orleans
Sam Lord's Castle Resort	Marriott Marquis	Los Angeles (2)	*Maryland*
Future Hotels	*North Carolina*	Ontario	Baltimore (2)
Colorado	Charlotte '84	San Diego	*Massachusetts*
Denver	*Texas*	San Francisco (2)	Boston (2)
West '84	Houston	San Jose	*Michigan*
Florida	Medical Center '84	*Colorado*	Detroit
Orlando	Town & Country '85	Denver	

Cruise Lines

Marriott also owns, through Oceanic Sun Line Shipping Company, two cruise ships which contain 490 rooms and a 45% interest in a third ship with a capacity of 650. All three ships operate under the Greek flag and sail the Aegean and Mediterranean from April to November and the Caribbean from December to March. The cuise business has had its ups and downs, and Marrriott learned that operating a cruise ship was not the same as operating a hotel. The company had some large losses in the cruise business due to the Greek-Turkish War on Cyprus in 1975.

Competition

Marriott considers its competition from other hotels, whether independent or chain-affiliated, to be strong. The hotel industry expects that demand will continue to exceed supply through 1986 due to high construction costs and limited capital. However, Fred Malek, head of the hotel group, exclaimed:

We can't maintain our rate of room growth at 20%. We see a compound growth of 16 to 17% for the next three years. But beyond 1986, the markets will be fully supplied and our growth rate would decline to 10 to 12%.[9]

Thus far, Marriott has stayed away from casinos, while competitors have flocked to Atlantic City. Bill Marriott, Jr., a Mormon, thinks "gambling is a depressing business."

FIGURE C23.5 MARRIOTT CORPORATION AND SUBSIDIARIES CONSOLIDATED INCOME, FISCAL YEARS ENDED DEC. 31, 1982, JAN. 1, 1982, AND JAN. 2, 1981
(In $1000s Except per Share Amounts)

	1982	1981	1980
Sales:			
Hotels	$1,091,673	$ 860,134	$ 690,038
Contract food services	819,824	599,050	529,768
Restaurants	547,403	446,475	414,086
Theme parks	82,453	94,655	84,833
Total sales	2,541,353	2,000,314	1,718,725
Operating income:			
Hotels	132,648	117,561	106,832
Contract food services	51,006	45,552	39,875
Restaurants	48,492	38,533	29,697
Theme parks	20,004	17,714	16,630
Total operating income	252,150	219,360	193,034
Interest expense, net	66,666	52,024	46,820
Corporate expenses	31,801	28,307	26,126
Income before income taxes	153,683	139,029	120,088
Provision for income taxes	59,341	52,893	48,058
Net income	$ 94,342	$ 86,136	$ 72,030
Earnings per share			
Primary	$ 3.46	$ 3.21	$ 2.61
Fully diluted	$ 3.44	$ 3.20	$ 2.60

He had to talk his father into serving alcohol at Marriott hotels back in 1961. He has indicated, however, a willingness to enter the gambling-hotel business if competition pressure so dictates.

Nevertheless, Marriott has consistently outperformed competitors. Marriott has defied recession by enjoying steadily rising operating income. Its major competitors, such as Hyatt, Sheraton, Hilton, Westin, and Holiday Inns, have not had similar results. While Marriott increased its operating income through the 1981 recession, operating income of all the others (excluding their casino hotels) declined (see Figure C23.5). Indeed, Marriott makes more money from fewer rooms than Hilton, and it is approaching Holiday Inns. In 1982, Marriott made in excess of $132 million with around 50,000 rooms, while Hilton made around $90 million with approximately 75,000 rooms and Holiday Inns made $150 million with over 300,000 rooms. However, with casinos, Hilton and Holiday Inns made an additional $52.2 million and $74.6 million, respectively, in 1982.

Marquis and Courtyard . . . A New Direction?

In February 1984, Bill Eggbeer, vice president for Business Development, stated, "We are not going after all hotel markets, . . . the Marquis represents a different thrust in that we have not had too many large convention hotels. We sensed a need for them in large cities and felt that our strong position in selling group business was an advantage.''[10] Thus far, the company has Marquis-type hotels in Orlando and one in Copley Plaza in Boston and another in the Yerba Buena development of San Francisco.

"The Courtyard by Marriott," Mr. Eggbeer declared, "reflects a careful, intensive analysis of the hotel business." A decision was based on extensive market research which showed that the "moderate-priced segment offered profit potential and that the established competition had become outmoded." The findings were that this segment had a need for a comfortable, attractive room with more room to work (larger desk) and a simple restaurant with straightforward food. Marriott took these findings and developed the Courtyard concept. Mr. Eggbeer said that both moves, Marquis and Courtyard, had been "pretty specifically targeted."

CONTRACT FOOD SERVICES

The trucks bearing the Marriott name which pull up to airplanes dispense carefully prepared quality food for over 100 airlines from more than 75 flight kitchens in over 43 airports throughout the world. The food is prepared according to airline specifications.

The company engages in licensing agreements with airport facilities and often leases land from the airport for the flight kitchens. The agreements are subject to cancelation within 30 days' notice, and some airlines have decided to curtail meal service.

In the past the air traffic controllers' strike had negative effects. Deregulation has pushed some airlines into difficult situations. Eastern Airlines, a Marriott In-Flight customer, for example, was experiencing difficulties in 1984.

Food Service Management

The FSM division provides food service and catering management to businesses for their cafeteria and executive dining rooms. Hospital and college food service management is also provided. In addition, the division provides cleaning services to some clients and also has a consulting business relating to food service management.

Terminal and Highway Restaurants

The company operates 66 terminal concessions at airports throughout the United States, the Caribbean, and Saudi Arabia and a terminal restaurant at Union Station in Washington, D.C. These facilities include restaurants, cafeterias, snack bars, and gift shops and typically provide around-the-clock food service to travelers. As a result of the Host International acquisition, 37 airport-terminal food service operations and 16 gift shops at locations other than airport terminals were added to this division in 1982. The company also operates 14 highway restaurants on the New Jersey and Delaware turnpikes under contracts with the turnpike authorities.

RESTAURANTS

At the beginning of 1982, the company included 549 company-operated and 1083 franchised units serving food in 46 states, Japan, and Canada. The majority of the division is composed of Roy Rogers family restaurants and Big Boy restaurants. Marriott is the franchisor of Big Boy.

Roy Rogers has a regional leadership position in the Northeast. In 1982, the company spent $300 million acquiring Gino's and Host International. Many of Gino's restaurants (175) were converted to Roy Rogers restaurants.

Big Boy is the largest coffee-shop franchise network. The intent of the company is to strengthen what is now a loose network and thereby take advantage of economies of scale.

Part of the Gino's acquisition was sold because it did not fit Marriott expansion plans. Recently, Marriott became a franchisor of Popeye's Fried Chicken.

With the acquisition of Host International, Marriott entered the specialty restaurant business. The company intends to expand the Charlie Brown's and Casa Maria dinner-house themes "opportunistically," moving from a West Coast base to an East Coast expansion.

THEME PARKS

In 1984, Marriott was completing sale of its regional Great America theme parks. The company was running into trouble regarding the sale of its Santa Clara theme park. The Cas Development Corporation had paid Marriott $10 million in 1983 for an option to buy the 137-acre amusement park for $86.5 million by March 31, 1984. In January, the City of Santa Clara agreed to buy the park for $101 million. The Cas Development Company therefore sued Marriott for damages, saying that although Marriott had obtained permission from the developers to give the city a chance to buy the park, the company had agreed not to solicit an offer. Cas, in February 1984, claimed that Marriott sought an offer from the city and used their agreement to raise the price. Marriott claimed the developers understood that the agreement was subordinated to the city's rights.

The parks have done well, attracting a daily capacity of over 40,000 people in both California and Illinois, and have been a valuable source of cash flow since opening. However, no new theme parks are planned.

OBJECTIVES OF THE MARRIOTT CORPORATION

Mr. Bill Eggbeer, director of corporate planning, stated, "Our objective is to be the premier company in the lodging, food service, and related areas business . . . the related areas evolve as we move ahead."[11] (See Figure C23.6.) Basically, Marriott has always been a growth company, and therefore the major element of its strategy is to grow in established businesses through policies such as expanding the hotel group or adding either more restaurants or more flight kitchens. Also, the company wishes to develop internally its "close in skills" of managing the hospitality and service businesses.

Marriott will acquire companies but only when they add "real economic value." The company does not wish to have a "diverse portfolio" or "to acquire for acquisition's sake."

According to Mr. Eggbeer, the company has had an average growth of 24% in the last 5 years. The company's objective was to grow at 20% in earnings per share and at 20% in return of equity for the next 5 years. Mr. Eggbeer explained that there occurs a point "when a company can't grow at 20% and we do not intend to force that growth. If we can't do it we'll just roll back those objectives because we are not going to grow in marginal businesses."[12]

FIGURE C23.6 LODGING, FOOD SERVICE, AND RELATED AREAS BUSINESS

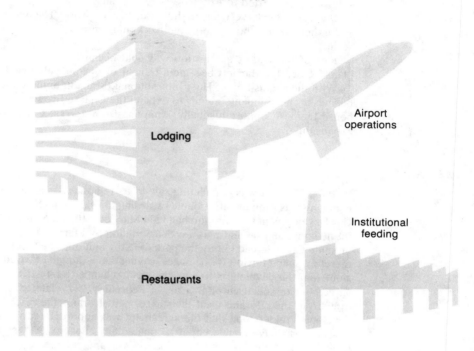

Mission

To assist senior management in building and strengthening the competitive strengths and profitability of Marriott's business portfolio

Corporate planning at Marriott:

Project- vs. process-oriented

Mix of resources
  Outside vs. inside
  Staff and line

Focus on basic strategic issues
  Customer
  Competitors
  Costs

Arrive at comprehensive program for each business
  Investment
  Pricing policy
  Product/service offerings
  Cost management
  Realistic financial expectations

STRATEGIC PLANNING AT MARRIOTT

In February 1984, Bill Eggbeer was 1 week away from being promoted to vice president, Business Development, or as he jokingly put it, "the product champion." Mr. Eggbeer explained that strategic planning was both a top-down and bottom-up process at Marriott. As he explained, the corporate office sets the objectives and major strategies and then the specific strategies are arrived at by the business groups through an annual planning process.

Each separate business develops its own objectives. And, as Mr. Eggbeer explained, although Marriott is a growth company, the business need not choose a growth strategy. "We have divisions that don't grow 20% usually because they already have a leading market share."

The individual SBUs (strategic business units) develop plans which are then reviewed at the corporate level. Sometimes they are returned from the corporate level for revisions, but "the meat and potatoes" of the plans are done by the SBUs. (See Figure C23.7.)

Planning Structure

Strategic planning really began at Marriott in 1975 when Mr. Gary Wilson, then treasurer, got the company into strategic planning by hiring half a dozen key people, including a strategic planner from McKinsey & Co.

In 1984, the planning structure was undergoing some decentralization changes. Up to that time there had been a vice president of Corporate Planning and three directors. The three directors concentrated on new business development and restaurants, and a "utility" person handled everything else. In 1984, Mr. Eggbeer explained that each

FIGURE C23.7 STRATEGIC PLANNING AT MARRIOTT

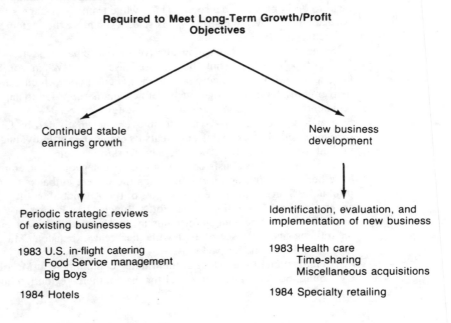

Required to Meet Long-Term Growth/Profit Objectives

Continued stable earnings growth

New business development

Periodic strategic reviews of existing businesses

1983 U.S. in-flight catering
Food Service management
Big Boys

1984 Hotels

Identification, evaluation, and implementation of new business

1983 Health care
Time-sharing
Miscellaneous acquisitions

1984 Specialty retailing

major group (hotels, in flight, and restaurants) now has a vice president of Business Planning. In addition, there is a vice president of Business Planning at the corporate level who deals with "major ad hoc planning efforts that don't fit neatly into one of the groups and has primary responsibility for new business and acquisitions." Over all of them is the senior vice president of Planning, who coordinates all planning at Marriott. Planning at Marriott also serves a coordinated and facilitating role for projects taken on by ad hoc task forces.

Certain aspects of strategic planning at Marriott were necessarily kept secret during the development stages. Mr. Eggbeer indicated that he had spent most of 1983 working on a secret new business venture and would now head the venture team for that project. Mr. Eggbeer had worked with Phil Kotler, the famed marketing/management professor, while earning a masters degree in management and marketing from Northwestern University and, before joining Marriott, had been doing strategic planning consulting for Booz, Allen & Hamilton.

HUMAN RESOURCES AND STRATEGY

Marriott believes relations with its managers and employees are good. The company had 109,200 full-time employees at the end of 1982. Only about 10% of Marriott employees are unionized, and those employees are from acquired businesses. Marriott has had many run-ins with unions and had an especially tough time with the opening of its hotel in downtown Chicago. The company was one of the first in the hospitality industry to engage in annual employee surveys, in which employees comment confidentially about working conditions, supervisors, and so on.

The company has been a proponent of a more participative style of management, but it is highly centralized at the same time. It also has tight controls, policies, and procedures. There are standard operating procedures for every facet of operations. Job task manuals have each job broken down. There are, for example, 66 steps for a hotel maid to do in making up a room. Thus, while training managers to be consultative and participative, J. W. Marriott, Jr., has said, "The more the system works like the Army, the better."

Some would say that a consultative or participative style is not consistent with "Army-type" systems, but Bill Eggbeer disagrees. "When you have a workforce as large as we do, with as many face to face encounters with customers, the only way to deliver consistently is to rigorously define what is supposed to happen . . . without that regimentation there is no consistency," states Eggbeer.[13]

Marriott's policies vis-à-vis its employees are motivated by fairness. The company recognizes employees' rights and treats its employees as individuals. This, Marriott has proved, can be done in a "well-defined working system."

The company has consistently believed in management and employee training. There have been times during recessions when there were cutbacks on management training programs. Stan Bruns, general manager of the Atlanta Marriott, after returning from a general manager's meeting at Marriott's Rancho Las Palmas in Palm Springs, California, indicated that he thought the company had learned its lesson and would not cut back on training again. It seems that with the great expansion, Marriott had run out of managers due to the cutbacks.

An indication of the extent of the training commitment at Marriott was given by Mr. Cy Young, head of hotel personnel for the southern region (20 hotels). The company, now divided into 10 world regions, would soon split into 12. Each region would have a head of training, who would have a direct reporting relationship with the regional director of operations and a dotted-line relationship with headquarters' human resource development office. Mr. Young explained why this was so necessary for Marriott: "When I joined the company we only had 22 hotels, now we have over 120. I have opened 23 hotels myself since being with the company and now am responsible for almost as many hotels as we had when I joined the company."[14]

In 1937, Bill Marriott, Sr., set the tone for the way Marriott employees would be treated and this policy has continued to the present day. Robert O'Brien, in a biography of Bill Marriott, writes,

Employees were trained in company programs and policies, were encouraged to work for promotion, and knew by example that Bill would always promote from within rather than seek outside, and when a curber was promoted to supervisor, or a supervisor to an assistant managership, Bill wrote him a personal letter of appreciation and congratulations. When an employee's relative died, he wrote a personal letter of condolence. When the Connecticut Avenue curber who won the Washington city public links golf championship could not afford the trip to New York to play in the regional championship, Bill paid his way. When the black chef in the Philadelphia store needed $200 for an eye operation, Bill paid it. Bill and Allie instituted the custom of giving every employee a Christmas present of a day's pay for every year of service. When an employee completed five years of service, he or she received a gift from the company—a radio, a refrigerator, an electric stove, the longer the service, the bigger the gift.[15]

The executive officers of the company are:

J. Willard Marriott	Chairman of the Board
J. W. Marriott, Jr.	President and Chief Executive Officer
(J. W. Marriott, Jr., and Richard E. Marriott are sons of J. Willard Marriott)	
Frederic V. Malek	Executive Vice President
Gary L. Wilson	Executive Vice President and Chief Financial Officer
Francis W. Cash	Senior Vice President
Sterling D. Colton	Senior Vice President and General Counsel
James E. Durbin	President, Marriott Hotels
Clifford J. Ehrlich	Senior Vice President, Personnel and Organization Development
Richard E. Marriott	Group Vice President—Corporate
Howard E. Varner	Group President, Host
Stephen F. Bollenbach	Vice President and Treasurer
William J. Shaw	Vice President and Corporate Controller
Robert E. Koehler	Senior Vice President and Corporate Secretary

FINANCIAL RESOURCES AND STRATEGY

History

In the last 10 years Marriott changed the way it structured its capital base. This resulted in a doubling of the return on capital between 1975 and 1980, and the return has remained healthy into 1984. Spearheading the financial changes was Mr. Gary Wilson, chief financial officer, who explains, "We made a capital-intensive business into a non-capital-intensive one."[16]

The strategic steps involved in the change were:

1 *Liquidation of $100 million of Marriott's marginal assets.* The assets included land, 38 restaurants, 16 dinner houses, a security business, two European flight kitchens, and a travel wholesale division. The funds were used to "pay down" debt.

2 *Installation of an inflation-adjusted system for measuring returns on future investments.* A higher ROI was required for new investments.

3 *Transition from hotel ownership to management contractors.* This enabled faster growth. Insurance companies bought hotels and contracted the management out to Marriott.

Wilson also changed financing from the use of traditional mortgages based on secured debt to the use of unsecured revolving credit with major banks. Wilson states that Marriott "is a major diversified company and major companies don't borrow with secured debt."

By 1979, the above strategies had worked so well that Marriott had cash-flow riches or, from an alternative perspective, an unused debt capacity. "We have a tremendous cash-flow machine here today," said Wilson in 1980. In order to utilize excess cash effectively, Wilson was instructed by Marriott's board of directors to make a $250 million investment. Nothing looked good, so the company decided its own stock was the best "buy" around. So Marriott put its "money where our mouth is" and made the second-biggest buy-back in U.S. corporate history, purchasing $250 million of its own stock on the open market.

The stock repurchase "recapitalized" the company by improving its return on equity, raised its earnings per share, but also increased its debt ratio to 70% and net interest coverage to 4 times, one under the company's target. Wilson commented, "My feeling is when there is a good opportunity to invest you should. You can always bring the debt down."

1984

Earnings through the third quarter of 1983 were up to 22.7% to $36.7 million. Indeed, earnings and ROE performance place Marriott among the top 20% of Standard and Poor's 500 firms. The 1982 annual report states, "Marriott plans to continue performing at these levels through the 1980s."

Financing will continue to be done by the new syndication process. The Potomac Hotel Limited Partnership (PHLP) eliminated Marriott's capital investment in 11 hotels with a total cost of $365 million. The syndication will earn Marriott long-term management fees, and Marriott's position as a general partner will derive substantial tax benefits.

Marriott's growth in the future will be based on target debt levels based on cash-flow coverage of four times interest expense. Lenders require this ratio to approve debt financing at prime rates.

Marriott has maintained coverage of debt at its targeted levels despite rapid growth. The growth is financed both by internal cash flow and by hotel dispositions.

The company's high cash flow and policy of management contracts rather than ownership of hotels (less capital-intensive basis) "allows Marriott to expand at 20% annually without commensurate capital requirements." In 1984, Marriott did have a good record of reinvesting its cash flow in businesses with high returns and had confidence in planned profit growth of at least 20% through the mid-1980s.

THE COMPANY'S CHALLENGES

Marriott faced many challenges in 1984, some of which were:

1 Would the company's late entry into the super-size architecturally different convention hotel in expensive cities like New York prove profitable?

2 Would the Courtyard concept be successful enough to warrant expansion after test marketing? And, even if successful, could the company obtain the financial support to go into head-on competition with franchised giants such as Holiday Inns and Ramada Inn? Should Marriott franchise the Courtyards or finance and control the expansion through management contracts derived from syndications?

3 Could the company expect to be a 20% growth company for the coming 5- to 7-year plan when the hotel, restaurant, and airline businesses are becoming overbuilt in many markets and extremely competitive?

REFERENCES

1 Thomas Moore, "Marriott Grabs for More Room," *Fortune*, Oct. 31, 1983, pp. 106–122.
2 Ibid.
3 Christopher H. Lovelock, "Marriott's Rancho Las Palmas Resort," in *Services Marketing*, Prentice-Hall, Englewood Cliffs, N.J., 1984.
4 Moore, op. cit., p. 118.
5 Robert O'Brien, *Marriott: The J. Willard Marriott Story*, Deseret, Salt Lake City, Utah, 1977, p. 180.
6 Ibid.
7 Lisa Bergson, "The CFO as a Corporate Strategist," *Institutional Investor*, September 1980, pp. 181–188.
8 Moore, op. cit., p. 112.
9 Ibid.
10 William Eggbeer, telephone interview with case writer, February 1984.
11 Ibid.
12 Ibid.
13 Ibid.
14 Cy Young, telephone interview with case writer, February 1984.
15 O'Brien, op. cit.
16 Bergson, op. cit., p. 181.

NEW COKE: COCA-COLA'S RESPONSE TO THE PEPSI CHALLENGE

Prepared by Patricia P. McDougall, Georgia State University,
and Manfred Huebner, Jon Morris, and Patricia A. Timms.

THE ANNOUNCEMENT OF THE NEW TASTE—APRIL 23, 1985

> Shortly before 11:00 a.m. the doors of the Vivian Beaumont Theater at Lincoln Center opened to two hundred newspaper, magazine, and TV reporters. The stage was aglow with red. Three huge screens, each solid red and inscribed with the company logo, rose behind the podium and a table draped in red. The lights were low; the music began. "We are. We will always be. Coca-Cola. All-American history." As the patriotic song filled the theater, slides of Americana flashed on the center screen—families and kids, Eisenhower and JFK, the Grand Canyon and wheat fields, the Beatles and Bruce Springsteen, cowboys, athletes, the Statue of Liberty—and interspersed throughout, old commercials for Coke. No political candidate would have gotten away with such patrioteering without howls of protest, and the members of the press weren't seduced by the hype. (Thomas Oliver, *The Real Coke, The Real Story*, New York: Random House, 1986, p. 131.)

Chairman Goizueta came to the podium and boasted "the best has been made even better. Some may choose to call this the boldest single marketing move in the history of the packaged-goods business. We simply call it the surest move ever made because the taste of Coke was shaped by the taste of the consumer."

New Coke was launched. The American people reacted immediately and violently. After three months of vigorous, unrelenting protest, stunned and humbled Coca-Cola executives called a second press conference to tell the American people that Coke was sorry. The corporate giant announced that it would reissue the original Coca-Cola formula as Coke Classic and asked the forgiveness of the American people.

Huebner, Morris, and Timms researched Coca-Cola as an MBA project. © Patricia P. McDougall. Used by permission.

How could a $7 billion corporation with a sterling track record commit such a blunder? How could this giant international company so totally misread consumers' feelings? How dare they tamper with an American institution? Or, did Coca-Cola orchestrate the entire affair as a huge publicity stunt to get millions of dollars of free advertising for its new Coke and boost the sales of the old one?

INDUSTRY ANALYSIS

The soft drink industry is dominated by two main competitors, the Coca-Cola Company and Pepsi-Cola. Both depend on a network of bottling companies to distribute their bottled soft drinks. Coca-Cola uses its own network of wholesalers for their fountain syrup distribution, while Pepsi distributes its fountain syrup through its bottlers.

A principal concern of the industry is long-term growth potential, and how this growth is affected by changing population demographics, per capita saturation, and changing consumer preferences. Changes in these variables have caused changes in the channels of distribution which are likely to change the cost structure of the industry.

Industry Growth

Growth in the soft drink industry can be increased by consumption per individual and by population growth. Total consumption in the industry over the last two decades has risen 6.5 percent compound annual growth rate. Since the population of the United States is growing at only about 2 percent a year, the strongest potential for growth in the U.S. industry is through per capita growth. As reflected in Figure C24.1, per capital growth has risen steadily from about 16.2 gallons per year in 1965 to where Americans now drink over 40 gallons of soft drinks per year.

Industry analysts view the aging population and the approaching of the point of saturation in per capita consumption as the two main issues influencing the prospects for future growth. Some analysts have argued that these factors may even reverse the industry's historical growth rate.

The 15- to 24- and 25- to 34-year-old age groups have been the heaviest pop drinkers. Figure C24.2 graphs the age composition trends of the U.S. population. These heavy consumption groups are becoming a smaller percentage of the total population, while older groups which have historically consumed fewer soft drinks will grow rapidly. The real question is whether the present younger-age, heavy consumption groups will retain their consumption patterns as they get older.

Optimistic analysts cite industry data such as Figure C24.3, which shows soft drink consumption for three sample periods. While the chart does show that older people drink less than younger people at any given time period, people are increasing their consumption even as they age. For example, today's 50 to 59 group consumed more in 1980 than when they were 40 to 49 years old in 1970, and 10 years earlier when they were 30 to 39 years old in 1960.

Perhaps the more critical issue is the fear that the market may be approaching the point of saturation in per capita consumption. Just how many gallons of soft drinks can Americans drink per year? A tapering off of the growth rate in per capita consumption appears to have already started. From 1965 to 1971 the annual growth rate was 6.9 percent, but the following 1971 to 1977 period shows a drop to 5.4 percent, and another

FIGURE C24.1 GROWTH IN PER CAPITA CONSUMPTION OF SOFT DRINKS, 1965–1990

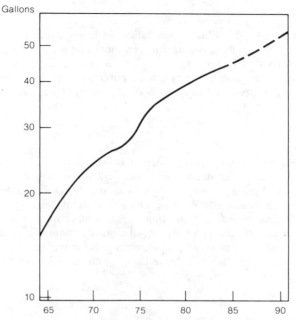

Sources: NSDA Sales Survey Beverage Marketing Corporation, The Boston Consulting Group.

FIGURE C24.2 PROJECTED AGE COMPOSITION OF U.S. POPULATION

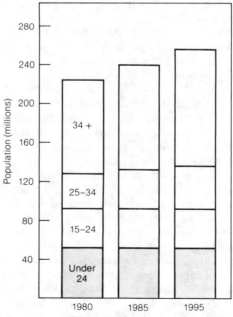

Source: Predicasts Composite Forecasts.

FIGURE C24.3   SOFT DRINK PER CAPITA BY AGE GROUP
(8-Ounce Servings)

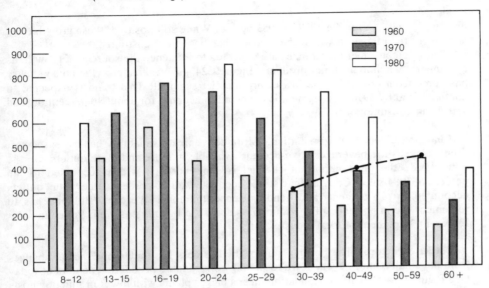

Source: Coca-Cola U.S.A. (*Beverage Digest,* August 17, 1984).

FIGURE C24.4   GROWTH OF DIET VERSUS NATURALLY SWEETENED SOFT DRINKS

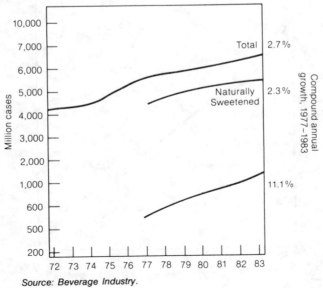

Source: *Beverage Industry.*

drop to 3.7 percent for the 1977 to 1983 period. While still positive, these growth rates are slower than those to which the industry has become accustomed.

Changing consumer preferences are expected to influence the sources of growth, as consumers switch to healthier products. Figure C24.4 shows that growth in the industry has come from growth in the low-calorie or diet segment. This trend is expected to continue, and by 1990 this segment is expected to account for about 40 percent of total soft drink consumption.

Changing Channels of Distribution More convenient availability has increased soft drink sales, as the beverages have become available in more and more outlets. On the bottled side the most important channel is supermarkets, which accounted for 46 percent of 1984 sales. Convenience stores accounted for 20 percent, other retail outlets accounted for 17 percent, and vending accounted for 17 percent. But one has to remember the importance of the fountain side of the business as well. Fountain sales represent 33 percent of total industry sales.

Bottler Structure The bottling side of the business has undergone radical changes from the small plant in every town to the big consolidated production centers of today (see Figure C24.5). This consolidation means bigger plants with lower production costs that can compete more aggressively in the marketplace. Substantial scale economies exist as both labor and factory expenses decrease as size increases. All this translates into lower cost per case as seen in Figure C24.6. This cost savings has helped offset the increase in cost due to the proliferation in brands.

FIGURE C24.5   CONSOLIDATION OF U.S. SOFT DRINK PRODUCTION FACILITIES

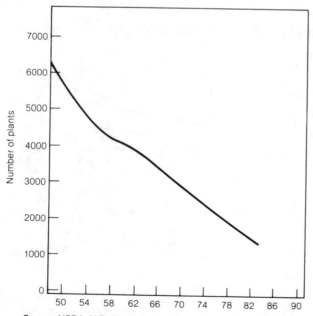

Source: NSDA. U.S. County Business Patterns. BCG Estimates.

FIGURE C24.6   IMPACT OF HISTORICALLY INCREASING PLANT SIZE ON AVERAGE SOFT DRINK
BOTTLING COSTS

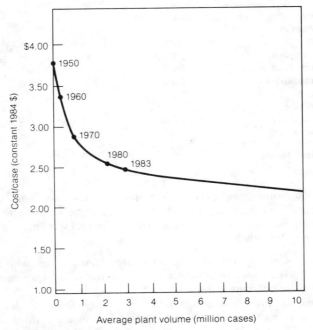

Source: The Boston Consulting Group.

Product Introductions   Starting in the 1980s there has been a barrage of new products or product reformulation changes. There have been few entrants into the sugared cola category, as most product introductions have principally occurred in such segments as diet colas, lemon-lime, and juice-containing drinks.

Competitors   The two major competitors—Coke and Pepsi—controlled 68 percent of the market in 1985. Most significant of the smaller competitors were Dr. Pepper, 7-Up, and Royal Crown. The top 10 soft drink companies and each's corporate market share is given in Figure C24.7.

As reflected in Figures C24.8 and C24.9, Coke and Pepsi dominate the top soft drink brands. A comparison of the top 10 brands for 1984 (Figure C24.8) and 1985 (Figure C24.9) offers many insights into the nature of competition in the soft drink industry. While Coke ranked as number 1 in 1984, the division of Coke sales between new Coke and Coke Classic allowed Pepsi to capture the number 1 spot in 1985, although Pepsi's market share fell from 18.1 percent in 1984 to 17.3 percent in 1985. The 1985 combined market share of new Coke and Coke Classic was 23.3 percent. While Coke occupied only 2 of the top 5 spots in 1984, the introduction of new Coke allowed the company to seize 3 of the top 5 spots in 1985. The phenomenal growth rates of Diet Coke and Diet Pepsi should also be noted.

FIGURE C24.7 TOP 10 SOFT DRINK COMPANIES IN 1985

Company	1985 Market share
1. Coca-Cola	38.8%
2. Pepsi-Cola	29.2%
3. 7-Up	5.9%
4. Dr. Pepper	5.1%
5. Royal Crown	3.1%
6. Canada Dry	2.0%
7. Crush	1.2%
8. A & W	1.1%
9. Sunkist	1.0%
10. Shasta	1.0%

Source: Beverage Digest.

Although marketing very similar products, the two giants of the industry differ significantly in their strengths and weaknesses. Coke's major strengths and weaknesses are first detailed, followed by Pepsi's strengths and weaknesses.

Coke's strengths:

1 Coca-Cola has a strong lead in the international arena, with about 60 percent of its profits derived from overseas soft drink operations. Pepsi, its nearest competitor, is far behind in international sales.

2 Decentralized management allows Coke to make quick decisions in the domestic international markets. Coke's domestic operations are divided into bottling and fountain. Bottling is divided into 5 selling areas with all responsibility at the area level.

3 Coke has a well-diversified product line and is the top seller in most of the flavor segments—brand Coca-Cola, Coca-Cola Classic, Diet Coke, Sprite, Caffeine-Free Diet Coke, and Minute Maid. These products allow the Coca-Cola system to better segment the market and better position itself in the different segments.

FIGURE C24.8 TOP 10 SOFT DRINK BRANDS FOR 1984

Brand	1984 Market share	1984 Brand growth
1. Coke	24.8%	+3.3%
2. Pepsi	18.1%	+5.0%
3. Diet Coke	6.9%	+60.0%
4. 7-Up	5.3%	+1.0%
5. Dr. Pepper	4.7%	+8.0%
6. Sprite	3.3%	+27.0%
7. Diet Pepsi	3.1%	+31.0%
8. Mountain Dew	2.8%	+3.5%
9. Royal Crown	2.2%	−5.0%
10. Tab	2.1%	−24.0%
Top 10	73.3%	+8.0%
Other brands	26.7%	+1.0%

Source: Beverage World.

FIGURE C24.9   TOP 10 SOFT DRINK BRANDS FOR 1985

Brand	1985 Market share	1985 Brand growth
1. Pepsi	17.6%	+5.1%
2. Coca-Cola Classic	17.3%	−25.0%
3. Diet Coke	8.0%	+26.0%
4. Coke	6.0%	—
5. Dr. Pepper	4.7%	+9.0%
6. 7-Up	4.6%	−7.0%
7. Diet Pepsi	3.6%	+25.0%
8. Sprite	3.4%	+10.3%
9. Mountain Dew	2.6%	+2.2%
10. Royal Crown	2.1%	+4.0%
Top 10	69.9%	+6.0%
Other brands	30.1%	+4.3%

Source: *Beverage World.*

4 Coke is the number 1 supplier of syrup for fountain sales. Coke is especially strong in sales to fast food restaurants. Their network of wholesalers is considered top notch.

Coke's weaknesses:

1 Much of the original bottler's contract which was developed in the early 1900s is still in effect today. Because the contract fixes the price of syrup, Coke has no control over the price. Despite some amendments, this contract still represents an obstacle to the company.

2 Many small bottlers lacking the economies of scale to compete in today's marketplace still exist in the system.

3 The extensive product line could be considered a weakness as well as a strength, as more products and more fragmentation result in a higher cost of production, inventory, and distribution. In addition, cannibalizing existing products has become an important factor.

Pepsi's strengths:

1 Pepsi-Cola has strong, concentrated bottlers, which because of their large size have good economies of scale and are thus low-cost producers.

2 Pepsi has more flexibility in its pricing policies since the company is not hampered by a fixed price contract with its bottlers.

3 The lack of diversity in its product line helps control production costs, and advertising can be more focused. Only recently, with the introduction of Slice, did Pepsi enter the flavored category.

4 By acquiring Pizza Hut, Kentucky Fried Chicken, and Taco Bell, Pepsi has become the largest fast food restaurant chain in America. Ownership of these outlets secures distribution for its fountain syrup.

5 Advertising has been the most effective in the industry. The use of superstars like Michael Jackson has heightened the Pepsi image and has resulted in a strong position in the youth segment of the market.

Pepsi's weaknesses:

1 Pepsi lacks substantial diversification into the international market. Most of its revenues come from domestic operations.

2 With only about 30 percent of its total revenue coming from soft drinks, management's attention may be diverted from this important aspect of the business.

3 Pepsi's weakness in the fountain side of the business is evident, with only a 20 percent share of the market. Pepsi lacks Coke's huge network for distribution and is trying to secure distribution by buying fast food restaurant chains.

4 Pepsi's diversification into fast food chains has made their existing syrup customer very unhappy. Wendy's recently switched to Coke because they view Pepsi as a competitor, not a supplier.

THE COCA-COLA COMPANY

As related by Thomas Oliver in *The Real Coke, The Real Story*, an Atlanta pharmacist registered a trademark for "French Wine Cola—Ideal Nerve and Tonic Stimulant" in 1885. The name for the brew was appropriate, as it is said to have contained cocaine, along with wine and a few other ingredients. After about a year, the formula was changed and the name was changed to Coca-Cola because it was thought that the two C's, written in the Spencerian script that was popular at the time, would look good in advertising. Coke was sold by traveling salesmen as a cure for hangovers and headaches.

Asa Candler bought the rights to Coca-Cola in 1889 and expanded the business by selling syrup to wholesalers, who in turn sold to drugstores. The syrup was mixed with carbonated water and served at soda fountains.

Later that year, two Tennessee businessmen purchased for $1.00 the right to bottle throughout nearly all of the United States. Feeling that drugstore fountain sales would predominate, Candler wanted no part of the expensive bottling operation. The two men promptly sold regional bottling rights to other businessmen in the South, and later in the rest of the country. By 1930 there were approximately 1,000 independent bottlers.

Ernest Woodruff purchased the Coca-Cola company in 1919 for $25 million. Woodruff was president of what was later to be known as the Trust Company of Georgia, the bank whose vault still guards the secret recipe for Coke. The formula was so secret that no more than three people at any time ever know the proper mixture of its ingredients.

By the 1920s the company was embroiled in legal battles against imitators and facing bankruptcy. Profits were falling, sugar prices were rapidly increasing, and because of the contract, syrup was sold to bottlers at the fixed cost set in 1899. Robert Woodruff, Ernest's son, was brought in as president in 1923 to restore morale and profits.

When Woodruff took control Coke was sold in the U.S., Canada, Cuba, and Puerto Rico, but was otherwise unknown around the world. Woodruff outlined a plan to test Coke in Europe, and when the board refused to grant approval, he proceeded in secrecy to establish a foreign sales department. Within 3 years the foreign department showed a profit.

During World War II Coke became a morale booster to the overseas troops. Initially the drink was shipped from a base in Iceland, but this became impractical as demand increased. In 1943, General Dwight Eisenhower requested that the War Department establish 10 bottling plants in North Africa and Italy. The War Department supplied the machinery and personnel, usually soldiers who had worked for Coca-Cola prior to the war. At the end of the war there were 64 worldwide plants which had been built at government expense. These were incorporated without cost into the company. By 1985 Coke was distributed to 155 countries and consumed more than 303 million times a day. Coke is as much a symbol of the U.S. as the Statue of Liberty. It is so strongly identified with the U.S. that when an ambassador is expelled for political reasons Coke is sometimes soon exiled as well.

Management

Past Players

Robert Woodruff—"The Boss." Robert Woodruff, known as "The Boss," became president of the Coca-Cola Company in 1923. In 1954 he "officially retired," but many felt he effectively controlled the company until his death in 1985. At the time of the announcement of the new Coke formula, it was speculated that management had waited for Woodruff's death to make the change. In fact, he endorsed the change.

J. Paul Austin—Chairman of the Board 1970–1981. Lingering a year beyond his expected retirement in 1980, he created an Office of the Chairman whose vice chairmen essentially operated the company on a day-to-day basis.

J. Lucian Smith—President and COO of The Coca-Cola Company 1976–1980. He was against the annual price cap on syrup. Disputes with bottlers over the escalating syrup costs pitted him against Austin and Keough.

Present Players

Roberto C. Goizueta—Chairman and CEO of The Coca-Cola Company. Goizueta joined Coca-Cola in 1961 after fleeing Cuba when Castro came to power. A chemist by training, Goizueta did not come up through the traditional marketing route.

Donald R. Keough—President and COO of The Coca-Cola Company. Keough was president of Coca-Cola USA, the domestic soft drink arm of The Coca-Cola Company, when the FTC challenged Coke in 1971, as well as in the late 1970s during confrontations with bottlers. He and Goizueta were considered the prime contenders as Austin's replacement.

Brian Dyson—President of Coca-Cola USA. In 1978 Dyson was lured by Keough from his native Argentina, where he worked for the international sector, to head up Coca-Cola USA. Dyson led the company's involvement in the refranchising efforts. He argued effectively that the success of the Coca-Cola company depended on the success of its bottlers.

Sergio Zyman—Senior Vice President of Marketing for Coca-Cola USA. Mexican-born Zyman defected from Pepsi-Cola in 1979. He has been vice president of bottler operations, director of fountain sales, and Keough's executive assistant. In September 1983, Zyman was selected to head Project Kansas—an experiment to explore the possibility of a reformulation of Coke.

Roy Stout—Director of Marketing Research. In 1979 Stout was given the first of several new colas to test. As early as 1976 Stout had compiled a top-secret report that showed leadership over Pepsi as no longer a given. Research by Stout's department forced management to consider that decline in market share might be related to taste. Stout was an active participant in Project Kansas.

The Beginnings of Trouble

In spite of an outwardly healthy image, behind-the-scenes troubles in the 1970s began to distract Coke executives from their primary mission. Beginning with the 1971 salvo fired by the FTC charging that the bottlers' contract restricted competition, to the fight with bottlers over the price of syrup, a dispute which eventually resulted with the chairman and the company president not speaking with each other, many say Coke executives just lost sight of the heart of the matter—selling Coke. Critics charge that Coke's personnel decisions began to reflect the good-old-boys' regime. Keough has been quoted as saying that compensation was awarded "not on performance, but perfect attendance."

Coke executives seemed to forget more and more that Coke was not a private company, but a public company responsible to its shareholders. Profits fell to a compound annual rate of only 7 percent between 1978 and 1981, and net income for 1980 increased a mere .5 percent.

Walls Down

In 1971, the FTC challenged Coke, charging that the bottlers' contracts granting territorial exclusivity violated antitrust laws by restricting competition. If the government prevailed, anyone could invade a bottler's territory. This concept was known as "walls down" at Coke headquarters. This would make a bottler's future uncertain, thus reducing the value of the franchise, with anarchy predicted to result. The bottlers' contract granted each bottler an exclusive right *in perpetuity* to bottle Coke in his area, and with the exception of soda fountains, no one else could sell Coke in that market, and the company could not refuse to sell them syrup.

An administrative law judge ruled in October 1975 that the bottlers' territorial exclusivity was not a violation of federal trade regulations, but 2½ years later the ruling was reversed and the FTC reinstituted the complaint. By 1978 little else was discussed at company headquarters. Long-range planning was prevented, the system Coke knew might not exist. Keough later complained that after he assumed office in 1974, the first 50 meetings he attended were legal briefings on the FTC battle. Admitting that he had made a mistake, Keough said, "I should have hired a roomful of lawyers and told them to deal with it and we could have gotten on with the business."

It was not until 1980 that the complaint was ruled in favor of Coca-Cola. The years of turmoil had caused the company to lose sight of its main objective.

Escalating Syrup Costs

Dating back to 1899, the original bottlers' contract set syrup at a fixed price. In 1921, the contract was modified to fix the price of syrup at the 1921 current price, subject to quarterly adjustments based on the price of sugar. Only the rising cost of sugar could be passed on to the bottler. This agreement worked well for 50 years, until the seventies when the spiraling costs of the other syrup ingredients made it barely possible for the company to make a profit on Coke. So once again, Coke found itself in conflict with the bottlers over modifying the contract.

Even within the company there was disagreement as to how the contract should be amended. Lucian Smith, the president and COO at the time, advocated a totally flexible price that would reflect future inflation, while others felt some accommodation to the bottlers was necessary and favored an annual cap on how much the company could raise the price of syrup.

As to be expected, the bottlers put up a fierce resistance to any amendment. Keough described the fight as like trying to talk someone out of a birthright as "Every bottler on his dying bed calls his son to his side, and speaking his last words says 'Don't you ever let them mess with that contract.'"

In the end Keough went around Smith and convinced Austin and Woodruff to favor an annual cap. The board of directors agreed soon after. As a result, Smith and Austin's relationship became so strained that the two highest-ranking executives of the company didn't even speak to each other. Because of his preoccupation with the syrup amendment at the expense of day-to-day business, Austin reduced Smith's power by his creation of an Office of the Chairman, in which seven executive vice presidents, in essence, assumed Smith's duties as COO. A slighted Smith resigned a year later.

Changes in Bottling—Franchise Ownerships

One of Dyson's first goals as the new head of Coca-Cola USA in 1978 was to alter the company's laissez-faire attitude toward changes in bottling-franchise ownerships. It had always been company policy not to get involved with franchise transfers. If a bottler decided to sell, Coca-Cola could not stop him from transferring the contract to a new owner who had all rights in perpetuity. Thus, the company had no real control over who was selling its products or how well the products were being sold. Dyson argued effectively that the Coca-Cola company should involve itself in franchise ownership since the owner's performance determined the company's performance.

So in 1979, the Washington, D.C., franchise was purchased by the managers of the franchise through a leveraged buyout structured by Keough and Dyson. Dyson's strategy was that each time a franchise came up for sale, Coca-Cola would either find a friendly buyer or purchase and later resell it. This would allow Coke to organize regional companies into larger distributorships that made more sense geographically.

The Pepsi Challenge

While Coca-Cola was absorbed in legal and internal battles, Pepsi had its eye on sales. In the 1960s Pepsi made a major change in their advertising strategy: they stopped talking about the product and started talking about the user. The 1963 "Pepsi Generation" advertising campaign captured the imagination of the baby boomers. It enhanced the image of Pepsi-Cola and anyone who chose to drink it.

Pepsi took the lead in 1975 supermarket sales and has led in every year since, except 1976. Supermarket sales are regarded as the freedom of choice segment, since in other segments the customer often has limited choice—he can buy only the brand that is offered.

Supermarket sales represent about a third of Coke's total market, with fountain sales and vending sales making up the other two-thirds. Since contracts with major fountain clients, such as McDonald's, are based on Coke's status as the number 1 cola, Coke felt it imperative to lead in all categories; otherwise, fountain clients might switch to Pepsi.

The "Pepsi Challenge" shook The Coca-Cola Company to its foundation. It all started in 1975 when Larry Smith was sent to Dallas to crack the market in Coke's heartland, the South. Pepsi was number 3 in Dallas, lagging behind Coke and the homebrew Dr. Pepper. Smith could not even entice a major grocery chain with an offer to finance a Pepsi promotion. Pepsi would pay the chain money and sell them Pepsi at a discount in exchange for newspaper ad promotion and prominent in-store displays. The chain was not interested. They didn't need Pepsi.

Coke had a 35 share, Dr. Pepper had 25, and Pepsi had 6. The nationwide Pepsi Generation theme wasn't working in Texas. Convinced that people were drinking Coke for its name, not its taste, Smith requested a custom-made advertising campaign for his market. Alan Pottasch, the advertising mastermind of the Pepsi-Cola Company, was opposed to local campaigns because they were always product-oriented and would interfere with his carefully built emphasis on the user rather than the beverage. If it succeeded in one area, bottlers in other areas would hear of it and want it for their territories, and a campaign that works in one place might not in another.

Putting his job on the line Smith hired the in-house advertising agency of the Southland Corporation's 7-Eleven convenience store chain to help him come up with a campaign. Field tests to determine how people felt about Pepsi gave consumers a choice between two unmarked colas and asked them which tasted better. Pepsi was chosen by most of the people. A couple of hundred taste tests gave a slim advantage to Pepsi, 52 to 48. In comparative advertising a valid test that demonstrates a preference, however slim the margin, gives a company the legal right to claim superiority.

Pepsi ran its Dallas TV commercial showing loyal Coke drinkers selecting Pepsi as the better-tasting drink of the two unmarked colas. Coke tried to disprove the claim, but found when they ran their own test that it wasn't false. Coke had never tested its soda against any competitive product. Coke's counteradvertising was unsuccessful; in fact, they played into Pepsi's hands, mentioning Pepsi in an ad for the first time. Pepsi's share quickly went from 6 to 14. The Challenge extended to Houston and moved to Los Angeles and by 1983 was spread across the country. Only Atlanta, Coke's headquarters, was spared the insult of the Challenge.

Both Coke and Pepsi now agree that Coke's sales were not significantly hurt by the Challenge. Pepsi's sales did increase, but the increased share came from the shares of other soft drink producers, as the beverage industry developed more and more into a two-horse race.

Wounded pride led to an obsession with Coke's image as number 1. What concerned Coke the most was the loss in share in the food store segment of the business. Even when Coke outspent Pepsi in advertising, Pepsi still maintained their share leadership in supermarket sales (see Figure C24.10 for a comparison of Coke and Pepsi shares in food stores). Pepsi used its lead in supermarket sales to claim superiority over Coke.

These two giants do not fight for market share for the fun of it. One point of overall market share represents $250 million in sales at the wholesale level. So, one can easily see why Coca-Cola management was concerned about Coke's poor share performance in the supermarket segment.

Coke's Market Research and Project Kansas

In the mid-1950s Coke was outselling Pepsi by a 2 to 1 margin; however, this wide margin was gradually narrowed by Pepsi long before the introduction of new Coke. As early as 1976, Coke's marketing department compiled a top-secret report that showed leadership over Pepsi was no longer a given. The report was largely ignored by executives.

FIGURE C24.10   SHARE OF SUGAR COLAS
(Total Food Stores)

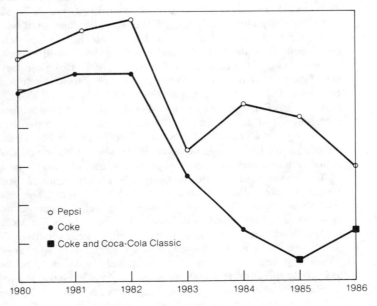

○ Pepsi
● Coke
■ Coke and Coca-Cola Classic

1980   1981   1982   1983   1984   1985   1986

A later report claimed that while in 1972, 18 percent of soft drink users were exclusive Coke drinkers and a mere 4 percent drank only Pepsi, 10 years later the tally was 12 percent to 11 percent in Coke's favor. One suggested reason for Coke's tenuous lead was Coke's greater availability. Even if someone wanted Pepsi, in some places he or she might find only Coke.

Stout developed a complicated formula to measure the effect of advertising on sales. The results of the formula indicated that despite the fact that Coke spent far more on advertising than Pepsi, Coke's advertising programs were not effective enough. Pepsi, on the other hand, had very effective ad campaigns, most notably the "Pepsi Generation" and the Michael Jackson spots. Coke had earlier turned down Michael Jackson as a candidate for its advertising because he was considered too flashy and his appearance didn't jibe with the company's image as the all-American boy.

Pepsi's relentless attacks had narrowed Coke's once large lead down to a mere 4.9 percent. Even more disturbing to Coke executives was that Coke was actually trailing in the grocery store segment by 1.7 percent. Coke finally decided that the loss in its market share basically boiled down to one factor—taste.

In September 1983 Zyman became manager of a special project, Project Kansas, so named after a newspaper article by William Allen White in the *Emporia* (Kansas) *Gazette*: "Coca-Cola is the sublimated essence of all that America stands for. A decent thing, honestly made, universally distributed and conscientiously improved with the years." Perhaps because of his newness to headquarters or because of his foreign background, Zyman had little problem with the idea of changing the formula, and he was quick to accuse reluctant managers of an inability to act with the times.

Coke had previously begun to investigate the public's willingness to accept a different Coke, conducting 1,000 interviews in 10 major markets to test the public's response. Two key findings were: (1) exclusive Pepsi drinkers would be interested in a new Coke, and (2) many people didn't think Coke should be tampered with.

A year after Project Kansas was born the technical department finally felt they had developed the right formula, and Coke initiated blind taste tests between the new formula and Pepsi. According to *Beverage Digest*, Coke conducted 190,000 tests among the 13- to 59-year-old group. The tests centered on two key questions: (1) how consumers responded to a new formula in taste tests versus old Coke, and (2) how new Coke faired versus Pepsi. New Coke beat Pepsi 47 to 43 percent with 10 percent expressing no preference, and new Coke outscored old Coke 55 to 45 percent.

Throughout all their studies, researchers never made it clear to the consumers they tested that old Coke could be taken off the shelves if the new Coke was introduced. No actual research was done as to whether Coke should merely introduce a line extension.

Top management reaction to the new formula was mixed. Some wanted to introduce a second Coke. Others pointed out that Coke's product line was already unwieldy and bottlers would not be happy about adding yet another. Concern over the fountain business raised questions as to which Coke companies like McDonald's would choose. If McDonald's chose the new taste over old Coke, executives felt it would damage the flagship brand. The obsession with being number 1 in all phases rules out the idea of a second cola since two cokes would most likely split Coke's market share, allowing Pepsi to become the number 1 soft drink, an intolerable possibility for Coke.

Finally, Coke's market share decline (refer to Figure C24.10) and Stout's taste tests, which continued to show new Coke winning out over old Coke and Pepsi by staggering margins, forced Keough to ignore his gut reaction against toying with America's heritage. Keough, Chairman Goizueta, Director of Corporate Marketing Herbert, and Dyson met and agreed to give Coke a new taste.

How to handle the introduction of new Coke was carefully considered. Since Coke's corporate culture wouldn't let the company admit in any way that Pepsi was superior, the introduction couldn't say that in taste tests new Coke beat Pepsi, because someone might then ask how old Coke did versus Pepsi. By not being more candid about taste, taste became the focal issue as the public judged new Coke against old Coke.

Reaction to the Announcement and the Return of Old Coke

Pepsi Declares a Holiday   Pepsi placed full-page ads of Pepsi President Roger Enrico's congratulatory letter to Pepsi bottlers in the nation's major newspapers the same day as the Coke press conference. The letter read in part:

> It gives me great pleasure to offer each of you my heartiest congratulations. After seventeen years of going at it eyeball to eyeball, the other guy just blinked. Coca-Cola is withdrawing their product from the marketplace, and is reformulating brand Coke to be more like Pepsi. . . . Maybe they finally realized what most of us have known for years, Pepsi tastes better than Coke . . . we have earned a holiday. We're going to declare a holiday on Friday. Enjoy!

Public Reaction   Public reaction to the introduction of new Coke was swift, and for the most part, very negative. To many consumers, changing Coke's formula was like rewriting the constitution. Many Americans, especially those who lived in the South, saw Coke as an institution, and a link to a simpler past. In short, these mainstream middle Americans felt betrayed by an old friend. Many frenzied consumers rushed to grocery stores and bought huge supplies of the soon to be scarce old Coke. Some people spent hundreds of dollars stockpiling old Coke.

Newspapers all over the country ran negative articles about the new product, adding more fuel to the fire. By the middle of May, over 5,000 calls per day were being received by Coke's consumer affairs department. Coke answered over 40,000 letters in the spring of 1985. The vast majority of the calls and letters were negative. Most people were more upset with the fact that the taste had been changed rather than the new taste per se. By the end of spring, Coke came to the painful realization that they had vastly underestimated the sentimental feelings millions of consumers had for Coke.

Bottlers' Reaction   Initially, most of Coke's bottlers supported the introduction of new Coke. Even the southern bottlers were at least convinced of long-term gains. However, the short-term effects were not viewed with optimism. As one Coke bottler put it, "Getting from here to there could be a little rough."

Some Coke bottlers reported immediate acceptance by their customers. Most of these bottlers were located in the northeastern part of the country. In these markets, the introduction of new Coke actually increased the bottlers' market shares. However, in order to gain wide acceptance, new Coke was going to have to be welcomed by consumers in the South, as the South represented Coke's high per capita markets.

Those bottlers who feared negative short-term effects saw their fears realized when the full force of public resentment hit. Frank Barron, whose territory in Georgia led the world in per capita sales of Coke, saw his volume "go to hell in a handbasket" by mid-June. His experience was hardly unique. On July 3 several large bottlers met with Brian Dyson, president of Coca-Cola USA, to tell him that they had to come back with the old Coke. But the later reintroduction of Coke Classic did not offer the bottlers a panacea. A July 29, 1985, *Leisure Beverage Insider* article stated that the extension of brand Coke with Coke Classic meant an 18 percent increase in costs due to packaging, warehouse space, production capability, truck space, ingredients, labels, crowns, point-of-purchase materials, and labor. Despite this rather gloomy outlook, virtually all of Coke's bottlers hailed the reintroduction of the old Coke.

Fountain Sales   McDonald's is Coke's number 1 customer, selling Coke as its only cola product. At Coke's request, McDonald's was the first major customer to run a promotion for Coke. McDonald's use of Coca-Cola brand identified cups in the promotion marked the first time McDonald's had ever used a supplier's package. The purpose behind the promotion was to get a quick trial run for the new formula. McDonald's, with over 7,200 restaurants in the U.S., was an obvious choice. It was never disclosed how much Coke paid for the promotion, but it seems likely that the cost was not small.

McDonald's stayed with the new Coke for about a year, but in May 1986 they decided to go back to the old formula. The decision was made quietly as McDonald's issued a simple statement saying that their marketing research results indicated that Coke Classic was the choice of the majority of their customers, and based on that finding McDonald's had no choice but to change. The option of carrying two colas was never considered. McDonald's felt it would be too confusing and expensive to carry both Coke and Coke Classic.

The key issue for food service restaurants was the limited number of fountain heads. Most dispensing units have only four heads, thus if a restaurant were to offer Coke

FIGURE C24.11 CONSOLIDATED BALANCE SHEETS
(In Thousands Except per Share Data)

	December 31	
	1985	1984
Assets		
Current		
Cash	$ 495,672	$ 307,564
Marketable securities, at cost (approximates market)	369,491	474,575
	865,163	782,139
Trade accounts receivable, less allowances of $19,479 in 1985 and $20,670 in 1984	897,200	872,332
Inventories and film costs	913,293	740,063
Prepaid expenses and other assets	294,628	241,326
Total current assets	2,970,284	2,635,860
Investments, film costs, and other assets		
Investments (principally investments in affiliates)	470,575	334,220
Film costs	536,112	341,662
Receivables and other assets	364,581	408,324
	1,371,268	1,084,206
Property, plant and equipment		
Land	139,450	130,883
Buildings and improvements	771,088	645,150
Machinery and equipment	1,742,118	1,518,264
Containers	358,354	337,993
	3,011,010	2,632,290
Less allowances for depreciation	1,127,301	1,009,715
	1,883,709	1,622,575
Goodwill and other intangible assets	672,445	615,428
	$6,897,706	$5,958,069

Classic and new Coke, two of the four heads would be for a sugared cola product. This would likely mean dropping one flavored offering such as an orange or a root beer. In essence, restaurants were forced to choose one brand of Coke over the other. At least in the fountain segment, the reintroduction of the old formula cannibalized new Coke's sales.

Wall Street   The introduction of new Coke, and the subsequent introduction of Coke Classic, barely caused a twitter in Coke's stock price. Despite their proclamations of victory, Pepsi's stock price showed no sudden upward or downward movement that could be traced to either of the two announcements. Coca-Cola's balance sheets are presented in Figure C24.11, and selected financial data are provided in Figure C24.12.

Asked to summarize what happened in the soft drink industry in 1985 and to make predictions for 1986, three top analysts offered the following thoughts in a 1986 issue of *Beverage World*.

FIGURE C24.11   *(CONTINUED)*

	December 31	
	1985	**1984**
Liabilities and shareholders' equity		
Current		
Accounts payable and accrued expenses	$1,108,964	$1,020,807
Loans 'and notes payable	391,629	502,216
Current maturities of long-term debt	34,495	120,300
Entertainment obligations	215,249	192,537
Accrued taxes—including income taxes	253,507	186,942
Total current liabilities	2,003,844	2,022,802
Entertainment obligations	270,676	175,234
Long-term debt	889,201	740,001
Deferred income taxes	320,832	241,966
Deferred entertainment revenue	434,096	—
Shareholders' equity		
Common stock, no par value—		
Authorized: 180,000,000 shares in 1985 and 1984;		
Issued: 137,699,566 shares in 1985 and 137,263,936		
shares in 1984	69,227	69,009
Capital surplus	602,617	532,186
Reinvested earnings	3,092,255	2,758,895
Foreign currency translation adjustment	(181,440)	(234,811)
	3,582,659	3,125,279
Less treasury stock, at cost (9,039,031 shares in 1985;		
6,438,873 shares in 1984)	603,602	347,213
	2,979,057	2,778,066
	$6,897,706	$5,958,069

Emmanuel Goldman of Montogomery Securities:

1. New Coke can't just be yanked from the shelf. Some consumers actually liked it.

Martin Romm of Boston Corporation:

1. Given the current numbers, Coke seems to be showing reasonably good results with the two brands together. The sum of the parts is greater than the whole.
2. Pepsi-Cola has definitely benefitted from the current situation. In a sense, the new and the old versions of Coke are competing with one another.
3. Consumers have embraced the Pepsi brand while rejecting new Coke.

Allan Kaplan of Merrill Lynch:

1. Coke took a chance. What it refers to right now as its fighting brand (new Coke) is going to go head to head with Pepsi for the new generation of soft drink consumers who like sweeter drinks. The new Coke is as sweet, if not slightly sweeter, than Pepsi.

FIGURE C24.12 SELECTED FINANCIAL DATA
(In Millions Except per Share Data)

		Year Ended December 31		
		1985	1984	1983
Summary of Operations*†	Net operating revenues	$7,904	$ 7,152	$6,641
	Cost of goods and services	4,194	3,823	3,618
	Gross profit	3,710	3,329	3,023
	Selling, administrative and general expenses	2,665	2,287	2,041
	Operating income	1,045	1,042	982
	Interest income	148	129	83
	Interest expense	168	123	72
	Other income (deductions)—net	68	7	(2)
	Income from continuing operations before income taxes	1,093	1,055	991
	Income taxes	415	433	438
	Income from continuing operations	$ 678	$ 622	$ 553
	Net income	$ 722	$ 629	$ 559
Per Share Data§	Income from continuing operations	$ 5.17	$ 4.70	$ 4.06
	Net income	5.51	4.76	4.10
	Dividends	2.96	2.76	2.68
Year-end position	Cash and marketable securities	$ 865	$ 782	$ 611
	Property, plant and equipment—net	1,884	1,623	1,561
	Total assets	6,898	5,958	5,228
	Long-term debt	889	740	513
	Total debt	1,315	1,363	620
	Shareholders' equity	2,979	2,778	2,921
	Total capital¶	4,294	4,141	3,541
Financial ratios	Income from continuing operations to net operating revenues	8.6%	8.7%	8.3%
	Income from continuing operations to average shareholders' equity	23.5%	21.8%	19.4%
	Total debt to total capital	30.6%	32.9%	17.5%
	Dividend payout	53.7%	58.0%	65.3%
Other data	Average shares outstanding§	131	132	136
	Capital expenditures	$ 542	$ 391	$ 384
	Depreciation	178	159	147
	Market price per share at December 31§	84.50	62.375	53.50

  * Operating results for 1975–1984 have been restated to exclude the results of Presto Products, Incorporated, and Winkler/Flexible Products, Inc., which were sold in December 1985 and accounted for as discontinued operations.
  † In June 1982, the company acquired Columbia Pictures Industries, Inc., in a purchase transaction.

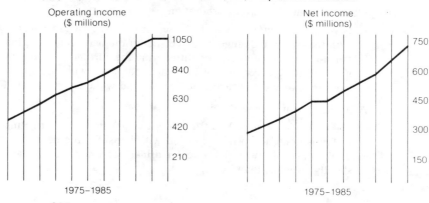

668

	Year Ended December 31							
	1982‡	**1981**	**1980**	**1979**	**1978**	**1977**	**1976**	**1975**
	$5,862	$5,540	$ 5,327	$4,472	$ 3,938	$3,265	$2,877	$ 2,726
	3,189	3,062	2,988	2,431	2,148	1,790	1,574	1,598
	2,673	2,478	2,339	2,041	1,790	1,475	1,303	1,128
	1,810	1,706	1,620	1,367	1,159	915	802	689
	863	772	719	674	631	560	501	439
	106	70	40	36	35	29	29	22
	74	38	35	10	7	6	6	6
	7	(23)	(10)	(2)	(14)	(10)	(4)	(8)
	902	781	714	698	645	573	520	447
	408	349	320	312	294	263	242	214
	$ 494	$ 432	$ 394	$ 386	$ 351	$ 310	$ 278	$ 233
	$ 512	$ 482	$ 422	$ 420	$ 375	$ 331	$ 294	$ 249
	$ 3.81	$ 3.50	$ 3.19	$ 3.13	$ 2.84	$ 2.52	$ 2.25	$ 1.89
	3.95	3.90	3.42	3.40	3.03	2.68	2.38	2.20
	2.48	2.32	2.16	1.96	1.74	1.54	1.325	1.15
	$ 261	$ 340	$ 231	$ 149	$ 321	$ 350	$ 364	$ 389
	1,539	1,409	1,341	1,284	1,065	887	738	647
	4,923	3,565	3,406	2,938	2,583	2,254	2,007	1,801
	462	137	133	31	15	15	11	16
	583	232	228	139	69	57	52	42
	2,779	2,271	2,075	1,919	1,740	1,578	1,434	1,302
	3,362	2,503	2,303	2,058	1,809	1,635	1,486	1,344
	8.4%	7.8%	7.4%	8.6%	8.9%	9.5%	9.7%	8.5%
	19.6%	19.9%	19.7%	21.1%	21.2%	20.6%	20.3%	18.7%
	17.3%	9.3%	9.9%	6.8%	3.8%	3.5%	3.5%	3.1%
	62.8%	59.5%	63.2%	57.6%	57.4%	57.5%	55.7%	56.9%
	130	124	124	124	124	123	123	123
	$ 382	$ 330	$ 293	$ 381	$ 306	$ 264	$ 191	$ 145
	138	128	123	103	86	76	66	63
	52.00	34.75	33.375	34.50	43.875	37.25	39.50	41.125

‡ In 1982, the company adopted Statement of Financial Accounting Standards No. 52, "Foreign Currency Translation."
§ Adjusted for a two-for-one stock split in 1977.
¶ Includes shareholders' equity and total debt.

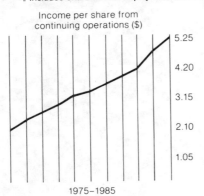

Income per share from continuing operations ($)

1975–1985

Return on shareholders' equity (%)

1975–1985

2. Coke feels it has retained the people who liked the old Coke with Coca-Cola Classic. It will use the new Coke to attack the new generation. New Coke will be around for a while.

Two Cokes

When the return of old Coke as Coke Classic was announced at a news conference on July 11, 1985, the scene of this conference was entirely different. Goizueta told those present:

Today, we have two messages to deliver to the American consumer. First, to those of you who are drinking Coca-Cola with its great new taste, our thanks. . . . But there is a second group of consumers to whom we want to speak today and our message to this group is simple, we have heard you.

In the months following the decision to sell new Coke and Coke Classic, the company's marketing strategy shifted emphasis from specific brands to categories—the megabrand strategy was developed. All drinks with the name Coke were grouped together—Coke, Coke Classic, Cherry Coke, Diet Coke, Caffeine-Free Coke, Caffeine-Free Diet Coke, and later, Diet Cherry Coke—thus, providing a new way to read the numbers.

By the end of 1985, Pepsi had become the number 1 soft drink, but Coke Classic was gaining rapidly. The switch of McDonald's and Hardee's back to Coke Classic presented a crippling blow to new Coke's projections of success. The following year *Beverage World* reported that Coke Classic returned to its number 1 spot, Pepsi followed in second place, and sales for new Coke stabilized as the new Coke finished the year ranked as number 9, with 2.3 percent of the overall market.

Commenting on Coca-Cola's decision to change the formula Keough said, "Some critics will say Coca-Cola made a marketing mistake. Some cynics will say that we planned the whole thing. The truth is we are not that dumb and we are not that smart."

NUCOR CORPORATION

Prepared by Frank C. Barnes, University of North Carolina at Charlotte.

INTRODUCTION

Nuclear Corporation of America had been near bankruptcy in 1965, when a fourth reorganization put a 39-year-old division manager, Ken Iverson, into the president's role. Iverson began a process which resulted in Nucor, a steel mini-mill and joist manufacturer which rated national attention and reaped high praise. (See Figure C25.1.)

In a 1981 article subtitled "Lean living and mini-mill technology have led a one-time loser to steel's promised land," *Fortune* stated:

> Although Nucor didn't build its first mill until 1969, it turned out 1.1 million tons of steel last year, enough to rank among the top 20 U.S. producers. Not only has Nucor been making a lot of steel, it's been making money making steel—and a lot of that as well. Since 1969, earnings have grown 31% a year, compounded, reaching $45 million in 1980 on sales of $482 million. Return on average equity in recent years has consistently exceeded 28%, excellent even by Silicon Valley's standards and almost unheard of in steel. The nine-fold increase in the value of Nucor's stock over the last five years—it was selling recently at about $70 a share—has given shareholders plenty of cause for thanksgiving.

The Wall Street Journal commented, "The ways in which management style combines with technology to benefit the mini-mill industry is obvious at Nucor Corp., one of the most successful of the 40 or more mini-mill operators." Ken Iverson was featured in an NBC special, "If Japan Can, Why Can't We?" for his management approach. As *The Wall Street Journal* commented, "You thought steel companies are only a bunch of

FIGURE C25.1   KEN IVERSON AND NUCOR CORPORATION

Ken Iverson

A joist plant

A steel mill

losers, with stodgy management, outmoded plants and poor profits?'' Well, Nucor and Iverson were different.

However, the challenges hadn't stopped. The economy made the 1980s a horrible time for the steel industry. All companies reported sales declines, most lost profitability, and some, in both major and mini-mill operations, closed or restructured. Nucor's 30% plus return on equity hit 9%. Iverson, however, was one of 52 recipients of the bronze medal from *Financial World* in 1983 for holding onto profitability; they kept costs down but not at the expense of laying off their people—a near-religious commitment at Nucor.

By 1987 Nucor was the ninth largest steel producer in the U.S. and number 372 on the Fortune 500 list. (See Appendixes A and B for financial performance.) But the easy gains scored by the new mini-mill operations over the integrated mills were over. The historical steel companies were arousing from their twenty-year slumber, adding modern technology, renegotiating with their equally aged unions, and closing some mills. They were determined to fight back. Mini-mill was fighting mini-mill, as well as imports, and a number had closed. Thus the industry faced a picture of excess capacity which would be the backdrop in the battle for survival and success over the next years.

Iverson and Nucor knew how to fight the battle. By 1986 they had $185 million in cash at their disposal. An expansion program in steel was started. Analysts, however, moved away from their stock, worrying about expansion in an industry facing overcapacity and intense competition. Among their moves, Nucor announced a revolutionary new steel mill based on an advanced technology unique in the world, planned a joint-venture mill with a Japanese steel company, and shocked analysts by entering the fastener business, which had become 90% imported. ''We're going to bring that business back.'' The battle was joined.

BACKGROUND

Nucor was the descendant of a company which manufactured the first Oldsmobile in 1897. After seven years of success, R. E. Olds sold his first company and founded a new one to manufacture the Reo. Reo ran into difficulties and filed for voluntary reorganization in 1938. Sales grew 50 times over the next 10 years, based on defense business, but declined steadily after World War II. The motor division was sold and then resold in 1957 to the White Motor Corporation, where it operates as the Diamond Reo Division. Reo Motors' management planned to liquidate the firm, but before this could be done, a new company gained control through a proxy fight. A merger was arranged with Nuclear Consultants, Inc., and the stock of Nuclear Corporation of America was first traded in 1955. Nuclear acquired a number of companies in high-tech fields but continued to lose money until 1960 when an investment banker in New York acquired control. New management proceeded with a series of acquisitions and dispositions; they purchased U.S. Semi-Conductor Products, Inc.; Valley Sheet Metal Co., an air conditioner contractor in Arizona; and Vulcraft Corp., a Florence, South Carolina, steel joist manufacturer. Over the next four years, sales increased five times, but losses increased seven times. In 1965, a New York investor purchased a controlling interest and installed the fourth management team. The new president was Ken Iverson, who had been in charge of the Vulcraft division.

Ken Iverson had joined the Navy upon graduation from a Chicago-area high school in 1943. The Navy first sent him to Northwestern University for an officer training program but then decided it needed aeronautical engineers and transferred him to Cornell. This had been "fine" with Iverson because he enjoyed engineering. Upon receiving his Bachelors degree in 1945 at age 20, he served in the Navy for six months, completing his four-year tour.

He wasn't too excited about an A.E. career because of the eight years of drafting required for success. Metals and their problems in aircraft design had intrigued him, so he considered a Masters degree in metallurgy. An uncle had attended Purdue, so he chose that school. He married during this time, gave up teaching geometry so he could finish the program in one year, and turned down an offer of assistance toward a Ph.D. to "get to work."

At Purdue he had worked with the new electron microscope. International Harvester's research physics department had just acquired one and hired Iverson as assistant to the chief research physicist. Iverson stayed there five years and felt he was "set for life." He had great respect for his boss, who would discuss with him the directions businesses took and their opportunities. One day the chief physicist asked if that job was what he really wanted to do all his life. There was only one job ahead for Iverson at International Harvester and he felt more ambition than to end his career in that position. At his boss's urging he considered smaller companies.

Iverson joined Illium Corporation, 120 miles from Chicago, as chief engineer (metallurgist). Illium was a 60-person division of a major company but functioned like an independent company. Iverson was close to the young president and was impressed with his good business skill; this man knew how to manage and had the discipline to run a tight ship, to go in the right direction with no excess manpower. The two of them proposed an expansion which the parent company insisted they delay three to four years until it could be handled without going into debt.

After two years at Illium, Iverson joined Indiana Steel Products as assistant to the vice president of manufacturing, for the sole purpose of setting up a spectrographic lab. After completing this within one year, he could see no other opportunity for himself in the company, because it was small and he could get no real responsibility. A year and a half later, Iverson left to join Cannon Muskegon as chief metallurgist.

The next seven years were "fascinating." This small ($5–6 million in sales and 60–70 people) family company made castings from special metals which were used in every aircraft made in the U.S. The company was one of the first to get into "vacuum melting" and Iverson, because of his technical ability, was put in charge of this. Iverson then asked for and got responsibility for all company sales. He wasn't dissatisfied but realized that if he was to be really successful he needed broader managerial experience.

Cannon Muskegon sold materials to Coast Metals, a small, private company in New Jersey which cast and machined special alloys for the aircraft industry. The president of Coast got to know Iverson and realized his technical expertise would be an asset. In 1960 he joined Coast as executive vice president, with responsibility for running the whole company.

Nuclear Corporation of America wished to buy Coast; however, Coast wasn't interested. Nuclear's president then asked Iverson to act as a consultant to find metal businesses Nuclear could buy. Over the next year, mostly on weekends, he looked at potential acquisitions. He recommended buying a joist business in South Carolina. Nuclear said it would, if he would run it. Coast was having disputes among its owners and Iverson's future there was clouded. He ended his two years there and joined Nuclear in 1962 as a vice president, Nuclear's usual title, in charge of a 200-person joist division.

By late 1963 he had built a second plant in Nebraska and was running the only division making a profit. The president asked him to become a group vice president, adding the research chemicals (metals) and contracting businesses, and to move to the home office in Phoenix. In mid-1965 the company defaulted on two loans and the president resigned. During that summer Nuclear sought some direction out of its difficulty. Iverson knew what could be done, put together a pro-forma statement, and pushed for these actions. It was not a unanimous decision when he was made president in September 1965.

The new management immediately abolished some divisions and went to work building Nucor. According to Iverson the vice presidents of the divisions designed Nucor in hard-working, almost T-group type, meetings. Iverson was only another participant and only took charge whenever the group couldn't settle an issue. This process identified Nucor's strengths and set the path for Nucor.

By 1966 Nucor consisted of the two joist plants, the Research Chemicals division, and the Nuclear division. During 1967 a building in Ft. Payne, Alabama, was purchased for conversion into another joist plant. "We got into the steel business because we wanted to be able to build a mill that could make steel as cheaply as we were buying it from foreign importers or from offshore mills." In 1968 Nucor opened a steel mill in Darlington, South Carolina, and opened a joist plant in Texas. Another joist plant was added in Indiana in 1972. Steel plant openings followed in Texas in 1975 and in Nebraska in 1977. The Nuclear division was divested in 1976. A fourth steel plant was opened in Utah in 1981 and a joist plant was opened in Utah in 1982. By 1984 Nucor consisted of six joist plants, four steel mills, and a Research Chemicals division.

In 1983, in testimony before the Congress, Iverson warned of the hazards of trade barriers, that they would cause steel to cost more and that manufacturers would move overseas to use the cheaper steel shipped back into this country. He commented, "We have seen serious problems in the wire industry and the fastener industry." *Link* magazine reported that in the last four years, 40 domestic fastener plants had closed and that imports had over 90 percent of the market.

In 1986 Nucor began construction of a $25 million plant in Indiana to manufacture steel fasteners. Iverson told the *Atlanta Journal*, "We are going to bring that business back." He told *Inc.* magazine, "We've studied for a year now, and we decided that we can make bolts as cheaply as foreign producers and make a profit at it." He explained that in the old operation two people, one simply required by the union, made one hundred bolts a minute. "But at Nucor, we'll have an automated machine which will manufacture 400 bolts a minute. The automation will allow an operator to manage four machines." Hans Mueller, a steel industry consultant at East Tennessee State University, told the *Journal*, "I must confess that I was surprised that Iverson would be willing to dive into that snake pit. But he must believe that he can do it because he is not reckless."

Before making the decision, a Nucor task force of four people traveled the world to examine the latest technology. The management group was headed by a plant manager who joined Nucor after several years' experience as general manager of a bolt company in Toronto. The manager of manufacturing was previously plant manager of a 40,000-ton melt shop for Ervin Industries. The sales manager was a veteran of sales, distribution, and manufacturing in the fastener industry. The plant's engineering manager transferred from Nucor R&D in Nebraska. The Touche-Ross accountant who worked on the Nucor account joined the company as controller. The first crew of production employees received three months of in-depth training on the bolt-making machines, with extensive cross-training in tool making, maintenance, and other operations.

In what *The New York Times* called their "most ambitious project yet," Nucor signed an agreement in January 1987 to form a joint venture with Yamato Kogyo, Ltd., a small Japanese steelmaker, to build a steel mill on the Mississippi River with a 600,000-ton-per-year capacity. The $200 million plant would make very large structural products, up to 24 inches. Structural steel products are those used in large buildings and bridges. Iverson noted, "These are now only made by the Big Three integrated steel companies." The Japanese company, which would own 49% of the stock, had expertise in continuous casting, in which Nucor was interested. Their 1985 sales totaled $400 million, with approximately 900 workers. They would provide the continuous-casting technology while Nucor would provide the melting technology and management style.

In August 1986, Iverson told Cable News Network, "We are talking about within the next two years perhaps building a steel mill to make flat roll products, that would be the first time a mini-mill has been in this area." It was expected that approximately $10 million would be needed to develop this process. The thin-slab would also produce feed stock for Vulcraft's 250,000-tons-per-year steel deck operation. Although the project was considered pure research at the time and projected for "late 1988," the division manager stated, "The more we look into it, the more we feel we'll be able to successfully cast those slabs." This process would be the most significant development in the steel industry in decades and would open up the auto and appliance businesses to the mini-mills. Then in January 1987 plans were announced to build the $200 million, 800,000-ton mill for the production of high-grade flat rolled steel by the first half of 1989. They stated, "We've tested numerous approaches . . . this one is commercially feasible. It's been tested and it can do the job."

In December 1986 Nucor announced its first major acquisition, Genbearco, a steel bearings manufacturer. At a cost of more than $10 million, it would add $25 million in sales and 250 employees. Iverson called it "a good fit with our business, our policies and our people." It was without a union and tied pay to performance.

Nucor's innovation was not limited to manufacturing. In the steel industry, it was normal to price an order based on the quantity ordered. In 1984, Nucor broke that pattern. As Iverson stated, "Sometime ago we began to realize that with computer order entry and billing, the extra charge for smaller orders was not cost justified. We found the cost of servicing a 20-ton order compared with a 60-ton order was about 35 cents a ton and most of that was related to credit and collection. We did agonize over the decision, but over the long run we are confident that the best competitive position is one that has a strong price to cost relationship.'' He noted that this policy would give Nucor another advantage over foreign suppliers in that users could maintain lower inventories and order more often. ''If we are going to successfully compete against foreign suppliers, we must use the most economical methods for both manufacturing and distribution.''

THE STEEL INDUSTRY

The early 1980s had been the worst years in decades for the steel industry. Data from the American Iron and Steel Institute showed shipments falling from 100.2 million tons in 1979 to the mid-80 levels in 1980 and 1981. Slackening in the economy, particularly in auto sales, led the decline. In 1986, when industry capacity was at 130 million tons, the outlook was for a continued decline in per capita consumption and movement toward capacity in the 90- to 100-million-ton range. The chairman of Armco saw ''millions of tons chasing a market that's not there; excess capacity that must be eliminated.''

The large, integrated steel firms, such as U.S. Steel and Armco, which made up the major part of the industry, were the hardest hit. *The Wall Street Journal* stated, ''The decline has resulted from such problems as high labor and energy costs in mining and processing iron ore, a lack of profits and capital to modernize plants, and conservative management that has hesitated to take risks.''

These companies produced a wide range of steels, primarily from ore processed in blast furnaces. They had found it difficult to compete with imports, usually from Japan, and had given up market share to imports. They sought the protection of import quotas. Imported steel accounted for 20% of the U.S. steel consumption, up from 12% in the early 1970s. The U.S. share of world production of raw steel declined from 19% to 14% over the period. Imports of light bar products accounted for less than 9% of U.S. consumption of those products in 1981, according to the U.S. Commerce Department, while imports of wire rod totaled 23% of U.S. consumption. ''Wire rod is a very competitive product in the world market because it's very easy to make,'' Ralph Thompson, the Commerce Department's steel analyst, told the *Charlotte Observer*.

Iron Age stated that exports, as a percent of shipments in 1985, were 34% for Nippon, 26% for British Steel, 30% for Krupp, 49% for USINOR of France, and less than 1% for every American producer on the list. The consensus of steel experts was that imports would average 23% of the market in the last half of the 1980s.

Iverson was one of very few in the steel industry to oppose import restrictions. He saw an outdated U.S. steel industry which had to change.

About 12% of the steel in the U.S. is still produced by the old open hearth furnace. The Japanese shut down their last open hearth furnace about five years ago. . . . The U.S. produces about 16% of its steel by the continuous-casting process. In Japan over 50% of the steel is continuously cast. . . . We Americans have been conditioned to believe in our technical superiority. For many generations a continuing stream of new inventions and manufacturing techniques allowed us to far outpace the rest of the world in both volume and efficiency of production. In many areas this is no longer true and particularly in the steel industry. In the last three decades almost all the major developments in steel making were made outside the U.S. There were 18 continuous-casting units in the world before there was one in this country. I would be negligent if I did not recognize the significant contribution that the government has made toward the technological deterioration of the steel industry. Unrealistic depreciation schedules, high corporate taxes, excessive regulation, and jawboning for lower steel prices have made it difficult for the steel industry to borrow or generate the huge quantities of capital required for modernization.

By the mid-1980s the integrated mills were moving fast to get back into the game; they were restructuring, cutting capacity, dropping unprofitable lines, focusing products, and trying to become responsive to the market. The president of USX explained: "Steel executives, in trying to act as prudent businessmen, are seeking the lowest-cost solutions to provide what the market wants." Karlis Kirsis, director of World Steel Dynamics at Paine-Webber, told *Purchasing Magazine,* "The industry as we knew it five years ago is no more; the industry as we knew it a year ago is gone."

Purchasing believed that buyers would be seeing a pronounced industry segmentation. There would be integrated producers making mostly flat-rolled and structural grades, reorganized steel companies making a limited range of products, mini-mills dominating the bar and light structural product areas, specialty steel firms seeking niches, and foreign producers. There would be accelerated shutdowns of older plants, elimination of products by some firms, and the installation of new product lines with new technologies by others. There would also be corporate facelifts as executives diversified from steel to generate profits and entice investment dollars. They saw the high-tonnage mills restructuring to handle sheets, plates, structurals, high-quality bars, and large pipe and tubular products which would allow for a resurgence of specialized mills: cold-finished bar manufacturers, independent strip mills, and mini-mills.

Wheeling-Pittsburgh illustrated the change under way in the industry. Through Chapter 11 reorganization it had cut costs by more than $85/ton. They divided into profit centers, negotiated the lowest hourly wage rate ($18/hour) among unionized integrated steel plants, renegotiated supply contracts, closed pipe and tube mills, and shut 1.6 million tons of blast furnace capacity in favor of an electric furnace with continuous casting.

Paine Webber pointed out the importance of "reconstituted mills," which they called the "People Express" of the industry. These were companies which had reorganized and refocused their resources, usually under Chapter 11. These include Kaiser Steel, The Weirton Works, Jones and Laughlin, Republic, Youngstown, Wheeling, LTV, and others.

Joint ventures had arisen to produce steel for a specific market or region. The chairman of USX called them "an important new wrinkle in steel's fight for survival" and stated, "If there had been more joint ventures like these two decades ago, the U.S. steel industry might have built only half of the dozen or so hot-strip mills it put up in that time and avoided today's overcapacity." *Purchasing* observed "The fact is that these combined operations are the result of a laissez-faire attitude within the Justice Department under the Reagan administration following the furor when government restrictions killed the planned USS takeover of National Steel (which later sold 50% interest to a Japanese steelmaker)."

However, the road ahead for the integrated mills would not be easy. While it was estimated they would need $10 billion to improve their facilities, the industry had lost over $7 billion since 1982. *Purchasing* pointed out that tax laws and accounting rules are slowing the closing of inefficient plants. Shutting a 10,000-person plant could require a firm to hold a cash reserve of $100 million to fund health, pension, and insurance liabilities. The chairman of Armco commented: "Liabilities associated with a plant shutdown are so large that they can quickly devastate a company's balance sheet."

THE MINI-MILL

A new type of mill, the "mini-mill," emerged in the U.S. during the 1970s to compete with the integrated mill. The mini-mill used electric arc furnaces to manufacture a narrow product line from scrap steel. In 1980 *The New York Times* reported:

> The truncated steel mill is to the integrated steel mill what the Volkswagen was to the American auto industry in the 1960's: smaller, cheaper, less complex and more efficient. Although mini-mills cannot produce such products as sheet steel [flat-rolled] and heavy construction items, some industry analysts say it is only a matter of time before technological breakthroughs make this possible.

Since mini-mills came into being in the 1970s, the integrated mills' market share has fallen from about 90% to about 60%, with the loss equally divided between mini-mills and foreign imports. While the integrated steel companies averaged a 7% return on equity, the mini-mills averaged 14%, and some, such as Nucor, achieved above 25%.

The leading mini-mills were Nucor, Florida Steel, Georgetown Steel (Korf Industries), North Star Steel, and Chaparral. Nucor produced "light bar" products: bars, angles, channels, flats, smooth round, and forging billets. It was beginning to make more alloy steels. Florida Steel made mostly reinforcing bar for construction (rebar) and dominated the Florida market. Korf Industries had two mini-mill subsidiaries which used modern equipment to manufacture wire rod.

The mini-mills were not immune to the economic slump in the early eighties. Korf Industries, which owned Georgetown Steel, found its interest charges too large a burden and sought reorganization in 1983. In March of 1983 Georgetown followed the historic wage-cutting contract between the United Steel Workers of America and the major steel companies and asked its union to accept reductions and to defer automatic wage increases. In 1982 Nucor froze wages and executives took a 5% pay cut. Plants went to a four-day schedule in which workers would receive only base rate if they chose to work a fifth day doing cleanup.

Florida Steel, with two-thirds of its sales in Florida, also felt the impact. At its headquarters in Tampa, a staff of over 100 handled accounting, payroll, sales entry, and almost all other services for all its facilities. Their division managers did not have sales responsibilities. Florida Steel experienced a sales decline for 1982 of 22% and an earnings drop from $3.37 per share to a loss of $1.40. The next year was also a year of losses.

Florida Steel employees had faced periodic layoffs during the recession. The firm was nonunion (although the Charlotte plant lost an election in 1973) and pay was based on productivity. A small facility at Indian Town, near West Palm Beach, never became productive, even with personnel changes, and had to be closed. A new mini-mill in Tennessee was completed in late 1983.

Mini-mills had tripled their output in the last decade to capture 17% of domestic shipments. Paine Webber predicted the big integrated mills' share of the market would fall to 40%, the mini-mills' share would rise to 23%, "reconstituted" mills would increase from 11% to 28%, and specialized mills would increase their share from 1% to 7%. Iverson stated mini-mills could not go beyond a 35% to 40% share due to technical limitations; mini-mills could not produce the flat-rolled sheet steel used in cars and appliances.

Iverson told *Metal Center News* in 1980:

> We are very interested in the development of a thin slab, which would then allow mini-mills to produce plate and other flat rolled products . . . actually, the thinnest slab that can now be produced is about 6 inches thick. . . . (That results in a plant that is too large.) There are a number of people working to develop the process. . . . We have done some work, but our primary efforts at the moment are in connection with other people who are working on it. . . . The likelihood is it would be developed by a foreign company. There are more efforts by foreign steel companies in that direction than in the United States. . . . I'd say probably a minimum of three to five years, or it could take as much as 10 to achieve this.

In 1983 Iverson described the new generation of mini-mills he foresaw:

> If you go way back, mini-mills got started by rolling reinforcing bar. With the advent of continuous casting and improvements in rolling mills, mini-mills gradually got into shape. Now they have moved in two other directions: one being to larger sizes, and the other being a growing metallurgical expertise for improved product quality and production of special bar quality in alloys. Both of these represent expansion of markets for mini-mills.

By 1986 the new competitive environment was apparent. Four mini-mills had closed their doors within the year and Iverson saw that more shutdowns were ahead. The overcapacity of steel bar products and the stagnant market had made it difficult for some companies to generate the cash needed to modernize and expand their product lines.

> The mini-mills are going through the same kind of restructuring and rethinking as the integrated mill. They know the problem of overcapacity isn't going to go away quickly. And, for some of the remaining firms to survive, they will have to move into more sophisticated products like special quality and clean-steel bars and heavier structurals and, once the technology is perfected, flat-rolled products. You won't see the market growth by the mini-mills the way it was in the past until the overcapacity issue is resolved and the mills begin entering new product areas.

ORGANIZATION

Nucor, with its 16-person corporate office located in Charlotte, North Carolina, had divisions spread across the U.S. The 11 divisions, one for every plant, each had a general manager, who was also a vice president of the corporation, directly responsible to Mr. Iverson. The divisions were of two basic types, joist plants and steel mills. The corporate staff consisted of a single specialist in personnel and a four-person financial function under Mr. Sam Siegel. Iverson, in the beginning, had chosen Charlotte "as the new home base for what he had envisioned as a small cadre of executives who would guide a decentralized operation with liberal authority delegated to managers in the field," according to *South Magazine*.

Iverson gave his views on organization:

You can tell a lot about a company by looking at its organization charts. . . . If you see a lot of staff, you can bet it is not a very efficient organization. . . . Secondly, don't have assistants. We do not have that title and prohibit it in our company. . . . In this organization nobody reports to the corporate office, the division managers report directly to me. . . . And one of the most important things is to restrict as much as possible the number of management layers. . . . I've often thought that when a company builds a fancy corporate office, it's on its way down.

Each division is a profit center and the division manager has control over the day-to-day decisions that make that particular division profitable or not profitable. We expect the division to provide division contribution, which is earnings before corporate expenses. We do not allocate our corporate expenses, because we do not think there is any way to do this reasonably and fairly. We do focus on earnings. And we expect a division to earn 25% return on total assets employed, before corporate expenses, taxes, interest or profit sharing. And we have a saying in the company—if a manager doesn't provide that for a number of years, we are either going to get rid of the division or get rid of the general manager, and it's generally the division manager.

A joist division manager commented:

I've been a division manager four years now and at times I'm still awed by it: the opportunity I was given to be a Fortune 500 vice-president. . . . I think we are successful because it is our style to pay more attention to our business than our competitors. . . . We are kind of a "no nonsense" company. That is not to say we don't have time for play, but we work hard when we work and the company is first and foremost in our minds. . . . I think another one of the successes of our company has been the fact that we have a very minimum number of management levels. We've been careful to avoid getting top heavy and so consequently we put a great deal of responsibility on each individual at each level. It has often been said, jokingly, that if you are the janitor at Vulcraft and you get the right promotions, about four promotions would take you to the top of the company.

Mr. Iverson's style of management is to allow the division manager all the latitude in the world. His involvement with the managers is quite limited. As we've grown, he no longer has the time to visit with the managers more than once or twice a year. . . . Whereas in many large companies the corporate office makes the major decisions and the people at the operating level sit back to wait for their marching orders, that's not the case at Nucor. . . . In a way I feel like I run my own company because I really don't get any marching orders from Mr. Iverson. He lets you run the division the way you see fit and the only way he will step in is if he sees something he doesn't like, particularly bad profits, high costs or whatever. But in the years I've worked with him I don't believe he has ever issued one single instruction to me to do something differently. I can't recall a single instance.

The divisions did their own manufacturing, selling, accounting, engineering, and personnel management. (See Figure C25.2.) A steel division manager, when questioned about Florida Steel, which had a large plant 90 miles away, commented, "I really don't

FIGURE C25.2 ORGANIZATION CHART

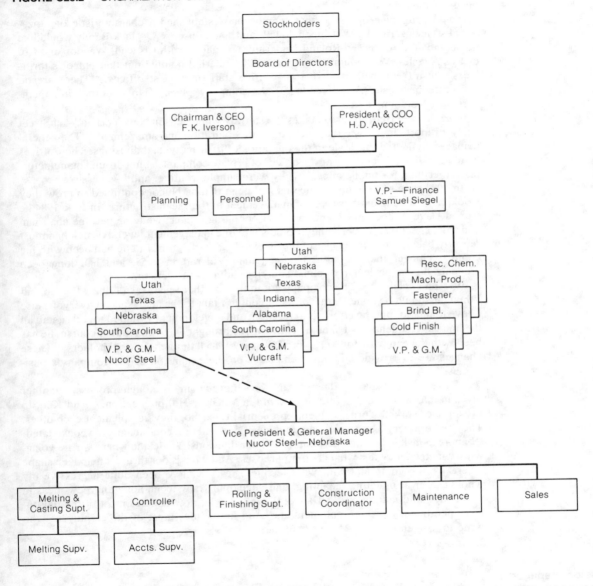

know anything about Florida Steel. . . . I expect they do have more of the hierarchy. I think they have central purchasing, centralized sales, centralized credit collections, centralized engineering, and most of the major functions.'' He didn't feel greater centralization would be good for Nucor. ''The purchasing activity, for example, removed from the field tends to become rather insensitive to the needs of the field and does not feel the pressures of responsibility. And the division they are buying for has no control over what they pay. . . . Likewise centralized sales would not be sensitive to the needs of their divisions.''

South Magazine observed that Iverson had established a characteristic organizational style described as ''stripped down'' and ''no nonsense.'' ''Jack Benny would like this company,'' observed Roland Underhill, an analyst with Crowell, Weedon and Co. of Los Angeles, ''so would Peter Drucker.'' Underhill pointed out that Nucor's thriftiness doesn't end with its ''spartan'' office staff or modest offices. ''There are no corporate perquisites,'' he recited. ''No company planes. No country club memberships. No company cars.''

Fortune reported, ''Iverson takes the subway when he is in New York, a Wall Street analyst reports in a voice that suggests both admiration and amazement.'' The general managers reflected this style in the operation of their individual divisions. Their offices were more like plant offices or the offices of private companies built around manufacturing rather than for public appeal. They were simple, routine, and businesslike.

In 1983, one of Iverson's concerns had been that as Nucor continued to grow they would have to add another layer of management to their lean structure. In June 1984 he named Dave Aycock president and chief operating officer, while he became chairman and chief executive officer—they would share one management level. Aycock had most recently been division manager of the steel mill at Darlington. But he had been with the company longer than Iverson, having joined Vulcraft in 1955, and had long been recognized as a particularly valued and close advisor to Iverson.

Iverson explained: ''The company got to the size that I just wasn't doing the job that I thought should be done by this office. I couldn't talk to the analysts and everyone else I have to talk to, put the efforts into research and development I wanted to, and get to all the units as frequently as I should. That's why I brought Dave in. And, of course, he has been with the company forever.'' In a February 1985 letter he told stockholders: ''These changes are to provide additional emphasis on the expansion of the company's businesses.''

''Dave is a very analytical person and very thorough in his thought process,'' another division manager told *33 Metal Producing,* a McGraw-Hill publication. ''And Ken, to use an overworked word, is an entrepreneurial type. So, they complement each other. They're both very aggressive men, and make one hell of a good team.'' Aycock stated: ''I am responsible for the operations of all our divisions. To decide where we are going, with what technologies; what are our purposes. And what is our thrust. I help Ken shape where we are going and with what technologies. . . . I've been quite aggressive my whole career at updating, adapting, and developing new technology and new ideas in production and marketing.'' ''Dave's the fellow who now handles most of the day-to-day operations,'' Iverson commented. ''And he handles most of the employees who write to us—about 10 to 15% of his time.''

Division Managers

The general managers met three times a year. In late October they presented preliminary budgets and capital requests. In late February they met to finalize budgets and treat miscellaneous matters. Then, at a meeting in May, they handled personnel matters, such as wage increases and changes of policies or benefits. The general managers as a group considered the raises for the department heads, the next level lower of management. As one of the managers described it:

In May of each year, all the general managers get together and review all the department heads throughout the company. We have kind of an informal evaluation process. It's an intangible thing, a judgment as to how dedicated an individual is and how well he performs compared to the same position at another plant. Sometimes the numbers don't come out the way a general manager wants to see them, but it's a fair evaluation. The final number is picked by Mr. Iverson. Occasionally there are some additional discussions with Mr. Iverson. He always has an open mind and might be willing to consider a little more for one individual. We consider the group of, say, joist production managers at one time. The six managers are rated for performance. We assign a number, such as +3 to a real cracker jack performer or a −2 to someone who needs improvement. These ratings become a part of the final pay increase granted.

The corporate personnel manager described management relations as informal, trusting, and not "bureaucratic." He felt there was a minimum of paperwork, that a phone call was more common, and that no confirming memo was thought to be necessary. Iverson himself stated:

Management is not a popularity contest. If everybody agrees with the organization, something is wrong with the organization. You don't expect people in the company to put their arms around each other, and you don't interfere with every conflict. Out of conflict often comes the best answer to a particular problem. So don't worry about it. You are always going to have some conflict in an organization. You will always have differences of opinion, and that's healthy. Don't create problems where there are none.

A Vulcraft manager commented: "We have what I would call a very friendly spirit of competition from one plant to the next. And of course all of the vice presidents and general managers share the same bonus system so we are in this together as a team even though we operate our divisions individually." The general managers are paid a bonus based on a total corporate profit rather than their own divisions' profits. A steel mill manager explained:

I think it's very important for the general managers to be concerned with contributing to the overall accomplishment of the company. There is a lot of interplay between the divisions with a flow of services, products, and ideas between divisions. Even though we are reasonably autonomous, we are not isolated. . . . We don't like the division managers to make decisions that would take that division away from where we want the whole company to go. But we certainly want the divisions to try new things. We are good copiers; if one division finds something that works, then we will all try it. I think that's one of our strengths. We have a lot of diverse people looking at ways to do things better.

Iverson revealed his view of management in his disdain for consultants:

They must have a specific job to do because they can't make your decisions. . . . The fellow on the line has to make decisions. . . . First he has to communicate and then he has to have the intestinal fortitude and the personal strength to make the decisions, sometimes under very difficult conditions. . . . A good manager is adaptable and he is sensitive to cultural, geographical, environmental, and business climates. Most important of all he communicates. . . . You never know if someone is a good manager until he manages. And that's why we take people as young as we possibly can, throw responsibility at them and they either work or they don't work. In a sense it's survival of the fittest. But don't kid yourself; that's what industry is all about.

A steel division manager commented in comparing the Nucor manager to the typical manager of a large corporation:

We would probably tend to have managers who have confidence in their abilities and, very importantly, have confidence in other people in their division. And people who are very sensitive to the employees of their division. . . . But, I think if you saw four or five different division managers you'd have four or five different decision-making styles.

A Vulcraft general manager in his early forties who had been promoted to the division manager level nine years earlier said:

The step from department manager to division manager is a big one. I can't think of an instance when a general manager job has been offered to an individual that it has been passed up. Often it means moving from one part of the country to another. There are five department heads in six joist plants, which means there are 30 people who are considered for division manager slots at a joist plant. Mr. Iverson selects the division managers.

His own experience was enlightening:

When I came to this plant four years ago, we had too many people, too much overhead. We had 410 people at the plant and I could see, because I knew how many people we had in the Nebraska plant, we had many more than we needed. That was my yardstick and we set about to reduce those numbers by attrition. . . . We have made a few equipment changes that made it easier for the men, giving them an opportunity to make better bonuses. Of course the changes were very subtle in any given case but overall in four years we have probably helped the men tremendously. With 55 fewer men, perhaps 40–45 fewer in the production area, we are still capable of producing the same number of tons as four years ago.

The divisions managed their activities with a minimum of contact with the corporate staff. Each day disbursements were reported to Siegel's office. Payments flowed into regional lockboxes. On a weekly basis, joist divisions reported total quotes, sales cancelations, backlog, and production. Steel mills reported tons rolled, outside shipments, orders, cancelations, and backlog. Mr. Iverson graphed the data. He might talk to the division about every two weeks. On the other hand Iverson was known to bounce ideas off the steel division manager in Darlington with whom he had worked since joining the company.

The Vulcraft manager commented on the communications with the corporate office: "It's kind of a steady pipeline. I might talk to the corporate office once a day or it might be once a week. But it generally involves, I would not say trivial information, just mundane things. Occasionally I hear from Sam or Ken about serious matters."

Each month the divisions completed a two-page (11″ × 17″) "operations analysis" which was sent to all the managers. Its three main purposes were (1) financial consolidation, (2) sharing information among the divisions, and (3) Iverson's examination. The summarized information and the performance statistics for all the divisions were then returned to the managers.

VULCRAFT—THE JOIST DIVISIONS

Half of Nucor's business was the manufacture and sale of open web steel joists and joist girders at six Vulcraft divisions located in Florence, South Carolina; Norfolk, Nebraska; Ft. Payne, Alabama; Grapeland, Texas; St. Joe, Indiana; and Brigham City, Utah. Open web joists, in contrast to solid joists, were made of steel angle iron separated by round bars or smaller angle iron (see Figure C25.3). These joists cost less, were stronger for many applications, and were used primarily as the roof support systems in larger buildings, such as warehouses and stores.

The joist industry was characterized by high competition among many manufacturers for many small customers. The Vulcraft divisions had over 3,000 customers, none of whom dominated the business. With an estimated 25% of the market, Nucor was the largest supplier in the U.S. It utilized national advertising campaigns and prepared competitive bids on 80% to 90% of buildings using joists. Competition was based on price and delivery performance. Nucor had developed computer programs to prepare designs for customers and to compute bids based on current prices and labor standards. In addition, each Vulcraft plant maintained its own engineering department to help customers with design problems or specifications. The Florence manager commented, "Here on the East Coast we have six or seven major competitors; of course none of them are as large as we are. The competition for any order will be heavy, and we will see six or seven different prices." He added, "I think we have a strong selling force in the marketplace. It has been said to us by some of our competitors that in this particular industry we have the finest selling organization in the country."

Nucor aggressively sought to be the lowest-cost producer in the industry. Materials and freight were two important elements of cost. Nucor maintained its own fleet of almost 100 trucks to ensure on-time delivery to all states, although most business was regional due to transportation costs. Plants were located in rural areas near the markets they served.

FIGURE C25.3   ILLUSTRATION OF JOISTS

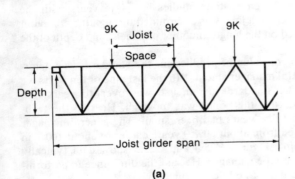

(a)

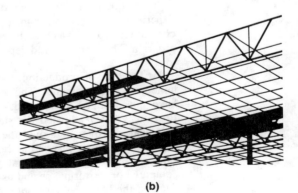

(b)

The Florence manager stated:

I don't feel there's a joist producer in the country that can match our cost. . . . We are sticklers about cutting out unnecessary overhead. Because we put so much responsibility on our people and because we have what I think is an excellent incentive program, our people are willing to work harder to accomplish these profitable goals.

Production

On the basic assembly line used at Nucor, three or four of which might make up any one plant, about six tons per hour would be assembled. In the first stage eight people cut the angles to the right lengths or bent the round bars to the desired form. These were moved on a roller conveyor to six-man assembly stations where the component parts would be tacked together for the next stage, welding. Drilling and miscellaneous work were done by three people between the lines. The nine-man welding station completed the welds before passing the joists on roller conveyors to two-man inspection teams. The last step before shipment was the painting.

In the joist plants, the workers had control over and responsibility for quality. There was an independent quality-control inspector who had the authority to reject the run of joists and cause them to be reworked. The quality control people were not under the incentive system and reported to the engineering department.

Daily production might vary widely since each joist was made for a specific job. The wide range of joists made control of the work load at each station difficult; bottlenecks might arise anywhere along the line. Each workstation was responsible for identifying such bottlenecks so that the foreman would reassign people promptly to maintain productivity. Since workers knew most of the jobs on the line, including the more skilled welding job, they could be shifted as needed. Work on the line was described by one general manager as "not machine type but mostly physical labor." He said the important thing was to avoid bottlenecks.

There were four lines of about 28 people each on two shifts at the Florence division. The jobs on the line were rated on responsibility and assigned a base wage, from $6 to $8 per hour. In addition, a weekly bonus was paid on the total output of each line. Each worker received the same percent bonus on his base wage.

The amount of time required to make a joist had been established as a result of experience; the general manager had seen no time studies in his 15 years with the company. As a job was bid, the cost of each joist was determined through the computer program. The time required depended on the length, number of panels, and depth of the joist.

At the time of production, the labor value of production, the standard, was determined in a similar manner. The general manager stated, "In the last nine or ten years we have not changed a standard." The standards list in use was over 10 years old. Previously, they adjusted the standard if the bonus was too high. He said the technological improvements over the last few years had been small. The general manager reported that the bonus had increased from about 60% 9 years earlier to about 100% in 1982 and had stabilized at that point. Figures C25.4 and C25.5 show data typically computed on performance and used by the manager. He said the difference in performance on the line resulted from the different abilities of the crews.

FIGURE C25.4   TONS PER MANHOUR, 52-WEEK MOVING AVERAGE

1977	.163	1983	.215
1978	.179	1984	.214
1979	.192	1985	.228
1980	.195	1986	.225
1981	.194	1987	.218
1982	.208		

FIGURE C25.5   A SAMPLE OF PERCENTAGE PERFORMANCE, JULY 1982

	Line	1	2	3	4
	1st	117	97	82	89
Shift					
	2nd	98	102	94	107

We don't have an industrial engineering staff. Our engineering department's work is limited to the design and the preparation of the paperwork prior to the actual fabrication process. Now, that is not to say they don't have any involvement in fabrication. But the efficiency of the plant is entirely up to the manufacturing department. . . . When we had our first group in a joist plant, we produced 3½ tons an hour. We thought that if we ever got to 4 tons, that would be the Millennium. Well, today we don't have anybody who produces less than 6½ tons an hour. This is largely due to improvements that the groups have suggested.

Management

In discussing his philosophy for dealing with the work force, the Florence manager stated:

I believe very strongly in the incentive system we have. We are a nonunion shop and we all feel that the way to stay so is to take care of our people and show them we care. I think that's easily done because of our fewer layers of management. . . . I spend a good part of my time in the plant, maybe an hour or so a day. If a man wants to know anything, for example an insurance question, I'm there and they walk right up to me and ask me questions which I'll answer the best I know how. . . . You can always tell when people are basically happy. If they haven't called for a meeting themselves or they are not hostile in any way, you can take it they understand the company's situation and accept it. . . . We do listen to our people. . . . For instance last fall I got a call from a couple of workers saying that the people in our Shipping and Receiving area felt they were not being paid properly in relation to production people. So we met with them, discussed the situation, and committed ourselves to reviewing the rates of other plants. We assured them that we would get back to them with an answer by the first of the year. Which we did. And there were a few minor changes.

The manager reported none of the plants had any particular labor problems, although there had been some in the past.

In 1976, two years before I came here, there was a union election at this plant which arose out of racial problems. The company actually lost the election to the U.S. Steelworkers. When it came time to begin negotiating the contract, the workers felt, or came to see, that they had little to gain from being in the union. The union was not going to be able to do anything more for them than they were already getting. So slowly the union activity died out and the union quietly withdrew.

He discussed formal systems for consulting with the workers before changes were made:

Of course we're cautioned by our labor counsel to maintain an open pipeline to our employees. We post all changes, company earnings, changes in the medical plan, anything that might affect an employee's job. Mr. Iverson has another philosophy, which is, "Either tell your people everything or tell them nothing." We choose to tell them everything. We don't have any regularly scheduled meetings. We meet whenever there's a need. The most recent examples were a meeting last month to discuss the results of an employee survey and three months before was held our annual dinner meetings off site.

We don't lay our people off and we make a point of telling our people this.

In the economic slump of 1982, we scheduled our line for four days, but the men were allowed to come in the fifth day for maintenance work at base pay. The men in the plant on an average running bonus might make $13 an hour. If their base pay is half that, on Friday they would only get $6 to $7 an hour. Surprisingly, many of the men did not want to come in on Friday. They felt comfortable with just working four days a week. They are happy to have that extra day off.

Recently the economic trouble in Texas had hurt business considerably. Both plants had been on decreased schedules for several months. About 20% of the people took the 5th day at base rate, but still no one had been laid off.

In April 1982 the executive committee decided, in view of economic conditions, that a pay freeze was necessary. The employees normally received an increase in their base pay the first of June. The decision was made at that time to freeze wages. The officers of the company, as a show of good faith, accepted a 5% pay cut. In addition to announcing this to the workers with a stuffer in their pay envelopes, meetings were held. Each production line, or incentive group of workers, met in the plant conference room with all supervision—foreman, plant production manager, and division manager. The economic crisis was explained to the employees by the production manager and all questions were answered.

STEEL DIVISIONS

Nucor had steel mills in four locations: Nebraska, South Carolina, Texas, and Utah. The mills were modern "mini-mills," all built within the last 20 years to convert scrap steel into standard angles, flats, rounds, and channels using the latest technology. Sales in 1985 were 1,152,000 tons, a 16% increase over that of 1984. This figure represented about 70% of the mills' output, the remainder being used by other Nucor divisions. In recent years, Nucor had broadened its product line to include a wider range of steel chemistries, sizes, and special shapes. The total capacity of the mills reached 2,100,000 tons in 1985.

A case writer from Harvard recounted the development of the steel divisions:

By 1967 about 60% of each Vulcraft sales dollar was spent on materials, primarily steel. Thus, the goal of keeping costs low made it imperative to obtain steel economically. In addition, in 1967 Vulcraft bought about 60% of its steel from foreign sources. As the Vulcraft Division grew, Nucor became concerned about its ability to obtain an adequate economical supply of steel and in 1968 began construction of its first steel mill in Darlington, South Carolina. By 1972 the Florence, South Carolina, joist plant was purchasing over 90% of its steel from this mill. The Fort Payne plant bought about 50% of its steel from Florence. The other joist plants in Nebraska, Indiana, and Texas found transportation costs prohibitive and continued to buy their steel from other steel companies, both foreign and domestic. Since the mill had excess capacity, Nucor began to market its steel products to outside customers. In 1972, 75% of the shipments of Nucor steel was to Vulcraft and 25% was to other customers.

Iverson explained in 1984:

In constructing these mills we have experimented with new processes and new manufacturing techniques. We serve as our own general contractor and design and build much of our own equipment. In one or more of our mills we have built our own continuous-casting unit, reheat furnaces, cooling beds, and in Utah even our own mill stands. All of these to date have cost under $125 per ton of annual capacity—compared with projected costs for large integrated mills of $1,200 to $1,500 per ton of annual capacity, ten times our cost. Our mills have high productivity. We currently use less than 4 manhours to produce a ton of steel. This includes everyone in the operation: maintenance, clerical, accounting, and sales and management. On the basis of our production workers alone, it is less than three manhours per ton. Our total employment costs are less than $60 per ton compared with the average employment costs of the seven largest U.S. steel companies of close to $130 per ton. Our total labor costs are less than 20% of our sales price.

In contrast to Nucor's less than 4 manhours, similar Japanese mills were said to require more than five hours and comparable U.S. mills over six hours. Nucor's average yield from molten metal to finished products was over 90%, compared with an average U.S. steel industry yield of about 74%, giving energy costs of about $39 per ton compared with their $75 a ton. Nucor ranked 46th on *Iron Age*'s annual survey of world steel producers. They were second on the list of top 10 producers of steel worldwide based on tons per employee, at 981 tons. The head of the list was Tokyo Steel at 1,485. U.S. Steel was 7th at 479. Some other results were: Nippon Steel, 453; British Steel, 213; Bethlehem Steel, 329; Kruppstahl, 195; Weirton Steel, 317; and Northstar Steel, 936. Nucor also ranked 7th on the list ranking growth of raw steel production. U.S. Steel was 5th on the same list. U.S. Steel topped the list based on improvement in tons per employee, at 56%; Nucor was 7th with a 12% improvement.

THE STEEL MAKING PROCESS

A steel mill's work is divided into two phases, preparation of steel of the proper "chemistry" and the forming of the steel into the desired products. The typical mini-mill utilized scrap steel, such as junk auto parts, instead of the iron ore which would be used in larger, integrated steel mills. The typical mini-mill had an annual capacity of 200,000 to 600,000 tons, compared with the 7 million tons of Bethlehem Steel's Sparrow's Point, Maryland, integrated plant.

A charging bucket fed loads of scrap steel into electric arc furnaces. The melted load, called a heat, was poured into a ladle to be carried by overhead crane to the casting machine. In the casting machine the liquid steel was extruded as a continuous red-hot solid bar of steel and cut into lengths weighing some 900 pounds called "billets." In the typical plant the billet, about four inches in cross section and about 20 feet long, was held temporarily in a pit where it cooled to normal temperatures. Periodically billets were carried to the rolling mill and placed in a reheat oven to bring them up to 2,000°F at which temperance they would be malleable. In the rolling mill, presses and dies progressively converted the billet into the desired round bars, angles, channels, flats, and other products. After cutting to standard lengths, they were moved to the warehouse.

Nucor's first steel mill, employing more than 500 people, was located in Darlington, South Carolina. The mill, with its three electric arc furnaces, operated 24 hours per day, 5½ days per week. Nucor had made a number of improvements in the melting and casting operations. The former general manager of the Darlington plant had developed a system which involved preheating the ladles, allowing for the faster flow of steel into the caster and resulting in better control of the steel characteristics. Less time and lower capital investment were required. The casting machines were "continuous casters," as opposed to the old batch method. The objective in the "front" of the mill was to keep the casters working. At the time of the Harvard study at Nucor each strand was in operation 90% of the time, while a competitor had announced a "record rate" of 75% which it had been able to sustain for a week.

Nucor was also perhaps the only mill in the country which regularly avoided the reheating of billets. This saved $10 to $12 per ton in fuel usage and losses due to oxidation of the steel. The cost of developing this process had been $12 million. All research projects had not been successful. The company spent approximately $2 million in an unsuccessful effort to utilize resistance heating. They lost even more on an effort at induction melting. As Iverson told *Metal Producing,* "That costs us a lot of money. Timewise it was very expensive. But you have got to make mistakes and we've had lots of failures." In the rolling mill, the first machine was a roughing mill by Morgarshammar, the first of its kind in the Western Hemisphere. This Swedish machine had been chosen because of its lower cost, higher productivity, and the flexibility. Passing through another 5 to 9 finishing mills converted the billet into the desired finished product. The yield from the billet to finished product was about 93%.

The Darlington design became the basis for plants in Nebraska, Texas, and Utah. The Texas plant had cost under $80 per ton of annual capacity. Whereas the typical mini-mill cost approximately $250 per ton, the average cost of all four of Nucor's mills was under $135. An integrated mill was expected to cost between $1,200 and $1,500 per ton.

The Darlington plant was organized into 12 natural groups for the purpose of incentive pay: 2 mills, each had two shifts with 3 groups—melting and casting, rolling mill, and finishing. In melting and casting there were three or four different standards, depending on the material, established by the department manager years ago based on historical performance. The general manager stated, "We don't change the standards." The caster, the key to the operation, was used at a 92% level—one greater than the claims of the manufacturer. For every good ton of billet above the standard hourly rate for the week, workers in the group received a 4% bonus. For example, with a common standard of 10 tons per run hour and an actual rate for the week of 28 tons per hour, the workers would receive a bonus of 72% of their base rate in the week's paycheck.

In the rolling mill there were more than 100 products, each with a different historical standard. Workers received a 4% to 6% bonus for every good ton sheared per hour for the week over the computed standard. The Darlington general manager said the standard would be changed only if there was a major machinery change and that a standard had not been changed since the initial development period for the plant. He commented that, in exceeding the standard the worker wouldn't work harder but would cooperate to avoid problems and moved more quickly if a problem developed: "If there is a way to improve output, they will tell us." Another manager added: "Meltshop employees don't ask me how much it costs Chaparral or LTV to make a billet. They want to know what it costs Darlington, Norfolk, Jewett to put a billet on the ground—scrap costs, alloy costs, electrical costs, refactory, gas, etc. Everybody from Charlotte to Plymouth watches the nickels and dimes."

The Darlington manager, who became CEO in 1983, stated:

> The key to making a profit when selling a product with no aesthetic value, or a product that you really can't differentiate from your competitors, is cost. I don't look at us as a fantastic marketing organization, even though I think we are pretty good; but we don't try to overcome unreasonable costs by mass marketing. We maintain low costs by keeping the employee force at the level it should be, not doing things that aren't necessary to achieve our goals, and allowing people to function on their own and by judging them on their results.

> To keep a cooperative and productive workforce you need, number one, to be completely honest about everything; number two, to allow each employee as much as possible to make decisions about that employee's work, to find easier and more productive ways to perform duties; and number three, to be as fair as possible to all employees. Most of the changes we make in work procedures and in equipment come from the employees. They really know the problems of their jobs better than anyone else. We don't have any industrial engineers, nor do we ever intend to, because that's a type of specialist who tends to take responsibility off the top division management and give them a crutch.

> To communicate with my employees, I try to spend time in the plant and at intervals have meetings with the employees. Usually if they have a question they just visit me. Recently a small group visited me in my office to discuss our vacation policy. They had some suggestions and, after listening to them, I had to agree that the ideas were good.

THE INCENTIVE SYSTEM

The foremost characteristic of Nucor's personnel system was its incentive plan. Another major personnel policy was providing job security. Also all employees at Nucor received the same fringe benefits. There was only one group insurance plan. Holidays and vacations did not differ by job. The company had no executive dining rooms or restrooms, no fishing lodges, company cars, or reserved parking places.

Absenteeism and tardiness were not problems at Nucor. Each employee had four days of absence before pay was reduced. In addition to these, missing work was allowed for jury duty, military leave, or the death of close relatives. After this, a day's absence cost them bonus pay for that week, and lateness of more than a half hour meant the loss of bonus for that day.

Employees were kept informed about the company. Charts showing the division's results in return on assets and bonus payoff were posted in prominent places in the plant. The personnel manager commented that as he traveled around to all the plants, he found everyone in the company could tell him the level of profits in their division. The general managers held dinners at least twice a year with their employees. The dinners were held with 50 or 60 employees at a time. After introductory remarks the floor was open for discussion of any work-related problems. The company also had a formal grievance procedure. The Darlington manager couldn't recall the last grievance he had processed.

There was a new employee orientation program and an employee handbook which contained personnel policies and rules. The corporate office sent all news releases to each division where they were posted on bulletin boards. Each employee in the company also received a copy of the Annual Report. For the last several years the cover of the Annual Report had contained the names of all Nucor employees. Every child of every Nucor employee received up to $1,200 a year for four years if they chose to go on to higher education, including technical schools.

The average hourly worker's pay was $31,000, compared with the average earnings in manufacturing in that state of slightly more than $13,000. The personnel manager believed that pay was not the only thing the workers liked about Nucor. He said that an NBC interviewer, working on the documentary "If Japan Can, Why Can't We?" often heard, "I enjoy working for Nucor because Nucor is the best, the most productive, and the most profitable company that I know of."

"I honestly feel that if someone performs well, they should share in the company and if they are going to share in the success, they should also share in the failures," Iverson stated. There were four incentive programs at Nucor, one each for production workers, department heads, staff people such as accountants, secretaries, or engineers, and senior management, which included the division managers. All these programs were on a group basis.

Within the production program, groups ranged in size from 25 to 30 people and had definable and measurable operations. The company believed that a program should be simple and that bonuses should be paid promptly. "We don't have any discretionary bonuses—zero. It is all based on performance. Now we don't want anyone to sit in judgment, because it never is fair . . . ," said Iverson. The personnel manager stated: "Their bonus is based on roughly 90% of historical time it takes to make a particular joist. If during a week they make joists at 60% less than the standard time, they receive a 60% bonus." This was paid with the regular pay the following week. The complete paycheck amount, including overtime, was multiplied by the bonus factor. Bonus was not paid when equipment was not operating: "We have the philosophy that when equipment is not operating everybody suffers and the bonus for downtime is zero." The foremen are also part of the group and received the same bonus as the employees they supervised.

The second incentive program was for department heads in the various divisions. The incentive pay here was based on division contribution, defined as the division earnings before corporate expenses and profit sharing are determined. Bonuses were reported to run as high as 51% of a person's base salary in the divisions and 30% for corporate positions.

Officers of the company were under a single profit sharing plan. Their base salaries were approximately 75% of comparable positions in industry. Once return on equity reached 9%, slightly below the average for manufacturing firms, 5% of net earnings before taxes went into a pool, that was divided among the officers based on their salaries. "Now if return on equity for the company reaches, say, 20%, which it has, then we can wind up with as much as 190% of our base salaries and 115% on top of that in stock. We get both." In 1982 the return was 9% and the executives received no bonus. His pay in 1981 was approximately $300,000 but dropped the next year to $110,000. "I think that ranked by total compensation I was the lowest-paid CEO in the Fortune 500. I was kind of proud of that, too." In 1986, Iverson's stock was worth over $10 million dollars. The young Vulcraft manager was likewise a millionaire.

There was a third plan for people who were neither production workers nor department managers. Their bonus was based on either the division return on assets or the corporate return on assets.

The fourth program was for the senior officers. The senior officers had no employment contracts, pension or retirement plans, or other normal perquisites. Their base salaries were set at about 70% of what an individual doing similar work in other companies would receive. More than half of the officers' compensation was reported to be based directly on the company's earnings. Ten percent of pretax earnings over a preestablished level, based on a 12% return on stockholders' equity, was set aside and allocated to the senior officers according to their base salary. Half the bonus was paid in cash and half was deferred.

In lieu of a retirement plan, the company had a profit sharing plan with a deferred trust. Each year 10% of the pretax earnings was put into profit sharing. Fifteen percent of this was set aside to be paid to employees in the following March as a cash bonus and the remainder was put into trust for each employee on the basis of percent of their earnings as a percent of total wages paid within the corporation. The employee was vested 20% after the first year and gained an additional 10% vesting each year thereafter. Employees received a quarterly statement of their balance in profit sharing.

The company had an Employer Monthly Stock Investment Plan to which Nucor added 10% to the amount the employee contributed and paid the commission on the purchase of any Nucor stock. After each 5 years of service with the company, the employee received a service award consisting of 5 shares of Nucor stock. Additionally, if profits were good, extraordinary bonus payments would be made to the employees. In 1978, each employee received a $500 payment.

According to Iverson:

I think the first obligation of the company is to the stockholder and to its employees. I find in this country too many cases where employees are underpaid and corporate management is making huge social donations for self-fulfillment. We regularly give donations, but we have a very interesting corporate policy. First, we give donations where our employees are. Second, we give donations which will benefit our employees, such as to the YMCA. It is a difficult area and it requires a lot of thought. There is certainly a strong social responsibility for a company, but it cannot be at the expense of the employees or the stockholders.

Nucor had no trouble finding people to staff its plants. When the mill in Jewett, Texas, was built in 1975, there were over 5,000 applications for the 400 jobs—many coming from people in Houston and Dallas. Yet everyone did not find work at Nucor what they wanted. In 1975, a Harvard team found high turnover among new production workers after start-up. The cause appeared to be pressure from fellow workers in the group incentive situation. A survival-of-the-fittest situation was found in which those who didn't like to work seldom stuck around. "Productivity increased and turnover declined dramatically once these people left," the Harvard team concluded. Iverson commented: "A lot of people aren't goal-oriented. A lot of them don't want to work that hard, so initially we have a lot of turnover in a plant but then it's so low we don't even measure after that."

The Wall Street Journal reported in 1981:

Harry Pigg, a sub-district director for the USW in South Carolina, sees a darker side in Nucor's incentive plan. He contends that Nucor unfairly penalizes workers by taking away big bonus payments for absence or tardiness, regardless of the reason. Workers who are ill, he says, try to work because they can't afford to give up the bonus payment. "Nucor whips them into line," he adds. He acknowledges, though, that high salaries are the major barrier to unionizing the company.

Having welcomed a parade of visitors over the years, Iverson had become concerned with the pattern: "They only do one or two of the things we do. It's not just incentives or the scholarship program; its all those things put together that results in a unified philosophy for the company."

AS 1987 BEGAN

Looking ahead in 1984, Iverson had said: "The next decade will be an exciting one for steel producers. It will tax our abilities to keep pace with technological changes we can see now on the horizon." Imports didn't have to dominate the U.S. economy. He believed the steel industry would continue to play a pivotal role in the growth of American industry. He pointed out comparative advantages of the U.S. steel industry: an abundance of resources, relatively low energy costs, lower transportation costs, and the change in the government's attitude toward business.

The excitement he had predicted had occurred. Imports were a challenge for steel, just as for textiles, shoes, machine tools, and computers. The old steel companies were flexing their muscle and getting back into the game. Overcapacity hadn't left the mini-mill immune, there was no safe haven for anyone. Nucor was no longer a small company, David, with free shots at Goliath.

The honeymoon appeared over. Wall Street worried about what Nucor should do. Cable News Network posed the position of some on Wall Street: "They say basically you guys are selling to the construction companies, you are selling to some fairly depressed industries. They also say, Nucor, they were a specialized little niche company. They did what they did very well; but now all of a sudden, they are going out, building these big mills to make huge pieces of steel and they are talking casted cold, all that stuff. They're worried that you may be getting into deals that are a little too complicated from what they perceive you as being able to do well."

The New York Times pointed out that expansion would certainly hurt earnings for the next several years. They quoted a steel consultant. "It is hard to do all that they are trying to do and keep profits up. With the industry in the shape it's in, this is not the time to expand beyond the niche they've established."

With $185 million in cash, Iverson told *Inc.* "It (going private) has been mentioned to us by a number of brokerage firms and investment houses, but we wouldn't even consider it. It wouldn't be fair to employees, and I don't know whether it would be fair to the stockholders. . . . You're going to restrict the growth opportunities. . . . You either grow or die. . . . Opportunities wouldn't be created for people within the company."

Iverson told *CNN*:

We've decided that really we want to stay in that niche (steel). We don't want to buy any banks. . . . All of the growth of the company has been internally generated. We think there are opportunities in the steel industry today. . . . There are ample opportunities, although they are somewhat harder to find than they used to be.

Another of my strengths is the ability to stick to my knitting. The reason executives make a lot of mistakes is that sometimes they get bored—they think the grass is greener on the other side so they go out and buy a bank or an oil company or they go into businesses where they have no expertise. . . . I have never gotten bored with this company. I've done this job so long that I think I have some insight into the needs and the capabilities of the company. I'm not misled into thinking we can do something that we can't.

An economics professor and steel consultant at Middle Tennessee State University told the *Times*, "You're not going to see any growth in the steel market, so the only way to make money is to reduce costs and have new technology to penetrate other companies' business."

The New York Times stated: "Critics question whether it is wise to continue expanding production capabilities, as Nucor is doing, when there is already overcapacity in the steel industry and intense competition already exists between the mini-mills." Iverson insisted the strategy would pay off in the long term. He told the *Times,* "The company's strategy makes sense for us. To gain a larger share in an ever-shrinking market, you've got to take something from someone else."

Iverson's position was clear:

We're going to stay in steel and steel products. The way we look at it, this company does only two things well, builds plants economically and runs them efficiently. That is the whole company. We don't have any financial expertise, we're not entrepreneurs, we're not into acquisitions. Steel may not be the best business in the world, but it's what we know how to do and we do it well.

APPENDIX A
Nucor Corporation
Sales, Earnings, and Statistical Data
1976–1986

	1976	1977	1978	1979
For the Year				
Sales, costs and earnings:				
Net sales	175,768,479	212,952,829	306,939,667	428,681,778
Costs and expenses:				
Cost of products sold	142,235,949	168,247,627	227,953,309	315,688,291
Marketing and administrative expenses	14,744,882	19,729,586	28,660,033	36,724,159
Interest expense (income)	2,290,757	2,723,024	1,877,476	1,504,791
	159,271,588	190,700,237	258,490,818	353,917,241
Earnings before federal income taxes	16,496,891	22,252,592	48,448,849	74,764,537
Federal income taxes	7,800,000	9,800,000	22,600,000	32,500,000
Net earnings	8,696,891	12,452,592	25,848,849	42,264,537
Net earnings per share	.45	.64	1.30	2.10
Dividends declared per share	.03	.05	.07	.11
Percentage of earnings to sales	4.9%	5.8%	8.4%	9.9%
Return on average equity	17.6%	20.7%	32.6%	37.5%
Return on average assets	8.2%	10.1%	16.1%	19.4%
Average shares outstanding	19,119,669	19,481,464	19,855,210	20,152,914
Sales per employee	76,421	88,730	115,826	145,316
At Year End				
Working capital	30,914,076	30,853,297	45,277,360	53,826,193
Current ratio	2.0	2.0	1.8	1.8
Stockholders' equity per share	2.78	3.37	4.59	6.58
Shares outstanding	19,447,677	19,701,946	20,065,257	20,261,631
Stockholders	24,000	22,000	22,000	23,000
Employees	2,300	2,500	2,800	3,100

Source: Company financial report.

	1980	1981	1982	1983	1984	1985	1986
For the Year							
	482,420,363	544,820,621	486,018,162	542,531,431	660,259,922	758,495,374	755,228,939
	369,415,571	456,210,289	408,606,641	461,727,688	539,733,252	600,797,865	610,378,369
	38,164,559	33,524,820	31,720,377	33,988,054	45,939,311	59,079,802	65,900,653
	(1,219,965)	10,256,546	7,899,110	(748,619)	(3,959,092)	(7,560,645)	(5,288,971)
	406,360,165	499,991,655	448,226,128	494,967,123	581,711,471	652,317,022	670,990,051
	76,060,198	44,828,966	37,792,034	47,564,308	78,548,451	106,178,352	84,238,888
	31,000,000	10,100,000	15,600,000	19,700,000	34,000,000	47,700,000	37,800,000
	45,060,198	34,728,966	22,192,034	27,864,308	44,548,451	58,478,352	46,438,888
	2.21	1.67	1.06	1.32	2.11	2.74	2.17
	.15	.16	.17	.20	.24	.27	.31
	9.3%	6.4%	4.6%	5.1%	6.7%	7.7%	6.1%
	29.0%	17.8%	10.0%	11.4%	16.0%	17.8%	12.5%
	16.9%	10.3%	5.9%	7.0%	9.8%	11.2%	8.2%
	20,414,109	20,756,583	20,912,577	21,066,448	21,169,492	21,345,852	21,405,440
	150,756	155,663	133,156	148,639	176,069	197,011	181,983
At Year End							
	48,872,282	58,349,979	66,439,942	105,402,367	152,919,639	213,513,319	177,297,282
	1.7	1.8	2.0	2.2	2.5	2.8	2.5
	8.64	10.17	11.07	12.21	14.10	16.65	18.16
	20,549,991	20,890,521	20,987,823	21,135,272	21,241,618	21,472,508	21,131,298
	22,000	22,000	22,000	21,000	22,000	22,000	22,000
	3,300	3,700	3,600	3,700	3,800	3,900	4,400

Nucor Corporation
Balance Sheet Data
1976–1986

	1976	1977	1978	1979
Assets				
Current assets:				
Cash	8,156,215	3,346,196	6,286,583	8,716,950
Short-term investments	3,875,000	3,750,000	21,131,652	27,932,854
Accounts receivable	13,493,692	18,897,191	26,580,943	35,203,909
Contracts in process	3,428,026	4,494,418	5,316,522	5,004,091
Inventories	32,643,688	30,410,685	41,548,920	40,007,532
Other current assets	219,423	256,812	245,674	496,854
	61,816,044	61,155,302	101,110,294	117,362,190
Property, plant and equipment:				
Land and improvements	2,209,289	2,696,502	3,526,812	4,915,078
Buildings and improvements	15,138,400	18,441,047	22,229,110	29,875,783
Plant machinery and equipment	44,212,629	55,992,359	68,677,667	91,865,271
Office and transportation equipment	1,637,493	1,803,511	2,579,600	5,478,870
Construction in process	8,516,708	7,739,163	18,240,643	28,326,555
	71,714,519	86,672,582	115,253,832	160,461,557
Less accumulated depreciation	15,778,779	20,733,060	26,722,157	35,879,558
	55,935,740	65,939,522	88,531,675	124,581,999
Other assets	1,343,797	916,158	3,812,724	1,167,325
Total assets	119,095,581	128,010,982	193,454,693	243,111,514
Liabilities and Stockholders' Equity				
Current liabilities:				
Long-term debt due within one year	438,462	438,462	463,462	1,245,764
Accounts payable	16,220,543	12,077,514	24,150,147	26,414,666
Federal income taxes	5,465,824	4,440,824	15,640,824	15,913,361
Accrued expenses and other current liabilities	8,777,139	13,345,205	15,578,501	19,962,206
	30,901,968	30,302,005	55,832,934	63,535,997
Other liabilities:				
Long-term debt due after one year	31,667,308	28,132,692	41,473,077	41,398,138
Deferred federal income taxes	1,819,563	2,619,563	4,019,563	4,919,563
Deferred compensation and other liabilities	621,772	661,317	—	—
	34,108,643	31,413,572	45,492,640	46,317,701
Stockholders' equity:				
Common stock	885,143	1,261,644	1,795,698	2,721,040
Additional paid-in capital	9,211,839	9,855,410	10,743,090	11,125,185
Retained earnings	44,088,406	55,497,968	79,934,950	119,891,199
Treasury stock	(100,418)	(319,617)	(344,619)	(479,608)
	54,084,970	66,295,405	92,129,119	133,257,816
Total liabilities and stockholders' equity	119,095,581	128,010,982	193,454,693	243,111,514

Source: Company financial report.

	1980	1981	1982	1983	1984	1985	1986
				Assets			
	5,753,068	8,704,859	10,668,165	6,384,795	2,863,680	8,028,519	11,008,879
	16,000,000	—	34,224,381	72,669,615	109,846,810	177,115,954	117,727,705
	35,537,959	42,983,058	34,685,498	51,110,372	58,408,244	60,390,448	61,268,892
	7,985,985	5,719,121	3,656,643	7,058,803	8,462,815	10,478,296	9,120,533
	49,599,265	72,996,664	48,831,434	56,555,102	73,797,302	78,641,805	96,474,278
	489,450	978,590	476,527	110,475	74,522	114,125	137,968
	115,365,727	131,382,292	132,542,648	193,889,162	253,453,373	334,769,147	295,738,255
	5,806,711	12,142,613	12,215,375	12,577,104	12,918,519	12,818,723	15,041,782
	34,853,546	53,037,722	53,668,523	55,971,208	58,909,921	61,709,286	75,217,588
	139,182,579	245,037,510	244,143,769	258,305,715	277,553,868	279,579,407	331,945,921
	5,711,199	6,868,069	9,565,667	9,736,448	8,643,752	14,883,272	16,358,988
	33,541,819	1,776,106	3,260,329	2,071,147	1,944,670	7,238,325	13,700,338
	219,095,854	318,862,020	322,853,663	338,661,622	359,970,730	376,229,013	452,264,617
	46,021,581	66,245,946	83,782,273	107,356,805	131,867,940	150,954,339	181,431,475
	173,074,273	252,616,074	239,071,390	231,304,817	228,102,790	225,274,674	270,833,142
	2,781,867	783,761	18,903	373,073	632,302	267,367	5,036,247
	291,221,867	384,782,127	371,632,941	425,567,052	482,188,465	560,311,188	571,607,644
			Liabilities and Stockholders' Equity				
	1,696,815	1,654,784	1,603,462	2,402,462	2,402,462	2,402,462	3,052,462
	36,640,991	32,237,889	22,948,867	37,135,084	32,691,249	35,473,011	53,165,551
	4,362,619	10,733,627	12,535,096	14,813,909	23,705,195	27,597,464	14,309,565
	23,793,020	28,406,013	29,015,281	34,135,340	41,734,778	55,782,891	47,913,395
	66,493,445	73,032,313	66,102,706	88,486,795	100,533,684	121,255,828	118,440,973
	39,605,169	83,754,231	48,229,615	45,731,000	43,232,384	40,233,769	42,147,654
	7,519,563	15,619,563	25,019,563	33,219,563	38,819,563	41,319,563	27,319,563
	—	—	—	—	—	—	—
	47,124,732	99,373,794	73,249,178	78,950,563	82,051,947	81,553,332	69,467,217
	2,758,713	2,797,948	2,802,796	5,642,727	5,669,757	5,732,382	8,665,397
	13,353,856	16,531,759	17,696,568	17,022,043	18,991,334	24,299,195	25,191,988
	161,952,033	193,355,403	211,921,654	235,569,108	275,035,788	327,816,850	367,575,659
	(460,912)	(309,090)	(139,961)	(104,184)	(94,045)	(346,399)	(17,733,590)
	177,603,690	212,376,020	232,281,057	258,129,694	299,602,834	357,502,028	383,699,454
	291,221,867	384,782,127	371,632,941	425,567,052	482,188,465	560,311,188	571,607,644

26

OVERSEAS NATIONAL AIRWAYS, INC.

Prepared by Melvin J. Stanford, Mankato State University.

The extensive reorganization of Overseas National Airways, Inc. (ONA), which had taken place in late 1977, was the subject of a thorough review by ONA's management early the following year. The company, which was a major U.S. charter airline and which had worldwide operating authority except for Japan, Australia, and New Zealand, had encountered some severe turbulence in the events of recent years. In addition to some earlier aircraft accidents, three serious crashes between 1975 and 1977 had destroyed two DC-10 aircraft and one DC-8. Because of these accidents and large financial operating losses, and in the face of increasing competition in the airline passenger industry, ONA's major stockholders had brought in new leadership in 1977.

Mr. Edward Ory became chairman of ONA's executive committee in April 1977. A complete reorganizational plan was developed during mid-1977. The plan called for ONA to divest all auxiliary and diversified activities. Moreover, the plan was to standardize to DC-10 aircraft operation and to dispose of all other aircraft and spare parts.

These moves would involve a drastic reduction in personnel and scope of operation. In October of 1977, Mr. G.F. Steedman Hinckley resigned as chairman of the board of directors of ONA after 18 years as chief executive. Following the election of Mr. Ory as chairman of the board of directors, the company proceeded to implement the reorganizational plan in November and December of 1977. The fleet of DC-8 aircraft and spare parts was sold. While this resulted in an accounting loss, the company's cash flow was improved for indebtedness commitments and future cash requirements. This move left ONA operating two DC-10-30 jet aircraft, down from a fleet of 21 jet aircraft in 1975. In addition, ONA still subleased out to other operators four DC-8 and one DC-9 aircraft

Note: Copyright © 1980 by Brigham Young University. This case was prepared as a basis for class discussion. Used by permission.

functional Styl.

which it had on lease. Drastic reductions were also made in the number of employees from about 900 to 361.

A third DC-10-30 aircraft was on order from McDonnell-Douglas Corporation for delivery in June of 1978. It was expected that this aircraft would be placed in service in time for the summer peak season in air passenger charter. With this in mind, ONA was projecting a near break-even operation for 1978 (as compared to a loss in excess of $12 million in 1977), and an expected profit of about $2.5 million in 1979 and $5.6 million in 1980.

objective

A consulting firm which had undertaken a thorough study of ONA after its re-organization had reported to ONA's insurance companies that the transformation had appeared to be successful and that when the third DC-10-30 was delivered to ONA in June, the company should be as well organized and managed as any charter airline. While this was very encouraging to ONA's management, Mr. Ory and his staff were also concerned with the changing conditions in the air charter market and were continuing to review all available options. *threat*

COMPANY BACKGROUND

Overseas National Airways, Inc., was organized in 1950. From its base in California it began charter flight operations with a fleet of five DC-4 aircraft. The outbreak of the Korean conflict in 1950 greatly expanded ONA's operations, flying cargo and military personnel between the United States and Japan. This was followed later by participating in the evacuation of Dutch nationalists from Indonesia, the immigration of Hungarian refugees, and transport of supplies to the French in Viet Nam, as well as other charter flight operations.

In 1958, ONA pioneered the transatlantic charter market with a fleet of DC-6 aircraft. The following year, ONA received one of the largest U.S. military air transport service contracts ever awarded to a single carrier. Twelve DC-7's and another DC-6 were required for military passenger operations, both domestic and international, over the Atlantic and Pacific oceans for military contract flights. This large contract, however, proved to be ONA's undoing. The company had been low bidder on the contract and had found that it couldn't make a profit. Consequently, ONA went into bankruptcy and suspended operations in 1963.

weakness

Two years later, ONA was refinanced and resumed commercial flight operations utilizing the DC-7 aircraft. Two DC-8 jets and four DC-9 jet aircraft were also ordered, with the two DC-8's being delivered in mid-1966. The Civil Aeronautics Board awarded ONA in 1966 long-term authority for transatlantic charter operations, including tour flights. The transatlantic market developed into the largest tourist flight market for ONA and other charter airlines, as well as a principal market for all the scheduled passenger airlines of the world. Passenger charter flights to London, Paris, and Rome were initiated in 1967 and the CAB certificate was extended to include the Caribbean and Hawaii. In 1968 ONA acquired a fleet of eight Lockheed L-188 Electras which were modified for military and domestic cargo operations. By 1969, ONA was operating a fleet of 21 aircraft in commercial passenger and cargo as well as military contract flights. A considerable amount of military business involved passenger and cargo airlifts between the United States and other bases in Viet Nam.

answer mkt

strength

The first two DC-10 wide-bodied jet aircraft were acquired by ONA in mid-1973. At that time, the Electra cargo aircraft were sold. Additional DC-8 aircraft were acquired during 1975. Then in November 1975 and January 1976, two DC-10 aircraft were lost in serious accidents. Later in 1976 the DC-9 aircraft were taken out of service, and three DC-10-30's were ordered, two of which were delivered in May and June of 1977, with the third to be delivered in June of 1978. By 1977, the emphasis had shifted more from military to commercial business, with predominantly passenger operations. The following table shows amounts of ONA's net operating revenues attributable to airline services during recent years.

	1977	1976	1975	1974	1973
Commercial:					
Aircraft leasing	$1,657	$2,632	$4,520	$4,460	$2,584
Passenger	67,885	52,467	53,543	47,056	38,395
Cargo	492	9,825	9,977	6,406	6,247
Total	$70,034	$64,924	$68,040	$57,992	$47,226
Military:					
Passenger	$9,963	$10,988	$13,200	$7,765	$5,165
Cargo	—	7,005	8,414	15,757	21,509
Total	$9,963	$17,993	$21,614	$23,522	$26,674

Note: Dollar amounts in 1000s.

Some diversification had been attempted in recent years. ONA had owned the Delta Queen Steamboat Company, which owned and operated the riverboat *Delta Queen* for pleasure cruises on the Mississippi River. ONA had also owned Great Ocean Cruise Line, Inc., a nonoperating company which had contracted for the construction of another riverboat, the *Mississippi Queen*. Both of these subsidiary companies had been exchanged by ONA for stock in the Coca-Cola Bottling Company of New York, Inc., in 1976, after the latter had made an unsuccessful attempt to acquire ONA. The Coca-Cola stock was later sold by ONA for $3.4 million, most of which was used to repay bank loans that had funded the riverboats. ONA had also owned Chippewa Land Company, Ltd., which owned land and buildings in California. Chippewa was sold in early 1977 at a loss of about $350,000.

Alaska International Industries, Inc., had also tried to acquire ONA. However, that attempt was "deferred indefinitely" because of financing problems, according to the *Wall Street Journal*.

MARKETING

Flights between the United States and Europe over the North Atlantic were ONA's primary market. In addition, during 1977, 11% of the company's total revenues came from flying Islamic pilgrims from several African countries to Saudi Arabia during the Haj, or the Moslem holy season. The best non-transatlantic markets were the long-range ones: Hong Kong, Tahiti, Rio de Janeiro, Lima, and South Africa, which were all emerging as off-season charter destinations.

Most of ONA's charter business was sold through about 20 established wholesale tour agencies who contracted for their flight services twice a year, generally at the rate of about $12.65 per mile for the DC-10 aircraft. Due to the increasing volume of civilian tour travel, ONA had sold out nearly all its available flight time for the entire year 1978, to fully utilize its present two DC-10 aircraft and after May to utilize all three DC-10 aircraft, for an average daily utilization between 11 and 14 hours. In addition, ONA contracted with the U.S. military for transport of military personnel around the world on a flexible basis, which amounted to approximately 20% of ONA's business. From time to time, foreign airlines were also seeking additional aircraft for charter flights over their routes as seasonal peak traffic occurred for them, such as Moslem travel to Mecca during the Haj.

ONA marketing operations were concentrated at its New York headquarters at the JFK International Airport, with sales offices in San Francisco, Detroit, and Germany. Other offices in various cities had been closed down as a result of the reorganization, but it was believed by management that the three sales offices plus the headquarters would be sufficient for DC-10 operation.

FLIGHT OPERATIONS

Passenger revenue miles for ONA were about 2.14 billion in 1977, holding fairly steady since 1973 despite the change in fleet configuration. Cargo ton miles, however, had declined steadily and by 1978 ONA was out of the charter cargo business (see aircraft operating statistics, Exhibit C26.1).

The director of the flight operations department was Captain Marshall, who was a long-time pilot and experienced flight captain. The flight training managers, pilots, and flight engineers reported to the director of flight operations. A number of ONA flight crews had been retired or separated during the recent reorganization, reportedly those who were the least qualified. The pilots' union contract allowed for dismissal of any crew member who did not meet ONA standards on all training and proficiency requirements. Crew qualifications were considerably higher in ONA than average U.S. scheduled airlines operating DC-10 aircraft. The ONA DC-10 captains all averaged over 22,000 total flight hours.

The flight operations manual had been revised for DC-10-30 operations only, and the newly printed manual had been approved by the Federal Aviation Administration. Emphasis on operating discipline among flight crew personnel was strong.

Training was an important part of ONA's flight operations. The transition from DC-9 and DC-8 aircraft to exclusively DC-10 required considerable transition training on the part of flight crews. ONA obtained the American Airlines ground-school curriculum built around slides and tapes which American furnished. All the training manuals were upgraded to the DC-10-30 series aircraft that ONA operated. ONA established very high standards for its flight training, and a federal safety inspector assigned to the company attended all the ground training classes along with ONA crews. Arrangements had also been made with United Airlines to provide DC-10 cockpit procedure training and DC-10 flight simulator training. All the flight personnel realized that the future of the company and the success of the new operation depended upon a greatly improved safety record.

Each DC-10 required a cabin staff of 10 attendants. Training for these attendants was largely on a classroom basis, with some involvement in the aircraft when they were available at JFK airport between flights and during maintenance. The trainees would fly as crew members for observation only for their first major flight and then would gradually be integrated into the cabin crew as experience improved their ability. ONA

EXHIBIT C26.1 OVERSEAS NATIONAL AIRWAYS, INC.: AIRCRAFT OPERATING STATISTICS

	1977	1976	1975	1974	1973
Aircraft days operated:					
DC-10-30	434	—	681	728	424
DC-8-63	937	1,164	584	673	1,187
DC-8-61	788	1,276	916	432	296
DC-8-20/30*	—	1,966	1,415	547	14
DC-9-30†	—	1,189	1,557	1,820	1,968
L-188 cargo	—	—	—	2,285	3,526
Average daily utilization (block hours):					
DC-10-30	12.3	—	9.7	10.1	12.0
DC-8-63	11.1	8.7	9.2	11.2	12.0
DC-8-61	9.6	9.3	10.0	10.2	10.0
DC-8-20/30*	—	2.2	3.9	4.2	8.6
DC-9-30†	—	9.6	9.7	4.2	9.3
L-188 cargo	—	—	—	5.3	5.9
Passenger revenue miles (000):					
Commercial	1,866,244	1,620,595	1,659,117	1,492,760	1,959,373
Military	276,389	330,198	349,163	319,295	227,682
Total	2,142,633	1,950,793	2,008,280	1,812,055	2,187,055
Cargo ton miles (000):					
Commercial	3,063	17,132	19,943	21,192	22,385
Military	—	28,806	41,722	84,042	106,233
Total	3,063	45,938	61,665	105,234	128,618
Number of employees (end of year):					
Flight	213	268	447	399	507
Nonflight	148	321	536	433	541
Subsidiary companies	—	—	105	106	135
Total	361	589	1,088	938	1,183

* The DC-8-20/30 aircraft were removed from service during 1976.
† The DC-9-30 aircraft were retired and the related cargo operation was discontinued during 1976.
Source: ONA annual reports.

employed about 150 flight attendants, all of whom had been with the airline for an extensive period. Consequently, the need for additional training was not great.

Flight control was an impressive part of ONA's operations. This included crew and flight scheduling, flight dispatch, and worldwide communications. A licensed airline dispatcher and maintenance engineer were both on duty 24 hours a day 7 days a week to provide and maintain constant flight watch of every segment of every flight. No ONA flight could be initiated from any part of the world without dispatch clearance and an approved flight plan by this central flight operations dispatcher at JFK airport in New York.

ONA used the United Airlines computer which was directly connected to the ONA flight control center through a keyboard and display printer for flight planning of all flights everywhere in the world. When a flight was contemplated, whether domestic or international, there were more than 20 separate pieces of flight plan information typed into the UAL computer on a terminal located at the flight planning dispatch center of ONA at JFK airport. Within a matter of seconds, the computer would print back the *strength*

entire flight plan with the best routes to fly, upper winds between any two points, the most economical speed to fly, the flight time between all checkpoints, the weight of fuel consumed at each checkpoint, the remaining fuel aboard, the ground speed to be expected, time at each checkpoint, the alternative airport, the fuel at arrival, the most economical power setting, and the most economical and safe fuel load, etc.

The computer flight plan was checked by the dispatcher, and then on signal command, the computer typed a copy of the flight plan message on a teletype circuit to any en route station in the world requested by the controlling dispatcher, plus a copy for the captain of the flight, wherever he may be located in the world.

The U.S. Weather Bureau's principal weather station in Maryland was connected directly into the United Airlines computer. Weather and upper wind reports from all over the world were fed into the computer on a continuous basis. This weather and wind information and forecasts were constantly passed on to the aircraft crews in flight, and were immediately available to the flight planners and dispatchers. All flight operations dispatch personnel were extremely capable and experienced. Flying a worldwide operation would not be possible without the availability of present day communications facilities.

MAINTENANCE

strength

ONA had a highly qualified and experienced maintenance organization. The DC-10 line maintenance was being performed by ONA personnel at JFK airport in New York for the 250-hour and 750-hour services. All 1500-hour and 3000-hour major DC-10 heavy maintenance services were being done by United Airlines under contract. ONA had maintenance contracts with United Airlines for both major airframe maintenance services and a 100% spare parts exchange program. This arrangement eliminated time out of service for accessories, rotatables, and time components. All replacement parts were immediately available from UAL on an exchange basis. In addition, ONA had approximately $4 million invested in DC-10 maintenance spare parts other than engines.

ONA also had a contract with General Electric for all of its heavy engine maintenance and overhauls. Daily engine parameter monitoring data were fed into a GE control computer on a daily basis, and continuous monitoring of all engine operating data was conducted by GE. When a flight terminated at any place in the world, the engine log of monitored parameter data was telexed back to ONA at JFK and fed immediately into GE's computer. Oil Spectro-analysis was made at each 250-hour engine service as an additional control over all engine operations. GE engine reliability on the ONA DC-10 aircraft had been excellent.

Maintenance for ONA's DC-10 aircraft was also performed by Pan-American, Lufthansa, BTA, UAL, Continental, and other experienced major airlines as required in various places in the world by ONA and under ONA maintenance personnel supervision. ONA presently had one maintenance engineer based in Los Angeles, two in Detroit, and four in Frankfurt, Germany. All these engineers were highly trained and experienced with DC-10 aircraft, which had so many double and triple systems that maintenance dispatch reliability of those aircraft was phenomenal as compared to the older generation of DC-8's. ONA had also adopted a special stringent and conservative tire and wheel inspection and maintenance to avoid tire failures and reduce the risk from abortive takeoffs from tire failures. ONA had closed its maintenance base in Wilmington, Ohio, following the recent disposal of its fleet of DC-8 aircraft.

ACCIDENTS

Strength

& weakness

ONA had experienced one major accident with propeller-driven aircraft just two years after it began doing business. In 1952, at Oakland, California, a DC-4 aircraft on a training flight was struck by another aircraft in a midair collision, resulting in a total loss of the aircraft. The next major accident did not occur until 17 years later. In 1969, an ONA DC-9 landing at Sacramento, California, from a military cargo flight suffered a broken fuselage due to a premature wing spoiler deployment during landing. Although there was major damage involved, it was repairable. The next year, in 1970, a DC-9 in the vicinity of the Virgin Islands was diverted toward an alternative airport due to bad weather. The aircraft ran out of fuel and ditched at sea with a load of passengers. Twenty-three passengers were killed, and the aircraft was a total loss.

At Bangor, Maine, in 1973, three tires in succession blew out on a DC-8 taking off, and the takeoff was aborted. The aircraft caught fire, and it burned through the wing. Although there was major damage, the aircraft was repaired.

The first loss of a ONA DC-10 occurred in November of 1975. During a takeoff from JFK airport in New York, seagulls were ingested into the engine, resulting in engine fire. Number three engine disintegrated, the takeoff was aborted, and the main landing gear collapsed. All passengers and crew were safely evacuated, with 32 passengers injured. The engine fire spread to the entire aircraft, resulting in a total loss.

A second ONA DC-10 was lost in January of 1976 at Istanbul, Turkey. The aircraft touched down 45 feet short of the runway overrun during a night instrument landing and broke off its landing gear. All 364 passengers and 13 crew members were successfully evacuated. However, the aircraft sustained major damage resulting in total loss.

The following year, at Niomey, Niger, Africa, a DC-8 cargo flight touched down 1750 feet short of the runway during a night approach on instruments. After the impact, the aircraft rolled over. It was totally destroyed and the two crew members were killed. The cause of that accident had not yet been determined.

business level.

one strategy

All the accidents had been covered by insurance. However, in order to avoid future accidents and qualify for continued insurance and air charter certification, ONA had reviewed all its operating procedures and modified them for increased safety provisions. Management believed that standardization on DC-10 aircraft would facilitate an improved safety program and reduce or eliminate future accidents.

ORGANIZATION AND PERSONNEL

weakness.

Prior to joining ONA, Mr. Ory's experience had been principally in investment and transportation management and had included more than two years (1974–1976) as president of U.S. Banknote Corporation in New York. He had spent more than 14 years managing private investments and was still a partner in a New York investment firm. Mr. Ory was a graduate of the U.S. Merchant Marine Academy and had served as a licensed deck officer on the *S.S. America.* Later he had become controller and assistant to the president of Grace Line Steamship Company.

Following the reorganization in late 1977, ONA was structured in five operating departments, each of which was directly responsible to the president, Mr. J. W. Bailey, who had previously been president under Mr. Hinckley and now reported to Mr. Ory.

The five departments were:

Financial division with 17 total employees
Maintenance division with 50 total employees

Flight operations division with 231 total employees
Passenger services division with 20 total employees
Marketing division with 17 total employees

In addition, there was an insurance department and a labor relations department reporting directly to the president.

All the key personnel in ONA were considered to exceed the normal requirements in credentials and background experience for their respective positions. Notwithstanding the drastic reductions that had recently been made in the number of employees, the morale and spirit of those remaining was considered to be very high.

FINANCIAL SITUATION

Operating revenues of ONA had reached a peak of nearly $90 million in 1975 and had declined to just under $80 million in 1977 (see Exhibit C26.2).

The company entered 1978 with a relatively strong cash position (see balance sheets, Exhibit C26.3). Minimum annual payment of principal on the company's long-term debt was $3.66 million in 1978 and $3.52 million in each year 1979 through 1982. Although the balance sheet reflected the aircraft equipment at cost, management believed that with rising prices the DC-10's might be worth as much as $20 million more than the book value.

The company had recently disclosed, in a report filed with the Securities and Exchange Commission, that it had made $3.1 million in questionable payments from 1971 through 1976. The report said that payments and allowances to domestic and foreign passenger charter operators and uncollected money owed by the charter operators amounted to $1,675,000 through 1975. Additionally, charter flight commissions that exceeded the 5% allowed by the Civil Aeronautics Board (CAB) rules, together with discounts below tariff levels, amounted to $945,000 through 1976. ONA had previously disclosed payments of $420,000 involving the company's flight operations between foreign points. ONA also said that it gave less than $10,000 a year in facilitating payments, such as money given customs officials to expedite clearance of goods.

The charter transactions, according to the report, constituted rebates, excess commissions, and failure to collect the full tariff filed with the CAB. Most of the payments and allowances were made under an understanding with the charter operators of their agents that if all seats on a flight weren't filled the charter price would be reduced proportionately.

All the payments mentioned were not accurately disclosed on ONA's books. While those payments wouldn't require additional payment of income taxes, they might require adjustment of loss carryovers. In 1976 the CAB had brought charges against ONA in connection with the payments. The proceeding was settled in 1977 with the CAB agreeing that it wouldn't bring further action against ONA if the company discontinued any illegal practices discovered by the director's committees. ONA also paid the CAB $50,000 to settle possible civil penalties that could have been imposed.

The largest single stockholder of ONA was Louis Marks Jr., a venture capitalist and member of the Marks Toy family. Mr. Marks owned 20% of ONA stock. Marline Resources Company, which was controlled by Mr. Marks, owned an additional 15.5% of ONA stock. The third largest stockholder was Dan W. Lufkin, a Wall Street entrepreneur and former investment banker. Messrs. Marks and Lufkin had controlled ONA for about 15 years. Together with several members of management, they owned

EXHIBIT C26.2 OVERSEAS NATIONAL AIRWAYS, INC. FIVE-YEAR FINANCIAL SUMMARY
(Dollars in Thousands Except for per Share Data)

	Year ended				
	1977	**1976**	**1975**	**1974**	**1973**
Operating revenues:					
Charter revenues	$ 78,340	$ 80,285	$ 85,134	$ 76,984	$ 71,316
Aircraft rentals	1,657	2,632	4,520	4,460	2,584
Total	79,997	82,917	89,654	81,444	73,900
Operating expenses:					
Flight operations	72,778	86,109	81,159	71,364	69,414
Marketing, general and administrative	6,725	7,025	6,313	5,896	6,186
Depreciation	3,385	2,901	3,378	4,072	4,841
Total	82,888	96,035	90,850	81,332	80,441
Operating income (loss)	$ (2,891)	$ (13,118)	$ (1,196)	$ 112	$ (6,541)
Other income (expenses):					
Interest and debt expense	(4,260)	(2,052)	(683)	(793)	(1,345)
Capitalized interest and debt expense	—	1,512	—	—	267
Interest income	374	597	1,277	1,146	955
Gain (loss) on disposition of equipment	(3,092)	10,913	2,523	1,991	1,987
Other—net	(137)	(90)	(36)	2	(1,287)
Total	(7,115)	10,880	3,081	2,346	577
Income (loss) before taxes, discontinued business and cumulative accounting changes	$(10,006)	$ (2,238)	$ 1,885	$ 2,458	$ (5,964)
Federal income taxes (benefit)—deferred	(208)	513	(518)	(585)	1,347
Income (loss) from operation of discontinued business	—	(152)	161	33	45
Loss on disposal of discontinued business (net of applicable federal income tax of $760,000)	—	(1,975)	—	—	—
Cumulative effect of changes in accounting principles	(2,640)	—	—	392	—
Net income (loss)	$ (12,438)	$ (3,852)	$ 1,528	$ 2,298	$ (4,572)
Income (loss) per share of common stock:					
Continuing operations	$ (4.20)	$ (0.74)	$ 0.59	$ 0.81	$ (1.93)
Discontinuing operations	—	(0.92)	0.07	0.02	0.02
Cumulative changes in accounting principles	(1.13)	—	—	0.17	—
Net income (loss)	$ (5.33)	$ (1.66)	$ 0.66	$ 1.00	$ (1.91)
Dividend payable per share of common stock	—	—	0.50	—	—
Average number of common shares outstanding	2,330,801	2,317,929	2,305,370	2,305,370	2,394,344

Source: ONA annual reports.

EXHIBIT C26.3   OVERSEAS NATIONAL AIRWAYS, INC. BALANCE SHEETS, DEC. 26, 1977, AND DEC. 31, 1976

	1977	1976
Assets		
Current assets:		
Cash including marketable securities of $6,200,000 in 1977	$ 9,649,000	$ 4,876,000
Cash and marketable securities securing surety bonds for advance charter deposits	2,665,000	2,021,000
Accounts and notes receivable (net of allowance for doubtful accounts of $1,422,000 in 1977 and $952,000 in 1976)	8,434,000	3,398,000
Expendable parts, materials, and supplies	—	1,202,000
Prepaid expenses and other assets	591,000	972,000
Nonoperating assets and investment in subsidiary held for resale	3,363,000	549,000
Total current assets	24,702,000	13,018,000
Security deposits	156,000	2,930,000
Equipment, at cost:		
Airframes, engines, parts and assemblies	64,089,000	11,068,000
Airframe overhaul costs	—	3,786,000
Other property and equipment	2,575,000	3,782 ,000
Total	66,664,000	18,636,000
Less accumulated depreciation	4,082,000	6,611,000
	62,582,000	12,025,000
Progress payments on flight equipment	9,771,000	29,229,000
Total equipment—net	72,353,000	41,254,000
Nonoperating equipment held for resale	—	5,640,000
Developmental and pre-operating costs, net of amortization	—	1,128,000
Noncurrent receivable	222,000	—
Total assets	$97,433,000	$63,970,000
Liabilities and shareowners' equity		
Current liabilities:		
Accounts payable and accrued expenses	$12,251,000	$13,744,000
Advance charter deposits	2,665,000	1,750,000
Progress notes payable and current maturities of long-term debt	8,987,000	17,546,000
Total current liabilities	23,903,000	33,040,000
Long-term debt:	38,976,000	2,307,000
Senior	19,229,000	1,650,000
Total long-term debt	58,205,000	3,957,000
Other liabilities	1,158,000	503,000
Commitments and contingent liabilities		
Shareowners' equity:		
Common stock par value $1 per share; shares authorized, 10,000,000 in 1977 and 5,000,000 in 1976; issued, 2,456,830	2,457,000	2,457,000
Additional paid-in capital	25,560,000	25,425,000
Accumulated deficit	(13,252,000)	(814,000)
Total	14,765,000	27,068,000
Less 126,029 shares of treasury stock at cost in 1977 and 1976	(598,000)	(598,000)
Total shareowners' equity	14,167,000	26,470,000
Total liabilities and shareowners' equity	$97,433,000	$63,970,000

Source: ONA annual reports.

about 49% of ONA stock. The other 51% was owned by the public and was traded in the over-the-counter market. Price quotations for ONA stock in 1976 and 1977 were:

	1st Quarter	2nd Quarter	3rd Quarter	4th Quarter
1977 range:				
Low closing bid	2¼	2½	3⅛	3¼
High closing bid	3¾	3⅞	4¼	5⅞
1976 range:				
Low closing bid	6	5	3¼	3¼
High closing bid	9¼	7⅜	5½	4½

THE AIR CHARTER INDUSTRY

Charter air passenger transportation serves primarily pleasure as opposed to business travelers. As such it is generally seasonal in nature, with the greatest traffic occurring during the summer months. Since tourist travel is also dependent upon economic prosperity to some degree, the industry is also somewhat cyclical. U.S. passenger miles and revenue are shown in Exhibit C26.4, both for commercial charter operations and for scheduled international and domestic operations.

The air charter industry was highly regulated by the Civil Aeronautics Board of the United States. An airline was permitted to fly only to those areas where it held operating certificates from the CAB. However, a charter operator could fly on any schedule of his own choosing between the authorized points.

The marketing of a certified supplemental (charter) airline was completely different than a scheduled air carrier. The charter airline did not make any direct sales effort to the public nor any direct advertising to the public. All sales were made through a

EXHIBIT C26.4   OVERSEAS NATIONAL AIRWAYS, INC.: U.S. PASSENGER AIRLINE MILES AND REVENUE
(All Figures in Millions)

Year	Scheduled domestic		Scheduled international		Commercial charter	
	Revenue passenger miles	Passenger revenue	Revenue passenger miles	Passenger revenue	Revenue passenger miles	Passenger revenue
1970	104,156	$ 6,246.4	27,563	$1,380.4	6,044	$182.4
1971	106,438	6,736.4*	29,220	1,484.0*	7,772	218.7*
1972	118,138	7,564.8	34,268	1,706.5	7,783*	212.2
1973	126,317	8,379.4	35,640	1,894.9	10,161	279.5*
1974	129,732	9,757.5	33,186	2,121.7	9,016*	312.1
1975	131,728	10,113.1	31,082	2,230.1	6,885	287.3
1976	143,271*	11,855.3	33,717	2,411.0	6,647	291.2
1977	156,609	13,487.6	36,610	2,785.7	8,352	359.9

* Revised.
Source: FAA Statistical Handbook of Aviation.

network of established travel agents. There were thousands of well-established travel agencies in the United States who relied on small local travel agents in each city, town, or community to generate interest and business from their general area public to take low-cost travel tours all over the world. This kind of charter tour business had been built up in the United States primarily since World War II. The increased standard of living and affluency had created a strong demand for vacation and convention travel both domestically and abroad.

opportunity

There were approximately 250 large travel tour agencies in the United States who promoted and generated charter tour business, all fed by thousands of small agencies. These wholesalers would plan, promote, and schedule package tours for 12 months of the year by bidding for transportation, hotels, meals, guides, etc., on a highly sophisticated and organized basis, usually twice a year, utilizing smaller widespread travel agencies to sell volume travel business for them at rates less than 50% cheaper than vacationers or conventioners could provide for themselves individually by traveling at conventional airline and hotel standard rates.

COMPETITION IN AIR CHARTER

The increase in the air charter business has not gone unnoticed by scheduled airlines, who were also experiencing increased traffic over the primary tourist routes, the greatest of which was the North Atlantic route. In 1977, the charter revenue of the domestic trunk and international trunk airlines in the United States totaled about the same as the supplemental or charter airlines in the United States (see Exhibit C26.5).

Scheduled carriers serving the United States were authorized to perform charter flights on their routes without prior approval. Off-route charters could also be performed without prior approval by U.S. and most foreign scheduled carriers, although in the case of U.S. scheduled carriers there were restrictions as to volume, frequency, and regularity.

There were more than 40 carriers (both domestic and foreign) authorized to operate scheduled and/or charter services on the prime commercial routes between the United States and Europe over the North Atlantic. These carriers included 11 scheduled U.S. carriers and 6 U.S. supplemental carriers. Beginning in 1977 the scheduled carriers began to offer large fare discounts within the United States, based on deregulation by the CAB and encouragement by the Carter administration. Low fares began also to appear on the North Atlantic and Hawaii routes. The Sky Train that began between London and New York on a very low fare basis had prompted other transatlantic carriers to cut their fares. All these reduced fares by the scheduled carriers added to the competition faced by the charter airlines.

threats

The competitive impact of these very low scheduled fares had been offset to some extent by the efforts of the CAB to liberalize United States charter regulations to enable the supplemental carriers to compete more effectively with the low fares on the scheduled airlines. The result had been to reduce the advance purchase period requirement of some charters and to eliminate that requirement for others. Also reduced was the minimum size of charter groups from 40 to 20 in most programs, to eliminate the minimum stay requirement and to permit sale by tour operators of a greater percentage of the charter flight seats up to the day of departure. Further proposed liberalizations of charter rules had been resisted by many of the foreign governments. However, the United States had been making a strong and continuing diplomatic effort to gain acceptance of the new rules by the foreign governments.

opportunities

EXHIBIT C26.5   OVERSEAS NATIONAL AIRWAYS, INC.: U.S. AIR CARRIER DATA, 1976 AND 1977
(Dollars in Millions)

	Domestic trunks		International trunks		Local service		Supplementals (charters)	
	1976	1977	1976	1977	1976	1977	1976	1977
Passenger revenue (scheduled)	10,239	11,365	2,412	2,790	1,387	1,616		
Charter revenue:								
Civilian							291	370
Military							107	114
Total							398	484
Freight revenue (scheduled)	215	238	248	251	32	46		
Mail revenue (scheduled)	721	824	381	425	71	83		
Subsidy payments	183	217	85	88	18	39		
	—	—	—	—	70	67		
Operating profit	469	514	134	222	90	129	-.06	6.6
Net income	275	379	171	160	51	84	2.6	-2.8
Long-term debt	3,841	3,316	1,311	1,257	514	567	133	103
Stockholder equity	3,224	3,684	747	883	319	380	213	198
Revenue passenger miles (billions)	131.4 Sched.	141.3 Sched.	33.7 Sched.	36.6 Sched.	12.1	13.5	6.7 civilian 1.6 military	8.4 civilian 1.6 military

Source: "Airline Industry Economic Report," Civil Aeronautics Board, Vol. X-4, February 1978.

The Civil Aeronautics Board had publicly expressed that for years air charter carriers were the only source of low-fare air transportation for the price-conscious traveler and should not be allowed to be driven out of business by the recent rash of scheduled low fares. The CAB added that distinctions would remain between charter and scheduled services because of continuing differences such as requirements that charter tickets must be sold by charter operators and charter flights could be canceled for non-operational reasons including inadequate sales. The liberalized charter system proposed by the CAB would allow discount pricing and one-way ticketing without requiring advance purchase or minimum group size. It would also replace advance booking charters. The CAB proposal followed a policy established in 1977 to drop unnecessary restrictions on charter airlines.

Another development that might help offset intensified competition from the scheduled carriers was the decline of charter operations of the scheduled carriers. In 1976 the scheduled carriers accounted for nearly half of the charter passengers in the transatlantic market as compared to only 37% in 1977. This decline was thought by the industry to be due to the fact that a number of the scheduled carriers had been selling their excess narrow-bodied aircraft and had reduced the number of aircraft devoted to charter activity. It was believed in the industry that no scheduled carrier in early 1978 currently had wide-body aircraft dedicated to the charter market, which increasingly demanded such equipment to operate profitably.

There were, however, three other developments that might further heighten competitive pressure on the charter market by the scheduled carriers. First, some scheduled carriers had been offering unusually high commissions to travel agents on individual ticket sales. Second, the rights of scheduled carriers to operate charter flights off their regular routes were recently expanded by the elimination or reduction of various limitations on the volume, frequency, and regularity of such off-route charter flights. Third, the CAB had under consideration a proposal that would authorize part charter services on scheduled flights. Although in the past the CAB had rejected various part charter proposals, if it were to approve the scheduling of part charter groups on scheduled flights at charter rates it would heighten the competitive impact on the charter airlines.

There were four major participants in the U.S. air charter passenger industry. They are shown below together with their revenue passenger miles in 1977.

Capitol International Airways	2.205 billion
Evergreen International	146 million
McCulloch	20 million
ONA	2.142 billion
TIA (Trans-International Airlines)	3.095 billion
World Airways	2.373 billion
Total	9.981 billion

While these air carriers were mostly involved in passenger operations, they did carry some freight. In addition, there were two major freight charter airlines in the United States: Tiger International and Seaboard. Comparative financial data for some of the charter airlines and scheduled air carriers are shown in Exhibit C26.6. Tiger International, which operated the Flying Tiger Line (originating from the Flying Tigers in China

EXHIBIT C26.6 AIRLINE STATISTICS, COMPARATIVE FINANCIAL DATA, 1977
(Dollars in Millions)

Airline (FY)	1977 Revenue	1977 Net income (Est)					Net income as % of revenue	1976 net worth	Net income as % of net worth	1976 Long-term debt	Long-term debt as % of net worth
		Mar	Jun	Sep	Dec	Total					
American	$2,230	$ 1	$36	$59	$(21)	$ 75	3%	$610	12%	$416	68%
Braniff	770	1	10	11	7	35	5	189	19	242	128
Continental	655	7	7	17	3	28	4	157	18	328	209
Delta	1,720	22	34	31	23	110	6	542	20	357	65
Eastern	2,005	19	3	9	9	40	2	339	12	556	167
KLM	1,130	(9)	17	40	(9)	39	3	311	13	429	138
National	495	2	3	3	3	11	2	195	6	141	72
Northwest	1,045	12	27	32	23	94	9	666	14	122	18
Pan Am	1,890	(24)	18	67	(9)	52	3	352	15	727	207
Seaboard	135	5	1	1	2	9	7	42	21	59	140
Tigers Intl.	480	1	7	8	8	24	5	239	10	698	292
TWA	2,300	(54)	31	67	4	48	2	377	13	908	241
UAL	3,260	(23)	31	76	2	86	3	800	11	932	117
Western	690	2	2	9	1	14	2	117	12	110	94
World	109	(1)	1	3	1	4	4	107	4	18	17
ONA	80	(3)	(3)	2	(2)	(6)	(8)	25	(32)	21	84

Source: ONA company report.

during World War II), provided scheduled air freight service to key cities in the U.S. and Asia and freight charters on a worldwide basis. Flying Tiger previously purchased some of ONA's DC-8 jet aircraft in order to serve new U.S. domestic markets that were added as a result of air freight deregulation approved by Congress late in 1977.

Capitol International Airways operated a fleet of DC-8 jets. It did not have any wide-bodied jet aircraft. In 1977, Capitol's revenues were slightly greater than ONA's, reflecting a sharp growth over 1976 (see operating summary, Exhibit C26.7). Capitol had a relatively low level of long-term debt (see balance sheets, Exhibit C26.8). Capitol Airways had been founded by Jesse F. Stallings, who in 1978 was the president, chairman, and chief executive officer and also a major stockholder.

Trans-International Airways (TIA) was one of several operating subsidiaries of the Trans-America holding company. TIA was the largest U.S. air charter line for passengers, with over 3 billion revenue passenger miles in 1977. Its passenger services were handled by a fleet of wide-bodied jet aircraft. TIA earned $9.5 million profit on $199 million revenue in 1977 and had total assets of $162 million (see financial summary, Exhibit C26.9). Its financial resources were backed by its parent company, Trans-America, which had total assets of $1.26 billion and consolidated net income in 1977 of $169 million (see Exhibit C26.10).

World Airways, Inc., operated a fleet of 747, DC-10, and DC-8 jet aircraft. In terms of revenue passenger miles it was slightly larger than ONA, and its aircraft operating revenues were near $100 million in 1977 (see Exhibit C26.11). World Airways for several years had been owned as a subsidiary of First Western Bank and Trust Company, which was sold in 1974 to Lloyds Bank, Ltd., for $115 million. The gain from the sale of the bank resulted in a profit of nearly $16 million after taxes. World Airways then had a very large amount of funds invested in marketable securities (see balance sheets, Exhibit C26.12). World's management stated that it was retaining its resources and marketable securities and looking for suitable diversification opportunities. World Airways' stock was traded on the New York Stock Exchange, but 82% of it was owned by Edward J. Dailey, who was president and chairman of the company.

RECENT DEVELOPMENTS

During the first quarter of 1978, several events were of serious concern to ONA's management. Although the reorganization of the company had been proceeding smoothly, ONA received notification in February that due to a strike at the McDonnell-Douglas plant the third DC-10, which was scheduled for delivery in May of 1978, would not be delivered on time but would be delivered later that year, perhaps in October. Such a late delivery would entirely miss the most profitable summer peak season during which time about two-thirds of the company's annual profits were made. Loss of the revenue from this aircraft for which charters were already booked could significantly reduce the operating results below the planned break-even operation for 1978.

Additional pressure from competition due to deregulation was also of increasing concern to ONA's management. Congress had deregulated domestic airline operations to a large degree in November 1977, and the CAB was proposing further deregulation of the airline industry, both charter and scheduled, which would adversely affect ONA's competitive position in international operations if the legislation were to pass. Moreover, the foreign exchange rate was a matter of concern. The increasing pressure against the dollar in foreign markets proved to be a disadvantage to ONA's profitable operations.

EXHIBIT C26.7 CAPITOL INTERNATIONAL AIRWAYS, FIVE-YEAR OPERATING SUMMARY
(Dollars in Thousands)

	Years ended December 31				
	1977	1976	1975	1974	1973
Commercial revenues:					
Transportation revenues:					
International	$64,827	$38,488	$26,177	$31,677	$27,327
Domestic	9,692	7,253	7,034	8,547	7,034
Maintenance	889	433	468	354	1,357
Aircraft rentals	13	1,161	1,859	255	
Total commercial	75,421	47,335	35,538	40,833	35,718
Military revenues:					
International:					
Fixed annual contracts	1,228	1,041	5,274	2,968	4,116
Individual service orders	4,172	3,515	3,459	3,885	5,630
Domestic	171	103	61	528	789
Total military	5,571	4,659	8,794	7,381	10,535
Total revenues	$80,992	$51,994	$44,332	$48,214	$46,253
Operating revenues	$80,992	$51,994	$44,332	$48,214	$46,253
Operating income (loss)	348	1,447	536	(1,730)	2,145
Nonoperating (expense):					
Interest, principally on long-term debt	(382)	(606)	(959)	(1,195)	(1,306)
Gain on sale of aircraft	—	2,536	2,414	2,127	—
Other, net	378	238	110	(75)	(49)
Income before federal income tax and cumulative effect of change in accounting principle and retroactive application of Statement of Financial Accounting Standards No. 13	344	3,615	2,101	(873)	790
Provision (credit) for federal income tax	45	723	519	(209)	188
Income before cumulative effect of change in accounting principle and retroactive application of Statement of Financial Accounting Standards No. 13	299	2,892	1,582	(664)	602
Cumulative effect of change in accounting principle	705	—	—	—	—
Retroactive application of Statement of Financial Accounting Standards No. 13	—	—	—	—	(555)
Net income (loss)	$1,004	$2,892	$1,582	$(664)	$47

Source: Capitol annual reports.

EXHIBIT C26.8 CAPITOL INTERNATIONAL AIRWAYS CONSOLIDATED BALANCE SHEETS

	1977	1976
Assets		
Current assets:		
Cash (including certificates of deposit of $2,500,000 in 1977 and U.S. Treasury notes of $1,400,000 in 1976)*	$ 3,483,622	$ 1,742,327
Accounts receivable		
U.S. government	552,911	180,155
Commercial and other	1,639,458	798,771
Federal income tax recoverable	190,333	
Maintenance parts and supplies, at average cost	1,688,495	1,467,589
Prepaid expenses	1,186,020	858,814
Total current assets	8,740,839	5,047,656
Property and equipment, at cost	49,068,739	47,581,318
Less accumulated depreciation	25,868,907	21,744,024
Net property and equipment	23,199,832	25,837,294
Deferred charges and other assets	3,096,502	913,623
	$35,037,173	$31,798,573
Liabilities and stockholders' equity		
Current liabilities:		
Accounts payable	$ 9,849,918	$ 6,168,825
Unearned transportation revenue*	583,260	1,207,006
Accrued expenses	2,512,722	1,170,858
Federal income tax		931,985
Long-term debt due within one year	1,091,864	1,834,057
Total current liabilities	14,037,764	11,312,731
Long-term debt due after one year	3,092,966	4,184,830
Deferred federal income tax	4,887,515	4,286,515
Commitments		
Stockholders' equity:		
Common stock, $1 par value 7,000,000 shares authorized, 3,072,000 shares issued	3,072,000	3,072,000
Additional paid-in capital	664,375	664,375
Retained earnings	9,282,553	8,278,122
Total stockholders' equity	13,018,928	12,014,497
	$35,037,173	$31,798,573

* Excludes deposits in escrow of $3,654,000 in 1977 and $2,083,000 in 1976.
Source: Capitol annual reports.

EXHIBIT C26.9   TRANS-INTERNATIONAL AIRLINES, INC.
FINANCIAL SUMMARY
(Dollars in Thousands)

	1977	1976
Assets		
Cash and short-term investments	$ 19,983	$ 31,185
Accounts receivable	8,014	9,300
Flight and other equipment (collateral for notes payable)	130,748	145,140
Other assets	3,206	5,798
	$161,951	$191,423
Liabilities and capital		
Notes payable	$ 23,555	$ 65,038
Accounts payable and other liabilities	47,095	46,826
Income taxes	15,016	12,815
Capital	76,285	66,744
	$161,951	$191,423
Revenues		
Commercial transportation	$122,259	$107,233
Military transportation	72,853	24,806
Other income	3,608	836
	198,720	132,875
Expenses		
Flight operations and maintenance	147,082	97,296
Depreciation	15,211	11,159
Selling administrative and general	16,431	12,977
Interest	2,576	5,626
Income taxes	7,878	2,690
	189,178	129,748
Net income	$ 9,542	$ 3,127
Source of funds		
Net income	$ 9,542	$ 3,127
Depreciation and amortization	15,370	11,318
Other noncash income items	14,454	3,522
Contribution by Transamerica Corporation for purchase of Saturn Airways, Inc.		29,755
Other	2,936	13,806
	$ 42,302	$ 61,528
Application of funds		
Cash dividends		$ 6,500
Additions to flight and other equipment	$ 819	1,280
Payments of notes	41,483	23,582
Acquisition of Saturn Airways, Inc. assets, including equipment of $27,855—net of liabilities assumed		30,166
	$ 42,302	$ 61,528

EXHIBIT C26.10 TRANSAMERICA CORPORATION (PARENT COMPANY OF TRANS-INTERNATIONAL)
FINANCIAL STATEMENTS
(Dollars in Thousands)

	1977	1976
Assets		
Investments in subsidiaries—at cost plus equity in undistributed earnings since acquisition:		
Occidental Life Insurance Company of California	$ 456,595	$ 417,348
Transamerica Insurance Company	166,640	142,092
Transamerica Financial Corporation	175,541	179,477
United Artists Corporation	108,661	100,130
Trans International Airlines, Inc.	76,289	66,659
Delaval Turbine, Inc.	105,185	86,461
Other subsidiaries	12,881	3,183
	1,101,792	995,350
Accounts with subsidiaries	121,508	78,229
Cash and short-term investments	25,301	12,271
Other	12,310	5,965
	$1,260,911	$1,091,815
Liabilities and shareholders' equity		
Notes payable	$ 147,799	$ 138,588
Income taxes payable, net or deferred tax benefits of $7,679 in 1977 and $25,542 in 1976	66,954	10,552
Other	24,592	21,415
	239,345	170,525
Shareholders' equity—including $516,870 in 1977 and $414,099 in 1976 representing equity in undistributed net income of subsidiaries	1,021,566	921,290
	$1,260,911	$1,091,815
Revenues		
Dividends from subsidiaries	$ 83,073	$ 71,841
Interest—principally from subsidiaries	1,874	1,964
Net realized gain (loss) on investment transactions and foreign exchange transaction adjustments	580	(603)
Amounts received from subsidiaries for income taxes over amounts due on a consolidated return basis	11,844	6,319
	97,371	79,521
Expenses		
Interest	17,366	10,342
General and administrative	13,673	10,600
	31,039	20,942
Net income of parent company	66,332	58,579
Equity in undistributed net income of subsidiaries	102,771	55,158
Consolidated net income	$ 169,103	$ 113,737

EXHIBIT C26.10 *(CONTINUED)*

	1977	1976
Source of funds		
Net income of parent company	$ 66,332	$ 58,579
Depreciation and amortization	240	229
Increase in income taxes payable	56,402	29,844
Proceeds from new debt financing		50,000
Increase in bank loans	9,241	(11,876)
Stock issued for merged company		29,624
	$ 132,215	$ 156,400
Application of funds		
Cash dividends	$ 48,904	$ 42,356
Investment in subsidiaries	5,074	29,473
Payments of long-term debt		15,000
Increase in cash and accounts with subsidiaries	56,309	66,225
Cost of reacquired common shares	16,665	1,548
Other	5,263	1,897
	$ 132,215	$ 156,400

Although ONA supported aviation regulatory reform, certain proposals pending before the Senate essentially would destroy the vital distinction between supplemental and scheduled air carriers. ONA was opposed to the following proposals:

1 To permit a supplemental carrier to get scheduled authority and a scheduled carrier to get supplemental authority.

2 To freeze the "unrealistic" definition of off-route charter trips as that term was applied by the board on January 1, 1977.

3 To allow scheduled carriers to charge fares after July 1, 1978, as much as 10% more or, immediately, 35% less than the standard industry fare level. ONA believed that the permissible range of fare change should be no more than 5% added nor less than 30% deducted from the standard industry for coach service, because it was important to restrict the ability of scheduled carriers to offer uneconomic and predatory fares which are subsidized by economy and first class service. The pending legislation did not provide the protection that ONA felt was required to the charter industry.

ONA supported the various proposals which would make air service more competitive, including empowering the Civil Aeronautics Board to issue interstate and overseas charter authority to an applicant filing after June 30, 1981, merely on a determination of fitness. ONA believed, however, that charter authority should be a certificate and not a license.

ONA also believed that supplemental air carriers provided the consumer with the lowest-cost air transportation, provided the U.S. government with a rate yardstick vis-à-vis foreign and U.S. flag scheduled carriers, provided a competitive spur to the international air transport association cartel, and added the most responsive backup military airlift capability. It was believed to be in the public interest to insure that the

EXHIBIT C26.11   WORLD AIRWAYS, INC. AND SUBSIDIARIES SUMMARY OF OPERATIONS
(Dollars in Thousands)

	Year ended December 31				
	1973	1974	1975	1976	1977
Revenues:					
Commercial transportation	$ 60,608	63,922	64,981	50,193	77,505
Military contracts	20,833	19,891	28,207	18,664	16,586
Aircraft leasing	6,735	7,700	10,785	13,075	14,403
Maintenance	5,771	6,187	6,339	6,871	6,196
Net gain (loss) on disposition of assets	6,859	7,070	(25)	971	2,660
Interest and dividends	2,629	7,453	7,737	6,362	7,030
Total	103,435	112,223	118,024	96,136	124,380
Expenses:					
Operating	77,137	75,818	78,040	70,094	89,957
Selling, general, and administrative	11,679	11,578	10,316	10,153	10,033
Depreciation	8,103	6,942	6,749	6,606	6,642
Aircraft rentals	7,084	11,443	11,076	10,423	9,493
Interest	2,743	2,488	2,545	1,666	1,789
Total	106,746	108,269	108,726	98,442	117,914
Income (loss) before income taxes, discontinued operations and cumulative effect of accounting change	(3,311)	3,954	9,298	(2,806)	6,466
Income tax expense (credit)	(2,059)	(1,288)	1,822	2,964	2,882
Income (loss) before discontinued operations and cumulative effect of accounting change	(1,252)	5,242	7,476	158	3,584
Discontinued operations	2,254	155,990	—	—	—
Cumulative effect of accounting change (net of income taxes of $1,863,000)	—	—	—	3,018	—
Net income	1,002	21,232	7,476	2,176	3,584
Retained earnings at beginning of period	66,366	67,368	88,600	96,076	98,252
Retained earnings at end of period	67,368	88,600	96,076	98,252	101,836

Source: World annual reports.

supplemental or charter carriers continued to provide those benefits. The supplemental airlines had provided those benefits because they were a distinct class of air carriers whose sole business was to offer low-cost charter air transportation. It was believed that there was no economic way to provide air transportation at a lower cost than charter because the air carrier got paid for operating the aircraft based on a 100% load factor, whereas the scheduled carriers accepted the load factor risk which averaged 55% and had significant selling and marketing expenses which resulted in higher fares.

ONA management was continuing to evaluate its operations and was considering all options available to it, including the sale or lease of its DC-10 aircraft. ONA had recently received an offer from another airline to purchase its third (undelivered) DC-10. ONA's management believed that the sale of that aircraft and the sale of its present two DC-10 aircraft could result in a significant gain to the company.

EXHIBIT C26.12 WORLD AIRWAYS, INC. BALANCE SHEETS, DECEMBER 31, 1976 AND 1977

	1976 Consolidated	1977 Consolidated
Assets		
Current assets:		
Cash	$ 2,576,000	$ 777,000
Short-term investments, at cost, plus accrued interest (market value $33,739,000 in 1976 and $80,003,000 in 1977)	33,219,000	80,062,000
Accounts receivable, trade (U.S. government and other; $2,191,000 and $7,312,000 in 1976 and $1,349,000 and $7,741,000 in 1977, respectively)	9,503,000	9,090,000
Notes receivable, current portion	1,471,0000	1,446,000
Prepaid expenses and other current assets	4,524,000	6,481,000
Total current assets	51,293,000	97,856, 000
Investments, at cost (market value, $51,292,000 in 1976 and $23,103,000 in 1977)	52,854,000	23,103,000
Operating equipment, at cost:		
Flight equipment	105,800,000	97,176,000
Other	3,786,000	3,867,000
	109,586,000	101,043,000
Less accumulated depreciation	39,510,000	38,982,000
	70,076,000	62,061,000
Notes receivable	1,249,000	
Deferred charges and other assets	296,000	1,720,000
Total assets	$175,768,000	$184,740,000
Liabilities and stockholders' equity		
Current liabilities:		
Current portion of notes payable	$ 2,102,000	$ 3,845,000
Accounts payable	7,250,000	10,699,000
Accrued payroll	1,506,000	1,917,000
Income taxes payable	1,058,000	9,628,000
Deferred flight revenue	3,101,000	4,452,000
Other current liabilities	3,066,000	1,781,000
Total current liabilities	18,083,000	32,322,000
Long-term portion of notes payable	18,178,000	17,103,000
Accrued airworthiness reserves—flight equipment	4,069,000	3,631,000
Deferred federal income tax	22,821,000	17,133,000
Deposits securing lease rentals	300,000	675,000
Minority interest in partnership	5,061,000	3,036,000
Total liabilities	68,512,000	73,900,000
Stockholders' equity		
Capital stock, $1 par value:		
Authorized: 15,000,000 shares; issued: 10,000,000 shares	10,000,000	10,000,000
Retained earnings	98,252,000	101,836,000
	108,252,000	111,836,000
Less cost of 200,000 treasury shares	(996,000)	(996,000)
	107,256,000	110,840,000
Total liabilities and stockholders' equity	$175,768,000	$184,740,000

Source: World annual reports.

Another item of concern for ONA's management was operating costs, fuel cost in particular. In commenting on the situation, Mr. Ory observed that airlines had a very high fixed cost. "Jet fuel is about the only variable cost we have." "In fact," he said, "most costs in any business tend to be fixed. Charter is becoming less important with more direct flights between points added by scheduled airlines. Charter is a cyclical business on a worldwide basis. We have a plan to stay in business with the DC-10 fleet, but the delay in the delivery of our third DC-10 together with the competitive pressure of deregulation and various pressures on profit are causing us to re-evaluate our position."

Threat

could diversify into scheduled to spread the risk & even out the seasonal nature of current business.

A.H. ROBINS AND THE DALKON SHIELD

Prepared by Elizabeth Bogdan, Tracy Cox, Joan LeSoravage,
Elizabeth Ghaphery, Marisa Hausmann, and Larry Rosenberger
(under the direction of Neil H. Snyder), McIntire School of
Commerce, University of Virginia.

Founded in 1866, A.H. Robins is a diversified, multinational company with base operations in Richmond, Virginia. Robins is primarily a manufacturer and marketer of two types of pharmaceuticals: those marketed directly to the consumer and those dispensed solely through the medical profession (commonly known as ethical pharmaceuticals). However, Robins is more than a pharmaceutical company. Pet care products, health and beauty aids, and perfumes are among the many products manufactured by the company under brand names which include Robitussin* cough syrup, Sergeant's* pet care products, Chap Stick* lip balm, and Caron* perfumes.

In 1866, Albert Hartley Robins opened a tiny apothecary shop for the purpose of providing to the medical profession research-formulated, clinically proven, and ethically promoted pharmaceuticals. Over a century later, the Robins philosophy remains unchanged. After three generations of operation, Robins is still led by members of the Robins family. Currently, the company has almost 6,000 full-time employees. Making employees feel like family has long been recognized as important to the overall success of the company. The ability to "converse as decision makers and to be treated as first-class" causes Robins employees to take great pride in their company and to demonstrate a very high degree of loyalty to the firm. As an example of this concern for the views of employees, one Robins salesman said "that his advice often carries greater weight than that of the firm's market research department."[1]

This sense of family extends beyond work, too. The company sponsors activities that include a company softball team and company trips, and it offers employees little things that tend to make a big difference, such as free coffee and birthday holidays. Claiborne

---

* Trademark of A.H. Robins

Robins believes that "his greatest assets are the people that work for him."[2] According to the *Richmond Times-Dispatch* (June 23, 1985), "When a person is employed by A.H. Robins, it's almost for life. Only on rare occasions do people not reach retirement with this company."

THE INTRAUTERINE DEVICE ENVIRONMENT

The market for birth control devices in the 1970s was very volatile. Before the inception of intrauterine devices (IUDs), several artificial methods of birth control were available to consumers. Included in this group were the diaphragm, the condom, and the pill. Each of these methods offered women significantly better birth control protection than afforded by natural measures. However, the diaphragm and the condom lacked what women seemed to want most from birth control devices—spontaneity. Thus, the pill was viewed by consumers as the ultimate form of contraception. Unquestioned, because it solved the perennial problems of birth control, the pill enjoyed a prosperous existence. The pill was convenient and safe, and it offered exceptional birth control protection.

The discovery of the pill's harmful side effects caused many women to lose confidence in oral contraceptives. The realization of problems like an increased risk of heart disease, dramatic mood swings, and excessive weight gain gave rise to a national concern over the safety of the pill. This concern was the focus of the Gaylord Nelson hearings of the early 1970s. These hearings publically exposed the harmful side effects of oral contraceptives. "It is estimated . . . that within six months of the Gaylord Nelson hearings . . . up to one million women went off the birth control pills."[3]

Since the pill was no longer viewed as the ultimate answer to birth control, women returned to traditional methods of contraception. However, they refused to sacrifice convenience and almost foolproof protection. What could have been better than a device—not a "dangerous" drug—that offered the same protection as the pill at a comparable price with more convenience? The stage was set for the introduction of the IUD. Previously, IUDs had been used only on a small scale in various planned parenthood clinics. It was not until the harmful side effects of the pill were made public that IUDs were viewed as commercially viable.[4]

An IUD is a "small, flexible piece of sterile plastic which is inserted into the uterus by the physician to prevent pregnancies."[5] The minute the device is inserted it is effective. "Once an IUD has been inserted, it entails no further costs, no daily protective procedures. It works only inside the uterus—without effects on your body, blood, or brain; it doesn't cause you to gain weight, have headaches or mood changes. And it provides the user with a most satisfying method of contraception."[6]

Because of the simplicity of the device, manufacturing costs are low and profits can be high. When volume is sufficient, an IUD can be manufactured, sterilized, and packaged for 35 to 40 cents, and it can be sold for $3.00 to $3.50.[7] Due to the size and profit potential of the birth control market, the manufacturers of IUDs were well positioned to reap a bountiful harvest, but competition was tough. The secret to success was timing, and the winners would be the first in the market. Firms competing in the market realized that "unlike most consumer products, new drugs and delivery devices must first gain acceptance among a small group of specialists. If the specialists accept this their patients will too."[8] Therefore, the marketing effort was directed at physicians, knowing that they would refer the device to their patients.

THE DALKON SHIELD

Dr. Hugh Davis, an assistant professor of medicine at John Hopkins University and an expert in birth control, was instrumental in developing the Dalkon Shield. Dr. Davis conducted research on patients using the shield, and he reported a pregnancy rate of 1.1% (comparable with the pill). The competitive advantage the Dalkon Shield had over other IUDs was the "larger surface area designed for maximum coverage and maximum contraceptive effect."[9] The potential of the Dalkon Shield was great, and drawing from its already established reputation and distribution channels in the pharmaceutical industry, the IUD seemed to be a logical addition to Robins' product offerings.

On June 12, 1970, A.H. Robins paid $750,000, a royalty of 10% of future net sales, plus consulting fees to acquire the Dalkon Shield. At the time of purchase, Robins had no expertise in the area of birth control. Although they did hire consultants, Robins had neither an obstetrician nor a gynecologist on its staff.[10] They assigned assembly of the shield to the corporate division of the company that manufactures Chap Stick lip balm. Before buying the product, however, Robins medical director, Frederick A. Clark, Jr., reviewed statistical tests performed by Dr. Davis on the shield.[11] These tests showed that in 832 insertions, 26 women became pregnant. Dr. Davis's tests, however, were done on the original shield, not the one ultimately sold by Robins. The major difference between the original shield and the one sold by Robins was the addition of a multifilament tail.[12]

When they went to the market, Robins was excited about their product. "Possibly no other IUD has received the benefit of such ecstatic claims by its developer, its manufacturer, and the admiring multitude."[13] Robins used promotional methods that were designed especially for acceptance of the shield within the medical profession. Foremost among these promotions was a text written by Dr. Davis, *Intrauterine Devices for Contraception—the IUD*. The appendix of his book lists complications reported with the use of ten major IUDs. The shield was presented in a very good light with only a 5.4% complication rate. The complication rate of the competition range from 16.9% to 55.7%.

Difficulties Emerge

A.H. Robins began selling the Dalkon Shield on January 1, 1971. On June 22, 1971, when a doctor reported that his shield-wearing daughter suffered a septic spontaneous abortion, miscarriage caused by infection, the company was particularly concerned about the safety aspects of the shield. The main concern was the shield's unique multifilament tail, which has since been accused of actually drawing infection from the vagina into the normally sterile uterus.[14] Ironically, the product that was thought to be the ultimate form of birth control turned sour (36 alleged deaths and 13,000 alleged injuries), and it had a devastating effect on A.H. Robins.

Difficulties with Research[15]   Although the text written by Dr. Davis had been accepted by the medical profession as a major textbook on IUDs, the problems with IUDs raised many concerns, and the text was referred to as a "thinly disguised promotion of the shield."[16] Examination revealed that Robins possessed data on five formal studies based on the experience of about 4,000 shield users. Three of these five studies were performed by people with financial interests in the shield. The foremost of these studies was done by Dr. Davis. He claimed a pregnancy rate of 1.1%, an expulsion rate of 2.3%, a medical removal rate of 2.0%, and a total complication rate of 5.4%. However, another study conducted over an 18-month period that was dated October 25, 1972, showed a 4.3% pregnancy rate.

In an interview broadcast on *60 Minutes,* Paul Rheingold, a New York attorney who has represented 40 Dalkon Shield users, said that "this IUD got on the market with no animal tests, and with whatever minimal clinical . . . or testing on human subjects . . . the company wanted to do, which turned out to be practically nothing."[17]

Financial Implications Approximately 4.5 million Dalkon Shields were sold by Robins, producing an estimated profit of $500,000.[18] "The product generated total revenues to the company of $13.7 million in 4.5 years. But during the first six months of 1985, Robins paid out $61.2 million in Dalkon-related expenses."[19] By June 30, 1985, Robins and Aetna Life and Casualty Company (Robins' insurance company) had paid $378.3 million to settle 9,230 Dalkon Shield cases. This exhausted all but $50 million of Robins' product liability insurance. Legal fees and other costs related to the shield have totaled $107.3 million. Robins' portion of the total Dalkon claims has been $198.1 million. Robins announced an anticipated minimum cost to handle future Dalkon expenses of $685 million, excluding punitive damages.

Exhibits C27.1 through C27.12 present financial information on the company contained in its 1984 annual report.

BANKRUPTCY

On August 21, 1985, A.H. Robins filed for bankruptcy under Chapter 11 of the Federal Bankruptcy Code. "When it filed its request for reorganization on August 21, Robins listed $2.26 in assets for each $1 in debts and talked publicly about the strengths of the company when items related to the Dalkon Shield birth control device were excluded."[20]

EXHIBIT C27.1   NET SALES
(In Millions of Dollars)

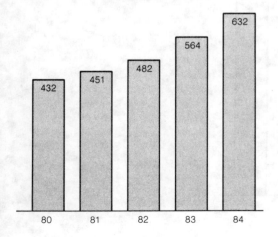

EXHIBIT C27.2   NET EARNINGS OR LOSS
(In Millions of Dollars)

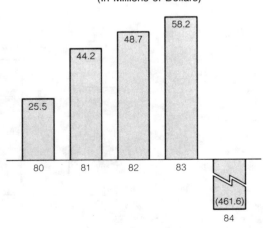

EXHIBIT C27.3   EARNINGS OR LOSS PER SHARE
(In Dollars)

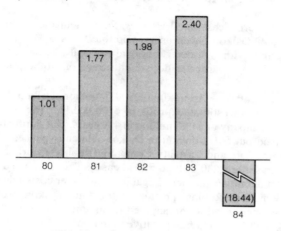

Robins noted that it had a profit of $35.3 million from net sales of $331.1 million in the first six months of 1985. What the sales and profits did not show was the extent to which Robins was having to dip into its retained earnings to pay Dalkon-related bills. "Dalkon payments had taken away only 1.7 cents from each $1 in Robins sales from 1974 through 1983, but then jumped to 12.3 cents in 1984. And when it jumped to 18.5 cents in the first six months of this year (1985) there wasn't enough left from sales to meet other expenses."[21]

"The petition in bankruptcy court stops the flow of Dalkon payments. A perceived advantage for Robins in seeking the Chapter 11 route is that the company's reorganiza-

EXHIBIT C27.4   DIVIDENDS PER SHARE
(In Dollars)

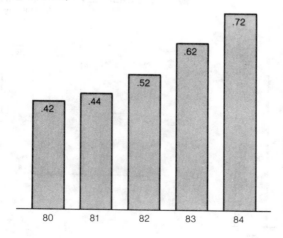

EXHIBIT C27.5   WORLDWIDE R&D EXPENDITURES
(In Millions of Dollars)

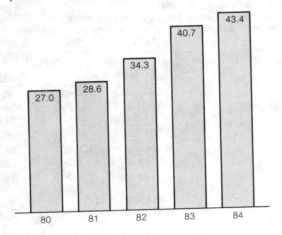

tion plan would likely stretch out Dalkon payments so that a cash-flow problem wouldn't recur."[22] "The action was taken [in bankruptcy court] in an effort to ensure the economic vitality of the company, which is, of course, critical to our ability to pay legitimate claims to present and future plaintiffs."[23]

A.H. Robins' petition in bankruptcy court has been at the center of a heated debate. Those in support of the company have argued that "A.H. Robins' move into bankruptcy court could ensure that there is money for all who are suing the company instead of letting 'the first wolves who tear at the carcass' get it all."[24] On the other hand, Aaron

EXHIBIT C27.6   CAPITAL ADDITIONS
(In Millions of Dollars)

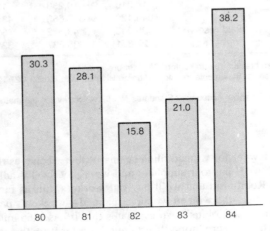

EXHIBIT C27.7
A.H. Robins Company, Incorporated and Subsidiaries
Selected Financial Data
(Dollars in Thousands Except per Share and Ratio Data)

	1984	1983	1982	1981
Operations				
Net sales	$631,891	$563,510	$482,324	$450,854
Cost of sales	237,508	220,628	195,008	190,759
Marketing, administrative and general	222,939	196,495	168,963	157,852
Research and development	43,352	40,686	34,279	28,572
Total operating costs and expenses	503,799	457,809	398,250	377,183
Operating earnings	128,092	105,701	84,074	73,671
Interest income	7,560	8,350	8,085	8,437
Interest expense	(3,240)	(5,441)	(10,308)	(3,564)
Litigation settlement income	1,205	2,256	3,135	3,379
Reserve for Dalkon Shield claims	(615,000)			
Litigation expenses and settlements	(77,950)	(18,745)	(7,091)	(3,318)
Provision for losses on disposition of businesses				
Other, net	(13,190)	(144)	(3,740)	(4,997)
Earnings (loss) before income taxes	(572,523)	91,977	74,155	73,608
Provision for income taxes (benefits)	(110,910)	33,756	25,462	29,380
Net earnings (loss)	$(461,613)	$ 58,221	$ 48,693	$ 44,228
Per share data				
Earnings (loss) per share	$(18.44)	$2.40	$1.98	$1.77
Dividends per share	.72	.62	.52	.44
Stockholders' equity (deficit) per share	(5.23)	14.69	13.29	12.52
Weighted average number of shares outstanding	25,037	24,295	24,552	25,015
Balance sheet data				
Cash and cash equivalents	$ 91,627	$133,381	$ 79,986	$ 89,024
Working capital	122,344	229,525	200,810	177,259
Current ratio	1.7 to 1	3.2 to 1	4.0 to 1	3.1 to 1
Property, plant and equipment, net	$135,685	$107,651	$ 98,079	$ 96,457
Depreciation and amortization	16,310	10,253	10,384	10,096
Total assets	648,129	509,663	439,983	443,942
Long-term obligations, exclusive of Dalkon Shield reserve	25,330	48,322	51,040	48,232
Stockholder's equity (deficit)	(127,851)	335,837	321,085	310,201

Amounts for 1983 and prior years have been reclassified to conform to 1984 presentation.
See Note 12 of Notes to Consolidated Financial Statements for information on litigation; see Exhibit C27.12.
* Results were computed on a FIFO basis.
† Results preceded adoption of Statement of Financial Accounting Standards No. 52 which revised the method of translating foreign currency.

M. Levine, a lawyer for women filing against Robins, believes that "this is a company that's saying, 'we'll pay our suppliers and we'll pay for TV ads and we'll pay for the syrup for the Robitussin and we'll pay our workers, but as far as this one particular group of creditors—the women we have maimed—we won't pay.'"[25]

Levine pointed to Robins' own estimates that it has $466 million in assets and only $216.5 million owed to creditors. "Certainly this is far from the usual type of debtor who

1980†	1979†*	1978†*	1977†*	1976†*	1975†*	1974†*
$432,328	$386,425	$357,070	$306,713	$284,925	$241,060	$210,713
187,496	157,895	146,636	122,374	108,519	89,304	71,233
160,477	139,782	131,195	114,490	101,568	85,378	77,128
27,033	20,522	18,951	16,107	12,729	10,690	9,568
375,006	318,199	296,782	252,971	222,816	185,372	157,929
57,322	68,226	60,288	53,742	62,109	55,688	52,784
5,614	5,767	3,469	2,033	2,355	1,726	2,465
(4,741)	(4,194)	(3,469)	(2,106)	(1,719)	(1,189)	(1,134)
3,590	28,934					
(4,616)	(6,005)	(9,560)	(3,331)	(1,146)	(5,065)	
(9,129)						
(4,112)	(13,539)	901	(2,675)	(2,710)	(2,518)	(1,209)
43,928	79,189	51,629	47,663	58,889	48,642	52,906
18,458	34,443	21,713	20,862	27,534	23,095	25,989
$ 25,470	$ 44,746	$ 29,916	$ 26,801	$ 31,355	$ 25,547	$ 26,917
$1.01	$1.71	$1.15	$1.03	$1.20	$ .98	$1.03
.42	.40	.34	.32	.30	.27	.26
11.16	10.52	9.20	8.39	7.69	6.79	6.04
25,314	26,107	26,127	26,127	26,127	26,127	26,126
$ 49,705	$ 69,381	$ 72,058	$ 43,611	$ 50,769	$ 41,763	$ 29,228
146,258	153,411	156,632	128,838	126,904	100,387	89,459
3.0 to 1	2.9 to 1	3.7 to 1	3.5 to 1	4.1 to 1	3.5 to 1	4.5 to 1
$ 80,511	$ 59,994	$ 55,350	$ 49,751	$ 39,066	$ 34,640	$ 30,418
10,950	8,806	8,427	6,837	6,076	5,007	4,322
390,570	379,597	326,073	287,045	262,668	223,544	190,263
35,346	26,518	27,809	16,718	20,412	6,740	5,620
280,394	272,673	240,275	219,242	200,802	177,275	157,695

files a bankruptcy court petition. According to Levine's motion, Robins' petition was instituted not to benefit a corporation in distress, as the laws are intended, 'but to enable the petitioner to escape the jurisdiction of another court when the day of reckoning for their alleged acts of misconduct was at hand.'"[26] The National Woman's Health Network, for instance, said at a news conference that the company is financially healthy, but is trying to duck its responsibility to women who have filed lawsuits. On the other hand, Roscoe E. Puckett, Jr., a spokesman for Robins, contends that "the best hope for all concerned is for A.H. Robins to remain financially healthy. To do that, we had to stop the financial hemorrhaging that threatened to destroy the company to the detriment of everyone, including the legitimate Dalkon Shield claimants."[27] "Other

EXHIBIT 27.8
A.H. Robins Company, Incorporated and Subsidiaries
Consolidated Statements of Operations
(Dollars in Thousands Except per Share Data)

	Year ended December 31		
	1984	**1983***	**1982***
Net sales	$ 631,891	$563,510	$482,324
Cost of sales	237,508	220,628	195,008
Marketing, administrative and general	222,939	196,495	168,963
Research and development	43,352	40,686	34,279
Total operating costs and expenses	503,799	457,809	398,250
Operating earnings	128,092	105,701	84,074
Interest income	7,560	8,350	8,085
Interest expense	(3,240)	(5,441)	(10,308)
Litigation settlement income	1,205	2,256	3,135
Reserve for Dalkon Shield claims	(615,000)		
Litigation expenses and settlements	(77,950)	(18,745)	(7,091)
Other, net	(13,190)	(144)	(3,740)
Earnings (loss) before income taxes	(572,523)	91,977	74,155
Provision for income taxes (benefits)	(110,910)	33,756	25,462
Net earnings (Loss)	$(461,613)	$ 58,221	$ 48,693
Earnings (loss) per common share	$(18.44)	$2.40	$1.98
Average number of shares outstanding	25,037	24,295	24,552

* Reclassified to conform to 1984 presentation.
The Notes to Consolidated Financial Statements are an integral part of these statements; see Exhibit C27.12.

factors include our desire to ensure that all persons to whom the company has an obligation are treated fairly, to preserve the assets of the company and maintain its current operations."[28]

To supplement Dalkon expenses and to alleviate the tight cash-flow position that Robins has experienced recently, they requested a $35 million credit limit "to meet $25 million of cash needs of its U.S. operations, $2 million in letters of credit for foreign suppliers, and $8 million of credit for its foreign units."[29] This credit limit was the subject of heated debate among the Internal Revenue Service, the attorneys for more than 10,000 women who have filed suit against Robins, and various Robins' creditors. "The IRS contends that Robins owes about $61 million in corporate income taxes from as far back as 1978. Arguing on behalf of the agency, Assistant U.S. Attorney S. David Schiller told the judge that Robins had failed to prove that it needs the entire $35 million of credit or that it couldn't get the loans elsewhere under more favorable terms."[30] The credit line requested by Robins was ultimately approved by a federal court judge. "Under the agreement, Robing will receive $23 million from Manufacturers Hanover Trust Co., New York, and $12 million from Bank of Virginia. The arrangement, which

EXHIBIT C27.9

A.H. Robins Company, Incorporated and Subsidiaries
Consolidated Statements of Stockholders' Equity (Deficit)

(Dollars in Thousands Except per Share Data)

	Common stock ($1 par value)	Additional paid-in capital	Retained earnings (deficit)	Cumulative translation adjustments	Treasury stock (at cost)	Total
Balance—January 1, 1982	$26,127	$ 700	$ 295,851	$ 84	$(12,561)	$ 310,201
Net earnings			48,693			48,693
Cash dividends—$.52 per share			(12,696)			(12,696)
Translation adjustment for 1982				(16,559)		(16,559)
Purchase of treasury stock—644,000 shares					(8,844)	(8,844)
Issued for stock options—24,550 shares	24	266				290
Balance—December 31, 1982	26,151	966	331,848	(16,475)	(21,405)	321,085
Net earnings			58,221			58,221
Cash dividends—$.62 per share			(14,997)			(14,997)
Translation adjustment for 1983				(9,250)		(9,250)
Issued for stock options—61,900 shares	62	716				778
Balance—December 31, 1983	26,213	1,682	375,072	(25,725)	(21,405)	335,837
Net loss			(461,613)			(461,613)
Cash dividends—$.72 per share			(17,936)			(17,936)
Translation adjustment for 1984				(10,051)		(10,051)
Purchase of treasury stock—1,040,404 shares					(17,070)	(17,070)
Issued for stock options—20,300 shares	21	201				222
Shares reissued with acquisition—1,243,707 shares		9,427			13,333	22,760
Balance—December 31, 1984	$26,234	$11,310	$(104,477)	$(35,776)	$(25,142)	$(127,851)

The Notes to Consolidated Financial Statements are an integral part of these statements; see Exhibit C27.12.

EXHIBIT C27.10
A.H. Robins Company, Incorporated and Subsidiaries
Consolidated Balance Sheets
(Dollars in Thousands)

	December 31		
	1984	**1983**	**1982**
Assets			
Current assets			
Cash	$ 1,792	$ 1,534	$ 5,792
Certificates of deposit and time deposits	13,426	57,700	14,349
Marketable securities	76,409	74,147	59,845
Accounts and notes receivable—net of allowance for doubtful accounts of $2,613 (1983—$2,560, 1982—$2,473)	111,313	112,260	107,790
Inventories	84,611	82,714	72,219
Prepaid expenses	5,643	6,674	5,136
Deferred tax benefits	15,800		3,537
Total current assets	308,994	335,029	268,668
Property, plant and equipment			
Land	6,313	6,552	6,940
Buildings and leasehold improvements	106,165	89,374	75,933
Machinery and equipment	90,260	70,169	68,453
	202,738	166,095	151,326
Less accumulated depreciation	67,053	58,444	53,247
	135,685	107,651	98,079
Intangible and other assets			
Intangibles—net of accumulated amortization	82,502	50,201	53,140
Note receivable, less current maturity			8,044
Deferred tax benefits	106,700		
Other assets	14,248	16,782	12,052
	203,450	66,983	73,236
	$648,129	$509,663	$439,983

was opposed vigorously by the Internal Revenue Service and others with claims pending against Robins, assigns the two banks priority for payments among all Robins creditors."[31]

"In approving the credit agreement, Judge Robert R. Merhige Jr. acknowledged that some of the terms 'could be questioned.' But he said he felt compelled to 'give way to the business judgment' of the company's managers. He also expressed concern that denying the request might harm the company's prospects for obtaining credit."[32]

EXHIBIT C27.10
(CONTINUED)

	December 31		
	1984	**1983**	**1982**

Liabilities and Stockholders' Equity (Deficit)

	1984	1983	1982
Current liabilities			
Notes payable	$ 16,129	$ 7,116	$ 5,419
Long-term debt payable within one year	21,600	3,225	1,325
Current portion of reserve for Dalkon Shield claims	51,000		
Accounts payable	23,855	23,989	20,807
Income taxes payable	11,850	28,589	12,269
Accrued liabilities:			
Dalkon Shield costs	22,653	11,094	2,134
Other	39,563	31,491	25,904
Total current liabilities	186,650	105,504	67,858
Long-term debt	11,400	33,000	36,225
Reserve for Dalkon Shield claims, less current portion	564,000		
Other liabilities	13,930	12,270	14,022
Deferred income taxes		3,052	793
Stockholders' equity (deficit)			
Preferred stock, $1 par—authorized 10,000,000 shares, none issued			
Common stock, $1 par—authorized 40,000,000 shares	26,234	26,213	26,151
Additional paid-in capital	11,310	1,682	966
Retained earnings (deficit)	(104,477)	375,072	331,848
Cumulative translation adjustments	(35,776)	(25,725)	(16,475)
	(102,709)	377,242	342,490
Less common stock in treasury, at cost— 1,793,347 shares (1983—1,996,650 shares, 1982—1,996,650 shares)	25,142	21,405	21,405
	(127,851)	355,837	321,085
	$648,129	$509,663	$439,983

The Notes to Consolidated Financial Statements are an integral part of these statements; see Exhibit C27.12.

THE FUTURE

"In October (1984), the company filed in federal district court in Richmond a motion seeking a class action to resolve all punitive damage claims arising from Dalkon Shield litigation. The goal is a single trial for the purpose of determining if A.H. Robins should,

A.H. Robins Company, Incorporated and Subsidiaries
Consolidated Statements of Changes in Financial Position
(Dollars in Thousands)

	Year ended December 31		
	1984	1983*	1982*
Cash provided by operations			
Net earnings (loss)	$(461,613)	$ 58,221	$ 48,693
Non-cash expenses			
Depreciation and amortization	16,310	10,253	10,384
Deferred tax benefit, reserve for Dalkon Shield claims	(125,933)		
Reserve for Dalkon Shield claims	615,000		
Other, net	6,140	2,477	3,201
	49,904	70,951	62,278
Operating requirements, (increase) decrease			
Accounts and notes receivable	1,686	(7,212)	(18,172)
Inventories	125	(10,424)	(4,647)
Accounts payable, income taxes payable and accured liabilities	(147)	36,279	(13,936)
Other, net	2,955	4,910	5,477
	4,619	23,553	(31,278)
Investments			
Capital additions	(38,155)	(20,955)	(15,815)
Acquisitions	(51,809)	(5,700)	(2,035)
	(89,964)	(26,655)	(17,850)
Cash flow from operations	(35,441)	67,849	13,150
Cash provided by (utilized in) financial activities			
Notes payable and long-term debt	5,933	543	(648)
Purchase of treasury shares	(17,070)		(8,844)
Issuance of treasury shares for acquisition	22,760		
	11,623	543	(9,492)
Less cash dividends paid	17,936	14,997	12,696
Net increase (decrease) in cash and cash equivalents	$(41,754)	$ 53,395	$ (9,038)

* Reclassified to conform to 1984 presentation.
  The Notes to Consolidated Financial Statements are an integral part of these statements; see Exhibit C27.12.

A.H. Robins Company, Incorporated and Subsidiaries
Notes to Consolidated Financial Statements

1. Significant Accounting Policies

Consolidation

The consolidated financial statements include the accounts of A.H. Robins Company, Incorporated and all majority-owned subsidiaries. Accounts of subsidiaries outside the U.S. and Canada are included on the basis of a fiscal year beginning December 1 (or date of acquisition) and ending November 30. All significant intercompany accounts and transactions have been eliminated.

Inventories

Inventories are valued at the lower of cost or market. The cost for substantially all domestic inventories is determined on the last-in, first-out (LIFO) method while cost for foreign inventories is based on the first-in, first-out (FIFO) method.

Property, Plant and Equipment

Property, plant and equipment are recorded at cost and are depreciated over their estimated useful lives. Depreciation for all companies is computed on the straight line method for assets acquired after 1979. Depreciation on assets acquired in 1979 and prior years is computed on the declining balance method for domestic companies and on the straight line method for foreign companies.

Intangible Assets

Excess of cost over net assets of subsidiaries acquired after October 31, 1970 is being amortized over a period of 40 years or less. Excess cost of $17,357,000 relating to companies acquired prior to that date is not being amortized. Expenditures for development of patents are charged to expense as incurred. Patents purchased and trademarks are being amortized over their determinable lives.

Income Taxes

The Company provides for deferred income taxes on items of income or expense reported for tax purposes in different years than for financial purposes. The investment tax credit is included in earnings in the year the credit arises as a reduction of any provision for income taxes.

The Company files a consolidated Federal income tax return with its domestic subsidiaries. Income taxes, if any, are provided for on earnings of foreign subsidiaries remitted or to be remitted. No provision is made for income taxes on undistributed earnings of foreign subsidiaries reinvested in the companies.

Retirement Plans

The Company and certain of its subsidiaries have retirement plans for their employees. Costs of the plans are funded when accrued except for the plans of certain foreign subsidiaries. Unfunded prior service costs are provided for over periods not exceeding 40 years. Certain medical and life insurance benefits are provided for qualifying retired employees. The annual costs for these programs are not material and are expensed when paid.

Earnings (Loss) Per Share

Earnings (loss) per share are based on the weighted average number of common shares and common share equivalents outstanding during each year.

2. Acquisitions and Divestitures

On January 5, 1984, the Company acquired all of the outstanding stock of Quinton Instrument Company, Inc. for which the Company issued 1,243,707 shares of its common stock valued for accounting purposes at $18.30 per share and paid $20.1 million in cash. The total acquisition cost was $42.9 million, which consisted of the assigned value of the above-mentioned shares, the cash paid and acquisition expenses. The Company accounted for the acquisition as a purchase and accordingly has included Quinton's results of operations in its financial statements beginning January 5, 1984. On an unaudited pro forma basis, assuming the acquisition had occurred on January 1, 1983, the Company's net sales, net earnings and earnings per share would have been $587,328,000, $56,992,000 and $2.23, respectively. The pro forma amounts reflect estimated adjustments for goodwill amortization, depreciation and interest expense. Goodwill of $27,118,000 is being amortized on a straight line basis over a period of 40 years.

On April 2, 1984, the Company acquired substantially all of the assets associated with radio stations WRQK-FM and WPET-AM in Greensboro, North Carolina. The acquisition price was $7.6 million.

In December 1984, the Company acquired all of the outstanding stock of Lode B. V., an established ergometer manufacturer located in the Netherlands. Lode B. V., an addition to the Company's Medical Instruments Division, has been accounted for by the purchase method and did not result in a significant impact on 1984 financial results.

In March 1983, the Company acquired substantially all of the assets of Scientific Protein Laboratories, a company primarily engaged in the manufacture of animal-derived pharmaceutical products.

Also in March 1983, the Company sold its Quencher cosmetics line at an after-tax gain of $801,000.

In November 1982, the Company acquired the assets of U.S. Clinical Products, Incorporated, located in Richardson, Texas. U.S. Clinical Products engages primarily in the manufacturing and marketing of tamper-resistant seals used in hospitals on intravenous containers after the manufacturer's closure has been removed.

3. Foreign Operations

At December 31, 1984, undistributed earnings of foreign subsidiaries totaled approximately $70,981,000 including amounts accumulated at dates of acquisition. Of this amount, $14,600,000 might be subject to net additional Federal income taxes if distributed currently. No provision has been made for income taxes on these undistributed earnings.

Foreign currency exchange losses included in earnings amounted to $1,187,000 in 1984 (1983—$938,000, 1982—$2,436,000). Net foreign assets included in the consolidated financial statements at December 31, 1984 were $75,098,000 (1983—$93,011,000, 1982—$101,271,000).

4. Inventories

	(Dollars in thousands)		
	1984	**1983**	**1982**
Finished products	$41,814	$43,462	$38,467
Work in process	18,425	16,186	8,221
Raw materials and supplies	24,372	23,066	25,531
	$84,611	$82,714	$72,219

Substantially all domestic inventories were valued on the last-in, first-out (LIFO) method while most foreign inventories were valued on the first-in, first-out (FIFO) method. Approximately 68% of inventories was valued under LIFO in 1984 (1983—70%, 1982—65%) and the remainder under FIFO. Current cost (FIFO method) of inventories exceeded the LIFO values by $3,281,000 in 1984; $4,424,000 in 1983; and $3,546,000 in 1982.

5. Long-Term Debt

Long-term debt, net of amounts payable within one year, is summarized as follows:

	(Dollars in thousands)		
	1984	**1983**	**1982**
8¾% promissory note due annually to 1988		$19,700	$21,025
Bonds, interest rate 55% of prime, due annually from 1984 to 1991	11,400	13,300	15,200
	$11,400	$33,000	$36,225

Annual maturities of long-term debt for the next five years are: 1985—$21,600,000; 1986—$1,900,000; 1987—$1,900,000; 1988—$1,900,000; and 1989—$1,900,000.

The 8¾% promissory note was redeemed at par subsequent to year end and therefore has been reclassified as long-term debt payable within one year.

Interest incurred during 1984 of $2,500,000 was capitalized and included in property, plant and equipment. No interest was capitalized in 1983 or 1982.

6. Lines of Credit

At December 31, 1984, unused lines of credit which do not support commercial paper or similar borrowing arrangements and may be withdrawn at the banks' option amounted to $12 million with domestic banks. Aggregate compensating balances were not material.

7. Stock Options

The Company has stock option plans for officers and certain key employees. The qualified stock option plan of 1973 as amended in 1982 was terminated on January 31, 1983 except as to outstanding options. A new incentive stock option plan was approved by the stockholders on April 26, 1983 under which 1,000,000 shares of common stock were made available for the granting of options. The plans are administered by a committee, subject to certain limitations expressly set forth in the plan, with authority to select participants, determine the number of shares to be allotted to a participant, set the option price, and fix the term of each option.

Transactions of the qualified and nonstatutory stock option plans are summarized below:

	Shares available for option	Options outstanding	
		Shares	Price per share
Balance—			
Dec. 31, 1981	1,355,300	241,350	$10.19 to $11.38
Exercised		(24,550)	10.19 to 11.38
Canceled and expired	4,150	(4,150)	10.19
Balance—			
Dec. 31, 1982	1,359,450	212,650	10.19 to 11.38
Terminated—			
1973 Plan	(602,450)		
Exercised		(61,900)	10.19 to 11.38
1983 Plan	1,000,000		
Balance—			
Dec. 31, 1983	1,757,000	150,750	10.19 to 11.38
Granted	(488,500)	488,500	13.69
Exercised		(20,300)	10.19 to 13.69
Canceled and expired	13,700	(13,700)	11.38
Balance—			
Dec. 31, 1984	1,282,000	605,250	10.19 to 13.69

The options are exercisable at any time until their expiration dates, which are in 1986 (136,550 shares) and 1994 (468,700 shares).

8. Provision for Income Taxes

The provision for income taxes includes:

	(Dollars in thousands)		
	1984	1983	1982
Currently payable:			
Domestic	$ (4,061)	$13,563	$ 1,572
State	1,580	2,745	3,639
Foreign	9,234	10,947	11,859
	$ 6,753	$27,255	$17,070
Deferred:			
Domestic	$(110,009)	$ 5,917	$ 8,238
State	(8,648)	270	292
Foreign	994	314	(138)
	$(117,663)	$ 6,501	$ 8,392
Total provision	$(110,910)	$33,756	$25,462
Earnings (loss) before income taxes consist of:			
Domestic	$(590,925)	$71,613	$52,974
Foreign	18,402	20,364	21,181
	$(572,523)	$91,977	$74,155

Note 12 in the Notes to Consolidated Financial Statements discusses a minimum reserve established by the Company in 1984 for pending and future claims related to the Dalkon Shield. These claims are deductible for tax purposes as incurred by the Company. It is the Company's belief that the currently recognized claims will be fully deductible against its future taxable income. However, generally accepted accounting principles limit the recognition of future tax benefits to those amounts assured beyond any reasonable doubt. Accordingly, the Company has recognized for financial statement purposes only those benefits arising from the carryback of product liability expenses against income tax expenses previously recognized by the Company. At December 31, 1984, the Company had, for financial statement purposes only, unrecognized loss carryforward deductions in the amount of $138,132,000 and unrecognized foreign and investment tax credits carryforward of $86,939,000.

Should the realization of product liability claims produce a taxable loss in a future period, the Company is permitted under provisions of the U.S. Internal Revenue Code to carry such loss back as a deduction against previous taxable income for a period up to 10 years. Such loss may also be used to reduce future taxable income for a period up to 15 years.

In 1984, the Company realized net tax benefits of $5,206,000, primarily in the form of investment tax credit and depreciation, from its investment in tax benefit leases under the "safe harbor" leasing provisions enacted in 1981 and 1982. These benefits reduced the 1984 provision or domestic taxes currently payable and increased the provision for deferred taxes. As current tax benefits are realized, the Company has reduced its purchase cost of the leases and established a deferred tax liability for the leases' future taxable income. Interest income is accrued on the unrecovered purchase cost. The excess of the purchase cost and accrued interest over the cumulative tax savings expected is amortized on an interest method during the years temporary excess tax savings are produced. The interest accrued and investment amortized during the lease terms have no material effect on earnings. At December 31, 1984, the balance of unrecovered investment and accrued interest was $1,071,000.

Deferred income taxes result from tax leases and from income and expense items reported for financial accounting and tax purposes in different periods. The source of these differences and the tax effect of each is shown below:

	(Dollars in thousands)		
	1984	1983	1982
Reserve for Dalkon Shield claims	$(125,933)		
Discounted portion of install- ment note receivable	574	$1,106	$1,520
Tax depreciation in excess of books	2,134	1,480	1,096
Other	356	988	585
Tax benefit from tax leases	$ 5,206	2,927	5,191
	$(117,663)	$6,501	$8,392

Reconciliation of the effective tax rate and the Federal statutory rate is as follows:

	Percent of Pretax Income (Loss)		
	1984	1983	1982
Statutory Federal tax rate	(46.0)%	46.0%	46.0%
Product liability claims in excess of amounts carried back	15.2		
Foreign, investment and other tax credits not recognized after loss carryback	11.1		
Federal tax on foreign earnings	1.4	(1.1)	(3.1)
State taxes on income, net of Federal tax benefit	(1.3)	2.8	3.6
Investment and other tax credits		(2.1)	(2.8)
Foreign earnings taxed at higher (lower) effective tax rate	.1		.3
Puerto Rican earnings exempt from tax	(1.1)	(6.7)	(9.0)
Tax exempt interest	(.1)	(.3)	(1.2)
All other, net	1.3	(1.9)	.5
	(19.4)%	36.7%	34.3%

A wholly owned subsidiary in Puerto Rico operates under partial income tax exemptions granted for periods through 1999. The estimated tax saving from the Puerto Rican operation was $6,200,000 in 1984 (1983—$6,200,000, 1982—$6,700,000). Puerto Rican withholding taxes are provided on those earnings expected to be repatriated prior to expiration of the exemptions.

During 1983, the Internal Revenue Service completed its examination of the Company's tax returns for the years 1978 through 1980 and proposed a deficiency of income taxes of approximately $6,400,000. The Company is con-testing the proposed deficiency which arises from a proposed reallocation of income from the Company's Puerto Rico subsidiary. It is likely that a similar deficiency will be proposed for the years 1981 and 1982.

Management believes that any additional income taxes that may result from the proposed deficiency, and from the probable proposed deficiency related to the same issues for the years 1981 and 1982, should not have a material adverse effect on the consolidated financial position of the Company.

9. Business Segment Information

Information about operations in different business segments and in various geographic areas of the world is included on page 32 of this report and incorporated herein by reference.

10. Retirement Plan

The Company and certain of its subsidiaries have retirement plans covering substantially all of their employees. The total retirement expense for 1984 was $6,908,000 (1983—$6,246,000, 1984—$5,435,000). The actuarial present value of accumulated plan benefits, assuming a weighted average rate of return of 8% in 1984 (1983—8%, 1982—6.5%), and plan net assets available for benefits of domestic defined benefit plans as of January 1, 1984, 1983 and 1982 are as follows:

	(Dollars in thousands)		
	1984	1983	1982
Actuarial present value of accumulated plan benefits:			
Vested	$40,895	$35,601	$30,925
Nonvested	3,472	3,250	4,351
	$44,367	$38,851	$35,276
Net assets available for benefits	$55,621	$47,287	$36,017

Assets available for benefits and the actuarial present value of accumulated benefits have not been determined for several minor foreign pension plans which are not required to report such information to government agencies.

Other liabilities include $6,635,000 of accrued pensions and severance benefits in foreign subsidiaries (1983—$7,063,000, 1982—$7,100,000).

11. Commitments

Rentals of space, vehicles and office and data processing equipment under operating leases amounted to

$6,718,000 in 1984 (1983—$6,428,000, 1982—$5,843,000).

Minimum future rental commitments under all noncancelable operating leases at December 31, 1984 with remaining terms of more than one year are as follows:

	(Dollars in thousands)
1985	$2,515
1986	1,804
1987	1,634
1988	1,265
1989	822
Later years	1,853
Total minimum future rentals	$9,893

The Company has agreed to repurchase, at the option of the shareholder until such time as the securities are registered, the shares of the Company issued to the former Quinton Instrument Company, Inc. shareholders. Upon tender of the shares, the Company will repurchase the shares at the current market price. At December 31, 1984, there were 1,017,103 shares subject to this agreement.

As of December 31, 1984, the Company had outstanding commitments of $8 million for the construction of plant, office and research and development facilities.

12. Litigation

Dalkon Shield—In June 1970, the Company acquired the rights to the Dalkon Shield, an intrauterine contraceptive device. Approximately 2.8 million devices were sold in the U.S. through June 1974. Approximately 1.7 million of the devices were sold abroad.

Numerous cases and claims alleging injuries claimed to be associated with use of the device have been filed against the Company in the U.S. ("Claims"). Only a few claims have been filed in foreign jurisdictions. The alleged injuries fall under the following general groups: perforation of the uterus or cervix, infection of the female reproductive system, pregnancy, ectopic pregnancy, spontaneous abortion which may be accompanied by sepsis, death, sterility, fetal abnormality and premature delivery, painful insertion and removal, and miscellaneous injuries. In addition to compensatory damages, most cases also seek punitive damages.

As of December 31, 1984, there were approximately 3,800 Claims pending against the Company in Federal and state courts in the U.S. The Company expects that a substantial number of new Claims will be filed against the Company in the future.

Through December 31, 1984, the Company had disposed of approximately 8,300 Claims. In disposing of these Claims, the Company and its insurer have paid out approximately $314.6 million. Prior to 1981, substantially all disposition costs (including legal expenses, but excluding punitive damages) were charged to applicable products liability insurance carried by the Company. The Company incurred costs in excess of insurance in the following amounts: 1981—$3.3 million; 1982—$7.1 million; 1983—$18.7 million; and 1984—$78.0 million (exclusive of the reserve described below).

Of the Claims disposed of prior to December 31, 1984, 50 were tried to conclusion. Of that number, 27 resulted in verdicts for compensatory damages in favor of plaintiffs and 23 in verdicts in favor of the Company. Seven of the plaintiff verdicts (involving compensatory awards aggregating approximately $5 million) and one verdict in favor of the Company are the subject of pending appeals. Eight of the plaintiff verdicts also included awards of punitive damages in an aggregate amount of $17,227,000. Six of these punitive awards aggregating $8,827,000 have been paid; two are the subject of appeals. Punitive damage awards are not covered by insurance and are payable by the Company.

The Company is unable to assess its potential exposure to additional punitive damage awards. It has recently filed a motion in the United States District Court for the Eastern District of Virginia seeking certification of a class of present and prospective claimants in both Federal and state courts for the purpose of determining and finally resolving in a single proceeding whether the Company should be liable for punitive damages by reason of the Dalkon Shield and, if so, the aggregate amount of additional punitive damages that should be awarded.

The Company had product liability insurance covering compensatory awards with respect to the Dalkon Shield for pertinent periods prior to March 1978. In October 1984, the Company settled its suit, commenced in 1979, against its insurer concerning coverage of Dalkon Shield liability. From existing coverage and some additional coverage resulting from the settlement of this suit the Company had at December 31, 1984, approximately $70 million of insurance coverage that it expects to be able to use.

In anticipation of the conclusion of the insurance coverage suit, the Company commissioned a study, the purpose of which was to provide management of the Company with data to establish a loss reserve for the future costs in compensatory damages and legal expenses of the disposition of pending and future Claims. The study estimated the amount of this future disposition cost based on the following: (1) an estimate of total injuries based on an epidemiological analysis of published literature regarding the Dalkon Shield and other IUDs; (2) a statistical analysis of all Claims filed during the period 1981 through 1983 which constitute 51% of all Claims filed since the inception of the litigation through December 31, 1983; and (3) a statistical analysis of disposition timing and costs of all Claims filed during the period January 1, 1979 through December 31, 1983 and disposed of prior to October 1, 1984. The information on claims filed and disposition timing and costs was extracted from a database which contains information on Claims filed through December 31, 1983. The study utilized information from the periods discussed above, which was believed to be more representative of future experience, rather than the entire litigation period which would have produced a materially higher estimate of disposition cost.

Based on the study's estimate of disposition cost and a review of 1984 fourth-quarter settlement cost data, management established a reserve, net of insurance, of $615 million against 1984 earnings in the accompanying consolidated financial statements. Management believes this represents a reasonable estimate of a minimum reserve for compensatory damages and legal expenses for pending and future Claims. The reserve does not provide for any punitive damages or damages from Dalkon Shield litigation abroad since there is no substantive basis to quantify such exposures. In taking into account 1984 fourth quarter settlement cost data, management excluded the cost of a single group settlement which management believes is reasonable to assume is not representative of the expected future disposition of Claims. If the excluded settlement cost had been factored as an increasing trend into projected future cost of disposition of Claims, the reserve would have been increased by a material amount.

Based on the study's projected schedule of disposition of pending and future Claims, the payout of the reserve will take place over many years. The Company has reduced its 1984 provision for income taxes by $125.9 million, representing the expected minimum tax benefit to be realized by loss carrybacks to 1983 and prior years, plus reductions in deferred taxes expected to turn around in the tax loss carryforward period. The net effect of the reserve, less estimated tax benefits, is $489.1 million or $19.53 per share.

Continuing uncertainties associated with the litigation preclude a determination of the ultimate cost of the Dalkon Shield litigation to the Company. There has been a significant increase in the number of new Claims filed per month and additional pressure on and a resulting increase in some settlement values which, if continued, would result in a greater Claim disposition cost than the amount estimated by the study. Whether this represents a long term trend or is, as management believes is reasonable to assume, the temporary result of publicity associated with several Dalkon Shield related events in 1984 and 1985 causing a temporary acceleration in the rate of filing of Claims with a subsequent leveling to those shown in the study will only be determined by future experience.

In addition to these uncertainties, there are other factors which could affect, either favorably or unfavorably, the ultimate outcome of the Dalkon Shield litigation and the resulting financial impact on the Company. Among them are:

- The Dalkon Shield removal campaign initiated on October 29, 1984
- The types of injuries alleged in future Claims
- The effect of the passage of time, including the effect of statutes of limitations
- The level of litigation activity relating to devices sold abroad
- The method of disposition of Claims
- The class action intended to resolve the question of punitive damages.

Accordingly, the reserve may not necessarily be the amount of the loss ultimately experienced by the Company. It is not likely, however, that the ultimate loss will be less than the amount reserved. Further, the exposure of the Company for additional compensatory and punitive damages awards over and above this reserve, although not presently determinable, may be significant and further materially adversely affect the future consolidated financial condition and results of operations of the Company.

Other—In December 1982, the United States District Court for the Southern District of New York determined that the suit filed in 1977 by Kalman and Anita Ross, stockholders of the Company, should be certified as a class action for damages on behalf of persons who purchased the Company's Common Stock during the period March 8, 1971 through June 28, 1974. In addition to the Company, certain of its present and former officers and directors are defendants. This suit alleges dissemination of false and misleading information and failure to disclose other information concerning the Dalkon Shield. After completion of discovery, an agreement was reached under which the Company will pay $6.9 million in settlement of this class action. This agreement is subject

EXHIBIT C27.12   *(CONCLUDED)*

to final judicial approval. The action against the individual defendants will be dismissed, subject to final judicial approval. A provision for this settlement has been recorded in 1984 and included in Other, Net.

In March 1980, Zoecon Corporation filed a civil action against the Company and Miller-Morton Company, a subsidiary since merged into the Company, alleging unfair competition (a claim since abandoned) and patent infringement in connection with the marketing of the Sergeant's Sentry V flea and tick collar. The Company counterclaimed alleging patent invalidity on the part of Zoecon Corporation. The case has now been disposed of by way of a settlement having no material financial impact on the Company.

in fact, be liable for punitive damages and, if so, the amount of those damages in respect to all present and future Dalkon Shield claimants. It is our view that this is the only fair means of settling this issue. In addition to the class action, the court has been requested to establish a voluntary opt-in proceeding to dispose of claims for compensatory damages on a facilitated basis. Such a proceeding would allow those plaintiffs who so desire to advance their claims with a minimum of delay and expense."[33]

Additionally, the company initiated an advertising campaign for the purpose of persuading women using the shield to have them removed at the company's expense. As of the publication date of the company's 1984 Annual Report, "More than 18,250 inquiries (had) been received, . . . the Company (had) paid for 777 examinations and 4,437 removals."[34]

REFERENCES

1 Product Management, October 1972.
2 75th Anniversary Book.
3 Subcommittee hearing before Congress. June 13, 1973, Dr. Thomsen testimony.
4 Ibid.
5 SAF-T-COIL informational pamphlet.
6 Ibid.
7 Subcommittee hearing, op. cit.
8 Ibid.
9 Ibid.
10 *Richmond Times-Dispatch*, June 23, 1985.
11 Ibid.
12 Ibid.
13 Subcommittee hearing, op. cit.
14 *Richmond Times-Dispatch*, op. cit.
15 Most of the information in this section was taken from Dr. Thomsen's testimony before the Committee on Government Operations, House of Representatives, May 30–31, 1973; June 1, 12–13, 1973.
16 Subcommittee hearing, op. cit.
17 *60 Minutes*, CBS Television Network, Sunday, August 5, 1984.
18 *Richmond Times-Dispatch*, August 25, 1985.
19 *Richmond Times-Dispatch*, August 22, 1985.

20 *Richmond Times-Dispatch*, September 1, 1985.
21 *Richmond Times-Dispatch*, September 1, 1985.
22 *Richmond Times-Dispatch*, August 24, 1985.
23 *Richmond Times-Dispatch*, September 1, 1985.
24 *Richmond Times-Dispatch*, August 25, 1985.
25 *Richmond Times-Dispatch*, August 24, 1985.
26 Ibid.
27 Ibid.
28 *Richmond Times-Dispatch*, August 22, 1985.
29 *Wall Street Journal*, October 2, 1985.
30 *Wall Street Journal*, October 10, 1985.
31 *Wall Street Journal*, October 2, 1985.
32 Ibid.
33 A.H. Robins 1984 Annual Report.
34 Ibid.

ROSS JOHNSON MANUFACTURING COMPANY

Prepared by William R. Allen, Suffolk University, in collaboration with Marvin A. Franklin.

At the end of the fall semester Robert Tinsley was in the process of completing his M.B.A. at the university. In August, he had completed four years of active duty as an officer in the U.S. Navy. The majority of his degree work had been done at night school over the last year and a half while he was on shore duty. His undergraduate degree was in business, making it possible for him to take an accelerated program. During the summer, Bob had received an interesting offer from a former employer, Ross Johnson, to work for him in a small manufacturing company that he was starting in central New Jersey.

BACKGROUND

In the 1920s, Ross Johnson's father had founded a small pump manufacturing firm in northern New Jersey. After graduation from college Ross turned down his father's offer to go into business with him and decided instead to get a "graduate degree in experience." Shortly afterward, with the prospect of war ahead, Ross submitted to his father's calls for help to meet increased production requirements. As fate would have it, the draft age was raised to 26 in 1942, and Ross served his country at the Philadelphia Naval Shipyard for the next three years. Just as the war ended and Ross was being separated from the service, his father died unexpectedly. Ross found himself at age 29 the president of a two million dollar per year pump manufacturing concern, and he didn't even have an idea where the checkbook was! Over the next ten years, through the infusion of young energetic blood into the company, sales revenues tripled. In 1956, he

Note: This case was prepared as a basis for class discussion rather than to illustrate either effective or ineffective handling of a management situation. Used by permission.

sold the company to a large U.S. conglomerate desiring to expand its hydraulics division.

Self-imposed retirement did not last long. Ross, who always preferred the engineering end of the business, developed some new designs and was soon back in the pump manufacturing business. Starting from scratch, he built an international marketing organization and over the next fourteen years developed a business even more profitable than the former. This time he thought he had hung up his entrepreneurial desires forever, even though he continued to be active in pump design and consulting work.

In the spring Ross received a letter from Robert Tinsley concerning possible employment. Having recently decided to start up a new pump manufacturing company, Ross decided that Bob, with his Navy experience and M.B.A., would be the ideal person to operate the business. Then he could return again to his consulting status.

THE FIRST MEETING

In August, shortly before Bob's separation from the Navy, Ross met with him for the first time. It was more of a reunion at first. They talked over old times and caught up on the families over the last three years. Then, as the wives talked, the men got down to business.

"I was very flattered by your offer, Mr. Johnson, but you do not know anything about me besides the time I did yard work for you and the fact that I have been a Navy officer and will be getting an M.B.A.," began Bob.

"That may be true," responded Ross, "but I know a good man when I see one, and no matter how tight the job market gets there will never be enough good people to go around. Besides, you remember how I had to take over my father's business. I did not have any experience whatsoever. In fact, the company virtually stagnated the first two years while I was working as hard as I knew how. After I finished my trial by fire and gained some experience, I was able to triple sales. I believe I can teach you what you need to know, and hard work on your part will take care of the rest. But do not worry about that so much. I have a lot of time and money tied to this venture, so you can rest assured I will not let you sink."

"Well then, exactly what might I be getting myself into, Mr. Johnson?" asked Bob. "I really do not know anything about the new company."

"As you know, Bob, I have been a pump consultant for the last ten years. However, all along I have been working to develop a revolutionary new pump out of plastic that would perform to the specifications of traditional cast iron pumps but be measurably lighter and less expensive. About three years ago, I began seriously testing a prototype. Over the last two years I have developed what I believe to be the only all-plastic, self-priming, self-lubricating, fully corrosion resistant, multiuse centrifugal pump," explained Ross. Ross handed Bob a copy of the promotional brochure he had developed for the pump. (Exhibit C28.1 shows the promotional literature developed by Mr. Johnson for the Johnson Pump.)

"But is that the only plastic pump on the market?" interrupted Bob.

"Yes," continued Ross. "The other plastic pumps are specialty types only: swimming pool pumps, dishwasher pumps, etc. This is the only multiuse industrial plastic pump available now. But let me continue. Once I had decided that this was a quality product from exhaustive personal testing and testing by reputable engineering firms, and I was satisfied there was sufficient demand for such a pump on the basis of my previous

BASIC PUMP AND
ENGINE SET →

for construction, irrigation, estates,
chemicals, liquid fertilizers,
farms, swimming pools, firefighting
sprinkling systems
. . . a NEW superior pump . . .
built to last longer and take
more on-the-job punishment

WITH CONNECTION
NIPPLES AND
DISCHARGE ELBOW →

EXCLUSIVE FEATURES . . .

LIGHT WEIGHT: Move from job to job
with ease

SUPERIOR PERFORMANCE: Higher pressures plus higher flows

LONGER LIFE: Rust and wear resistant
throughout.

HIGH SUCTION LIFTS: Rapid prime on
lifts to 28 feet.

LOW MAINTENANCE: Parts subjected to
wear easily and inexpensively replaced.

AND WITH
RUBBER FEET →

1½" or 2" INLET-OUTLET SELF-PRIMING
3 H.P. - 4 CYCLE ENGINE ● 9000 GALLONS PER HOUR

ENGINE SPECIFICATIONS:

Make & Model: Briggs & Stratton 80232
Type 0035: 4 Cycle Single Cylinder
Displacement: 7.75 Cu. In.
Fuel Tank Capacity: 2 Quarts
Type Air Cleaner: Oil — foam
Oil Reservoir Capacity: 1¼ Pints
Cooling Method: Air Cooled
Starting Method: Automatic Recoil Rope
Rated: 3 B.H.P. @ 3600 R.P.M.

PUMP SET SPECIFICATIONS:	1½"	2"
Rating in U.S. Gal./hr.	6M	9M
Overall length, inches	17.5	17.5
Overall length, m.m.	444	444
Overall width, inches	15	15
Overall width, m.m.	381	381
Overall height, inches	12.7	12.7
Overall height, m.m.	323	323
Weight, lbs.	30	30
Weight, kilos.	13.6	13.6

experience, I was ready to start all over again. In order to share the capital outlays and risks involved, I sold one-half of the company to a venture capital and overseas brokerage organization. They were needed for their cash and for their access to overseas markets. It was understood that there would not be any interest paid on notes or dividends paid from revenues until the company was properly established.

"Over the past six months we have been selling the pumps in kit form to pump manufacturers overseas. All the work is jobbed out. At this time we perform only the marketing function.

"However, we are currently setting up an assembly operation in a warehouse in central New Jersey. I chose the location to get away from the crowded, high-rent area in northern New Jersey. Besides, the warehouse is only one hour from Newark Airport, two hours from LaGuardia Airport, and one and one-half hours from the Philadelphia Airport. It is still essentially a distribution center until we can gear up for kit assembly this fall. We're planning pump and engine assembly in the spring. We will continue to buy parts, instead of making them, during the initial stages in order to maintain flexibility. Also, we want to keep a low-overhead and low-debt position.

"I have just completed the hiring and the setting up for the initial process. Two men have been hired at a total of $27,750 per year to assemble kits and pack them for distribution. Another man has been hired to run the office and handle orders, shipments, accounting procedures, and so on. I was surprised at the difficulty I had in hiring people. There is supposed to be gross unemployment, but it took me two weeks to find anyone suitable to hire. We have had some difficulty obtaining assembly parts for the kits, other than the plastic parts. However, through proper purchasing procedures this should not hold up distribution. The only other headache at present has been the necessity to build a paint room for $3,000 in order to meet Occupational Safety and Health Administration standards. Also, for some reason many of the buyers want different-colored pumps. Any questions, Bob?"

"Yes," remarked Bob, "one big one. What does it cost you to make the pump and what is your profit margin?"

"I'm glad you asked that," replied Ross, as he turned to the financial section of his project notebook. (Exhibit C28.2 shows selected financial information.) "Here are the figures. I have worked out a decent profit margin. Of course, in some areas we have had to take a smaller margin in order to penetrate the market. Once we have firmly established our market position, it will be possible to readjust prices. Well, what do you think, Bob?"

"It sounds almost too good to be true," smiled Bob. "From what I can tell, you have the hottest item on the market, at the lowest price, and yours is the only show in town. The most appealing part to me is the opportunity to be virtually my own boss. I am really too overwhelmed to think straight now, Mr. Johnson. Let me think it over and come see your setup next month."

Bob was initially very impressed. He had had very little actual experience in the business world, so the opportunity seemed perfect for him. But at the same time, being a somewhat risk-averse individual, Bob knew the value of some research on his own.

At first, he approached the Small Business Administration (SBA) and found they had

EXHIBIT C28.2   SELECTED FINANCIAL INFORMATION—ROSS JOHNSON MANUFACTURING COMPANY

	Mr. Johnson	Partners
Capitalization		
Stock certificates	$ 25,000	$ 25,000
Ross Johnson notes	100,000	100,000
	$125,000	$125,000
Fixed costs per month		
Rent and utilities	$2,500.00	
Mr. Johnson (consulting fee)	2,500.00	
Office manager	1,875.00	
Assembly and packing workers	2,312.50	
Total fixed costs	$9,187.50	
Contribution margin per pump kit		
Variable cost (includes cost of packing, parts, tools, etc.)	$33.75	
Royalty fee to Mr. Johnson	5.00	
Total variable costs	$38.75	

Contribution margin = selling price *minus* total variable cost
= $48.75 − $38.75
= $10.00

a wealth of information to aid small businesses. In addition, they had financed several studies with regard to the success and failure variables inherent in starting a small manufacturing company. (Exhibit C28.3 shows the success and failure factors determined by the Small Business Administration.) Bob analyzed the variables and the company, concluding that the only areas of doubt in his mind were the market and the competition. Before he saw Mr. Johnson again, he wanted to do some research on the industry.

His search led him, with the assistance of the university library's business bibliographer, through a myriad of references: *Moody's, Standard and Poor's, Sweet's Industrial Construction Catalogue, Dun and Bradstreet, Fortune's Plant and Product Catalogue, Thomas' Register, The Value Line of Investment Survey, Conover Nast Purchaser's Guide, Bureau of Commerce Industry Census,* and many others. (Exhibit C28.4 shows selected industry data for pump manufacturers.)

The information available left something to be desired. But this in itself told Bob something. He found out that the majority of pump manufacturers are subsidiaries of conglomerates such as ITT, Ingersoll Rand, FMC, Sundstrand, etc. Most of the manufacturers have relatively few employees and sell only a few million dollars' worth of pumps per year. Thus the industry is very competitive. The large conglomerates have enough capital to sink into their hydraulics division to counter any marketing efforts by smaller manufacturers such as the Ross Johnson Manufacturing Company. In addition, they have the distribution network to grab market share and squeeze out the smaller manufacturer. Yet there is still that large percentage of small pump manufacturers who are surviving quite well. Unfortunately, reference sources do not usually analyze the

EXHIBIT C28.3   MANAGEMENT FACTORS CONTRIBUTING TO SUCCESS OR FAILURE OF NEW SMALL MANUFACTURERS

Success factors	Failure factors
Market	*Market*
Good knowledge of the market	Strong competition
Wide consumer base	Cyclical industry
Competitive price advantage	*Experience*
Product	Poor knowledge of markets and marketing
Uncommon product	Inadequate overall experience
Good product engineering and	*Marketing*
development	Lack of aggressive selling
Financing	Weak pricing policy
Ready capital	Slow collection of accounts receivable
Low overhead	Dependence on a few personal contacts
Low labor costs	Small customer base
Experience	*Financing*
Technically skilled owners	Shortage of total capital
Good experience in the industry	Shortage of working capital
Good managerial ability	High debt level
Previous ownership of related business	Chief owner and/or partner uninsured
Attitude	*Management*
Realistic plans for growth	Dependence on survival of principal manager
Hardworking	Little drive or ambition
Use of outside consultants	Understaffed
Personnel	
Skilled work force	
High-quality work	
Good personnel relations	
Plant	
Excellent machinery and equipment	
Room for expansion	
Marketing	
Aggressive selling	
Good service to customers	
Fast delivery	

pump market at such a low level or, in fact, at any level because it is so closely tied to other, larger industries. But again something can be culled from the scarcity of data. The majority of the manufacturers are in large metropolitan areas near the industrial centers of the United States, where they most likely specialize in different pumps for different industries. Thus there are enough different markets to support many suppliers.

Ultimately, Bob decided that there was some doubt about the future of the Ross Johnson Manufacturing Company, despite its rating on the SBA success variables. He formulated three very penetrating questions for Ross Johnson: What is the demand for the Johnson Pump? What is the competitive situation? What is the company's marketing strategy with respect to the demand situation and the competition situation?

EXHIBIT C28.4   INDUSTRY DATA

Location of pump manufacturers	
New England	154
North Central	246
South	130
West	130
Total in U.S.	660

Size of pump manufacturers	
Number of employees	**Sites**
1–4	189
5–9	79
10–19	93
20–49	97
50–99	60
100–249	62
250–499	43
500–999	22
1000–2499	13
2500 +	2
	660

THE SECOND MEETING

In September, Bob drove to central New Jersey to meet with Ross Johnson to question him concerning the doubts that had developed about the market and the competition.

"It's good to see you again," began Bob, greeting Ross Johnson. "To be honest, I have had some second thoughts about your offer, and I have some questions that I need answered before I can make my final decision."

"That sounds good to me, Bob," responded Ross. "I am glad you have been thinking before you make up your mind. What are your questions?

"First of all, Mr. Johnson, I am rather concerned about the economic situation and what effect this will have on demand. What is your estimation of the demand for the Johnson Pump in the current economic conditions?" questioned Bob.

"That sounds like a good place to start to me," replied Ross. "As you know, this is not the first economic uncertainty I have ever endured. There is, of course, the potential for an energy crisis, which might lead you to believe that there could be a cutback in the petrochemical-dependent plastics market. The industrial plastics which we use will continue to be produced under virtually all conditions. Although there may be some difficulty in obtaining parts for the kits, foresighted purchasing should alleviate any problems. Also, you may not be aware that the president of Briggs and Stratton is a personal friend of mine and has already promised 7,000 engines for next year. So we at least will have pumps to sell. But to answer your question with respect to demand, let me continue. It is precisely because of current economic conditions that the demand for our pump is so high. I can buy all the parts for $33.75 and sell the kit for $48.75. If you will look at my break-even figure here, you will see that because of the low overhead and high profit margin, I have to sell only 919 pumps per month before I begin to turn a profit. That's an amazingly small number of pumps. The key point is the low unit cost. My pump performs all the same functions as the leading cast iron pumps and, at the same time, has a much lower price. In August, I sold 1,000 kits; in September, I will sell 1,000. I have orders for 1,100 in October, 1,500 in November, and 2,000 in December. But, most significantly, with the help of my partner I have orders and verbal commitments for next year for 10,000 kits domestically and 40,000 kits overseas. In addition, I am confident I can sell the 7,000 assembled pumps. I am going on a three-week sales promotion trip in October which should give me an even better picture of the demand next year. Overall, the high quality and low price of the product, aided by the distribution connections of my partners and their inherent interest in the survival of the company, says to me that the Ross Johnson Manufacturing Company has a very bright future."

"That all sounds fine," rebutted Bob, "but what about the competition? Won't the big conglomerates duplicate the pump and eventually squeeze you out of the market?"

"That is another thoughtful question, Bob," replied Ross. "Let me begin by admitting that there will eventually be some competition. As a matter of fact, one of my old enemies recently sent for a kit, with the obvious intentions of testing it and possibly duplicating it. I have sent him one of the older models without any directions. But he will eventually get one of the new models and start to work on duplicating it. I believe it will take at least one year for them to duplicate the pump and go into production. This includes the time to perfect a mold, make drawings, and do tests and, probably most important of all, the time to approve the capital allocation necessary for a production run. In the meantime, I will be improving the pump. I have already developed several types of shafts that will permit the pump to be driven by everything from electric motors to hand cranks."

"I am sure that there will be some delay," agreed Bob, "but how will your marketing strategy be set up for the eventual competition?"

"I believe," continued Ross, "that there is almost an inexhaustible market, for a low-cost, multiuse centrifugal pump. This, of course, will eventually mean serious competition. Even though I have patent rights, the slightest alteration by another manufacturer will get around them. Thus, I feel marketing is really the most important factor in meeting future competition. Time is of the essence, which is why I am doing so much of the sales work myself. If we are to get good market penetration, then it is essential that I establish a strong distribution system by convincing wholesale and retail distributors to take on a relatively unproven, revolutionary pump. If a national distributor such as Sears, Taylor Rental, or Black and Decker decides to include our pump in their distribution mix, we will have the volume necessary to keep our costs and prices low enough to maintain our market share. Once established, we should be able to compete with anyone. What do you say, Bob?"

THE ROXY
DINNER THEATRE

Prepared by John Oliver, Valdosta State College, and Steven J. Anderson, Christoph Nussbaumer, Albert J. Taylor, and Jeanne Whitehead, Austin Peay State University.

Tom Thayer sat alone in the dark of the empty stage. "I really love this business," he thought, "but some changes have to be made if we are to survive." Tom was president of South Stage Theatre Corporation, owners of the Roxy Dinner Theatre. He had just left the cast party that celebrated the first full month of operation at the Roxy. The cast was still celebrating its artistic success when Tom left. Now he must consider the business side of the Roxy's first month.

The Roxy Theatre is located in downtown Clarksville, Tennessee. Constructed in the 1930s, the Roxy enjoyed many years of profitable operation as a motion picture theatre showing first-run cinema classics like *Casablanca, Gone With the Wind*, and Roy Rogers Westerns. In 1974, the Roxy was forced to close its doors due to lack of business. Shopping center cinemas had taken most of the old theater's patrons. The Roxy lay dormant and fell into a state of disrepair until June 1980, when a minor renovation was attempted by a community theater group. This attempt failed and the Roxy once again closed its doors in January 1981. It seemed there was little hope for the Roxy, and it was slated for demolition to make room for parking in the downtown area. It was then that a group of young entrepreneurs decided to establish a theater in Clarksville, saving the old building in the historic downtown location.

SOUTH STAGE THEATRE CORPORATION

In July 1981, a group of five young people from varied theatrical backgrounds formed the South Stage Theatre Corporation and leased the Roxy building. Each of the five

This case was presented to the North American Case Research Association, November 1987. Copies of this case can be obtained from John E. Oliver, School of Business, Valdosta State College, Valdosta GA 31698. The case was designed for classroom discussion only. It was not meant to depict effective or ineffective handling of administrative situations.

owners held an equal $2,000 share in the corporation and occupied a seat on the board of directors. Each had unique qualifications and played a personal role in the operation of the Roxy.

Tom Thayer, age 27, was the president of the corporation. He was selected to serve in this role by his colleagues only because officers were necessitated by the articles of incorporation. Tom graduated from Clarksville Northwest High School in 1975, attended the American Musical and Dramatic Academy in New York on scholarship, and studied acting with Sally Welch, a protégé of Lee Strasberg. He had been in the theater since age 12, both locally and in New York. Tom taught dramatic arts at the Rhodes School in Maine. He functioned as primary director, choreographer, designer, writer, coach, carpenter, and general business manager.

Carmello Roman, age 27, also graduated from Clarksville Northwest High School in 1975, attended Austin Peay State University briefly, then studied graphic arts at Stephens College, Missouri, on scholarship. Like Tom, Carmello studied acting with Sally Welch and performed extensively in local area productions. When not working in New York as a graphic artist, Roman designed makeup and costumes for the Roxy and assisted in direction, acting techniques, and choreography. Roman did all the graphics, brochures, and posters for the Roxy.

Ginger Mulvey, age 28, was vice president for marketing and general house manager. Ginger graduated from Clarksville High School in 1974. She had extensive acting experience in the Clarksville area and worked as an actress sporadically for five years in New York. Ginger returned to Clarksville to open the Roxy. Her duties included the hiring of staff, inventory, serving as hostess, reservations, some accounting and marketing, and publicity photos.

Tom Griffin, age 26, was the technician. A native Clarksvillian, Tom graduated from Clarksville High School in the mid-1970s. He was the son of a long-time theater professional who taught at the local state university. Tom did a stint in the U.S. Air Force in Germany where he handled lighting for the oldest English-speaking theater in that country. Griffin was in charge of all the technical aspects of the Roxy, including the design of lighting for plots and sets, construction of sets, lighting of performances, inventory and procurement of set materials, directing, and performing.

John McDonald, age 38, was a native of Memphis, Tennessee. John had acting experience in soap operas and off-Broadway shows. He taught acting at the American Academy of Performing Arts and at the Rhodes School in Maine where he met Tom Thayer. McDonald was primary director of the children's theater and workshops, selected plays, helped design sets, and directed about one-third of the shows.

The Roxy group was tightly knit with a great cumulative drive to make the Roxy a success. The group's primary objective, as evidenced by the Statement of Purpose in Exhibit C29.1, was to bring the performing arts to Clarksville and the surrounding community. Profit was necessary but was not the primary motivation of the group.

PERFORMING ARTS IN THE MIDDLE-TENNESSEE AREA

Clarksville, Tennessee, is a town of about 60,000 people located in Montgomery County, which adds another 30,000 people to the available market population. The primary employer in the area is Fort Campbell, the home of the U.S. Army's 101st Airborne Division, where 20,000 military personnel plus additional civilian support personnel work, bringing the total area market population to 110,000. Austin Peay State

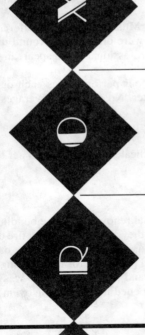

ROXY DINNER THEATRE

We are the newly established South Stage Theatre Corporation composed of Clarksville residents who have been working throughout the country in professional theatres and related industries. We have decided to return to Clarksville to establish a professional dinner theatre company in our home town.

Before we go any further, let us give you some information about the Clarksville area.

Clarksville is located in Middle Tennessee on the scenic Cumberland River with a population of over a quarter of a million people within a 50 mile radius.

Its residents are active in civic, religious, athletic and cultural organizations with a strong interest in visual and performing arts.

Clarksville is the home of Austin Peay State University with a student/faculty population of approximately 5000. There are 4 high schools, 3 junior high schools and various elementary and private schools.

Surrounding the city are: the Fort Campbell Military Reservation, home of the 101st Airborne Division; Hopkinsville, Kentucky; Nashville, the state capital, home of the Grand Ole Opry and recording capital of the world, and a well-populated rural community.

The presence of the Fort Campbell Military Reservation and neighboring colleges, as well as a strong tourist industry, provides a large influx of people from surrounding states and the nation as a whole.

We, the South Stage Theatre Corporation, are proposing to bring a new concept in theatre and entertainment to this active area.

The growing populus can support and deserves to have in its boundaries this professional theatre. The community has always been very supportive of The Arts and will welcome this addition to its cultural outlets.

This entertainment complex is located near the public square in Clarksville's historic downtown district, across from the new First National Bank and the proposed Rodeway Inn. This centrally-located site has convenient parking and access to all major thoroughfares.

We intend to renovate and restore the old Roxy Movie Theatre at 100 Franklin Street into a new and exciting entertainment complex augmented by interested community members and artists from around the country.

With the support and cooperation of the Clarksville community, we know this endeavor will provide a much needed entertainment service, while being a community-oriented force and integral business partner.

The following outlines our intentions and beliefs for establishing the new Roxy Dinner Theatre.

I. PURPOSE

(a) To provide the community with an entertainment facility that incorporates an evening of sophisticated dining and theatrical enjoyment at a reasonable price.

(b) To provide local artists with the opportunity to showcase their talents.

(c) To incorporate the professional standards developed by many successful theatres around the nation. Professional artists will be hired to work with this theatre in cooperation with the Actors' Equity Association and the resident staff.

II. ARTISTIC DESIRE

(a) To serve the community by providing professional productions of American plays and musicals.

(b) The season will encompass a revolving showcase of mediums including:

1. Musical Plays
2. Revues
3. Dramas
4. Comedies
5. Local talent: i.e., orchestras, cabaret bands and supper club style entertainment.

III. DINNER

(a) Each ticket includes a complete dinner, with a choice of cuisines.

(b) Alcoholic beverages will be available at an additional charge.

IV. ADDITIONAL SERVICES

We plan to expand in the future into the following areas:

(a) Gallery space for the visual arts
(b) Daytime Aerobics classes
(c) Children's Theatre
(d) Theatrical program directed toward the elderly and disabled
(e) "The Lillian," a members club upstairs at the Roxy. Members will be invited to preview openings, select seating, hold membership in the "Reel Club," a club devoted to films of a bygone era, and other special attractions.

We hope that the Clarksville community will be as excited about the South Stage Theatre Corporation at the Roxy as we are.

The possibilities of this new endeavor are boundless. The community is important in the success of this theatre, and we hope that our cooperation will create an atmosphere of high artistic values and lively community involvement.

Once established, this union of local talent and professional involvement will surely heighten the cultural experience of all who become involved.

Join us in the creation and celebration of the opening of the new Roxy, Clarksville's first professional dinner theatre.

University has approximately 5,000 students, faculty, and staff. Forty different plants employ approximately 5,000 people in manufacturing. Agriculture is a major contributor to the economy, with beef and dairy cattle, dark-fired tobacco, corn, wheat, and soybeans leading the list of commodities produced in the area. The rest of the population is employed in either government or retail establishments serving the military, education, manufacturing, and agricultural communities. Nashville, Tennessee, is 40 miles away.

The Roxy faced competition from primary as well as secondary competitors. The following is a list of these:

1 The Barn Dinner Theatre was located in Nashville, Tennessee, 40 miles from Clarksville. For $17.25 patrons were provided with a catered meal similar to those offered by the Roxy. The schedule was similar to the Roxy's, but nationally known talent was sometimes featured.

2 The Fort Campbell Cabaret Dinner Theatre charged $11 for a ticket that included a meal. They were open year round on Friday and Saturday nights and showcased local Fort Campbell talent in modern plays similar to the Roxy's fare.

3 The Soldier Show Theatre at Fort Campbell was a motion picture cinema that charged $2 per ticket.

4 The Tennessee Performing Arts Center in Nashville was usually open on Friday and Saturday evenings featuring Broadway shows with the original casts like Mickey Rooney in *Sugar Babies*. Five shows per year-round season were usually offered at prices that varied from $10 to $25. No meals were served, but cocktails and other beverages were offered during intermissions.

5 The Austin Peay State University Theatre and Music Department offered free performances with no meals or refreshments. Shows were offered year round usually featuring student talent, but occasionally featuring a professional Shakespearean group or other special talent.

6 The Kiwanis Club Community Theatre offered four performances each of three different plays per year at a cost of $8 to $10 per ticket. No meals or beverages were available.

7 The high school drama club offered three free performances of two modern plays each year.

8 The Capri Twin and Martin Four motion picture theaters charged $3.75 per ticket.

THE ROXY OPENS

Before the Roxy could be opened, an extensive physical renovation of the building was necessary. In fact, the doors could not be opened until they were replaced by fire doors. The proscenium (the area located between the curtain and the orchestra) of the original stage was struck, the theater seats were removed, and platforms for new seating were built. The neon green and red interior was repainted and a projected stage was built. After much work, planning, and training, the Roxy opened its doors on November 3, 1981, as a fully operational dinner theater.

OPERATING THE ROXY

The Roxy staff established a production schedule of 144 performances per year based on 12 performances per month of 12 different shows per year. Six of the 12 shows were to be musicals. Each show would run three weeks with four performances per week. This left one week per month between shows to prepare for the next show's three-week run.

A Thursday night show was available without dinner for $8 a person. On Friday and Saturday nights, patrons could dine or not as they wished. The price was $8 without a meal and $13, $15, or $17 with a meal depending upon seating. On Sundays, a brunch performance was featured for $11. Dinners were catered by a local restaurant. Waiters were hired to serve all meals. While the Roxy had a bar and maintained a bartender, it did not have a liquor license and sold only beer and soft drinks. "Brown bagging" by patrons was permitted. Seating was highly flexible, consisting of small tables and chairs which would be clustered to create many different seating arrangements.

Open auditions were held and performers, selected from the community, donated their time and talents. The supply of talent was entirely dependent upon those persons in the area willing to volunteer their time to rehearsals and performances. This would limit the types of performances the Roxy could present in the future, especially musicals.

The primary promotional tool for the Roxy was advertising in the entertainment section of the local newspaper. This advertising was "donated" in exchange for tickets. There was no other charge if the finished copy was provided. Very little additional advertising was available or sought by the staff. Limited funds were a major constraint. An example of an ad is shown in Exhibit C29.2.

The five members of the Roxy staff performed a variety of tasks that were often rotated and shared. Specialization was not possible due to the mercurial nature of theater operations. One day might require intensive work on costumes or choreography, while another might require greater attention to sets or rehearsal. The flexibility of the members was a plus, and the feelings of cohesiveness and comraderie were strong within the group. Members worked in the cold of winter to save on utility bills and often relied on "happy hour" at a nearby hotel for food.

The freewheeling, flexible style of the group, while positive in most respects, caused problems in some areas of operations. For instance, there was often confusion concerning reservations, advertising, and cash disbursements. In fact, accounting records for purchases, bills to be paid, receipts, and disbursements were not kept on a regular basis. Check stubs often showed amounts with no explanations or explanations with no amounts. The Roxy operated on a shoestring. Often, when bills were due, funds were not available to pay them. The Roxy staff discovered, by accident, that it was less expensive to bounce a check at the bank than to pay a reconnection fee for utilities. It became their unwritten policy to write checks on insufficient funds to pay bills. This allowed the Roxy to continue operations while they scrambled to produce funds to cover the check. Funds were provided from several sources—the sale of tickets, meals, and beverages; cash donations of patrons, who were noted in the programs as angels and saints according to the size of the donation; and donations of old clothes, furniture, rugs, etc., by concerned friends.

Expenses for a performance consisted of costumes, sets, script rentals, royalty payments, advertising, printing, food, labor costs, musicians (for musicals), and overhead items such as utilities. Cash was limited so expenditures were made only for the most necessary items. Often, old sets were cannibalized to create new ones. Additional props or parts were sometimes borrowed from local businesses in exchange for tickets, sometimes donated by concerned patrons, or, if absolutely necessary, purchased at the lowest possible cost often with tickets proffered to sweeten the deal.

For musicals, the Roxy staff made a verbal agreement with a pianist to provide music for $600 per show. Royalties for musicals were expected to average $975 per show while royalties for a play averaged $250. The first production was a play, not a musical.

EXHIBIT C29.2   A SAMPLE AD

Labor expense included the cost of a bartender at $75 per week and four waiters who worked approximately 16 hours a week at $2.05/hour plus tips during the run of the show (three weeks). The cost of a catered meal was $6.50 per plate.

The fixed costs associated with operating the Roxy included a $910 monthly lease payment, $540 per month to repay a renovation loan (half of which was interest), and $150 per month for insurance. The principals paid themselves a total of $1,175 per month. This included the $235 rent for two of the members' apartment. In addition, they retained an attorney to keep track of royalties, entertainment taxes, and other required record keeping and reporting. Entertainment taxes were 6.75 percent of ticket sales.

Utilities expenses included telephone, gas for heating, and electricity for lighting. The telephone bill was expected to average $220 per month. Gas expense would probably average $1,000 per month during the four months of winter and $50 per month during the warmer months. Electricity averaged $400 per month.

Because of the informality of the Roxy staff, two of the owners have elected to have the corporation pay their rent of $235 per month rather than draw salaries.

THE FIRST MONTH

November 1981 had been an exciting time for the members of the Roxy group. Ticket sales amounted to $10,734, even though an average of only 118 of the 200 available seats were filled at most performances. However, Tom was concerned about a number of things. He could not tell how many of the seats at a performance were filled by free-ticket holders. He also had no record of how many meals were sold, given away, or spoiled. He also did not know how many tickets of each price had been sold.

He had a cigar box filled with notes, receipts, bills, and canceled checks. Upon examination of the contents, Tom found the following information:

1 A bill for $303.33 for graphic design of advertising and programs.

2 A bill for $460.00 for the printing of programs.

3 A receipt from the U.S. Post Office for $88.

4 A bank statement indicating monthly service and NSF charges of $57.75.

5 A note from Tom that the corporation owed him $33.37 for the use of his personal auto for business trips.

6 Receipts totaling $331.74 for props.

7 A laundry receipt for $300.28 for cleaning costumes.

8 Several bills from plumbers and electricians for repairs to the old building totaling $893.45. Tom wasn't sure whether such expenses might be incurred every month.

9 Canceled checks indicating several purchases of supplies (napkins, cleaning supplies, etc.) totaling $391.82.

10 Other miscellaneous items totaling $312.50.

11 Canceled checks to the caterer totaling $4,722.92.

12 A bill for $115 for attorney fees.

Tom believed that he could construct an income and expense statement and that he could find out the number of tickets the Roxy must sell to break even. But he was more concerned about how to control disbursements, free tickets, meals, and other operational problems. More importantly, Tom was concerned about filling the house with a paying audience. When audiences didn't just appear, Tom had begun questioning whether the market for the Roxy's productions was as rosy as the group imagined in its statement of purpose in Exhibit C29.1. An economics professor from the university had mentioned something about regional node theory to Tom. According to the professor, people from small towns would travel to larger regional population centers for shopping and entertainment, but it was questionable whether people from the larger city would travel to the smaller town for the same purposes. Since the Roxy had not advertised outside Clarksville, it was difficult for Tom to know whether audiences would travel from Nashville to the Roxy.

In his discussions with friends, Tom found that many believed that the majority of area residents were apathetic toward the arts and support of the arts, especially the performing arts. The statement that, "If it's in Clarksville, it can't be very good," was expressed by more than one acquaintance. One person responded that there was a limited audience for anything more intellectually stirring than a tractor pull and an inherent distrust of any form of entertainment out of the norm. Others expressed a hesitancy to spend more than the price of a movie ticket for any form of entertainment. Some thought the transient population with wide cultural backgrounds afforded by Fort Campbell was unaware of cultural events in the local community.

Tom wondered whether serving meals was a good idea, and whether serving alcoholic beverages might increase the audience size. He had obtained some information from the State Alcoholic Beverage Commission indicating that, following an inspection of a business's premises, a liquor license could be granted under the following constraints:

For businesses seating 75 to 125 persons, the minimum fee per year was $600, which was paid to the Alcoholic Beverage Commission. The business must also procure business tax licenses from the city and county which would equal the fee paid to the Alcoholic Beverage Commission ($600) and put up a $10,000 bond. The fee for a business seating 126 to 175 persons was $750 in addition to the $10,000 bond.

Once the liquor license was secured an outlay of up to $5,000 would be necessary to stock liquor and mixers. An experienced bartender would be required at a wage of $5 an hour.

A study of some local restaurants which served both dinner and liquor showed 25 to 30 percent of their total profits came from business at the bar. Bars usually earned a 70 percent profit per dollar on liquor sales. This was an after-tax profit estimate.

Tom was perplexed as he wondered what needed to be done to operate the Roxy profitably, fill the house, solve the money problems, and keep the group together. One thing was certain though. The Roxy team had never enjoyed life as much as they had in the last 30 days. They all agreed that they wanted to continue their poor—but full-filled—artist lifestyle even if the Roxy didn't return a profit.

SEAGRAM COMPANY, LTD.

*Prepared by Jodi Guhman, Andrea Hunnicutt, Mark McClellan,
and Carmen Andino-Aquino under the direction of Leslie W.
Rue, Georgia State University.*

HISTORY

In 1909 there were 613 distilleries in the United States. From 1909 to 1914 approximately 200 of these companies went out of business, and by 1919 only 34 distilleries were operating in the United States. The Temperance movement can claim credit for a large percentage of this decline in American distilleries. The movement gained strength in the 1890s when groups such as the Anti-Saloon League successfully obtained passage of local and state legislation against liquor. Beginning in 1910, these groups focused their efforts on obtaining national legislation. The political efforts of the Temperance movement gained an unexpected boost from the wartime spirit of sacrifice, thus aiding the passage of the Eighteenth Amendment.

In the meantime, a man named Sam Bronfman, son of a Russian immigrant, started off selling firewood and fish to the villages of central Manitoba, Canada. By World War I, he and his brother Allan were selling whiskey by mail—a legal activity, though every Canadian province was dry except Quebec. In the early twenties, as all provinces began to legalize liquor sales, the Bronfmans became distillers. The first distillery was built near Montreal. The name of the original firm was Distillers Corporation Limited.

The Bronfmans began to prosper as suppliers to U.S. bootleggers during the Prohibition years. It was this situation that actually brought the business its success. When it appeared that Prohibition's days were numbered, Sam made the decision to stop supplying the market. He reasoned that if the company stockpiled its production and properly aged its products, the company would be able to establish a lead over U.S. distillers. Therefore, Bronfman was anxious to obtain additional inventories, and he began expanding plant capacity by acquiring existing distilleries mainly in the United States. The Lawrenceburg Distillery in Indiana was the first purchase, followed by the purchase of the Calvert Distillery in Maryland. The most significant acquisition was the Joseph E. Seagram and Sons distillery started in 1857 and acquired by Bronfman in

1928. This not only added additional stock to Bronfman's inventories but also increased the prestige of his company. The new organization became known as the Distillers Corporation—Seagram Limited. When Prohibition ended on December 5, 1933, Seagram's products flowed freely—and legally. The repeal legitimized and expanded the company's U.S. market. While Bronfman was refurbishing the newly acquired distilleries, he began importing part of his Canadian inventories and blending them in the states. The first products introduced on the U.S. market were Seagram's 5 Crown and Seagram's 7 Crown. Both proved to be very popular and sold well from the start. Seagram established its market lead and never lost it.

Bronfman's acquisitions were not limited to North America. During the 1930s and 1940s he built one new distillery in Puerto Rico and acquired several smaller operations as well. A significant acquisition during this period was the Fromm and Sishel Company, which was Seagram's first exposure to wine. It was followed by the acquisitions of Paul Masson Vineyards and the Brown Vintners Company. Other acquisitions included Chivas Brothers Ltd. in 1935 and the Henry McKenna Distillery in 1941.

Today, Seagram holds 20 percent of the industry market, twice as much as its closest competitor, Hueblein, Inc.

ALCOHOLIC BEVERAGE TRENDS

Per capita consumption of most alcoholic beverages is dropping (see Exhibit C30.1). 1983 was the fourth consecutive annual sales decline for distilled spirits. Poor market-

EXHIBIT C30.1   DRINKING TRENDS: CONSUMPTION PER PERSON
(In Gallons)

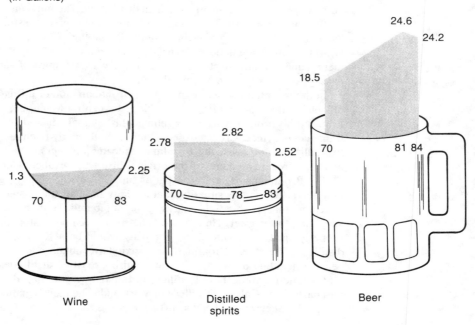

ing, the fitness boom, increased excise taxes, and concern over drunk driving have hurt sales.

Industry critics charge that marketers have not figured out how to capitalize on the nation's concern with health and fitness, as well as the move toward more natural, lighter food and drinks, such as soft drinks with fewer calories or caffeine-free sodas and "light" beer and wine.

Industry marketers would like to be able to promote "light" or "mild" spirits. That kind of labeling could spur dramatic changes in the industry. "We could sell 50-proof whiskey as a before-dinner drink," says a Seagram spokeman. He maintains that Seagram's 7 Crown at 50 proof would taste the same as at 80 proof. "What you lose in the lower-proof drinks is the 'bite,' but sure, you can take out alcohol like you can take out caffeine."[1] But current regulations of the Bureau of Alcohol, Tobacco and Firearms require that any liquor of less than 80 proof must be labeled "diluted," a less-than-appealing word that is more likely to turn consumers off than attract them.

A recent Seagram ad campaign confronts the competition from beer and wine by showing that the alcohol content of four 10-ounce glasses of beer or four 3-ounce glasses of wine is equal to that of four 1-ounce jiggers of 80-proof spirits. The ad's message is, "Sometimes when you think you're drinking less, you may actually be drinking more."[2] (Note that all the recipes that are in the Seagram pamphlet call for at least 1½ ounces of liquor, and many liquors are more than 80 proof. Indeed, as previously mentioned, anything below 80 proof is diluted, so 80 proof is the lowest alcohol concentration found among liquors.)

Distillers were dealt a double blow by Congress in 1984. In addition to acting on the drinking age, Congress hiked excise taxes on distilled spirits from 24 percent to 26.3 percent of the average retail price of a bottle—an additional 35 cents on an 86-proof fifth or about $1.25 on a 100-proof gallon. Currently, state and federal taxes on liquor account for nearly one-half of its retail selling price.[3]

So distillers are faced with the worst kind of marketing problem: increased prices (with excise taxes) for a product with an increasingly negative image (national mood shifting toward sobriety) in an intensely competitive, declining market.

The liquor industry is at a disadvantage by not being able to market its products through television advertising as can the beer and wine industry. As mentioned earlier, new product introductions that have benefited the beer and soft drink industries (low-calorie and no-caffeine offerings) have been largely absent from the liquor industry.

In 1983, apparent consumption of distilled spirits amounted to 431.1 million gallons, down 1.5 percent from the 437.7 million gallons sold in 1982. The figures in Exhibit C30.2 are based on compilations of state tax collections, shipments from wholesalers to retailers, and control-state sales, most of which are at retail.[4]

Though some analysts claim that the increase in the adult population will counterbalance the decline in consumption, the numbers indicate otherwise. Exhibit C30.2 shows that even though the adult population has increased, per adult consumption has fallen from 1982 to 1983.

Within the liquor industry itself, the white-goods segment (rum, vodka, gin, etc.) has benefited at the expense of brown goods (whiskies). Rum has accounted for a healthy portion of the growth in white goods, with consumption rising by 141 percent during the period 1972 to 1982 and its share of the distilled spirits market increasing from 3.5 to 7.6 percent. The only brown liquor to exhibit growth (although modest) in recent years is Canadian whiskey. Brands such as Lord Calvert Canadian and James Foxe convey the prestige of an imported label, but at a moderate price.

EXHIBIT C30.2 U.S. CONSUMPTION OF DISTILLED SPIRITS, 1982 VS. 1983

	1982	1983
Population (000)		
Total	231,786	233,891
Adult	159,673	162,415
Consumption		
Total (000 gallons)	437,659	431,132
Per capita	1.89	1.84
Per adult	2.74	2.65
Per $1 million income (gallons)	172	158

Source: U.S. Bureau of Census and DISCUS.

Today, the hottest liquor products on the market are cream liqueurs (see Exhibit C30.3). Cordials and liqueurs represent nearly 9 percent of the distilled spirits market, having grown 77 percent over the past decade. As yet, no dominant brand has emerged. The leading seven brands hold only 42 percent of the market.

Particularly in vogue are white table wines (see Exhibit C30.4) and sparkling wines, both perceived as less filling and more fashionable than beer and liquor. Wine coolers—

EXHIBIT C30.3 BIGGEST VOLUME GAINERS BY CATEGORY DURING 1983 (Thousands of Cases)

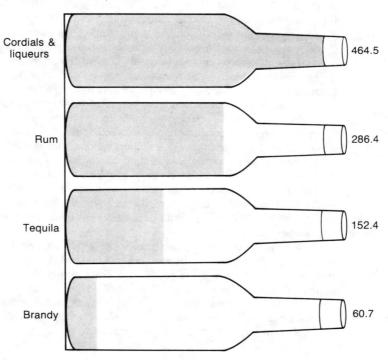

Cordials & liqueurs	464.5
Rum	286.4
Tequila	152.4
Brandy	60.7

EXHIBIT C30.4   TABLE WINE SHARE OF MARKET

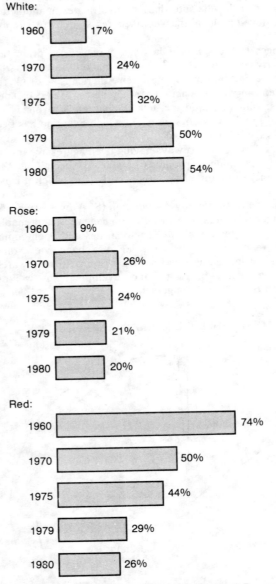

White:

1960 17%
1970 24%
1975 32%
1979 50%
1980 54%

Rose:

1960 9%
1970 26%
1975 24%
1979 21%
1980 20%

Red:

1960 74%
1970 50%
1975 44%
1979 29%
1980 26%

Source: IMPACT American Wine Market Review & Forecast, 1961 ed.

blends of wine, fruit juice, and carbonated water—are selling well, as is cognac, whose growth is tied closely to that of wine. With more than a 20 percent increase in sales from 1979 to 1980, the cognac market is opening up to a growing audience that appreciates fine food and wine.

SEAGRAM IN THE 1980S

The Seagram Company, Ltd., provides export markets for distilled spirits and wines produced by its worldwide subsidiaries and affiliates, manufactures products locally for exportation, develops local markets, secures sources of supply, and concentrates on innovation.

The changes in the spirits industry are even more dramatic for Seagram than for many of its rivals. The North American market comprises 70 percent of Seagram's liquor sales (see Exhibit C30.5), and when Americans do drink, they are not drinking the kinds of liquors in which Seagram predominates. Malts, blended whiskeys, and other brown goods, which bring in the bulk of Seagram's revenues, have fallen off. Vodka, rum, gin, and specialty liquors, areas in which Seagram has been weak, are attracting more buyers (see Exhibit C30.6).

Seagram is described as always having been aggressive in the familiar brown-goods market, rarely excelling in products outside its specialty.[5] Whether it can be as aggressive in wine, or in any of the other markets in which it lags behind, remains to be seen.

In 1950 the Seagram Family Association (SFA) was established. SFA was designed to help younger members of distributor management and enable distributors and Seagram executives to maintain close personal ties and open communication on industry concerns. SFA members meet each spring to exchange views on current business issues ranging from the installation of security systems to new warehouse financing. They discuss sales, marketing programs, and developments as well as current and potential problems with Seagram's management.

EXHIBIT C30.5   1984 SEAGRAM'S REVENUE ALLOCATION

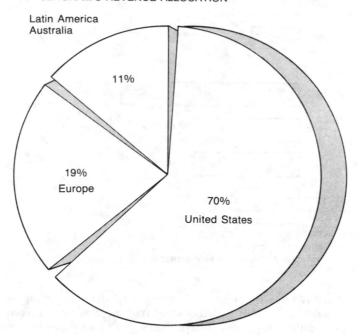

EXHIBIT C30.6 BIGGEST VOLUME GAINERS BY CATEGORY, 1983 VS. 1968
(Millions of Cases)

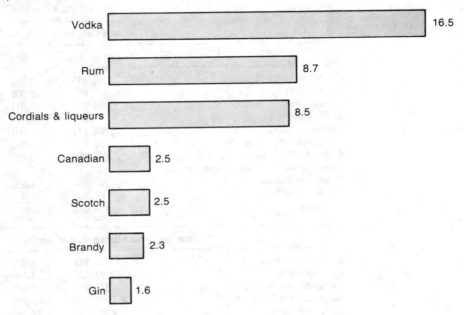

Vodka	16.5
Rum	8.7
Cordials & liqueurs	8.5
Canadian	2.5
Scotch	2.5
Brandy	2.3
Gin	1.6

Also, in 1961 the Seagram's Distributor Consulting Service was formed. It has provided distributors with operations-related support in such areas as warehouse design, inventory management, security, accounting, and order processing. The goal is to increase mutual profitability through more effective distribution of Seagram's products.

A similar program was launched for distillers. This program assists distillers in training their salesmen. In the last 7 years, Seagram distillers have worked actively with their retailers to enhance distribution.

Therefore, the sense of family maintained in the company through various forms of action—people working together to meet common goals—has reinforced the same entrepreneurial spirit that launched Seagram.

FINANCIAL POSITION

Seagram's dominant position in the liquor distilling industry is easily seen by examining the financial statements. Not only is the company the industry leader in terms of total dollar amounts, but it also consistently falls above industry averages for most balance sheet and income statement items. Exhibits C30.7 and C30.8 show Seagram's balance sheet and income statement, converted to common-size percentages.

Particular areas of the financial statements in which the Seagram Company enjoys advantages over the competition are inventories, long-term investments, current liabilities, and gross margin. In each of these areas Seagram is ahead of the industry average. When the composite data for the industry is converted to financial ratios, this advantage is even more apparent.[6] Exhibit C30.9 lists the financial ratios of the industry

EXHIBIT C30.7   BALANCE SHEET, 1983 AND 1984
(With Percentages)

	1984		1983	
	In $1000s	%	In $1000s	%
Assets				
Cash and investments	89,091	(1.68)	132,323	(2.61)
Receivables	351,465	(6.63)	360,549	(7.12)
Inventories	1,064,500	(20.01)	1,023,736	(20.22)
Other current assets	25,379	(0.48)	29,446	(0.58)
Common stock, Du Pont	2,762,441	(52.08)	2,621,856	(51.80)
Note receivable, Sun Co.	90,000	(1.69)	90,000	(1.77)
Property, plant, and equipment	724,735	(13.66)	630,438	(12.48)
Investments & advances—spirits and wine companies	101,075	(1.91)	84,721	(1.65)
Other noncurrent assets	95,959	(1.81)	88,727	(1.76)
Total	5,304,645	(100)	5,061,796	(100)
Liabilities and shareholders' equity				
Short-term debt	364,315	(6.87)	446,391	(8.82)
U.S. excise tax	71,426	(1.35)	75,818	(1.50)
Payables and accrued liabilities	345,430	(6.51)	243,636	(4.81)
Other current liabilities	94,359	(1.78)	131,078	(2.59)
Long-term debt	760,750	(14.34)	742,288	(14.66)
Deferred taxes	872,817	(16.45)	817,506	(16.15)
Minority shareholders of subsidiaries	12,967	(0.24)	38,655	(0.76)
Total shareholders' equity	2,782,581	(52.46)	2,566,424	(50.71)
Total	5,304,645	(100)	5,061,796	(100)

Source: Annual Reports.

as a whole, broken into upper and lower quartiles. In addition, it should be noted that the equity interest in Du Pont accounts for 31 percent of reported earnings per share, as shown in Exhibit C30.8. This is obviously a significant factor which has helped Seagram's stock rise from $9.79 per share in 1979 to $35 per share in 1983 (see Exhibits C30.10 and C30.11).

CORPORATE STRATEGIES

Acquisitions and Divestitures

The potential for growth in the mature liquor industry is limited. Most of the major companies in the distilling industry are combating industry trends by diversifying. Brown-Forman Distillers Corporation, makers of Jack Daniels, has recently acquired Lenox, Inc., the manufacturer of Lenox fine china and crystal. American Brands, Inc., owner of James B. Beam Distilling Company, also controls Sunshine Biscuits, Inc.,

EXHIBIT C30.8 INCOME STATEMENT FOR THE 12 MONTHS ENDED JANUARY 31, 1984
(With Percentages)

	In $1000s	%
Sales and other income	2,647,552	(100)
Cost of goods sold	1,705,507	(64.42)
Gross margin	942,045	(35.58)
Selling, general, and administrative expenses	711,015	(26.85)
Operating income (EBIT)	231,030	(8.73)
Interest expense	67,906	(2.56)
Income before taxes	163,124	(6.16)
Provision for income taxes	43,732	(1.65)
Income from spirits and wine operations	119,392	(4.51)
Miscellaneous income	101,307	(3.83)
Equity in unremitted earnings of Du Pont	96,847	(3.66)
Net income	317,546	(11.99)
Per share data:		
Income from operations	2.45	(69)
Equity interest in Du Pont	1.08	(31)
Total per share	3.53	(100)

Source: Annual Report.

EXHIBIT C30.9 FINANCIAL RATIOS OF THE LIQUOR INDUSTRY

		Industry norms*		
	Seagram	Upper quartile	Median	Lower quartile
Liquidity ratios:				
Current	1.748	3.0	1.4	1.2
Quick	0.532	0.8	0.3	0.2
Efficiency ratios:				
Total asset turnover	49%	26.5%	54.7%	97.8%
Inventory turnover	1.6	na	na	na
Leverage ratios:				
Debt ratio	31%	na	na	na
Times interest earned	3.4	na	na	na
Profitability ratios:				
Net profit margin	11.99 %	10.5	4.9	3.5
Return on total assets	5.98	12.0	5.4	3.3
Return on equity	11.41 %	38.2	26.1	10.5

* Industry data are taken from *Guide to Industry Norms and Financial Ratios*, Dun and Bradstreet, New York.

EXHIBIT C30.10   END-OF-YEAR PRICE PER SHARE OF COMMON STOCK

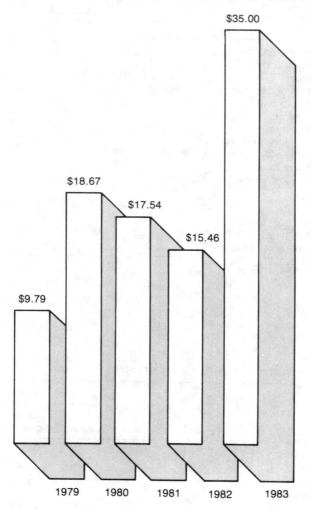

Master Lock Company, and several other unrelated companies. Seagram's top competitor, Heublein, Inc., is owned by R. J. Reynolds, which also owns Del Monte Corporation and Kentucky Fried Chicken.

Seagram's chairman Edgar Bronfman had been shopping for an acquisition in the United States after having received $2.3 billion from the sale of a Seagram subsidiary to the Sun Company in 1981. Texas Pacific Oil Co. of Pennsylvania was the only big nonliquor asset Seagram had. Although Texas Pacific had rich potential in acreage and undeveloped reserves, Bronfman wanted a mature resources company that was pouring out current profits, which Seagram needed for its capital-intensive distilleries (see Exhibit C30.12).

EXHIBIT C30.11   INCOME
(Millions)

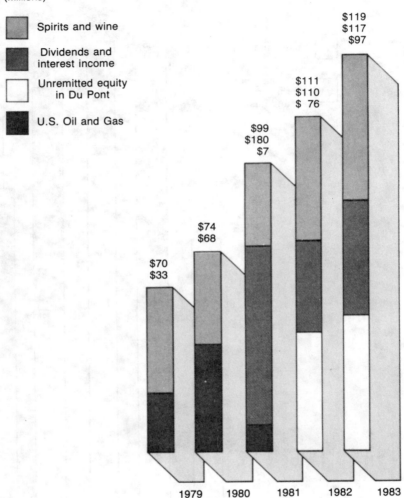

Seagam's first bid was for the St. Joe Minerals Corporation, but the offer was withdrawn because the price was more than Seagram thought the company was worth. Seagram had purchased 446,000 shares of the mineral company and, after bowing out, sold them for a profit of approximately $10 million.

Seagram then considered such consumer-goods companies as Colgate-Palmolive, Bristol-Myers, and Gillette. Finally, Conoco, Inc., the nation's ninth-largest oil company, became the target.

Seagram's bid for Conoco ranged from $70 per share to $92 per share. Conoco resisted this move and desperately searched for a merger partner. E. I. Du Pont de

EXHIBIT C30.12   CAPITAL EXPENDITURES
(Millions)

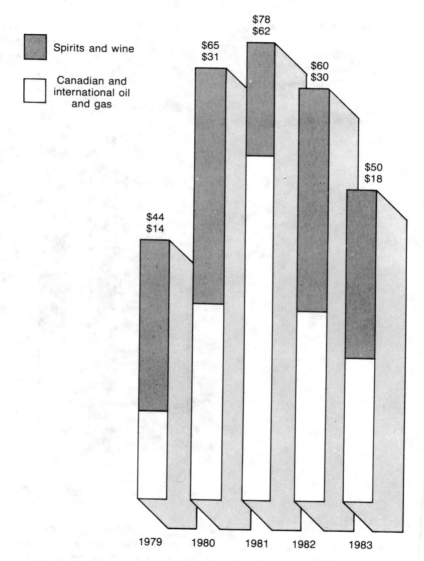

Spirits and wine

Canadian and
international oil
and gas

$78
$62

$65
$31

$60
$30

$50
$18

$44
$14

1979   1980   1981   1982   1983

Nemours & Company and the Mobil Oil Corporation joined in on the bidding. On
August 5, 1981, after 4 months of negotiations, Du Pont acquired Conoco at $98 per
share, making it the most expensive takeover in history at that time.[7] Seagram then
exchanged the 32 percent of Conoco that it had acquired on the open market for 20
percent of Du Pont–Conoco.

The question remains: Is owning a part of Du Pont a good deal for Seagram?
Bronfman admits that the opportunity came along "more or less by accident." As oil

supplies dwindle, Bronfman argues, having a supply of Conoco coal to use as feedstock for Du Pont chemicals will provide a tremendous competitive advantage.[8] Approximately one-third of Seagram's net income and reported earnings per share is derived from its unremitted equity interest in Du Pont. Still, Seagram's intention was to obtain a source of cash, and this is yet to be realized.

Seagram's two highest-ranking executives under Edgar Bronfman may not be as enthusiastic about the Du Pont connection as he is. The Bronfman family owns 39 percent of Seagram, and Edgar's younger brother Charles—the company's vice chairman—recently claimed that Seagram may attempt another oil company acquisition. Charles, a Canadian citizen, favors a Seagram buy-out of a U.S. oil interest in Canada. This is particularly attractive since the introduction of the Canada National Energy Program in 1981. The program limits foreign investors to 50 percent of any new oil development, while favoring Canadians with cash grants of 80 percent of exploration costs and offering Canadian companies preferential access to lucrative new oil acreage. Edgar, a U.S. citizen since 1955, declares that the company's "redeployment of assets" is essentially completed. Seagram President Philip E. Beekman, credited with a vast improvement in the company's liquor business, said that he is "still interested in a consumer products acquisition outside the liquor business."[9] Beekman came to Seagram from Colgate-Palmolive, and last year reportedly lobbied against buying a U.S. resources company. Beekman lacks the family connection but is admired as the liquor tactician whose marketing brilliance has been largely responsible for the company's improved profitability. Seagram earned $286 million on sales of $2.8 billion in the fiscal year ended July 31, 1981, compared with profits of $142 million on sales of $2.5 billion in 1980. Beekman wants an acquisition because he knows this kind of improvement cannot last.

Seagram's problem was that it no longer had the financial might to do anything as big as it could have done just a few months earlier. Which of its more modest options it would choose would depend largely on which Seagram executive had his way.

In November 1983, Joseph E. Seagram and Sons, Inc., acquired Coca-Cola's Wine Spectrum for over $200 million in cash. The purchase moved Seagram from sixth to second place among U.S. vintners, trailing only Gallo. The company is credited with the foresight to continue its investment in the wine business at a time of industrywide shakeout and uncertainty. Coke cringed when the Wine Spectrum continued to generate a return on assets of less than 5 percent a year in wine, compared with the 10 to 15 percent ROA its soft drink business yields.

Most experts predict that wine industry growth will rebound to the 5 to 7 percent levels it enjoyed in the years leading up to 1982, making it an attractive investment again. Says Bronfman, "It seemed to us that by acquiring the Wine Spectrum we could have a shortcut to profitability simply by economies of scale—more products spread over the same, or slightly increased overhead."[10] Under Coke, Taylor California Cellars wines became one of the fastest-growing domestic labels. Seagram is excited because there are a lot of possibilities, such as blending wines or creating wine cocktails.

Moderation

There is a trend toward moderation in drinking because of increased interest in self-improvement and health. Companies within the spirits industry are united by their desire to counteract antidrinking sentiment by educating people against abuse.

Seagram is a company that accepts its responsibility to the consumers of its products and to the public at large. It is the only distiller in the world that has consistently, since 1934, counseled moderation in the use of its products.

The first Seagram moderation message appeared in October 1934, less than a year after the end of Prohibition. Beneath the headline "We who make whiskey say: 'Drink moderately,'" the text explains:

> There is nothing new about drinking whiskey. Through generations, it has always occupied a natural place in gracious living; the House of Seagram believes that whiskey, properly used, is deserving of that position. . . . We feel that you will agree with us that the desirable way of life is thoughtful, informed by experience, guided by common sense. Realizing this, we feel sure you will prefer moderation in the enjoyment of the finest. . . .[11]

Along with the other messages, there has been—from the earliest years—a continuing series of ads on the perils of drinking and driving. A variety of approaches have been used to drive home the point, including a shadowed headline suggesting the double vision of an intoxicated driver and several ads dramatizing the very real consequences of accidents through photographs of shattered windshields or an ambulance stretcher.

Hence, its series of moderation messages, published widely throughout the United States and Canada, has been recognized and honored as an unmatched example of corporate responsibility.

BUSINESS STRATEGY

Brewers, wine growers, and distilleries are responding to new tastes with lighter and more flavorful drinks. Distillers must introduce a lot of new products to attract the consumers who are switching to wines and low-alcohol beers.

Seagram is now making a marketing assault on virtually all the liquor categories that it has never breached. Seagram's Imported Vodka, a significant new entry in a highly competitive category, has already become the largest-selling import in its introductory markets. But with this move Seagram is taking on a top competitor. Heublein's Smirnoff sold about 7.2 million cases last year—more than double that of its nearest rival, which happens to be another Heublein brand, Popov. Seagram's Wolfschmidt sold about 1.1 million cases. Seagram hopes to distinguish its new product with the cachet of an import and stylish packaging, "Imported vodka without the imported price."[12]

Seagram has reformulated its Myers's Platinum White and Gold Rich Rums as Jamaican, rather than Puerto Rican, rums. The repositioning allows Myer's to differentiate itself from the Puerto Rican brands—most obviously Bacardi, the largest-selling single liquor brand in the United States. Rather than go head-to-head with Bacardi, possibly a suicidal undertaking, Seagram appears to be using the super-premium brands from Myer's to lure rum drinkers up to the next step.

In addition to Seagram's new vodka and rum, the company is expanding its line of brandies and cordials. Seagram's most recent offering in the cordial liqueurs category is Dr. McGillicuddy's Mentholmint Schnapps. This new entry from Seagram has successfully competed with Beam's, Trenais and with imported french liqueurs introduced early in 1983. Currently, Seagram markets 28 liqueurs and 9 flavored brandies under its popular Leroux label. Seagram also markets 20 additional liqueurs and brandies under assorted labels such as Vandermint Minted Chocolate and Myer's Original Rum Cream.

Seagram is moving ahead with its nonalcoholic St. Regis Blanc wine. St. Regis is aimed at regular drinkers who, from time to time, don't want alcohol. The product is being tested in Phoenix, Arizona, and Sacramento and Stockton, California. In addition to advertising with television commercials showing young, affluent-looking drinkers in a variety of drinking situations, Seagram is undertaking extensive promotional and sampling programs for St. Regis. One report said that the company might spend as much as $15 million to roll out St. Regis.[13]

Another concept which has been highly successful in the U.S. market is the importation of Scotch and Canadian whiskies at high strength which are then reduced to bottling strength with specially treated water. This method has made it possible to sell such products as Lord Calvert Canadian and Passport Scotch at moderate prices because there are significant savings on handling costs.

JOINT VENTURES

"The first mixers good enough to be called Seagram's" were introduced in the New York metropolitan area in late February 1983.[14] The Seagram's mixers are the result of a partnership agreement between the Coca-Cola Bottling Company of New York and Joseph E. Seagram and Sons, Inc. Seagram agreed to license its name for a line of mixers that would be formulated and distributed by Premium Beverages, Inc., a new unit of Coke New York.

The Seagram's mixer product line includes ginger ale and sugar-free ginger ale, club soda, tonic and sugar-free tonic, seltzer, bitter lemon, collins, and a grapefruit-lemon combination called Half and Half.

Venezuela is an example of a successful partnership between Seagram and local businessmen. A jointly owned distillery produces whiskey, rum, gin, vodka, brandy, liqueurs, and wines, which have major shares of the market. In addition to the local products, Seagram's jointly owned enterprise in Venezuela sells very successfully such Seagram imports as Chivas Regal Scotch and 100 Pipers Scotch.

Another example of a successful partnership is "Kirin-Seagram," the company's joint venture with Kirin, the largest brewery in Japan. Kirin-Seagram recently completed a large, modern distillery capable of producing Scotch-type and U.S.-type whiskies, gin, vodka, and liqueurs. The current bottling capacity of 12 million liters annually has been designed for easy expansion as sales increase.

The Kirin-Seagram sales force aggressively markets the Seagram brands imported into Japan as well as the products of the new distillery. Kirin-Seagram, owned 50 percent by each company, is the first such joint venture in Japan's beverage industry— an industry which is already among the largest in the world.

Operations in Japan and Venezuela typify the advantages of Seagram's partnership concept, which adds local knowledge and local participation to Seagram's experience and expertise in both producing and marketing huge volumes of very high quality beverage products. Both local products and imports benefit from the combination of resources and supervision.

Captain Morgan Rum, from Seagram's Jamaica operations, is a dominant seller in Canada and the United Kingdom. In Venezuela, Seagram's Cacique Rum is one of the leading brands. In Brazil, Seagram's Montilla brand is the number-one rum. French, Austrian, Italian, German, and Alsatian wines, brandies, champagnes, and spirits are distributed in world markets by Seagram.

EXHIBIT C30.13 LONG-TERM TRENDS—U.S. PER CAPITA SPIRITS CONSUMPTION VS. PER CAPITA INCOME

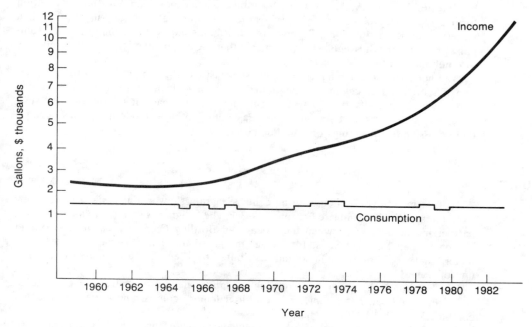

EXHIBIT C30.14 LONG-TERM TRENDS—CONSUMER EXPENDITURES ON ALCOHOLIC BEVERAGES

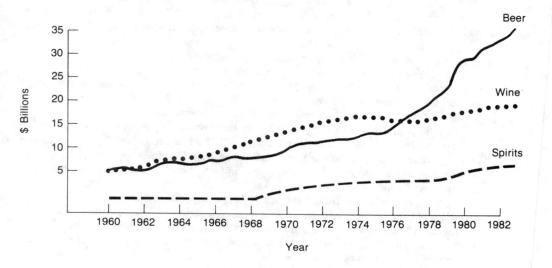

As stated earlier, the corportion has purchased or established companies in over 20 countries to produce and sell wines and spirits through local enterprises. This, together with a policy of encouraging local management, has been one of the keys to Seagram's marketing success.

THE FUTURE

Though it is true that per capita consumption of alcoholic beverages in the United States is on the decline (see Exhibit C30.13), the adult population is increasing and it is not yet known how much this will offset the downturn in liquor sales.

Because the American fitness trend has yet to take hold overseas, acquisition of local distillers abroad are likely to move sales up outside of North America in places where drinking habits have not yet begun to decline.

Of all the segments of the beverage industry, the wine sector has the most promising growth potential. The consumption of white wine has grown 513 percent over the past decade (see Exhibit C30.14).

REFERENCES

1 "Annual Liquor Survey: Why Consumption Is Down," *Business Week*, May 7, 1984, p. 120.

2 *The Liquor Handbook 1984*, Jobson, New York, 1984, p. 3.

3 "How Seagram Is Scrambling to Survive the Sobering of America," *Business Week*, Sept. 3, 1984, p. 94.

4 *Liquor Handbook*.

5 "How Seagram Is Scrambling."

6 *Industry Norms and Financial Ratios, 1982–83*, Dun and Bradstreet, New York, p. 148.

7 "Seagram's Bid for Conoco," *Hermes: Columbia Business School Magazine*, fall 1981, p. 7.

8 Kraar, "Seagram Tightens Its Grip on DuPont," *Fortune*, Nov. 16, 1981, p. 77.

9 "Seagram: Its Cash Hoard Is Spent, and Its Future Is Up in the Air," *Business Week*, Dec. 21, 1981, p. 98.

10 di Cagno, "Edgar Bronfman: A Conversation," *Hermes: Columbia Business School Magazine*, Dec. 21, 1981, p. 9.

11 Brady, "50th Anniversary for Seagram Moderation Campaign," Joseph E. Seagram and Sons, Inc., New York, p. 2.

12 Brady, "Seagram Introduces 'Imported Vodka without the Imported Price,'" Joseph E. Seagram and Sons, Inc., New York, p. 3.

13 "Seagram Slips the Alcohol out of Wine," *Business Week*, July 9, 1984, p. 46.

14 Dawson, "Seagram Soft Drinks: A New Media Mixer," *Marketing and Media Decisions*, April 1983, p. 70.

TEXAS AIR CORPORATION

Prepared by Faramarz Parsa, West Georgia College, and Leslie W. Rue, Georgia State University.

Texas Air Corporation, a Delaware corporation organized in 1980, is a holding company with investments in airlines and related businesses. Texas Air Corporation owns all the common stock of Continental Airlines, Inc., Eastern Air Lines, Inc., People Express, Inc., New York Airlines, Inc., Frontier Airlines Inc., and SystemOne Holdings, Inc. Since February 1, 1987, Continental, People Express, New York Air, and Frontier have been marketed by Continental as a single integrated airline under the "Continental Airlines" name.

Both Continental and Eastern are major U.S. certified air carriers with headquarters in Houston and Miami, respectively. SystemOne manages and coordinates the marketing of airline reservations and computer processing systems and telecommunications facilities. Texas Air is headquartered in Houston and its securities are traded on the American Stock Exchange and the Pacific Stock Exchange and trade under the ticker symbol "TEX." On September 25, 1987, the closing sale price of the common stock on the American Stock Exchange was $26.00 per share.

POSTDEREGULATED AIRLINE INDUSTRY

Hardly a day goes by without news of an airline that has merged, purged its work force, or simply gone bankrupt. But this has not always been the case. This was once a cozy industry for the fat and sassy. How it changed is a story of some of the best—and worst—cases of business strategy and management.

The U.S. airline industry consists of some 250 individual commercial air carriers operating approximately 4,500 aircraft and employing over 355,000 people. In 1985, the industry served 380 million passengers and carried 6 billion cargo ton-miles.

Used by permission.

The industry is highly concentrated. The six largest carriers account for 84 percent of all revenue passenger miles. (A revenue passenger mile equals one revenue-paying passenger flying 1 mile. A major airline is one with at least $1 billion in annual revenue.) The remaining passenger revenue is shared by 16 carriers classified as nationals (each with annual revenues between $75 million and $1 billion) which account for about 12 percent, and by the regionals/commuters, which account for 4 percent of all revenue passenger miles.

The Airline Deregulation Act of 1978 brought drastic legal and regulatory changes to the airline industry. Deregulation caused a shift in the perspective of management, marketing, and operations and, in fact, was accompanied by more change than the industry had seen in the previous 40 years.

Under deregulation, the way airlines were viewed changed dramatically. Prior to deregulation, airlines were thought of as public utilities with government protection. Under deregulation, however, airlines became businesses that are subject to the forces of the free market. The government no longer decides which airline will fly where, and if a city should have service. Rates and services are now determined by competition. The theory is that without government regulation, the efficient companies will prosper and the inefficient ones will die out, with the end result being better service to the public.

Deregulation has affected many elements of the airline marketplace, including: freedom of market entry and exit, freedom of pricing, use of automation as a competitive weapon, alteration in the relationships between airlines, lifting of restrictions on promotional activities, and shifts in labor-management relationships. The overall intent of deregulation was to put a greater premium on efficiency, cost control, production, marketing, and handling of employees and to cause airline executives to behave more like managers in other industries.

There is another side to deregulation, however. It was believed in the late 1970s and early 1980s that the free market forces would increase competition, enhance productivity, and lower prices. In fact, airline fares have decreased and operating efficiencies have improved. However, in the past few years there has been concern that increasing concentration in the airline industry is beginning to undermine the benefits of deregulation. One of the original goals of deregulation was to discourage the airline monopolies that had existed, but just the opposite has actually happened. Another failure of deregulation has been in encouraging new competitors in the market. Many thought People Express would capture a large market share, but instead it floundered and was subsequently absorbed by Continental. Texas Air Corporation is the only new major competitor to enter the market since deregulation. It is possible that the concentration of the nation's jet service in the hands of a few "mega-carriers" will discourage price competition through oligopoly.

Secrets of Success

Carriers that survive what now seems to be the last phase of deregulation are likely to have a few characteristics in common:

Cost Control   Fuel and labor are the two major operating expense components for airlines. In the last few years the entire industry has benefited from the lower fuel prices which generally account for about 25 percent of an airline's total operating expenses. Labor costs have also yielded to cost-control efforts by the airlines. Compelled primarily by the emergence of such low-cost entities as People Express, the major airlines have resorted to a variety of labor cost-containment measures, including permanent or temporary reductions in wage rates, lower pension funding rates, filing for protection under Chapter 11 of the Federal Bankruptcy Code to escape onerous labor contracts (Continental Airlines), and, most widespread, the negotiation of two-tier wage contracts. Pioneered by American Airlines in 1983, this type of contract imposes a lower wage scale (usually called a B scale) on newly hired workers, typically 30 percent to 50 percent below former starting rates.

A Hub System   Since the airline industry was deregulated in late 1978, and especially since full route freedom became effective at the beginning of 1982, the carriers' route systems have been in constant flux. The intense competitive battle has prompted old and new carriers alike to experiment with different operating strategies, eliminate marginal segments, and take advantage of new opportunities, such as the demise of another airline or its withdrawal from a particular route.

In this period of exposure to free-market forces, the most successful strategy by far has been based on the use of hub-and-spoke systems. This approach establishes a number of routes connected to a central hub where passengers can be collected from feeder flights, transferred to other flights of the same line, and carried to their ultimate destinations. Its advantages to the airline are numerous: a large number of points are connected without the need to schedule individual flights between them; the passenger is retained on the system for longer distances; average revenue per passenger is raised, and lightly traveled point-to-point segments are avoided.

In addition to pursuing the hub strategy generally, the major airlines have undertaken other moves in formulating their route systems. Their objectives include improving geographical and seasonal balance of traffic; penetrating new, attractive areas; changing the mix of business and leisure traffic; and improving the coordination of international and domestic routes.

The principal hubs of the major airlines are as follows:

American	Dallas/Ft. Worth and Chicago
Continental	Houston and Denver
Delta	Atlanta and Dallas/Ft. Worth
Eastern	Atlanta, Miami, and Kansas City
Northwest	Minneapolis/St. Paul
Piedmont	Charlotte, Baltimore, and Dayton
Pan Am	New York and Miami
Republic	Detroit, Memphis, and Minneapolis/St. Paul
TWA	St. Louis and New York
United	Chicago, Denver, and San Francisco
US Air	Pittsburgh
Western	Salt Lake City and Los Angeles

Marketing   The industry's highly competitive environment necessitates vigorous marketing efforts to make it successful. Among the most widely used tactics are the "frequent flier" programs that most carriers have now adopted. These plans, which offer bonuses for various totals of mileage flown at full fares, are designed to build carrier loyalty among customers and increase the number of full-fare tickets.

Computer Reservation Systems   Computer Reservation Systems (CRSs) constitute another potent tool. Approximately 90 percent of all travel agent–generated reservations are made through these systems. Although there are five such systems currently in operation (owned by American, United, TWA, Eastern, and Delta), American's Sabre and United's Apollo system together account for about 70 percent of the market. Considerable controversy developed during 1983 over the operation of these systems. Although the reservation systems have been available to all carriers as co-hosts for a fee, there were widespread accusations by smaller airlines that the systems offered unfair advantages to the host company in methods of display and in ticketing. In November 1984, the CAB adopted new rules governing CRS operations. Among other things, these rules cover (1) display bias (the display must show schedules, fares, rules, and availability of all airlines in an unbiased way); (2) contracts (unjust discrimination in setting fees charged to co-hosts is prohibited); and (3) marketing information and service enhancements (boarding passes and seat selection will be available to all subscriber airlines if available to any). CRS fees were substantially increased under the new rules.

Growth through "Horizontal Integration"   The airline industry is undergoing a period of consolidation. In addition to Texas Air's acquisition of Eastern, People Express, and Frontier, recent consolidations include Northwest Airlines' acquisition of Republic Airlines, Trans World Airlines' acquisition of Ozark Air Lines, Delta Air Lines' acquisition of Western Air Lines, U.S. Air's agreement to acquire Pacific Southwest Airlines, and American Airlines' agreement to acquire Air Cal. Such consolidations may result in attractive advantages for the respective airlines' becoming stronger competitors. Some of the advantages of "bigness" include:

Economies of scale. Since oil prices are lower than in the late 1970s and early 1980s, the carriers are less eager to buy fuel-efficient but costly new planes. Instead, for the price of three or four new 747s a carrier can get an entire fleet of used aircraft by buying out a competitor. For example, TWA gained 50 DC-9s when it purchased Ozark Airlines. Acquiring the same number of seats in new planes would have cost about $775 million, more than three times the entire Ozark purchase price.

Efficient operations. Combining fleets can also make for more efficient operations. Because Republic had few large planes, it was forced to schedule 19 flights a day that were essentially duplicates. Several went to the same destination at exactly the same time as another Republic flight. Northwest has a large fleet of big jets, some of which are underutilized. The combined airlines can now schedule big jets to take care of passengers on those duplicate flights, reducing the number of flights and slashing costs.

Reduced overhead. Airlines expect further savings from reduced overhead in ground operations. Carriers can spread the costs associated with ticket agents and other employees over a greater number of passengers.

Controlling traffic at "hub" airports. Hubs give carriers the ability to fill the greatest possible number of seats on each flight. For example, an airline might schedule ten or more flights to arrive at its hub from various feeder airports within a one-hour period. Drawing on this groups of arriving passengers, the airline can then fill up a couple of jumbo jets for very profitable trips to major cities.

Slots. In some cases, the acquiring airline has also gained a hidden strategic asset: slots—the takeoff and landing rights—at crowded airports. Until recently, these slots were rigidly allocated by an industry committee to airlines at busy airports. Starting in April 1986, however, airlines were allowed to buy and sell slots. As a result, slots owned by carriers like Eastern, with its 164 at LaGuardia, suddenly have a tremendous cash value. —*opportunity to sell & make money to over loss.*

FRANK LORENZO AND TEXAS AIR

Mission

Frank Lorenzo is the chairman and chief executive officer of the Texas Air Corporation. He once said that by 1990 there will be only six major airlines and he intends to own one of them. Texas Air's acquisition of Eastern Airlines in 1987 has given Lorenzo the controlling interest of the largest air carrier in the free world. The following is the chronology of Lorenzo's climb to the top (see Exhibit C31.1).

1940:   Born in Queens, N.Y., the son of Spanish immigrants who operated a beauty parlor. He buys his first stock at age 15—in TWA.

1966:   After working as an analyst at TWA and Eastern, he forms an airline financial advisory firm with Harvard business school classmate Robert Carney.

1966:   Partnership with Carney evolves into Jet Capital, set up ostensibly to get into aircraft leasing. Raises $1.5 million in a public stock offering.

1972:   Jet Capital buys the floundering airline that became Texas International, restructures debt, and offers "peanuts" fares—long before deregulation. Brings the company back to profitability in less than two years.

1978:   Uses modest cash cushion to make two runs at National Airlines; is outbid by Pan Am but pockets $40 million on sale of his National stock.

Strength of Lorenzo

1979:   Invites TWA Chairman L. Edwin Smart to breakfast and offers to buy TWA. Smart, infuriated, stalks out without eating.

1980:   Creates nonunion New York Air to take a bite out of Eastern's lucrative East Coast shuttle service. Texas Air, newly formed holding company for Texas International, retains 64 percent of New York Air. Remaining stock offered to the public.

EXHIBIT C31.1   FRANK LORENZO'S EMPIRE

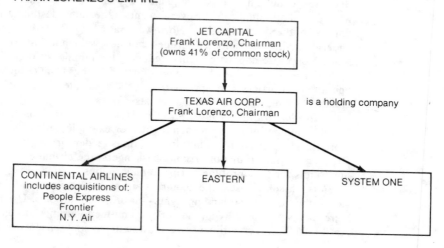

1982: Wins Continental Airlines after years of legal fights and stock maneuvers, merging it with Texas International. Losses mount rapidly at Continental despite layoffs and employee concessions.

1983: Continental files for Chapter 11, spuring pilots, mechanists, and flight attendants to walk off the job. Lorenzo replaces strikers, cuts work force by two-thirds. Continental reemerges as low-fare carrier.

1985: With Continental rejuvenated, Lorenzo proposes full payment to creditors—except disputed labor claims. Makes new offer for beleaguered TWA but loses out to Carl Icahn, who is backed by unions that are adamantly opposed to Lorenzo. Lorenzo incurs a similar rebuff at Frontier. Frontier sells instead to People Express, which is headed by disenchanted Lorenzo protégé Donald Burr.

1986: Continental emerges from Chapter 11, agrees to repay creditors 100 cents on the dollar, plus interest. Acquires People Express and merges it and its Frontier Airlines unit into Continental. Acquires Eastern Airlines and makes Texas Air the largest air carrier in the free world.

Continental Airlines

Texas Air acquired the troubled Continental Airline in 1981, in a bitter takeover battle and against the wishes of Continental's management and employees. While industry experts questioned why Lorenzo wanted the airline which had lost $21 million in 1980, he argued that a merger with Continental was needed to obtain hubs at Denver, Houston, and Los Angeles. Shortly after Texas Air acquired Continental, Lorenzo started to reduce labor costs and proposed a 30% cut in payroll. The unions subsequently went on strike. Claiming burdensome labor contracts, Continental filed for Chapter 11 bankruptcy on September 24, 1983.

From September 24, 1983, to September 2, 1986, Continental operated as a debtor-in-possession under Chapter 11 of the Federal Bankruptcy Code. Continental emerged from bankruptcy on September 2, 1986, less than three years after it had filed for bankruptcy. At this time, Continental arranged for payment of 100 cents on the dollar to holders of all the $1 billion of debts the company took with it into bankruptcy, plus interest, with no dilution of shareholder equity. In 1986, the airline generated a net profit of $17.9 million on revenues of $2.0 billion as compared to a net profit of $60.9 million on revenues of $1.7 billion in 1985. However, without $84 million in reorganization-related costs, which were charged against 1986, Continental would have reported a $103 million pretax profit. One of the key factors that contributed to Continental's 1986 profitability in the face of the company's rapid growth and the dramatic fare competition was its low unit operating cost, which averaged only 5.95 cents per available seat mile.

Merging People Express, Frontier, and New York Air into Continental in 1986 resulted in Continental growing from the nation's seventh-largest carrier, with 133 aircraft serving 81 cities, to the third-largest, with 314 aircraft serving 141 cities.

New York Air

Frank Lorenzo created nonunion New York Air in 1980 as a shuttle service between New York's LaGuardia Airport and Washington, D.C.'s National Airport. As a subsidiary of Texas Air, New York Air was originally started to compete with Eastern's East

Coast shuttle service. Because of its low labor costs and high load factor, New York Air became very profitable. It subsequently expanded its hub complexes around the high-density Northeastern corridor cities of New York, Boston, and Washington, D.C.

In 1986, as a part of its approval to acquire Eastern, the U.S. Department of Transportation required Texas Air to sell many of New York Air's valuable slots at LaGuardia and National airports to Pan Am. Texas Air integrated New York Air into Continental in 1987.

weakness

People Express

Donald C. Burr, chairman and founder of People Express Airlines Inc., spent 14 years working for Lorenzo as president of Texas International before he left the company with a dozen of his collegues to launch his own airline. People Express took off quietly on April 30, 1981, from a deserted terminal at Newark Airport.

The airline began with a simple concept. Burr hoped to build his airline by using low fares for "no-frills" flights to attract car and bus riders who would not ordinarily fly.

Later on the airline shifted its "no-frills" low-fare strategy to a full-service operation and expanded its route service by purchasing of the Frontier Airlines on November 1985. Because of its strong hub in Denver, Frank Lorenzo had made several attempts to buy the troubled Frontier before it was purchased by People Express. Not being able to reverse Frontier's losses, People Express fell into financial despair, and was acquired by Texas Air on December 1986.

Eastern Air Lines

The acquisition of Eastern Air Lines, on November 25, 1986, was perhaps the most important of Texas Air's recent moves. This acquisition made Texas Air the largest air carrier holding company in the free world. Eastern, which was the fourth-largest U.S. air carrier measured in terms of available seat miles, brought to Texas Air a broad network of operational facilities, advanced information-processing capabilities, and substantial human resources. Eastern provided Texas Air with a work force of 39,000, a fleet of more than 280 modern aircraft, prime air travel markets, and long-standing public identity.

In spite of the above attributes, Eastern has not been able to capitalize on these strengths and translate them into profits in recent years. Eastern had incurred net losses of $66 million in 1981, $75 million in 1982, $184 million in 1983, $38 million in 1984, net income of $6.3 million in 1985, and a net loss of $131 million in 1986.

SystemOne Corporation

Computerization has overtaken the airline industry in unparalleled fashion, to the point that a sophisticated telecommunications network is necessary to compete in the marketplace. In June 1986, Texas Air Corporation established SystemOne Corporation as a wholly owned, stand-alone subsidiary, charged with providing information management, data processing, and telecommunications services to Texas Air subsidiary airlines, as well as other airlines, corporations, and travel agents throughout the world.

By combining the entities that operated the automated systems and services at Eastern and Continental, as well as acquiring additional expertise, Texas Air established a subsidiary with composite 1986 revenues of $300 million. In terms of passenger processing, SystemOne is the largest vendor of computer reservations and passenger-handling systems. More importantly, SystemOne solidifies Texas Air's position in the travel automation marketplace and helps to ensure the marketing and distribution of its airline subsidiaries' products.

SystemOne provides a comprehensive computer reservation system (CRS) to over 5,500 travel agents. Computer reservation systems utilize display screens to provide travel agents with information ranging from flights, fares, hotels, and car rental to currency exchange rates and ski conditions in a matter of seconds.

In terms of reservations, SystemOne is the third-largest such system in the country and is available in over 20 percent of the domestic travel agent locations. Competition is fierce among CRS vendors for agency placement, and SystemOne plans to aggressively increase its market share. SystemOne is headquartered in Houston and employs 2,400 highly trained people.

Operations

In 1986, Texas Air more than tripled the size of its airline operations through the acquisitions of Eastern, People Express, and its subsidiary Frontier Airlines. As of March 1, 1987, the aggregate fleet size of Texas Air's subsidiaries (not including regional carriers) had increased to 603 aircraft, as compared to 160 aircraft at the end of 1985. Exhibits C31.2 through C31.5 show a comparison of flight composition, daily departures from hub cities, load factors, and cost per available seat mile for the two airlines.

EXHIBIT C31.2   CONTINENTAL AND EASTERN COSTS PER AVAILABLE SEAT MILE

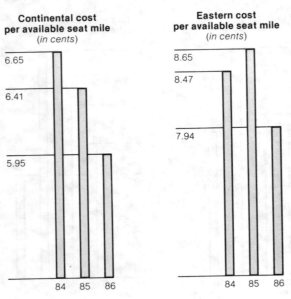

Continental cost per available seat mile *(in cents)*

6.65
6.41
5.95

84   85   86

Eastern cost per available seat mile *(in cents)*

8.65
8.47
7.94

84   85   86

EXHIBIT C31.3   CONTINENTAL AND EASTERN'S DAILY DEPARTURES

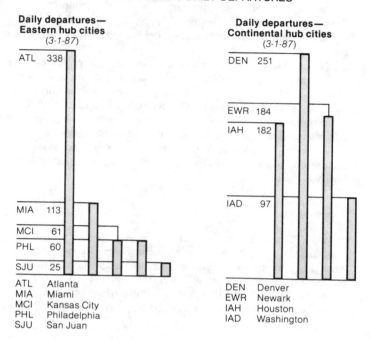

Daily departures—
Eastern hub cities
(3-1-87)

ATL   338

MIA   113
MCI   61
PHL   60
SJU   25

ATL   Atlanta
MIA   Miami
MCI   Kansas City
PHL   Philadelphia
SJU   San Juan

Daily departures—
Continental hub cities
(3-1-87)

DEN   251
EWR   184
IAH   182

IAD   97

DEN   Denver
EWR   Newark
IAH   Houston
IAD   Washington

EXHIBIT C31.4   CONTINENTAL AND EASTERN'S LOAD FACTORS

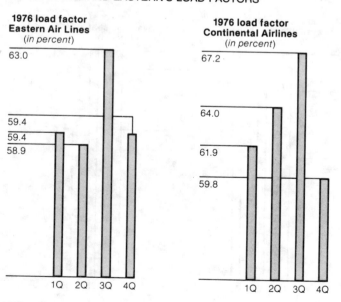

1976 load factor
Eastern Air Lines
(in percent)

63.0
59.4
59.4
58.9

1Q   2Q   3Q   4Q

1976 load factor
Continental Airlines
(in percent)

67.2
64.0
61.9
59.8

1Q   2Q   3Q   4Q

786

EXHIBIT C31.5   CONTINENTAL AND EASTERN'S FLEET COMPOSITION

Eastern fleet composition
(3-1-87)

DC10	2
L1011	24
B757	25
A300	34
DC9	79
B727	122

Total 286

Continental fleet composition
(3-1-87)

A300	6
B747	8
DC10	16
MD80	45
DC9	47
B737	86
B727	106

Total 314

Employees

appears threats

Continental and Eastern have approximately 25,500 and 40,200 employees, respectively. While more than 81 percent of Continental employees are nonunion, the majority of the Eastern employees are represented by three major unions—International Association of Mechanists (IAM), the Airline Pilots Association (ALPA), and the Transport Workers Union (TWU). Continental, with a labor cost of 23 percent of total operating expense, enjoys one of the lowest labor costs in the industry. On the contrary, Eastern's labor cost of 39.4 percent is among the highest.   *strength*

weakness

Marketing

present performance

present strategy to?

Eastern is currently building its marketing efforts to attract and retain customers. Frequent flier programs have been implemented as part of strategy to serve this purpose. These programs award "credits" based on miles traveled. These "credits" can be accumulated and later used for free travel. In the summer of 1986, Eastern's frequent flier program was integrated with Continental's to allow travelers to earn credits on, and apply them to, either airline.   *present strategy to?*

Continental and Eastern Airlines have also introduced MaxSaver, which is a highly restricted discount fare designed to attract incremental business to fill seats that otherwise would remain empty. MaxSavers are sometimes priced up to 80 percent below full coach fares. This program has helped both airlines achieve higher load factors; however, it is not yet clear if this has resulted in higher profits.

opportunity to spread O/H costs

Significant numbers of airline tickets are sold by travel agents. Travel agents generally receive commissions based by the prices of tickets sold. A potential problem for

— Threat

Continental and Eastern is that travel agents may favor writing tickets on other, higher-priced airlines.

Finance

The common stock of Texas Air is listed for trading on the American Stock Exchange, which is its principal market, and also on the Pacific Stock Exchange. The high and low prices for the common stock during each quarter commencing after December 31, 1984, are as follows:

	High	Low
1985		
1st Quarter	11⅝	8⅞
2nd Quarter	17⅜	9¾
3	20	15¼
4	19¾	14⅛
1986		
1	31	14¼
2	40⅞	29⅜
3	35½	25⅛
4	40	32½
1987		
1	51½	33¾

On September 25, 1987, the closing price of the common stock on American Stock Exchange was $26 per share. Texas Air has not paid dividends on common stock since the second quarter of 1983.

As of December 31, 1986, Texas Air and its consolidated subsidiaries had total cash and marketable securities of $1,211,053,000. Texas Air, has sought to build these high levels of liquidity in order to provide for contingencies. Texas Air and its consolidated subsidiaries also had $4,893,218,000 of long-term indebtedness. Exhibits C31.6 and C31.7 contain Texas Air's consolidated balance sheet and income statement.

Challenges Ahead

While there is some evidence of deteriorating service across the industry since deregulation (delayed flights, lost baggage, overbooked flights, cancelations, lack of legroom), almost all surveys have ranked Continental's service as by far the worst in the industry, with Eastern being ranked second worst. One Chicago travel agent was quoted as saying, "we get complaints about everybody these days, but my agents tell me we can't give away space on Continental to business clients. About half our vacation travelers won't fly it again at any price" (*Wall Street Journal*, July 24, 1987, p. 1).

Quality service is an issue that Mr. Lorenzo must be concerned with. A reputation for shoddy service can scare away all but the most marginal passengers. Although the company has roughly $1.5 billion in cash, which gives it some breathing space, it has to preserve every part of its 20 percent U.S. market share in order to service its $4.5 billion debt.

EXHIBIT C31.6
Texas Air Corporation and Subsidiaries
Consolidated Statement of Operations
(Dollars in Thousands, Except per Share Data)

	For the years ended December 31,		
	1986	1985	1984
Operating revenues:			
Passenger	$4,026,464	$1,765,570	$1,231,985
Cargo, mail, and other	380,433	178,620	139,717
	4,406,897	1,944,190	1,371,702
Operating expenses:			
Wages, salaries, and related costs	1,352,798	408,359	272,023
Aircraft fuel	694,294	476,115	364,419
Depreciation and amortization	277,583	88,087	81,776
Other	1,844,844	806,926	546,284
	4,169,519	1,779,487	1,264,502
Operating income	237,378	164,703	107,200
Other income (expense):			
Interest and debt expense	(306,996)	(106,515)	(91,393)
Interest income	77,373	34,200	19,370
Gain on disposition of property, equipment, and other assets, net	110,984	1,325	9,592
Gain on sale of investments	50,340	36,451	546
Gain (loss) on subsidiaries' equity transactions	20,817	—	(92)
Minority interest in (income) losses of subsidiaries, net	(6,574)	1,134	3,134
Chapter 11–related expenses	(64,410)	(36,500)	(2,500)
Equity in losses of Eastern Air Lines, Inc. and People Express, Inc.	(29,316)	—	—
Other, net	(10,263)	(2,421)	4,480
	(158,045)	(72,326)	(56,863)
Income before provision for income taxes and extraordinary credit	79,333	92,377	50,337
Income tax provision	37,096	43,762	22,545
Income before extraordinary credit	42,237	48,615	27,792
Extraordinary credit: Utilization of net operating loss carryforwards	30,466	42,366	22,545
Net income	$ 72,703	$ 90,981	$ 50,337
Primary earnings per share:			
Income before extraordinary credit	$ .65	$ 2.49	$ 1.24
Extraordinary credit	1.10	2.54	1.59
Net income	$ 1.75	$ 5.03	$ 2.83
Fully diluted earnings per share:			
Income before extraordinary credit	$ .68	$ 1.81	$ 1.20
Extraordinary credit	.99	1.78	1.01
Net income	$ 1.67	$ 3.59	$ 2.21

Source: 1986 Annual Report.

EXHIBIT C31.7
Texas Air Corporation and Subsidiaries
Consolidated Balance Sheet
(Dollars in Thousands)

	December 31,	
	1986	**1985**
Assets		
Current assets:		
Cash	$ 78,923	$ 6,774
Marketable securities, at lower of cost or market	1,132,130	650,105
Accounts receivable, less allowance for doubtful receivables ($16,662 and $11,272)	715,685	225,765
Inventories of spare parts and supplies, less allowance for obsolescence ($21,181 and $17,771)	284,729	52,516
Prepayments and other	99,098	42,341
Total current assets	2,310,565	977,501
Property and equipment, at cost:		
Flight equipment	3,630,066	877,095
Aircraft purchase deposits	50,308	31,092
Other	1,120,081	185,583
	4,800,455	1,093,770
Less: Accumulated depreciation	(408,332)	(342,391)
	4,392,123	751,379
Property and equipment under capital leases:		
Flight equipment	988,203	187,352
Other	65,499	6,531
	1,053,702	193,883
Less: Accumulated amortization	(62,035)	(57,858)
	991,667	136,025
Total property and equipment	5,383,790	887,404
Other assets	500,256	71,433
	$8,194,611	$1,936,338

weakness

The work force is highly factionalized, and this presents a big obstacle for Lorenzo. The mergers have thrown together young, enthusiastic employees with jaded veterans. Mr. Lorenzo faces the challenges of integrating and unifying these diverse cultures.

long range objective

The most challenging issue facing Lorenzo, which some say could determine the survival of the company, is the negotiation of contracts with his largest union at Eastern—the International Association of Machinists and Aerospace Workers. If Lorenzo can settle the machinists' contract, which expires December 31, 1987, he may be able to secure the labor peace and lower costs he needs to operate Eastern smoothly and profitably. If he fails, Eastern workers may strike, shutting down the airline and cutting off its cash flow. Without that cash, Texas Air may not be able to pay the interest on its enormous debts, causing the entire enterprise to unravel.

opportunity

threat

	December 31,	
	1986	1985

Liabilities and Stockholders' Equity

Current liabilities:		
Current maturities of long-term debt	$ 333,700	$ 34,204
Current obligations under capital leases	97,592	7,862
Accounts payable	641,264	137,300
Air traffic liability	567,102	91,212
Accrued payroll and pension costs	396,142	63,816
Accrued interest	90,330	18,911
Accrued taxes	50,823	12,056
Other accrued liabilities	98,941	39,221
Total current liabilities	2,275,894	404,582
Estimated liabilities subject to Continental's Chapter 11 reorganization proceedings	—	648,245
Long-term debt, net	3,337,901	548,435
Obligations under capital leases, net	1,174,455	161,030
Deferred credits	210,834	16,221
Minority stockholders' equity in subsidiary companies (aggregate liquidation value—$221,793 and $20,475)	10,796	20,656
Commitments and contingencies		
Redeemable preferred stock (aggregate liquidation value—$471,976 and $26,087)	380,862	22,012
Nonredeemable preferred stock and common stockholders' equity:		
Nonredeemable preferred stock (liquidation value—$150,000)	600	—
Class A common stock—$.10 par value; 4,080,000 shares authorized; 2,040,000 shares outstanding	204	204
Common stock—$.01 par value; 75,000,000 shares authorized; 35,659,856 and 19,913,909 shares issued	357	199
Additional paid-in capital, net of notes receivable of $825 and $296 and deferred compensation of $12,869 at December 31, 1986	860,198	245,326
Retained deficit	(55,399)	(118,717)
Common treasury stock, 161,105 and 958,139 shares, at cost	(2,091)	(11,855)
Total nonredeemable preferred stock and common stockholders' equity	803,869	115,157
	$8,194,611	$1,936,338

Source: 1986 Annual Report.

TOYS 'R' US (A)

Prepared by Caron St. John, Clemson University.

In 1948, Charles Lazarus began selling baby furniture in the back of his father's Washington, D.C., bicycle repair shop, located below the apartment where Lazarus's family lived. Within a few months, and in response to customer requests, he added a few toys to his line of baby furniture. Before long he realized parents who bought toys returned for more toys—but parents who bought furniture rarely came back. "When I realized that toys broke," he said, "I knew it was a good business."[1] Soon his entire business was focused on toys.

His first store was successful, and he opened his second store in Washington as a self-serve, cash-and-carry business. In 1958, he opened his third store—a 25,000-square-foot "baby supermarket" with discount prices and a large selection of products. Within a few years, a fourth supermarket-style store was introduced. By 1966, the four stores in the Washington, D.C., area were achieving $12 million in annual sales.

In order to have the capital necessary for continued growth, Lazarus sold his four stores in 1966 to Interstate Stores, a retail discount chain, for $7 million. Lazarus stayed on with Interstate and maintained operating control over the toy division. Between 1966 and 1974, the Toys 'R' Us division of Interstate Stores grew from 4 to 47 stores through internal growth and a merger with Children's Bargain Town.

In 1974, the parent company, Interstate Stores, filed for bankruptcy. When Interstate completed reorganization and emerged from bankruptcy in 1978, the new company name was Toys 'R' Us (TRU) and Charles Lazarus was chief executive officer. Since then, all but four of the Interstate Stores have been divested and all creditors have been paid.

Between January 1979 and January 1984, Toys 'R' Us grew from 63 stores with sales of just under $350 million to 169 stores with sales of over $1.3 billion, for a compound annual growth rate of 30%. During the same years, profits increased from $17 million to $92 million for a compound annual growth rate of 40%. TRU stock, which traded for $2 per share in 1978, split 3 for 2 for 4 years in a row and consistently trades above $40 per share. A $2 TRU stock investment made in 1978 was worth $200 in the spring of 1984.

Toys 'R' Us is currently the largest toy retailer in the world, with an estimated 12.5% share of the U.S. market.[2] With 169 retail toy supermarkets, Toys 'R' Us is now represented in all but six of the top-20 retail toy areas in the United States.

Charles Lazarus has consistently been the motivating force behind the growth of Toys 'R' Us. Lazarus, a man without a college education, is now worth over $75 million. His vision is for Toys 'R' Us to become the McDonald's of toy retailing: "We don't have golden arches, but we're getting there."[3] He credits his success in toy retailing to his love of the business. "What we do is the essence of America—making a business grow," he says. "If you're going to be a success in life you have to want it. I wanted it. I was poor. I wanted to be rich. . . . My ego now is in the growth of this company."[4]

TOY INDUSTRY

Retail toy sales in the United States were $10.5 billion in 1983. Primarily because of the national interest in electronic games, sales growth in the previous years had exceeded 18% per year. Excluding the electronic games category, industry sales growth has averaged 11% since 1980. Exhibit C32.1 shows the percent of total dollar sales by product category for 1980 through 1982.

In 1980, electronic games accounted for 18.4% of total U.S. toy market sales. By 1982, electronic games represented 30.9%, or almost one-third, of total toy sales. Industry analysts estimate that sales of traditional toys, such as Slinky, Silly Putty, and Etch-A-Sketch, account for 50% of nonelectronic games sales each year.[5] Highly publicized toys, like Cabbage Patch dolls and ET products, account for the remaining 50% of sales.

Toy retailing is a very seasonal business. Well over 50% of toy sales are reported in the fourth quarter—with much of those sales generated in the 6 weeks before Christmas. To balance the unevenness of toy sales, most toy stores sell other seasonal items like swimming pool supplies and lawn furniture.

EXHIBIT C32.1 PERCENTAGE OF U.S. RETAIL TOY DOLLAR SALES BY PRODUCT

Product	1980	1981	1982
Preschool	11.2	9.6	8.8
Arts/crafts/models/kits	6.6	7.1	5.1
Activity	10.9	10.8	8.5
Dolls	11.3	11.4	10.4
Games/puzzles	12.2	12.3	9.5
Infant toys	2.3	1.7	1.9
Nonriding toys	12.5	14.6	12.0
Riding trans.	7.1	6.5	7.0
Electronic games	18.4	18.5	30.9
All other	7.4	7.4	5.9

Source: "National Toy Chains Increase Market Share; Discounters Decline," *Playthings,* October 1983.

EXHIBIT C32.2 PERCENTAGE OF U.S. RETAIL TOY DOLLAR SALES BY STATE

State	1982*
California	11.72
Texas	7.75
New York	6.66
Illinois	5.01
Florida	4.99
Ohio	4.86
Pennsylvania	4.66
Michigan	4.19
Remaining 42 states	50.16

* Column will not sum to 100%, due to rounding.
Source: "U.S. Retail Toy Sales Up Slightly," *Playthings,* December 1983.

Retail toy sales are tied to population. In 1982, the state with the largest share of retail sales was California (see Exhibit C32.2). The states with the smallest shares of retail sales were Vermont (.18% of sales), Wyoming (.21%), and Alaska (.23%). The metropolitan areas with the largest retail toy sales were New York, Los Angeles, Chicago, Detroit, and Houston.

Discount stores are the primary outlet for toy sales in the United States (see Exhibit C32.3). Although all categories of retailers compete with each other, they use different approaches to appeal to customers. The larger department stores compete on the basis of convenience—the customer can purchase toys while shopping for other items. The national toy chains offer a much larger selection of products at lower prices with a minimal level of in-store service. The discount stores frequently offer similar low prices and minimal service, but their selection is not as extensive as that of the toy chains. The small, independent toy stores provide personalized service and specialty items but ask higher prices.

With 169 stores, Toys 'R' Us is the largest national toy chain. Child World, a division of Cole National, follows TRU with 89 stores. Lionel Corporation, a company reorganizing under Chapter 11 in 1984, operates 59 stores.

EXHIBIT C32.3 PERCENTAGE DISTRIBUTION OF UNIT SALES BY TYPE OF OUTLET

Type of outlet	1980*	1981*	1982*
Discount	37	36	35
Sears-Penney's-Wards	5	5	6
Other department stores	6	6	6
Variety	11	10	9
National toy chains	10	11	12
All other toy stores	4	3	3
Catalog showrooms	3	3	3
Other	25	25	26

* Columns will not sum to 100% due to rounding.
Source: "National Toy Chains Increase Market Share; Discounters Decline," *Playthings,* October 1983.

Industry Trends

Some demographic and industry trends that are expected to continue to influence in a positive way the demand for toys in the next several years are:

1 *Increased numbers of children.* Since the late seventies, members of the baby boom generation, who delayed having children while in their twenties, have started having babies. Consequently, the 2 to 5 age group has been growing steadily for several years.

2 *More money to spend on toys.* These older parents are having children after their households are formed and careers are established, so family incomes are higher. In many families, both parents are employed full-time. The higher family incomes mean there is more money for discretionary items like toys.

3 *Broader market appeal of toy stores.* As noted earlier, the toy market has joined with the video games and home electronics markets to form a broader category of "toys." The objective is to appeal to the teen and young adult market segment and draw this new group of buyers into the toy stores.

4 *Increased visibility of toys because of licensing.* Licensing, or basing a product on a motion picture, television program, or comic strip character, has accelerated in importance in the eighties and is expected to continue. Toys based on popular characters appeal to an already established market.

TOYS 'R' US

The aim of Toys 'R' Us is to be the customer's only place of purchase for toys and related products.[6] Management is proud that TRU attracts the least-affluent purchasers because of the everyday discount prices and also attracts the most-affluent purchasers because of the extensive product selection. In order to provide total service to all customer segments, the company maintains tight operating procedures and a strong customer orientation.

Retailing Operations

According to Charles Lazarus, "Nothing is done in the stores."[7] What he means is that all buying and pricing decisions are made at corporate headquarters in Rochelle Park, New Jersey. The corporate buying and pricing decisions are made using an elaborate computerized inventory control system where sales by item and sales by store are monitored daily. Those actual sales numbers are compared to forecasts, and when substantial differences exist, the slow items are marked down to get them out of the stores and the fast-selling items are reordered in larger quantities.

By closely following the buying habits of the consumer, TRU is able to pick up on trends before the crucial Christmas buying season and to maintain more flexibility than competitors. In 1980, when sales of hand-held video games fell off sharply before Christmas, Toys 'R' Us had been forewarned by its extensive monitoring system and had moved much of its stock of video games, at reduced prices, before the Christmas season. TRU was fully stocked with the big Christmas items that year—the Rubik's Cube and Strawberry Shortcake—unlike virtually all its competitors.

The TRU stores are regionally clustered with a regional warehouse within 1 day's driving distance of every store (see Exhibit C32.4). The company also owns a fleet of

Rochelle Park, N.J.
WASH. D.C. WHSE
- Marlo Hts., MD
- Rockville, MD
- Baileys Crossroads, VA
- Adelphi, MD
- Fairfax, VA
- Lanham, MD
- Catonsville, MD
- Towson, MD
- Richmond (South), VA
- Glen Burnie, MD
- Tyson's Corner, VA
- Hampton, VA
- Norfolk, VA
- Richmond (North), VA
- Golden Ring, MD
- Salisbury, Md

L.A. WHSE
- Van Nuys, CA
- Torrance, CA
- Covina, CA
- Anaheim, CA
- Ontario, CA
- La Mesa, CA
- Rosemead, CA
- San Diego, CA
- Woodland Hills, CA
- Cerritos, CA
- San Bernadino, CA
- Culver City, CA
- Burbank, CA
- Oceanside, CA
- Bakersfield, CA
- Santa Ana, CA
- Chula Vista, CA
- La Mirada, CA
- Las Vegas, NV

S.F. WHSE
- Sunnydale, CA
- Pleasant Hill, CA
- Colma, CA
- Hayward, CA
- San Jose, CA
- Arden Way, CA
- Citrus Heights, CA
- Redwod City, CA
- Newark, CA
- Fresno, CA
- Sacramento, CA
- E. San Jose, CA
- Santa Rosa, CA

CHICAGO WHSE
- Burbank, IL
- Melrose, IL
- Niles, IL
- Calumet City, IL
- Highland Park, IL
- Schaumburg, IL
- Downers Grove, IL
- Chicago (Southeast), IL
- Milwaukee (South), WI
- Milwaukee (North), WI
- Moline, IL
- Merrilville, IN
- N. Riverside, IL
- Aurora, IL
- Joilet, IL
- Riverview, IL
- Bloomingdale, IL
- Matteson, IL
- W. Dundee, IL
- Orland Park, IL
- Rockford, IL

N.Y./N.J. WHSE
- Levittown, NY
- Commack, NY
- Totowa, NJ
- E. Brunswick, NJ
- Paramus, NJ
- Watchung, NJ
- Brooklyn, NY
- Massapequa, NY
- Valley Stream, NY
- Carle Place, NY
- Staten Island, NY
- Eatontown, NY
- Colonie, NY
- Jersey City, NJ
- Huntington Station, NY
- Lake Grove, NY
- Woodbridge, NJ
- Livingston, NJ
- Yonkers, NY
- Toms River, NJ
- Douglaston, NY
- Bay Parkway, NY
- Bayshore, NY
- Nanuet, NY
- Milford, CT

HOUSTON WHSE
- Houston (Gulf), TX
- Houston (North), TX
- Houston (Katy), TX
- San Antonio (NW), TX
- Beaumont, TX
- San Antonio (NE), TX
- Houston (SW), TX
- Willowbrook, TX
- Austin, TX

DETROIT WHSE
- Southgate, MI
- Madison Heights, MI
- Southfield, MI
- Livonia, MI
- Roseville, MI
- Flint, MI
- Saginaw, MI
- Grand Rapids, MI
- Lansing, MI
- Toledo, OH
- Dearborn, MI
- Sterling Heights, MI

BOSTON WHSE
- Warwick, RI
- Peabody, MA
- Auburn, MA
- Framingham, MA
- Woburn, MA
- Dedham, Ma
- Springfield, MA
- Waterbury, CT
- Corbins Corner, CT
- Manchester, NH
- Swansea, MA
- Newington, NH
- Portland, ME

DALLAS WHSE
- Fort Worth, TX
- Dallas, TX
- Oklahoma City, OK
- Mesquite, TX
- Arlington, TX
- Tulsa, OK
- Red Bird, TX
- Hurst, TX
- Shreveport, LA

SEATTLE WHSE
- Clackamas, OR
- Jantzen Beach, OR
- Seattle, WA
- Tukwila, WA
- Tigard, OR
- Spokane, WA
- Tacoma, WA

PHILA. WHSE
- Montgomeryville, PA
- King of Prussia, PA
- Lawrence Township, NJ
- Port Richmond, PA
- Deptford, NJ
- Cherry Hill, NJ
- Phila. (NE), PA
- Phila. (So.), PA
- Granite Run, PA
- Oxford Valley, PA
- York, PA

MIAMI WHSE
- Palm Beach, FL
- Altamonte Springs, FL
- Hollywood, FL
- Hialeah, FL
- Plantation, FL
- Tampa, FL
- Cutler Ridge, FL
- Miami, FL

ATLANTA WHSE
- Nashville, TN
- Montgomery, AL
- Birmingham, AL
- Cumberland, GA
- Northlake. GA
- Southlake, GA

KUWAIT CITY, KUWAIT

CINCINNATI WHSE*

TORONTO, CANADA whse*

*Opening in 1984.

Source: "Welcome to Toys 'R' Us," booklet prepared by Toys 'R' Us for new employees.

trucks to support its warehousing operations. The 15 regional warehouses allow TRU to keep the stores well stocked and make it possible for TRU to order large quantities of merchandise early in the year, when manufacturers are eager to ship. Since most manufacturers will defer payments for 12 months on shipments made in the months immediately following Christmas, TRU is able to defer payment on about two-thirds of its inventory each year. TRU's competitors typically buy closer to Christmas, when buying terms are tighter.

All 169 TRU stores have the same layout with the same items arranged on exactly the same shelves—all according to blueprints sent from the corporate office. A TRU store is typically 43,000 square feet and is characterized by wide aisles and warehouse-style shelving stocked to the ceiling with over 18,000 different items. A substantial percent of the floor space is devoted to computers and computer-related products and to nontoy items like diapers, furniture, and clothing. However, toys, games, books, puzzles, and sports equipment are the major focus of the stores.

Each store is jointly managed by a merchandise manager and an operations manager. The merchandise manager has full responsibility for the merchandising effort in the store: content, stock level, and display. The operations manager is responsible for the building, personnel, cash control, customer service, and everything else that is not directly related to merchandise. Area supervisors oversee the total operations of three or four stores in a given area, and area general managers are responsible for the performance and profitability of all the TRU stores in a given market.

Marketing

As indicated earlier, each Toys 'R' Us store carries over 18,000 items. Although toys represent, by far, the majority of the items stocked, other products include baby furniture, diapers, and children's clothing. The feeling at TRU is that the parent will go to the store to buy a necessity or nonseasonal item and will leave with at least one toy purchase. The average TRU customer spends $40 per visit.[8]

In recent years, TRU expanded its product line to include home computers and software in addition to the traditional toys. The move has served to broaden the company's customer base to include teenagers and adults, and to create add-on business at each retail unit. According to company statistics, products for these "older children" accounted for 18% of sales in 1983 compared with 11% in 1982.[9] TRU strongly feels this is not a change in its basic business—computers and software are toys for adults.

This strategy of carrying a wide selection of merchandise has benefited TRU in another way. The company has been successful in encouraging year-round buying at its stores (see Exhibit C32.5). In 1980, 7.5% of profits were made in the 9 months of January through September compared with 20% in 1982 (see Exhibit C32.6).[10]

TRU has a strong policy of year-round discount prices. Because TRU buys most of its merchandise during the off-season, when manufacturers are offering discounts, the company is able to pass the discounts on to the customer. TRU has a policy of not having store sales. Individual items will be marked down if they are not selling, but TRU does not have sales that are categorywide or storewide.

Virtually all the Toys 'R' Us stores are located on an important traffic artery leading to a major shopping mall. A location of this type serves two purposes: it allows TRU to attract mall patrons without paying high mall rents, and it gives TRU the space to do business the way it wants to—as a large "supermarket" for toys, complete with grocery-type shopping carts.

EXHIBIT C32.5   NET SALES BY QUARTER
(In $1000s)

End of fiscal year	First quarter	Second quarter	Third quarter	Fourth quarter	Total
1/29/84	$181,717	$213,945	$220,689	$703,291	$1,319,642
1/30/83	138,523	167,781	189,930	545,501	1,041,735
1/31/82	97,349	123,730	132,938	429,268	783,285
2/1/81	70,247	92,660	101,922	332,503	597,332
2/3/80	56,515	75,768	78,304	269,730	480,317
1/28/79	38,000	53,583	57,478	200,038	349,099

Source: Annual reports and 10-K reports for fiscal years 1979 through 1984.

Other customer conveniences include the stock availability and return policy. Product availability is virtually guaranteed. Because of extensive inventory monitoring and attention to consumer buying habits, TRU rarely has a "stock out." Also, TRU boasts of a liberal return policy. The company claims it will accept all returns with no questions asked—even if a toy with no defect is broken by a child after several months of play.

Since TRU is not represented in all regions of the United States (see Exhibit C32.4), it does no national advertising. Before opening stores in a new region, TRU does concentrated television and newspaper advertising. Once the stores are open, TRU may continue very limited television and newspaper advertising.

Domestic and Foreign Expansion

Toys 'R' Us pursues a corporate objective of 18% expansion of retail space per year. In order to meet this objective, it has opened 24 or 25 new stores each year for the last few years.

All the expansions are made as a total entry into a new region. First, TRU builds a warehouse, then it clusters several stores within 1 day's driving distance of the warehouse so that prompt merchandise delivery is ensured. Typically, the warehouse and all the stores are up and running within the same fiscal year and in time for the Christmas

EXHIBIT C32.6   NET EARNINGS (OR LOSS) BY QUARTER
(In $1000s)

End of fiscal year	First quarter	Second quarter	Third quarter	Fourth quarter	Total
1/29/84	$5,357	$7,113	$6,061	$73,786	$92,317
1/30/83	2,516	4,431	4,734	52,481	64,162
1/31/82	618	3,221	3,182	41,899	48,920
2/1/81	(193)	298	44	28,744	28,893
2/3/80	(180)	1,552	725	24,800	26,897
1/28/79	(1,556)	183	564	18,017	17,208

Source: Annual reports and 10-K reports for fiscal years 1979 through 1984.

season. Once TRU enters a local market with more than one store, it immediately becomes the low-price leader in the area—forcing competitors to bring down their prices.

Charles Lazarus keeps a file of 300 locations that have already been selected as potential sites for future U.S. stores.[11] The regions are selected on the basis of demographic patterns and toy buying statistics. The individual store locations are decided after an analysis is completed of the area shopping malls, traffic patterns, and local retail toy competition. The fiscal 1984 and 1985 plans call for regional expansion into the midwest, upstate New York, and Pennsylvania.

In addition to domestic expansion, TRU is embarking on a plan of growth into the large non-U.S. toy market. The first Canadian and European stores are scheduled to open in late 1984. Arrangements are under way for a store in Singapore, and plans have been made with Alghanim Industries, a major Kuwait-based corporation, to provide technical and buying assistance for a series of toy stores that Alghanim has planned for the Middle East.

TRU is ranked as one of the top-20 U.S. retailers in annual capital expenditures (see Exhibit C32.7). It finances expansions exclusively with internally generated funds. It is able to build the capital necessary for expansion by not paying dividends (see Exhibit C32.8 and C32.9).

KIDS 'R' US, TOO

TRUs only venture outside of toy retailing has been into children's clothing—a $6 billion industry in the United States alone. According to a TRU press release, the corporate objective in creating Kids 'R' Us was to ''provide one stop shopping with an overwhelming selection of first quality, designer and brand name children's clothing in the seasons' latest styles at everyday prices. . . . We have taken the knowledge and systems we have refined for our toy stores over the past 30 years and applied some of these principals to our Kids 'R' Us stores.''[12]

In 1983, TRU opened two Kids 'R' Us stores in the New York area. Corporate plans call for a total of eight to ten Kids 'R' Us stores by the end of 1984. Each store offers a full assortment of first-quality, discount-priced clothing and accessories for children up

EXHIBIT C32.7   COMPANY RANKINGS BY CAPITAL EXPENDITURES, 1983
(In $1000s)

1.	Safeway	$500,000	11.	Lucky	140,000
2.	Dayton Hudson	475,000	12.	Carter Hawley Hale	138,000
3.	Kroger	410,000	13.	Stop & Shop	125,000
4.	Sears, Roebuck	400,000	14.	Supermarkets General	110,000
5.	J.C. Penney	395,000	15.	Allied Stores	100,000
6.	Federated	325,000	16.	Albertsons	95,000
7.	K Mart	320,000	17.	Toys 'R' Us	90,000
8.	Winn-Dixie	176,600	18.	Wal-Mart	90,000
9.	Jewel Cos.	166,000	19.	Melville	85,000
10.	May	140,000	20.	Associated Dry Goods	85,000

Source: Prepared by case writer.

EXHIBIT C32.8 STATEMENTS OF CONSOLIDATED EARNINGS
(In $1000s)

	End of fiscal year					
	Jan. 29, 1984	Jan. 30, 1983	Jan. 31, 1982	Feb. 1, 1981	Feb. 3, 1980	Jan. 28, 1979
Net sales	$1,319,642	$1,041,735	$783,285	$597,332	$480,317	$348,099
Costs and expenses:						
Costs of sales	881,258	705,260	522,808	409,886	319,964	234,389
Selling, advertising, general & admin.	254,448	206,378	166,930	131,430	101,548	71,867
Depreciation and amortization	13,428	11,060	8,900	7,124	5,457	4,658
Interest expense	2,404	4,285	4,086	2,933	4,502	6,398
Interest income	(10,138)	(9,570)	(11,649)	(4,997)	(4,065)	(3,413)
Gain on sale of property			(1,910)	(1,507)	(355)	(202)
	1,141,400	917,413	689,165	544,869	427,051	313,687
Earnings before tax	178,242	124,322	94,120	52,463	53,266	35,402
Taxes on income	85,925	60,160	45,200	23,570	26,490	18,255
Net earnings	$ 92,317	$ 64,162	$ 48,920	$ 28,893	$ 26,776	$ 17,147

Source: Annual reports and 10-K reports for fiscal years 1979 through 1984.

EXHIBIT C32.9   CONSOLIDATED BALANCE SHEETS
(In $1000s)

	End of fiscal year		
	Jan. 29, 1984	Jan. 30, 1983	Jan. 31, 1982
Assets			
Current assets:			
Cash and short-term investments	$235,838	$134,516	$123,383
Accounts and other receivables	17,909	17,508	14,524
Merchandise inventories	264,192	191,950	140,657
Prepaid expense and other	1,537	705	4,010
Total current assets	519,476	344,679	282,574
Property and equipment less dep.			
Real estate	184,500	120,836	78,625
Other	85,264	65,882	53,892
Leased property under capital leases net dep.	15,998	17,138	18,685
Other assets	14,990	10,473	8,721
	$820,228	$559,008	$442,497
Liabilities and stockholders' equity			
Current liabilities:			
Accounts payable	$184,504	$ 82,278	$ 65,740
Accrued expenses, taxes	79,281	66,011	47,051
Federal tax payable	33,167	36,948	30,853
Current portion:			
Long-term debt	1,260	1,281	788
Oblig. under capital leases	822	756	962
Total current liabilities	299,034	187,274	145,394
Deferred income tax payable	8,708	8,540	5,414
Long-term debt	30,913	17,047	62,177
Obligations under leases	21,850	22,671	23,663
Stockholders' equity	5,405	3,600	2,115
Additional paid-in capital	191,732	147,745	90,902
Retained earnings	274,205	183,750	120,674
Less: Treasury shares at cost	(4,352)	(4,352)	(4,352)
Receivables from exercise of stock options	(7,267)	(7,267)	(3,490)
	459,723	323,476	205,849
	$820,228	$559,008	$442,497

Source: Annual reports and 10-K reports for 1982 through 1984.

to age 12. The surroundings are spacious and well decorated with neon signs, color-coded departments, fitting rooms with platforms for small children, changing areas for infants, play areas for children, and color-coded store maps.

Some observers feel TRU will meet more resilient competition in children's clothing than it did in toys. Department and discount stores make more money on children's clothing than they do on toys and are not willing to give up that market easily. "Department stores fight when it comes to soft goods. That's their bread and butter, it's the guts of their business."[13] Some department store managers feel the purchase of children's clothing sets a family's buying patterns for years—so the implication of losing the children's departments as a way to draw in families goes beyond the immediate loss of profits in that area.[14]

COMPETITOR REACTION

TRU has an excellent reputation with consumers—a reputation that precedes the company into new market areas. Toys 'R' Us also has a reputation—one that is feared and respected—with its competitors. Examples of comments from competitors include:

Toy store owner:
"We were going, 'oh, nooo,' because they were coming in right across the street from us."

(*The Miami Herald*, Nov. 22, 1982)

President of a buying guild about a children's store owner:
"All I can tell you is his face turned white. You come up against a giant like this, with every major line discounted, and where do you go? If you're the average kiddy shop next door, do you take gas or cut your throat?"

(*The Wall Street Journal*, Aug. 25, 1983)

Manufacturer about a buyer:
"One department store buyer, arriving at the [TRU] store, said it caused her instant depression."

(*The Wall Street Journal*, Aug. 25, 1983)

Atlanta toy retailers about TRU's entry into the Atlanta market:
"I admire Toys 'R' Us. They will own the town."
"I hope they take the business from Zayre, Richway, Lionel and not us. We may have to start looking outside Atlanta for locations."
"The new Toys 'R' Us will saturate the market."

(*Toys, Hobbies & Crafts*, May 1983)

Michael Vastola, chairman of the board of Lionel Corporation:
"They have paid a lot of attention to real estate and location, and it has paid off. You have got to say that they have a very disciplined, well-managed operation."

(*The New York Times*, Sept. 4, 1983)

REFERENCES

1 Stratford P. Sherman, "Where the Dollars 'R'," *Fortune*, June 1, 1981 pp. 45–47.
2 TRU annual report and 10-K report for fiscal year ended January 1984.

3 Dan Fesperman, ''Toys 'R' Us Is a Giant in Kids' Business,'' *The Miami Herald*, Nov. 22, 1982.

4 Subrata N. Chakravarty, ''Toys 'r' Fun,'' *Forbes*, Mar. 28, 1983 pp. 58–60.

5 Paul B. Brown, ''Staying Power,'' *Forbes*, Mar. 26, 1984 pp. 186–188.

6 Chakravarty.

7 Sherman.

8 Sherman.

9 TRU annual report for fiscal year ended January 1983.

10 Chakravarty.

11 Chakravarty.

12 ''Kids 'R' Us—The Children's Clothing Store Both Parents and Kids Will Choose,'' press release from Toys 'R' Us, July 1983.

13 Claudia Ricci, ''Children's Wear Retailers Brace for Competition from Toys 'R' Us,'' *The Wall Street Journal*, Aug. 25, 1983.

14 Peter Kerr, ''The New Game at Toys 'R' Us,'' *The New York Times*, July 4, 1983.

TOYS 'R' US (B)

Prepared by Caron H. St. John, Clemson University.

When its 1987 fiscal year ended on February 1, Toys 'R' Us had once again achieved record sales and profits. Between January 1984 and February 1987, sales grew from $1.3 billion to over $2.4 billion and profits increased from $92 million to $152 million. By the end of fiscal 1987, the company's store holdings had increased to 271 toy stores in the U.S., 25 toy stores outside the U.S., and 43 Kids 'R' Us stores. The company's share of the $12 billion U.S. toy market was over 15%.

OPERATIONS

In 1986, Toys 'R' Us instituted some new programs to help control costs. As a result, expenses as a percentage of sales declined from 20.7% to 18.8%. The company planned to implement even more programs to reduce costs in fiscal 1987. For example, UPC scanning was implemented at checkout lanes in some stores in 1986 and was planned for half of all U.S. toy stores by fall of 1987. Toys 'R' Us expects the scanning system to allow lower payroll costs, better control over inventory, and faster customer checkouts. The idea behind all the cost reduction efforts is to position the company to offer lower prices without hurting profit margins. Charles Lazarus wants the price reductions so the company can increase its market share in its existing markets.

The company's emphasis on broad selection and year-round discount prices has continued to help spread sales throughout the year. As shown in Exhibit C33.1, over 50% of sales and roughly 25% of earnings were made during the first three-quarters of fiscal years 1986 and 1987.

Used by permission.

EXHIBIT C33.1
Quarterly Sales and Net Earnings

Quarter	Net sales	Cost of sales	Net earnings
	Year ended February 1, 1987		
lst	$ 368,367	$ 251,539	$ 10,340
2nd	426,031	298,336	13,062
3rd	471,728	328,426	12,755
4th	1,178,777	789,908	116,060
Year	$2,444,903	$1,668,209	$152,217
	Year ended February 2, 1986		
1st	$ 326,058	$ 221,208	$ 12,179
2nd	349,949	241,914	11,843
3rd	376,090	259,209	7,644
4th	924,037	600,611	88,108
Year	$1,976,134	$1,322,942	$119,774

Source: 1987 annual report.

INTERNATIONAL EXPANSION

Between 1984 and 1987, Toys 'R' Us opened 24 toy stores in Canada, Britain, Singapore, and Hong Kong. Following the formula of the U.S. operations, the international stores are freestanding, warehouselike buildings with discount-priced toys stacked from floor to ceiling. Although concessions are made to local tastes, most of the merchandise sold in the overseas stores is the same as in the United States. Even overseas the company successfully uses its time-proven strategy of selling low-priced infant items such as diapers to win over the first-time mother.

It is still unclear whether the international operations are doing well. Although sales performance is as good as domestic stores, the international stores may not be profitable yet. Competitors have chosen to avoid head-on price competition with Toys 'R' Us and, in some cases, are trying to position themselves as less visually intimidating and more sympathetic to the shopper.

FUTURE PLANS

For fiscal year 1988, Toys 'R' Us is planning further expansion. The company is scheduled to open 45 new toy stores in the U.S. including several in the two new market areas of Pittsburgh, Pennsylvania, and Phoenix, Arizona. The Kids 'R' Us clothing stores division is also scheduled for further expansion in fiscal 1988. The company plans to open 30 new stores, bringing its total number of clothing stores to 73.

International expansion is a top priority. In fiscal 1988, Toys 'R' Us plans to open 13 toy stores in Canada, Britain, and West Germany. The company expects to open at least 200 stores overseas in the next 10 years. (See Exhibits C33.2 and C33.3.)

EXHIBIT C33.2
Toys 'R' Us, Inc. and Subsidiaries
Statements of Consolidated Earnings
(In Thousands Except per Share Information)

	Fiscal year ended		
	February 1, 1987	February 2, 1986	February 3, 1985
Net sales	$2,444,903	$1,976,134	$1,701,700
Costs and expenses:			
Cost of sales	1,668,209	1,322,942	1,138,862
Selling, advertising, general and administrative	458,528	408,438	344,237
Depreciation and amortization	33,288	26,074	18,378
Interest expense	7,890	6,999	5,018
Interest income	(7,229)	(8,093)	(10,969)
	2,160,686	1,756,360	1,495,526
Earnings before taxes on income	284,217	219,774	206,174
Taxes on income	132,000	100,000	94,750
Net earnings	$ 152,217	$ 119,774	$ 111,424
Net earnings per share	$1.17	$.93	$.87

Source: 1987 annual report.

REFERENCES

1 Annual report and 10-K report for fiscal year ended Feb. 1, 1987.
2 Mark Maremont, Dori Jones Yang, and Amy Dunkin, "Toys 'R' Us Goes Overseas— And Finds That Toys 'R' Them, Too," *Business Week*, Jan. 26, 1987.
3 Ibid.

Toys 'R' Us, Inc. and Subsidiaries
Consolidated Balance Sheets
(In Thousands)

	February 1, 1987	February 2, 1986
Assets		
Current assets:		
Cash and short-term investments	$ 84,379	$ 136,171
Accounts and other receivables, less allowance		
for doubtful accounts of $1,133 and $1,077	37,502	25,971
Merchandise inventories	528,939	413,493
Prepaid expenses	3,566	3,246
Total current assets	654,386	578,881
Property and equipment:		
Real estate, net of accumulated depreciation of		
$22,400 and $16,304	600,747	422,729
Other, net of accumulated depreciation and		
amortization of $86,207 and $61,833	240,218	191,047
Leased property under capital leases, net of		
accumulated depreciation of $15,797 and		
$14,708	12,440	13,529
Other assets	15,175	19,730
	$1,522,966	$1,225,916
Liabilities and Stockholders' Equity		
Current liabilities:		
Accounts payable	$ 305,705	$ 248,976
Accrued expenses, taxes and other liabilities	118,260	93,665
Federal income taxes	73,059	52,001
Current portion:		
Long-term debt	973	2,113
Obligations under capital leases	968	964
Total current liabilities	498,965	397,719
Deferred income taxes	40,321	26,137
Long-term debt	63,966	65,024
Obligations under capital leases	18,673	19,642
Commitments		
Stockholders' equity		
Common stock par value $.10 per share:		
Authorized 200,000,000 shares issued		
127,110,608 and 84,053,916	12,711	8,405
Additional paid-in capital	239,721	216,930
Retained earnings	650,499	502,595
Foreign currency translation adjustments	8,449	2,052
Treasury shares, at cost	(5,571)	(4,423)
Receivable from exercise of stock options	(4,768)	(8,165)
	901,041	717,394
	$1,522,966	$1,225,916

Source: 1987 annual report.

TURNER BROADCASTING SYSTEM, INC.

Prepared by Neil H. Snyder, McIntire School of Commerce,
University of Virginia, and Melanie D. Sheip, Morgan Guaranty
Trust.

TED TURNER: ENTREPRENEUR

In 1962, at age 24, Ted Turner faced some very difficult decisions—more difficult, in fact, than most people, including businesspeople, ever face. His father committed suicide and left an outdoor (billboard) advertising business that was $6 million in debt and short of cash. Rejecting the advice of the company's bankers who believed Turner was too inexperienced to run the company, he chose not to sell the firm, but instead, to build it. Immediately, he sold some of the company's assets to improve its cash position, refinanced its debt, renegotiated contracts with customers, hired new salespeople, and turned the company around. By 1969, the company's debt was paid off, and in 1970, having secured the future of Turner Advertising, Ted Turner purchased Channel 17, an Atlanta independent/UHF television station. Although Channel 17 is widely recognized today as a profitable business, in 1970 it was two years old, losing $50,000 per month, and competing in a market dominated by three firmly rooted network stations in Atlanta.

Recently, due in large measure to his phenomenal financial success, journalists have begun to explore Ted Turner, the man. Below are excerpts from a *Wall Street Journal* article:

> Associates of broadcaster Ted Turner like to retell the story of his victory in a 1979 yachting race because they think it says it all about the man.
>
> Mr. Turner's boat, *Tenacious,* battled 40-foot waves whipped by 65-knot winds in the Irish Sea to win the Fastnet race. Of the 306 boats that started the race, only 87 finished, and in one of ocean racing's greatest tragedies, 19 sailors drowned.

After his extraordinary display of skill and courage, Mr. Turner at dockside callously reminded his somber British hosts that in the 16th century the Spanish Armada ran into similar trouble. "You ought to be thankful there are storms like that," he said, "or you'd all be speaking Spanish." . . .

The flamboyant Southerner, called a visionary by some and a buffoon by others, seems a bit of both. Widely referred to as "Terrible Ted" and "The Mouth of the South," he has been charged with hypocrisy for preaching family values and then appearing drunk in public, and for criticizing the networks' TV "garbage" while boasting to Playboy magazine that he has photographed nude women. . . .

Friends and colleagues attribute both Mr. Turner's successes and his excesses to a personality riddled with contradictions. "Ted is a brilliant person," says Irwin Mazo, a former Turner accountant, "but he also borders on egomania." Although he often talks hard-line conservatism, Mr. Turner seems genuinely concerned about pet liberal issues like overpopulation, world hunger and nuclear proliferation. He presides over a major news organization but says he limits his newspaper reading to glances at *USA Today* and the Atlanta papers' sports section. He professes to admire the courtly values of the Old South yet often treats his senior executives like servants.

The conflicting sides are cemented by an overwhelming tenacity. "He competes in everything he does," says Jim Roddey, a former Turner executive and sailing buddy who has known him for 25 years. "He sails like he conducts business—it's all or nothing." Indeed, when he saw an Atlanta Braves game-night promotion threatened by lack of participants, he jumped into the contest: He rolled a baseball around the infield with his nose and emerged with blood streaming from forehead to chin.

That incident, his friends say, demonstrates both Mr. Turner's love of publicity and his willingness to sacrifice his dignity in his drive to win. . . .

Mr. Turner was thrust into the business world more than 20 years ago, when his father committed suicide immediately after selling most of the family billboard business. Then 24 years old, Mr. Turner challenged the would-be buyers and regained control of the company. "He could have lost it all," recalls Mr. Mazo, the accountant. But then as apparently now, says Mr. Mazo, "Ted is willing to put all his chips on the table and roll the dice."

In 1970, with the billboard business reestablished, Mr. Turner gambled next on buying a floundering Atlanta UHF television station. In 1976, he transformed it into one of the nation's most profitable stations by having its signal bounced off a satellite and into the nation's cable-TV systems. He channeled Turner Broadcasting's profits from the superstation into a round-the-clock news service dubbed Cable News Network. Five years later, as CNN approaches profitability, Mr. Turner is looking for a new challenge.

Throughout, Mr. Turner's revolutionary moves have been scoffed at by the broadcasting establishment, just as brokers now are scoffing at his CBS takeover bid. Even Turner confidants have been skeptical about his moves. "He's made about $500 million and at least $400 million of that was on deals I told him not to do," chuckles Mr. Roddey, the former Turner executive who admits to advising the company to stick with billboards. . . .

Mr. Turner's management technique isn't any more conventional. "He's not a manager," says Mr. Roddey. "He's not hands-on. He always used to tell me I was getting bogged down in the details, like making the payroll."

But the volatile executive is "a very tough guy to work for," says Reese Schonfeld, the first president of CNN, who left after a dispute with Mr. Turner over hiring and firing. "I've seen him abuse a lot of people. Once you let him humiliate you, he'll walk all over you." Mr. Schonfeld says Mr. Turner has a habit of ordering his senior executives to fetch drinks for him.

Not all Turner employees have such gripes. Lower-level workers at CNN, housed in the basement of Turner Broadcasting's Atlanta headquarters, say their encounters with Mr. Turner are infrequent and non-confrontational. But life in Turner's executive suite looks stressful: In June 1983, for example, when Mr. Bevins was 36, he was struck by a heart attack while in Mr. Turner's office. Mr. Bevins declines to discuss the incident. . . .

In recent years, however, both Mr. Turner and his company have toned down. Aides say the change began when Mr. Turner began to realize that obtaining control of a network might someday be within his grasp. He began to position himself for an eventual combination, they say.

For Mr. Turner, that meant dropping off the interview trail and scaling down his public excesses. He repeatedly declined to be interviewed for this story, for instance. While hardly prim these days, "he's become more discreet," says one longtime Turner employee. And with age, his friends say, has come a dose of maturity. "Lately he talks a lot about world peace, nuclear war, improving the environment," says Gary Jobson, tactician aboard many of Mr. Turner's winning yachts.[1]

Turner's perspective on business is interesting to say the least. He is quoted as saying,

I don't think winning is everything. It's a big mistake when you say that I think trying to win is what counts. Be kind and fair and make the world a better place to live, that's what's important. . . . I think the saddest people I've ever met were people with a lot of wealth. If you polled 90 percent of the people and asked them what they want most, most would want to be millionaires. I'll tell you, you've got to be one to know how unimportant it is. . . . I'm blessed with some talents. I've made a lot of money, more than I ever thought I would. . . . But if I continue to be successful, I would like to serve my fellow man in some way other than doing flips at third base. . . . People want leadership, somebody to rally around, and I want to be a leader.[2]

CREATING A NETWORK: WTBS, THE SUPERSTATION

WTBS is the pioneer of the superstation concept. Owned and operated by the Turner Broadcasting System Inc., it is an independent UHF television station, Channel 17 in Atlanta, Georgia, whose signal is beamed via satellite to television households nationwide. Ted Turner, TBS president and chairman of the board, purchased Channel 17 in January 1970. By merging the then Turner Communications Corporation with Rice Broadcasting, he gained control of the television outlet, which became WTCG, flagship station of the Turner Communications Group.

Realizing that WTCG's programming could be made available by satellite to millions of television viewers throughout the country, Turner originated the superstation concept. In short, the "SuperStation" is a reworking of the traditional television network concept, in which one station acts as original programming supplier for a multiplicity of distant cable markets. On December 16, 1976, WTCG made history, as its signal was beamed to cable systems nationwide via a transponder on RCA's Satcom I satellite. Satcom I was replaced by Satcom III-R in January 1982, and by Galaxy I in January 1985.

In 1979, the Turner Communications Group was renamed Turner Broadcasting System Inc., and, to reflect this change, the WTCG call letters became WTBS. The company estimates that, as of February 29, 1984, WTBS was beamed into approximately 75% of U.S. cable homes and 35% of U.S. television homes.

WTBS broadcasts 24 hours per day, acquiring its programming primarily from film companies, syndicators of programs that have run successfully on television networks, and its sports affiliates. WTBS currently has available 4,100 film titles for its programming needs, the majority of which are available for multiple runs. In addition, approximately 500 titles are under contract and will become available for programming purposes in the future. Approximately 23% of the purchased programming has been obtained from Viacom International, Inc. and 17% from MCA. WTBS has not obtained more than 10% of its purchased programming needs from any other single supplier, and approximately 1,900 hours of programming broadcast on WTBS during 1983 were produced internally, or under contract. Exhibits C34.1 through C34.6 are descriptions of internally produced programs. WTBS plans to produce more programs internally in the future.

WTBS derives revenue from the sale of advertising time, and advertising prices depend on the size of WTBS' viewing audience and the amount of available time sold. Since February 1981, the A.C. Nielsen Company has been measuring the audience level of WTBS for use by the company and its advertisers. The demand for advertising time on cable television is significantly lower than that for advertising time on the three major networks because of the relatively small size of the cable network audiences and the fact that cable has not penetrated significantly in many of the major urban markets. The board of directors of TBS anticipates that the continued growth of the cable television (CATV) industry, particularly in the major urban markets, will result in increased demand on the part of advertisers.

The revenues of WTBS also include amounts obtained from "direct response" advertising, which represent fees received by the company for the sale of products it promotes by advertisement. The company broadcasts advertisements for the products during unsold advertising time, and the products are ordered directly by viewers through the company by mail or telephone. WTBS collects a fee for each order. In 1983, these fees amounted to 6.6% of total advertising revenues for WTBS.

Advertising time for WTBS as well as the company's cable news services is marketed and sold by the company's own advertising sales force consisting of approximately 101 persons located in sales offices in New York, Chicago, Detroit, Los Angeles, and Atlanta.

According to the *Wall Street Journal*,

It's hard to laugh at Mr. Turner's operations now, or at least the WTBS operation. His superstation, one of the nation's most popular cable services, now beams a steady diet of sports, movies and reruns into almost 34 million U.S. households, or about 84% of all homes equipped for cable.

It has revolutionized the cable-television business, says Ira Tumpowsky, a Young & Rubicam Inc. senior vice president who oversees the agency's cable-TV buying. "He's the person who moved cable from a reception industry to a marketing industry," the advertising executive says.[3]

PORTRAIT OF AMERICA

PORTRAIT OF AMERICA, an in-depth, 60-part documentary series exploring each of the United States and U.S. territories, highlights the SuperStation program lineup. Filmed on location, this ambitious, five-year series of hour-long specials marks the most comprehensive look ever at the pieces which make up the greatest nation on earth.

Hosted and narrated by award-winning television, film and stage star Hal Holbrook, *PORTRAIT OF AMERICA* reveals unusual characters, depicts interesting places and delves into the ingenuity, beauty and heritage of American life with insatiable curiosity. Each episode focuses on a single state, commonwealth or territory, painting a close-up, modern picture of the land and its people, framed in the flavor of local culture and the strength of American history.

"We're taking an insightful look at the diversity of people and resources of this nation, rather than dwelling on its weaknesses," says WTBS President Robert Wussler.

PORTRAIT OF AMERICA, originated by TBS Board Chairman and President R.E. "Ted" Turner, has been cited by numerous organizations for outstanding television achievement. The series has been honored with a George Foster Peabody Award, one of electronic journalism's most prestigious prizes, and a variety of top film festival awards.

Recommended by the National Education Association for viewing by students, the award-winning *PORTRAIT OF AMERICA* airs four times a month to ensure viewing availability. The SuperStation presents the first telecast during prime time, with replays scheduled for late night, weekend early fringe and weekend daytime. The series successfully debuted in January 1983 with a profile of Virginia, followed in the first 18 months by programs featuring Nevada, Georgia, Puerto Rico, Florida, Texas, Oregon, Iowa, Indiana, New Jersey, New Mexico, Connecticut, Idaho, Wisconsin, Missouri, North Dakota, Louisiana and Maine. A new *PORTRAIT OF AMERICA* episode will be introduced every month, with the entire series continuing for five years.

"This project is yet another example of the impact cable television can have on viewers across the nation," says *PORTRAIT OF AMERICA* Executive Producer Ira Miskin. "TBS intends to make a tangible contribution to a nation long starved for reinforcement of its faith in what makes America great."

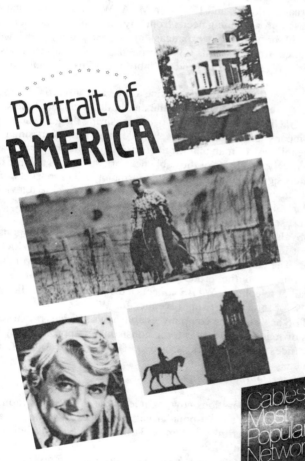

Portrait of AMERICA

Cable's Most Popular Network

SuperStationWTBS

JACQUES COUSTEAU

In the Turner Broadcasting System tradition of quality family programming, the SuperStation offers exciting first-run Cousteau Society specials and a regularly scheduled series of hour-long documentaries, *THE UNDERSEA WORLD OF JACQUES COUSTEAU.*

Scheduled for 1985 is a seventh and final hour to the successful *COUSTEAU/AMAZON* series. The special explores the cocaine and drug trafficking problem in Amazonia, a major source of cocaine brought into the United States.

Also new from The Cousteau Society in 1985 is a two-hour documentary on the 2,348-mile Mississippi River, offering the most comprehensive look Cousteau has ever made at a water system in the United States.

In 1984, the SuperStation aired *COUSTEAU/ AMAZON*, a six-hour documentary covering the

"Calypso's" 18-month expedition into South America's Amazon River Basin, where teams of environmental scientists explored the uncharted. Narrated by Joseph Campanella, the series gives new insight into the world's second longest river, its abundant lifeforms, its people and its future.

An encore presentation of the entire seven-hour *COUSTEAU/AMAZON* series is scheduled for early 1985.

COUSTEAU/AMAZON has received national acclaim, being called "an extraordinary video venture" by the *Chicago Tribune*. The *Philadelphia Inquirer* has said, "What makes a Cousteau show utterly different from any other is the decency, humanity and worth of the man himself. His character shines through the screen." The series is "as gorgeous as you'd expect it to be," said the *Atlanta Constitution,* while *The Hollywood Reporter* applauded it as "uplifting and entertaining." *Daily Variety* said of the documentary, which took two years to produce, "It's been worth the wait."

During past seasons, the SuperStation debuted two more beautiful Cousteau films: *ST. LAWRENCE: STAIRWAY TO THE SEA,* a fascinating study of the Great Lakes-Inland Waterway System; and *CRIES FROM THE DEEP,* a stirring investigation of the struggle for survival between men and animals in the Canadian North Atlantic.

THE UNDERSEA WORLD OF JACQUES COUSTEAU, which airs Sundays at 5:35-6:35 PM (ET), combines scientific knowledge with beauty and aquatic adventure to create one of television's most highly acclaimed documentary series.

Captain Jacques-Yves Cousteau and son Jean-Michel have devoted their lives to making people aware of nature and its processes. They have set the tone for many of today's environmental action efforts and are symbols of mankind's concern for the health and well-being of future generations.

Jacques Cousteau

Jean-Michel Cousteau

Cable's Most Popular Network

SuperStationWTBS

GOOD NEWS

Liz Wickersham
GOOD NEWS

GOOD NEWS, an innovative, uplifting and positively entertaining approach to the news, airs on SuperStation WTBS Sundays at 10:05 AM (ET). The half-hour program recaps the week's most inspiring news from around the world, with host Liz Wickersham reporting the positive, healthy and creative side of human events.

Now in its second year, *GOOD NEWS* has become basic cable's highest rated, originally produced, regularly scheduled, non-sports program. It offers lifestyle features, revealing interviews with some of the entertainment industry's most celebrated stars and unique looks at the hottest box office attractions and music videos.

News items designed to evoke smiles and boost spirits are gathered for *GOOD NEWS* through the worldwide resources of Turner Broadcasting's Cable News Network. *GOOD NEWS* is an original WTBS production, conceived by TBS Board Chairman R.E. "Ted" Turner, and produced by WTBS' award-winning writers/producers, Bonnie and Terry Turner.

Liz Wickersham became known to Super-Station viewers as host of *THE LIGHTER SIDE*. Prior to joining TBS in March 1982, she was a successful model and actress. She has been seen in many popular publications, including *Glamour, Mademoiselle* and *Cosmopolitan,* and has appeared in episodes of television's "One Life to Live," "The Edge of Night," "B.J. and the Bear" and "Magnum, P.I."

GOOD NEWS airs Sundays at 10:05-10:35 AM (ET) on SuperStation WTBS.

Cable's Most Popular Network

SuperStationWTBS

Carol Mansell

Dick Sargent

Ronnie Schell

DOWN TO EARTH

DOWN TO EARTH, SuperStation WTBS' first made-for-cable situation comedy, offers fun for the whole family on Fridays at 6:35-7:05 PM (ET).

Produced in Los Angeles by The Arthur Company in association with Procter & Gamble Productions Inc., *DOWN TO EARTH* follows the mishaps of a zany, endearing angel named Ethel MacDoogan, sent to earth for one final chance to win her wings. Through her daily efforts as their housekeeper, Ethel brings the Preston family, a widower and his three children, closer together and finally has earned her wings.

Ethel, who wants to remain on earth, now is assigned the task of aiding others, in addition to her role with the Prestons. Ethel (born 1887, died 1925) must report her earthly activities to Lester Luster, one of the head angels who can recall Ethel to heaven if she makes too many major blunders.

Modern living, from aerobics to home computers, is a revelation to this angel. Mix a large portion of naivete with a healthy dash of curiosity and a pinch of mischief and that's Ethel, *DOWN TO EARTH* with her late 20th century entourage. The Preston family consists of Richard, 38, an inventor's agent; Duane, 16, who is primarily concerned with his image; Lissy, 14, who begins to date; and Jay Jay, 8, the only one who knows Ethel is an angel.

Carol Mansell, who appeared in the title role of the Kennedy Center production "Really Rosie," stars as Ethel Methel MacDoogan. Ronnie Schell, who portrayed Gomer Pyle's best friend "Duke" on the hit television series "Gomer Pyle, USMC" is Lester Luster. Dick Sargent, who starred as Darrin Stephens on the long-running comedy "Bewitched," plays Richard Preston.

David Kaufman (Duane), Kyle Richards (Lissy) and Randy Josselyn (Jay Jay) round out the cast.

Cable's Most Popular Network

SuperStationWTBS

THE CATLINS

THE CATLINS is a fascinating weekday series aired exclusively on SuperStation WTBS, and brought to you in part by the Brands at Procter & Gamble. Each exciting half-hour episode of *THE CATLINS* airs Monday through Friday at 11:05 AM (ET).

Set in Atlanta, the action centers around the wealthy and powerful Catlin family, whose feuds, romances, intrigues, laughs and triumphs weave a captivating contemporary drama.

Headed by Catherine Catlin, a tough-minded matriarch, the family consists of eight core members. T.J. Catlin is Catherine's son and Chairman of the Board of the family's financial empire. He and his wife Annabelle, an aristocratic Southern Belle, have five children. Matthew, their oldest child, is a handsome and highly respected cardiologist. Maggie is a brilliant and beautiful lawyer. Jonathan is the middle son, a straight-laced man who is desperate to prove himself. Beau is the family's dashingly attractive, devil-may-care black sheep. And Jennifer, the youngest Catlin, is a beautiful but naive young woman.

The Catlins are a rich and politically influential group, but they face major and minor complications in their efforts to stay on top. Most of their foils are generated by the antagonistic Quinn family, consisting of Medgar and his sons Seth and Cullen. The mutual dislike between the Catlins and the Quinns creates an electric and suspenseful atmosphere throughout their lives.

Other continuing characters on *THE CATLINS* include Dirk Stack, a slick-talking entrepreneur; Stacy Manning, a journalist whose first priority is herself; Woody Thorpe, a hardworking "good ol' boy" trying to become a success; and Babe Chalifoux, an undercover F.B.I. agent.

Tune in and keep up with *THE CATLINS* as the adventures unfold, weekdays on the SuperStation.

Danny Nelson is
Medgar Quinn

Joseph Rainer is
Dirk Stack

Mary Nell Santacroce is
Catherine Catlin

Cable's
Most
Popular
Network

SuperStationWTBS

WORLD OF AUDUBON

WORLD OF AUDUBON is an exciting new environmental series telecast on SuperStation WTBS. Airing quarterly throughout 1985, *WORLD OF AUDUBON* explores and celebrates the beauty and majesty of nature in fast-paced magazine format programs guaranteed to be soaring experiences.

The National Audubon Society, in its first long-term television effort, joins Turner Broadcasting System and the SuperStation in bringing the bracing and bewildering vitality of the great outdoors into focus as a fragile and beautiful treasure. *WORLD OF AUDUBON* highlights the splendors of the earth as cameras capture the teeming wildlife realm, showing that the world is full of glorious things.

"But," warns the National Audubon Society, "the wonders of wildlife are in danger!"

Cliff Robertson

Hosted by veteran actor and environmentalist Cliff Robertson, each hour-long edition of *WORLD OF AUDUBON* uses remarkable on-location photography and interviews with noted conservationists to cover a variety of issues.

"The preservation of our planet's environment and its wildlife is one of the most important issues facing mankind today," says TBS Board Chairman and President R.E. "Ted" Turner. "We must be deeply concerned about the type of world we leave for future generations." National Audubon Society President Dr. Russell Peterson declares, "Of all the projects Audubon is working on, few compare in importance to this initiative with Ted Turner. It is a great opportunity for the National Audubon Society to reach the public with our very important message."

WORLD OF AUDUBON includes magnificently photographed segments on sea otters in Big Sur, CA; rare pink flamingos in Great Inagua, West Indies; bald eagles in Alaska; and grizzly bears in Yellowstone National Park. There are revealing interviews with actor Richard Chamberlain, who is working to preserve California's scenic Tuolumne River; with actress Pam Dawber ("Mork and Mindy"), who is a solar energy proponent; and with Margaret Owings, who is founder of "Friends of the Sea Otter."

WORLD OF AUDUBON's Academy Award-winning host Cliff Robertson is an active conservationist. His stage, film and television credits are numerous. He was selected personally by President John F. Kennedy to portray the President as a young World War II Navy Lieutenant in "PT-109." Robertson displayed his acting versatility by portraying a mentally-retarded man in the 1968 film, "Charly," for which he won an Academy Award.

WORLD OF AUDUBON is originated by R.E. "Ted" Turner and is a co-production of Turner Broadcasting System and the National Audubon Society.

Cable's Most Popular Network

SuperStationWTBS

TBS Sports

In January 1976, TBS acquired the Atlanta Braves professional baseball club, and on December 29, 1976, the Atlanta Hawks professional basketball club was acquired. Although both teams have consistently lost money, they have provided TBS with excellent sports programming, and the Atlanta Braves, "America's Team," have a national following. TBS aired 150 Braves games and 41 Hawks games in 1984.

Along with a full schedule of Atlanta Braves baseball and Atlanta Hawks basketball, TBS Sports offers NCAA basketball, NBA basketball, NCAA football, Southeastern Conference football, and a variety of special sports presentations. For example, TBS Sports telecast the NASCAR circuit's Richmond 400, college football's Hall of Fame Bowl, and World Championship Wrestling during 1984.

Recently, baseball Commissioner Peter Ueberroth persuaded Ted Turner to make annual payments to other major league teams if he continued to broadcast Braves games across the nation over his cable station. Turner has agreed to make these payments, totaling more than $25 million, into a central fund for five years.[4] This agreement is a compromise. Ueberroth had wanted to end nationwide cable broadcasts of baseball games, since they were hurting the profits of teams in other cities. Ueberroth is reported to have said that superstations are the most serious problem facing professional baseball.[5]

Ted Turner is said to be as creative with his sports franchises as he is with TBS. For example, the *Wall Street Journal* concluded that:

Even in the stodgy game of baseball, Mr. Turner has displayed some business acumen. The Atlanta Braves franchise that he bought in 1976 was mired in mediocrity. Mr. Turner beefed up its farm system, paid top dollar to lure stars from elsewhere, and transmitted across the nation practically every game the team played. Average attendance at Braves' home games last year was 21,834, triple the figure for 1975. The Braves are widely considered pennant contenders this season.

In baseball, as in his other businesses, Mr. Turner has managed to outrage both his employees and his peers. Mr. Turner once tried to demote a slumping star to the minor leagues. At another point, he named himself manager of the team. Such antics led to a collision with the then-commissioner of baseball, Bowie Kuhn, and to Mr. Turner's temporary suspension from the game. According to one biography, Mr. Turner pleaded with Mr. Kuhn: "I am very contrite. I would bend over and let you paddle my behind, hit me over the head with a Fresca bottle."[6]

CNN

Through its subsidiary Cable News Network, Inc. (CNN), which began broadcasting on June 1, 1980, TBS provides a 24-hour news programming service which is available to CATV systems throughout the United States and in some foreign countries. The programming includes comprehensive reporting of domestic and international news, sports, business, and weather, plus analysis, commentary, and reports by its staff of experts and investigative reporters. CNN obtains news reports from its bureaus in various U.S. and foreign cities. Each of these bureaus is equipped to provide live reports to CNN's transmission facility in Atlanta thereby providing the capability for live coverage of news events around the world. In addition, news is obtained through wire services, television news services by agreement with television stations in various locations worldwide, and from free-lance reporters and camera crews.

CNN employs over 160 journalists, executives, and technicians. The news channel was initially received by 193 CATV systems serving approximately 1.7 million subscribers. As of December 31, 1983, 4,278 CATV systems serving approximately 25.1 million subscribers received CNN's programming.

According to the *Wall Street Journal*,

> During its five years of losses, CNN has grown to become the nation's most popular cable service, available in some 32 million homes. And this year, the company indicates, CNN should move into the black. Though still not an equal of the high-powered network news operations, CNN is nipping at their heels, and doing it on a bargain-basement budget.
>
> CNN is weak on features says Jim Snyder, News vice president of Post-Newsweek Stations Inc., the broadcasting division of the Washington Post Co., but it covers breaking news "as well as anybody." A recent *Washington Journalism Review* assessment of the channel carried the headline "CNN Takes Its Place Beside the Networks."[7]

CNN Headline News

CNN offered another 24-hour news service to cable operators effective December 31, 1981. Referred to as CNN Headline News (CNN HN), this service utilizes a concise, fast-paced format, programming in half-hour cycles throughout the day. CNN HN employs approximately 225 people, and its start-up required the construction and furnishing of a studio facility and additional transmitting facilities. The resources and expertise of CNN is utilized by CNN HN for accumulation of news material. Its revenues are derived from the sale of advertising on CNN HN and from fees charged for the syndication of CNN HN directly to over-the-air television and radio stations.

The number of cable homes receiving the CNN HN signal increased from approximately 5,400,000 in October 1983 to approximately 9,100,000 as a direct result of TBS' agreement to acquire CNN HN's major cable news competitor (The Satellite News Channel). Despite this increase in cable homes, TBS executives do not expect CNN HN to be profitable in 1984.

Cable Music Channel

On October 26, 1984, TBS launched its own brand of video-clip programming to compete with MTV. The Cable Music Channel started with 2.5 million households, about half the expected subscriber count company executives had predicted. However, by November 30, 1984, the Cable Music Channel's title and affiliate list was sold to MTV Networks Inc. for $1.5 million in cash and advertising commitments at a loss of $2.2 million. Cable Music Channel President/TBS Executive Vice President Robert Wussler acknowledges that operator resistance was largely responsible. "We didn't get the homes and we weren't about to get 3 or 5 million homes. We surveyed the field, felt we had a good product, but the industry obviously embraced MTV, the future in terms of acquiring subs was bleak and we felt strongly that this was our best course of action."[8]

KEY EXECUTIVES AND OWNERSHIP

Ted Turner is aided by highly qualified, experienced men. Robert J. Wussler, executive vice president, had 21 years' experience with CBS, including his appointment as president of the CBS Sports Division, before joining TBS in August 1981.

William C. Bevins, Jr., is vice president of finance, secretary and treasurer, as well as a director of the company. Previously, he was affiliated with Price Waterhouse for 10 years, most recently as senior manager.

Henry L. (Hank) Aaron has been vice president-director of player development for the Atlanta Braves since 1976, the vice president of community relations, and a director of the company since 1980. He was previously a professional baseball player with a total of 28 years of experience in professional sports, and he holds the world's record for the most home runs hit by a professional baseball player.

Burt Reinhardt became president of CNN in 1982 and a director of CNN in 1983. He was employed by the company in 1979 and was instrumental in organizing CNN. Previously, he served as executive vice president of UPI Television News and executive vice president of the Non-Theatrical and Educational Division of Paramount Pictures.

Gerald Hogan joined the company in 1971 and served as general sales manager of WTBS from 1979 until 1981. He became senior vice president of Turner Broadcasting Sales, Inc. in 1982.

Henry Gillespie joined TBS in 1982 as chairman of the board of Turner Program Services, Inc. Prior to that, he served as president of Columbia Pictures Television distribution and president of Viacom Enterprises.

J. Michael Gearon has been a director of the company, president of Hawks Management Company, and general partner of Atlanta Hawks, Ltd., operator of the Atlanta Hawks professional basketball team, since 1979. He previously owned a real estate brokerage and development firm in Atlanta, Georgia.

Ownership Philosophy

Currently, Ted Turner owns 86% of the common shares outstanding. Exhibit C34.7 presents TBS common stock ownership of selected individuals. Most of the stockholders besides Turner and his family are either directors or executive officers of TBS.

FINANCIAL ISSUES

Debt Philosophy

TBS is a highly leveraged company that emphasizes the building of asset values. Presently, the company has a $190 million revolving credit agreement extending until 1987, and $133 million of this credit line has been borrowed. Concerning long-term debt, the company has incurred debt restructuring fees which it expenses as interest based on the weighted average of the principal balance outstanding throughout the term of the agreement. The company paid restructuring fees of $3,650,000 during 1983, and the balance due at year-end is classified as current and long-term in accordance with the payment terms of the agreements.

Under terms of its 1983 debt agreement, the company is limited with regard to additional borrowings, cash dividends, and acquisition of the company's common stock.

EXHIBIT C34.7   TBS COMMON STOCK OWNERSHIP

Name of beneficial owner	Amount	Percent of class
R.E. Turner	$17,579,922	86.2%
William C. Bevins, Jr.	20,000	0.1
Peter A. Dames	98,910	0.5
Karl Eller	1,000	—
Tench C. Coxe	128,285	0.6
J. Michael Gearon	31,500	0.2
Martin B. Seretean	20,800	0.1
William C. Bartholomay	210,700	1.0
Allison Thornwell, Jr.	215,912	1.1
All directors and officers as a group (27 persons)	$18,421,489	90.4%

Source: 1984 annual 10-K reports.

TBS is also required, among other things, to maintain minimum levels of working capital and to meet specified current ratio requirements. It is important to note that the company was not in compliance with certain restrictive covenants of its loan agreement on December 31, 1983. TBS received waivers of these restrictions from lenders; accordingly, the amounts due have been classified in accordance with the original terms of the agreement.

Owner's Equity

Characteristic of firms in the growth stage of the business life cycle, TBS has experienced mostly negative earnings since its inception (see Exhibit C34.8). Most of its losses have resulted from the high start-up costs associated with the divisions that have been created in the past 10 years. Exhibit C34.9 shows balance sheet information for the years 1977 to 1983.

Working Capital

During 1983, the company was unable to generate sufficient cash flow from operations to meet its needs. Working capital deficits were primarily funded through short-term credit lines and financing agreements with vendors, program suppliers, and others during the first three-quarters of the year. A large percentage of cash outflow resulted from the debt restructuring fees.

TBS faces several uncertainties that could arise out of normal operations that might require additional cash. However, management feels that the current financing program will be adequate to meet the company's anticipated needs. In the unlikely event that these uncertainties do materialize and require cash in excess of the anticipated amounts, because of limitations in existing loan agreements, there is no assurance that the company can obtain additional borrowings which might be needed to meet these excess needs.

EXHIBIT C34.8 TURNER BROADCASTING COMPANY HISTORICAL COMMON SIZE INCOME STATEMENT
(Dollars in Thousands)

	1977	1978	1979	1980	1981	1982	1983
Revenue:							
Broadcasting	$ 19,573	$23,434	$ 27,789	$ 35,495	$ 55,329	$ 96,647	$136,217
Cable production	0	0	0	7,201	27,738	49,708	65,169
Sports	6,706	8,181	7,395	9,211	8,840	16,263	21,401
Management fees	1,782	2,094	2,285	2,473	2,835	2,717	1,462
Other	738	134	252	230	305	306	283
Total revenue	$ 28,799	$33,843	$ 37,721	$ 54,610	$ 95,047	$165,641	$224,532
Cost of expenses:							
Cost of operation	$ 12,767	$13,219	$ 16,997	$ 35,124	$ 49,036	$ 81,187	$105,695
S, G & Admin.	10,729	12,736	14,460	25,218	37,067	60,343	80,722
Amortization film contracts	1,178	1,571	2,290	2,803	4,010	7,497	8,674
Amort. player/other contracts	1,556	1,599	1,508	1,210	0		
Depreciation of P, P & E	934	1,037	1,222	2,172	3,469	4,182	4,706
Interest expense/ amort. debt	1,291	1,323	2,098	4,437	9,673	13,084	14,383
Other	1,251	0	0	0	0	0	0
Total costs & expenses	$ 29,706	$31,485	$ 38,575	$ 70,964	$ 103,255	$166,293	$214,170
Income (loss) from operation	$ −907	$ 2,358	$ −854	$ −16,354	$ −8,208	$ −652	$ 10,362
Equity loss-limited partners	−1,053	−1,225	−2,014	−2,905	−5,215	−2,698	−3,350
Income before gains or dispos.	−1,960	1,133	−2,868	−19,259	−13,423	−3,350	7,012
Gain on disposition of prop.	0	395	312	15,694	0		
Income bef. tax & extra. items	−1,960	1,528	−2,556	−3,575	−13,423	−3,350	7,012
Provision (benefit) for taxes	−728	669	−1,060	200	0		
Income bef. extra. items	−1,232	860	−1,496	−3,775	−13,423	−3,350	7,012
Gain on prepay- ment of debt	0	343	0	0	0		
Net income (loss)	$−1,232	$ 1,203	$−1,496	$−3,775	$−13,423	−3,350	$ 7,012

EXHIBIT C34.9 TURNER BROADCASTING COMPANY HISTORICAL COMMON SIZE BALANCE SHEET
(Dollars in Thousands)

	1977	1978	1979	1980	1981	1982	1983
Current assets							
Cash	$ 1,351	$ 154	$ 342	$ 489	$ 504	$ 538	$ 594
Accounts receivable	3,537	4,951	6,322	10,662	18,868	25,728	34,186
Less: allow for doubt accts.	431	547	415	793	1,164	1,997	2,418
Net accounts receivable	3,106	4,404	5,907	9,869	17,704	23,731	31,768
Prepaid expenses	1,250	563	585	552	1,086	1,378	2,177
Notes payable—S-T	0	0	0	0	0	0	0
Curr. port. def. prog. prod. cost						2,490	2,660
Film contract rights—current	1,128	2,055	2,570	2,521	3,495	4,516	12,163
Other current assets	1,359	528	644	1,591	1,433	2,585	2,305
Total current assets	$ 8,194	$ 7,704	$10,048	$ 15,022	$ 24,222	$ 35,238	$ 51,667
Film contract rights	$ 3,193	$ 5,632	$ 7,537	$ 5,660	$ 9,464	$ 15,633	$ 26,057
Inv. in limited partnerships	1,000	2,578	2,480	2,027	900	1,900	1,633
Net prop., plant & equipment	6,543	7,784	13,381	26,647	28,698	67,555	71,505
Notes receivable—L-T	1,146	404	514	920	0	0	0
Deferred program prod. costs						4,460	11,432
Deferred charges	0	0	0	0	9,623	6,585	13,926
Net contract rights	6,165	4,947	3,628	2,784	2,084	1,583	1,246
Intangible assets	0	0	0	0	0	0	25,567
Other assets	1,624	1,349	1,696	958	1,970	2,232	2,805
Total assets	$27,865	$30,398	$39,284	$ 54,018	$ 76,961	$ 135,186	$ 205,838
Current liabilities							
Accounts payable	$ 2,043	$ 2,615	$ 1,351	$ 2,079	$ 3,926	$ 7,548	$ 6,954
Accrued expenses	0	0	1,752	7,196	11,152	16,750	22,551
Deferred income	0	0	216	700	2,226	7,220	7,083
Short-term borrowings	0	0	6,642	17,907	42,783	49,924	0
Long-term debt—current	5,411	4,910	2,704	8,430	3,005	4,266	14,473
Obligation-film RTS (current)	0	0	3,344	2,456	3,465	5,613	11,317
Debt restructure fees (cur.)	0	0	0	0	2,253	3,000	3,650
Income taxes payable	0	0	0	163	0	0	0
Total current liabilities	$ 7,454	$ 7,525	$16,009	$ 38,931	$ 68,810	$ 94,321	$ 66,028

EXHIBIT C34.9   *(CONTINUED)*

	1977	1978	1979	1980	1981	1982	1983
Long-term debt	$15,968	$16,329	$14,158	$ 9,825	$ 7,165	$ 42,802	$ 122,404
Unfunded pension cost	283	283	283	283	283		
Deferred income taxes	1,076	1,980	918	918	2,834		
Deferred income	0	0	0	0	1,313	646	562
Debt restructure fees payable	0	0	0	0	4,207	3,000	650
Obligations—emp. contracts	0	0	1,410	2,221	2,560	3,442	5,201
Obligations—film rights	0	0	3,631	2,662	3,943	7,379	13,959
Other liabilities						1,097	7,507
Total liabilities	$24,781	$26,117	$36,409	$ 54,840	$ 91,115	$ 152,687	$ 216,311
Common stock, par .125	$ 1,024	$ 1,024	$ 2,663	$ 2,663	$ 2,663	$ 2,663	$ 2,663
Capital in excess	1,541	1,572	291	602	1,508	1,508	1,508
Retained earnings (deficit)	1,095	2,298	802	−2,973	−16,396	−19,746	−12,734
	$ 3,660	$ 4,894	$ 3,756	$ 292	$−12,225	$−15,575	$ −8,563
Less shares of stock— treasury						−474	−754
Notes rec.—sales of CS— treas.						−1,452	−1,156
Treasury stock	$ −576	$ −613	$ −881	$−1,114	$ −1,929	$ −1,926	$ −1,910
Total stockholders' equity	$ 6,744	$ 9,175	$ 6,631	$ −530	$−26,379	$−17,501	$−10,473
Total liabilities & S.E.	$31,525	$35,292	$43,040	$ 54,310	64,736	$ 135,186	$ 205,838

Dividend Policy

TBS has not paid a cash dividend since 1975. In view of the unavailability of funds to the company and restrictions in its loan agreements against any dividend payments, it is not anticipated that dividends will be paid to holders of its common stock in the foreseeable future.

Capital Structure

Presently, 97% of TBS' capital structure consists of long-term debt. In the fourth quarter of 1984, TBS was considering a public offering to raise $125 million to pay off its bank debt. The company planned to use a combination of 10-year notes, stocks, and warrants to raise the capital. Based on preliminary plans, the offering would boost the number of shares outstanding from the current 20.3 million to 22.2 million, reducing the percentage of shares held by Turner from 87% to 79%.

INDUSTRY AND COMPETITION

The dramatic increase in the number of alternative sources of television broadcasting has led to a measurable drop in the audience shares of the three major networks.

Consequently, there is a great deal of pressure for change in the television industry. Pay and ad-supported cable, independent broadcast stations, and videocassettes are all seen as contributing to the decline. In the next decade, it is believed that television entertainment may shift toward a broader range of outlets including ad hoc and regional networks, pay-per-view networks, and more reasonably priced videocassette recorders.

Networks

Although television audience viewing is growing, the big three networks are concerned about the decline in their audience shares and about when the decline will stop. The availability of syndicated programs is becoming scarce as new broadcasters race to buy up existing shows. However, networks have an advantage in this competition because of their programming expertise and facilities. Exhibit C34.10 shows how precipitous the decline in network television audience share was between 1975 and 1976, and 1981 and 1982.

Independents

Independent television stations have experienced phenomenal growth in the past 15 years. In 1971, there were 65 independent broadcasters serving 30 markets in the United States with losses of $24 million. In 1980, 179 independent stations served 86 markets

EXHIBIT C34.10   DECLINE IN NETWORK TV AUDIENCE

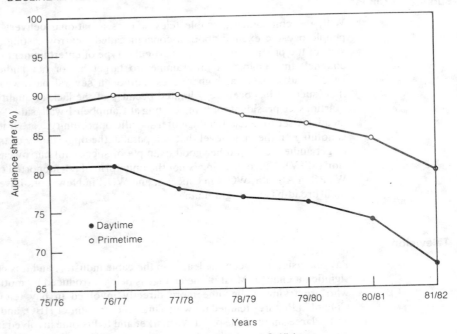

Source: Needham Harper Steers, based on data from A.C. Nielsen.

with profits of $158 million. This growth can be largely attributed to the FCC's financial interest rule which prohibits the big three networks from syndicating programs that they originally aired and from owning any financial interest in programming produced by others. The independents thus have been able to compete against the networks by airing former network hit shows at key times during the day, including prime time.

Cable

The cable industry is in the midst of a gigantic building boom which can be attributed to two advances. First, there was an increase in the number of channels picked up by cable operators from 12 to 54. Second, in 1975 Home Box Office (HBO) started sending its signal via satellite, and other stations, including WTBS, followed and were able to easily attain national distribution for their cable programming.

The fall 1984 Cable Study Report conducted by Mediamark Research, Inc. found that the median age of pay television subscribers was 35.2 years with an average yearly income of $29,879. *Cablevision,* the trade magazine of the cable industry, projects that the percentage of pay television subscribers will jump from 23% of the population in 1984 to 27% in 1986. Most of the cable industry's profits will be invested in the wiring of additional homes, particularly those in major urban areas. The high costs associated with wiring these areas had kept cable operators out previously. Now, cities represent more than four-fifths of the potential market.

Ad-Supported Cable

With the emergence of cable television as a national delivery system, many media people became excited about a concept called "narrowcasting." Narrowcasting consists of the programming of one particular type of entertainment (e.g., ESPN—a sports channel) that enables a programmer to target his or her audience and thus attract specific advertisers at higher rates. Although several narrowcasting networks exist, their success has been very limited because of the lack of quality programming. Dave Martin, vice president for broadcasting at Campbell-Ewall, said, "Narrowcasting allows an advertiser to take advantage of a specific opportunity. . . . If it works, though, there is nothing on the mass level that will parallel the opportunity of true narrowcasting to a target audience." Another good example of successful narrowcasting is Music Television (MTV). Narrowcasting is not the only form of ad-supported cable. Stations such as WTBS in Atlanta, WGN in Chicago, and WOR in New York have been successful with their broad-based program.ning.

Pay Television

Pay television has been the leader in the cable industry, and it is currently experiencing significant change. Most of the change is being introduced by motion picture companies who are trying to become more directly involved in pay television. For example, Columbia Pictures teamed up with Time, Inc., parent of HBO, and CBS in an attempt to grab a large share of the pay T.V. market and to become involved in pay-per-view (PPV) television. PPV requires a subscriber to pay an additional fee to view certain major programs. Thus far, most PPV has not been profitable because of the high prices viewers must pay for the programs.

A major threat to large pay television systems comes from smaller private delivery systems. For example, SMATV is a private system that picks up cable signals using a satellite disk and sends the signal via cable to a group of apartment houses, hotels, or clusters of private homes. SMATV has been extremely effective in urban areas previously ignored by other cable systems. This system does not offer the potential, however, of other systems such as MDS (multipoint distribution system) or DBS (direct broadcast satellite).

FCC Rulings

Television broadcasting is subject to the jurisdiction of the Federal Communications Commission (FCC) under the Communications Act of 1934, as amended. Among other things, FCC regulations govern the issuance, term, renewal, and transfer of licenses which must be obtained by persons to operate any television station. The FCC's recent proposal to repeal its network syndication and financial interest rules is strongly supported by the three major networks. Currently, the networks cannot syndicate their own programs, nor can they have a financial interest in programs produced by others. This rule prevents the networks from making money from their shows in syndication. Independent television stations, on the other hand, have grown substantially under this rule because of their ability to air former hit shows.

Independent broadcasters argue that repeal of the financial interest rule will increase the possibility of the networks' monopolizing and withholding off-network, syndicated, prime-time entertainment programming. However, CBS, NBC, and ABC contend that this possibility would not materialize, since the networks have neither the incentive nor the opportunity to discriminate against the independents.

To make the television industry more competitive, the FCC is preparing to adopt a plan to expand the 7-7-7 rule to the 12-12-12 rule. Currently, television station owners are allowed to own only seven AM and seven FM radio stations in addition to seven television stations. This limitation was adopted in the 1950s to encourage program diversity in the marketplace. Under the new plan, media companies would be allowed to own as many as 12 television stations only if the audience reach of the stations does not exceed 25% of the national viewing audience. This plan would eventually result in an increase in the number of television station owners capable of competing with the three major broadcast networks.

Another important issue facing the FCC concerns the reexamination of the fairness doctrine, the 35-year-old requirement that broadcasters cover "controversial issues" and air contrasting views. FCC Chairman Mark S. Fowler says that "the government shouldn't be the one to decide what's fair and what isn't."[9] However, defenders of the fairness doctrine counter that the airwaves are a scarce public resource that must be protected from abuse. Under Fowler's administration, the FCC has continued to expand its deregulatory efforts by abolishing regulations and relaxing rules that restrict regional concentration and multiple ownership of broadcast stations. "These are the areas where the agency must regulate, but in the choice between competition and regulation, competition is far better for the consumer," says Fowler.[10]

The Changing Landscape of Competiton

Clearly, competition in the home entertainment industry, in general, and television, in particular, are changing. VCRs are the hottest items going. Exhibit C34.11 shows how rapidly factory sales of VCRs have risen since 1982. Exhibit C34.12 shows that firms competing in the cable industry have made significant progress over the last 20 years "wiring" homes in our nation. Finally, Exhibit C34.13 shows how rapidly sales of videocassette tapes have increased. There can be no doubt that the landscape of competition is changing.

OUTLOOK FOR THE FUTURE

The future of the cable industry is still bright. According to Robert J. Wussler, executive vice president of TBS, "I don't think the momentum is out of the game, although I certainly think the bloom is off the rose. But all you have to do is come to a couple of cable conventions and see that there's still enough money around and there are still enough young people around to execute all the ideas people can dream up. No, there's still a lot of momentum around, even if it's not the gold rush."[11] Wussler believes broadcasting in general has hit a plateau or is shrinking. Due to the rise of independents, cable, direct broadcast satellites, videocassette recorders, and our various lifestyles, he does not believe broadcasting is becoming more powerful. According to Wussler, broadcasters do not need to worry about getting bigger again, but instead they must worry about getting smaller and about how they are going to manage being smaller. As for cable industry growth, Wussler does not see many limitations. Although it is a tough business to get into today because it requires a lot of capital and there are channel capacity problems, the future is bright.

If the cable industry continues to grow and superstations proliferate, TBS will face more competition. According to the *Wall Street Journal*,[12] some industry observers

EXHIBIT C34.11   FACTORY SALES IN BILLIONS OF DOLLARS

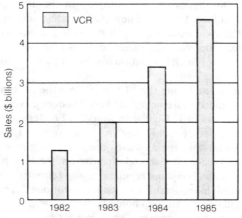

Source: Richmond Times-Dispatch, July 5, 1985. (Electronic Industries Association figures for 1985 are projected.)

EXHIBIT C34.12 HOMES WITH CABLE TV
(In Millions, Rounded)

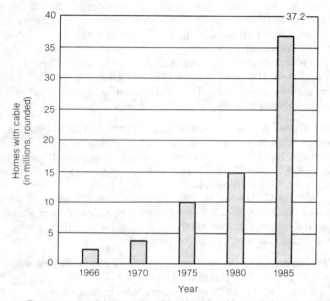

Figures are as of Jan. 1 except for 1985, when May statistics were used.
Source: Richmond-Times Dispatch, July 4, 1985. (National Cable Television Association using Arbitron estimates for 1985.)

EXHIBIT C34.13 SALES TO DEALERS
(In Millions of Units)

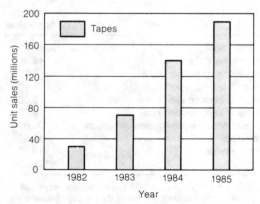

Source: Richmond-Times Dispatch, July 5, 1985. (Electronic Industries Association figures for 1985 are projected.)

have questioned whether Turner Broadcasting could hold up if superstation imitators proliferated beyond the handful now operating. But Bonnie Cook, an analyst for J.C. Bradford & Co. in Nashville, dismisses that notion. She believes that anybody can transform a television station into a superstation, but cable systems can carry only a limited number of channels. Thus, it is unlikely that the number of superstations will increase dramatically.

Television broadcasting is changing. In early 1985, Capital Cities Communications, Inc. purchased ABC, and in April 1985 Ted Turner made a move to acquire CBS for $5.4 billion including no cash. This acquisition attempt attracted praise, criticism, and ridicule. According to the *Wall Street Journal*,

> Mr. Turner has long broadcast his drive to run a network. Some associates contend that this desire became almost an obsession after Capital Cities Communications Inc. last month agreed to acquire American Broadcasting Cos. CBS thus was seen as Mr. Turner's last chance, because RCA, the parent of NBC, was probably too big to be taken over.
>
> William C. Bevins Jr., the financial vice president of Turner Broadcasting, denies that the ABC acquisition move forced Mr. Turner's hand. But he concedes that the transaction "certainly crystallized where the various regulatory agencies stood and that the timing was propitious."[13]

The package offered by Turner, which is reputed to be made up primarily of junk bonds, is presented in Exhibit C34.14.

CBS rejected Turner's offer as inadequate and took steps to prevent a takeover. Andy Rooney, a regular on the television program *60 Minutes*, had this to say about Turner's offer,

> Ted Turner, the Atlanta, Ga., money operator, yachtsman and baseball team owner, has applied to the Federal Communications Commission for its approval

EXHIBIT C34.14 TURNER BROADCASTING SYSTEM INC.'S PACKAGE FOR CBS

For each of CBS's 30 million shares, Turner offers the following package:

Type of security	Face value
$46 of 15% 7-year senior note	$ 46.00
$46 of 15½% 15-year senior debenture	46.00
$10.31 of 5-year Series A zero coupon note	5.00
$11.91 of 6-year Series B zero coupon note	5.00
$15.90 of 8-year Series C zero coupon note	5.00
$18.38 of 9-year Series D zero coupon note	5.00
$30.00 of 16¼% 20-year senior subordinated debenture	30.00
1 share of $2.80 preferred	16.50
0.75 share of Class B common	16.50
Total	$175.00*

* This is the face value of the offer for each CBS share. Analysts say there isn't any way of currently evaluating the market value of the package because the issues don't yet exist.

Source: Wall Street Journal, April 19, 1985.

of his scheme to take CBS away from its present owners. He has offered CBS stockholders a grabbag of what are known on Wall Street as "junk bonds" for their shares in CBS. . . .

I offer my services in trying to locate a new anchorman for the CBS Evening News and someone else to do pieces at the end of "60 minutes" because if Ted Turner takes over CBS, I doubt very much that Dan Rather will want his job and I know darn well I won't.[14]

On May 7, 1985, TBS announced a first-quarter loss of $741,000, compared with a $5.3 million loss a year earlier.

REFERENCES

1 *Wall Street Journal,* April 19, 1985, pages 1 and 6.
2 *Atlanta Constitution,* January 8, 1977.
3 *Wall Street Journal,* April 19, 1985.
4 Ibid.
5 *Richmond Times-Dispatch,* January 28, 1985.
6 *Wall Street Journal,* April 19, 1985.
7 Ibid.
8 *CableVision,* December 10, 1984.
9 *Business Week,* May 7, 1984.
10 Ibid.
11 *Broadcasting,* December 12, 1983.
12 *Wall Street Journal,* April 19, 1985.
13 Ibid.
14 *Richmond Times-Dispatch,* April 25, 1985.

WHEELING-PITTSBURGH STEEL COMPANY (B)

Prepared by Neil H. Snyder, Deborah Albro, Eileen Gordon, Connie Lett, Martha Parker, and Susan Pendergast, McIntire School of Commerce, University of Virginia.

INTRODUCTION

On December 5, 1968, Wheeling Steel Corporation merged with Pittsburgh Steel Company to form Wheeling-Pittsburgh Steel Company (W-P). W-P is engaged in the manufacturing, processing, and fabricating of steel and steel products. Exhibits C35.1 through C35.4 contain pertinent information about W-P's products. The firm is currently the seventh largest integrated steel company in the United States. W-P has eleven

EXHIBIT C35.1   PERCENTAGE CONTRIBUTIONS TO SALES REVENUES

Products	1984	1983	1982
Hot- & cold-rolled sheet & strip	41.9%	35.8%	25.5%
Coated sheet	16.6	19.6	16.6
Fabricated	14.9	15.3	15.7
Tin mill	11.1	18.0	17.0
Rail products	8.9	5.3	4.2
Seamless tubular	1.2	0.2	8.4
Welded tubular	0.3	1.5	4.8
Other	5.1	4.3	7.8
	100.0%	100.0%	100.0%

EXHIBIT C35.2 SHIPMENTS BY PRODUCT CLASS
(Net Tons)

Products	1984	1983	1982
Hot- & cold-rolled sheet & strip	53.6%	47.1%	37.3%
Coated sheet	13.2	16.7	17.1
Fabricated	10.5	10.9	12.1
Rail products	10.4	7.1	6.0
Tin mill	8.7	14.9	16.8
Seamless tubular	0.7	0.1	4.0
Welded tubular	0.4	1.3	4.3
Other	2.5	1.9	2.3
	100.0%	100.0%	100.0%

operating plants and fourteen subsidiaries. Exhibits C35.5 and C35.6 show the location of W-P's plants and its subsidiary companies, respectively.

HEADING FOR A CRISIS

In 1978, Dennis J. Carney became chairman of W-P, and he faced several major problems including the company's low market share, poor reputation with its customers, erratic earnings, and old equipment. To deal with these problems, Carney embarked on a campaign to upgrade the company's facilities with funds obtained from a multitude of sources (see Exhibit C35.7). By increasing W-P's debt to modernize, a very heavy burden was placed on an already struggling organization. In 1983, W-P's bank credit lines expired and the company ended 1984 with its tenth loss in eleven quarters. Exhibits C35.8 through C35.10 show selected financial data, stock price information, and financial ratios, respectively.

Twice in two years Carney had persuaded the United Steel Worker's Union (USW) to help W-P by granting wage concessions in excess of $150 million. However, these concessions were not necessarily a sign of good labor/management relations. In fact, the USW and Chairman Carney were constantly at odds. Carney was viewed by the union

EXHIBIT C35.3 SHIPMENTS BY MAJOR MARKET CLASSIFICATION
(Net Tons)

Market Class	1984	1983	1982
Automotive	11%	15%	15%
Intermediate markets	45	38	27
Construction	13	15	17
Containers	10	13	14
Appliances	5	7	8
Oil & gas	1	1	7
Rail transportation	10	7	5
Other	5	4	7
	100%	100%	100%

EXHIBIT C35.4 PRINCIPAL MARKETS AND MAJOR MARKET CLASSIFICATIONS TO WHICH RESPECTIVE CLASSES OF PRODUCTS WERE SOLD, BASED UPON SHIPMENTS
(Net Tons)

Products	Automotive			Construction			Containers		
	1984	1983	1982	1984	1983	1982	1984	1983	1982
Hot- & cold-rolled sheet & strip	11%	17%	25%	4%	6%	7%	8%	8%	9%
Tin mill	7	6	6	—	—	2	60	62	69
Coated sheet	38	38	28	10	15	16	—	—	—
Fabricated	—	—	—	79	82	88	—	—	—
Seamless tubular	—	—	1	—	1	1	—	—	—
Welded tubular	—	1	—	—	32	21	—	—	—

EXHIBIT C35.5 WHEELING-PITTSBURGH STEEL CORPORATION'S PLANTS

Canfield, Ohio
Martins Ferry, Ohio
Mingo Junction, Ohio
Steubenville, Ohio
Yorkville, Ohio

Allenport, Pennsylvania
Monessen, Pennsylvania

Benwood, West Virginia
Follansbee, West Virginia
Beech Bottom, West Virginia
Wheeling, West Virginia

EXHIBIT C35.6 WHEELING-PITTSBURGH SUBSIDIARY COMPANIES

Consumers Mining Company*
W-P Coal Company*
Ft. Duquesne Coal Company*
Gateway Coal Company
Harmar Coal Company
Mingo Oxygen Company*
Monessen Southwestern Railway Company*
Pittsburgh-Canfield Corporation*
Three Rivers Coal Company*
Wheeling-Empire Company
Wheeling Gateway Coal Company
Wheeling-Itasca Company
Wheeling-Pittsburgh Trading Company
WMI, Inc.

* These wholly owned subsidiaries filed petitions for relief under Chapter 11 of the federal bankruptcy laws in the U.S. bankruptcy court for the western district of Pennsylvania.

Appliances			Oil and gas			Intermediate		
1984	1983	1982	1984	1983	1982	1984	1983	1982
7%	11%	14%	—%	—%	—%	65%	53%	36%
10	8	9	—	—	—	21	22	22
6	5	6	—	—	—	43	38	44
—	—	2	—	—	—	20	18	10
—	—	—	96	99	97	4	—	1
—	—	1	23	31	23	77	33	46

EXHIBIT C35.7   WHEELING-PITTSBURGH DEBT

Secured long-term debt holders (in millions)

Mitsubishi Corporation*	$177.4
Prudential	51.7
Metropolitan Life	51.7
Aetna	20.7
Connecticut General	18.0
New York Life	15.1
Mutual of New York	13.2
Northwestern Mutual	13.2
Teachers	10.3
Pennsylvania IDA	9.0
Equitable	6.7
Massachusetts Mutual	4.2
John Hancock	3.4
Total	$394.6

Revolving working capital loans (in millions)

Manufacturers Hanover	$24.8
Royal Bank of Canada	20.7
Security Pacific	16.5
Pittsburgh National Bank	8.3
Manufacturers National—Detroit	8.3
Continental Illinois	8.3
Canadian Imperial Bank	8.3
National Bank of Canada	8.3
Bank of Nova Scotia	8.3
First Pennsylvania Bank	4.1
North Carolina National	4.1
Total	$120.0

* Guaranteed in event of default by eleven bank lenders.

EXHIBIT C35.8   WHEELING-PITTSBURGH'S FINANCIAL SITUATION

	1981	1982	1983	1984
Net sales	$1,151,112,000	$755,083,000	$772,320,000	$1,049,215,000
Net income	60,059,000	(58,769,000)	(54,080,000)	(59,376,000)
NI/Sh com. stock	14.28	(15.98)	(15.74)	(14.12)
Pref. div. declared	3,763,000	4,976,000	8,373,000	8,308,000
Depreciation	42,989,000	38,219,000	40,361,000	48,729,000
Plant imprvmnts.	110,177,000	160,211,000	91,905,000	26,878,000
Working capital	195,477,000	230,026,000	101,216,000	124,968,000
Long-term debt	358,733,000	495,915,000	513,928,000	527,291,000
Raw steel prod-uctn.	2,944,000	1,818,000	2,222,000	2,804,000
Shipments (tons)	2,146,000	1,368,000	1,642,000	2,320,000

EXHIBIT C35.9   WHEELING-PITTSBURGH'S STOCK PRICES

	6% Prior Preferred		$5 Cumulative Preferred		Common Shares	
	High	Low	High	Low	High	Low
1978	58.75	45.00	49.50	40.50	14.00	9.00
1979	48.00	42.75	38.875	34.125	20.00	15.625
1980	42.75	38.25	38.75	31.50	23.375	17.625
1981	40.00	38.00	34.00	30.00	32.50	25.625
1982	38.50	34.00	33.00	28.00	17.00	13.0
1983	42.50	38.25	34.00	31.00	28.00	22.25
1984	38.00	32.00	36.00	25.00	22.50	13.625

EXHIBIT C35.10   WHEELING-PITTSBURGH'S FINANCIAL RATIOS

	1981	1982	1983	1984
Current	1.86	2.57	1.42	1.61
Debt	.58	.63	.69	.71
Debt-equity	.77	1.15	1.39	1.56
Times interest earned	2.93	(1.93)	(.92)	(.03)
Inventory turnover	6.74	4.73	5.09	6.30
Total assets turnover	1.03	.63	.62	.86
Gross profit margin	.0852	(.0086)	(.0137)	.0779
Profit margin on sales	.0522	(.0778)	(.0700)	(.0566)
Return on total assets	.0713	(.0194)	(.0133)	(.0016)
Return on equity	.1283	(.1363)	(.1468)	(.1761)

as a highly controversial, autocratic, and abrasive leader. In the four years during which Carney was chairman, five top-level W-P executives resigned, and he is reported to have alienated a W-P director, and the company's largest stockholder, Allen Paulson, with his management style.

W-P's losses during 1982, 1983, and 1984 totaled more than $172 million. In addition, the company's long-term debt increased to more than $500 million in 1983, and its interest expense approached $60 million per year. To avoid bankruptcy, Carney turned to the USW and W-P's creditors for help in meeting the company's principal and interest payments. Exhibit C35.11 shows W-P's debt repayment schedule.

The USW stated that it was the creditors' turn to help the company, but the creditors were unwilling to do so unless the USW agreed to help as well. Eventually, the USW relented. However, this time they presented a list of demands that included a complete restructuring of the company's long-term debt, two union seats on the company's board of directors, and a large share of W-P's common stock. W-P's creditors agreed to defer $90 million of debt due in 1985 and in 1986 in exchange for a lien on the company's $300

EXHIBIT C35.11   W-P'S DEBT REPAYMENT FOR THE NEXT FIVE YEARS
(In Thousands*)

	1985	1986	1987	1988	1989
First-mortgage bonds:					
5.45% Series A due 1985	$12,600	$ —	$ —	$ —	$ —
9.50% Series D due 1994	3,187	3,187	3,187	3,187	3,187
4% Mortgage due 2001	376	391	407	423	447
Senior secured notes:					
11% Series A due 2001	3,493	3,493	3,493	3,493	3,493
11% Series B due 2001	2,007	2,007	2,007	2,007	2,007
11% Series C due 1994	2,590	2,710	3,250	3,250	3,250
Notes payable to banks	—	40,000	40,000	40,000	—
8% Supplier loan due 1985	2,412	—	—	—	—
8.5% Supply contract, 1987	14,000	14,000	14,001	—	—
Loan agreement:					
"A" Tranche 12.875%, 1991	—	7,300	14,600	14,600	14,600
"B" Tranche 13% due 1991	—	—	—	10,000	20,000
Long-term leases:					
Revenue bond lease obligations at 6.75% to 9.25% due 2005	1,470	505	535	570	610
Other lease obligations due 1991	497	563	349	312	310
11% Notes of W-P Coal Company due 1993	1,864	1,864	1,864	1,864	1,864
14% Notes of Ft. Duquesne Coal Company due 1992	697	798	914	1,046	1,198
Amount reclassified due to filing a petition for reorganization under Chapter 11	(39,495)	—	—	—	—
Total	5,698	76,818	84,607	80,752	50,960

* Represents debt scheduled for payment in the indicated years prior to the corporation's filing a petition for reorganization under Chapter 11 of the bankruptcy laws except for the amount reclassified for 1985.

million in current assets. The USW found the creditor's offer unacceptable, because it provided too little help and because it would have given them a major claim on W-P's assets. The impasse in negotiations continued until April 16, 1985, when Wheeling-Pittsburgh filed for Chapter 11 bankruptcy.

The repercussions of W-P's bankruptcy and the implications for the steel industry, as a whole, are far-reaching. Foremost is the issue of wage renegotiation. After declaring bankruptcy, W-P made it clear that it would not continue to honor previous labor agreements, and the company entered into negotiations with the union which culminated in the union's rejection of W-P's proposed 30% wage and benefit cut. Finally, the bankruptcy court was asked to rule on the wage issue. If the court ruled in W-P's favor, the company's lower wage rates coupled with court protection from its creditors would place W-P in an excellent competitive position when it emerged from Chapter 11. Moreover, the ruling might set a downward trend in steel industry wage rates, thus making the domestic steel industry more competitive with foreign producers. Ultimately, the court ruled in W-P's favor.

After the ruling, W-P proposed to cut labor costs by 18%, or to about $17.50 an hour on the average. Previously, the USW had stated that if the average hourly wage were set lower than $18.50, the union would strike. Additionally, W-P indicated that it would not be able to make a $5 million pension fund payment due at the end of July 1985. For all practical purposes, this would end the health and life insurance benefits of W-P workers and place those pensioned in a precarious position. On July 21, 1985, the steel industry experienced its first major strike in twenty-six years. Eight thousand three hundred W-P employees walked off their jobs.[1]

THE STEEL INDUSTRY

The steel industry is confronted with a host of problems which have caused several companies in the industry to contemplate bankruptcy. Included in this list are high labor costs, weak prices, and increasing foreign competition. Part of the problem is the product. Demand for steel is derived demand, meaning that its demand is contingent upon the demand for products in which it is used. Manufacturers of cars, bridges, ships, machine tools, and appliances are end-use buyers of steel. Since they are durable goods, purchases of these products can be postponed by consumers during economic downturns. Thus, steel demand is highly sensitive to inventory cycles, business cycle changes, the long-term investment outlook, and the rate of overall economic growth.[2]

Price Elasticity

The cost of steel usually represents only a small percentage of the cost of the end-use products in which it is used. However, steel producers are faced with extremely price-elastic demand because of the homogeneity of the product and the lack of brand name differences. Thus far, steel producers have not differentiated their products effectively. To maintain market share and compete, steel producers must discount their prices when the demand for steel declines or competition intensifies. This practice has caused a steady decrease in steel prices over the past several years (see Exhibit C35.12). The

EXHIBIT C35.12   COMPOSITE REAL PRICES RECEIVED BY U.S. PRODUCERS

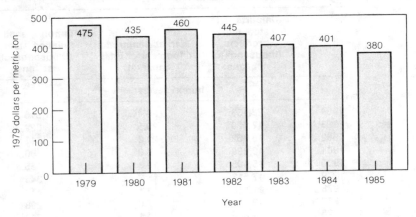

problem is worsened by foreign steel producers who engage in "dumping," or selling steel products in the U.S. at prices below production costs.

Imports

Recently, the steel industry has experienced a surge in imports which, in 1984, claimed 26.4% of the U.S. domestic steel market (see Exhibits C35.13 and C35.14). Government-imposed restrictions have attempted to help the domestic industry. For example, during 1964 to 1974 Voluntary Restraint Agreements between the U.S. and foreign steel–producing nations were in force. It was hoped that U.S. steel companies would use this period of protection to modernize their facilities. Yet, the industry's capital outlays fell below the 1968 level for each of the following six years, while wages and dividend payments rose considerably.[3]

In 1983 and 1984, when steel imports were approaching their highest levels of U.S. market share, many U.S. firms reacted by filing lawsuits charging foreign producers with dumping. President Reagan responded by announcing a new voluntary agreement in October 1984, which was designed to hold steel imports to a little over 20% of U.S. market share until 1989. As of October 1985, Voluntary Restraint Agreements had been reached with fourteen nations. The result of President Reagan's actions became visible in July 1985, when imports declined sharply. From June to July, steel imports fell from 2.3 million tons to 1.5 million tons.[4]

Capacity

Domestic steel production capacity experienced almost no growth between 1960 and 1980. Furthermore, the capacity of U.S. steel producers has been cut drastically since 1980 in an effort to bring it in line with demand. In 1980, domestic steel production capacity was 154 million tons; it was 134 million tons in 1984; and it is expected to fall to 120 million tons by 1987. Even though U.S. producers have reduced their capacity, they

EXHIBIT C35.13   U.S. STEEL INDUSTRY IMPORTS

	Imports, all steel mill products (thousands of net tons)	Market penetration (percent of total market)	Imports, semi-finished steel* (thousands of net tons)
	Import levels		
1984	26,163	26.4%	1,516
1983	17,070	20.5	822
1982	16,662	21.8	717
1981	19,898	18.9	790
1980	15,495	16.3	155
1979	17,518	15.2	345
1978	21,135	18.1	414
1977	19,307	17.8	298
1976	14,285	14.1	240
1975	12,012	13.5	243
	Percent increase (decrease)		
1983–84	53.3%		84.4%
1982–83	2.4		14.6
1981–82	(16.3)		(9.2)
1980–81	28.4		409.7
1979–80	(11.5)		(55.1)
1978–79	(17.1)		(16.7)
1977–78	9.5		38.9
1976–77	35.2		24.2
1975–76	18.9		(1.2)

* Examples of semifinished steel are ingots, billets, and slabs.
Source: American Iron and Steel Institute (AISI) Annual Statistical Report—1984.

continue to use only a portion of that capacity. Exhibit C35.15 shows that the capacity utilization problem is one that is becoming more severe.

Cost Control

Cost control is another major concern of domestic steel producers. Labor and energy costs represent a large portion of total costs, and they have become the target of manufacturers' cost reduction efforts. Since a large part of their labor force is unionized, steel producers must bargain with the United Steel Workers' Union (USW) to set wage and benefit rates for labor contracts. Labor costs in the steel industry exceeded the manufacturing sector average by more than 90% in 1982. Additionally, although energy consumption per ton of steel produced decreased by 2% between 1973 and 1981 for U.S. firms, Japanese firms cut their energy consumption per ton by 11% during this time.[5]

EXHIBIT C35.14 U.S. STEEL INDUSTRY IMPORTS BY COUNTRIES OF ORIGIN

	1984	1983	1982	1981	1980
Import volume (thousands of net tons)					
Canada	3,167	2,379	1,844	2,899	2,370
Latin America	3,132	2,415	974	782	630
Europe	9,963	5,310	6,775	8,077	4,744
Asia & Africa	9,685	6,761	6,939	8,011	7,620
Australia & Oceania	216	206	130	129	132
Total imports of steel mill products	26,163	17,070	16,662	19,898	15,495
Percent of total imports					
Canada	12.1%	13.9%	11.1%	14.6%	15.3%
Latin America	12.0	14.2	5.8	3.9	4.1
Europe	38.1	31.1	40.7	40.6	30.6
Asia & Africa	37.0	39.6	41.6	40.3	49.2
Australia & Oceania	0.8	1.2	0.8	0.6	0.8
Total imports of steel mill products	100.0%	100.0%	100.0%	100.0%	100.0%
U.S. market penetration					
Canada	3.2%	2.9%	2.4%	2.7%	2.5%
Latin America	3.2	2.9	1.3	0.8	0.7
Europe	10.1	6.4	8.9	7.7	5.0
Asia & Africa	9.8	8.1	9.1	7.6	8.0
Australia & Oceania	0.2	0.2	0.2	0.1	0.1
Total imports of steel mill products	26.4%	20.5%	21.8%	18.9%	16.3%

Source: AISI Annual Statistical Report—1984.

In 1982, the aggregate net loss of the six largest domestic steel producers reached over 3 billion dollars, and only slight improvements have been made since 1982 (see Exhibit C35.16). These firms experienced losses in the first quarter of 1985 which amounted to an average of $17 per ton. In 1984, their average loss was $6 per ton. Exhibits C35.17 through C35.20 provide additional information about the global steel industry.

Due to the depressed condition of the steel industry, some companies are selling their most profitable units to improve their financial position. Other firms are seeking mergers with foreign steel producers. In April 1984, an agreement was reached between Nippon KoKan (NKK), Japan's second largest steel producer, and National Steel, the U.S.'s fourth largest producer. NKK bought 50% of National, and it plans to spend $1 billion to modernize National's facilities. The improvement project is expected to cut National's

EXHIBIT C35.15 RAW STEEL CAPACITY VS. PRODUCTION

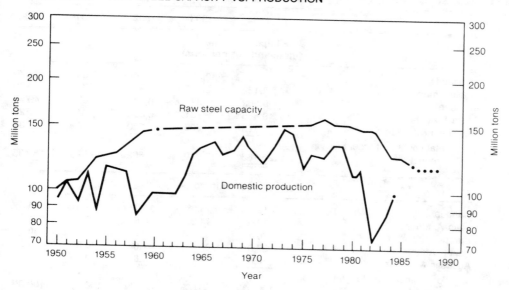

EXHIBIT C35.16 AGGREGATE NET PROFITS OF THE SIX LARGEST DOMESTIC PRODUCERS
(Billions of Dollars)

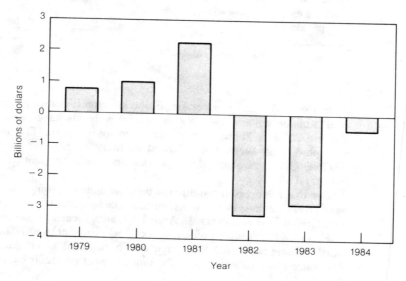

EXHIBIT C35.17   MARKET SHARE BY FIRM

	1950			1960			1970			1981		
	A	B	C	A	B	C	A	B	C	A	B	C
U.S. Steel	22.6	28.4	28.0	18.7	26.3	25.2	21.0	23.1	20.2	16.6	19.1	15.5
Bethlehem	10.9	13.7	13.5	11.4	16.0	15.3	13.8	15.2	13.2	11.6	13.3	10.9
Republic	6.4	8.0	7.9	5.4	7.6	7.3	6.7	7.4	6.4	6.5	7.5	6.1
J&L	6.8	8.5	8.4	7.0	9.8	9.4	8.4	9.3	8.1	7.6	8.7	7.1
Youngstown } merged 1978												
National } merged	4.0	5.0	5.0	5.3	7.5	7.1	7.3	8.0	7.0	6.6	7.6	6.2
Granite City } 1971												
Armco	3.0	3.8	3.7	5.0	7.0	6.7	5.4	5.9	5.2	5.8	6.7	5.4
Inland	3.3	4.1	4.1	5.1	7.2	6.9	4.7	5.2	4.5	5.8	6.7	5.4
Wheeling } merged												
Pittsburgh } 1968	3.3	2.9	2.9	2.6	3.7	3.5	2.9	3.2	2.8	2.1	2.4	2.0
Total of above	60.3	74.5	73.5	60.5	85.1	81.4	70.2	77.3	67.4	67.6	72.0	58.6
Other domestic	20.3	25.5	25.2	10.6	14.9	14.3	20.6	22.7	19.8	24.4	28.0	22.8

Note: A = Millions of net tons
B = Percent of domestic shipments
C = Percent of domestic and imported shipments

Source: Barnett and Schorsch, Steel: Upheaval in a Basic Industry, Cambridge, Mass., Ballinger, 1983.

EXHIBIT C35.18   U.S. STEEL INDUSTRY
INTERNATIONAL COMPARATIVE COST STRUCTURE
(Costs per Metric Ton—at Actual Operating Rates)

	U.S.	Japan	W.Germany	U.K.*	France
1980					
Revenue	$507.24	$426.66	$506.96	$ 514.23	$501.61
Labor	$175.11	$ 93.88	$164.56	$ 452.81	$172.87
Raw materials	292.12	259.61	289.68	456.63	299.96
Financial costs	39.93	82.85	63.04	159.57	105.53
Total costs/ton	$507.16	$436.33	$517.28	$1,069.02	$578.36
Exogenous cost factor				−342.70	
				$ 726.32	
Pretax profit/ton	$ 0.08	$ 26.32	($ 10.33)	($ 212.09)	($ 76.74)
1981					
Revenue	$574.28	$496.52	$440.60	$ 456.59	$433.64
Labor	$185.19	$108.11	$145.10	$ 144.76	$143.14
Raw materials	320.58	287.85	284.26	384.86	296.39
Financial costs	39.76	93.32	57.28	77.06	90.60
Total costs/ton	$545.52	$489.28	$486.63	$ 606.68	$530.13
Pretax profit/ton	$ 28.75	$ 7.24	($ 46.03)	($ 150.10)	($ 96.49)
1982					
Revenue	$581.17	$453.79	$463.15	$ 453.11	$447.73
Labor	$214.54	$ 96.99	$162.08	$ 134.94	$146.08
Raw materials	359.18	279.30	289.84	342.07	293.42
Financial costs	65.34	84.04	66.03	76.32	94.33
Total costs/ton	$639.06	$460.33	$517.95	$ 553.32	$533.83
Pretax profit/ton	($ 57.89)	($ 6.54)	($ 54.80)	($ 100.21)	($ 86.10)

operating costs by about $44 million per year. Mergers and joint ventures are two of the
most attractive alternatives for domestic steel producers to acquire badly needed capital
for improvements, since many of them are highly leveraged. Additionally, mergers and
joint ventures give foreign firms easier access to the U.S. market.

A JOINT VENTURE

After two unsuccessful attempts to form joint ventures, in February 1984 W-P and
Nisshin Steel Corporation of Japan reached an agreement. W-P registered to offer 1
million shares of common stock at $35 per share, and Nisshin Steel agreed to purchase
500,000 shares under the preemptive rights offering. Allen E. Paulson, chairman and
president of Gulfstream Aerospace Corporation, and a member of W-P's board, agreed

EXHIBIT C35.18   (*CONTINUED*)

	U.S.	Japan	W.Germany	U.K.*	France
			1983		
Revenue	$533.37	$467.43	$436.64	$ 413.48	$419.49
Labor	$173.08	$101.27	$152.94	$ 93.96	$156.80
Raw materials	345.44	274.54	268.17	290.01	257.52
Financial costs	64.62	96.08	60.86	53.40	91.47
Total costs/ton	$583.14	$471.89	$481.97	$ 437.36	$505.78
Pretax profit/ton	($ 49.77)	($ 4.47)	($ 45.33)	($ 23.89)	($ 86.29)
			1984		
Revenue	$542.56	$450.30	$405.02	$ 378.95	$387.79
Labor	$149.10	$ 91.73	$117.18	$ 81.43	$128.20
Raw materials	347.00	256.84	245.17	262.86	235.42
Financial costs	66.85	88.71	46.63	46.21	72.77
Total costs/ton	$562.95	$437.28	$408.98	$ 390.51	$436.39
Pretax profit/ton	($ 20.39)	$ 13.02	($ 3.95)	($ 11.56)	($ 48.61)
			1985 (Jan.–June average)		
Revenue	$523.90	$425.43	$387.11	$ 359.20	$368.03
Labor	$139.10	$ 83.05	$ 95.33	$ 64.66	$105.44
Raw materials	329.98	242.50	231.57	252.08	224.59
Financial costs	64.85	82.34	39.17	36.33	57.25
Total costs/ton	$533.93	$407.89	$366.07	$ 353.07	$387.38
Pretax profit/ton	($ 10.03)	$ 17.54	$ 21.04	$ 6.14	($ 19.36)

* Strike year in the U.K.
Source: World Steel Dynamics (WSD) Price/Cost Monitor Report #7.

to purchase the remaining 500,000 shares. This transaction increased Paulson's holdings in W-P from 31.7% to 35.3% and gave Nisshin a 10% interest in the company. As part of the joint venture agreement, W-P invested approximately $10 million in the Japanese steel maker's stock. As a result of this agreement, a $40 million production line will be constructed at one of W-P's existing plants in the Ohio River Valley. The line is expected to be operating by 1986 and will produce rust-resistant galvanized steel for the auto industry. The production of rust-resistant steel is one of the few markets that is growing in the industry.[6]

MODERNIZATION PROGRAM

Over the last six years, W-P has been heavily involved in a modernization program that will enable the firm to satisfy its customers' demands for better quality and service, while remaining competitive with foreign and domestic steel producers. Between 1979 and 1983, W-P spent approximately $536 million modernizing its facilities. During this

EXHIBIT C35.19   U.S. STEEL INDUSTRY
INTERNATIONAL COMPARATIVE UNIT LABOR COSTS, 1980–1985
(At Actual Operating Rates)

	Man-hours per ton shipped	× Labor cost per hour =	Unit labor cost (Labor cost per ton shipped)
U.S.			
1980	9.17	$19.06	$174.78
1981	8.90	20.78	184.94
1982	8.65	24.67	213.40
1983	7.28	23.70	172.54
1984	6.67	22.36	149.14
1985 (Jan.–June)	6.02	23.10	139.06
Japan			
1980	9.15	$10.25	$ 93.79
1981	9.36	11.55	108.11
1982	8.90	10.90	97.01
1983	8.47	11.96	101.30
1984	7.71	11.89	91.67
1985 (Jan.–June)	7.51	11.06	83.06
UK			
1980	46.02	$ 9.96	$458.36
1981	15.06	9.57	144.12
1982	14.86	9.14	135.82
1983	11.87	7.92	94.01
1984	11.68	6.98	81.53
1985 (Jan.–June)	10.49	6.18	64.83
W.Germany			
1980	11.04	$14.93	$164.83
1981	11.00	13.19	145.09
1982	12.26	13.28	162.81
1983	12.05	12.71	153.16
1984	10.21	11.49	117.31
1985 (Jan.–June)	9.25	10.30	95.28
France			
1980	11.22	$15.39	$172.68
1981	11.31	12.66	143.19
1982	12.04	12.15	146.29
1983	12.14	12.87	156.24
1984	11.59	11.01	127.61
1985 (Jan.–June)	10.86	9.71	105.45

Source: WSD Price/Cost Monitor Report #7.

EXHIBIT C35.20 U.S. STEEL INDUSTRY
WORLD PRODUCTION AND GROSS CAPACITY UTILIZATION
(Percent of Capacity)

	U.S.	Japan	EEC	Developing world	Communist world
1973	97.0	88.4	85.8	65.7	89.7
1974	94.4	84.9	87.4	68.0	88.0
1975	76.8	73.1	63.5	68.4	88.5
1976	80.7	73.0	68.4	71.8	88.3
1977	79.0	64.9	62.1	70.2	87.2
1978	86.9	65.0	65.6	73.9	90.2
1979	87.9	71.5	69.2	78.1	87.4
1980	72.8	70.1	64.1	79.1	85.3
1981	77.5	63.9	63.7	72.5	81.1
1982	48.5	63.0	56.8	70.1	80.0
1983	55.3	61.6	59.0	67.6	83.1
Forecast:					
1984	70.0	66.3	66.3	67.1	83.9
1985	80.8	70.8	73.2	68.5	85.3
1986	91.3	79.7	81.8	68.2	92.2
1987	71.8	78.7	76.9	64.9	89.2
1990	78.3	86.0	75.5	70.5	90.0

Source: World Steel Dynamics, *The Steel Strategist #10,* Paine Webber, Inc., December 1984.

time, the company's spending to enhance production facilities grew more than 5 times faster than the domestic industry average and more than 4 times faster than the average for Japanese firms. The construction of a new railroad rail mill utilizing the most advanced technology available in the world at a cost of $105 million consumed the lion's share of the firm's investment capital. Another component of the modernization plan was the construction of a new two-strand continuous slab caster and a new five-strand continuous bloom caster at a cost of $175 million.

These two casters employ the most advanced technology for quality control available in the world. The technology was obtained from Japan and Germany, and it utilizes automated and computerized equipment that will enable W-P to increase quality, expand production, conserve energy, and decrease operating costs. Mitsubishi financed the project, and the equipment was supplied by Hitachi Corporation of Japan and Mannesmann Demag AG of West Germany. Technical assistance and engineering for the slab caster was provided by the Nippon Steel Corporation. Technical assistance for the bloom caster was provided by August Thyssen-Hutte AG of West Germany.[7]

Additionally, as a part of their modernization program, W-P spent $15.7 million upgrading its 80-inch hot strip mill at its Steubenville plant. This expenditure was necessary for W-P to comply with Environmental Protection Agency (EPA) requirements. Since 1979, W-P has invested over $100 million to comply with other EPA regulations dealing with air and water quality control measures, and the company anticipates the promulgation of additional environmental regulations that will result in significant increases in its overall capital and operating expenditures.

THE FUTURE

On September 19, 1985, the *Wall Street Journal* reported that Dennis Carney was expected to resign on September 20 to pave the way for a strike settlement. Although it was suggested that Carney might change his mind, they said it "is extremely unlikely, chiefly because of the severance guarantee. The United Steel Workers union, whose protests in part contributed to Mr. Carney's anticipated resignation, have informally agreed to resume bargaining in earnest if Mr. Carney departs."[8]

According to Jerry Flint, the Steel Industry could be on the verge of an amazing recovery. Says he,

It's easy to be negative about steel. Turnarounds that never came. Write-offs of $4.4 billion in assets and $7 billion in losses in four years. The six largest companies lost $325 million in the fourth quarter alone and this is in a strong economy. For the price of a couple TV stations, you could buy the great Bethlehem Steel Co. with its $5 billion in sales and 45,000 employees. . . .

Drop steel imports 3 million tons to 4 million tons. Let the capital goods business improve, not a boom, just a normal upswing, enough to add another couple million tons to steel sales. Let the United Steelworkers union cooperate to cut labor costs in the bargaining this spring. You know what happens? The bloodletting in the steel industry ends, and the profits begin to flow, this year. . . .

First, ask about productivity. This may be the untold miracle of American industry. "We're producing steel at fewer man-hours per ton in America than anybody else in the world now," Says Lynn Williams, president of the United Steelworkers' of America. "We have 4.6 man-hours in a ton, and by the end of this year it will be 4," says David Roderick, chairman of U.S. Steel. At Bethlehem productivity last year improved 5% from 1984, which was improved 12% from 1983, which was improved 15% from 1982. . . .

Quality is another major plus. It's no secret that U.S. steel wasn't matching up. A few years ago the reject rate on Japanese steel was 1% to 1.5%, while American-made metal was running 5% to 10%, says George Ferris, who once headed Ford Motor Co.'s steel operations and now runs Wheeling-Pittsburgh Steel. In an auto plant example, a bad coil means taking down the press for half an hour to change it, and losing production of 300 to 450 stampings. Today the American Steelmakers say they are as good as anybody. "We're all [U.S. and Japan] around a 2% reject rate," says Ferris. "Yes, we've seen the quality of steel improve," says Roger Smith, chairman of General Motors. But he asks for even better quality, plus better steels, lighter, rustproof, more dent-resistant. . . .

Right now the biggest "if" in the turnaround is the union question. While U.S. productivity is high, wages and benefits are even higher—$17.18 an hour pay and $24.84 with benefits at Bethlehem. One product study on hot-rolled band, for example, showed 3.6 man-hours per ton in the U.S. to 3.4 in Japan, 6.9 in Brazil, 4.6 in Britain and 5.5 in Korea. But the $20-plus labor cost meant $84 per ton for that hot-rolled against $16 for Korea and $37 for Japan.[9]

REFERENCES

1 *Wall Street Journal*, February 5, 1985 to July 21, 1985.
2 Bossong, "Industry Perspective: The Steel Industry—Stagnation, Decay, or Recovery," *Business Economics*, July 1985.

3 Kawahito, "Relative Profitability of the U.S. and Japanese Steel Industries," *Columbia Journal of World Business,* Fall 1984.

4 *Iron Age,* October 4, 1985.

5 Kawahito, loc. cit.

6 Wheeling-Pittsburgh 1984 10K Report.

7 1983 10K Report.

8 *Wall Street Journal,* September 19, 1985.

9 *Forbes,* March 10, 1986.

THE AIRLINE INDUSTRY

Prepared by Patricia P. McDougall, Georgia State University.

Since the first scheduled passenger service of the 120-mile distance between Los Angeles and San Diego, the airline industry has undergone dramatic changes. Today, the U.S. airline industry employs more than 355,000 people, operates over 4,500 aircraft, and serves over 380 million passengers.

Tremendous growth has occurred in the industry, as evidenced in Table N1.1. Flying, once a glamorous experience, has become today's mass transportation. Since 1975, the number of available seat miles (one airline seat transported 1 mile) has increased by 80 percent, and the number of passengers has increased 85 percent. Capacity utilization has improved, with load factors rising from 53.7 percent to 61.4 percent. With the exception of a slight dip in 1982, passenger revenues have steadily increased.

Net operating profit has followed a more erratic course, with the 1978 record profits exceeding $1 billion in sharp contrast to the red ink that flowed in the 1981 to 1983 time period. The industry returned to profitability in 1984, and earned profits in excess of $860 million in 1985.

This industry note will concentrate on domestic operations of passenger airlines, and as such, will not focus on air cargo or international operations. International operations are subject to regulation by both the U.S. and foreign governments, thus adding a degree of complexity beyond the scope of this discussion. Although a secondary source of revenue for the scheduled passenger airline, air cargo remains a somewhat unique operation served by a small group of specialized carriers.

THE COMPETITORS

Airlines are classified into three principal groups—majors, nationals, and regionals. The majors (sometimes referred to as trunks) have annual revenues exceeding $1 billion.

TABLE N1.1 1975–1985 HIGHLIGHTS
U.S. SCHEDULED AIRLINES

	1975	1976	1977	1978	1979
Traffic—scheduled service					
Revenue passengers enplaned (000)	$ 205,062	$ 223,318	$ 240,326	$ 274,719	$ 316,863
Revenue passenger miles (000)	162,810,057	178,988,026	193,218,819	226,781,368	262,023,375
Available seat miles (000)	303,006,243	322,821,649	345,565,901	368,750,530	416,126,429
Revenue passenger load factor (%)	53.7	55.4	55.9	61.5	63.0
Passenger revenue ($000)	12,353,501	14,265,947	16,273,355	18,806,247	22,791,390
Freight and express revenue ($000)	1,309,779	1,497,123	1,718,529	1,986,820	2,211,321
Mail revenue ($000)	303,022	320,121	390,762	386,639	452,021
Charter revenue ($000)	489,856	572,580	644,381	578,285	520,916
Total operating revenues ($000)	15,355,921	17,501,215	19,924,800	22,883,955	27,226,665
Total operating expenses ($000)	15,228,042	16,779,282	19,016,760	21,519,092	27,026,610
Operating profit ($000)	127,879	721,933	908,040	1,364,863	199,055
Interest expense ($000)	402,041	371,634	373,206	538,642	618,446
Net profit ($000)	(84,204)	563,354	752,536	1,196,537	346,845
Revenue per passenger mile (c)	7.6	8.0	8.4	8.3	8.7
Rate of return on investment (%)	3.1	8.5	10.2	6.5	6.5
Operating profit margin (%)	0.8	4.1	4.6	6.0	0.7
Net profit margin (%)	(.5)	3.2	3.8	5.2	1.3
Employees	289,926	303,006	308,068	329,303	340,696

Source: Air Transport Association of America, Washington, DC.

Nationals are those carriers with annual revenues between $75 million and $1 billion. Regional airlines' revenues are less than $75 million.

The term "national" is somewhat misleading, as the operating territory of these airlines is normally regional. The nationals typically operate shorter segments and may serve smaller cities than the majors do. Aloha, Braniff, and Southwest are examples of national carriers.

Selected 1985 statistics are provided in Table N1.2 on the top 12 airlines in operating revenues (airlines with more than a billion dollars in revenues).

The intense competition which has occurred since deregulation has contributed to the erratic performance of several major carriers. Table N1.3 compares the net operating profit or loss for 11 major carriers between 1985, 1986, and the first quarter of 1987.

THE PRE-DEREGULATION ERA

Government action has impacted the structure of the industry since its earliest days. In the industry's infant days, postal service air mail subsidies served to promote development. In the 40 years between 1938 and 1978, the Civil Aeronautics Board (CAB) was given broad power in regulating entry, exit, subsidy allocation, route structure, pricing,

	1980	1981	1982	1983	1984	1985
$	296,903	$ 285,976	$ 294,102	$ 318,638	$ 344,683	$ 380,024
	255,192,114	248,887,801	259,643,870	281,829,148	305,115,855	335,897,966
	432,535,103	424,897,230	440,119,206	464,537,979	515,323,339	546,994,334
	59.0	58.6	59.0	60.7	59.2	61.4
	28,048,689	30,722,629	30,549,719	32,744,618	36,939,345	39,235,809
	2,431,926	2,596,850	2,437,703	2,592,567	2,859,419	2,680,715
	610,996	653,996	688,675	653,129	712,070	889,575
	1,160,524	1,175,154	1,085,537	1,075,428	1,112,050	1,279,812
	33,727,806	36,662,555	36,407,635	38,953,672	43,825,047	46,664,414
	33,949,421	37,117,325	37,141,070	38,643,262	41,673,536	45,238,150
	(221,615)	(454,770)	(733,435)	310,410	2,151,511	1,426,264
	967,719	1,209,461	1,384,084	1,482,352	1,540,377	1,588,306
	17,414	(300,826)	(915,814)	(188,051)	824,668	862,715
	11.0	12.3	11.8	11.6	12.1	11.7
	5.3	4.7	2.1	6.0	9.9	9.8
	(0.7)	(1.2)	(2.0)	8.0	4.9	3.1
	1.3	(0.8)	(2.5)	(0.5)	(1.9)	1.8
	340,696	360,517	330,495	328,648	345,079	355,113

TABLE N1.2   TOP 12 AIRLINES IN 1985 IN OPERATING REVENUES

Airline	Total operating revenues (000)	Passengers (000)	Break-even*	Net profit (loss) ($000)
American	$5,859,334	41,229	47.8	$322,640
United	4,920,132	38,101	56.5	(88,223)
Eastern	4,815,070	41,766	56.8	6,310
Delta	4,738,168	39,805	44.9	156,775
Transworld	3,860,695	20,871	60.0	(193,092)
Pan American	3,156,988	13,040	54.4	40,474
Northwest	2,650,008	14,538	51.5	72,961
U.S. Air	1,749,126	19,278	47.7	109,850
Republic	1,734,397	17,442	NA†	177,006
Continental	1,731,054	16,143	NA	64,280
Piedmont	1,366,641	18,053	46.6	66,710
Western	1,306,546	11,908	51.4	67,134

* Percent of capacity that must be sold to cover all expenses.
† NA—not available.
Source: Air Transport 1986: The Annual Report of The U.S. Scheduled Airline Industry.

TABLE N1.3 MAJOR CARRIER PERFORMANCE

Carrier	Net profit (loss) (000)		
	1985	**1986**	**1987—1st Quarter**
American	$ 322,640	$ 529	$ 25,210
Continental	64,280	(13,626)	(97,835)
Delta	156,775	(6,375)	27,076
Eastern	6,310	(110,626)	2,098
Northwest	72,961	(16,455)	(25,981)
Pan American	40,474	(125,274)	(87,690)
Piedmont	66,710	(6,918)	5,662
TWA	(193,092)	(169,363)	(54,813)
United	(88,223)	(107,284)	(35,120)
U.S. Air	109,850	(10,360)	18,701
Western	67,134	10,883	(15,795)

Source: U.S. Department of Transportation.

mergers and acquisitions, and quality of service. Unlike other regulatory agencies such as the Interstate Commerce Commission, the CAB had the explicit responsibility not only for the regulation of the air transport industry, but also for its promotion and development. The CAB was not given responsibility for safety, as this was and still is the province of the Federal Aviation Administration (FAA) formed in 1958. Since the formation of the Department of Transportation (DOT) in 1966, the FAA has been housed within the DOT.

Under regulation, airlines operating in interstate markets were required to obtain a certificate from the CAB that they had been found "fit, willing, and able" to provide air transportation. In its 40 years of regulation, the board did not approve a single one of scores of proposals to form new carriers to serve major markets. The only significant entry into scheduled service came when the board certified the local service carriers after World War II. Although several local service airlines were later permitted to serve major markets, they initially were granted certificates only to replace the trunks in providing subsidized service to smaller communities.

During regulation, a carrier's route map was among its most valuable assets. Route competition was tightly controlled by the CAB through issuance of route certificates. Some routes were highly competitive, while others were protected and became the virtual property of one or two carriers. In assigning routes, the CAB often sought to maintain the status quo of the industry. A financially weak carrier was often awarded a profitable route. This type of action maintained competition and avoided bankruptcies. When an airline was forced to service unprofitable routes, the CAB often assigned a more profitable route as well.

Mergers were also used to maintain status quo in the industry and to avoid disruption in passenger services. Financially weak carriers were often allowed to merge in order to avoid bankruptcy.

Since deregulation virtually removed competition on pricing and routes, the various carriers competed principally on scheduling convenience and service.

DEREGULATION

Limited competition and the refusal of the board to permit new carriers into the industry provoked complaints from entrepreneurs who wanted to enter the industry, and from critics who argued that the industry had developed into an oligopoly that charged consumers higher prices than were necessary and offered few price or service options. Proponents of deregulation cited the lower fares of smaller, unregulated intrastate operators such as Southwest Airlines operating in Texas and Air California and Pacific Southwest Airlines operating in California.

In light of the protected environment to which carriers had become accustomed, it was not surprising that the Airline Deregulation Act of 1978 transformed the industry. The act removed almost all market entry barriers and price controls. However, the government did retain control of safety and controlled air traffic through the FAA.

With deregulation new airlines entered the industry, and with the aid of a deep recession, they recruited experienced airline personnel and purchased aircraft at bargain prices. Unencumbered by union wage contracts, the new entrants operated on a lower cost basis, and in turn were able to cut fares below those of the majors. A major shakeup of the industry followed.

COSTS

Labor

As shown in Table N1.4, labor represents the single largest expense. During regulation, wage increases were typically passed on to the consumer in fare increases. Following deregulation, the new entrants operated with significantly lower wage costs. This disparate situation was created by a number of conditions. The new entrants entered the industry at a time when there was a surplus of airline personnel, the new entrants were unencumbered with union wage contracts, and their employees had no seniority. The starting pay of an airline pilot at a new airline was about $30,000, whereas the average union pilot's wage was about $71,000 per year. New entrant People Express was able to operate on a cost basis of 5.3 cents per seat mile, compared to an 11 cents average for major carriers.

Airlines with comparatively low operating costs became the industry's price leaders, forcing the higher cost carriers to lower costs so they could reduce prices. Western Airlines and Pan American both received 10 percent wage cuts from its employees, with workers receiving company stock in exchange. Some airlines drastically cut their work

TABLE N1.4   PRINCIPAL ELEMENTS OF AIRLINE OPERATING EXPENSES

	Percent of total operating expense	
	1982	1983
Labor	35.8	36.6
Fuel	27.8	25.0
Traffic commissions	6.2	6.9

forces and sought higher productivity. For example, United pilots increased their flying time 15 percent. More extreme measures occurred at some airlines. With Continental's bankruptcy in 1983, Chairman Lorenzo reduced pilots' salaries of $89,000 to $43,000, and flight attendants' salaries dropped from $29,000 to $15,000.

As airline executives attempted to rachet down wages, the controversial two-tier wage system developed. The economic recovery and resultant expansion in the industry changed a labor surplus into a tight labor market, and by the mid-1980s, the two-tier systems began to be modified or eliminated. New entrants were forced to increase wages to retain their personnel. Industry giants, as well, found themselves subject to wage competition. A 29-day strike by United pilots in 1985 prevented the carrier from achieving its objective of permanent lower wages. American, finding its pilot salary scales lagged United, hastened to match United. American abandoned its two-tier wage scale for mechanics and proposed to abandon it for flight attendants.

Fuel

Fuel costs represent the second most significant cost to the carrier. Carriers have attempted to reduce fuel costs through the purchase of more fuel-efficient aircraft, speed reduction, and weight reduction. Lighter seats and carpets, the elimination of 125 to 450 pounds of exterior paint, a change from glass to plastic mini-bottles, and carrying a reduced quantity of drinking water have all contributed to weight reduction. Even small reductions in speed bring large fuel savings. For example, a reduction of 14 miles per hour on a DC-8 in a flight from Chicago to Los Angeles saves 164 gallons of fuel, but adds only 4 minutes of flight time.

Following deregulation, fuel costs skyrocketed. The average price per gallon in 1978 was $.392; in 1979 it rose to $.578. It continued to rise in 1980 to $.894, and by 1981 was $1.042. For some airlines, fuel costs escalated to more than one-third of operating expenses. The reaction of some major carriers of purchasing more fuel-efficient aircraft and selling off older, less fuel-efficient aircraft, created a glut of airplanes. New entrants purchased these aircraft at fire sale prices and were able to offset their higher fuel costs with lower labor costs. People Express purchased 17 737s for only $62 million. That same amount would have purchased only 4 new 737s.

The drop in fuel costs since the early 1980s and the fuel conservation measures have benefited the industry. From June 1985 to June 1986, aviation fuel costs plummeted 35 percent to $.52 a gallon—one half the 1981 cost. Each one-cent change in the price of jet fuel affects operating costs by about $100 million.

BARRIERS TO ENTRY

Hub and Spoke System

In the hub and spoke system an airline uses connecting flights to and from smaller "spoke" cities to generate traffic for flights from hubs in larger cities. This ability to feed passengers from one flight to another has allowed large airlines to dominate traffic at major airports, reaping economies of scale and enormous market clout. For example, U.S. Air, Inc. in Pittsburgh and TWA in St. Louis control more than 80 percent of the flow through these hubs.

The spoke flights may be flown by the carrier's own planes, or increasingly, major carriers are linking with smaller, commuter lines to generate traffic for flights from hubs in larger cities. The advantages of the system are numerous: a large number of points are connected without having to schedule individual flights between them; lightly traveled point-to-point segments are avoided; the passenger is retained in the system for a longer distance without interlining; and the carrier has a centralized location for maintenance, control, and crew base.

Facilities

Sufficient facilities (air traffic control personnel and airports) have not kept pace with the increased air traffic following deregulation. The 1981 Professional Air Traffic Controllers Organization (PATCO) strike added pressure to the system. New entrants and airlines wishing to expand often find that established carriers already control terminal facilities such as ticket counters and gates at congested airports. Landing slots may be allocated by the FAA.

Antitrust immunity has been granted to established airlines for meetings to allocate slots and gates. With demand exceeding supply, agreements have been difficult to reach, and their allocations have not pleased new entrants and small commuters. No easy solution is seen in the short term, as additional airports and massive additions to the air traffic control system require a long lead time.

Computer Reservation Systems

The unfairness of computer reservation systems (CRSs) have long been argued by the small carriers. These systems handle approximately 90 percent of flights booked by travel agents. The systems are available to all carriers for a fee. In response to charges that the systems offered unfair advantages to the host company in methods of display and ticketing, the CAB adopted antibias rules in 1984. Even so, Delta Air Lines complained to the Transportation Department that American Airlines, who owns the largest CRS, had "abused its CRS market power to the detriment of air transportation."[1] American has denied the charge.

Five CRSs are currently in operation. These are owned by American, United, TWA-Northwest, Texas Air, and Delta. American's Sabre and United's Apollo, together, account for about 70 percent of the market. The CRSs have become an important source of revenues for their owners. Some of the systems have been extended to other kinds of reservations, such as hotels and rental cars.

Frequent Flier Programs

Frequent flier programs have probably become the most widely used and successful marketing effort in the industry. These plans offer points for various totals of mileage which can then be traded for free airline tickets. The plans are designed to build carrier loyalty among customers. Since the programs were introduced in 1981, airlines have issued about 30 million memberships. Julius Maldutis, an airline analyst with Salomon Brothers, estimates that if the rewards were claimed, the potential lost revenue would amount to over $300 million for the industry. Triple award programs increase the

TABLE N1.5   FREQUENT FLIER PROGRAMS

Airline	Membership (millions)	Extra potential revenue loss* (millions)
American	6.3	$190
Continental/Eastern	3.0	170
Delta	4.0	140
Northwest	3.0	90
Pan Am	1.0	30
TWA	4.0	15
United	6.0	215
USAir/Piedmont	3.0	90
TOTAL:	30.3	940

* Includes direct losses (cost of meals, baggage handling, etc.) and potential lost ticket sales if members cashed in their miles.

Source: Salomon Brothers, Inc., estimates.

potential for lost revenue to $940 million. As seen in Table N1.5, the potential revenue lost to American, the program's innovator and largest membership, is $190 million.

Wall Street analysts, who try to predict the financial performance of the industry, contend that the airlines don't have a consistent method of accounting for the value of frequent flier rewards. One of the Financial Accounting Standards Board (FASB) proposals for measuring frequent flyer liabilities called for airlines to set aside 10 percent of their revenues to cover potential losses from the reward programs. Such an accounting change could have a devastating impact on earnings.

CODE-SHARING—NEW OPPORTUNITY FOR THE COMMUTERS AND REGIONALS

Deregulation allowed the major carriers to abandon lower-density routes they were previously required to serve, thus abandoning service to many smaller cities. This created opportunities for the commuter and regional carriers. In the first 5 years following deregulation, they increased their service from less than 175 cities to over 850 cities. Airplanes belonging to this group typically accommodate about 19 passengers, although a small percentage hold more than 30 passengers. The number of cities they serve has remained fairly constant since this time, as the majors have, for the most part, completed their route abandonments.

Recent growth for the commuters and regionals has resulted primarily from marketing agreements with major carriers. Table N1.6 lists some of the larger airlines and their partners. The commuters or regional airlines feed traffic from smaller cities into the major's hub airport, and in return the smaller airline code-shares the major's flight schedule. In code-sharing the smaller carrier's flight schedule is listed with that of the larger carrier in the commuter reservation system. The smaller carrier may also benefit from shared advertising and the handling of flights at the larger airline's gate. The larger carrier benefits by the added development of their hub operation at a minimal cost.

TABLE N1.6   MAJOR AIRLINES' CODE-SHARING AGREEMENTS
(As of March 1987)

American Airlines	Air Midwest, AVAir, Chaparral, Command Airways, Executive Air Charter, Metro Airlines, Simmons Airlines, Wings West
Continental Airlines	Air New Orleans, Britt Airways, Colgan Airways, Emerald Airlines, Gull Air, Mid Pacific Air, PBA, Presidential Airways, Rocky Mountain Airlines, Royale Airways, Trans-Colorado
Delta Air Lines	Atlantic Southeast, Business Express, Comair, Skywest
Eastern Air Lines	Air Midwest, Atlantis Airlines, Aviation Associates, Bar Harbor, Britt Airways, Metro Airlines, Precision Valley Aviation
Northwest Airlines	Big Sky Airlines, Express Airlines, Fischer Brothers, Mesaba Aviation, Simmons Airlines
Pan American	Air Atlanta, Pan Am Express (Ransome), Presidential Airways
Piedmont Aviation	Brockway Air, CCAir, Henson Aviation, Jetstream International
Trans World Airlines	Air Midwest, Piedmont, Resort Air, Resort Commuter
United Airlines	Air Wisconsin, Aspen Airways, Westair Commuter
USAir	Air Kentucky, Chautauqua Airlines, Crown Airlines, Pennsylvania Airlines, Pocono Airlines, Southern Jersey Airways, Suburban Airlines

Source: Travel Weekly.

Passengers can be carried beyond the major hub airport without the cost of providing support operations at the smaller city.

AIRLINE OLIGOPOLY—THE RECONCENTRATION OF THE INDUSTRY

The fierce competition by new entrants which followed deregulation appears to be about over as the industry returns to the conditions which brought on regulation in the first place. With more than half of the airlines operating in 1978 and two-thirds of the new entrants having failed, the industry is dominated by six megacarriers controlling 80 percent of the market, versus 73 percent in 1978. Ten airlines control 96 percent of the market. Airlines consultant Lee Howard of Airline Economics, Inc. predicts a share of more than 90 percent by 1990. Market shares of the 10 largest carriers for 1985 and 1986 are shown in Table N1.7.

Industry analysts cite the following seven major factors as contributing to this reconcentration:

- Hub and spoke development by major and national airlines
- Marketing alliances between large and regional/commuter airlines
- Control of traffic by such mechanisms as computerized reservation systems and code-sharing
- Innovative marketing plans such as bonus miles for frequent fliers
- Control of airport access gates, landing slots, ticket counters, and hangars
- Mergers and acquisitions
- Bankruptcies[2]

TABLE N1.7 CONCENTRATION AMONG CARRIERS INCREASING

1986 Rank	Company	Market share	1985 Rank	Company	Market share
1.	Texas Air System	19.6%	1.	American	13.3%
2.	United	16.4%	2.	United	12.5%
3.	American	14.1%	3.	Eastern	10.0%
4.	Delta	11.7%	4.	TWA	9.6%
5.	NWA	10.1%	5.	Delta	9.0%
6.	TWA	8.2%	6.	Pan Am	8.1%
7.	USAir	7.1%	7.	NWA	6.7%
8.	Pan Am	6.0%	8.	Continental	4.9%
9.	Southwest	2.0%	9.	People Express	3.3%
10.	America West	0.9%	10.	Republic	3.2%
	Others	3.9%		Others	19.4%

Source: Department of Transportation and S&P.

As indicated from Table N1.8, 19 of the 36 scheduled carriers operating before deregulation are no longer in operation, having been acquired, merged, or declared bankruptcy. The operating percentages of the other categories are even lower. Of the 4 former intrastate carriers, only 1 remains in operation. All 10 of the former supplementals have ceased operation. Thirty-eight of the 59 former commuters have disappeared. Of the new entrants, 84 of the 119 have fallen from the industry. The 6 all-cargo lines have been reduced to 1.

Rampant merger activity characterized the industry in the 1980s. The 22 mergers shown in Table N1.9 represent over $7 billion spent in pursuing concentration. Texas Air, which has accounted for much of the activity, has combined Continental Airlines, New York Air, Eastern, People Express, and Frontier Airlines to become the largest airline in the free world.

The increased importance of the hub and spoke system has been an impetus for merger activity, as a merger is often viewed as the cheapest and most efficient manner to

TABLE N1.8 AIRLINE ATTRITION UNDER DEREGULATION, OCTOBER 1978–DECEMBER 31, 1986

Category	Total	No longer operating	Currently operating	Percent operating
Certified prior to regulation	36	19	17	47%
Former intrastate	4	3	1	25
Former supplemental charter	10	10	0	0
Former commuters	59	38	21	36
New entrants	119	84	35	29
Former all cargo	6	5	1	17
Total	234	159	75	32%

Source: Frank A. Spencer and Frank H. Cassell, "Airline Oligopoly Reemerges from Deregulation," *Airline Pilot,* vol. 56, no. 5, 1987, p. 13.

TABLE N1.9   MERGER/ACQUISITION ACTIVITY, 1980–1987

Year	Companies	Price (millions)
1980	Pan Am–National	$ 373.7
	Republic-Airwest	38.5
1981	Texas Air–Continental (50 percent)	80.8
1985	Southwest-Muse	61.8
	People Express–Frontier	309.0
	United-Pan Am Pacific Routes	750.0
	Texas Air–Continental (19 percent)	81.1
1986	Northwest-Republic	884.0
	Texas Air–Eastern	607.5
	Trans World–Ozark	224.0
	People Express-Britt	36.0
	People Express–PBA	UNK
	Delta-Western	860.0
	Alaska–Jet America	19.8
	Texas Air–People/Frontier (September 16)*	298.0
	Texas Air–Rocky Mountain Airways	3.0
	American-AirCal (November)	225.0
	Alaska-Horizon	68.0
	USAir-PSA	400.0
1987	USAir-Piedmont	1,600.0
	Total	$7,365.2

* Note: Texas Air later reduced its offering for People Express from $138.4 million to $113.7 million, a decrease of about $25 million. A proposed $146 million merger of Frontier and United Airlines was aborted because of lack of agreement on Frontier pilot pay after absorption into United.
Source: Frank A. Spencer, "The Creeping Shadows of Re-regulation," *The Airline Quarterly.*

enter a market dominated by a competitor's hub. Delta's acquisition of Western added a valuable western hub in Salt Lake City to Delta's major hub in Atlanta.

DECLINING SERVICE, CONCERN FOR SAFETY, AND RECONCENTRATION FOSTER THE MOVE TOWARD RE-REGULATION

The American public's increasing concern with flight safety and the declining quality of service has made re-regulation at some minimum level more amenable. Complaints by passengers to the Department of Transportation, flight delays, and the bumping of passengers from overbooked flights have increased.

Reports of near midair collisions involving at least one commercial airliner jumped 48 percent in 1987. Airline pilots filed 487 reports of near collisions with the Federal Aviation Administration (FAA) in 1987, compared with 329 in 1986. Sixty-six of these were classified as critical, that is, the planes passed within 100 feet of each other.

Many pilots believe that the air traffic control system has not fully recovered from the 1981 Professional Air Traffic Controllers Organization Strike, and that the federal government has failed to provide sufficient facilities to handle the increased traffic. FAA officials dismiss the charges that the system is not back up to standards. The FAA is quick to note that despite the record number of near miss reports, the actual number of in-flight collisions dropped from 27 in 1986 to 21 in 1987.

Unprecedented fines have been levied by the FAA on American Airlines, Continental, and Eastern Air Lines for maintenance violations. To correct faulty maintenance practices which earned Eastern $9.5 million in fines in 1985, the airline increased its spending on maintenance to $500 million in 1987. Maintenance problems on aircraft may entail serious safety concerns which are not obvious to the consumer. For instance, American was fined for a leaky toilet, a problem more than merely hygienic. Water escaping to the outside of the plane formed a chunk of ice that knocked off an engine in midflight.

Calls for some form of reregulation are being heard from diverse quarters. Alfred E. Kahn, former chairman of the CAB and considered to be deregulation's granddaddy, has expressed serious concerns about anticompetitive side effects of deregulation. In a June 1987 speech, Robert Crandall, chairman and president of American Airlines, suggested that the government should allocate airport capacity. New entrants, as well, are beginning to suggest a return to regulation as they find it more and more difficult to protect themselves in the concentrating industry. Code sharing is seen by many of the commuters as a form of domination by the majors in which the commuter airline is forced to lose its independence in order to survive in an oligopoly market. Environmentalists want greater regulation in noise and particulate emissions.

Just as the industry appears to be returning to some stability, many industry analysts predict that the Department of Transportation or Congress may be forced to return the airline industry to some form of regulation.

REFERENCES

1 "Is Deregulation Working?" *Business Week*, December 22, 1986, p. 53.
2 Frank A. Spencer and Frank H. Cassell, "Airline Oligopoly Reemerges from Deregulation," *Airline Pilot*, vol. 56, no. 5, 1987, pp. 10–14.

THE COMPUTER INDUSTRY

Prepared by Faramarz Parsa, West Georgia College.

Computers seem to be everywhere today, performing every conceivable function and directly changing all aspects of the society—education, communication, health care, work, manufacturing, service, national defense, . . .—It is taking us from an industrial era to an information age, and no one can say where it will all lead.

The industry which had remained virtually unchanged since the 1950s and 1960s is coming undone. The powerful external forces—technological, economic, societal—are forcing the industry to recast from top to bottom. The job of predicting the future of computers was never more difficult than today.

The computer business, the world's newest mega-industry, has come a long way since the Univac 1, the world's first commercial computer, was introduced in the early 1950s. Computers blossomed in the 1960s and 1970s, emerging as the industry to watch. Revenues generated by the computer industry in 1987 exceeded $200 billion, well surpassing the steel and auto industries and only second to the oil companies (IBM is the second largest company after Exxon). By the end of this century computers will become the world's leading business.

The computer industry is no longer a one-product business. It is fragmenting. Twenty years ago the industry had just one basic product, the general purpose mainframe computers. Today we see numerous forms of computers—automated teller machines in banks, point-of-sales terminals at supermarkets, home computers, word processors, workstations, automated manufacturing systems—the list goes on and they all represent computer products specialization.

Because of wide range in both processing capability and price, the computer industry is usually broken into four different segments: large-, medium-, and small-scale systems, and personal computers. The following table shows the characteristics of each segment as defined by International Data Corporation (IDC).

Segment	Description	Price	User support	Industry sale—1986 (in billions)	% of Total industry	Major companies
Large-scale	Include mainframe and super computers used for general purpose and scientific application	$1 mil. and up	128 and up	$17.6	26.5	IBM, Unisys, Honeywell, ANDAHL
Medium-scale	Include mid to high end 32-bit super-minicomputers	$100,000 to $1 mil.	17–128	15	22.7	IBM, Digital, Honeywell, Hewlett-Packard, Unisys
Small-scale	Includes 16-bit minicomputers, 16- and 32-bit superminicomputers and super-microcomputers	$10,000 to $100,000	2–16	13	19	DEC, IBM, Data General, Hewlett-Packard, Tandy, T.I., WANG, NCR, Unisys
Micro-Computers	Includes inexpensive home computers for games, PCs for office, desktops, and workstations	$400 to $40,000	single	22	31.8	Commodore, IBM, Apple, Compaq, Tandy, Atari, H.P.

THE INDUSTRY LEADER

International Business Machines is the giant of the data processing industry. With revenues of $51.3 billion and net income of $4.8 billion in 1986, it accounted for an estimated 40% of the U.S. computer industry's sales and 70% of its profits. In contrast, IBM's two largest competitors—Unisys Corp. and DEC—had combined revenues of only $17 billion. As the table below indicates, IBM holds significant shares in all the major computer markets and has a virtual monopoly in the large-scale systems sector. Because of this dominance, Big Blue has set industry standards, most notably for mainframes but also for personal computers and local area networks.

IBM's 1986 MARKET SHARE IN VARIOUS PRODUCT MARKETS

Category	Market share
Large-scale	63%
Medium-scale	27
Small-scale	13
Personal computers	37

ANALYSIS

Large-Scale Systems

As recently as 1975, seven mainframe companies (IBM, Burrough, Univac/Sperry, NCR, Control Data, Honeywell, and Xerox) were responsible for over 80% of all revenues generated in the industry. Since 1975, Xerox and Honeywell dropped out of the mainframe market, and Burrough acquired Sperry to create Unisys Corp. The fortunes of all but IBM have been in steady decline. Mainframe sales, which used to grow by 15 to 20% a year, now increases only at 5% rate. In addition to showing signs of maturity, the mainframes in the past few years have also been attacked by the minicomputers. Because of technological advances, minicomputers now perform, at a tremendously reduced cost, many of the tasks once reserved for large-scale systems. For example, DEC's VAX8700 priced at $2.6 million is comparable to IBM's 3090-200E, which lists at $4.6 million.

The prognosis for large scale systems over the remainder of this decade is not encouraging. The growth rate is expected to slow down to 4% annually. Most U.S. orders would be for replacement systems rather than new products. However, aided by positive currency effects, the shipment value of international sales may rise slightly to a 10% pace.

Worldwide, Japan, with its strong technological resources, is IBM's strongest challenger in the mainframe sector. According to *Datamation* magazine, Fujitsu Ltd. and NEC Corp. were the No. 2 and No. 3 players, respectively, in the worldwide markets in 1986, while Hitachi Ltd. ranked fifth. (See Figure N2.1.)

FIGURE N2.1   1986 MARKET SHARES—LARGE-SCALE SYSTEMS
(U.S. Vendors' Share of Worldwide Installation Base)

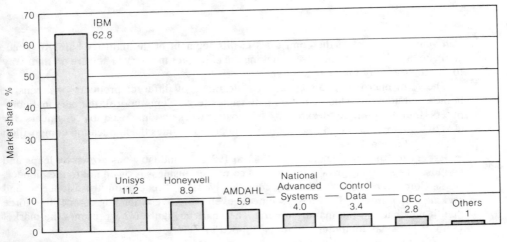

Source: IDC.

Medium-Scale Systems

The medium-scale segment, like large-scale systems, is maturing and slower growth of about 9% projected (as compared to 12% annual growth in 1980 to 1985). The three major companies in this segment are IBM, Digital Equipment, and Honeywell, which in 1986 had 27.4%, 23.6%, and 8.8% market share, respectively.

While IBM has had a large slip in market share from 1981 to 1986 in midrange systems for both medium- and small-scale computers, Digital is steadily gaining dominance in this segment. DEC finished out its fiscal year ended June 27, 1987, with record sales of $9.4 billion and net income of $1.1 billion. With its new VAX generation, the company has been not only satisfying the demands of its traditional engineering/scientific markets, but addressing the commercial markets as well. During fiscal 1987, the company claimed that it had doubled its market share in the financial service industry. DEC's strength lies in its networking capabilities. Users are very interested in tying together the various computers throughout their organizations and DEC has proven to do this job better than any competitor.

Small-Scale Systems

Small-scale systems have been very popular in recent years as departmental processors. With the proliferation of personal computers (PCs) on office desktops, companies have been employing minicomputers and superminicomputers to link the PCs to one another so that they can communicate and share resources. In addition, small-scale computers are well suited to act as intermediaries between PCs and corporate mainframes. These computers can also perform such departmental applications as: office automation, inventory control, accounts payable, general ledger, and project management.

Digital Equipment Corp. (DEC) and IBM with 19.3% and 12.7% share, respectively, are the two major forces in the small-scale market, followed by Hewlett-Packard (6%) and Data General (5.2%).

Microcomputers

Ten years ago, most of the companies in this segment of the industry barely existed, some not at all. Today, they are remaking the computer industry. They are on their way to the top—if only they can survive.

The term microcomputer covers a wide range of different products: inexpensive home computers on which children play games (e.g., Commodore); the personal computers found in office desktops, and costly workstations used by engineers for CAD/CAM applications. The chart in Figure N2.2 provides the application composition of personal computers.

Except for the relative slump of 1983 to 1985, the industry has grown by leaps and bounds. The stunning growth in personal computer business is owed not to the pioneer, Apple Computer, but to the Johnny-come-lately, IBM. Freed of antitrust concerns and seeking faster growth, IBM has become an even more overwhelming competitive force than it was back in the mainframe era. The chart in Figure N2.3 presents the market share of personal computers by units shipped in 1987.

In recent years large companies, such as IBM, have lost ground to the no-name "clones" as the skepticism toward purchasing lesser-known brands has diminished and

FIGURE N2.2   1986 PERSONAL COMPUTER DOLLAR SHIPMENT BY APPLICATION MARKET

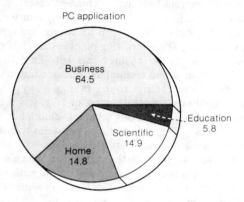

the quality and performance of such machines have improved. To regain control of the market, IBM is departing from its original strategy of building PCs with easily obtained off-the-shelf components. Marked as the most important event of 1987 for the personal computer industry, IBM introduced its new line of PS/2, which incorporates customized features and proprietary technology, making it more difficult and expensive for the clone markets to imitate. The top of the line of PS/2 family is using INTEL's new 32-bit 80386 microprocesser. This new line of PCs, featuring 2MB of memory, one 1.44MB 3½-inch floppy disk drive, and a 115MB hard disk drive, is in sharp contrast to the first IBM PC introduced in mid-1981, which featured only 64KB of memory, and one 160 KB floppy disk drive.

FIGURE N2.3   1987 PC VENDORS SHARE OF MARKET

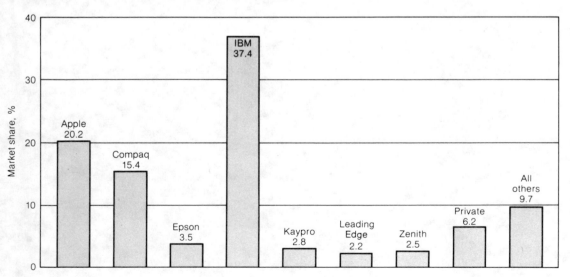

The distribution of personal computers is made through various channels: direct sales, independent computer retail chains, exclusive dealers, and catalog mail order. The direct sales channel is targeted to the business segment which is representing the largest segment of the PC market. IBM, with its strong and already established sales force, dominates this segment. The interesting point is that IBM can effectively use two different sales groups to target the business market. First, it sells its PCs to data processing personnel as stand-alone computers, and second, its typewriter and office products division appeals to secretaries to use PCs as word processors. Apple, which has not been taken seriously by corporate users of PCs, has recently formed a strong 350-person sales force to make gains in this segment. Zenith has also been strong in this segment and in recent years has been providing its systems to government agencies and in 1987 signed a large volume contract with IRS.

In the retail market, there are those independent stores such as Computerland, which has over 250 stores in the United States, and also some nationwide department store chains such as Macy's and Sears Business Centers. Computer manufacturers compete vigorously for shelf space in these stores and offer the dealers very attractive profit margins (25 to 50%), training material, brochures, point-of-sales displays, and education. Both Apple and IBM are very strong in this segment and use prime-time TV advertising to target individuals and small businesses.

Tandy is selling its computers through its Radio Shack retail outlets and can be considered the strongest in exclusive stores' sale. The mail-order catalog stores are also very active in direct sales, especially to price-sensitive customers. "Clones" sell very strongly through this channel. Even though Apple and IBM do not authorize sales of their products through the mail, the mail-order companies still sell a good sum of these brands. Apple's prohibition of the sale of its products by mail-order houses was challenged in court.

Competition in the education market remains intense. Apple dominates this market with roughly a 58% share, followed by Tandy Corp. IBM is making a major push to increase its presence in this segment. However, Apple has cultivated excellent relations with school systems, and in its quest, IBM faces a tough fight.

THE FAST-FOOD INDUSTRY

Prepared by Derrick Dsouza, Georgia State University.

INTRODUCTION

Fast-food restaurants are characterized by simplified/limited menus, and a high level of standardization with regard to service, training of personnel, and decor. In addition to delivering what their name suggests, i.e., quick customer turnaround, they compete with each other for customers on the basis of quality, service, cleanliness, and convenience offered. Fast-food service, therefore, provides drive-ins, take-outs, home delivery, drive-throughs, and self-service catering.

To appreciate the fast-food phenomenon, we need to understand the structure of the retail food industry, of which fast-foods is a part. We first need to distinguish between the food service industry and the retail grocers. The food service industry provides prepared foods, and essentially services the "eat-out" market; the retail grocers primarily provide unprepared or semiprepared foods that cater to what has been termed the "at home" market. This should not be construed to mean that these are noncompeting segments. Both segments in fact compete for customer sales in many areas. This industry structure is illustrated in Figure N3.1. Fast-food restaurants are part of the local restaurant subindustry (see Figure N3.1) that includes coffee shops, specialty (family) service restaurants, and full-service restaurants.

Local restaurants may be defined as public restaurants that sell prepared foods and beverages for consumption at or near the premises and are classified under the Department of Commerce SIC Code 5812. It may be noted, however, that such a classification of fast foods does not include those units that cater to the travel food service market (i.e., sales at hotels, air and bus terminals, etc.) or those catering to vending and contract food services.

The local restaurant subindustry is the largest and most dynamic segment of the food service industry because of (1) the high level of competition, (2) fragmentation of the market, (3) the continually changing consumer tastes, and (4) the size of the market. The fast-food segment forms a dominant part of the local restaurant subindustry.

FIGURE N3.1 STRUCTURE OF THE RETAIL FOOD INDUSTRY

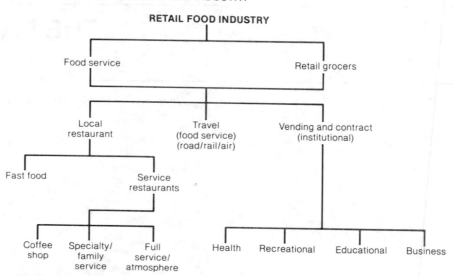

Source: Adapted from D. D. Wyckoff and E. W. Sasser, *The Chain-Restaurant Industry*, Lexington, Mass., Lexington Books, 1978.

Restaurant Business estimates that the size of the food service industry, as a whole (excluding military and school food service), to have been about $186.8 billion in 1986, and projects it to rise to about $268.3 billion by 1991. This provides for an average compound growth rate of 7.5 percent over these years. When adjusted for projected inflation, this growth rate drops to about 3.1% per year. A breakdown of *Restaurant Business'* projections has been provided in Figure N3.2.

Figure N3.2 illustrates how eating places with limited menus (of which fast-food operations forms a major portion) accounted for 39.3% of the sales rung up by major eating and dining places in 1985. Its share of this market increased marginally to 39.9% in 1986, and is predicted to reach around 41.9% by 1990.

Steady growth during the 1960s and the 1970s enabled the fast-food industry to carve out an appreciable share of the total food service market. Over the past few years, however, growth of the fast-food segment has plateaued, leading some industry analysts to believe that the industry is in the "mature" stage of its life cycle. Figure N3.3 provides some indication of growth trends in the fast-food industry over the last 8 years.

HISTORICAL BACKGROUND

The cook houses and coffee shops of Europe were the forerunners of the American restaurants of today. These cook houses and coffee shops were popular in colonial America. However, the nineteenth century saw a slow but steady metamorphosis of these cook house and coffee shops to the predecessors of the restaurants of today. Delmonico's, established in New York City in 1827, is generally credited as being the first true restaurant in the U.S. Delmonico's offered high cuisine at high prices. Nine-

FIGURE N3.2   SEGMENT-WISE SALES IN THE FOOD SERVICE INDUSTRY

	$ in billions		
	1985	**1986**	**1990**
Major eating and drinking places	$120.03	$128.94	$186.05
Eating & drinking places	$14.4	$15.23	$20.59
Eating places:			
Full menu	58.44	62.22	87.56
Limited menu	47.19	51.49	77.90
Hotel/motel market	10.70	11.48	16.87
Transportation market	2.73	3.00	4.89
Leisure market	4.94	5.19	7.07
Retail market	6.20	7.09	14.29
Business & industry market	10.11	10.54	14.05
Student market	8.60	9.11	11.76
Health care market	11.29	11.44	13.32
Total food service industry sales	$194.6	$186.79	$268.30

Source: Adapted from *Restaurant Business,* 20th Annual Restaurant Growth Index, September 20, 1987.

teenth-century America could not support high cuisine and prices like Delmonico's except in a few large cities. This gave rise to what may be termed "American style" restaurants. These restaurants catered to a much larger segment of the population and displayed varying characteristics. These were the coffee shops, cafeterias, economical but good table-service restaurants, and other similar types that met the customers' needs of the late 19th and early 20th centuries.

FIGURE N3.3   FAST-FOOD SERVICE SHARE OF THE TOTAL FOOD SERVICE MARKET

Year	Market share
1988*	30.06%
1987*	30.06
1986	30.03
1985	29.21
1984	28.87
1983	26.73
1982	24.78
1981	21.51
1980	20.10

* Estimated.
Source: Restaurants and Institutions, January 8, 1988, p. 62.

Thus the public restaurant business grew rapidly. By the 1920s, the automobile made the concept of drive-ins viable. Drive-ins were followed by customer demands for more convenience. Thus began a whole new industry—the fast-food industry. The concept of fast service, as such, is not a new one and in fact can be found to have existed in the roadside inns of ancient Rome. What makes today's fast-food industry so unique and such a huge success story is another critical factor—franchising.

FRANCHISING

The word franchise comes from the French "francer," which means "to free." Franchising seems to have appeared in the United States just after the Civil War, with dealership franchises being offered by manufacturers of consumer durables. By the turn of the century, franchises were being offered by many automakers, gasoline suppliers, and soft drink manufacturers. World War II saw the opening of numerous ice cream franchises and, of course, fast-food franchises.

Fast-food franchising can be traced to the 1920s and the 1930s. However, it did not gain momentum until the late 1950s and the 1960s, when economic factors played their part in helping the rapid expansion of the fast-food industry.

Technically a franchise is an agreement between two parties, the franchisor and the franchisee. The franchisor grants the franchisee rights to market goods and services with certain constraints on operations and territory. Through franchising, the small business acquires an instant "image," extended power, and a higher probability of success through a packaged set of manufacturing, marketing, and finance plans. The primary advantage of franchising is that it greatly reduces the chances of failure. This of course does not mean that franchising in the restaurant industry is failure-free. *Restaurant Business* magazine estimates that a total of 78 franchises, operating 5,667 outlets and worth around $574 million, failed during 1986. However, compared to the total franchising industry sales for 1986, this is a very small portion.

The cost of obtaining a franchise can vary considerably, and so can the mode of payment. The franchisee can generally expect to pay one or more of the following:

1 An initial fee
2 Royalty payments, normally a percentage of gross sales,
  a To the franchisor
  b For regional and/or national advertising
3 Equipment/training package purchase
4 Rent/fixed costs

Figure N3.4 provides some examples of typical costs that are involved when one starts a franchise in the fast-food industry.

Franchising and Fast Food

Franchising provides the franchisor with a viable and often very successful way of expanding operations. Growth in terms of sales revenues and geographical expansion are the primary goals in franchising. Growth resulting from a concerted effort to franchise has resulted in what is now called the "chain" industry. Statistics indicate that the largest chains have attained high levels of growth primarily through franchising. This

FIGURE N3.4 AVERAGE FRANCHISING COSTS FOR THE TOP FOUR FAST-FOOD CHAINS

	McDonalds	Burger King	Wendy's	Hardee's
Initial franchise fee	$ 12,500	$ 40,000	$ 25,000	$ 15,000
Refundable deposit	15,000			
Kitchen equipment	135,000		317,000	
Seating & decor	35,000	275,000	−500,000	470,000
Other expenses	78,000–132,000			
Total	$ 300,000	$315,000	$ 342,000	$485,000
(excluding cost of land)	$−350,000		$−525,000	
Royalties/rent on land	11.5%	3.5%	4%	3.5%–4%
Advertising contribution	NA	4%	4%	>5%
Average sales of typical unit in 1985	1.3 Million	1.0 Million	848,000	803,000

Source: Compiled from "New Directions in Franchising," *Restaurant Business,* March 20, 1987.

is particularly true of the restaurant industry. The fast-food chains are striking examples of how quickly chains can grow through franchising. When *Nations' Restaurant News* (*NRN*) ranked the top 100 food service chains (based on systemwide sales), 36 of the top 100 chains were from the fast-food sector. Some statistics on the top-ranked fast-food chains for the fiscal year 1986–1987 have been presented in Figure N3.5.

COMPETITION AND CONSOLIDATION IN THE RESTAURANT BUSINESS

Americans continue to eat out. According to the Department of Commerce's industry survey, per capita consumer spending on eating and drinking was around $675 in 1985. The fast-food sector is estimated to have accounted for about $50 billion of the $162.9 billion that consumers spent at commercial service outlets in 1986. Nevertheless, the restaurant industry, and especially the fast food segment of this industry, faces serious hurdles in the future.

According to government statistics, there were 409,453 commercial eating establishments and 296,654 noncommercial eating houses (e.g., military, day-care, etc.) in 1984. This provides individuals with a wide choice of where and what to eat. In an effort to attract customers, fast-food chains therefore have to rely heavily on advertising and other promotions to increase their visibility. The variety of food and the convenience offered, associated with the size and advertising clout of the chains, make this a very competitive industry. In addition, past trends seem to indicate that individuals are increasingly choosing to spend more of their disposable personal income on food eaten at home rather than away from home.

These problems are being reflected in the bottom line for some of the major chains. Some analysts suspect market saturation is taking its toll on the industry. One might, however, question whether saturation is systematically prevalent in all the segments of the restaurant industry. Some industry analysts argue that it might be occurring only selectively based on geographic region, type of food or "concept," the time factor, and the market segment.

FIGURE N3.5   VITAL STATISTICS OF THE TOP 20 FAST-FOOD CHAINS

Top 100 rank (by sales)		Chain	Concept	Sales system-wide ($ in millions)	Number of units	Sales per unit
1986	1987					
1	1	McDonalds	Burger	$14,110.0	9,900	$1.451
2	2	Burger King	Burger	5,590.0	5,579	1.080
3	3	Kentucky Fried Chicken	Chicken	3,700.0	6,905	0.641
4	5	Hardee's	Burger	3,030.0	3,013	0.875
5	4	Wendy's	Burger	2,800.0	3,900	0.767
6	6	Pizza Hut	Pizza	2,450.0	6,000	0.500
7	7	Dairy Queen	Ice cream	2,028.0	4,945	0.377
8	8	Domino's	Pizza	1,800.0	4,225	0.500
9	9	Taco Bell	Taco	1,500.0	2,700	0.550
10	16	Arby's	Roast beef	950.0	1,883	0.560
19	30	Little Caesars	Pizza	770.0	1,864	0.413
21	19	Long John Silver	Fish	741.0	1,430	0.515
23	20	Dunkin' Donuts of America	Doughnuts	712.0	1,650	0.454
27	26	Jack in the Box	Burger	645.7	905	0.795
28	27	Church's	Chicken	599.0	1,622	0.387
29	28	Roy Rogers	Burger	591.0	592	0.927
36	36	Baskin-Robbins	Ice cream	471.5	2,628	0.173
37	38	Popeye's	Chicken	460.0	730	0.730
43	45	Carl's Jr.	Burger	382.5	461	0.830
45	46	Rax Restaurants, Inc.	Burger	370.0	522	0.689

Source: Compiled from "Focus: Chain Analysis," *Nation's Restaurant News,* August 3, 1987.

Using growth as an indicator of industry status, the restaurant industry (with a sustained but low growth rate of 2.2% in 1985, 3.2% in 1986, and 2.7% in 1987) may be viewed as a mature industry. However, the status of individual segments of the market might differ. Using the life cycle format, the restaurant industry can be analyzed based on the type of meal served. Using this approach, one can characterize the take-out segment at one end of the spectrum as being in its infancy and the lunch segment, at the other end of the spectrum, as being very mature. Between these two lies the new breakfast segment and the more established dinner segments. The fast-food industry has traditionally catered to the lunch segment but in recent years is actually pursuing the take-out segment and has also entered the breakfast segment in force.

One of the strategies for survival in a saturated market such as the lunch segment of the fast-food service industry is to consolidate. This can take the form of horizontal integration, i.e., increasing the number of conventional stores through mergers and/or acquisitions of similar chains; or through concentric diversification, i.e., contracts/mergers with firms having product lines that afford synergy in the marketplace.

Industry Segmentation

There are ways other than "type of meal" to segment the fast-food restaurant market. In fact, most business analysts prefer to use the primary "concept" or "product" as the basis for segmenting the market. While this does create some controversies and gray areas, it essentially provides for a convenient method of providing well-defined markets. Ten such "concept"/"product" segments can be identified: (1) hamburgers/franks/roast beef; (2) chicken; (3) pizza; (4) Mexican; (5) seafood; (6) sandwich; (7) pancakes/waffles; (8) ice cream; (9) doughnuts, and (10) other (e.g., steak houses, etc.).

Figure N3.6 provides some idea of franchise restaurant sales by product segment. Each of these ten industry segments is described in the following paragraphs.

The Hamburger Segment   This is one of the most competitive segments of the fast-food business and one that is dominated by large chains (see Figure N3.7 for details). In 1986 rivalry reached such intensity that many competitors sought to redefine their business in terms of organization, operations, and even the basic concept. Major changes in top-level management were subsequently made in both large and small firms in this segment. McDonalds, Burger King, Wendy's, Hardee's, Arby's, and a host of other firms made changes at various managerial levels in their organizations. Product changes have also been implemented by many of these companies. Burger Bundles by Burger King is one example and Wendy's Classic is another. Prepacked salads rather than salad bars are increasingly being seen by fast-food operators as more convenient and cost-efficient. The emphasis on new-product innovation in this industry segment is thus clearly visable and is often found to be strongly supported by advertising and heavy expenditures on research and development.

The trend toward operating dual units under a single roof is also steadily gaining ground. For example, Wendy's and Baskin-Robbins are experimenting with such a contract, Hardee's is negotiating with 7-Eleven, and Coca-Cola is believed to be considering a joint agreement contract with Wendy's. Stores in the hamburger segment, which

FIGURE N3.6   FRANCHISE RESTAURANT SALES BY RESTAURANT TYPE

Major sales activity	$ in millions			
	1982	1983	1984*	1985*
Chicken	$ 3,308.0	$ 3,422.0	$ 3,947.4	$ 4,700.0
Burgers/franks/roast beef/etc.	15,990.8	18,940.0	21,230.0	23,800.0
Pizza	3,605.8	4,620.0	5,200.0	6,100.0
Mexican	1,305.3	1,720.0	1,919.1	2,127.0
Seafood	1,027.2	938.0	1,038.7	1,200.0
Pancakes/waffles	913.3	838.0	922.6	999.0
Steak/full menu	7,043.0	7,720.0	8,044.2	9,200.0
Sandwich/other	398.6	502.0	598.0	774.0
Total	$33,592.0	$38,700.0	$42,900.0	$48,900.0

* 1984 and 1985 estimated by respondents.
Source: Standard & Poor, *Industry Surveys 1987;* U.S. Department of Commerce.

FIGURE N3.7 TOP-RANKED CHAINS BY FAST-FOOD SEGMENT IN 1986–1987

Chain	Number of units	Market share	Average spent per person	Menu price increase
Top-ranked chains in the burger segment				
McDonalds	9,900	47.51%	NA*	NA
Burger King	5,579	18.8	$ 3.08†	NA
Hardee's	3,013	10.2	NA	NA
Wendy's	3,900	9.4	4.18	2.5%
Arby's	1,883	3.2	3.60	1.0
Jack in the Box	905	2.2	3.45	3.0
Roy Rogers	592	2.0	3.60	5.0
Carl's Jr.	461	1.3	NA	NA
Rex Restaurants	522	1.3	3.00	0.0
Sonic Drive-In Rest.	970	1.1	2.07	0.2
White Castle	234	1.0	NA	NA
Whata Burger	412	0.9	NA	NA
Krystal	242	0.6	2.55	2.0
A&W	540	0.5		
Top-ranked chains in the chicken segment				
Kentucky Fried Chicken	6,905	69.47	$ 5.20	1.0
Church's	1,622	11.25	3.65	0.0
Popeye's	730	8.64	4.10	NA
Chick-fil-A	370	3.80	3.08	NA
Bojangle's	235	3.75	2.80	1.2
Grandy's	227	3.10	3.20	0.4
Top-ranked chains in the pizza segment				
Pizza Hut	6,000	37.4	$10.50	2.0
Domino's	4,225	27.4	9.50	0.0
Little Caesars	1,864	11.7	3.00	0.0
Pizza Inn	770	4.6	4.50	1.0
Godfather's	700	4.6	10.80	3.0
Round Table Pizza	600	4.6	5.50	1.0
Showbiz/Chuck E. Cheese	270	4.3	5.50	0.0
Shakey's Pizza	383	3.2	4.50	1.0
Mr. Gatti's	338	2.2	7.87	0.0

* Not available.
† Previous year.
Source: Compiled from "Focus," *Nation's Restaurant News,* August 3, 1987.

traditionally have concentrated on the lunch market, are now increasingly looking toward the breakfast market to sustain growth. As an example, McDonalds has introduced breakfast sandwiches and has toyed with the idea of introducing pizzas.

The Chicken Segment Statistics provided by the U.S. Department of Commerce indicate that in 1986 there were 9,883 "units" specializing in chicken and generating about $4.9 billion in sales, as compared to 9,256 units with $4.4 billion in sales in 1985. Details on the top-ranked chicken chains are presented in Figure N3.7. The great majority of the chicken units are owned by the six large chains shown in Figure N3.7, with Kentucky Fried Chicken far in front of the pack with 6,905 units.

Statistics provided by the U.S. Department of Agriculture (which are in agreement with the National Broiler Council's findings) indicate that per capita consumption of poultry has been steadily increasing. In fact, they estimate that in 1987 per capita consumption of poultry (78.6 lbs./person) would for the first time surpass consumption of beef (73.8 lbs./person).

Despite the increasing trends in the per capita consumption of chicken, competition within the chicken segment of the fast-food industry is intense. One reason for this is that much of the chicken is consumed at home and therefore the share of the total chicken market captured by the fast-food restaurants is relatively low. Another reason is that growth in the chicken segment has been attained primarily by the "Big 6," with the smaller units being squeezed out in the process. Figure N3.8 provides some indications of how the top six units grew between 1985–1987.

In 1986–1987, this industry experienced an intense shakeout, with the smaller chains being forced to curtail growth. Industry analysts attribute this to many factors including: (1) oversupply, (2) consumer unwillingness to pay more for fast-food purchases, and (3) declining sales in certain geographic regions, particularly those where the oil market slump had a strong effect on the local economy. These competitive pressures have forced many chain operators in the chicken segment to close down troubled units and open up units in more lucrative areas.

In order to meet these changes in the industry, operators are now expanding menus, sprucing up images, and changing ad campaigns with increasing regularity. Some of these efforts have been paying dividends. For example, Kentucky Fried Chicken's 39-cent Chicken Littles, backed by a $40 million advertising campaign, has proved to be quite successful. By providing a chicken-based "burger," Kentucky Fried Chicken has also successfully attacked the huge quick-service sandwich business, hitherto dominated by the beef-based hamburger.

The Pizza Segment The pizza segment of the market has shown consistent growth trends over the past few years and was, in 1987, the fastest-growing segment of the fast-food industry. Much of this growth can be attributed to the innovations and enthusiasm

FIGURE N3.8 GROWTH IN THE CHICKEN SEGMENT OF THE FAST-FOOD INDUSTRY

Chain	Number of units in		Change over 2 years	
	1987	1985	Units added	% Growth
Kentucky Fried Chicken	6905	6396	509	7.8%
Church's	1622	1549	73	4.7%
Popeye's	730	521	209	39.5%
Chick-fil-A	370	319	51	16.0%
Bojangle's	235	328	(93)	(28.4%)
Grandy's	227	169	68	42.8%

Source: Compiled from "Focus," *Nation's Restaurant News,* August 3, 1987.

of the pizza chain operators. When Ann Arbor–based Domino's pizza successfully introduced the "home delivery" service, the move radically changed the complexion of the competition within the industry, and created what many see as an entirely new industry segment—the home-delivered fast foods. Many other pizza chains were quick to follow Domino's lead. Industry analysts, however, believe that the market is still in the growth stage and there is room for expansion and new entrants. The key to success in the pizza segment seems to be to carve out a niche and consolidate one's position. This is the approach that the pizza chains are successfully employing today.

Domino's strengths lie in its high quality, limited menu, and delivery-only concept. The company targets families and singles in the lower age groups. More than two-thirds of their units are franchised. The cost of setting up a franchise at $85,000–$140,000 is well below the initial investment required to start most hamburger franchises.

Not all pizza houses subscribe to the delivery-only concept. In fact, most have sit-ins and some, like Pizza Hut, offer full service. In such cases the menu becomes a crucial factor in building up sales. Chains have developed ingenious ways of building on the basic pizza. Pizza Hut's express-lunch program, for example, helps them position their product as a lunch item rather than only a dinner item as pizzas have traditionally been viewed.

In order to develop their niche, pizza chains have turned to advertisements and promotions. Domino's "Noid" commercials have been rated as very successful in increasing sales as well as customer perceptions of their product quality. Their "30-minute guarantee" is another success story. Other chains are also using discount promotions in order to build all-day traffic. Discounts, coupons, two-for-ones, and choice of toppings are some of the types of promotions that are being used by pizza chains to corner portions of the market.

Pizza Hut is by far the largest chain in the pizza segment, with 6,000 units. It is followed by Domino's with 4,225 units (see Figure N3.7 for more details). Third-ranked, Little Caesars is at a much lower level of 1,864 units but has shown impressive growth. In 1983 Little Caesars was ranked 21st in NRN's top 100 restaurants. In 1987, it had jumped to 14th place in terms of number of units.

The Mexican Segment   The Mexican segment is another fast-growing segment of the fast-food business. Unlike the other segments, however, this segment is not well defined. One of the reasons is that while some units in this segment cater specifically to Mexican specialities, many others also include burgers, fries, pizzas, and other fast-food entrees to their menu to draw in add-on customers. In addition, many units not generally included in this segment serve Mexican dishes. *Restaurant Business* magazine reports that as many as 79% of all restaurants serve at least one Mexican item on their menu.

Taco Bell is the major operator in this market segment with 2,700 units and sales of $1.5 billion. The company (a Pepsico subsidiary based in Irvine, California) continues to grow through acquisition of smaller chains. It recently completed an agreement to purchase 9 units of Atlanta-based D'lites of America, Inc. In addition, 100 units of the Zantigo chain were added following Pepsico's acquisition of Kentucky Fried Chicken. The West Coast–based Taco Bell now plans to expand along the East Coast.

Another major competitor in the field is Del Taco, a Costa Mesa, California–based firm with 199 units in California and 131 units outside California. Del Taco's units outside California are owned by Creative Fun 'N Foods, a W. C. Grace subsidiary. Del

Taco's agreement with Creative Fun 'N Foods gives the W. C. Grace subsidiary exclusive rights to develop Del Taco's outside California.

The Mexican market segment is particularly competitive in California where segment leaders like Taco Bell and Del Taco face strong competition from smaller chains like the 176-unit Nougles, Inc. and Taco Viva, a 60-unit chain.

The Seafood Segment   The demand for seafood has been steadily rising and provides a potential for growth in this segment of the fast-food industry. The national Marine Fisheries Services reported that U.S. per capita consumption of fresh and frozen seafood rose to about 9.3 lbs. per year in 1987. In a related study, conducted by the International Resource Development Corporation, 60 percent of fresh and frozen seafood was found to be eaten away from home and 14 percent was in fast-food outlets. The current overall market for seafoods is around $10 billion, giving the fast-food units a $1.4 billion slice of the pie. It has been projected that this slice will increase to around $3.9 billion by 1995. In 1985, there were a total of 2,423 seafood restaurants in the country, many of which provided fast-food service; of these, 1,362 were company-owned units and 1,061 were franchised (U.S. Dept. of Commerce).

Kentucky-based Long John Silvers is the largest of the seafood chains with sales of $741 million and 1,430 units. About 550 of these units are franchised. It is the only seafood chain that has gone truly national. Captain D's, seafood chain based in Tennessee, has 539 units (of which 234 are franchised). Some of the other smaller chains include Ohio-based Arthur Treachers, with 103 units, Skippers Seafood and Chowder Houses along the West Coast, and Miami-based Captain Crab in the South.

The seafood segment is not as competitive as the hamburger or chicken segment. Some of the reasons for this are the barriers to entry into this market: high product price, selected market segments, and high customer loyalty. Most operators, therefore, resort to niche marketing, with each chain or unit specializing in a few select seafood entrees.

Sandwich, Ice Cream, Doughnut, Pancake Segments   Some statistics on these segments have been provided in Figure N3.9.

THE CONSUMER

In 1982–1983, the National Restaurant Association conducted a two-part study on consumer attitudes and behavior. The objective was to find out why consumers eat out and how they go about making the decision to eat out. The two most frequently mentioned reasons for eating out were (1) convenience, and (2) enjoyment (see Figure N3.10).

The study also provided some idea of when and where these meals were eaten. These statistics are presented in Figure N3.11. It may be noted that the bulk (57.6%) of the meals eaten at fast-food restaurants were consumed at lunch.

The study found that in general, the decision to eat at fast-food restaurants was usually made on the "spur of the moment" and that the choice of fast-food restaurant to patronize was also made immediately before the visit.

FIGURE N3.9 SANDWICH, ICE CREAM, DOUGHNUT, AND PANCAKE SEGMENT STATISTICS

	Sandwich	Ice cream	Doughnut	Pancake
Total units (1985)	3,135	8,781	3,719	
Company-owned	NA	274	1,072	
Franchised	NA	8,507	2,647	
Total sales (1986)	$821 million	$1.4 billion	$1.168 billion	
Largest chain	Subway (1,011 units)	Dairy Queen (4,900 units)	Dunkin' Donuts (1,539 units)	International House of Pancakes (458 units)
Other operators	Blimpie (241 units) Schlotzsky's (200 units)	Baskin-Robbins (3,135 units) Yonkees (900 units) Swensen's Ice Cream (365 units)		Elmer Pancake & Steakhouse (28 units)
Industry characteristics	Emphasis on internationalization	New yogurt market		Fairly strong industry competition

Even though Americans are eating more meals away from home than ever before, they spend a smaller percentage of their disposable income on meals than do people from other countries. Figure N3.12 provides an indication of food spending habits in 18 different countries.

The American attitude toward meals is also changing. According to a recent study done by the Roper Organization, only 51% of the population eat three square meals

FIGURE N3.10 REASON FOR EATING OUT BY RESTAURANT TYPE

Reason	All restaurants	Restaurant type		
		Fast food	Family	Atmosphere
Lack of time	18.1%	39.7%	7.8%	1.4%
Convenience	37.3	40.8	53.4	16.1
Celebration	6.9	0.3	2.3	20.2
Enjoyment	23.4	5.9	23.0	46.0
Business meeting	1.7	0.9	1.6	2.8
Shopping	1.7	3.1	1.6	—
Traveling	2.4	2.5	2.9	1.7
Other	8.2	6.4	7.1	11.6

Note: Totals may not add to 100% due to rounding and exclusion of nonresponses.
Source: Consumer Attitude and Behavior Study, National Restaurant Association, 1983.

FIGURE N3.11   HOW MEALS WERE EATEN OUT

Meal	All restaurants	Restaurant type		
		Fast food	Family	Atmosphere
Breakfast	3.8%	3.3%	7.6%	0.5%
Lunch	31.9	57.6	25.9	5.3
Dinner	62.5	36.4	65.5	92.8
Other	1.6	2.4	0.8	1.3

Note: Totals may not add to 100% due to rounding and exclusion of non-responses.
Source: Consumer Attitude and Behavior Study, National Restaurant Association, 1983.

daily; 35% of the population do not eat breakfast; 5% do not eat dinner; and 11% exist on only one square meal per day.

DEMOGRAPHICS

The fast-food restaurant phenomenon is essentially an urban occurrence. The great majority of fast-food units are located in midsized to large towns and cities. The future potential of such an industry is therefore strongly linked to the growth potential of urban America, particularly the major metropolitan areas. Figure N3.13 provides some data on population and consumer buying power in the top 20 cities in the country in 1986. The table also provides projected figures for these cities in the year 1990.

The fast-food industry has traditionally targeted customers in their teens or twenties—typically the 15–25 age group. The baby boom of the 1950s and 1960s considerably enhanced the size of this market segment during the 1970s and the early 1980s. However, by the mid-1980s the baby boomers had moved to the 25–44 age group (see Figure N3.14), and the 14–24 market segment therefore shows a decrease in size. In fact between 1980–1985 the 14–17 age population segment decreased by 7.9% and the 18–24

FIGURE N3.12   PERCENTAGE OF DISPOSABLE INCOME SPENT ON FOOD AT HOME IN 20 COUNTRIES

Country	Percentage	Country	Percentage
United States	10.9%	Norway	19.0%
Canada	12.3	Japan	19.5
Netherlands	12.7	West Germany	20.0
United Kingdom	13.5	Italy	21.3
Australia	14.0	South Africa	24.4
France	15.7	Spain	26.5
Austria	17.2	Thailand	34.9
Sweden	18.1	Korea	37.5
Finland	18.7	Philippines	46.7

Source: U.S. Department of Agriculture.

FIGURE N3.13   PROJECTED TRENDS IN POPULATION AND CONSUMER BUYING POWER

	Population (millions)		Consumer buying power index	
	1986	**1990**	**1986**	**1990**
New York, NY	8.43	8.57	3.53	3.35
Los Angeles/Long Beach, CA	8.09	8.63	3.61	3.58
Chicago, IL	6.13	6.17	2.73	2.68
Philadelphia, PA	4.81	4.88	2.07	2.04
Detroit, MI	4.36	4.35	1.89	1.80
Boston/Lawrence/Salem, MA	3.70	3.74	1.86	1.80
Washington, DC	3.49	3.70	1.85	1.88
Houston, TX	3.21	3.64	1.49	1.53
Nassau/Suffolk, NY	2.70	2.79	1.40	1.37
Atlanta, GA	2.46	2.75	1.14	1.21
St. Louis, MO	2.42	2.44	2.06	1.03
Dallas, TX	2.30	2.61	1.11	1.19
Baltimore, MD	2.29	2.37	0.97	0.95
Minneapolis/St. Paul, MN	2.25	2.36	1.10	1.14
Pittsburgh, PA	2.18	2.14	0.89	0.80
San Diego, CA	2.14	2.40	0.98	1.04
Anaheim/Santa Ana, CA	2.12	2.29	1.07	1.08
Oakland, CA	1.90	2.02	0.94	0.94
Riverside/San Bernardino, CA	1.90	2.20	0.77	0.84
Newark, NJ	1.88	1.88	0.89	0.86

Source: Compiled from 1986 Survey of Buying Power, *Sales and Marketing Management,* 1986.

age segment dropped by 5.3%. This clearly indicates shrinkage in size of the fast-food industry's primary target market. The silver lining, however, is that many baby boomers are now beginning to settle down and have children and can once again be expected to frequent restaurants that provide convenience and quick service at moderate prices.

While restaurants and fast-food services have placed great importance on the baby boomer/yuppie segment of the population, another segment seems to be emerging as a potential market. The 50–60 segment, labeled the "ultras," consisting of 33 million Americans in 1986, is expected to increase to about 41 million by the year 2000. The ultras tend to eat out frequently due more to habit than from making conscious decisions. They tend to be more brand/restaurant loyal and are estimated to spend around 20% of their income on nonessentials, compared to the national average of 16.5%.

Another factor that has had a considerable impact on the fast-food industry is the increasing number of women in the work force. The U.S. Bureau of Labor Statistics projects that by 1990, 81% of the women in the age group of 25–44 will be working as compared to 66% in 1980. The implications are twofold. First, this will increase the number of meals eaten outside the home due to time constraints. Second, the increased disposable income will provide the means to eat out more frequently. In a related issue, the *American Demographic Magazine* has projected that families headed by single women will increase 26% by the year 2000. This again would steer members of single-parent households toward convenience-oriented, fast-service eating places.

FIGURE N3.14 POPULATION CHANGES IN VARIOUS AGE CATEGORIES, 1950–1985

Years	Total all ages	Under 5 years	Percent change							
			5–13 Years	14–17 Years	18–24 Years	25–34 Years	35–44 Years	45–54 Years	55–65 Years	65 Years and over
1950-1955	9.0%	13.1%	24.5%	9.5%	−6.9%	1.0%	5.9%	8.2%	9.2%	17.2%
1955-1960	8.9	9.6	18.0	21.3	7.7	−5.6	5.7	9.0	6.9	14.8
1960-1965	7.5	−2.5	8.5	26.2	25.8	−2.0	0.9	6.1	9.3	10.7
1965-1970	5.4	−13.5	2.5	12.4	21.6	12.6	−5.3	6.7	9.3	8.9
1970-1975	4.2	−7.4	−8.7	6.4	11.8	22.2	−1.4	1.9	5.9	11.5
1975-1980	5.4	2.0	−8.4	−5.8	8.5	19.5	13.4	4.3	8.5	13.3
1980-1985	5.1	9.9	−3.1	−7.9	−5.3	12.3	23.0	−0.6	2.7	11.0

Source: U.S. Department of Commerce, Bureau of the Census.

In a survey conducted by *Restaurants and Institutions,* a sizable 32% of Americans ate out more often in 1987 than in 1986. They spent more on eating out as well. According to the survey, in 1986 the average weekly eating-out budget was $28.68. By 1987 it had increased to $31.07; 40.3% of the population were found to eat out more than 7 times per week. Only 16.7% indicated that they ate out 1–2 times a week. A related study found that 31% of those who chose to eat out preferred to purchase "take-out" foods. The National Restaurant Association has estimated that 50% of this take-out food is eaten at home. The rest is eaten either in the car, at work, or at other places such as schools or parties.

THE MENU

To a large extent, the success of a restaurant can be attributed to its menu. For a fast-food operation, the choice of menu items is crucial. Fast-food operators, particularly the larger chains, spend millions, pretesting new products in selected markets before these products are added to the regular menu. A great deal of research efforts have been invested in designing menus, and some academic models have even been developed for menu making and menu pricing.

THREATS FROM OUTSIDE THE FAST-FOOD INDUSTRY SEGMENT

The Grocery Stores

Competition within the fast-food industry is intense. Not only do operators compete within their segment of the market (e.g., hamburger segment, chicken segment, etc.) but they also compete across segments (for example, McDonalds' Chicken McNugget cuts across two segments). In addition to industry competition, fast-food units face the threat of competition from other areas. Grocery stores and supermarkets, for example, stock frozen pizzas and burgers as well as items like breaded shrimp. They also stock T.V. dinners and other heat-and-serve entrees. The introduction of the microwave oven has much to do with this phenomenon. Prices of microwave ovens have dropped considerably over the years to a level that is now generally affordable. This trend is expected to boost sales of frozen convenience entrees from groceries and can be expected to adversely affect fast-food sales.

Grocery stores and supermarkets are no longer restricting themselves to frozen entrees. Many have chosen to meet the fast-food industry head-on. K-Mart, for example, has in-store, fast-food service in most of its stores. Many supermarkets already have an extensive deli. Industry analysts predict that by the year 2000, 80% of supermarkets will be selling ready-to-eat fast foods.

The Convenience Store

The convenience store segment is another force with which the fast-food operators have to contend. Catering to the same basic needs of the customers that the fast-food industry has capitalized on (convenience and quick service), these units are ideally placed to provide competition similar to that from supermarkets. 7-Eleven, the largest convenience store chain, has 8,000 outlets across the country. It is believed to be actively considering introducing fast food chain products. Convenience Food Mart, Inc., the third largest convenience food chain after 7-Eleven and Circle K, has recently introduced fresh muffins in its 1,500 locations.

Gourmet Fast Foods

Another segment that has recently developed is the upscale or gourmet fast-food restaurants that service both the take-out and particularly the meal-at-home market. This segment provides high-quality, freshly prepared foods for take-out. The target population is the older Yuppie population in a high income bracket who would like a quick meal yet frown on hamburgers and fries as an option! Although this market is currently small, there is good reason to believe that it will expand.

Pricing

Competition in the fast-food industry is rapidly increasing, leading industry analysts to believe that the market is saturated. This saturation is most prominent at the product or "concept" level and is most vividly illustrated by what has been termed as the "burger battle." The large chains are well entrenched all over the country, leaving little potential for further market development. Competitors therefore turn to product innovation in an attempt to maintain a competitive edge. However, while new-product innovation is one part of the burger battles, pricing plays a crucial role in developing or maintaining market share in the short run. This is due primarily to the fact that this industry serves the low-priced food market where margins are low. Chain operators have, therefore, found it extremely difficult to pass on price increases to the customer (Figure N3.7). Few operators have made any major changes in price over the period 1986–1987. Improper pricing could have extremely adverse effects on the sales revenues of large operators.

Another related critical factor is the average per customer sales. While the customer is inclined to think primarily in terms of the main course ordered, say a hamburger, the markups are highest on side dishes like fries and soft drinks. Thus, from the operator's point of view, it is the add-on sales that generate most of the profits. Pricing strategies for such add-ons is therefore crucial to maintaining profitability.

Decor

High volume sales backed by continuous quality control has assisted chains in standardizing their operations with particular emphasis being given to kitchens and front-end spatial layouts. The interior decor at fast-food restaurants has traditionally been spartan with little or no changes being introduced over the years. Increased competition, combined with the need to modernize older units in the chain, is making some fast-food chain operators rethink the issue of interior design. For example, the McDonalds restaurant at Rockefeller Center in Manhattan was designed to "reflect the center's landmark status . . . all that remains of the traditional McDonalds' decor are the uniforms of the employees and, of course, the menu." (*Restaurant Business*, April 10, 1980, p. 152.) While across-the-board changes of this sort may not be immediately forthcoming, instances such as this may induce operators to progressively introduce decor changes.

FIGURE N3.15   TELEVISION ADVERTISING EXPENDITURES BY LARGE CHAINS IN 1986

Chain	Amount ($ in millions)	% Increase over previous year
McDonalds	$321.2	9%
Burger King	165.2	6
Kentucky Fried Chicken	79.9	7
Wendy's	79.6	−5
Hardee's	29.5	−9
Pizza Hut	71.3	13
Domino's Pizza	33.8	94
Dairy Queen	16.0	35
Taco Bell	50.3	30

Source: Adapted from *Nation's Restaurant News*, March 23, 1987, p. 2.

Advertising

In a competitive industry which uses only a moderate level of production "technology" and where the customer is the individual or the household, advertising plays an important part. Much of the advertising is through television and radio commercials. The restaurant chains spent nearly $1.2 billion on T.V. advertising in 1986. Expenditures of some of the top chains are presented in Figure N3.15.

REFERENCES

Lundberg, D. E. (1979). *The hotel and restaurant business*. CBI Publishing Co., Inc., Boston, MA.

National Restaurant Association (August 1982). *Consumer attitude and behavior study—Part I*.

National Restaurant Association (November 1983). *Consumer attitude and behavior study—Part II*.

Nations Restaurant News (January 4, 1988). Facing a year of slow growth, p. F3.

Nations Restaurant News (August 3, 1987). The top 100, pp. F1–F88.

Restaurant Business (September 20, 1987). 20th Annual restaurant growth index, pp. 105–125.

Restaurant Business (August 10, 1987). Advertising: Sizzle that sells, pp. 157–172.

Restaurant Business (May 1, 1987). The saturation syndrome, pp. 189–197.

Restaurant Business (March 20, 1987). New directions in franchising. pp. 115–166.

Wyckoff, D. D., & Sassee, W. E. (1978). *The chain restaurant industry*, Lexington Books, Lexington, MA.

Restaurant and Institutions (December 9, 1987). How America loves to eat out, pp. 30–52.

Restaurant and Institutions (January 7, 1987). Ultras: The overlooked market, pp. 20–21.

INDEXES

NAME INDEX

Agee, William, 90
Andrews, Kenneth, 26
Ang, J. S., 19
Ansoff, H. I., 4, 18, 19
Avener, J., 4, 19

Bhatty, E. F., 92–93
Bonaparte, Napoleon, 3
Bracker, J. S., 4, 19
Brandenberg, R. G., 4, 19
Byars, Lloyd L., 220

Cathy, Truett, 44
Chua, J. H., 19

David, Fred, 68
Davis, Martin S., 53
Deane, Richard, 87
DeLorean, John Z., 55

Eisner, Michael D., 41
England, George, 85

Fireman, Paul, 41
Flavin, Joseph B., 53

Goldsmith, James, 53
Gray, Daniel, 25
Grinyer, P. H., 19
Gupta, A. K., 199
Guth, William D., 85
Guynes, C. S., 18, 19

Harrigan, Kathryn R., 167
Henry, Harold W., 18, 19
Herold, D. M., 19
House, Robert J., 4, 18, 19

Iacocca, Lee, 197

Johnson, Ross, 53

Karger, Delman, 18, 19
Kennedy, Allan, 142
Kudla, Ronald J., 19

Leontiades, James, 241

Macpherson, René, 198
Malik, Zafar, 18, 19
Mellinger, Frederick, 60
Mercer, Robert E., 53
Mintzberg, Henry, 22, 88, 208
Mock, Valerie, 87

Najjar, M. A., 18, 19
Naylor, Michael E., 25
Norburn, D., 19

Pearson, J. N., 4, 19
Peters, Thomas, 46
Pierce, John A., 68
Porter, Michael, 109
Portner, F. E., 4, 19
Posner, Victor, 202–203

Radosevich, R., 4, 19
Rhyme, Lawrence C., 4, 19
Robinson, Richard B., Jr., 4, 19
Rose, Michael, 46,
Rue, Leslie W., 18, 19, 220

Sapp, Richard W., 19
Seiler, Robert E., 19
Shein, Edgar, 136

SUBJECT INDEX

COMPANY INDEX